AF809634

DeSouza's

Forms and Precedents of

Conveyancing

Kolkata
Eastern Law House Private Ltd.
54 Ganesh Chunder Avenue
Kolkata 700 013

New Delhi
Eastern Law House Private Ltd.
36 Netaji Subhash Marg, Daryaganj
New Delhi 110 002

The spirit of legal doctrine

DeSouza's
Forms and Precedents of
Conveyancing

Thirteenth Edition

C.R. Datta
M.N. Das

Download of Forms
is at
www.elh.co.in > Resource menu

DeSouza's

Forms and Precedents of

Conveyancing

Thirteenth Edition

by

C.R. Datta
MA (Com), LLB (Cal), ATII (England), DIA (London)
Barrister-at-Law, Lincoln's Inn

M.N. Das
Former District & Sessions Judge and
Member-Secretary, State Law Commission, West Bengal

Economy VERSION

Kolkata New Delhi
EASTERN LAW HOUSE

Published and processed by
EASTERN LAW HOUSE PRIVATE LTD.
54 Ganesh Chunder Avenue
Kolkata 700 013
Tel: (033) 4063-2301 Email: mail@elh.co.in
www.elh.co.in

First Edition 1933
Second Edition 1935
Third Edition 1941
Fourth Edition 1948
Fifth Edition 1952
Sixth Edition 1958
Seventh Edition 1963
Eighth Edition 1968
Ninth Edition 1973
Tenth Edition 1976
Eleventh Edition 1980
Twelfth Edition 1983
Thirteenth Edition 1999
SECOND REVISED IMPRESSION 2001
THIRD REVISED IMPRESSION 2004
FOURTH IMPRESSION 2008
FIFTH IMPRESSION 2010
SIXTH IMPRESSION 2013
SEVENTH IMPRESSION 2014
EIGHTH IMPRESSION 2017
NINTH IMPRESSION 2019
TENTH IMPRESSION 2023

Whilst all reasonable care has been taken to ensure accuracy of the contents of this book, no person associated with the creation or publishing of this book shall have responsibility for any loss or damages that may be caused to any person due to errors or omissions which may have crept in inadvertently in this publication. Disputes, if any, are subject to Kolkata jurisdiction.

©
EASTERN LAW HOUSE PRIVATE LTD.
THE ESTATE OF C.J. DESOUZA
1999

ISBN 978-81-7177-394-7

Printed at
Dey's Offset, Kolkata

Preface to the Thirteenth Edition

The special and technical subject of Conveyancing which forms an integral part of the legal profession has been given a practical shape in *DeSouza's Conveyancing* which can claim to be a book on the subject with a difference.

While revising the work we have been conscious of the fact that it has earned a reputation of being the only book of its kind throughout the last six decades and we have tried to be as careful as possible to maintain its standard of excellence and the object of the book.

Enlarged and reoriented this revised edition is enriched with an abundance of materials distributed in several chapters with appropriate models and precedents. Each chapter deals with a specific subject and is prefaced with an adequate exposition of the legal principles involved and suitable guidelines have been indicated with a view to their practical application.

We have added several new subjects including Joint Venture, Foreign Collaboration, Franchising, Lease Financing of Equipment, Consumer Protection Act, Apartment Ownership, Promoters' Loan Agreement with relevant model forms in the background of the fact that India is a member of the WTO and multinationals and NRI's have become a part of the industrial and commercial scenario of the country.

Case laws have been updated as far as possible incorporating recent decisions of the Supreme Court and of the different High Courts. We are confident that the book will be of immense assistance not only to the members of the legal profession besides draftsmen and general practitioners but also to the corporate sectors including companies and firms.

We must thank Mr. Asok De, Director of Eastern Law House and its staff for the valuable assistance afforded to us in preparing this work followed by its processing.

Calcutta
8th September 1999

C.R. DATTA
M.N. DAS

Preface to the First Edition

The Publication of this book, the first of its kind, is intended to supply a long standing want felt both by Legal Practitioners and business men, for a suitable guide in drawing up their documents, such as used in British India, in a precise and correct manner.

The book is divided into two parts, the first containing model forms of all kinds of documents and legal instruments, very carefully selected and arranged into different chapters, and the second being a set of the most important petitions to Courts.

As the book is designed for the use of laymen as well, comprehensive notes embodying all the important law regarding the documents and petitions have been given at the foot of each chapter, and at the end of the second part, so that every educated person will be in a position to prepare his own documents independently of any professional aid.

My best thanks are due to Mr. M.K. Padhey, Pleader, Nagpur, for helping me with his valuable suggestions in the course of the preparation of the book, and also to my other friends, who have been so kind as to give me their assistance in various ways.

Suggestions from kind readers for further improvement of the book in the subsequent editions will be most gratefully acknowledged, and it is hoped that its publication will prove to be very useful, and will meet with appreciation and encouragement from the public.

8th September, 1933 L.C.D.

Contents

Table of Cases

1

Introduction

So early as in the Seventeenth Century the Common Law of England with its Statutory modifications and the doctrines of the English Courts of Equity and the System of Judicial Administration of England were applied mainly to the British subjects in certain parts of India which were then popularly known as the Company's Territories. The Privy Council as the highest Court of Appeal from India applied the principles of English jurisprudence as the rules of decision all over the country. Although the law and jurisprudence of this vast country and her model of judicial administration were in many respects different from those of England, nevertheless the massive structure of Indian law and jurisprudence as we now have resembles the common law and statute of England.[1]

The expression "Common Law of England" covered those unwritten legal doctrines embodying English habits, practise, customs and traditions which developed over centuries and were recognised by the English courts. The English people introduced into India not only the mass of legal rules strictly known as the common law of their own but also their traditions, outlook and techniques in establishing, maintaining and developing the judicial system of this country.

The Charters of Queen Elizabeth and James I granted to the Company in the years 1600 and 1609 gave them power to make, ordain and constitute such and so many reasonable laws, constitutions, orders, ordinances, etc. as to them shall seem fit and necessary bearing in mind always that the said laws, orders, constitutions, ordinances, etc. be reasonable and not contrary or repugnant to the laws, statutes and customs of this realm.[2] The

1 *Advocate General of Bengal* v *Rani Surnamooye Dassi* (1863)9 Moor Ind App 424.

2 Cowell's *Tagore Law Lectures* 1872, pp. 12-13.

Statutes of Elizabeth relating to fraudulent conveyances[3] were in force in Calcutta, Bombay and Madras and they applied to British subjects other than Hindus and Mahamedans.[4]

The Presidency Towns and the City of Rangoon played the leading role in the introduction of the common law into India. The courts were modelled entirely on the English pattern with jurisdiction extended to all British subjects all over Bengal, Bihar and Orissa (Rules of the High Court).[5]

After the attainment of independence and the adoption of the Constitution of India, judicial administration and the Constitution of the law courts remained fundamentally unchanged, except in matters such as the abolition of appeals to the Privy Council, the Constitution of the Supreme Court of India as the Apex Court, the conferment of writ jurisdiction on all the High Courts, etc. The concept, structure and organisation of courts, the substantive and procedural laws, the adversial system of trial and other proceedings and the function of judges and lawyers remained basically unaltered and rooted in the common law traditions in contradistinction to those prevailing in the civil law or other system of law.[6]

In England an equitable right or estate as recognised was somewhat different from a legal right or estate. The interest of a beneficiary in the trust property in England is an equitable interest while the legal interest in the estate remains vested in the trustee. This doctrine of the Court of Equity once not recognised in India after the advent of the British Rule was incorporated in the Indian Trusts Act of 1882 (s. 3) as trustee and beneficiary. Again in England when a person agrees to sell land, he creates an equitable interest in the land in favour of the buyer, an equitable interest recognised by the Court of Chancery. The law in India never recognised any distinction between legal and equitable interests. As early as 1872 the Judicial Committee in *Tagore* v *Tagore*,[7] observed "The Law of India, speaking broadly knows nothing of the distinction between legal and equitable property in the sense in which it was understood when equity was administered by the Court of Chancery in England." The same view was expressed in 1931[8] when it said that by the law of India "there can be but one owner and where the property is vested in a trustee, the owner must be the trustee." Another doctrine

3 13 Eliz C 5 and 27 Eliz C 4 is now replaced by s. 53 of the Transfer of Property Act.

4 6 Mad HC Rep 474, The Wills Act 1861; 24 and 25 Vict C 114 and the Naturalisation Act 1872; 35 and 36 Vict C 17.

5 OS, 4th Ed. 1941, p. 87.

6 *Byram Pestonji* v *Union Bank* AIR 1991 SC 2234; 1991 AIR SCW 2567; JT 1991(4) SC 15.

7 1872 Ind App Supp 47, 71.

8 *Rani Chitro Kumari* v *Mohan Bikram* (1931)589 App 279.

which is now a rule of estoppel and based on the equitable doctrine *He who seeks equity must do equity,* was recognised in India and the same has been incorporated in s. 51 of the Transfer of Property Act 1882, *e.g.* when improvements are made on third party's land by a stranger or *bona fide* holder of defective title.[9]

Some of the significant equitable doctrines however were not found acceptable by the Indian courts, *e.g.* purchase of property in favour of children or other persons for their advancement. The Indian Succession Act, did not enact the rule of English law by which a child who have had received a benefit out of the estate of his father must account for it on distribution of the same in the event of the father dying intestate. The rule has, however, been held to apply to persons subject to English law in India.[10] The equity of part performance which in England mitigated the rigours of the statute of fraud by taking a parole contract out of it when it had been partly performed seemed at one time to apply to India to the extent of taking away the application of the laws requiring registration and other formalities in such cases.[11] The doctrine has now been incorporated in a partial form into the statute governing transfer of property (s. 53A of the Transfer of Property Act 1882).

However, the statute law of India has incorporated in itself to a substantial extent equitable rules and doctrines. The Indian Trusts Act of 1882 embodies in a concise form the whole structure of trusts built up by the equity courts in England. The Act also deals with "certain obligations in the nature of trusts". There are attempts to enumerate broadly, circumstances under which a person may be placed in the position of a trustee with reference to another. These "obligations in the nature of trusts" are no different from the implied and constructive trusts found in the decisions of the English equity courts.

Another instance of an almost transplantation of the doctrines of English equity courts is to be found in the Specific Relief Act of 1877 since repealed and re-enacted by the Specific Relief Act 1963. It deals with cases in which courts will order restitution of specific property and order contracts to be specifically performed. It also enumerates the circumstances in which the courts will grant the relief of rectification and cancellation of instruments. The Act is in a sense a blend of common law and equity. The doctrine of the equity of redemption was held by the Privy Council in 1870 as not originally recognised in India.[12] It has received statutory recognition under s. 60 of the Transfer of Property Act 1882. The rights and liabilities of the lessor and

9 *Lake* v *Gibson* 1 Eq Ca Ab 290.
10 *Kerwick* v *Kerwick* 1920 Ind App 273.
11 *Mahamed Musa's* case (1914)421 App 75.
12 *Pattabhirameer* v *Vincatarow* (1870)13 Moor Ind App 560 (571-72).

lessee as incorporated in s. 108 of the Transfer of Property Act 1882, are based on well settled principles of the law in England.[13] The common law rule against transfer or bequest to unborn person is enacted in s. 13 of the Transfer of Property Act and in s. 113 of the Indian Succession Act. So the English Rule against perpetuity is incorporated in s. 114 of the Indian Succession Act in a modified form and as also in s. 14 of the Transfer of Property Act 1882.

The property clauses in the Constitution of India, contained in Art. 19(1)(*f*) and Art. 31, have been repealed by s. 2 and s. 6 of the Constitution (Forty-fourth Amendment) Act 1978, with effect from the 20th June 1979.

In other words, the right to property ceased to be a fundamental right and became only a legal right. Thus, Art. 19 had been amended and Art. 31 deleted. However, the new provision does not affect the right of minorities to establish and administer educational institutions of their choice. Similarly, the right of persons holding land for personal cultivation and within the ceiling to receive compensation at the market price has been ensured. Property has, accordingly, been given express recognition by Art. 300A in the Constitution as a legal right in that no person will be deprived of his or her property save in accordance with the law. Remedy against any violation of this legal right may be obtained under Art. 226 of the Constitution or by a civil suit but not under Art. 32 of the Constitution.

A short history of conveyancing in England. Conveyance means the action of conveying. John Austin in his lectures on jurisprudence said that it is by no means easy to define "ownership of property". Ownership of property which can be acquired by contract, inheritance and prescription is a right *in rem* against the whole world (*jus-ad-rem*) over a determinate thing but indefinite in point of user, unrestricted in point of disposition and unlimited in point of duration (Austin's *Jurisprudence,* p. 835). The word "property" owes its origin to the French word *propre* which means "one's own" and in its fullest significance signifies four distinct groups of rights, *viz.*, of—

(*i*) enjoyment;
(*ii*) destruction;
(*iii*) alienation; and
(*iv*) possession.

The expression "conveyancing" is of English origin. It means land transfer *inter vivos*. Section 205 of the Law of Property Act 1925, defines "conveyance also as including mortgage, charge, lease, assent and release, also any other document of transfer relating to property except will". Section 2(10) of the

13 *Indu Bhusan v Moazam Ali* AIR 1929 Cal 272.

Indian Stamp Act (Act 11 of 1899) defines it as including a sale and every instrument by which property whether movable or immovable, is transferred. Conveyance is a transfer within the meaning of s. 5 of the Transfer of Property Act 1882. But a transfer does not import always any species of contract by which all real rights in a property are passed from one living person to another.[14] English law, recognised property but not the absolute ownership of land.[15] In most ancient times in England, a corporeal hereditament, which means land in actual possession, was transferred by the method popularly known as *"Feoffment"* and *"livery of seisin"*. *"Feoffment"* could be made orally or in writing. All that was necessary, were appropriate words to denote the quality of the estate intended to be transferred which was followed by the ceremony, *i.e.* physical delivery of possession. This was known as Common Law Conveyance, whereas an incorporeal hereditament, which was a bundle of rights in land short of possession, *e.g.* right of way, right of pasture of cattle on another's land and other easement rights as then understood, meant the gift of a "fee" by use of appropriate expression and *"livery of seisin"*—the delivery of freehold to a tenant to be held by him according to feudal system. Although the transfer of an incorporeal hereditament was made by grant, such a grant in early days could be effected orally or in writing, which was done only in matters of importance to add solemnity to the transaction because of the seal to be affixed: Conveyances were required to be public and formal.[16]

Although originally a *feoffment* was always understood to mean not only seisin to feoffee (transferee) but nevertheless, with the development of Chancellor's jurisdiction and invention of equitable estate by the origin of the word "use" and in particular after the "Statute of Uses"[17] came in force, the expression "unto and to the use of" was considered necessary to indicate transfer of equitable estates as well. The *feoffment* mode of conveyance was followed by a new method known as "Lease and Release" which became popular by reason of the secrecy of the transfer it involved and this continued up to the year 1841, which was the year of origin of Modern Conveyance. Thus, when the transferor released his remaining interest in the property, the transferee became a tenant in fee simple. Thus, down to the time of King Henry VIII, nothing more was required to effect a valid *feoffment*. The Parliament then passed an Act in 1935 known as the "Statute of Uses"[17]

14 *Narandas* v *Parsoram* 4 BLR 500; *Ramkinkor* v *Satya Charan* (1939)43 CWN 281.

15 William's *Real Property*, 20th Ed., p. 7—Grantees regarded as holding the property of the king on obligation of fidelity and service to him (p. 13). See also Topham's *Real Property*, 11th Ed., p. 2.

16 Cheshire's *Modern Law of Real Property,* 12th Ed., p. 42.

17 State 27 Hen VIII C 10.

which required a consideration for the gift or gifts to be made unto and to the use of the feoffee and enacted further that where the land is held by one person for the use of another, the legal title was in that other.

Even then the use of writing remained optional until the time of King Charles II particularly in cases which did not require any deed under seal.[18] Writing was only employed in matters of very great importance, more so because the presence of a Charter, which required the seal of the executant, added solemnity to the transaction.

Deed poll. Thus, two types of deeds, *viz.* "Deed Poll" and "Indenture", mainly came gradually into use in England. Deed Polls are those made by and expressing the active intention of one party, they are drawn in first person and in which there is usually one party only and are so called because at times they were polled or cut levelled. It is a muniment of title of an executed contract conveying a property, Power of Attorney, declaration, disclaimer of title, declaration of trust, deed of adoption, will etc., are examples of deed polls.

Indentures. Indentures are documents having more than one and at least two parties. They were so called in ancient times because they, though engrossed on the same parchment, were indented or cut at the top with uneven edges so as, to fit or join with its counterpart. The idea was to safeguard against fraudulent substitution of different writings, but the practice has ceased long ago. Mortgages, conveyances, leases, etc., are all still called indentures. They all come under the definition of "conveyance" which, as defined in s. 205(1)(*ii*) of the Law of Property Act 1925, includes mortgage, charge, lease, assent, vesting declaration, disclaimer, release and every kind of assurance. An indenture is a conveyance of title.

Grant. A third type of deed was "Grant" which, though originally signified transfer of incorporeal rights, became gradually a synonym of conveyance. It was during the reign of King Charles II that the Parliament enacted, in 1677, a legislation to prevent fraud and perjuries commonly called the "Statute of Frauds",[19] which required writing for creation and transfer of landed interests and also for contracts for sale of land, the only exception being in case of lease for less than three years where the landlord kept reserved for himself a rent of at least two-third of the full improved value.[20] Thus common law conveyance was replaced by statutory conveyance and a single release was considered a sufficient conveyance of land, thus dispensing with the former lease.

Delivery—meaning of. A deed is very different from contract. On a contract for sale of land the contract is not binding on the parties until they have

18 William's *Real Property*, 20th Ed., p. 153.
19 29 Char 11 C 3.
20 William's *Real Property*, 20th Ed., p. 153.

exchanged their parts. But with a deed it is different. A deed is binding on the maker of it, even though the parts have not been exchanged as long as it has been signed, sealed and delivered. "Delivery" in this connection does not mean "handed over" to the otherside. It means delivered in the old legal sense, namely an act done so as to evince an intention to be bound. Even though the deed remains in the possession of the maker, or his solicitor, he is bound by it if he has done some act evincing an intention to be bound as by saying. I deliver this by act and deed. He may, however, make the "delivery" conditional: in which case the deed is called an "escrow" which becomes binding when the condition is fulfilled.[1]

This type of document called "escrow" was a simple writing not effective until certain conditions shall have been performed and not immediately.[2]

The Real Property Act 1845,[3] required all grants of landed interests to be effected by writing which thus became known as "conveyance".[4] Then followed the Law of Property Act 1922,[5] which, as amended in 1925, repealed the Statute of Frauds[6] and made it compulsory for all deeds to be signed and sealed. Under s. 52(1) of the Law of Property Act 1925, all transfers of land or of any interest are void unless made by deed.

The Conveyance of Land Act 1854 of England[6] is regarded as the authority on the form and the several clauses which are incorporated in the present form of conveyance, *i.e.* covenant as to good title, non-encumbrances, peaceful possession, further assurance and indemnity clause (vide s. 55 of T.P. Act 1882, in India). The Law of Property Act 1925, is the authority on the present form of conveyance. Under s. 44(1) of the Law of Property Act 1925, the statutory period for a good root of title, which was 40 years under s. 1 of the Vendor and Purchaser Act 1874, was reduced to 30 years and now it reduced to 15 years.[7] In India there is no such law. Although Art. 65 of the Limitation Act 1963, prescribes a period of 12 years as the period of limitation for suit for possession of immovable property nevertheless such a title cannot be certified as marketable title in the absence of other evidence.

1 *Vincent* v *Premo Enterprises* (1969)2 QB 609; (1969)2 All ER 941 *per* LORD DENNING MR.
2 Halsbury's *Laws of England*, 3rd Ed., vol. 2, p. 318.
3 Stat 8 & 9 Vic. C 106 S. 2.
4 A.C. Dutt on *Real Property*, 4th Ed., p. 165.
5 12 & 13 Geo V C 16.
6 Stat 44 & 45 Vic. C 41.
7 A.C. Dutt on *Real Property*, 4th Ed., p. 332; Cheshire's *Modern Law of Real Property*, 12th Ed., p. 732.

Land systems in ancient England. In conveyancing, the lawyers are most familiar with the word "fee simple". It had its origin in England and it means "absolute ownership" and being granted to a man and his heirs. So it never passed to the Crown for want of heirs. The word "fee" denotes "inheritability" and the word "simple" connotes that it passes to the general body of heirs no matter whether they are ascendants, descendants or collaterals. It is equivalent to free-hold tenure. It was originally the only type of real property known to English law until the decline of the feudal system. Though the largest interest in land yet having been created by the use of the words "and his heirs" it was considered not alienable without their consent. This restraint began to fall off gradually with the growth and development of constitutional Government and a time soon came when the words were construed as words of limitation, *i.e.* words which mark the estate to be taken by the grantee and not words of gift conferring any interest upon the heirs. This is the Rule in *Shelly's* case.[8] This is a Rule of Law and not of interpretation. Although the largest estate, *viz.* "the fee simple" was nevertheless subject to certain limitations and restrictions both under the common law as also under the statute on the rights of the owner, *e.g.* that he had no right to misuse the land to the prejudice of others, and had to obtain permission from appropriate authorities for its development. Moreover, his rights were subject to the right of support as against the neighbouring property and, lastly, the easement rights of the adjacent owners.[9] The other types of tenures, which lawyers often come across, are "copy hold" or as it was sometimes called in the past the "villein tenure" traced back up to Anglo-Saxon days and "leasehold". The former was an estate at the will and pleasure of the feudal lords who used to retain a portion of their military tenures granted by the king and made over the surplus to villagers in return for services who cultivated these lands on joint field system of husbandry subject to conditions fixed by customs, having no title deeds; the only muniment of the title being a copy of the roll or book in which account was kept by the court held by the lords. All 'copy hold' lands have been converted into freehold lands with effect from 1st February 1926 (ss. 128, 136 and s. 189 of the Law of Property Act 1925). A leasehold estate, although considered as heritable for the purpose of descent, was nevertheless regarded as a "Chattel real" and was never recognised as a real property as a tenant for years was 'possessed' and not seized and if dispossessed he could originally bring a personal action for recovery of damages.[10] The English Common Law thus recognised three types of estates, *viz.* estate in fee simple, estate in fee tail and estate for life. The first type of estate represented complete ownership. The second was

8 *Shelly's* case 1 Rep 24; William's *Real Property*, 20th Ed., pp. 336-338.
9 Glasgow: *Modern View of Conveyancing*, pp. 12-13.
10 Pollock & Maitland's *History of English Law*, vol. 11, p. 113.

more or less of a limited character. So it was an estate limited to the heirs of the grantor. It descended in the chain of the lineal descendants of the grantee failing which it used to revert to the original grantor or his heirs. A life estate is a mere right of enjoyment, so it is not heritable. A tenant by courtesy as cited in *Eager* v *Furnivall,*[11] whereby the husband of a lady seized in fee simple of an estate and having children by her was allowed to hold the same after her death was abolished by the Administration of Estate Act 1925.

Ownership of land and soil—Indian scenario. The English theory of Crown ownership of land was not applicable to India. A field, says Manu,[12] is his who clears the jungle. This is not, however, corroborated by epigraphic evidences. A subject could acquire proprietorship in the soil and the King had the right only to a share of the produce by way of tax by reason of protection afforded to the subjects. The Hindu theory of ownership of soil was upheld in *Secretary of State* v *Vira Rayan.*[13] It was observed that under the Hindu common law the first person making beneficial use of the soil acquires the right of ownership subject however to the right of the Crown as to a share of the crops. Yajnavalka says of three stages in the land economy of ancient India, *viz.* Mahapati (King), Kshetra Swami (landowner) and Krishak (cultivator). Partial feudalism was not completely unknown particularly during the Gupta Period as the Gupta Kings, in particular Samudra Gupta, was famous for having settled large areas of land with temples and Brahmins in return for religious and spiritual services. A major portion, however, remained with the free peasants who paid revenue to the King.[14] This was the Hindu idea of the ownership in land.[15] Another theory was that the ownership of land was collective, royal, individual and based upon early land settlements. The Mahomedans also recognised the right of the subject in the soil and what the rulers imposed was called *Mal*. According to Abu Hanifa the right of a sovereign even in conquered countries was limited to a tribute from the land. So the Mahomedan Rulers had to purchase lands from the cultivators when they required for their own purposes. Akbar purchased lands for construction of his forts.[16] The village communities of ancient India were organised patriarchal societies and an assemblage of co-proprietors. Though their property was blended, nevertheless, their rights were distinct, separate and continuous indefinitely.[17] They did not do away with the fiscal system

11 (1881)17 Ch D 115 at p. 120.
12 Chapter IX, v. 44.
13 9 Mad 175 at p. 179.
14 Ram Sharan Sharma: *Light on Early India Society and Economy*, pp. 78-115.
15 *Secretary of State* v *Vira Rayan* 9 Mad 175 (179).
16 Field: *Landholdings*, p. 741.
17 Maine: *Ancient Law*, p. 216.

based on old Brahminical ideas. It will not be out of place to say here a few lines about ownership of waste land and forests.[18] In the Privy Council the State was recognised as the owner of waste lands. This conception is correct so far as lands in ryotwari villages are concerned but in zamindary villages waste lands were conveyed to zamindars under the permanent settlement. The case of forests is the same. The British Administration introduced Permanent Settlement in India based on feudal doctrine of English land laws, that the soil was the property of the sovereign and they could confer upon and vest their interest upon the landlords of their creation. When the Permanent Settlement was gone, the State became the owner of all lands. The Estate Acquisition Acts have completely wiped away the feudal pattern of land tenure by abolishing all intermediaries in all the States. A raiyat, however, became the owner of his holding with heritable and transferable right under s. 4 of the West Bengal Land Reforms Act 1955. The intermediary system of landowning people has been abolished also in other States. Under s. 5 of the Bihar Land Reforms Act 1948, all homestead land of proprietors and tenure holders are held by the proprietors as rent-free under the State, other lands in *khas* possession as raiyats with rights of occupation. The Madras Estate (Abolition and Conversion in Ryotwari) Act 1948 (Madras Act XXVI of 1948), confers the status of a raiyat on every ryot and declares them each as entitled to a *pattah*. Although the feudal doctrine about the ownership of land was not applied in India, nevertheless the idea was not foreign to this country. The ghatwali tenures were created by the Muslim rulers which prevailed in Santhal Parganas, Birbhum and other places to ensure police and military services against invasion of mountain passes by lawless tribes, at low rent or no rent and also by the zamindars.[19] Chowkidari Chakran lands of the united Bengal were lands assigned to people to provide for police and military service. The jaigir grants to military officers and their subordinates in U.P. and Rajasthan were originally life grants but became gradually estates of inheritance in the latter part of the Mahomedan Rule. These lands were generally inalienable.[20] But with the progress of time, they lost their character for the reasons *inter alia* abolition of military service and/or computation in money. The State, however, was regarded as the owner of all waste lands except in zamindari villages which prevailed chiefly in Bengal, Bihar and Orissa.

Through the provisions of the Land Acquisition Act 1894 which is of an exceptional character Government has the power to take any land in any area for a public purpose and this exercise of the State's power of eminent

18 *Collector of Muslepatam* v *Covoly* 8 MIA 500 at p. 525.
19 *Thakur Rudheshwari Prasad* v *Rani Probhati* 1952 SCR 64; AIR 1952 SC 1.
20 Sir Jadunath Sarkar's *Ain-i-Akbori,* vol. 11, p. 63.

domain does not offend the right to livelihood etc. guaranteed by Art. 21 or Art. 300A of the Constitution.[21]

According to ryotwari village system which, though not exclusively but chiefly prevailed in the Madras presidency, the revenue settlement was made with the actual cultivators of the soil who were thus regarded as its owners.

Concept of absolute ownership. It was observed by the Calcutta High Court[1] that the concept of absolute ownership is out of date. The concept has changed from pre-feudal and feudal societies to industrial and post-industrial societies. An extended meaning of ownership appears from s. 2(62) of the Calcutta Municipal Corporation Act 1980 where it has been defined as to include the person for the time being receiving the rent of any land or building or of any part of any land or building, whether on his own account or as agent or trustee for any person or society or for any religious or charitable purpose or as a receiver who would receive such rent if the land or any part of the land or building were let to a tenant. Exactly similar is the definition of 'owner' appearing in s. 2(45) of the West Bengal Municipal Act 1993. A property may be subject to conditions and/or limitations, but it does not detract from the ownership on that ground. A lessee for 30 years or more is deemed to be the owner as defined in s. 3(*ia*) of the W.B. Apartment Ownership Act 1972. Section 3A of the said Act further contemplates double ownership in cases where any cooperative society is the owner of the building and members of such society are also owners of the apartments.

Conveyancing in India. In India conveyancing cannot be claimed to have reached that standard of efficiency and compactness needed to meet the challenges of the time, as legal education is still confined mostly to the study of substantive law and personal law governing Hindus, Muslims and others. There is a class of people known as DEED WRITERS in the *muffasil* who hold themselves out as conveyancing experts. There was no statutory law on the subject before the T.P. Act of 1882 came into force. The Act itself is not even now exhaustive and so is not a complete Code, as the preamble says "To amend certain parts of law relating to transfer of property by the act of parties". The Contract Act, Registration Act, West Bengal Apartments (Regulation of Construction and Transfer) Act 1972, Indian Trusts Act, Land Reforms Act, etc., contain provisions as to transfer of the property. Further s. 9 of the Act reads as follows: "A transfer of property may be made without writing in every case in which a writing is not expressly required by law". So in cases not covered by the Act, the courts in India are guided by the Contract

21 *New Reviera* v *Special LAO* (1996)1 SCC 731.
1 *Saha Institute of Nuclear Physics Co-operative Housing Society Ltd.* v *Corporation of Calcutta* AIR 1977 NOC 362 (Cal).

Act, Registration Act, etc., and also by the rules of justice, equity and good conscience in so far as they are not inconsistent with the Acts.[2] The said Act does not extend to whole of India. The Exemption Rule of Mahomedan law is still outside the purview of its operation [vide s. 2(*d*) of the Transfer of Property Act] but it refers to such rules as differ from the general rules contemplated in Chapter II of the Act. There is no statutory period up to which the intending purchaser shall make necessary searches and particularly in the muffasil, searches are very seldom carried on beyond 12 years. This is the usual search unless there are reasons for searches for longer period.[3] Title deeds are more often lost or misplaced not having been kept with the solicitor or the banker. The practice of *benami* transaction, the joint and undivided Hindu family system and the tenancy-in-common among the Mahomedan heirs, the right of pre-emption followed among the people in different areas are among other several causes which make investigation of title all the more a difficult job. The Transfer of Property Act, as it stood before the amending Act 20 of 1929, also saved Hindu law and Buddhist law. The word "Hindu" has been omitted by the amendment of 1929 as the difference between the Law and the Act has been abolished. So was the word "Buddhist". In the result Chapter II of the Act now applies to Hindu as also to Buddhists since 1929. Nevertheless the solicitors who do the conveyancing work in Presidency towns follow English precedents.

In India the Sanskrit literature recognised several types of documents, *e.g.* partition, gift, purchase, agreement, bond, etc.[4] Ancient documents like "Patni Taluq Grant" of Bengal were of the nature of a permanent managing lease for a fixed rental value and the sub-infeudations created, *e.g. "dar patindar"*, *"shidarpatnidar"*, *"pattahs"* granted by the Emperors, Nawabs, Collectors, "Charpatra" (redemption of rent), jaigir grants, Kabuliyats, etc., were all of the nature of deed polls on parchment expressing active intention of and the seal of the grantor. So it can be inferred that interest in land was created and also transferred in writing. Nevertheless, it was held so far back as in 1876 that no writing was necessary under the Hindu law as to the validity of any transfer, as it was transfer of possession which was essential.[5] The land system in India was really a complex one; it consisted of several other types of tenures, *viz*. Jagir, Ayma, Altamga, Chatwali, Brahmattar Lakhraj, Pirattar, Mahatran etc.

Although at present, the sale, exchange and mortgage of value above Rs. 100, except mortgage by deposit of title deeds, in Presidency towns

2 *Maharaja of Joypore* v *Rukmini* (1919)42 Mad 589 (598); 46 IA 109; 50 IC 631.

3 *Mazahar* v *Mukhtar* AIR 1938 All 64.

4 *Ebrahim* v *Fulbai* 26 Bom 577.

5 *Hurprashad* v *Sheo Dyal* (1876)26 WR 55; 3 IA 259 (278).

lease exceeding one year or reserving an annual rent and gifts and transfer of actionable claims and also transfers under special enactment (*vide* s. 5 of the West Bengal Land Reforms Act 1955), partition of agricultural holding under s. 14 of the said Act are all made by writings, nevertheless a partition of the joint family properties can by conduct of the parties and mutual agreement be effected orally.[6] A partition is not a transfer.[7] It is called partition by conduct of the parties. Parties enter into separate possession of their respective allotments, enjoy the same in severalty and have their respective names recorded in the books of the Municipality and Collectorate. If however any partition is effected with some fraudulent design or *mala fide* motive, *e.g.* with intent to delay or defeat creditors it is in that event a transfer under s. 53 of the Transfer of Property Act and may be impeached.[8] An endowment in favour of any deity or temple can be created by clear and unambiguous declaration of the settlor by his intention to dedicate followed by renunciation of ownership; such dedication whether to any idol or temple is not treated as a transfer to any living person but a gift to God and can be made even without any writing or registration.[9] The provisions of Transfer of Property Act are not strictly applicable in the case of Hindu endowment. A wakf *inter vivos* is also completed by dedication and delivery of possession unless it is a family settlement.[10] No writing is, therefore, necessary to create any Hindu endowment, in case of clear intention, (1927)54 IA 136. These are some transfers where no writing is necessary. A surrender is quite distinct from merger or abandonment.[11] Indian Trusts Act 1882 does not apply to endowments (*vide* s. 1).

The amending Act (20 of 1929) deleted the words "Hindu" and "Buddhist" from s. 2 of the T.P. Act 1882, and thus made writing compulsory in case of transfer of land of the value of Rs. 100 and upwards.

In Mahomedan law, a sale could be completely effected by mutual delivery of the property and payment of consideration but the principles of the Mahomedan law applicable to sales have been practically abrogated by the Contract Act and the Transfer of Property Act.[12] A gift may be made orally or in writing. This portion of the Mahomedan law is untouched by s. 123 of the

6 *Satya Kumar* v *Satya Kripal* (1909)10 CLJP 503.
7 AIR 1965 SC 866; AIR 1966 SC 432.
8 *Waman Ramkrishna* v *Ganapat* AIR 1936 Bom 10; see also ILR (1944) Nag 342; AIR 1934 Nag 44 (FB).
9 *Ramlingha* v *Sivachidambera* 42 Mad 440 (443).
10 Mulla's *Mahomedan Law*, 19th Ed., p. 153.
11 *Daip Sing* v *Kishno* ILR (1968)1 Punj 755.
12 Syed Ameer Ali's *Mahomedan Law*, 2nd Ed., p. 115.

Transfer of Property Act. So is the case of wakf. According to Abu Yusuf, a wakf *inter vivos* is completed by declaration of endowment by the owner and this view was accepted by the High Courts at Calcutta,[13] Patna,[14] and Madras,[15] nevertheless the Privy Council[16] held that inasmuch as it operates as extinction of the rights of the owner, any wakfnama involving property of the value of Rs. 100 or upwards requires registration under s. 17(1) of the Registration Act. A Hiba-bil-iwaz of a property of the value of Rs. 100 and upwards can be effected by a registered deed.

Suggestion. All endowments and wakfs be made in writing and registered like other transfer of property.

Capacity to convey. Section 7 of the Transfer of Property Act is to be read with s. 11 of the Indian Contract Act 1872. This is dependent on the capacity of the person(s) to enter into contracts to convey any property. Infants and lunatics are therefore, as a rule, incapable of selling their property. So are disqualified proprietors.

A person, who left India for Pakistan after partition in 1946 and has not returned since then becomes a Pakistani National whose property in India vests in the Custodian of Enemy Property under the Enemy Property Act read with the Defence of India Rules, has no right to convey the same.[17]

Aliens under the common law could not hold freehold lands in England nor fill any public office nor possess civil rights. Now they are not subject to any of those disabilities.[18] In India, they are competent to buy or sell property so long as they are not enemies. It was held by the Privy Council as early as 1836[19] that the English common law incapacitating aliens from holding any real property never applied in India. It is however significant to mention here the effect of s. 31(1) of Foreign Exchange Regulation Act (Act 46 of 1973). No person who is not a citizen of India and no company other than a banking company which is not incorporated under any law in force in India shall, except with the previous general or special permission of the Reserve Bank, acquire or hold or transfer or dispose of by sale, mortgage, lease, gift, settlement or otherwise an immovable property situate in India.

The Foreign Exchange Regulation Act 1973 has since been replaced by the Foreign Exchange Management Act 1999 (Act 42 of 1999). It received

13 *Jinjira* v *Mohammed* (1922)49 Cal 477.
14 *Mohd. Ibrahim* v *Bibi Mariam* (1929)8 Pat 148.
15 *Pathu Kutti Umma* v *Nedungadi Bank Ltd*. (1938) Mad 148.
16 *Muhammed Rustam Ali* v *Mushtaq Hussain* (1920)47 IA 224; 57 IC 329.
17 *Abdul Rauf* v *Janab Ali* 82 CWN 5.
18 *R.* v *Arnad* (1946)19 QB 806.
19 *Mayer of Lyons* v *East India Co.* 1 Moor Ind App 175.

the assent of the President on 29th December 1999 and came into effect on and from 1st June 2000. The changes made therein may be carefully noted.

In England, a person attains the age of majority when he completes the age of 21 years. In India, under s. 3 of the Indian Majority Act, the age of majority is 18 years except in the case where the minor was under the protection of the Court of Wards or Encumbered Estate Act (both of which have been now dead letters) or where he has a statutory guardian appointed by the court in which event his minority continues until he completes the age of 21 years. It was held by the Privy Council in *Mohori Bibi* v *Dharmadas*[20] that a contract by a minor is void and incapable of being validated by ratification and further there is no estoppel as against the minor. On this principle a lease to a minor was held[21] void. A lease by a minor is also void as under s. 107 of the Transfer of Property Act as it stands after the amendment of 1929. It must be executed by both the parties. Nevertheless, a minor may be a purchaser[22] or mortgagee.[1] No guardian can, however, bind a minor by a contract for purchase of any immovable property.[2] The powers and authorities of the natural guardian of a minor are now clearly defined under s. 8 of the Hindu Minority and Guardianship Act 1956. So a natural guardian can no longer create any mortgage charge nor transfer by sale, gift, exchange or otherwise nor create any lease beyond one year after the date of attainment of majority or for term exceeding five years without the order of the court to that effect first had and obtained. The rule does not apply to the undivided share of the minor in the Mitakshara coparcenery property (s. 12 of the said Act). *De facto* guardians have no power under any circumstances (s. 11). In England, the property of a lunatic can be dealt with by his statutory agent, a committee of his estate or receiver of the income appointed under the Lunacy Act 1890, but an infant cannot be transferee of a legal estate in land (s. 16 of the Law of Property Act 1925). In India, the law on lunacy was almost identical under the Indian Lunacy Act (IV of 1912). The Act of 1912 has since been repealed by the Mental Health Act 1987. Sections 50 to 74 of the 1987 Act make elaborate provisions for appointment of guardian or manager of the mentally ill person and of his properties and the management thereof. The manager has been given the power to execute conveyances on behalf of the mentally ill person only under orders of the District Court. The Official Assignee in the Presidency towns and the Receiver in the Muffasil have, by virtue of s. 68 and s. 19 of the Presidency Insolvency Act and s. 59 of the Provincial Insolvency Act

20 (1903)30 Cal 539 (PC); 30 IA 114.
21 *Pramila Bala Das* v *Jogeswar* (1918)3 Pat LJ 518.
22 *Ulfat Rai* v *Gourisankar* (1911)33 All 657.
1 *Raghava* v *Srinivasa* (1917)40 Mad 308.
2 *Mir Sarwarjan* v *Fakhruddin* (1911)39 IA 1; 30 Cal 232.

have power to deal in the property of an insolvent. Among the Mahomedans the following persons only are entitled to be guardians of the property of the minor: (*i*) father; (*ii*) executor appointed by the father's will; (*iii*) father's father; (*iv*) executor appointed by the will of father's father.[3] A *de facto* guardian has no power to sell any property belonging to the minor. The authority of the legal guardian is also most restricted. He can sell if such sale fetches its double value or in the event such sale is necessary for payment of the debts and/or legacies there being no other resources in cases where the costs charges and expenses of management exceed the income or where the property is falling into decay or has been usurped. A mutawalli has no power to sell, mortgage or otherwise deal in wakf property unless expressly authorized by the deed or by an order of the court or competent authority.[4] In England, the property of a lunatic can be dealt by his statutory guardian as any property is vested him and he is recognized as persons juristic capable of transferring and accepting transfer of property[5] but not to involve into any covenant. The transfers of a debutter property can be effected by the *shebaits* who are actually managing and administering the property of the deity and for good reasons and in the interest and for the benefit of the deity. This question was raised before the Judicial Committee in *Hanuman Persaud* v *Massamat Babooee*.[6] It was held that a *shebait* or a *mohunt* has no power to alienate the debutter property except in cases of legal necessity but he cannot convert any immovable property into cash investment even for better return by way of interest or dividend. The original concept of shebaitship as a mere right to manage the property has now been changed. It was held by a Full Bench of Calcutta High Court in *Monohar* v *Bhupendra*[7] that shebaitship is not merely office but also property and therefore can be a subject-matter of bequest, *shebaiti* rights can be transferred by custom, or renouncement but not by sale.

An executor, though the statutory owner of the property, has no beneficial interest in the estate. He can, however, sell any property in due course of administration (s. 307 of the Indian Succession Act 1925) in the absence of any restriction in the will. A Receiver does not acquire any proprietary right or title in the property over which he has been appointed as such. The Official Assignee as in the case of insolvency is similarly placed. The title remains vested in the person lawfully entitled to the estate.[8] He cannot sell any property unless authorized by the court (vide Or. 41, r. 1 of CPC) and execute the conveyance on behalf of the defaulting party or parties and he is

3 Mulla's *Mahomedan Law*, 19th Ed., pp. 292-293.
4 Section 51 of the Wakf Act 1995.
5 *Pramathanath* v *Pradhyamma* 67 IC 309.
6 (1856)6 MIA 393.
7 60 Cal 432.
8 *Ram Lachun* v *Hogg* 10 WR 930.

devoid of any estate or interest in the property himself. Although the Receiver sells the property under order of the court, nevertheless it is not a sale by the court but it binds and operates upon the estate of the persons who are parties to the order. No sale certificate is granted and no confirmation by the court is necessary.[9] The Receiver executes a conveyance along with the parties.

A firm cannot transfer any property unless the act is done by all the partners [s. 19(2)(*g*) of the Partnership Act] and further the same must be in the firm's name and with intent to bind the firm (s. 22).

Before the Constitution of India came into force all executive authority was exercised by the Governor-General in Council (s. 7 of the Government of India Act), while that of the province by the Governor (s. 49 of the said Act). All transfers were made and contracts were signed by persons so authorized and for and on their behalf. After the enforcement of the Constitution, all transfers and contracts in respect of properties vested in the Union of India are executed in the name of the President, while those vested in the State in the name of the Governor [Art. 299(1) of the Constitution of India]. The Board of Directors of a public company or a private company which is subsidiary to a public company cannot, under s. 293 of the Companies Act 1956, sell, mortgage, lease or otherwise dispose of the whole or a substantial portion of the undertaking of the company without a resolution of the share-holders passed in a general meeting. When any partnership assets stands in the name of a partner, he is a mere trustee and has no beneficial interest until dissolution of the firm and the account is taken. He cannot make any beneficial use thereof by its sale.[10]

The Hindu Succession Act 1956 which came into force on 17th June 1956 has improved the status of the Hindu female and her capacity to deal with the property. It was held by the Supreme Court[11] that unless the property is given for the first time without recognition of any pre-existing right she will have an absolute estate. It was held by the Bombay High Court[12] that "where the female Hindu was in possession of the joint family property after her husband's death in exercise of the powers of lien as to provisions to be made for her maintenance she was in possession of the property within the meaning of s. 14. It is not necessary that the possession by the female must be as that of an owner or as a limited owner. She would be the absolute owner under s. 14 of the said Act". A female Hindu possessed of

9 *Golam* v *Fatima* 16 CWN 394.
10 In re, *Adharji Mancharji* 55 Bom 795; 133 IC 845.
11 *Vaddeboyina* v *Vaddboyina* AIR 1977 SC 1944.
12 *Limba* v *Manikrao* AIR 1978 Bom 83.

the property on the date the Act came into force could become absolute owner only if she was a limited owner.[13]

Transfer by limited owners (vide s. 38 of the Transfer of Property Act). This section embodies the principle laid down in *Hanuman Persaud* v *Mst. Babooee.*[14] Such a transfer is valid if for adequate consideration and the purchaser after proper enquiry is satisfied as to *bona fide* existence of the legal necessities and/or justifying circumstances behind the sale.[15] This section is applicable in judging transfers by natural guardians of minors, widows, managers of a Hindu joint family, father or karta of a Mitakshara joint family.

The karta of Mitakshara joint family has power to sell the joint family property for legal necessities and justifying circumstances.[16] As regards other coparceners they can sell their share in Bombay, Madras and Madhya Pradesh but in other places with the consent of the other coparceners.

In case of alienation by a Hindu, prior to the 1956 Act, without legal necessity the reversioners were not bound to institute a declaratory suit during the lifetime of the widow. They could wait till her death and then sue the alienee for possession of the alienated property treating the alienation as a nullity. The alienee could not acquire any right by adverse possession against the reversioner during the lifetime of the widow.[17]

Transfer of family dwelling-house and its effect on right of residence.[18] The position on and rights of a widow, daughter, predeceased son's wife and certain other female heirs of a Hindu have been materially changed by the Hindu Succession Act 1956, and the question of the right of residence of such persons must now be considered in the context of the provisions of that Act. Section 23 of that Act lays down a special provision respecting the family dwelling-house.

Widow of undivided coparcener. (*a*) Where an undivided family consists of two or more males related as father and son or otherwise, and one of them dies leaving a widow, she is entitled to reside in the family dwelling-house in which she lived with her husband. (*b*) If the house is sold by the surviving coparcener or coparceners without necessity, the sale does not affect her right, and the purchaser cannot evict her, in any event until another suitable residence is found for her. (*c*) If the purchaser buys the house with full

13 *Kalawatibai* v *Soiryabai* AIR 1991 SC 1581.
14 6 MIA 393.
15 *Bhagwat* v *Debi Dayal* 35 Cal 420 (PC).
16 Mulla's *Hindu Law,* 17th Ed., p. 379.
17 *Radha Rani* v *Hanuman* AIR 1966 SC 216; *Kalawatibai* v *Soiryabai* AIR 1991 SC 1581.
18 Mulla's *Hindu Law,* 17th Ed., p. 787.

knowledge that the widow is residing and is being maintained in it, the purchaser is not entitled to oust her even though there may be other property belonging to the family out of which her maintenance can be derived. (*d*) But if the sale is for a family necessity, she is liable to be evicted even though the purchaser had notice at the time of purchase that she was in occupation of the house. (*e*) Similarly the right of residence cannot prevail against the husband's debts.

Government Grants Act 1895. The effect is to exclude operation of not merely the Transfer of Property Act. Such grant can be resumed without interference by the court under Art. 226 of the Constitution of India.[19] But no condition can validly be annexed to a grant which will have the effect of creating an estate unknown to law.[20] Where no restrictions are imposed in the grant itself, the transfer made in favour of a third person by the lessee cannot be ineffective and invalid in law.[1]

Cantonment tenure—nature. The Secretary of States (now the Union of India) is the absolute owner of all Cantonment lands (*vide* the Cantonment Act 1924). Unless he has parted with the ownership, there cannot be any adverse possession.[2] A person occupying land in Cantonments not specifically transferred to him can only hold it as a licensee from him, who could eject him at will by revoking his licence.[3] The mere fact that certain lands are declared by the Government to be within a Cantonment area does not vest their ownership in the Government unless it is shown that the lands were acquired by the Government for that purpose.[4] All lands within the Cantonment area do not necessarily belong to the Government. It is not the necessary implication of the second paragraph of cl. (6) of Bengal Cantonment Regulations though the rules suggest that the greater part of the land was at that time the Government property.[5]

Where subsequent to the establishment of a Cantonment the ownership of the land within it becomes vested in the Secretary of State (now the Union of India) and the prior owners of the land were compensated for the loss of such rights as they may have actually suffered, it is a fair presumption that the amount of compensation would vary according to whether the prior owners were deprived wholly of ownership and possession or whether they

19 *State of West Bengal* v *Birendranath Basunia* AIR 1955 Cal 601.
20 AIR 1945 PC 156; AIR 1948 PC 33.
1 (1994)1 Cal HN 15; AIR 1984 Del 224; (1992)2 CLJ 260; AIR 1988 Del 184.
2 *Ghatwala* v *Secretary of State* 12 IC 117; 15 CWN 909; 38 IA 204 (PC).
3 66 IC 582.
4 31 CWN 1033.
5 57 IA 339; 58 IC 854; 60 MLJ 142 (PC).

were deprived only of the ownership and allowed to remain in possession as licensee without payment of any rent.[6]

Disqualified transferee. A Judge, legal practitioner or others connected with the court are disqualified from purchasing any actionable claim (s. 136, Transfer of Property Act).

Unborn person. A transfer in favour of an unborn person is completely void in Mahomedan law.[7] The rule has been modified by statute, e.g. ss. 13 and 14 of the Transfer of Property Act which require that the transfer shall extend to the entirety of the entire remaining interest of the transferor in the subject-matter of transfer and further the same shall be operative not beyond the life or lives in existence on the date thereof and the minority of an unborn person who must be born in their life time. This is known as the rule against perpetuity and is also applicable to Mahomedans.[8]

Fiduciary relationship between the parties. Such relationship arises when one party is in a position of active confidence so as to dominate the will of another, e.g. guardian and ward, trustee and beneficiary, doctor and patient, preceptor and disciple and others. The court watches zealously all transactions between them and calls upon the party in position of active confidence to discharge the onus of good faith. Draftsmen entrusted with preparation of conveyances will take special care to avoid the facing such comments. In view of s. 88 of the Trust Act when a trustee, executor, partner, director, legal adviser or any other person standing in fiduciary capacity enters into any dealings and thereby gains any pecuniary benefit the transaction is highly suspected. The case of wife is the solitary exception.[9] Undue influence is presumed in the case of a sale by the client to his solicitor.[10]

The law in India as to undue influence is also contained in s. 16 of the Indian Contract Act. It is based upon English Common Law as observed by the Supreme Court in the case of *Ladli Prosad Joiway* v *Kernal Distillery Co. Ltd*.[11] It was held that the presumption of undue influence arises generally speaking in transactions between solicitor and client, trustee and beneficiary, spiritual adviser and devotee medical attendant and patients and parents and child (s. 111 of the Evidence Act 1872).

Operation and restraint on transfer. Under s. 8 of the Transfer of Property Act, a transfer passes the whole of the interest of the transferor in the absence

6 128 IC 441.
7 *Mahomed Shah* v *Official Trustee of West Bengal* 36 Cal 431.
8 *Abdul Fata* v *Russomoy* (1894)22 Cal 619.
9 *Mackenin* v *Royal Bank* 151 IC 981 (PC).
10 *Demera Bauxite Co.* v *Hubbard* 1923 AC 673.
11 AIR 1963 SC 1279 (1290).

of contrary intention. The English Common Law Rule—a woman's property becomes her husband's property on her marriage—was made inapplicable to India by s. 4 of the Indian Succession Act 1865, re-enacted as s. 20 of the Indian Succession Act 1925. The Married Women's Property Act 1874 was passed to establish separate property of women married before 1st January 1866 with reference to their wages and earnings. Under s. 10 of the Transfer of Property Act 1882, a property may be transferred to or for the benefit of a woman (not being a Hindu, Mahomedan, Buddhist) so that she shall not have power during her marriage to transfer or charge the same or her beneficial interest therein. A restraint in a lease is valid where the condition is for the benefit of the lessor or person or persons claiming under him. A restraint in a deed of partition as against the sale of any lot to a third party without offering same first among the co-sharers is valid. Conditions subsequent and precedent *e.g.* in a deed of gift for the residence of the donee in the property is valid (ss. 28, 31 and 126 of the Transfer of Property Act).[12] So also in the case of a gift of any property under whose terms the donee is to pay for the maintenance of the donor out of the income of the property. These documents are however of the nature of settlement or trust. So also is the case of the trust. The rule against perpetuity and the rule against accumulation as embodied in ss. 14 and 17 of the Transfer of Property Act do not apply to gifts for the benefit of any public charity so a restraint is valid in transfers of this type (see also s. 118 of the Indian Succession Act).

Ownership of superstructure and ownership of soil may be different. It is a part of the customary law, *i.e.* law of the land.[13] Buildings and structures constructed by any person on land to which he had no legal title does not by reason of their attachment to the land become the property of the owner of the land.[14] But in cases where such a person is in possession of the land under a *bona fide* title or claim of title he is protected in this sense, *viz.* he can remove the structure or claim compensation against the owner of the land. But a trespasser has no such right under any circumstances. The case of a husband constructing structure on land belonging to the wife is quite different in as much as the structures all become the property of the wife. The above proposition was first laid down[15] in 1886 and upheld by the Judicial Committee in *Vallabdas Naranji* v *Development Officer, Bandra*.[16]

12 *Ambica Charan* v *Sasitara* (1915)22 CLJ 613; 80 IC 868. See also *Sirish* v *Kadambini* 44 CLJ 18; 97 IC 685.
13 *Mretunjai* v *Hinja* AIR 1933 Oudh 468.
14 *K.K. Das* v *Anima Khatoon* 44 CWN 247.
15 *Thakoor Chandra Pormanick's* case 6 WR 229 (FB).
16 LR 56 IA 259.

The principle received statutory recognition under s. 51 of the Transfer of Property Act 1882. The English law on the subject was discussed in *Ramsden* v *Dyson*.[17]

There is however no absolute Rule of Law in India and so the maxim of jurisprudence that whatever is affixed to or built upon the soil becomes part of the soil has, if at all, a limited application in India. It was held by the Privy Council[18] that on a sale of a holding under the Bengal Land Revenue Sales Act 1859 for arrears of Government revenue by the Collector the auction purchaser acquired the interest of the Crown limited to the land and not the building. The owner was entitled to remove the materials unless the purchaser agreed to pay for the costs of the building.[19] The sale of a building only did not pass the land on which it stands.[1] Revenue sales under the Bengal Land Revenue Sales Act stood on a different footing. But under s. 8 of the Transfer of Property Act, where the land is transferred, the building also passes by implication[2] as property of the transferor with the legal incidents thereof—things attached to the earth if the owner is the same person. A sale of land includes sale of mineral rights as observed by the Supreme Court in *Raja Ananda* v *State of U.P.*[3] But a permanent lease does not pass any mineral rights.[4] Under s. 108(*h*) of the Transfer of Property Act, a lessee may even after determination of the lease remove, so long as he is in possession of the property, whatever he has attached to the earth but he must leave the property in the condition in which he received it. This is, however, subject to the terms of the lease which may provide that all such things shall be the property of the lessor. It was held in *Secretary of State for Foreign Affairs* v *Charlsworth Pudding & Co.*[5] The owner of a land is not the owner of a building constructed by a third party. The English law as to fixtures does not in *toto* apply to India. So a tenant can remove the fixtures brought by him in the property for his convenient use without at all intending to improve the property. As regards trade fixtures, the rule in the English law is also much more relaxed, so much so, that machinery and buildings in the colliery are regarded as accessories to the business and not annexations

17 (1865)1 HL 129.
18 *Maharaja Surja Kanta* v *Sarat Chandra Roy* 18 CWN 1281; 25 IC 309 (PC). See also *Narayan Deo* v *State of Orissa* AIR 1953 SC 383.
19 *Jwan Chand* v *Jugal Kishore* AIR 1960 Cal 331.
1 *Katikar Jute Mills* v *Calcutta Match Works* AIR 1958 Pat 133.
2 *Asgar* v *Mahomed Mehdi Hossein* (1903)30 Cal 566.
3 (1967)1 SCR 873.
4 *Giridhari Singh* v *Megh Lal Pandey* (1918)45 Cal 87; 44 IA 246; 42 IC 651.
5 26 Bom 1 (PC).

to the property[6] made to improve it. Section 51 of the Transfer of Property Act is the statutory recognition of the law as regards improvements done by *bona fide* holders.

Requirements of deeds of transfer in general. A conveyance begins with the names of the parties and ends with the execution and attestation clauses. There are some general requirements of all kinds of deeds of transfer. The special requirements of different kinds of transfer, like sale, mortgage, lease, exchange, gift etc., will be dealt in detail while dealing with each specific kind of transfer. The following are the necessary parts of a deed of transfer:

(i) *Description of the Deed.* "This Deed of Sale", "This Deed of Mortgage", "This Deed of Lease", etc., may be written in capital letters.

(ii) *Date on which it is executed.* "This Deed of Mortgage made on the 1st day of January 1976". It is the date of execution which is most material for the purpose of limitation, mutation, registration and passing of title. When several persons execute a deed, the date of execution by each person may be noted under his signature.

(iii) *Parties to the deed.* All proper parties to a deed; inter-parties must be impleaded more so because in common law only parties to the contract can take the benefits under the same. The transferor should be mentioned first and then the transferee. When there is a confirming party he may be joined and placed next after the transferor.

The name comes first, then the surname and thereafter the address followed by other descriptions such as "son of", "wife of", "daughter of" etc. Where a woman is divorced, she is described as "feme sole". Caste and religion are to be mentioned.

Their profession or occupation comes next, *e.g.* "Medical practitioner", "grocer" carrying on business etc. Change in a name whether a forename or surname or merely the spelling only is nevertheless a blot on the title.[7] Such changes shall be accounted for after the name of the conveying party.

In the case of juridical persons, *e.g.* companies and registered societies, after their names—registered under the Indian Companies Act, Societies Registration Act or incorporated under special statute with address of the head office are to be stated.

In the case of an idol—name of the idol—after that—acting and represented by its "shebait" so and so is to be mentioned and case of persons under disability, *e.g.*, minor, lunatics and others—represented by "so and so".

6 *Wake* v *Hall* (1886)8 App Cas 195.

7 Stanley Robinson's *Drafting*, p. 92.

In the case of trustees—their names and as trustees to the estate of "so and so" appointed under the Deed of Trust etc., etc., should be mentioned. If trustees are appointed by any court, the date of the order and number of proceedings in which they are appointed, have to be stated accordingly.

In the case of firm, all the partners should join as under s. 19 of the Indian Partnership Act (IX of 1932) one or more partners cannot transfer any immovable property belonging to the firm in the absence of express authority or by virtue of customs or usage to the contrary except in the case of the trading assets of a firm whose business is to buy and sell lands, the managing partner may sell as the partner of and acting on behalf of the firm carrying on business under the name and style of .... any such land or lands.

In the case of the Government—names of persons authorized under Art. 229(1) of the Constitution of India are to be stated and transfer shall be expressly made on behalf of or in the name of the President or the Governor as the case may be.

(iv) *Recitals.* Recitals shall contain a short history of the property up to its vesting in the transferor. Recitals should be short and intelligible. Recitals are of two kinds, *e.g.*, narrative recitals, *i.e.*, facts and circumstances which show the nature of interest to be dealt with and introductory recitals which show the motive or intention behind the execution of the deed and are immediately followed by the operative part. The doctrine of estoppel has an important bearing on recitals (s. 115, Evidence Act). A recital of seisin is a cornerstone of a conveyance. It acts as warranty of title.

Introductory recitals may contain facts culminating in the execution of the deed beginning from the agreement up to the motive for transfer, if any.

(v) *Habendum.* It is that part of the deed which states the interest that the purchaser is to take in the property such phrases as "To Have and To Hold" are used but not essential to make the transfer effective.

(vi) *Covenants.* A covenant is an agreement under seal, whereby one or more of the parties to the deed stipulate for the truth of certain facts, or is bound to do or not to do a specified thing. A covenant may be in express terms, or is inferred on the construction of the entire instrument. An implied covenant, or covenant in law, is one which the law implies either from the nature of the transaction or from the use of certain technical words.[8]

COVENANTS RUNNING WITH THE LAND. A covenant runs with the land where it touches and concerns and is annexed to and creates an interest in the land and which is an exception to the general rule that all covenants are personal. A covenant runs with the land when the benefit or burden of it, whether at

8 Halsbury's *Laws of England*, 3rd Ed., vol. 23, p. 598.

law or in equity, passes to the successors in title of the covenantee or the covenantor, as the case may be (Law of Property Act, 1925, s. 80). Such a covenant at times affects the nature and value of the land. A covenant may very well have reference to the land, but unless it is reasonably incidental to the relation of landlord and tenant, it cannot be said to touch and concern the land so as to be capable of running therewith or with the reversion. Tested by this principle, covenants *e.g.* to pay rents and taxes, to repair or keep in repair, not to assign or under-let are covenants which run with the land.[9]

Covenants as to title implied in sales under s. 55(2) of the Transfer of Property Act and implied covenants in mortgages under s. 65 and implied covenants for quiet enjoyment under s. 108(*c*) and restrictive covenants referred to in the first paragraph of s. 40 of the Transfer of Property Act 1882, are all instances of statutory covenants running with the land, while s. 40 contemplates negative covenants, s. 11 contemplates both positive and negative covenants. In England the development of the restrictive covenants was the work of the court of equity. The common law courts stood against the burden of covenants other than those made upon a demise of the property but nevertheless they made an exception in *Spencer's* case[10] as to covenants between the landlord and the tenants in regard to which the burden of the covenants was allowed to run with the land.

Before the passing of the Conveyancing Act 1881 (SC 44 and 45 Vic), a purchaser in England was entitled to following covenants from the vendor: (*i*) covenant as to good title; (*ii*) peaceful possession; (*iii*) free from encumbrance; and (*iv*) further assurance. These covenants are not now required to be expressly entered into as they are implied under s. 76 and Schedule II, Part I of the Law of Property Act 1925. In India, s. 55 of the Transfer of Property Act provides for the relevant covenants and under s. 55(2) of the Act the benefits of the covenants, which run with the land can be enforced by the transferees from time to time except however the covenant as to indemnity. Section 76(6) of the Law of Property Act 1925 of England contains provisions similar to s. 55 of the Transfer of Property Act in India. These covenants should therefore be expressly inserted in gift, exchange, marriage settlement, etc., more so because they are not implied by the statute. Section 108(*c*) of the Transfer of Property Act provides for the covenants on the part of the lessor as to peaceful possession of the demised premises upon the lessee paying the rent and performing the contract on his part. This section gives an absolute and unqualified right for quiet enjoyment. Section 65(*a*) of the Transfer of Property Act, which provides for statutory covenants on the part of the mortgagor, is similar to s. 55(2) of the said Act.

9 Cheshire's *Modern Law of Real Property*, 12th Ed., p. 451.
10 77 ER 72.

Persons in fiduciary character, e.g., trustee, executor, official assignee, guardian of an infant, manager of a lunatic shall enter into covenant only to the extent that they themselves have not done any act or thing nor suffered anything to the contrary whereby or by reason or means whereof they are in any way prevented from executing the deed or deeds in question. The implied statutory covenants are limited to his own act encumbering the property or hindering its transfer (Proviso to s. 55 of the Transfer of Property Act).

If a covenant has both positive and negative elements in it, the negative element may bind the land even though the positive cannot. Even a positive obligation may be binding if it is no more than a condition of a negative one; thus a covenant to submit plans before building may be enforceable against a purchaser as a covenant not to build without first submitting plans. The restrictive covenants most frequently met with in practice are covenants against building on land, and against carrying on any trade or business (or certain specified trades or businesses) on the premises. It is common to find such covenants inserted in conveyances or leases of urban property.[11]

RESIDENTS IN FLATS. In modern days peculiar questions arise when a resident in a flat in a multi-storied building uses his flat or the terrace of the building in a manner which would cause annoyance or nuisance affecting the other occupants. Covenants of various types besides those for the maintenance of the property or making contributions to the maintenance of common facilities and services are usually put in. In a case from Bombay the facts disclosed that one such occupier of a flat as a tenant erected a textile printing mill on its terrace and ran it during night, unauthorisedly utilised the water stored in the common overhead tanks on the terrace meant for domestic use of the other occupiers, removed the radio aerials and TV antennas of other occupiers and prevented these persons and their workers from reaching the common terrace for repairs of the radio aerials and TV antennas and telephone lines of the other tenements by blocking the staircase. The Supreme Court held that all these amounted to 'nuisance' and 'annoyance' though there were no statutory definitions of these expressions in the Bombay Rents, Hotel and Lodging House Rates Control Act of 1947 and the occupier was liable to be evicted.[12] Such a situation as disclosed by the facts of this case certainly invites incorporation of both positive and negative covenants, in a specific manner, in the relevant documents though all the contingencies cannot be anticipated.

(vii) *Testimonium.* This is that part of a deed which states that the parties have signed the deed. This clause is superfluous as what is necessary is the fact of proper execution of the deed.

11 Megarry & Wade: *Law of Real Property,* 5th Ed.
12 *Narpatchand* v *Shantilal* AIR 1993 SC 1712.

In the case of companies or corporations sealing and attestation would be necessary. The provisions of the Articles of Association should also be followed. Attestation as defined in s. 3 of the Transfer of Property Act and s. 63 of the Indian Succession Act is necessary in the case of gift, mortgage, lease and will. Before a deed is executed, the executant should read the deed. If he cannot, then it should be read over and explained to him by a competent person. In case of a *purdanashin* lady, care should be taken that she fully understands the terms, implications and effect of the deed. The fact of so explaining should be endorsed on the deed itself.

(viii) *Testatum.* This is the witnessing clause saying "the deed witnesseth". The word "witnesses" may be adequate. Address of each witness must be written under each signature.

In the case of conveyance it contains two essentials—consideration and receipt of the purchase money.

At the conclusion of the testatum, a statement of the character in which the vendor is conveying the property, *e.g.*, as trustee, executor or receiver or mortgagee is necessary.

(ix) *Operative words.* They differ in cases of different kinds of transfer. In the case of sale, such operative words are used as are necessary to pass the estate of the vendor unto the purchaser.

(x) *Parcels.* It means the description of the property following the operative words. Sometimes minute details of easements and incidents are mentioned but s. 8 of the Transfer of Property Act makes a transfer necessarily implying transfer of certain legal incidents. Anything intended to be transferred, which is not impliedly transferred under s. 8, should be specifically mentioned, *e.g.*, in the case of a transfer of a house, a garden is to be specifically mentioned. Boundaries on all sides must be given. It is safe always to say "now or lately butted and bounded" and to add at the end of the schedule "or howsoever otherwise the same may be butted, bounded, called, known, numbered, described or distinguished." Those involved in the negotiations need to satisfy themselves that the description in the document, including any plan that may be annexed, is such that there could never be a dispute as to the extent of the premises demised. Any ambiguity must be resolved before the final wording is agreed. All too often this is not done, and the parties become the victims of sloppy conveyancing. Commercial men talk in areas, while lawyers all too often do not, and thus dimensions and areas ought to be referred to whenever possible.[13]

(xi) *Exceptions and reservations.* These are possible only in cases not prohibited either by the letter or policy of law. In any event they must not be

13 Murray Ross: *Drafting and Negotiating Commercial Leases*, 4th Ed., 1994, p. 32.

uncertain, repugnant or contrary to the grant, *e.g.* sale of a house without land.[14] Section 8 of the Transfer of Property Act provides for transfer of the entire interest of the transferor and s. 10 of the said Act prohibits any condition restraining alienation except in the case of lease and transfer to a woman other than a Hindu, Mahomedan or Buddhist. A transferor of a land may retain absolute ownership of all mines and minerals and so on.[15] The rights of an absolute owner may be curtailed by easement rights vested in others irrespective of the fact of notice or no notice. A covenant running with the land may enure to the benefit of the owner of the property for the time being. A vendor may reserve full and free right of way and passage for all times to come over the land sold for purposes connected with the property. Similarly the right to take water from a well which falls within the property sold may be reserved and excluded from the conveyance. These are reservations and exceptions by way of necessity and are exceptions to the rule in *Wheeldor* v *Burrowes*[16] as observed in *London Corporation* v *Riggs*.[17] The other exceptions are (*i*) reciprocal easements, *e.g.* right of support as between two adjacent buildings mutually subservient and dependant on each other, the reciprocal right of support is presumed to have been reserved[18]; (*ii*) simultaneous conveyances of dwelling house and land adjacent by the same owner to different purchasers. In *Allen* v *Tayor*,[19] it was held the purchaser is not entitled to build so as to obstruct the light of the house. In India such reservations and exceptions are permissible as and by way of easements of necessity under the Indian Easements Act 1882, both with regard to transfer and bequest and also in a deed of partition. The vendor of a flat in a multistoreyed building though sells the same with all transferable and irrevocable right of use, can nevertheless exclude from such sale and/or reserve for him and for other co-owners easements and quasi-easements, *e.g.*, right of way and passage in common, right to use the open roof, right of access into the flat sold, with or without workman for repairing essential services such as drains, wires, pipes etc. The right of demolition or committing waste is also excluded in conveyances of such a type. The transfer of an apartment under the West Bengal Apartment Ownership Act 1972, read with the West Bengal Apartment (Regulation of Construction and Transfer) Act (West Bengal Act XVII of 1972) is subject to exceptions and reservations as regards the common areas and facilities which shall remain undivided and against partition thereof unless the property is

14 *Glasgow* v *Glasgow* 221 SC 322.
15 *Purnendu* v *Narendra* AIR 1943 Pat 3.
16 (1879)12 Ch D 89.
17 (1880)13 Ch D 798.
18 *Richard* v *Rose* (1858)9 Exch 218; 158 ER 98.
19 (1880)16 Ch D 355.

withdrawn from the provisions of the Act. An exception must relate to some property or definite right in existence on the date of the conveyance which would pass with the transfer if not expressly excluded, *e.g.*, underground minerals in case of absolute transfer of the land, but in the case of a lease on permanent tenure basis, the right to subsoil minerals depends much upon the terms of the grant.[20] A zamindar having the largest interest in the land is entitled to mineral right.[1] A reservation is something not in existence but created at the time of transfer, *e.g.* right of way over transferred land. A reservation operates as a new grant by the transferee to the transferor and the relevant deed shall be executed also by the transferee.[2]

(xii) *Completion of transaction.* The deed should be properly stamped under the Indian Stamp Act and registered where registration is necessary under the Indian Registration Act or other enactments.

It should be noted as to by whom the stamp is payable. In the absence of an agreement to the contrary, the expense for providing the proper stamp shall be borne, in the cases of the following instruments, *by the person drawing, making or executing such instruments*—administration bond; agreement relating to deposit of title-deeds, pawn or pledge; bill of exchange; bond; bottomry bond, customs bond, debenture; further charge, indemnity bond; mortgage deed; promissory note; release; respondentia bond; security bond; settlement; transfer of shares in an incorporated company or other body corporate; transfer of debentures, being marketable securities; transfer of any interest secured by a bond, mortgage deed or policy of insurance.

The stamp duty is payable in the case of a policy of insurance other than fire insurance by the person effecting the insurance; in the case of a policy of fire insurance by the person issuing the policy; in the case of a conveyance (including reconveyance of mortgaged property) by the grantee; in the case of a lease or agreement to lease, by the lessee or intended lessee; in the case of a counterpart of a lease, by the lessor; in the case of exchange, by the parties in equal shares; in the case of a certificate of a sale, by the purchaser of the property; and in the case of an instrument of partition, by the parties thereto in proportion to their respective shares in the whole of the property partitioned; or where the partition is made by the order of Revenue authority or civil court or arbitrator in such proportion as directed by the authority concerned.

Execution. It means signing of the document by the parties. Special care should be taken when any deed is signed by any illiterate or blind person or

20 *Rowbothem* v *Wilson* (1860)8 HLC 348 (360).

1 *Rageshwari* v *Kumar Kamakya* 58 IA 9.

2 *May* v *Beloona* (1905)2 Ch 605.

pardanashin lady. The solicitor or advocate entrusted with the work must see that the contents and effects thereof are truly and correctly read over, explained to and understood by the executant. In case any document is signed by some person by putting a mark or thumb impression, the document is also to be signed by the person taking the same. Execution is proved by calling attesting witnesses (s. 68 of Evidence Act). In cases where any map or plan is annexed to the document, the same shall also be signed by the parties.

Attestation. Attestation of a document after its execution. Though a formality is imperative in such cases, as—(*i*) mortgage (s. 59 of the Transfer of Property Act); (*ii*) gift (s. 124 of the said Act); and (*iii*) will (s. 63 of the Indian Succession Act). Section 69 of the Indian Evidence Act is the law as to proof of execution of documents required to be attested. Section 3 of the Transfer of Property Act defines what is meant by attestation. There is no set form for it but a party to a deed cannot be an attesting witness nor the holder of a power of attorney when he executes the document on behalf of the person who had given him the power of attorney. The essential conditions of a valid attestation are that two or more witnesses have seen the executant sign the instrument, or have received from him a personal acknowledgment of his signature, and each of them has signed the instrument in the presence of the executant to bear witness to this fact. It is essential that the attesting witness put his signature *animus attestandi i.e.* for the purpose of attesting the signature. A scribe may be an attesting witness as well as the signatures of the registering officer and the identifying witnesses endorsed on a deed (here a mortgage deed) can be treated as these of attesting witnesses if they had so signed in conformity with the essential conditions of attestation. A non-testamentary instrument creating a charge of the value of Rs. 100 or upwards, must be registered under s. 17(1)(*b*) of the Indian Registration Act but there is no provision of law that an instrument creating the charge must be attested by witnesses.[3]

The Madras High Court held in *N. Ramswamy* v *C. Ramdswamy*[4] that a deed of gift cannot be proved unless each of the attesting witnesses saw the other sign in his presence. A mortgage not validly attested operates neither as a mortgage nor as a charge.[5]

Possession of the property. It does not always mean actual physical possession but such possession as the nature of the property permits.[6]

3 *Abdul Jabbar* v *Venkata Sastri* (1969)1 SCC 573; (1969)2 SCJ 784; (1969)2 SCA 129; (1969)3 SCR 513.

4 AIR 1975 Mad 88.

5 *Prannath* v *Jadhunath* 32 Cal 729.

6 See *State of West Bengal* v *Subodh Gopal* AIR 1954 SC 92; 1954 SCR 587.

Acquisition of any property with notice that a person other than the vendor is in actual possession is based upon the principle of constructive trust (vide Expl. II to s. 3 of the Transfer of Property Act). If any purchaser fails to enquire he shall have to take subject to all equities.[7]

Registration of deeds. The Indian Registration Act lays down a detailed procedure for registration of documents and the various statutory duties that the registering officer has to perform. If an instrument is not compulsorily registrable, it is complete without registration; but if it is compulsorily registrable, it must be presented for registration before an officer competent to register documents (s. 17 of the Indian Registration Act). The real purpose is to secure every person dealing with property against fraud and to maintain a public register.

Under the Indian Registration Act (XVI of 1908), the registration of the following classes of documents is compulsory:

(a) Instruments of gift of immovable property;

(*b*) other non-testamentary instruments which purport or operate to create, declare, assign, limit, or extinguish, whether in present or in future, any right, title or interest, whether vested or contingent, of the value of one hundred rupees and upwards, to or in immovable property;

(*c*) non-testamentary instruments which acknowledge the receipt or payment of any consideration on account of the creation, declaration, assignment, limitation, or extinction of any such right, title or interest;

(*d*) leases of immovable property from year to year, or for any term exceeding one year, or reserving a yearly rent;

(e) non-testamentary instruments transferring or assigning any decree or order of a court or any award when such decree or order or award purports or operates to create, declare, assign, limit or extinguish, whether in present or in future, any right, title or interest whether vested or contingent, of the value of one hundred rupees and upwards, to or in immovable property and agreements between promoters and flat owners (s. 4 of the Maharashtra Act XLV of 1963);

(*f*) authority (not conferred by a will) to adopt a son.

But nothing in cls. (b) and (c) applies to—

(*i*) any composition deed; or

7 Mulla's *Transfer of Property Act*, 6th Ed., p. 15.

(*ii*) any instrument relating to shares in a joint stock company even if the assets of such company consist in whole or in part of immovable property; or

(*iii*) any debenture issued by any company and not creating, declaring, assigning, or extinguishing any right, title, or interest to or in immovable property, except in so far as it entitles the holder to the security afforded by a registered instrument whereby the company has mortgaged, conveyed, or otherwise transferred the whole or part of its immovable property, or any interest therein, to trustees upon trust for the benefit of the holders of such debentures; or

(*iv*) any endorsement upon or transfer of any debenture issued by any such company; or

(*v*) any document not itself creating, declaring, assigning, limiting, or extinguishing any right, title or interest of the value of one hundred rupees and upwards to or in immovable property, but merely creating a right to obtain another document, which will, when executed, create, declare, assign, limit, or extinguish any such right, title, or interest; or

(*vi*) any decree or order of a court except a decree or order expressed to be made on a compromise and comprising immovable property other than that which is the subject-matter of the suit or proceeding; or

(*vii*) grant of immovable property by the Government; or

(*viii*) instrument of partition made by the Revenue Officer; or

(*ix*) order granting loans and instruments of collateral security granted under the Land Improvement Loans Act; or

(*x*) orders granting loans and instruments for securing repayment, under the Agriculturists' Loans Act; or

(*xi*) any endorsement on a mortgage deed acknowledging payment of the whole or any part of the mortgage money, and any other receipt for payment of money due under a mortgage when the receipt does not purport to extinguish the mortgage; or

(*xii*) a certificate of sale granted to the purchaser of any property sold by public auction by a Civil or Revenue Officer;

Registration of the following documents are now considered compulsory—

(*i*) all instruments relating to declaration, amendment, withdrawal or acquisition of apartments or transfers thereof under the W.B. Apartment Ownership Act 1972; or

(*ii*) any transfer of a holding of a raiyat under s. 5 of the W.B. Land Reforms Act 1955; or (*iii*) partition of a holding among co-sharers under s. 14 of the said Act;

(*iv*) compromise decree or order creating any tenancy or lease[8] of any immovable property or agreement to lease [s. 17(1)(*d*) of the Registration Act];

(*v*) authority to adopt;

(*vi*) will, if operates as a family settlement;[9]

(*vii*) deed of dissolution of partnership where any immovable property of the value above Rs. 100 is given to the retiring partner;

(*viii*) agreement for sale between a promoter and prospective buyer of a flat.

A document purporting or operating to effect a contract for the sale of immovable property will not require registration by reason only of the fact that such document contains a recital of the payment of any earnest money or of the whole or any part of the purchase money unless of course a charge is created on the property on that account.

Registering Officer. It is important to see that the officer is duly qualified to register documents, and that the document is not presented in a wrong registration circle, as otherwise the registration would be of no validity.

In order that a document may be presented for registration, it is necessary that any interlineation, blank, erasure, or alteration should be signed or initialled by the executant, for otherwise the registering officer has the option of refusing its registration. No non-testamentary document relating to immovable property will be accepted for registration, unless it contains a description of such property sufficient to identify the same (ss. 20 and 21 of the Indian Registration Act). Houses in the town are described by their municipal numbers. Holding, blocks, division, sub-division, etc., and properties in the muffasil are described by reference to the *dags, mouzas, Khatians,* J.L. Numbers, R.S. Numbers, districts, etc. The description must in any event be sufficient to identify the property. The Indian Registration Act is not a complete Code. Although under the Transfer of Property Act a partition can be effected without writing, nevertheless under s. 14 of the West Bengal Land Reforms Act 1955, a partition of a raiyati holding can be done only by a registered instrument so also a transfer (s. 5 of the said Act).

Under the West Bengal Building (Regulation of Promotion of Construction and Transfer by Promoters) Act 1993 any agreement for sale of a flat between the promoter and the prospective purchaser of the flat must be registered

8 AIR 1977 SC 2425.
9 Murty's *Law of Wills,* 3rd Ed., p. 198.

in accordance with s. 7 of the Statute, failing which the agreement will be void.

Arbitration. Tripartite agreement between the principal and two contractors that bills shall be paid to one contractor and subsequently changing the procedure by requiring consultations with another contractor before settling the bills the principal is estopped from claiming that he is not bound by it.[10]

Mortgage by deposit of title deeds. A trust relating to immovable property can be created by a registered document (s. 5 of the Indian Trusts Act). It will not be out of place to say a few words regarding mortgage by deposit of title deeds under s. 58(*f*) and s. 59 of the Transfer of Property Act; such a mortgage can be created in the Presidency towns and other places mentioned therein by simply depositing the title deeds with intent to create a security thereon. This is based upon the equitable maxim—"equity looks at the intention rather than the form". If, however, such a mortgage is accompanied by a memorandum which constitutes the bargain, *i.e.*, the contract between the parties, it will have to be registered otherwise not. The leading authorities on the subject are *Pranjivandas Mehta* v *Chan Ma Phea*.[11]

Time limit for presentation of documents. Ordinarily, a document other than a will must, under s. 23 of the Indian Registration Act, be presented for registration within four months from the date of its execution, provided that, where there are several persons executing a document at different times, such document may be presented for registration and re-registration within four months from the date of each execution. In case a document is not presented within this time, owing to urgent necessity or unavoidable accident, another four months are allowed by way of grace, but then the document can be registered only on payment of a fine up to the limit of ten times the amount of the proper registration fee (s. 25 of the Indian Registration Act). Documents executed outside India are allowed four months' time from the date of their arrival in India (s. 26 of the said Act).

Enforcement to register. Parties refusing to register any document can be sued to enforce registration (s. 77 of the said Act).

A document must be presented for registration by some person executing or claiming under the same or by the representative or assignee of such person, or by the agent of such person, representative or assignee, duly authorized by power-of-attorney executed before and authenticated by a Registrar or Sub-Registrar or any Magistrate or a Notary Public, etc., as the case may be (s. 33 of the Indian Registration Act).

10 *Rolls Royce* v *Urmila & Co.* AIR 1998 Del 411.

11 1916 IA 122; 43 Cal 895; *Rao* v *Andhra Bank* AIR 1971 SC 1613.

Delivery of deeds. It is the duty of the vendor in all cases to hand over the deed and the title deeds to the purchaser. In cases where the original title deeds may be retained, *e.g.*, sale of a large estate by lots, the deed should mention the special condition as to the detention of the title deeds. A purchaser is entitled to copies of the title deeds at his expenses and to a covenant for production of the original deeds [s. 55(3) of the Transfer of Property Act]. There are similar provisions in s. 45(9) of the Law of Property Act 1925, in England.

Essence of drafting. Essence of drafting include (*i*) law, (*ii*) effect, and (*iii*) language. Drafting calls upon all the skill of lawyers; good draftsmen are they who have a comparatively wide experience of law and life, not acquired overnight and also of drafting techniques, who readily understand their clients' thoughts, intention and desire, quickly appreciate the manner in which proposed document will be operative, responsive to changes particularly those in relation to business and social condition; they seldom use any word without fully considering the purpose for which the same is meant; they possess wide experience of life and law adequate understanding principles governing the construction of provisions.[12] Drafting is the process of synthesis of law and facts in the language form. A document is a communication of the thoughts of both the parties. Nevertheless it is not open to the parties to divert or deflect the course of succession in case of intestacy as required by law.[13]

Information Technology Act 2000. It is important to note that this statute, which received the assent of the President on 9th June 2000, while providing legal recognition to electronic commerce involving use of alternatives to paper based methods of communication lays down in s. 1(4) that nothing in this Act shall apply to,—a negotiable instrument as defined in s. 13 of the Negotiable Instruments Act 1881, a power-of-attorney as defined in s. 1A of the Powers-of-Attorney Act 1882, a trust as defined in s. 3 of the Indian Trusts Act 1882, a will as defined in cl. (*h*) of s. 2 of the Indian Succession Act 1925 including any other testamentary disposition by whatever name called, any contract for the sale or conveyance of immovable property or any interest in such property, any such class of documents or transactions as may be notified by the Central Government in the Official Gazette.

12 Stanley Robinson's *Drafting*, p. 9.

13 In re, Willcock's *Settlement* (1875)1 Ch D 225.

2

Adoption

On failure of any male issue a Hindu may take a child from another family and adopt the child as his own. This is done with the object of securing the performance of funeral rites and to preserve the continuity of the lineage of the adoptive person. A person adopts a child mainly for securing the spiritual benefit and incidentally to secure an heir or perpetuate the adoptor's name. The person to be adopted may be a male or female. The person who is adopting may be a male or female. The person who is adopting may be a bachelor or a spinster or a widower or a widow or a divorcee.

The Hindu Adoptions and Maintenance Act 1956 has codified the law on adoption and it applies to all Hindus, Buddhist, Jaina and Sikh by religion. The requirements of a valid adoption are that: (*a*) the person adopting must have the capacity and right to take in adoption; (*b*) the person giving in adoption must have the capacity to do so; (*c*) the person adopted must be lawfully capable of being taken in adoption; and (*d*) conditions relating to adoption are fulfilled.

For a valid adoption certain conditions must be fulfilled. If the adoption is of a son then the adoptive father or mother must not have a Hindu son, son's son, or son's son's son living at the time of adoption. If the adoption is of a daughter, the adoptive father or mother must not have a Hindu daughter or son's daughter or son's son's daughter living at the time of adoption. To adopt a female, the adoptive father must be 21 years older than the female child to be adopted. If the adoption is by a female and the child to be adopted is a male, the adoptive mother must be at least 21 years older than the child. The same child may not be adopted simultaneously by two or more persons of different families though the husband and wife together can jointly adopt the same child. The child to be adopted must not be a married one and has not completed the age of 15 years and must be given over by the natural parents or lawful guardian and taken in adoption by the adoptive father or mother with the intention to transfer the child from the family of its birth to the family of its adoption. In case of orphans or abandoned child or whose parentage is not known, the consent of the person or persons caring for the child will be adequate for giving out the child in adoption. In case of a foreigner the intention of taking in adoption of such a child the consent of the person or association of persons caring for the child by first being appointed as guardian of the child concerned and thereafter by taking the child to the foreign country and then adopting it according to the laws of that country. These rules have been settled by the Supreme Court.

After adoption the child loses all its claims against its natural parents and their properties and acquires all the rights and privileges of a child in the adoptive family. The adoptive father or mother by virtue of adoption is not deprived of their usual rights relating to their properties or disposal thereof *inter vivos* or by Will. In other words, the adopted child does not divest any person of any property which vested in him or her prior to adoption.

Adoption validly made cannot be cancelled by the adoptive father or mother or any other person. The adopted child cannot renounce his adoption and cannot return to his or her family of birth.

No consideration should pass in relation to the adoption of a child. Adoptive father or mother shall not pay any money and the person who is giving in adoption shall not receive any payment or reward or consideration. Any party to such consideration will be punishable with imprisonment upto six months or fine or both.[1]

FORMS

Adoption of Male Child

THIS DEED OF ADOPTION is made on this 25th day of May 2000 BETWEEN AF son of B by caste Kayastha, by religion Hindu, aged 30 years residing at 38 Mc'Leod Street, Calcutta 700 017 (hereinafter called the FIRST PARTY) and GS son of D by caste Kayastha, by religion Hindu residing at 2/1 Ariff Road, Calcutta 700 067 (hereinafter called the SECOND PARTY).

WHEREAS the FIRST PARTY has no son or son's son or son's son's son living and the SECOND PARTY has five sons.

AND WHEREAS the FIRST PARTY approached the SECOND PARTY for taking one of his sons, JK, in adoption to which the SECOND PARTY agreed.

1 Section 17 of the Hindu Adoptions and Maintenance Act 1956.

NOW THESE PRESENTS WITNESSETH as follows:

1. That the FIRST PARTY on this day, the 25th May 1999 in the forenoon has taken in adoption JK who is an unmarried son of the SECOND PARTY and is aged about 6 years as his son with the consent of his wife WF.
2. That the SECOND PARTY has with the consent of his wife SF on the date and time aforesaid given the said JK in adoption to the FIRST PARTY.
3. That the ceremony of giving and taking in adoption has been duly performed in respect of the said JK along with other customary religious ceremonies in the presence of relatives and friends of the parties, besides the attesting witnesses.
4. That the said JK has and shall have all the legal rights of an adopted son of the FIRST PARTY from the date aforementioned and the execution of these presents.

IN WITNESS WHEREOF we the said AF and GS have signed this deed and WF and SF as consenting parties on the day month and year written above in the presence of friends and relatives and the following two attesting witnesses.

Signed and delivered by AF	Sd/-
and GS as executant and WF	Sd/-
and SF as consenting parties	Sd/-
in the presence of:	Sd/-

1.

2.

3. Friends and Relations Sd/-

Adoption of Male Child

THIS DEED OF ADOPTION is made on this 20th day of May 1999 BETWEEN AF son of B by caste Kayastha, by religion Hindu residing at 3 S.N. Banerjee Road, Calcutta 700 012 (hereinafter called the FIRST PARTY) and GS son of D by caste Kayastha, by religion Hindu residing at BC 64 Salt Lake, Calcutta 700 064 (hereinafter called the SECOND PARTY).

WHEREAS AF the FIRST PARTY has no issue, male or female, and on account of his advanced age has no expectation of having any issue.

AND WHEREAS AF and his wife WF have been anxious to adopt a suitable boy as their son.

AND WHEREAS the SECOND PARTY has seven sons and AF approached the SECOND PARTY for giving in adoption his son JK to which the SECOND PARTY agreed.

AND WHEREAS WF the wife of AF has consented to the taking in adoption of JK, aged 7 years, by AF.

AND WHEREAS the mother of JK and wife of GS, SF has also consented to her son being given in adoption to AF.

AND WHEREAS AF has on this day 20th day of May 1999 in the forenoon taken in adoption JK son of the SECOND PARTY as his son.

AND WHEREAS on this day the physical act of giving and taking of JK in adoption and other customary ceremonies including the DATTAKA HOMAM were performed in the presence of gathering of friends and relations of the parties, besides the attesting witnesses.

AND WHEREAS the parties considered it expedient and necessary that a proper DEED OF ADOPTION be executed as an authentic record of adoption.

NOW THIS DEED WITNESSES as follows:

1. Both the parties do hereby declare and confirm that the said AF has duly adopted the said JK as his son.
2. The said JK has and shall have from the date of adoption all the legal rights of an adopted son.
3. AF the FIRST PARTY shall be responsible for the maintenance and education of the said JK and he agrees to bring up his adopted son according to his status in life.
4. GS the SECOND PARTY shall have no claim and responsibility hereinafter as to the custody of or any other right against JK.

IN WITNESS WHEREOF the parties hereto have signed this deed on the day, month and year above-written.

Signed and delivered by AF and GS
in the presence of:

1.

2.

Signed by WF as a token of her giving consent to adoption of JK

Signed by SF as a token of her consent to give JK in adoption to AF

All in presence of friends and relations of the parties herein including.

Adoption by a Hindu Widow

THIS DEED OF ADOPTION is made on the 1st day of June 1999 by WF, widow of AF, a Hindu by caste Kayastha, aged 55 years residing at 1559 Chittaranjan Park, New Delhi 110 019.

WHEREAS my husband, the said AF died on 15th May 1996 without any issue.

AND WHEREAS the said AF has given before his death an authority to me by a deed dated 10th January 1996 to adopt a suitable boy belonging to the caste of Kayastha.

AND WHEREAS I have adopted JK son of GS by caste Kayastha, aged 8 years and residing at 30 Netaji Subhash Marg, Daryaganj, New Delhi 110 002 on the day 25th of May 1999 acting under the aforesaid authority.

AND WHEREAS the said JK aged 8 years and more than 21 years younger than myself has been given to me in adoption by his father GS with the consent of his wife GF on the aforesaid date in the forenoon at 30, Netaji Subhash Marg, Daryaganj, New Delhi 110 002.

AND WHEREAS the ceremony of giving and taking in adoption and the other necessary religious ceremonies have been duly and simultaneously performed on the aforesaid date and time and place in presence of ....

NOW I, the said WF hereby declare and confirm that I have duly adopted the said JK as a son to my deceased husband AF and the said JK shall from the date of adoption have all the legal rights of an adopted son.

IN WITNESS WHEREOF I have executed these presents on the date, month and year first above-written.

Signed by WF in presence of:

Adoption by Unmarried Hindu Woman

THIS DEED OF ADOPTION is made on the 26th day of May 1999 by AB daughter of CD by caste Kayastha aged 40 years residing at 10 Park Street, Calcutta 700 016.

WHEREAS I, AB am the only living daughter of CD.

AND WHEREAS I have remained unmarried and have attained the age of 40 years.

AND WHEREAS I approached GS who has four sons to adopt one of them named JK of 8 years age and GS and his wife SF agreed to such adoption.

NOW, I, the said AB state and declare that

1. On my free will and consent I have adopted JK aged 8 years, son of GS, a Hindu by caste Kayastha and residing at 14 Golf Green, Calcutta 700 095, on this 26th day of May 1999 in the forenoon as

my son on the said child being given over to me by the said GF and SF together.

2. That the aforesaid ceremony of giving to and taking in adoption and other necessary religious ceremonies have been duly performed on the aforesaid date and time in presence of friends and relatives of both parties.

3. That the said JK shall have all the legal rights as my adopted son from the day of adoption.

IN WITNESS WHEREOF I, AB, GS and SF, both being parents of the said JK have executed these presents on the day, month and year first above-written.

Signed and delivered by AB, GS
and SF in presence of:

Adoption of Son by Hindu Male without Wife's Consent

KNOW ALL MEN BY THESE PRESENTS that I, AH aged 45 years by caste Kayastha, by religion Hindu, residing at 33/5/5 Block B, New Alipore, Calcutta 700 053 have no son, son's son or son's son's son living and I have in the forenoon of 26th May 2000 in presence of relatives of both the families concerned adopted JK aged 8 years, son of GS of 8 Royd Street, Calcutta 700 016. The said Shri GS with intent to transfer his said son from the family of his birth to my family has, with the consent of his wife, Smt. SF willingly handed over his said son, JK, to me and I have taken the said JK into my lap as my adopted son. As my wife Smt. WF has completely and finally renounced the world her consent is neither available nor required by law. The said JK shall be treated as my son for all purposes with effect from the date of adoption *i.e.* the forenoon of 26th May 2000.

IN WITNESS WHEREOF I, AH, and GS execute these presents and SF signs these presents as a token of her consent to the said adoption on this 16th day of June 2000.

Signed and delivered by AH and
GS in presence of:

Signed by SF as a token of her
consent to giving her son in
adoption to AH in presence of:

Declaration by Guardian

KNOW ALL MEN BY THESE PRESENTS that I, GD, by religion Hindu son of MN residing at 15/1/B, G.T. Road, Howrah 711 002 hereby declare that I being Court appointed Guardian of JK a Hindu, aged 10 years, being son of CD of ...., Howrah and having obtained the permission of the District Judge, Howrah on 5th June 1999 have given my ward JK in adoption to AH after performance of the ceremony of giving and taking this day 15th June 1999 in presence of witnesses. Henceforth JK shall be the adopted son of AH.

Sd/ GD

as Guardian of JK appointed by
order dated 5th April 1999 of
District Judge at Howrah.

WITNESSES:

Consent given by Wife to Adopt

KNOW ALL MEN BY THESE PRESENTS that I, WF, wife of AF residing at 6 Janpath Road, New Delhi 110 010, hereby consent to the adoption of JK aged 8 years, son of GS of B-10-D, Hauz Khas, New Delhi 110 016 by my husband AF the said JK as our son.

IN WITNESS WHEREOF we the said WF and GS have execute these presents on 10th May 1999 at New Delhi.

WITNESSES: WF

GS

Authority given to Wife to Adopt

I, AF, son of D, residing at 6 Ballygunge Circular Road, Calcutta 700 019 do hereby authorise my wife, Smt. WF, to adopt to me and to herself in DATTAKA son of GS of 10 N.S.C. Bose Road, Calcutta 700 040, after my death and in case the said boy JK dies she is fully authorised to adopt any other boy from my caste.

Signature of 'AF'
10th April 1999
Calcutta

WITNESSES:

Deed by Adoptive Father and Natural Guardian

KNOW ALL MEN BY THESE PRESENTS that I AF, (being childless) son of B, residing at 33 Sham Sheth Street, Mumbai 400 002 and WF, wife of late GS, residing at 10 Kalvadevi Road, Mumbai 400 002, hereby DECLARE that I, the said AF have this day the 6th of June 1999 in a meeting of relatives, caste fellows and friends held at 33 Sham Sheth Street, in Mumbai duly with the consent of my wife CD, adopted JK aged 12 years son of late MN as my son and I, the said WF, being the natural guardian and mother of the said JK, his father GS having already died on .... have given the said JK in adoption to the said AF AND WE ALSO declare that the ceremony of giving and taking in adoption and other customary religious ceremonies necessary under the Hindu Law to which we are subject have been duly performed at the date and time of the said adoption AND WE FURTHER DECLARE that henceforth the said JK has ceased to be the member of the family of his birth, and that he shall have all the rights of an adopted son of the said AF and CD.

IN WITNESS WHEREOF the said AF and WF have executed these presents on this 6th day of June 1999 at Mumbai.

Signed and delivered by AF and
WF in presence of:

Adoption from Guardian

THIS DEED OF ADOPTION made on this 10th day of July 1999 BETWEEN AH, son of BH, residing at 5 Rayapethah High Road, Chennai 600 014 (hereinafter called the FIRST PARTY) of the FIRST PART and GD, son of MN, residing at 10 Thyagaraya Road, T. Nagar, Chennai 600 017 (hereinafter called the SECOND PARTY) of the SECOND PART.

WHEREAS the FIRST PARTY has no son, son's son or son's son's son living and was desirous of adopting a son a male child and approached the SECOND PARTY who has been appointed a Guardian of JK son of KL aged about 8 years (hereinafter called the ADOPTEE) by the Court of District Judge at .... in order to give JK in adoption to the FIRST PARTY.

AND WHEREAS the SECOND PARTY competent to give the adoptee in adoption because of the death of the child's parents in an accident on .... has agreed to give him in adoption to the FIRST PARTY.

AND WHEREAS the SECOND PARTY has been permitted by Order No. .... dated .... in Act VIII case No. .... of .... Judge, Howrah to give the adoptee in adoption to the FIRST PARTY.

AND WHEREAS the physical act of giving and taking JK in adoption and other customary ceremonies including the DATTAKA HOMAM were performed on 15th June, 1999 in the presence of relatives and friends of both the parties at ....

AND WHEREAS the parties considered it expedient and necessary that a proper Deed of Adoption be executed as an authentic record of such adoption.

NOW THIS DEED WITNESSETH as follows:

1. The parties do hereby declare that the adoptee, JK, has been duly adopted by the FIRST PARTY as his son on the 15th June 1999 at the time and place mentioned above.
2. That the said adoptee JK has and shall have from the date of the said adoption all the legal rights of an adopted son as conferred by the Hindu Law.
3. That the FIRST PARTY shall be responsible for the maintenance and education of the said JK and the FIRST PARTY hereby agrees to bring up his adopted son as his natural born son and according to his status in life.
4. That the SECOND PARTY shall have no claim hereinafter to the custody of the said JK or in relation to him.
5. That the FIRST PARTY has neither paid nor shall make any payment or give other reward in consideration of giving the adoptee JK in adoption, to the SECOND PARTY.

IN WITNESS WHEREOF AH and GD have executed these presents on the day, month and year first abovewritten.

Signed and delivered by AH and
GD in presence of:

Adoption without Consent of Step-mother

THIS DEED OF ADOPTION is made this 6th day of September 1999 BETWEEN AB, son of MN aged 30 years by religion Hindu, residing at BC 22 Salt Lake, Calcutta 700 064 (hereinafter referred to as the ADOPTIVE FATHER) of the one part and CD, son of LK aged 28 years, by religion Hindu, residing at 18 C.R. Avenue, Calcutta 700 069 (hereinafter referred to as the NATURAL FATHER), of the OTHER PART.

WHEREAS the ADOPTIVE FATHER has no son, grandson or great-grandson living and he is desirous of adopting a male child to be his son and the son of his wife, WF.

AND WHEREAS the ADOPTIVE FATHER approached CD the NATURAL FATHER for adopting one of his sons, now aged about 3 years.

AND WHEREAS the NATURAL FATHER has agreed to give his son EF in adoption to the ADOPTIVE FATHER.

AND WHEREAS the ADOPTIVE FATHER has obtained the consent of his wife WF to the said adoption.

AND WHEREAS the NATURAL MOTHER of the said child EF is dead and the NATURAL FATHER being married to MN who is the step-mother of the child EF and the consent of the step-mother MN not being necessary for the said adoption.

AND WHEREAS there is no impediment either in law or in fact for taking in adoption by the ADOPTIVE FATHER or giving in adoption by the NATURAL FATHER of the said EF.

NOW THESE PRESENTS WITNESSETH and the parties hereby record and agree as follows:

The said NATURAL FATHER after performing the necessary religious ceremony before a gathering of friends and relatives of both the parties held at the residence of NATURAL FATHER on 5th September 1999 at 7 p.m. has given the said EF his son to the ADOPTIVE FATHER who has taken the said EF in adoption as his son.

The said EF the adopted child shall have all the legal rights of a natural son of the ADOPTIVE FATHER from this day.

IN WITNESS WHEREOF the said AB the ADOPTIVE FATHER, his wife WF and the said CD the NATURAL FATHER have executed these presents after the said ceremony was over and in presence of their friends and relatives on the day, month and year first above-written.

WITNESSES:

1.

2.

Signature of AB

WF

CD

Adoption of Female Child where getting Consent of Wife Impossible

THIS DEED OF ADOPTION is made this 10th day of October 1999 BETWEEN AB, son of LK aged 45 years by religion Hindu, residing at 10/B, Civil Line, Delhi 110 006 (hereinafter referred to as the ADOPTIVE FATHER) of the one part and CD, son of DK aged about 43 years, by religion Hindu, residing at 15 Metcalf Road, Delhi 110 007 (hereinafter referred to as the NATURAL FATHER) of the OTHER PART.

WHEREAS the ADOPTIVE FATHER has neither any son or daughter and whereas the ADOPTIVE FATHER is desirous of adopting a daughter to look after the ADOPTIVE FATHER inasmuch as the ADOPTIVE FATHER'S wife is dead and there is no other relative to look after the household.

AND WHEREAS the NATURAL FATHER has 5 daughters all unmarried aged between 5 and 20 years of age.

AND WHEREAS the ADOPTIVE FATHER approached the NATURAL FATHER for taking in adoption one of the daughters of the NATURAL FATHER.

AND WHEREAS the NATURAL FATHER cannot maintain properly all his daughters and his wife is invalid and of unsound mind and in consideration thereof has agreed to give in adoption his second daughter MN aged 13 years to the ADOPTIVE FATHER.

AND WHEREAS the said daughter, MN is not married and consent of the wife of ADOPTIVE FATHER cannot be obtained as she is dead and the consent of the wife of the NATURAL FATHER is impossible to obtain inasmuch as she is of unsound mind.

AND WHEREAS the difference in age between the adoptive father and the daughter to be taken in adoption is more than twenty one years, and there is no impediment in giving the said daughter MN in adoption to the ADOPTIVE FATHER.

NOW THIS DEED WITNESSETH and the parties hereby record and agree as follows:

The NATURAL FATHER in the circumstances, has this day before a gathering of friends and relatives of both the parties held at the NATURAL FATHER'S residence at 1 p.m. given the said MN his second daughter in adoption to the ADOPTIVE FATHER.

The ADOPTIVE FATHER has taken the said MN in adoption as his daughter.

The said daughter MN shall have all the legal rights of a Hindu daughter of the ADOPTIVE FATHER as if MN were the ADOPTIVE FATHER'S Natural Daughter.

IN WITNESS WHEREOF the ADOPTIVE FATHER and the NATURAL FATHER have executed these presents in the presence of the friends and relatives after the ceremony was over and two of the friends and relatives have hereunto signed as attesting witnesses on the day, month and year first abovewritten.

WITNESSES:

1.

2. Signature of

AB (ADOPTIVE FATHER)

CD (NATURAL FATHER)

Adoption of Male Child from Orphanage

THIS DEED OF ADOPTION made this 18th day of November 1999 BETWEEN AB son of JK aged about 45 years, by religion Hindu, residing at 3 Park Street, Calcutta 700 016 (hereinafter referred to as the ADOPTIVE FATHER) of the one part and CD, son of DK aged about 50 years by religion Hindu, residing at 4 J.L.Road, Calcutta working as Superintendent of Jyoti Orphanage having its registered office at 3 Sainik Place, West Bengal and Guardian of MN aged 10 years, one of the orphans, duly appointed by the Dist. Judge of Nadia by an Order dated 5th May 1999 (hereinafter referred to as the GUARDIAN) of the other part.

WHEREAS the ADOPTIVE FATHER has no son, grandson or great grandson.

AND WHEREAS the ADOPTIVE FATHER intends to adopt a son who would look after him in his old age and offer oblations to the ADOPTIVE FATHER and his ancestors.

AND WHEREAS the ADOPTIVE FATHER approached the said GUARDIAN who is in-charge of the Jyoti Orphanage, a voluntary Social and Welfare Organisation, situate at Nadia giving shelter and maintaining orphan children abandoned by their parents to give the ADOPTIVE FATHER in adoption a suitable male child to be his adopted son.

AND WHEREAS the said GUARDIAN being satisfied about the *bona fide* intention of the ADOPTIVE FATHER and also being satisfied that such adoption will be for the welfare and benefit of the child proposed aged 10 years named MN.

AND WHEREAS the ADOPTIVE FATHER approved the selection of MN the GUARDIAN agreed to give MN in adoption and MN expressed his willingness to be the adopted son of the said ADOPTIVE FATHER.

AND WHEREAS the said MN met the ADOPTIVE FATHER and had discussions and expressed his willingness and gave his consent to be adopted by the ADOPTIVE FATHER as his son.

AND WHEREAS the GUARDIAN applied to the Dist. Judge at Nadia for the necessary permission to give the said MN in adoption to the ADOPTIVE FATHER and the said Dist. Judge gave permission to give MN in adoption to the ADOPTIVE FATHER by an Order dated 10th June 1999 in Act VIII Case No. .... of ....

AND WHEREAS WF the wife of the ADOPTIVE FATHER has also given her consent to the said adoption of MN by the ADOPTIVE FATHER.

NOW THESE PRESENTS WITNESSETH and the parties hereby record and agree as follows:

The said CD, the GUARDIAN as the Superintendent of Jyoti Orphanage being fully satisfied after enquiries being made and reports obtained from reliable sources about the *bona fide* intentions of the ADOPTIVE FATHER and that such adoption would be for the benefit and welfare of MN has this day before the respectable persons and officials of the Jyoti Orphanage put the said child in the possession of ADOPTIVE FATHER who has physically received the said MN in adoption as his son and that the said MN shall have from this day full and complete right, title and interest in the property of the said ADOPTIVE FATHER and his Joint Family and shall have all obligations of a son including the offering of oblations to the said ADOPTIVE FATHER and his ancestors as required by Hindu Law and custom.

IN WITNESS WHEREOF the said AB, the ADOPTIVE FATHER and the said CD the GUARDIAN have hereunto executed these presents in the presence of several respectable persons and officials of the Jyoti Orphanage on 18th day of November 1999 at 11 A.M. in the office of the Jyoti Orphanage at Nadia, West Bengal.

WITNESSES: Signature of ADOPTIVE FATHER, AB.

1. Signature of Superintendent and GUARDIAN, CD.

2. Signature of ADOPTIVE MOTHER

3

Agreement

Introductory observations. By the Statutes of 1781 and 1797, it was enacted that the courts in Calcutta, Bombay and Madras would be guided by the personal law or customs of the parties in matters such as inheritance and succession to lands, rents and goods, as also in matters of contract and dealings between the parties. In other words, in cases where both parties were Hindus, the Hindu Law of Contract and so in cases where both parties were Mahomedans the Mahomedan Law of Contract was applied. But if the parties were subject to different personal laws, then the law of the defendant was applied.

This unsatisfactory state of affairs was set at rest by the enactment of the Indian Contract Act 1872, which came into force on 1st September 1872. A contract is an agreement enforceable by law. Even then the same is not exhaustive. There are statutes like the Transfer of Property Act 1882, as amended in 1929. Specific Relief Act 1963, Sales of Goods Act 1930 etc., which deal with other branches of the law of contract.

An agreement is defined in s. 2(e) of the Indian Contract Act 1872. Every promise and every set of promises, forming the consideration for each other is an agreement.

In other words, an agreement is an act in the eye of law whereby two persons being *ad idem* declare their common intention to do or not to do any act, deed or thing. An agreement is the combined product of offer and acceptance for some consideration passed between them.[1] It creates an outstanding obligation or legal liability.[2]

1 Halsbury's *Laws of England*, 4th Ed., vol. 9, para 206.
2 Section 10 and s. 73 of the Indian Contract Act.

State actions. In contractual sphere as in all other State actions, the State and all its instrumentalities have to conform to Art. 14 of the Constitution of which non-arbitrariness is a significant facet. There is no unfettered discretion in public law. This imposes a duty to act fairly and to adopt a procedure which is fairplay action. To satisfy this it is necessary for the State to consider and give due weight to the reasonable or legitimate expectation of the persons likely to be affected by such decision.[3]

Formation. (a) *Proposal*. When a person signifies to another his willingness to do or not to do anything, he is called the *proposer*.[4]

(b) *Communication of the proposal and its acceptance (s. 3 of the Indian Contract Act)*.[5] When the person to whom the proposal is made signifies his assent thereto, the proposal is said to be accepted. A proposal, when accepted, becomes a *promise*. Otherwise it has no legal effect.

The person making the proposal is called the *promisor*, and the person accepting the proposal is called the *promisee*.

Promises which form the consideration of each other are called *reciprocal promises*.[6]

(c) *Consideration*. When, at the desire of the promisor, the promisee or any other person has done or abstained from doing, or does or abstains from doing, or promises to do or to abstain from doing something, such act or abstinence or promise is called a *consideration* for the promise.[7] An informal promise made without consideration, however strong may be the motive, is not enforced in a court of law. A promise to contribute money to a charitable institution is not a contract.[8]

(d) *Past consideration*. According to English law, the doctrine laid down by Lord Mansfield in *Earl* v *Oliver*,[9] that a past consideration is not a good consideration is still unsettled among the authorities whereas in India an executed consideration is good consideration.[10]

The question whether the contract is concluded or not, depends upon the circumstances of each case, having regard to the nature of the documents

3 *Food Corporation* v *Kamdhenu* AIR 1993 SC 1601.
4 Section 2(c) of the Indian Contract Act.
5 *Harvey* v *Facey* (1893) AC 552. H sent a wire to F enquiring of lowest price. Answer by F. Lowest price is £ 900. Reply by H. Agreed to buy at £ 900. Send title deeds. No answer. Court held that there was no contract.
6 Section 2(*f*) of the Indian Contract Act.
7 Section 2(*d*) of the Indian Contract Act.
8 Mulla: *Contract*, 11th Ed., p. 8.
9 (1848)2 Ex 71 at p. 90.
10 *Taluk Board* v *Sentha* AIR 1936 Mad 709.

produced and also the evidence on record. Where a purchase order was not accepted by the plaintiff nor any contract agreement was executed it was not a concluded contract and the question of forfeiting the security deposit would not arise.[11]

(e) *Consent*. Two or more persons are said *to consent* when they agree upon the same thing, and in the sense, this is known as *consensus ad idem* in English law. Consent is said to be free when it is not caused by coercion, undue influence, fraud, misrepresentation or mistake.[12]

(f) *Contract—voidable contract—contingent contract*. An agreement enforceable by law is a contract. All agreements are contracts if they are made by the free consent of parties both being *ad idem* competent to contract, for a lawful consideration, and with a lawful object, and are not by law expressly declared to be void.[13]

An agreement which is enforceable by law at the option of one or more of the parties thereto but not at the option of the other or others is a *voidable contract*.[14]

A *contingent contract* is a contract to do or not to do something if some event collateral to such contract does or does not happen.

(g) *Competency to contract*.[15] Every person is competent to contract who is of the age of majority according to the law to which he is subject, and who is of sound mind, and is not disqualified from contracting by any law to which he is subject. The Privy Council held in *Mohari Bibi* v *Dharmadas Ghosh*,[16] that a contract by a minor is void.[17] The following rules were laid down by decided cases as regards valid contracts for service rendered to a minor, *viz* (*i*) service must be personal to the minor; (*ii*) suitable to the minor's station of life; and (*iii*) actually needed by the minor.[18]

It will not be out of place to say something about the effect of contract entered into on behalf of the minor for sale and purchase of property as observed by the Privy Council in *Subbarao's* case.[19] Whatever be the law on the subject earlier since the passing of the Hindu Minority and Guardianship Act,[1] a natural guardian cannot enter into a contract for sale of any property

11 *Rajasthan* v *Dayal Woods* AIR 1998 AP 381.
12 Section 14 of the Indian Contract Act.
13 Section 2(*j*) and s. 10 of the Indian Contract Act.
14 Section 2(*i*) of the Indian Contract Act.
15 Section 11 of the Indian Contract Act.
16 (1903)30 Cal 539 (PC); 7 CWN 441.
17 Section 11 of the Indian Contract Act.
18 *Cowern* v *Nield* (1912)2 KB 419.
19 AIR 1948 PC 95.
1 Section 8 of the Act 32 of 1956.

belonging to the minor. So the law laid down in *Subramanyam's* case[2] that a contract for purchase even could not be specifically enforced is no longer good law inasmuch as a minor is not debarred from acquiring any valuable estate, so a conveyance of a property in favour of a minor is not void, so also a gift.[3] A lease to a minor is void.[4] So is a sale by the father to his minor son. An agreement for sale which passes no property, in favour of the minor is not binding on the minor more so because it cannot be enforced by the vendor.[5] The principles applicable to a minor as regards service contracts and necessities supplied are applicable to lunatics.[6]

In England, persons are incapable of entering into or enforcing contract by reason of (*i*) political status, *e.g.* aliens; (*ii*) infancy; (*iii*) corporate personality; (*iv*) lunacy or drunkenness. Minors are designated as infants and they attain majority on completion of 21 years. In common law, minors' contracts are divided into three classes— (*a*) those for necessaries, (*b*) those for his benefit, and (*c*) other contracts. The Infant Relief Act 1874,[7] rendered all contracts other than those for necessaries void. An alien in England has contractual capacity like a natural born British subject except that he cannot acquire any property in a British ship.[8]

In India, aliens are competent to buy and sell property, both movable and immovable, but their capacity to contract exists so long as they are 'friends'. So there can be no partnership between subjects of different hostile powers and the outbreak of a war between them determines the partnership.[9]

(h) *Communication—when complete*. The communication of a proposal is complete when it comes to the knowledge of the person to whom it is made. The communication of an acceptance is complete, as against the proposer, when it is put in a course of transmission to him so as to be out of the power of the acceptor; or against the acceptor, when it comes to the knowledge of the proposer. The communication of a revocation is complete, as against the person who makes it when it is put into a course of transmission to the person to whom it is made, so as to be out of the power of the person who makes it, as against the person to whom it is made, when it comes to

2 *Subramanyam* v *Subba Rao* AIR 1948 PC 95. See also *Mohari Bibi* v *Dharmadas Ghosh* (1903)30 Cal 539— Privy Council held that all contracting parties must be competent to contract.
3 Section 127 of the Transfer of Property Act.
4 *Satyadeva* v *Trebeni* 161 IC 579.
5 *Moang Aunj* v *Gyi* 32 IC 638.
6 Re, *Rhodes* 44 Ch D 94.
7 37 and 38 Vict. C. 62.
8 Merchant and Shipping Act 1894 (57 & 58 Cict, c. 60) S.I. See also Anson's *Contract*, 27th Ed., p. 212.
9 *Rodriguez* v *Speyer Brothers* (1919) AC 59.

his knowledge.[10] Payment made under a mistake can be claimed by way of refund provided it is not barred by limitation. Section 72 of the Contract Act applies.[11] Illegalities are incurable. Where the plea is of illegality or invalidity the conduct of the parties become irrelevant and earlier consent should not come in the way.[12]

(i) *Revocation of proposal and acceptance*. A proposal can be revoked at any time before the communication of its acceptance is complete as against the proposer, but not afterwards.[13] An acceptance can be revoked at any time before the communication of the acceptance is complete as against the acceptor, but not afterwards.

(j) *Revocation how made*. A proposal is revoked—

(1) by the communication of notice of revocation by the proposer to the other party;

(2) by the lapse of the time prescribed in such proposal for its acceptance or, if no time is prescribed, by the lapse of a reasonable time without communication of the acceptance;

(3) by the failure of the acceptor to fulfil a condition precedent to acceptance; or

(4) by the death or insanity of the proposer if the fact of his death or insanity comes to the knowledge of the acceptor before acceptance.

It is interesting to note here that the dictum in *Dickinson* v *Dodds*[14] is not applicable to India as the communication of the revocation of the proposal has to proceed from the proposer. It will be also interesting to note that the revocation of the authority of an agent does not affect third parties before they have knowledge of the same[15] and the revocation of a continuing guarantee is only as to future transaction.[16]

(k) *Compensation for breach of contract*. When a contract has been broken, if a sum is named in the contract as the amount to be paid in case of such breach, or if the contract contains any other stipulation by way of penalty,

10 Section 3 of the Indian Contract Act.
11 *Nagar Mahapalika* v *Sai Ram* AIR 1990 SC 274.
12 *Union Carbide* v *Union of India* AIR 1992 SC 248.
13 Sections 5 and 6 of the Indian Contract Act 1872.
14 (1876)2 Ch D 463. Dodds made an offer to sell a house to Dickinson for £ 800. The offer was kept open till 9 a.m. on Friday 12th June; on 11th June, Dodds entered into a contract with *A* for sale of the house. One *B* presumably not acting under authority from Dodds reported the matter to Dickinson who then handed over his acceptance in writing to Dodds which he refused. It was held by the Court of Appeal that there was no contract.
15 Section 208 of the Indian Contract Act.
16 Section 130 of the Indian Contract Act.

the party complaining of the breach is entitled, whether or not actual damage or loss is proved to have been caused thereby, to receive from the party who has broken the contract, reasonable compensation not exceeding the amount so named, or, as the case may be, the penalty stipulated for.[17]

A stipulation for increased interest from the date of default may be a stipulation by way of penalty.[18]

STIFLING OF PROSECUTION. The essence of the doctrine of stifling of prosecution is that no private person should be allowed to take the administration of criminal justice out of the hands of the Judges and place it in his own hands. The distinction between the 'motive' for entering into agreement and the 'consideration' for the agreement must be clearly maintained. Where the dropping of the criminal proceedings is a motive for entering into the agreement—and not in consideration—the doctrine of stifling of prosecution is not attracted. Where there is also a pre-existing civil liability, the dropping of criminal proceedings need not necessarily be a consideration for the agreement to satisfy that liability.[19]

EXCEPTIONS. When any person enters into any bail bond, recognizance or other instrument of the same nature, or, under the provisions of any law or under the orders of the Government of India, or of any State Government, and gives any bond for the performance of any public duty or act in which the public are interested, he will be liable, upon breach of the condition of any such instrument, to pay the whole sum mentioned therein. Nevertheless, the court has discretion to consider the nature of the bond and the breach.[20]

LIQUIDATED DAMAGES AND PENALTY. The rule of English law as to distinction between liquidated damages and penalty does not apply to India. A liquidated damage is a genuine covenanted pre-estimate of damage. A penalty is a lump sum payable as compensation on the happening of some event or events. The courts in India have always the power to ascertain the actual loss and award damages which they consider reasonable.[21]

If a party to the contract is required to suffer the consequences for his failure to abide by the terms by a stipulated date such a consequence would be penal but on the other hand if that party gets some benefit by complying with the requirement by the stipulated date such a clause granting benefit can never be treated as penal in character.[1]

17 Section 74 of the Indian Contract Act.
18 *Bhimji* v *Bombay Trust Corporation* (1930)54 Bom 381, 404, 405.
19 *Union Carbide* v *Union of India* AIR 1992 SC 248; see also *Deb Kumar* v *Anata Bandhu* AIR 1931 Cal 421.
20 *Secretary of State* v *Dilsizian Freres* (1921)45 Bom 1212.
21 *Fateh Chand* v *Balkishan Dass* AIR 1963 SC 1405.
1 *Prithvichand* v *S.Y. Sindhe* AIR 1993 SC 1929.

Forfeiture of Deposit. Earnest money or deposit signifies *bona fide* conclusion of the contract. It is liable to be forfeited on breach of contract. So if the sales go off by reason of the sellers' default he must return the deposit, but if the buyer is in fault he shall suffer on that account.[2]

The rule as to forfeiture of deposit is not applicable where the contract is not carried out.[3]

In a suit upon an agreement for sale it is not always necessary to deposit the money unless the court so directs. Not depositing the money along with the plaint cannot be taken as a factor to deprive the plaintiff of his relief nor is indicative of the fact that the plaintiff had not been ready and willing to perform his part of the contract.[4] A subsequent transferee with notice stands in a feduciary capacity and holds the property in trust to the prior agreement-holder, but the prior agreement-holder cannot automatically become the owner by seeking declaratory relief and has necessarily to file a suit for specific performance impleading both the vendor and the subsequent transferee.[5] Once a decree for specific performance is granted it includes the term for delivery of possession as the court was directing the enforcement of the entire agreement including the agreement to deliver possession.[6]

(l) *Execution and attestation—registration*. Agreements are executed and attested as a bond. It is not, however, essential that the signature of a party to an agreement should be attested by a witness.

Registration of agreements is not compulsory; but if an agreement by itself creates an interest in immovable property of the value of Rs. 100 and upwards, its registration will be compulsory. The vendor of any immovable property is not a trustee for the purchaser as in English law even under a registered agreement for sale.[7] Writing is necessary in several cases. A contract to sell the products of any particular land is to be registered inasmuch as it creates an interest in the land.[8]

(m) *Acknowledgement of liability under s. 18 of the Limitation Act, sec. 5 of the Indian Trusts Act.* Trust of Immovable Property—Lease, Gift, Sale, Mortgage under ss. 107, 123, 54 and 59 of the Transfer of Property Act.

Voidable and void agreements. Section 2(*i*) of the Indian Contract Act 1872, defines what is voidable agreement. An agreement is enforceable at the

2 Section 74 of the Indian Contract Act.
3 *Sudarshan* v *Chuba Singh* AIR 1956 HP 28.
4 *N. Venkatappa* v *Lingappa* AIR 1998 Kant 372.
5 *Kondapalli* v *Kondapalli* AIR 1999 AP 170.
6 *K.M. Rajendran* v *Arul Prakasam* AIR 1998 Mad 336.
7 *Ariff* v *Jadunath* 58 IA 91.
8 *Ali* v *Janabali* 62 CLJ 534.

instance of one party but not the other. Section 64 of the said Act provides for restoration of the benefits by the party avoiding the contract. The principles laid down under this section are not applicable to insurance policies which are discovered to be void by reason of concealment of facts[9] or to the benefits received by a minor or other incompetent persons.[10]

Where a sale deed was executed under no undue influence even though the vendor was old, blind, illiterate and tribal woman totally at the mercy of the person with whom she had been living till her death such person was in a position to dominate the will of the woman and obtain unfair advantage over her, the onus lies on that person to prove that sale deed was not executed under undue influence.[11]

A void contract is defined under s. 2(*j*) of the Indian Contract Act—a contract which has no legal effect. It may be classified as follows:

(a) *Consideration and object—unlawful.* If any part of a single consideration for one or more objects, or any one, or any part of any one, of several considerations for a single object, is unlawful, the agreement is void.[12]

The consideration or object of an agreement is unlawful, when—

(*i*) it is forbidden by law, *e.g.* (*a*) partnership with illegal object, (*b*) trading with alien enemy,[13] agreement involving traffic in public office,[14] contract regarding sale and purchase of jute goods among persons not being habitual dealers, are void under the Jute Goods Act.[15]

(*ii*) it is of such a nature that, if permitted, it would defeat the provisions of any law, e.g. agreement to defeat the provisions of insolvency law or the statute laws or common law among Hindus and Mahomedans, *e.g.* agreement in restraint of legal proceedings except reference to arbitration;

(*iii*) it is fraudulent e.g. excessive high rate of interest,[16] agreement for sale which is hit by section 53 of the T.P. Act; and

(*iv*) it involves or implies injury to the person or property of another; or the court regards it as immoral or opposed to public policy, e.g.

9 *Mithoolal Nayak* v *Life Insurance Corporation* AIR 1962 SC 814.
10 *Mohari Bibi* v *Dharmadas Ghosh* (1903)30 Cal 539 (PC).
11 *Sethani* v *Bhora* AIR 1993 SC 956.
12 Section 24 of the Indian Contract Act.
13 *Rodriguez* v *Speyers Brothers* (1919) AC 59.
14 *Saminatha* v *Muthusami* (1907)30 Mad 530.
15 Section 3C(1) of Jute Goods Act 1950.
16 Section 74 of the Indian Contract Act.

an agreement to purchase the share of company with a view to making others believe in a *bona fide* market.[17]

(b) *Agreement without consideration*. An agreement made without consideration is void,[18] unless—

(*i*) it is a deed of gift, duly executed and registered, and made on account of natural love and affection between the parties; or unless

(*ii*) it is a promise to compensate for something voluntarily done for the promisor; or unless

(*iii*) it is promise in writing to pay a debt barred by the law of limitation.

(c) *Agreements in restraint of marriage, trade and legal proceedings*. An agreement in restraint of marriage of any person, other than a minor, is void.[19]

An agreement by which one is restrained from exercising a lawful profession, trade or business of any kind is void unless it is an agreement not to carry on business within a specified area, of which goodwill is sold, or such agreement (*i.e.* not to carry on business), between partners prior to dissolution of, or during continuance of, partnership.[20]

An agreement in restraint of legal proceedings is void unless it is an agreement to refer a dispute to arbitration.

(d) *Agreements with uncertain meaning, by way of wager and under mistake of fact*. An agreement, the meaning of which is not certain, or capable of being made certain, is void.[1]

An agreement by way of wager is void unless it is an agreement involving prize or sum of money of the value or amount of Rs. 500 or upwards, to be awarded to the winners of any horse race.

Where both the parties to an agreement are under a mistake as to a matter of fact essential to the agreement, the agreement is void.[2]

The following are necessary to bring this section in operation:

(*i*) Mutual mistake (vide s. 22 of the Indian Contract Act);

(*ii*) Mistake of fact and not law except foreign law (s. 21 of the Indian Contract Act); and

(*iii*) Mistake of facts essential to the contract.

17 *Scott* v *Brown Doering McNab & Co.* (1892)2 QB 724.
18 Section 25 of the Indian Contract Act.
19 Section 26 of the Indian Contract Act.
20 Section 27 of the Indian Contract Act.
1 Section 29 of the Indian Contract Act.
2 Section 20 of the Indian Contract Act.

(e) *Contract with Governments.* When it is not in compliance with Art. 299(1) of the Constitution of India.

(f) *Contract of corporation.* It is the doctrine of English common law that all contracts by corporation shall be made under the common seal except small matters of daily occurrence.[3] Modern authorities are however following the principle of convenience and are liberal in cases of trading corporations as regards contracts made in the ordinary course of business. In India the courts do not recognise the rights of individuals interested in the corporation but the rights of the corporation. A contract *ultra vires* the company cannot be ratified even unanimously by all its members.[4]

(g) *Contract of employment.* A contract of employment cannot ordinarily be enforced by or against an employer. The remedy is to sue for damages. There are of course certain exceptions such as in the case of a public servant dismissed in contravention of Art. 311 of the Constitution; reinstatement of a dismissed worker under the Industrial Law; a statutory body acting in breach of statutory obligations. Courts do not ordinarily force an employer to recruit or retain in service an employee not required by the employer.[5]

(h) *Commercial contract.* In commercial contracts between parties belonging to two different countries the governing law is determined by the intention of the parties. The true intention of the parties, in the absence of express selection, is to be ascertained by applying sound ideas of business, convenience and sense to the language of the contract itself.[6]

When the parties enter into an agreement with each other, it is the agreement alone which determines their rights and obligations *qua* each other. Neither the rule of promissory estoppel nor the doctrine of legitimate expectation can be applied to amend, alter or vary express terms of the contract between the parties.[7]

FORMS

Loan Agreement with Bank

THIS AGREEMENT is made the .... day of .... in the year .... BETWEEN the .... AB Bank Ltd., a banking company having its registered office

3 Mulla: *Contract*, 11th Ed., pp. 168-169.
4 *Ashbury Ry. Co. v Riche* LR 7 HL 651.
5 *Nandganj v Badri Nath* AIR 1991 SC 1525.
6 *National Thermal v Singer & Co.* AIR 1993 SC 998.
7 *AAA Film v Union of India* AIR 1999 Del 178.

.... at .... (hereinafter called the BANK) of the ONE PART *and* Mr. .... son of .... residing at .... and carrying on business under the name and style of .... at .... hereinafter called the BORROWER of the OTHER PART.

WHEREAS the BANK through its branch at .... has at the request of THE BORROWER agreed to grant him financial accommodation against his said business and for that purpose to allow him overdraft facilities through a cash credit account in the name of .... up to the maximum limit of Rs. ....

NOW IT IS HEREBY AGREED by and between the parties as follows:

1. The BANK shall accommodate the BORROWER from time to time against his said business by overdraft as and when required by the BORROWER up to a maximum limit of Rupees .... only inclusive of all interest and other charges, but nevertheless the liability of the BORROWER shall not be limited to the above maximum amount, if the borrowings inclusive of interest and other costs, charges and expenses exceed the aforesaid agreed limit.

2. The BORROWER shall pay interest on the said loan or advance at the rate of .... per cent .... on the daily balance of the said account and the same shall be debited in his said account on the last working day of each English month and form part of the principal and carry further interest at the said rate. In case the aforesaid limit is not availed of by the BORROWER or if for any reason whatsoever there is a credit balance in favour of the BORROWER, the BORROWER shall nevertheless remain liable to pay interest at the stipulated rate on Rs. ....

3. That the account in the books of the BANK shall be conclusive proof against the BORROWER of the amount or amounts of the BANK. In addition to the stipulated interest the BORROWER shall pay to the BANK the following further charges also:

(*i*) usual incidental charges every six months;

(*ii*) usual commissions on foreign, that is, outstation cheques, drafts, etc. and other usual; and

(*iii*) customary charges.

4. The BORROWER has executed a relative pronote for the maximum limit of Rs. .... only carrying interest at the stipulated rate in favour of the BANK and has handed over the same to the BANK as security for the payment of any sum which may at any time be due to the BANK on the said cash credit account.

5. This agreement shall remain in force for a period of .... years from the date hereof, unless otherwise extended or determined by the BANK. The BANK shall be at liberty to refuse overdraft and stop making advances at any time without assigning any reasons whatsoever even without any prior

notice in which event the BANK shall not be liable to pay any damages if suffered by the borrowers on that account.

6. On the expiry of the period specified in Para 5 above or at any time later or earlier, the BORROWER shall pay or cause to be paid to the BANK on demand the balance then outstanding and owing to the BANK on the said cash credit account (inclusive of interest and all other charges and expenses) as appearing from the books of the BANK which the BORROWER has agreed to accept as sufficient and conclusive evidence as against him of the amount due from him and in the event of the said demand being neglected and/or not complied with, the BANK shall realise the amount or amounts due through civil process with all expenses and charges actually incurred.

IN WITNESS WHEREOF the parties hereto have at .... affixed their signature the day and the year first above-written.

WITNESSES:

1. .... BORROWER

Address:

2. .... Agent/Manager

Address:

Agreement for Cash Credit

The .... Bank .... (hereinafter called the BANK) through their office at .... having at the request of .... (hereinafter called the BORROWERS) undertaken to open in the books of the bank at ....a cash credit account with the BORROWERS up to the maximum limit of Rs. ....

It is agreed as follows:

1. That the BANK shall not, under this agreement, be required to make advances of such an amount that the total dues in this account including interest and other charges may, at any time, exceed the sum of Rs................

The BORROWERS shall, however, be responsible for the payment of the entire amount that may at any time be due in this account although such amount may exceed the above-mentioned limit.

2. That interest at the rate of .... per cent per .... shall be calculated on the daily balance of the said account and shall be charged to the account on the last working day of each month and it will form part of the principal and will carry interest at the above-mentioned rate.

3. That on the .... day of .... 19 .... next or on demand being made by the BANK on any earlier date, the BORROWERS shall pay to the

BANK the balance then outstanding and owing to the BANK on the said account inclusive of interest at the rate above mentioned to the date of payment together with all the charges and expenses charged or incurred by the BANK as ascertained by the books of the said bank which the BORROWERS agree to accept as sufficient proof of the correctness thereof, without the production of any voucher or paper.

4. That the head office of the BANK or the said Branch will be at liberty to sue the borrowers at .... or at ....

5. That the BORROWERS will be liable for all costs of recovery incurred by the BANK before filing a suit and also for all costs in connection with the suit till recovery of full amount, whether such costs may be allowed by rules of court or not.

6. That a relative pronote dated .... has been given to the BANK by the BORROWERS to secure payment of any sum which may at any time be due to the BANK on such account.

7. That the BORROWERS agree that when the Reserve Bank rate of discount is .... per cent or above, they will pay as interest 1 per cent above the said Reserve Bank rate.

8. That the BORROWERS agree to pay incidental charges for every six months or part thereof (according to labour involved) during the time the account remains open.

9. That the BORROWERS shall not be entitled to any interest for any sum which may at any time stand to their credit in this account.

10. That the BANK will always be at liberty to stop making advances at any time without previous notice and without assigning any reason, even though the said limit of Rs. .... has not been fully availed of.

11. That the BORROWERS further agree to pay interest at the stipulated rate on .... portion of the aforesaid limit even if the limit is not availed of at all or an amount less than the aforesaid portion is borrowed.

WITNESSED BY:	Signature of BORROWER or BORROWERS
....	....
Address	Address ....
Dated	Dated ....
	For the .... Bank
WITNESSED BY:	*Manager*
....	
Address	Dated ....
Dated	
....	
....	

Agreement between Producers and Distributors

MEMORANDUM OF AGREEMENT made on this .... day of .... in the year .... BETWEEN .... of No................, a Registered Partnership Firm consisting of.................... partners hereinafter called the PRODUCERS (which expression shall, unless excluded by or repugnant to the context, be deemed to include his/their heirs, executors, administrators, representatives and assigns) of the One Part and AB & Co. Ltd. a company registered under the Indian Companies Act (Act 1 of 1956) having its office at .... hereinafter called the Distributors (which expression shall unless excluded by or repugnant to the context, be deemed to include their representatives and assigns) hereinafter referred to as PARTY of the Other Part:

WHEREAS PRODUCERS have made a preliminary arrangement of producing a Bengali Talkie picture tentatively called Approach written by ....

AND WHEREAS the PRODUCERS need financial assistance and co-operation and therefore approached the PARTY hereto of the other part for such help and assistance AND whereas the PARTY agreed to render such financial assistance to the PRODUCERS to the extent and upon the terms and conditions hereinafter following

NOW THEREFORE THIS INDENTURE WITNESSETH as follows:

1. That the PRODUCERS undertake to complete the shooting for the aforesaid picture .... for an approximate cost of Rupees .... only, including print and publicity at least with three top-rank artists.

2. That the PRODUCERS hereof shall arrange and bear the necessary amount required for the payment to the artists, workers and other costs necessary for the production except those hereinbelow mentioned.

3. That the PRODUCERS undertake to deposit with the PARTY as security the sum of Rupees .... to be paid by instalments of Rs. .... on the date of signing of the contract and Rs. .... only on the date of the first shooting. If the PRODUCERS fail to complete one-fourth of the said picture approximately three thousand feet edited shots within two months from the first shooting date, then in that case the PRODUCERS shall also have to deposit a further sum of Rs...... as security with the PARTY. The amount so deposited shall remain to the credit of the PRODUCERS and would be returned to them within six months from the date of the last deposit to be made as aforesaid.

4. That the PARTY agrees to advance to the PRODUCERS for the production and completion of the aforesaid Bengali talkie picture a sum of Rs. .... to be paid in the following manner:

(*a*) That the PARTY shall arrange the studio, laboratory and raw film for the production by the PRODUCERS of the aforesaid picture and shall pay the necessary costs thereof by debiting the amount to the PRODUCERS from the first shooting date, provided that the PARTY shall arrange with the studio for allotting to the PRODUCERS at least eight days in a month and every month till the completion of the picture and shall, whenever necessary, enter into and sign a deed or documents in this behalf in which the PRODUCERS shall be a confirming party.

(*b*) That the PRODUCERS shall arrange for the .... editing and processing of the said film in any laboratory they may choose and the PARTY shall pay for the cost thereof and debit the amount to be paid to the PRODUCERS. The selection of the editor would be entirely with the PRODUCERS.

(*c*) That the PARTY after providing the expenses as in cls. (*a*) and (*b*) with an approximate amount of Rs. .... shall pay to firstly the balance of Rs. .... out of Rs. .... so agreed to be advanced, up to the rush prints along with the progress of the shooting of the aforesaid picture by instalments as and when required by the PRODUCERS provided however, that the PRODUCERS shall not be entitled to demand from the PARTY any such advance of money unless and until the PRODUCERS has completed approximately three thousand feet edited shots of this picture aforesaid.

5. That in consideration of the financial help agreed to be rendered hereinbefore by the PARTY to the PRODUCERS, the PARTY shall receive a commission of 20% on the net collection of the PRODUCERS' share of the aforesaid picture "Approach".

6. That the PARTY shall further be the sole distributor of the aforesaid picture and shall have rights, privileges and benefits of the said picture and shall have a first charge on it till realization of the advance made by the PARTY as aforesaid to be approved of by the PRODUCERS or by their authorized agent.

7. That the PARTY undertakes to arrange for public exhibition of the said picture .... within three months from the completion of the rush print in at least two best possible houses in Calcutta, *i.e.,* one in the north and one in the south and four houses outside the municipal limits of the city of Calcutta area and the proceeds thereof shall be distributed as under—

(*i*) after deducting .... commission of the PARTY of the net collection on producer's share, the PARTY shall also deduct .... from the balance therefrom to liquidate the principal of the amount of the advances made and the balance .... shall be paid to the PRODUCERS direct or to its authorized agent, persons or company monthly showing in a statement the collection received from the date of release.

8. That if the sale proceeds of the said picture after public exhibition does not cover the dues of the PARTY within two years, the signatory of this agreement on behalf of the PRODUCERS shall be jointly and severally liable to pay back to the PARTY of the balance amount remaining unrealized as and when called upon to do so provided satisfactory exploitation of the said film is made by the PARTY.

9. That the PRODUCERS will keep necessary accounts and papers customary in this business and the PARTY will have the right to inspect and take copies or extracts therefrom at any time during office hours and a monthly statement of account should be submitted by the PRODUCERS to the PARTY.

10. That the PRODUCERS undertakes to complete the production of the said film within six months from the first shooting date in conformity with cl. 4(*c*) mentioned above

(*a*) That the PRODUCERS will have the right to raise loan for the balance amount of Rs. .... or such amount as may be necessary for the completion of the said picture over and above the sum of Rs. .... to be advanced by the PARTY as aforesaid and the PARTY shall have no objection to that and will be added as a confirming party to the said transaction.

(*b*) That the PARTY undertakes not to charge, mortgage, or hypothecate the picture without the written consent of the PRODUCERS.

11. That if the PRODUCERS fail to comply with any of the terms and conditions entered into by this agreement, the distributor will have the right to complete the picture and the money paid by the PRODUCERS will be repaid by the PARTY after the release of the picture and from the releasing houses.

12. That if the PARTY fails to comply with the terms and conditions of this agreement, the PRODUCERS shall have the right to complete the picture from such source as they may think fit and to cancel the PARTY as the distributor and have also the right to appoint another distributor and to accept advances from other sources and the money to be advanced by the PARTY will be repaid to them after release of the picture and from the releasing houses.

13. In the event of either party failing to act in accordance with the provisions of the agreement, the aggrieved party shall at the first instance try to settle the disputed points mutually and amicably, failing such attempt the point in dispute shall be referred to arbitration in accordance with the provisions of the Arbitration and Conciliation Act 1996. If, however, the arbitrator declines to make any decision or award on the point referred to him then the parties concerned may settle the dispute by having recourse to appropriate legal proceedings.

IN WITNESS WHEREOF the parties to these presents hereunto set and subscribed their respective hands and seals the day, month and year first above-written.

Signed, sealed and delivered by *A* duly authorised by the partnership firm X & Co. in the presence of:

Signed and delivered by Mr. .... pursuant to the Board Resolution dated .... of AB & Co. Ltd. in the presence of:

Advertising Agreement

THIS ADVERTISING AGREEMENT made this 15th day of May 2000 BETWEEN ELH Ltd. a company registered under the Companies Act 1956 and carrying on business at 54 Ganesh Chunder Avenue, Calcutta 700 013 (hereinafter referred to as the 'OWNER' which term shall include its successors and assigns) of the One Part and Advertising Co. Ltd. a company registered under the Companies Act 1956 and carrying on business at 11 Park Street, Calcutta 700 016 (hereinafter referred to as the ADVERTISER which term shall include its successors and permitted assigns) of the Other Part.

WHEREAS the OWNER is seized and possessed of the land and building being premises No. 54 Ganesh Chunder Avenue, Calcutta 700 013, having frontage on the open main road with 10 ft. wide open space.

AND WHEREAS the ADVERTISER has approached the OWNER for utilising part of this open space facing the road for the purpose of erecting structures, fixing the Board or hoarding and advertising the products for its customers.

AND WHEREAS the ADVERTISER has agreed to obtain the necessary permission of the concerned authorities at its own expenses and costs and the OWNER has agreed to sign and/or join in signing all applications and documents necessary for the purpose of obtaining permission for erecting the Board and/or hoarding and advertising.

AND WHEREAS the ADVERTISER has agreed to pay a monthly licence fee from the date of execution of these presents and to increase such payment by 10% on obtaining the necessary permission for erecting the structure and fixing the Board and writing the advertisement thereon.

AND WHEREAS the OWNER has agreed to the proposals.

NOW THESE PRESENTS WITNESSETH and the parties hereto agree as follows:

1. The ADVERTISER will obtain necessary sanction and permission from the authorities concerned for fixing two pillars of iron and steel within the open space of premises No. 54 Ganesh Chunder Avenue, Calcutta 700 013

on the North-Western corner and to fix the Board made of wood and tin of a size of 10 ft. wide and 20 ft. in height and to write on the Board such matters as are permissible under law for the purposes of advertising the products of the advertiser or the Advertiser's customers.

2. ADVERTISER will pay and bear all the costs, charges and expenses for the erection of the Board, writings and all rates taxes and levies payable in relation thereto.

3. The ADVERTISER will keep the OWNER harmless from and indemnified against all actions, proceedings, claims, losses damages and expenses for such erections, setting up of the Board for advertisements or any act of the ADVERTISER.

4. In consideration of the OWNER having agreed to allow the ADVERTISER to erect the pillars, fixing the Board and writing the advertising matters the ADVERTISER would pay to the OWNER a Licence fee of Rs. 10,000 per month in advance by the 10th day of each month commencing from May 2000.

5. The ADVERTISER will keep in deposit with the OWNER a sum of Rs. 1 lakh free from any interest by way of Security.

6. The ADVERTISER agrees that it will not display any objectionable matter or any matter which may cause annoyance to the public or in a manner which will cause nuisance to the locality or cause any injury to the building of the owner or to any next building.

7. The OWNER agrees to allow the authorised employees of the ADVERTISER and its authorised representatives to enter the said premises for erection of the poles and/or pillars, fixing of the board and writing the advertising matters on proper notice and during the hours that may be mutually agreed to without causing any inconvenience to the premises or to the neighbours.

8. The ADVERTISER shall maintain the said erection and advertising board in good condition and repair, make it absolutely safe for the inmates of the premises and others who may happen to be inside or outside the premises, with or without licence or any member of the public who may happen to be near the said Advertising Unit.

9. This AGREEMENT will be for a period of 5 years commencing from 15th May 2000 with the option of renewal for another five years at an enhanced licence fee to the extent of 30% of the then existing rate on terms and conditions to be mutually agreed upon.

10. The ADVERTISER agrees to pay all costs, charges and expenses and Stamp Duty, if any, for registering this Agreement.

11. The ADVERTISER may use Neon Signs or any other Visual Signs on the Board to be fixed or otherwise on the structure in a manner permissible under law and for this purpose make an arrangement to take electric connection from the OWNER'S lines with the permission of CESC Ltd. and having a sub-meter for that purpose at the cost and expenses of the

ADVERTISER and the ADVERTISER would be liable to pay the bills for the consumption of electricity, and other charges, according to the readings of the sub-meters.

12. The ADVERTISER hereby agrees and undertakes to attend to any repairs or any other defects within 24 hours of the complaint made by the OWNER or other aggrieved person and on failure to do so the OWNER will get the repairs done at the cost and expenses of the ADVERTISER which the ADVERTISER undertakes to pay to the OWNER within 3 days of the submission of the bills.

13. All disputes and differences arising out of or in relation to these presents or the subject-matter hereof shall be referred to the Arbitration of Mr. P.K. Lekhi whose decision shall be final and binding on the parties and in accordance with the provisions of Arbitration and Conciliation Act 1996.

IN WITNESS WHEREOF the parties hereto have executed these presents on the day, month and year first above-written.

Signed, sealed and delivered by
Mr. ....
pursuant to the Board Resolution
dated .... of ELH Ltd., the
OWNER in the presence of: Signature

Signed, sealed and delivered by
Mr. ....
pursuant to the Board Resolution
of Advertising Co. Ltd., the
ADVERTISER dated ....
in the presence of: Signature

Agreement for Appointment of Sales Agent

THIS AGREEMENT is made on this 7th day of June 1999 BETWEEN Computer Company Ltd., a company registered under the Companies Act 1956 having its registered office at 7 N.S. Road, Calcutta 700 001 (hereinafter referred to as the COMPANY which expression shall unless the context requires otherwise include its successors) of the ONE PART and Mr. S. Tandon of 5 Bangalore Road, Bangalore, Karnataka (hereinafter referred to as the AGENT) of the OTHER PART.

WHEREAS the COMPANY is carrying on business as manufacturer of and dealer in Computers, Computer Hardwares and Computer Softwares for the last 10 years and selling its products both in domestic and export markets.

AND WHEREAS the AGENT was working with another company as the Chief Mechanic of the Computers and has acquired knowledge of repairs of

Hardwares and Softwares and is capable of rendering after sales service and maintaining Computers in good working condition.

AND WHEREAS the AGENT after leaving his employment has approached the COMPANY for agency to sell the products of the COMPANY on commission basis.

AND WHEREAS the AGENT has declared that he is not working for any other company and that he intends to work as agent for sale of computers and computer accessories as an independent contractor.

AND WHEREAS the COMPANY and the AGENT had discussions and negotiations relating to the sale of COMPANY'S products by the AGENT in the territories covered by the States of Karnataka, Kerala and Andhra Pradesh.

AND WHEREAS the parties herein have mutually agreed to the terms and conditions in regard to the sale of COMPANY'S products.

NOW THESE PRESENTS WITNESSETH and the parties hereby agree as follows:

1. The COMPANY hereby appoints the AGENT as the agent of the COMPANY in the States of Karnataka, Kerala and Andhra Pradesh for the sale of the COMPANY'S products including Computers, Computer Hardwares and Computer Softwares for a term of three years commencing from 1st July 1999 on terms and conditions mentioned hereinafter.

2. The AGENT shall:

(*a*) use his best endeavours to promote and expand the sales of the COMPANY'S Computers, Hardwares and Softwares (hereinafter referred to as the "PRODUCTS") in the State of Karnataka, Kerala and Andhra Pradesh (hereinafter called the "TERRITORIES") to all potential purchasers thereof and work diligently to obtain orders therefor;

(*b*) act loyally and faithfully and obey the orders and instructions of the COMPANY and if in any case it is not possible to obtain instruction in a particular matter to act in such a manner as the AGENT reasonably considers to be most beneficial to the interests of the COMPANY;

(*c*) refrain for engaging or being interested directly or indirectly as the principal, AGENT, partner, director or employee in the production, sale or advertisement of goods of any description or kind or similar to or competitive with the products of the COMPANY without the prior written consent of the COMPANY;

(*d*) not to take orders for the sale to any person of the products which he knows or has reason to believe are intended for re-sale outside the TERRITORIES without prior consent of the COMPANY;

(*e*) refer to the COMPANY all enquiries for the products received from outside the territories as also from addresses in the territories for re-sale outside the territories;

(*f*) take orders for sale of goods only subject to confirmation and acceptance by the COMPANY and on the usual terms and conditions;

(*g*) not make any representation in selling the goods nor to give any warranties or concessions other than those contained in the COMPANY'S conditions of sale;

(*h*) keep proper books of accounts and records of all enquiries and transactions relating to the products separate from other transactions outside the agency and submit reports from time to time to the COMPANY and allow the COMPANY'S authorised officer to inspect and take copies of such books of accounts and records;

3. The AGENT shall make market-survey and proper enquiries as to the financial stability of the intending purchasers of goods and furnish reports to the COMPANY. The AGENT shall attend and promote the sale of the products at all Sales Exhibitions and Trade Shows after properly apprising the COMPANY the particulars thereof.

4. The AGENT shall not assign, transfer or charge his rights under these presents and in all correspondence and commercial documents in relation to the products shall describe himself as the Selling Agent for the COMPANY'S products.

5. The AGENT shall defray all expenses of and incidental to the Agency, shall not make directly or indirectly any profit or take any benefit in the sale of the products and shall not divulge any information in relation to the COMPANY'S trade secrets or know-how or marketing technique or any method of manufacturing, selling or dealing in its products.

6. The AGENT agrees and covenants that the AGENT shall not act as the Selling Agent for any other company in Computer goods similar to the COMPANY'S products for three years within the said territories after termination of the present agreement.

7. The COMPANY shall at its own expense supply to the AGENT samples, patterns, catalogues, operating manuals, repairing manuals, particulars of parties and advertising materials as the COMPANY considers reasonably sufficient with a view to enable the AGENT to conveniently render after-sales-service to the purchasers of the products in the said territories.

8. Notwithstanding anything to the contrary contained herein the COMPANY reserves to itself its right:

(*a*) to decline at its absolute discretion without giving any reason therefor any order or to submit any quotation or tender on any enquiry transmitted to the COMPANY by the AGENT;

(*b*) to sell and supply the COMPANY'S products direct to customers in the said territories;

(*c*) to transfer and assign its rights and obligations under this Agreement to any other concern after giving 15 days' notice to the AGENT.

9. It is agreed that if in the reasonable opinion of the COMPANY the AGENT is not producing adequate sales coverage in or through the said territories, the COMPANY may exclude a portion of the territories or otherwise vary the extent of the territories on prior notice to the AGENT.

10. In consideration of the services to be rendered by the AGENT the COMPANY will pay to the AGENT a commission of 10% on the invoice price of products sold in the territories upto a sale of Rs. 10 lakhs and thereafter 5% up to the sale of Rs. 20 lakhs and 2.5% on sale proceeds in excess of Rs. 20 lakhs. Such commission shall be paid on furnishing of accounts every three months.

11. The COMPANY shall reimburse every month actual expenses of travelling, advertisements, repairs to the computers sold and such other expenses as the AGENT might reasonably spend in relation to rendering of after-sales-service and promoting sales of the COMPANY'S products.

12. If any customer does not make payment or makes short-payment or returns the goods in respect of which the COMPANY has paid commission to the AGENT, the AGENT hereby undertakes and covenants to refund the commission received for such products.

13. In addition to any other rights herein or under the law, the COMPANY shall have the right at any time to give notice in writing to the AGENT terminating the Agreement forthwith if the AGENT commits a breach of any of the terms herein or it does any act of insolvency or the AGENT is prevented from performing his duties hereunder for 3 months for any reason whatsoever or the AGENT is guilty of any conduct prejudicial to the interests of the COMPANY or the AGENT purports to assign the burden or benefit or charge the benefit of this Agreement.

14. After termination of this Agreement the AGENT shall at his own expenses promptly return to the company all samples, patterns, catalogues, advertising materials, specifications and other materials, documents and papers relating to the business of the COMPANY which the AGENT might have in his possession or under his control.

15. The waiver by the COMPANY of any breach of any of the terms of this Agreement shall not prevent the subsequent enforcement of that term and shall not be deemed a waiver of any subsequent breach.

16. There are no other promises, terms and conditions other than those contained in these presents.

17. This Agreement shall be renewable after the expiry of three years on the terms and conditions which might be mutually agreed upon.

IN WITNESS WHEREOF the parties have executed these presents on the day, month and year first above-written.

Signed, sealed and delivered by Mr. .... pursuant to Board Resolution of Computer Co. Ltd. dated 5th June 1999 in the presence of: Signature

Signed, sealed and delivered by Mr. S. Tandon, the AGENT in the presence of: Signature

Agreement between Manufacturer and Dealer

THIS AGREEMENT is made on this .... day of .... 1999 BETWEEN AB carrying on business at .... under the name and style of AB & Co. (hereinafter called the MANUFACTURER which term shall include its successors-in-interest) of the One Part and CD carrying on business at .... (hereinafter called the DEALER which term shall include his successors and assigns) of the Other Part to the following effect:

1. The MANUFACTURER shall supply and the DEALER shall sell the whole of the seller's existing stock of .... and other goods to be manufactured hereafter without any exception or reservation thereof.

2. The goods to be supplied shall be sold by the DEALER strictly at listed prices to retailers for which he will be entitled to a commission of ....% on all listed prices exclusive/inclusive of all railway freight (*as may be agreed*).

3. In case any portion of the goods shall remain unsold for over ..... months after supply and delivery, the DEALER shall return the stock to the MANUFACTURER.

4. The DEALER guarantees a minimum sale of the value of Rs. .... per year. In case the same falls short by 25% or more for any consecutive two years or more, this agreement may at the option of either party be rescinded.

5. The MANUFACTURER shall not, during the continuance of this agreement, appoint any other wholesale DEALER in respect of identical or renovated products nor make nor supply nor to anyone sell any portion thereof other than the DEALER.

6. Subject to what is stated in paragraph 4 hereof, this agreement shall remain in force for five years subject to the option of either party as provided therein and also subject to the condition that the DEALER shall not, during the currency of this agreement sell or encourage the sale of identical or similar products of any other manufacturer.

7. Any differences and disputes relating to these presents or the rights or obligations of the parties hereto in relation to transactions covered by

this agreement or arising out of or in relation to these presents shall be referred to the sole arbitrator Mr. XY for decision whose award shall be final and binding on the parties.

IN WITNESS WHEREOF the parties hereto have executed these presents on the day, month and year first above-written.

Signed, sealed and delivered by AB
the manufacturer in the presence of:

Signed, sealed and delivered by CD
the dealer in the presence of:

Agreement between Merchant and Travelling Agent

THIS AGREEMENT is made on this .... day of .... 1999 BETWEEN AB son of .... residing at .... (hereinafter called EMPLOYER which term shall include his successors) of the One Part and CD son of .... residing at .... (hereinafter called the AGENT) of the Other Part.

WHEREBY IT IS AGREED as follows:

1. In consideration of good and faithful service to be rendered, the EMPLOYER hereby appoints the said CD as travelling agent for .... years from the date hereof in the employer's business of manufacture and sale of detergents, on terms hereinafter mentioned.

2. The AGENT will, during the said period, diligently and faithfully serve the EMPLOYER in such capacity as aforesaid and will at all times obey and carry out the instructions of the EMPLOYER in regard to such service and all affairs ancillary or incidental thereto.

3. The AGENT will travel in the districts of, etc., and in such other district or districts as the EMPLOYER may at any time require for introducing new customers and/or pushing the sale of the products of the employer its trade or business.

4. The AGENT shall use his utmost endeavours to secure orders for the EMPLOYER'S goods and shall at regular intervals call on and report to the present and also future customers of the EMPLOYER in the district or districts concerned and also endeavour his best to secure fresh order or orders for such goods and to establish a market thereof and shall pass on all such orders obtained by him to the employer for execution without the least delay.

5. The AGENT shall at all times keep full and accurate accounts of all orders secured by him and of all other transactions and things done by him in connection with the said business, and forward to the EMPLOYER daily a statement of all business done by him during each day, specifying the persons or firms on whom he has called and the orders secured and moneys collected and spent by him.

6. If so directed by the EMPLOYER, but not otherwise, the AGENT shall collect debts and receive money on behalf of the EMPLOYER and give receipts for the same. Any money received by the AGENT shall be transmitted by him to the EMPLOYER on the day of receipt.

7. The AGENT will not at any time except under legal process divulge any trade or business secrets relating to the said business of the EMPLOYER or any customer or any AGENT of the said business which may become known to him by virtue of his position as AGENT or otherwise however save in so far as such disclosures are necessary in the interest and for the benefit of the said business and will be true and faithful to the EMPLOYER in all dealings and transactions whatsoever relating to the said business.

8. All moneys received by the AGENT on any weekday shall be deposited with the EMPLOYER on or before the close of office of the EMPLOYER.

9. During the continuance of his service the AGENT shall not serve any other concern nor be directly or indirectly interested therein and will not solicit orders in any other district than those specified in cl. 3 hereof without direction in writing of the EMPLOYER.

10. As consideration for the services to be rendered, the EMPLOYER will pay the agent a salary of Rs. .... per annum by monthly instalments of Rs. .... each, the first such instalment to be paid on the .... day of .... next, and will also pay to him a commission on the moneys actually received by the EMPLOYER in respect of all original orders obtained by the AGENT, at the rate of .... per cent, and in respect of all subsequent orders for such customers at the rate of .... per cent. The EMPLOYER shall have full discretion as to executing or non-executing any such order or orders secured without making himself liable to damages on that account in which event the AGENT shall have no claim against the EMPLOYER.

11. In addition to what is stated in cl. 10 hereof, the EMPLOYER shall also pay to the AGENT a fixed sum of Rs. .... per month to cover all expenses of travelling, board, lodging and otherwise (*or* the actual expenses incurred by him in connection with the business of the EMPLOYER).

12. In the event of the AGENT falling sick or being otherwise prevented from doing his work by reason of any accident or otherwise, he shall at the first instance be entitled to such leave with full pay as is provided for by the service rules governing the trade of the EMPLOYER whether of its own or of allied industries, but if his illness or incapacity is found to be incurable then the EMPLOYER may determine this agreement on payment of a sum equivalent to one ....'s salary, in addition to all arrears of salary and commission earned by him at the date of such determination, provided that if the agent is dismissed for misconduct, the AGENT shall not be entitled to anything in excess of arrears of salary and commission as aforesaid.

13. Either party may at any time determine this agreement by giving to the other .... calendar months' notice in writing, provided the

EMPLOYER may, in the event of any breach by the AGENT of this agreement, determine the same without notice or payment in lieu of notice.

14. After the determination of this agreement, the AGENT shall not for .... years, directly or indirectly, carry on any similar trade and business or be interested or concerned in any way within any district or districts in which the agent has at any time travelled on behalf of the EMPLOYER, in any business similar to that carried on by the EMPLOYER at the date of such determination, and shall not solicit the customers of the EMPLOYER for orders.

IN WITNESS WHEREOF the parties hereto have signed these presents on the day, month and year first above-written.

Signed, sealed and delivered by
AB in the presence of:

Signed, sealed and delivered by
CD in the presence of:

Agreement between Businessman and Manager

THIS AGREEMENT is made on this .... day of .... BETWEEN AB son of .... residing at .... (hereinafter called the EMPLOYER which term shall include his successors) of the One Part and CD son of .... residing at .... (hereinafter called the MANAGER) of the Other Part.

By THESE PRESENTS it is hereby agreed as follows:

1. In consideration of true, faithful and loyal service to be rendered, the EMPLOYER appoints the said CD as MANAGER in his trade carried under the name and style of .... at .... on terms hereunder mentioned.

2. The appointment will be effective from the day of .... and the MANAGER will be paid a sum of Rs. .... per month as his salary with yearly increment of Rs. .... up to the limit of Rs. .... depending on faithful and efficient service.

3. The MANAGER shall keep in deposit with the EMPLOYER a sum of Rs. .... as security deposit on which he will be entitled interest at ....% per annum to be repaid at the end of his service under the EMPLOYER after adjustment of all his accounts.

4. The MANAGER shall, during the continuance of his service under this agreement, properly and faithfully serve the EMPLOYER in such capacity as aforesaid, and will always devote his whole time, attention and energy honestly and diligently in managing, superintending and improving the

said business to the utmost of his power, skill and ability, and will do and perform all such services, acts, matters and things connected therewith as the EMPLOYER shall from time to time direct.

5. The MANAGER will not at any time, except under legal process, divulge any trade or business secret relating to the said business of the EMPLOYER or any customer or agent of the said business, which may become known to him by virtue of his position as MANAGER or otherwise, save in so far as such disclosure shall be necessary in the interest and for the benefit of the said business and will be true and faithful to the EMPLOYER in all dealings and transactions whatsoever relating to the said business.

6. The MANAGER will keep and maintain or cause to be kept and maintained as may be approved by the EMPLOYER all files, documents and papers as also all such books of account or other books as the EMPLOYER shall provide for that purpose, and will enter, or cause to be entered therein, the usual accounts or particulars of all goods, merchandise, articles and things, bought, received and sold or delivered upon credit or otherwise in the course of the said business, and the rates and prices at which the same shall be so bought, received, sold or delivered in the course of the said business, and will at all times render faithful information concerning the said business and all transactions therein to the EMPLOYER, and furnish him from time to time with accurate accounts of all business dealings and also with a daily statement of the bank balance of the said business.

7. The said books of account shall all be kept at the office of the said business at, etc., and shall remain open at all reasonable times to the inspection of the EMPLOYER and any person authorised by him in writing in that behalf.

8. All moneys received by the MANAGER on any weekday, except such sum as shall be required to be retained as petty cash, shall be deposited in the account of the EMPLOYER at .... Bank, on or before the close of the business hours and every payment exceeding Rs. .... made by the MANAGER on behalf of the said business shall be made by cheque drawn on the said bank.

9. The MANAGER shall, on completion of his service for one year, be entitled to .... weeks' holiday during the following year and to casual leave not exceeding 15 days per year and in case of sickness to a further leave for another month per year, all with full pay and other benefits of service.

10. The MANAGER shall observe the rules of conduct of service of the establishment as may be in force from time to time.

11. During the continuance of his service, the MANAGER shall not serve under any other concern nor be directly or indirectly interested (except as a shareholder of any limited liability company, whose business may not compete with that of the EMPLOYER).

12. In the event of illness of the MANAGER, or other cause incapacitating him from attending to his duties for .... consecutive weeks, the EMPLOYER may determine this agreement without notice on payment to the MANAGER of Rs. .... in lieu of notice, in addition to all arrears of salary and commission calculated up to the date of such determination.

13. Either party may determine this agreement by giving to the other .... calendar months' notice in writing, but without prejudice to any right or claim which may have then accrued to either of the said parties by virtue hereof.

14. If the MANAGER enters into any plot or conspiracy against the EMPLOYER or misappropriates the funds and assets of the trade or commits a breach of any of the stipulations hereof, or shall commit an act of insolvency or compound with his creditors or if he otherwise misconducts himself (of which the EMPLOYER shall be the sole judge), it shall be lawful for the EMPLOYER to dismiss the MANAGER summarily from his employment without any such notice or payment.

15. After determination of this agreement, the MANAGER shall not for .... years thereafter, be directly or indirectly interested in any business of the kind carried on by the EMPLOYER within a radius of .... miles from the places of business of the EMPLOYER.

IN WITNESS WHEREOF the parties hereto have signed these presents on the day, month and year first above-written.

Signed, sealed and delivered by
AB in the presence of:

Signed, sealed and delivered by
CD in the presence of:

Agreement with Agent for Procuring Purchaser

From AB (*intended vendor*)

To CD *(agent)*.

Re: Premises No. ....

Dear Sir

In consideration of your procuring a purchaser by your initiative and labour for my property known as, etc., before the .... day of .... at the price not below the sum of Rs. ...., or such less price, if any, to which I may hereafter agree, I agree to pay you a commission at the rate of .... per cent on the amount of the purchase money actually received by me. You shall not be entitled to any commission on such part of the said purchase money as shall be paid to the mortgagee to redeem property, such part not exceeding Rs......... in all. All unpaid sums kept outstanding by the purchaser on security of the said property or otherwise shall be deemed to have been actually received by me. I shall not engage nor appoint any other agent or agents for procuring a purchaser or purchasers so long as the authority hereunder given to you will remain valid. The above-mentioned commission shall not be payable in case the intended sale falls through or otherwise does not materialise for any reason whatsoever. This authority shall remain valid until .... day of .... when it shall automatically lapse and stand cancelled.

I agree and accept
CD

Yours faithfully
AB

Agreement between Principal and Monopoly Agent

To

....

Re: Works Order No. .... U/S. .... of ....

Dear Sirs

Referring to my personal discussions with your Mr. .... I write to confirm that I have had this day irrevocably appointed you as my sole and monopoly agent for the purpose of financing, clearing, lifting and handling the goods to be indented against Works Order quoted above and I hereby further nominate and appoint you as my constituted attorney in that behalf on *inter alia* the following terms and conditions:

1. That as handling agents you would operate the above indent and arrange with the manufacturers for early despatch of the goods and delivery thereof direct to you or your nominee (which I hereby consent) for which purpose you would arrange for the requisite finance, including carriage and delivery charges, at the first instance, all to be reimbursed out of the proceeds of sale thereof as hereunder contemplated.

2. You will furnish me with regular reports about the progress made by you, keep and maintain proper account of all receipts and expenses which shall be available for my inspection, once a week.

3. That for the purpose of handling and lifting the goods, you would also represent me to all intents and purposes before the manufacturers, *viz*, ... in all its offices and also before other appropriate authorities including Banks, Post Offices, Railways, Roadways and Carrying Companies etc., so as to make the goods to be indented readily available to you straightway and to negotiate for and complete the sale and disposal thereof

in lots or altogether at price or prices acceptable to you directly or through brokers and/or agents. You will also collect and keep in your custody all proceeds of such sale or sales and give good, valid receipts and discharges thereof.

4. You will immediately be intimated of the receipt of despatch, advice from the producers by me and when you are to make and/or arrange for the requisite payment and obtain release of the necessary documents (and storage of the goods at your godown for which purposes you are also hereby expressly authorized) which shall be endorsed and/or transferred by me simultaneously in your favour.

5. If, however, there occurs any demurrage or damages to the goods due to any act, default or negligence on your part in making and/or arranging the payments and/or in obtaining release of documents, the same will be borne and paid by you personally. Similarly, I shall remain liable for any loss or mischief to the goods, if those are caused by any act, default or negligence or error in judgment on my part. Such loss shall be debited to my account with you.

6. I shall deliver or cause to be delivered to you such further or other deeds or writings if any when necessary addressed to appropriate authorities to enable you to pay the requisite money and obtain delivery of documents and also the goods concerned and shall not take any delivery of the documents nor the goods myself nor authorize anybody to do the same on my behalf or charge nor encumber them or any portion thereof in any way.

7. In case of any short delivery or non-delivery of the goods, you shall have the right to lodge claims and sue the railways or roadways or carrying companies for necessary reliefs and recover damage or compensation on that account.

8. Under all circumstances, the relative documents will be handed over to you directly by the manufacturers immediately against payment and I shall remain responsible to reimburse you for all losses, suffered on account of any act, negligence, default on my part in effecting delivery of the documents or withholding the same and otherwise dealing with the materials without your consent in writing first had and obtained, which consent you may refuse in your absolute discretion.

9. You will continue to act as my handling agents until the entire consignment (which is at present decontrolled) is sold by you.

Yours faithfully

Agreement between a Cinema Artiste and Producer

An agreement made this the .... day of .... 2000 between Mr. .... son of etc. .... the proprietor/partner ....

a film producing concern named .... having its office at .... (hereinafter called the PRODUCER) of the One Part and CD son/wife/daughter of etc................. of .... Road .... (hereinafter called the ARTISTE) of the Other Part.

In consideration of good, faithful and diligent services to be rendered and the covenants and conditions to be observed and performed, the PRODUCER hereby engages and appoints the ARTISTE (who has passed the requisite sound and screen tests) as .... in the film or picture named and styled as .... to be produced by the PRODUCER (or in such films or pictures as may be produced from time to time) on *inter alia* terms hereunder mentioned, *viz.*:

1. That the ARTISTE will maintain himself/herself physically fit and act in any role to be selected by the director, answer and obey all notices and calls and regularly and punctually attend at the studio and/or the office of the PRODUCER or such other place or places as required by the PRODUCER .... for rehearsals and the shootings of the said film and other purposes in connection therewith and observe and submit to all rules and regulations of the establishment in force from time to time in that behalf.

2. The ARTISTE shall devote exclusively and work solely for the PRODUCER during the subsistence of this agreement and shall on no account act in any capacity elsewhere nor pose for photograph or be interested in any other shooting free or on payment.

3. That the ARTISTE shall whenever required speak, act, sign, dance and play on instruments as the case may be and act and perform to the best of his/her ability, also allow the PRODUCER to take her photographs in any costumes, dress and poses, and to get her voice recorded either on tape, gramophone, disc, etc. and do all other acts, deeds and things, make all such services available as may be required by the producer for completion of the said film and exploitation thereof.

4. The PRODUCER shall be the sole proprietor of .... and so entitled to the copyright and other rights of all pictures, photographs, both positive and negative, sketches, records of songs and other music in which the ARTISTE shall appear in connection with production and the ARTISTE shall have no claim whatsoever to any one of them on any account.

5. The ARTISTE shall not object to his/her name or any other name chosen by the PRODUCER as her film name or his/her photographs to be printed and published in all advertisements, posters, cards, booklet and other literature as desired by the PRODUCER.

6. As remuneration for all the services to be rendered, the PRODUCER shall pay a sum of Rs. .... to the ARTISTE of which Rs. .... is to be paid simultaneously with the execution of this agreement and a sum of

Rs. .... when the shootings of the film have been completed and a similar sum of Rs........... immediately after the day of release of the said film. The total sum of Rs........... thus to be paid under this contract constitutes the full consideration of the agreement paid or to be paid by the PRODUCER to the ARTISTE. The ARTISTE shall have a lien on the picture for all amounts unpaid.

7. In case any prearranged shooting engagement or rehearsal has to be cancelled, postponed or otherwise become infructuous owing to any act, default or negligence or inefficiency, irregularity on the part of the artiste or if he/she otherwise fails and/or neglects to perform his/her part of the agreement in the manner provided herein, he/she shall be liable for all costs thrown away and also further for all loss or damages sustained by the PRODUCER including loss of goodwill of the PRODUCER in addition to the termination of his/her services under this contract at the option of the PRODUCER. This clause, however, will not be operative in cases of absence on the part of the ARTISTE on medical grounds certified by a qualified doctor or in case where he/she suffers any injury in course of employment while in performance of his/her part under this agreement.

8. In the event of shootings at any place or places outside the studio, the PRODUCER shall bear and pay for all costs, charges and expenses of travelling by .... rail, car, bus or air at the discretion of the PRODUCER and shall also arrange for his/her free board and lodging.

9. In the event of loss or deterioration of health or personal injuries to the ARTISTE by reason by fire accident or any act of default or negligence on the part of the PRODUCER in course of shooting or its rehearsal but not arising out of any wilful act, default or negligence on his/her part, the PRODUCER shall be liable to pay his/her compensation as provided by the law in force from time to time.

10. In case any differences or disputes shall arise between the parties hereto in relation to these presents or the rights or obligations of the parties the same shall be referred to Mr. Z for decision and award which shall be binding and conclusive upon the parties. The provisions of the Arbitration and Conciliation Act 1996 and any modifications thereof shall be applicable.

IN WITNESS WHEREOF the parties hereto have executed these presents on the day, month and year first above-written.

Signed and delivered by AB
the PRODUCER

Signed and delivered by CD
the ARTISTE

WITNESS:

Publicity Agreement with a Cinema for Advertisement by Slide or Film

THIS AGREEMENT is made this .... day of .... 1999 BETWEEN AB son of .... residing at .... (hereinafter called the ADVERTISER) of the One Part and Joy Cinema situate at .... represented by its proprietor CD son of .... residing at .... (hereinafter called CINEMA) of the Other Part.

WHEREAS the ADVERTISER is the sole proprietor of the Trade and business carried on under the name and style of AD Co. at...... AND WHEREAS for the popularity and/or publicity of the trade the ADVERTISER is desirous of advertising his products and/or business through the medium of cinema slides/cinema films and for that purpose approached the owner of the CINEMA who on terms and conditions hereunder mentioned has agreed to do so at the cinema aforesaid.

NOW THEREFORE THIS AGREEMENT WITNESSES as under:

1. This AGREEMENT will remain in force for a period of .... years from the date of its execution.

2. That the ADVERTISER shall supply the CINEMA with a standard size slide measuring .... inches by .... inches containing exclusively matters and things relating to his said trade or business previously approved by the .... CINEMA (which the CINEMA may reject at its discretion without assigning any reason) and the said CINEMA shall exhibit the said slide by projecting the same on its screen for not less than .... seconds at a time in each show (or twice or thrice per week as may be agreed by and between the parties).

That the ADVERTISER shall supply .... millimetre standard size film of length not more than .... metres containing matter exclusively relating to his said trade or business for advertisement duly certified by the Board of Censors for exhibition which shall be exhibited by projecting the same on the screen of the said CINEMA at each show (or twice or thrice as may be agreed).

3. That the ADVERTISER shall pay to the said CINEMA for the exhibition of the advertisement a sum of Rs. .... only for each day the said slide/film is exhibited; such payment shall in all cases be made in advance weekly but not in cases where the CINEMA remains closed and the slide/film is not exhibited.

4. That the CINEMA shall not be liable to any damage to the slide/film due to natural wear and tear, heat or defect in the projector, but shall take every reasonable precaution for the safety and safe custody of the slide/film so long it is in the possession thereof. Any damage to the slide/film

necessitating its replacement or resulting in its loss shall be reported immediately to the ADVERTISER and no charges shall be made for its exhibition for the period it cannot be projected for any reason whatsoever.

5. That the ADVERTISER shall indemnify and keep indemnified the CINEMA, its proprietor, partner, servants, agents and business against all claims for damages and/or compensation or fine arising out of any action or prosecution at the instance of third parties or the authorities by reason of any prejudical or injurious matter contained in the slide/film or its exhibition.

6. That the CINEMA shall have full right and liberty to refuse exhibition of the slide/film without assigning any reason and without any notice and without being answerable for any loss or damages caused to the advertiser.

7. That the CINEMA shall return the said slide or film to the ADVERTISER on determination of this agreement or when the exhibition is stopped on account of any injunction obtained by any third party otherwise against its exhibition in cases where any objection to its exhibition is raised by the authorities.

8. If the ADVERTISER shall become insolvent or compounds with his creditor or fails and/or neglects to make the weekly payment, the CINEMA shall be entitled to discontinue further exhibition without prejudice to its right to recover any sum due by the ADVERTISER.

9. In case any dispute or difference shall arise between the parties during the pendency of this agreement or after its termination or earlier determination as to its meaning and construction or to any other matter or thing arising directly or indirectly under this contract then and in such an event the same shall be referred to arbitration and the final decision of a single arbitrator to be mutually agreed between the parties who alone shall consider and determine the same and whose decision or award shall be binding and conclusive upon both the said parties, and this clause shall be deemed a submission within the meaning of the Arbitration and Conciliation Act 1996 or statutory modification or re-enactment thereof.

IN WITNESS WHEREOF the parties hereto have executed these presents on the day, month and year first above-written.

Signed and delivered by AB

Signed and delivered by CD
representing the CINEMA

WITNESS:

Loan Agreement re. Production of a Picture

Dear Sir

Re: ....

With reference to the sum of Rs. .... advanced by you this day under a hundi drawn in your favour and also all costs of realization thereof as between attorney and client, I am writing to you this letter to record the transaction as follows:

1. I am the sole producer of the above picture now under production at .... and the same is free from all encumbrances, lien and charges and that I alone am entitled to enter into this agreement.

2. I shall utilize the said sum of Rs. .... in the production, preparation and completion of the said picture only.

3. Subject to the provisions of cl. 7, I shall deliver to you all prints (negative and positive copies) duly passed by the Board of Censors at my own costs and expenses after completion of the film and you shall keep the same in Government-approved places at my costs. If you do otherwise and if any loss is occasioned to me you will be held liable.

4. The said picture together with all prints, both positive and negative, and all duplicate and other copies and all moneys due and payable by exhibitors and other persons on account of hire or otherwise in connection with the said film and all the deposits in bank, furniture, fittings, tools, implements, dress materials, playrights and other properties, assets and credit connected with the said picture shall stand charged in your favour as security for due repayment of the moneys due by me to you under these presents.

5. Subject to the provisions of cl. 7, I shall keep the said film with all accessories duly insured against loss or damage by fire, theft, etc., with some insurance company approved by you and hand over to you receipts obtained by me as and when payments are made for insurance premiums.

6. I shall not appoint any distributor or agent or otherwise part with the said picture except with your consent.

7. As soon as any distributor is appointed as per terms of cl. 6 or if you are asked to deliver the film directly to any show house you will have to release all prints (negative and positive copies) delivered to you in terms of cl. 3 provided always that all the conditions in this agreement will not be in force if you are paid the sum of Rs. .... plus all interest due thereon. If no money is paid to you at the time of release I undertake and authorise you to accept all sale proceeds till your dues are fully paid off.

8. If in working out this agreement or in any matter relating to this transaction, any dispute arises, each party will be entitled, without interfering

in any way with the production, publication, or exhibition of the film in question, to notify the other party for referring the dispute to arbitration in accordance with the Arbitration and Conciliation Act 1996.

9. If due to your laches in any way, I suffer loss, you will be held liable to compensate me.

Yours faithfully

Agreement between a Solicitor and Articled Clerk*

THIS ARTICLED CLERKSHIP DEED, made the .... day of .... 20..... BETWEEN AB of etc., a solicitor of the High Court .... (hereinafter called the SOLICITOR) of the First Part, and CD of etc., (hereinafter called the ARTICLED CLERK) of the Second Part:

WITNESSETH, and it is hereby agreed and declared as follows:

1. The ARTICLED CLERK, of his own free will and accord hereby places and binds himself to the SOLICITOR as a candidate to serve under him honestly and faithfully in his profession of a solicitor from the date hereof for the term of .... years.

2. The ARTICLED CLERK do hereby covenants with the SOLICITOR as follows:

(*i*) That the ARTICLED CLERK will faithfully and diligently serve the SOLICITOR as his assistant and will not at any time cancel, spoil, destroy, waste, spend nor tamper with or destroy or do any other mischief to any of the books, papers, writing, stamps or other property belonging to the solicitor or his firm or to any of his clients.

(*ii*) That the ARTICLED CLERK shall not serve under any other SOLICITOR nor in any other commercial or industrial firm or company nor participate in any trade or business nor otherwise carry on any business in competition with that of the SOLICITOR.

(*iii*) That the ARTICLED CLERK will, at all times during the said term of article period, preserve the secret of the SOLICITOR and his firm, and readily and cheerfully obey and execute the lawful and reasonable commands of the SOLICITOR and his partners, behave properly with the SOLICITOR and his partners and their staff employed by them and their clients and will not absent himself nor keep aloof from his duties at any time during the said term without the previous consent of the SOLICITOR, but will, from time to time, and at all times during the said term, conduct himself with all due loyalty, obedience, diligence, honesty and propriety.

* May be adapted to suit any other employer.

3. That in case the ARTICLED CLERK shall commit a breach of the foregoing covenant or if the solicitor or his firm shall sustain or suffer any loss, damage or prejudice by reason of any wilful act, default, neglect or improper conduct on his part, then and in such an event the articled clerk shall be liable to indemnify the solicitor and his firm on that account.

4. In consideration of the foregoing covenants and of the sum of Rs. .... now paid as premium to the SOLICITOR (the receipt of which sum the solicitor, hereby acknowledges), the SOLICITOR hereby covenants with the ARTICLED CLERK that the SOLICITOR will accept and take the ARTICLED CLERK as his assistant and will by best manner, and the utmost of his skill and knowledge give lessons on and teach and instruct him or cause to be taught and instructed in the practice or profession of a SOLICITOR, and also will give him all reasonable facilities to learn the work of a SOLICITOR and allow him while serving under these articles to study the course of legal education at the Law College as provided or approved by statute in force from time to time.

5. The SOLICITOR will at the expiration of the said term use his best endeavours to cause him to be admitted and enrolled as a solicitor of the High Court, provided the clerk shall have well, faithfully and diligently served his said clerkship, and shall have successfully passed all such examinations as articled clerks are by law or custom bound to pass before being admitted to practise as SOLICITORS.

6. The SOLICITOR hereby further covenants that if the SOLICITOR or the clerk dies within the first three years of the said term, then the SOLICITOR or his representatives will repay to the ARTICLED CLERK or his personal representative such portion of the said premium of Rs. .... as is hereinafter mentioned (that is to say).

(*i*) If such death happens before the expiration of the first year of the said term the sum of Rs. ....

(*ii*) If such death happens after the expiration of the first year and before the expiration of the second year of the said term the sum of Rs. .... and

(*iii*) If such death happens after the expiration of the second year and before the expiration of the third year of the said term, the sum of Rs. ....

IN WITNESS, the SOLICITOR and the ARTICLED CLERK have hereunto set and subscribed their respective hands and seals the day, month and year first above-written.

Signed, sealed and delivered

Agreement between Master and Workman

AN AGREEMENT made the .... day of ....20 ..... BETWEEN AB of, etc. (hereinafter called the EMPLOYER) of the One Part and CD of etc., (hereinafter called the WORKMAN) of the Other Part.

WHEREBY IT IS AGREED as follows:

1. In consideration of good and faithful service promised to be rendered and the duties to be performed and the covenants and conditions to be observed and fulfilled by the workman the EMPLOYER has appointed the WORKMAN as his assistant and/or to serve under him in his trade or business of export of goods on *inter alia* terms and conditions as follows:

2. The WORKMAN will serve the EMPLOYER as an assistant for a period of........ months (*or* years) from the .... day of ...., and will do, execute and perform with all due despatch and punctuality according to the best of his intelligence, skill and ability, all such works as the EMPLOYER shall require him to do in such capacity and at all times, will conduct himself and behave honestly, faithfully and properly in the course of such service towards the EMPLOYER, his customers and his other workmen.

3. The WORKMAN will in no case during the continuance of this agreement (and even at any time thereafter) serve under any person or persons or company or firm carrying similar trade or business or himself carry on or be otherwise interested in any trade or business similar to and identical with that now carried on by the employer within a radius of five miles from the business premises or from its the then place or places without the written consent of the EMPLOYER.

4. The EMPLOYER will pay the WORKMAN a weekly *or* monthly wages of Rs. ...., payable on Saturday of every week (*or* on the last day of every month) so long as he shall do his duties faithfully, honestly and diligently and/or otherwise shall duly fulfil the terms of the agreement on his part herein contained.

5. If the WORKMAN shall make himself absent from the service of the EMPLOYER without notice or leave of absence or be found guilty of misconduct or commit any breach of this agreement or any act of indiscipline, it shall be lawful for the EMPLOYER to dismiss him summarily forthwith without prejudice to his other rights and remedies as against him when and in such an event he shall lose and forfeit all wages which may then be due to him, but if this agreement be otherwise determined as hereinafter provided, the WORKMAN shall be entitled to the said wages up to the time of such determination.

6. If the WORKMAN shall at any time be incapacitated by illness or accident arising out of any act, default, negligence on the part of the owner or other unavoidable causes, from efficiently performing his duties pursuant to this agreement, his wages shall not be payable during the time of such incapacity,

except according to the provisions of the Workmen's Compensation Act or any other law in force.

7. Either party may determine this agreement at any time by giving to either of them .... days' previous notice in writing for that purpose.

IN WITNESS WHEREOF the parties hereto have signed these presents on the day, month and year first above-written.

Signed, sealed and delivered by AB

Signed, sealed and delivered by CD
in the presence of:

Agreement between Master and Domestic Servant

In consideration of good, faithful and honest service promised to be rendered, the undersigned AB of, etc., (MASTER) hereby agrees to appoint CD of, etc., (SERVANT), as domestic servant at the monthly wages of Rs. .... and I, the undersigned CD, hereby agree to serve the said AB honestly, soberly and faithfully at all times and in all respects and obey all his commands during my service, and conform to the rules of his establishment and conduct myself with propriety towards him, his family and friends and guests and not to absent or otherwise keep aloof from such service at any time without leave.

This agreement may be terminated at any time by either party giving the other one month's notice, or on payment by the said AB of a month's wages in advance, except in case of any act of indiscipline or breach of duty or misconduct on the part of the said CD when and in such an event notice to terminate such service may forthwith be given by the said AB without payment in lieu of notice or compensation whatsoever.

(Date)

AB

CD

Agreement between Parent and Resident Governess

THIS AGREEMENT made the .... day of ....BETWEEN AB of, etc., (hereinafter called the EMPLOYER) of the One Part and CD of etc., (hereinafter called the GOVERNESS) of the Other Part. WHEREBY IT IS AGREED as follows:

1. The EMPLOYER will employ the GOVERNESS to take care of and look after moral welfare, discipline, good habits and health of the children and

enrich their mind with other accomplishments and best thoughts and teach them in such branches of arts and science and general education as are usually required by or given to children of their respective ages.

2. The hours of instructions shall be ...... hours daily excluding Sundays or other holidays as shall be fixed by the employer.

3. The GOVERNESS shall take sole charge of the said children between the hours of .... and .... each day, except during the vacation and impart education to them.

4. The GOVERNESS shall be entitled to a ....'s continuous vacation in each year at such time as the EMPLOYER shall approve.

5. In consideration of the service so to be rendered as aforesaid, the EMPLOYER will pay to the GOVERNESS an annual sum of Rs. .... as her salary by quarterly *or* monthly payments of Rs. .... each and a further sum of Rs. .... per week for her washing allowance.

6. The EMPLOYER shall provide the GOVERNESS with suitable accommodation with necessary furniture, fittings, etc., and also books and instruments for coaching the children.

7. The GOVERNESS will duly and faithfully perform the duties aforesaid during her engagement to the utmost of her ability, and conform in all respects to the reasonable requirements of the EMPLOYER or his wife and the rules and regulations of his establishment.

8. The GOVERNESS shall accompany and will never refuse to accompany the EMPLOYER to any place or places wherever the EMPLOYER shall be staying with the children.

9. The GOVERNESS shall be entitled to one month's privilege leave and sick leave not exceeding 30 days in the aggregate with full pay during the continuity of her service under the EMPLOYER and not otherwise.

10. This agreement may be determined at any time by either party by giving either of them .... month's notice in writing. PROVIDED, HOWEVER, if the GOVERNESS fails and/or neglects to take proper care of the children to the reasonable satisfaction of the EMPLOYER or does any act jeopardising their mind, health, safety or education, then and in such an event the EMPLOYER shall be entitled to dismiss her forthwith upon payment of her salary up till date irrespective of the service of any notice upon her.

IN WITNESS, etc.

Signed, sealed and delivered AB

CD

Agreement between a School and a Teacher

THIS AGREEMENT made the .... day of .... 2000 BETWEEN AB School represented by its President/Secretary of, etc., (hereinafter referred to as the SCHOOL) of the One Part and CD of etc., (hereinafter called the TEACHER) of the Other Part. WHEREBY IT IS AGREED as follows:

1. In consideration of efficient service as a qualified teacher, offered by the TEACHER, the SCHOOL hereby engages the TEACHER to instruct the pupils of the SCHOOL at, etc., in such subjects as the SCHOOL shall from time to time prescribe (*or state the subjects*), and also to take such part in the internal organisation and discipline of the said school as it shall from time to time direct.

2. The SCHOOL shall pay the TEACHER, during the continuance of this agreement, a basic salary of Rs. .... per year (or a salary commencing at the rate of Rs. .... per year with annual increments of Rs. .... a year subject to a maximum salary of Rs. .... a year. Such salary shall be paid by equal instalments on the expiry of the month for which the same is due or before the 7th of every following month.

3. The TEACHER shall also be entitled to other payments, *e.g.* gratuity, dearness allowance, etc., as may be prescribed by the rules and in the absence thereof by rules governing Government institutions in that behalf unless otherwise provided therein simultaneously with his salary as aforesaid.

4. The TEACHER shall observe strict discipline, attend the classes regularly and punctually and impart such lessons and instructions, as the Secretary/Headmaster shall allot to him from time to time, all through school hours and also attend tutorial and special coaching classes as may be allotted to him even after school hours.

5. The TEACHER shall observe the rules and regulations of the University/Board of Secondary Education, submit to and obey all decisions of the Managing Committee, Headmaster and Secretary as may be given or imposed from time to time.

6. In addition to the duties of teaching, organisation and discipline the TEACHER shall, when required to do so, supervise and direct the regular games and pastimes of pupils and attend religious services held in the SCHOOL as social functions among students.

7. The TEACHER shall do his best to enforce and maintain discipline, good habits and morals among the pupils, and reform their character, but shall not be entitled to personally chastise or give corporal punishment any pupil without the sanction of the Headmaster or his or their guardian.

8. The TEACHER shall be entitled to such leave as is prescribed under the rules of the SCHOOL or observed in Government institutions.

9. Clauses (2) and (8) in so far as the increment and leave are concerned shall be operative only upon confirmation of service on completion of full one year of the educational session and subject to the teacher rendering satisfactory service and fulfilment of the terms of this agreement.

10. The TEACHER shall not do any private tuition to any student whether of this school or other school nor carry on any trade or business or profession nor be interested in any other educational institution unless otherwise expressly permitted by the school nor be concerned in plots or conspiracies against the school or the Government or the Managing Committee.

11. This agreement may be determined at the end of any school term by either party giving the other notice in writing to that effect within two weeks after the beginning of such term or at any time by the SCHOOL upon paying to the TEACHER, in addition to the proportion of his salary due up to the date of such determination, one third (*or*, etc.) of the said yearly salary. PROVIDED, HOWEVER in cases of gross misconduct or dereliction of duty or breach of any of the terms of this agreement (notwithstanding any waiver or condonation thereof) the school may determine this agreement forthwith without notice or compensation in lieu of notice, on paying the TEACHER the portion of salary due up to the date of determination.

IN WITNESS WHEREOF the parties here have executed these presents on the day, month and year first above-written.

Signed, sealed and delivered by AB
President of AB School in the
presence of:

Signed, sealed and delivered by CD,
the Teacher in the presence of:

Agreement between Firm of Solicitors and Managing Clerk

AN AGREEMENT, made the .... day of .... 1999 BETWEEN AB, CD and EF etc., practising as solicitors at, etc., under the style of the firm of AB & Co. (hereinafter called the SOLICITORS) of the One Part, and GH of, etc., (hereinafter called the MANAGING CLERK), of the Other Part: WHEREBY IT IS AGREED as follows:

1. In consideration of good, faithful and diligent services to be rendered and the duties to be performed, the SOLICITORS hereby engage the MANAGING CLERK to serve the said SOLICITORS in their profession as aforesaid for the term of .... years with effect from the .... day of ...., or earlier determination thereof as hereunder provided any time during the continuity of such service by either party upon giving to the other .... calendar months' notice in writing of their intention to that effect.

2. The working hours of the MANAGING CLERK shall be normally from 10.30 am to 6 pm on week days and from 10.30 am to 2 pm on Saturdays. PROVIDED, HOWEVER, the MANAGING CLERK shall whenever required by the SOLICITORS attend on counsel and also clients even after the normal hours of business without, however, any extra remuneration on that account.

3. The MANAGING CLERK will devote his whole-time attention, and all his abilities and energies during office hours (subject to the usual or reasonable holidays) exclusively to the work of the said SOLICITORS and will not absent himself therefrom without the consent of the SOLICITORS.

4 The MANAGING CLERK shall remain responsible for safe custody and preservation of all case papers and evidences and will not under any circumstances cancel, obliterate, injure, embezzle, waste or do away with any of the books, deeds, papers, writings or other property of the SOLICITORS or their clients, nor, without their leave, lend the same to others or remove them or any of them elsewhere.

5. The MANAGING CLERK shall not, at any time hereafter without the consent in writing of the SOLICITORS, divulge or make known any of the trusts, secrets, accounts, matters or transactions of or relating to the said firm of SOLICITORS but will keep with inviolable secrecy all matters entrusted to him and faithfully and diligently serve the SOLICITORS and shall never take any gratuity or reward in any case without the express consent of the SOLICITORS.

6. The MANAGING CLERK shall at all times remain true and faithful to the SOLICITORS in all matters, dealings and transactions whatsoever, and shall, whenever, required, give to the SOLICITORS and each and every person constituting the firm a just and true account of the same and shall not enter into plots and conspiracies against them.

7. The MANAGING CLERK shall, all through his service under the said SOLICITORS, attend their office regularly and punctually and do all work such as keeping of day books, preparation of brief for counsel, attend references before the Registrar, Master and other officers, check up the work of the court clerk, bill clerk, typist and others and do other work required of him and will not, during the period of employment, render any legal or professional service to any other person or persons, directly or indirectly, whether for reward or free of charges.

8. The MANAGING CLERK shall not, after retirement or termination of the said employment, solicit the clients to any new solicitor nor do or suffer any act, deed or thing which may be prejudicial to or injuriously affect the interest of the SOLICITORS nor associate him with the opposite parties in respect of cases which he handled with a view to helping them nor secure any advantage by reason of his special knowledge of the secrets of the cases.

9. The SOLICITORS will pay the MANAGING CLERK a salary of Rs. .... per month.

10. In case the MANAGING CLERK shall commit any breach of this agreement or neglect any of his duties, or shall become insolvent or make any arrangement with his creditors, or is guilty of any such misconduct, whether in his said employment or towards the solicitors or any of the partners of the said firm as would, in the absence of any agreement in writing between the said parties, entitle the said firm or any partner thereof to dismiss him from their or his employment, it shall not be necessary for the SOLICITORS to give the MANAGING CLERK any notice whatsoever of their intention to determine his said employment, but they shall have power to dismiss him forthwith on paying such a proportion of his salary only as shall be due in respect of the then current quarter (*or* month) up to the date of such dismissal together with arrears (if any).

IN WITNESS WHEREOF the parties herein have signed these presents on the day, month and year first above-written.

Signed, sealed and delivered by AB, CD and EF partners of the firm AB & Co. in the presence of:

Signed, sealed and delivered by GH the Managing Clerk in presence of:

Agreement between Solicitor and a Company

AN AGREEMENT made the .... day of .... 2000 BETWEEN AB & Co., whose registered office is situate at, etc. (hereinafter called the CLIENT), of the One Part, and CD of etc. (hereinafter called the SOLICITOR), of the Other Part: WHEREBY IT IS AGREED as follows:

1. The CLIENT does hereby appoint the SOLICITOR, and the SOLICITOR accepts the appointment to act for the CLIENT as SOLICITOR in all its legal affairs requiring the employment of a SOLICITOR, including all matters relating to conveyancing, compensation, litigation proceedings and otherwise.

2. The remuneration of the SOLICITOR, for all his work and labour as aforesaid shall be a sum of Rs. .... fixed per annum, payable by monthly instalments of Rs. ....

3. All disbursements and out-of-pocket expenses incurred by the SOLICITOR in or relating to the CLIENT'S business shall be paid by the CLIENT for which the SOLICITOR shall submit proper bills accompanied by vouchers.

4. The SOLICITOR shall, during the continuance of this agreement devote himself solely and exclusively to the legal business of the CLIENT, and shall not act as SOLICITOR for any other person or persons except his own relations.

5. The SOLICITOR shall, during the continuance of this agreement, conduct the said business of the CLIENT to the best of his skill and ability, and shall be entitled to employ, at the CLIENT'S expense, and with his approval, a sufficient number of staff of competent clerks and servants to carry on the said business promptly and satisfactorily.

6. Either party may determine this agreement by a notice in writing to the other party stating his or their intention to determine the same on the expiration of .... months from the date of such notice, and the client may determine this agreement forthwith in the event of any fraud, misconduct or neglect of duties on the part of the solicitor. Upon the determination of this agreement and payment of the said salary due up to such determination, and payment of all disbursements and out-of-pocket expenses incurred up to the date thereof, the SOLICITOR shall deliver all deeds, documents and papers in his possession relating to the business of the CLIENT or as the CLIENT shall direct, and shall continue to afford him all reasonable assistance for concluding pending matters at the date of such determination without making any charge therefor.

IN WITNESS etc.

Signed, sealed and delivered, etc. AB
CD

Agreement between Publisher and Author

MEMORANDUM OF AGREEMENT made this 15th day of July 2000 BETWEEN Eastern Law House Private Ltd, a Company with limited liability, incorporated under the Indian Companies Act and having its registered office at No. 54 Ganesh Chunder Avenue, Calcutta 700 013 (hereinafter called the PUBLISHERS) which expression shall, unless excluded by or repugnant to the context, include the said Eastern Law House Private Ltd., its successors in the business (as the case may be) of the One Part AND Mr. P. Gupta of No. 5 C.R. Avenue, Calcutta 700 071 (hereinafter called the AUTHOR which expression shall, unless excluded by or repugnant to the context, include the said Mr. P. Gupta and his heirs, executors, administrators and assigns) of the Other Part.

WHEREAS the AUTHOR has written an original work entitled Publishers' Companion and is the owner of the copyright therein.

NOW IT IS HEREBY AGREED by and between the parties hereto as follows:

1. The AUTHOR grants to the PUBLISHERS the sole and exclusive right to print and publish the said work in book form in the territories of the world for all the editions and reprinted editions.

2. The AUTHOR warrants that the said work is an original work and that the AUTHOR is the owner of the copyright therein and that he has not made

any assignment of or granted any licence in respect of any of the rights relating to the subject-matter of this agreement and that the said work has not been published.

3. The AUTHOR shall not make any assignments of the rights to print and publish the said work in the territories of the world or grant any licence to print and publish the said work or any part thereof in the territories of the world without the consent in writing of the PUBLISHERS.

4. The time when a new edition or reprinted edition will be published is to be decided by the PUBLISHERS. The terms and conditions for such new edition or reprinted edition will be the same as those of this agreement. In such events, however, the AUTHOR shall have the option of editing and preparing the same for the press.

PROVIDED ALWAYS THAT in case of the AUTHOR'S inability or death, the publishers shall be at liberty to have it revised by any other person of the PUBLISHER'S choice and will have the right to use the name of the AUTHOR in that and all subsequent editions as previously used in the first edition. The revision charges and editing charges will, however, be debited to the AUTHOR.

5. The AUTHOR undertakes to deliver the complete typescript in duplicate of the said work to the PUBLISHERS ready for the printers.

6. The PUBLISHERS agree to print and publish the said work at their own cost, subject however to the approval of the typescript.

7. The number of copies of the said work to be printed, distributed and/or presented in each edition will be decided by the PUBLISHERS.

8. That prior intimation of, at least one year, should be given by the AUTHOR to the PUBLISHERS in writing in the event the AUTHOR decides to sell or present the copyright of the said work to anyone and in such case such transfer shall be subject to the terms and conditions as to the publication of future editions and reprinted editions contained herein.

9. The AUTHOR will neither write nor revise any other rival book against the said work for any other PUBLISHERS or publish any rival book against the said work either by himself or otherwise.

10. The PUBLISHERS shall pay to the AUTHOR during the legal period of his copyright the following royalties and fees:

(*a*) On each edition published in the territories of the world, except as otherwise provided in this agreement, a royalty at the rate of 10% (ten per cent) of the published price for the first seven hundred copies sold in India;

$12^1/_2$% (twelve and one half per cent) of the published price for the next seven hundred copies sold in India; and

15% (fifteen per cent) for all copies sold in India thereafter.

(*b*) On each copy sold outside India 10% (ten per cent) of the actual amount received from sale.

PROVIDED ALWAYS THAT royalties and fees shall only be payable upon amounts actually received by the PUBLISHERS AND no royalties and fees shall be payable in respect of any copies given away for review or other purposes, destroyed by fire, water, enemy action, in transit or accident.

11. The PUBLISHERS will prepare every year a statement of accounts showing the sales of the said work and will make payment to the AUTHOR, or his legal representatives.

12. That the AUTHOR warrants that the said work:

(*a*) contains nothing of a defamatory, libellous or obscene character or of an otherwise actionable nature; and

(*b*) is in no way whatever a violation or infringement of any existing copyright or of any proprietary or other actionable rights of others and that the AUTHOR and the author's legal representatives shall and will indemnify the PUBLISHERS against all loss and damage whatsoever to be incurred or sustained including any legal costs or expenses incurred by the PUBLISHERS by reason of any breach of this warranty.

Provided always that the PUBLISHERS shall have the right without prejudice to their other rights under this clause to alter the text of the said work as may appear to them appropriate for the purpose of removing any passage which in their absolute discretion or on the advice of their legal advisers may be considered actionable at law.

13. The copyright in the said work will remain the property of the AUTHOR.

14. The proof sheets of the said work shall be corrected by the AUTHOR.

15. The PUBLISHERS shall present the AUTHOR 20 (twenty) copies of the said work in each edition free of cost.

16. The AUTHOR shall prepare the contents, the table of cases, the table of statutes and the subject index, etc., ready for the printers and will deliver the same to the PUBLISHERS within two weeks from the date of receiving the printed pages of the text of the said work.

PROVIDED ALWAYS THAT in the case of the author's inability or failure to do the same, the PUBLISHERS shall be at liberty to appoint any other person of their choice to do the same and to fix his remuneration and such charges shall, however, be debited to the AUTHOR.

17. If the PUBLISHERS shall consider that the copyright in the said work has been infringed, the PUBLISHERS shall be at liberty to take such steps as they may consider necessary for dealing with the matter, and if they desire

to take proceedings they shall on giving the AUTHOR an understanding to pay all costs and expenses and to indemnify the AUTHOR against all liabilities for costs, be entitled to use the author's name as a party to such proceedings, but at the same time to control, settle or compromise as they think fit. Any profits or damages which may be recovered in respect of any such infringement of the copyright shall, after deduction of all costs and expenses, be divided equally between the AUTHOR and the PUBLISHERS.

18. If at any time any dispute or question shall arise touching the construction or effect of this Agreement or any clause or thing therein contained or respecting the rights or liabilities of the parties hereunder, the same shall be referred to the arbitration in accordance with provisions of the Arbitration and Conciliation Act 1996.

IN WITNESS WHEREOF the parties hereto have executed these presents on the day, month and year first above-written.

Signed, sealed and delivered by
Director Mr. .... pursuant to
Board resolution of Eastern Law
House Private Ltd., dated ....
in the presence of:

Signed, sealed and delivered by
Mr. P. Gupta the author in
presence of:

Tenancy Agreement re. Residential House

AN AGREEMENT made this the 20th day of July 1999 BETWEEN AB, son of, WX residing at 3 Queen's Road, Calcutta hereinafter called the LANDLORD of the One Part and CD, son of YZ, residing at 5 Mott Street, Calcutta hereinafter called the TENANT of the Other Part witnesseth as follows:

1. That the LANDLORD shall let out and the TENANT shall take on monthly tenancy basis all that double-storeyed dwelling-house being premises No. 3 Queen's Road, Calcutta with bath, privies, garage, kitchen, store, compound, out-houses and all fittings and fixtures including electricity and water connection on terms and conditions hereunder contained.

2. That the TENANT shall keep in deposit with the LANDLORD a sum of Rs. 2 lakhs as security deposit or caution money and pay a sum of Rs. 5,000 only as rent per month which will increase progressively by 10% every five years in advance on the 7th of every current month without any delay or default and it is hereby recorded that the TENANT has this day paid to the LANDLORD the security money and also a further sum of Rs. 5,000 as rent for the month of August 1999 which the LANDLORD doth hereby admit, acknowledge and confirm.

3. That it is further agreed, declared and covenanted by and between the parties that the house will be used and occupied on the following conditions:

(*a*) The LANDLORD shall keep the house in wind and watertight condition, whitewash all walls once in three years and paint all wood work once in five years.

(*b*) Save and except as aforesaid, the TENANT shall otherwise maintain and preserve the property in good condition and order, protect the same against moth and white ants, replace all broken fittings and fixtures by substitutes of equally good quality.

(*c*) All taxes (both owner's and occupier's share) at present existing shall be paid by the LANDLORD, but all increased or additional taxes, if and when imposed and other charges, if any levied by the municipality, shall be borne and paid by the TENANT without any right of reimbursement against the LANDLORD.

(*d*) That the TENANT shall not make any material alteration to the property unless approved in writing and sanctioned by the LANDLORD and in any event such alteration, if permitted, shall be made by the TENANT at his own costs, expense and on such terms and conditions as may be imposed by the landlord. Such alterations and additions shall in all cases become the property of the LANDLORD and the TENANT shall not be entitled to any contribution by the LANDLORD or to any compensation on that account.

(*e*) That the TENANT shall use the property as his residence with the members of his family and shall not transfer the tenancy or sublet the whole or any portion thereof nor keep any paying guests nor share accommodation nor carry on any trade or business nor store any inflammable or combustible goods except kerosene, coal, etc., in small quantities required for domestic consumption.

(*f*) If the TENANT fails or neglects to pay the rent as hereinbefore stated or otherwise commits any breach of the covenants, conditions and stipulations hereunder imposed or is adjudicated an insolvent, it shall be lawful on the part of the LANDLORD to determine the TENANCY hereunder created by appropriate notice and to sue for recovery of possession notwithstanding any waiver of condition of the said breach.

(*g*) The TENANT has had inspection of the property and is fully satisfied about its condition and internal arrangement and has thereafter freely and voluntarily agreed to the terms of tenancy hereunder provided and shall not hereafter make any grievance on any account whatsoever.

4. Save as aforesaid, the rights and obligations between the parties shall be governed by the law relating to statutory tenancy in force for the time being.

IN WITNESS whereof, etc.

Signed, sealed and delivered, etc.

Agreement for Carriage of Goods

THIS AGREEMENT is made this 30th day of November 1999 BETWEEN ELH Manufacturers Ltd., a company registered under the Companies Act 1956 and having its registered office at 56 Karl Marx Sarani, Calcutta 700 023 (hereinafter called the EMPLOYER) of the one part and Carriers Co. Ltd., a company registered under the Companies Act 1956 and carrying on transport business, *inter alia*, at 5 Diamond Harbour Road, Calcutta 700 023 (hereinafter called the CONTRACTOR) of the Other Part.

WHEREAS the EMPLOYER manufactures and carries on business in structural engineering and mechanical equipment of various kinds and sizes.

AND WHEREAS the CONTRACTOR is a Common Carrier owning several trucks lorries and trailers for carriage of heavy materials by road from place to place having all-India permit and/or Road Licence and spare capacity and approached the EMPLOYER for carriage of its goods at competitive charges to which the EMPLOYER agreed.

NOW THESE PRESENTS WITNESSES and the parties hereby agree as follows:

1. This agreement will remain valid for a period of one year commencing from 1st December 1999 to 30th November 2000 after which date, the agreement will automatically stand terminated by the efflux of time unless extended further by mutual agreement.

2. The CONTRACTOR shall keep with the EMPLOYER a sum of Rs. 5 lakhs as interest-free security deposit. The Security Deposit shall be retained by the EMPLOYER as security for the due performance of the agreement on the part of the CONTRACTOR. On any breach of any of the terms of this agreement the Security Deposit shall forthwith become liable to be forfeited. The Security Deposit shall, unless forfeited, be liable to meet any damage, loss or avoidable expenditure caused to the EMPLOYER by any act of the CONTRACTOR.

3. On receipt of Notice from the EMPLOYER notifying to the CONTRACTOR the fact of the forfeiture of the Security Deposit either in full or in part, as compensation towards any loss or damage suffered by the EMPLOYER, the CONTRACTOR shall replenish the Security Deposit so that the same is always available to the EMPLOYER during the performance of the contract.

4. The EMPLOYER shall be at liberty to sue or recover the amount of damages and losses including all costs and expenses which the EMPLOYER

may have sustained, incurred or be put to in consequence of the default or failure on the part of the CONTRACTOR in due performance thereof. The EMPLOYER shall also be at liberty to retain, set off and appropriate all and every sum, which may, at any time, be due and owing to the EMPLOYER by the CONTRACTOR against the earnest money or any money payable or due to the CONTRACTOR.

5. The amount of Security Deposit will be refunded to the CONTRACTOR without interest on the expiry of the agreement after adjustment of dues of the EMPLOYER if any, against the CONTRACTOR. In case, however, the agreement is renewed or extended by mutual consent, the amount will not be refunded but kept as the Security Deposit against the renewed or extended agreement.

6. The CONTRACTOR shall furnish one copy of the Consignment Note priced Invoice to the Consignee of the goods within "THREE" days from the date of loading of Truck/Trailer at destination for the purpose of West Bengal Sales Tax Permit and Octroi Exemption Certificate. In case of failure to comply with the above the EMPLOYER or the Consignee will not be liable for payment of any detention or demurrage or any other charges incurred on this account. The CONTRACTOR shall not pay any Octrois / Municipal Taxes on any account for transportation of any materials for and on behalf of the EMPLOYER without the written permission from the EMPLOYER. If any amount is paid without EMPLOYER'S permission, the liability will be with the CONTRACTOR only.

7. The nature of work to be performed by the CONTRACTOR and the charges payable to him for the services to be rendered shall generally be in accordance with the schedule given hereunder.

8. The CONTRACTOR guarantees the supply of vehicles requisitioned every day, including on holidays. The Trucks will be placed at such point as the EMPLOYER shall direct from time to time. All the Trucks/Trailers shall be in proper order and conditions and shall be driven by a properly qualified and experienced driver and shall be accompanied by at least one Cleaner, who will be required to assist in the loading and unloading of the said Truck/Trailer and stacking where necessary. All expenses incurred for running the said Trucks/Trailers and the salary and wages of the drivers and cleaners shall be borne and paid for by the CONTRACTOR.

9. The EMPLOYER will inform the CONTRACTOR over the phone or otherwise about the lifting of goods on the following day. On receipt of the lifting programme, specified number of Trucks/Trailers will be placed by the CONTRACTOR at the appointed date, time and place. Should the CONTRACTOR fail to supply the number of Trucks/Trailers requisitioned the EMPLOYER will arrange the number of Trucks/Trailers short supplied and any loss to the EMPLOYER on this account will be debited to CONTRACTOR'S account and will be recovered from the CONTRACTOR.

10. After the loading at the starting point is completed, the CONTRACTOR will be required to sign the office copy of the challan/ Materials/ Packages

loaded on the lorry in good order and conditions and of the weight mentioned in the Challan. The CONTRACTOR shall also be handed over three copies of the said Challan. After delivery of the Stores/ Materials/ Packages at the destination, the Contractor shall keep two copies of the Challan signed by the Consignee and further obtain Rubber Stamp of the Consignee thereon and handover one copy of the Challan to the Consignee. The CONTRACTOR shall submit one of such signed copies to the EMPLOYER immediately and the second copy shall be attached to the Bill of the CONTRACTOR to be submitted.

11. The CONTRACTOR shall duly cover the Stores/Materials/Items/ Packages carried by it as aforesaid with Tarpaulin and shall properly secure the same so that they may not be damaged or lost en route.

12. In case any Road Permit or other permit from Civil, Police or other authorities is necessary for the transport of the consignment, it shall be the responsibility of the Contractor to arrange for and obtain the same from the authorities concerned. The EMPLOYER, however, agrees to render necessary assistance by way of issuing letters, recommendations etc. in favour of the CONTRACTOR.

13. The CONTRACTOR'S Trucks/Trailers should reach destination within a reasonable time of their release from the loading stations. The CONTRACTOR'S representatives attending the Employer or Loading station must carry Identity Cards with them and they must help the EMPLOYER'S officials in inspecting the Road Permit, Licence etc. when required.

14. The CONTRACTOR shall remain responsible to make good any damage or loss caused to the EMPLOYER due to negligence, lack of proper care and caution on the part of any of the employees or men of the contractor or employees in the Truck/Trailer. The driver of the Truck/Trailer which might be hired by the CONTRACTOR from the market will also be deemed to be the CONTRACTOR'S man so far as this clause is concerned.

15. The CONTRACTOR shall be responsible for the protection and safe custody of the EMPLOYER'S stores, stocks and goods entrusted to it till such stock is duly delivered at the destination and shall also be responsible for any loss or damage to EMPLOYER'S stock while in transit, except in case of an accident. In the event of any accident happening before the stock is duly delivered which caused or is likely to cause damage to the stocks carried or is calculated in any manner detrimental to the EMPLOYER'S interest, the CONTRACTOR shall be held wholly responsible for reporting the accident to the nearest Police Station and/or nearest Office of the EMPLOYER within 24 hours of the actual occurrence.

16. Disputes regarding non-delivery/short delivery and any other dispute related to the despatch of the consignment from the Employer's premises and brought to the notice of the Carrier by the EMPLOYER should be settled within a period of four weeks from the date of intimation to the CONTRACTOR

failing which the agreement will be liable to be suspended/cancelled without prejudice to any liabilities that the CONTRACTOR is subject to under the terms and conditions of the agreement.

17. The CONTRACTOR shall assume all liabilities and keep the EMPLOYER wholly indemnified against any action or suits, claim, cost, damages, charges and expenses arising howsoever out of the work covered by the agreement.

18. The CONTRACTOR shall be fully responsible for complying with all the Acts, Regulations, etc. in regard to its workmen or vehicles and shall fully indemnify the Employer against any liability or action by the Contractor's workmen and others. The CONTRACTOR shall reimburse the Employer either from the "Security Deposit" or the Bills pending with the EMPLOYER for payment.

19. The EMPLOYER does not guarantee to the CONTRACTOR about the number of vehicles required per day, month nor does the EMPLOYER guarantee about the nature or quantities of stores or materials that will be made available to the CONTRACTOR for transportation.

20. The EMPLOYER reserves the right to appoint more than one CONTRACTOR for the same services. The EMPLOYER also reserves the right to amend/revise or modify the terms and conditions of the Contract or part hereof or cancel it any time during the currency of the Contract, without assigning any reason whatsoever.

21. The CONTRACTOR will submit its bills in triplicate along with receipted challans on completion of such transactions or services rendered by him to the EMPLOYER for arranging payment on verification within 90 days from the date of submission of the bills provided the bills are in order in all respects.

22. The CONTRACTOR shall at the starting point or the site of work, place and keep at such point or site a duly authorised representative empowered to act on its behalf, who will receive instructions from the EMPLOYER or its officers in relation to the carriage of the Stores/Materials/Packages. Provided, however, the entire responsibility for the transport and safe delivery of the Stores/Items/Materials/Packages shall be of the CONTRACTOR, who shall also be fully responsible for giving proper and adequate instructions to the Drivers, Cleaners and other staff and for providing the fuel, spare parts and other accessories that may be required for the purpose of the work entrusted to it under this Agreement. The CONTRACTOR or his duly authorised representative shall duly attend the office of the EMPLOYER whenever desired.

23. The CONTRACTOR shall not assign or sublet the Contract or any part thereof in any manner whatsoever without the previous permission in writing from the EMPLOYER.

24. Without prejudice to any other provision, the CONTRACTOR shall be bound to keep the EMPLOYER fully indemnified against any action, claim or

proceeding under the provision of any Act, Rules, regulations, bye-laws, notifications, direction or order having the force of law for anything done or committed by the CONTRACTOR in contravention of such provisions or for the infringement or violation by it, in the course of the execution or completion of the work under the Contract. If as a result of such action, claim or proceeding the EMPLOYER is adjudged liable to any penalty or to pay any compensation such liability shall be deemed to be the liability of the CONTRACTOR and the CONTRACTOR shall be wholly liable for all such penalties.

25. The CONTRACTOR shall be paid a sum of Rs. 250.00 per day per vehicle as “Detention Charges” in case its vehicle is held up either for loading or unloading for more than six working hours and an amount of Rs. 200.00 will be paid if the Vehicle requisitioned is not utilised but returned empty.

26. Each truck shall be required to carry upto 10 M.T. and Trailer 18 M.T. and *pro rata* rates will be payable for materials carried in excess of these weights. Items weighing 10 M.T. which can be carried within the standard size of the truck will be considered as normal load. Other items exceeding in height/width/length/weight will be considered as overdimensional and will be dealt with separately. Any item which can be carried by the trailer with maximum height and width of 8'-0" with weight of 18 M.T. length up to 43'-0" will be considered as normal trailer load. Other items exceeding in height/width/length/weight will be considered as overdimensional items and will be dealt with separately.

27. All disputes shall be subject to the jurisdiction of Calcutta High Court.

The Schedule

IN WITNESS WHEREOF the parties herein have executed these presents on the day, month and year first above-written at the Employer’s office in Calcutta.

Signed, sealed and delivered by
Mr. ....
pursuant to Board Resolution
dated .... of the EMPLOYER
in the presence of:

Signed, sealed and delivered by
Mr. ....
pursuant to Board Resolution
dated .... of the CONTRACTOR
in the presence of:

4

Apartment Ownership

The West Bengal Apartment Ownership Act 1972. The owner of a building having apartments for residential purposes may submit the building to the provisions of the West Bengal Apartment Ownership Act 1972. Along with the application an agreement has to be submitted to the authorised officer. The owners of the building may withdraw the property from the provisions of,the Act with the permission of the State Government.

The advantages of submitting the building to the provisions of the West Bengal Apartment Ownership Act 1972 are that each apartment owner will be assessed to municipal tax separately but such apartments and Association of Apartment Owners or Condominium or Co-operative Society has to be formed by the apartment owners for maintenance of the apartments and common services and that all disputes among the members or apartment owners or between the apartment owners and Association or Condominium or Society should be decided by the Authorised Officer appointed under the West Bengal Apartment Ownership Act 1972 and his decision will be final.

The declaration submitting the building to the provisions of the said Act and the agreement are to be registered under the Registration Act 1908. The Association or Condominium or Society shall be governed by its bye-laws which will define the rights and obligations of the members as also the functioning of the Association or Condominium or Society.

FORMS

Declaration under section 2, read with section 10 of the West Bengal Apartment Ownership Act 1972

[*See* Rules 3(1) and 4(1) of the West Bengal Apartment Ownership Rules 1974]

1. In pursuance of section 2 of the West Bengal Apartment Ownership Act 1972, read with sub-section (1) of section 10 of the Act, I/we............hereby declare that I/we/am/are the owner/owners of the property situated at....................city/town/village..............in the district.................and do hereby further declare that I/We submit the said property, comprising a building or buildings...............containing apartment, together with the common areas and facilities, mainly meant for residential purpose, to the provisions of the West Bengal Apartment Ownership Act 1972 (West Bengal Act XVI of 1972) and all amendments thereto.

Authenticated copies of the building plan and site plan, prepared by....................and sanctioned by..............are appended herewith and marked respectively as Annexures 'A' and 'B'. The relevant title deed is also appended herewith and marked Annexure 'C'.

2. I/We, ... do hereby furnish further the following particulars as required under sub-section (1) of section 10 of the said Act:

A. Description of the property:

(*i*) Area and description of the land upon which the building/buildings is/are constructed:

(*ii*) Area and description of the building/buildings. Building No. ..... :

(*a*) Total plinth area:

(*b*) Number of storeys:

(*c*) Number of apartments:

(*d*) Other particulars, if any:

(*iii*) Area and description of common areas and facilities:

(*a*) Lawn, Parks etc.:

(*b*) Road, Pathways:

(*c*) Other common areas, if any:

(*d*) Water Supply arrangements:

(*e*) Street light within the property:

(*f*) Internal drainage:

(*g*) Other common facilities, if any:

(*iv*) Description of the limited common area and facilities, if any stating to which apartments their use is reserved:

(*v*) Value of the property:

(*vi*) Nature of interest of the owner/owners of the property:

(*vii*) Existing encumbrances, if any, affecting the property:

B. Description of common areas and facilities in respect of each building—

(*a*) Foundation and main wall of the building/buildings:

(*b*) Stairway:

(*c*) Water Tank:

(*d*) Plumbing Network:

(*e*) Electric wiring network:

(*f*) Other common areas:

C. Description of each Apartment or each building .... Apartment No. .... or Building No. ....

(*a*) Location:

(*b*) Approximate area:

(*c*) Number of rooms:

(*d*) Immediate common area to which it has access:

(*e*) Any other information necessary for its proper identification:

(*f*) Value of the Apartment:

D. Percentage of individual interest in the common areas and facilities appertaining to each apartment and its owner for all purposes including voting.

E. Other particulars, if any

3. I/We.....................do hereby further declare, covenant and undertake as follows:

(*i*) that each apartment constitutes a single residential unit, transferable and heritable as such, but shall not be partitioned or sub-divided for any purpose, whatsoever;

(*ii*) that each apartment owner, present or future, shall be entitled to an undivided interest in the common areas and facilities in the percentage expressed in the Declaration and appurtenant to such Apartment;

(*iii*) that the common areas and facilities, general or restricted, shall remain undivided and that no owner shall bring any action for partition or division thereof so long as the property remains submitted to the provisions of the said Act;

(*iv*) that the percentage of the undivided interest in the general or restricted common areas and facilities, as expressed in the Declaration, shall not be altered except with the consent of all the apartments owners expressed in an amended Declaration duly executed and registered as provided in the said Act;

(*v*) that during the period the property remains subject to the said Act, no encumbrance of any nature shall be created against the property, though such an encumbrance may be created only against each apartment and the percentage of undivided interest in the common areas and facilities appurtenant to such apartment in the same manner as in relation to any other separate parcel of property subject to individual ownership;

(*vi*) that the percentage of the undivided interest in the common areas and facilities shall not be separated from the apartment in which it appertains and shall be deemed to be conveyed or encumbered with the apartment even though such interest is not expressly mentioned in the conveyance or other instrument;

(*vii*) that no apartment owner shall do anything which would be prejudicial to the soundness and safety of the property or reduce the value thereof or impair any easement or hereditament or shall add any material structure or excavate any additional basement or cellar;

(*viii*) that no apartment owner shall sell, otherwise transfer or rent out his apartment for any purpose other than residential; and

(*ix*) that for the proper and effective administration of the property and for the due maintenance, repair and replacement of the common areas and facilities the apartment owners shall strictly comply with the provisions of the said Act and the bye-laws made thereunder and shall pay their share or common expenses as assessed by the Association of Apartment Owners and that the failure to comply with any such requirement shall be a ground for action for damages or for other relief or reliefs at the instance of the Manager or the Board of Managers on behalf of the Association of Apartment Owners or in a proper case, by an aggrieved apartment-owner.

IN WITNESS I/we have set out our hands this........... day of .... and solemnly declare that what is stated in .... is true to my/our knowledge and what is stated in .... is my/our information received from ....

(1) Shri/Smt. .... Sole owner/or all the owners of the property

(2) Shri/Smt. ....

(3) Shri/Smt. ....

and so on

In the presence of:

(1) ....

and

(2) ....

solemnly affirmed before me

this....................................day

of .... 19 ....

(Signature of the Magistrate/or person competent to administer oath)

Agreement for Transfer of a Flat by a Member of a Co-operative Housing Society to Another

THIS AGREEMENT MADE at .... this .... day of .... 1999 BETWEEN Mr. T.R. hereunder referred to as the TRANSFEROR of the One Part and Mr. P.R. of .... hereinafter referred to as the TRANSFEREE of the Other Part.

WHEREAS the TRANSFEROR is a member of Popular Co-operative Housing Society Ltd., registered under No. 2368 of 1989 under the West Bengal Co-operative Societies Act 1983 and as such member he is occupying as Owner Flat No. 4 on First Floor in the building known as COSY standing on Plot No. 3 on K.P. Road, Calcutta 700009 belonging to the said Society having a carpet area of about 500 sq. meters.

AND WHEREAS the TRANSFEROR intends to transfer his right to occupy the said flat with all his right, title and interest in the said society to the Transferee.

Now therefore these presents witnesseth and the Parties hereto have agreed as follows:

1. The TRANSFEROR will transfer and the TRANSFEREE will purchase the Transferor's right to occupy and his right, title and interest to and in the said Flat together with all its fixtures and fittings at the price of Rs. 5 lakhs calculated at the rate of Rs. 1,000 per sq. ft. The TRANSFEREE has inspected the flat and is satisfied in all respects.

2. The TRANSFEREE will pay to the TRANSFEROR on the execution of this agreement as earnest money Rs. 1 lakh and the balance against delivery of possession of the said Flat.

3. The TRANSFEROR shall obtain the consent of the Board of Directors of the said Society and of the Registrar of Co-operative Societies, West Bengal as required under Rule 142 of the West Bengal Co-operative Societies Rules 1987 to the transfer of the flat and of the five shares held by him in the said Society to the TRANSFEREE, before completion of the transfer. The transfer shall be completed within 6 months of execution of this Agreement.

4. The TRANSFEREE has taken inspection of all the documents in possession of the TRANSFEROR to title to the said Flat and is satisfied therewith.

5. After obtaining the requisite consents the TRANSFEROR shall deliver vacant possession of the Flat to the TRANSFEREE against payment of the said balance amount of Rs. 4 lakhs and execute transfer form in respect of the said five shares bearing Nos. 120 to 124 held in the Society and represented by Share Certificate No. 3 dated ....

6. The TRANSFEROR will take the Flat in the condition as it is and the TRANSFEROR will not be liable to do anything in respect thereof.

7. After vacant possession of the said Flat is given to the TRANSFEREE he will be the absolute owner thereof with all rights of occupation thereto as a member of the Society and thereafter the TRANSFEROR will have no right, title or interest therein.

8. The TRANSFEROR shall pay all the Society's dues upto the date of delivery of possession and thereafter the TRANSFEREE will be liable to pay the same and will be subject to the bye-laws and Resolutions of the Society.

9. It has been represented by the TRANSFEROR that (*i*) he is the absolute owner of the said Flat and no other person has any interest therein, (*ii*) there is no encumbrance or claim of any person on the said Flat, (*iii*) that he has been in exclusive and peaceful possession and occupation of the said Flat since it was purchased by him, (*iv*) on taking possession of the said Flat the TRANSFEREE will be entitled to occupy and enjoy the same without any claim or interruption from the TRANSFEROR or anybody claiming under him.

10. The TRANSFEROR undertakes that on completion of the transfer he will hand over to the transferee (*i*) the Certificate of Shares together with the share transfer form duly filled in and executed, (*ii*) the agreement for purchase of flat between the Developer and the TRANSFEROR all other documents relating to the Flat, if any, in the possession of the Transferor.

11. The TRANSFEROR shall sign and execute, any deed or writing and do all acts required to be signed executed or done to complete the title of the TRANSFEREE to the said Flat as and when requested at the cost and expense of the Transferee.

12. Any fee or donation or money required to be paid to the Society for its consent to the transfer of the said Flat and/or the shares under Rule 142(2) of the West Bengal Co-operative Societies Rules 1987 or any other Rules and if any stamp duty is required to be paid on the share transfer

form the same will be borne and paid by the TRANSFEROR and the TRANSFEREE in equal shares.

13. If any clearance under the Income-tax Act 1961 or compliance with any provision thereof is required then this agreement will be subject to the approval or clearance or certificate of the Income-tax authorities concerned.

14. In case of refusal of the society to give its consent to the transfer or the refusal of the Income-tax authority to give its approval or for any reason beyond the control of the TRANSFEROR or the TRANSFEREE this Agreement becomes impossible of performance the TRANSFEROR shall refund the earnest money to the TRANSFEREE forthwith without any interest. But if the TRANSFEROR commits any default in completing the transfer, the TRANSFEREE will be entitled to cancel this agreement by giving 30 days' notice and in that event the TRANSFEROR will be liable to refund the amount of earnest money and all other monies received with interest thereon at 12% p.a. from the date of this Agreement till payment. If the TRANSFEREE makes any default in completing this Agreement the TRANSFEROR will be entitled to cancel this Agreement by giving 30 days' notice to the TRANSFEREE and in that event the earnest money only will be forfeited. This is without prejudice to the right of any party to file a suit for specific performance of this contract and/or for further damages, if any.

IN WITNESS WHEREOF the parties have executed these PRESENTS on the day, month and year above-written.

Signed and Delivered by the within
named TRANSFEROR in the presence of:

Signed and Delivered by the within
named TRANSFEREE in the presence of:

Agreement for Sale of Apartment

AGREEMENT MADE at .... this .... day of .... 2000 BETWEEN Mr. V of .... hereinafter referred to as the VENDOR (which term shall include unless repugnant to the context his successors and assigns) of the one part and Mr. P of .... hereinafter referred to as the PURCHASER (which term shall include unless repugnant to the context his heirs and successors) of the other part.

WHEREAS the VENDOR is absolutely seized and possessed of the land and premises situate at..................and more particularly described in the Schedule hereunder written.

AND WHEREAS on the said land described in the First Schedule hereunder written there are certain buildings or structures.

AND WHEREAS the VENDOR proposes to develop the said land by demolishing the existing structures and by constructing a new building in their place, according to the Building Plans hereinafter mentioned and to sell the flats in the said Building on Apartment Ownership basis.

AND WHEREAS the VENDOR has obtained permission of the Competent Authority under the Urban Land (Ceiling and Regulation) Act 1976.

AND WHEREAS the PURCHASER has agreed to purchase one flat or apartment in the said building being Apartment No. 3 on the First Floor of the said building and having the specifications mentioned in the 2nd Schedule hereunder written at the price of Rs. 25 lakhs only but subject to the provisions herein contained.

AND WHEREAS the PURCHASER has examined the title of the VENDOR to the said land and has seen the documents of title in the Vendor's possession and is satisfied with the Vendor's title to the said property.

AND WHEREAS the VENDOR declares that the said property is free from any encumbrances.

AND WHEREAS the VENDOR proposes to enter into an agreement for sale with the said PURCHASER pending the construction of the said building.

AND WHEREAS the PURCHASER has agreed to purchase and the VENDOR has agreed to sell on ownership basis the said Apartment No. 3 on the First Floor in the said building hereinafter referred to as "the Apartment" on the terms and conditions mentioned herein.

NOW THEREFORE THESE PRESENTS WITNESSETH and the parties agree as follows:

1. Unless prevented by any circumstances beyond his control, the VENDOR shall construct a building on the said plot of land more particularly described in the First Schedule hereunder written in accordance with the plans and specifications sanctioned by the Municipal Corporation. The PURCHASER agrees that the VENDOR shall be entitled to make such variations therein as the Government or the Municipal Corporation or other local body or authority may require and as may be necessary by the exigencies of the circumstances from time to time.

2. Inspection of the Plan and Title Deeds have been given to the PURCHASER and he has satisfied himself as to the title of the VENDOR to the said land and premises and accepts the same.

3. The VENDOR shall sell and the PURCHASER shall purchase the apartment being Apartment No. 3 having a carpet area of approximately 500 sq. ft. on the First Floor of the building to be constructed on the said property and delineated on the plan and thereon shown by red coloured boundary line at or for a lump-sum price of Rs. 25 lakhs (subject to what is provided hereinafter) and this lump-sum price shall (subject to aforesaid) be final and binding and shall be independent and irrespective of the actual carpet area of the Apartment on completion of the building. Out of the said amount

a sum of Rs. 5 lakhs has been paid by the PURCHASER to the VENDOR on the execution of these presents and the balance will be paid by instalments as follows:

(1) Rs. 5 lakhs on or before..................

(2) Rs. 5 lakhs on or before..................

(3) Rs. 5 lakhs on or before..................

(4) Rs. 5 lakhs being the balance against delivery of possession of the Flat to the Purchaser.

The time will be of the essence of the contract in case of each instalment.

4. The PURCHASER shall be liable to pay interest at the rate of 12% p.a. on all the amounts due and payable by the PURCHASER under this Agreement if such amounts remain unpaid for more than 7 days after becoming due. This is without prejudice to the rights and remedies of the VENDOR under these presents and/or in law.

5. Possession of the Apartment shall be given to the PURCHASER after the said building is ready for occupation and the building occupation or completion certificate obtained from the Municipal Corporation or other concerned authority. The VENDOR shall give possession of the said Apartment to the PURCHASER on or before the .... day of .... The PURCHASER shall, within the seven days of the receipt by him of the written notice from the VENDOR that the said Apartment is ready for use and occupation and that the building completion certificate or occupation certificate has been obtained from the concerned authority, take possession of the said Apartment.

6. On the PURCHASER duly observing and performing all the obligations and stipulations contained in this Agreement and on his part to be observed and performed and on payment to VENDOR all amounts payable by him under this Agreement, the PURCHASER shall be entitled to the possession of the said Apartment.

7. The VENDOR shall not incur any liability if he is unable to deliver possession of the said Apartment on or before the...........day of..............or the completion of the said building is delayed by reason of non-availability of steel, cement or any other building material or on account of civil commotion, riot or any act of God or on account of any notice, order, rule, or notification of the Government and/or public body or authority or on account of withholding of or delay on the grant of the building completion or occupation certificate, water connection and/or any other necessary facilities, permission or sanctions by the Government, the Municipal Corporation and/or any such other or similar public body or authority or on account of any Order of any Court.

8. No act of the VENDOR shall be construed as a grant in law to the PURCHASER of the said plot and building to be constructed thereon or any

part thereof until a formal Deed of Sale of Apartment or Conveyance is executed as hereinafter provided.

9. After the VENDOR informs the PURCHASER that the VENDOR obtained occupation Certificate or completion certificate from the Municipal Corporation, the PURCHASER shall not be entitled to refuse to take possession or delay taking possession thereof on the ground that in the opinion of the PURCHASER some work still remains to be done or completed in or in respect of the said Apartment or building. After 30 days of taking possession the PURCHASER shall have no claim against the VENDOR as to any item of work *viz.*, construction, designs, finishing or any other items or quality of work in the said Apartment. On the delivery of possession it shall be the sole responsibility of the PURCHASER to maintain the Apartment in good and tenantable repairs in all respects.

10. The PURCHASER shall have no claim save and except in respect of the said Apartment hereby agreed to be purchased by him. All the other structures of the said land, open spaces, parking places, lobbies, staircases, lifts, terrace etc. will remain the property of the VENDOR until all the Apartments are sold and transferred to the PURCHASERS thereof and the Declaration and Deeds of Apartment are executed and the association is formed as provided in the West Bengal Apartment Ownership Act 1972 (West Bengal Act XVI of 1972).

11. Notwithstanding anything herein contained, upon notice in writing from the VENDOR calling upon the PURCHASER to take possession of the said Apartment, the PURCHASER shall be liable to contribute a monthly sum equivalent to 10% of all outgoings in respect of the said property such as all rates, taxes, assessment, dues, duties and impositions of any kind or nature whatsoever in respect of the said land and/or the building thereon or any part thereof as may be charged or imposed by Government, Municipality and/or any other competent authority and wages of watchmen, malee, and sweeper and other expenses of common benefit irrespective of the fact whether or not the PURCHASER has actually taken possession of the Apartment upon notice as aforesaid and until such time all the flats to be constructed are sold to the buyers thereof. Thereafter the purchasers shall also continue to be liable to contribute to all such common expenses as aforementioned during all the time he would be entitled to the said apartment and his contribution shall be in proportion to the area of the Apartment and as the Association of Apartment Owners shall from time to time decide.

12. The purchasers of all the flats and the premises in the said building including the PURCHASER herein shall join and form an Association and the PURCHASER agrees to join such association or society. On completion of the building and receipt by the VENDOR of the full price of all the flats/car parking places and other premises in the said building under this and similar agreements in respect thereof and all other charges and deposits payable

by each purchaser to the VENDOR under this Agreement and similar agreements with other Purchasers in respect of each Apartment the VENDOR shall convey and/or cause to be conveyed to each purchaser including the PURCHASER herein title to the respective Apartment free from all encumbrances. However, the VENDOR will not be obliged to execute the Deed of Apartment till such time as all the flats and premises are sold. The PURCHASER shall be liable to contribute to and at the time of execution of this Agreement and deposit and keep deposited with the VENDOR a sum of Rs. 50,000 towards legal costs (exclusive of stamp duty and registration charges of the Deed of Apartment) in connection with the execution of this and other documents required to be executed. All the legal expenses including the expenses of Stamp Duty and Registration charges will be borne by the PURCHASER alone.

13. The costs charges and expenses of preparing, engrossing, stamping and registering all the Agreements, Conveyances, Deeds or any other document or documents required to be executed by the VENDOR or by the PURCHASER as well as the entire professional costs of the advocates of the VENDOR in preparing and approving all such documents shall be borne by the PURCHASER in proportion to the area which the flat agreed to be sold bears to the total built up area of the building.

14. VENDOR will prepare the draft Deed of Apartment to be executed in favour of the PURCHASER. The form will be common to all the flat purchasers in the said building. The VENDOR will furnish a copy of such draft Deed of Apartment and after approval the PURCHASER shall get the same engrossed and stamped and the VENDOR will sign the same. It will be the responsibility of the PURCHASER to lodge the same for registration.

15. Without prejudicing the rights of the PURCHASER under the Deed the VENDOR will be at liberty to sell, assign or otherwise deal with his own interest in the said land and building or any part thereof.

16. No delay or indulgence by the VENDOR in enforcing any of the terms of this Agreement or any forbearance or giving of time to the PURCHASER shall be construed as a waiver on the part of the VENDOR. Any breach or non-compliance of any term or condition of this Agreement by the PURCHASER shall not in any manner prejudice the right of the VENDOR.

17. Until transfer of the said Apartment to the PURCHASER and all dues payable to VENDOR have been paid and without previous written consent of the VENDOR the PURCHASER shall not agree to or let, transfer or assign or give on Leave and Licence the said Apartment. The consent shall not however be unreasonably withheld.

18. Upon the PURCHASER paying the VENDOR'S dues and performing the terms and stipulations of this Agreement the PURCHASER shall peacefully hold and enjoy the Apartment for ever without any interference by the VENDOR or any person claiming under him.

19. The PURCHASER on getting possession of the said Apartment shall not demolish or cause to be demolished any construction work in or about the said apartment nor at any time make or cause to be made any new construction or work of whatsoever nature in or about the said Apartment nor will he make any additions or alterations in the said Apartment without the previous consent in writing of the VENDOR or in contravention of any Municipal Rules and Regulations nor without such consent or in such contravention as aforesaid, close lounges and any balcony, effect any alteration in the elevation or change the colour scheme of the exposed walls of the various lounges or external walls.

20. The PURCHASER covenants to do all acts, and things and sign and execute all other documents and papers as shall be incidental to the due carrying out the performance of the terms of this Agreement and for safeguarding the interests of the VENDOR and other purchasers of apartments in the said building as the VENDOR may require him to do and execute from time to time at the costs and expenses of the VENDOR.

21. The PURCHASER covenants to observe and perform all the Rules and Regulations which the Association of Apartment Owners may adopt at its inception and from time to time and at all times for fully and effectively vesting the management in the Association and otherwise to observe all stipulations and conditions in respect of the use and occupation of the particular flats by particular members and to ensure regular and punctual payment of contributions and charges. The PURCHASER shall observe all the rules and regulations which the VENDOR may frame and bring into force including rules and regulations regarding parking of cars, storing of materials and goods outside the Apartments, playing games likely to cause damages, injury, nuisance and other similar matters during the interim period until all the apartments are sold and building is completed and the Association is formed.

22. The VENDOR shall pay the balance if any of the deposits paid by the PURCHASER to the VENDOR under clauses 11 and 12 above after defraying the expenses mentioned in the said clauses and after transfer of the property is complete shall be paid to the respective flat owners. The said deposits shall not carry any interest.

23. Service of all letters, receipts and notices by the VENDOR shall be under certificate of posting to the address given by the PURCHASER. Such despatch will be sufficient proof of receipt of the same by the PURCHASER.

24. The PURCHASER shall not use or permit to be used the said Apartment for any purpose other than residential purpose or for a purpose approved by the Association. The PURCHASER shall not cause or permit to be caused any nuisance or annoyance to the occupiers of other flats and Apartments in the said building. The PURCHASER shall not be entitled to use any parking

or other space in the compound of the building for parking vehicles, except any parking space he may have agreed to purchase, and his right to park the vehicle will be subject to the rules and policy of the Association.

25. Subject to the other provisions of this Agreement the sale of the said Apartment will be completed within 6 weeks from the date of completion of the building and the occupation certificate being issued by the Municipal Corporation and notice whereof is given by the VENDOR to the PURCHASER.

26. All the outgoings including ground rent, taxes, etc. pertaining to the property up to the date of the occupation certificate of the flat payable and paid by the VENDOR may be apportioned between the VENDOR on the one hand and the PURCHASER and the other purchasers of the other Apartments on the other.

27. The VENDOR and all other necessary parties interested in the said property shall make and execute the Deed of Apartment (Deed of Conveyance) in terms of the draft to be prepared by the VENDOR.

28. It is declared by the VENDOR that no notice had been issued by the Government or Municipal Corporation or any other Public Body for carrying out repairs to the said property and if such notice is issued prior to the completion of the sale the VENDOR shall comply with the same at his expenses.

29. Before completion of the sale of the said Apartment to the PURCHASER if the whole building including the said flat is notified by the Government or any other authority for acquisition or requisition the PURCHASER will not be entitled to cancel the Agreement but will be entitled to refund of the amount paid by him to the VENDOR or a proportionate part thereof in case the compensation awarded for the property is less than the cost incurred by the VENDOR in the construction of the building including the price of the land, out of the compensation if and when awarded and paid by the Government or other authority. In the case of requisition of the said Apartment the PURCHASER will be entitled to the compensation that will be awarded by the requisitioning authority and save as aforesaid all his liabilities under this Agreement and subsequently as the owner of the said Apartment will continue to subsist.

30. The said and other Apartments shall be subject to the provisions of West Bengal Apartment Ownership Act 1972 and the Rules made thereunder and execute or join in executing a Declaration to the effect that he or they submits his Apartment or their Apartments to the provisions of the West Bengal Apartment Ownership Act 1972, in the form prescribed by or under the said Act and will abide by the terms thereof.

31. On the purchaser's failure to complete the purchase of the said Apartment in terms of this Agreement within the time stipulated herein the PURCHASER shall forfeit the said earnest money and will be liable to pay

proportionate costs, charges and expenses and damages incurred by the VENDOR.

32. On the VENDOR'S failure to complete the sale within the stipulated time he shall be liable to refund to the PURCHASER the amount of earnest money and all other moneys with interest at 12% p.a. till repayment and all costs, charges and expenses incidental to this agreement and incurred by the PURCHASER.

33. The original Apartment Agreement given to the PURCHASER will be lodged for registration under the Registration Act 1908 within 4 weeks from the date of delivery of possession of the Apartment by the VENDOR to the PURCHASER and the VENDOR will admit execution before the Registering Authority (Sub-Registrar) on receiving intimation that this agreement is so lodged.

34. All disputes and differences whatsoever arising between the parties hereto or persons claiming under them touching this Agreement or any matter or things contained or the construction thereof or as to any matter in any way connected therewith or arising thereout or the operation thereof or the rights and liabilities of either of the parties shall be referred to arbitration and such arbitration shall be governed by and be subject to the provisions of the Arbitration and Conciliation Act 1996 as modified from time to time or re-enactment thereof for the time being in force.

IN WITNESS WHEREOF the parties hereto have hereunto put their respective hands on the day, month and year first above-written.

The Schedules above referred to

I

II

Signed and delivered by the within
named VENDOR ....
in the presence of:

1.

2.

Signed and delivered by the within
named PURCHASER ....
in the presence of:

1.

2.

5

Apprenticeship

Introductory observation. A contract of apprenticeship is a contract for personal service and is usually, though not necessarily, effected by a deed. The apprentice must signify his consent except in cases when he is a minor and enters into the contract through his guardian. The contract being for personal service terminates by death or permanent incapacity of either party. An apprenticeship agreement need not be in writing unless it is one under the Apprentices Act (Act XIX of 1850) which has been replaced by Act LII of 1961. Section 4 of the Apprentices Act provides that no person shall be engaged as an apprentice to undergo apprenticeship training in a designated trade, i.e., a trade which the Central Government specifies as designated trade for the Act (*a*) unless such person or, if he is a minor, his guardian has entered into a contract of apprenticeship with the employer, and (*b*) the contract of apprenticeship has been registered with the Apprenticeship Adviser. Every contract of apprenticeship may contain such terms as agreed by the parties provided no term or condition shall be inconsistent with the provisions of the Act. In other cases, no written document is necessary but sometimes for a long period of apprenticeship or where terms are complicated, a deed is executed embodying the articles of apprenticeship. An apprenticeship deed is generally executed and attested.

FORMS

Apprenticeship Deed

THIS APPRENTICESHIP DEED, made the .... day of .... 2000 BETWEEN AB of, etc. (hereinafter called the MASTER), of the first part, CD of, etc. (hereinafter called the FATHER), of the second part, and EF, son of CD, aged .... years (hereinafter called the APPRENTICE), of the third part, WITNESSES as follows:

1. The APPRENTICE, of his own free will and accord and with the knowledge and consent of the FATHER, hereby agrees to be bound as a good and regular apprentice to the MASTER in the trade (*or*, etc.), of, etc., and to serve the MASTER for a term of ...... years from the date hereof.

2. As consideration for imparting technical knowledge and education to the apprentice the FATHER of the APPRENTICE has paid to the MASTER a sum of Rs. ....as premium (the receipt of which the MASTER hereby acknowledges).

3. THE MASTER HEREBY AGREES with the FATHER and the APPRENTICE jointly and severally as follows:

(*a*) The MASTER shall throughout the said term teach, give instruction and lessons and train the APPRENTICE to the best of his knowledge and/or cause him otherwise efficiently trained and instructed, in the trade or business of, etc., as carried on by the MASTER and in all matters and things appertaining thereto, PROVIDED that the APPRENTICE shall always be regular and punctual and make his best services available to the MASTER and obey all lawful commands of the MASTER, and commit no breach of duty or act of indiscipline or any of the conditions of the contract by the APPRENTICE herein contained.

(*b*) The MASTER shall, during the period of apprenticeship, pay the APPRENTICE Rs. ....each week (*or* month) during the first year and Rs. ....a week (*or* month) during the second and every subsequent year of the apprenticeship as his allowance.

(*c*) The MASTER shall give all facilities and always provide the APPRENTICE during the period of apprenticeship with adequate tools and implements to work with as may be necessary or requisite to receive lessons and instructions in the particular trade and with suitable board and lodging, and also medical attendance and medicines during sick periods.

(*d*) The MASTER shall not require the APPRENTICE to work at the said trade on Sundays or other public holidays, or more than.........hours during any other week/days.........hours during any Saturday.

4. THE FATHER HEREBY AGREES with the MASTER as follows:

(*a*) The FATHER shall provide the APPRENTICE during the period of apprenticeship with suitable clothing and all other necessaries of life, except board, lodging, medical attendance, medicine, tools and materials.

(*b*) The FATHER shall pay the MASTER as premium *(if it is payable by instalments)* in the following manner, namely, etc.

5. AND THIS DEED FURTHER WITNESSES and the FATHER AND THE APPRENTICE jointly and severally agree with the MASTER as follows:

(*a*) That the APPRENTICE shall faithfully and obediently serve the MASTER during the period of apprenticeship in the said trade and shall obey all lawful and reasonable commands of the master and behave himself properly, honestly and diligently in all respects.

(*b*) That the APPRENTICE shall at all times cautiously handle all tools and implements provided for by the MASTER and never cause any mischief or damage nor wilfully waste or spoil or remove any property nor divulge, otherwise make known, to others any trade secret nor injure the MASTER in his trade nor neglect his duty or make himself absent therefrom without leave except in case of sudden illness of which immediate notice should be given to the MASTER.

(*c*) The APPRENTICE shall not work nor serve elsewhere during the period of apprenticeship and shall always preserve and maintain the secrets of the trade imparted to him.

(*d*) That the MASTER shall have power to reimburse himself against loss caused by absence, negligence or misconduct of the apprentice out of the allowance payable to him.

6. PROVIDED, however, and notwithstanding anything herein before contained, it is hereby further agreed by and between the parties as follows:

(*a*) The MASTER shall have the power always by one week's notice in writing to determine this agreement in case of gross negligence, misconduct, dereliction of duty on the part of the apprentice, or in the event of default being made in payment of any instalment or instalments of the said premium.

(*b*) In case the MASTER or the apprentice shall die or become permanently incapacitated during the said term, or the MASTER shall cease to carry on the said trade, the MASTER or his executors or administrators shall refund the FATHER a part of the premium, proportionate to the period of the said term then unexpired, and all liabilities hereunder of the parties hereto or their executors or administrator, shall thereupon stand determined.

(*c*) If the APPRENTICE shall duly and faithfully serve the MASTER throughout the said term, the MASTER will employ the APPRENTICE as a, etc., in his said trade for the period of .... years at wages of no less than Rs. ....per month.

IN WITNESS WHEREOF the parties hereto have executed these presents on the day, month and year first above-written.

Signed, sealed and delivered
by AB, CD and EF

Deed of Cancellation of Apprenticeship

THIS DEED is made the .... day of .... 1999 BETWEEN AB of, etc. (hereinafter called the MASTER), of the first part, CD of, etc. (hereinafter called the FATHER), of the second part, and EF, son of CD, aged ...... years (hereinafter called the APPRENTICE) of the third part.

WHEREAS by a deed dated the .... day of .... and made between the said AB, CD and EF, the APPRENTICE was, in consideration of Rs. ...., duly apprenticed to the MASTER to learn the trade (or, etc.) of, upon the terms and stipulations therein expressed; AND WHEREAS disputes and differences have lately arisen between the said parties which could not be adjusted. *Now this deed witnesses* and it is hereby agreed between the parties as follows:

1. In consideration of Rs. .... to be paid by the FATHER to the MASTER (the receipt whereof the MASTER hereby acknowledges), the said deed shall stand cancelled, determined and made void in all respects and to all intents and purposes whatsoever and it is hereby recorded that the said sum has been paid.

2. The MASTER hereby accepts the sum of Rs. .... in full discharge of all claims and demands whatsoever, which he may have or might set up against the FATHER, either under or by virtue of the said deed, or otherwise howsoever.

3. No action or other proceedings whatsoever, civil or criminal, shall hereafter be taken by or on behalf of either of the said parties, against the other or his or their executors or administrators, under or by virtue of the said deed either for performance or non-performance of its terms, covenants and conditions or in respect of cancellation of the same or for or in respect of any other act, matter, complaint or thing whatsoever touching or relating to the said apprenticeship.

4. The APPRENTICE shall not enter into the service or employment of any other person or persons in the town of, etc., or within an ambit of .... miles thereof, nor divulge or disclose any of the secrets of the MASTER, or of his trade or dealings, or any other matter or thing whatsoever which may be injurious, prejudicial or derogatory either to the business or to the character or reputation of the MASTER or any of his family, friends, servants or customers.

IN WITNESS, etc.

Signed, sealed and delivered AB

CD

EF

6

Arbitration and Award

THE OLD ACT

The Arbitration Act 1940

Introductory observations. The law relating to arbitration in India was codified and standardized and the same is contained in the Arbitration Act (X of 1940) mainly based on the English law as amended by the Amending Act.[1] It repealed, among others, the Indian Arbitration Act (Act IX of 1899) which had only a restricted application only in the Presidency towns and in notified areas and was based upon the English Arbitration Act 1899,[2] and the Schedule II of the Code of Civil Procedure (Act V of 1908) and other provisions therein relating to arbitration modified after the Common Law Procedure Act 1854.[3]

In ancient India, the decisions of panchayats had been accepted as binding long before regular courts were established.[4] To refer matters to such a bench was one of the natural ways of settlement of disputes in India which resembled judicial courts. The panchayati system fell into disuse with the advent of British Rule and in 1850 the Civil Procedure Code (Act VIII of 1850) was placed in the statute book and in 1899 the old Arbitration Act was enacted and courts in India followed the English Rules or the Private International Law. Since attainment of a sovereign independent status, courts are free to follow their own principles as consonant with their own ideas of justice, equity and good conscience.[5]

1 24 and 25 Geo Vict C 14.
2 52 & 53 Viet C 49.
3 17 and 18 Vict C 125.
4 *Amir Bibi* v *Arokiam* 45 IC 813; 34 MLJ 184.
5 *India and General Duvests Trust Ltd.* v *Ramchandra* AIR 1952 Cal 508.

The Arbitration Act 1940 has since been repealed and replaced by the Arbitration and Conciliation Act 1996 which has come into force on 25th January 1996. But as s. 85 of the new Act provides, notwithstanding such repeal of the 1940 Act its provisions shall apply in relation to arbitral proceedings which commenced before the 1996 Act came into force unless otherwise agreed by the parties. Accordingly, some of the provisions of the 1940 Act are noted below. Details of the Act follow hereafter.

"Arbitration agreement" or submission means, according to cl. (*a*) of s. 2 of the Arbitration Act 1940 (hereinafter referred to as the Act), "is a written agreement to submit present or future disputes and differences to arbitration, whether to one arbitrator or more arbitrators named therein or not."

The authority of the arbitrator or umpire is irrevocable except with leave of the court. The principles laid down by the Privy Council in *Pestonjee's* case[6] are of universal application. A submission can be revoked only if the court is satisfied *prima facie* that some manifest injustice will be the consequence of binding the parties to the contract, so it is not revocable without just and sufficient causes.

Arbitration is of three types: (*i*) private arbitration; (*ii*) Arbitration with the intervention of court; and (*iii*) court arbitration.

A reference to arbitration may be made without the intervention of a court. The provisions relating to such arbitration are to be found in Chapter II, ss. 3 to 19 of the Act.

Any of the parties to an arbitration agreement may desire to have the difference to which the agreement applies, referred to arbitration with the intervention of a court having jurisdiction in the matter, even though no suit is pending. The provisions for such arbitration are to be found in Chapter III, s. 20 of the Act.

In a pending suit also, all the parties interested may agree that any matter in difference between them in the suit shall be referred to arbitration. The procedure in such cases is laid down in Chapter IV, ss. 21, 23, 25 of the Act.

Authority of appointed arbitrator or umpire. An arbitrator is a judge appointed by the consent of the parties. The authority of an appointed arbitrator or umpire cannot be revoked except with the leave of the court and, in cases of sufficient cause, unless a contrary intention is expressed in the arbitration agreement.[7]

Effect of death of a party to an arbitration agreement. Arbitration agreement is not discharged by the death of any party thereto, either in respect of the

6 *Pestonjee* v *D. Manickjee & Co.* 12 MIA 112; 10 WR 51 (PC).
7 Section 5 of the Arbitration Act 1940.

deceased or any other party, but shall in such event be enforceable by or against the legal representative of the deceased. Nor does the death of any party, by whom the arbitrator was appointed, revoke his authority.[8]

Power of arbitrator. Section 13 of the Arbitration Act (Act X of 1940). Unless a different intention is expressed in the agreement, the arbitrator or umpire has power to—

(*i*) administer oath to the parties and witnesses appearing;

(*ii*) state a special case for the opinion of the court on any question of law involved or state the award, wholly or in part, in the form of a special case of such question for the opinion of the court;

(*iii*) make the award conditional or in the alternative;

(*iv*) correct in an award any clerical mistake or error arising from any accidental slip or omission; and

(*v*) administer to any party to the arbitration such interrogatories as may, in the opinion of the arbitrators or umpire, be necessary.

Award. When the arbitrators or umpire have made their award, they are to sign it and file it in the court in accordance with the provisions of s. 14 of the Act. As stated by Russell,[9] the arbitrator shall decide neither more nor less than the dispute referred to him, otherwise the award is liable to be set aside. An award though at times is attested but such attestation is not essential except in Bombay under the Bombay High Court Rules.[10] An award may be set aside on the ground laid down in s. 30 of the Act.

FORMS

Award made under an Order of the Court

In the matter of the Arbitration Act

and

In the matter of Suit No. ....
of ....

This is the award of the Arbitrator made this ....day of .... 2000.

WHEREAS in pursuance of an order of reference dated the................ day of .... made by the court in Suit No. .... of 2000 of the court

8 Section 6 of the Arbitration Act 1940.

9 Russell on *Arbitration*, 15th Ed., p. 257.

10 Paruek's *Arbitration*, 3rd Ed., p. 132.

of .... etc., the following matters in difference between the above-named AB and CD, namely, etc. (*state the matter in difference*), were referred to us for arbitration and determination: NOW WE THE UNDERSIGNED having heard and examined the parties and considered all allegations and counter-allegations and submissions made against each other and all documents and other evidences produced and laid before us, made our award as follows:

WE AWARD ....

(1) that, etc.

(2) that, etc.

Date: Arbitrator

Award by Arbitrator Appointed by Parties

In the matter of the Arbitration Act (Act X of 1940) and in the matter of an Arbitration Agreement dated................ BETWEEN AB, of, etc., and CD, of etc.

THIS is the award of the Arbitrator made this .... day of .... 2000.

WHEREAS in pursuance of an agreement and/or submission in writing dated the .... day of .... and made between the above-named AB and CD, the said AB and CD referred to me, XY, for my decision and award the matters in dispute and difference between them (*state the matters in difference)*: Now I, the said XY, having heard and examined the parties and considered the pleadings and all allegations and counter-allegations made by them against each other and also all books, papers, writings and other evidences produced before me, do hereby make my award as follows:

I AWARD

(1) that, etc.

(2) that, etc.

(3) that the cost of this reference be paid by the said CD (or AB).

IN WITNESS WHEREOF I have hereunto set and subscribed my hand and signature this .... day of .... 2000.

XY (Arbitrator)

Award by Umpire

In the matter of the Arbitration Act (Act X of 1940) and In the matter of Arbitration Agreement dated .... BETWEEN AB etc. and CD etc.

WHEREAS by an agreement in writing and/or submission dated the .... day of .... made between AB of, etc., and CD of, etc., the matters in disputes and differences between them as specified therein were referred to the decision and arbitration of X and Y as joint arbitrators who thus appointed me as the umpire at the commencement of the reference on the .... day of ....19.........

And the said X and Y having disagreed and differed as between themselves over the subject-matter of the arbitration and the award to be made thereon during the pendency of the proceeding, I, the said umpire, took upon myself the reference and having examined the pleadings and heard the parties and considered allegations and counter-allegations and all documents and evidences produced before me, do hereby make my award as follows:

I AWARD ....

(1) that, etc.

(2) that, etc.

(3) that, etc.

Dated this .... day of .... 19........

IN WITNESS, etc. Z (Umpire)

THE NEW ACT
The Arbitration & Conciliation Act 1996

This Act applies to arbitral proceedings commencing on or after 22nd August 1996.

No judicial intervention. No judicial authority shall intervene unless specifically asked to do so.

Parties to be referred to arbitration

(a) *Domestic disputes.* A judicial authority before which an action is brought the subject-matter of which is covered by an arbitration agreement shall, on an application by a party, refer it to arbitration. The application praying for such reference to arbitration shall be accompanied by a certified copy of the Arbitration Agreement. However, the pendency of such an action in court will not prevent the commencement or continuation of the arbitration proceedings or making of an Award.

(b) *International disputes.* If an action is brought in case of an international dispute covered by New York Convention in any court then on the application of a party the court may refer the parties to arbitration. The court may refuse to refer the dispute to arbitration if it finds that the agreement is void or incapable of being performed.

When an international dispute covered by Geneva Convention is brought before a court then on an application of a party the court shall refer the parties to arbitration. However, if the arbitration cannot be proceeded with or it becomes inoperative then the court may proceed with the action before it.

In respect of international contractual or commercial legal relationship if any action is brought before a court in India covered by the Geneva Convention the court will refer the parties to arbitration. However, there must be a written valid agreement for referring the dispute to arbitration and both the parties must have adopted the Convention.

Procedure. For referring the matter in a pending proceeding before a court to arbitration an application has to be made by a party for referring the dispute to arbitration setting out the facts and circumstances of the case. The application is to be accompanied by a duly authenticated copy of the agreement containing the arbitration clause, particulars of the parties and cause of action and as to the jurisdiction of court. The Chief Justice of High Court will appoint the Arbitrator in case of domestic arbitration. The Chief Justice of Supreme Court will appoint the Arbitrator in case of an international arbitration. If a party to an arbitration agreement either of his own or in spite of direction of the court fails to appoint its Arbitrator within 30 days or each party appoints an Arbitrator but the Arbitrators fail to appoint a third Arbitrator within 30 days then a party may make an application to Chief Justice of the High Court of the State having the jurisdiction for appointment of an Arbitrator. Such an application can be made if the parties fail to appoint an Arbitrator, one party appoints the Arbitrator but the other party does not accept the appointment or the sole Arbitrator does not enter into reference. If the parties have agreed to appoint an Arbitrator according to the procedure laid down in the agreement but fail to do so then a party may apply to the Chief Justice for appointment of an Arbitrator. The Chief Justice may delegate his powers to an individual or an Institution in which case the application has to be made to that delegate.

The decision of the Chief Justice is final. The Chief Justice will frame a scheme for the purpose of the application for appointment of an Arbitrator.

Interim orders

(a) *By Court.* Before the arbitration starts or during arbitration proceeding or after the Award is made, a party may apply to the court for interim protection. Such interim protection may include appointment of a guardian for a minor or for a person of unsound mind or for the preservation or sale of goods or to secure the amount under dispute or for detention, preservation and protection of the subject-matter of the dispute. The court may issue interim injunction or appoint a receiver. The court may make the interim order for protection as may appear to the court to be just and convenient. The power of the court is the same as in any other proceeding before the court.

(b) *By Arbitrator.* An Arbitrator may make interim orders if the parties have not agreed to the contrary. The Arbitrator may at the request of a party order the opposite party to take any interim measure of protection as the arbitrator may consider necessary in respect of the subject-matter of the dispute. The Arbitrator may require a party to furnish security which may appear to the Arbitrator to be just and convenient for the protection and preservation of the subject-matter of the dispute.

During the pendency of the arbitration proceeding a party to the arbitration may therefore apply either to the court or to the Arbitrator for interim reliefs subject to any agreement between the parties.

Jurisdiction. Except for the appointment of an Arbitrator for which an application has to be made to Chief Justice or his delegate all other applications are to be made to the Principal Civil Court of the District or the High Court within whose jurisdiction the cause of action arose or the respondent resides or carries on business or the first application was validly made. Whether an Arbitrator has become legally or factually unable to function or he has failed to act without undue delay shall be decided by the parties. If they cannot agree then an application lies to court for decision on such a point. Once an application is made in respect of arbitration agreement to a court having jurisdiction all other subsequent proceedings should be before that court in respect of the said matter.

Court assistance. A party with the approval of the Arbitrator or the Arbitrator may apply to the court for assistance in taking evidence. On such an application the court may direct that evidence be given directly before the Arbitrator. The court may issue process to witnesses to appear before the Arbitrator in accordance with the rules of taking evidence before the court itself. Failure of the witnesses to comply with the direction of the court will amount to contempt of the court.

Application for setting aside of an Award. An application can be made by a party to the court for setting aside the Award. The party has to show that he was (*i*) under some incapacity or (*ii*) the Arbitration Agreement is not valid or (*iii*) he was not given proper notice of the appointment of the Arbitrator or (*iv*) of the arbitration proceedings or (*v*) otherwise he was unable to present his case. He may show that (*vi*) the Award deals with a dispute not within the scope of the Arbitration or (*vii*) that the composition of the Arbitral Tribunal or (*viii*) the arbitration proceeding was not in accordance with the agreement. The court may set aside the Award (*ix*) if the subject-matter of the dispute is not capable of settlement by arbitration or (*x*) the Award is in conflict with the public policy of India. Where the valid portion of the Award can be separated the court will set aside the invalid portion only. An Award if (*xi*) induced by or affected by fraud or corruption or (*xii*) there has been breach of confidentiality or (*xiii*) reliance on evidence in other proceedings then it would be void as being against public policy of India.

Limitation. The limitation for making the application for setting aside the Award is 3 months from the date of receipt of the Award or the corrected Award or the additional Award, as the case may be. The court has the discretion to extend this period by another 30 days for sufficient causes being shown.

Refer back to arbitrator. In appropriate cases at the request of a party the court may adjourn the hearing of the application to give an opportunity to the Arbitrator to resume the proceedings or to take such action as would eliminate the grounds for setting aside the Award.

Award is decree. In absence of a setting aside application, the Award shall be final and binding on the parties and can be enforced under the Code of Civil Procedure as a decree.

Enforcement of domestic Award. The Award is treated as a decree and can be executed in accordance with the provisions of Or. 21 read with s. 36 of the Code of Civil Procedure 1908. Both the domestic Award and the foreign Award are binding on the parties without any further Order of the court. Such an Award may be used as a defence or by way of set-off or otherwise in any legal proceedings in India.

Enforcement of foreign Award. For enforcing a foreign Award an application has to be made annexing an authenticated copy of the Award, a certified copy of the Agreement of Arbitration and necessary evidence that the Award is a foreign Award. Where the Award is in a foreign language, an English translation certified as correct by the Diplomatic or Consular Agent is to be annexed. The court means a District Court or the High Court. A foreign Award may not be enforced if the opposite party objects on the ground that (*i*) he was under incapacity or (*ii*) the agreement was not valid or (*iii*) he was not given proper notice of the appointment of the Arbitrator or the proceedings and (*iv*) he was unable to present his case or (*v*) that the Award deals with a dispute beyond the arbitration agreement or (*vi*) beyond the jurisdiction of the Arbitrator or (*vii*) the procedure was not in accordance with the agreement of the parties or (*viii*) was contrary to law of the country where the arbitration took place or (*ix*) that the Award is not yet binding on the parties or (*x*) has been set aside or (*xi*) suspended by a competent authority of the country in which the Award was made or (*xii*) that the subject-matter is not capable of settlement by arbitration or (*xiii*) the enforcement of the Award would be contrary to the public policy of India. An Award obtained by inducement or fraud or corruption is against the public policy of India.

On an application for enforcement of a foreign Award the court may adjourn the matter and order the other party to give suitable security. If the Award is severable the court may enforce the valid portion and set aside the invalid portion. If the court is satisfied about the validity of the foreign Award it shall enforce it as a Decree of that court.

Appealable orders. An appeal shall lie to the Appellate Court from an order of the Court granting or refusing to grant an interim order on an application before, during or after the arbitration proceedings. An appeal would lie from the order setting aside an Award or refusing to set aside an Award. Similarly, an appeal would lie from an order of Arbitrator granting an interim order or refusing to grant an interim order. The appeal will be to the court having the jurisdiction over the subject-matter of the arbitration. There is no second appeal. The parties however may approach the Supreme Court under the procedure available including by way of Special Leave Petition.

Schemes under s. 11 of the Arbitration and Conciliation Act 1996. The Calcutta High Court by a Notification published in the Calcutta Gazette of 25th January 1997 issued a Scheme for appointment of Arbitrators. The request to the Chief Justice under s. 11(4), (5) or (6) of the Act has to be made in writing. The application shall be accompanied by the original Arbitration Agreement or a duly certified copy thereof, the names and addresses of the parties and Arbitrator, if any, the name and address of the person, if any, to whom any function has been entrusted by the parties to the Arbitration Agreement under the appointment procedure agreed upon by them, the qualification required for the new Arbitrator, description of general disputes, point of common issue, the requirements and remedies sought. The application is to be supported by an affidavit with relevant documents that the conditions of sub-sec. (4) or (5) or (6) of s. 11, as the case may be, have been satisfied. The Chief Justice of Calcutta High Court has not delegated this authority to any other Judge or person or Institution.

The Delhi High Court by a Notification dated 2nd February 1996 issued under s. 11 of the Arbitration and Conciliation Ordinance 1996 has also provided for a request by an application in the above lines. But it has additionally provided that if the original Arbitration Agreement or a true copy thereof is not available then the applicant should make a prayer that the opposite parties should produce the original Arbitration Agreement or a true copy thereof. The Delhi High Court also delegated power to appoint Arbitrator to Civil Judge where the value of the subject-matter does not exceed Rs. 1 lakh, to the District Judge/Additional District Judge where the value of the subject-matter does not exceed Rs. 5 lakhs and to the Judge of the High Court exercising Ordinary Original Civil Jurisdiction where the value of the subject-matter exceeds Rs. 5 lakhs. The application fee has been fixed at Rs. 250, Rs. 500 and Rs. 1000 respectively.

Public works contracts arbitration. Some of the State Governments have set up Tribunals for resolution of disputes relating to Public Works Contracts. The Gujarat Public Works Contracts Disputes Arbitration Tribunal Act 1992 provides the procedure for resolution of disputes by the Tribunal. Reference of all disputes regarding Public Works Contracts are to be made to the Tribunal. The jurisdiction of the Civil Courts has been barred. Even the Award cannot be challenged. The operation of Arbitration Act has been excluded.

Some aspects of the Act. For amicable settlement of commercial disputes the General Assembly of the United Nations recommended to all countries adoption of Model Law on Arbitration based on the United Nations Commission on International Trade Law (UNCITRAL).

The Government of India has enacted the Arbitration and Conciliation Act 1996 on that model.

The Arbitration and Conciliation Act 1996 (Act) modelled on the UNCITRAL Model Law, consolidates and amends the existing law relating to domestic arbitration, international commercial arbitration and enforcement of foreign arbitral awards.

The underlying object of the Act is to galvanise the system of arbitration and to facilitate the conciliation in business matters. The Act recognises the autonomy of the parties in the conduct of arbitral proceedings. It promotes transparency in the matter of decision making by the arbitral tribunal by providing that the arbitral tribunal gives reasons for the arbitral Award.

The Act restricts the scope of judicial scrutiny of the award and minimises the supervisory role of courts. The grounds for challenging an award are (*a*) lack of capacity of a party (*b*) invalidity of the arbitration agreement (*c*) violation of principles of natural justice and (*d*) the arbitrator exceeding his terms of reference. The scope of judicial review is limited. The only residuary ground which empowers the courts to go into the merits of the award is that the award is in conflict with the public policy of India.

The Act dispenses with the requirement of making the arbitral award a rule of the court before it is enforced. The arbitral award itself, once it becomes final, is deemed to be a decree of the court for enforcement. A settlement agreement reached by the parties and signed by them with the help of the conciliator will be final and binding on them.

The Act allows resort to arbitration by parties for resolution of their disputes except certain disputes which cannot be submitted to arbitration under the Act.

The Act gives maximum freedom to the parties in the appointment of arbitrators by providing for institutional arbitration if parties agree to abide by the rules of procedure for appointment of arbitral institution.

A significant feature of the new law is that the Chief Justice of India or the Chief Justice of a High Court has been empowered to designate any person or institution to take the necessary steps for the appointment of arbitrators.

The Act empowers the arbitral tribunal to decide on its own jurisdiction and to consider the objections with regard to the existence or validity of the arbitration agreement. It provides that an arbitral tribunal will not be bound by the Code of Civil Procedure 1908 or the Indian Evidence Act 1872.

The Act provides that parties can agree to the rules for settlement of their disputes, on the procedure to be followed by the arbitral tribunal and the time schedule for the award. The idea is to eliminate delays and long procedure. This procedure Fast Track Arbitration (FTA) is suitable in cases which can be decided on the basis of the documents and where oral hearings and examination of the witnesses are not required such as preventing infringement of patent, trade mark, brand, copyright, licence, francise, etc. and falsification, concealment or destruction of evidence. The Fast Track Arbitration (FTA) can also supplement normal arbitration, for example, in a large infrastructural project, an urgent dispute can be resolved of FTA whereas normal issues can be settled by the conventional mode of arbitration.

The Rules of Arbitration of the Indian Council of Arbitration also provides that the parties may opt for FTA and request the bench, before the commencement of the arbitration proceedings, to decide the reference in a fixed time frame agreed between the parties.

Generally an arbitration tribunal is constituted in accordance with the terms of contract, claimant submits his statement of facts and claims and the respondent submits his defence and counter claims. Both parties file documentary evidence with the pleadings. The arbitration tribunal applies its mind and may ask for further documents/information for making an award.

The main features of the Act are (1) restriction of judicial intervention with the process and product of arbitration. It provides that the judiciary too should give due credence to an arbitration agreement. The judicial authority has to direct the parties to resort to arbitration as mentioned in the agreement;

(2) the grounds on which award of an arbitrator may be challenged before the judiciary have been drastically reduced. The arbitration award can be challenged only on the basis of invalidity of the agreement, want of jurisdiction on the part of the arbitrator or lack of proper notice to a party about the appointment of the arbitrator or of arbitral proceedings or that it is in conflict with "the public policy of India" including fraud and corruption;

(3) the powers of the arbitrator relating to the application of law, venue of arbitration, appointment of experts and acting on their report, seeking assistance of the court in taking evidence, award of interest etc. have been amplified;

(4) it puts a check on the tendency of parties to withhold evidence for a period and then suddenly raise the procedural objection to thwart arbitration proceedings;

(5) it recognises the role of institution in promoting and organising arbitration;

(6) it provides for filling up vacancies in arbitrators if there is a difference of opinion between the parties by the Chief Justice or an institution or person designated by Chief Justice;

(7) it has deleted the time limit for making of award but enjoins an arbitrator to act expeditiously;

(8) it has deleted the provisions relating to arbitration through intervention of court;

(9) it recognises the importance of transnational commercial arbitration by providing that even where the arbitration is held in India, the parties to the contract are free to designate the law applicable to the substance of the dispute.

(10) (*a*) Unless the agreement provides otherwise, the arbitrator must give reasons for the award and (*b*) the award is executable as a decree.

The Act for the first time provides a detailed statutory framework for the conduct of independent conciliation proceedings outside the court. It encourages the arbitral tribunals to use mediation conciliation or other Alternative Dispute Resolution (ADR) procedure during the arbitral proceedings to encourage settlement of disputes.

A conciliation proceeding can be initiated by a party inviting the other party to conciliate under the provisions of the Act. Once the opposite party accepts in writing the invitation to conciliate the conciliation proceedings start. It is for the parties concerned to decide on the number of conciliators.

The role of the conciliator will be to assist the parties in resolution of disputes amicably in an independent and impartial manner. A conciliator is not a judge but only a facilitator. He derives authority from the parties. He is to be guided by the principles of objectivity, fairness and justice. He is to give due consideration to the usage of trade and the facts and circumstances of disputes.

At an appropriate stage of conciliation proceedings, the conciliator may make proposal for settlement of the dispute.

A settlement agreement reached by the parties and signed by them with the help of the conciliator will be final and binding on the parties. It will have the same status and effect as if it is an arbitral award on agreed terms and will be enforceable like a decree of court.

Since conciliation is a consensual proceeding, it is entirely dependent on the continued good will of the parties and can be terminated by any of the parties at any time before the signing of the settlement agreement.

The parties to a conciliation proceeding cannot initiate any arbitral or judicial proceeding during the continuance of the conciliation proceeding. The only exception being the resort to such proceedings for preserving the parties' rights.

A conciliator cannot, unless otherwise agreed to by the parties, act as an arbitrator, representative or counsel of a party in any arbitral proceeding by the parties at a later stage.

The confidentiality principle applies to all persons. The conciliator and the parties are under obligation to keep all matters relating to conciliation proceedings confidential, whether it has resulted in a settlement agreement or not. The law provides that notwithstanding anything contained in any other law, the principle of confidentiality shall be maintained by the parties as well as the conciliator except where its disclosure is necessary for parties for the implementation and enforcement of the settlement agreement.

The essential features of a valid arbitration agreement as observed by Russell[1] are that (*i*) it must be in writing intended to bind the parties; (*ii*) it must contemplate some disputes and differences already arisen between the parties to the agreement or one which may arise in future between them with regard to some specific subject-matters which they intend to conclude by the decision of a third party; (*iii*) the parties must be *ad idem*; and (*iv*) intention of the parties to have the dispute adjudicated by private tribunal. The element of dispute, whether in common law or under any statute relating to the agreement, gives the private tribunal jurisdiction.[2] There must be a right asserted by one party and denied and disputed by another. The arbitrator or arbitrators may be named by the parties in the body of the agreement itself or they may agree upon the method of choosing one or more arbitrators. Normally, when the agreement is in respect of some present dispute, the parties nominate one person as the sole arbitrator or more as they like, one on each side, and they may as well do the same in case of future disputes and differences. Unless a sole arbitrator is agreed upon, the arbitrators shall appoint an umpire at the commencement of the

1 15th Ed., p. 1.

2 *Nandram* v *Raghunath* AIR 1954 Cal 245.

proceedings who shall take upon the reference only in case the arbitrators shall differ as between themselves.

Sometimes trade associations like a Chamber of Commerce, Institute or Association, which are empowered under the provisions relating to their respective constitutions of which the parties or either of them are members, are named as the authorities to nominate or select an arbitrator when any dispute or difference shall arise as between them. In agreements to which the Government is a party, particularly in building and manufacturing contracts, arbitration under the Defence of India Act, etc., etc., the arbitrator or arbitrators are often designated not by the name of any individual or individuals but by the name of the office. In the result the individual or individuals holding that particular office or offices at the time when the dispute arises become the arbitrator or arbitrators by virtue of their office.

FORMS

(Validity of the Forms be checked with the Department)

Notice under section 11 of the Arbitration and Conciliation Act 1996

To
Builders India Private Ltd.
7A, Camac Street
Calcutta 700 016

Dear Sirs

Re: Arbitration of the disputes arising out of Contract No. 3 entered with us.

You had entered into a Contract No. 3 with us undertaking to construct certain flats and guest houses on terms and conditions contained in said contract.

You have failed to complete construction and to make over delivery of possession of houses you had agreed to construct on our behalf.

We have paid you advances and also all your running bills. In spite of this, you are inordinately delaying the matter. Time was of the essence of the contract. You have failed to keep the time schedule.

The few apartments and guest houses that you have constructed and agreed for joint inspection were found to be defective and not suitable for occupation of the staff and they have not yet been made habitable.

In spite of requests you have failed and neglected to complete the work. As a result of your breach of the agreement we have suffered losses and we are still suffering losses every day. Our huge investment has been blocked and we have to pay interest to our Banker for the finance obtained to make payment to you.

Under the clause of the said contract, there is an agreement to refer the disputes to Arbitration of Mr. Rajib Khaitan, Advocate of 6 S.P. Mukherjee Road, Calcutta 700 025.

Under the provisions of section 11 of the Arbitration and Conciliation Act 1996 we hereby give you notice to concur with the appointment of Mr. Rajib Khaitan, Advocate, as the Sole Arbitrator in the matter of the differences and disputes that have arisen between the parties herein and the same be referred for adjudication to him.

The said disputes are, *inter alia,* the following:

(*a*) Whether the construction of houses and guest-houses under the said Contract No. 3 have been in accordance with the contract?

(*b*) Whether the construction has been completed in accordance with the specification and the terms and conditions of the contract?

(*c*) Whether the contractor has delivered completed houses, flats?

(*d*) Whether the Eastern India Enterprise has suffered any loss or damages due to non-compliance of the terms and conditions of the contract by Builders India Private Ltd?

(*e*) What is the damage and compensation that the employer is entitled to get from the contractor?

Please give your concurrence within 7 days of receipt of this letter.

Yours faithfully

Application for Cancellation of Arbitration Agreement

In the High Court at Calcutta Ordinary Original Civil Jurisdiction

In the matter of Arbitration and Conciliation Act 1996

And

In the matter of an application under section 7 of the said Act

And

Builders India Private Ltd., a company registered under the Companies Act 1956 and carrying on business in 7A, Camac Street, Calcutta 700 016

Petitioner

And

S.N. Udyog Private Ltd. a company registered under the Companies Act 1956 and carrying on business at 6 S.P. Mukherjee Road, Calcutta 700 025

Respondent

To

The Hon'ble Mr. ....

Chief Justice and His Companion Justices of the said Hon'ble Court

The humble petition of the petitioner above-named most respectfully

SHEWETH:

1. Your petitioner received on 15th November 1999 a notice dated 10th November 1999 from the respondent requesting the petitioner to appoint an arbitrator under an alleged Agreement of Arbitration contained in a Contract No. 3 dated 5th September 1995.

2. Your petitioner states that the alleged agreement to refer disputes to arbitration was invalid and not binding on the petitioner, *inter alia,* for the following reasons:

(*a*) ....

(*b*) ....

3. Your petitioner states that the subject-matter of the alleged disputes between the parties is within the jurisdiction of the Court at Mumbai.

4. Your petitioner reasonably apprehends that if the said agreement is allowed to remain outstanding further proceedings may be taken by the respondent pursuant to the said notice or otherwise and in that event your petitioner would be seriously prejudiced.

5. The existence and validity of the alleged Arbitration Agreement alleged to be in possession of the respondent have to be determined by this Hon'ble Court on production thereof by the respondent.

6. The respondent be directed to produce the alleged Arbitration Agreement before this Hon'ble Court for scrutiny and for cancellation.

7. Unless orders are made as prayed for your petitioner will suffer loss and prejudice.

8. This application is made *bona fide* and in the interest of justice.

Your petitioner therefore humbly prays to Your Lordships for the following Orders:

(*a*) Direction on the respondent to produce the Arbitration Agreement to this Hon'ble Court;

(*b*) Declaration that the said Arbitration Agreement is invalid, void and of no effect;

(*c*) Cancellation of the alleged Arbitration Agreement as a nullity;

(*d*) Direction that the said notice dated .... is invalid, void and of no effect;

(*e*) Injunction restraining the respondent from giving any effect or further effect to the said notice;

(*f*) Costs of this application be paid by the respondent;

(*g*) Further Orders be made and directions be given as to this Hon'ble Court may deem fit and proper to afford complete relief to your petitioner.

And your petitioner as in duty bound shall ever pray.

Signature of Advocate for the petitioner

Signature of petitioner

Verification

I, ... son of .... aged about .... years, by occupation service, working for gain at 7A, Camac Street, Calcutta 700 016 do hereby solemnly affirm and say as follows:

(1) I am a Director of Builders India Private Ltd. and a principal officer and a Constituted Attorney. I know and I have made myself acquainted with the facts and circumstances of the case and I am able to depose thereto. I am authorised and competent to verify and I do verify the aforesaid petition on behalf of Builders India Private Ltd.

(2) The statements in paragraphs 1 to 8 herein are true to my knowledge based on information derived from records maintained by the petitioner Builders India Private Ltd. and believed by me to be true.

Solemnly affirmed by the said Mr. .... pursuant to a Board Resolution dated .... of

Builders India Private Ltd. in the Court House at Calcutta this .... day of November 1999.

Petition for Appointment of an Arbitrator

Special Suit No. .... of ....

In the High Court at Calcutta Ordinary Original Civil Jurisdiction

In the matter of Arbitration and Conciliation Act 1996

And

In the matter of an application under section 8 of the Arbitration and Conciliation Act 1996

And

Builders India Private Ltd., a company registered under the Companies Act 1956 and carrying on business at 7A, Camac Street, Calcutta 700 016

Petitioner

versus

S.N. Udyog Private Ltd., a company registered under the Companies Act 1956 and carrying on business at 6 S.P. Mukherjee Road, Calcutta 700 025

Respondent

To
The Hon'ble Mr. ....
.... Chief Justice and
His Companion Justices of the
said Hon'ble Court

The humble petition of Builders India Private Ltd., the petitioner above-named, most respectfully

SHEWETH:

1. Your petitioner entered into a contract with the respondent for construction of certain flats and guest houses on terms and conditions contained in an Agreement dated 5th September 1995.

2. Your petitioner completed the work and offered delivery of flats and guest houses duly constructed and demanded from the respondent payment of the final bill.

3. The respondent failed and neglected to pay the outstanding amount and your petitioner in accordance with the arbitration clause in the agreement referred the disputes to the arbitration of Mr. Rajib Khaitan, Advocate and gave notice accordingly to the respondent.

4. No reply was received to the said notice and the arbitration proceedings could not commence.

5. Your petitioner has now been served with a Summons to appear and defend a suit which has been filed by the respondent for damages against the petitioner for breach of the said contract.

6. Your petitioner has to enter appearance and file a statement in the said suit. Your petitioner states that the said suit is in respect of the contract for construction of house, flats and guest houses which work the petitioner has completed and submitted the final bill but payment has not been received. The disputes and differences arose by and between the petitioner and the respondent in relation to the construction and also payment of bills of your petitioner.

7. By virtue of the arbitration clause in the said contract your petitioner duly served a notice on the respondent and appointed the Advocate as the sole arbitrator.

8. Your petitioner was and is still ready and willing to have the disputes and differences adjudicated upon by the Arbitrator to be appointed under the Arbitration Clause in the agreement notice whereunder was served on the respondent. However because of its failure to appoint the sole Arbitrator as stated by your petitioner, this Hon'ble Court will be pleased to appoint an Arbitrator under section 11 of the Arbitration and Conciliation Act 1996.

9. Your petitioner states that in the facts and circumstances of the case the proceedings in the said suit be stayed, an Arbitrator be appointed to resolve the disputes between the parties covered by the said suit and the Award be made.

10. Unless orders are made as prayed for your petitioner will suffer loss and prejudice.

11. This application is made *bona fide* and in the interest of justice.

Your petitioner therefore humbly prays Your Lordships for the following orders:

(*a*) Stay of further proceedings in the above suit;

(*b*) An Arbitrator be appointed to resolve the disputes raised in the suit or otherwise in the arbitration proceedings;

(*c*) Costs of this application be the costs in the arbitration proceedings;

(*d*) Further orders be made and directions be given as to this Hon'ble Court may deem fit and proper.

And your petitioner, as in duty bound, shall ever pray.

Verification

I, ... son of .... aged about .... years, working for gain at 7A, Camac Street, Calcutta 700016 do hereby solemnly affirm and say as follows:

(1) I am the Manager of Builders India Private Ltd., and a principal officer and a Constituted Attorney. I know and I have made myself acquainted with the facts and circumstances of the case and I am able to depose thereto. I am competent to affirm and I do affirm and declare and verify on behalf of the petitioner.

(2) The statements contained in paragraphs 1 to 11 of the foregoing petition are true to my knowledge based on records maintained by the petitioner and believed by me to be true.

Solemnly affirmed by the said Mr. .... pursuant to a Board Resolution dated .... of Builders India Private Ltd. in the Court House at Calcutta on this .... day of November 1999.

Before me
Commissioner

Petition Praying for Interim Measures

In the High Court at Calcutta Ordinary Original Civil Jurisdiction

In the matter of:
The Arbitration & Conciliation Act 1996

And

In the matter of:
An application under section 9 of the said Act

And

In the matter of:
An Arbitration Agreement contained in the Contract No. 3 dated ....

And

In the matter of:
Builders India Private Ltd., a company registered under the Companies Act 1956

and carrying on business at 7A, Camac Street, Calcutta 700 016

Petitioner

versus

S.N. Udyog Private Ltd., a company registered under the Companies Act 1956 and carrying on business at 6 S.P. Mukherjee Road, Calcutta 700 025

Respondent

To

The Hon'ble Mr. ....
Chief Justice and His Companion
Justices of the said Hon'ble Court

The humble petition of the petitioner above-named most respectfully

SHEWETH:

1. The petitioner is engaged in construction of houses, flats, guest houses and other apartments.

2. The petitioner has a good reputation as a contractor in the construction business.

3. By and under a contract No. 3 dated .... entered into with the respondent, your petitioner agreed to build and construct several houses, flats and guest houses for and on behalf of the respondent in accordance with the specifications and on terms and conditions contained in the said contract.

4. Your petitioner carried out the work of construction in accordance with the said agreement and completed the work and obtained the completion certificate from the respondent.

5. Your petitioner submitted running bills from time to time but the respondent wrongfully deducted 10% from the same purported to be as Security Money.

6. The respondent also obtained the Performance Guarantee, from the petitioner issued by the petitioner's Banker. The respondent also obtained from the petitioner Bank Guarantees for the Earnest Money that were required to be deposited with the respondent.

7. The respondent has wrongfully refused to take delivery of the completed houses, flats and guest houses on some flimsy pretext and has withheld payment of the outstanding bills amounting to Rs. 50 lakhs.

8. In breach of the said agreement, the respondent has invoked the said Bank Guarantees but the same has not yet been paid by the bank concerned.

9. Your petitioner gave due notice to the respondent regarding the dispute to the sole Arbitrator Mr. Rajib Khaitan an Advocate in terms of the arbitration clause in the said Contract No. 3. The respondent has not yet replied to the said notice appointing the said sole Arbitrator by the petitioner.

10. The said Bank Guarantees were furnished pursuant to fraud practised by the respondent on your petitioner inasmuch as your petitioner was led to believe that the respondent intended to act in accordance with the terms of the agreement and that it would not create problems for any oblique motives. The said Guarantees were issued on terms and conditions dictated by the respondent unilaterally and were burdensome. The petitioner was not aware of such terms and conditions dictated by the respondent to the bank without any intimation to the petitioner.

11. There is special equity that the said Bank Guarantee should not be enforced or encashed inasmuch as your petitioner has duly complied with the terms and conditions of the said Contract No. 3 and the respondent cannot have any genuine grievance in relation to the performance of any obligation of the petitioner under the Contract No. 3.

12. The respondent is commercially insolvent and several petitions are pending for windingup of the respondent company.

13. If the company goes into liquidation then your petitioner being an unsecured creditor will not get any payment in the winding up proceedings from the Official Liquidator. If in the meantime the Bank Guarantees were encashed then on the one hand, your petitioner's huge amount will be taken away by the respondent and on the other hand, the outstanding bills amounting to Rs. 50 lakhs would remain outstanding and would never be recovered. The petitioner has a special equity in its favour for an Order of Injunction restraining invocation or encashment of the Bank Guarantees issued in relation to the Contract No. 3 namely Bank Guarantees Nos. 1 and 2 dated 5th and 10th January 1999 for Rs. 20 lakhs and Rs. 5 lakhs issued by State Bank of India, Camac Street Branch in favour of the respondent on behalf of the petitioner.

14. By reasons of the aforesaid, your petitioner prays for an Order of Injunction restraining the respondent from encashing the said Bank Guarantees until settlement of the disputes between the parties by the Arbitrator.

15. Unless Orders are made as prayed for herein your petitioner will suffer loss and prejudice.

16. This application is made *bona fide* and in the interest of justice.

Your petitioner, therefore, humbly prays Your Lordships for the following Orders:

(*a*) Injunction restraining the respondent from enforcing the Bank Guarantees Nos. 1 and 2 issued by the State Bank of India, Camac Street Branch for Rs. 20 lakhs and Rs. 5 lakhs or encashing the same or receiving payment until the disposal of the arbitration proceedings in terms of the arbitration clause in the said contract;

(*b*) Ad-interim Order in terms of prayer (*a*) above;

(*c*) Costs incidental to this application be the costs in the proceedings.

And your petitioner, as in duty bound shall ever pray.

Signature of Advocate for the petitioner — Signature of the petitioner

Verification

I, ... son of .... aged about .... years, by occupation service working for gain at 7A, Camac Street, Calcutta 700 016 do hereby solemnly affirm and say as follows:

(1) I am the Manager of Builders India Private Ltd. and a Principal Officer and a Constituted Attorney. I know and I have made myself acquainted with the facts and circumstances of this case and I am able to depose thereto. I am authorised and competent to verify the aforesaid petition and I do verify the same on behalf of the petitioner.

(2) The statements contained in the paragraphs No. 1 to 16 hereinabove are true to my knowledge based on information derived from records maintained by the petitioner company and I believe them to be true.

Solemnly affirmed by the said Mr.. pursuant to Board Resolution of the Builders India Private Ltd. dated .... in the Court House at Calcutta on the 5th day of November 1999.

Before me

Commissioner

Petition for Appointment of a Sole Arbitrator

In the High Court at Calcutta Ordinary Original Civil Jurisdiction

In the matter of:

The Arbitration & Conciliation Act 1996

And

In the matter of:
An application under section 11 of the said Act

And

In the matter of:
An Arbitration Agreement contained in the Contract No. 3 dated ....

And

In the matter of:
Builders India Private Ltd., a company registered under the Companies Act 1956 and carrying on business at 7A, Camac Street, Calcutta 700 016

Petitioner

versus

S.N. Udyog Private Ltd., a company registered under the Companies Act 1956 and carrying on business at 6 S.P. Mukherjee Road, Calcutta 700 025

Respondent

To

The Hon'ble Mr. ....
Chief Justice and His Companion Justices of the said Hon'ble Court

The humble petition of the petitioner above-named most respectfully

SHEWETH:

1. Your petitioner is engaged in construction business and has a good reputation.

2. By and under an agreement dated .... entered into with the respondent your petitioner agreed to build and construct specified houses, flats and guest houses for and on behalf of the respondent. The terms and conditions and the specifications will appear from the said agreement. Your petitioner carried out the work of construction in terms of the agreement and offered to deliver possession of the completed work to the respondent.

3. The respondent on some pretext or the other failed to take delivery of the houses flats and guest houses constructed by your petitioner, and to pay the final bills of your petitioner duly submitted to the respondent.

4. The said agreement contained a clause to the effect that all disputes and differences shall be referred to an Arbitrator to be appointed by the parties.

5. The disputes and the differences have arisen between the parties on or about .... Your petitioner requested the respondent to concur in the appointment of a sole Arbitrator and your petitioner appointed Mr. Rajib Khaitan, an Advocate of Old Post Office Street, Calcutta. A copy of the notice in this regard sent to the respondent is annexed hereto marked 'A'.

6. The respondent is carrying on business at the address given above within the said jurisdiction of this Hon'ble Court and the disputes arose and the respondent failed to give concurrence for the appointment of sole Arbitrator at the address of the respondent within the jurisdiction of this Hon'ble Court.

7. Your petitioner states that this Hon'ble Court will be pleased to appoint a sole Arbitrator as provided in the Arbitration Agreement dated .... a certified copy whereof is annexed hereto marked 'B'.

8. Unless Orders are made as prayed for herein, your petitioner would suffer loss and prejudice.

9. This application is made *bona fide* and in the interest of justice.

Your petitioner, therefore, humbly prays to Your Lordships for the following orders:

(*a*) A suitable person be appointed as the sole Arbitrator to arbitrate in the disputes arising from the said agreement and to give his Award;

(*b*) Costs of this application be the costs in the arbitration proceedings;

(*c*) Further orders be made and directions be given as to this Hon'ble Court may deem fit and proper to afford complete relief to your petitioner.

And your petitioner as in duty bound shall ever pray.

Signature of the Advocate of the petitioner

Signature of the petitioner

Verification

I, ... son of .... aged about .... years, by occupation service, working for gain at 7A, Camac Street, Calcutta 700 016 do hereby solemnly affirm and say as follows:

(1) I am the Manager of Builders India Private Ltd. and Principal Officer and Constituted Attorney. I know and I have made myself acquainted with the facts and circumstances of this case and I am able to depose thereto. I am authorised and competent to verify the aforesaid petition and I do verify the same on behalf of the petitioner.

(2) The statements contained in the paragraphs 1 to 9 herein are true to my knowledge based on information derived from records maintained by the petitioner and I believe them to be true.

Solemnly affirmed by the said Mr. .... pursuant to Board Resolution dated .... of the Builders India Private Ltd. in the Court House at Calcutta on the 10th day of November 1999.

Before me
Commissioner

Petition for Substitution of Arbitrator upon Challenge

In the High Court at Calcutta Ordinary Original Civil Jurisdiction

In the matter of:
The Arbitration & Conciliation Act 1996

And

In the matter of:
An application under section 12 read with section 15 of the said Act

And

In the matter of:
An Arbitration Agreement contained in the Contract No. 3 dated ....

And

In the matter of:
Builders India Private Ltd., a company registered under the Companies Act 1956 and carrying on business at 7A, Camac Street, Calcutta 700 016

Petitioner

versus

1. S.N. Udyog Private Ltd., a company registered under the Companies Act 1956 and carrying on business at 6 S.P. Mukherjee Road, Calcutta 700 025

2. Mr. D.N. Banerjee of 15 Old Post Office Street, Calcutta 700 001

Respondent

To

The Hon'ble Mr. ....
Chief Justice and His Companion
Justices of the said Hon'ble Court

The humble petition of the petitioner above-named most respectfully

SHEWETH:

1. By and under an agreement dated .... the petitioner undertook to construct houses, flats and guest-houses, for the respondent on agreed specifications, terms and conditions and price.

2. Your petitioner completed the work, obtained payment of the running bills, offered delivery of houses, flats and guest-houses and claimed payment of the final bill.

3. The respondent raised various minor objections with a view to withhold payment of the outstanding bills.

4. Some disputes and differences arose under the Agreement of Reference to arbitration dated .... The parties referred the disputes to the arbitration of Mr. Rajib Khaitan, an Advocate appointed by the petitioner and to Mr. S. Gupta an Engineer appointed by the respondent. The said arbitrators appointed Mr. D.N. Banerjee as the Umpire.

5. The Arbitrators entered into reference dated .... and held certain sittings.

6. At the sixth sitting differences of opinion arose between the said arbitrators. The matter was referred to the Umpire on .... who commenced the proceedings and held five sittings.

7. Since .... the said Umpire has not held any meeting or hearing of the said arbitration proceedings. The Umpire is not proceeding with the reference nor has made his Award although more than 4 months have passed since he entered on the reference.

8. The petitioner states that the said Umpire has no intention to complete the proceedings and he is incapable of doing so and as such this Hon'ble Court would be pleased to remove him from further acting as Umpire in the said arbitration proceedings.

9. Your petitioner states that a declaration be made that the Arbitration Agreement shall cease to have effect with respect to the differences and disputes referred to the said arbitrators and ultimately to the said Umpire.

10. Without prejudice to the aforesaid, but in the alternative, your petitioner states that this Hon'ble Court would be pleased to appoint a Sole Arbitrator to adjudicate the disputes among the parties. A Copy of the issues settled by the Arbitrators is annexed hereto marked 'B', from which it will appear the nature of the disputes among the parties to be settled by the Arbitrators to be appointed. The Arbitrator to be appointed be directed to enter into reference and complete the proceedings and give his Award within the time to be specified by this Hon'ble Court.

11. Unless orders are made as prayed for herein your petitioner will suffer loss and prejudice.

12. This application is made *bona fide* and in the interest of justice.

Your petitioner, therefore, humbly prays Your Lordships for the following orders:

(*a*) The Umpire Mr. D.N. Banerjee be removed from further acting as Umpire in the reference made by the parties herein;

(*b*) Declaration that the Arbitration Agreement has ceased to have any effect in respect of the disputes and differences referred to the said Arbitrators and/or the Umpire;

(*c*) A suitable person be appointed as the sole Arbitrator to adjudicate the disputes among the parties and give his Award within the time that may be specified by this Hon'ble Court;

(*d*) Costs of this application be the costs in the Arbitration proceedings;

(*e*) Further orders be made and directions be given as to this Hon'ble Court may deem fit and proper to afford complete relief to your petitioner.

And your petitioner as in duty bound shall ever pray.

Signature of Advocate for the petitioner

Signature of the petitioner

Verification

I, ... son of .... aged .... years, by occupation service, working for gain at 7A, Camac Street, Calcutta 700 016 do hereby solemnly affirm and say as follows:

(1) I am the Manager of Builders India Private Ltd. and Principal Officer and Constituted Attorney. I know and I have made myself acquainted with the facts and circumstances of this case and I

am able to depose thereto. I am authorised and competent to verify the aforesaid petition and I do verify the same on behalf of the petitioner.

(2) The statements contained in the paragraphs 1 to 12 herein above are true to my knowledge based on information derived from records maintained by the petitioner company and I believe them to be true.

Solemnly affirmed by the said Mr. .... pursuant to Board Resolution dated ....of the Builders India Private Ltd. in the Court House at Calcutta on the 15th day of December 1999.

Before me
Commissioner

Petition for Substitution of Arbitrator upon Termination of Mandate

In the High Court at Calcutta Ordinary Original Civil Jurisdiction

In the matter of:

The Arbitration & Conciliation Act 1996

And

In the matter of:

An application under section 15 of the said Act

And

In the matter of:

An Arbitration Agreement contained in the Contract No. 3 dated ....

And

In the matter of:

Builders India Private Ltd. a company registered under the Companies Act 1956 and carrying on business at 7A, Camac Street, Calcutta 700 016

Petitioner

versus

1. S.N. Udyog Private Ltd., a company registered under the Companies Act 1956 and carrying on business at 6 S.P. Mukherjee Road, Calcutta 700 025

2. Mr. Somnath Banerjee of 7 Hindustan Park, Calcutta 700 029

Respondents

To

The Hon'ble Mr. ....
Chief Justice and His Companion
Justices of the said Hon'ble Court

The humble petition of the petitioner above-named most respectfully

SHEWETH:

1. By and under an agreement dated .... the petitioner undertook to construct houses, flats and guest-houses, for the first respondent on agreed specifications, terms and conditions and price.

2. Your petitioner completed the work, obtained payment of the running bills, offered delivery of houses, flats and guest-houses and claimed payment of the final bill.

3. The first respondent raised various minor objections with a view to withhold payment of the outstanding bills.

4. Disputes and differences arose in relation to the said agreement. The said agreement contained an arbitration clause. According to the terms of the agreement, Mr. Anil Chaudhury was appointed as the sole arbitrator in respect of the matters in dispute between the parties.

5. The said arbitrator failed to enter into reference in spite of requests.

6. On application being made by the petitioner in this Hon'ble Court the said arbitrator was removed by an Order dated .... and respondent No. 2 was appointed in place and stead of Mr. Anil Chaudhury.

7. The disputes between the parties concerned fraud and forgery of the documents which form the foundation of the claims and contentions of the parties.

8. Your petitioner states that such disputes involved complicated questions of Criminal Law and detailed evidence to be taken including opinion from experts for that purpose and several witnesses have to be summoned, which could not be appropriately done and the matter adjudicated upon by the present arbitrator. In the premises, it will be more appropriate and convenient that his mandate be terminated.

9. The present arbitrator appointed by the said order removing the earlier arbitrator is a non-legal person and he will not be able to adjudicate the present disputes between the parties which involves complicated questions

of forgery of documents and fraud a new arbitrator be appointed interims of sub-section (2) of section 15 of the Act.

10. Unless orders are made as prayed for herein your petitioner will suffer loss and prejudice.

11. This application is made *bona fide* and in the interest of justice.

Your petitioner therefore humbly prays Your Lordships for the following orders:

(*a*) Terminate the mandate of the present arbitrator;

(*b*) Appoint by substitution a new and competent arbitrator in terms of section 15(2) of the Act;

(*c*) Costs of this application be the costs in the court proceedings;

(*d*) Further Orders be made and directions be given as to this Hon'ble Court may deem fit and proper.

And your petitioner as in duty bound shall ever pray.

Signature of the Advocate for the petitioner — Signature of the petitioner

Verification

I, ... son of .... aged .... years by occupation service, working for gain at 7A, Camac Street, Calcutta 700 016 do hereby solemnly affirm and say as follows:

1. I am the Manager of Builders India Private Ltd., and its Principal Officer and Constituted Attorney. I know and I have made myself acquainted with the facts and circumstances of this case and I am able to depose thereto. I am authorised and competent to verify the aforesaid petition and I do verify the same on behalf of the petitioner.
2. The statements contained in paragraphs 1 to 13 hereinabove are true to my knowledge based on information derived from records maintained by the petitioner company and I believe them to be true.

Solemnly affirmed by the said Mr. .... pursuant to Board Resolution dated .... of the Builders India Private Ltd. in the Court House at Calcutta on the 15th day of December 1999.

Before me

Commissioner

Petition seeking for Interpretation of Award

In the High Court at Calcutta Ordinary Original Civil Jurisdiction

In the matter of:
The Arbitration & Conciliation Act 1996

And

In the matter of:
An application under section 33 of the said Act

And

In the matter of:
An Arbitration Agreement contained in the Contract No. 3 dated ....

And

In the matter of:
Builders India Private Ltd., a company registered under the Companies Act 1956 and carrying on business at 7A, Camac Street, Calcutta 700 016

Petitioner

versus

1. Impressions India Private Ltd., a company registered under the Companies Act 1956 and carrying on business at 6 S.P. Mukherjee Road, Calcutta 700 025

2. Mr. D.N. Banerjee of 7 Hindusthan Park, Calcutta 700 029

Respondents

To

The Hon'ble Mr. ....
Chief Justice and His Companion
Justices of the said Hon'ble Court

The humble petition of the petitioner above-named most respectfully

SHEWETH:

1. By and under an agreement dated .... the petitioner undertook to construct houses, flats and guest-houses for the first respondent on agreed specifications, terms and conditions and price.

2. Your petitioner completed the work, obtained payment of the running bills, offered delivery of houses, flats and guest-houses and claimed payment of the final bill.

3. The first respondent raised various minor objections with a view to withhold payment of the outstanding bills.

4. Disputes and differences arose between the parties and under the arbitration clause contained in the agreement these disputes and differences were referred to the respondent No. 2 for adjudication.

5. After hearing the parties, respondent No. 2 the sole arbitrator gave the Award dated ....

6. Your petitioner received a copy of the said Award on .... under section 31 of the Arbitration & Conciliation Act 1996.

7. The said Award a copy whereof is annexed hereto and marked 'A' is incomplete in several respects. Respondent No. 2 has not given his decision on the disputes as to escalation of costs. Respondent No. 2 failed to consider and decide the disputes as regards extra work done by the petitioner and the liability of first respondent to pay for the work duly accepted by the first respondent. For non payment of the outstanding bills under the agreement interest @ 18% per annum was payable by the first respondent. Though this issue was raised subsequently on this point the respondent No. 2 failed to adjudicate this issue.

8. Your petitioner states that this is a fit case that this Hon'ble Court will be pleased to remit the Award dated .... to the respondent No. 2 for determination of the disputes regarding escalation of costs, payment for extra work done benefit of which was received by the first respondent and the contracted rate of interest payable by the first respondent to the petitioner on the outstanding amount payable by the first respondent in respect of the final bill which included the escalation costs, costs for additional work done and interest on the outstanding amount upto the date of submission of the final bill. The respondent No. 2 is further required to adjudicate on the question of interest for the subsequent period till payment of the petitioner's claims by the first respondent.

9. In the facts of the case, your petitioner states that the Award be remitted to the respondent No. 2 with a direction to give his decision on the aforesaid points after hearing the parties if necessary even though all the relevant documents are on record of the said arbitration proceeding.

10. This Hon'ble Court will be pleased to fix a time within which the respondent No. 2 will give his Award including his decision on the above points.

11. Unless orders are made as prayed for herein, your petitioner will suffer loss and prejudice.

12. This application is made *bona fide* and in the interest of justice.

Your petitioner, therefore prays Your Lordships for the following orders:

(*a*) Award dated .... given by respondent No. 2 be remitted to respondent No. 2 for submission of his decision on following points:

(*i*) whether the petitioner is entitled to and if so, to what extent, the escalation costs in the execution of the agreement?

(*ii*) whether the petitioner is entitled to payment for additional work done and if so upto what extent?

(*iii*) whether the petitioner is entitled to interest on its outstanding amounts, if so, the period for the same and the rate at which the petitioner is entitled to such interest?

(*b*) A time limit be fixed within which respondent No. 2 has to give his decision on the issues mentioned in prayer (*a*) above.

(*c*) Further orders be made and directions be given as to this Hon'ble Court may deem fit and proper in the facts of the case.

And your petitioner as in duty bound shall ever pray.

Signature of the Advocate for the petitioner

Signature of the petitioner

Verification

I, ... son of .... aged about .... years by occupation service, working for gain at 7A, Camac Street, Calcutta 700 016 do hereby solemnly affirm and say as follows:

1. I am the Manager of Builders India Private Ltd., and its Principal Officer and Constituted Attorney. I know and I have made myself acquainted with the facts and circumstances of this case and I am able to depose thereto. I am authorised and competent to verify the aforesaid petition and I do verify the same on behalf of the petitioner.

2. The statements contained in paragraphs 1 to 12 hereinabove are true to my knowledge based on information derived from records maintained by the petitioner company and I believe them to be true.

Solemnly affirmed by the said Mr. .... pursuant to Board Resolution dated .... of the Builders India Private Ltd. in the Court House at Calcutta on the 15th day of December 1999.

Before me
Commissioner

Application for Setting Aside an Award

In the High Court at Calcutta Ordinary Original Civil Jurisdiction

In the matter of:
The Arbitration & Conciliation Act 1996

And

In the matter of:
An application under section 34 of the said Act

And

In the matter of:
An Arbitration Agreement contained in the Contract No. 3 dated ....

And

In the matter of:
Builders India Private Ltd., a company registered under the Companies Act 1956 and carrying on business at 7A, Camac Street, Calcutta 700 016

Petitioner

versus

1. Eastern India Enterprise, a company registered under the Companies Act 1956 and carrying on business at 6 S.P. Mukherjee Road, Calcutta 700 025

2. Mr. D.N. Banerjee of 7 Hindusthan Park, Calcutta 700 029

Respondents

To
The Hon'ble Mr. ....
Chief Justice and His Companion
Justices of the said Hon'ble Court

The humble petition of the petitioner above-named most respectfully

SHEWETH:

1. By and under an agreement dated .... the petitioner undertook to construct houses, flats and guest-houses, for the first respondent on agreed specifications, terms and conditions and price.

2. Your petitioner completed the work, obtained payment of the running bills, offered delivery of houses, flats and guest houses and claimed payment of the final bill.

3. The first respondent raised various minor objections with a view to withhold payment of the outstanding bills.

4. Pursuant to the arbitration clause in the said agreement the parties herein that is the petitioner and respondent No. 1 appointed respondent No. 2 as the sole arbitrator to settle and adjudicate all the disputes and differences, between the petitioner and the first respondent arising out of the construction work done by the petitioner for the first respondent.

5. The differences and disputes arose on .... and thereafter the same were referred to the arbitration of respondent No. 2 on .... and respondent No. 2 entered into the reference on ....

6. Thereafter several sittings were held and both the petitioner and the first respondent adduced both documentary and oral evidence.

7. Respondent No. 2 gave his award on .... notified the same to the parties with a copy thereof on .... A copy of the Award is annexed hereto marked 'A'.

8. The said award is invalid and be set aside for, *inter alia*, the following reasons:

(*a*) the said award deals with a dispute not contemplated by the parties;

(*b*) the said award deals with a matter not falling within the terms of submission to arbitration;

(*c*) the said award contains decisions on matters beyond the scope of the submission to arbitration.

(*d*) the award does not deal with issue No. 5 raised and settled.

9. The disputes referred to respondent No. 2 for arbitration will appear from the statement of facts and counter statement of facts. Copies of those documents are annexed hereto marked 'B' and 'C' respectively.

10. The parties raised several issues. Thereafter respondent No. 2 settled these issues and the parties did not object.

11. After the award is given it is found that the award deals with issues not raised and the award omits to adjudicate on issue No. 5 which was raised and settled by respondent No. 2.

12. Your petitioner states that the said Award is bad in law and in fact. The said award is invalid and should be set aside.

13. Your petitioner states that this Hon'ble Court will be pleased to scrutinise the Award and documents filed along with award and direct further enquiry as may be necessary and thereafter set aside the said award.

14. Unless orders are made as prayed for herein your petitioner will suffer loss and prejudice.

15. This application is made *bona fide* and in the interest of justice.

Your petitioner therefore humbly prays Your Lordships for the following orders:

(*a*) The Award given by respondent No. 2 on .... be set aside;

(*b*) Costs of this application be paid by respondent No. 1;

(*c*) Further orders be made and directions be given as to this Hon'ble Court may deem fit and proper;

And your petitioner as in duty bound shall ever pray.

Signature of the Advocate for the petitioner	Signature of the petitioner

Verification

I, ... son of .... aged about .... years by occupation service, working for gain at 7A, Camac Street, Calcutta 700016 do hereby solemnly affirm and say as follows:

1. I am the Manager of Builders India Private Ltd. and its Principal Officer and Constituted Attorney. I know and I have made myself acquainted with the facts and circumstances of this case and I am able to depose thereto. I am authorised and competent to verify the aforesaid petition and I do verify the same on behalf of the petitioner.
2. The statements contained in paragraphs 1 to 15 hereinabove are true to my knowledge based on information derived from records maintained by the petitioner company and I believe them to be true.

Solemnly affirmed by the said Mr. .... pursuant to Board Resolution dated .... of the Builders India Private Ltd. in the Court House at Calcutta on the 15th day of December 1999.

Before me

Commissioner

Application for Setting Aside an Award and Interim Relief

Matter No. .... of 1999

In the High Court at Calcutta Ordinary Original Civil Jurisdiction

In the matter of:

The Arbitration and Conciliation Act 1996

And

In the matter of:

An application under section 34 of the said Act

And

In the matter of:

An Award dated 3rd July 1999 made and published by Mr. S. Roychoudhury, the Learned Sole Arbitrator

And

In the matter of:

Clarion Marketing Agency, carrying on business at 99 Chowringhee Road, Calcutta 700 071 within the said jurisdiction

Petitioner

versus

1. Eastern India Publishers Ltd., a company registered under the Companies Act 1956 and carrying on business at 78 Mission Row, Calcutta 700 013 within the said jurisdiction

2. Mr. S. Roychoudhury residing at 5 Alipore Road, Calcutta 700 070 outside the said jurisdiction

Respondents

To
The Hon'ble Mr. ....,
Chief Justice and His Companion
Justices of the said Hon'ble Court

The humble petition of Distributors Ltd. the petitioner above-named most respectfully

SHEWETH:

1. Your petitioner carries on business as distributor of and dealer in books and other publications.

2. The first respondent is the publisher of the book called Principles and Forms of Pleading. Under an agreement your petitioner was appointed the distributor of the said book and the first respondent agreed to deliver 10,000 copies of 1998 Edition of the said book.

3. The first respondent delivered 8,000 copies of the said books of the said edition which the petitioner distributed and sold and paid the sale price of the said books to the first respondent after deducting the agreed commission. There is no dispute so far as these 8,000 copies of the said book are concerned.

4. In breach of the agreement the first respondent failed to deliver the balance 2,000 copies in spite of requests on the plea that these had been sold out and there was no stock of the said publication.

5. Under the said agreement the disputes and differences were to be referred to respondent No. 2 for settlement of the dispute by arbitration.

6. The dispute was referred to the respondent No. 2 and your petitioner filed the statement of claim and the respondent filed the counter-statement of claim.

7. At the arbitration proceedings your petitioner gave evidence that if the balance 2,000 copies were delivered by the first respondent then your petitioner would have earned an income of Rs. 50,000.

8. Your petitioner contended that your petitioner was entitled to receive the delivery of the said 2,000 copies of the said book from its next edition in addition to the agreed 10,000 copies of the next edition of the said book.

9. After hearing the parties the Learned Arbitrator gave an Award for Rs. 40,000 and interest at 10% per annum from the date of breach of agreement by the first respondent for not delivering 2,000 copies of the said book.

10. Your petitioner states that the said Award is invalid and could not be given effect to and is liable to be set aside as invalid.

11. The Learned Arbitrator acted beyond the scope of the agreement, did not consider the provisions of the Specific Reliefs Act and acted contrary to law applicable to the said arbitration proceedings and it contains decisions on matters not submitted to arbitration.

12. Your petitioner states that the said purported Award published by respondent No. 2 is bad, illegal, without jurisdiction and is a nullity. The said purported Award contains errors on the face of the Award, the respondent No. 2 misconducted the matters and/or the proceedings. The said purported Award is liable to be set aside on the grounds, *inter alia*, the following:

(*i*) For that the purported Award contains errors both of fact and of law.

(*ii*) For that the purported Award is invalid, illegal and without jurisdiction inasmuch as the Arbitrator did not grant the reliefs to the petitioner which the petitioner was entitled to under the contract.

(*iii*) For that the respondent No. 2 failed to adjudicate upon the main issue as to whether the respondent No. 1 was liable to deliver to the petitioner 2,000 copies of the next edition of the book in addition to the contractual 10,000 copies of the book.

(*iv*) For that the purported Award is vitiated by reason of violation of the principles of natural justice inasmuch as the petitioner was absent at two meetings though your petitioner's Advocate appeared and the respondent No. 2 proceeded with the proceedings in spite of the absence of your petitioner.

(*v*) For that the Learned Arbitrator held the meetings behind the back of the petitioner.

(*vi*) For that the subsequent opportunity given to your petitioner did not cure the defects of hearing *ex parte*.

(*vii*) For that the Learned Arbitrator misconducted himself and/or the proceedings by purporting to curtail the scope of claim and confining the claim of your petitioner to monetary compensation.

(*viii*) For that the said Award is otherwise wrong both in fact and in law and is not a reasoned one.

13. Your petitioner will crave leave to refer to and rely on the proceedings, meetings and documents used before the Learned Arbitrator at the time of hearing of the application.

14 In the facts and circumstances your petitioner states that the said Award be set aside and cancelled and be taken off the file.

15. An Order of Injunction be issued restraining the respondents from taking any further steps or any step prejudicial to the petitioner.

16. This application is made within 30 days of the said Award.

17. The orders prayed for are necessary and unless they are passed your petitioner will suffer loss and will be prejudiced.

18. This application is made *bona fide* and in the interest of justice.

Your petitioner, therefore, humbly prays Your Lordships for the following orders:

(a) The purported Award be set aside and cancelled;

(*b*) An order of Injunction be passed restraining the respondents from taking any steps prejudicial to your petitioner;

(*c*) *Ad interim* orders in terms of prayers (*a*) and (*b*) above;

(*d*) Costs of and incidentals to this application be paid by the first respondent;

(*e*) Further orders be made and directions be given as to this Hon'ble Court may deem fit and proper.

And your petitioner as in duty bound shall ever pray.

Verification

Application for Appointment of an Arbitrator

In the High Court at Calcutta Ordinary Original Civil Jurisdiction

In the matter of:

The Arbitration and Conciliation Act 1996

And

In the matter of:

An application under section 11(6) of the said Act read with the scheme framed by the Hon'ble Chief Justice of the High Court at Calcutta by a Notification published in the Calcutta Gazette of 25th January 1997 for the appointment of Arbitrator

And

In the matter of:

Global Distributors Private Ltd., a company registered under the Companies

Act 1956 and carrying on business at 52 India Exxhange Place, Calcutta 700001 within the said jurisdiction

Petitioner

versus

Ruma & Company, a company registered under the Companies Act 1956 and carrying on business at 9 Old Court House Street, Calcutta 700 001 within the said jurisdiction

Respondent

To

The Hon'ble Mr. ....
Chief Justice and His Companion
Justices of the said Hon'ble Court

The humble petition of the Global Distributors Private Ltd., the petitioner above-named most respectfully

SHEWETH:

1. Your petitioner is carrying on business as distributor of and dealer in books, journals and allied publications.

2. The respondent is the publisher, *inter alia,* of a book .... on Computers.

3. By an agreement dated 15th September 1998, it was agreed by and between the parties that the respondent would deliver to the petitioner 50,000 copies of each edition or re-print of the said book for distribution and sale on a commission of 25% of the published price of the book.

4. The said agreement also contains an arbitration clause providing that all disputes and differences between the parties in relation to the said book and/or the said agreement and the rights, duties and claims of the parties would be referred to the arbitration of Mr. XY for decision in the arbitration proceedings.

5. In respect of the sixth edition of the said book published in March 1999 the respondent delivered to your petitioner only 2,000 copies of the said book which copies your petitioner has already sold and distributed within two months and paid the last published price of the book less the commission of your petitioner to the respondent for which the respondent has issued a receipt to your petitioner.

6. In breach of the said agreement the respondent failed to deliver the balance copies of the said book to your petitioner on the plea that all copies of the said book had been sold out within the first four months of its publication.

7. Your petitioner claimed compensation by way of commission at 25% of the published price of balance 48,000 copies of the said book not delivered to your petitioner.

8. The claim of your petitioner against the respondent for breach of the agreement is Rs. 15 lakhs. Your petitioner also claims interest at the applicable rate of 18% per annum.

9. The respondent has not paid the claims of the petitioner in spite of demand.

10. Disputes and differences arose between the petitioner and the respondent. Your petitioner by a letter dated .... requested the respondent to refer the disputes to a named Arbitrator for adjudication. More than 30 days have elapsed but the respondent has not concurred in such an appointment.

11. Your petitioner by a letter requested the named Arbitrator to enter into reference and commence the arbitration proceedings but no reply has been received and more than 30 days have elapsed.

12. A certified copy of the agreement containing the arbitration clause is annexed hereto and marked "A". A copy of the letter addressed to the respondent requesting to concur in referring the dispute to the arbitration of the named Arbitrator is annexed hereto marked "B". A copy of the letter requesting the named Arbitrator to enter into reference relating to the disputes between the parties is annexed hereto marked "C".

13. Your petitioner's cause of action arose at 32 India Exchange Place, Calcutta 700 001 and the respondent is carrying on business at the aforesaid address at Calcutta both within the jurisdiction of this Hon'ble Court.

14. The respondent has raised certain untenable defences. The respondent has suggested that it would print the next edition of the said book and deliver 48,000 copies of the same to your petitioner for distribution and sale as promised in the said agreement.

15. In the facts and circumstances of this case, your petitioner states that this Hon'ble Court will be pleased to take necessary measure for securing the appointment of an Arbitrator.

16. As the said Arbitrator to be appointed will have to decide a question mainly under the Indian Contract Act, no special knowledge or

technical knowledge will be required for the personnel to be appointed as Arbitrator.

17. Your petitioner states that an Arbitrator be appointed as prayed for herein with directions to enter into reference, complete the proceedings and give the Award within the time that might be fixed.

18. Unless orders are made as prayed for your petitioner will suffer loss and will be prejudiced.

19. This application is made *bona fide* and in the interest of justice.

Your petitioner, therefore, humbly prays Your Lordships for the following orders:

(*a*) An Arbitrator be appointed with directions to enter into reference, complete the proceedings and give the Award within such time as this Hon'ble Court will be pleased to determine;

(*b*) Further Orders be made and directions be given as to this Hon'ble Court may deem fit and proper.

And your petitioner as in duty bound shall ever pray.

Signature of the Advocate
for the petitioner Signature

Verification

I, ... son of .... aged about .... years by occupation service, working for gain at 32 India Exchange Place, Calcutta 700 001 do hereby solemnly affirm and say as follows:

1. I am the Manager of Global Distributors Private Ltd., and its Principal Officer and Constituted Attorney. I know and I have made myself acquainted with the facts and circumstances of this case and I am able to depose thereto. I am authorised and competent to verify and I do verify this aforesaid petition on behalf of the Global Distributors Private Ltd.
2. The statements in paragraphs 1 to 19 hereinabove are true to my knowledge based on information derived from the records maintained by the petitioner Global Distributors Private Ltd. and believed by me to be true.

Solemnly affirmed by the said Mr. .... pursuant to a Board Resolution dated .... of Global Distributors Private Ltd. in the Court House at Calcutta on the 5th day of December 1999.

Application for Court Assistance in taking Evidence

In the High Court at Calcutta Ordinary Original Civil Jurisdiction

In the matter of:
The Arbitration and Conciliation Act 1996

And

In the matter of:
An application under section 27 of the said Act

And

In the matter of:
Global Distributors Private Ltd., a company registered under the Companies Act 1956 and carrying on business at 32 India Exchange Place, Calcutta 700 001 within the said jurisdiction

Petitioner

versus

1. Eastern Law House Private Ltd., a company registered under the Companies Act 1956 and carrying on business at 54 G.C. Avenue, Calcutta 700 013 within the said jurisdiction

2. Mr. S.N. Chawla, Advocate of 5 Old Post Office Street, Calcutta 700 001

Respondent

To
The Hon'ble Mr. ....
Chief Justice and His Companion Justices of the said Hon'ble Court

The humble petition of Global Distributors Private Ltd., the petitioner abovenamed most respectfully

SHEWETH:

1. Your petitioner is carrying on business as distributor of and dealer in books, journals and allied publications.

2. The first respondent is the publisher of, *inter alia,* of a book on Computers.

3. By an agreement dated 15th September 1998, it was agreed by and between the parties that the respondent would deliver to the petitioner 50,000 copies of each edition or reprint of the said book for distribution and sale on a commission of 25% of the published price of the book.

4. The said agreement also contains an arbitration clause. Pursuant to the said arbitration agreement on failure of the parties to appoint an Arbitrator an application was made to this Hon'ble Court under section 11(6) of the Arbitration & Conciliation Act 1996. On such application respondent No. 2 has been appointed as the Sole Arbitrator. Respondent No. 2 has duly entered into reference and has been proceeding with the arbitration matter.

5. During the arbitration proceedings it appeared that the evidence of the printer, the book printing company of 6A, S.N. Banerjee Road, Calcutta 700 013 will be necessary. It further transpired that the evidence of the proof reader who gave the print order is also necessary.

6. The person who gave the print order, namely, Mr. Ajoy Gupta is unable to move freely about in view of injury to his legs. In view of this, a Commission is necessary to examine Mr. Ajoy Gupta at his residence.

7. By reasons of the aforesaid your petitioner states that a Summons be issued on the printer Mr. P. Goenka of 6A, S.N. Banerjee Road, Calcutta 700 013 to appear before the respondent No. 2 and give evidence in the proceedings before him.

8. Your petitioner states that a commission be issued for examining Mr. Ajoy Gupta at his residence as regards the subject-matter of the said arbitration.

9. This application is being made with the consent of respondent No. 2.

10. Your petitioner states that the Orders prayed for herein be made for quicker and expeditious adjudication and disposal of the matter before respondent No. 2.

11. Unless Orders are made as prayed for your petitioner will suffer prejudice.

12. This application is made *bona fide* and in the interest of justice.

Your petitioner therefore humbly prays Your Lordships for the following orders:

(*a*) Summons and processes be issued by this Hon'ble Court commanding Mr. P. Goenka to appear before respondent No. 2 to give evidence with reference to the subject-matter of the arbitration proceedings pending before him;

(*b*) Commissioner be appointed to take evidence of Mr. Ajoy Gupta at his residence with liberty to the parties to examine and cross-examine the said Mr. Ajoy Gupta with direction to the Commissioner to submit his report direct to the respondent No. 2;

(*c*) Costs of the witness and the commission be paid by the parties in equal proportion;

(*d*) Further Orders be made and directions be given as to this Hon'ble Court may deem fit and proper.

And your petitioner as in duty bound shall ever pray.

Signature of the Advocate
for the Petitioner Signature

Verification

I, ... son of ....
aged about .... years, by occupation service working for gain at 32 India Exchange Place, Calcutta 700 001 do hereby solemnly affirm and say as follows:

1. I am the Manager of Global Distributors Private Ltd., and its Principal Officer and Constituted Attorney. I know and I have made myself acquainted with the facts and circumstances of this case and I am able to depose thereto. I am authorised and competent to verify and I do verify this aforesaid petition on behalf of Global Distributors Private Ltd.

2. The statements in paragraphs 1 to 12 hereinabove are true to my knowledge based on information derived from the records maintained by the petitioner Global Distributors Private Ltd. and believed by me to be true.

Solemnly affirmed by the said Mr. .... pursuant to a Board Resolution dated .... of Global Distributors Private Ltd. in the Court House at Calcutta on the 5th day of December 1999.

Before me

Commissioner

Award made by Arbitrator Appointed by Court under section 11 of the Arbitration and Conciliation Act 1996

In the matter of the Arbitration and Conciliation Act 1996

And

In the matter of Application No. ...... of 1999

This is the Award of the Arbitrator made this .... day of .... 1999.

WHEREAS in pursuance of an Order dated .... made by the Hon'ble High Court at Calcutta in Application No. .... of .... 1999 I was appointed Arbitrator and I entered into the reference, the parties filed Statement of claim, counter-statement and documents and the parties have adduced both documentary and oral evidence, issues were framed and arguments were heard from both sides and ultimately there were only two issues raised namely,

(*a*) whether the Executive Engineer of the State Government received 500 M.T. of Bitumen and

(*b*) whether the Contractor—Claimant is entitled to carrying charges amounting to Rs. 2 lakhs.

I have considered the averments in the statement of claim and in the counter-statement, the documentary evidence produced and oral evidence given by the Executive Engineer as also the Contractor. I deal with the two issues as follows:

Issue No. 1. From the documents and from the evidence of the Executive Engineer it is clear that the Contractor transported 500 M.T. of Bitumen from Haldia and offered delivery to the Executive Engineer, P.W.D. but he directed to deliver the goods to Assistant Engineer, P.W.D. at some other place specified by him. The Contractor delivered the goods to the specified Asstt. Engineer. The Asstt. Engineer did not issue any receipt for the goods delivered on the ground that there was no office order for purchase of the Bitumen by his section and as such he could not give the receipt. The Executive Engineer has admitted that he also could not issue any receipt for the Bitumen inasmuch as payment for the goods would be made by the Section of the Asstt. Engineer. He has stated that unless the higher authorities gave definite direction as to who would issue the receipt and who would be responsible for payment the Executive Engineer could not do anything in the matter. It was admitted that the goods were received by the P.W.D. of the State Government and that the Asst. Engineer was accountable to the Executive Engineer. It is further admitted by the Executive Engineer that the Bitumen in question was used by the P.W.D. of the State Government. In the premises I hold that the contractor delivered 500 M.T. of Bitumen to the Chief Engineer/Executive Engineer/ P.W.D. and the P.W.D. received and appropriated the goods.

Issue No. 2. As the P.W.D. has received the goods it is apparent that the Contractor has discharged his obligations of carriage of goods from Haldia to the destination and is entitled to carriage charges. The Contractor is entitled to payment of Rs. 2 lakhs being the agreed carriage charges with interest at 18% per annum on Rs. 2 lakhs from .... till payment.

I award Rs. 2 lakhs to be paid by the Executive Engineer, P.W.D. State Government to the Contractor with interest thereon at 18% per annum from .... till payment.

I award Rs. 20,000 as costs to be paid to the Contractor by the Executive Engineer, P.W.D. State Government.

Dated this .... day of ....

Arbitrator

(Name ....)

Award by Arbitrator Appointed by Party

In the matter of the Arbitration and Conciliation Act 1996 and In the matter of an Arbitration Agreement dated .... BETWEEN AB of .... and CD of ....

This is the Award of the Arbitrator made this .... day of ....

In pursuance of an agreement and/or submission in writing dated .... day of .... and made between the above-named AB and CD, the said AB and CD referred to me, XY for my decision and award on the matters in dispute and difference between them. The dispute was as to whether CD carried 500 M.T. of Bitumen from Haldia to the place of AB and delivered the same and as to whether CD is entitled to payment of carriage charges interest and costs.

I entered into the reference, the parties filed their statement of claim counterstatement and documents, the issues were framed. The parties adduced both documentary and oral evidence and arguments were heard at length.

By consent of the parties, two issues were raised namely:

(*a*) whether AB received 500 M.T. of Bitumen carried by CD, and

(*b*) whether CD is entitled to carrying charges amounting to Rs. 2 lakhs, interest and costs.

I have considered the statements in the pleadings, examined the documents and the oral evidence given by AB and CD. I deal with the two issues as follows:

Issue (a). From the documents and evidence of AB it is clear that CD carried 500 M.T. of Bitumen from Haldia and offered delivery to AB. AB however directed CD to deliver the goods to Assistant of AB at another place. CD delivered the goods to the Assistant at the other place. The said Assistant however did not issue any receipt on the plea that he has no authority to issue the receipt or to make payment for the goods. The said AB also did not issue any receipt for the goods on the plea that he did not physically receive the goods and he could not make payment without orders from the higher authorities, and after the question of liability to pay *inter se* AB and his Assistant holding charge of two different sites be settled no payment could be made to CD for carrying charges. From the evidence on record and from the oral evidence of AB it is clear that the CD carried the goods from Haldia and delivered the same to AB and/or to his order. I answer the issue No. (*a*) in favour of CD and against AB and hold that AB received 500 M.T. of Bitumen carried by CD from Haldia and delivered to the order of AB.

Issue (b). From the documentary evidence and from the oral evidence of AB and CD it is established that CD carried 500 M.T. of Bitumen from Haldia and delivered the same to AB and/ or to his order. CD has performed his part of the contract and is entitled to the carrying charges of Rs. 2 lakhs, as also interest and costs.

I award against AB and in favour of CD Rs. 2 lakhs as carrying charges and interest at 18% per annum from .... till payment.

I award Rs. 20,000 against AB and in favour of CD as Costs of the arbitration proceedings.

Dated ....

Arbitrator

(Name XY)

Award by Umpire

In the matter of the Arbitration and Conciliation Act 1996

And

In the matter of Arbitration Agreement dated .... BETWEEN AB and CD

WHEREAS by an Agreement in writing and/or submission dated .... day of .... made between AB residing at .... and CD residing at .... the matters in dispute and differences between them as specified therein were referred to the decision and arbitration of X and Y as Joint Arbitrators who thereafter appointed me Z, as the Umpire at the commencement of the Reference on the .... day of ....

AND WHEREAS the said X and Y having disagreed and differed as between themselves over the subject-matter of the Arbitration and the Award to be made thereon during the pendency of the proceeding I the said Umpire took upon myself the reference.

From the statement of claim counter-statement and documents the Arbitrators raised two issues namely,

(*a*) whether AB received 500 M.T. of Bitumen, and

(*b*) whether CD is entitled to carrying charges amounting to Rs. 2 lakhs.

At the hearing before the Arbitrators CD wanted to raise a third issue as to whether CD was entitled to additional carrying charges from the specified place of delivery to AB to the place where actual delivery was made at the direction of AB. The Arbitrators did not agree to raise the issue and as such the matter has come before me.

I have gone through the statement of claim, counter-statement documentary evidence produced by the parties and I have considered the oral evidence adduced by AB and CD before me.

It is admitted by AB in his oral evidence that the carriage contract was from Haldia to the residence of AB where he has a godown and the carrying charges was fixed at Rs. 2 lakhs for a distance of 200 miles. At the direction of AB the goods brought by CD to the address of AB was diverted to another place 100 miles away with direction to deliver the goods to the godown-keeper there. Admittedly CD carried the goods from the residence of AB to the said godown 100 miles away, and delivered the same to the godown-keeper there. The godown-keeper there refused to give any receipt. AB also did not give any receipt for the goods delivered by CD.

In view of the pleadings, documentary evidence on record and the oral evidence of AB and CD the following issues arise:

(*a*) whether AB received 500 M.T. of Bitumen;

(*b*) whether CD is entitled to the agreed carrying charges of Rs. 2 lakhs for the distance of 200 miles from Haldia to the residence of AB;

(*c*) whether CD is entitled to further carrying charges of the further 100 miles from the residence of AB to the specified godown in proportion to the agreed rate;

Issue (a). From the evidence on record and as admitted by AB I hold that CD carried 500 M.T. of Bitumen and delivered the same to or to the Order of AB and AB received the same.

Issue (b). From the evidence and oral evidence of the parties and admission of AB I hold that CD is entitled to the carrying charges from Haldia to the residence of AB a distance of 200 miles at the agreed rate of Rs. 2 lakhs.

Issue (c). From the documentary evidence and also the oral evidence of the parties and admission of AB I hold that CD carried the goods for extra 100 miles from the residence of AB to the godowns specified by AB and this CD did not do gratuitously but under an implied term that CD would be paid at the agreed rate of Rs. 2 lakhs per 200 miles. I hold that CD is entitled to payment for the extra 100 miles carriage of the goods at the request of AB at the agreed rate.

I therefore award against AB in favour of CD Rs. 2 lakhs for carriage of 500 M.T. of Bitumen from Haldia to the residence of AB and offering to deliver the same.

I hold that CD carried 500 M.T. of Bitumen from Haldia to residence of AB and thereafter another 100 miles at the direction of AB to the godown and delivered the said goods. I award Rs. 1 lakh in favour of CD and against AB for such extra carriage at the agreed rate of Rs. 2 lakhs for 200 miles.

I award interest at 18% per annum on the said sums of Rs. 2 lakhs and Rs. 1 lakh from the date of filing of statement of claim till realisation.

I award the cost of Rs. 20,000 in favour of CD and against AB.

Dated this .... day of ....

Umpire
(Name Z)

Application Seeking for Interim Measures

In the High Court at Calcutta Ordinary Original Civil Jurisdiction

In the matter of:
Arbitration and Conciliation Act 1996

And

In the matter of:
Section 9 of the said Act

And

In the matter of:
An Agreement of Lease bearing No. 2 dated 10th January 1999 entered into between the parties

And

In the matter of:
21st Century Finance Limited, a Company registered under the Companies Act 1956 having its Corporate Office at 5 N.S. Road, Calcutta 700 001 within the said jurisdiction

Petitioner

versus

1. Duncans Tea Co. Limited, a Company registered under the Companies Act 1956 having its registered Office at 6 A.T. Road, Dibrugarh 1, Assam

2. S. Bardhan, working for gain at 6 A.T. Road, Dibrugarh 1, Assam

3. K. Barua, working for gain at 6 A.T. Road, Dibrugarh 1, Assam all outside the said jurisdiction

Respondents

To
The Hon'ble .... Chief Justice and His Companion Justices of the said Hon'ble Court

The humble petition of the petitioner above-named most respectfully

SHEWETH:

1. The petitioner has its corporate office at 5 N.S. Road, Calcutta 700 001 within the said jurisdiction.

2. Under a Lease Agreement your petitioner leased out to the first respondent Tea Processing Machinery with attachments and accessories described in Schedule I. A copy of the said Lease Agreement is annexed hereto marked "A". The said Agreement was entered into at the office of the petitioner at 5 N.S. Road, Calcutta 700 001 within the said jurisdiction.

3. By reason of your petitioner leasing out the said machinery to the respondent No. 1 at the request of the respondents Nos. 2 and 3, the respondents Nos. 2 and 3 executed the said agreement and unconditionally and irrevocably guaranteed due performance of the obligations of first respondent in payment of instalments, costs and expenses and compensation recoverable by your petitioner from the respondent No. 1 under the said lease agreement.

4. By way of security the respondents executed a Demand Promissory Note and made over the same to your petitioner at Calcutta within the said jurisdiction.

5. Under the Agreement the respondents were liable to pay .... monthly instalments of rent at the rate of Rs. .... each commencing from ....

6. The first respondent committed default and failed to pay the instalment on and from .... and a sum of Rs. .... has now become due and payable by the respondents to your petitioner particulars of whereof are given hereunder:

Particulars	
Monthly instalment of rent which fell due on .... and thereafter	Rs. ....
Agreed overdue interest and/or compensation from the respective due dates	Rs. ....
Lease Rental for unexpired lease period	Rs. ....
Total	Rs. ....

7. On the defaults of the respondent No. 1 your petitioner became entitled to claim overdue charges from subsequent period and to terminate and did terminate the said Agreement by a notice dated .... A copy of the aforesaid letter together with acknowledgment cards evidencing receipt by the respondents are annexed hereto and collectively marked "B".

8. After termination of the said Agreement your petitioner became entitled to take possession of the said machinery. The respondents have not given back possession of the machinery to your petitioner. The respondents are wrongfully utilising the said machinery and are liable to pay damages and/or compensation to your petitioner at the rate of Rs. .... per day till possession of the machinery is given to the petitioner for which notice has been given.

9. Your petitioner is the owner of the machinery and is entitled to have possession thereof and claims specific delivery of the same in good condition. In the event specific delivery of the same cannot be had by your petitioner then your petitioner will claim a sum of Rs. .... being the approximate value of the said machinery.

10. In spite of demands the respondents have failed and neglected to pay your petitioner's claims herein and to make over possession of the machinery.

11. The said Lease Agreement contained an Arbitration Clause to which your petitioner will refer. In the facts and circumstances aforesaid disputes

and differences have arisen in relation to and/or concerning and/or touching the said Lease Agreement which are referable to Arbitration. Under section 9 of the Arbitration and Conciliation Act 1996, this Hon'ble Court is empowered to pass orders for the purpose of preservation and protection of the assets and properties of the petitioner prior to commencement of the Arbitration Proceedings.

12. The said machinery require proper handling, constant maintenance and expert care. The first respondent is using the petitioner's machinery at its factory at Tinsukhia, Assam but not keeping them in good condition and repair. Your petitioner being the owner is entitled to take possession of the machinery and deal with the same in such manner as it thinks fit and proper. The said machinery are being used unauthorisedly and illegally by the respondents. Your petitioner prays that an order of injunction be passed restraining the respondents from dealing with, disposing or, alienating, encumbering and/or using the said machinery in any manner whatsoever. Further more, the facts and circumstances of this case justify passing an order appointing a Receiver as prayed for with a direction to take possession of the machinery and remove the same at your petitioner's godown.

13. The said Agreement provides that your petitioner is entitled to enter the premises of the Lessee and take possession of the machinery, but in order to avoid any complications, your petitioner is praying for appointment of a Receiver to take possession of the machinery and remove the same. The said Agreement further provides that on the Agreement being determined before expiry of the full term, the respondents would deliver to your petitioner all certificates and policy of insurance and other documents relating to the said machinery and your petitioner prays that appropriate directions be given accordingly in this regard. If notice of this application is served upon the respondents, they would immediately take steps to render the proceedings infructuous. Facts of this case justify passing of an *ex parte Ad interim* Order.

14. The respondents are disposing of and depleting their assets and properties and the sale proceeds are being diverted and secreted. They are likely to deal with, sell or remove the machinery of your petitioner as well as their own assets to prevent execution of the Award which is likely to be passed in favour of your petitioner after the disputes are referred to arbitration in terms of the agreement. In the circumstances your petitioner prays that the respondents be directed to furnish security for Rs. .... within .... days from the date of passing of the order and in default thereof the assets and properties of the respondents be attached. Particulars of such assets and properties are given in the first respondent's Balance Sheet a copy whereof is annexed hereto marked "C". The particulars of assets and properties of respondents Nos. 2 and 3 are given in a Schedule annexed hereto marked "C-1".

15. Your petitioner prays that an order of injunction be passed restraining the respondents, their servants and agents from disposing of, alienating, encumbering or dealing with any of their assets and properties until further order.

16. The subject-matter of the relief claimed is valued at more than Rs. 10 lakhs. Part of the cause of action as pleased in paragraphs .... and .... arose within the jurisdiction of this Hon'ble Court. The Agreement was executed at the petitioner's office and breaches and defaults were committed by non-payment of instalments at the petitioner's Calcutta Office within the said jurisdiction. The respondents are wrongfully detaining the machinery at Tinsukhia outside the said jurisdiction. In the premises your petitioner prays for leave under Clause 12 of the Letters Patent to institute these proceedings before this Hon'ble Court. Arbitration will be held in Calcutta and the Award will be filed in this Hon'ble Court. This Hon'ble Court has the jurisdiction to entertain this application.

17. Unless orders are made as prayed for your petitioner will suffer irreparable loss and injury.

18. This application is made *bona fide* and in the interest of justice.

Your petitioner, therefore, humbly prays Your Lordships for leave under Clause 12 of the Letters Patent and for an order that:

(*a*) A Receiver be appointed over the leased-out machinery and fully described in Schedule I to the Lease Agreement which is now lying at Tinsukhia, Assam or wherever the same may be found with a direction to take possession of the same forthwith with the help of an Agent, if necessary, make inventory and remain in symbolic possession thereof;

(*b*) Receiver be authorised to take police help and Officer-in-Charge of the local Police Station in Tinsukhia, Assam do render such assistance to the Receiver or his Agent, as may be required;

(*c*) Injunction restraining the respondents, their servants and agents from disposing of, alienating, encumbering or dealing with the machinery mentioned in the Schedule to the Lease Agreement;

(*d*) Respondents be directed to show cause as to why they should not be asked to furnish security within a period to be specified by this Hon'ble Court for Rs. 90 lakhs;

(e) In case of respondents showing cause or showing insufficient cause they be directed to furnish security for Rs. 90 lakhs within 15 days and in default, their assets and properties mentioned in the Balance Sheet and Schedule annexed hereto be attached and kept attached till they are sold;

(f) *Ad interim* Orders in terms of the prayers above;

(g) Costs of and incidental to this application be paid by the respondents;

(h) Such further or other Orders be made and/or directions be given as to this Hon'ble Court may seem fit and proper.

And your petitioner as in duty bound shall ever pray.

Advocates on Record Signature

Verification

I, ... Constituted Attorney and the Law Officer of the petitioner do hereby solemnly affirm and say that the statements made in paragraphs 1 to .... of the foregoing petition are true to my knowledge based on information derived from records maintained by the petitioner and I believe them to be true and those made in paragraphs .... hereinabove are my respectful submissions before this Hon'ble Court.

Solemnly affirmed by the said .... in the Court House at Calcutta this .... day of .... 1999.

Before me
Commissioner

Notice for Hearing of Application

In the High Court at Calcutta Ordinary Original Civil Jurisdiction

In the matter of:
Arbitration & Conciliation Act 1996

And

In the matter of:
Section 9 of the said Act

And

In the matter of:

An Agreement of Lease bearing No. 2 dated 10th January 1999 entered into between the parties

And

In the matter of:

21st Century Finance Limited, a company registered under the Companies Act 1956 having its Corporate Office at 5 N.S. Road, Calcutta 700 001 within the said jurisdiction

Petitioner

versus

1. Duncans Tea Co. Limited, a Company registered under the Companies Act 1956 having its registered office at 6 A.T. Road, Dibrugarh 1, Assam

2. S. Bardhan, working for gain at 6 A.T. Road, Dibrugarh 1, Assam

3. K. Barua, working for gain at 6 A.T. Road, Dibrugarh 1, Assam all outside the said jurisdiction

Respondents

To

1. Duncans Tea Co. Ltd.
2. S. Bardhan
3. K. Barua

All of 6 A.T. Road
Dibrugarh 1, Assam

Dear Sirs

PLEASE TAKE NOTICE THAT on .... the .... day of .... 2000 at the hour of 10-30 o'clock, in the forenoon or so soon thereafter as Counsel can be heard an application will be made on behalf of the petitioner above-named before the Hon'ble Judge taking Arbitration and Conciliation Act 1996 matters for the following orders:

(*a*) A Receiver be appointed over the Tea Processing Machinery with attachments and accessories described in the Agreement of Lease with a direction to take possession of the same with the help of an Agent, if necessary;

(*b*) Injunction restraining the respondents, their servants, and agents from dealing with, disposing of, alienating and/or encumbering the machinery mentioned in the Schedule to the Agreement;

(*c*) Receiver be authorised to take police help and officer-in-charge of the local Police Station in Dibrugarh, Assam do render such assistance to the Receiver or his agent as may be required;

(*d*) Respondents be directed to show cause as to why they should not be asked to furnish security in favour of the Registrar, Original Side of this Hon'ble Court to the extent of Rs. 90 lakhs within 10 days from the date of order;

(*e*) In default of showing cause or showing insufficient cause the respondents be directed to furnish securities for Rs. 90 lakhs within 15 days and in default the entire assets and properties of the respondents be attached;

(*f*) *Ad interim* orders in terms of prayers above;

(*g*) Costs of and incidentals to this application be paid by the respondents;

(*h*) Further orders be made and/or directions be given as to this Hon'ble Court may deem fit and proper.

Dated this .... day of 2000

Yours faithfully
Advocate-on-Record

Grounds: Petition of the petitioner verified by an affidavit of S. Ghose, affirmed on .... day of .... 2000 and the records and proceedings of the above matter.

PLEASE TAKE FURTHER NOTICE that this application being moved on .... before the Hon'ble Justice .... when His Lordship was pleased to pass the following order:

"Leave is given under Clause 12 of the Letters Patent.

Liberty to serve by Courier, Returnable on ....

This matter will appear as New Motion on .... Parties shall act on a xerox of the signed copy of the minutes of this order on the usual undertaking."

Advocate-on-Record
of the petitioner

Sd/–
Asstt. Registrar
High Court O.S.
Calcutta

Notice under Arbitration and Conciliation Act 1996

By Speed Post with A./D.

Date ....

Dhillon Industrial Corporation Ltd.
15/1/A, J.P. Nagar
Bangalore 560 078

Dear Sirs

Client: Smart Finance Co. Ltd. of Calcutta
Re: Lease in respect of Computer machinery

Under instructions from and on behalf of my client, Smart Finance Co. Ltd., I address you as follows:

You entered into a Lease Agreement dated 5th December 1999 with our client above-named in respect of machinery referred to above and agreed, *inter alia*, to pay to them monthly Lease Rent of Rs. 50,000 commencing from 5th January 2000. The tenure of the said Lease was for 3 years from the date of commencement.

You have failed and neglected to perform your part of the obligation, defaulted in payment of the lease rentals and in furnishing the Security Deposit. You have, therefore, committed breaches of the Agreement and defaults in payment and are liable to the consequences, thereof.

My client has, therefore, instructed me to terminate and determine the said Lease Agreement which I hereby do. You have also become liable to pay lease rentals for the unexpired period of lease and other charges.

After giving credit for all sums paid by you, a sum of Rs. 20 lakhs is due and payable by you to my client.

Particulars	
Monthly Instalment which fell due on 5th January 2000	Rs. 50,000.00
Monthly lease rentals from 5th February 2001 to 5th December 2001	Rs. 5,50,000.00
Interest at the agreed rate provided under the Agreement from the respective due dates calculated up to 5th December 2001	Rs. 1,50,000.00
Expenses incurred in attempting to collect the rentals	Rs. 50,000.00
Lease rentals for the unexpired period of the Lease	Rs. 12,00,000.00
Total:	Rs. 20,00,000.00

My client has, therefore, instructed me to call upon you which I hereby do that if you fail to pay the aforesaid sum with further overdue compensation at the agreed rate from .... until payment within 7 days from the receipt hereof, my client will be compelled to initiate appropriate legal proceedings including referring the matter to arbitration in terms of the relevant Arbitration Clause contained in the Agreement without any further reference to you.

Your are not entitled to use or possess the said equipment. Your are hereby requested to forthwith deliver the said machinery to my client, failing which you will be held liable to pay compensation and/or mesne profits at Rs. 2,000 per day till delivery thereof to my client for wrongful use or possession or depriving my client of the benefit of the same.

Yours faithfully

Advocate

Copy forwarded to:

By Speed Post with A/D.

1. Mr. ....

2. Mr. ....

Both of:

Copy forwarded to: Smart Finance Co. Ltd.

7

Assignment of Copyright etc.

In England, a debt was looked upon as a personal obligation and an assignee could only bring an action at law against the debtor. The Court of Equity, however, recognised the title of an assignee of a debt regarding it as a piece of property. The Transfer of Property Act has effected an important change in the law having recognised an actionable claim as a valuable property. An assignment of an actionable claim in order to be valid must be in writing and signed by the transferor or his authorised agent.

Assignment of Actionable Claims

Actionable claim.[1] Actionable claim means a claim to any debt, other than a debt secured by a mortgage of immovable property, or by hypothecation or pledge of movable property, or to any beneficial interest in the movable property not in the possession, either actual or constructive, of the claimant, which the Civil Courts recognize as affording grounds for relief, whether such debt or beneficial interest be existent, accruing, conditional or contingent.

Transfer of actionable claim how effected.[2] The transfer of an actionable claim, whether with or without consideration, can be effected only by the execution of an instrument in writing signed by the transferor or his duly authorized agent (attestation and registration not being compulsory), and will be complete and effectual upon the execution of such instrument, and thereupon all the rights and remedies of the transferor, whether by way of damages or otherwise, will vest in the transferee, whether such notice of the transfer as hereinafter provided be given or not:

Provided that every dealing with the debt or other actionable claim by the debtor or other person, from or against whom the transferor would, but

1 Section 3 of the Transfer of Property Act.
2 Section 130 of the Transfer of Property Act.

for such instrument of transfer as aforesaid, have been entitled to recover or enforce such debt or other actionable claim, will (save whether the debtor or other person is a party to the transfer or has received express notice thereof as thereinafter provided) be valid as against such transfer. The transferee of an actionable claim may, upon the execution of such instrument of transfer as aforesaid, sue or institute proceedings for the same in his own name without obtaining the transferor's consent to such suit or proceeding, and without making him a party thereto.

Every notice of transfer of an actionable claim must be in writing, signed by the transferor or his agent duly authorised in this behalf, or in case the transferor refuses to sign, by the transferee or his agent, and must state the name and address of the transferee.[3]

Warranty of solvency of debtor. Where the transferor of a debt warrants the solvency of a debtor, the warranty, in the absence of a contract to the contrary, applies only to his solvency at the time of the transfer, and is limited, whether the transfer is made for consideration to the amount or value of such consideration.[4]

Incapacity of officers connected with Courts of Justice. No judge, legal practitioner, or officer connected with any Court of Justice can buy, or traffic in, or stipulate for, or agree to receive any share of, or interest in, any actionable claim.[5]

Saving of negotiable instruments, etc. The above provisions relating to assignment of actionable claims do not apply to stocks, shares or debentures, or to instruments which are for the time being by law or custom negotiable, or to any mercantile documents of title to goods.[6]

Assignment of Copyright

Copyright. Copyright in India is a purely statutory right. In the United Kingdom, the first Copyright Act (8 Anne C 19) was passed in the year 1709. The statute gave the author of books already then printed the right of publication for a continuous period of 20 years and for books not published for 14 years. The statute curtailed considerably the protection granted under the Common Law in published works. All enactments were finally repealed by the Copyright Act 1842 (5 & 6 Vict C 45). In India, the Indian Copyright Act (XX of 1847) was correspondingly placed on the statute book. The Copyright Act 1957, amended and consolidated the law on the subject. The Act fixed the time of copyright in published literary, dramatic, musical and

3 Section 131 of the Transfer of Property Act.
4 Section 133 of the Transfer of Property Act.
5 Section 136 of the Transfer of Property Act.
6 Section 137 of the Transfer of Property Act.

artistic works to 60 years next after the death of the author since the beginning of the following calendar year[7] and prescribed the mode of its assignment under s. 18 of the said Act. An assignment must be in writing and signed by the assignor or his authorised agent.

Rectification. It is an equitable relief granted by the Court of Equity on the doctrine of mistake. In order that rectification may be granted there must be mutual mistake and that the document does not represent the true intention between the parties[8] and the mistake relates to some facts and not of law.[9] A mistake of foreign law has the same force as mistake of facts.[10] When parties to a deed agree to modify or vary, add to or subtract from the terms of any previous deed, it is necessary that the intention of the parties should be expressed in a written instrument, as oral testimony of such agreement is not admissible in evidence. Such deeds require registration if the principal deed was registered. A relief action may be granted by the court even in the case of fraud to carry out the real intention of the parties. This is entirely discretionary and when granted the order does not prejudice the rights acquired by third parties in good faith and for value.[11]

Patent and Trade Mark

The law on Patents as contained in the Patent & Design Act 1911 and the Patent Act 1970 has since been replaced by Patents (Amendment) Act 1999 and the Designs Act 2000 (Act 16 of 2000). Similarly the Trade and Merchandise Marks Act 1958 has been repealed and replaced by the Trade Marks Act 1999 (Act 47 of 1999).

FORMS

Deed of Assignment of Business Debts

THIS DEED OF ASSIGNMENT made the .... day of ...., BETWEEN AB of, etc. (hereinafter called the ASSIGNOR), of the one part, and CD of, etc. (hereinafter called the ASSIGNEE), of the other part.

7 Section 22 of the Copyright Act 1957 as amended by Act 13 of 1992 wef 28.12.1991.
8 *Amanti Bibi* v *Lachman* 14 Cal 308.
9 Section 20 of the Indian Contract Act 1872.
10 Section 21 of the Indian Contract Act.
11 Section 26, Specific Relief Act 1963.

WHEREAS the ASSIGNOR has for some time past carried on the trade or business, of, etc., at, etc., in the course whereof the several persons, whose names, addresses and occupations are mentioned in the schedule hereunder written, have become lawfully indebted to him in respect of the several sums of money written opposite to their respective names, AND WHEREAS the ASSIGNOR has contracted with the ASSIGNEE for the absolute sale to him of the said business debts at and for the sum of Rs. .... NOW THIS DEED WITNESSES that in consideration of the sum of Rupees .... now paid to the ASSIGNOR by the ASSIGNEE (the receipt of which sum the ASSIGNOR hereby acknowledges), the said AB, as beneficial owner, do hereby grant, transfer, sell and assign unto and to the use of the said CD ALL the several said debts, and/or sums of money specified in the said schedule which are now lawfully due and owing to the ASSIGNOR together with all interest due thereon and all benefits of the security or securities held on account therefor, if any, TO HAVE AND TO RECEIVE AND APPROPRIATE them for his absolute use and benefit with absolute power, authority and liberty to enforce payment thereof by suit or otherwise AND that the ASSIGNOR do hereby covenant with the ASSIGNEE that all several debts are lawfully due and payable to him and further that the parties by whom they are payable are alive and not insolvent, and furthermore that he has not entered into any compromise agreement or arrangement with any of them nor committed himself in any way as to any time, indulgence or concession nor written off any of them with a view to exonerate any of them from all liability on that account. AND that the ASSIGNOR shall at all times hereafter co-operate with the ASSIGNEE and do, execute and perform all such further and other acts, deeds, things or writings as may be reasonably required for realisation of the said debts and/or further and better and more effectively transferring and/or assuring them or any of them unto and in favour of the ASSIGNEE as may be reasonably required.

Schedule above referred to

Name and address of the debtor	*Amount of debt*	*Securities if any*	*Remarks*	*Other particulars*

IN WITNESS WHEREOF the parties herein have executed these presents on the day, month and year first above-written.

Signed, sealed and delivered by AB
the ASSIGNOR in the presence of:

Signed, sealed and delivered by CD
the ASSIGNEE in the presence of:

Deed of Assignments of Bond Debt

THIS DEED OF ASSIGNMENT is made the .... day of .... BETWEEN AB of, etc., (ASSIGNOR), of the one part, and CD of, etc. (ASSIGNEE), of the other part.

WHEREAS by a bond bearing date, ... executed by one EF described therein as obligor in favour of the said AB, the said EF (OBLIGOR) became bound to the said AB in the sum of Rs. .... subject to the condition for discharge as thereunder provided AND WHEREAS the said bond is still in full force and virtue AND WHEREAS the principal sum secured under the said bond together with arrears of interest thereon at present, amounts to Rs. .... AND WHEREAS the said AB has agreed to transfer, assign and sell the said bond debt to the said CD at and for the sum of Rs. .... NOW THIS DEED WITNESSES that in consideration of the sum of Rs. .... now paid to AB by the said CD the receipt whereof the said AB do hereby admit, acknowledge and confirm the said AB as the beneficial owner, hereby transfers and assigns unto the said CD ALL THAT the principal sum of Rs. .... secured by the said bond, and the sum of Rs. .... now due for arrears of interest thereon and all further interest hereafter to become due and payable from time to time for the same, and all his right, title, interest, claim and demand whatsoever under the said bond and the full benefit and advantage thereof: TO HAVE AND HOLD the same to the CD absolutely with full authority, liberty and power to enforce the bond and realise all moneys due and payable thereunder by suit or otherwise.

AND the said AB hereby declares that the said bond is still in full force and virtue and the said principal sum of Rs. ...., together with the sum of Rs. .... due for arrears of interest thereon is lawfully due and payable to the ASSIGNOR under and by virtue of the same. And that the ASSIGNOR had and still has good right, full power and absolute authority to grant, transfer and assign the same in the manner hereinbefore indicated. AND further that the ASSIGNOR shall at all times hereafter do, execute and perform all such acts, deeds, things as may be reasonably required for further and better transferring or assigning the same at the cost and expenses of the ASSIGNEE.

IN WITNESS WHEREOF the parties herein have executed these presents on the day, month and year first above-written.

Signed, sealed and delivered by AB
the ASSIGNOR in the presence of:

Signed, sealed and delivered by CD
the ASSIGNEE in the presence of:

Assignment of a Bond Debt

(SHORT FORM)

IN CONSIDERATION of the sum of Rs. .... paid by the ASSIGNEE Sri .... to me the ASSIGNOR Sri .... the receipt whereof is hereby acknowledged, the ASSIGNOR as beneficial owner do hereby transfer to the ASSIGNEE all that the debt due and payable to the transferor by CD and to become due thereon under the bond dated .... executed by CD in his favour TO HAVE AND TO HOLD the same absolutely and forever.

The said debt is still due and owing to the assignor from the said CD.

IN WITNESS WHEREOF

Assignment of a Bond Debt

(SHORT FORM)

IN CONSIDERATION of the sum of Rs. ...., paid by the ASSIGNEE Sri .... to the ASSIGNOR Sri .... the receipt whereof is hereby acknowledged, the ASSIGNOR as the beneficial owner do hereby transfer to the ASSIGNEE all that the debt due and payable to the transferor by CD on a bond dated .... and all interests due and to become due thereon: TO HAVE AND TO HOLD the same absolutely and forever. The said debt is still due and owing to the ASSIGNOR from the said CD.

IN WITNESS WHEREOF the parties have executed these presents on the 15th day of December 1999.

Signed, sealed and delivered by
AB in the presence of:

Signed, sealed and delivered by
CD in the presence of:

Deed of Assignment of Bond Debt

THIS DEED OF ASSIGNMENT is made this .... day of .... BETWEEN AB son of .... residing at .... (hereinafter referred to as the ASSIGNOR which term shall include his heirs and legal representatives) of the one part and CD son of .... residing at .... (hereinafter referred to as the ASSIGNEE of the other part.

WHEREAS by a Bond bearing .... executed by one EF described therein as obligor in favour of the said AB, the said EF (obligor) became bound to the said AB in the sum of Rs. .... subject to the condition for discharge as thereunder provided and whereas the said bond is still in full force and virtue and whereas the principal sum secured under the said bond together with arrears of interest thereon, at present amounts to Rs. .... and whereas the said AB has agreed to transfer, assign and sell the said bond debt to the said CD at, and for the sum of Rs. .... : Now this deed witnesses that in consideration of the sum of Rs. .... now to the said AB paid by the said CD (the receipt whereof the said AB does hereby admit and acknowledge), the said AB, as beneficial owner, hereby transfers and assigns unto the said CD the principal sum of Rs. .... secured by the said bond, and the sum of Rs. .... now due for arrears of interest thereon and all interests henceforth to become due and payable for the same, and all his right, title, interest, claim and demand whatsoever under the said bond and the full benefit and advantage thereof: TO HAVE AND HOLD the same to the CD absolutely with full authority, liberty and power to enforce the bond and realise all moneys due and payable thereunder by suit or otherwise.

IN WITNESS WHEREOF the parties have executed these presents on the day, month and year first above-written.

Signed, sealed and delivered by AB — AB
in the presence of:

Signed, sealed and delivered by CD — CD
in the presence of:

Deed of Assignment of Business Debts

THIS DEED OF ASSIGNMENT is made this .... day of .... BETWEEN AB son of .... residing at .... (hereinafter referred to as the ASSIGNOR which term shall include his heirs and legal representatives) of the one part and CD son of .... residing at .... (hereinafter referred to as the ASSIGNEE) of the other part.

WHEREAS the ASSIGNOR has for some time past carried on the trade or business of, etc., at, etc., in the course whereof the several persons whose names, addresses and occupations are mentioned in the schedule hereunder written, have become lawfully debtors to him and so for the several sums of money set opposite to their respective names, and whereas the ASSIGNOR has contracted with the ASSIGNEE for the absolute sale to him of the said business debts at and for the sum of Rs. .... NOW THIS DEED WITNESSES that in consideration of the sum of Rs. .... now paid to the ASSIGNOR by the ASSIGNEE (the receipt of which sum the ASSIGNOR hereby acknowledges), the said AB, as beneficial owner, does hereby transfer, sell and assign unto and to the use of the said CD all the several said debts, and sums of money specified in the said schedule which are now due and owing to the ASSIGNOR TO HAVE AND TO RECEIVE them for his absolute use and benefit with absolute power, authority and liberty to enforce payment thereof by suit or otherwise AND that the ASSIGNOR does hereby covenant with the assignee that all the several debts are lawfully due to him and the parties by whom they are payable are alive and, further, that he has not entered into any arrangement with any of them AND that the ASSIGNOR shall at all times hereafter do, execute and perform all such and other acts, deeds, things or writing as may be reasonably required for further and better transferring and/or assuring them or any of them.

Schedule above referred to

Signed, sealed and delivered, etc. AB
CD

Assignment of Cinematograph Rights in a Play or Novel

AN AGREEMENT made the .... day of .... BETWEEN AB .... of etc., (hereinafter called the AUTHOR) of the one part and CD of etc., (hereinafter called the ASSIGNEE) of the other part.

Whereas the AUTHOR is the sole proprietor of the playright or copyright in the play or story or novel entitled "..............." AND WHEREAS the AUTHOR has agreed to sell the right of making film and/or cinematograph rights in the said play (or story or novel) NOW IT IS HEREBY AGREED by and between the parties as follows:

1. In consideration of the sum of Rs. .... paid by the assignee to the AUTHOR (the receipt whereof the AUTHOR hereby admits and acknowledges) the AUTHOR does hereby grant, sell, assign, transfer and assure to the ASSIGNEE the sole, exclusive and monopoly right to produce cinematographic films, scenes, scenary and other reproductions of the said play (story or novel) or any part thereof and to present, exhibit or perform the said play, story, or rewrite the novel or any part thereof in public by means of sound or silent films or any other similar contrivance which may be mechanically represented, exhibited or performed in all parts of the world in which the said rights are subsisting or may be acquired by the ASSIGNEE.

2. The AUTHOR warrants to the ASSIGNEE that he is the sole owner of the valid and subsisting copyright and playright in the said play (story or novel) and that he has not granted any licence or otherwise parted with any interest in the right to produce the same by means of cinematograph films or other similar contrivances.

3. The ASSIGNEE shall at all times hereafter be entitled to produce or cause to be produced and exhibited for sale or hire any film of the said play (story or novel) and, in case he fails to do so, it shall be optional on the part of the AUTHOR, by notice in writing and subject to repayment of the purchase money to terminate this agreement and the cinematograph rights in the said play (or novel) shall forthwith be reassigned to the AUTHOR.

4. The ASSIGNEE agrees to the publication of the AUTHOR'S name in conjunction with the title of the film of the said play (story or novel) in all books, literature advertisements, programmes and notices under his control.

5. The ASSIGNEE agrees not to make any alteration of a substantial nature in the story of the said play (story or novel) or in climax situations or in the characterisation thereof without the previous consent in writing of the AUTHOR.

IN WITNESS WHEREOF THE parties hereto have executed these presents on the day, month and year first above-written.

Signed, sealed and delivered by
AB in the presence of:

Signed, sealed and delivered by
CD in the presence of:

Apology for Infringement of Copyright

Dear Sirs

I am extremely sorry to learn the infringement of your copyright in the .... which have been published in my book.

At the time when the publication of the book first commenced I was not at all aware that you are the owner of its copyright and, in fact, until I received your letter of complaint I was completely ignorant of the same. I was first approached only as far back as .... last when a representative of the .... offered me the series on certain terms to which I readily agreed more so because the series has been already published in that journal without being aware of the fraud practised on me.

However, I deeply regret for the innocent infringement of your rights and undertake not to publish any more of these series in future in any book, journal, literature or other publications.

Yours very truly

....

Assignment of Copyright of Book Reserving Royalty

THIS DEED OF ASSIGNMENT is made this 5th day of December 1999 BETWEEN CD son of .... residing at .... (hereinafter called the AUTHOR) of the one part and Eastern Law Ltd. a company registered under the Companies Act 1956 having its Registered Office and carrying on business of Publishers and Booksellers at 54 Ganesh Chunder Avenue, Calcutta 700 013 (hereinafter called the PUBLISHER which term shall include its successors and assigns) of the other part. WHEREAS the AUTHOR is entitled to the copyright of the book known as .... AND WHEREAS the PUBLISHERS approached the author for assignment thereof which the AUTHOR has agreed to do on terms hereunder contained.

Now THIS DEED OF ASSIGNMENT WITNESSES as follows:

(1) In consideration of and subject to the covenants on the part of the publishers as hereinafter contained, the AUTHOR does hereby grant, convey, transfer, sell, assign and assure unto and to the use of the PUBLISHERS all that copyright as defined in section 14 of the Copyright Act 1957, of the book entitled .... on the subject of .... TO HAVE AND TO HOLD the same as absolute owners thereof for the full term of copyright as prescribed by law.

(2) The PUBLISHERS shall, so long as the said work or any adaptation, modification or translation thereof is published and sold, submit to the AUTHOR twice every year, once during the month of January and the other by June, a statement of account showing details of the copies printed, published, held in stock and sold or disposed of (except otherwise by sale of damaged or destroyed copies) and of the profits, if any, earned thereunder.

(3) The PUBLISHERS shall pay or cause to be paid to the author or his nominee or nominees a royalty at the rate of .... per cent on the sale proceeds of the copies of the work or adaptations or translations thereof that may be actually published and as disclosed in the statement of account referred to in clause (2). No royalty shall be payable on any copies of work that may be damaged or destroyed or disposed of otherwise than by regular sale.

(4) That the PUBLISHERS shall also pay to the AUTHOR half the net profits earned by them, if any, from transfer, sale or assignment of any of the rights comprising the copyright or from grant of any interest or licence therein: PROVIDED THAT the PUBLISHERS shall not be entitled to and shall not do or cause anything to be done in derogation of the AUTHOR'S other rights, particularly the right to royalty reserved hereunder.

(5) That the AUTHOR does hereby agree to revise the work and bring it up to date or otherwise modify, alter, adapt or translate it or get it translated whenever reasonably required by the PUBLISHERS: PROVIDED ALSO THAT the PUBLISHERS will not normally require the AUTHOR to do so more than once in two years; PROVIDED FURTHER THAT in case the AUTHOR shall fail and/or neglect,

and/or refuse to revise, modify, alter, translate the work or get it translated as and when reasonably required by the PUBLISHERS, they shall be at liberty to get the same done on his account by any person or persons of their choice after due notice to the AUTHOR and deduct all costs, charges and expenses out of moneys payable to the author. PROVIDED ALSO THAT in selecting the person proposed to revise, modify, alter, adapt or translate the work and in fixing the remuneration to be paid therefor, the author's wishes, if any, shall so far as possible be respected by the PUBLISHERS.

(6) That the AUTHOR has delivered or shall deliver (within a period of .... months from the date hereof) the manuscript of the said work to the PUBLISHERS.

(7) That the AUTHOR does hereby declare that the work of which the copy is being hereunder assigned is entirely original work of the AUTHOR and that the same does not in any manner whatsoever violate or infringe any existing copyright or any other right of any other person or other persons; and further that it does not contain anything which may be considered as obscene, libellous, scandalous or defamatory.

(8) The AUTHOR HEREBY AGREES to indemnify and keep the PUBLISHERS indemnified against all claims, demands, suits and other actions and proceedings, if any, that may be instituted or taken and also against all damages, costs, charges, expenses which the publishers shall or may suffer, on account of printing, publication or sale of the said work or any part thereof, or by reason of such printing, publication and/or sale being an infringement of some other person's copyright or other rights in the work or by reason of its containing anything which may in any sense be obscene, libellous, scandalous or defamatory.

(9) The PUBLISHERS shall print and publish the work or cause the same to be printed and published as soon as practicable within a period of 12 months from the date of this contract, and in default thereof the AUTHOR may, by a notice in writing, call upon the publishers to print and publish the work within two months of the receipt of the said notice; and if the publishers shall still fail and/or neglect to print and/or publish the work within the said period, save and except in so far as they are prevented from doing so by circumstances beyond their control, the AUTHOR shall be at liberty to rescind the contract on giving a notice to that effect to the publishers when the copyright shall revert fully to the author and all the rights of PUBLISHERS shall, as from that date, stand determined.

(10) That in case of dispute or difference arising between the parties touching the meaning, construction, interpretation, breach or fulfilment or non-fulfilment of the terms of these presents or any clause or condition thereof, the same shall be referred to the decision of arbitrator(s) in accordance with the provisions of Arbitration and Conciliation Act 1996.

(11) That the words AUTHOR and PUBLISHERS, "party" or "parties", unless there be something contrary in the context, include their respective heirs, survivors, successors, representatives, executors, administrators and assigns and successors in business.

IN WITNESS WHEREOF the parties hereto have executed these presents, the date, month and year first hereinbefore mentioned.

Signed, sealed and delivered by
CD the AUTHOR in the presence of:

Signed, sealed and delivered
by Mr. M.K. Chawla pursuant to
Board Resolution of Eastern Law
Ltd. dated .... in the
presence of:

Deed of Assignment of Growing Crops

THIS ASSIGNMENT is made the ...., day of .... BETWEEN AB of etc. (VENDOR), of the one part, and CD of, etc. (PURCHASER), of the other part.

WHEREAS the said AB has agreed to sell to the said CD the crops of, etc., and grass now growing on the pieces of land hereinafter described, and all the benefits and advantages thereof, at the price of Rs. .... NOW THIS DEED WITNESSES that in consideration of the sum of Rupees ...., the receipt whereof the said AB hereby acknowledges, the said AB, as beneficial owner, hereby grants, sells and assigns to the said CD ALL the crops of, etc., and grass, which are now growing, arising and being on the pieces of land, etc. (*describe the pieces of land specifically*); TOGETHER WITH full right, liberty and powers for the said CD and the servants, agents, labourers and other person or persons employed by him for that purpose either with or without cattle, carts, etc., from time to time, and at any time during the ensuing months of, etc., to enter upon the said piece of land or any part thereof for the purpose of checking the condition of the said crops and for the purpose of reaping, mowing and cutting the said crops, of, etc., and grass and removing the same, AND ALSO to do all such other acts and things as may be necessary or required for the purpose of obtaining the full benefit of this deed: TO HOLD the same to the said CD absolutely.

IN WITNESS WHEREOF etc.

Signed, sealed and delivered AB

Assignment of Copyright and Trade Name in a Newspaper by a Limited Company to the Trustee of an Intended Association

THIS DEED OF ASSIGNMENT made this .... day of .... 2000 BETWEEN ...., a company registered under the Companies Act 1956 having its registered office at .... (hereinafter called the ASSIGNOR which expression shall where the subject or context allows or admits of be deemed to include its successors and assigns) of the one part and Mr. .... son of...........residing at...........(hereinafter called the ASSIGNEE which term shall where the subject or context allows or admits of be deemed to include his heirs and successors and assigns and persons being members of the intended association) of the other part.

WHEREAS the ASSIGNOR is the sole proprietor and owner of the newspaper known as .... for over .... years free from all encumbrances with all rights hereby assigned which are valid and subsisting.

NOW THIS DEED OF ASSIGNMENT witnesseth as follows:

1. In consideration of a sum of Rs. .... paid by the ASSIGNEE to the ASSIGNOR (the receipt whereof the ASSIGNOR doth hereby admit, acknowledge and confirm) the ASSIGNOR as beneficial owner of the copyright in the said newspaper do hereby grant, convey, sell, transfer, assign, assure the same unto and to the use of the ASSIGNEE absolutely and for ever and other right, title and interest and claim therein AND all goodwill, benefits and other advantages and connections of the newspapers throughout the world together with all contracts and orders outstanding on this day with full and absolute right to print, reproduce, multiply, circulate and sell the same or any translation thereof to the intent and with the object that the ASSIGNEE shall own the said newspaper as trustee for the members of the intended association and for the benefit of all its members.

2. The ASSIGNOR doth hereby covenant with the ASSIGNEE and agree as follows:

(*i*) Notwithstanding any act, deed or thing whatsoever heretofore done or executed, performed or knowingly suffered to the contrary, the assignor had good right, full power and absolute authority to grant, convey, transfer, assign and sell the copyright and the trade name of the said newspaper unto and to the ASSIGNEE in the manner hereinbefore indicated.

(*ii*) The said copyright and also the trade name and also the goodwill are free from encumbrances and attachments and there is no injunction or prohibitory order.

(*iii*) The ASSIGNOR shall hereafter do execute and perform any further or other act, deed or thing and writings for further and better assuring the said copyright and trade name unto and to the use of ASSIGNEE as may be reasonably required.

Description

ALL THAT the copyright of the ASSIGNOR, the trade mark and trade name in the daily newspaper in .... named "........." now printed and circulated from the premises No. ...... and its goodwill, benefits and other advantages and all pending orders and contracts and business connections together with the right to print, reproduce, multiply, publish, circulate and sell the same or any translation or version thereof.

IN WITNESS WHEREOF the common seal of the company is hereunto affixed and these presents are also executed by the ASSIGNEE at Calcutta in the presence of:

The common seal of the ASSIGNOR company is hereunto affixed pursuant to the resolution of the Board of Directors dated the ....day of .... by Mr. .... in the presence of:

EXECUTED by the ASSIGNEE Mr. .... at Calcutta in the presence of:

Assignment of Patent

THIS DEED OF ASSIGNMENT OF PATENT is made this .... day of .... 1999 BETWEEN AB son of .... residing at .... (hereinafter called the ASSIGNOR which term shall include his heirs, legal representatives and assigns) of the one part and CD son of .... residing at .... (hereinafter called the ASSIGNEE which term shall include his heirs, successors and assigns) of the other part.

WHEREAS the ASSIGNOR is the inventor and patentee in respect of a machine (state here the nature of the patent).

AND WHEREAS the said patent was duly registered on the .... day of .... 19 .... as number.........in the Patent Office at .... and the patentee, *viz.,* the said AB has thus the exclusive privilege and authority to use the same for a period of .... years from the aforesaid date subject to payment of prescribed fee within time.

AND WHEREAS the said AB has agreed to assign and the said CD has agreed to purchase the benefit of the said invention and the patent at and for the price of Rs. .... :

NOW THIS DEED OF ASSIGNMENT WITNESSES that in pursuance of the said agreement and in consideration of the said sum of Rs. ...., paid by the said CD to the said AB which the ASSIGNOR AB doth hereby admit, acknowledge and confirm as having had and received from the ASSIGNEE CD the said AB as beneficial owner hereby grant, transfer and assign unto CD the said ASSIGNEE, all that the said invention and patent and the full and exclusive benefit and advantage thereof AND all and every improvement, extension or renewal thereof TO HAVE AND TO HOLD the same AND the said ASSIGNOR hereby covenants with the said ASSIGNEE that notwithstanding anything done or omitted or knowingly suffered the said patent is now valid and subsisting.

AND the said ASSIGNOR further covenants with the said ASSIGNEE that he will at the cost of the person requiring the same do all such things for further assuring this transfer unto the said ASSIGNEE as may be required for the registration of assignment with the authorities under the provisions of the Designs Act 1911 and the Patent Act 1970.

The Schedule

IN WITNESS WHEREOF the parties have executed these presents on the day, month and year first above-written.

Signed, sealed and delivered by AB
the ASSIGNOR in the presence of:

Signed, sealed and delivered by CD
the ASSIGNEE in the presence of:

Assignment of Policy of Life Insurance by Nomination

(*For endorsement on policy*)

I, AB of, etc. holder of Policy No. .... issued by the Life Insurance Corporation of India pursuant to section 39 of the Indian Insurance Act 1938, do hereby nominate CD of, etc. as the person to whom the money secured by this Policy of Insurance shall be paid in the event of my death and request the Life Insurance Corporation to register this my nomination and issue a written acknowledgment thereof in accordance with section 39(3) of the said Insurance Act.

Signed AB

Deed of Assignment of Policy of Life Insurance by way of Gift with Reservation

THIS DEED OF ASSIGNMENT made the .... day of .... BETWEEN AB of, etc. (ASSIGNOR), of the one part and CD of, etc. (ASSIGNEE), of the other part

WITNESSES that in consideration of natural love and affection between the said AB and CD, the said AB does hereby and hereunder transfer and assign as and by way of gift to the said CD all the benefits of and all moneys now due or shall hereafter become payable under the Policy of Insurance No. .... dated .... on the life of the said AB PROVIDED ALWAYS that in the event of the said CD predeceasing the said AB the benefit of and right to receive moneys under the said policy shall to all intents and purposes revert to the said AB as if this assignment had never been made nor intended. AND THAT the said AB do hereby covenant with the said CD that the said policy is still in *force* and further that the said AB has not charged *nor* encumbered the same in any way and furthermore there is no injunction or prohibitory order against him from assigning the same in the manner hereunder effected.

IN WITNESS, etc.

Signed, sealed and delivered AB

Deed of Assignment of Policy of Life Assurance

THIS ASSIGNMENT made the .... day of .... BETWEEN AB of, etc. (ASSIGNOR), of the one part, and CD of etc. (ASSIGNEE), of the other part.

WHEREAS a policy of assurance being No. .... for Rs. ....was issued by the Life Insurance Corporation of India on the life of the ASSIGNOR on the .... day of .... to be paid to the ASSIGNOR on maturity or to his nominee or heirs, the executors, administrators or assigns after his death, subject to payment of the annual premium of Rs. .... AND WHEREAS the said AB has agreed to transfer and assign unto and in favour of the said CD the said policy of assurance for a sum of Rs. .... NOW THIS DEED WITNESSES that in consideration of the sum of Rupees ...., paid by the said CD the receipt whereof the said AB does hereby admit and acknowledge, the said AB does hereby transfer and assign unto and to the use and for the benefit of CD the above recited policy of assurance together with the benefit of the said sum of Rs. ....thereby assured and all the other moneys, profits, benefits and advantages thereof to be had, recovered or obtained under or by virtue of the said policy: TO HAVE AND TO HOLD the same unto and to the use of the said CD absolutely, subject to the conditions as to payment of future premiums and otherwise to be henceforth observed in respect of the said policy: AND the said AB hereby covenants with the said CD that he, the said AB, shall not do, execute or perform or knowingly suffer anything to the contrary whereby or by reason or means whereof the said policy may be rendered void or voidable, or the said CD or his heirs, executors, administrators or assigns may be prevented from receiving the said sum of Rs. .... or any benefit or advantage thereunder.

IN WITNESS WHEREOF the parties herein have signed these presents on the day, month and year first above-written.

Signed, sealed and delivered by AB
the ASSIGNOR in the presence of:

Signed, sealed and delivered by CD
the ASSIGNEE in the presence of:

Deed of Assignment of Shares in a Company

THIS ASSIGNMENT is made the ...... day of .... BETWEEN AB of, etc. (hereinafter called the ASSIGNOR), of the one part, and CD of, etc. (hereinafter called the ASSIGNEE), of the other part, WITNESSES that in consideration of the sum of Rupees .... paid by the ASSIGNEE to the ASSIGNOR, the receipt whereof the assignor hereby acknowledges, the said AB hereby assigns and transfers to the said CD .... ordinary shares of Rs. .... each, numbered .... to ...., under Folio number .... which stand in the name of the ASSIGNOR in the books of......Co., Ltd.: TO HAVE AND TO HOLD the same to the ASSIGNEE absolutely, subject nevertheless to the conditions of the Memorandum and Articles of Associations of the company on which the ASSIGNOR held the same up to date. AND the ASSIGNEE hereby agrees to take the said shares subject to such conditions.

IN WITNESS, etc.

Signed, sealed and delivered AB

Assignment of a Registered Trade Mark

THIS DEED OF ASSIGNMENT OF TRADE MARK made this .... day of .... 1999 BETWEEN AB son of .... residing at .... (hereinafter referred to the ASSIGNOR which term shall include his heirs, successors and legal representatives) of the one part and CD son of .... residing at .... (hereinafter called the ASSIGNEE which term shall include his heirs, legal representatives and assigns) of the other part.

WHEREAS the said AB is the owner and the proprietor of a Trade Mark number......duly registered in the Register of Trade Marks maintained by the Trade Mark Registration Office at ....

AND WHEREAS the said AB has made actual and *bona fide* use of the said Trade Mark in India in relation to the toilet goods manufactured by him at his factory in ....

NOW THIS DEED OF ASSIGNMENT WITNESSES that in pursuance of the said agreement and in consideration of the said sum of Rs. .... paid by the said CD to AB the receipt whereof he the said AB hereby admits, acknowledges and confirms, he the ASSIGNOR AB does hereby grant, transfer and assign upon the terms hereinafter mentioned, the exclusive use and all benefits of the aforesaid Trade Mark in relation to the goods of toiletry manufactured by him at his factory at ....

AND the said ASSIGNOR hereby covenants with the ASSIGNEE that he will not infringe nor use a mark identical with the Trade Mark hereby assigned nor use another Trade Mark nearly resembling it as to be likely to deceive or cause confusion, in the course of trade, in relation to the goods in respect of which it is registered and in a manner as to render the use of this mark likely to be taken either as being a use of the said Trade Mark or to import a reference to the ASSIGNOR.

AND the ASSIGNOR further covenants that he, the ASSIGNOR, shall at the costs of CD or any person claiming through him do or cause to be done any other act, deed or thing as may be required for more perfectly assuring the aforesaid assignment.

The Schedule

IN WITNESS WHEREOF the parties hereto have executed these presents on the day, month and year first above-written.

Signed, sealed and delivered by AB the
ASSIGNOR in the presence of:

Signed, sealed and delivered by CD the
ASSIGNEE in the presence of:

Deed of Assignment of Rent

THIS DEED OF ASSIGNMENT OF RENT made this .... day of .... 2000 BETWEEN AB son of .... residing at .... (hereinafter referred to as the VENDOR which term shall unless the context requires otherwise include his heirs, legal representatives and assigns) of the one part and CD son of .... residing at .... (hereinafter called the PURCHASER which term shall include his heirs, successors and assigns) of the other part.

WHEREAS by a Deed of Sale dated the ...... day of ...... AB has sold and conveyed to CD absolutely the land (*describe the property*), subject to the existing tenancy or tenancies of person or persons named in the schedule hereunder AND WHEREAS it has been agreed by and between AB and CD that the said AB shall also transfer and assign unto and to the use of the said CD all rents payable by all such tenants accrued up to and inclusive of the date of sale at and for the sum of Rs. .... NOW THIS DEED WITNESSES that in pursuance of the said agreement and in consideration of the sum of Rs. .... paid by CD the receipt whereof the said AB hereby admits, acknowledges and confirms, the said AB does hereby grant, transfer and assign unto and in favour of the said CD ALL those rents and sums of money particulars whereof are specified in the Schedule hereunder and all benefits and advantages thereof and empower and authorise, CD TO HAVE, receive, collect and realise the same either amicably or through court and appropriate the same for his absolute use and benefit. AND THIS Indenture further witnesses that the said AB does hereby covenant with the said CD that all and every item of such rents and sums of money are still lawfully due and payable by the said respective tenants AND that the said AB never received any advance against such rent or rents nor any part payment or any other deposit or deposits adjustable with the said rents nor released or committed to release or remit the same or any portion thereof nor written off any amount with intent to exonerate any tenant or tenants from his or their liability on that account. AND FURTHER there is no injunction or prohibitory order against him from realising the same or any portion thereof nor from assigning all such amounts in the manner hereunder effected.

The Schedule above referred to

Serial No.	*Name of tenants*	*Monthly rent*	*Due for*	*Amount due*	*Remarks*

IN WITNESS WHEREOF the parties herein have executed these presents on the day, month and year first above-written.

Signed, sealed and delivered by AB
the VENDOR in the presence of:

Signed, sealed and delivered by CD
the PURCHASER in the presence of:

8

Bail Petition

Any person arrested by police in connection with a bailable offence is entitled to bail as a matter of right (s. 436, Cr PC). The Officer-in-Charge of police station on arresting an accused on bailable offence shall offer him bail. If he can furnish bail the officer shall release him on bail on condition of his appearing before the Magistrate concerned on a date fixed. If the person is unable to furnish bail he shall be produced before the Magistrate within twenty-four hours of his arrest. The Magistrate has to release him on bail with or without surety or on personal bond.[1]

In case of non-bailable offence the bail is granted at the discretion of the Magistrate. Under the conditions mentioned in s. 437, Cr PC the person may be released on bail. Magistrate may impose appropriate conditions. If, however, the investigation is not completed within (*a*) ninety days of the first order of detention and the offence is punishable with death, imprisonment for life or imprisonment for a term of not less than seven years or (*b*) within sixty days when investigation relates to any other offence, the Magistrate will release him on bail on his furnishing a bail bond. The Magistrate cannot postpone his release to enable the police to submit charge-sheet.[2] It is not defeated by lapse of time or subsequent filing of charge-sheet.[3]

An affidavit may be filed in support of the petition for bail or the petition may be sworn. When the bail is refused by the Magistrate under s. 437, Cr PC the petitioner may approach the Sessions Judge first and also the High Court for bail. Normally the petitioner approaches the Sessions Judge first for bail under s. 439, Cr PC and then the High Court. When the power

1 *Dharma* v *Rabindra Nath* 1978 Cr LJ 864.
2 *Umashankar* v *State* 1982 Cr LJ 1186 (MP).
3 *Raghubir Singh* v *State* AIR 1987 SC 149; 1987 Cr LJ 157.

of the Sessions Judge and of High Court under s. 439, Cr PC is concurrent there is no bar to the petitioner first moving High Court. But some High Courts expressed the view that when concurrent power is there in two forums the lower forum should be approached first unless the applicant can assign reasons as to why he was approaching the higher forum. There is however no legal bar for the High Court entertaining the bail petition even if the petitioner did not approach Sessions Judge first.[4]

The Appellate Court, including High Court as Appellate Court, may order release of the accused on bail pending hearing of an appeal. When the hearing of an appeal is likely to be delayed bail should be granted by the Appellate Court.[5] When the accused is likely to serve out the full or substantial part of the sentence pending hearing of the appeal bail should be granted.[6]

Forms

Application for Anticipatory Bail before High Court

In the High Court at Calcutta
(Criminal Miscellaneous Jurisdiction)

In the matter of an Application for anticipatory bail under section 439, Cr PC

AB son of MN residing at ....,
.... *Petitioner*

versus

The State .... *Respondent*

To

The Hon'ble Mr. ....
Chief Justice and His Companion
Justices of the said Hon'ble Court

The humble petition of AB, the petitioner above-named

4 *Abdul Kasim* v *State* AIR 1960 MP 54; *Daini* alias *Raju* v *State* 1989 Cr LJ (NOC) 149 (MP); *Thakur Prasad* v *State* 1977 Cr LJ 471; *Chajjuram* v *State* 1977 Punj LR 619.

5 *Anurag* v *State* AIR 1987 Pat 274 (FB).

6 *Harbhajan* v *State* 1977 Cr LJ 1424 (P&H).

MOST RESPECTFULLY SHEWETH:

1. That the petitioner is a reputed businessman having a long-standing business in Calcutta and is an income-tax and sales-tax assessee.

2. That the petitioner has his permanent residence in Calcutta.

3. That due to business rivalry, his business rival, Z Co. Ltd., lodged a false complaint against the petitioner before the police alleging cheating and forgery.

4. That the intention of the *de facto* complaint is only to harass and humiliate the applicant and to tarnish his clean image in business circle.

5. Your petitioner apprehends that pursuant to the said complaint the police may arrest your petitioner and thereby put the petitioner to harassment and mental agony and physical inconvenience.

6. That the petitioner undertakes to abide by all the terms and conditions that may be imposed upon him in the order of bail.

7. That if the anticipatory bail is not granted the petitioner shall suffer irreparable injury.

8. That the application is made *bona fide* and in the interest of justice.

In the circumstances the petitioner humbly prays that Your Lordships may be graciously pleased to direct that in the event of the petitioner being arrested in connection of this case the petitioner will be released on bail forthwith and/or may pass such other order or orders as Your Lordships may deem fit and proper.

And your petitioner as in duty bound, shall ever pray.

Advocate of AB — Sd. AB

Verification

I, AB, son of MN, by occupation business, residing at ...., Calcutta .... do hereby solemnly affirm and say as follows:

1. I am the petitioner above-named. I know the facts of this case and I am able to depose thereto.
2. The statements in paragraphs 1 to 8 in the foregoing petition are true to my knowledge and belief.
3. I sign this verification on the 11th day of June 2000 in Calcutta.

Solemnly affirmed by the said AB on 11th day of June 2000 in the Court House at Calcutta.

Before me — Sd. AB

Commissioner

Application for Anticipatory Bail before Sessions Judge

In the Court of Sessions Judge at ....

Criminal Misc. Case No. ...... of ......

In the matter of:

An application for anticipatory bail under section 438 of the Code of Criminal Procedure 1973

And

In the matter of:

AB .... *Petitioner*

versus

The State of West Bengal ... *Respondent*

The humble petition of the petitioner above-named

MOST RESPECTFULLY SHEWETH:

1. That the petitioner is a senior Government servant working under the Central Government in the Department of Customs and Excise.

2. That in connection with his official duties he has to undertake various raids against criminals and anti-socials.

3. That some known criminals of the area, namely, ... hatched a conspiracy to harass and malign your petitioner in public by implicating him by and in lodging an FIR at the Police Station at ....

4. That the petitioner being a permanent Government servant has no chance of going underground and if necessary he shall co-operate with the police in investigation and anticipatory bail be granted to your petitioner.

5. That if no anticipatory bail is granted he shall suffer irreparable injury.

6. That the petitioner undertakes to abide by all the terms and conditions of the order of bail if passed.

Hence it is prayed that Your Honour will be pleased to grant the petitioner anticipatory bail and pass such other order or orders as Your Honour deem fit and proper.

And for this act of kindness your petitioner shall ever pray.

Advocate of AB AB

Verification

I, AB, son of MN, residing at .... do hereby solemnly affirm and say as follows:

1. I am the petitioner above-named. I know the facts and circumstances of this case.
2. The statements in paragraphs 1 to 6 hereinabove in the petition are true to my knowledge and belief.
3. I sign this verification on this 7th day of June 2000 at Howrah.

Solemnly affirmed by the said AB
on this 7th day of June 2000 at
Court House at .... AB

Before me
Notary/Magistrate

Application for Anticipatory Bail under section 438, Cr PC

In the Court of the Sessions Judge at Howrah

AB son of MN resident of ... *Petitioner*

versus

The State of West Bengal ... *Respondent*

The humble petition of the petitioner above-named

MOST RESPECTFULLY SHEWETH:

1. That a burglary was said to have been committed in a village which is contiguous to the village Dhubli where the petitioner's house is situated on the night of 6th June 2000.

2. That the owner of the house, in which the burglary had been committed, has enmity with the petitioner for several years over landed properties and he is trying to implicate the petitioner in the said dacoity case falsely.

3. That the petitioner has reasons to believe that your petitioner may be arrested on accusation of having committed the said offence of burglary which is a non-bailable offence by police at the instance of the said owner of the house where burglary is said to have been committed.

4. That the petitioner undertakes to obey all the conditions mentioned in clauses (*i*) to (*iii*) of sub-sec. (2) of section 438, Cr PC and to obey any other conditions if imposed by Your Honour.

In the circumstances your petitioner prays that Your Honour may be graciously pleased to issue a direction to the Officer-in-Charge of Police Station Dhubli that in the event of your petitioner being arrested he may be released on bail on any conditions that Your Honour may be pleased to impose on your petitioner.

And your petitioner, as in duty bound, shall ever pray.

Verification

I, AB, son of MN, residing at ...., Howrah .... do hereby solemnly affirm and say as follows:

1. I am the petitioner above-named. I know the facts and circumstances of the case.
2. The statements in paragraphs 1, 2, 3 and 4 of the foregoing petition are true to my knowledge and belief.
3. I sign this verification on this 7th day of June 2000 at the Court House in Howrah.

Solemnly affirmed by the said AB
on this 10th day of June 2000 at
Court House in Howrah.

Before me
Notary/Magistrate

Application for Bail before High Court under section 439, Cr PC

In the High Court at Calcutta
(Criminal Miscellaneous Jurisdiction)

In the matter of:

An application for bail under section 439, Cr PC

And

In the matter of:

AB .... *Petitioner*
(in Jail Custody)

versus

The State of West Bengal ....
Respondent

To
The Hon'ble Mr. ....
Chief Justice and his companion
Justices of the said Hon'ble Court

The humble petition of AB the petitioner above-named

MOST RESPECTFULLY SHEWETH:

1. The petitioner is a respectable person having his own business. He is an income-tax payer.

2. Shri CM being the *de facto* complainant in order to harass and humiliate the petitioner has engineered a false case against the petitioner because of business rivalry and got him arrested by the police.

3. The evidence collected during investigation so far against the petitioner is very meagre.

4. The petitioner applied for bail before the Sub-divisional Judicial Magistrate .... on 2nd May 2000 but his bail was refused.

5. That the petitioner then applied for bail before the Sessions Judge, Alipore in Criminal Misc. Case No. ...... of ...... on .... but the Sessions Judge has also refused bail.

6. The petitioner is in custody over a month and the police duly interrogated him during the police custody and his further detention in custody is not necessary for the purpose of investigation of the case.

7. That the petitioner has his permanent residence at ...., and carries on business and he has no chance of absconding.

8. The petitioner undertakes to abide by the terms and conditions that may be imposed upon him by the Hon'ble High Court and shall attend the Court of the Learned Magistrate as and when required.

9. That the petition is *bona fide* and made in the interest of justice.

In the circumstances the petitioner humbly prays Your Lordships may be graciously pleased to direct the release of the petitioner on bail or pass such other order as Your Lordships may deem fit and proper.

And your petitioner as in duty bound shall ever pray.

Advocate of AB Sd. AB

Verification

I, AB, son of MN, by occupation business, resident of .... at preset in Alipore Jail custody do hereby solemnly affirm and say as follows:

1. I am the petitioner above-named and I know the facts and circumstances of this case.
2. The statements in paragraphs 1 to 9 of the foregoing petition are true to my knowledge and belief.
3. I sign this verification on ....

Solemnly affirmed by the said AB
on .... at the Court
House in ....

Before me
Commissioner

Petition for bail under section 389, Cr PC

In the Court of the Sessions Judge at Alipore, 24-Parganas
Case No. ... of ...... under s. 379, IPC

The State
versus

Accused AB .... Son of MN,
Village: ...., Thana: ....

In the matter of petition for bail of the accused-petitioner pending the hearing of the appeal.

The humble petition of the accused in the above case

MOST RESPECTFULLY SHEWETH:

1. That your petitioner was convicted by the Sub-Divisional Judicial Magistrate of Alipore under s. 379, IPC on 5th March 2000 and sentenced to undergo three months Rigorous Imprisonment.

2. That your petitioner has this day filed an appeal before Your Honour against the said order of conviction and sentence.

3. That the cycle alleged to have been stolen by the petitioner was purchased by him at an auction held by court on 28th February 2000 for Rs. 300 and that the fact was proved by no less than six witnesses.

4. That your petitioner was a *bona fide* purchaser of the cycle for value and had no knowledge or even suspicion that the cycle was a stolen property.

5. That your petitioner is a newspaper hawker of fairly good means and he has a stall at .... and there is no apprehension of your petitioner absconding pending the hearing of the appeal.

6. Your petitioner states that bail be granted to your petitioner pending disposal of the appeal in which your petitioner has a good chance of success.

7. Unless bail is granted your petitioner will lose all the regular customers and the main source of livelihood.

Your Petitioner prays that Your Honour may be pleased to grant *ad interim* bail to your petitioner pending the hearing of the appeal.

And your petitioner, as in duty bound, shall ever pray.

Verification

I, AB, son of MN, by occupation business, residing at ...., do hereby solemnly affirm and say as follows:

1. I am the accused petitioner above-named and I know the facts and circumstances of this case.
2. The statements in paragraphs 1 to 7 hereinabove petition are true to my knowledge and belief.
3. I sign this verification on this 3rd April 2000 at Alipore.

Solemnly affirmed by the said AB
on this 3rd day of April 2000 at the
Court House in Alipore.

Before me

Notary/Magistrate

Petition for Bail under section 439, Cr PC before Sessions Judge

In the Court of the Sessions Judge at Alipore
Case No. 10 of 1999 pending in the Court of
the Sub-divisional Magistrate of Alipore

The State ....

versus

Accused AB son of GH, Village: ....
Thana: ....

In the matter of an application of AB the accused for bail

The humble petition of AB the accused above-named

MOST RESPECTFULLY SHEWETH:

1. That it was alleged that there was a burglary in the house of ZEE on the night of 3rd May 2000 and your petitioner was arrested by the police some two weeks afterwards on 18th May 2000 at his house. The charge-sheet was submitted on 16th June 2000. Your petitioner's prayer for bail was rejected by Mr. JM, Sub-divisional Judicial Magistrate at .... on 10th July 2000. Being aggrieved by the order of the Learned Magistrate refusing to grant bail to your petitioner, he begs to move your Honour for bail on the following amongst other grounds.

Grounds

(*i*) That the name of your petitioner does not appear in the First Information Report.

(*ii*) That no incriminating article was found in the house of your petitioner on a search by the police, and that he was arrested on mere suspicion and that your petitioner is perfectly innocent of the charge.

(*iii*) That no inmate of the house of ZEE identified your petitioner in the identification parade held inside the Alipore Jail by Mr. M, a Second Class Magistrate.

(*iv*) That the accused has a Ration Shop at .... and that he resides there with his wife and children.

2. Your petitioner states that there is no possibility of your petitioner escaping or absconding during trial or otherwise.

3. Your petitioner has a good defence and the prosecution case is based on false allegations.

4. That your petitioner is willing to furnish proper security for appearance in the court to take his trial.

5. In view of the aforesaid your petitioner states that the bail be granted to your petitioner as prayed for herein in the interest of justice.

Your petitioner therefore prays that Your Honour may be pleased to call for the records and issue notice to the Public Prosecutor and on hearing the parties be graciously pleased to pass an order directing release of your petitioner on bail.

And your petitioner, as in duty bound, shall ever pray.

Dated .... Signature

Advocate

Verification

I, AB, son of GH, by occupation business, residing at ...., do hereby solemnly affirm and say as follows:

1. I am the accused petitioner above-named and I know the facts and circumstances of this case.
2. The statements in paragraphs 1 to 5 in the above petition are true to my knowledge and belief.
3. I sign this verification on this 4th day of August 2000 at the Court House at Alipore.

Solemnly affirmed by the said AB
on this 4th August 2000 at the
Court House at .... AB

Before me
Notary/Magistrate.

Bail Petition before a Magistrate during Police Enquiry under s. 437, Cr PC

In the Court of .... Magistrate ....

The State ....

versus

Accused AB son of TZ, Village: ....
Thana: ....

In the matter of petition for bail of accused AB, during police enquiry

The humble petition of AB the accused above-named

MOST RESPECTFULLY SHEWETH:

1. That your petitioner was arrested by the police on 5th March 2000 on mere suspicion. That nearly a month has passed after the arrest but still the Investigating Police Officer has not submitted a charge-sheet.

2. That your petitioner was not identified by any inmate of the house of CM where the burglary is alleged to have taken place, nor any incriminating article was found in his house.

3. That your petitioner has reason to believe that one GS with whom your petitioner is on bad terms and who is looking after the case for the complainant has falsely implicated your petitioner in the case out of grudge.

4. That your petitioner shall fully co-operate with the police.
5. That your petitioner is not likely to abscond or leave the country.

Your petitioner prays that your Honour may be pleased to call for police papers and after perusing the same be pleased to direct the release of your petitioner on bail.

And your petitioner, as in duty bound, shall ever pray.

Advocate AB

Verification

I, AB, son of TZ, residing at ...., by occupation business, do hereby solemnly affirm and say as follows:

1. I am the petitioner above-named. I know and I have made myself acquainted with the facts and circumstances of the case and I am able to depose thereto.
2. The statements in paragraphs 1 to 5 of the foregoing petition are true and correct to my knowledge and belief.
3. I sign this verification on the 6th day of May 1999.

Solemnly affirmed by the said AB on 6th May 2000 at the Court House at .... AB

Before me

Notary/Magistrate.

Bail Petition before a Magistrate in a Pending Case under section 437, Cr PC

In the Court of .... Magistrate of ....

Case No. ... of ...... under section .... IPC

The State ....

versus

Accused AB son of MN, residing at ....

In the matter of petition for bail of accused AB

The humble petition of AB the accused in the above case

MOST RESPECTFULLY SHEWETH:

1. That your petitioner was arrested by the police on 5th April 1999 on suspicion. That he was not named in the FIR nor was he identified by any inmate of the house, where the burglary is said to have taken place during the identification parade by Mr. JM, a Judicial Magistrate.

2. That nothing incriminating was found in the house on search by the police.

3. That your petitioner is a family man and is not likely to abscond.

4. Your petitioner be granted bail inasmuch as there is no valid ground for continued detention and the trial is not likely to be completed within the near future.

Your petitioner prays that after issuing the notice to the State and hearing both sides Your Honour may be pleased to pass Order for releasing your petitioner on bail.

And your petitioner as in duty bound, shall ever pray.

Advocate AB

Verification

I, AB, son of MN, aged about 30 years, by occupation business, residing at ...., do hereby solemnly affirm and say as follows:

1. I am the petitioner above-named and I know the facts and circumstances of this case.
2. The statements in paragraphs 1 to 4 in the foregoing petition are true and correct to the best of my knowledge and belief.
3. I sign this verification on this 20th day of June 1999.

Solemnly affirmed by the said AB
on 20th day of June 2000 at the
Court House at .... AB

Before me
Notary/Magistrate

Bail Petition

In the Court of the Sub-Divisional Judicial
Magistrate at ....

The State ....

versus

1. AB
2. CD

3. EF
4. GH

Case—under section 188, IPC; section 116, Cr PC; section 29, Police Act; section 151, Cr PC

The humble petition of the accused persons named-above

MOST RESPECTFULLY SHEWETH:

1. That your petitioners were arrested by .... Police under section 151, Cr PC on 5th May 2000 at 3 P.M. and were kept in the lock up in the police station and the bail offered by your petitioners was refused by the police.

2. That your petitioners have been produced before Your Honour this day and they have been charged under section 188, IPC.

3. That the offences mentioned in the paragraph 2 above are all bailable.

Under the circumstances, your petitioners pray that they be released on bail pending the disposal of the case.

And your petitioners, as in duty bound, shall ever pray.

Advocate AB, CD, EF & GH

Verification

We, AB, CD, EF and GH, sons of MN, by occupation business, residents of ...., do hereby solemnly affirm and say as follows:

1. We are the petitioners above-named and know the facts and circumstances of the case.
2. The statements made in paragraphs 1, 2 and 3 of the foregoing petition are true to our knowledge and belief.
3. We sign this verification on 15th May 2000.

Solemnly affirmed by AB, CD, EF and GH on 15th May 2000 at the Court House at ....

AB
CD
EF
GH

Before me

Notary/Magistrate

9

Bonds

Bonds. The dictionary meaning of the word 'bond' is a writing of an obligation to pay a sum or perform a contract. A bond according to s. 2(5) of the Stamp Act means—

(*i*) any instrument whereby a person obliges himself to pay money to another, on condition that the obligation shall be void if a specified act is performed, or is not performed, as the case may be;

(*ii*) any instrument attested by a witness, and not payable to order or bearer, whereby a person obliges himself to pay money to another; and

(*iii*) any instrument so attested, whereby a person obliges himself to deliver grain or other agricultural produce to another.

A simple bond is distinguished from a promissory note inasmuch as no money is payable under a bond to the order of the obligee or to the bearer of the instrument. A simple bond is also distinguishable from the mere acknowledgment of indebtedness inasmuch as in an acknowledgment there is usually no undertaking to pay in expressed terms. Bottomry bonds are contracts of the nature of mortgage of the ship for money borrowed by the owner or the master in case of unforeseen necessity, distress, to execute repairs, or to pay for repairs executed and to complete the voyage against security of the bottom of the ship. The lender shall also undertake sea risk. This is now obsolete in practice.[1]

A bond is either single or double, *i.e.* with a condition. If a bond be merely for the payment of money, or for the performance of some particular act, without any condition annexed to it, the bond is said to be single. In a bond with a condition, the obligor binds himself to pay, by way of penalty or

1 Halsbury's *Laws of England*, 4th Ed., vol. 43, p. 138.

liquidated damages, an amount larger (usually double) than he actually borrows, or an amount equivalent to the amount of damages that he would be liable to pay if he fails to perform a specified act, on condition that the bond will become void if he repays the loan with interest, or only performs the specified act, as the case may be, on a specified date, otherwise that it will remain in full force.[2]

A conditional bond contains explanatory recitals which follow the obligation and precedes the condition.[3]

The obligation of a double bond is in the same form as intended to operate as in a single one except that the sum of money which is the subject-matter is described as penalty or liquidated damages according to the true intention of the parties. The distinction between the penal bond and other bonds flows from the well-known principles of law and equity as to reliefs against penalty. The question as to whether any particular clause in an obligation bond is penalty or not depends upon the intention of parties to be gathered from the interpretation of the whole document in the light of circumstances under which it was executed. In England, a bond acknowledging debt must bear the seal of the obligor, but the law is not rigid in India. Bonds in India are of various types: (*a*) Money Bond; (*b*) Indemnity Bond; (*c*) Customs Bond; (*d*) Administration Bond; (*e*) Security Bond; (*f*) Bottomry Bond; (*g*) Respondentia Bond; and (*h*) Hypothecation Bond.

The person who binds himself to pay money or to perform a particular act is called the *obligor*; and the person in whose favour a bond is executed is called the obligee.

Instruments amounting to agreements only. If a party to an instrument binds himself, in the event of a breach on his part of any of the conditions of the instrument, to pay the other party thereto a penalty not being a certain sum of money, the instrument amounts to an agreement only; and so also an indemnity note passed to a railway company by a consignee in respect of goods delivered to the consignee, and for which he is unable to produce the railway receipt, by which note he undertakes to keep the railway company, its agents and servants, harmless and indemnified against all claims to the said goods, since the indemnity note does not contain a contract that the indemnification should be in *money* necessarily, as the company might have been indemnified in some other way, such as by delivering the goods in perfect order to the real owner.

Execution and attestation—registration—signature by scribe. A bond must be signed, or a mark made on it, by the executant at the end on the right

2 Section 74 of the Indian Contract Act 1872.
3 Halsbury's *Laws of England*, 4th Ed., vol. 12, p. 557.

side of the instrument, in the presence of the witness or witnesses, who should sign on the opposite left side, also in the presence of the executant. Registration for any kind of bond is not compulsory; but if a bond by itself creates an interest in immovable property of the value of Rs. 100 and upwards, its registration will be compulsory.

Signature by the writer of the bond, as in any other instrument, in itself, is not an attestation, and the scribe is not an attesting witness, though there is nothing to prevent a scribe from being a witness provided he signs in the proper place. Attestation must appear, as such, on the face of the instrument.

FORMS

Simple Money Bond

BY THIS BOND I, AB of, etc., am hereby held and firmly bound to CD of etc. in the sum of Rs. .... only to be paid to the said CD, his heirs, executors or administrators or assigns, for which payment faithfully and truly to be made, I bind myself, my heirs, executors or administrators by these presents.

SIGNED and delivered by me at .... this .... day of ....

THE CONDITION of this bond is such that, if the above bound AB, his heirs, executors or administrators, do and shall faithfully and truly pay or cause to be paid, to the said CD, his heirs, executors, administrators or assigns, the sum of Rs. .... only, with interest thereon at the rate of .... per cent. per annum, on the .... day of ...., THEN the above-written bond or obligation shall be void and of no effect, otherwise the same shall remain in full force and value.

Signed, sealed and delivered AB (*Debtor*)

ANOTHER FORM

KNOW ALL MEN by these presents I, AB son of etc., am hereby held and firmly bound unto and in favour of CD son of etc., in the sum of Rs. .... for which payment to be truly and faithfully made. I bind myself, my heirs, executors and administrators. Sealed with my seal. Dated this .... day of ....

Now the condition of the bond, etc. (see PREVIOUS PRECEDENT).

Signed, sealed and delivered etc.

Instalment Money Bond

KNOW ALL MEN by these presents, we the undersigned, *viz.*, AB, son of etc., hereinafter referred to as the borrower of the first part and CD, son of etc., hereinafter referred to as the surety of the second part are by these presents held and firmly bound unto and in favour of EF, son of etc., hereinafter referred to as the lender in the sum of Rs. .... of good and lawful money of the Republic of India for which payment to be truly and faithfully made by instalments in the manner provided in the schedule below and for that purpose we, the undersigned AB and CD, bind ourselves, our respective heirs, executors, administrators and representatives.

Sealed with our seal, dated this .... day of .... 19.........

WHEREAS the borrower AB approached the lender EF for a loan and/or accommodation of Rs. .... to be repaid with interest of ....% per annum by instalments in the manner hereunder indicated and secured by a bond in terms hereunder contained. Now the condition of this above-written bond or obligation is such that if the borrower AB or the surety CD or either of them shall repay or cause to be repaid the said sum of Rs. .... with interest thereon at ....% in the manner hereunder indicated, then and in such an event the bond or obligation shall be void and stand automatically cancelled, otherwise the same shall remain in full force and virtue.

Schedule of Instalments

Signed, sealed and delivered AB

Money Bond with Surety

This BOND is made the .... day of ...., by AB, son of etc.

(*Debtor*) and CD, son of, etc. (*Surety*).

WHEREAS EF, son of etc., has this day lent and advanced to me, *viz.*, the said AB, a sum of Rupees .... (Rs. ......) only at the request and on the assurance and guarantee of the said CD, the surety, as to its repayment personally with interest at ....% per annum in case of default on my part. Now by this bond we, the said AB and CD, hereby and hereunder jointly and severally hold and bind ourselves, our respective heirs, executors, administrators and representatives unto the said EF his heirs, executors, administrators, representatives and assigns for payment to him or them, as the case may be, of the sum of Rupees .... (Rs. ....) only, on demand (or, on or before the .... day of .... or, by instalments, etc.) with interest thereon at the rate of .... per cent per annum from the date hereof until such payment.

IN WITNESS whereof, we, the said AB and CD, have set and subscribed our respective hands and seals the day, month and year first above-written.

In the presence of:

Signed, sealed and delivered AB
CD

Administration Bond under section 291 of the Indian Succession Act[4]

KNOW ALL MEN by these presents we, AB son of etc. (ADMINISTRATOR) and CD son of, etc., (SURETY), are held and jointly and severally bound to EF the .... Judge, etc., in the sum of Rs. .... only, of lawful good money to be paid to the said Judge, or to his successor in office, for which payment to be truly and lawfully made, we do hereby bind ourselves, and each of us and also our respective heirs, executors, administrators or assigns firmly by these presents for the whole of the amount.

Sealed with our seals, this .... day of ....

WHEREAS by an order of the Court of .... Judge, etc., made on the .... day of .... under section 290 of the Indian Succession Act, the above-named AB has been appointed administrator of the estate of GH (*deceased*), subject to his furnishing security by execution of a bond of Rs. ...., with one surety: AND WHEREAS the said CD has agreed to stand surety for the said AB and was approved by the court subject to his entering into the above-written bond as surety for the said AB: NOW THE CONDITION of this bond or obligation is such that, if the said AB, do and shall, within six months from the grant to him of letters of administration of the estate of GH deceased, or such further time as the said court may allow, do make or cause to be made a full and true inventory containing a full and true estimate of all the property, assets and credits of the estate which have or shall come in his hands, possession or to his knowledge in course of administration and also all the debts and outstandings due and payable by the estate and exhibit the same in the said court and do and shall, within one year from the said grant or such further time as the said court may allow, exhibit an account of the estate of the said deceased, showing the assets which have

4 *Surendra Nath Pramanik* v *Amrita Lal Pal Chowdhury* 47 Cal 115, 120. Bond taken to ensure due administration of the estate. The court may dispense with the surety altogether taking only the bond from the Administrator (Coote: *Probate Practice*, 16th Ed., p. 154).

come to his hands and the manner in which they have been applied, appropriated or disposed of, and do and shall well and truly administer the property, assets and credits of the deceased according to law, and all and every the rest and residue of the said property, credits and estate, which shall be found remaining and shall assent to and deliver and pay to such person or persons as shall be lawfully entitled thereto, THEN and in such an event the above-written bond or obligation shall be void and of no effect, otherwise the same shall remain in full force and virtue.

Signed, sealed and delivered AB

CD

Administration Bond under section 34 of the Guardians and Wards Act 1890

KNOW all men by these presents I, AB of, etc. (GUARDIAN), am held and firmly bound to CD, the Civil Judge, etc., in the sum of Rs. .... of lawful and good money to be paid to the said CD or to his successors in office, for which payment to be faithfully and truly made we, EF, of, etc., and GH, of etc. (*sureties*), are hereby also jointly and severally held and firmly bound to the said CD in the said sum of Rs. .... and further I, the above-bound AB and we, the above-bound EF and GH, bind ourselves and each of us, jointly and severally, and also our respective heirs, executors, administrators or assigns firmly by these presents.

Sealed with our seals this .... day of ....

WHEREAS by an order of the Court of the Civil Judge, etc., made on the .... of ...., under the Guardians and Wards Act, the above-named AB has been appointed certificated guardian of the property of IJ, minor son of KL, subject to furnishing security to the satisfaction of the court as provided therein AND WHEREAS the said EF and GH have been approved of as sureties by the court subject to their executing a bond jointly with the said AB as herein contained to which they both have agreed: NOW THE CONDITION of this bond or obligation is such that, if the said AB does and shall justly and truly account for, whenever called upon to do so, for what he may have received in respect of the property, assets and credits of the said minor and otherwise act according to and observe and perform all orders and directions of the court and in all matters and things conduct himself properly, THEN and in such an event the above-written bond or obligation shall be void and of no effect, otherwise the same shall remain in full force and virtue.

Signed, sealed and delivered AB

EF

GH

Security Bond on Grant of Succession Certificate

(The Indian Succession Act 1925, section 375)

BY THE BOND we, AB of, etc. (PRINCIPAL), and CD of, etc., (SURETY), are jointly and severally held and firmly bound to EF .... Judge, etc., in the sum of Rs. .... of lawful and good money to be paid to the said .... Judge, or to his successors in office for the time being as the case may be for which payment to be truly and faithfully made, we bind ourselves and also our respective heirs, executors, administrators and representatives jointly and severally by these presents.

Sealed with our seals this .... day of ....

WHEREAS by an order dated .... made in Case No. .... of .... of the Court of .... Judge, etc., a succession certificate in respect of the estate of MN deceased has been ordered to be issued under section 373 (read section 375) of the Indian Succession Act, to the above-named AB subject to his entering into a bond for Rs. .... with one surety as herein contained and WHEREAS the said AB has agreed to enter into the above-written bond AND WHEREAS the said CD has agreed to join with the said AB in the same bond as surety for the said AB and has been approved by the court: NOW THE CONDITION of this bond or obligation is that, if the said AB does and shall justly and truly account for the debts and securities for which the certificate is granted, indemnify and keep indemnified against all the claims brought by the lawful heirs of the deceased GH and do otherwise administer according to law the said properties and credits and deliver and pay and/or cause to be delivered and paid the same to person or persons lawfully entitled thereto and otherwise act and conduct himself properly in all other respects THEN the above-written bond or obligation shall be void and of no effect, and shall automatically stand discharged, otherwise the same shall remain in full force and virtue.

Signed, sealed and delivered AB

CD

Security Bond from Receiver

KNOW all men by these presents we, AB of, etc. (RECEIVER), and CD of, etc. (SURETY), are jointly and severally bound to EF .... Judge, etc., in the sum of Rs. .... to be paid to the said .... Judge, or to his successors in office, as the case may be, for which payment to be truly and faithfully made, we bind ourselves, and each of us, as also our respective heirs, executors or administrators, jointly and severally, by these presents.

Sealed with our seals this .... day of ....

WHEREAS a suit being T. Suit No. of .... (cause title) has been instituted in this court by the said GH against IJ for reliefs *inter alia* as appearing from the plaint, (*state the object of the suit*): AND WHEREAS by an order dated .... made in the said suit by the said court the said AB has been appointed Receiver of the rents, issues and profits of the immovable property and all the outstanding movable property of KL as mentioned in the plaint of the said suit subject to his furnishing security for Rs. .... with one surety: AND WHEREAS the said AB offered the said CD as such surety which was approved and accepted by the said court subject to his joining with the said AB in a bond on terms herein appearing: NOW THE CONDITION of this bond or obligation is such that, if the above-bound AB shall duly account for all and every sum or sums of money or moneys and other property or properties which he shall so receive as Receiver and also on account of the rents, issues and profits of the immovable property at such periods as the said court shall appoint, and shall duly pay the balance or balances, which shall from time to time be due from him, as the said court has directed or shall hereafter direct, THEN and in such an event this bond or obligation shall be void and of no effect, otherwise it shall remain in full force and virtue.

Signed, sealed and delivered AB

CD

Bond by Manager of Property of Mentally ill Person[5]

WHEREAS AB son of .... has been adjudged as a mentally ill person and by an Order dated .... passed in Case No. .... of .... CD has been appointed as Manager of the properties of the said AB by the District Judge, Alipore who has, under section 56 of the Mental Health Act directed CD to enter into a Bond for Rs. 50,000 with one Surety unto and in favour of the District Judge, Alipore or his Successor in office.

AND WHEREAS the said CD as Manager of the properties of the said and EF as surety hereby furnish the said Bond as called for.

NOW THE CONDITION of the Bond or obligation is that if the said CD shall honestly and faithfully manage the properties of the said AB and otherwise administer the same according to law and act and conduct himself properly in all respects then the above-written Bond shall be no effect and shall stand automatically discharged, otherwise it shall remain in full force and virtue.

5 Section 56 of the Mental Health Act provides for appointment of Manager of the properties of a mentally ill person; sections 59 to 64 of the Act lay down the duties and powers of the Manager.

I, EF son of .... do hereby declare myself surety for the above-named CD and that I will have the said CD properly discharge his duties and responsibilities as Manager of the properties of the aforesaid AB and in case of his failure or default or negligence in so doing, I bind myself to forfeit to the District Judge, Alipore or his successor in office the sum of Rs. 50,000 (Rupees fifty thousand) only.

Signed, sealed and delivered
this .... day of ...... at Alipore CD
EF

Security Bond for Stay of Execution of Decree

(Or. 41, r. 5 of CPC)

KNOW ALL MEN by these presents we, AB son of etc. (JUDGMENT-DEBTOR) and CD son of etc., (SURETY) hereby and hereunder are held and firmly bind ourselves jointly and severally to Sri .... or his successor in office for the time being in the sum of Rs. .... of lawful good money to be truly and faithfully paid, for which payment we bind ourselves and our respective heirs, executors and administrators and representatives as hereunder stated.

Sealed with our seals this .... day of ....

WHEREAS a decree for Rs. .... was made on the .... day of .... against the said AB in a suit being Suit No. .... of .... the court etc. (*cause title*) AND WHEREAS the said AB has preferred an appeal against the said decree being Appeal No. .... of .... of the court of .... which is now pending. AND WHEREAS by an order dated .... made in the said appeal the Court of Appeal has granted stay of execution of the said decree upon the said AB furnishing security to the satisfaction of the court for the sum of Rs. .... AND WHEREAS the said AB has offered the said CD as surety he having been approved by the court subject to his entering into a bond for Rs. .... creating thereunder a first charge on the undermentioned property for satisfaction of the said decree as may be confirmed or varied by the Court of Appeal.

NOW THE CONDITION of the above-written bond or obligation is such that in the event the said decree being eventually passed and/or confirmed and/or upheld in appeal, the said AB and/or CD shall pay or cause to be paid to the decree-holder the full decretal amount inclusive of interest and costs and/or shall otherwise satisfy and/or discharge the same or in case the suit is ultimately dismissed, then and in all such events the above-written bond or obligation shall stand cancelled and be of no effect and the property charged shall stand redeemed, otherwise the same shall remain in force and virtue.

PROVIDED, HOWEVER, in case the decree is modified by the Court of Appeal, the property hereunder charged shall continue to remain charged as security for whatever amount is due and payable to the decree-holder.

Schedule of the property charged

Signed, sealed and delivered AB

CD

Bond to a Firm with Surety for Securing the Faithful Service of an Employee

KNOW ALL MEN by these presents that we, M (EMPLOYEE) son of .... residing at .... and N (SURETY) son of .... residing at .... are hereby held and firmly bound unto AB and CD carrying on business in co-partnership under the name and style of .... at premises No. .... in the sum of Rs. .... (Rupees ....) of lawful good money to be paid to the said AB and CD or their successors and assigns constituting the said partnership firm for which payment is to be truly and faithfully made we bind ourselves and also our respective heirs, executors, administrators and representatives.

SEALED with our respective seals this .... day of .... 19...... WHEREAS the above-named firm has agreed to provide the EMPLOYEE with a job and for that purpose appointed him at present as the cashier and accountant combined provisionally on terms and conditions contained in an agreement bearing the same date with these presents and executed almost simultaneously and upon the said employee and the above SURETY entering into a bond in favour of the said AB and CD for the amount and on terms hereunder contained.

NOW THE CONDITION of the above-written bond or obligation is such that if the said EMPLOYEE while in employment whether in the original or in any promotion or transferred post under the said partners or the survivor of them or other person or persons for the time being constituting the firm shall duly and faithfully devote to and execute, perform and discharge all the duties of his office without causing any injury, loss or damage by reason of any act, default, negligence or error in judgment to the employer or in the alternative if the said EMPLOYEE and/or the SURETY or either of them shall from time to time and at all times hereafter indemnify and keep indemnified the said partners and other persons constituting the firm for the time being against all loss, damages, costs, charges and expenses which he or they or any of them shall or may sustain by reason of any act, default, misconduct, negligence, error in judgment, breach of duty, embezzlement and mismanagement on the part of the said employee, then and in such an event the above-written bond shall stand void and cancelled and be of no effect, otherwise the same shall remain in full force.

Signed, sealed and delivered M
In the presence of: N

Guarantee, Deposit and Charge as Security for Advances to a Third Person

To
ELH & Co.
XY Road, Calcutta

IN CONSIDERATION of your having lent and advanced to AB of etc. at my request a sum of Rs. .... (Rupees ....) as a loan or accommodation bearing interest at the rate of .... per cent per annum and such further or other sum or sums to be hereafter advanced as the said AB may require from time to time not exceeding in any case the sum total of Rs. .... (Rupees ....), all such sums to carry interest at the aforesaid rate and shall be repaid on or before the .... day of .... 2000.

I, the undersigned, do hereby stand surety for and guarantee repayment of the aforesaid loan or loans to you personally and place on record as follows:

1. I have deposited with you the title deeds/securities mentioned in the schedule hereto as collateral security for repayment of the said loan or loans with interest as aforesaid.

2. The said title deeds/securities which are all hereby pledged by me for repayment of the said loan(s) with interest or any of the properties shall not be charged, encumbered nor otherwise dealt with by me in any way without your consent first had and obtained in writing so long as the said loan(s) or any part thereof shall remain outstanding to you or any account in respect thereof unsettled.

3. I shall, whenever required by you so to do, execute at my own costs and expenses a deed or deeds of transfer such as mortgage, charge, etc., of such of the said property or properties/security or securities together with power of sale and all other necessary powers for securing and/or enforcing the payment of the said loan(s) and interest or otherwise for liquidation of the same.

4. No change whatsoever in the constitution of your firm shall impair or discharge my liability hereunder notwithstanding section 38 of the Partnership Act 1932, or any other enactment.

List of title deeds/securities

Dated this .... day ....19......

Yours faithfully
MN

Bond to Preserve Trade Secret

KNOW ALL MEN by these presents that I, B son of A hereinafter referred to as the obligor hereby firmly hold and bind myself unto X son of Y hereinafter referred to as the obligee in the sum of Rs. .... of lawful good money as agreed and liquidated damages and not as a penalty which sum to be truly and sufficiently paid for which payment I, the said B bind myself, my heirs, executors, administrators and representatives.

Dated this .... day of .... 2000.

WHEREAS the said obligee has imparted and is still to impart special knowledge to the said obligor about the secret of art or process of manufacturing a 'Patent' known as .... on the assurance and guarantee of the obligor as to preservation and maintenance of strict secrecy and confidence thereof for which purpose to give a bond or obligation as is hereafter given.

Sealed with my seal this .... day of .... 2000.

NOW THE ABOVE-WRITTEN BOND OR OBLIGATION is conditioned to be void in case the said obligor shall at all times hereafter whether in service or not under or otherwise connected with or not with the obligee well and truly keep, preserve and maintain or cause to be kept, preserved and maintained the secrecy of the said art or process and never to reveal the same to anyone under any circumstances, otherwise the same shall remain in full force and virtue.

Signed, sealed and delivered B

Indemnity Bond in Case of Loss or Non-production of Title Deeds

KNOW ALL MEN BY THESE PRESENTS that I, AB (VENDOR) of etc. hereby hold and firmly bind myself unto CD .... (PURCHASER) of etc. in the sum of Rs. .... of good and lawful money to be paid to the purchaser, his heirs, etc., for which payment to be truly and faithfully made, I bind myself, my heirs, executors, administrators and representatives.

Sealed with my seal this .... day of .... 19 ....

WHEREAS by an agreement dated etc. and made between the parties hereto, it was witnessed that the said AB (vendor) agreed to sell and the said CD (purchaser) agreed to purchase subject to a good and marketable title being made out All That Piece or Parcel of land, hereditament etc. fully mentioned and described in Schedule A hereto as an estate in fee simple and free from encumbrances, attachments, trust and lien, etc. at and for the sum of Rs. .... AND WHEREAS in course of the investigation of the title of the said vendor it appeared that certain documents, namely, the documents mentioned or described in Schedule 'B' to these presents which are essential and necessary links in the chain of title were reported as missing not being in the possession of the vendor or anybody else on his behalf to his knowledge and it is not further known up till now in whose possession or custody and power the same were or are or likely to be at present. AND WHEREAS in answers to the Requisitions on Title the vendor has declared them as lost or mislaid and not pledged or deposited anywhere as security for any debt or claim AND WHEREAS the said purchaser on such declaration and assurance of the vendor as aforesaid has agreed to complete the said purchase upon the said vendor executing the conveyance of the said premises in favour of the said purchaser with all usual covenants including the covenant as to indemnity but nevertheless and in addition thereto upon the vendor entering into the above-written obligation conditioned as hereinafter expressed for the protection and indemnity of the purchaser. Now the above-written bond or obligation is conditioned to be void only in either of the cases following, that is to say:

1. In case all the said documents be hereafter discovered anywhere and shall be delivered to the said purchaser or his heirs, executors, administrators or assigns free of any costs, charges and expenses on that account and be effectually discharged from any estate, right, title interest or claim, demand etc. whatsoever if any in, to or upon the said premises acquired by any third party or parties adverse to or in derogation of the title of the said purchaser, his heirs, executors, administrators or assigns under or by virtue of the said documents or any of them.

2. Alternatively if for a period of 12 years or more from the date of these presents the purchaser, his heirs, etc., shall peacefully and quietly hold, possess and enjoy the said lands, hereditaments and premises, etc., without any claim, demand, interruption or disturbance whatsoever by any person or persons claiming any right, title or interest in the said property under or by virtue of the said documents or any of them, otherwise the same shall remain in full force and virtue and the said AB (*vendor*), his heirs, executors, administrators shall at all times hereafter remain liable for and shall fully and effectually indemnify and keep indemnified the said CD (*purchaser*), his heirs, executors, administrators and assigns against all loss and damage, costs, charges and expenses which he or they or any one of them may be put to or reasonably incur or suffer by reason thereof the said documents not having been delivered to the purchaser simultaneously with the completion of the said purchase.

A

Schedule of the property sold

B

Schedule of the title deeds not delivered

Signed, sealed and delivered
at .... in the presence of: AB

Indemnity Bond

In case of non-production of Title Deeds (another form)

BY THE PRESENT INDEMNITY BOND executed by me on this .... day of ....2000, I, AB s/o MN residing at .... (hereinafter called the OBLIGOR) my successors and legal representatives in favour of C s/o XY residing at .... hereinafter called the OBLIGEE, which expression shall mean and include his heirs, successors and legal representatives, in the sum of Rs. .... of lawful money paid to me by the said C.

Signed by me with my seal this .... day of .... 2000.

WHEREAS by an agreement dated .... made between the parties, I, the OBLIGOR, agreed to sell and the said OBLIGEE agreed to purchase subject to a good and marketable title being made out the property situated in which is fully mentioned and described in Schedule 'A' annexed hereto and which is free from all encumbrances, attachments, trust and lien, etc. for the sum of Rs. .... (Rupees .... only) AND WHEREAS in course of the investigation of my title it has transpired that the documents described in Schedule 'B' to these presents which are essential and necessary to complete the title are missing and are not being in my possession or anybody else on my behalf to my knowledge and it is not further known up till now in whose possession or custody and power the same were or are likely to be at present.

AND WHEREAS in answer to the requisitions on title I have declared them as lost or mislaid and not pledged or deposited anywhere as security for any debt or claim.

AND WHEREAS the said OBLIGEE on such declaration given by me as aforesaid agreed to complete the said purchase upon my executing the conveyance of the said premises in his favour with all usual covenants including the covenant as to indemnity but nevertheless and in addition thereto upon my entering into the above-written obligation conditioned as hereinafter expressed for the protection and indemnity of the purchaser. Now the above-written bond or obligation is conditioned to be void only in either of the cases following, that is to say:

1. In case all the said documents shall be hereafter discovered anywhere and delivered to the said purchaser or his heirs, executors, administrators or assigns free of any costs, charges and expenses on that account.

2. Alternatively if for a period of over twelve years from the date of these presents the purchaser, his heirs, etc. shall peacefully and quietly hold, possess and enjoy the said lands, hereditaments and premises, etc., without any claim, demand, interruption or disturbance whatsoever by any person or persons claiming any right, title or interest in the said property under or

by virtue of the said documents or any of them, otherwise the same shall remain in full force and virtue and I, my heirs, executors, administrators, shall at all times hereafter remain liable for and shall fully and effectually indemnify and keep indemnified the said (PURCHASER) his heirs, executors, administrators and assigns against all losses and damages, costs, charges and expenses which he or they or any one of them may be put to or reasonably incur or suffer by reason of the fact of the said documents not having been delivered to the purchaser simultaneously with the completion of the said purchase.

Schedule 'A'

Schedule 'B'

Signed, sealed and delivered AB

Indemnity Bond with a Surety in Favour of a Bank on the Death of an Account-holder

By the present indemnity bond, I, namely, P, s/o .... r/o .... hereinafter called the PRINCIPAL OBLIGANT and S, s/o .... r/o .... hereinafter called the SURETY, are hereby held and firmly bind ourselves to People's Bank Limited, Chandni Chowk Branch, New Delhi, in the sum of Rs. .... (Rupees .... only) of lawful good money for which payment to be truly and faithfully made, we bind ourselves as well as our respective heirs, executors, administrators and representatives.

Sealed with our seal this .... day of .... 19......

WHEREAS one E since deceased had at the time of his death which occurred on the day of .... 2000, the following accounts with the said bank (or etc.) namely (GIVE PARTICULARS).

AND WHEREAS one C claims the proceeds of the said accounts as sole heir of the said late E and further represent that inasmuch as the deceased had died intestate, no representation to the estate was necessary.

AND WHEREAS the bank has agreed to pay the proceeds of the said accounts to the said C aggregating to Rs. .... on his furnishing security with one surety in terms hereunder contained. Now the condition of the above-written bond or obligation is such that in the event of any claim being at any time hereafter made to the proceeds of the said accounts by any other person or persons whomsoever if the said P and S shall forthwith pay or cause to be paid to the bank the said sum of Rs. .... with interest at 12% per annum and further pay for all losses, damages, costs, charges and expenses which bank may suffer and/or otherwise indemnify and keep indemnified the bank, its officers and agents in all other respects on account therefor, then and in such an event the above-written bond or obligation shall be void, otherwise the same shall remain in full force and virtue.

IN WITNESS, whereof the said P and S have signed, sealed and delivered this bond on day, month and the year first above-mentioned.

Signed, sealed and delivered in the
presence of the witnesses:

WITNESSES:

1. Name .... P
   Address ....
2. Name .... S
   Address ....

Indemnity to a Company and its Directors on Issue of a Duplicate to Replace Lost Share Certificate (O)

To ELH Limited and AB, CD
and EF its Directors

Gentlemen

I have lost or mislaid the certificate of title dated .... and numbered .... relating to .... (fully paid up) (Ordinary) Shares Folio number in the above-named Company of (Rs. 10) each numbered .... to .... both inclusive and of which I am the registered holder.

The said certificate has not been pledged or deposited by me by way of security, nor have I sold or transferred any of the shares to which it relates, and I am entitled to the custody of the certificate of title relating to such shares.

I request you to issue to me a fresh certificate of title to the said shares and I hereby undertake to indemnify you and each of you against all proceedings, claims, expenses and liabilities whatsoever which may be taken or made against or incurred by you or any of you by reason of the issue of such fresh certificate or the registration of a transfer of the said shares or any of them without the production of the said original certificate.

Dated the .... day of .... 2000.

WITNESS to the Signature
of the said .... Signed XY (Shareholder)

Deed of Guarantee by a Bank on Behalf of a Company for the Performance of a Contract in Favour of State Government

THIS DEED OF GUARANTEE MADE THIS .... day of .... BETWEEN the Bank of Credit (hereinafter called the BANK) of the one part and the State of West Bengal represented by its Governor Sri .... (hereinafter called the STATE) of the other part.

WHEREAS by Acceptance of Tender No. .... dated .... made between X Ltd. a COMPANY incorporated under the Indian Companies Act having its registered office at .... (hereinafter called the COMPANY) it was witnessed that the COMPANY agreed with the State of West Bengal for supply of plants, machinery and equipment in accordance with terms, specifications and conditions therein contained which *inter alia* provided for an advance of Rs. 2 lakhs being equivalent to 10% of the total F.O.B. value of the contract price (such payment to be secured by a Bank Guarantee);

AND WHEREAS the BANK has at the request of the COMPANY agreed to stand surety for and guarantee refund of the said advance in case the plants, machinery and equipment of the value 20 lakhs aforesaid is not delivered to the State of West Bengal in accordance with the terms and conditions of the said agreement, and the STATE of .... agreed to make the said advance on such bank's guarantee as aforesaid:

NOW THIS DEED WITNESSES AS FOLLOWS:

1. In consideration of the STATE of .... having agreed to advance a sum of .... to the COMPANY, through the BANK, for the purpose hereinbefore indicated, the BANK do hereby guarantee that in case the COMPANY shall fail and/or neglect to supply the STATE the plants, machinery and equipment of the value of ....in accordance with the specifications and conditions contained in the Acceptance of Tender dated the .... subject to any amendments or modifications thereof, if any, when made, the BANK shall repay to the STATE such amount or amounts, as the BANK may be called upon to pay subject to the maximum limit of ....

2. This guarantee of the BANK shall be effective immediately upon receipt of the sum of .... from the STATE for and on behalf of the COMPANY and shall continue in force until and unless the supply of plants, machinery and equipment of the value of .... aforesaid is fully effected.

3. The guarantee hereinbefore contained shall not be affected by any change in the constitution of the BANK or of the company nor in the event of any winding-up order being made against the COMPANY.

IN WITNESS WHEREOF the parties hereto have set and subscribed their respective hands and seals the day, month and year first above-written.

For and on behalf of the State
of West Bengal Bank of Credit

1. ....
2. ....

Guarantee for the Performance of a Contract

THIS DEED OF GUARANTEE made the .... day of ....BETWEEN GB son of etc. (hereinafter called the GUARANTOR) which expression shall .... of the one part and PD son of .... etc. (hereinafter called the PRINCIPAL) which expression shall .... of the other part.

WHEREAS BY AN AGREEMENT dated .... made between CF son of etc., therein referred to as *the contractor* of the one part and the said PD therein referred to as PRINCIPAL of the other part, it was *inter alia* agreed by and between the parties as follows:

(*State the nature of work to be done by the contractor*).

AND WHEREAS the said work was entrusted to the contractor upon the GUARANTOR having agreed with the PRINCIPAL as to its guarantee of performance by the contractor and to indemnify and keep indemnified the principal against all losses, damages, costs, charges and expenses arising out of performance or non-performance thereof. Now it is agreed and declared by and between the parties as follows:

1. The GUARANTOR will see that the contractor unless relieved from the performance by operation of any clause of the contract or by statute or by virtue of the decision of any tribunal or court of competent jurisdiction, shall carry out, execute and perform the contract without any exception or reservation and in case he commits any breach thereof the guarantor will indemnify and keep indemnified the PRINCIPAL and his estate against all losses, damages, costs, expenses, or otherwise which he may suffer or otherwise incur by reason of any act, negligence, default or error in judgment on the part of the contractor in performing or non-performing the contract.

2. In case of any dispute or difference as regards the quantum of such losses or damages or costs, charges and expenses, the same shall be decided by reference to arbitration of one architect or engineer if the parties so agree or otherwise of two architects or engineers, one to be appointed by each, the two would appoint an Umpire and whose decision shall be final and binding on all parties.

In witness whereof the parties hereto have hereunto set and subscribed their respective hands and seals the day, month and year first above-written:

Signed, sealed and delivered GB
in the presence of:

General Form of Security Bond to be Executed by an Employee with Two Sureties

Know all men by this Security Bond we, AB (employee) of, etc. etc. and CD (*first surety*) of etc. etc. and EF (*second surety*) of etc. are firmly held and bound unto GH (employer) of etc., in the sum of Rupees .... (Rs. ....) only of lawful good money to be paid to the said employer, or his heirs, executors, administrators and representatives for which payment will and truly to be made, we bind ourselves and our respective heirs, executors, administrators and representatives jointly, severally and respectively.

Sealed with our seals this .... day of .... 2000.

Whereas the above-bound AB was on the .... day of .... 2000 provided with a job under the employer and now holds and exercises the office of Cashier in terms of an agreement dated .... made between the said AB and the employer (or in terms of the letter of appointment dated .... issued by the employer) and whereas by virtue of such office and other office or offices so which the employee may hereafter be promoted or transferred or appointed the said employee is presently and in future will be entrusted with the care and responsibility of handling and keeping in safe custody of various money, currency, shares and other valuable securities, papers, documents and also property and goods belonging to the employer subject to the supervision and check of the employer or any person appointed by him and whereas the employee in such course of employment is also bound to keep and maintain or cause to be kept and maintained a true and faithful account of the said money, shares, securities etc.

Now the condition of the above-written bond or obligation is such that if the employee shall all along during the continuity of his service under the employer whether, in the original or in any promoted or transferred post, keep and maintain or cause to be kept and maintained a true and proper account of all such money, cash, shares, securities, etc., and/or otherwise always duly and faithfully perform and discharge the duties of such office or offices which he shall hold and exercise for the time being or in the alternative if the said AB, CD and EF shall indemnify and keep indemnified the employer, his heirs, executors, administrators or assigns against all and every loss and damage or injury caused to and costs, charges and expenses incurred by the employer by reason of any act, default, error in judgment on the part of the said AB, then the above-written bond or obligation shall be void and of no effect, otherwise the same shall be and remain in full force and virtue.

PROVIDED, HOWEVER, notwithstanding anything hereinbefore contained, it is hereby mutually agreed and declared by and between the parties that none of the two sureties, viz., the said CD and EF shall in any case be at liberty or shall have the power to terminate their suretyship under this bond except upon giving to the employer three weeks' prior notice in writing of his or their intention so to do and in any event such termination shall not take effect and so be without prejudice to the right of the employer to seek redress on all claims then already arisen and this bond shall, accordingly, continue and remain valid in respect of all acts, defaults, omissions, error in judgment on the part of the employee as against them as their past liability under this bond.

IN WITNESS WHEREOF we have hereto set our respective hands and seal this .... day of .... 2000.

Signed, sealed and delivered CD
in the presence of: EF

Indemnity Bond by Building Contractor

BY THIS BOND we, AB of, etc., (BUILDER), and CD of, etc., (*surety*), are jointly and severally held and firmly bound unto EF of, etc., (OWNER), in the sum of Rupees ...., to be paid to the said EF or his heirs, executors, administrators or assigns, for which payment to be truly and faithfully made, we bind ourselves, and each of us, and also our respective heirs, executors, administrators or assigns, jointly and severally, by these presents.

Sealed with our seal ...., this .... day of ....

WHEREAS the said AB has entered into a contract with the said EF to build and complete a certain dwelling house with buildings and out-buildings thereto (*or*, etc.) in accordance with the plans and specifications which have already been agreed upon and kept signed by the said AB and EF within .... calendar months from the date hereof, upon a piece or parcel of land, situate at, etc., for the sum of Rs. .... AND WHEREAS it is expressly provided in the said contract that the said AB would enter into a bond with one surety in terms hereinbefore contained: NOW THE CONDITION of the above-written bond or obligation is such that, if the said AB shall duly and punctually, within .... calendar months aforesaid, build, complete and finish the said dwelling-house with the out-buildings thereto (*or*, etc.) in accordance with the said plans and specifications to the reasonable satisfaction of the said EF and his architect, or surveyor (delay caused by fire accident, mob violence, attack from the air or strikes of workmen or other major disturbances only excepted), THEN, and in such an event the above-written bond shall be void, but otherwise it shall remain in full force and virtue.

IN WITNESS WHEREOF ETC.

Signed, sealed and delivered AB
CD

Indemnity Bond against Possible Claim of a Co-sharer believed to be Dead

THIS DEED OF INDEMNITY made this .... day of BETWEEN AB son of etc. (VENDOR) of the one part and CD son of etc. (PURCHASER) of the other part.

WHEREAS by a conveyance bearing even date with these presents made between the parties hereto the property mentioned and described in the schedule below was granted, conveyed, sold, transferred and assigned by the said AB unto and in favour of the said CD.

AND WHEREAS the said property was owned by the said AB jointly with his brother EF who left home on or about the 5th day of ...... and has not since returned nor been heard of at all in spite of diligent enquiries and is believed to be dead AND WHEREAS the said EF was unmarried at the time when he left home and as such he could not have left any heir other than the vendor. AND WHEREAS ever since the said EF left home, the vendor was at all times and is still now openly in exclusive use, possession, control and enjoyment of the entirety of the said property to all intents and purposes and thus declared himself to be its sole and absolute owner. AND WHEREAS the vendor agreed to sell the said property and the purchaser agreed to purchase the same subject to the vendor executing a separate deed of indemnity in favour of the purchaser in terms hereunder contained.

NOW THIS DEED OF INDEMNITY witnesseth that in consideration of the purchaser having purchased the property on the assurance and guarantee of the vendor as to protection and indemnity against any possible claim by the said EF if he is discovered to be still alive or by any person or persons through or under him the vendor do hereby and hereunder agree to indemnify and at all times keep indemnified the purchaser and his heirs, executors, administrators and representatives and also estate against all such possible claims or demands made or any actions and proceedings, if any, commenced by the said EF if alive or by any person or persons claiming through or under him in respect of the said property and also against all costs, charges and expenses reasonably incurred for defending any such claim, action or proceedings

The Schedule of the property sold

IN WITNESS WHEREOF, etc.

Signed, sealed and delivered AB

Indemnity Bond in favour of Bank or Limited Company

KNOW ALL MEN by these presents we, AB of, etc., (PRINCIPAL DEBTOR), and CD of, etc. (SURETY), are hereby held and firmly bind ourselves unto .... bank, a company etc., in the sum of Rs. .... of lawful good money for which payment to be truly and faithfully made, we bind ourselves as well as our respective heirs, executors, administrators and representatives.

Sealed with our seal this day of .... 2000.

WHEREAS one EF since deceased had at the time of his death which occurred on the day of 2000 the following accounts with the said bank (or, etc.), namely, etc.: AND WHEREAS the said AB claims the proceeds of the said accounts as the sole heir of the said late EF and further represented that inasmuch as the deceased had died intestate, no representation to the estate was necessary and, as such, the same has not been taken out. AND WHEREAS the bank has agreed to pay the proceeds of the said accounts to the said AB aggregating to Rs. .... on his furnishing security with one surety in terms hereunder contained. Now the condition of the above-written bond or obligation is such that in the event of any claim being at any time hereafter made to the proceeds of the said accounts by any other person or persons if the said AB and CD shall forthwith pay or cause to be paid to the bank the said sum of Rs. .... with interest at 18% per annum and further pay for all losses, damages, costs, charges and expenses which the bank may reasonably incur or suffer and/or otherwise indemnify and keep indemnified the bank, its officers and agents in all other respects on account therefor, then and in such an event the above-written bond or obligation shall be void, otherwise the same shall remain in full force and virtue.

IN WITNESS, etc.

Signed, sealed and delivered AB

CD

Bottomry Bond[6]

BY THIS BOND, I, AB of, etc., Master of the ship, etc., of the port of, etc., official number ...., am held and firmly bound to CD of, etc., in the sum of Rupees ...., for which payment will and truly to be made to the said CD, his heirs, executors, administrators and assign, I hereby bind myself, my heirs, executors and administrators firmly by these presents.

AND for further security of the said CD, I, the said AB, do by these presents pledge the said ship and her freight, together with her tackle and apparel

6 Now obsolete in practice. See Halsbury's *Laws of England*, 4th Ed., vol. 43, p. 138.

(*if necessary, add*—and also the cargo now on board the said ship); AND IT IS HEREBY DECLARED that the said ship and her freight (and cargo) are thus pledged for the security of the money advanced to me, and shall not be pledged or mortgaged to any other person until payment of this bond is first made, with the interest that may become due thereon. Sealed with my seal at ...., this .... day of ....

WHEREAS the above-named ship having been compelled to put into the port, of, etc., for repairs and necessaries AND WHEREAS the owners of the said ship and her freight, and the shippers and consignees of the cargo on board of her, having refused to provide the money required to pay for the said repairs and necessaries, the above-bound AB has been compelled to borrow at bottomry and has received from the said CD the sum of Rs. ...., which sum is to run at bottomry on the hull and freight of the said ship from the port of, etc., on a voyage to the port of, etc., (*if necessary add*—having permission to touch, stay at and proceed to all ports and places within the limits of the voyage), at the rate of .... per cent. for the voyage: Now THE CONDITION of this bond is such that, if the above-bound AB, his heirs, executors or administrators shall pay or cause to be paid to the said CD, his heirs, executors, administrators or assign, the sum of Rs. .... being the principal of the bond, together with the interest which shall become due thereon, within 30 days after the safe arrival of the ship at her place of discharge in the port of, etc., or in case the said ship be lost during the said voyage THEN and in such an event this obligation and pledge shall be void and of no effect, otherwise it is to remain in full force and effect.

Three bonds of the same tenor and date have been signed, the one of which being accomplished, the others to be void and of no effect.

Signed, sealed and delivered
at .... in
the presence of:

Signature of the Master

10

Cancellation of Documents

When the parties to a deed agree that the deed should not operate, it is necessary that the deed should be returned to the executant and a deed of cancellation should be executed. Such a deed should be registered if the original deed had been registered.

Forms

Agreement to Rescind a Contract

THIS AGREEMENT is made this .... day of...........BETWEEN AB son of .... residing at .... of the one part and CD son of .... residing at............of the other part.

WHEREAS by an agreement dated the .... day of ...., and made between the said AB and the said CD, the said CD agreed to erect, construct and build for the said AB at .... a dwelling house etc. on the terms and conditions therein mentioned: AND WHEREAS differences having arisen between the said AB and the said CD regarding the terms, conditions and implications of the said agreement, the parties hereto have agreed to rescind the said agreement: NOW IT IS HEREBY AGREED as follows:

1. The aforesaid agreement made on the .... day of ...., be and is hereby rescinded.

2. That on adjustment of the account between the parties of all sums paid by the said AB and all work done, executed or performed by the said CD a further sum of Rs. .... is found due and payable to the said CD which the said CD doth hereby admit, acknowledge and confirm to have received from the said AB.

3. Each party releases the other from the obligation arising out of performance or non-performance of the contract under the aforesaid agreement.

IN WITNESS WHEREOF the parties hereto have executed these presents on the day, month and year first above-written.

Signed and delivered by AB

Signed and delivered by CD

WITNESS:

Deed of Cancellation

THIS DEED OF CANCELLATION made this .... day of .... 2000 BETWEEN P (hereinafter referred to as the PURCHASER) of the one part AND V (hereinafter referred to as the VENDOR) of the other part:

WHEREAS by an Agreement ...... made between the parties hereto and registered in the office of the Sub-Registrar of .... Book No. I, Vol. ...... Pages ...... being No. .... for the year 1998 it was witnessed that the party hereto of the 1st part agreed to purchase the property fully mentioned in the Schedule thereto as also in the Schedule hereunder written and hereinafter referred to as the said property at and for the sum of Rs. .... on terms contained therein.

AND WHEREAS the party of the 1st part paid to the party of the 2nd part a sum of Rs. ...... as earnest money ...... on the basis of the said agreement.

AND WHEREAS the said sum of Rs. .... was in terms of the said agreement secured by a charge on the said property.

AND WHEREAS the said agreement is in full force and virtue.

AND WHEREAS it has now been agreed by and between the parties hereto that the party of the 2nd part shall refund to the party of the 1st part the said sum of Rs. .... and also pay a further sum of Rs. .... on account of all his costs, charges and expenses for searches, investigation of title and on other accounts whereupon the said agreement shall stand cancelled.

AND WHEREAS the party of the 2nd part has refunded to the party of the 1st part the said sum of Rs. ...... and paid Rs. .... as aforesaid which the party of the 1st part doth hereby as also by the receipt hereunder written, admit, acknowledge and confirm.

AND WHEREAS the party of the 2nd part has also returned to the party of the 1st part the said agreement for sale dated the .... endorsed as cancelled. NOW THIS INDENTURE WITNESSETH that for the consideration as aforesaid the party hereto of the 1st part doth hereby agree, declare and confirm that he has no longer any right, title, claim or interest in the said property under and by virtue of the hereinbefore recited agreement for sale which stands cancelled with immediate effect and shall hereafter be of no force and effect whatsoever AND FURTHER that the party of the 1st part doth hereby and hereunder grant, release, discharge, reassure the said property and every part thereof unto and to the party of the 2nd part freed and discharged from the charge, security, claim, created thereon under and by virtue of the said recited agreement for sale as aforesaid and all claims, demand, cause of action arising out of or in connection with the same AND the party of the 1st part doth hereby covenant with the party of the 2nd part that he has not done any act, deed or thing whereby or by reason or means whereof he is prevented or hindered from cancelling the said agreement for sale and/or releasing and reassuring the said property in the manner as aforesaid.

The Schedule above referred to

OR HOWSOEVER OTHERWISE the same may be butted, bounded, called, known, numbered, described or distinguished.

IN WITNESS WHEREOF the party of the 1st part doth hereunder set and subscribe his hand and seal the day, month and year first above-written.

Signed, sealed and delivered
at .... in the presence of: P

Deed of Cancellation of a Conveyance

THIS INDENTURE made this .... day of .... 1999 BETWEEN AB son of .... etc. hereinafter referred to as the PURCHASER which expression shall .... of the one part AND CD son of .... hereinafter referred to as the VENDOR which expression shall ...... of the other part WHEREAS by conveyance dated ...... day of ...... 19......... made between the parties hereto and registered in Book I, Vol. ...., Pages ...... to ...... being No. .... for the year .... in the Office of the Registrar of ...... it was witnessed that the VENDOR had for the consideration mentioned therein purported to grant, convey, sell, transfer, assign and assure the under mentioned property unto and to the use of the PURCHASER absolutely and for ever so as to enable the purchaser to have, hold, own, possess and enjoy the same peacefully and quietly without any claim, demand, interruption by any person or persons on behalf of and/or claiming under the VENDOR and to receive the rents, issues and other profits and benefits of the property AND WHEREAS the said conveyance though contained *inter alia* all the necessary covenants as are usual on the part of a VENDOR in the case of a sale of the property of that nature, viz. the covenant as to good title, peaceful possession, non-encumbrance, further assurance and indemnity, but nevertheless, the same could not be acted upon or otherwise given effect to inasmuch as the VENDOR did not and further could not deliver possession of the property up till now owing to obstruction and/or resistance as to such delivery of possession created by several persons still residing in the said property. AND WHEREAS the PURCHASER has in the circumstances aforesaid been kept out of possession of the said property and so deprived of all its rents, issues and other profits and other benefits thereof and also of all benefits of the moneys invested AND WHEREAS in the event hereinbefore stated the conveyance has been infructuous to all intents and purposes AND WHEREAS in the circumstances hereinbefore stated the parties have mutually agreed and decided to be relieved of their respective liabilities arising out of the transaction of sale by having the said conveyance cancelled against refund of the consideration money only all other accounts between them having been settled and adjusted AND WHEREAS the said PURCHASER has returned the said conveyance to the VENDOR endorsed as "cancelled" thereon and the VENDOR has also refunded the consideration money to the PURCHASER which the PURCHASER do hereby admit, acknowledge and confirm NOW THIS INDENTURE WITNESSETH that for the consideration as aforesaid the parties hereto do hereby mutually agree and declare the said conveyance shall be and has in fact and truth been cancelled with immediate effect (as if the same was never executed or brought into existence) and as such the same was and shall be of no force and effect hereafter and This Indenture Further Witnesseth that parties hereto further agree and declare that in consequence of such cancellation as hereunder made all right, title, interest and claim, demand, etc. of the purchaser in the property concerned under and by virtue of the purported deed of conveyance are hereby retransferred, reassigned, and reassured shall be deemed as completely divested, extinguished and discharged and reverted fully to and vested in the VENDOR as his former estate and they are both placed in the same position in which they were before the sale and This Indenture furthermore witnesseth that the parties hereby mutually agree and covenant to each other that neither of them has done, executed or performed any act, deed or thing or suffered anything to the contrary whereby or by reason or means whereof the said property may in any way be affected or prejudiced in title or estate or the parties or any of them may be hindered or prevented from cancelling the said Indenture of Conveyance and releasing and re-transferring the said property unto and to the use of the VENDOR in the manner hereinbefore indicated.

The Schedule above referred to

IN WITNESS WHEREOF:

Signed, sealed and delivered AB
at .... in the presence of: CD

Deed of Revocation of Trust

THIS DEED OF REVOCATION OF TRUST is made this the .... day of ...., BETWEEN AB of, etc., (hereinafter called the SETTLOR), of the one part and CD of etc., and EF of etc. (hereinafter called the TRUSTEES) of the other part.

WHEREAS by a deed of trust made the ...... day of .... I, the SETTLOR, transferred the properties described therein as also in the schedule hereto upon trust for the objects specified therein AND WHEREAS XY a beneficiary under the said deed of trust having since died the said objects failed AND whereas, I, the SETTLOR, having also reserved free power and authority to revoke the trust am desirous of creating a fresh trust after revoking the said trust NOW THIS DEED OF REVOCATION OF TRUST WITNESSES that in the exercise of the power of revocation expressly reserved in the said deed of trust and all other powers enabling me, I, the said AB hereby and hereunder revoke and determine the trust created by the aforesaid deed of trust to all intents and purposes as if the same was never created nor intended.

IN WITNESS, etc.

The Schedule above referred to

Signed, sealed and delivered AB

CD

EF

Deed of Cancellation

THIS AGREEMENT IS MADE at Calcutta the 10th day of January 2000 BETWEEN Mr. X of .... hereinafter referred to as the first party and Mr. Z of .... hereinafter referred to as the second party.

WHEREAS the first party has executed a Deed of Conveyance on the .... day of .... in favour of the second party in respect of the land and premises situated at .... and more particularly described in the Schedule to the said Deed.

AND WHEREAS the second party had agreed to pay to the first party a sum of Rs. 5,00,000 as consideration for the sale of said land and premises for the said amount but the second party failed and neglected to pay and has admitted his inability to pay the said sum.

AND WHEREAS the title to the said property was intended to be passed to the second party on payment of the said amount.

AND WHEREAS the possession of the said property has not yet been given to the second party.

AND WHEREAS the said Deed of Conveyance has been lodged for registration with the Registrar of Assurances at Red Cross Place, Calcutta but the first party has not yet admitted the execution thereof.

AND WHEREAS the second party was unable to make arrangement for payment of the said consideration money, the first party and second party have therefore agreed to cancel the said Deed of Conveyance and they have also agreed to cancel the said agreement and do hereby record the said agreement of cancellation.

NOW IT IS AGREED AND DECLARED by the parties hereto that in view of inability of the purchaser to pay the consideration money the parties hereto by mutual consent do hereby cancel the said Deed of Conveyance and agree and confirm that the same is cancelled and shall be deemed to be and treated as cancelled and never to have been acted upon.

AND it is agreed and confirmed that the said property has not passed to the second party and second party does not claim any right, title or interest in the said property under or by virtue of the said Deed of Conveyance.

AND it is further agreed and declared that all costs, charges and expenses including the stamp duty and registration fees in respect of the Deed of Conveyance and of these presents are to be borne and paid by the second party wholly.

IN WITNESS WHEREOF the parties have executed these presents on the day, month and year first above-written.

Signed and delivered by the
within-named first party Mr. X
in the presence of: Signature

Signed and delivered by the
within-named second party Mr. Z
in the presence of: Signature

11

Clubs and Societies

Halsbury in his *Laws of England* has defined club as a club except a proprietary club or an investment club may be defined as a society of persons associated together, not for the purposes of trade, but for social reasons, the promotion of politics, sport, art, science or literature, or for any other lawful purpose; but trading activities will not destroy the nature of a club if they are merely incidental to the club's purposes. The association must be private and have some element of permanence. The purposes for which a club exists may be altered or modified, and there is no rule of law which requires a club to fulfil each and every separate purpose for which it was originally formed. Once the mutual assent of the members has been secured, the doctrine of *ultra vires* has no place with respect to the activities of such an association.[1]

A club may be of two kinds, *viz.*—(*i*) a members' club or (*ii*) a proprietary club. The properties of the club generally vest in the members, while in the latter case an individual or a limited company or a society as the case may be owns the property nevertheless the members are allowed to make use of that property on certain terms. The members' club may be an unincorporated society or may be registered under the Companies Act (Act 1 of 1956) or Societies Registration Act (Act XXVI of 1981). A proprietary club is run by the owner or the owners, as the case may be, for purposes of gain, while in a members' club it is not so. It is necessary in a society or club so registered that the Memorandum of Association should contain the name of the society, the objects of the society, the names, addresses and occupations of the governors, council, directors, committee or other governing body to whom, by the rules of the society, the management of its affairs is entrusted. A copy of the rules and regulations of the society, certified to be a correct copy by not less than three members of the governing body has to be filed

1 Halsbury's *Laws of England*, 4th Ed., vol. 6, p. 56.

with the Memorandum of Association with the Registrar of Companies or Society as the case may be of the State. The proceedings of such a society must conform to the provisions of the Societies Registration Act. If the members' club is registered under the Companies Act 1956 it must also conform with the provisions of that Act.

In an unincorporated club the liability of an individual member (even if he be a secretary or other office-bearer of the club) for debts incurred by the club depends upon whether he has in any way pledged his personal credits.

FORMS

Memorandum for Businessmen's Club

(1) The name of the club shall be .... Businessmen's Club.

(2) The objects of the club are:

(*a*) to provide for a common place for meeting of the members of the club for the purposes of recreation, discussion of common problems, encouragement of thrift, advancement of social welfare ideas, mutual assistance, protection of interests of the members, etc.;

(*b*) to provide for instruction and diffusion of knowledge amongst the families of members, their dependants and employees;

(*c*) to provide for medical assistance and other relief measures for the members, their dependants and employees;

(*d*) to develop civic consciousness, to raise standard of living and to take steps for development and enactment of appropriate legislation for the interests of the members and the business community;

(*e*) and for other objects and purposes which may be conducive to and beneficial for the members and the business community.

(3) No person other than a businessman shall be eligible to be a member of the club.

(4) The subscribers to this Memorandum of Association shall be the original members of the club. The total number of members of the club shall not exceed 200 unless in a special general meeting the number is altered by a three-fourth majority of the members present.

(5) There shall be a committee of management consisting of seven members (besides Chairman, Secretary and Treasurer) elected at the annual general meeting of the club to be held in the month of April each year or as early as possible thereafter. Three members of the committee shall retire every year voluntarily or by lot. There shall be elected also a chairman, a secretary and a treasurer respectively at the annual general meeting after

the election of the members of the managing committee who shall hold office till the termination of the next annual general meeting at which the office-bearers inclusive of the members of the managing committee have been elected for the next ensuing year. The property of the club shall vest in the managing committee and in the event of any member of such committee dying or having been expelled or having become incapable of acting the said properties of the club shall continue to vest in the remaining members of the managing committee which may include also any member annually added thereto.

(6) No new member shall be elected unless he has deposited a proposal fee of Rs. .... and subscription for the first three months. This deposit shall be known as proposal fee which shall belong absolutely to the club irrespective of the fact whether the proposed candidate has been elected or not. In the event of the proposed candidate not being elected the subscription aforementioned shall be returned to him and he will not be eligible for being elected till the expiry of six months from the date of such rejection of his proposal for election. No new deposit, however, will be required to be made by him if he seeks election at a subsequent time. A member shall be deemed to be duly elected if three-fourths of the members present vote in his favour for election. A person who has ceased to be a member and desires to be re-admitted to the club as a member may be so admitted by deposit of any proposal fee provided he had not been expelled from the club and provided there is no objection to his readmission by one-fourth of the total number of members of the club who signify their dissent to his re-admission in writing. Candidates for admission must be proposed by one member and seconded by another, and the name of the candidate in full with his address shall be inserted in the candidate's book, and placed in some conspicuous part of the club for 14 days. The election of the member shall be by ballot.

(7) There shall be payable by each member a monthly subscription of Rs. .... which is subject to alteration in an annual general meeting at which at least three-fourths majority must be more than one-half of the total number of members of the club.

(8) A member may resign in writing at any time and his resignation shall take effect immediately but without prejudice to any liability or obligation incurred by him theretofore while he was a member. He shall cease to have any interest in the property of the club or exercise any rights in respect thereto at such resignation submitted by him in writing to the secretary.

(9) If the conduct of any member either in or out of the club houses shall in the opinion of the committee or of any 21 members of the club who shall certify the same in writing, be injurious to the character, reputation and interests of the club or who is alleged to be guilty of any dishonourable or disreputable conduct in his dealings with a member of the club, the committee after such enquiry as may be necessary and after giving

opportunity to the member concerned to explain his conduct in writing, shall be empowered to request such member to resign, and if such member shall not resign within one month, the committee shall order his name to be erased from the list of members, and he shall cease to be a member; provided that no such request be sent to any member unless the resolution to send the same be agreed to by two-thirds of the committee actually present at a meeting convened for the purpose: provided also that in such meeting of the committee it is unanimously resolved that immediate expulsion of the member whose conduct in question be advisable the committee shall be empowered forthwith to expel such member, should it, however, be the opinion of any 21 members that the case of the members so expelled might be reconsidered without damage to the club, the committee shall call an extraordinary general meeting, to which the matters shall be submitted, such meeting to consist of at least two-thirds of the total number of members of the club, and if a majority of not less than three-fourths of such meeting shall agree to the reinstatement of that member he shall be reinstated. Any member expelled from the club shall be deemed to have forfeited his proposal fee and subscription, and shall subject to the above provisions, be for ever after ineligible for re-election. The rules of natural justice demand that a man is not to be removed from office or membership or otherwise dealt with to his disadvantage without having a fair and sufficient notice of what is alleged against him and an opportunity of making his defence; and that the decision whatever it is must be arrived at in good faith with a view to the common interest of the society or institution concerned. If these conditions are satisfied a Court of Justice will not interfere with the decision.

The expression 'dishonourable' or 'disreputable' conduct shall include:

(*a*) wilful and intentional non-fulfilment of contract, or fraudulent and flagrant breach of contract;

(*b*) frivolous repudiation of contract;

(*c*) refusal to refer any question in dispute to arbitration or to abide by an arbitration or appeal award, unless arbitration is specifically excluded by the contract.

(10) The club shall be opened to the members between 6 p.m. and midnight every day unless otherwise determined in a special general meeting. A member of the committee (including the chairman, secretary and the treasurer), however, shall be entitled to visit the club premises at any hour of the day and inspect any place, book or article at all reasonable hours.

(11) There shall be an annual general meeting of the members to be held in April or as early as possible thereafter in each year at which the member of the committee and the officers of the club shall be elected, the accounts shall be passed and other agenda as proposed by the committee or by any seven members after a previous notification thereof for at least fourteen

days shall be taken into consideration and adopted as required. The account shall be audited annually and the annual balance-sheet shall be submitted to the members at least fourteen days before the said annual general meeting.

(12) The management of the affairs of the club shall be in the discretion of the committee inclusive of the said office-bearers whereof the chairman of the club shall preside if present and in his absence a member of the committee as proposed, seconded and assented to by the majority of the members present shall preside. The committee shall be entitled to hold extraordinary of special general meetings from time to time as the committee may think fit. The extraordinary general meeting may be required to be held by 21 members of the club and special general meeting may be called by the chairman as and when necessary. The members of the committee may also call an extraordinary general meeting by directing the secretary to issue the notices therefor. No extraordinary general meeting shall be called without seven days' previous notice therefor. A special general meeting may be called by the chairman after a two days' notice therefor. The notices shall be sent per peon or under a certificate of posting, by post to the members at the address given to the secretary therefor.

(13) A member shall be entitled to invite not more than two guests at the premises of the club but such guests shall not be entitled to be present at any general special or extraordinary meeting of the members or of the meeting of the committee. No expelled member shall be invited as a guest into the club nor shall such a guest be allowed to remain in the club if more than 21 members desire his eviction from the premises of the club.

(14) The members shall not be liable personally for goods supplied to or obligation incurred by any officer of the club on behalf of the club but the property of the club shall be liable to meet such debt or obligation in the hands of the managing committee. The managing committee shall be entitled to sue and be sued in the name of the club provided the rules relating thereto embodied in the Code of Civil Procedure regarding such matters are complied with.

(15) The aforementioned rules shall be liable to alteration by a majority of three-fourths of the members present in a meeting specially convened therefor whether in the extraordinary or special general meeting or whether embodied in the agenda for the annual general meeting provided, however, that a majority of the total number of members of the club adopt the said alteration. The managing committee is empowered to frame bye-laws for the conduct of the proceedings and affairs of the club or as may be conducive to the fulfilment of objects of the club and are in conformity and not in conflict with the rules aforementioned.

(16) On the dissolution of the club the properties of the club shall be transferred to such other club or association or party as may be determined

by the members at the meeting where the resolution of dissolution is passed, provided that such a resolution shall not take effect unless confirmed by another meeting of the members held after 21 days of the prior resolution for dissolution and disposal of the properties of the club.

Memorandum of Association of the ...... Club Ltd.

(*Limited Club*)

1. The name of the Company shall be "THE .... CLUB LIMITED".

2. The Registered Office of the Company shall be situated in West Bengal.

3. The objects for which the Company is established are:

(*a*) to provide facilities for games, sports and pastimes in the neighbourhood of and to afford to its members all the usual privileges, advantages, conveniences and accommodation of a residential Club;

(*b*) to take over the effects and liabilities of the present unincorporated Association, known as the .... including its outstanding debts;

(*c*) from time to time to borrow or raise moneys which may be required for the purpose of the Club upon Bonds, Debentures, Bills of Exchange, Promissory Notes or other obligations or securities of the Company or by mortgage or charge of the Company's property, including its uncalled Capital (if any), and the amount guaranteed by the members of the Company for the time being, as mentioned in the fourth clause hereof;

(*d*) to purchase, take on lease or hire or otherwise acquire, any movable or immovable property, or any right, or privileges necessary or convenient for the purposes of the Club;

(*e*) to lay out and prepare, adopt, and improve any lands, for the purpose of riding, holding, horse and other shows, horse racing, shooting, playing golf, tennis, croquet or other sports or games thereon, or for any kind of athletic sports, entertainment, amusements or recreations and to construct, alter, keep in repair houses, pavilions, refreshment rooms, stables and other buildings erections and conveniences whether of a permanent or temporary nature which may seem directly or indirectly conducive to the Company's objects, and to pull down or demolish, sell, or otherwise dispose of, any buildings or erections not so required;

(*f*) to invest the money of the Company, not immediately required, in such securities as may from time to time, be determined by the Committee including any Debentures issued by the Company;

(*g*) to sell, improve, manage, develop, lease, mortgage, dispose of or otherwise deal with all or any part of the property of the Company with power especially to sell, deal in, and distribute all kinds of apparatus required for any game, sport or pastime, and all kinds of provisions, wines, spirits, tobacco and other stores among Members and Honorary or Temporary Members, for consumption either inside or outside the premises belonging to or used by the Club, and to give and contribute towards prizes, cups, medals, stakes and other rewards whether competed for by members or others;

(*h*) to subscribe to, become a member of or otherwise co-operate with any other Association, whether incorporated or not, whose objects are altogether or in part similar to those of this Company;

(*i*) to remunerate any person or Company for services rendered, or to be rendered, in placing or assisting to place or guaranteeing the placing of any Debentures or other Securities of the Company;

(*j*) to do all or any of the above things through trustees, agents or otherwise, and either alone, or in conjunction with others;

(*k*) generally to do all such other things as are incidental or conducive to the attainment of the above objects.

4. Every member of the Company undertakes to contribute to the assets of the Company in the event of it being wound up during the time that he is a member, or within one year afterwards for payment of the debts and liabilities of the Company contracted before the time at which he ceases to be a member, and of the costs, charges, and expenses of winding up the same, and for the adjustment of the rights of the contributories amongst themselves, such amount as may be required not exceeding Rs. ....

5. If upon the winding up or dissolution of the Company, there remains after the satisfaction of all debts and liabilities, any property whatsoever the same shall be paid to or distributed among the members of the Company, in equal shares.

We, the several persons whose names and addresses are subscribed are desirous of being formed into a Company in pursuance of this Memorandum of Association.

Names, addresses & descriptions
of subscribers

Names, addresses & descriptions
of witnesses

Dated this .... day of 2000

Model Bye-laws of a Club

1. **Guests.** Non-members, other than permanent Guests, may be admitted to the Club premises only when accompanied by a Member or his permanent Guest. The Committee reserves the right to check all persons entering the Club premises to ensure that only Members and their genuine guests are admitted.

A Visitors' Book is kept in the main Entrance Hall of the Club House in which, in order to comply with the Excise regulations members are requested to enter the names of their guests other than golfing and tennis guests, for whom separate books are provided.

Members introducing guests are responsible for all charges incurred on their account. Any individual, particularly a resident of Calcutta should not normally be introduced as a guest more than six times in a year.

Members' dependent children upto the age of 21 years only may use their membership; special application to be made in respect of their children between the ages of 21/23 years. Beyond the age of 23 years, members' children must conform to guest rules.

2. **Children.** Members or their permanent Guests bringing children to the Club premises are particularly requested to see that they do not interfere with the convenience of other members.

Ayahs are not allowed on the gravelled area or on the Tea Lawn, other than in the children's playground.

On Race mornings and afternoons, only those children who are accompanied by their own parents may use the precincts of the Club other than the children's playground.

3. **Dogs.** Dogs must be kept under proper control, and when within the precincts of the Club House they must be on a leash. Dogs may not be taken into any of the Club buildings.

Any dog in the neighbourhood of the Club House which barks or otherwise causes annoyance to members must be sent to the garage in charge of a dog boy.

Dogs brought into the Club compound on track must be under control at all times and when in the vicinity of the Race Course they must be on a lease.

On Race mornings and afternoons they may not be brought into the Club Grounds even in cars.

4. **Closing hours.** The Club House will be closed at 8 p.m. on week days and 10 p.m. on Saturdays, Sundays and Public Holidays or at such times as the Committee may decide.

5. **Motor Cars.** Are not allowed to stand in the porch or in the roadway near the Club House, on Saturdays, Sundays and Public Holidays.

Members are requested to assist the Committee by ensuring that their cars are parked between the white lines in the covered garage area or the parking spaces defined in the uncovered area to the North of the new tennis courts. Under no circumstances may cars be parked along the verges of the 'IN' and 'OUT' roads.

The route to the Garage it via the Club House. Cars or other vehicles may not be driven direct to the garage from the main Entrance Gate except on Race Afternoons and on track mornings.

Members are requested to see that their cars are driven slowly inside the Club Grounds and they do not interfere with golfers when passing in front of the 13th tee. Horns should not be sounded within the Club Grounds.

6. **Transistors & Radios** may not be played in the vicinity of the Club House. Music is available in A.C. Bars over weekends and holidays.

7. **Tipping** of any Club Staff is strictly forbidden except only when an individual is employed as a Caddy. Appreciation of service may be shown by a contribution to the Gratuity Fund for which a book is maintained by the Club Stewards.

8. **Complaints** should be addressed to the Managing Member in writing or entered in a book which is kept for that purpose in the lounge.

9. **Suggestions.** Constructive suggestions are welcomed, and may be entered in 'SUGGESTION BOOK' which is kept in the lounge.

GOLF

1. **Caddies.** Caddies must be engaged through the Caddy Master, and the Caddies' Engagement Register must be signed before commencement of play or practice.

2. **Payment due to caddies** must, in all cases, be made by cash.

3. The employment of Forecaddies is permitted except where expressly disallowed, *e.g.* when playing in competition.

4. **A match between a member and a playing caddy** has the same standing on the course as other Two-Ball Matches.

5. **Starting sheet.** Matches will start in the order written on the Starting Sheet.

A match may not be entered on the Starting Sheet until two players in the match are within the Club premises, except as provided for under Bye-laws 6 hereunder.

6. **Booking of times.** Starting times for Saturdays, Sundays and holidays will be allotted, and Members may apply for times on those days not more than 14 days before the day of play. All timings for competitions will be allotted.

Applications for starting times must specify the names of the players in the match. Where a guest is one of a match, his name and the designation 'GUEST' must be entered on the slip.

7. **Allotment of times.** The allotment of times in the case of Three and Four Ball matches, Fixed matches, will be subject to the limits laid down from time to time by the Committee. This chart will be posted on the Club Notice Board and Members will be notified of changes periodically when they occur.

8. **Forward times.** Subject to Bye-law 9 hereunder, any match may start at the 8th or any subsequent Tee, provided that the following match has not reached the preceding Tee. A forward booking may be made at the 1st Tee—But only for alternate times—on the Starting Sheet and, if ready to start at such times on the 1st Tee, such match will be entitled to play. Under no circumstances are three or four-ball matches, mixed matches and mixed foursomes permitted to commence play outside the times laid down by the Committee.

9. **Cutting in.** Members may not at any time cut in unless there is a clear hole behind them; for example, no match may start from the 8th Tee when there are players on the 7th hole or when players have moved off the 6th green. Similarly, no match may start from the 11th, 12th, 13th, 15th or 17th Tees when the next following match has left the 9th, 10th, 11th, 13th or 15th green respectively.

10. **Shamianas.** Players must leave the shamianas and be on the Tees at the 5th and 15th holes before the match ahead has left the green, and be on the 10th tee before the match ahead has played a second shot.

11. **Golfing guest.** Members may introduce, as Golfing Guests, visitors to, or residents of Calcutta, provided that no resident non-Member shall be introduced on more than six occasions in one calendar year in all, irrespective of the Members introducing him. Guests must play either with their introducer or his Permanent Guest.

Names of guests must be entered in the Guest Book in the 18th Bar prior to commencing a round.

12. **Green Fees.** Green Fees will be charged to Members of Golfing Guest introduced by them or playing with the Permanent Guest as follows:

		On Saturdays Sundays and Holidays		*Other days*
Gentlemen	......	Rs.	......	Rs.
Ladies	......	Rs.	......	Rs.
Visiting Members	......	Rs.	......	Rs.

13. **18th Shamiana Bar.** Ladies are not permitted in this Bar before 1 p.m. on Sundays and Holidays.

14. **Dogs.** Dogs, if brought on the course, must be kept under control. Dogs are not allowed to be brought into the Club compound on Race days.

15. **Closure of Course.** The gold course, or any part thereof, may be closed, owing to weather conditions at the discretion of the Managing Member or a Member of the Golf Sub-Committee.

CATERING

1. Breakfast, Lunch, Tea and Supper are served daily on demand, according to the standard menu. Members are asked to give 24 hours' notice of any special menus, lunch parties, etc. Except for Club evenings and special dinner parties booked in advance, the kitchen will normally be closed at 9 p.m.

2. Large and small Cakes, Shortbreak, Club Biscuits and Fudge may be purchased from the Club Bakery on giving 24 hours' notice.

Sausages, Bacon, Pate and other items can also be obtained from the Club Deep Freeze.

3. Members may not have picnics within the Club grounds without the previous sanction of the Managing Member.

4. The Club House and/or the Air Conditioned Bars may be engaged by Members for private parties.

5. Under Excise Regulations, children under the age of 18 years are not permitted in the A.C. Bar.

TENNIS

1. **Booking.** A member desiring to reserve a court or to book the marker should either enter his name personally in the book kept for that purpose, or apply by letter or telephone .... A chart of bookings made will be displayed each day in the tennis court area, and this may be referred to by all players.

Courts may be reserved not more than 14 days in advance, and it is helpful if 24 hours' clear notice of bookings is given.

2. **Cancellations.** If a court has been booked and is not required it will be charged for unless (*a*) notice of cancellation is received 24 hours before the time for which it has been booked, or (*b*) the court is used by some one else, or (*c*) it is closed under Bye-law 3 below.

Cancellation of Tennis Courts in the book must be initialled by the Member who booked the court.

3. **Closing of Courts.** The Courts may be closed on any day or days at the discretion of the Managing Member or a Member of the Tennis Sub-Committee.

4. **Tennis Balls.** Members must make their own arrangements for Tennis Balls, which are also available for purchase at the Club Shop.

5. **Tennis Guests.** A fee of Rs. 3 will be charged to members for each guest introduced by them or playing with their Permanent Guest.

6. **Signing.** Members are asked to ensure that they sign for their guests, marker, ball boys, before vacating the court.

SWIMMING BATH

1. **Hours.** The Swimming Bath is open daily from 6-30 a.m. to 8 p.m. except only for annual painting in January/February.

2. **Children** using the Swimming Pool must be accompanied at all times by either a Member or Permanent Guest and under no circumstances should be left unattended in the Swimming Pool where, if not under control, they can be in danger of injury or cause nuisance to other Members.

3. **Towels.** Bath Towels are provided by the Club. They should on no account be removed from the area of the Pool and Changing Rooms.

4. **Servants.** No servants are allowed inside the Swimming Bath premises other than Club attendants.

5. **Dogs.** Dogs are not allowed within the precincts of the Swimming Bath under any conditions whatever.

ACCOMMODATION

1. **Reservation.** Booking of the Club Suites may be made through the Head Steward at the Club.

2. **Charges.** The rates for the Air-Conditioned room with attached bath have been kept intentionally low, currently @ Rs. 40 per day for Permanent Members and Rs. 70 per day for Reciprocal and Temporary Members. These charges cover electricity and service, with additional Rs. 10 for a third occupant in any room.

3. **Duration.** Two Suites are available for extended occupation by firms, whilst the others are intended for reservation for short periods. No member

may normally occupy for more than 10 days at a stretch unless there is no pending booking for the room.

4. **Accounts.** Bills in respect of occupants will be submitted weekly for payment on presentation.

5. **General.** Residents at the Club are particularly requested to abide by all Rules and covenants pertaining to .... CLUB.

Hacking—Bridle Path

MEMBERS and their guests are requested to refer to the Sketch Map posted on the Club Notice Boards. When using the Bridle Path they are requested to give right of way to golfers when crossing any fairway or approaching any tee.

Constitution of a Rotary Club

ARTICLE I

Name

The name of this organisation shall be .... of ....

ARTICLE II

Territorial Limits

The territorial limits of this club shall be as follows.

*** *** ***

ARTICLE III

Object

The object of Rotary is to encourage and foster the ideal of service as a basis of worthy enterprise and, in particular, to encourage and foster:

First: The development of acquaintance as an opportunity for service;

Second: High ethical standards in business and professions; the recognition of the worthiness of all useful occupations; and the dignifying by each Rotarian of his occupation as an opportunity to serve society;

Third: The application of the ideal of service by every Rotarian to his personal, business and community life;

Fourth: The advancement of international understanding, goodwill and peace through a world fellowship of business and professional men united in the ideal of service.

ARTICLE IV
Meetings

Section 1. This club shall meet regularly once each week on the day and at the time provided in the bye-laws, provided that in an emergency, or for good cause, the BOARD OF DIRECTORS of the club may change the regular meeting of any week to a different day of the same week or to a different hour of the regular day, or to a different place, or cancel the regular meeting of any week when it falls on a legal holiday, or because of the death of the club President or an epidemic or a disaster affecting the entire community.

Section 2. An annual meeting for the election of officers of this club shall be held not later than the thirty-first day of March in each year as provided in the bye-laws of this club.

Article V
Membership

Section 1. *Kinds.* There are four kinds of membership, namely, active; senior active; past service and honorary.

Section 2. *Active membership.* Each active member shall be an adult male person of good character and good business or professional reputation—

(*a*) engaged as proprietor, partner, corporate officer, or manager of any worthy and recognized business or profession; or

(*b*) holding an important position in an executive capacity with discretionary authority in any worthy and recognized business or profession; or

(*c*) acting as the local agent or branch representative of any worthy and recognized business or profession, having charge of such agency or branch in an executive capacity; and

personally and actively engaged in the business or profession in which he is classified in the club and having his place of business or residence located within the territorial limits of the club, except as otherwise provided in Article 7, section 2A of this Constitution.

Section 3. *Classifications.* (*a*) Each active member of this club shall be classified in accordance with his business or profession.

(*b*) The classification of each active member will be that which covers the principal and recognized activity of the firm, company or institution with which he is connected, or if he be independently engaged in a business or profession his classification shall be that which covers his principal and recognized business or professional activity.

(*c*) *How corrected.* The Board, in its discretion, may correct or adjust the classification of any member, whose membership has not terminated, if the circumstances warrant such action. Due notice of such proposed correction or adjustment shall be given to the member and he shall be allowed a hearing thereon.

Section 4. *Limitation.* The active membership shall consist of but one man from each classification of business or profession, excepting the newspaper and religion classifications, and excepting the provision for additional active members as provided in sections 5 and 6 of this Article.

Section 5. *Additional active member.* (*a*) Any active member of this club may propose for and the club may elect to active membership one additional man from the concern or establishment with which the proposer is connected, whose classification shall be the same as that of the proposer. The qualifications of such additional member shall be those required for active membership. An additional active member is in all respects an active member except that the membership of an additional active member elected under the foregoing provisions of this section shall automatically terminate with the termination of the active membership of the active member who proposed him.

(*b*) The club may, subject to the approval of the holder of the classification, elect to additional active membership in the club any former active member of a Rotary Club whose place of business whereat he is actively engaged in within the territorial limits of the club and who otherwise qualified for membership, provided—

(1) that there shall, in no case, be more than one additional active member elected under this paragraph of this section in respect of any one classification,

(2) that any member so elected shall have terminated membership of his former club only because he ceased to be actively engaged within the territorial limits of that club in the classification of business or profession under which he was classified in that club, and

(3) that an additional active member elected under this paragraph of this section shall cease to be a member when the classification becomes vacant, provided that when the classification is again filled, he may [without prejudice to the right of the holder of the classification to propose an additional active member under para (*a*) of this section] then be re-elected.

Section 6. *Religion and newspaper classifications.* Representatives of more than one denomination and of more than one newspaper published within the territorial limits of this club may be eligible to active membership under the same classifications, provided that they otherwise possess the qualifications for active membership.

Section 7. *Public office holder.* Persons elected or appointed to public office for a specified time only shall not be eligible to active membership in this club under the classification of such office. This shall not apply to persons holding a position or office in schools, colleges or other institutions of learning.

An active member of this club who is elected or appointed to public office for a specified period may during the period in which he holds such office continue as such active member in the club under the classification represented by him in the club immediately prior to such election or appointment.

Section 8. *Local preference.* No man engaged as the local agent or branch representative of an outside concern shall be eligible to active membership when a suitable prospective member may be available whose principal place of business is within the territorial limits of this club.

Section 9. *Senior active membership.* (*a*) Any active member of this club—

(1) who has been an active member of this or other clubs for a total of fifteen or more years; or

(2) who is of the age of sixty or more after having been an active member of one or more clubs for a total of ten or more years; or

(3) who is of the age of sixty-five or more after having been an active member of one or more clubs for a total of five or more years; or

(4) who is a present or a past officer of Rotary International; or

Any past service member of this club—

(*i*) who has been an active member of this club and who, at the time he ceased to be an active member of this club, had the qualifications for senior active membership as hereinbefore set forth; or

(*ii*) who has been an active and past service member of this and/or other clubs for a total of fifteen or more years; or

(*iii*) who is a present or past officer of Rotary International shall automatically and forthwith become a senior active member.

(*b*) This club may, at its option, elect to senior active membership in this club any former member of any club, who was a senior active member or was eligible to become senior active member at the time he ceased to be member of a club, provided such former member resides within the territorial limits of this club or within the surrounding area.

(*c*) A senior active member shall have all the rights, privileges and responsibilities of an active member, except that—

(*i*) he shall not be considered as representing a classification, and

(*ii*) he shall not have the right to propose an additional active member.

This club may admit to membership a qualified person in the classification of business or profession in which such senior active member may be engaged.

Section 10. *Past service membership.* (*a*) A former active member of a club whose active membership was terminated because of his retirement from active business or professional life, may be elected a past service member in this club provided he has been an active member in one or more clubs for or more years. Such former member may be elected to past service membership at the time of, or at any time after, the termination of his active membership, provided he has all the other qualifications of a past service member. If his retirement from business or professional life occurs after he has ceased to be a member of a Rotary club, he is not eligible to past service membership. He must reside and continue to reside within the territorial limits of this club or within the surrounding area, unless he has been an active member in this club in which event he may reside and continue to reside in the locality of his residence at the time he ceased to be an active member in this club.

(*b*) A past service member shall have the rights, privileges and responsibilities of an active member except that—

(*i*) he shall not be considered as representing a classification,

(*ii*) he may not become a senior active member (except as provided in section 9A of this Article), and

(*iii*) he does not have the right to propose an additional active member.

Section 11. *Honorary membership.* (*a*) A male person who resides within or who has resided within the territorial limits of the club and who has distinguished himself by meritorious services in the furtherance of Rotary ideals there or elsewhere may be elected to honorary membership in the club.

(*b*) Honorary members shall be exempt from payment of admission fees and dues, shall have no vote and shall not be eligible to hold any office in the club; shall have no interest in any property of the club; shall not be considered as representing a classification, but shall be entitled to attend all meetings and enjoy all other privileges of the club. No honorary member of this club is entitled to any rights or privileges in any other club.

Article VI
Officers and Directors

Section 1. The governing body of this club shall be a Board of Directors to be constituted as the Bye-laws of the club may provide.

Section 2. Except as herein otherwise specifically provided, the decision of the Board in all club matters shall be final, subject only to an appeal to the club. The Board shall have general control over all officers and all committees and may, for good cause, declare any office vacant. It shall constitute a board of appeal from the rulings of all officers and actions of all committees. Appeal may be taken from any decision of the Board to the club. On such appeal, the decision appealed from shall be reversed only by a two-thirds vote of the members present, at a regular meeting specified by the Board, a quorum being present, notice of such appeal having been given by the Secretary to all members of the club at least five days previous to such meeting.

Section 3. The officers of this club shall be a President, one or more Vice-Presidents, all of whom shall be members of the Board, and a Secretary, a Treasurer, and Sergent-at-arms, any or all of whom may or may not be members of the Board of Directors as the Bye-laws of the club shall provide.

Section 4. Each officer shall be elected as provided in the Bye-laws of the club and, except as may otherwise be provided in relation to the President, shall take office on the first day of July immediately following his election and shall serve for the period of his election or until his successor shall have been elected and qualified.

The President shall be elected at any time within the two-year period immediately preceding the year for which he is elected to serve as President. The President shall take office on the first day of July in the Rotary year for which he is elected to serve as President and shall serve for the period of his election or until his successor shall have been elected and qualified. In the event that the President is elected prior to the Rotary year immediately preceding the year in which he is to serve as President, such President-elect shall, if he is not otherwise a member of the Board, serve as an *ex-officio* member of the Board in the year immediately preceding the year in which he is to serve as President.

Each officer and each director shall be an active (including additional active), senior active, or a past service member in good standing of this club.

Article VII

Admission Fees and Dues

Section 1. Each active, senior active, and past service member of this club shall pay, as an admission fee and as annual dues, such sums as may be prescribed in the Bye-laws of this club, except that a senior active or past service member who has held active membership in this club shall not be required to pay a second admission fee.

Article VIII

Duration of Membership

Section 1. *Period.* Membership shall continue during the existence of the club unless terminated as hereinafter provided.

Section 2. *How terminated.* (*a*) Active membership shall automatically terminate, if, and when, an active member ceases to be personally and actively engaged in the classification of business or profession under which he is classified in the club or ceases to have his place of business or residence located within the territorial limits of the club, or his connection with his business establishment is severed.

Except that by permission of the Board of Directors, an active member, moving from the territorial limits of the club, may be given special leave of absence for a period not exceeding one year to enable him to visit and become known to a Rotary Club in the community to which he moves, providing he is still active in the same classification of business or profession and continues to comply with the attendance and all other conditions of Rotary membership. The termination of his membership would take effect only at the end of the period of leave granted to him.

In the event an active member of the club, after having been an active member of the club for five or more years, ceases to have his place of business or residence within the territorial limits of the club, he may retain his membership in the club provided his new place of business or residence is located within the corporate limits of the city in which the club is located.

(*b*) The membership of an additional active member elected under the provisions of Article 5, section 5A of this Constitution shall automatically terminate with the termination of the membership of the active member who proposed him, or in the event such active member becomes a senior active member of this club. If such additional active member is promptly re-elected to active membership in this club, he shall not be required to pay a second admission fee.

An additional active member elected under Article 5, section 5B shall cease to be a member when the classification becomes vacant provided that when the classification is again filled he may (without prejudice to the right of the holder of the classification to propose an additional active member under Article 5, section 5A of this Constitution) then be re-elected.

(*c*) Past service membership shall automatically terminate on the thirtieth day of June next after the date of election. However, the Board in its discretion may, by resolution from year to year, continue such honorary membership for the ensuing year. Such honorary membership may be continued by the Board although the person so elected has ceased to reside within the territorial limits of the club.

Section 3. *How to rejoin.* When the membership of an active member has terminated as provided in the foregoing section 2, such person may make new application for membership, under the same classification or another classification. Such application by an additional active member elected under the provisions of Article 5, section 5A of this Constitution shall be considered, before any other, for membership under the classification in which he applies. If elected to membership he shall not be required to pay a second admission fee.

Section 4. *Termination—non-payment of dues.* Any member failing to pay his dues within thirty (30) days after the prescribed time shall be notified in writing by the Secretary at his last known address. If the dues are not paid on or before ten (10) days from the date of notification, said membership shall automatically terminate.

Such former member, at the discretion of the Board, may be reinstated to membership upon his petition, and upon the payment of all his indebtedness to the club, provided that no former member can be reinstated to active membership if his former classification has been filled.

Section 5. *Termination—non-attendance.* (*a*) The membership of any active, senior active, or past service members except as provided in this article, who is absent from four consecutive regular weekly meetings of this club shall automatically terminate, unless such absence is made up as hereinafter provided, or he is excused by the Board for good and sufficient reason.

Any member absent from a regular meeting of this club may make up such absence by attendance at a regular meeting of any other Rotary Club or a provisional Rotary Club at any time between the usual time of the regular meeting of this club immediately preceding the day of absence and the usual time of the regular meeting of this club immediately following the day of absence and be given full credit for attendance in this club, provided notice of such attendance is given to this club by the secretary of the club visited or the member may make his own report.

In the event an active, senior active, or past service member of this club presents himself at the regular time and place of meeting of any other club for the purpose of attending the meeting of such club, and such club has omitted, postponed or changed the time or place of its meeting for the said week, then such member shall be credited with attendance by this club for the week for which he would be entitled to credit had such meeting been held at the regular time and place, provided notice of such circumstances is given to this club by the secretary of the club visited or the member may make his own report.

Any active, senior active or past service member of this club, who is serving as an officer of Rotary International, or a committee-man of Rotary

International, or as a SPECIAL REPRESENTATIVE OF THE DISTRICT GOVERNOR, or who is in the employ of Rotary International, absent from a regular meeting of this club on Rotary business shall be credited with attendance at such meeting missed while on such business, provided notice of such circumstances is given to this club by the member.

Any active, senior active, or past service member of this club absent from a regular meeting of this club while travelling with reasonable directness to or from a convention of Rotary International, an international assembly, a Rotary Institute for past and present officers of Rotary International, a Rotary regional conference, a Rotary International committee meeting, a Rotary district conference, Rotary district assembly any district meeting held by direction of the board of directors of Rotary International, or a regular announced intercity meeting of Rotary clubs, shall be credited with attendance at such regular meeting of this club, provided notice of such circumstances is given to this club by the member.

Any active, senior active, or past service member of this club absent from a regular meeting of this club who attends a convention of Rotary International, an international assembly, a Rotary Institute for past and present officers of Rotary International. A Rotary regional conference, a Rotary International committee meeting, a Rotary district conference, a Rotary district assembly, any district meeting held by direction of the board of directors of Rotary International, or a regularly announced intercity meeting of Rotary clubs, at any time between the usual time of the regular meeting of this club immediately preceding the day of absence and the usual time of the regular meeting of this club immediately following the day of absence shall be credited with attendance at such regular meeting of this club, provided notice of such attendance is given to this club by the member.

(*b*) The membership of any active, senior active or past service member, except as hereinafter provided, whose percentage of attendance is less than sixty per cent during the first or second six months of this club's fiscal year shall automatically terminate, unless he is excused by the Board for good and sufficient reason.

(*c*) Any senior active or past service member who, because of protracted ill-health or impairment, is physically unable to comply with the provisions of this section may, during the period of its continuance, upon application to the Board be excused from complying with attendance requirements and his absence shall not be computed in the attendance record of the club.

(*d*) Any senior active or past service member who has been a member of one or more Rotary clubs for in the aggregate twenty years or more, and has reached the age of sixty-five years, may notify the secretary in writing of his desire to be excused from complying with attendance requirements. If approved by the Board such member's attendance or absence shall not be computed in the attendance record of the club.

Section 6. *Termination for other causes.* (*a*) The membership of any member who shall cease to have the qualifications for membership in this club may be terminated by the Board by the votes of not less than two-thirds of the members thereof, at a meeting called for that purpose.

(*b*) The membership of any member may be terminated by the Board, for a reason which the Board may deem to be sufficient by the votes of not less than two-thirds of the members thereof, at a meeting called for that purpose.

(*c*) In either case (*a*) or (*b*) the member shall be given at least ten days' notice in writing of such pending action and an opportunity to submit to the Board a written answer. He shall also have the privilege of appearing before the Board to state his case. Service of such notice shall be made by personal delivery or by registered letter to his last address.

(*d*) In case of a decision to terminate membership, the secretary shall, within seven days after the date of the Board's decision, notify the member in writing of the decision of the Board. Such member may, within fourteen days after the date of such notice, give written notice to the secretary of his intention either to appeal to the club or to arbitrate as provided in Article 12 of this Constitution. In the event he appeals, the Board shall set a date for the hearing of the appeal at a regular meeting of the club, to be held within twenty-one days after the receipt of such written notice of appeal. At least five days' notice of such club meeting and its special business shall be given in writing to every member of the club, and only members of the club shall be permitted to be present when such appeal is considered at such meeting.

(*e*) When the Board has terminated the membership of an active member as provided for in this section, the club shall not elect any member under his former classification, until the time for hearing the appeal, if any, has expired and the club's decision or the arbitrators has been announced.

(*f*) The action of the Board shall be final if no appeal to the club is taken and no arbitration is requested. If an appeal is taken, the action of the club shall be final.

Section 7. *Resignation.* The resignation of any member from this club shall be in writing (addressed to the President or Secretary) and shall be accepted by the Board, provided that all indebtedness of said member to the club has been paid.

Section 8. *Property interest—forfeiture of.* Any person whose membership in this club has been terminated in any manner shall forfeit all interest in any funds or other property belonging to the club.

ARTICLE IX

Community, National and International Affairs

Section 1. The general welfare of the community, the nation and the world is a concern to the members of this club, and the merits of any public question involving such welfare shall be proper subjects of fair and intelligent study and discussion before a club meeting for the enlightenment of its members in forming their individual opinion. However, this club shall not express an opinion on any pending controversial public measure.

Section 2. This club shall not endorse or recommend any candidate for public office and shall not discuss at any club meeting the merits or demerits of any such candidate.

Section 3. (*a*) This club shall neither adopt nor circulate resolution or views, nor take corporate action, dealing with world affairs or international policies of a political nature.

(*b*) This club shall not direct appeals to clubs, peoples or governments, or circulate letters, speeches, or proposed plans for the solution of specific international problems of a political nature.

ARTICLE X

Official publication

Section 1. By acceptance of active, senior active, or past service membership in this club, such member voluntarily becomes a subscriber to the monthly publication of Rotary International. His subscription shall be handled in six-month periods and shall continue as long as he is a member of the club and to the end of any six-month period during which he may cease to be a member of the club.

Section 2. The amount of the subscription shall be collected by the club from each member, semi-annually, in advance. The secretary shall enter such subscriptions and amounts so collected in a special subscription account and remit to Rotary International.

Section 3. The Board of Directors of Rotary International may prescribe this standard club constitution without this article for the use of clubs outside of the United States of America and Canada.

ARTICLE XI

Acceptance of object and compliance with Constitution and Bye-laws

A member by payment of his admission fee and dues thereby accepts the principles of Rotary as expressed in its object and submits himself to and agrees to comply with and be bound by the Constitution and Bye-laws of this club, and on these conditions alone is entitled to the privileges of the club. No member shall be absolved from the observance of the Constitution and Bye-laws on the plea that he has not received a copy of them.

Article XII
Arbitration

Should any dispute arise between any member or members, or a former member or members, and the club, or any officer or the Board of the club, relating to membership or any officer or the Board of the club, relating to membership or to any alleged breach of the Constitution or Bye-laws, or the expulsion of any member from the club, or on any account whatsoever which cannot be satisfactorily settled under the procedure already provided for such purpose, the matters in difference shall be settled by arbitration. Each party shall appoint an arbitrator and the arbitrators shall appoint an umpire. Only members of a Rotary club may be appointed as umpire or as arbitrators all functioning in accordance with the Arbitration and Conciliation Act 1996. The decision arrived at by the arbitrators, or in the event of their disagreement, by the umpire, shall be final and binding on all parties.

Article XIII
Bye-laws

This club shall adopt Bye-laws not inconsistent with the Constitution and Bye-laws of Rotary International (and the rules of procedure for and area administration where established) and with this Constitution, embodying additional provisions for the Government of this club. Such Bye-laws may be amended from time to time as therein provided.

Article XIV
Amendments

Section 1. *Time.* This Constitution, except in an emergency as provided for in Article 6, section 2 of the Bye-laws of Rotary International, and except as provided in section 4 of this Article, may be amended only by action of the Council on legislation as part of the Convention of Rotary International held in an even-numbered year, and except that in the event a sufficient number of votes are cast by clubs against approval of action by the Council on any proposed enactment to amend this Constitution, which will require action by the Convention, as provided in Article 9, section 8G of the Bye-laws of Rotary International, this Constitution may be amended by the Convention in an odd-numbered year by a majority vote of the electors present and voting at the time such amendments are submitted to the Convention.

Section 2. *Who may propose.* Amendments to this Constitution, except as provided in section 4 of this Article, may be proposed only by a club, by a district conference, by the general council or the conference of Rotary International in Great Britain and Ireland, by the Council-on-legislation, or by the board of directors of Rotary International.

Section 3. *Procedure.* Any proposal to amend this Constitution shall be delivered to the General Secretary of Rotary International not later than the first day of August, in the Rotary year in which the Council-on-legislation is to meet.

The General Secretary of Rotary International shall mail a copy thereof to the Secretary of each club by the first day of November in the Rotary year in which the Council-on-legislation is to meet.

The General Secretary of Rotary International shall transmit directly to the Council all duly proposed amendments.

The Council shall consider and act upon each such duly proposed amendment and any preferred amendment thereof.

Section 4. Article 1 (Name) and Article 2 (Territorial Limits) of this Constitution may be amended at any regular meeting of this club by the affirmative vote of a majority of members present and voting, provided that notice of such proposed amendment shall have been mailed to each member at least ten (10) days before such meeting, and provided further, that such amendment shall be submitted to the Board of Directors of Rotary International for its approval and shall become effective only when so approved.

Societies

Societies in India were originally registered under Societies Registration Act 1860 (Act XXI of 1860) unless there is some local legislation in the State. The old Act (Act XXI of 1860) was repealed in its application to West Bengal with effect from 1st April 1963. The old Act was modelled after the Library and Scientific Institution Act 1854 of England.[2] In West Bengal they are now registered under the W.B. Societies Registration Act 1961 (West Bengal Act XXVII of 1961). Any seven or more individuals associated with any of the objects—religious, charitable or literary, prescribed under sub-section 2 of section 4 of the Act—form a society by filing with the Registrar a Memorandum of Association and a copy of the Regulations.

2 17 and 18 Vict C 112, in England.

The society so registered is neither a corporation nor a limited company incorporated under the Companies Act.[3] It is an independent registered association but not a partnership of individuals which has acquired a legal status by virtue of its registration with the Registrar appointed by the State Government under the provisions of the Societies Registration Act. It enjoys the status of a legal entity apart from the members constituting the same. Every member of a corporation or an incorporated company join the same on that basis. The majority of the members is entitled to exercise its powers and control its operation generally. The same would be the position in the case of unincorporated associations of individuals whether the same be registered under the Societies Registration Act or not. The rule of majority is the normal basis of these associations. The members join these associations whether incorporated or unincorporated, whether registered or unregistered, knowing fully well that affairs of these associations would be conducted normally by the vote of the majority of the members thereof. In the absence of any specific rules and regulations governing the conduct of these affairs, this would be normal presumption and no member who joins any association would be heard to contend to the contrary. The properties belonging to any society vest in the trustees and in the absence thereof are deemed to vest for the time being in the governing body.

SOCIETIES REGISTRATION ACT XXVI OF 1961

Memorandum of Association

1. The name of the society shall be "..............."

2. The Registered Office of the society shall be situated at ...., ... in the State of West Bengal.

3. The aims and objects of the society are as follows:

(*a*) To perpetuate the memory of ....

(*b*) To help and give relief to the poor and indigent and other deserving person or persons by providing food, shelter, periodical distribution of cloth, medicine and money and other necessities, also to provide books to deserving students and *sanyasis* and to distribute alms in cash or kind annually out of the funds of the society.

(*c*) To give lessons and instructions on the *Geeta, Bible, Koran* and other religious scriptures and arrange for and provide all suitable and necessary ways and means for the daily worship and

3 *Satyavarat* v *Arya Samaj* AIR 1946 Bom 516 (519); 48 Bom LR 34.

periodical festivals of .... according to the wishes of ...... and offering of Puja and Bhoga to ...... and for observance of such other occasional religious festivals at the Samadhi Mandir at .... as may be decided by the society from time to time.

(*d*) To perpetuate, keep and maintain the aforesaid Samadhi Mandir and other premises and the land attached thereto at .... in good state and condition and make such additions, alterations and repairs thereto as may be necessary.

(*e*) To construct, maintain, extend, alter, repair or improve any temple building and premises that may be acquired by the Ashram. To undertake administration of any religious or charitable institution or endowment, *e.g.* church, temple, math or others.

(*f*) To receive and collect any gifts, subscriptions and donations either in cash or in kind, or acquire by any other lawful ways and means and spend the same in fulfilment of all or any of the aims and objects of the society. The income and properties of the society shall be applied solely for the promotion and fulfilment of the aims and objects of the society, provided if any donor intends that his contributions, donation or subscription shall be applied to the attainment of any particular object or objects of the Ashram, such contribution, donation, subscription shall be spent towards the promotion of that particular object or objects only.

(*g*) To acquire by purchase, take on lease, hire or by gift or otherwise and hold any movable or movables and also any immovable property or properties or any rights or privileges that may be deemed necessary or useful for the advancement of the objects of the Ashram or any of them.

(*h*) To arrange and/or provide for the long-standing practice of annual observation of .... Utsava at the Samadhi Mandir of .... at ....

(*i*) To do all such other lawful acts, deeds and things as are incidental and conductive to the attainment of the objects or any of them.

(*j*) To manage and administer any orphanage, nursing home, hospital, library, reading room, trust, school, college and other institution irrespective of caste, creed or social status.

(*k*) To take over, absorb or amalgamate with any other society or association or institution whose objects are similar to the objects of the society.

(*l*) To apply the income and properties of the society for the fulfilment of its objects and not to pay any portion thereof by way of profit or dividend or bonus.

4. Without prejudice to the generality of the above objects and for effectively carrying out the same the society shall have power to receive, hold and possess any property including securities of any kind and to construct and maintain any building, to manage transfer or otherwise dispose of or deal in any property of security and to enter into any contract for or in connection with the purposes of the society to raise moneys and funds including debentures and to establish provident fund or funds for the benefit of the employees of the society and to accept the management of any trust or endowment in which the society may be interested. The society shall have also the power to frame rules and bye-laws under its Constitution.

5. The management and control of the .... shall be in the hands of a Committee of Management of the society to be elected annually by the Mantra Sishyas of .... and shall be carried on in accordance with the rules as may be framed or modified from time to time by the said Committee of Management, whose names, addresses and descriptions are subscribed hereunder:

The following persons shall be the members of the first governing body of the society:

	Name	*Address*	*Description*
1.	Sri	....	President
2.	"	....	Secretary
3.	"	....	Treasurer
4.	"	....	Assistant Secretary
5.	"	....	"
6.	"	....	Member
7.	"	....	"
8.	"	....	"
9.	"	....	"

We the undersigned are desirous of forming a society named "................................." in pursuance of this Memorandum of Association:

Signature	*Address*	*Occupation*
....	....	....
....	....	....
....	....	....
....	....	....
....	....	....

WITNESS:

Signature	*Address*	*Occupation*
....	....	....
....	....	....
....	....	....
....	....	....
....	....	....

Rules and Regulations

1. **Definition.** In these Rules and Regulations unless there be anything repugnant to or inconsistent with the subject or context:

(*a*) *Society* means............

(*b*) *Committee of Management* means the Committee of Management of .... duly appointed annually by the Mantra Sishyas of ....

(*c*) *Member* means any of the members forming the Committee of Management.

(*d*) .... means an assemblage of Mantra Sishyas both male or female of .... over 18 years of age.

(*e*) *A Meeting of the Sishya Sangha* means a meeting of the Mantra Sishyas both male or female of .... over 18 years of age present at a meeting duly convened and held under the rules of the Ashram.

(*f*) *Financial Year* means the year commencing from 1st Baisakh to the last date of Chaitra in one year.

(*g*) *Mantra Sishya* means a direct disciple either male or female of Shree .... over 18 years of age and eligible under these rules to participate and vote in a meeting of the Sishya Sangha.

(*h*) *President* means the President of the .... Ashram elected annually in a meeting of the Sishya Sangha.

(*i*) *Treasurer* means the Treasurer of ....

(*j*) *Assistant Secretary* means the Assistant Secretary of ....

(*k*) .... means premises at ...., ...

2. **Committee of Management.** The Committee of Management shall consist of:

(*a*) President, (*b*) Secretary, (*c*) two Assistant Secretaries, (*d*) Treasurer and 16 members duly elected annually at a meeting of the Sishya Sangha convened for the purpose in the manner hereinafter provided for.

3. All properties of the Ashram, both movable and immovable, as well as the management of the affairs and concerns of the Ashram shall vest in the Committee of Management subject to the rules and regulations of the Ashram.

4. No one except a Mantra Sishya above 18 years of age shall be eligible to be a member.

5. The members shall hold office for a term of one year, but any of them shall be eligible for re-election.

6. In the case of any casual vacancy in the post of any of the members on account of death, resignation, expulsion or any other incapacity to work as a member, a new member will be co-opted by the Committee of Management from amongst the Sishyas within four weeks from the date of such casual vacancy of the Sangha. Such a new member will hold office till the next election of the Committee of Management. Pending filling up of the vacancy as stated above the remaining members in the Committee will carry on the work of the Ashram and the properties both movable and immovable of the Ashram shall vest in the remaining members.

7. For the proper conduct of the affairs of the Ashram the Committee of Management shall hold meetings as and when necessary, but there shall be at least one meeting in every two months and it shall keep proper records of all proceedings of such meetings. Five members present at a meeting shall form the quorum.

8. The Committee of Management shall, out of the funds and income of the Ashram, spend money for the fulfilment of the objects of the Ashram according to the budget as sanctioned by the Sishya Sangha at the annual general meeting. The Committee of Management shall appoint and, whenever necessary dismiss any sevak, pujari, durwan and other menial servants for the work of the Ashram and shall make all suitable arrangements for the protection of the Samadhi Mandir etc.

9. The Committee of Management may frame rules and bye-laws not inconsistent with the rules and regulations hereof for the internal management of the Ashram and the conduct of its meetings and may alter and amend the same when necessary.

10. All deeds and documents by or in favour of the Ashram shall be in the name of the Ashram.

11. In case any member shall desire to tender resignation from the membership before the expiry of his term, he shall have to give at least one month's notice in writing to the Secretary of the Committee of Management

and in case he himself happens to be the Secretary then at least three months' notice to the President of the society. Such a letter of resignation will be placed at a meeting of the Committee of Management especially convened for the purpose within one month from the receipt of the letter. No resignation shall be deemed to have taken place until accepted at the said meeting. Similar procedure will be followed in the case of any casual vacancy due to death or incapacity of a member to work as a member.

12. The members shall not be entitled to any remuneration.

13. **President.** The President shall preside over every meeting of the Committee of Management. In his absence, one of the members shall be elected as Chairman of the meeting.

14. **Secretary.** The Secretary or one of his Assistant Secretaries duly authorised by him shall look after the daily worship and Bhogarag of .... and also conduct the day-to-day affairs as resolved and passed by the Committee. He shall incur all necessary expenses in connection with his work mentioned above.

The Secretary to the Committee of Management will be in charge of the office of the Ashram and amongst others do the following acts and things:

(*a*) To check and verify accounts in the cash book and sign the same.

(*b*) To sign and issue notices for the meeting of the Committee of Management and the annual meeting of the Sishya Sangha.

(*c*) To look after and conduct all correspondence relating to or in any way concerning the Ashram other than those which may be allocated to any member or members in charge of any department of the society.

(*d*) To keep or cause to be kept in proper order and custody all documents and all papers and files belonging to the Ashram.

(*e*) To operate or cause to be operated by one of his assistant secretaries duly authorised by him on current account in one or more bank or banks as approved by the Committee of Management in conjunction with the Treasurer of the society.

(*f*) To sign in token of sanction all vouchers for necessary expenses of the Ashram within the limit sanctioned by the Committee before payment by the Treasurer.

15. **Treasurer.** (*a*) To receive subscriptions, donations and pronamis in cash and record the receipts in the Cash Book maintained for the purpose.

(*b*) To arrange for investment of surplus assets of the Ashram as approved by the Committee of Management in conjunction with the Secretary of the society.

(*c*) To operate on current account in one or more bank or banks as approved by the Committee of Management in conjunction with the Secretary or one of the Assistant Secretaries duly authorised by the Secretary of the Ashram.

(*d*) To submit all books and papers relating to the Ashram's receipts and expenditures, cash books, bank pass books, etc., to the Secretary of the Ashram once in a month for his scrutiny and signature.

(*e*) To prepare yearly accounts of receipts and expenditures and have the same audited by the Auditor appointed by the Committee of Management and approved at the general meeting and present the same before the annual meeting of the Sishya Sangha.

16. **Auditors.** At the annual meeting of the society, one or two Mantra Sishya, or outsiders be elected Auditors or Jt. Auditors who will audit the accounts of the Ashram for the ensuing year. Such appointment will be made for one year, but the same Auditor or Auditors will be eligible for re-election.

The Auditor or Auditors shall have at all reasonable time access to the books of accounts of the Ashram and to all papers, vouchers, receipt books, etc., and for this purpose of verifying any accident examine any office-bearer of the Ashram to make any enquiry from any member.

The Auditor or Auditors shall not be entitled to any remuneration.

17. **Assistant Secretary to the Committe of Management.** The Assistant Secretary will assist the Secretary in all matters relating to the duties of the Secretary and in the absence of the Secretary shall function according to his (Secretary's) instructions.

18. **Proceedings of the Committee of Management.** All proposals put to any meeting of the Committee of Management must be decided and passed by majority of votes of the members present at the meeting.

19. All resolutions duly passed in any meeting of the Committee of Management shall duly be recorded in the Proceedings Book either in Bengali or in English and shall be signed by all members present at the meeting.

20. The President may request any Mantra Sishya, who is not a member of the Committee or any of the persons who is not a Mantra Sishya, to attend a meeting of the Committee of Management to give their valuable and considered opinion regarding any matter relating to the Ashram. Such non-members of the Committee shall have, however, no power to cast vote at the meeting.

21. **Proceedings of the meeting of annual Sishya Sangha.** The Annual General Meeting of the society will be held on a date to be decided by the Committee of Management not later than four months after the date of

financial year of the Ashram. Necessary notice to all Mantra Sishyas shall be issued 15 days in advance by the Secretary. The notice will be in Bengali mentioning the date, time and place and the agenda of the meeting.

22. The business of the Annual Meeting of the society shall be:

(*a*) to consider the Ashram's annual report presented by the Secretary on behalf of the Committee of Management;

(*b*) to consider and pass the audited accounts of receipts and expenditure for the previous year;

(*c*) to elect the President and other members of the Committee of Management for the ensuing year; and

(*d*) to consider any other matter brought before the meeting either by the Committee of Management or by any member present at the meeting concerning the management and welfare of the Ashram.

23. **Quorum of meeting of Sishya Sangha.** Fifteen members of the Sishya Sangha personally present in any meeting of the Sishya Sangha shall form the quorum.

24. If for want of quorum any meeting of the Sishya Sangha cannot be proceeded with, then the meeting will be adjourned to some other date as the Committee of Management may think proper. No new matter shall be considered at the adjourned meeting except those mentioned in the agenda of the meeting which has been adjourned.

25. **Chairman.** At every meeting of the Sishya Sangha, one of the Mantra Sishyas present at the meeting shall be duly elected Chairman of the meeting.

26. Every resolution submitted to a meeting of the Sishya Sangha shall be determined by the majority votes of the Mantra Sishyas present, every Mantra Sishya having one vote. In case of equality of votes, the Chairman will have the casting vote. Votes will be taken by show of hands or by ballots as decided by the Sishya Sangha.

27. An attendance book shall be kept and as far as possible it should be signed by all Mantra Sishyas present at the meeting of the Sishya Sangha. The proceedings of all meetings of the Sishya Sangha shall be duly and properly recorded or caused to be recorded in the proceedings book either in English or Bengali by the then Secretary or in his absence by any member and shall be signed by the Chairman of the meeting.

28. An extraordinary meeting of the Sishya Sangha shall be convened at such place and time as the Committee of Management may deem fit on the written requisition of at least 10 Mantra Sishyas showing the reasons for calling of the same and shall be convened within 15 days of the receipt of requisition. A week's notice to be served to the Mantra Sishyas for the purpose will suffice.

29. It shall be lawful for the Sishya Sangha at an annual meeting duly convened for the purpose in the manner herein to amend, vary, alter, modify or repeal all or any of the rules and regulations of the Ashram.

Certified to be the true copy of the rules and regulations of ....

1. ....

2. ....

3. ....

Members of the Committee of Management

.... Society

(Registered under the West Bengal Societies Registration Act 1961)

(Act XXVI of 1961)

Memorandum of Association

1. The name of the society is ....

2. The registered office of the society will be situated at No. .... for the time being. The said office may be removed to such other place or places as the COUNCIL OF PROMOTERS shall think fit and proper from time to time. It may open and close any branch office or offices at any other place or places as it may decide from time to time.

3. The objects for which the society is established are:

(*i*) To preach the Message of Jesus Christ, to hold meetings, Crusades and Campaigns, to pioneer and support Gospel work in Virgin Areas, to print and publish religious literature such as tracts, magazines, pamphlets, books and booklets.

(*ii*) To train workers for Gospel outreach, to support Christian workers, for the propagation of the Gospel.

(*iii*) To co-operate with Christian Organisations or Associations in India and abroad to work within the scope of the 'India Evangelistic Crusade'.

(*iv*) To help local churches in the construction of Church and to administer the same and to establish community halls and support social work through schools and orphanages and to provide for stipends, scholarships, prizes, library, reading-room, lectures etc., and to provide and give medical relief and monetary help and shelter to poor and deserving children. To administer any trust or endowment.

(*v*) The receive any sum or sums of money as gifts or donations in cash or kind or subscriptions given to or acquired by any other means by the Crusade and to spend in fulfilment of all or any of the objects of the Crusade.

(*vi*) To purchase or to acquire on lease or in exchange or hire or to acquire by gift or otherwise and to hold and deal in whenever necessary in movable and immovable property or any right or privilege that may be deemed necessary for the promotion and advancement of the objects of the Crusade or any of them and to enter into any contract or contracts and to execute such conveyance or conveyances as may be necessary or required.

(*vii*) To borrow or raise money whenever necessary for some urgent and important work of the Crusade or for its maintenance and uplift or for any other religious or charitable purpose by the issue of or upon Bond, Promissory Notes, Debentures or other securities or by mortgaging the property of the Crusade, or to meet other obligations as may be determined by the Crusade from time to time. The value of such loan shall in no case exceed half of the total value of the properties.

(*viii*) To do all such lawful things as are incidental or conducive to the attainment of the above objects or any of them.

4. If upon the dissolution or winding-up of the society there remains after satisfaction of all debts and liabilities any property whatsoever the same shall not be paid to or distributed among the members of the society but shall be given or transferred to some other institution or institutions having objects similar to those of the society to be determined by the votes of three-fourths of the members of the society for the time being present personally at the time of dissolution or in default thereof, by the court having jurisdiction in the matter.

5. No portion of the income and property of the society shall be paid, applied or transferred directly or indirectly by way of dividends, bonus or otherwise howsoever by way of profit to any member of the society or any person claiming through any of the members PROVIDED THAT nothing hereto contained shall prevent the payment in good faith of remuneration or reward to any officer, employee or servant of the society or any member of the society or other persons in return for any service actually rendered to the society.

6. The management and control of the affairs of the society and/or of the branches of the society shall be carried on in accordance with the Articles of Association of the society and/or the rules and bye-laws and regulations framed by the COUNCIL OF PROMOTERS for the said purpose.

7. The names and addresses of members and office-bearers of the First Council of Promoters are:

Council of Promoters

1.	President
2.	Secretary-cum-Treasurer
3.	Member
4.	Member
5.	Member
6.	Member
7.	Member

8. We the several persons whose names and addresses are subscribed hereto are desirous of being formed into a society in pursuance of this Memorandum of Association and under the provisions of the West Bengal Societies Registration Act 1961 (Act XXVI of 1961).

Names and Addresses	*Occupation*	*Signature*	*Witness*
1.	....	....	....
2.	....	....	....
3.	....	....	....
4.	....	....	....
5.	....	....	....
6.	....	....	....
7.	....	....	....

Dated the 22nd day of October 1983

Rules and Regulations

(Registered under the West Bengal Societies Registration Act 1961)

1. **Interpretation.** In these Rules and Regulations unless there be anything in the subject or context inconsistent therewith:

(*a*) The *Society* means ....

(*b*) The *Members* means the members of the society for the time being.

(*c*) The *President* and *Secretary-cum-Treasurer* mean those respective office-bearers for the time being of the society.

(*d*) The *Annual General Meeting* and a *Special General Meeting* mean such general meetings of the society as are convened and held only under the rules of the society in force.

(*e*) The *Meeting* means all meetings other than Annual and Special General Meetings of the society.

(*f*) A *Resolution* means a Resolution of the Society duly passed and adopted.

(*g*) The *Seal* means the seal of the society.

(*h*) *Year* means the official year of the society as may be determined by the Council of Promoters from time to time.

(*i*) *Life Members* and *Ordinary Members* means the life members and ordinary members respectively of the society.

2. **Membership.** All persons who belong to the Christian community and profess Christian religion and who have attained 21 years of age and have subscribed to the aims and objects of the society subject to the approval of the Council of Promoters will be entitled to be its Ordinary Members and Associate Members on payment of their subscriptions as hereinafter provided. The decisions of the Council of Promoters in this regard shall be final and binding.

3. **Clauses of Membership and Fees:** (i) *Ordinary Members.* Those members as aforesaid who shall pay an yearly subscription of Rs. 10 per year shall be admitted as an ordinary member of the society subject to the approval of the Council of Promoters.

(ii) *Associate Members.* Those members as aforesaid who shall pay an yearly subscription of Rs. 5 will be Associate Members of the Society subject to the approval of the Council of Promoters.

Explanation. (*a*) Those persons, who have paid till the date of registration of the society the respective membership fees applicable to the respective clauses, shall be deemed to have been admitted to the respective clauses, and shall be deemed to be the Founder Members.

(*b*) Any ordinary member, whose subscription has remained in arrears before the holding of the Annual General Meeting or Extraordinary General Meeting shall not be entitled to exercise the voting rights at the Annual General Meeting or the Extraordinary General Meeting, as the case may be.

4. **Patrons.** The Council of Promoters may, according to such terms and conditions as it shall decide from time to time, admit as PATRONS those persons who are likely to help in furthering the objects and cause of the society either through their professional knowledge and experience and/or through financial assistance.

5. **Register of Members.** The society shall maintain at its registered office a register of its members and shall enter therein, within 15 days after the admission of a member or the cessation of his membership as the case may be, the following particulars:

(*a*) The name and address of the member.

(*b*) The date on which the member was admitted.

(*c*) The date on which a member ceased to be such member.

6. **Rights of Members.** (*a*) Each Ordinary Member shall have one vote at every meeting.

(*b*) All Ordinary and Associate Members of the society shall be entitled to participate in the meetings and religious functions and gatherings of the society and after the expiry of one month of his or her/their membership elect or be elected to its Council of Promoters.

(*c*) All the Ordinary Members shall have right to inspect the books of account, book containing minutes of proceedings of general meetings and register of members of the society on any working day during business hours by giving reasonable notice.

(*d*) All the members—Ordinary and Associate—of the society shall be bound by the Rules and Regulations and/or bye-laws which may be framed from time to time.

7. **Council of Promoters.** (*a*) The members of the First Council of Promoters of the society shall hold the offices for a period of five years, after the expiry of which the Council of Promoters shall be composed and constituted from among the members of the society as follows:

(*i*)(*a*) Seven members to be elected at every Annual General Meeting.

(*b*) Two members to be co-opted by the members as in (*a*) above.

(*ii*) The Council of Promoters thus composed and constituted shall from amongst themselves elect the following office bearers:

"President" and "Secretary-cum-Treasurer".

8. A member or an office-bearer of the Council of Promoters may resign by making a request addressed to the President or the Secretary-cum-Treasurer of the Council of Promoters in that respect in writing before the expiry of his term.

9. A member who is an undischarged insolvent or who has been convicted of any offence in connection with the formation, management or of the affairs of the society or of any offence involving moral turpitude shall not be entitled to be a member or office-bearer of the Council of Promoters.

10. In case of any vacancy in the Council of Promoters, including the office-bearer, caused by the removal of disqualification under these rules or by death or by resignation of any member or office-bearer during his

term as a member or office-bearer another member or office-bearer during his term as a member or office-bearer may be appointed in his place and stead by the remaining members and the office-bearers of the Council of Promoters and such appointed member or office-bearer shall hold the office only for the unexpired portion of the said member's or office-bearer's term.

11. Members of the Council of Promoters shall be eligible for re-election.

12. **Proceedings of the Council of Promoters.** The Council of Promoters shall meet at least twice in a year. Other meetings may be held either upon the advice of the President, or request of at least three members of the Council of Promoters.

13. (*a*) The quorum for the meeting of the Council of Promoters shall be three members present in person.

(*b*) If within half an hour of the time appointed for a meeting a quorum is not constituted, the meeting shall stand adjourned for one hour at the same time and place, and if at the meeting a quorum be not constituted within half an hour of the time appointed for the meeting, the members present shall constitute the quorum.

(*c*) The absence, without leave of any member of the Council of Promoters for 3 (three) consecutive meetings and/or for a continuous period of 6 months whichever is more, shall entitle the Council of Promoters to remove such member from the Council of Promoters.

(*d*) The Council of Promoters may pass a resolution by circulation. Such resolution passed whether by majority or unanimously by circulation amongst the members of the Council of Promoters shall be equally valid and shall be construed as if passed at a meeting duly called and convened for the purpose and such resolution shall be entered by the Secretary-cum-Treasurer in the minute-books of the meetings of the Council of Promoters.

14. The Council of Promoters shall be empowered with any, every and all functions pertaining to the administration, control and management of the society and will decide on all questions and more particularly the Council of Promoters acting collectively shall have power to:

(*a*) Represent the society.

(*b*) Acquire and transfer property, movable, immovable or both, assume obligations and conclude agreements of any nature.

(*c*) Appoint the personnel of the society, determine their remuneration, salaries and other service conditions and also to terminate their services, dismissal or otherwise and take disciplinary action as necessary.

(*d*) Open and operate bank accounts, deposit, withdraw or invest funds, issue, accept, sign, endorse and deliver cheques, drafts, letters of credit and in general any other negotiable instruments. Such banking account or accounts as and when opened shall be operated jointly by the President and Secretary-cum-Treasurer.

(*e*) Determine and incur expenses in general and administer the finances of the society and to raise, receive and accept funds, subscriptions, donations and money and all kinds of gifts and charities.

(*f*) Decide on the establishment of branch offices of the society.

(*g*) Exercise control over the books and funds of the society, prepare and submit to the General Meeting the annual report, the balance-sheet, income and expenditure account of the society.

(*h*) Frame bye-laws relating to the internal administration of the society.

(*i*) Decide on any, every and all matters pertaining to or in connection with the administration of the society and the successful pursuance of aims and objects.

(*j*) To make arrangements or appointments of the council or such other bodies for organising and publishing regular bulletins, journals or other publications and to hold and organise classes, lectures, meetings etc., under the direct supervision and guidance of the Council of Promoters.

15. The President shall preside over and direct the meetings of the Council of Promoters. But if at any meeting the President be not available to preside within 30 minutes of the time fixed for the meeting, the members of the Council of Promoters present shall elect one of them as Chairman of the meeting.

16. The Secretary-cum-Treasurer shall be the Executive Officer of the Council of Promoters. He or she shall carry on the administrative work of the society, receive all letters and documents addressed to the society, prepare correspondence, keep all books and records of the society.

17. The Secretary-cum-Treasurer shall collect all dues to the society and effect all its payments, keep appropriate records and books and help the Council of Promoters in financial administration of the society.

18. **Delegation of Authorities.** The Council of Promoters may delegate any of its powers and authorities referred to in rules to a sub-committee of two or more persons appointed from amongst the members of the society, if necessary. In each of such sub-committees, the President and the Secretary of the Council of Promoters shall always remain *ex officio* members.

19. **General Meetings.** The general body of the members shall be the supreme authority of the society in respect of all its activities and more particularly to decide on:

(*a*) Amendments and/or additions to the memorandum of society and these rules.

(*b*) Election of not more than seven members of the Council of Promoters every year after the expiry of the period of the First Council of Promoters and appointment of auditors and fix up their remuneration.

(*c*) Approval with or without amendments of the annual report, the Annual Balance-sheet and the Income and Expenditure Account.

(*d*) Collaboration or amalgamation of the society with any other society or fund pursuing similar objects.

(*e*) Dissolution of the society and disposal of fund upon dissolution as hereinbefore mentioned.

20. The Annual General Meeting shall be convened by the Council of Promoters regularly once a year within the three months following the end of the society's accounting year provided that for any reason if it be not practicable to convene the Annual General Meeting within the aforesaid period, the Council of Promoters shall have power to extend the date of such Annual General Meeting for a further period not exceeding three months and it will not continue to act during this period but not more than 15 months shall elapse between the two Annual General Meetings.

21. The Council of Promoters may, whenever it deems necessary call an Extraordinary General Meeting.

22. The notice for the General Meeting shall be delivered personally or sent by post to the members of the society at least 10 days prior to the date of the meeting and at least five days in the case of an adjourned meeting. The notice must indicate the place, date and hour hereof, as well as the items of agenda.

23. The General Meeting whether Annual or Extraordinary shall not discuss or decide on any matter which are not included in the agenda, save and except with the permission of the President.

24. The quorum for the General Meeting shall be one-fifth of the membership strength or 20 whichever is less. In the event such quorum is not present within half an hour of the time appointed for the meeting the General Meeting shall stand adjourned for one hour at the same place and at such adjourned meeting the members present shall constitute a quorum.

25. The decision of the General Meeting including the election of the members of the Council of Promoters shall be taken by show of hands or secret ballot as the President may desire by majority of the votes of the members present.

26. The General Meeting shall be presided over by the President and in his absence the members present shall elect from amongst themselves a

President of the Council of Promoters for the meeting. The decision of the General Meeting shall be recorded in minutes, entered into a special book maintained for the purpose, duly signed by the President of the meeting.

27. **President.** (*i*) The President shall guide and supervise the various activities of the society. He shall preside over the Council of Promoters and at the Annual General and other General Meetings. He shall be the Head of the society. The ruling of the President at the Council of Promoters shall be final and binding on all questions raised.

(*ii*) The President in case of emergency may exercise all the powers and perform all the functions required to be exercised and performed under the Rules and Regulations by the Managing Committee provided always that all the actions taken by the President shall be placed before the Council of Promoters in the next meeting immediately failing the exercise of such powers and functions by the President.

(*iii*) The President in case of emergency if he thinks fit may also dissolve the Council of Promoters and appoint an *ad hoc* Council of Promoters provided, however, that the Council of Promoters appointed by the President under this sub-rule shall function only until the new Council of Promoters is elected at the next Annual General Meeting immediately failing the appointment of such *ad hoc* Council of Promoters.

28. **Secretary-cum-Treasurer.** The Secretary-cum-Treasurer shall be in charge of all executive work of the society. He shall keep records of the affairs of the society and issue calls for various meetings. He will not act under the guidance, supervision and advice from the President and the Council of Promoters.

29. **Audit.** At each Annual General Meeting a qualified Auditor/Auditors as provided in Explanation to s. 15(2) of the West Bengal Societies Registration Act 1961, shall be appointed. The Auditor shall submit a report on the income and expenditure, account and balance-sheet of the society presented by the Council of Promoters. The minutes of the meeting of the Council of Promoters and of the General Meeting, books of accounts, the correspondence and in general, all records of the society as well as any date required for the carrying on of the audit shall, upon a requisition by the auditors, be submitted to them.

30. **Casting Vote.** In all matters to be decided by a simple majority in General Meetings, casting vote of the PRESIDENT shall prevail in case of equality of votes.

31. **Financial Year.** The financial year of the Society shall commence on the 1st day of January and end with the 31st day of December according to English calendar year.

32. **Investments.** The funds of the society, besides being invested in the investment authorised by law for the time being in force relating to the investment of the TRUST FUNDS may also be invested in fixed deposit account with a scheduled bank or banks as may from time to time be directed by the Council of Promoters.

33. The name of a member of the society whose fees shall be in arrears may be removed from the register of members of the society on three months' notice to such member unless in the meantime such arrears are paid. Any member, whose name has been so removed from the register of members, shall not be eligible for readmission as a member unless he pays all arrears for which his name has been so removed from the register of members.

34. Any member may resign his membership by serving a written notice to that effect on the Secretary, but any dues payable by the member to the society on the date of resignation shall be payable by him.

35. **Suits and Proceedings.** The society may sue or be sued in the name of its secretary.

36. **Indemnity.** Every member of the Council of Promoters or any sub-committee, auditor, and other officer or servant of the society shall be indemnified against all liabilities arising out of acts and things done by him in performance of the duties entrusted, by way of damages otherwise, and all losses, costs, charges and expenses which he may incur or become liable by reason of any contract entered into or any act or deed done by him as such member, auditor, officer or servant in any way or about the discharge of his duties.

CERTIFIED to be a true copy of the Rules and Regulations of ....

1. .... President
2. .... Secretary-cum-Treasurer
3. .... Member

Council of Promoters

Date ....

Trade Union

A trade union is an association of wage earners for maintaining and/or improving the conditions of their employment. As defined in the *Chamber's Encyclopaedia* "it is an association of wage-earners or salary earning people primarily for the purpose of collective action for forwarding or defending its professional interests". It is defined under s. 2A of the Indian Trade Union Act 1926. It has not grown out of old caste system or craft guilds though they contained rudiments of trade unionism. It was not originally created by law. Its struggle for recognition and realisation of its objectives and the problems of regulating its activities have been modified by law.

Article 19(1)(*c*) of the Constitution of India gives all citizens the right to form associations and unions. The right to form a union is given by sub-cl. (*c*) of Art. 19, the right of the members to meet is guaranteed by sub-cl. (*b*) of Art. 19, their right to move from one place to another place within India by sub-cl. (*d*), their right to discuss their problems and to inter-change their views by sub-cl. (*a*), their right to hold property by sub-cl. (*f*) and so on each however being subject to such reasonable restrictions as may be imposed by cls. (2) to (6) of Art. 19.[4] An association of citizens cannot, however, claim the right and powers nor the facilities which are not guaranteed to citizens nor freedom from restrictions to which the citizens composing it are subject. The right to form a union under sub-cl. (*c*) of Art. 19 does not by any means carry with it a concomitant right that the unions formed for protecting the interest of labour shall be free from all interference except those justified on grounds of public order or morality. They are always subject to and governed by such laws, rules and ordinances as might from time to time be enacted to impose limitations and restrictions, the union of citizens might legitimately engage themselves. In any event trade unions have under Art. 19(1)(*c*) no guaranteed right to an effective, collective bargaining or to strike either as part of its collective bargaining or otherwise. The right to strike or the right to declare a lock-out is controlled or restricted by legislation, standing orders, ordinances and the validity of such legislation, standing order or ordinance is tested not with reference to the criteria laid down in cl. (4) of Art. 19 but by totally different consideration.[5]

The enjoyment and fulfilment of the purposes of the trade union are not in all cases guaranteed by sub-cl. (*c*) of Art. 19(1). The right to be recognised and/or to represent the workmen is never an absolute right guaranteed by Art. 19(1)(*c*) though every member has the right to join a union of his own choice or refuse to be member of a union.[6]

Trade Union with reference to the law of contract. Section 27 of the Indian Contract Act 1872, declares any agreement by which anyone is restrained from exercising a lawful trade or profession, or business of any kind to that extent void. Agreements in restraint of trade are also bad as opposed to public policy under ss. 23 and 24 of the Indian Contract Act. Nevertheless s. 19 of the Trade Unions Act 1926, protects such agreement from being void or voidable on the ground that any of its objects is in restraint of trade when the same is between the members of a registered trade union. But no

4 J.L. Mallick's *Trade Union Law*, p. 24.

5 *All India Bank Employees' Association* v *The National Industrial Tribunal* AIR 1962 SC 171.

6 *Uttar Pradeshiya Shramik Maha Sangha* v *State of Uttar Pradesh* AIR 1960 All 45; see also *Keshoram Rayon Workmen's Union* v *Registrar of Trade Unions* AIR 1967 Cal 507.

suit or any other action lies for recovery of damage for breach of conditions on which any member or members shall or shall not sell their goods, transact business work or employ or be employed in any trade. The English Act, *i.e.* s. 3 of the Trade Union Act 1871, gives complete protection to all unions whether registered or not.

A trade union can act through agents and, in doing so, it remains liable for costs, charges and expenses, negligence and defaults of agents.[7]

Nevertheless s. 18(2) of the Indian Trade Unions Act protects the trade union from any liability on account of acts of agents in cases when done without knowledge or against express instructions as registration of a union gives it a separate legal entity from its members. The union acts as agents of the members.

Section 23 of the Payment of Wages Act 1936, provides that any agreement or contract whereby any employee relinquishes any right conferred upon him by the Act is void in so far as the same deprives him of such a right.

Government servants have the right under Art. 19(1)(c) to form associations. The Government can control recognition in the interest of or efficiency and discipline of the employees. There is no fundamental right to obtain recognition of the Government.[8]

Trade union with reference to law of crime. Although s. 17 of the Indian Trade Unions Act 1926, protects all officers and members against offence under s. 120(B) of the Indian Penal Code (which refers to criminal conspiracy other than conspiracy to commit an offence) in connection with any contract or agreement as between them for promotion of the objects of the union (s. 15 of the Act) but nevertheless the immunity does not extend to criminal trespass, intimidation, molestation or violence (ss. 143, 340, 342, 352, 425, 447 and 506, IPC).[9] In the result peaceful strike or gathering together though permitted, unlawful confinement, criminal trespass, force, assault are not exempt from liability. In any event an agreement to commit an offence is never exempted under the criminal law of the land.[10] A strike is illegal against contract to the contrary in the contract of employments.

The trade union is mainly a post-war organisation; nevertheless the idea dates back to early part of the 18th century. Before 1918, workers engaged in the industry were in an unorganised state. Working hours were inordinately long and wages were pitiably poor, education was practically nil and the conditions of workers were in fact humiliating so much so that workers were treated mere adjuncts of the machinery rather than human

7 *Taffvale's* cases 1901 AC 420 (429).
8 *Raghubir* v *Union of India* AIR 1962 SC 263.
9 *Rooke* v *Barnad* 1964 AC 1129.
10 *Joy Engineering Works* v *State* AIR 1969 Cal 407.

beings. The import of the World War which resulted in the rise in prices and wages and costs of living, contributed to the cause of labour consciousness and established occupational units in the repealing and amending Act of 1942 (Act 25 of 1942) and, came into operation on 1st June 1917, was the earliest legislation on the subject. It was subsequently amended by the Indian Trade Unions Amendment Act XV of 1928 and again by the repealing and amending Act of 1942 (Act 25 of 1942) and, lastly, by the Amendment Act 1947, which received the assent of the Governor-General on 20th December 1947. The Act protects the members of the trade union against civil action in respect of any act done in furtherance of the trade and from liability for criminal conspiracy for any agreement or understanding as between themselves. Various temporary or permanent organised bodies were set up primarily for the purpose or regulating the relation between workmen and which imposed restricted conditions on the conduct of any trade or business and included any federation of two or more unions. The Act achieved success in every State in respect of anything done in furtherance of trade so much so that regulations were enacted to help its implementation in West Bengal, Bombay United Province, Andhra, Madhya Pradesh, Assam and Madras. The labour courts were set up to hear disputes arising out of the refusal of the employers to recognise particular unions. A trade union was not entitled to recognition under any order of the labour court until and unless it fulfilled certain conditions. The Amendment Act specified certain acts for recognition of the trade union. The act also specified certain acts as unfair practice on the part of the employer. A trade union is an association completely different from the company and, even though registered as such, cannot be a trade union. It, however, does not follow that a combination which purports to be registered as a company is not a trade union. A trade union can be registered only under the Trade Unions Act but not under the Societies Registration Act 1860 (XXI of 1860) or the Co-operative Societies Act 1972 (Act II of 1972) or under the Companies Act 1956 (Act 1 of 1956); registration of the trade union under any of those Acts is void *ab initio* (s. 14 of the Trade Unions Act).

The mode of registration is simple. Any seven or more persons by subscription of their respective names to the rules of the trade union and also by applying under the provisions of the Act may apply for registration under this Act. Chapter 2 of the Trade Unions Act contains full particulars as to how a trade union may be registered. It also provides for the regulations as are contemplated in s. 29 of the Trade Unions Act.[11] The condition of registration being that the trade union becomes a body corporate and so without registering it cannot have a real and perpetual succession. It can acquire and own property; it can contract to achieve and, lastly, it can sue and be sued when registered.

11 The Trade Unions Act 1926 as amended by Amendment Act of 1947.

FORM A

(Regulation 3)

Application for Registration of a Trade Union

Dated the .... day of .... 19.........

1. We hereby apply for the registration of a trade union under the name of ....

2. The address of the head office of the union is ....

3. The union came into existence on the .... day of .... 19......... (and has on its roll on the date of his application .... members).[12]

4. The union is a union of employers/workers engaged in the .... industry (or profession).

5. The particulars required by s. 5(1)(*c*) of the Indian Trade Unions Act 1926, are given in Schedule I.

6. The particulars given in Schedule II show the provision made in the rules for the matters detailed in s. 6 of the Indian Trade Unions Act 1926.

7. (To be struck out in the case of unions which have not been in existence for one year before the date of application). The particulars required by s. 5(2) of the Indian Trade Unions Act 1926, are given in Schedule III.

8. We have been duly authorised to make this application by ....

		Signature	*Occupation*	*Address*
Signed	1	....	....	....
	2	....	....	....
	3	....	....	....
	4	....	....	....
	5	....	....	....
	6	....	....	....
	7	....	....	....

12 *Vide* Notification No. 2474 Com., dated the 9th August 1939.

State here whether the authority was given by a resolution of a general meeting of the union, or, if not, in what other way it was given.

To
The Registrar of Trade Unions, West Bengal

SCHEDULE I

List of officers

NOTE. Enter in this Schedule the names of all members of the executive (including all honorary or temporary members)[13] of the union; shown in column 1 the names of any posts held by them (*i.e.*, President, Secretary, Treasurer, etc.,) in addition to their office as members of the executive.

SCHEDULE II

Reference to Rules

The numbers of the rules making provision for the several matters detailed in column 1 are given in column 2 below:

1 *Matter*	2 *Number of Rules*
Name of union	
The whole of the objects for which the union has been established	
The whole of the purposes for which the general funds of the union shall be applicable	
The maintenance of a list of members	
The facilities provided for the inspection of the list of members by officers and members	
The admission of ordinary members	
The admission of honorary or temporary members	
The conditions under which members are entitled to benefits assured by the rules	
The conditions under which fines or forfeitures can be imposed or varied	
The manner in which the rules shall be amended, varied or rescinded	
The manner in which members of the executive and the other officers of the union shall be appointed and removed	
The safe custody of the fund	
The annual audit of the accounts	
The facilities for the inspection of the account books by officers and members	
The manner in which the union may be dissolved	

13 *Vide* Notification No. 2474, dated the 9th August 1939.

SCHEDULE III

(This need not be filled in if the union came into existence less than one year before the date of application for registration) Statement of liabilities and assets on the .... day of .... 19.........

Liabilities	*Rs. P.*	*Assets*	*Rs. P.*
Amount of general fund		Cash	
Amount of political fund		In hand of Treasurer	
		In hands of Secretary	
		In hands of	
Loans from		In the ...... Bank	
....		In the ...... Bank	
....		Securities as per list below	
....		Unpaid subscriptions due	
Debts due to		Loans to	
....		....	
....		....	
Other liabilities (to be specified)		Immovable property	
		Goods and furniture	
....		Other assets (to be specified)	
....		....	
		....	
Total liabilities		Total assets	

List of Securities

Particulars	*Nominal value*	*Market value*	*In hands of*

Signed 1 ....

2 ....

3 ....

4 ....

5 ....

6 ....

7 ....

Model Constitution of a Trade Union

Rules and Regulations of .... (name of the union)

1. The name of the union shall be the .... and hereinafter referred to as "the union".

2. The registered office of the union shall be ....

3. The aims and objects of the union shall be—

(*i*) to redress the grievances of members;

(*ii*) to secure for the members proper conditions of service;

(*iii*) to persuade the employers to standardise at a fair level the wages of their workmen;

(*iv*) to prevent any reduction of wages below the permissible level;

(*v*) to organise and unite the persons engaged in the .... industry in the .... city and to regulate the relations of employers and of employees, *inter se*;

(*vi*) to provide against sickness, unemployment, infirmity, old age and death;

(*vii*) to secure compensation for members in cases of accidents under the Workmen's Compensation Act;

(*viii*) to make efforts at settlement of disputes between employers and workmen in an amicable manner in the interest of continuity of work;

(*ix*) to provide legal assistance to members in respect of matters or disputes arising out of, or incidental to, their employment;

(*x*) to render necessary help to the members during the period of any strike brought about with the permission of the union or a lock-out;

(*xi*) to obtain adequate information relating to the .... industry in India and outside;

(*xii*) to co-operate and federate with labour organisations having similar objects in India and outside;

(*xiii*) to help, in accordance with the Indian Trade Unions Act, the working classes in India;

(*xiv*) generally, to take such other steps as may be necessary to ameliorate the social, economic, civic and political conditions of the members;

(*xv*) to open permanent or temporary centres for the achievement of all or any of the above objects.

4. Any person engaged in the .... industry in the .... (in .... District) who has attained the age of 15 years shall be entitled to

become an ordinary member of the union on payment of an admission fee of annas .... and a monthly subscription of .... provided he agrees to abide by these rules and regulations and such other rules and bye-laws as may from time to time be framed by the union.

5. A member running in arrears of his monthly subscriptions for a period of three months shall be declared a defaulter and, in the event of his not clearing up the arrears within one month of such declaration, he shall cease to be a member and his name shall be removed. He may, however, rejoin on payment of arrears and fresh admission fee.

6. **Benefits.** No member of the union shall be entitled to any benefits that the union may decide to give to its members unless he has been a member for at least six months and has paid all contributions.

7. A member of the union who is in arrears with his subscription or dues shall not be entitled to any benefits until all arrears have been paid and a period of two months has elapsed from the date of payment of such arrears.

8. Should the members of the union go on strike without the sanction or approval of the Managing Committee, they shall not be entitled to any benefits whatever.

9. The union shall keep a register of all its members containing their names and particulars of their place of work, their residence, etc.

10. The register shall be open to inspection by any member or officer of the union at the head office during the hours during which the office of the union is open on any weekday excluding holidays.

11. **Executive.** The executive of the union shall consist of a President, not more than two Vice-Presidents, a General Secretary, two Secretaries, a Treasurer, and four more members. All of them shall be elected at the Annual General Meeting of the union and they shall be eligible for re-election.

The Executive so constituted shall have power to co-opt two more members.

12. **Management of the union.** The management of the affairs of the union shall be carried on by the Executive constituted as above.

13. In the event of a vacancy occurring among the office-bearers or the members of the Executive, it shall be filled by the Managing Committee by co-option.

14. Any office-bearer of the union or a member of the executive can be removed at the General Meeting of the members by a three-fourths majority for committing any fraud or having acted against the interests of the union, provided the office-bearer or the member to be removed is given reasonable opportunity to explain his conduct.

15. The Executive shall meet once a month or as often as found necessary on such days and at such place as may be fixed by the General Secretary in consultation with the President.

16. The presence of at least one-third members of the Managing Committee shall be necessary to form a quorum. No quorum is necessary for adjourned meetings.

17. At least five days' notice shall be given for a Managing Committee meeting.

18. The President shall preside over all meetings of the union and the Executive, preserve order, sign all minutes and shall be allowed to give a casting vote only. The President shall have power if necessary, to call special meetings of the Executive or of the union, whenever necessary. One of the Vice-Presidents shall function in place of the President in his absence.

19. The General Secretary shall record minutes of all union and committee meetings, conduct all correspondence, convene all meetings, keep all accounts, exercise a supervision over the affairs of the union and shall also keep a correct account of all receipts and expenditure. He shall prepare a balance-sheet annually showing clearly every item of receipts and expenditure. He shall be responsible for submitting to the Registrar of Trade Unions all returns and notice that should be sent to that officer under the Indian Trade Unions Act 1926. He shall have power to engage, in consultation with the President and subject to the approval or confirmation of the Managing Committee, any assistants for organising and clerical purposes if he considers necessary, and all such assistants shall be under the control of the General Secretary.

20. The Secretaries shall generally help the General Secretary. One of them shall perform the duties of the General Secretary in his absence.

21. The Treasurer shall be responsible for all moneys which may from time to time be paid into the union and for duly banking them. He shall make payments towards all expenditure sanctioned by the Managing Committee. He shall not have the power to draw money from the bank without first having the cheque signed by the President or the General Secretary.

22. There shall be held in the month of April or May an Annual General Meeting of all the members of the union to transact the following business:

(*a*) to adopt the report of the work done by the union and the audited statement of accounts;

(*b*) to elect the office-bearers and other members of the Managing Committee for the current year; and

(*c*) to transact such other business as may be brought forward with the permission of the Chairman.

23. The President may call a General Meeting of the members of the union whenever he thinks necessary by giving 15 days' notice to the members and shall call it on a requisition signed by one-fifth of the total strength of the union within 20 days of the receipt of the requisition. The quorum for the General Meeting shall be one-third of total membership. No quorum is necessary for adjourned meetings.

24. The general funds of the union shall consist of the admission fees, subscriptions from members, donation etc. They shall be deposited in a bank or banks, approved by the Managing Committee in the name of the union and the account may be operated by the Treasurer and either the President or the General Secretary. The General Secretary or the Treasurer shall not keep more than Rs. 50 with him for current expenses.

25. The union shall make the provision for the annual audit of the accounts of the union by competent auditors appointed by the Executive in accordance with the provisions of trade regulations applicable to the union.

26. The rules may be amended, altered, rescinded or added to at any time by a majority of the members present at a General Meeting provided a previous notice of at least seven days is given to the members of the proposed amendments, etc.

27. (*a*) The union shall not be dissolved except by the vote of a majority of three-fourths members present at a General Meeting called for the purpose, provided the total number of votes cast at such a meeting is not less than two-thirds of the total number of the members then on the rolls of the union.

(*b*) On the dissolution of the union the executive shall send a notice of dissolution to the Registrar in the manner provided by s. 28 of the Trade Unions Act and shall also make arrangements for winding up the union and to distribute its assets.

Dated this .... day of 2000

12

Companies

A company is a separate person or entity having independent existence from its members. A company may be a private company or a public limited company. The liability of its members may be limited by shares held by them or by guarantee.

Any two persons may form a private company. The maximum number of members of a private company shall not exceed fifty. A public company may be formed by any seven persons. No limit has been prescribed as to the maximum number of members of a public company.

The constitution of a company is contained in the Memorandum of Association which is required to be registered with the Registrar of Companies. The internal regulations of the company are contained in its Articles of Association registered with the Registrar of Companies. The provisions of the Companies Act 1956 will override any provisions in the Memorandum of Association or the Articles of Association of the company.

If a company acquires any property subject to a charge, this fact has to be registered with the Registrar of Companies. When a company creates a charge over any of its assets (other than Pledge) such charge has to be registered with the Registrar of Companies. The creditor or the charge-holder may register such charge with the Registrar of Companies if the company delays or fails to do so.

All notices and documents may be served on a company or an officer thereof sending them to the company or at the registered office of the company. The service of notice may be by post under Certificate of Posting, by Registered Post or by leaving it at the registered office. Other modes of service at the registered office will also be valid.

The management is in the hands of the Board of Directors. The Board can exercise all the powers of the company for running the business. The Board acts by Resolution and by a majority vote.

The Board of Directors can exercise the powers on behalf of the company by issuing Debentures and to borrow moneys by passing appropriate resolution at a meeting of the Board. However, in the case of a public company or a private company which is the subsidiary of a public company, the Board requires consent of the General Meeting to sell, lease or dispose of the whole or substantially the whole of the undertakings of the company or to borrow moneys exceeding the aggregate of the paid-up capital of the company and its free reserves.

All the important contracts and execution of documents shall be pursuant to authorisation at a general meeting wherever necessary and the Board Resolution. Such Board Resolution may authorise the Secretary and a Director of the company to affix the Official Seal of the company on the documents and to execute the same and also specify the person who will execute the documents.[1]

A company may appoint a Sole Selling Agent for any area for a term of five years or less at a time. The appointment is renewable for a similar period. Such appointment has to be approved by the first general meeting of the company after the appointment. If the general meeting does not approve then from the date of the meeting the agreement becomes void. The Central Government may regulate the appointments or terms and conditions of the appointment of Sole Selling Agent for any area or for any goods.[2]

A company may propose to amalgamate with another company. The other company in such a case takes over all the assets and liabilities of the first (amalgamating) company. The two companies may amalgamate on terms and conditions agreed upon by them and on obtaining the consent of the respective shareholders at a General Meeting and on notice to the Central Government with the sanction of the High Court concerned.[3]

FORMS

Memorandum of Association

.... Private Ltd.

(Incorporated under the Companies Act 1956)

1. The name of the company is ....

2. The Registered Office of the company will be situated at .... in the State of ....

1 Sections 292 and 293 of the Companies Act 1956.
2 Sections 294 and 294AA of the Companies Act 1956.
3 Sections 391 to 396A of the Companies Act 1956.

3. The objects to be pursued by the company immediately after incorporation are:

To acquire by purchase the business of publishers of journals and periodicals carried on under the names and styles of Indian Journal of Power and River Valley Development and Indian Mining Journal as going concerns with all the assets and liabilities, pending contracts, rights, privileges and goodwill attached thereto.

4. The objects incidental to and ancillary to attainment of the main objects are:

(*a*) To carry on the business of printers and publishers of books, journals, periodicals, newspapers, magazines, etc., in different languages and to organise their sales in India and outside India directly or through agents.

(*b*) To carry on the business of advertising agents for publicity through journals and periodicals, cinema slides, neon signs, and all other modes of advertisement.

(*c*) To carry on the business of importers, exporters, traders, agents, printers, contracts, brokers, and dealers of all commodities that may be found profitable by the company.

(*d*) To initiate, promote, encourage, facilitate and support financially or otherwise research of all kinds of scientific or natural phenomena whether directly or indirectly connected with any of the above subjects.

5. The other objects for which the company is established are as follows:

(*i*) To acquire and undertake the whole or any part of the business of any concern either private or public company, firm or individual which may in the opinion of the company be carried on conveniently.

(*ii*) To apply for, purchase or otherwise acquire any patents, licences, concessions and the like conferring any exclusive or non-exclusive or limited right to use, make or deal with or the acquisition of which may be calculated directly or indirectly to benefit the company.

(*iii*) To enter into partnership or any other arrangement for sharing profits, union of interests, co-operation, joint venture, reciprocal concessions with any person, firm or company carrying on or engaged in or about to carry on or engage in any business or transaction which the company is authorised to carry on or engage in or any business or transaction capable of being conducted so as to benefit the company directly or indirectly.

(*iv*) To enter into any agreement with any Government, railway, body corporate, corporation or other authorities supreme, municipal, local or otherwise and private or public bodies that seem competent or undertake operations similar to those undertaken by this company and conducive to the company's objects or any of them and to obtain from any such Government, railway, body concessions which the company may think desirable to obtain and to carry out, exercise and comply with any such arrangements, rights, privileges and concessions.

(*v*) To advance and lend money upon such security as may be thought proper or without taking any security and to invest and deal with the money of the company not immediately required upon such securities.

(*vi*) To borrow or raise or secure payments of money in such manner as the company shall deem fit and in particular by issue of debentures charged upon all or any of the company's properties, both present and future, including its uncalled capital and to purchase, redeem and to pay off any such securities or debentures.

(*vii*) To draw, accept, make, endorse, discount and negotiate bills of exchange, promissory notes and other negotiable instruments, coupons, drafts, bills of lading, railway receipts, debentures, certificates, securities, and other instruments and securities whether transferable or negotiable or not.

(*viii*) And generally to do all such other things as are incidental or conducive to the attainment of the objects or any of them and the intention is that the objects set forth in all the paragraphs of this clause shall have the widest possible construction and shall be in no way limited or restricted by reference to or in reference from the terms of any other paragraphs of this clause.

6. The liability of the members is limited.

7. The capital of the company is Rs. 21,000 divided into 2,100 Equity shares of Rs. 10 each with the power to increase or reduce the capital as may be determined by the company in General Meetings from time to time.

We, the several persons whose names, addresses and descriptions are subscribed hereto are desirous of being formed into a private limited company in pursuance of this Memorandum of Association and we are respectively agreeable to take the number of shares in the capital of the company set opposite to our respective names.

Serial No.	*Names, Addresses and Description*	*Number of Shares taken*	*Witness*

Dated the .... day of .... 2000.

Articles of Association

.... Company Ltd.

(Incorporated under the Companies Act 1956)

1. The provisions of Table A in the first schedule of the Companies Act 1956, shall apply to this company so far as they are applicable to private limited Companies and are not expressly provided otherwise in these articles.

2. **Share Capital.** The capital of the company is Rs. 21,000 divided into 2,100 Equity shares of Rs. 10 each payable Rs. 5 on application and the balance on allotment.

3. **Private Company.** The company shall be a private limited company and accordingly:

(*a*) No invitation shall be made to the public to subscribe its share capital or debenture, if any.

(*b*) The number of members of the company shall not exceed 50 excluding the employees of the company and the joint holders of one or more shares shall be considered for the purpose of this sub-clause as one member.

(*c*) The right to transfer its shares shall be restricted as hereinafter provided.

4. **Agreement.** As soon as possible after the registration of the company the Directors shall give effect to the agreement between the firms Indian Journal of Power and River Valley Development and Indian Mining Journal of the one part and the company of the other part to acquire the business as stated in the Memorandum of Association of the company, by proper entries in the books of account.

5. **Shares.** Subject to and without prejudice to the other provisions of these articles, the shares of the company shall be under the control of the Directors who shall allot to the members its shares at such time and in such manner and for such consideration as Directors shall determine.

6. **Transfer and Transmission of Shares.** Shares of the company may be transferred by the holders thereof to their sons, daughters, wives or other legal heirs or any other member or members of the company in the usual way, but such transferrer shall be deemed to remain the holder of any share transferred until the name of the transferee is entered in the Register of Members as the holder thereof.

7. In case a shareholder of the company expresses his intention to transfer all or any part of the shares held by him to any other person except those referred to in the above article, he is to signify his such intention by proposal in writing to the Directors of the company giving the name, address and description of such proposed transferee and the Directors will convene a meeting forthwith to consider such proposal and the Directors will be at

liberty to either take in such transferee as a member of the company or arrange the sale of such shares to some of the members of the company.

8. Any member wishing to transfer his shares shall give notice in writing (hereinafter called the SALE NOTICE) to the company of his intention to do so specifying and denoting the number of shares he intends to sell. Every such notice shall constitute the company the agent of the member proposing to sell (hereinafter called the VENDOR) for the sale of such shares as a *fair value* to any member of the company (hereinafter called the PURCHASER) or in the absence of any member agreeing to purchase, to any outsider whom the Directors in their meeting may nominate. No sale notice may be withdrawn without the written sanction of the Directors.

9. On receipt of a SALE NOTICE the Directors shall offer the shares comprised in such notice at their "fair value" in the first instance to the existing members of the company and shall set a limit of time not less than 30 days within which such offer, if not accepted, shall be deemed to have been declined. Should more than one member accept the offer, the Directors may either divide the shares between them as nearly as may be in proportion to their holding in the company.

10. If the Directors are unable within 60 days after the receipt of the SALE NOTICE by them to find any member willing to purchase any or all of such shares offered for sale at a "fair value", then they may by resolution nominate an outsider, as PURCHASER of such shares and the VENDOR shall be bound upon payment of the "fair value" to transfer the shares to such purchaser be he a member or outsider, within seven days from the receipt of the notice of the transaction.

11. If the Directors fail within 90 days after service of the sale notice to find a PURCHASER for any or all of the shares comprised therein at a "fair value", they shall give notice to this effect to the vendor within seven days thereafter stating the best value, if any, that they are able to obtain for the said shares.

12. The VENDOR shall then be at liberty to either accept the offer or to sell and transfer the said shares to any person he may select without the sanction of the Directors provided that the sale be effected at a figure higher than that offered in writing by the Directors, and the company shall thereafter be bound by such transfer. In the absence of any notice to the vendor as prescribed here, he shall conclude that no offer is forthcoming for the said shares and may proceed to deal with them in the manner prescribed above.

13. Before the ordinary General Meeting of each year, the auditors of the company shall make out a valuation of the company and assign a "fair value" to each share and on the basis of such valuation at the ordinary General Meeting in each year, the company shall by resolution fix the price of the shares (but such price must not be less than the value reported by the auditor).

14. **Directors.** The number of Directors shall not be less than two and more than five.

15. The qualification of a Director shall be the holding of at least 100 shares in the company. The Directors shall get such remuneration as may be determined by the company in general meeting from time to time.

16. The following persons shall be the first Directors of the company:

(1) Mr. ....

(2) Mr. ....

17. The Board of Directors may appoint additional Directors who will hold office up to the date of the next Annual General Meeting of the company but the number of the Directors and additional Directors together shall not exceed five.

18. The business of the company shall be managed by the Managing Director under the supervision of the Board of Directors.

19. The Board of Directors shall appoint one of the them to the office of the Managing Director for such terms and conditions as they think fit but not exceeding five years at a time.

20. **Rotation of Directors.** All the Directors shall retire every year but they will be eligible for re-election.

21. **Disqualification of Directors.** The office of Director shall be vacated if he:

(*a*) fails to obtain within the time specified in sub-sec. (1) of section 27 of the Companies Act 1956 or any time thereafter ceases to hold the share-qualification necessary for his appointment, or

(*b*) is found to be of unsound mind by a competent court of law having jurisdiction; or

(*c*) is adjudged an insolvent; or

(*d*) applies to be adjudged an insolvent; or

(*e*) is convicted by a court in India of any offence and is sentenced in respect thereof to imprisonment for not less than six months;or

(*f*) fails to pay any calls made in respect of shares of the company held by him whether alone or jointly with others within six months from the date of such calls being made; or

(*g*) is found to be interested directly or indirectly in any business almost similar to that of the company without having previous consent of the Board of Directors in writing.

22. **Meetings.** A meeting of the Board of Directors shall be held at least once in every three calendar months. Two Directors present in person shall form the quorum.

23. Notice of every meeting of the Board of Directors shall be given in writing to every Director at his usual address.

24. An Annual General Meeting of the company shall be held within 18 months from the date of its incorporation and thereafter once at least in every year at such time (not being more than nine months after the expiry of the financial year of the company).

25. Notice of an Annual General Meeting shall be given to each member in writing to his usual address at least 21 days before the date of the meeting specifying the place, day and hour of the meeting and also a statement of the business to be transacted thereat.

26. No business shall be transacted at any General Meeting unless a quorum of two members is present in person at the time when the meeting proceeds to transact business.

27. On show of hands every member present in person shall have one vote; on a poll every member present in person or by proxy shall have one vote for each share held by him. In the case of an equality of votes the chairman shall have a casting vote.

28. **Accounts.** The Board of Directors shall keep or cause to be kept proper books of accounts.

29. The books of accounts shall be kept at the registered office of the company and shall be open to inspection by the Directors during the usual office hours.

30. The Board of Directors shall, as required by sections 210 and 211 of the Companies Act 1956, cause to be prepared and to be laid before the Company in the General Meeting such Profit and Loss Accounts and Balance-Sheet and Reports as are referred to in those sections.

31. **Audit.** Once at least in every year the accounts of the company shall be examined and the correctness of the Balance-Sheet and Profit and Loss Accounts be ascertained by a Chartered Accountant.

We, the several persons whose names, addresses and descriptions are subscribed hereto, are desirous of being formed into a private limited company in pursuance of this Memorandum of Association and we are respectively agreeable to take the number of shares in the capital of the Company set opposite to our respective names.

Serial No.	*Names, Addresses and Description*	*Number of Shares taken*	*Witness*

Dated the .... day of .... 1999.

Agreement of Amalgamation of One Company with Another

THIS AGREEMENT is made on this 5th day of June 2000 BETWEEN AB Co. Ltd., a company registered under the Companies Act 1956 and having its registered office at .... (hereinafter called the VENDOR) of the One Part and XY & Co. Ltd., a company registered under the Companies Act 1956 and having its registered office at .... (hereinafter called the PURCHASER) of the Other Part.

WHEREAS the VENDOR is a company limited by shares with a capital of Rs. 50 lakhs divided into 50,000 shares of Rs. 100 each;

AND WHEREAS the VENDOR has under its Memorandum of Association the necessary rights and powers to sell, transfer or convey the business of the company in whole or in part with all its undertakings, assets, pending contracts and other rights whatsoever for adequate consideration in cash, shares, debentures or such other securities;

AND WHEREAS the PURCHASER is a company limited by shares with a share capital of Rs. 100 lakhs divided into 1,00,000 shares of Rs. 100 each;

AND WHEREAS all the shares of PURCHASER have been allotted and paid-up and the PURCHASER is authorised under its Memorandum of Association to increase its share capital;

AND WHEREAS the PURCHASER has the power under its Memorandum of Association to purchase the business of any other company similar to the one carried on by it as a running concern with all its assets, rights and liabilities whatsoever;

AND WHEREAS the VENDOR has agreed to amalgamate with the PURCHASER and it has passed necessary resolution for that purpose on .... and the PURCHASER has also passed the necessary resolution on .... for taking over the business of the VENDOR with all its undertakings, assets and liabilities.

NOW THESE PRESENTS WITNESSETH and the parties hereby agree as follows:

1. The PURCHASER shall forthwith pass the necessary resolution to increase its share capital to Rs. 150 lakhs by the creation and issue of 50,000 shares of the value of Rs. 100 each ranking *pari passu* in all respects with its present shares.

2. The VENDOR shall sell and the PURCHASER shall purchase and take over the entire business of the VENDOR with all its undertakings, rights, assets and liabilities whatsoever with effect from the .... day of

.... for consideration of Rs. 60 lakhs agreed to be paid to the VENDOR in the manner as follows:

(*a*) Rs. 10 lakhs in cash; and the balance

(*b*) Rs. 50 lakhs by issue of shares to the VENDOR

or to such persons as the VENDOR may direct, which shares shall be treated as fully paid-up.

3. As for the .... day of .... the PURCHASER shall be entitled to the business of the VENDOR with all its undertakings, rights, securities and liabilities whatsoever and wherever situate and shall thenceforward be entitled to carry on the business, realise the securities without any let or hindrance from the VENDOR company or any one claiming through or under it.

4. Upto the above said .... day of .... when the business of the VENDOR is taken over as above the VENDOR shall carry on its business for and on behalf of the PURCHASER.

5. On or before the expiry of .... days from the date of taking over of business as above the VENDOR shall deliver to the PURCHASER all title deeds of the properties and the premises belonging to it along with an abstract report regarding its title to the properties and premises. The defects, if any, to the title of the VENDOR to the said properties and premises shall be intimated to the VENDOR in writing within .... days after receipt of the title deeds and abstract of title and if no objection is lodged within the time prescribed as above the PURCHASER must be deemed to have accepted the title.

6. The purchase shall be completed on .... the .... to .... at the office of the PURCHASER'S Solicitors when the PURCHASER shall pay the said sum of Rs. 10 lakhs in cash or Bank Draft and shall hand over the Certificates for Rs. 50 lakhs of the said shares and thereupon the VENDOR and all other necessary parties shall execute all such deeds and do such things as may be reasonably required for vesting all the properties agreed to be sold in the PURCHASER.

7. The entire staff of the VENDOR company shall be taken over and maintained by the PURCHASER company with effect from the aforesaid date of taking over on the same terms and conditions as those are at present prevailing.

8. For the purpose of stamp duty the value of goodwill fittings and fixtures, book debts, contracts, patents, designs and trade marks, belonging to the VENDOR shall be taken as Rs. 10 lakhs and the value of all other properties of the VENDOR hereby agreed to be sold at Rs. 50 lakhs.

IN WITNESS WHEREOF the parties hereto executed these presents on the day, month and year first above-written.

Signed, sealed and delivered
by Mr. ....
pursuant to Board Resolution
dated .... of the VENDOR
AB Co. Ltd. in the presence of: VENDOR

Signed, sealed and delivered
by Mr. ....
pursuant to Board Resolution
dated .... of XY & Co. Ltd.
in the presence of: PURCHASER

Conversion of firm into Company

The Companies Act 1956 in Part IX, section 567 makes provision as to Companies and firms authorised to register under the Act. The section provides *inter alia* that before the Registration of a Joint-stock Company there shall be delivered to the Registrar of Companies a list containing the names, addresses and occupation of all persons who were the members of the firm, their shares, a copy of the Deed of Partnership, a Statement specifying the nominal share capital, number of shares taken by each of the members and the name of the company to be registered with the word "Limited". This section can be taken as the enabling provision for conversion of a partnership firm into a Limited Company. The existing partnership firm is required to execute a document in the line of the Memorandum of Association containing the requirements of this section.

SUGGESTED FORM

Company Limited by Shares

Memorandum and Articles of Association of Industrial Company Pvt. Ltd.

MEMORANDUM OF ASSOCIATION made this 15th day of September 2000 BETWEEN S. Tanton residing at .... by occupation business of the FIRST PART, T. Tanton residing at .... by occupation business of the SECOND PART, U. Tanton, residing at .... by profession business of the THIRD PART, V. Tanton residing at ....

.... by occupation business of the FOURTH PART, W. Tanton, residing at .... by occupation business of the FIFTH PART, X. Tanton residing at .... by occupation business of the SIXTH PART and Y. Tanton residing at .... by occupation business of the SEVENTH PART.

WHEREAS the parties on the FIRST PART to SEVENTH PART are carrying on business in partnership under the name and style of Industrial Company in Delhi having several branches in South, East and West of India under a Registered Deed of Partnership dated ....

AND WHEREAS the firm has been carrying on business as manufacturer of and dealer in all kinds of Computer Hardware and Softwares and import and export of all sorts of goods in connection therewith.

AND WHEREAS the said Partners have adjusted their rights and accounts with the intention to register a JOINT STOCK COMPANY under the name and style of INDUSTRIAL COMPANY PVT. LTD. for the purpose of carrying on the said business of Partnership with a nominal Share Capital of Rs. 7,00,000 divided into 70,000 Equity Shares of Rs. 10 each.

AND WHEREAS the said parties have agreed that the share-holding of each of them in the said JOINT STOCK COMPANY would be 10,000 shares each fully paid-up.

AND WHEREAS for the better and efficient management of and expansion of the said business the said parties have agreed that the said JOINT STOCK COMPANY be governed by the Articles of Association containing the regulations for the day-to-day management of the company particulars whereof is mentioned in Schedule 'A' hereto.

AND WHEREAS the assets and properties of the said partnership firm would be the assets and properties of the JOINT STOCK COMPANY, the particulars whereof are given in Schedule 'B' hereto.

AND WHEREAS the parties have agreed that the said partnership firm and the JOINT STOCK COMPANY would be and continue to be bound by the regulations and the parties among themselves will be governed by these presents and the said Articles of Association.

NOW THESE PRESENTS WITNESSETH that the said parties in relation to all acts and deeds hereby agree and undertake as follows:

1. The name of the company is INDUSTRIAL COMPANY PVT. LTD.

2. The Registered Office of the company will be situated in Delhi.

3. (*a*) The main objects to be pursued by the company on its incorporation are the manufacturing and dealing in all sorts of Computer, Hardware and Software and exporting thereof;

   (*b*) The objects incidental or ancillary to the attainment of the above main objects are the acquisition, construction, building, setting-up and provisions of establishment for the tool shops, assembly lines, packaging units and workshops for training the personnel and establishing infrastructure for the Computer industry as are conducive to the attainment of foregoing objects;

(*c*) The other objects for which the company is established are carrying on the business of, dealing in as exporter and importer of computer goods and in connection with the business to borrow moneys give Guarantees, make inter-corporate deposits, accept deposits, borrow money from banks and financial institutions and to do all other acts which are necessary for carrying on the business of company.

4. The liability of members is limited.

5. The share capital of the company is Rs. 7,00,000 divided into 70,000 Equity Shares of Rs. 10 each.

Schedule A

The Articles of Association of Industrial Company Pvt. Ltd. being the regulations for the management of the company as contained in Table 'A' of First Schedule of the Companies Act 1956 with necessary modifications to suit the members.

Schedule B

(Particulars of assets and properties taken over from the partnership firm after accounts being adjusted.)

We, several persons whose names and addresses are subscribed are desirous of being formed into a company in pursuance of this Memorandum of Association and we respectively agree to take the number of shares in the capital of the company set opposite our respective names.

Name, address and description of Subscribers		*No. of shares subscribed by each Subscriber*
1. S. Tanton, 3 White Street New Delhi 110 002	Businessman	10,000
2. T. Tanton 3 White Street New Delhi 110 002	do	10,000
3. U. Tanton 4 White Street New Delhi 110 002	do	10,000
4. V. Tanton 4 White Street New Delhi 110 002	do	10,000

Name, address and description of Subscribers		No. of shares subscribed by each Subscriber
5. W. Tanton 5 White Street New Delhi 110 002	Businessman	10,000
6. X. Tanton 5 White Street New Delhi 110 002	do	10,000
7. Y. Tanton 6 White Street New Delhi 110 002	do	10,000

Dated the ....
day of .... 2000 K.P. Joshi, Auditor

....

WITNESS to the above signatures

Contract between a Proprietor of Business and Promoter of a Company

AN AGREEMENT made this .... day of .... 1999 BETWEEN .... son of .... residing at .... in the District of .... by caste .... by occupation .... and .... son of .... residing at .... by caste .... by occupation .... hereinafter collectively referred to as the AGENTS AND TRUSTEES of .... a private limited company intended to be incorporated under the Indian Companies Act (Act VII of 1956) of the ONE PART and .... son of .... residing at .... in the District of .... hereinafter referred to as the proprietor of the OTHER PART:

WHEREAS the proprietor has been carrying on business at No. .... under the name and style of .... AND WHEREAS the agents and trustees intend to register a Company having similar objects by their own initiatives and efforts with a capital of Rs. .... divided into .... ordinary shares of Rs. .... each AND WHEREAS the proprietor intends to amalgamate and merge his said concern with the said company as and when registered AND WHEREAS at the treaty for such incorporation it was agreed by and between the parties that the trustees and agents shall accommodate the proprietor to the extent of Rs. .... to pay up its immediately payable debts and liabilities fully mentioned and described in Schedule "A" hereto to be adjusted, liquidated and reimbursed as hereinafter appearing and to be treated as loan advanced to the company for acquisition of the said concern now IT IS HEREBY AGREED AND DECLARED as follows:

1. A company shall forthwith be formed at the costs and expenses of the agents and trustees and duly incorporated under the Indian Companies Act as a private company limited by shares of Rs. .... having as one of its objects the acquisition and management and working of the concern of the proprietor.

2. The proprietor shall sell and the said company shall purchase.

(*i*) ALL THAT the goodwill of the said .... (with the exclusive right to use the name of .... & Co. as part of the name of the company and represent the company as carrying on such business in continuation of the proprietor or in succession thereto) and all trade and property marks connected therewith.

(*ii*) All the plant, machinery, office furniture, patents, licences, wagons, carts, lorries, implements and utensils to which the proprietor is entitled in connection with the said business.

(*iii*) All the book debts and other debts and actionable rights and claims due to the proprietor in connection with the said business and the full benefits of all securities for such debts and claims.

(*iv*) The full benefit of all pending contracts and engagements to which the proprietor is entitled to in connection with the said business.

(*v*) All bills, cheques and notes of the proprietor in connection with the said business.

(*vi*) All other property and benefits and advantages to which the proprietor is entitled in connection with the said business including the benefits of all insurance policies and other contracts.

An abstract list is set out in the Schedule "B" hereto.

3. The consideration money for which purchase shall be Rs. .... to be paid and satisfied by allotment of .... fully paid-up shares.

4. The sum or sums so spent by the agents and trustees for the repayments of the debts and liabilities of the concern as well as for preliminary and other expenses in connection with the incorporation of the company shall be treated as contributions by them towards the share capital and shall be adjusted by allotment of fully paid-up shares of the company when incorporated.

5. The parties hereto shall each subscribe the Memorandum of Association of the company for .... share in all. The other subscribers may be such persons as the parties hereto shall mutually agree upon.

6. The Memorandum and Articles of Association of the company shall provide that the directors of the company shall enter into an agreement

for purchase of the business of the proprietor a draft whereof has been prepared and signed by the parties hereto for the purpose of identification and the parties shall use their best endeavours to enable the company to enter into and carry out such agreement in terms of the agreement. Subject to what are hereinbefore stated the company shall be a private limited company to all intents and purposes.

7. The parties hereto shall be the first directors of the company. They shall continue as permanent directors except in case of fraud, lunacy, criminal conviction or any other offence, insolvency, moral turpitude.

8. The parties hereto shall not, during their respective lives, transfer any share of the company to be allotted to them without the previous consent in writing of the other parties.

9. The purchase shall be completed by the .... day of .... when possession of the office and all its equipment shall, as far as practicable be given to the company together with all books, papers and writings, and the consideration aforesaid shall be paid and satisfied subject to the provisions of this agreement and thereupon the proprietor and all other necessary parties, if any, shall at the expenses of the company execute and do all assurances and things for transferring and/or vesting the said concern in the .... company and giving to it the full benefit of this agreement as shall be reasonably required.

10. If from any cause whatsoever other than the wilful default of the proprietor the purchase shall not be completed by the said day of .... the proprietor shall pay interest on the said sum of Rs. .... at the rate of .... per cent per annum and as interim security thereof he will execute a *hundi* in favour of the agents and trustees.

11. Save as aforesaid the proprietor shall pay and discharge all other debts and liabilities in connection with the said business as on the .... day of .... and shall indemnify the company and the agents and trustees against all proceedings, claims and demands in respect thereof.

12. If the company is not formed and does not adopt these presents on or before the 5th day of May 2000, any of the parties may by notice in writing to the other parties determine this agreement.

13. Upon adoption of this agreement by the company as aforesaid, the agents and trustees shall be freed and discharged from all liabilities created by these presents and the *hundi* shall stand cancelled and discharged.

IN WITNESS WHEREOF the parties hereto have hereunto set and subscribed their respective hands and seals the day, month and year first above-written.

Signed, sealed and delivered Proprietor
at .... Agents & Trustees of Company

Agreement between a Company and its Employees

AB Ltd. 57 G.C. Avenue, Calcutta 700 013

General Rules for Service

1. EVERY EMPLOYEE shall perform his duty honestly and diligently and shall carry out any order or work entrusted or asked to do by his departmental senior or by a director. He shall have to do any work other than his general assignment if he is required to do. He may be transferred from one work to another.

2. GENERALLY office hours will be from 10 AM to 6 PM with a short recess for tea or lunch at a suitable time. However, any employee shall not refuse to work beyond above time if, sometimes, it is necessary to do so for office work.

3. YEARLY increment, if any, will be as stated in salary scale. However, any staff member may get promotion to a higher post if directors feel so, looking to his efficiency and higher responsibilities. Salary shall be paid according to English calendar months.

4. DIRECTORS may relieve any employee from his service with (*a*) one calendar month's notice in case of a permanent Staff; (*b*) one calendar month's notice in case of a temporary one; and (*c*) at any time without serving notice in case of an apprentice. Any employee may be dismissed any time without any previous notice if he is found guilty of gross indiscipline, fraud, misappropriation or acting against the interest of the company. He may be degraded to a lower scale of salary if he is not found competent for the work and duties assigned to him.

5. LEAVE: Generally there will be 12 days' casual leave in a year, and any further leave will be subject to deduction in salary. Employees going to their native places far away from West Bengal may be allowed additional leave with pay subject to the previous sanction of directors, who will decide whatsoever, looking to the circumstances stated in applications.

6. BONUS: There will be no hard and fast rules for payment of bonus which shall be in the absolute discretion of the directors who shall decide at the end of every year the bonus to be paid. However, there will be no liability on the part of the company to pay bonus if they cannot do so.

7. TEMPORARY EMPLOYEES: Employees appointed on temporary or apprentice basis may be made permanent generally after completion of two years' service or earlier in the absolute discretion of the directors if directors feel to do so. Any employee can be appointed on permanent basis from the beginning if it is felt to do so.

8. PROVIDENT FUND: All permanent staff members or such temporary members, who are specifically approved by the directors will get benefit of the Provident Fund Scheme if it is maintained by the company.

9. CHANGE: Directors have authority to make any changes at any time in the above general rules.

Appointment / Renewal of Service Order

Mr. XY
3 A.K. Road, Calcutta
is hereby informed that he has been appointed/his service has been renewed as an employee of this company subject to acceptance of general rules of service from 10th day of June 1999 under the following terms:

(1) General assignment of work.
(*Subject to changes*)

(2) Permanent, temporary or apprentice.

(3) Scale of Salary.

(4) Starting salary from ....

(To be signed by employers)

To
AB Ltd.
57 G.C. Avenue, Calcutta

I have read and understood thoroughly the rules of service and the above terms of my appointment/renewal of my service, and I do hereby agree with all terms as above and I shall abide by all general rules of service which are now or may hereafter be in force and accordingly I accept my appointment/the renewal of my service with you.

(To be signed by the employee)

Tea Co. Limited

(Incorporated under the Companies Act 1996)
Authorised Capital (Rs. 10,00,00,000 (Rupees Ten Crore)
5 Anna Salai, Chennai 600 005

DEBENTURE

Issued pursuant to clauses 78 and 112(3) of the Company's Memorandum and Articles of Association respectively and in pursuance of a resolution of the Directors of the Company passed on the 5th day of September 1999.

1. Tea Co. Limited (hereinafter called the COMPANY) hereby binds itself to pay to X Bank Ltd. (hereinafter called the DEBENTURE-HOLDER) at the time and the event of the principal money accrued becoming payable as provided by the conditions endorsed hereon the sum of Rs. 50 lakhs

(Rupees fifty lakhs) and until payment of the said sum of Rs. 50 lakhs to pay interest thereon at the rate of 12 per cent per annum by yearly payments on the 31st day of December in each year.

2. This DEBENTURE is issued subject to and with benefits of the conditions endorsed hereon which are to be deemed part of it.

3. The PAYMENT of the principal sum and interest secured in this debenture is unconditionally guaranteed by the Governor of Tamil Nadu.

Given under the Common Seal of the COMPANY on this 30th day of September One Thousand Nine Hundred Ninety-nine.

WITNESS :

Name : ....

Address: Tea Co. Ltd.
5 Anna Salai
Chennai 600 005

for Tea Co. Ltd.
Managing Director

Name : ....

Address : ....

Signed, sealed and delivered for and on behalf of the Governor of State of Tamil Nadu in the presence of:

Signed, sealed and delivered by X Bank Ltd. through its authorised agent Mr. .... in the presence of:

Conditions (Endorsed on the Debenture)

1. The company will redeem this debenture by allotment to the debenture-holder of equity shares of the company of the face value equal to the Principal sum of Rs. 50 lakhs hereby secured within 3 (three) months from the date when the company declares its first dividend on equity shares and in the meantime the debenture-holder will not transfer or alienate this debenture. The company will simultaneously with the allotment of shares as aforesaid pay in cash to the debenture-holder the accrued interest on this debenture upto the date of such allotment.

2. The company will also be entitled to redeem this debenture at any time prior to such conversion as aforesaid by payment to the debenture-holder of the principal sum hereby secured together with interest accrued due thereon upto the date of such payment. Such option however shall be exercisable by the company by giving one month's notice in writing in that behalf to the debenture-holder.

3. The debenture-holder shall be entitled to call in and compel payment of the principal sum hereby secured together with interest accrued thereon in any of the following events namely:

(*a*) If the company makes default for three months in payment to the debenture-holder of any interest due on this debenture after the date at which the same ought to have been paid and after one month's written notice is given to the company to that effect by the debenture-holder.

(*b*) If an order is made or an effective resolution is passed for winding up of the company.

(*c*) If the company ceases or threatens to cease to carry on the business.

(*d*) If the company fails to convert this debenture into equity shares of the company in the event and within the time specified in condition No. 1 above.

(*e*) If the company fails to make payment pursuant to any notice given to it by the debenture-holder in terms of condition No. 2 above on expiry of one month from the date of service thereof.

Tea Co. Ltd.
X Bank Ltd.
for Governor of State of Tamil Nadu

Debenture Trust

THIS DEBENTURE TRUST DEED is made this 29th day of May 1999 BETWEEN X Co. Ltd. a company registered under the Companies Act 1956 having its registered office at .... (hereinafter called the COMPANY which term shall include its successors) of the One Part and Mr. AB son of .... residing at .... and Mr. CD son of .... residing at .... (hereinafter called the trustees which term shall include their successors and the Trustee for the time being) of the Other Part.

WHEREAS by clause .... sub-clause .... of .... its Memorandum of Association, the COMPANY is authorised to borrow or raise or secure the payment of money by the issue of debentures charged upon any of the company's properties.

AND WHEREAS the Directors of the COMPANY being duly empowered in that behalf by para .... of the Articles of Association of the company have decided by a resolution passed by the Board of Directors in the meeting of the Board held on .... to raise a sum of Rs. .... by issue of .... First Mortgage Bearer Debentures of Rs. .... each, bearing interest at .... per cent per annum framed in accordance with the forms set forth in the First Schedule hereto and to secure the same by mortgaging with the trustees the properties described in the Second Schedule hereto.

AND WHEREAS the trustees above-mentioned have consented to act as *trustees* for the debenture-holders.

NOW THIS DEED WITNESSETH AND DECLARES AS FOLLOWS:

1. That in these presents unless there be something in the subject or context inconsistent therewith, the expressions following shall have the meaning hereafter mentioned, that is to say:

COMPANY means .... Ltd.

TRUSTEES means Mr. ....

or any other trustees hereof for the time being.

DEBENTURES means the debenture of the company in the form set out in the First Schedule hereto for the time being outstanding and entitled to the benefit of these presents.

DEBENTURE-HOLDERS means the persons for the time being entitled to the benefit of the debentures.

MORTGAGED premises means the property belonging to the Company described in the Second Schedule hereto and comprised in the security of the debenture-holders.

Words denoting the singular include the plural and *vice versa* unless the contrary appears from the context.

2. The debentures entitled to the benefit of these presents shall consist of a series of .... debentures of Rs. .... each, aggregating to Rs. .... in all to rank *pari passu* without any preference or priority by reason of the date of issue or otherwise and secured by the mortgage hereby created on the mortgaged premises.

3. The COMPANY hereby covenants with the TRUSTEES that the COMPANY will on the .... day of .... or such earlier day as principal moneys shall become payable under clause 7 hereof pay the debenture-holders the amounts secured by their debentures respectively, and in the meantime will pay interest to the debenture-holders on the day of .... 19...... in each year, the first payment of interest to be made on the day of .... 19......

4. Provided that the COMPANY shall be entitled, at the end of every year, to redeem .... per cent debentures by giving one month's notice to the debenture-holders by advertisement of its intention to do so, on payment of the amount due on such debentures with interest up to date. The debentures to be redeemed in this manner will be determined by lot.

5. In consideration of the debentures hereby authorised aggregating to Rs. ...... the company, as the beneficial owner, hereby mortgages unto the

TRUSTEES all the fixed plant and machinery and fixture at present existing at the company's factory and described in Para A of the Second Schedule hereto and which may be acquired by the COMPANY hereafter or fixed or erected hereafter at its factory for the benefit of the debenture-holders and the property described in Para B of the Second Schedule as security for the due payment of principal moneys amounting to Rs. .... in aggregate with interest and all other charges, expenses and other dues, the payment of which has been secured by a charge on the mortgaged premises under these presents. The charge hereby created on the property mentioned in Part A of the Second Schedule shall be the specified charge, while that on the property included in Part B of the Second Schedule shall rank as floating charges.

The TRUSTEES may, at any time, by notice in writing to the COMPANY, convert the said floating charge into a specific charge as regards any assets included in the Second Schedule and specified in the notice in case it is, in the opinion of the trustees, in danger of being seized or sold under any sort of distress or execution levied or threatened or in any other case.

6. The COMPANY shall hold and enjoy all the mortgaged premises and carry on therein and therewith the business or any of the business mentioned in the Memorandum of Association of the COMPANY until the security hereby constituted shall become enforceable under the terms of these presents, in which case the trustees may, in their discretion, without any such request as next hereinafter mentioned and shall upon the request in writing of the holder or holders of .... at least of the debentures, enter upon or take possession of the mortgaged premises, or any of them and may in the like discretion and shall upon the like request sell, call in, collect and convert into money the same or any part thereof with full power to sell any of the same premises either together or in parcels, and either by public auction or private contract, and either for a lump sum or for a sum payable by instalments or for a sum on account and a mortgage or charge for the balance and with full power upon every such sale to make any special or other stipulations as to title or evidence, or commencement of title or otherwise which the trustees shall deem proper and with full power to modify or rescind or vary any contract for sale of the said premises or any part thereof and to re-sell the same without being responsible for any loss which may be occasioned thereby and with full power to compromise and effect compositions and for the purposes aforesaid or any of them to execute and do all such assurance and things as they shall think fit.

7. The principal moneys due to the debenture-holders under this Indenture shall become immediately payable and the security hereby constituted shall become enforceable within the meanings of these presents in each and any of the following events:

(*a*) If the COMPANY makes default in the payment of any interest which ought to be paid in accordance with these presents.

(*b*) If the COMPANY ceases to carry on its business.

(*c*) If an order shall be made or a special resolution shall have been passed for winding up the company.

(*d*) If the COMPANY acts in contravention of clause .... of its Articles of Association.

Provided that on the happening of the events specified in sub-clause (*a*), the permission given by clause 6 to hold and enjoy the mortgaged premises shall not be determined unless and until the trustees shall have first served on the .... company a preliminary notice requiring the company to pay the interest in arrears and the company shall have neglected for the period of 30 days to comply with such notice.

8. As soon as the principal moneys shall become payable and the security enforceable under the last preceding clause No. 7 (and unless the time for payment and the security to be enforced has been expressly extended by the debenture-holders), the trustees shall enter upon and take possession of the mortgaged premises and shall forthwith take steps to consult the debenture-holders for the purpose of determining whether the business of the company may be allowed to be carried on or whether the mortgaged premises shall be realised by sale or otherwise.

9. Until the happening of some one of the events mentioned in clause No. 7 of this Indenture, the trustees shall not be in any manner bound to interfere with the management or affairs of the said business except to the extent they may consider necessary for the preservation of the mortgaged premises or any part thereof.

10. If the debenture-holders resolve not to allow the business of the COMPANY to be carried on as mentioned in clause No. 8 above but to realise the security, the trustees shall, after giving a notice of 30 days in writing to the company, proceed to realise the mortgaged premises by sale or otherwise and, in doing so, shall conform to directions, if any, given by debenture-holders.

11. The trustees shall apply the proceeds of such sale or other mode of realisation in the following manner, that is to say, that the trustees shall pay:

(*a*) In the first place all costs, charges and expenses incurred in or about such sale or the performance or execution of trust or otherwise in relation to these presents or otherwise in respect of the security including the remuneration of the trustees.

(*b*) Secondly, the interest for the time being due and owing on the debentures.

(*c*) Thirdly, the principal money then due and owing to debenture-holders.

(*d*) And lastly, the surplus, if any, to the company or its assigns.

Provided that if the said money shall be insufficient to pay all such interest or principal money in full, then the said moneys shall be paid rateably and without preference or priority among all debenture-holders of this series according to the amount of the face value of the debentures held by them, but all interest shall be paid before any principal moneys.

12. When all the principal moneys, secured by these presents shall have been paid and satisfied, the trustees shall forthwith, upon the request and at the cost of the COMPANY and on being paid all the costs, charges and expenses properly incurred by the TRUSTEES in relation to the security, reconvey, reassign, release and surrender the mortgaged premises or so much of the same as shall not have been sold or disposed of, unto the COMPANY or its assigns.

13. If the COMPANY shall, at any time during the continuance of the security, be desirous of selling, demising or otherwise disposing of or dealing with any part of the mortgaged premises otherwise than in respect of the floating charge the ordinary course of the company's business, the TRUSTEES may, if satisfied that the debenture-holders' security shall not be thereby prejudiced, assent to or concur in such sale, demise, disposal or other dealing, and may, if necessary, release the property in question from the trust under this deed on such terms as the trustees may determine.

14. The COMPANY hereby covenants with the trustees:

(*i*) That the moneys secured by this deed shall be the first mortgage and charge on the mortgaged premises and shall take precedence over all other moneys which may hereinafter be borrowed by the COMPANY against the security of the premises hereto mortgaged;

(*ii*) that the COMPANY shall maintain the mortgaged premises and any and every part thereof in a fit and efficient condition of repair and shall keep the said property duly insured against risk of fire, riot, civil and war risks with such insurers and in such manner as the TRUSTEES may determine from time to time and, to default, the trustees shall carry out repair and keep insured the mortgaged premises in the interest of the debenture-holders, and shall be entitled to the immediate payment of such expenditure in full; and

(*iii*) that the COMPANY shall pay the trustees remuneration for the services under this Indenture at the rate of Rs. .... per year, such remuneration to be a charge on the mortgaged property.

15. The debenture-holders may, by a resolution, remove the trustees or the TRUSTEES may, with the consent of the directors of the COMPANY and of the majority of the debenture-holders in writing resign or retire from trusteeship.

16. In the event of death, bankruptcy, disability or resignation of any TRUSTEE or TRUSTEES, another TRUSTEE or TRUSTEES shall be appointed who shall thereafter have and exercise all powers of the TRUSTEE or TRUSTEES under these presents. The power of appointing a new TRUSTEE or TRUSTEES shall be vested in the directors, but no such trustee shall be appointed by the company until his appointment has been approved by a resolution of the debenture-holders.

17. The TRUSTEES may by agreement with the directors of the COMPANY modify the terms of the deed in any manner that may be necessary to meet any requirement or contingency, provided that the TRUSTEES are satisfied that such modifications are in the interests of the debenture-holders.

18. If any debenture is proved to the satisfaction of the COMPANY to have been lost, the COMPANY will issue a fresh debenture on payment of a fee of Rs. .... for each such debenture and on such indemnity as the directors may think fit.

In witness whereof the company has caused its Common Seal to be affixed to these presents and the trustees have hereto set their hands the day and year above-written.

WITNESSES:

Common Seal of the ....
affixed in the presence of:

Directors
TRUSTEES

Agreement between Company and a Broker

THIS AGREEMENT made on the 10th day of May 2000 BETWEEN X Co. Ltd., a company carrying on the business of building contractors at 5 J.P. Nagar, Bangalore (hereinafter called the COMPANY) of the one part and B & Co. of 8 Joy Nagar, Bangalore (hereinafter called the BROKER) of the other part.

WHEREAS the COMPANY wants to sell the property described in the Schedule hereto and for the said purpose the services of the broker are required.

AND WHEREAS the said BROKER is agreeable to act as broker for the sale of the said property described in the Schedule hereto.

AND WHEREAS the COMPANY has agreed to pay to the BROKER a commission of 1 per cent on the sale price.

NOW THEREFORE THIS AGREEMENT WITNESSES and the parties hereby agree as follows:

1. The COMPANY hereby authorises the BROKER for a period of six months to sell the property described in the Schedule hereto at the price and on the terms and conditions hereinafter contained in these presents.

2. The BROKER will sell the property at the minimum price of Rs. 8,00,000 and out of this consideration the purchaser shall pay Rs. 2,00,000 in advance as earnest money and the balance of Rs. 6,00,000 shall be paid within 3 months hereof before the Registrar of Assurances at the time of registration of the sale deed.

3. The BROKER shall be authorised to sell the property at a price not less than Rs. 8,00,000 and on terms and conditions that may be acceptable to the COMPANY.

4. The COMPANY represents and warrants that the details of the property as described in the Schedule hereto are true and correct and the said property is free from all encumbrances.

5. The COMPANY undertakes to deliver to the purchaser within reasonable time an abstract of title showing that the COMPANY is the owner of the property having a good title and the said property is free from all encumbrances.

6. The COMPANY hereby agrees that the sale-deed to be executed by the COMPANY shall contain full covenants and warranties as are usual in similar cases.

The Schedule

IN WITNESS WHEREOF the parties herein have executed these presents on the day, month and year first above-written.

Signed, sealed and delivered by
Mr. ....
pursuant to Board Resolution
dated 2nd May 2000 of X Co. Ltd.
in the presence of:

Signed, sealed and delivered by
Mr. ....
as proprietor of B & Co. in the
presence of:

Underwriting of Issue of Shares and Debentures

A company cannot allot any shares offered to the public for subscription unless the minimum amount required as stated in the Prospectus has been applied for and the amount has been received in money. This is called minimum subscription.[4]

In the event enough shares are not applied for to raise the minimum subscription the application money has to be returned. To avoid the contingency of minimum subscription not being received by the issue of shares the company may enter into underwriting agreements with the financial institutions, banks and others whereby the bank, financial institutions or other persons assure the company that in case the public do not subscribe for adequate number of shares to raise the minimum subscription, such banks, financial institutions or other persons shall take up the requisite or agreed number of shares so that the minimum subscription or money for the entire issue be raised and allotment be made in accordance with the Prospectus, the provisions of the Companies Act 1956 and other Statutory provisions in this regard.

A company may pay a commission to any person in consideration of his agreeing to subscribe for any shares in or Debentures of the company or to procure such subscription. The payment of commission should be authorised by the Articles of the company and it should not exceed 5% of the Issue price or the amount mentioned in the Articles, whichever is less, and in case of Debentures 2.5% of the Issue price of Debentures or the rate mentioned in the Articles, whichever is less. These facts are to be disclosed in the Prospectus.[5]

This assurance to subscribe or procure subscription for the shares or Debentures of the company, if the minimum subscription is not raised or the entire issue is not subscribed, is called Underwriting. The term means an Agreement to subscribe to shares and/or Debentures of a company in the event the public or the existing shareholders do not subscribe as required by the company.[6]

To raise the required Capital a company issues shares and/or Debentures and unless such shares and Debentures are subscribed by the Investors the company's purpose will not be served. Underwriting of the shares and Debentures gives an assurance to the company against the risk of inadequate response from the investors and the risk of not obtaining even the minimum subscription.

A person who acts as an Underwriter must hold a certificate from the Securities & Exchange Control Board of India. Every stock-broker or Merchant Banker registered with the Board is entitled to act as an Underwriter without obtaining a Certificate.[7]

4 Section 69 of the Companies Act 1956.
5 Section 76 of the Companies Act 1956.
6 Rule 2 of Securities & Exchange Board of India (Underwriters) Rules 1993.
7 Rule 3 of SEBI (Underwriters) Rules 1993.

The Underwriters shall not derive any benefit directly or indirectly from the Underwriting of issue of shares and Debentures other than the commission or the brokerage payable under the agreement for Underwriting or Brokerage. An Underwriter shall not take up underwriting obligations exceeding twenty times of its Net Worth. In case of underwriting public issue when called upon to subscribe the Underwriter within 45 days shall subscribe to such shares or Debentures as agreed.[8]

Broker's Consent Letter

To
The Board of Directors
X Co. Ltd.
Bangalore

Dear Sirs

Re: Your public issue of 12% Secured Non-convertible Redeemable Debentures for the aggregate value of Rs. 2,000 Crores.

We, the undersigned, hereby agree to act as Brokers to the aforesaid issue and our name being inserted as Brokers to the issue in the Prospectus to be issued by the company. We hereby authorise the company to deliver this letter of consent to the Registrar of Companies, Bangalore pursuant to the provisions of section 60 of the Companies Act 1956.

We are agreeable to accept brokerage at 1% on the nominal value on allotment of the Debentures made in respect of applications bearing our stamps as brokers. We authorise you to deliver a copy of this letter to the Registrar of Companies pursuant to the provisions of section 76(1)(*v*) of the Companies Act 1956.

Yours faithfully
B & Co.

Underwriter's Consent

To
The Board of Directors
X Co. Ltd.

Dear Sirs

We have seen your draft prospectus offering for public-subscription 1,00,000 shares of your company of the nominal value of Rs. 100 each. We

8 Rule 15 of SEBI (Underwriters) Rules 1993.

are agreeable to underwrite the whole issue provided the shares are offered to the public in accordance with the conditions entered in the prospectus.

We shall put in a written application for allotment of such shares as remain unsubscribed on the closing day fixed for subscription of those shares. If all these shares are subscribed by the public on or before the closing day, our undertaking shall cease. If a smaller number of shares are subscribed by the public then our application and undertaking shall have effect in respect of the balance shares.

You shall pay us a commission at the rate of 5% on the face value of 1,00,000 shares to the issued. If we fail to apply for the shares which remain unsubscribed on the closing day fixed for subscription of those shares we hereby authorise you to appoint some of your officers to make an application on our behalf for the unsubscribed shares on the closing day fixed for subscription and the commission payable to us may be appropriated by you towards the application and/or allotment money. Please let us have your acceptance of this application.

Yours faithfully
Y & Co.

Letter of Acceptance

To
Y & Co.

Dear Sirs

With reference to your application dated .... we accept your offer to act as an underwriter to our issue of 1,00,000 ordinary shares of Rs. 100 each at a commission of 5% per cent upon the footing and subject to the conditions contained in your application and in the draft Prospectus.

Yours faithfully
X & Co. Ltd.

Underwriting Agreement for Shares

THIS AGREEMENT made on the 4th day of June 2000 BETWEEN X & Co. Ltd., a company having its registered office at .... (hereinafter called the COMPANY) of the one part and Merchant Bank Ltd., having its registered office at .... (hereinafter called the UNDERWRITER) of the other part.

WHEREAS the COMPANY is intending to offer for public subscription the issue of 1,00,000 shares of Rs. 100 each in accordance with terms of the draft prospectus a copy of which is annexed hereto with such modifications therein as may be mutually agreed upon BETWEEN the COMPANY and the UNDERWRITER.

AND WHEREAS the UNDERWRITER has agreed to underwrite the shares on the terms and conditions contained in the draft prospectus as also in these presents.

NOW THEREFORE THESE presents witnesseth and the parties hereby agree as follows:

1. If the said 1,00,000 shares shall on or before the 10th day of June 1999 (or such later date as shall be mutually agreed upon by the parties hereto but not after the 10th July 2000) be offered by the COMPANY for subscription by the public at par on the terms of such prospectus as aforesaid, the UNDERWRITERS shall on or before the closing of the subscription list apply at par for the said 1,00,000 shares.

The said prospectus shall be issued in the form already approved by the UNDERWRITER or with such modification, if any, as shall be mutually agreed between the company and the UNDERWRITER.

2. If on the closing of the lists under the said prospectus the said 1,00,000 shares shall be allotted in respect of applications from the public the responsibility of the UNDERWRITER will cease and no allotment is to be made under this agreement to the UNDERWRITER but if the said 1,00,000 shares be not allotted to the public or any smaller number of such shares be allotted, the undertaking of the UNDERWRITER is to take the balance shares.

3. The COMPANY shall pay to the UNDERWRITER in cash within 15 days from the allotment of the said 1,00,000 shares a commission at the rate of 5% on the nominal value of the entire issue of the shares.

4. This agreement is irrevocable on the part of the UNDERWRITER and authorises the COMPANY in the event of the UNDERWRITER not applying for the said 1,00,000 shares to cause application to be made for such shares or any part thereof in the name and on behalf of the UNDERWRITER in accordance with the terms of the said prospectus and UNDERWRITER authorises the directors of the COMPANY to allot the requisite shares of the COMPANY to the UNDERWRITER. In the event of the COMPANY causing an application to be made for such shares in the name of the UNDERWRITER, the UNDERWRITER shall hold the COMPANY, and the said applicants harmless and keep them indemnified in respect of all liabilities in relation to such application and/or shares.

IN WITNESS WHEREOF the parties hereto have executed these presents on the day, month and year first above-written.

Signed, sealed and delivered by
Mr. ....
pursuant to Board Resolution
dated 4th June 2000 of X & Co.
Ltd. in presence of:

Signed, sealed and delivered by
Mr. ....
pursuant to Board Resolution of
Merchant Bank Ltd. dated 4th
June 2000 in the presence of:

Underwriting Agreement for Debentures

THIS AGREEMENT is made on the 20th day of June 2000 BETWEEN X & Co. Ltd., of .... (Address) (hereinafter called the COMPANY) of the one part and B.R. & Co. Ltd. having its office at .... (Address) (hereinafter called the UNDERWRITER) of the other part.

WHEREAS THE COMPANY IS INTENDING TO OFFER for public subscription 50,000 12% mortgage debentures which are to be constituted and secured by a Trust Deed drawn up on terms and conditions contained therein and for the purpose of identification initialled by both the parties.

AND WHEREAS the COMPANY is desirous of obtaining assurance of such debentures being subscribed and/or taken up by the investors and the UNDERWRITER has given such assurance.

NOW THEREFORE THESE presents witnesseth and it is hereby agreed as follows:

1. The COMPANY will offer for public subscription the said 50,000 debentures of Rs. 1,000 each.

2. Such offer is to be made by a prospectus prepared in accordance with the terms of the draft prospectus annexed hereto but with full power for the COMPANY, prior to the publication of such prospectus, to modify the same in such a manner as the company shall think fit provided that such modification shall be approved by the said UNDERWRITER.

3. The UNDERWRITER shall take up and pay at par the whole of the debenture stock aforesaid which shall not have been taken up and allotted to other persons within 15 days after the first publication of the said prospectus and in consideration of the obligation so imposed on the UNDERWRITER it shall be entitled to 2.5% of the issue price of the said 50,000 debentures.

4. The UNDERWRITER shall pay up the full issue price of the debentures taken up by it as aforesaid by instalments and at the times specified in the prospectus aforesaid.

5. The UNDERWRITER may fix the premium at which the said debentures shall be offered for subscription by the said prospectus and if it does not within 10 days after notice in writing specify the same then the company may fix the premium.

6. Any notice to the UNDERWRITER may be given by sending the same through the post addressed at its above mentioned address and a notice so sent shall be deemed to have been received at the expiration of twenty-four hours after it is posted.

IN WITNESS WHEREOF the parties hereto have executed these presents on the day, month and year first above-written.

Signed, sealed and delivered by
Mr. ....
pursuant to Board Resolution
dated 18th June 2000 of X & Co.
Ltd. in the presence of:

Signed, sealed and delivered by
Mr. ....
pursuant to Board Resolution of
B.R. & Co. Ltd. dated 19th June
2000 in the presence of:

Petition for Rectification of the Register of Charges and for Other Reliefs

Before the Company Law Board Bench, Eastern Region
9 Old Post Office Street, Calcutta 700 001

Company Petition No. .... of 2000

In the matter of the Companies Act 1956 section 141 of the said Act and Regulation 44 of the Company Law Board Regulations 1991

And

In the matter of:

1. X Co. Ltd. a company registered under the Companies Act 1956 having its registered office at .... Calcutta

2. Y Co. Ltd. a company registered under The Companies Act 1956 having its registered office at .... Calcutta

And

ELH Bank Ltd. a Banking Company within the meaning of the Companies Act 1956 and carrying on business *inter alia*, at .... Calcutta

Petitioner

versus

1. X Co. Ltd. a company registered under the Companies Act 1956 and carrying on business at .... Calcutta

2. Y Co. Ltd. a company registered under the Companies Act 1956 and carrying on business at .... Calcutta

3. The Registrar of Companies West Bengal, having its office at Nizam Palace, 226 A.J.C. Bose Road, Calcutta 700 020

Respondents

The humble petition of ELH Bank Ltd., the petitioner above-named most respectfully

SHEWETH:

1. Particulars of the company. (*a*) The first respondent was incorporated on .... and the second respondent was incorporated on ....

(*b*) The registered offices of the respondents Nos. 1 and 2 are at .... Calcutta.

(*c*) The authorised, issued, subscribed and paid-up capital of the first respondent is Rs. 10,00,000. The authorised, issued, subscribed and paid-up capital of the second respondent is Rs. 15,00,000. The shares of both the companies comprise of equity shares of Rs. 10 each fully paid-up.

(*d*) The objects for which the respondents Nos. 1 and 2 were established are to manufacture and deal in jute goods and allied products. The objects of the two companies will appear from the Memorandum of Association of each of the two companies to which your petitioner will crave leave to refer.

(*e*) The management of the first respondent has been amalgamated with the second respondent and all the assets and liabilities of the first respondent are vested in the second respondent.

2. Particulars of the Petitioner. (*a*) The petitioner was incorporated as a Banking Company in 1982 and is carrying on banking business at .... Calcutta.

(*b*) The petitioner granted credit facilities to the first respondent against hypothecation of movable assets and mortgage of its immovable properties. The petitioner is a secured creditor.

(*c*) The second respondent has taken over the assets and liabilities of the 1st respondent and the petitioner has claims against the second respondent and is entitled to a charge over all its movable assets and mortgage on its immovable properties being the successor of the first respondent.

3. Particulars of the respondents. (*a*) The respondents Nos. 1 and 2 are public companies, the first respondent has been amalgamated with the second respondent. The first respondent has not yet been dissolved.

(*b*) The terms and conditions on which the first respondent has been amalgamated with the second respondent will appear from the order dated .... of the Hon'ble High Court at Calcutta sanctioning the scheme, a copy whereof is annexed hereto.

(*c*) The charges and modifications of charge created by the first respondent in favour of the petitioner have been filed with the Registrar of Companies, West Bengal but the respondent No. 3 has not yet issued the Certificates and the reasons for not issuing such Certificates could not be ascertained.

4. Jurisdiction of the Bench. The petitioner declares that the subject-matter of the petition and the respondents are all within the jurisdiction of this Hon'ble Bench.

5. Limitation. The petitioner further declares that the present petition is within the period of limitation laid down by the Companies Act 1956 and the petitioner's cause of action arises from day to day.

6. Facts of the case. (*a*) The petitioner bank granted credit facilities to first respondent against hypothecation of its movable assets and mortgage of its immovable properties. The first respondent executed several Banking documents. The Charge and Modifications thereof were filed with the Registrar of Companies, respondent No. 3.

(*b*) From time to time the limit of credit facilities was enhanced and further banking documents were executed by the respondents. The necessary forms were filed with the Registrar of Companies for Registration of Modification of Charges.

(*c*) Respondent No. 3 has not yet issued any Certificate either for the Original Charge created or for the subsequent Modification of Charges. On enquiries no specific explanation was given by the Registrar of Companies except that it was stated that there was some defects in the forms submitted.

(*d*) Your petitioner verbally requested the respondents Nos. 1 and 2 to look into the matter and regularise the same but nothing so far has been done.

(*e*) In the facts of the case your petitioner states that respondents Nos. 1 and 2 be directed to correct the defects, if any, in the forms submitted by them. In view of the said hypothecation and mortgage the Respondent No. 3 be directed to issue the necessary Certificate of Charges and Modification of Charges.

(*f*) The delay or omission in filling the requisite forms or incorporation of the particulars therein or annexing any documents thereto or furnishing any explanation asked for by the Registrar of Companies be condoned and the Register of Charges be correspondingly rectified and the requisite certificates be issued to the petitioner.

(*g*) The petitioner is ready and willing to do all such acts and things and make payment of such fees as this Learned Bench may direct.

7. **Matters not previously filed or pending with any other court.** Your petitioner declares that your petitioner has not filed any application, writ petition or suit regarding the matter in respect of which this petition has been made before any other court of Law or authority or Bench of the Board, and no such application, writ petition or suit is pending before any of them.

8. **Reliefs sought.** In the facts and circumstances mentioned hereinbefore your petitioner prays for the following reliefs:

(*a*) The delay in filing the particulars of Charge and Modification of Charge and modification thereof be condoned;

(*b*) The omission or misstatement in Form 8 and Form 13 or in any other Form filed with the Registrar of Companies be allowed to be rectified;

(*c*) Registrar of Companies be directed to specify reasons for not issuing the Certificate of Registration and Certificate of Modification of Charge to the petitioner;

(*d*) Leave be given and delay be condoned to comply with the requisition that may be made by the Registrar of Companies and/or to make good the defect and/or defects within such time as this Learned Bench may direct;

(*e*) The respondents be directed to comply with the provisions of law in regard to the Charge and/or Modifications thereof in respect of the assets and properties of the respondents Nos. 1 and 2 in favour of the petitioner;

(*f*) Further Orders be made as to this Learned Bench may deem fit and proper.

9. Interim Order, if prayed for. Pending final decision on the petition your petitioner seeks issue of the following Interim Orders:

(*i*) Registrar of Companies be directed to make an enquiry into the Registration and Modification of Charges in favour of the petitioner and submit a report to this Learned Bench;

10. Particulars of Bank Draft. Bank draft No. 56 dated ....for Rs. .... drawn by and payable at petitioner's branch at .... Calcutta.

(Cause Title as above)

Affidavit verifying the petition

I, ... son of ...., aged .... years, by occupation service working for gain at .... Calcutta do hereby solemnly affirm and say as follows:

1. I am the Branch Manager and a principal officer of ELH Bank Ltd. .... Calcutta. I know and I have made myself acquainted with the facts and circumstances of this case and I am able to depose thereto. I am authorised and competent to affirm and I do affirm this affidavit on behalf of the petitioner-bank.

2. The statements in paragraphs .... of the petition shown to me and signed by me and marked with letter X are true to my knowledge and those mentioned in paragraphs .... of the said petition are based on information derived from records maintained by the said bank and believed by me to be true, and those in paragraphs .... of the said petition are my humble submissions to this Learned Bench.

Solemnly affirmed by the said
.... at Calcutta this ....
day of .... 2000 Signature

Before me
Notary Public

Application by the Depositor under section 58A(9) of the Companies Act

Before the Company Law Board Bench, Eastern Region
9 Old Post Office Street, Calcutta 700 001

Company Petition No. .... of 2000

In the matter of the Companies Act 1956 section 58A read with the Regulation 37 of the Company Law Board Bench Rules 1991

And

In the matter of AB residing at .... Calcutta

Petitioner

versus

X Co. Ltd. a company registered under the Companies Act 1956 and having its registered office at .... Calcutta

Respondent

The humble petition of the applicant above-named most respectfully

SHEWETH:

1. Name and address of the depositor-applicant	:	AB residing at .... Calcutta.
2. Name of the company and address of its registered office	:	X Co. Ltd., having its registered office at .... Calcutta.
3. Name of the depositor and his address	:	AB residing at .... Calcutta West Bengal.
4. Amount of deposit	:	Rs. 10,00,000.
5. Fixed Deposit Receipt No. and date	:	Fixed Deposit Receipt No. 5 dated 6th September 1995. Xerox copy is enclosed.
6. Terms and conditions of deposit as also date of maturity of deposit	:	Interest at 25% per annum was payable quarterly. The principal amount was payable on 15th January 1999. Interest was payable every quarter.
7. Details of payment made by the company, if any	:	The company has not made any payment of interest or the principal amount in spite of demands.
8. Actual amount due as on the date of application	:	Principal amount: Rs. 10,00,000 Interest amount : Rs. 2,50,000.
9. Details of correspondence if any made between the company and the depositor	:	Copies of correspondence are enclosed.

10. Any other particulars as may be considered relevant	:	The company is carrying on business acquiring assets and shares in other companies and making inter-corporate deposits, and is commercially insolvent and several applications for winding-up are pending.

The depositor-applicant therefore prays:

(*i*) that the company above-named be directed to make payment of the aforesaid deposit along with interest due thereon in accordance with the terms and conditions of deposit contained in Fixed Deposit Receipt;

(*ii*) further Orders be made as the Company Law Board may deem fit and proper in the circumstances of the case.

Place ....
Date ....

Signature of the depositor-applicant

Verification

I, ..., son of ...., aged .... years, residing at ...., do hereby solemnly affirm and say as follows:

1. I am the depositor above-named. I know the facts and circumstances of the case.
2. The statements made in paragraphs .... hereinabove are true to my knowledge derived from records maintained by me and from the Board proceedings against the respondent company and I believe them to be true. I sign this Verification this .... day of .... 2000 at .... Calcutta.

Signature

Before me
Notary

Petition for Framing of Scheme for Management

Before the Company Law Board
Principal Bench, New Delhi
Company Petition No. ... of ......

In the matter of the Companies Act 1956

And

In the matter of an Application under sections 397, 398, 399, 402 and 403 of the Companies Act 1956

And

X Co. Pvt. Ltd. a company registered under the Companies Act 1956 having its registered office at ....

And

In the matter of:

1. AB, residing at ....
2. CD, residing at ....
3. EF, residing at ....
4. GH residing at ....
5. JK residing at ....

Petitioners

versus

1. X & Co. Pvt. Ltd., a company registered under the Companies Act 1956 and having its registered office at ....
2. MN, working for gain at ....
....
3. PQ, working for gain at ....
....

Respondents

The humble petition of the petitioners above-named most respectfully

SHEWETH:

A. Particulars of the company. (1) X & Co. Pvt. Ltd. (hereinafter referred to as the COMPANY) was incorporated on 15th May 1985 as a Private Limited Company. The registered office of the COMPANY is situated at .... in the State of West Bengal. The authorised capital of the COMPANY is Rs. 10 lakhs. The issued subscribed and paid-up capital of the COMPANY is Rs. 5 lakhs comprising of 50,000 Equity shares of Rs. 10 each.

(2) The main objects for which the COMPANY was incorporated are, *inter alia*, to take over the business of the firm X. & Co. and to manufacture and deal in all kinds of Computers, Hardwares & Softwares and as exporter and importer of all kinds of Electronic goods. The objects will appear from

the Memorandum and Articles of Association of the Company a copy whereof is annexed hereto marked "A".

(3) Soon after its incorporation the COMPANY commenced its business on taking over the assets and liabilities and business of the firm X & Co.

B. Particulars of petitioners. The petitioners and the respondents Nos. 2 and 3 were carrying on business in partnership in manufacturing diverse plant, machinery, tools and implements and other Electronic goods, Computers Hardware and Software and exporting the same. Due to expansion of business, the petitioners and respondents 2 and 3 converted their partnership business into a Private Limited Company, respondent No. 1 herein. Each of the petitioners subscribed 16% of the shares issued by the COMPANY. The petitioners together held 80% of the Equity Shares issued, subscribed and paid-up shares in the share capital of the COMPANY.

C. Particulars of the respondents. The respondents Nos. 2 and 3 along with the petitioners formed a partnership business under the name and style of X & Co. for manufacturing and dealing in all kinds of Computers, Hardware of Software and plant, machinery, tools, implements and other Electronic articles. After the partnership business was converted into a private limited company, the first respondent above-named, respondents Nos. 2 and 3 each subscribed and held 10% of the issued, subscribed and paid-up shares of the company. The respondents Nos. 2 and 3 together held 20% of the issued, subscribed, and paid-up capital of the COMPANY and the petitioners together held 80% of issued, subscribed and paid-up capital of the COMPANY.

D. Jurisdiction of the Bench. The petitioners declare that the subject-matter of the petition is within the jurisdiction of this Learned Bench.

E. Limitation. The petitioners further declare that the petition is within the limitation period inasmuch as the cause of action is arising day-to-day.

F. Facts of the case. (*a*) The respondents Nos. 2 and 3 and the petitioners were the subscribers to the Memorandum and Articles of Association of the COMPANY. The first directors were also the permanent directors of the COMPANY. The respondents Nos. 2, 3 and the petitioner No. 1 were the permanent directors.

(*b*) Before and at the time of incorporation of the COMPANY in reality it was a partnership firm, the petitioners and the respondents Nos. 2 and 3 were sharing profits and losses of the firm in the ratio of 80:20. Respondents Nos. 2 and 3 were managing the affairs of the COMPANY.

(*c*) Respondents Nos. 2 and 3 wrongfully issued shares and allotted the same to respondents Nos. 2 and 3 to the exclusion of the petitioners and thereby the total holding of respondents Nos. 2 and 3 increased to 40% each. Your petitioners became a minority of 20% and respondents Nos. 2 and 3 combined holding being 80%.

(*d*) Respondents Nos. 2 and 3 by virtue of the said purported 80% holding of shares in all matters ousted the petitioners from the management of the company.

(*e*) The COMPANY made huge business and the turnover increased substantially but the respondents Nos. 2 and 3 manipulated the transactions and did not enter in the books of accounts of the company the real transactions.

(*f*) The respondents Nos. 2 and 3 did not allow the petitioners to inspect the books of accounts and since last one year have not issued notice of any Board Meeting to the petitioners and thereby prevented the petitioners from attending any Board Meeting or participating in the management of affairs of the company.

(*g*) The petitioners by several letters from time to time requested the respondents to issue the notice of all Board Meetings by registered post and deposited in advance Rs. 500 towards the cost of such notices by registered post. The respondents have not issued any notice of any Board Meeting to the petitioners.

(*h*) The respondents have manipulated the accounts and syphoned the funds of the COMPANY for the benefit of the respondents Nos. 2 and 3 to the prejudice of the petitioners.

(*i*) Respondent No. 2 is also diverting the business of the COMPANY to another business in the name of MN Co. and thereby making undue profits at the cost of the company and to the prejudice of the petitioners.

(*j*) Respondents Nos. 2 and 3 have been acting in a manner harsh, burdensome and oppressive to the petitioners and have purported to conduct the affairs of the COMPANY in a manner prejudicial to public interest. Respondents Nos. 2 and 3 have been managing the affairs of the COMPANY in a manner oppressive to the petitioners and the COMPANY and conducting the affairs of the COMPANY in a manner prejudicial to the interest of the COMPANY and to the public interest. Some of the instances of the wrongful acts and conduct of respondents Nos. 2 and 3 are given hereunder:

(*i*) Respondents Nos. 2 and 3 purported to have held the Board Meetings without giving notice to the petitioners;

(*ii*) Respondents Nos. 2 and 3 have, with the assets, products, funds and know-how of the COMPANY, been carrying on their separate businesses with the company's customers and others;

(*iii*) Respondents Nos. 2 and 3 have been misappropriating the funds of the COMPANY and manipulating the accounts.

(*k*) The first petitioner informed the Regional Director, Department of Company Affairs, Eastern Region Bench of the said misconduct of the respondents Nos. 2 and 3 and the said Regional Director has asked the

Registrar of Companies to make enquiries and the Registrar of Companies has found certain irregularities in the management of the company.

(*l*) From the records of the Registrar of Companies, it appears that the respondents Nos. 2 and 3 have held several Board Meetings and purported to pass several Resolutions which were prejudicial to the interest of the petitioners and in respect of such Board Meetings no notice was served to your petitioners and your petitioners were prevented from attending the Board Meetings.

(*m*) The purported resolutions copies whereof are annexed hereto were passed in violation of the provisions of sections 299, 300 and 287 of the Companies Act 1956 and are thus void and liable to be set aside.

(*n*) Respondents Nos. 2 and 3 are lacking in commercial probity in relation to their dealings with the affairs of the COMPANY and also in relation to the petitioners and it is not safe to leave the affairs of the company in the hands of the respondents Nos. 2 and 3 any more.

(*o*) The whole object of the respondents Nos. 2 and 3 is to exclude the petitioners from the management of the company and to usurp absolute control of the management of the company so that the respondents Nos. 2 and 3 can continue with their acts of mismanagement and syphoning away the funds and assets of the company to the prejudice of the company, its shareholders, petitioners, employees and creditors of the company.

(*p*) Unless appropriate directions are given by this Hon'ble Board the company and its shareholders including the petitioners will be seriously prejudiced.

(*q*) The petitioners are being prevented from taking part in the conduct of the business of the company.

(*r*) Respondents Nos. 2 and 3 have caused loss to the company by fraudulent and unlawful conduct and are liable to indemnify the company to the extent of Rs. 90 lakhs which is the sum your petitioners have very conservatively assessed.

(*s*) All the Board Resolutions passed during the last one year are invalid and of no effect inasmuch as your petitioners were wrongfully excluded and prevented from attending any Board Meetings in spite of the fact that the cost of sending by registered post the notices of all such Board Meetings was deposited with the company.

(*t*) The conduct of the respondents Nos. 2 and 3 is wrongful and has been continuing and the same being oppressive and prejudicial to the petitioners and also to the interest of the company's creditors and employees call for intervention by this Hon'ble Board. Respondents Nos. 2 and 3 have failed to act with commercial probity and morality

G. Matters not previously filed or pending with any other Court or Bench. The petitioners further declare that they have not previously filed any application, writ petition or suit regarding the matter in respect of which this petition has been made before any Court of Law or any other authority or any other Bench of the Board, and no application, writ petition or suit is pending before any one of them.

H. Reliefs sought. In view of the facts mentioned in paragraph F above, and in view of the fact that the wrong-doers are in control and purporting to continue in control of the management of affairs of the company and denuding the petitioners of any say in the management of affairs of the company, and manipulating the accounts, misappropriating the funds of the company and as redressal of the petitioners' grievances is not possible in the domestic forum and it is a fit case for winding-up of the company but that would prejudicially affect the petitioners and employees and as such the petitioners pray for the following reliefs:

(*a*) A scheme be framed by this Hon'ble Bench for management and administration of affairs and assets of the company;

(*b*) An Administrator be appointed to manage the affairs of the company;

(*c*) A Committee of Directors be appointed consisting of the petitioners and respondents Nos. 2 and 3 to assist the Administrator;

(*d*) Declaration that the respondents Nos. 2 and 3 are liable to reimburse the company of the assets and funds syphoned by them;

(*e*) Enquiry into the losses and damages caused to the company by the wrongful acts of respondents Nos. 2 and 3;

(*f*) Declaration that the Board Meetings and Resolutions thereunder during the last one year are all invalid, illegal and null and void;

(*g*) All Minutes and Resolutions relating to the Board Meetings during the last one year be delivered up to this Hon'ble Bench and the same be cancelled and adjudged void;

(*h*) *Ad interim* Orders in terms of the prayers above be passed.

(*i*) Costs of this application be paid by the respondents Nos. 2 and 3;

(*j*) Further and other Orders be made and directions be given as to this Learned Bench may deem fit and proper to afford complete relief to the petitioners.

I. Interim Orders if any prayed for. Pending final decision on the petition, the petitioners seek issue of the following Interim Orders:

(*a*) Injunction restraining the respondents 2 and 3 from diverting any funds or assets of the COMPANY in any manner whatsoever;

(*b*) Injunction restraining the respondents Nos. 2 and 3 from utilising the funds and assets and properties of the COMPANY for their own business;

(*c*) That a Special Officer be appointed to make an inventory of the assets and properties of the COMPANY and to initial books and accounts and records of COMPANY;

(*d*) *Ad interim* Orders in terms of prayers above;

(*e*) Further and other Orders be made and directions be given as to this Learned Bench may deem fit and proper.

J. Particulars of Bank Draft Evidencing payment of fee for application made.

(*i*) Brabourne Road Branch, Calcutta of Punjab National Bank on which the bank draft has been drawn;

(*ii*) Brabourne Road Branch, Calcutta of Punjab National Bank issued the demand draft;

(*iii*) Demand Draft No. 1234 dated .... for Rs. ....

K. List of Enclosures

(*i*) ....

(*ii*) ....

(*iii*) ....

(*iv*) ....

Place .... Signature of the
Date .... Petitioners

(Cause Title of the Petition)

Affidavit verifying the Petition

We AB residing at .... CD, residing at ...., EF residing at ...., GH, residing at .... and JK residing at .... do hereby solemnly affirm and say as follows:

1. That we are the Petitioners. We know and we have made ourselves acquainted with the facts and circumstances of this case and we are able to depose thereto.

2. That the statements contained in paragraphs .... of the petition shown to us and signed by the petitioners and marked with the letter "X" are true to our knowledge and those mentioned in the paragraphs .... of the petition are based on information derived from the records in our possession and believed by us to be true and those mentioned in the paragraphs .... of the petition are our humble submissions to this Hon'ble Bench.

3. The statements in paragraphs 1 and 2 hereinabove are true to our knowledge.

Solemnly affirmed by the said AB,
CD, EF, GH & JK at Calcutta
this .... day of 2000

1. .... Signatures
2. .... of the
3. .... Deponents
4. ....
5. ....

Before me
Notary Public

Application for Relief from Certain Liabilities

Company Petition No. .... of 1999

In the High Court at Calcutta
Original Jurisdiction

In the matter of:
The Companies Act 1956

And

In the matter of:
An application under section 633(2) of the said Act

And

In the matter of:
X Company Ltd. a company registered under the Companies Act 1956 and having its Registered Office at .... Calcutta within the said jurisdiction

And

In the matter of:
An application by:

1. AB residing at .... Calcutta
2. CD residing at .... Calcutta
3. EF residing at ....Calcutta

.... *Petitioners*

To

The Hon'ble Mr. .... Chief
Justice and His Companion
Justices of the said Hon'ble Court

The humble petition of AB, CD and EF the petitioners above-named most respectfully

SHEWETH:

1. X Co. Ltd. (hereinafter referred to as the COMPANY) was incorporated in or about .... 1980 under the provisions of the Companies Act 1956.

2. The registered office of the COMPANY is at .... Calcutta.

3. The authorised, issued, subscribed and paid-up capital of the COMPANY is Rs. .... divided into .... Equity Shares of Rs. 10 each.

4. The objects for which the COMPANY was formed are set out in Clause III of the Memorandum of Association of the COMPANY to which your petitioners will crave leave to refer. The principal object of the COMPANY was to carry on trading business. Soon after incorporation the COMPANY commenced the business and is still carrying on the business.

5. Your petitioner No. 1 was the Director of the COMPANY till 1997. Your petitioner No. 2 was the Managing Director of the COMPANY but resigned in January 1998. Your petitioner No. 3 is an ordinary Director and excepting attending the Board Meetings did not take part in the management of affairs of the COMPANY. Since January 1997 a new set of directors were elected and they are in control and management of affairs of the COMPANY. The new management did not prepare the final accounts and Balance-sheets and Profit and Loss Accounts of the COMPANY for year-ending 30th March 1996, 30th March 1997 and 30th March 1998 and no such accounts have been published or was filed with the Registrar of Companies.

6. The said new management and the incoming directors have not held the Annual General Meeting for the last three years in spite of the requests of the petitioner No. 3 to that effect.

7. Your petitioners state that due to mismanagement of affairs of the COMPANY by the incoming Directors there have been violations of provisions of the Companies Act 1956 inasmuch as in respect of the last three years Annual General Meetings were not convened, Balance Sheets and Profit and Loss Accounts and Annual Returns were not filed with Registrar of Companies in compliance with the provisions of the Companies Act 1956.

8. Your petitioners reasonably apprehend that the Registrar of Companies might take legal action against your petitioners for the defaults of the incoming directors.

9. Your petitioners state and submit that your petitioners have repeatedly requested the said incoming directors to comply with the provisions of the said Act and final accounts and Returns be filed with the Registrar of Companies. The incoming directors and the present management have not yet complied with the provisions of the said Act and made defaults in filing the accounts and the Returns with the Registrar of Companies, West Bengal.

10. Your petitioners reasonably apprehend that the Registrar of Companies may start legal proceedings against your petitioners or either of them in respect of the said defaults in not holding the Annual General Meeting and/or not filing the Balance Sheets and Profit and Loss Account and the Annual Returns with the Registrar of Companies, West Bengal.

11. Your petitioners state and submit that the said defaults have been caused due to circumstances beyond the control of your petitioners and mainly due to mismanagement of affairs of the COMPANY by the incoming directors and in spite of your petitioners being diligent and vigilant in complying with the provisions of the Companies Act 1956.

12. Your petitioners have acted honestly and reasonably and have not committed any defaults and should not be made liable to any penalties or exposed to any legal proceedings and having regard to circumstances above-referred to, your petitioners ought fairly to be excused and relieved wholly from any liability for any such default in not convening the said Annual General Meetings, preparing the final accounts and laying them before the General Meetings or filing the final accounts and Returns with the Registrar of Companies, West Bengal.

In the premises your petitioners humbly pray Your Lordships for the following orders:

(*a*) Your petitioners be excused and/or relieved from any liability in respect of any defaults in convening and holding the Annual General Meetings for the years ending 30th March, 1996, 30th March 1997 and 30th March 1998 and in not laying the Audited Balance Sheets and Profit and Loss Accounts for the said years before the Annual General Meetings and in not filing the final accounts and returns in respect of the said years with the Registrar of Companies, West Bengal in compliance with the provisions of the Companies Act 1956;

(*b*) Further Orders be made and directions be given as to this Hon'ble Court may deem fit and proper to afford complete relief to your petitioners.

And your petitioners as in duty-bound shall ever pray.

Verification

I, AB, residing at .... do hereby solemnly affirm and say as follows:

1. I am petitioner No. 1 above-named and I know the facts and circumstances of the case and I am able to depose thereto. I am authorised by petitioners Nos. 2 and 3. I do affirm and verify the aforesaid petition for self and on behalf of petitioners Nos. 2 and 3.
2. The statements in paragraphs 1 to 12 of the foregoing petition are true to my knowledge based on information derived from records maintained by me and petitioners Nos. 2 and 3 and on inspection of the records of Registrar of Companies and I believe them to be true.
3. The statements in paragraphs 1 and 2 are true to my knowledge.

Solemnly affirmed by the said AB
at the Court House in Calcutta on
this .... day of 2000

Before me
Commissioner

Petition for Winding-up of a Company

Company Petition No. .... of 1999

In the High Court at Calcutta
Original Jurisdiction

In the matter of:
The Companies Act 1956

And

In the matter of:
An Application under sections 433, 434 and 439 of the Companies Act 1956

And

In the matter of:
X Co. Ltd., a company registered under the Companies Act 1956 and having its Registered Office at .... Calcutta within the said jurisdiction

And

In the matter of:
AB residing at .... Calcutta within the said jurisdiction

Petitioner

To
The Hon'ble Mr. ....
Chief Justice and His Companion
Justices of the said Hon'ble Court

The humble petition of AB the petitioner above-named most respectfully

SHEWETH:

1. The address of your petitioner for the purpose of service of notices, processes etc. is that of its Advocate-on-Record M/s EF & Co. having its office at .... Calcutta 700 001.

2. X Co. Ltd. (hereinafter referred to as the said COMPANY) was incorporated on 5th March 1982 under the Companies Act 1956.

3. The registered office of the COMPANY is at .... Calcutta within the said jurisdiction.

4. The authorised, issued subscribed and paid-up capital of the COMPANY is Rs. .... divided into .... equity shares of Rs. 10 each.

5. The main objects for which the COMPANY was formed and incorporated are contained in the Memorandum of Association of the COMPANY and include mainly trading business in all commodities and articles.

6. On or about .... at the request of the COMPANY your petitioners sold and delivered goods of certain quantity, at an agreed price. The COMPANY accepted the goods and appropriated the same.

7. Your petitioner submitted bills which were duly accepted and never disputed by the COMPANY.

8. The COMPANY paid a sum of Rs. 10,000 by way of part payment and promised to pay the balance of Rs. 90,000 within a month. This period has expired on 30th March 1998.

9. In spite of demand the COMPANY has failed to pay the said Rs. 90,000 or any part thereof and deferred payment thereof on some pretext or the other. By its letter dated .... the COMPANY requested for six months' time to pay the balance amount of Rs. 90,000. A copy of letter is annexed hereto. The COMPANY has not paid any further amount in spite of the said promise.

10. Your petitioner through its Advocate on Record issued a notice to the COMPANY demanding payment of Rs. 90,000 with interest at 18% per annum from the due date of payment till realisation. Such rate of interest is a part of the agreement, which will appear from the bills of your petitioner copies whereof are annexed hereto.

11. More than three weeks have passed but the COMPANY has not yet replied to the notice nor paid any portion to your petitioner.

12. The petitioner claims a sum of Rs. 90,000 with interest amounting to a sum of Rs. 5,000 aggregating to Rs. 95,000.

13. The COMPANY has failed and neglected and refused to pay the said sum of Rs. 95,000 or any portion thereof.

14. The COMPANY is unable to pay its creditors, its liability far exceeds its present and probable assets. It is commercially insolvent. In the premises it is just, fit and equitable that the company should be and be wound up under the provisions of the Companies Act 1956.

15. This application is made *bona fide*, in the interest of justice, and the balance of convenience is also in favour of passing the Orders prayed for herein.

The petitioner therefore humbly prays Your Lordships for the following Orders:

(*a*) X Co. Ltd. be wound up under the provisions of the Companies Act 1956;

(*b*) Official Liquidator be appointed as Liquidator of the company to take possession of the assets, properties, books and records of the company forthwith;

(*c*) Further Orders be made and directions be given as to this Hon'ble Court may deem fit and proper.

And Your petitioner as in duty bound shall ever pray.

Date: Sd/- AB
Place: (EF & Co.)
Advocates for the petitioner

(Same Cause Title)

Affidavit verifying the petition

I, AB residing at .... Calcutta do hereby solemnly affirm and say as follows:

1. That I am one of the creditors of the COMPANY. I know and I have made myself acquainted with the facts and circumstances of this case and I am able to depose thereto.

2. The statements contained in paragraphs 1 to 10 of the petition herein now shown to me and marked with the letter "X" are true to my knowledge and those contained in paragraphs 11 to 13 hereof are based on information derived from records in my possession, and believed by me to be true and correct and those contained in paragraphs 14 and 15 hereof are my humble submissions to this Hon'ble Court.

3. The statements contained in the foregoing paragraphs of this Affidavit are true to my knowledge.

Solemnly affirmed by the said AB
at the Court House in Calcutta
on this .... day of 2000

AB
(Signature)

Before me
Commissioner

Application for Relief from Certain Liabilities

In the Court of the Metropolitan Magistrate at Calcutta

In the matter of:
The Companies Act 1956

And

In the matter of:
An application under section 633(1) of the said Act

And

In the matter of:
An application by:

1. AB residing at ....
2. CD residing at ....
3. EF working for gain at .... Calcutta

Petitioners

The humble petition of AB, CD and EF the petitioners above-named

MOST RESPECTFULLY SHEWETH:

1. That the State through Registrar of Companies, West Bengal filed two complaints and two cases were started against your petitioners being Case Nos. .... and .... under sections 210(3) and 220(3) of the Companies Act 1956. In both the cases your petitioners pleaded guilty and the said pleas were accepted by the Learned Magistrate and your petitioners were fined Rs. 100 in each of the two cases and your petitioners were directed to file the relevant Returns with the Registrar of Companies,

West Bengal by 20th February 2000, with additional fees. Your petitioners have paid the fines.

2. Your petitioners in spite of the best efforts were unable to file the Balance Sheets and Annual Returns for the year-ended 30th March 1998 due to labour trouble and the factory and Head Office remaining closed, and the books of Accounts and records were not available to prepare the Balance Sheets or the Annual Returns.

3. In spite of negotiations your petitioners failed to get the requisite documents and access to the books of accounts. Any application for the Search Warrants would have aggravated the situation.

4. The State through the Registrar of Companies again filed two Complaints under section 614A(2) of the Companies Act 1956 complaining that the Order dated .... has not been complied with.

5. Your petitioners could not comply with the order in the circumstances mentioned above in spite of their best efforts and as such default or non-compliance has been caused due to circumstances beyond the control of the petitioners and mainly due to the labour trouble.

6. Your petitioners have acted honestly and reasonably and have not committed any default within the meaning of the Companies Act 1956 and could not be made liable to any legal proceedings and pray that your petitioners be excused and relieved fully from any liability for such defaults in filing the Balance Sheets and Annual Returns with the Registrar of Companies and/or non-compliance with the said Orders.

In the circumstances your petitioners therefore most humbly pray Your Honour that:

(*a*) The petitioners be excused and/or relieved from any liability in respect of any defaults in filing the Balance Sheets and Profit and Loss Accounts and the Annual Returns with the Registrar of Companies and/or complying with the Order dated .... of this Learned Court;

(*b*) The complaints filed and/or the Prosecution Cases Nos. .... be not proceeded with and your petitioners be discharged therefrom;

(*c*) Such further and other Orders be made and/or directions be given as to this Learned Court may seem fit and proper to afford complete relief to your petitioners.

And your petitioners as in duty bound shall ever pray.

Verification

I, AB, residing at .... do hereby solemnly affirm and say as follows:

1. I am the petitioner No. 1 above-named and I know the facts and circumstances of the case and I am able to depose thereto. I am authorised by petitioners Nos. 2 and 3. I do affirm and verify the aforesaid petition for self and on behalf of petitioners Nos. 2 and 3.
2. The statements in paragraphs 1 to 6 of the foregoing petition are true to my knowledge based on information derived from records maintained by me and petitioners Nos. 2 and 3 and on inspection of the records of Registrar of Companies and I believe them to be true.
3. The statements in paragraphs 1 and 2 are true to my knowledge.

Solemnly affirmed by the said AB
at the Court House in Calcutta on
this .... day of 2000

Before me
Commissioner

13

Construction Agreement

The owner of a land with a view to get construction made of a multistoried building on the land may invite tenders from one or more contractors. The tenderer in his tender will give general description of the proposed work, plans, drawings, specifications and other documents as may be necessary. The tenderer will also give an estimate of the quantity and cost of materials, labour charges and other costs and the terms of payment.

On consideration of the tender and after consulting the owner's architect, an agreement is entered into with the Contractor. The owner may show his architect the plans, drawings, specifications and other documents for the purpose of construction. Normally the agreement of construction entered into between the owner and the contractor will contain details of work to be done and the rights and obligations of the owner and the contractor and the part that the architect will play in completion of the work. The Agreement for construction will contain, *inter alia,* that the contractor will provide the required labour, materials, water, plant and machinery. The contractor shall execute the work in accordance with the plans, drawings, specification and documents agreed upon by the parties. Both parties will be guided by the instructions of the architect at every stage. The construction, nature of construction, defective construction, remedial work for any defective construction all will be decided and directed by the architect. The progress of construction and terms of payment to the contractor shall be specifically provided for. The time limit for completion of the work, the execution thereof and compensation payable for delayed work and escalation costs should be specified. The responsibility to obtain necessary sanction and the certificates for the construction, water and electricity connections should be on the contractor who shall be required to obtain the completion certificate from the Municipality concerned. The owner shall be liable to pay for any additions or alterations to the agreed plan at the same rate as for the work done under the contract. The owner should be exempted from the liability to third parties due to any accident during the execution of the work by the contractor and the sole responsibility for that would lie with the contractor who shall take all precautionary measures. Any materials brought on the site and used in construction shall be paid for and any unused material shall be removed immediately on construction being completed. No liability will lie on the owner to any labourer or to any supplier of goods or services or for payment of any bills or cesses or impositions in regard to the said construction. Until the contractor completes construction and completion certificate is obtained, the contractor shall not be entitled to payment of final bills. Any other special requirement of the owner including the mode of settlement of disputes and the work being continued even if settlement proceedings being continued are to be provided for. It is a contract under the Indian Contract Act and most of the provisions of the Act is applicable to such a contract.

FORMS

Agreement for Construction of Building

THIS CONSTRUCTION AGREEMENT is made on the 5th day of June 2000 BETWEEN LO, son of AB, residing at .... (hereinafter referred to as OWNER) of the First Part and XZ, son of MN, residing at .... (hereinafter called the CONTRACTOR) of the Second Part.

WHEREAS the party of the First Part is the owner of a plot of land measuring .... at .... and more particularly described in the plan attached and therein delineated in red.

AND WHEREAS the OWNER being desirous of erecting a building on the said plot has appointed Shri AK as the architect who has prepared plans, specifications and drawings for the said proposed building.

AND WHEREAS the plans, designs, drawings and elevations of the said intended building and specifications of the works to be done and of the materials to be provided in and for the erection of the said building have been prepared by the said architect sanctioned by the Authorities concerned and approved by the parties herein and have been subscribed for the purposes of identification by both the parties.

AND WHEREAS the CONTRACTOR is willing to enter into an agreement for the execution of the said works in accordance with the Architect's said plans, specifications and drawings at actual costs plus 20% profit basis.

NOW THESE PRESENTS WITNESSETH and the parties hereby agree as follows:

1. The CONTRACTOR shall erect on the said plot of land a building in conformity with the sanctioned plans, drawings and elevations and complete all the said works with the material of best quality and in the most substantial and workmanlike manner and to the satisfaction of the said architect and will in all respects comply with and abide by the true intent and manner of the said specifications, plans, drawings and elevations and of this agreement.

2. The CONTRACTOR will finish and complete the said building on or before the 5th day of June 2001 and if the said building shall not be completed on or before the said date the CONTRACTOR shall forfeit, out of the moneys which shall be due to him by virtue of this agreement, the sum of Rs. 1000 for every day which shall elapse after the 5th day of June 2001 until the said building shall be completed. Provided that if the CONTRACTOR is prevented by any strike among the workmen or by reason of any event beyond his control, the said architect may extend the time for the completion of the works for such reasonable period as he may think fit.

3. If the CONTRACTOR shall become bankrupt or from any cause whatsoever be prevented from or is delayed in proceeding with and completing the said works according to the terms and conditions of this agreement, or does not proceed with the said works to the satisfaction of the said architect, it shall be lawful for the said architect to leave or cause to be left at the usual place of abode or business of the CONTRACTOR, a notice in writing for the said CONTRACTOR to proceed forthwith and effectually with the said works. In case the said CONTRACTOR shall, for 7 days after such notice is so left as aforesaid, make default in forthwith and effectually proceeding with the said work it shall be lawful for the said architect to employ any other workmen either by CONTRACTOR or otherwise to proceed with the said works and complete the same and pay to the said workmen out of the moneys which shall be then due to the said CONTRACTOR on account of this agreement, the amount of their charges for the same and for all necessary materials to be found and provided for such completion; and if the amount of balance to the credit of the CONTRACTOR be insufficient to cover such charges for such workmen and materials then in such a case the said CONTRACTOR shall and will make good and pay such deficiency on demand.

4. If the said architect shall at any time or times consider any of the workmen employed by the said CONTRACTOR on the works as in any way incompetent or as acting improperly it shall in every such case be lawful for the said architect to discharge such workmen and the said CONTRACTOR shall without delay put another workman in his place.

5. In case any of the materials brought on the said premises by the said CONTRACTOR shall be considered by the said architect as unsound or in any respect improper, the said CONTRACTOR will upon notice in writing to him or his foreman on the premises given by the said architect cause the same to

be removed from the ground and proceed with the said works with materials corresponding with the specifications and instructions approved by the said architect and on default of such removal within 7 days after such last mentioned notice, it shall be lawful for the said architect to cause to be removed to such place as he may think proper without being in any way answerable or accountable for the loss or damage that shall happen to any materials so removed and to cause proper materials to be substituted for the same, and to pay all expenses in connection with such removal and substitution out of the moneys which shall become due to the said CONTRACTOR by virtue of this agreement.

6. In case the said architect shall consider any part of the said works to have been executed in an unsound and improper manner, the said CONTRACTOR will cause the same immediately to be taken down and executed in a proper manner to the satisfaction of the said architect without any extra charge or expense whatsoever.

7. If the said architect or the owner shall think proper at any time or times to make any alterations or additions or omission in the works hereby contracted for, he or they shall give to the said CONTRACTOR written instructions for such alterations or omissions signed by the said architect. Any additional charge by the CONTRACTOR with respect to such alterations if certified to be correct by the architect shall be paid for in the same manner and at the same time as hereinafter expressed for the payment of the ultimate balance of the said sum not exceeding the sum calculated at the agreed rate.

8. Any damage arising from accidents or carelessness of the workmen or otherwise to the said work hereby contracted for or to the materials or implements therein used or to the workmen shall be borne and effectually made good by the said CONTRACTOR at his own costs and charges.

9. The CONTRACTOR shall use in the construction best quality materials in accordance with the specifications mentioned herein.

10. The CONTRACTOR will not without the consent of the said architect make any sub-contract for the execution of the works hereby contracted for or any part thereof nor assign or underlet the present contract or any part thereof.

11. Notwithstanding anything contained herein it will be sole responsibility of the CONTRACTOR to comply with the provisions of law relating to the construction of the said building in accordance with these presents and the CONTRACTOR hereby undertakes to keep the OWNER harmless from and indemnified against any action, claim, loss, damages, expenses howsoever arising for any breach of any statutory provisions, rules or regulations or any term of this agreement.

12. The CONTRACTOR shall be paid Rs. 5 lakhs as his remuneration for the labour supplied and material used and supervision made by him for the aforesaid building. The payment towards the said construction will be made in the manner following:

Rs. 2 lakhs shall be paid per month of construction work continuing the first instalment to be paid on 10th July 1999 and thereafter by 10th of each succeeding month of construction work being done and the balance, if any, within three months of the completion of the building, provided that in case of each payment the architect certifies that the work and materials to a sufficient amount shall have been done executed or provided by the said CONTRACTOR to the satisfaction of the said architect. Provided also that the said CONTRACTOR shall not be entitled to payment or to receive the balance sum or his remuneration until the said architect shall certify under his own hand that the whole of the said works have been completed and finished to his satisfaction and Completion Certificate from the Authorities concerned has been obtained. The decision of the architect shall be binding on the parties and shall be final.

IN WITNESS WHEREOF the parties hereto have signed this agreement on the day month and year above-written.

Signed and delivered by LO, the
OWNER in the presence of : Sd/- (Owner)

1. ....

2. ....

Signed and delivered by XZ, the
CONTRACTOR in the presence of: Sd/- (Contractor)

1. ....

2. ....

Direct Contract to Build a House

THIS AGREEMENT is made the .... day of .... BETWEEN AB, son of etc. (hereinafter called the OWNER) of the one part and CD, son of etc. (hereinafter called the CONTRACTOR) of the other part.

WHEREAS the OWNER desires to have certain works as shown and indicated in the Specification/Schedule/Drawings/Plans/Designs/Rates and Acceptance of Tender executed each of which documents has been kept signed in duplicate by or on behalf of the parties hereto for the purpose of identification and shall be treated as part or parts of this agreement.

NOW IT IS HEREBY AGREED by and between the parties as follows:

1. For the consideration hereinafter mentioned the contractor shall, upon and subject to the conditions annexed hereto, execute and complete the works so shown and described.

2. The OWNER will pay the CONTRACTOR a lump sum amount of Rs. .... (or such other sum as shall become due and payable hereunder) in accordance with the quotation, rates or acceptance of the tender at the time and in the manner specified in the conditions.

CONDITIONS:

1. The said OWNER shall arrange for and supply the materials and the said CONTRACTOR shall construct and build and completely finish for the OWNER with his own labour on the plot of land described in the plan or plans annexed hereto a three-storeyed house according to the specifications, elevations and sections indicated therein and according to the directions of the owner or his consulting or supervising engineer, if any, or his duly appointed agent, given from time to time without any deviation from or modification of the said plans, drawings, specifications, elevations or sections except with written consent from the owner first had and obtained otherwise such deviation and work will be considered as gratuitously done and if required by the OWNER the CONTRACTOR shall at his own costs and expenses dismantle the same and complete the work according to the plans, drawings, specifications, elevations or sections.

2. The said CONTRACTOR shall build and completely finish and make the said house habitable on or before the .... day of .... 2001 unless prevented by any labour strike, fire, accident, earthquake, mob violence, attack from the air or any other major disturbances and in default thereof, he shall remain liable for and pay to the owner damages at the rate of Rs. .... (in words Rupees ....) per day for such breach of the contract so long as the said house shall remain unfinished or inhabitable.

3. The said CONTRACTOR shall build the said house under his direct personal supervision and in the best workmanlike manner and shall not, on any account whatsoever, employ a sub-contractor for the building or completing any portion thereof except with the written consent of the OWNER first had and obtained which the OWNER may in his absolute discretion withhold without assigning any reason.

4. The OWNER shall pay to the said CONTRACTOR on the .... day of .... each month against his running bills 90% of such sum as he claims or entitled to on the progress of the work and according to the approved rates mentioned in the Acceptance of Tender less 20 per cent thereof which will be adjusted at the time of settlement of his bills and final payment after completion of work and scrutiny of all the bills.

or

The OWNER shall pay to the CONTRACTOR portions of the said sum of Rs. .... on *pro rata* basis fortnightly/monthly less a sum of equivalent to

25% thereof which will all be adjusted at the time of final payment after completion of the work and scrutiny of all the bills.

5. All moneys which the said CONTRACTOR shall be liable to pay to the OWNER on account of the breach of this contract or on any other account shall be deducted by the said OWNER from and set off against any money or moneys which may be due to the said CONTRACTOR on account of the construction of the said house during the process or on completion.

6. Within .... months of the completion of the said house and adjustment of the account the OWNER shall pay to the CONTRACTOR such balance amount as he may then be entitled to according to the terms of this contract upon scrutiny of all his bills.

7. In case the OWNER shall desire for any deviation from the said plans and specifications, designs or any more or other building or buildings or any additional work or works to be done or executed, the CONTRACTOR shall duly execute such deviations or extra or additional work in a proper, substantial and workmanlike manner, in all respects according to such altered plans and specifications and within the time prescribed or any extension thereof as may be mutually agreed and to the satisfaction of the OWNER. The additional costs of such deviations, alterations and additions, if any, shall be estimated and paid in the manner provided by clause 4 hereof.

8. The CONTRACTOR shall remain liable to and shall indemnify the owner in respect of all causes of action, claims, damages, compensation or costs, charges and expenses arising out of any accident or injury, sustained by the OWNER or any member of his family or guest or by any workman or other person, whether in the employment of the CONTRACTOR or not while in or upon the said works or the site of the same arising out of any act, default or negligence, error in judgment on his part or on the part of his servants and agents.

9. The OWNER shall be entitled to determine this agreement and discharge the contract, without prejudice to other rights and remedies available to him, if the CONTRACTOR shall become insolvent or fails and/or neglects to carry out instructions on his behalf or to complete the work or suspend the same or delay the progress thereof without reasonable cause or suffers or allows any execution or attachment levied on the properties at the site or refuses or persistently neglects to make good the defective work, if any, or if without the written consent of the owner, he shall assign or sublet this contract.

10. In case of termination of this agreement and/or discharge of the contractor as hereinbefore stipulated, the OWNER shall be entitled to appoint a new CONTRACTOR OR CONTRACTORS to continue and complete the said dwelling house and buildings, or any additions to building or buildings and works, if any, according to the said plans and specifications or any deviations

therefrom and authorise him to use any plants, materials and property of the CONTRACTOR left upon the site and the CONTRACTOR shall in such case lose and forfeit all his rights whatsoever under this contract except his claim for moneys unpaid on settlement of account between the parties and scrutiny of all his bills.

11. In case any dispute or difference shall arise between the parties during the progress of or after construction or abandonment of the work as to the meaning or construction of this contract or touching or relating either to the said buildings or works, or to any other matter or thing arising directly or indirectly under this contract, then and in such an event the same shall be referred to arbitration and the final decision of a single arbitrator to be mutually agreed between the parties who alone shall consider and determine the same and whose certificate or award shall be binding and conclusive upon both the said parties, otherwise to two arbitrators, one to be appointed by each party who will appoint an umpire at the commencement of the proceedings and this clause shall be deemed a submission within the meaning of the Arbitration and Conciliation Act 1996 or statutory modification or re-enactment thereof.

IN WITNESS WHEREOF, the said OWNER and CONTRACTOR have hereto respectively signed on the day, month and year first above-written.

Signed, sealed and delivered by AB — AB
and CD in the presence of .... — CD

NOTE: If the building materials are to be supplied by the contractor, the following paragraph should be added: "The contractor will at the first instance and at his own costs and expenses, arrange for all bricks, lime, sand, cement, stone, timber, iron rods and other materials whatsoever necessary for the said works, all such materials being of the best quality available in the market, sound and well-seasoned, and also tools, implements, scaffolding whatsoever necessary for carrying out and/or completing of the said work according to the said plans and specifications; and in case any material or materials is or are not approved by the owner, he shall forthwith, at his own expenses, replace and substitute the same with better material and materials as approved by the owner.

Agreement between Builder and Artisan

THIS AGREEMENT is made on this .... day of .... BETWEEN AB son of .... residing at .... (hereinafter called the BUILDER which terms shall include his heirs, successors and permitted assigns) of the one part and CD son of .... residing at .... (hereinafter called the ARTISAN) of the other part.

WHEREBY IT IS AGREED and declared by and between the parties as follows:—

1. In consideration of good and faithful service promised to be rendered and the duties to be performed and of the covenants and conditions to be observed, performed and fulfilled as hereunder provided, the BUILDER has employed the ARTISAN as a, etc., at, etc., from the date hereof, at the rate of Rs. .... per week, and will pay him the same on the Saturday of every week so long as he shall faithfully, honestly and diligently serve the BUILDER and observe the rules of the establishment and obedience and discipline.

2. The ARTISAN will at all times hereafter obey the BUILDER and serve him diligently and faithfully in all matters and things during such service and will duly observe and keep the usual hours of attendance and work according to the rules and regulations of the establishment in force from time to time and to be observed by other workmen employed by the builder, and will properly and steadily perform all such work as shall be required by the BUILDER or his foreman, and will not absent himself nor otherwise keep aloof or sit idle from such work without the builder's or his foreman's express consent first had and obtained.

3. The ARTISAN will devote full time and whole-hearted attention to his works and shall not, during the period of such service as aforesaid, serve anywhere except for doing odd jobs during spare hours without detriment to the interest of the BUILDER nor leak out any trade or business secret of the BUILDER under any circumstances.

4. Either party may at his option determine this agreement by giving either of them one week's notice ending on the last day of the week.

5. Notwithstanding anything hereinbefore contained the BUILDER shall be at liberty to determine this agreement at any time for reason of any act of negligence, misconduct or breach of duty on the part of the artisan or on account of any act of indiscipline and dismiss him summarily forthwith.

IN WITNESS WHEREOF the parties hereto have executed these presents on the day, month and year first above-written.

Signed, sealed and delivered by	AB
AB and CD in the presence of:	CD

Agreement to Construct a Multi-storeyed Building

MEMORANDUM OF AGREEMENT made this 5th day of May 2000 BETWEEN AB son of MN by caste .... by occupation .... by religion .... residing at .... hereinafter referred to as the VENDOR (which term or expression shall unless excluded by or repugnant to the subject or context by deemed to include his heirs, executors, administrators, representatives and assigns) of the ONE PART AND CD son of PQ by caste .... by occupation .... residing at .... hereinafter referred to as the PURCHASER (which expression shall unless repugnant to the subject or context be deemed to include its successors representatives and assigns) of the OTHER PART:

WHEREAS the VENDOR as the sole and absolute owner is absolutely seized and possessed of or otherwise well and sufficiently entitled to all that the building with land and premises situate on the piece or parcel of land containing by estimation an area of 6 cottahs 6 chittacks and 6 square feet be the same a little more or less being premises No. ...., Calcutta, more, fully and particularly mentioned and described in the Schedule hereunder written and hereinafter for the sake of brevity collectively referred to as the *said property*. The premises is partly occupied by the VENDOR and his family and partly let out to tenants who pay a sum of Rs. .... as rent per month inclusive of taxes.

AND WHEREAS the PURCHASER approached the VENDOR with a proposal for construction of a multi-storeyed building on the site according to modern taste, design and architecture at their costs after demolition of the existing old building which will be sold to the purchaser who will pay in exchange of and as consideration for such sale (*i*) initially a token sum of Rs. .... as earnest money; (*ii*) a recurring sum of Rs. .... per month on the 7th of every month as compensation for loss of rent of the property to be demolished from the date of sale until completion of the building and delivery of possession of the flats as hereunder mentioned; (*iii*) allow the VENDOR and his family alternative accommodation in a flat measuring at least 500 square feet (carpet area) in the building promoted by his sister concern, *viz*. .... at premises No. .... free of rent and other charges; and (*iv*) finally allot and convey two flats as ownership flats at their respective book values in the said multi-storeyed building when completed duly equipped with all fittings and fixtures.

NOW THIS MEMORANDUM witnesseth and it is hereby agreed by and between the parties hereto as follows:

1. The VENDOR will sell and the PURCHASER will purchase all that the said property being premises No. .... in the town of .... as it is and where it is more fully and particularly mentioned and described in the Schedule hereunder written and the inheritance thereof in fee simple in possession or an estate equivalent thereto free from all encumbrances attachments trusts liens and other defects of title but subject to a good and marketable title to the reasonable satisfaction of the purchaser's solicitor (name) .... at or for the consideration as hereinbefore and hereunder stated, *viz*. (*i*) initial payment of Rs. .... as earnest money to be paid in cash simultaneously with the execution of this agreement;

(*ii*) a further recurring payment of Rs. .... per month as compensation for loss of rent of the property pending demolition thereof and construction of the multi-storeyed building such payment shall be regularly made on the 7th of each month until delivery of possession of the flats; (*iii*) free accommodation to the VENDOR and his family in a flat measuring 500 square feet (carpet area) in the building constructed by his sister concern (name) at premises No. ....; and (*iv*) finally allot and convey at their book values two residential self-contained flats, one in the ground floor and the other in the first floor of the building to be constructed, as ownership flats or apartments fully completed and equipped and habitable in all respects with all electric and sanitary fittings, fixtures and appurtenances, separate electric meter and connection measuring at least 800 square feet (carpet area) both to be delivered to the VENDORS on or before 15th day of May 2002 and each shall consist of at least the following accommodation, *viz*. (*a*) four bed with attached bath W.C. shower; (*b*) one kitchen and store, drawing room; (*c*) dining hall; (*d*) servants room; and (*e*) car parking space 50 square feet with right of ingress thereto and egress therefrom through the staircase and main entrance facing the municipal road.

2. The VENDOR shall within one week from the date of the execution of this agreement deliver to the purchaser's advocates on record on their accountable receipt all the original documents of title relating to the said property as are in possession of the VENDORS for investigation of title on behalf of the purchaser.

3. The VENDOR shall duly answer all requisitions and objections as to the title of the property as may be made from time to time by the purchaser's Advocate and also make out a good and marketable title thereto to the reasonable satisfaction of the said Advocate free from all encumbrances, attachment debts charges, trust, lien etc. when the purchaser's advocate shall inform the VENDOR within a fortnight from that date about his acceptance or rejection of the title of the vendor in respect of the said property subject however to the result of further searches and enquires and shall in case of approval of the title send to the VENDOR a draft of the proposed conveyance relating to the said property to enable the vendors to apply for and obtain necessary Income-tax Clearance Certificate under s. 230A of the Income Tax Act. The vendor shall make any other party or parties if any so required join in the conveyance so as to convey an absolute title to the purchaser or to redeem any charge or encumbrances.

4. The purchase shall be completed within one month from the date of obtaining of the Income-tax Clearance Certificate under s. 230A of the Income Tax Act by the Vendor and time for this purpose be deemed to be the essence of contract when the VENDOR shall execute and register a conveyance or conveyances in respect of the said property and deliver peaceful vacant

possession of the portion thereof in his occupation to the purchaser and the rest by attornment of tenancy. The purchaser shall bear and pay all costs of and incidental to stamp and registration of the conveyance.

5. The PURCHASER shall thereafter but before any action is taken for demolition of the existing building provide the VENDOR and his family with alternative accommodation in the building at .... promoted by his sister concern comprising at least a carpet area of 500 square feet for which the VENDOR shall not be liable to pay any rent or taxes or make any other contribution on any account whatsoever.

6. The PURCHASER shall thereafter be entitled to recover vacant possession of the entire premises by eviction of the tenants and other occupiers by legal process or by negotiations and settlement of terms as regards their rights and claims and demolish the existing building.

7. The PURCHASER shall carry out the demolition work in a most skilful manner with all precautionary safety measures without causing any damages, injury or other mischiefs to any other building or buildings or loss of life or limb of the people residing at the locality and shall remain fully liable for all his acts, deeds, things and error in judgment on that account.

8. In the event of the title of the VENDOR is not accepted by the purchaser's Advocate or the said property not being found free from attachments or encumbrances whatsoever or subject to any scheme of acquisition or requisition or any other defect as regards title or in the event of the VENDOR failing to procure the necessary income tax clearance certificate under the provisions of s. 230A of the Income Tax Act within a period of three months from the date of delivery of draft conveyance unless the time for that purpose is extended by mutual consent the purchaser shall be entitled to rescind this agreement when the vendor shall refund the earnest money of Rs. .... with interest at 12% per annum and shall further pay a sum of Rs. 5,500 as costs of and incidental to this agreement and searches and investigation of title when the proposed deal shall stand cancelled.

9. Immediately with the execution of this agreement the vendor will allow the purchaser to instal and fix a board on the said property who shall also publish advertisement inviting offers for purchase of the flats and/or apartments to be constructed on the site of the said property but will not charge any rent or occupation charges for fixing board on the site of the said property nor raise any objection to the same. The PURCHASER shall not conclude any final deal with any such party before completion of the conveyance.

10. After the execution of this agreement and even prior to the completion of the sale the PURCHASER shall be at liberty to prepare or cause to be prepared a plan and plans for constructing a multi-storeyed building or buildings on

the site of the said property by demolition of the existing structure standing thereon and the VENDORS shall as and when necessary sign such plan or plans and other papers and writings that may be required for the purpose of obtaining sanction of such plan or plans by the purchaser from the Corporation of Calcutta or obtaining permission from the Competent Authority under the provisions of the Urban Land (Ceiling and Regulation) Act 1976, it being expressly agreed that all costs, charges and expenses for obtaining sanction of such plan or plans whatsoever will be borne and paid by the purchaser and the VENDOR will not be liable for reimbursement of such costs, charges and expenses for any reason whatsoever.

11. The VENDOR declares that the quantum of vacant land contained in the said property is within the ceiling limit as prescribed under s. 27 of the Urban Land (Ceiling and Regulation) Act 1976 and it is not necessary to obtain any further permission under the provisions of the Urban Land (Ceiling and Regulation) Act 1976.

12. If at any time before the completion of the purchase it so appears that the said property or any portion thereof is affected by any scheme of alignment of the CORPORATION OF CALCUTTA, OR CALCUTTA IMPROVEMENT TRUST, OR CALCUTTA METROPOLITAN DEVELOPMENT AUTHORITY, or is notified to be acquired or requisitioned by the Government or any other public body or authority, the PURCHASER shall have the option of rescinding this agreement and upon such rescission the VENDORS shall forthwith refund the said earnest money paid by the purchaser to the VENDORS with interest at 12% per annum as also the costs of and incidental to the perusal and investigation of the VENDORS' title assessed at Rs. 2500 only in the aggregate.

13. The plan of the proposed building at .... showing the flats to be allotted to the VENDOR in accordance with this agreement will be signed by both parties.

14. The PURCHASER shall have the right of demolition renovation of the existing building and construction of the proposed building at .... and to sell, resell, lease out, let out other flats and spaces in the proposed building on plan basis from the date of conveyance without any objection from the VENDOR in so far as the same does not affect the rights of or conflict with the interest of the VENDOR as regards two flats hereunder agreed to be allotted and conveyed to him.

15. Any dispute or difference between the parties arising out of the meaning construction or import of this agreement or their rights and liabilities hereunder shall be adjudicated by reference to the arbitration of two independent arbitrators one to be appointed by each party who shall appoint an Umpire at the commencement of the reference and the award of the arbitrators or umpire shall be final and conclusive on the subject as

between the parties and this clause shall be deemed to be a submission within the meaning of Arbitration and Conciliation Act 1996 and its statutory modification or re-enactment thereof in force from time to time.

Schedule of property

IN WITNESS WHEREOF the parties hereto have hereunto set and subscribed their respective hands and seals the day, month and year first above-written.

Signed, sealed and delivered by the above-named vendors at Calcutta in the presence of:

Signed, sealed and delivered by the above-named purchaser at Calcutta in the presence of:

Received of and from the within-named purchaser the within-mentioned sum of Rs........................ only being the earnest money payable under these presents as per memo below:

WITNESS: Signed

MEMO OF CONSIDERATION

By A/c Payee Cheque No. ...... dated .... drawn on X Bank Ltd., Calcutta Branch in favour of the VENDOR. RS. ....

(Rs. ....)

WITNESS: Signed

14

The Consumer Protection Act 1986

The United Nations General Assembly by a resolution of 9th April 1996 adopted certain guidelines for strengthening consumer protection policies and legislation in the member countries. The Economic and Social Council of the United Nations had adopted a resolution urging all Governments to implement the guidelines.

In the United States of America there are a number of statutes to safeguard the interest of consumers but there is no consolidated statute covering all matters of protection to the consumers. In the United Kingdom there have been several Acts to protect the interests of the consumers and ultimately the Consumer Protection Act of 1986 has been passed which is wide ranging creating civil and criminal liability for products, unsafe goods, misleading price indications and allied matters.

In India there have been several statutes which indirectly protected the interest of consumers including the Monopolies and Restrictive Trade Practices Act 1969, Indian Contract Act 1876, Sale of Goods Act 1930, Drugs and Cosmetics Act 1940 and several other Acts relating to particular aspect of consumer interest.

Ultimately the Consumer Protection Act 1986 was passed. This is a comprehensive legislation providing simple, speedy and inexpensive redressal of grievances of the consumers. This Act is in addition to the provisions of other statutes. The Act of 1986 intends to promote and protect the rights of the consumers by making provisions to have the right to be informed about the quality, quantity, purity, potency, standard and price of goods and services. The Act prohibits marketing of goods and services hazardous to life and property. A consumer has been assured the right to access to variety of goods and services at reasonable prices. The Act provides for redressal against unfair or restrictive trade practices, exploitation and spread of consumer education and machinery at different levels for hearing complaints and granting reliefs.

The Act provides for three-tier machinery or Tribunal which are quasi-judicial, namely, District Forum, State Forum and National Forum.

The Consumer Protection Act 1986 applies to all goods and services in private, public and co-operative sectors for consumption by the consumer or for use in his business or occupation for earning his livelihood.

A person may file a complaint in relation to goods sold or delivered or agreed to be sold or delivered or any service provided or agreed to be provided. His complaint may be against unfair or restrictive trade practices or defective goods or the services suffer from deficiency or price charged is in excess of the price fixed under law or displayed on the goods or on its package or against goods which will be hazardous are being offered for sale to public.

District Forum. A complaint may be made to the District Forum if value of the subject-matter or claim does not exceed Rs. 5 lakhs and any part of cause of action arose within the territorial limits of the Forum or the opposite parties reside or carry on business within its territorial limits. Where there are several opposite parties but only some or one of them reside or carry on business within the territorial limits the complaint may be filed with the leave of the District Forum. The complaint may be filed by the consumer or by recognised Consumer Association or by Central or State Government or by one or more consumers where the general interests of consumers are involved with the leave of the Forum for and on behalf of all consumers so interested. District Forum after hearing the parties may direct the removal of the defect, replacement of the goods, return of the price, to pay compensation, to discontinue unfair or restrictive trade practice or discontinue sale of hazardous goods and withdrawal of the same from the market. The Forum may direct payment of cost to the complainant. If the Forum finds that the complaints are frivolous or vexatious it may on recording reasons dismiss the complaint and ask the complainant to pay costs.

From the order of the District Forum an appeal lies to the State Commission. The limitation for appeal is 30 days from the order. The State Commission may extend the date for preferring the appeal by another 30 days.

The jurisdiction of the State Commission is to hear the appeal from the order of the District Forum within the State and also to hear the original complaint where the value of goods or service and compensation or claim is more than Rs. 5 lakhs but does not exceed Rs. 20 lakhs.

The National Commission can hear appeals from the orders of the State Commission of any State in India and to hear original complaints where the value of the goods or services and compensation or claims exceed Rs. 20 lakhs. The appeal has to be preferred within 30 days from the order of the State Commission. National Commission may extend the period by another 30 days for sufficient cause shown.

The Supreme Court may hear an appeal from the order of the National Commission. The appeal has to be preferred within 30 days from the date of the order. The Supreme Court may extend the period by another 30 days for sufficient cause.

Limitation. The limitation period for making complaint to District Forum, State Commission or the National Commission is two years from the date of the cause of action. After this period of two years on sufficient cause being shown a complaint may be entertained on condonation of delay and recording reasons for condoning such delay.

Execution. The District Forum, State Commission and National Commission may execute its orders as if it is a decree. In case it fails to execute the decree it shall send such decree for execution to the Civil Court within whose jurisdiction the opposite party has its registered office or resides or carries on business or works for gain.

Rules. In exercise of the powers conferred by section 30 of the Consumer Protection Act several States have made Consumer Protection Rules for carrying out the objects and purposes of the Consumer Protection Act 1986.

Form of complaint. The complaint must contain the name, description and address of the complainant and opposite parties, the facts leading to the complaint, the time and place where cause for complaint arose and copies of documents, if any, in support of the complaint and the reliefs which the complaint is claiming. The Act has treated the complaint as an application for the purpose of the Limitation Act and impliedly section 5 of the Limitation Act has been made applicable and the District Forum. State Commission and National Commission have been given power to condone the delay in filing the complaint on sufficient cause being shown for the delay and on recording the reasons for condoning the delay.

FORMS

Applications for Deficiency of Service

DEFECTIVE WASHING MACHINE

In the District Consumer Disputes Redressal Forum
Darbhanga Collectorate, Darbhanga
Consumer Complaint No. ...... of ......

In the matter of:
A complaint under sections 11 and 12 of the Consumer Protection Act 1986 and the Rules made thereunder

And

Mr. X residing at ....
....

Complainant

versus

Machinery Company Limited, a company incorporated under the Companies Act 1956 and carrying on business at ....

Respondent

To
The Hon'ble President and His Companion Member of the District Consumer Disputes Redressal Forum

The complainant above-named most respectfully

SHEWETH:

1. The respondent is a manufacturer of electrical goods including Washing Machines and carries on business in ....

2. The claim of compensation and/or redressal of grievances of the complainant does not exceed Rs. 5 lakhs.

3. The complaint relates to the malfunctioning of the Washing Machine purchased by the complainant from the respondent about 18 months ago. This Application is being made within 2 years from the date of cause of action for making this application.

4. On 15th June 1998 the complainant purchased one Automatic Washing Machine from the respondent at Rs. 20, 000.

5. The complainant paid the price, took delivery of the machine and the respondent issued a cash memo and a Guarantee/Warranty Card guaranteeing the proper functioning of the machine. The guarantee was valid for 3 years.

6. After about 7 days of running the said machine in accordance with the printed instructions given by the respondent the machine did not work properly. The complainant by his letter dated 25th June 1998 complained to the respondent setting out the malfunctioning of the Washing Machine including the non-working of the spinning mechanism.

7. The respondent sent its mechanic who apparently repaired the defect. But after some time again there was the malfunctioning of the machine since its water pump was not properly functioning. Its spinning mechanism also did not work.

8. After several reminders the respondent sent its mechanic who tried to repair the machine and ultimately made the machine workable but stated that the defect was a manufacturing one and therefore the same could not be fully repaired.

9. The complainant requested the respondent by a letter dated 10th December 1998 to replace the said machine as there was a manufacturing defect and in spite of best efforts the respondent's mechanic could not repair the defects. The respondent received the said letter but neither replaced the machine nor repaired the defect nor replied to the said complaint. A copy of letter and copy of the receipt are annexed hereto marked "A" and "A-1".

10. Copies of the Cash Memo and the Guarantee Card are annexed hereto marked "B" and "C" respectively.

11. Copies of the previous complaints are annexed hereto marked "D".

12. By reasons of the breach of the agreement, breach of the Warranty and negligence of the respondent, the complainant has suffered loss and damages which the complainant assesses at Rs. 35, 000.

In the facts and circumstances of the case the complainant prays for the following reliefs:

(*a*) Refund of Rs. 20,000 paid to the respondent for the purchase of the said Washing Machine;

(*b*) Interest from date of purchase on Rs. 20,000 at 18% per annum;

(*c*) Damages for harassment, physical injury and mental agony assessed at Rs. 35,000;

(*d*) Costs of the present proceeding;

(*e*) Further and other reliefs as the complainant is entitled to

And the complainant as in duty bound shall ever pray.

Place: ....

Date: .... Signature of Complainant

Verification

I, Mr. X .... son of Mr. Y. residing at .... Darbhanga, Bihar do hereby solemnly declare and state that the statements contained in the preceding paragraphs of this complaint are true to the best of my knowledge and belief and nothing stated herein is false and I have not suppressed any material fact.

Verified at .... Collectorate on this ...... day of .... Deponent

Identified by me Advocate

ANNEXURES:

1. Cash Memo
2. Guarantee Card
3. Letters of complaint

Defective Computer

In the Bihar State Consumers Disputes Redressal Commission
12 North Srikrishnapuri, Patna, Bihar

Original Jurisdiction

Consumer Complaint No. .... of 2000

In the Matter of:
A complaint under section 17 of the Consumer Protection Act 1986 and the Rules made thereunder

And

Mr. X residing at 2 North Shrikrishnapuri, Patna, Bihar

Complainant

versus

Computer Limited a company registered under the Companies Act 1956 and carrying on business at 5 North Srikrishnapuri, Patna, Bihar

Respondent

To

The Hon'ble President and his Companion members of the State Commission

The humble complaint of the complainant above-named most respectfully

SHEWETH:

1. The respondent is the manufacturer of and dealer in Computers both Hardwares and Softwares and is carrying on business, *inter alia*, at Patna and New Delhi.

2. The claim of the complainant is less than Rs. 20 lakhs but more than Rs. 5 lakhs.

3. The complainant's cause of action for this complaint arose on and after 30th December 1998 within two years of the present application.

4. The complainant purchased a Computer from the respondent on 10th July 1998 at Rs. 6 lakhs on terms and conditions contained in the Guarantee Card given by the respondent.

5. Under the terms and conditions of the said sale of Computer by the respondent the respondent undertook to render free service for one year in relation to the said Computer.

6. Within six months of its installation at the office of complainant at 2 North Srikrishnpuri, Patna there was malfunctioning of the said Computer.

7. The complainant by a letter dated 15th December 1998 requested the respondent to replace the Computer as in spite of repairs by the respondent's mechanic, the Computer was malfunctioning and was of no use to the complainant.

8. The respondent again sent its mechanic who attended the Computer but could not repair it or remove the defect and the machine continued to malfunction.

9. The complainant by its letter of 5th January 1999 made a detailed complaint to the respondent about the machine and requested respondent to replace the said Computer.

10. The respondent by its letter of 28th January 1999 denied any defect in the Computer or that it was malfunctioning.

11. The complainant contacted an expert Mr. Z from Patna who was the Principal of Patna Computer College and got the Computer examined by him and received a certificate/report of his examination of the Computer.

12. According to the expert opinion there was a manufacturing defect in the Computer and it could not be repaired by any mechanic and required substantial replacement of certain parts of the Computer and reassembly thereof. A copy of the expert's report was sent to the respondent. In spite of this, the respondent did not take any effective steps. A copy of the expert's report is annexed hereto marked 'A'.

13. The complainant by a letter of 5th February 1999 requested the respondent to take back the Computer and refund the price paid therefor. A copy of the letter is annexed hereto marked 'B'.

14. The respondent in reply stated that there was no defect in the Computer and that the complainant is not entitled to any refund of the price for the Computer. A copy of letter is annexed hereto marked 'C'.

15. Copies of the receipt given by the respondent for purchase of the Computer and Guarantee Card are annexed hereto marked 'D' and 'D-1' respectively.

16. The complainant states that the contention of the respondent is untenable and unwarranted and in spite of several attempts the respondent has not been able to make the Computer function properly. The expert opinion is also to the effect that there was a manufacturing defect in the Computer.

17. In view of the aforesaid the respondent is bound to take back the Computer and refund the purchase price thereof and pay the costs and expenses incurred by the complainant in taking the expert opinion and incidentials thereto.

18. The respondent shall also pay the compensation due to the complainant for the harassment, troubles, loss of business, physical inconvenience and mental agony arising directly out of the breach of warranty, breach of the agreement and breach of duty on the part of the respondent. The complainant assesses such loss and damages at Rs. 5 lakhs.

19. Without prejudice to the aforesaid the complainant states that an enquiry be made as to the loss and damages the complainant has suffered due to the defective and malfunctioning Computer sold and delivered by the respondent to the complainant and its inability to repair the same and depriving the complainant of any use of the Computer and putting the complainant to harassment and mental agony and loss of business.

In the facts and circumstances of the case the complainant prays for the following reliefs:

(*a*) Refund of Rs. 6 lakhs paid as consideration for the said Computer;

(*b*) Interest from the date of payment of the said consideration money till realisation at 18% per annum;

(*c*) Payment of Rs. 5 lakhs by the respondent to the complainant by way of compensation for the loss and damages caused to the complainant by the wrongful acts of the respondent;

(*d*) Alternatively an enquiry into the loss and damages suffered by the complainant due to wrongful acts of the respondent and malfunctioning of the Computer and payment by the respondent to the complainant the amount so found due on such enquiry;

(*e*) Costs of the present complaint and proceeding be paid by respondent to complainant;

(*f*) Further and other reliefs that the complainant is entitled to.

And the complainant as in duty bound shall ever pray.

Place: Patna
Date: 5th March 2000

Verification

I, Mr. X, son of .... residing at 2 North Srikrishnapuri, Patna, Bihar do hereby solemnly declare and state that the statements contained in the complaint above are true to the best of my knowledge and belief and that I have not suppressed any material fact.

Verified at Patna
this 6th day of February 2000

Deponent

Identified by me Advocate

ANNEXURES:

1. Receipt
2. Guarantee Card
3. Expert Report
4. Copies of correspondence

Complaint before National Commission

MALFUNCTIONING COMPUTER

In the National Consumers Disputes Redressal Commission
5th Floor, Janpath Bhawan, New Delhi
Original Jurisdiction
Consumer Complaint No. .... of ......

In the matter of:

A complaint under section 21 of the Consumer Protection Act 1986 and the rules made thereunder.

And

Mr. X residing at ....
....

Complainant

versus

Computer Limited a company registered under the Companies Act 1956 and carrying on business at .... within the said jurisdiction

Respondent

To
The Hon'ble President and His Companion Members of the National Commission

The humble complaint of the complainant abovenamed most respectfully

SHEWETH:

1. The respondent is the manufacturer of and dealer in Computers both Hardwares and Softwares and is carrying on the business, *inter alia*, at Patna and New Delhi.

2. The claim of the complainant exceeds Rs. 20 lakhs.

3. The complainant's cause of action for this complaint arose on and after 30th December 1998 within two years of the present application.

4. The complainant purchased a Computer from the respondent on 30th December 1998 at Rs. 26 lakhs on terms and conditions contained in the Guarantee Card given by the respondent. The said Computer was sold and delivered by the respondent from its New Delhi Office.

5. Under the terms and conditions of the said sale of Computer by the respondent the respondent undertook to render free service for one year in relation to the said Computer.

6. Within six months of its installation at the office of the complainant at 2 North Srikrishnapuri, Patna there was malfunctioning of the said Computer.

7. The complainant by a letter dated 15th January 1999 requested the respondent to replace the Computer as in spite of repairs by the respondent's mechanic, the Computer was malfunctioning and was of no use to the complainant.

8. The respondent again sent its mechanic who attended the Computer but could not repair it or remove the defect and the machine continued to malfunction.

9. The complainant by its letter of 5th February 1999 made a detailed complaint to the respondent about the Computer and requested the respondent to replace the said Computer.

10. The respondent by its letter of 28th February 1999 denied any defect in the Computer or that it was malfunctioning.

11. The complainant engaged an expert Mr. Z from Patna who was the Principal of Patna Computer College and got the Computer examined by him and received a Certificate/report of his examination of the Computer.

12. According to the expert opinion there was a manufacturing defect in the Computer and it could not be repaired by any mechanic and required substantial replacement of certain parts of the Computer and reassembly thereof. A copy of the expert's report was sent to the respondent. In spite of this, the respondent did not take any effective steps. A copy of the expert's report is annexed hereto marked "A".

13. The complainant by a letter of 5th March 1999 requested the respondent to take back the Computer and refund the price paid therefor. A copy of the letter is annexed hereto marked "B".

14. The respondent in reply stated that there was no defect in the Computer and that the complainant is not entitled to any refund of the price for the Computer. A copy of the letter is annexed hereto marked "C".

15. Copies of the receipt given by the respondent for purchase of the Computer and the Guarantee Card are annexed hereto marked "D" and "D-1" respectively.

16. The complainant states that the contention of the respondent is untenable and unwarranted and in spite of several attempts the respondent has not been able to make the Computer function properly. The expert opinion is also to the effect that there was a manufacturing defect in the Computer.

17. In view of the aforesaid the respondent in bound to take back the Computer and refund the purchase price paid therefor and to pay the costs and expenses incurred by the complainant in taking the expert opinion and incidentals thereto.

18. The respondent is also liable to pay compensation to the complainant for the harassment, troubles, loss of business, physical inconvenience and mental agony suffered by and arising directly out of the breach of warranty, breach of the agreement and breach of duty on the part of the respondent. The complainant assesses such loss and damages at Rs. 15 lakhs.

19. Without prejudice to the aforesaid the complainant states that an enquiry be made as to the loss and damages the complainant has suffered due to the defective and malfunctioning of the Computer sold and delivered by the respondent to the complainant and its inability to repair the same and depriving the complainant of any use of the Computer and putting the complainant to harassment and mental agony and loss of business.

In the facts and circumstances of the case the complainant prays for the following reliefs:

(*a*) Refund of Rs. 26 lakhs paid as consideration for the said Computer;

(*b*) Interest from date of payment of the said consideration money till realisation at 18%;

(*c*) Payment of Rs. 15 lakhs by the respondent to the complainant by way of compensation for the loss and damages, harassment and mental agony caused to the complainant by the wrongful acts of the respondent;

(*d*) Alternatively an enquiry into the loss and damages suffered by the complainant due to wrongful acts of the respondent and malfunctioning, costs of expert opinion and payment by the respondent to the complainant the amount so found due on such enquiry;

(*e*) Costs of the present complaint and proceeding be paid by respondent to the complainant;

(*f*) Further and other reliefs that the complainant is entitled to be granted.

And the complainant as in duty bound shall ever pray.

Place: ....

Date: X

Verification

I, Mr. X, son of .... residing at 2 North Srikrishnapuri, Patna, Bihar do hereby solemnly declare and state that the statements contained in the complaint above are true to the best of my knowledge and belief and that I have not suppressed any material fact.

Verified at New Delhi
the 18th day of April 2000

Deponent

Identified by me
Advocate

ANNEXURES:

1. Receipt
2. Guarantee Card
3. Expert report
4. Copies of correspondence

15

Registration of a Co-operative Society

Co-operative Societies are governed by the Central Co-operative Societies Act 1912, where there is no State Act. In West Bengal they were governed by the West Bengal Co-operative Societies Act (Act XXI of 1940) as amended by the West Bengal Act XVII of 1970 until 1973, when the West Bengal Co-operative Societies Act 1973, came into force. The 1940 Act was expected to introduce a new life in the rural areas of West Bengal, but corruption, nepotism and vested interest struck at the very root of co-operative movement of the State. The Act was amended in 1970 and two successive ordinances were promulgated on 30th September 1972 and 27th January 1973 with a view to plugging the loopholes, but they failed to achieve much result. The West Bengal Co-operative Societies Act 1973, was enacted to consolidate and amend the law which introduced some major changes: (1) Bar to membership (s. 12); (2) refusal to register (s. 15); (3) disqualification for directorship (s. 23); (4) supersession of managing committee (s. 26); (5) seizure of books (s. 83); and (6) overriding power (s. 141) and several other changes. The rules framed under the 1940 Act continued until the 1974 Rules came not force. Sections 6 and 8 of the Central Act provide for conditions of registration and application for registration of co-operative societies. Sections 11 and 13 of the West Bengal Act of 1940 provided for what societies may be registered and application for such registration. The corresponding sections in 1973 Act are ss. 11 and 13, but the contents of the latter are different. The details about the formation of co-operative societies are given in the Bengal Societies Rules 1974. Rule 7 of 1940 Act provides that no primary society shall be registered unless it consists of at least 15 persons and where it is a credit society unless such persons reside in the same town or village or same group of villages or members of the same class or occupation. A co-operative farming society or housing society may be registered if it consists of eight or more persons. Rule 8 of 1973 Act requires that the applicants must reside or hold landed property in the same town or village and further that they must be members of the same class or occupation.

The provisions of the 1973 Act were found insufficient in the changed circumstances. There were lacunae, vagueness and omissions. By amendments these could not be removed. A Co-operative Law Committee was set up which submitted its report on the basis of which ultimately the West Bengal Co-operative Societies Act 1983 was passed and the West Bengal Co-operative Societies Rules 1987 were framed.

Application for registration must be in the prescribed Form and manner and be accompanied by a copy of the proposed by-laws.

FORMS

FORM NO. 1

Application for the Registration of a Co-operative Society with Limited/Unlimited Liability

[Rule 8(*i*)]

Part 1

To
The Registrar of Co-operative Societies
West Bengal

Dated .... 19......

Sir

We, the undersigned, agree to the enclosed by-laws, and under section 13 of the W.B. Co-operative Societies Act 1983 (West Bengal Act XLV of 1983), apply to be registered as a co-operative society with limited/unlimited liability under the title of .... the registered office being ...... post office ...... thana/ panchayat .... union board .... sub-division .... district ....

Serial No.	*Name of applicant for registration*	*Father's name*	*Occupation*	*Age*	*Permanent address*	*Present address*	*Whether member of any other society if so name and address of the society(ies)*	*Signature or LTI of the applicant*
1	2	3	4	5	6	7	8	9

Part II

1. Name of the proposed society ....
2. Nature of Liability of Members ....
3. On share basis or without shares ....
4. Number of applicants ....
   (*a*) Individuals
   (*b*) Co-operative Societies

5. Names of the members of the first Board (constituted under Rule 30):

(If it is desired that the Registrar should constitute the first Board by nomination, no name need be mentioned here).

(1) .... Chairman
(2) .... Vice-Chairman
(3) ....
(4) ....
(5) ....
(6) ....

6. Name and address of the person (Chief Promoter in the case of a co-operative hanging society) to whom communications, if any, are to be addressed till registration of the society.

7. Certified that the applicants belong to a different family as required under section 13(2) of the Act.

Signature of three applicants
authorised by the promoters to
sign and certify on their behalf.
1. ....
2. ....
3. ....

Date ....

N.B. A true copy of the proceedings of the promoters' meeting should be annexed with the application.

Bye-laws of General (Multipurpose) Co-operative Society

1. The society shall be called ....

2. The registered office shall be for the at .... in the city of ....

3. The objects for which the society is established are mainly to promote the financial and economic interests of its members and more particularly—

(*a*) To acquire by purchase land, develop the same and to distribute and sell the same in small plots to its members at a fair price on co-operative basis and apply the proceeds of such sale towards all and any of its objects.

(*b*) To undertake construction or maintenance of schools, churches, mission halls or roads, bridges, culverts, to maintain gardens, tanks etc.

(*c*) To promote and encourage the spirit and practice of mutual help, co-operation and collaboration among its members.

(*d*) To assist its members to obtain their necessities of life at a fair price and with that and in view to open stores and counters at different centres for sale of all commodities required by them.

(*e*) To carry on trade, both wholesale and retail, in all sorts of articles and to engage in any business or transaction conducive to the interest and convenience of its members.

(*f*) To subscribe and/or to become a member of or otherwise co-operate in any manner with any co-operative association having objects altogether or in part similar to those of the society.

(*g*) To create fund or funds, to receive deposits on interest and to lend the same to members at concessional rate of interest.

(*h*) To adopt other measures designed to encourage among the members the spirit and practice of thrift, mutual co-operation and self-help and to propagate co-operative ideas.

(*i*) To amalgamate with other society or societies, organisation or institution in pursuit of all or any of its objects.

(*j*) To print and publish books, manazine, literature, journals written by its members writers on co-operative basis.

(*k*) Without prejudice to the generality of the above and for the effective carrying out of the above objects, the co-operative society shall have the power to acquire, receive and hold property of any kind including securities and negotiable instruments, to construct and maintain buildings, including the rights to alter or improve them and to equip them suitably, to manage, sell, transfer or otherwise dispose of or deal with property of any kind belonging to the society, to enter into contract or contracts for and in connection with any of the purposes of the society, to raise moneys and funds in such a manner as may be deemed fit for and on behalf of the society to establish a provident fund for the benefit of the employees of the society and when considered necessary, and to accept the management or execution of any trust or fund or endowment in which the society may be interested.

(*l*) To mortgage charge lease or otherwise dispose of exchange or deal in any manner authorized by law any property. And generally to do all such acts, deeds and things as are incidental to the attainment of the aims and objects of the society.

4. The area of operation of the society will for the present be the State of ....

5. The share capital of the society shall be Rs. .... divided in .... shares of Rs. .... each. Each member shall subscribe for at least one share. The share capital shall be applied in pursuit of the objects of the society as the Managing Committee shall from time to time decide in that behalf. The share capital may from time to time be increased by resolution at the general meeting convened specially for the purpose with the sanction of the Registrar of Co-operative Societies.

6. The membership shall consist of:

(*i*) Persons who join in the application for registration of the society as prescribed by law.

(*ii*) Persons admitted as considered eligible by the Managing Committee of the society.

7. Every member of the society must be—

(*i*) of good character,

(*ii*) of not less than 18 years of age except a minor heir of a deceased member.

8. Every member on admission shall sign his name in the Register of members or thumb-mark the same, and shall pay Rs. .... as admission fee which shall not be refunded in any case. Every member shall subscribe for at least one share of the society of the value of Rs. .... Every member shall have one vote. The chairman shall have a casting vote. No member shall be entitled to transfer his share but to surrender the same.

9. Membership shall be terminated by—

(*i*) death,

(*ii*) ceasing to hold one full share,

(*iii*) expulsion by a two-third majority of the members of the society in an extraordinary general meeting convened for the purpose after service of three weeks' prior notice therefor,

(*iv*) withdrawal after three months' notice given to the society, provided the member is not indebted to the society and is not a surety for an unpaid debt,

(*v*) insolvency.

On such termination of membership, the admission fee and the share of the member shall be deemed to be forfeited to the society except that:

(*a*) in case of death, the Managing Committee may admit to membership the heir of the deceased member or return the book value of the share to the heir.

(*b*) in case of insolvency, the receiver shall be paid the book value of the share by the society.

10. A member may be expelled from the society for:

(*i*) failure to pay the share money or debt due from him to the society.

(*ii*) conviction of a criminal offence involving dishonesty or resulting in his imprisonment for three months or more,

(*iii*) applying to be adjudicated as an insolvent,

(*iv*) intentionally doing any act detrimental to the interest of the society or wilfully disobeying any bye-law or decision of the Managing Committee or of the general meeting.

11. The liability of the members is limited and for any deficit or shortfall in the assets of the society on liquidation thereof shall be limited to four times the value of the share purchased.

12. The supreme authority shall be vested in the general meeting which shall be held at least once a year. At the annual general meeting, the balance-sheet and the profit and loss account shall be available to the members; considered and passed, the members of the Managing Committee shall be elected and any other special business may be conducted, notice whereof shall be given to the members at least 10 days prior thereto.

13. Five members present in person shall form a quorum.

14. An extraordinary general meeting may be called by the President or by the Secretary at the direction of the Managing Committee and shall be called by the President on the written requisition of five members.

15. The bye-laws of the society shall not be amended unless 2/3rd majority of the total members are present and vote for such amendment, notice whereof is given to the members at least three weeks prior thereto.

16. The Managing Committee shall consist of nine members comprising a President, a Vice-President, a Secretary, a Treasurer and five other members elected at the annual general meeting, five members present shall constitute the quorum for such meeting. The Managing Committee shall exercise all the powers of the society except those reserved for the general meeting.

17. The first Managing Committee shall comprise:

1. Shri .... of .... President.
2. Shri .... of .... Vice-President.
3. Shri .... of .... Secretary.
4. Shri .... of .... Treasurer.
5. Shri .... of .... Member.
6. Shri .... of .... Member.
7. Shri .... of .... Member.
8. Shri .... of .... Member.
9. Shri .... of .... Member.

IN WITNESS whereof the following members have subscribed to the aforementioned by-laws in token of their being bound by the same.

No.	*Name*	*Address*	*Witness*

Co-operative Housing Society under the West Bengal Apartment Ownership Act 1972

Such a Co-operative Housing Society is different from a Co-operative Society registered under the Co-operative Societies Act 1983. It is a co-operative of the apartment owners no doubt, but nevertheless an association of the apartment owners and its formation is quite different from the former. Under the bye-law 3(2) framed under the West Bengal Act XVI of 1972, as published in the Calcutta Gazette on 23rd November 1974, the following procedure has been prescribed.

Within forty-five days from the appointed day or from the date of submission of the property concerned to the provisions of the Act, whichever is later, or within such further period as the competent authority may, on application made to it or of its own motion, allow, the apartment owners of each property, owned by four or more apartment owners, shall, in a general meeting to be held on such date and at such time and place as may be convenient to all such owners and to be presided over by an apartment owner chosen by the apartment owners present in such meeting, form an association under some specific name and style, and the apartment owner presiding over such meeting shall immediately communicate the formation of such an association along with the names of the members thereof, in Form No. 1, to the Competent Authority who shall register the association under a serial number, and cause the names of the members thereof to be entered in the book kept in its office for the purpose.

Explanation.—For the purpose of this clause, a person owning more than one apartment, shall be deemed to be one apartment owner.

FORM NO. 1

[*See* Bye-law 3(2) of the W.B. Apartment Ownership Bye-laws 1974]

To
The Competent Authority
Under the West Bengal
Apartment Ownership Act 1972
....

Sir

I hereby communicate that in a general meeting duly held on .... presided over by the undersigned, the Association of the Apartment Owners under the name and style of .... for our property at .... already submitted to the provisions of the West Bengal Apartment Ownership Act 1972, has been formed under the by-laws framed under the said Act with the following as members thereof:

Names of the members	No. of the apartments in the building owned by him/her
(1) Shri/Smt.	....
(2) Shri/Smt.	....
(3) Shri/Smt.	....
(4) Shri/Smt.	....
and so on	

Yours faithfully

....

Date ....

Place ....

Signature of the Apartment Owner presiding over the general meeting

Co-operative Housing Society

A Co-operative Housing Society is a Society registered generally with a limited liability of the members under the West Bengal Co-operative Societies Act 1983. One of the objects of the Act is to bring about better and happier conditions of living for the weaker sections of the community. The object of a Co-operative Housing Society is to provide its members a dwelling house, apartment or lands for construction of dwelling houses or apartments and maintenances of common services in connection therewith. It includes a Federation of such Societies. A Co-operative Society is formed generally with limited liability of its members. However, a Co-operative Society with unlimited liability of its members to contribute jointly or severally for any deficiency in the assets of the Society may be registered. The Companies Act 1956 does not apply to a Co-operative Society. Ten or more persons can make an application for registration of a Co-operative Society. The application is to be accompanied by bye-laws of the Society. The application is to be made to the Registrar of the Co-operative Societies concerned.

A Co-operative Housing Society has a perpetual succession and a common seal with power to acquire, hold and dispose of property, to enter into Contracts and to institute and defend suits and other proceedings in its name.

Instruments relating to shares or debentures without touching immovable property or any Mortgage Deed executed in favour of Co-operative Society are not compulsorily registrable under the Registration Act 1908.

Eight or more individual persons each belonging to a different family may make an application for registration of a Co-operative Housing Society.[1]

All disputes concerning the business of a Co-operative Housing Society capable of being the subject of civil litigation or relating to the affairs of the Society (except labour matters) shall be referred to the Registrar of Co-operative Societies in the prescribed manner. The Registrar or any authorised person exercising the power of Registrar may decide the dispute or he may refer the dispute to be decided by arbitration. From the Registrar's decision, an appeal lies to the Tribunal.

A member may apply for loan through the Co-operative Society from the West Bengal State Co-operative Housing Federation Limited. Such loan is given on the terms and conditions and at the rate of interest that might be specified by the Federation.

The functioning of Co-operative Housing Society is governed by the Act and the Rules made thereunder and the bye-laws and regulations of the Society. The application for registration is to be made in Form 1 with three copies of the bye-laws addressed to the Deputy Registrar of Co-operative Societies (Housing), CMA, 6A Subodh Mullick Square, Calcutta 700013 or to the Assistant Registrar of Co-operative Societies of the concerned area, as the case may be.

A Co-operative Housing Society provides its members with dwelling houses, apartments or lands for construction of dwelling houses, or apartments and maintains common services and collects each member's contribution towards such expenses. The Society is managed by a Board but the ultimate power is vested in the members at a General Meeting. All disputes including the winding up of the Society are to be decided by the Registrar and the Civil Courts will have no jurisdiction over matters relating to winding up of the Society or disputes amongst the members or the members and the Society in relation to the apartments.

An individual, a Co-operative Society and the State Government may apply for membership of the Society. An association may be a member with the approval of the State Government. The rights and obligations of the members among themselves and in relation to land or apartment are governed by the provisions of the Act and Rules and the bye-laws of the Society.

Construction Agreement between Promoter and Co-operative Housing Society

THIS AGREEMENT MADE on this 10th day of December 2000 BETWEEN Mr. XY of .... (hereinafter referred to as the PROMOTER)

1 Proviso to s. 13(2) of the West Bengal Co-operative Societies Act 1983.

which term shall include his successor and assigns) of the One Part and Delhi Co-operative Housing Society Ltd. registered under the Delhi Co-operative Housing Societies Act and having its registered office at .... (hereinafter referred to as the SOCIETY which term shall include its successors) of the Other Part.

WHEREAS the SOCIETY is seized and possessed of 15 cottahs of land in the premises No. .... of ....

AND WHEREAS the PROMOTER has offered to promote, develop and construct a multi-storeyed building on the said land for the purposes of the SOCIETY on ownership flats basis.

AND WHEREAS the PROMOTER has agreed to take up the work of promoting, developing and/or constructing the said multi-storeyed building on the said land and the Society has agreed to authorise the PROMOTER to take up the said work.

NOW THESE PRESENTS witnesseth and the parties hereby agree as follows:

1. The PROMOTER will prepare the plan for construction of multi-storeyed building on the said land of the SOCIETY and get it approved by the authorities concerned.

2. The PROMOTER shall obtain requisite permissions from the Urban Land Ceilings Authority, the Municipality, and other concerned authorities for the development and construction of the said multi-storeyed building.

3. After the PROMOTER obtains necessary sanction for construction of the said multi-storeyed building in the said land and submits the requisite particulars as to the nature and mode of construction and the materials to be used and the time to be taken, the SOCIETY would get the same examined through its nominated Engineer/Architect and Lawyers and subject to their approvals, the PROMOTER shall carry out any additions or alterations or modifications as might be suggested by them and will obtain further permission or consent or approval of the authorities concerned.

4. The PROMOTER shall construct the said building according to the sanctioned plan, specifications and drawings in self-contained flats of not less than 500 sq. ft. carpet area each flat.

5. The said multi-storeyed building will have the basement, ground floor and 4 upper floors with all modern amenities and facilities for the entire building as also for each flat, basement and each floor.

6. The PROMOTER should make arrangement for drainage, sewerage, water connection, electric connection, and obtain completion certificate and occupation certificate from the appropriate authorities.

7. In consideration of the PROMOTER completing the said multi-storeyed building in the manner aforesaid, the SOCIETY agrees to pay to the PROMOTER

a consolidated sum of Rs. 6 crores on a turnkey project basis and the PROMOTER shall not be entitled to any extra amount either for escalation of costs, labour or materials or otherwise inasmuch as the said construction amount includes a percentage thereof as the escalated cost.

8. The said sum of Rs. 6 crores shall be paid by the SOCIETY to the PROMOTER on the PROMOTER furnishing a Bank Guarantee for the due performance of these presents for Rs. 6 crores which would stand reduced as and when the PROMOTER progresses with the work of construction of each floor.

9. The said sum of Rs. 6 crores would be paid by the SOCIETY in the manner following:

(*a*) By way of advance on the execution of these presents Rs. 50 lakhs.

(*b*) On completion of Foundation of the said building Rs. 50 lakhs.

(*c*) On completion of the basement Rs. 1 crore.

(*d*) On completion of the first floor Rs. 50 lakhs.

(*e*) On completion of the second floor Rs. 50 lakhs.

(*f*) On completion of the third floor Rs. 50 lakhs.

(*g*) On completion of the fourth floor Rs. 50 lakhs.

(*h*) On completion of the fifth floor Rs. 50 lakhs.

(*i*) On completion of fittings and furnitures Rs. 50 lakhs.

(*j*) On completion of drainage, sewerage, water-connection and electric connection Rs. 50 lakhs.

(*k*) On completion of plastering and painting both inside and outside the said building Rs. 50 lakhs.

(*l*) On giving possession of the said building complete in all respects together with completion certificate and occupation certificate, balance amount of Rs. 1 crore.

10. The PROMOTER agrees and undertakes to complete the construction of the said building and hand over the same to the SOCIETY within a period of two years from the date of execution of these presents.

11. In the event there be any delay in the schedule of work of construction or making over the possession of the completed building to the SOCIETY, the PROMOTER would pay interest @ 18% per annum on the amount invested and paid by the SOCIETY to the PROMOTER inasmuch as the SOCIETY would have to pay interest to the Delhi Co-operative Housing Federation Ltd. for the loans obtained from that Federation.

12. In the event there is delay in releasing loans by the said Federation to the SOCIETY, and consequent delay by the SOCIETY in payment to the PROMOTER, the PROMOTER shall not be entitled to suspend or delay its work but has to carry on the construction and completion of the work at his own costs and for which no compensation would be paid by the SOCIETY in as

much as an element of compensation has been included in the lump sum amount of Rs. 6 crores.

13. It is agreed that in the event of delay in completion of the said building the PROMOTER shall give possession of flats or floors which be found complete and ready for occupation of the members of the SOCIETY.

14. The SOCIETY will be at liberty to enter into an agreement for sale and/or sell flats to its members whether such flats have been constructed or are in the process of construction or will be constructed.

15. It is agreed that the Society would be entitled to create charge or mortgage on the multi-storeyed building in favour of the said Federation for the loans obtained or that might be obtained for the purpose of construction of the said multi-storeyed building and/or for payment to the PROMOTER.

16. The PROMOTER shall construct the multi-storeyed building in accordance with the plan/sanctions and shall make such additions and alterations that might be required by the Society's Supervisor on the site provided these are within the sanctioned plan and for such extra work the SOCIETY would make payment as might be agreed upon by the SOCIETY and the PROMOTER before taking up such additions or alterations.

17. The PROMOTER on completion of the work and handing-over of possession of the said building would make over to the society all plans, drawings, specifications, permissions, approvals, clearance certificate, and execute all such documents and do all such acts as might be required by the SOCIETY.

18. After making over possession and handing over all relevant documents to the SOCIETY the PROMOTER shall remove all plant, machinery, tools, implements and clean the entire building including inside of the flats so that the entire building is ready for occupation and use by the Society's members and other occupiers.

19, The bank guarantee amount will be reduced in proportion to the work done by the PROMOTER each sixth month from the execution of the Bank Guarantee to the extent of Rs. 5 crores after which the Bank Guarantee would continue till one year after the delivery of possession of the said multi-storeyed building to the Society.

20. From the beginning of construction work till the handing-over of possession of the completed building, the Promoter at his own cost would keep the said building fully insured against all losses and damages to the building, against all possible risks as also against death, injury or other loss or damages to the workers engaged in the construction of said multi-storeyed building and other persons on or in the site or building or in the vicinity thereof.

21. The PROMOTER shall allow the Society's representative, supervisor, architect or engineer to inspect the site and the process of construction,

nature of construction, quality of materials being used and all other safety aspects of the construction of building.

22. The PROMOTER agrees and undertakes that the buildings would be constructed in such a manner and with such materials that there would be no danger to the occupiers or visitors to the said premises or any chance of collapse of any portion of the said building and for this purpose the PROMOTER should furnish a Bank Guarantee for Rs. 1 crore valid for five years after completion of the said multi-storeyed building.

23. The bank charge and/or commission for obtaining the said Bank Guarantee have been taken care of in the said sum of Rs. 6 crores.

24. In case of any differences or disputes arising during the construction or after construction but within the guarantee period of five years from the date of delivery or occupation of the said building without stopping the work or discharge of any obligation of the parties, such disputes shall be referred to the Registrar of the Co-operative Society under the Co-operative Societies Act whose decision shall be final and binding on the parties.

IN WITNESS WHEREOF the parties have executed these presents on the day, month and year first above-written.

Signed and delivered by the said Mr. XY, the PROMOTER in the presence of:

1. .... Signature

2. ....

Signed, sealed and delivered by Mr. .... pursuant to the Resolution of Delhi Co-operative Housing Society Ltd. dated .... in the presence of:

1. .... Signature

2. ....

Construction Agreement between Builder and Co-operative Society

THIS AGREEMENT MADE this 5th day of July 2000 BETWEEN ...., a partnership firm carrying on business at .... (hereinafter referred to as the BUILDER which expression shall include its present and future partners, their heirs, executors, administrators and assigns) of the One Part AND Mr. XY residing at and owner of ....

.... (hereinafter referred to as the CHIEF PROMOTER which expression shall include his successors and assigns) of the Other Part.

WHEREAS the BUILDER is a partnership firm engaged in construction of buildings.

AND WHEREAS the said Mr. XY is the CHIEF PROMOTER of the XY Co-operative Housing Society Limited, to be registered under the West Bengal Co-operative Societies Act 1983 comprising the proposed purchasers of flats of the building to be constructed on the plot at .... (hereinafter referred to as the said SOCIETY).

AND WHEREAS the members of the said SOCIETY are desirous of entrusting the task of construction and erection of a building on the plot .... on agreed terms and conditions.

NOW THIS AGREEMENT WITNESSETH and the parties agree as follows:

1. The BUILDER intends to purchase the plot of land at .... measuring 6 cottahs and thereafter to transfer it in favour of the SOCIETY.

2. The SOCIETY accepts the Certificate of title given to the BUILDER by Mr. XY's Advocate to the effect that the title to the property in question is marketable, free from encumbrances and reasonable doubts and that no requisitions will be made or objection taken by the SOCIETY as regards the title.

3. The CHIEF PROMOTER shall cause registration of the Society under the West Bengal Co-operative Societies Act 1983.

4. On its registration the CHIEF PROMOTER will apply for financial assistance by way of loan to the West Bengal Co-operative Housing Federation Ltd. (hereinafter referred to as 'Federation') for at least 75% of the estimated cost of the land and construction cost of the building.

5. Negotiation with the said Federation is already in progress and it is expected that 75% at least of the total finance required by the SOCIETY will be granted by way of loan by the said Federation on mortgage of the land by deposit of title deeds.

6. The copies of plan, specifications, list of amenities and the drawings in respect of the building to be constructed on the plot prepared by Mr. ...., Architect has been furnished to the BUILDER and the Builder has taken inspection of all documents necessary for the purposes of construction of the multi-storeyed building. The BUILDER has given to the Society two sets of the plans, specifications, list of amenities and drawings and one set whereof is returned signed by the CHIEF PROMOTER. The BUILDER shall present to the Calcutta Municipal Corporation the necessary plans for being sanctioned.

7. The BUILDER will purchase the land measuring 6 cottahs and the BUILDER shall construct for the SOCIETY according to the sanctioned or

approved plans, specification, amenities and drawings a five-storeyed building with parking space on the said plot of land.

8. The SOCIETY will pay to the BUILDER for the land and for construction of the building Rs. 78 lakh. The price will include the laying of drainage and water connections to the Municipal mains and electric connections to the CESC Ltd. mains and all the specified amenities.

9. The price will be paid to the BUILDER by the following instalments:

(*a*) Rs. 18 lakhs immediately on execution of agreement and satisfying the said SOCIETY that the conveyance of the said plot of land in the Builder's favour will be executed:

(*b*) A further sum of Rs. 18 lakhs will be paid to the Builder on or before 5th October 2000 or on commencement of construction work by the BUILDER whichever is earlier;

(*c*) A further sum of Rs. 1.5 lakhs will be paid to the Builder on or before 5th day of January 2001;

(*d*) As to a further sum of Rs. 1.5 lakhs (which sum when paid will be 50% of the total price of land, building and garage spaces to be constructed by the BUILDER) will be paid to the Builders on or before 5th April 2001;

(*e*) Over and above the sum specified in sub-clauses (*a*), (*b*), (*c*) and (*d*) above, all sums or advances which may be received by the SOCIETY from time to time from the Federation under its arrangement with them will be paid to the BUILDER as and when it is received;

(*f*) The balance price will be paid to the BUILDER on completion of the construction of the building on obtaining completion certificate and occupation certificate.

10. (*a*) In default of payment of any two of the payments referred to in clause 9 above, the BUILDER will be entitled to forfeit the sums already paid and the agreement will be terminated and the CHIEF PROMOTER or the SOCIETY shall have no claim against the BUILDER for specific performance or for compensation or for damages or otherwise;

(*b*) If within a year hereof the SOCIETY is not able to enter into an agreement with the West Bengal Co-operative Housing Federation Ltd. for obtaining loans by way of advance of not less than 75% of the estimated cost of land and construction cost of the building to be disbursed periodically against construction work as it proceeds then notwithstanding anything herein contained this agreement shall stand terminated and no claim for specific performance, damages, compensation or otherwise on either side would lie and the BUILDER shall return to the CHIEF PROMOTER and the SOCIETY the sums already received after deducting all costs and expenses incurred within a period of three months.

11. On receipt of Rs. 36 lakhs by the stipulated instalments the BUILDER will execute in favour of the SOCIETY a conveyance of the plot of land for a sum of Rs. 78 lakhs. All costs of and incidentals to the conveyance including stamp duty and registration charges will be paid by the SOCIETY. The SOCIETY will take no objection and make no requisitions as regards the builder's title thereto. The BUILDER will make a declaration that they have not themselves created any encumbrance on the land and that charge in favour of the West Bengal Co-operative Housing Federation Ltd. on the land will have a first charge and the Builder's right over the land will be subject to any such first mortgage in favour of the said Federation. Notwithstanding the Builder's right to retain possession of the building to be constructed until the full price and all other moneys due to the BUILDER are paid all the Builder's legal rights under this Agreement and at law against the Society would remain unimpaired.

12. If any alterations are made in the plans at the instance of the Calcutta Municipal Corporation or any other authority the SOCIETY shall accept the same. The BUILDER will also not make any further charge on the SOCIETY on acceptance of such alterations. All outgoings of all kinds payable to the Calcutta Municipal Corporation or any other authority as from the day the land is conveyed in favour of the SOCIETY will be borne and paid by the SOCIETY and it shall accept the Builder's invoices or bills or vouchers and pay the same forthwith on presentation.

13. The SOCIETY shall engage and appoint Clerk of Works for the supervision of the construction work. Any difference of opinion as regards any matter arising in connection with the construction work between such clerk-of-works and the Builder will be decided in accordance with the directions of the said Architect whose decision shall be final and conclusive and binding on the parties.

14. The plans, drawings and specifications shall be and remain the Builder's property until the completion of the conveyance in favour of the SOCIETY. If any discrepancy arises between the specifications and the plans or drawings, the specifications shall prevail over and be deemed to be correct and binding notwithstanding the drawings. The BUILDER hereby agrees and undertakes that it shall remove all surplus material, plant and rubbish from the premises before handing over the possession of the Building and at the Builder's own cost. The BUILDER shall clean the entire site of all materials and make the compound level in good order cemented and/or tiled and usable. The BUILDER will lay the lawns and flower beds and get the passage in the compound as shown in the plans concreted before handing over possession. All plant, equipment and materials brought on the premises by the BUILDER shall be removed forthwith on completion of construction work.

15. The BUILDER hereby agrees and binds itself and its agents that it shall conform to the provisions of all Acts, rules and regulations and bye-laws for the time being in force and shall and will give all necessary notices to obtain sanction of the local authorities in respect of the construction work and generally will comply with the building and other regulations of such authority. For any such purposes, the Society's consent or authority if required will be promptly given.

16. The Builder hereby undertakes that it will not without the consent of the Society assign or sub-let the work of building or construction or any part thereof to any person except labour, planning, drainage, water supply and electric installations.

17. In the event of any accident or extra work to be done or variation made or Force Majeure, Acts of Gods, Civil Commotion, disturbance, conflict of any kind or non-availability of materials such as cement, steel, etc. the Builder will be entitled to an extension of time proportionate to the delay caused in order to enable the Builder to complete the constructions. In case of differences of opinion as to the time to be extended the said Architect will compute the period of delay and the extension of time for completion of the construction.

18. The Builder shall at all times during the period of construction keep all its labour and supervisory staff duly insured against all risks for workmen's compensation.

19. The Society will pay directly to Calcutta Municipal Corporation any amount that has to be paid towards consumption of water by the Society after the building is occupied and pay the CESC Limited for consumption of power.

20. The Society and its Architect will be entitled to inspect the building to be constructed by the Builder from time to time during the period of construction and after receipt of notice of completion. Any requisition or objection in respect of the construction work and/or whether it has been carried out in accordance with this agreement shall be taken and intimated to the Builder within 30 days of receipt of notice of completion and/or inspection whichever is later. If no requisition is made or objection taken within the said period of 30 days, the right to make requisition or take objections will cease and all objections shall be deemed to have been waived. Nothing herein contained shall however entitle the SOCIETY to delay or defer payments to the Builder of the balance of the moneys due to the BUILDER and the same shall be paid on the due dates therefor.

21. The SOCIETY shall as soon as it is registered under the West Bengal Co-operative Societies Act 1983 ratify this Agreement and if so required by the BUILDER will at its own cost execute proper documents to confirm and carry out the terms and conditions and other stipulations herein contained in conformity with the law.

22. All disputes, differences arising during the continuance of this Agreement or thereafter between or among the Builder, the SOCIETY, the CHIEF PROMOTER/Chief Promoter's representative touching or in relation to the Agreement between the BUILDER and the CHIEF PROMOTER and/or the SOCIETY or the construction or application thereof or any clause or thing in this agreement contained or as to any act, deed or omission of any party in any way relating to this agreement or the rights, duties or liabilities of any party under this agreement shall be settled through the arbitration under the Arbitration and Conciliation Act 1996 and if any dispute arises after the registration of the said SOCIETY, such dispute shall be referred to the Registrar of Co-operative Societies, West Bengal under sections 95 and 96 of the West Bengal Co-operative Societies Act 1983.

The First Schedule

Gr. Floor	1st Floor	2nd Floor	3rd Floor	4th Floor

The Second Schedule

Payment of amounts on following dates:

On signing of Agreement Rs. ......

.... 2000 Rs.

.... 2001 Rs.

.... 2002 Rs.

Amounts to be received from
Housing Federation Ltd. Rs.

IN WITNESS WHEREOF the parties hereto have executed these presents on the day, month and year first hereinabove written.

Signed, sealed and delivered by
Mr. ....
pursuant to Board Resolution of
Builders Limited dated ....
in the presence of: Signature

1. ....

2. ....

Signed and Delivered by Mr. XY
the CHIEF PROMOTER in presence of: Signature

1. ....
2. ....

Form I

Form of Application for the Registration of a Co-operative Society with Limited Liability

[Rule 8(1)]

PART I

To
The Registrar of Co-operative Societies

Dated ....

Sir

We the undersigned agree to the enclosed bye-laws and under section 13 of the West Bengal Co-operative Societies Act 1983 (West Bengal Act XLV of 1983), apply to be/registered as a Co-operative Society with limited liability under the title of .... the registered office being at .... Post Office .... Thana .... Town/Panchayat .... Sub-division .... District ....

1. Serial No.:
2. Name of applicant for registration:
3. Father's Name:
4. Occupation:
5. Age:
6. Permanent Address:
7. Present Address:
8. Whether member of any other society, if so name and address of the society(ies):
9. Signature/L.T.I. of applicant:

PART II

1. Name of the proposed society ....
2. Nature of liability of members ....
3. On share basis or without shares ....
4. Number of applicants ....
   (*a*) Individual: ....
   (*b*) Co-operative Societies: ....
5. Names of the members of the first Board (constituted under Rule 30)—(if it is desired that the Registrar should constitute the first board by nomination, no name need be mentioned here).

(1) .... Chairman

(2) .... Vice-Chairman

(3) ....

(4) ....

(5) ....

(6) ....

6. Name and address of the person (Chief Promoter in the case of a Co-operative housing society) to whom communication, if any, are to be addressed till registration of the society ....

7. Certified that each of the applicants belong to different family as required under section 13(2) of the Act.

Signature of three applicants authorised by the promoters to sign and certify on their belief.

(1) ....

(2) ....

(3) ....

Date ....

Deed of Release

(Used by the West Bengal State Co-operative Housing Federation Limited)

THIS INDENTURE MADE this .... day of .... 20........... BETWEEN the West Bengal State Co-operative Housing Federation Limited, a society registered under the West Bengal Co-operative Societies Act 1940 (West Bengal Act XXI of 1940 bearing registration No. 104/Cal of 1965 and having its registered Office at 'Todi Mansion', P-15 India Exchange Place Extension in the City of Calcutta hereinafter referred to and called the RELEASOR (which term or expression shall, unless excluded by or repugnant to the context, mean and include its successors and assigns) of the one part and .... Society Limited, registered under the Co-operative Society Act 1983, bearing Registration No. .... dated .... and having its registered office at .... hereinafter referred to and called the RELEASEE (which term or expression shall unless excluded by or repugnant to the context mean and include its successors and assigns) of the other part, WITNESSETH.

WHEREAS the RELEASEE executed and registered a Deed of Mortgage on .... which was registered at the office of the Registrar of Assurance, Calcutta, in Book No. .... Volume No. .... pages No. .... to .... Being No. .... for the year .... and the RELEASEE (Mortgagor in the said Deed of Mortgage) mortgaged the property described in the schedules to the said Deed of Mortgage for taking loan of Rs. .... Rupees ....) only from the RELEASOR (Mortgagee in the Deed of Mortgage) for the purpose of construction) of .... (...............) separate house/apartments at .... in the district of .... for .... members of the Releasee Society namely .... Society Limited, on the terms, conditions and covenants as fully stated and contained in the said Deed of Mortgage dated, ... (hereinafter referred to as the Principal Mortgage).

AND WHEREAS the said members included one member, namely .... of the Releasee Society.

AND WHEREAS for the said .... Rs. .... (Rupees ....) was sanctioned by the RELEASOR society on terms and conditions as fully described and set out in the said Principal Mortgage;

AND WHEREAS thereafter a further charge Deed for a sum of Rs. .... (Rupees ....) only in favour of the said member as in schedule B therewith was registered at the office of the Registrar of Assurances, Calcutta on .... (date) in Book No. .... Volume No. .... Pages .... to .... Being No. .... for the year .... wherein for the said .... a sum of Rupees .... (Rupees ....) only and thus the said .... became entitled to Rs. .... (Rupees ....) only;

AND WHEREAS the said Shri .... accordingly received a sum of Rs. .... (Rupees ....) only out of the sanctioned loan of Rs. .... from the releasor/society);

AND WHEREAS the property of the said member Shri .... was mortgaged in the said Principal Mortgage and in the said further charge by the RELEASEE Society in favour of the releasor Society as described and set out in Schedule 'A' herewith;

AND WHEREAS the releasee society has made payment of a sum of Rs. .... (Rupees ....) only and all interest and all other sums due and payable thereon to the RELEASOR on account of the said loan of Rs. .... (Rupees ....) only as paid to Shri .... by the releasor-society which payment the releasor society doth hereby admit and acknowledge;

AND WHEREAS the releasee society has accordingly as per provisions contained in the said Principal Mortgage has requested the releasor-society to release the mortgaged property as in Schedule 'A' hereunder;

AND WHEREAS accordingly the releasor society has decided to release the said property as in Schedule 'A' herein in favour of the releasee society;

NOW THIS DEED WITNESSETH as follows:

In pursuance of the aforesaid payment of Rs. .... (Rupees ....) only and all interest and all other sums due and payable thereon as received by the RELEASOR from the RELEASEE as aforesaid doth by this indenture release the mortgaged property on request of the said member, namely Shri .... as described in the said Schedule the said Principal Mortgage and also fully described and set out in the Schedule A herein from the mortgage charge and declare that the society property as in Schedule A herein covered by the said Principal Mortgage is now free from all encumbrances, charges, liabilities and obligations whatsoever and accordingly from this day, the property mentioned in Schedule A herein is released from the mortgage bond by the releasor in favour of and unto the RELEASEE.

The RELEASOR doth hereby declare and state that it has not made any transfer of its interest in the property released nor has it encumbranced or charged it in any way.

All deeds, documents etc. of the Releasee Society in respect of the said property described in the Schedule A herein are to be handed over and returned by the RELEASOR accordingly.

PROVIDED always and it is further agreed between the RELEASOR and the releasee society that this Deed of partial release is between the parties hereto without affecting and/or changing any of the terms, conditions, rights and obligations of the parties as contained and set out in the said principal Mortgage.

Schedule A referred to above

Description of the property regarding loanee member.

Under District .... Sub-Registry and Police Station .... Mouza .... J.L. No. .... Old Khatian No. .... Hal Khatian No. .... Dag No. .... Area and Land Decimals of land as per plan annexed to the said principal Mortgage dated .... along with the building and all other construction and structure standing thereupon.

IN WITNESS WHEREOF the parties herein execute these presents on the day, month and year first above-written.

For West Bengal State Co-operative Housing Federation Ltd. the Releasor	For .... Society Ltd. the Releasee

....

WITNESS:

1.

2.

16

Debutter Property

A debutter is an endowment and much less a trust although it can be created through the medium of trust in which event the ownership of the property vests in the trustees and the deity is the beneficiary. It is not however necessary that creation of the debutter must always be by a registered deed. It is a gift to the God so not a gift to a living person within the meaning of the Transfer of Property Act. God is a juristic person an invisible spirit but capable of holding property. No writing is necessary to create an endowment. The essential requirements are (*i*) intention to divest; (*ii*) Sankalpa; and (*iii*) Utsarga.[1]

A Hindu who is of sound mind, and not a minor, may dedicate his property for religious or charitable purposes. Although it is not necessary to effectuate the said purpose by a registered instrument but it is necessary for the validity of a deed of endowment that the executant should divest himself of the property. Such dedication may also be effected by a will which, however, must be duly executed and attested by at least two witnesses. The deed of endowment, however, would require registration if it purports to transfer the interest of the executant in the immovable property of the value of one hundred rupees and upwards. The dedication must be for an object which is not vague or uncertain, *e.g.* a gift or bequest for spreading of Hindu religion or to Dharma or for good work is void. A gift or bequest in favour of an idol, even though it is to be installed and consecrated after the donor's death is not invalid. All property which a Hindu is entitled to dispose of by gift or will may be dedicated for religious or charitable objects.

The effect of a valid deed of dedication is to place the property comprised in the endowment extra commercium. The dedication is not invalidated by

1 *Vide* Mukherjea on the *Hindu Law of Religious and Charitable Trusts*, 5th Ed., pp. 38, 104, 105, 158 and other pages.

reason of the fact that members of the settlor's family are nominated as *shebaits* and given reasonable remuneration out of the endowment and also rights of residence in the dedicated property. The dedication moreover may be either absolute or partial. The property may be given out and out to the idol or it may be subject to a charge in favour of the idol. Where a Hindu dedicated the whole of his property to a temple and got deed of dedication registered, which in subsequent clauses provided that after the death of the grantor certain female members of his family should succeed him as managers and that half the income should be applied to the temple purposes and the other half should be enjoyed by the managers without power of alienation and in default of such managers the Government should become the manager in which event the whole net income should then be applied to the expenses of the temple, such a deed was held to be a valid endowment of the whole property to the temple and the donor's heirs had no right in it against either the idol or the managers.[2] The Indian Trust Act is not applicable to Hindu endowments and Mahomedan wakfs.

A *shebait,* who is a manager but not a trustee, can nevertheless alienate a debutter property only in cases of legal necessity, justifying causes and for the benefit of the deity. His power to alienate debutter property is analogous to that of an infant's manager as defined by the Judicial Committee in *Hanuman Persaud* v *Massamat Babooee.*[3] But he must be in-charge, *i.e.* manager of the property having *de facto* possession, control and administration. "An order of the court giving a trustee or *shebait* leave to mortgage the property is *prima facie* evidence of legal necessity and cannot be questioned on grounds of defect in procedure or want of jurisdiction except in cases of fraud upon the court".[4]

In *Niladri Shahoo* v *Mahunt Chaturbhuj Das,*[5] it was held by the Privy Council, following the principle enunciated in *Prosanna* v *Golap Chand,*[6] that the court could in cases of necessity make an order for sale.

In the absence of legal necessity, the sale of a debutter property by a *shebait* is *prima facie* an act amounting to a breach of the trust. So a purchaser acquires no interest. A sale in execution of a decree against the *shebait* in his representative capacity stands on a different footing and the purchaser acquires a good title.[7] The case of a permanent lease is also the same,

2 *Jadu Nath* v *Sita Ram* 44 IA 187.
3 (1856)6 MIA 393.
4 *Pashupatinath Seal* v *Pradyumnakumar Malik* (1936)63 Cal 454.
5 LR 53 IA 252.
6 LR 2 IA 145.
7 *Subbaiya* v *Mustapha* LR 50 IA 295.

nevertheless the transfer is valid during the lifetime or tenure of the office of the transferor *shebait*. A transfer of a portion of the debutter property admittedly not for any legal necessity for which no declaration in Form B under the West Bengal Estates Acquisition Act 1935, was filed, was nevertheless held as not void but valid during the lifetime or tenure of the office of that particular *shebait*.[8]

In case of such a nature, the transferee can hold, possess and enjoy the property adversely until when the particular *shebait* or *shebaits* cease to be in the picture by reason of death, removal, retirement or otherwise, in other words, so long as he continues to be the manager. This proposition was laid down authoritatively by the Judicial Committee in *Ram Charan* v *Narayangilal*.[9] This doctrine was affirmed in *Mahadeo Prosad* v *Bharati*,[10] but if the entire property is solid, the transfer is totally void, even if the permission is granted under the Indian Trust Act or on principles underlying the Guardians and Wards Act, which are the guidelines for cases of transfer of debutter estate although they are not applicable to Hindu endowments,[11] the transferee is not completely protected as he is to establish legal necessity in case the sale is challenged.

Whether a Brahmottar land is transferable.[12]

If the land is granted burdened with the condition of service, it is not transferable. If in recognition of service transferable conversion of a debutter property into secular estate.[13]

A *thakurbati* is not divisible.[14]

A private debutter can be partitioned among the *shebaits* for better enjoyment provided the same does not destroy the debutter character of the estate.[15]

Contrary view was expressed in *Sukumar Bose* v *Abani Kumar Halder*.[16]

8 *Surendra Nath Pramanick* v *State of West Bengal* 83 CWN 525.
9 LR 60 IA 124.
10 LR 62 IA 47.
11 *Gostha Behari De* v *Purna Chandra De* AIR 1949 Cal 219.
12 *Jiban Chandra* v *Naren* AIR 1955 Ass 24.
13 *Gobinda* v *Debendra* 12 CWN 98; *Tulsidas* v *Siddique* 20 CLJ 315; *Appu* v *Karumba* 21 MLJ 588; *Chandi Charan Das* v *Dulal* 54 Cal 30.
14 57 Cal 570.
15 34 CWN 151; *Dharmadas* v *Gosta* 16 CWN 29; *Bhabatarini* v *Behari* 10 IC 399; *Madhab* v *Sarat* 15 CWN 126.
16 60 CWN 778.

FORMS

Sale of Debutter Property

THIS DEED OF SALE made this .... day of .... BETWEEN .... deity consecrated and established at premises No. .... Calcutta, hereinafter referred to as the SAID DEITY represented by its SHEBAIT of the first part .... son of .... by religion Hindu .... by occupation .... residing at No. .... and C.D. .... son of .... by religion Hindu, by occupation .... residing at .... hereinafter referred to as the PURCHASER which expression shall where the subject or context allows or admits of be deemed to include his heirs, executors, administrators, representatives and assigns of the second part.

WHEREAS .... (name) is at present SHEBAIT of the DEITY and so is fully in charge of and management and administration of the estate of the DEITY which consist of *inter alia* properties mentioned and described in SCHEDULE "A".

AND WHEREAS the temple that is place of worship of the DEITY is located at premises No. .... which is now lying in a most dilapidated condition for want of necessary repairs and maintenance for a long time.

AND WHEREAS the income of the estate of the DEITY that is the rent which is collected from other property belonging to the DEITY is hardly a sum of Rs. .... per month that is Rs. .... per year out of which the following disbursements are to be made, *viz.*

(*a*) Amount paid to the priest for performance for daily Seva and Puja of the DEITY at the rate of Rs. .... per month that is Rs. .... per year.

(*b*) Amount paid to the milkman for supply of milk to the DEITY at the rate of Rs. .... per month that is Rs. .... for the year.

(*c*) Amount paid to the maid-servant for the cleaning of the temple of the DEITY and utensils Rs. .... per month that is Rs. .... per year.

(*d*) Amount paid as costs of fruits and sweets of the DEITY every day Rs. .... per month that is Rs. .... per year.

(*e*) Amount spent for kerosene oil for one Hurricane lamp kept burning at night at the temple of the deity Rs. .... per month, *i.e.* Rs. .... per year.

(*f*) Miscellaneous and contingent expenses Rs. .... per year.

(*g*) Taxes payable to the Municipality per quarter Rs. .... that is Rs. .... per year. Total Rs. .... per year.

AND WHEREAS in the circumstances there is no such surplus income nor any reserve fund for the maintenance and repair of the temple and for essential services to the DEITY AND WHEREAS the said temple which is out of repair for a long time is liable to collapse before the ensuing monsoon unless urgent repairs are immediately executed the costs whereof are estimated at a sum of Rs. .... AND WHEREAS the estate of the DEITY having no funds to carry out repairs the party of the second part contracted for sale of the property namely the vacant land at premises No. .... yielding no income fully mentioned and described in the schedule below at and for a sum of Rs. .... which offer is the highest among others he received after advertisement in newspapers on two occasions AND WHEREAS the said PURCHASER is also satisfied about the *bona fides* of such sale and has agreed to purchase same at the price of Rs. .... to be paid to the party of the first part immediately on execution of the conveyance and to contribute a further sum of Rs. .... per month towards cost of Seva and Puja in perpetuity.

NOW THIS DEED OF SALE witnesses that in the circumstances aforesaid and for legal necessities and justifying causes SHEBAIT as representing the said DEITY and in exercises of all powers, authorities and liberties vested in him as such SHEBAIT do hereby and hereunder grant, convey, transfer, assign, and assure unto the other party of the third part the property fully mentioned and described in Schedule "B" hereto free from all charges for the performance of everyday Puja and periodical festivals of the DEITY but subject to the contribution of the sum of Rs. .... per month in perpetuity on that account. AND THAT the party of the first part do hereby covenant and agree with the party of the second part that the said property is free from encumbrances except the charge for the maintenance and Seva and Puja of the DEITY which is hereby extinguished and that the same is not otherwise prejudiced in title or estate and that the party of the first part has not done executed or performed anything whereby he is hindered or prevented from granting and/or conveying the same in the manner hereinbefore indicated.

Schedule above referred to

SCHEDULE "A"

List of properties belonging to the deity.

SCHEDULE "B"

Description of property sold under this Deed of Sale.

IN WITNESS WHEREOF the parties have executed this Deed of Sale on the day, month and year first above-written.

Signed, sealed and delivered by the within-mentioned AB the SHEBAIT as representing the DEITY in the presence of:

Signed, sealed and delivered by the within-mentioned CD, the PURCHASER in the presence of:

MEMO OF CONSIDERATION

NOTE: *Sale.* A sale by a *shebait* or mohunt of his right to manage debutter property is void, even though the transfer may be coupled with an obligation to manage the property in conformity with the trust attached thereto. Nor can the right be sold in execution of a decree against him. Even if a custom be proved which sanctions the sale of such a right, the courts should refuse to recognize it, as being against public policy, especially where the sale is made to a stranger for the pecuniary benefit of the vendor.

It is however competent for the *shebait* to renounce his right of management and transfer the same without receiving any consideration to a person standing in the line of succession provided the transferee is not disqualified by personal unfitness. A sale of the debutter not even for legal necessity is valid during the life of the transferor.[17]

Lease of Debutter Property

THIS DEED OF LEASE is made this 5th day of February 1999 BETWEEN Shree ...., Deity, represented by .... of .... the *shebait* (hereinafter referred to as the LESSOR) of the one part and Messrs. ...., a company registered under the Companies Act 1956 and having its registered office at .... (hereinafter referred to as the LESSEE) of the other part.

17 *Surendra Nath Pramanick* v *State of West Bengal* (1978-79)83 CWN 525.

WHEREAS by a Deed dated .... Sri .... dedicated, *inter alia*, his immovable property at .... to the DEITY absolutely and for ever and the said .... is the *shebait* and carries on the Seva Puja of the said deity and the management and administration of the said debutter property.

AND WHEREAS the income from debutter property became inadequate due to inflation to carry out the Seva Puja of the said deity and maintenance of the debutter property with the income thereof and there was urgent legal necessity for augmentation of the existing income and it was thought fit that a portion of building now used for residence of the *shebait* could be leased out and the rent from the said leased out portion of debutter property could sufficiently augment the income of the said deity.

AND WHEREAS the said *shebait* representing the said deity made an application to the Hon'ble High Court at Calcutta for permission to lease out for legal necessity 3 rooms on the ground floor used as residential quarters of the *shebait* but forming a part of the debutter property at the premises .... and after hearing the persons interested and after consideration of income and expenditure for the Seva Puja of the deity and maintenance of the debutter property the Hon'ble High Court at .... was pleased to sanction by an Order dated .... The granting of lease for a period of 5 years at a time renewable every 5 years subject to a minimum monthly lease rent of Rs. 3,000 which should be enhanced by 20% every 5 years.

AND WHEREAS THE LESSEE has made searches and inspected all relevant documents, court records including the certified copy of the said Order of the Hon'ble High Court at .... passed on .... and has satisfied himself with the authority and power of the LESSOR to grant the lease of the said 3 rooms of the debutter property (hereinafter referred to as the said PREMISES) and the validity of the present Deed of Lease and agreed to take on lease the said PREMISES at a monthly rent of Rs. 3,000 to be enhanced by 20% every 5 years for a period of 5 years in the first instance and thereafter renewable for 5 years at a time.

AND WHEREAS the LESSEE agrees that the *shebait* does not give any warranty as to his power or authority to grant the said lease save and except that the said dedication of the property to the said deity and Order of the Hon'ble Court and that up till now there is nobody else claiming to be the *shebait* of the said deity or the Manager of the said debutter property.

NOW THESE PRESENTS WITNESSETH and the parties hereby agree as follows:

1. In pursuance of the said Order of the Hon'ble High Court at .... and in consideration of the rent hereby reserved and on the terms, conditions,

covenants and agreements herein contained and on the part of the LESSEE to be observed and performed the LESSOR doth hereby demise unto the LESSEE all that the said 3 rooms each measuring 120 sq. ft. situated on the ground floor of the premises No. .... facing East having frontage on 30 ft. wide .... to hold the said PREMISES unto the LESSEE for a term of 5 years with option to renew for 5 years at a time on an enhanced lease rent of 20% commencing from the date of execution of these presents but subject to earlier determination as mentioned hereinafter.

2. The LESSOR shall pay by way of lease rent a sum of Rs. 3,000 per month payable in advance by the 10th of each month.

3. The LESSEE shall deposit Rs. 3,00,000 by way of security money free of interest which security money will be refunded on the LESSEE giving vacant possession the said premises to the LESSOR.

4. The LESSEE shall give notice 13 months before the expiry of lease as to whether it intends to renew the lease for another 5 years.

5. The LESSEE shall pay all present and future municipal rates, taxes, duties and levies and other outgoings, statutory or otherwise payable to Municipality or other authorities in respect of said leased out premises.

6. The LESSEE shall keep the leased-out premises in good and tenantable repairs but shall not carry out any additions or alterations or structural changes without the written consent of the LESSOR.

7. Within one month of the LESSEE getting possession of the said PREMISES, the LESSEE shall start the repairs or renovation of the said leased-out premises and paint the outside of the entire building used by the said *shebait* including the leased-out premises.

8. The LESSEE shall not use the said PREMISES for any unlawful purpose or bring into the PREMISES any inflammable or hazardous article, thing or goods or store them there.

9. The LESSEE shall use the said PREMISES only for the purposes of carrying on its business and in doing so undertakes not to create any nuisance or undue annoyance to the neighbours.

10. The LESSEE shall not sub-lease or grant any leave or licence to any person, firm or company or create any charge or mortgage over the said PREMISES without the prior written consent of the LESSOR.

11. The LESSEE shall make arrangements for separate Meters for water, electricity and gas as it may require at its own cost and the LESSOR would give the consent for such installation of Meters or connection for electricity or gas.

12. If the LESSEE makes any default in payment of lease rent for two months or commits any breach of any of the terms or conditions contained herein the LESSOR shall have the liberty to terminate the lease and to re-enter the said premises.

13. The LESSEE agrees and on enquiry has been satisfied that all necessary sanctions and permissions have been obtained, all formalities have been observed for the purposes of granting the lease and that the LESSOR shall have no liability or responsibility as to the validity or otherwise if questioned of the present demise.

14. The LESSEE agrees and undertakes to bear and pay the requisite stamp duty and registration charges and other legal and miscellaneous expenses in respect of present Deed of Lease.

IN WITNESS WHEREOF the parties have executed these presents on the day, month and year first above-written.

Signed and delivered by Sri ...., *shebait* representing Sree Sree Radha Gobinda pursuant to Order dated .... of the Hon'ble High Court at .... in presence of:

1. ....

2. ....

For Sree Sree Radha Gobinda
Shebait

Signed, sealed and delivered by Mr. .... pursuant to Board Resolution dated .... of Messrs. Business Ltd. in presence of:

1. ....

2. ....

For Business Ltd.
Director

Lease of Debutter Property

THIS DEED OF LEASE is made on this 30th day of May 1999 BETWEEN GODDESS DURGA installed in the Temple called "Durga Mandir" at .... (hereinafter referred to as the said DEITY) of the First Part, Swami Brahmananda, one of the trustees, residing at the premises adjoining the Durga Mandir, ... (hereinafter referred as the LESSOR which expression shall unless excluded by or repugnant to the context include his successors in office) of the Second Part and Sri Jubaraj by religion Hindu, by occupation business at present residing at .... (hereinafter referred to as the LESSER) of the Third Part.

WHEREAS by a Deed of Trust dated .... the land at .... and all funds were dedicated to the Goddess Durga with direction to construct a temple thereon and install the said Goddess Durga therein.

AND WHEREAS by the said deed five named persons were appointed as the Trustees who would constitute a Board and conduct the affairs of the said deity and the Trust Property.

AND WHEREAS the said property with the trust funds the said temple was constructed and the deity was installed and the said temple was named as "Durga Mandir".

AND WHEREAS the Board of Trustees agreed to act as the Trustees and agree to the directions contained in the said Trust Deed, constructed the said temple and named it as "Durga Mandir" and installed the said Goddess Durga therein.

AND WHEREAS due to inflation the costs of maintenance of the property and daily Seva Puja of the deity and holding of the periodical festivals have gone up considerably during the last nine years the income of the Trust property has become inadequate to meet the expenses in relation to the said Durga Mandir.

AND WHEREAS the Board of Trustees is empowered by the Trust Deed to manage and maintain the trust property along with its assets and funds with power for legal necessity to lease out or sell any portion of the Trust property so that the said Durga Mandir may be properly maintained and the Seva Puja of the deity continue.

AND WHEREAS the Board of Trustee had by a resolution passed unanimously at its meeting held on 16th April 1999 decided to lease out a portion of the debutter property as described in the Schedule below in the interest of the deity.

AND WHEREAS Sri Yubaraj is desirous of staying near the said Durga Mandir and devote his time in the worship of the said Goddess Durga and thereby became almost a part of the said Durga Mandir to have peace of mind and lead a life dedicated to the Goddess Durga.

AND WHEREAS the said Sri Yubaraj approached the Board of Trustees for a lease of a portion of vacant land adjacent to and belonging to the said deity not required for the purposes of deity or periodical Seva Puja or festivals for leasing out to him for construction of a small house in conformity with the design and structure of the said Durga Mandir and the Board in principle agreed to do so.

AND WHEREAS the said Sri Yubaraj has sold his property with a view to take on lease a portion of the property belonging to the said deity and make constructions thereon for his residential purposes.

AND WHEREAS the Board of Trustees have considered the proposal and taking into consideration the dire need for money for the maintenance of the existing property and for meeting the expenses of Seva Puja of the deity the existing income has to be augmented agreed to the proposal.

AND WHEREAS considering the legal necessity for leasingout a portion of the debutter property the Board of Trustees by a Resolution dated .... authorised Swami Brahmananda, a party of the Second Part to execute a Lease Deed on behalf of the Board of Trustees of the said party in favour of Sri Yubaraj for a period of 30 years on a lump sum premium of Rs. 10 lakhs and on a monthly rent of Rs. 500. All rates, taxes, levies, cesses and outgoings in respect of the said land proposed to be leased out measuring about 4 cottahs should be borne by the LESSEE and in respect of the said leased out land and the Board of Trustees of the property shall have no obligation to pay any money on any account whatsoever and all expenses and outgoings shall be borne by the LESSEE.

AND WHEREAS Sri Yubaraj has made enquiries and searches and examined the Trust Deed and has satisfied himself fully about the right, title and interest of the deity and the powers of Board of Trustees to authorise granting of such lease in the facts and circumstances stated herein and has agreed to accept lease of the said land of the deity on terms and conditions mentioned hereinbefore and contained hereinafter.

NOW THESE PRESENTS witnesseth and the parties hereby agree as follows:

1. In consideration of the sum of Rs. 10 lakhs paid by the LESSEE to the LESSOR as non-refundable premium and in consideration of a monthly rent of Rs. 500 the LESSOR hereby grants and the LESSEE hereby takes on rent a plot of land measuring more or less 4 cottahs for a period of 30 years from the date hereof.

2. The LESSEE would be at liberty to construct a two-storeyed building not taller than the temple and having a design in conformity with the said temple and should give it an appearance of a part of the temple.

3. The LESSEE shall pay and discharge and satisfy all taxes, rates, cesses, levies and impositions both existing and future in respect of the premises demised irrespective of the legal liability of the said deity.

4. The LESSEE shall take possession of the said building to be constructed and shall not use the same except for residential purposes of the LESSEE and his family members. In the event the lessee intends to dispose of the said leasehold property he should offer the same to the deity represented by the Board of Trustees at a price not more than the value of the unexpired period, total value being Rs. 10 lakhs for 30 years.

5. The LESSOR doth hereby covenants that the land comprising in the Lease Deed is not at present affected by any notice or scheme by any municipality or other local authority and the property is free from all encumbrances, attachment, charges and other claims and demands.

6. The LESSOR has a good and marketable title to lease out to the LESSEE the said property and the said leasing out is duly authorised by the Trust Deed and the Board of Trustees and the lessee has satisfied himself about these facts.

7. The LESSOR or the Board of Trustees has not done, executed or performed anything whereby the present lease is hindered or prevented from granting or executing or transferring the property in any manner.

8. In the event through inadvertence or error or by any other cause whatsoever if it is found to be incomplete in respect of the right, title and interest or possession of the LESSEE, the LESSOR shall be bound to execute any further Deed in favour of the LESSEE for further perfecting, ensuring and assuring the right, title and interest and possession of the LESSEE.

9. The LESSOR shall execute or cause to be done or executed all such lawful acts, deeds and things whatsoever for further and more perfecting, conveying and assuring the said property and every part thereof in the manner aforesaid according to the true intent and meaning of the deed.

10. The LESSOR doth hereby and hereunder grant, convey, transfer and assign and assure unto and to the use of the LESSEE full and free right and liberty of way and passages for ingress to and egress from the said premises for himself his family members and relations and visitors over the said plot measuring about 4 cottahs as indicated in the site plan attached hereto through the passage 15 ft. wide leading to the plot from .... to premises and to hold at all times hereafter for 30 years and for all purposes and telephone, electric, gas, water and sewage connections over and under the same and the same plot of land will also be used by all persons visiting or having any interest in the said Durga Mandir.

11. The parties have agreed and understood the nature of enjoyment of the demised premises herein situated and the surrounding areas and the

fact is that the demised premises is attached to the said Durga Mandir and the LESSEE agrees it will not object to or make any grievance of any noise or disturbance by virtue of usual Seva Puja of the deity and the periodical festivals and/or religious functions that might be held in or outside the said Durga Mandir.

12. The LESSEE shall have the right to surrender the lease in which case as also on termination of the lease the building constructed on the lease-hold property would belong to the said deity and that the LESSOR shall return a proportionate amount of the said amount of Rs. 10 lakhs depending on the unexpired period of the said lease and excepting that the LESSEE shall not have any right against the LESSOR on any account for whatsoever reason.

Schedule of the lease property

All that piece and parcel of land measuring about 4 cottahs, now lying vacant under Khatian No. ..., Dag No. ..., in Mouza Ganesh Bazar, J.L. No. ..., and butted and bonded.

by

on the North: ... .

on the South: ... 10 ft. wide ....

on the East: ... .

on the West: ... a portion of the property of the said temple.

IN WITNESS WHEREOF the parties hereunder have set out and subscribed their respective hands and seal, on the day, month and year first above-written.

For self as Shebayat and
Deity as authorised by
the Board of Trustees

Signature of the LESSOR
(by the pen of Shebayat)

WITNESSES:

1.

2.

3.

Signature of LESSEE

Sri Yubaraj (TRUSTEE)

WITNESSES:

1.

2.

3.

MEMO OF CONSIDERATION

Bank Draft in favour of deity drawn on .... Bank, ..., No. ...... dated .... for Rs. 10 lakhs.

Received the consideration
(Signature of the LESSOR)

WITNESSES:

1.

2.

3.

17

Development and Sale of Apartments

Statutes affecting apartment ownership. Developer's agreement, construction agreement, agreement with prospective flat or apartment owners and management of common amenities of the flats or apartments, transfer of flats and matters relating thereto are governed by several Statutes both Central and State. Before entering into any agreement it has to be ensured that these laws are complied with. Some of the Statutes are:

1. Companies Act 1956 (where company is a party);
2. Co-operative Societies Act 1912 and State Acts;
3. Co-operative Housing Society Acts of States;
4. Delhi Apartment Ownership Act 1986;
5. Gujarat Ownership of Flat Act 1972;
6. Income-tax Act 1961;
7. Karnataka Ownership Flat Act 1972;
8. Karnataka Ownership Flats (Regulation of the Promotion of Construction, Sale, Management and Transfer) Act 1972;
9. Maharashtra Ownership Flats (Regulation of Promotion of Construction, Sale, Management and Transfer) Act 1963;
10. Maharashtra Apartment Ownership Act 1970;
11. Registration Act 1908;
12. Stamp Acts both Central and States;
13. Transfer of Property Act 1882;
14. Urban Land (Ceiling and Regulations) Act 1976;
15. Uttar Pradesh Ownership Flats Act 1975;
16. West Bengal Apartment Ownership Act 1972;
17. West Bengal Building (Regulation of Promotion of Construction and Transfer by Promoters) Act 1993;

18. West Bengal Building Tax Act 1996;
19. West Bengal Co-operative Societies Act 1983;
20. West Bengal Government Land (Regulation of Transfer) Act 1993.

Apartment ownership regulations. Many of the States have enacted laws regulating ownership of flat or apartment and promotion of, construction, sale, management and transfer of flats.

Provisions have been made for control on planning and construction with a view to securing quality of raw materials to be used in construction, the security and stability of the apartments to be built and substantial responsibility have been imposed on Promoters. Provisions have been made for protection of buyers and compensation for loss to the buyers, requirement as to insurance of the constructed building and for violation of law or rules the Promoters have been made liable for cancellation of their registrations, imprisonment and fine apart from liability to pay compensation to the buyer of the flat.

"Promoter" means an individual, a firm and association of persons, a corporation or a company who constructs or causes to be constructed buildings on a plot of land for the purpose of transfer of such building or flats.

Every Promoter must register his name as a promoter with the Authorised Officer under the Act on payment of a fee. Without such registration a person is not a Promoter and cannot take up such construction work.

The Promoter should make an application for permission to begin house construction in the appropriate form to the Authorised Officer. For such permission a fee is payable according to the value of the cost of construction. In the application the Promoter is to give description of the land, site plan, proof of ownership of the land, authority to develop the land, the area of the land, the particulars of flats to be constructed, the facilities and amenities to be provided to the flat-owners, sanctioned plan of the building to be constructed, the approximate cost of construction and sources of funds. Further the details of agreement with the landowner regarding the construction of houses and the amount received and the period within which possession of the flat is to be given and a copy of the agreement between the Promoter and buyer of the flat are to be furnished. The names and addresses of the Architects, Engineers and Contractors are to be furnished to the Authorised Officer. Income Tax Clearance Certificate and Sales Tax Clearance Certificate are also to be submitted.

Buyers have been given the right to claim compensation in due process of law for any defective construction or sub-standard materials used for construction or any unauthorised change in the structure of the building has been done or the Promoter wrongfully encumbers the land or building without the permission of the buyer or fails to give possession to the buyer within the specified period or delays construction of the flat.

Generally the Act provides for a machinery for settlement of the disputes without going to Court or to arbitration. The Authorised Officer under the Act is authorised to receive complaints from the buyers and to decide the same.

After the construction is complete and the flats have been sold the buyers are required to form an Association or a Co-operative Society or a company which would be responsible for the maintenance of the building and to provide the common services to the flat-owners.

When an Association or Company or Co-operative Society is formed the Promoter shall transfer to it all his rights, title and interest in the land and building and make over all documents relating thereto.

The agreement between the Promoter and the buyer of the flat should contain certain minimum information or clauses such as description of the land, details of location of flat, total covered area of flat, carpet area, height, length and width of each room, constructional particulars and necessary details, electrification and sanitation arrangements common area for flat owners, total cost of flat, booking fee, instalment, rate of interest, refundable money in case the purchase falls through, when the Deed of Transfer of Flat would be completed and when the possession would be given.

The Promoter is required to obtain a Completion Certificate from the competent authority and submit the same to the Authorised Officer.

The Promoter is required to insure the land with building after completion of construction covering the liability for any loss of lives and properties and physical injuries. He shall submit a copy of the Policy to the Authorised Officer.

The Promoter is not entitled to alter or add to the structure without prior approval of the authority concerned. To protect the interest of the buyer and to give him quick remedy such Acts have made provisions for decision on a complaint of the buyer against the Promoter by the Authorised Officer under the Act and his decision would be final.

For breach of undertaking or agreement the Promoter is liable to imprisonment upto 3 years or fine up to Rs. 5,000 or both apart from his liability for breach of trust in his dealings with the buyers.

Development, Construction and Transfer of Apartments by Promoters in West Bengal. The West Bengal Building (Regulation of Promotion of Construction and Transfer by Promoters) Act 1993, the Rules made thereunder in 1995, the West Bengal Apartment Ownership Act 1972 and the rules made thereunder in 1974 regulate the promotion of construction and transfer of building by Promoters and Ownership of Apartment which is heritable and transferable and are applicable in whole of West Bengal. Similar Acts and Rules have been enacted by the State of Maharashtra and other States.

The Act provides that every Promoter who intends to construct a building for the purpose of transfer by sale, gift or otherwise, shall at least 90 days before the commencement of construction of such building make an application to the Authorised Officer of the State Government for registration of his name and for permission for construction of such building. The application should be in the prescribed form. The Promoter must be the owner or there must be an agreement between the owner of the land and the Promoter authorising the Promoter to undertake the construction of the building and such agreement should be duly registered. The application is required to be disposed of within 3 months by the Authorised Officer. The Authorised Officer will issue a Certificate of Registration and grant permission for construction and forward a copy to the authority who has sanctioned the Plan for construction of the building.[1]

The Certificate of Registration and the permission for construction of the building would remain valid for a period of 3 years which period can be extended by another maximum 2 years.[2] The Promoter may appeal against the order of the authorised officer within 30 days.[3]

Any dispute between the proposed purchaser of the flat and the Promoter may be referred to the prescribed officer of the State Government for adjudication.[4]

The State Government either *suo motu* or on the application of the aggrieved party within 60 days from the date of the order of the prescribed officer may revise the order after giving opportunity to the parties to show cause.[5]

A Promoter shall before taking any money or deposit enter into a written agreement for sale with each of the intended purchaser of such flat. The agreement shall be registered under the Registration Act 1908. The Promoter cannot take more than 40% of the sale price. The agreement shall contain

1 Section 3 of the West Bengal Building (Regulation of Promotion of Construction and Transfer by Promoters) Act 1993.

2 Section 4 of the West Bengal Building (Regulation of Promotion of Construction and Transfer by Promoters) Act 1993.

3 Section 5 of the West Bengal Building (Regulation of Promotion of Construction and Transfer by Promoters) Act 1993.

4 Section 6 of the West Bengal Building (Regulation of Promotion of Construction and Transfer by Promoters) Act 1993.

5 Section 6A of the West Bengal Building (Regulation of Promotion of Construction and Transfer by Promoters) Act 1993.

particulars mentioned in the Act and in the rules.[6] Once such agreement is entered into the Promoter cannot alter the structure of the flat or building or construct additional structure without the consent of the said intending purchaser and also without the permission of the Government Authority. The Purchaser within one year of taking possession may complain about any defect and if the defect is not rectified by the Promoter then the Promoter is liable to pay compensation to the purchaser for such defect or alteration. Any dispute between the purchaser and Promoter shall be referred to the Chief Engineer in the Housing Directorate, Housing Department of State Government for adjudication. The adjudication is to be made by the Chief Engineer or through his nominee within one year and his decision shall be final.[7]

After the agreement is entered into with the intending purchaser the Promoter shall not enter into any agreement, create any charge or mortgage on the flat or on the land without the consent of such purchaser. If the Promoter does any such thing then the flat purchaser is entitled to refund of the moneys paid for the flat with interest at 12% per annum. If the Promoter delays the construction or delivery of the flat he is liable to refund the moneys taken with interest at 25% per annum from the due date of delivery of possession if the purchaser is unwilling to take possession of the flat due to such delay.[8]

The Promoter shall take steps for formation of a Co-operative Society of the Owners of the flat and get it registered.[9]

Promoter shall take all necessary steps to complete his title and convey to the organisation of the persons taking flats, which is a registered Co-operative Society, his right, title and interest in the land and the building and shall execute all relevant documents and conveyances as agreed and he shall deliver all documents in his possession to the Co-operative Society.[10] The Promoter shall also obtain Insurance Policies covering the liability for any loss or death caused by any defect in land or building and the risks should cover 90% of the value or estimated value of building and for a

6 Section 7 of the West Bengal Building (Regulation of Promotion of Construction and Transfer by Promoters) Act 1993.

7 Section 8 of the West Bengal Building (Regulation of Promotion of Construction and Transfer by Promoters) Act 1993.

8 Section 9 of the West Bengal Building (Regulation of Promotion of Construction and Transfer by Promoters) Act 1993.

9 Section 10 of the West Bengal Building (Regulation of Promotion of Construction and Transfer by Promoters) Act 1993.

10 Section 11 of the West Bengal Building (Regulation of Promotion of Construction and Transfer by Promoters) Act 1993.

period of not less than 5 years from the date of giving delivery of last salable flat.[11] The Act provides that no Civil Court shall have any jurisdiction to entertain or decide any question relating to matters arising under any provisions of the said Act or Rules.[12]

The West Bengal Building (Regulation of Promotion of Construction and Transfer by Promoters) Rules 1995 provides for the form, fee for registration, permission for construction, services of all notices and processes, adjudication of disputes, appeals, particulars to be incorporated in the Agreement for Sale between the Promoter and the intending purchaser, the procedure for breach of agreement and the period within which the Promoter must execute the conveyance.

West Bengal Apartment Ownership Act 1972 is mainly applicable to building for residential purposes. The Act applies only when the owner of a building or the owner of apartments of a building by a declaration duly registered submits that the building be governed by the said Act. This Act has, therefore, no automatic application to the multistoreyed building. Similarly the owner or all the flat-owners may withdraw the said building from the operation of the said Act by another instrument to that effect executed by them.[13]

If the said Act is applicable to a building then the member of a Co-operative Society of that building, if the Society is the owner of the property, shall be the owner of apartment in his possession for a limited purpose. Such interest of the member shall be transferable and heritable property. If the apartment has been acquired in benami then the benamdar will be the real owner.[14]

Each apartment-owner shall be entitled to an undivided interest in the common areas and facilities on a percentage basis calculated on the area of the apartment in his possession.[15]

No encumbrance can be created against the multistoreyed building but each owner of each apartment may create encumbrance including the percentage of undivided interest in the common areas and facilities appurtenant to such apartment.

Any person acquiring by purchase or by inheritance or by lease for 30 years or more must execute an instrument in the prescribed form and register

11 Section 12 of the West Bengal Building (Regulation of Promotion of Construction and Transfer by Promoters) Act 1993.

12 Section 12A of the West Bengal Building (Regulation of Promotion of Construction and Transfer by Promoters) Act 1993.

13 Sections 2 and 11 of the West Bengal Apartment Ownership Act 1972.

14 Sections 3A, 4 and 4A of the West Bengal Apartment Ownership Act 1972.

15 Section 5 of the West Bengal Apartment Ownership Act 1972.

it undertaking to comply with the bye-laws, covenants, conditions and restrictions contained in the declaration. The declaration should be submitted in duplicate within 15 days from the date of its execution to the competent authority along with copies of site plan, building plan and relevant title deeds.[16] The instrument of declaration or any amendment thereto or withdrawal of the property are compulsorily registrable.[17] Each apartment including its percentage of undivided interest in the common areas and facilities is to be treated as a separate unit for the purpose of assessment of municipal rates and taxes.[18]

The Transfer of Property Act 1882 shall be applicable to the apartment subject to the provisions of the Act of 1972.

The West Bengal Apartment Ownership Rules 1972 provides for the form and manner in which the declaration is to be submitted to the competent authority, how it can be amended, the execution and registration of an instrument as referred to in section 4(3) of the Act and the forms.

The provisions of the Act are mainly to be complied with by the Promoter. The intending purchaser is mainly interested in the agreement for sale to be executed by the Promoter, Promoter's Power of Attorney or title to the property and the ultimate conveyance of the flat by the Promoter and, if possible, by the owner as a confirming party. All the documents are compulsorily registrable with the Registrar of Assurances, registration fee is payable and stamp duty on the instrument is payable on the value assessed by the registering authority.

Maharashtra. Section 4 of the Maharashtra Ownership Flats (Regulation of the Promotion of Construction, Sale, Management and Transfer) Act 1963 requires an agreement to be drawn up in respect of sale with each of the persons who have taken a flat or flats on ownership basis before accepting any money as advance or deposit and such advance payment of money or deposit cannot exceed 20% of the Sale price under the agreement. Section 4 (1A) provides that the agreement should be in the prescribed form and to contain several matters mentioned therin.

The duty in respect of an agreement covered by Explanation 1 to Art. 25 of Sch. I to the Bombay Stamp Act 1958 is leviable as if it is a conveyance. If there is an agreement to sell immovable property and possession of such property is transferred to the purchaser before the execution or at the time of execution or subsequently without executing any conveyance in respect

16 Sections 4(3) and 10A of the West Bengal Apartment Ownership Act 1972.
17 Section 12 of the West Bengal Apartment Ownership Act 1972.
18 Section 14 of the West Bengal Apartment Ownership Act 1972.

thereof, such an agreement to sell is deemed to be a conveyance. In the event of a conveyance is executed in pursuance of such agreement subsequently, the stamp duty already paid and recovered on the agreement for sale which is deemed to be a conveyance shall be adjusted towards the total duty leviable on the conveyance.[19]

Organisation and Registration of Co-operative Societies

The first point that has to be looked into in respect of organisation of a co-operative society is that the person who would be its members must be persons with needs and interest in common. One of the objects of the society would have to be the promotion of thrift, self-help and mutual and among the members (Preamble to the Act). There must be at least 15 persons to form a society except in the case of an Engineers' Co-operative where at least 7 persons are required. These persons may be individuals of a body of persons of an association approved by State Government (s. 59). In the case of individuals, the persons must be of the age of 18 years or above, *i.e.* those who are competent to contract. These is no age restriction in the case of Students' Co-operatives [s. 59(1)]. Some of the promotee-members have to be above the age of 21 years to form the committee of Management of the Society and number of such persons should at least be equal to the number meant to constitute the Managing Committee. This restriction is also non-existent in the case of Students' Co-operatives. When a society is meant to be a credit society, its members must reside in the same town or village or group of villages or they must be members of the same class or occupation. A Central or provincial society may be formed by at least 6 co-operative societies or 6 applicants including at least 4 co-operative societies. The ratio of individual members to society members is not to exceed one-third of the total number of applicants [r. 8(3)].

With regard to the question of liability it has been stipulated that a society may be of any type of liability—limited or unlimited. In respect of a society with limited liability, the last word in its name must be "Limited".

Next point is the procedure to be followed in submitting by-laws for registration. This has been provided in s. 13 and r. 9. Following papers have to be submitted to the Registrar of Co-operative Societies:

(*i*) An application in the form given in the Schedule of the West Bengal Co-operative Societies Rules 1974. This should be duly filled in and signed by the persons intending to form the society.

(*ii*) Two copies of by-laws which the society proposes to adopt, duly signed by the applicants and a third copy, if the society intends to be a member of a financing bank.

19 *Veena Hasmukh Jain v State of Maharashtra* AIR 1999 SC 807.

(*iii*) The applicants may mention the names of persons who would form the first Committee of Management including the names of Chairman and Vice-Chairman in the application or in the by-laws (r. 30). Whereby these names are not given, the Registrar shall appoint such persons while registering the society and such persons may or may not be members of the society.

The next point is the decision of the Registrar to register the society or his refusal to do so. Provisions of law in this respect are in ss. 14, 15 & 16 and r. 10.

On receipt of application and by-laws, the Registrar shall have to satisfy himself whether the application is in order and the by-laws are in conformity with the Act and Rules. He must also satisfy himself if the by-laws are suitable for (*i*) carrying out the objects of the society and (*ii*) for ensuring safe conduct of the society's business. If he is satisfied he is bound to register the society. But the decision in this respect lies with the Registrar and if he thinks he is not satisfied, he may refuse to register the society. In that case he has to record that in writing and communicate his decision to the applicant No. 1 within 15 days of the order. In this connection the Registrar has to comply with the Government direction contained in letter No. 2323, Co-operative, dated 6th July 1970 which lays down certain other criteria for registration in terms of r. 7 of the Rules 1940 and r. 8(2) of the Rules 1974. Under s. 13(4), the Registrar is bound to dispose of an application for registration within 3 months from the date of its receipt. The applicants may however prefer an appeal against the Registrar's refusal to register within a period of two months from the date of communication of this decision. The appeal has to be made to the Co-operative Tribunal. The provision relating to this appeal is in the Fourth Schedule of the Act.

If the Registrar registers the society, he must issue to the society a certificate of registration, which, from the viewpoint of law in particular, shall be conclusive evidence of the fact that the society is a registered society and its by-laws are its registered by-laws.

After registration, one copy of the by-laws duly stamped with the official seal of the Registrar shall be retained in the office of the Registrar and another copy together with the certificate of registration shall be forwarded to the society. Where a society intends to be a member of a financing bank, a third copy shall, after authentication, be sent to the financing bank.

On receipt of the by-laws and certificate of registration, the Committee of Management formed under r. 30 should hold a meeting. In this meeting, secretary and other office-bearers should be elected. Entrance fees and value of shares on first call, if not already realised from members, should be arranged to be realised. Books and registers to be maintained by a society have been given in r. 56. Some of the important books are Cash Book, Member Register, Share Ledger, Minute Book, Loan-ledger etc.

FORMS

FORM A

[*See* Rule 3(1)]

Application Form by the Promoter for Registration under section 3 of the West Bengal Building (Regulation of Promotion of Construction and Transfer by Promoters) Act 1993

(West Bengal Act XX of 1993)

From:

Address:

To
The Authorised Officer

Sir

I/We, being the sole proprietor/promoter intend to construct a block/ building containing .... flats for the purpose of transfer by sale, gift or otherwise do hereby apply for registration of my name/our names under sub-section (1) of section 3 of the West Bengal Building (Regulation of Promotion of Construction and Transfer by Promoters) Act 1993.

2. An attested copy of receipt No. .... dated .... showing the payment of prescribed fee of Rs. 500 (Rupees five hundred) only in enclosed herewith.

3. A duly signed statement showing the sources of fund for each construction is enclosed.

4. Registration number, if any, under any other Act (name of the Act to be specified and attested photo-copy of such registration is to be furnished).

5. Particulars of land, if already acquired, on which construction is proposed.

6. The manner in which the above land has been acquired (if purchased) the cost of the land to be mentioned.

7. Extent of applicant's interest in the land.

8. It is hereby declared that none of the applicants—

(*a*) is of unsound mind or stands so declared by a competent court, or (*b*) is an undischarged insolvent, or

(*c*) being a discharged insolvent has not obtained from the court having jurisdiction, a certificate that his insolvency was caused by misfortune without any misconduct on his part, or

(*d*) has been convicted of an offence of criminal breach of trust, or

(*e*) is otherwise incompetent to make any contract under any law for the time being in force, of

(*f*) the certificate of registration granted previously for construction of any other building was cancelled under section 4 of the Act.

Yours faithfully

(Signature of applicant with
Seal, wherever applicable)

FORM C

[*See* Rule 3(3)]

Form of Registration Certificate in Terms of sub-section (7) of section 3 of the West Bengal Building (Regulation of Promotion of Construction and Transfer by Promoters) Act 1993

(West Bengal Act XX of 1993)

Certified that Shri/Smt. M/s. .... of .... (address) has/have duly been registered under sub-section (5) of section 3 of the West Bengal Building (Regulation of Promotion of Construction and Transfer by Promoters) Act 1993 with effect from the .... day of .... (month) .... (year), the Registration number being ....

(Signature)

Authorised Officer

Dated .... (seal)

NOTE: This Certificate is valid for the period of 3 years from the date of issue.

Copy to the Authority sanctioning the plan.

FORM D

[*See* Rule 4(1)]

Application Form for Permission to Construct under sub-section (1) of section 3 of The West Bengal Building (Regulation of Promotion of Construction and Transfer by Promoters) Act 1993

(West Bengal Act XX of 1993)

To
The Authorised Officer
....

Sir

In terms of sub-section (2) of section 3 of the West Bengal Building (Regulation of Promotion of Construction and Transfer by Promoters) Act 1993 (West Bengal Act XX of 1993). I/We do hereby apply for permission for construction of building containing .... flats under the West Bengal Building (Regulation of Promotion of Construction and Transfer by Promoters) Act 1993, for the purpose of .... (details, *i.e.* sale, gift or otherwise).

2. I have been registered as a promoter in terms of the Act (an attested copy of certificate of registration as promoter bearing Regd. No. .... dated .... is enclosed herewith).

3. Required particulars are furnished below:

(*a*) Detailed description of the land with a site plan;

(*b*) The nature of my/our title to the land (copy of title documents to be annexed);

(*c*) Details of the agreement between the owner of the land and the promoter authorising the latter to undertake construction (copy of registered agreement to be annexed);

(*d*) The nature of encumbrances on such land including any right, title or interest or claim of any party in or over such land;

(*e*) The total covered floor area, the number of flats proposed to be constructed and the approximate size of the flats and facilities including common area facilities;

(*f*) Copy of the sanctioned plan;

(*g*) Details of specifications of the construction of building as approved by any Competent Authority under any law for the time being in force;

(*h*) The estimated expenditure for such construction and the sources from which the expenditure shall be financed;

(*i*) Details of financial arrangements made with any Bank or financial institution and of legal safeguards, if any, taken for such construction or transfer by sale, gift or otherwise;

(*j*) Details of advance payment or deposits proposed to be taken from intending purchasers of flats;

(*k*) The date within which possession of flats proposed to be handed over to the purchaser;

(*l*) Copies of agreements entered into or proposed to be entered into with the purchaser of flats;

(*m*) Name of Architect/Engineer/any other person authorised to submit such plan under any other law for the time being in force who have prepared/will prepare the plans and estimates of the proposed construction together with address;

(*n*) Name and address of the Contractor/Contractors engaged or proposed to be engaged for the construction;

(*o*) Certificate of up-to-date income tax/sales tax clearance of the applicant to be furnished.

4. I/We do hereby declare and affirm that the above particulars are true to the best of my/our knowledge and information and that nothing has been suppressed in this application. If any information is found to be incorrect or contrary to the provisions of the Act or any other law in force, if any suppression of any material and relevant information is subsequently detected, I/We shall be liable to be proceeded against under the law. Any change in the above information at any stage shall be brought to your notice in writing by me/us within a week from the date of such change with reasons thereof. I/We do hereby also undertake that when completed a completion certificate duly issued by the Competent Authority shall be sent to you within 15 (fifteen) days from the date of receipt.

Yours faithfully

(Signature and Seal,
wherever applicable)

Dated ....

FORM E

[*See* Rule 4(3)]

Form for according Permission under sub-section (5) of section 3 of the West Bengal Building (Regulation of Promotion of Construction and Transfer by Promoters) Act 1993

(West Bengal Act XX of 1993)

Permission is hereby granted to Shri/Smt./ M/s. .... of .... (address) duly registered as promoter under sub-section (1) of section 3 of the West Bengal Building (Regulation of Promotion of Construction and Transfer by Promoters) Act 1993, the registration number being .... dated .... valid upto .... for construction of building/buildings containing .... apartments at premises No. ....

This permission is subject to compliance of provisions under section 12 of the Act.

(Signature)

Authorised Officer

Dated .... (Seal)

NOTE: 1. This permission shall remain valid for a period of three years from the date of issue *vide* sub-section (1) of section 4 of the Act.

2. Regarding extension of validity of this permission, see the provisions under sub-section (1) of section 4 of the Act.

3. A copy of insurance policy to be furnished within one month after completion of construction.

4. This permission may be revoked under sub-section (2) of section 4 of the Act and in the event of non-compliance of the provisions under section 12 of the Act.

FORM F

[*See* Rule 6(1)]

Memorandum of Appeal under section 5 of the West Bengal Building (Regulation of Promotion of Construction and Transfer by Promoters) Act 1993

(West Bengal Act XX of 1993)

Before the Appellate Authority under section 5 of the West Bengal Building (Regulation of Promotion of Construction and Transfer by Promoters) Act 1993.

In the matter of appeal by Shri/Ms. ....

versus

The Authorised Officer under the West Bengal Building (Regulation of Promotion of Construction and Transfer by Promoters) Act 1993

And

In the matter of order dated .... passed by the Authorised Officer

THE APPELLANT MOST RESPECTFULLY SHEWETH:

1. That the appellant made an application for .... under section .... of the West Bengal Building (Regulation of Promotion of Construction and Transfer by Promoters) Act 1993, on .... to the Authorised Officer.

A copy of such application is annexed as Annexure I.

2. The appellant shall narrate his case paragraph-wise statement annexing the copy/copies of relevant document as referred. A copy of the order giving rise to the appeal shall also be annexed.

3. Grounds of appeal (The appellant shall state paragraph-wise the grounds for assailing the impugned order of the Authorised Officer).

4. The appellant may like to add any other relevant point.

5. Prayers (The appellant shall state the prayer/prayers).

Verification

I/We .... son of .... residing at .... in my/our capacity as .... of the appellant(s) do hereby verify that the statements made in paragraph(s) .... are matters of record and those of paragraph(s) .... are my submissions and I do hereby verify this memorandum of appeal on this .... (month) .... (year) at (place) ....

(Signature)

FORM G

[*See* Rule 7(1)]

Form of Application for Adjudication of Dispute regarding Purchase of any Flat in Terms of section 6 of the West Bengal Building (Regulation of Promotion of Construction and Transfer by Promoters) Act 1993

(West Bengal Act XX of 1993)

From:

To
The Authorised Officer
....

Sir

In terms of section 6 of the West Bengal Building (Regulation of Promotion of Construction and Transfer by Promoters) Act 1993, I do hereby beg to inform you that I had entered into an agreement with .... (Promoter) for purchase of a flat at ....

A copy of the Agreement made under section 7 of the Act and duly registered is enclosed for perusal.

Now I pray to you for adjudication of the following disputes (to be stated clearly).

1.
2.
3.

Dated .... Yours faithfully

Full Address:

Power of Attorney to Promoter

Know all men by these presents

WHEREAS, I, Mr. .... is the owner of a piece and parcel of land, hereditaments and premises with buildings, messuages and tenements standing thereon and situate lying and being premises No. ...., described in Schedule I hereunder.

AND WHEREAS by an Agreement for sale of even date executed by me as VENDOR of the one part and .... a company registered under the Companies Act 1956 having its office at .... as DEVELOPER-PURCHASER of the other part, I have agreed to sell the said property to the said DEVELOPER on terms and conditions contained in the said Agreement.

And WHEREAS to give effect to the said Agreement, it is necessary to give to the DEVELOPER a Power of Attorney to enable it to get the requisite exemption, permission, sanction etc. from the appropriate and/or competent authorities.

AND WHEREAS the said DEVELOPER has requested me to execute and grant the said Power of Attorney in favour of the DEVELOPER which I hereby do.

NOW THESE PRESENTS witnesseth that I, Mr. ...., do hereby nominate, constitute and appoint Builders Ltd. to be my true and lawful Attorney to do and execute and perform all or any of the following acts, deeds, matters and things namely:

1. To prepare plans for development of the said property and to submit the same to Calcutta Municipality Corporation and other concerned authorities for obtaining approval to the same and any amendments thereto.

2. To approach all concerned authorities under the Urban Land (Ceiling and Regulation) Act 1976 for the purpose of obtaining exemption under section 20 thereof in respect of the said property and for that purpose to sign such applications, papers, writings, undertakings as may be required and to carry out correspondence with the authorities concerned, to appear before them and also to prefer appeals from any order of the competent authority or any other authority made under the provisions of the said Act.

3. To approach, appear, represent and carry on correspondence with and pay the necessary fees or dues and to deposit the requisite amounts to or with all concerned authorities including Government Departments, Municipalities, Town Planning Departments and other concerned authorities in connection with the development, construction, sale of Apartments and Management thereof.

4. To enter upon the land and premises with men and material and to do all things necessary for demolition of existing structures and constructing the multistoreyed building and to apply for and obtain from the authorities concerned permits for cement, steel and other materials, water supply, electricity connection and all other things necessary for the carrying out the said construction work.

5. To apply for and obtain electricity and water connection from the WBSEB or CESC Ltd. and Municipality Corporation and to execute the necessary documents including lease agreement in respect of a portion of the said premises for installation of electrical equipment for supply to the entire apartments building and to instal separate meters for each apartment.

6. To apply for and obtain from Government Departments and Municipality NO OBJECTION CERTIFICATE, permission or sanction for carrying out the construction of the said buildings, completion thereof, Exemption Certificate, Completion Certificate and Occupation Certificate in respect of the said multistoreyed apartments buildings.

7. To enter into agreements for sale of the flats or apartments to be constructed at the said premises on ownership basis and to take advances or payments in respect thereof, give possession and execute conveyance as and when necessary on such terms and conditions as the Attorney may think proper and in consonance with the law and for this purpose to obtain the necessary permission, NO OBJECTION CERTIFICATE or Clearance from the authorities concerned and to get the documents, agreements, conveyances registered and to do all things in connection therewith.

8. To negotiate and enter into agreements with existing tenants, to arrange for the alternative accommodation if necessary and to assure them to give similar accommodation in the multistoreyed building when constructed on such terms and conditions as the Attorney may think appropriate and if necessary to take legal proceedings for eviction of tenants and to engage lawyers for that purpose and to sign Vakalatnama and all pleadings and affidavits and petitions necessary in that connection.

9. To insure the property against all risks such as fire, tempest, riots, civil commotion, malicious acts, explosions, bombs, short-circuits, bursting of gas cylinders and floods, earthquakes or otherwise causing any damage to the building or any portion thereof for the full value of the multistoreyed buildings and other assets and lives therein as the Attorney may think proper.

10. To ask, receive and realise from all occupiers or purchasers of flats, charges, expenses, rates, cesses and other sums due or that might become due and payable by them and on non-payment to take appropriate steps for realisation thereof.

11. To accept writ of Summons or other legal processes or notices, appear before any Officer, Authority, Department, Magistrate, Court, Tribunal, Judicial or Quasi-Judicial Officer and represent me and in connection therewith file appeals or revision or representation and appoint Advocates and lawyers to appear and act in all matters connected with or in relation to or arising out of the said development and construction and sale of the said flats and/or the said premises.

12. To sign and verify and execute all pleadings, affidavits, petitions, representations, applications, appeals, revision, review petitions in connection with any suit, proceeding, appeal, revision, review before any Officer, Authority, Court, Tribunal, Magistrate or any other person for and on my behalf.

13. To receive from any person, officer, authority, Tribunal or Court any document, money or other things and give release and receipt therefor.

14. Generally to do and perform all acts, deeds, things, matters necessary for all or any of the aforesaid purposes and to give full effect thereto.

15. To do all other acts, deeds, matters and things which may be necessary to be done for rendering these presents valid and effectual to all intents and purposes.

16. For performing and carrying out the purposes of these presents I hereby grant unto the said Attorney full and absolute authority and power to substitute and appoint in its place and stead one or more Attorneys to exercise all or any of the powers and authorities hereby conferred and to revoke any such appointment from time to time and to substitute or appoint another or others in place of such Attorney and on such terms and conditions as the Attorney shall think fit and proper.

17. I hereby agree to ratify and confirm whatsoever the said Attorney shall do in relation to the premises by virtue of these presents and I hereby declare that I shall not do anything inconsistent with the Power of Attorney.

18. I hereby declare that the powers and authorities hereby granted are irrevocable till the said property is fully and properly developed as per agreement for sale and in accordance with the statutory provisions, rules and regulations and that the transfer and/or conveyance of the land, buildings, flats are conveyed to the purchasers and Association of Apartment Owners is registered and starts functioning.

IN WITNESS WHEREOF I have executed these presents at Calcutta on the 5th day of June 1999.

The Schedule

All that piece and parcel of land measuring about 6 cottahs in Dag No. 5 Khatian No. 8, Mouza Old Road, with two-storeyed building being premises No. 3 New Road, Calcutta in the Municipal Ward No. 2 butted and bounded by in the North Corporation Road, South-Canal, East by Black Road, West by Drain.

Signed and delivered by the said
Mr. S. Tanton in presence of:

Signature

1.

2.

Accepted and signed by Mr. Z
pursuant to Board Resolution of
4th June 1999 of Builders Ltd.
in presence of:

Signature

Power of Attorney for Admitting Execution and Registration of Document

TO ALL TO WHOM THESE PRESENTS shall come, I, XY, of 3 Bank Street, Calcutta 700 027 Indian inhabitant send Greetings.

WHEREAS I have executed a Deed of Conveyance of the property of Premises No. 3 Bank Street, Calcutta 700 027 in favour of Mr. ML, the PURCHASER.

AND WHEREAS the said Deed is required to be lodged for Registration in the Office of Registrar of Assurances, Red Cross Place, Calcutta 700 001.

AND WHEREAS I am unable to appear before the Registrar for admitting execution of the said Deed relating to the said property as I am now residing at Mumbai.

AND WHEREAS I am desirous of appointing Mr. CA as my Constituted Attorney to attend office of the Registrar to admit execution of the said Conveyance on my behalf and which the said Attorney has agreed to do.

NOW KNOW YOU ALL AND THESE PRESENTS WITNESSETH that I do hereby nominate, constitute and appoint Mr. CA of 9 Bank Street, Calcutta 700 027 to be my true and lawful Attorney for the purpose expressed herein that is to say that to present and lodge in the office of Registrar of Assurances, Red Cross Place, Calcutta 700 001 and to admit execution of Deed of Conveyance dated 5th January 1999 executed by me in favour of Mr. ML the PURCHASER and do all acts, and things necessary for effectively registering the said Conveyance.

AND I DO HEREBY AGREE to ratify and confirm all and whatever my said Attorney shall do or purport to do or cause to be done by virtue of these presents.

IN WITNESS WHEREOF I have executed these presents on the 10th day of January 1999.

Signed and delivered by the
within-named Mr. XY in the
presence of:

Signature

Accepted by CA in the
presence of:

Signature

Before the Registrar of Assurances

(Registered)

Developer's Agreement

THIS AGREEMENT IS MADE this .... day of .... 2000 BETWEEN AB Ltd. a company registered under the Companies Act 1956 and carrying on business at .... (hereinafter referred to as the DEVELOPER) of the ONE PART and Mr. XY residing at .... (hereinafter referred to as the OWNER) of the OTHER PART.

WHEREAS the DEVELOPER has vast experience in developing lands and constructing multi-storeyed buildings and flats.

AND WHEREAS the OWNER is absolutely seized and possessed of a piece of land measuring 5 cottahs with structures thereon being premises No. .... and more fully described in Schedule I hereunder.

AND WHEREAS the OWNER intended to demolish the existing structures and to get constructed a multi-storeyed building at the said premises and approached the DEVELOPER for that purpose.

AND WHEREAS the DEVELOPER has agreed to develop the said land and on demolishing the existing structures to construct a multi-storeyed building with apartments or flats system with the object of selling such apartments or flats.

NOW THESE PRESENTS WITNESSETH and the parties hereby agree as follows:

1. This Agreement for development and construction is being made on the express understanding that the DEVELOPER would comply with and/or cause compliance with all the statutory provisions in relation to such development and construction and for this purpose the expenses that might be incurred would be solely borne by the DEVELOPER.

2. The DEVELOPER hereby agrees and undertakes to obtain necessary sanctions and permission for constructing a multi-storeyed building on the said premises after demolishing the existing structures.

3. The DEVELOPER undertakes to procure for the OWNER alternative accommodation from the date OWNER is required to vacate the said premises till construction is completed and the entire first floor apartment to be constructed is given possession to the OWNER. For such alternative accommodation no rent would be payable by the OWNER.

4. In consideration of the OWNER having agreed to entrust to the DEVELOPER the development of the land and construction of the said multi-storeyed building at the said premises and in connection therewith, authorising the DEVELOPER to exercise the rights, powers, privileges and benefits of the OWNER and the OWNER executing a Power of Attorney in its favour, the DEVELOPER agrees to pay the OWNER a sum of Rs. 50 lakhs and the entire first floor of the multi-storeyed building when constructed. Out of the said Rs. 50 lakhs the DEVELOPER would pay Rs. 25 lakhs on execution of these presents and balance in five quarterly instalments beginning from the month in which

the said premises is handed over to the DEVELOPER for the purpose of development and construction.

5. The development of the said land by demolishing the existing structures and construction of multi-storeyed buildings thereon would be according to plan to be sanctioned and subject to such sanction according to the specification and particulars given in Schedule II hereinunder.

6. The demolition of the existing structures, development of the said land and construction of the said multi-storeyed building would be at the sole risk and expense of the DEVELOPER and the DEVELOPER would comply with all statutory provisions, rules and regulations in relation thereto.

7. The DEVELOPER would acquire no right, title or interest in the said premises or the structures that are proposed to be constructed by the DEVELOPER apart from the rights, privileges and licences that might be granted by the OWNER under the Power of Attorney to be executed by the OWNER in favour of DEVELOPER to enable him to carry out the purposes and objects of these presents.

8. In default of payment of any instalment or any non-compliance of any of the terms and conditions of these presents or on the failure of DEVELOPER to obtain necessary plan, sanctions and other permissions required to be obtained or committing any other breach of these presents or non-compliance of any of the statutory obligations in relation to the said development and construction of the said premises, this agreement will stand terminated on the OWNER giving thirty days notice to the DEVELOPER.

9. The OWNER hereby gives permission to DEVELOPER to enter upon the said property for the purpose of development, demolition of the existing structures and construction of the multi-storeyed building subject to DEVELOPER arranging for the OWNER an alternative accommodation.

10. The OWNER agrees to execute the necessary Power of Attorney authorising the DEVELOPER to do all such acts and things that are necessary for the development of the said land, demolition of the existing structures, construction of the building and to obtain advance booking for the apartments or flats to be constructed on the said premises.

11. The OWNER agrees to sign and execute from time to time plans, applications for lay-outs, sub-division, construction of the building and other applications necessary to be submitted to the authorities concerned at the request of and at the cost of DEVELOPER.

12. The OWNER shall be indemnified from any action, fines, penalties or costs and expenses for any violation of any statutory provisions in relation to the said development and construction by the DEVELOPER.

13. The OWNER shall not object to any construction or laying of sewerage, drainage, water pipes, cables or other provisions made in accordance with the law and scheme of construction of the said multi-storeyed building.

14. Upon full payment of the said Rs. 50 lakhs to the OWNER, the DEVELOPER shall be at liberty to enter into agreements to sell or allot any of the flats or apartments as dwelling units in the said multi-storeyed building to be constructed except the 1st floor reserved for the OWNER and to give possession to any party of such units or flats and to enter into agreement with them or execute Conveyances in accordance with the statutory provisions applicable to such multi-storeyed apartments.

15. On receipt of full consideration including possession of the first floor of the said multi-storeyed building constructed by the DEVELOPER and the said sum of Rs. 50 lakhs, the OWNER will execute Deeds of Conveyance in favour of such purchaser of the dwelling units or flats or apartments or in favour of any co-operative society or company or association of purchasers of flats as the DEVELOPER may desire and as may be permissible under the law in force. Such Deeds of Conveyance shall be prepared by the DEVELOPER and approved by the OWNER. The cost of drafting and Stamp Duty on the conveyance, cost of registration and all other expenses shall be borne by the DEVELOPER and/or purchasers of the flats as may be agreed upon by and between the DEVELOPER and the purchasers of flats.

16. On and from the execution of these presents the DEVELOPER shall pay and discharge all taxes, outgoings, rates, cess and all other levies by the Municipality or Public Body or any other authority in relation to the said premises, the demolition of the said structures, development of the said premises and construction of the said multi-storeyed building and sale and allotment and giving possession to the prospective buyers of the said flats.

17. The OWNER takes no responsibility as regards title to the said property or compliance with any statutory obligations and makes no representation to the DEVELOPER in any respect whatsoever.

18. The DEVELOPER declares that it has made all necessary enquires from the places and authorities concerned about the title of the OWNER in the said premises, any liability of the said premises to any authority or any restrictions put on the said premises and declares that it has entered into agreement after fully satisfying itself about the title of OWNER and the feasibility and suitability of the said premises to be developed and the multi-storeyed building to be constructed and the apartments to be sold to the intending purchaser and that it would not hold the OWNER responsible for anything whatsoever.

19. The said development work and construction of the multi-storeyed building and the handing-over of the first floor of the said building to be constructed to the OWNER should be completed within three years from the date of execution of this agreement. The time will be of the essence of the agreement. In default, the OWNER shall be at liberty to enter into agreement with another Developer or Contractor or otherwise deal with the said

premises and all payments made and expenses incurred by the DEVELOPER shall stand forfeited.

20. The said development work and construction of multi-storeyed building should be carried out under the direct supervision and in presence of DEVELOPER and the DEVELOPER'S presence at the site of construction is a condition of this agreement. However, for the purposes of the said development and construction, the DEVELOPER may take the assistance of Architects, Building Contractors and others but the work should be carried out under the direct physical supervision of the DEVELOPER or its duly authorised Director.

21. The DEVELOPER undertakes to keep the OWNER fully indemnified against and harmless from any losses, costs, charges, expenses or claims by any of Developer's Contractors, Architects, workers or agents or for any breach of any statutory or contractual obligations.

IN WITNESS WHEREOF the parties herein have signed, sealed and delivered these presents on the day, month and year first above-written.

The Schedules above referred to

SCHEDULE I

Details of the premises to be developed.

SCHEDULE II

Detailed specifications of the multi-storeyed building to be constructed and details of statutory provisions to be complied with by the DEVELOPER.

Signed, sealed and delivered by
Mr. .... pursuant to
Board Resolution of AB Ltd. dated
.... in the presence of:

1. .... Signature

2. ....

Signed, sealed and delivered by
the said Mr. XY in the presence of:

1. .... Signature

2. ....

Agreement between Landowner and Promoter

THIS AGREEMENT IS MADE this 20th day of November 2000 BETWEEN Mr. AB of .... (hereinafter referred to as the OWNER) which term shall include his heirs, successors and assigns of the ONE PART and XY Ltd., a company registered under the Companies Act 1956 having its office at .... (hereinafter referred to as the PROMOTER which term shall include its successors and permitted assigns) of the OTHER PART.

WHEREAS the OWNER is seized and possessed of a piece of land measuring 5 cottahs with more or less being premises No. .... and more fully described in the Schedule hereunder.

AND WHEREAS the PROMOTER has approached the OWNER with an offer to develop the said land and has shown a plan for construction of a 5-storeyed building with self-contained 3 flats on each floor.

AND WHEREAS the OWNER has agreed to authorise the PROMOTER to develop the said land described in the schedule in accordance with the plan annexed hereto after demolishing the existing structures thereon for the purpose of sale of flats.

AND WHEREAS the OWNER has agreed to execute and/or join in execution of the Sale Deeds in favour of buyers of the flats to be constructed.

AND WHEREAS the PROMOTER has undertaken to take the necessary permission of the Urban Land Authorities, the Clearance Certificate from the Income Tax Authorities and necessary permission from the Authorised Officer appointed under the State laws and municipalities in relation to the development and construction of the said multi-storeyed building and to comply with all other provisions of law, both Central and State.

NOW, THEREFORE, THESE PRESENTS WITNESSETH and the parties hereby agree as follows:

1. The OWNER would hand over vacant possession of the said land and building to the PROMOTER and entrust the work and the right to develop the said property.

2. The OWNER hereby gives licence and permission to the PROMOTER to enter upon the land with full right and authority with men and material to commence carry on and complete development and construction thereon of the multi-storeyed building in accordance with the particulars given in the schedule annexed hereto.

3. In consideration of the OWNER having given licence and permission to the PROMOTER to enter upon the said land and in consideration of having agreed to entrust to the PROMOTER to develop and construct the multi-storeyed building on the said land and to confer upon the PROMOTER rights, powers, privileges and benefits mentioned in these presents the PROMOTER paid Rs. 15 lakhs on execution of these presents and agrees to give possession to the owner 2 flats on floor of the said multistoreyed building to be constructed and a further sum of Rs. 15 lakhs by quarterly instalments within 2 years from the date of execution of these presents.

4. In developing the said land and constructing the said multi-storeyed building the PROMOTER shall obtain the requisite sanctions, permissions, clearance and authority from the authorities concerned under the Urban Land (Ceiling and Regulations) Act 1976, Income-tax Act 1961 and the other relevant Central and State Acts and the rules and regulations in force at his own expense and costs.

5. The PROMOTER will develop the said land and construct the multi-storeyed building and complete the same in every respect at his own costs, expenses and risks and on his own account.

6. The OWNER shall however on request by the PROMOTER sign and execute the applications, plans and other documents necessary in relation to the said development and construction and the costs and expenses thereof would be borne by the PROMOTER.

7. In accordance with law and as required by the authorities concerned including the Municipal Corporation the PROMOTER shall bear all costs, charges and expenses, carry out the work of development of the said property and construction and completion of the said multi-storeyed building, including the drainage system, laying of cables, water pipes and obtaining connections for electricity as might be necessary and required under the plans, sanctions, permissions of the authorities concerned and would make the said property fit for occupation and use.

8. The PROMOTER shall be entitled to make advertisements, hung up advertisement boards upon the said property and do such other things as might be required for the purpose of sale of the flats in the said premises to be constructed without in any way prejudicing the interests of the OWNER.

9. The PROMOTER shall pay and discharge all taxes, rates and other levies on or in relation to the said land and building and payable by the OWNER or occupier thereof.

10. The PROMOTER shall be at liberty to sell or allot flats or apartments or units in the said building to be constructed on the said land and to enter into agreements with the prospective buyers or allottees individually or collectively on such terms and conditions as he might think fit and proper without affecting any right or interest of the OWNER.

11. The agreement to sell or allot flats or units that might be entered into by the PROMOTER shall be in accordance with the laws applicable and the rules and regulations governing the said building and flats and allow any of the parties to occupy any of the flats or dwelling units without affecting any right of the OWNER under these presents.

12. It will be the sole responsibility of the PROMOTER to deal with the authorities concerned and to comply with the rules and regulations of the said multi-storeyed building and transfer thereof to the intending purchasers

of the flats at his own costs and expenses and that the owner shall not be responsible in any manner whatsoever.

13. The PROMOTER agrees and declares that he has made searches and enquiries and has satisfied himself that the said land is free from encumbrances or restrictions and that it is suitable for construction of the said multi-storeyed building and the laws applicable thereto permit the sale of flats and to carry out the purposes and object of these presents.

14. The OWNER agrees to execute conveyances or sale deeds or join in the execution thereof in favour of the prospective purchasers of flats in the said building to be constructed. The Stamp Duty and Registration charges and all formalities in connection therewith will be paid and borne by the Promoter and/or the Purchasers and that the OWNER shall have no responsibility whatsoever in respect thereof. The PROMOTER shall arrange for payment of Stamp Duty and registration of Sales Deeds or Conveyances and arrange for payment of all expenses including the lawyer's fees.

15. The PROMOTER shall keep the OWNER fully indemnified against and harmless from all losses and damages, costs, charges, expenses, claims or the proceedings in relation to the said land, development thereof, construction, completion, occupation and sale of the flats or otherwise in relation to or touching the subject-matter of this agreement or for violation of any laws, rules or regulations or due to accident, mishap and other calamities, malicious damage, riots, thefts, burglary, fine, death or injury to any worker or person who is engaged in or near the construction site or arising from any other way whatsoever and the PROMOTER undertakes to take out appropriate Insurance Policies in this regard without in any way reducing his duty to the OWNER.

16. Without causing prejudice to the rights of OWNER, the PROMOTER will be at liberty to enter into separate contracts in his own name with a building contractor, architect and others including the prospective purchasers.

17. The time of performance of these presents is to be of the essence of the Contract and in default of the PROMOTER keeping the time schedule or committing any breach of any of the terms of these presents the OWNER shall be at liberty to give notice for compliance or to make good the breach within sixty days from date of receipt of notice and in default of such compliance, the OWNER shall be entitled to forfeit the moneys already paid by the PROMOTER and to terminate the agreement and to engage any other builder for completion of the work and that the PROMOTER shall have no claim against the OWNER or against the land or against the construction already made on the said land by the PROMOTER and the said licence and the permission shall automatically stand cancelled.

IN WITNESS WHEREOF the parties have executed these presents on the day, month and year first above-written.

Schedule

(Particulars of land on which the multi-storeyed building would be constructed).

Signed and delivered by Mr. AB
the OWNER in the presence of:

1. .... Signature

2. ....

Signed, sealed and delivered by
Mr. ....
pursuant to the Board Resolution
dated 5th July 2000 of XY Ltd.
in the presence of:

1. .... Signature

2. ....

Developer's Agreement with Tenant

THIS AGREEMENT IS MADE this 5th day of January 2000 BETWEEN AB Ltd. a company registered under the Companies Act 1956 and carrying on business at .... (hereinafter referred to as the DEVELOPER) of the One Part and Mr. MN residing at .... (hereinafter referred to as the TENANT) of the Other Part and Mr. XY of .... (hereinafter referred to as the OWNER) the confirming Party.

WHEREAS Mr. XY is the OWNER of the premises at .... under whom and in which premises on the ground floor Mr. MN is a monthly tenant in respect of a flat of 600 sq. ft. carpet area.

AND WHEREAS the said OWNER and DEVELOPER have agreed to demolish the existing structure at the said premises at .... and to construct a multi-storeyed building thereon.

AND WHEREAS it is necessary that the TENANT should vacate the said premises to facilitate demolition of existing structure and construction of the multi-storeyed building.

AND WHEREAS the TENANT has agreed to vacate the said premises on the assurance of DEVELOPER that the TENANT would be given a similar accommodation in the multi-storeyed building at a rent of Rs. 3 per sq. ft. of carpet area.

NOW THESE PRESENTS WITNESSETH and the parties hereby agree as follows:

1. The DEVELOPER shall provide the TENANT temporarily with a similar accommodation with similar facilities in the vicinity of the present locality at the same rent.

2. On such temporary accommodation being given the TENANT will shift to the new accommodation giving absolute vacant possession of the said flat to the DEVELOPER.

3. The TENANT shall continue in possession of the temporary accommodation till he is given a flat in the multi-storeyed building to be constructed.

4. On getting vacant possession of the premises the DEVELOPER shall with due dispatch demolish the existing structure and start construction according to sanctioned plan and on obtaining the requisite permissions of the authorities concerned and in accordance with the agreement with the OWNER.

5. After the construction has been completed or partly completed the DEVELOPER on obtaining the necessary certificate shall give to the TENANT in the building similar accommodation and the TENANT will shift from his temporary accommodation to the new building as a TENANT under the OWNER and pay the agreed rent at Rs. 3 per sq ft. of the carpet area.

6. The TENANT agrees to be a member of and/or join any association or body formed by other occupants, TENANTS or OWNERS of the flats or apartments and comply with the statutory provisions in relation to the multi-storeyed buildings.

7. The TENANT agrees that he made all necessary enquiries before entering into these presents and that he shall not be entitled to complain about the amenities and nature and quality of the construction if the same have been done according to the sanctioned plan.

IN WITNESS WHEREOF the parties have executed these presents on the day, month and year first above-written.

Signed, sealed and delivered by
Mr. ....
pursuant to Board Resolution of
15th December 1998 of AB Ltd.
the DEVELOPER in the presence
of:

1. .... Signature

2. ....

Signed and delivered by Mr. MN,
the TENANT in the presence of:

1. .... Signature

2. ....

Confirmed by the said Mr. XY, the OWNER in the presence of:

Signature

1. (Confirming Party)

2.

Transfer of Apartment by Developer

THIS DEED OF Transfer of Apartment made this ...... day .... 2000 BETWEEN AB Ltd. a company registered under the Companies Act 1956 and having its office at .... (hereinafter referred to as the VENDOR which term shall include its successors and assigns) of the First Part and Mr. MN .... (hereinafter referred to as the PURCHASER which term shall include his successors, heirs, Administrators, Executors and assigns) of the Second Part and Mr. XY of .... (hereinafter referred to as CONFIRMING PARTY) of the Third Part.

WHEREAS under an Agreement dated .... the VENDOR obtained the authority and right to demolish the existing structure and construct in its place a multi-storeyed apartment building at ....

AND WHEREAS the CONFIRMING PARTY gave the VENDOR a Power of Attorney, *inter alia*, to enter into agreement for sale of apartments in the said multi-storeyed building.

AND WHEREAS the PURCHASER has made searches and enquiries in respect of the relevant documents and satisfied himself in all respects and that the said multi-storeyed building since constructed is free from all encumbrances and all statutory provisions have been complied with and permissions have been obtained and completion certificate and occupation certificate have been obtained.

AND WHEREAS the VENDOR intends to sell and the PURCHASER intends to purchase 600 sq. ft. carpet area comprising in flat No. .... on the first floor of .... at a price of Rs. 1,000 per sq. ft. of carpet area.

AND WHEREAS the purchaser has agreed to pay and bear the stamp duty and registration charges of this Deed of Transfer of Apartment.

AND WHEREAS the VENDOR has complied with all statutory formalities and undertakes to comply with all statutory formalities required in relation to this agreement.

NOW THIS DEED WITNESSETH and the parties agree as follows:

1. In consideration of the PURCHASER paying the price of the said apartment of Rs. 6,00,000 (Rupees six lakhs) before execution of these presents to the VENDOR (the receipt whereof the VENDOR hereby admits) the VENDOR doth hereby grant and transfer by way of sale unto the PURCHASER forever all that the said Apartment No. .... on the first floor of premises No. .... having a carpet area of 600 sq. ft. and more particularly written in Schedule I hereunder together with 10% undivided interest in land appurtenant to the said Apartment, in the common areas and facilities of the said piece of land and the said building described in Schedule II hereunder TO HAVE AND TO HOLD the said flat hereby granted and sold unto the PURCHASER forever to be held as heritable and transferable according to law subject to the condition that the said flat is to be used for residential purpose and for no other purpose.

2. The VENDOR doth hereby covenant with the PURCHASER that (*a*) he has authority to grant and sell the said flat hereby granted and sold unto and to the use of the purchaser, (*b*) the PURCHASER shall at all times hereafter peaceably and quietly enter upon, hold, occupy, possess and enjoy exclusively the said premises hereby granted with appurtenances, (*c*) the said premises are free from any encumbrances, charges, rights, trusts and (*d*) the VENDOR shall from time to time execute or cause to be executed and do or cause to be done all reasonable acts, things, deeds, conveyances for better and further and even more perfectly granting the said premises unto and to the use of the purchaser as the purchaser shall reasonably require.

3. The PURCHASER doth hereby covenant with the VENDOR and other co-owners of the other flats or units in the said multi-storeyed building that, (*a*) the PURCHASER shall abide by the bye-laws of any Association of Apartment Owners of owners of flats or units and shall bear and pay his proportionate share in the common expenses required of him to be paid as his share of expenses as required by the Association of Apartment Owners, (*b*) shall use the said flat for residential purpose only, (*c*) the PURCHASER shall not do any work or bring any heavy material in the flat which would jeopardise the soundness or safety of the property or reduce the value thereof or impair any easement or add any material, tiles or structure or execute or alter any wall or put up any cellar without the unanimous consent of all other apartment-owners and the Association being first obtained.

4. The VENDOR hereby covenants with the PURCHASER that the VENDOR shall, unless prevented by fire or accident, from time to time and at all times hereafter at every reasonable request and at the cost of the PURCHASER produce or cause to be produced to the PURCHASER his Advocate or in any legal or other proceedings all or any deeds and writings mentioned in Schedule III hereunder for the purpose of showing the title to the said land and/or buildings and deliver to the PURCHASER attested copies or extracts of

the said documents, drawings and writings as the purchaser may require and in the meantime keep the said documents safe, unobliterated and uncancelled.

5. It is hereby further declared and agreed that in case the said Deeds and Writings to be produced or delivered by the VENDOR to any other person the VENDOR shall thereupon enter into a covenant with that person for production and furnishing copies of the said Deed and Writings by the said person to the PURCHASER as and when required as aforesaid.

IN WITNESS WHEREOF the parties herein have executed these presents on the day, month and year first above-written.

Schedule I

Schedule II

Schedule III

Signed, sealed and delivered by
Mr. ....
pursuant to Board Resolution of
..................of AB Ltd. the VENDOR
in the presence of:

1. .... Signature

2. ....

Signed and delivered by Mr. MN
the PURCHASER in the presence of:

1. .... Signature

2. ....

Signed and delivered by Mr. XY the
OWNER and CONFIRMING PARTY in the
presence of:

1. .... Signature

2. ....

Agreement for Sale of Flat by the Original Purchaser to Another

THIS AGREEMENT IS MADE on this 10th day of July 2000 BETWEEN Mr. AB of .... (hereinafter referred to as the VENDOR, which term shall include his successor, heirs, administrators, executors and assigns) of the One Part and Mr. XY of ....(hereinafter referred to as the PURCHASER, which term shall include his successors, heirs, administrators, executors and assigns) of the Other Part.

WHEREAS by an Agreement for sale between the VENDOR and MN Ltd. of .... the VENDOR has agreed to purchase the flat No. .... on the first floor in premises No. .... and the said agreement has been duly registered.

AND WHEREAS the VENDOR has paid the consideration money and/or made arrangements for payment thereof to the said owner of the said building.

AND WHEREAS the VENDOR is no more interested in occupying the flat and is intending to sell his right, title and interest therein.

AND WHEREAS the PURCHASER has approached the VENDOr for purchasing the said flat No. .... on the first floor at premises No. .... at a price of Rs. 6 lakhs plus interest at 20% per annum on the respective instalments paid by VENDOR to the said MN Ltd.

AND WHEREAS the VENDOR has agreed to sell his right, title and interest in the said flat No. .... on the first floor of premises No. .... in the said multi-storeyed building to be constructed and/or under construction.

AND WHEREAS the PURCHASER has agreed to purchase the said flat No. .... on the first floor of the said premises on the same terms and conditions on which the VENDOR agreed to purchase the said flat from MN Ltd.

AND WHEREAS the MN Ltd. has given its consent to transfer of the said agreement and the said flat by the VENDOR to the PURCHASER.

NOW THESE PRESENTS WITNESSETH and the parties agree as follows:

1. The VENDOR agrees to assign to the PURCHASER and the PURCHASER agrees to take over all the rights and benefits of the VENDOR to acquire by purchase the said flat No. ...... on the first floor in the multi-storeyed building under construction in premises No. .... and particulars thereof contained in the agreement BETWEEN the said MN Ltd. and the VENDOR, a copy whereof has been made available to the PURCHASER and the substance whereof are given in Schedule I hereunder.

2. In consideration of the VENDOR having agreed to assign his right title and interest in the said agreement with MN Ltd., the PURCHASER has agreed to pay a consolidated sum of Rs. 7,50,000 to the VENDOR on the execution of this agreement, the receipt whereof the VENDOR doth hereby admit.

3. The VENDOR hereby agrees, declares and covenants that all his rights, title, interest and benefits in the said agreement with the MN Ltd. belonging to him and available to the VENDOR will hereafter belong and be available to

the PURCHASER as if the said agreement was entered into by and between said MN Ltd. and the PURCHASER herein in place of VENDOR and MN Ltd.

4. The VENDOR does not and will not claim any right, title or interest in the said agreement between VENDOR and MN Ltd. in the said flat No. .... on the first floor of the multi-storeyed building under construction at No. ....

5. The PURCHASER has inspected all agreements, declarations, permissions, documents and has satisfied himself about the right, title and interest of the VENDOR and compliance of all statutory provisions by the VENDOR and the MN Ltd. in relation to the said flat.

6. The PURCHASER agrees and undertakes to take over and be bound by all terms and conditions of the said agreement between the VENDOR and MN Ltd. and be bound by all the obligations undertaken or agreed to by the vendor in the said agreement including the obligations to join and become a member of the proposed Association of Apartment-owners that will be formed by or on behalf of the purchaser in the said building and to sign all forms and papers in connection therewith.

7. The VENDOR and PURCHASER agree that each one of them would execute all necessary deeds and documents and do all such acts and things which would be necessary for effective possession and enjoyment of the said flat by PURCHASER and for protecting the right, title and interest of the PURCHASER in the said flat.

IN WITNESS whereof the parties hereto do execute these presents on the day, month and year first above-written.

Schedule I

Schedule II

Signed and delivered by Mr. AB
in the presence of:
1. .... Signature
2. ....

Signed and delivered by Mr. XY
in the presence of:
1. .... Signature
2. ....

Signed, sealed and delivered by
Mr. .... pursuant of Board
Resolution of 8th July 2000 of MN Ltd.
as confirming party in the presence of: Signature

Agreement for Sale of Flat

THIS AGREEMENT FOR SALE made this the 5th day of September 2000 BETWEEN (1) Sri AB son of Sri CD, by faith Hindu, by Occupation Business, residing at present at .... hereinafter referred to as the LAND OWNER (which expression shall unless excluded by or repugnant to the context be deemed to mean and include his heirs, executors administrators, representatives and legal assigns) of the First Part and MN a partnership firm represented by its partners and carrying on business as Builders, Promoters, Developers and Constructors having its office at .... hereinafter referred to as the DEVELOPER (which term or expression shall unless excluded by or repugnant to the context be deemed to mean its successors and assigns) of the Second Part and Sri PQ son of Sri XY residing at .... by occupation Service (hereinafter referred to as the PURCHASER (which expression shall unless excluded by or repugnant to the context shall mean and include his heirs, executors, administrators, legal representatives and/or nominees) of the Third Part.

WHEREAS the party hereto of the First Part herein is the absolute Owner and is seized and possessed of and/or otherwise well and sufficiently entitled to ALL THAT piece and parcel of land measuring an area of 5 (five) cottahs be the same a little more or less being the Development Scheme of the Government of West Bengal popularly known as .... being Scheme plot No. ...., Block ...., ..., comprised in a portion of C.S. plot No. .... within J.L. No. ...., Mouza ...., Police Station .... at present ...., Municipal Holding No. ......, Ward No. ...., within the limit of .... known as premises No. .... by virtue of a Registered Deed of Sale dated .... and registered with the Registrar of Assurances, Calcutta recorded in Book No. 1, being Nos. 10 for the year 1996.

AND WHEREAS the LAND OWNER has entered into an agreement on .... with the DEVELOPER/Second Party for construction of residential flats on terms and conditions mentioned therein.

AND WHEREAS by virtue of the said Deed of Agreement the said LAND OWNER First Party has delivered peaceful vacant possession of the said property to the DEVELOPER/Second Party for the purpose of construction of multi-storeyed building at the cost of the DEVELOPER/Second Party comprising of residential apartments on the said plot of land for selling out ownership flats/apartments to the intending purchaser for valuable consideration.

AND WHEREAS by virtue of the said Deed of Agreement executed on .... the LAND OWNER/First Party agreed to sign any document if required for conveying the flat to the intending PURCHASER with proportionate share of land at the cost of the intending PURCHASER Third Party and the said LAND OWNER also declares that he shall have no objection to the matter of realisation of advance amount from the intending PURCHASER of the plot by the DEVELOPER.

AND WHEREAS by virtue of the said Deed of Agreement dated .... the LAND OWNER agreed to sign any document if required by conveying the flat to the intending purchaser at his cost and the said LAND OWNER/VENDOR also declares that he shall have no objection in the matter of realisation of advance amount from the intending purchaser/s of the plots.

AND WHEREAS by virtue of the said agreement dated .... the LAND OWNER/VENDOR agreed not to receive any other consideration from the DEVELOPER or from the PURCHASER except which were provided in the said agreement dated .... executed between the said VENDOR/LAND OWNER and the DEVELOPER.

NOW THIS AGREEMENT WITNESSETH and it is hereby agreed by and between the parties hereto as follows:

1. The DEVELOPER/Second Party will construct and complete the multi-storeyed building as per sanctioned plan No. .... dated .... and shall plan, design, supervise and construct as per Indian Standard Code and the Development Scheme of the Government of West Bengal popularly known as ...., being Scheme plot No. .... Block ...., ..., comprised in a portion of C.S. plot No. .... within the Limit of .... as per specification mentioned hereunder.

2. The VENDOR and the DEVELOPER have jointly represented before the PURCHASER that the said premises is free from all encumbrances and *lis pendens.*

3. 'Covered Area' shall according to the context mean the plinth area of the said unit or all units in the building including bath rooms and balcony or terrace and also the thickness of the boundary walls, internal walls and pillars columns PROVIDED THAT IF ANY WALL BE COMMON BETWEEN two units then $1/2$ of the area under such wall shall be included in each unit and also including a proportionate share of the area of the common portion of the building and/or as per the analysis given by the architect of the DEVELOPER.

4. The DEVELOPER shall arrange for separate electric meter for the owner of the respective flat from the CESC and also for water connection and drainage connection from the .... and the respective flat owner shall be liable to pay a sum of Rs. 10,000 (Rupees Ten Thousand only) to the developer for the same PROVIDED THAT if all the

purchasers want Generator for supply of electricity the DEVELOPER will arrange the same and the purchasers will be liable to pay the cost of Generator and the charges for running thereof.

5. The Land: All that piece or parcel of land measuring 5 (five) cottahs be the same a little more or less within the Development Scheme of the Government of West Bengal popularly known as .... being Scheme plot No. ...., comprised in a portion of C.S. plot No. .... within J.L. No. ......, Mouza .... Police Station .... at present ...., Municipal, Holding No. ...., Ward No. .... within the limit of .... and known as .... which is butted and bounded as follows:

On the North by 20 ft. wide road.

On the South by Scheme plot No. ......, owned by Mr. ....

On the East by Scheme plot No. ......, owned by Sri ....

On the West by Scheme plot No. ......, owned by Sri ....

6. Common Portions Common to the Owners of the Flats

(*a*) The land comprised in the premises but excluding those reserved for parking of car/cars marked by the DEVELOPER exclusively to any Unit or the PURCHASER and those mentioned herein.

(*b*) Only general light point/points of the common portions shall be provided.

(*c*) Drains, sewers main water connections from the South Dum Dum Municipality the underground reservoir main water delivery pipe line from underground reservoir to overhead water tanks lift and distribution pipe-line to kitchen and toilets of different units/and or to the common portions.

(*d*) Last roof for use only, staircases and landings of different units and to the common portions.

(*e*) Water pumps and motors, Electrical wiring and Main Switch-box, Main electrical distribution-board, Sub-distribution boards, Electrical wirings, Main electrical meter, and other installations and fittings.

(*f*) Water and sewage evacuation pipes from the units to the main drains and sewers common to the buildings, water reservoir pipe lines septic lines, septic tank overhead tank etc.

(*g*) Boundary wall, Main gates, Drive ways are common to the said building including the roof of the said building.

7. Declarations of the said unit and/or Flat No. .... intended to be purchased by the PURCHASER:

ALL THAT the said Unit being the Flat No. .... on first floor containing a total super-built-up area of .... sqft. (approx.) inclusive of common area facilities in the proposed building.

APARTMENT .... premises No. .... together with the proportionate share in the land on which the said entire building has been constructed.

8. Type of Construction and Specification of Building:

Foundation	:	Stone column/isolated footings with the beams connecting the column (Specially designed to suit the soil condition).
Structure	:	RCC-framed structure.
Roof	:	RCC Slab with proper water proofing treatment.
Walls	:	1st class burnt bricks in suitable cement sand mortar plastered.
Wall Finish	:	Plaster of paris on internal walls and super snowcem on outer walls.
Floors	:	Drawing/Dining/Bed Room/Balcony with Mosaic Tiles/ Kitchen/Toilets with Marble Finish.
Door	:	One side teak factory made Flush Door with Eye piece Mortice Lock and Stopper, Main Entrance door will be Fire Resistant.
Window	:	Wooden and MS Grills with Glass.
Sanitary	:	Bath Room walls upto 5' Marble Tiles coloured/ White ceramic ware fittings C.P./ Royal Tap shower/ Towel Rod/Mirror.
Kitchen	:	Marble sink and Forking Top in Marble and wall of working Top upto 2' Granite.
Electricals	:	Concealed wiring and points in all Rooms, Kitchen, toilets, Balcony using standard quality conductors, plug points in all Rooms, Kitchen, Toilets, etc. TV and Telephone outlet in living Room.
Water	:	Deep Bore well with O.G. Tank for 24 Hours water Supply.
Lift	:	24 hours Automatic Lift service.
Security	:	Separate Security Control Room, Pump Room.
Entertainment	:	Dish Antenna at extra cost.
Fire Protection	:	Fire extinguishing equipment at common place, Lightening Arrestor at suitable place.

Parking extras : Car-parking space available at extra cost.

Extras : To be notified and separately paid for by purchaser.

9. Consideration money for the proportionate undivided share/interest in the said land cost of construction of the said Unit.

A. Consideration for transfer of proportionate undivided $^1/_{10}$th Owner's share in the land	...	Rs.	5,00,000
B. Consideration for construction and cost of the said Unit and the common portions proportionately shall be	...	Rs.	6,00,000
	...	Rs.	11,00,000

The Third Party/PURCHASER agrees to purchase the flat being No. 2 on the 1st floor of the said building at a total price of Rs. 11,00,000 (Rupees Eleven Lakhs only). The said flat intended for sale has not yet been booked earlier to any person. The mode of payment by the purchaser to the DEVELOPER/Second Party will be in the following manner:

(*i*) At the time of booking (*ii*) First Instalment (*iii*) Second Instalment (*iv*) Third instalment	...	Rs.	4,50,000
(*v*) Before possession within 31st December 1999	...	Rs.	6,50,000

Before date of possession the PURCHASER shall pay all amounts becoming due to the DEVELOPER.

10. The DEVELOPER/Second Party shall complete the construction of the building in all respects and make ready for possession of the said apartment to the PURCHASER/Third Party on or before 5th December 1999 subject to compliance of terms and conditions written hereunder.

11. In case of default, in the matter of payment of advance money and/ or instalment as stated in clause 9 of this Agreement by the PURCHASER/ Third Party to the DEVELOPER/Second Party, the purchaser/Third Party shall be liable by way of compensation to pay interest at the rate of 2% per annum on the outstanding amount after 15 days on failing to pay the instalment/advance money to be paid to DEVELOPER/Second Party from the date of demand notice in addition to the payments as written in clause 9 hereinabove.

12. In the event the PURCHASER/Third Party defaults in the matter of payment of the instalments in accordance with clause 9 of this Agreement for more than 30 (thirty) days from the date of demand notice then the

DEVELOPER/Second Party will be at liberty to forfeit the said right to the flat and also to sell out the said flat No. 2 to anybody at its sweet will and the repayment will be as per clause No. 13 of this agreement.

13. The PURCHASER/Third Party may get refund of the amount already paid on account of the his booking of the said flat subject to intimation in writing to the DEVELOPER/Second Party who shall return in such case 75% of the total amount deposited subject to minimum deduction of Rs. 50,000 and the said reduced amount will be refunded within six months from the date of the intimation and/or cancellation of this agreement.

14. The PURCHASER/Third Party shall not sell, transfer and/or assign any of his right, title or interest with respect to the said flat, particularly stated in clause 7 of this Agreement to anybody before taking delivery of possession of the said flat without written consent of the Developer/Second Party.

15. The DEVELOPER/Second Party shall not be liable for any loss caused by acts of God or other unforeseen circumstances making it impossible for the Developer to construct the said building and to deliver possession of the said flat in the said building to the PURCHASER/Third Party on or before the stipulated date. Save and except the aforesaid reasons, the DEVELOPER/Second Party shall be liable to deliver possession of the said flat in the said building to the PURCHASER/Third Party on or before the said stipulated date, otherwise the DEVELOPER/Second Party shall be liable to pay the damages at the rate of Rs. 4,500 per month to the PURCHASER/Third Party till the delivery of the said flat in the building.

16. The PURCHASER/Third Party shall become the absolute owner in respect of the said flat after mutation of the said flat and/or after registration of the said deed of conveyance. The PURCHASER/Third Party shall be bound to make registration of his flat.

17. The DEVELOPER shall arrange for execution and registration of the Deed of Conveyance by the Registered Power of Attorney of the LAND OWNER in respect of the said flat in favour of the PURCHASER but the purchaser agrees to bear and/or pay the cost of registration of Deed of Conveyance including the stamp duty and all charges separately.

18. In the event the DEVELOPER/Second Party fails or neglects to complete the sale as aforesaid or otherwise to carry out any one or more of the obligations on its part as provided in this Agreement or otherwise required by law the PURCHASER/Third Party shall be at liberty to enforce specific performance of this Agreement by institution of legal proceedings or at his option sue the DEVELOPER/Second Party for recovery of the advance amount unless the DEVELOPER affected under clause 16 of this agreement.

19. The PURCHASER/Third Party agrees to bear all the common expenses with other flat-owners as will be settled among themselves.

20. General specification as agreed by and between the parties is written as hereinabove mentioned.

IN WITNESS WHEREOF the party of the First Part being the OWNER, the party of the Second Part, being the DEVELOPER, and the party of the Third Part being the PURCHASER hereto have set and subscribed their respective hands on the day, month and year first above-written.

Signed, sealed and delivered by
the LAND OWNER at Calcutta in the
presence of:

Signed, sealed and delivered by
the DEVELOPER at Calcutta in the
presence of:

Signed, sealed and delivered by
the PURCHASER at Calcutta in the
presence of:

Sale to a Co-operative Society

THIS INDENTURE IS MADE at .... this .... day of .... in the year two thousand and .... BETWEEN .... of .... inhabitant hereinafter called the VENDOR (which expression shall mean and include his heirs, executors and administrators) of the One Part AND .... and .... all inhabitants of .... hereinafter referred to as the CONFIRMING PARTIES of the Second Part AND THE .... CO-OPERATIVE HOUSING SOCIETY LIMITED, a Co-operative Society registered under the Maharashtra Co-operative Societies Act 1960, under No. Bom/HSG .... of 1966 having its registered office at Plot No. .... Road, ... hereinafter called the PURCHASERS (which expression shall, unless repugnant to the context or meaning thereof, include its successors and assigns) of the Third Part whereas by a Deed of Conveyance dated the ....day of .... 20........... made and entered into BETWEEN the VENDOR and Shri .... and such of the CONFIRMING PARTIES as mentioned hereunder .... on the .... 20......... all that vacant piece or parcel of land being at .... in the registration sub-district of .... and more particularly described in the Schedule hereunder written was conveyed unto the VENDOR AND WHEREAS by an agreement dated the .... day of .... 20......... made and entered into between the VENDOR and MESSRS .... BUILDERS, a partnership firm having its office at No. .... Road, ... and the said firm agreed to purchase the said plot of land measuring about .... square yards bearing plot .... situate at .... Road, ... for a consideration of Rs. .... AND WHEREAS by the said agreement it was confirmed that the entire consideration of Rs. .... was paid by the said firm to the VENDOR and the VENDOR has delivered possession of the said plot of land to the said firm who were allowed to construct a building thereon as per the plans passed and sanctioned by the .... municipality and the CONFIRMING PARTIES were allowed by the VENDOR to sell the various flats in the said building on ownership basis as proposed pending transfer of the said property to the nominee of the said firm AND WHEREAS after entering into the said agreement dated the .... day of .... 20........... and obtaining possession of the said plot of land, the said firm commenced constructing a building thereon consisting of several flats and the CONFIRMING PARTY entered into agreements with diverse persons in respect of such flats in such building AND WHEREAS the construction of the aforesaid building was completed by the said firm and the said building is now known as "......................." (the said land together with the building standing thereon being more particularly described in the Schedule hereunder written) AND WHEREAS on the aforesaid building being constructed the said firm gave to the holders of the respective flats in the said building possession of the respective flats as per agreements entered into between the said firm and the individual flat-holders and such holders accepted possession thereof in terms of cl. (6) of their respective agreements AND WHEREAS the holders of all the flats in the said building known as ".............." formed themselves into a Co-operative Housing Society, viz. the PURCHASERS herein AND WHEREAS the CONFIRMING PARTIES are the present partners of the said agreements which the said firm had entered into with the holders of diverse flats, *inter alia,* provided that the aforesaid building which the said firm was then constructing would consist of a ground and .... upper floors initially and that if and when the Municipal Corporation for .... allowed the erection of a further floor on such building the CONFIRMING PARTIES would be entitled to do so and the CONFIRMING PARTIES reserved unto themselves the right to dispose of the flats on such additional floor, *viz.* the .... floor, or such building if and when erected and that the said land and the said building consisting of a ground floor and .... upper floors would be transferred to such Co-operative Housing Society and that such conveyance would contain a condition reserving to the said firm the rights in respect of the said .... floor as aforesaid AND WHEREAS the PURCHASERS being the Co-operative Housing Society formed by the holders of all the flats of the aforesaid building consisting of a ground floor and .... upper floors known as "................." and the said land and building being already in possession of the PURCHASERS and the full purchase price in respect of the said flats and the said garages in the said building (aggregating to Rs. ....) having been paid to the said firm, the PURCHASERS requested the CONFIRMING PARTIES to procure a Deed of Conveyance from the VENDOR in favour of the PURCHASERS reserving unto the CONFIRMING PARTIES the right in respect of the floor as aforesaid which the VENDOR and the CONFIRMING PARTIES have agreed to do in the manner hereinafter appearing NOW THIS INDENTURE WITNESSETH that in pursuance of the said agreement and in consideration aforesaid the VENDOR doeth hereby grant, convey and assure and the CONFIRMING PARTIES do and each of them does hereby confirm unto the PURCHASERS all that piece or parcel of land with the messuages, tenements and the building consisting of a ground floor and ...... upper floors known as "..................." standing thereon situate lying and being at .... Road, in the .... Taluka of the .... District containing by admeasurement about .... square yards and more particularly described in the Schedule hereunder written TOGETHER WITH all and singular the said building known as "..............." consisting of one ground floor and .... upper floors (which said land, hereditaments and premises are hereinafter referred to for brevity's sake as "the said premises"), courts, yards, areas, ways, compounds, paths, passages, waters, watercourses, sewers, ditches, drains, trees, plants, lights, liberties, easements, profits, privileges, advantages, rights, members and appurtenances whatsoever to the said premises belonging or any wise appertaining to or with the same or any part thereof now or at any time heretofore usually held, used, occupied or enjoyed or reputed or known as part or member thereof or be appertaining thereto and also, TOGETHER WITH ALL the deeds, documents writings, vouchers, and other evidence of title relating to the said premises or any part thereof and ALL the estate, right, interest, use, inheritance, property, possession, benefits, claim and demand whatsoever both at law and equity of the VENDOR into and out of or upon the said premises or any part thereof TO HAVE HOLD AND POSSESS the said premises and every part thereof described in the Schedule hereunder written and all and singular and other the premises hereby granted, conveyed and assured or intended so to be with their and other their rights members and appurtenances unto and of the use and benefit of the PURCHASERS for ever SUBJECT nevertheless to the payment by the PURCHASERS of all rents, taxes, assessments, rates, dues and duties now chargeable upon the same or which may hereafter become payable in respect thereof to the Government or the Municipality AND ALSO subject and reserving the right in favour of the CONFIRMING PARTIES to erect and put up one further floor (*i.e.*, the .... floor) on the said building known as "................." if and when the Municipal Corporation for .... allows such erection AND ALSO reserving unto the confirming parties the right to dispose of the flats of such additional floor (*viz.*, the ....floor) if and when erected as also the right of approach to such .... floor with the right to lay and connect drains, water and other pipes, electric and other cables, wires and connections and conveniences and all other access through or over the remaining part of such building and land in connection with such .... floor to be erected by the CONFIRMING PARTIES, and the VENDOR doth hereby covenant with the purchasers that notwithstanding any act, deed, matter or things whatsoever by him the VENDOR or any person lawfully or equitably claiming by, from, through, under or in trust for him made, done, committed or omitted or knowingly suffered to the contrary, he the vendor now hath in himself good right, full power and absolute authority to grant, convey and assure the said premises hereby conveyed and assured and intended so to be unto and to the use of the PURCHASERS in the manner aforesaid AND it shall be lawful for the purchasers from time to time and at all times hereafter peaceably and quietly to enter upon, possess and enjoy the said premises described in the Schedule hereunder written and to receive all rents, issues and profits thereof and of every part thereof to and for their own use and benefit without any suit, lawful eviction, interruption, claim and demand whatsoever for or by him the VENDOR or by any person or persons lawfully or equitably claiming or to claim by under or in trust for him and that free and clear and freely and clearly and absolutely acquitted, exonerated and for ever discharged or otherwise by the VENDOR well and sufficiently saved, defended and kept harmless and indemnified of, from and against all former and other estates, titles, charge and encumbrances whatsoever, had, made, executed, occasioned or suffered by the VENDOR or any other person or persons lawfully or equitably claiming or to claim by, from, under or in trust for him AND further that He the VENDOR and all persons having or lawfully or equitably claiming any estate or interest whatsoever in the said premises or any of them or any part thereof from, under or in trust for the VENDOR shall and will from time to time and at all times hereafter at the request and cost of the PURCHASERS do and execute or cause to be done and executed all such further and other lawful reasonable acts, deeds, things and assurances in the said land, hereditaments and premises whatsoever for the better and more perfectly assuring the said premises described in the Schedule hereunder written and every part thereof unto and to the PURCHASERS in the manner aforesaid as by the PURCHASERS shall be reasonably required AND the PURCHASERS do hereby covenant with the VENDOR and the CONFIRMING PARTIES that they the PURCHASERS shall and will at all times hereafter allow the CONFIRMING PARTIES to erect one further floor, *viz.*, the .... floor on the said building known as "............" if and when the Municipal Corporation of .... allows such erection and the confirming parties shall have the right to dispose of the flats on the .... floor if and when erected and the stamp duty and registration charges are to be borne by the Purchasers' Society.

IN WITNESS WHEREOF the VENDOR and the CONFIRMING PARTIES hereto have set their respective hands and seals and the PURCHASERS have affixed its Common Seal to the original and duplicate thereof the day and the year first hereinafter written.

The Schedule above referred to

Signed, sealed and delivered by
the within-named VENDOR in the
presence of:

Signed, sealed and delivered by the confirming parties Shri .... Shri .... in the Shri .... and Shri .... in the presence of:

The common seal of Co-operative Housing Society Limited has been hereunto affixed .... pursuant to the Resolution of its Managing Committee .... bearing date the .... day of .... 20... in the presence of Shri .... the Chairman of the said Society, Mr. ...., a member of the Managing Committee of the said Society and Mr. .... the Secretary of the said Society who have each signed these presents in the presence of:

RECEIVED of and from the within-named purchasers herein the within-named consideration money to be paid by them to me sum of Rs. .... (Rupees .... only) being the consideration money by cheque No. .... of X Bank Ltd.

WITNESSES: I say received.

Sale to a Co-operative Society

THIS INDENTURE IS MADE this .... day of .... BETWEEN .... son of .... etc., or a partnership firm duly registered under the Indian Partnership Act having its registered office at No. .... hereinafter referred to as the VENDOR (which expression where the subject or context allows or admits of shall mean and include his heirs, executors and administrators or successor or successors in business as the case may be) of the One Part AND .... son of etc., ... and .... son of etc., ... hereinafter referred to as the CONFIRMING PARTIES of the Second Part AND THE ....CO-OPERATIVE HOUSING SOCIETY LIMITED, a Co-operative Society registered under the Co-operative Societies Act, ... having its registered office at No. .... Road, ..., hereinafter called the PURCHASERS (which expression shall, unless repugnant to the context or meaning thereof, include its successors and assigns) of the Third Part WHEREAS by a deed of conveyance dated the .... day of 20 .... made between the VENDOR described therein as PURCHASER and Shri .... (described therein as VENDOR) and registered with the Sub-Registrar of Assurances of .... in Book .... pages to .... being No. .... for .... it was witnessed that the vacant piece or parcel of land or ground measuring .... situate, lying and being at .... in the district of .... and more particularly described in the Schedule hereunder written was granted, conveyed, sold, transferred, assigned and assured unto the VENDOR absolutely and for ever AND WHEREAS by an agreement dated the .... day of .... 20...... made between the VENDOR and .... BUILDERS, a Partnership firm having its office at No. .... Road, ... the said firm agreed to build upon and construct a multi-storeyed building on the said land upon terms thereunder contained. AND WHEREAS the said firm commenced with and constructed a building thereon consisting of several flats and the CONFIRMING PARTIES have entered into agreements with the VENDOR for purchase in respect of such flats in such building AND WHEREAS the construction of the aforesaid building having been completed by the said firm the VENDOR has delivered possession of the respective flats in the said building to the respective purchasers as per agreements entered into with them. AND WHEREAS the individual flat-holders and such PURCHASERS have accepted the said flats and possession thereof in terms of clause (.................) of their respective agreement AND WHEREAS the holders of the flats in the said building known as "................." formed themselves into a Co-operative Housing Society.

NOW THIS INDENTURE WITNESSETH that in pursuance of the said agreement and for the consideration aforesaid, the vendor do hereby grant, convey, transfer, sell and assure and the confirming parties do and each of them join with the VENDOR in effecting such transfer and sale and do hereby confirm unto the PURCHASERS the said multi-storeyed building consisting of ground floor and .... upper floors known as ".............." standing thereon situate lying being at .... Road, in the .... District of .... together with the land thereunder containing by measurement .... more or less and more particularly mentioned and described in the Schedule hereunder written TOGETHER WITH the hereditaments and premises are hereinafter referred to for brevity's sake as ("the said premises"), courts, yards, areas, ways, compounds, paths, passages, waters, watercourses, sewers, ditches, drains, trees, plants, lights, liberties, easements, profits, privileges, advantages, rights, members and appurtenances whatsoever to the said premises belonging or any wise appertaining to or with same or any part thereof now or at any time heretofore usually held, used, occupied or enjoyed or reputed or known as part or member thereof or be enjoyed or reputed or known as part of member thereof or be appertaining thereto and also TOGETHER WITH ALL the deeds, documents, writings, vouchers, and other evidence of title relating to the said premises or any part thereof and ALL the estate, right, interest, use, inheritance, property, possession, benefits, claim and demand whatsoever both at law and equity of the VENDOR and CONFIRMING PARTIES into and out of or upon the said premises or any part thereof TO HAVE AND TO HOLD, POSSESS AND ENJOY the said premises described in the Schedule hereunder written and all and singular and other the premises hereby granted, conveyed and assured or intended so to be with their and other their rights, members and appurtenances unto and to the use and benefit of the PURCHASERS for ever SUBJECT nevertheless to the payment by the PURCHASERS of all rents, taxes, assessments, rates, dues and duties now chargeable upon the same or which may hereafter become payable in respect thereof to the Government or the Municipality and that the VENDOR doth hereby covenant with the PURCHASERS that notwithstanding any act, deed, matter or thing whatsoever by him the VENDOR or any person lawfully or equitably claiming by, from, through, under or in trust for him made, done, committed or omitted of knowingly suffered to the contrary the VENDOR now has in himself good right, full power and absolute authority to grant, convey and assure the said premises hereby conveyed and assure and intended so to be unto and to the use of the PURCHASERS in the manner aforesaid AND it shall be lawful for the PURCHASERS from time to time and at all times hereafter peaceably and quietly to enter upon, possess and enjoy the said premises and every part thereof described in the Schedule hereunder written and to receive all rents, issues and profits thereof and of every part thereof to and for their own use and benefit without any suit, lawful eviction, interruption, claim and demand whatsoever for or by him the VENDOR or by any person or persons lawfully or equitably claiming or to claim by, under or in trust for him and that free and clear and freely and clearly and absolutely acquitted, exonerated and for ever discharged or otherwise by the VENDOR well and sufficiently saved defended and kept harmless and indemnified of, from and against all former and other estates, titles, charge and encumbrances whatsoever, had, made, executed, occasioned or suffered by the VENDOR and the CONFIRMING PARTIES or any other person or persons lawfully or equitably claiming or to claim by, from, under or in trust for him or them AND further that the VENDOR and the confirming parties and all persons having or lawfully or equitably claiming any estate or interest whatsoever in the said premises or any of them or any part thereof from under or in trust for the VENDOR and/or the CONFIRMING PARTIES shall and will from time to time and at all times hereafter at the request and cost of the purchasers do and execute and perform or cause to be done and executed all such further and other lawful reasonable acts, deeds, things and assurances in respect of the said land, hereditaments and premises whatsoever for the better and more perfectly assuring the said premises described in the Schedule hereunder written and every part thereof unto and to the PURCHASERS in the manner aforesaid as by the PURCHASERS shall be reasonably required.

IN WITNESS WHEREOF the VENDOR and the CONFIRMING PARTIES hereto have set their respective hands and seals and the PURCHASERS have affixed its Common Seal to the original and duplicate thereof the day and the year first hereinabove written.

The Schedule above referred to

Signed, Sealed and Delivered by the within-named VENDOR .... in the presence of:

Signed, Sealed and Delivered by the CONFIRMING PARTIES Shri .... Shri .... in the ....Shri .... and Shri .... in the presence of:

THE COMMON SEAL .... OF ....CO-OPERATIVE HOUSING SOCIETY LIMITED has been hereunto affixed .... pursuant to the resolution of its Managing Committee bearing date .... the .... day of .... 20...... in the presence of Shri .... the Chairman of the said Society, Mr. ...., a member of the Managing Committee of the said Society and Mr. ...., the secretary of the said Society who have each signed these presents in the presence of:

RECEIVED OF and from the within-named PURCHASERS herein the sum of Rs. .... (Rupees .... only) being the within-named consideration money by cheque No. ...... on X Bank Ltd.

WITNESSES: VENDOR

Deed of Assignment of Ownership Flat

THIS DEED OF ASSIGNMENT made this .... day of .... 20........ BETWEEN Shri .... son of .... by faith .... by occupation .... hereinafter referred to as the ASSIGNOR (which expression shall mean and include his heirs, executors and administrators) of the one part

AND Shri .... son of .... by faith .... by occupation .... hereinafter referred to as the ASSIGNEE (which expression shall mean and include his heirs, executors, administrators and assigns) of the other part.

WHEREAS the ASSIGNOR has acquired by purchase Flat No. .... on the building known as .... Plot No. ...., ... Road, ... under an Agreement dated the day of .... 20........... between himself as Party of the Second Part and .... of the First Part after paying Rs. .... as purchase price and having deposited certain sums of money as mentioned therein.

AND WHEREAS the ASSIGNEE has deposited a sum of Rs. .... (Rupees .... thousand only) with the ASSIGNOR for the purchase of the said Flat No. .... and the ASSIGNOR had delivered vacant possession of the said Flat No. .... to the ASSIGNEE in pursuance of an Agreement of Sale dated .... day of ....20......... made between the parties thereto.

AND WHEREAS the assignor has agreed to assign all his right, interest, title and benefits under the said agreement dated the .... day of ....20......... to the ASSIGNEE free from all encumbrances.

NOW THIS INDENTURE WITNESSETH that in pursuance of the said Agreement and in consideration of the sum of Rs. .... (Rupees .... thousand only) paid by the ASSIGNEE to the ASSIGNOR (the receipt whereof the ASSIGNOR doeth hereby admit, acknowledge and confirm and for ever discharge, acquit and release the ASSIGNEE of the same and every part thereof) the ASSIGNOR doeth hereby grant, convey, sell, assign and transfer all his estate, right, interest, title in and all benefits of the flat in terms of the said Agreement dated the .... day of .... 20 .... mentioned hereinabove including the deposits standing to the credit of the ASSIGNOR with the said Shri .... and others being the party of the First Part referred to in the Agreement dated the .... day of ....20............ TO HAVE AND TO HOLD the same unto and to the use of the ASSIGNEE absolutely and enjoy all benefits thereof but subject to the conditions on which the ASSIGNOR held the same under the Agreement dated .... day of .... 20............ and the ASSIGNEE doth hereby agree to take the said flat subject to such conditions contained therein AND the ASSIGNOR doeth hereby covenant, with and agree to indemnify and keep indemnified the ASSIGNEE his estate, heirs, executors, administrators and representative against all loss and damage occasioned as a result of any defect in title or want of title to the said flat or for any reason the said flat is not transferred in the name of the ASSIGNEE or in the event the ASSIGNEE is not made a member of the proposed Co-operative Housing Society of the said building known as "........." or refused membership of the said proposed Co-operative Housing Society for any reason whatsoever or the ASSIGNEE is dispossessed of the said flat by said

Shri .... and others being the party of the First Part referred to in the said Agreement dated the .... day of .... 20...... as a result thereof and the ASSIGNOR further agrees and covenants with the ASSIGNEE to do, execute any further or other document or documents and/or deeds and to do all acts, things and deeds as may be necessary to complete and make perfect the title of the ASSIGNEE in respect of the said flat.

Schedule above referred to description of the flat

IN WITNESS WHEREOF the parties hereto have set and subscribed their respective hands and seals the day, month and year first hereinabove written.

Signed and delivered by the within-named ASSIGNOR Shri .... in the presence of:

Signed and delivered by the within-named ASSIGNEE Shri .... in the presence of:

RECEIVED of and from Shri .... the sum of Rs. .... (Rs. .... thousand only) being the balance of the purchase money of Flat No. .... floor, Plot No. ...., Road .... making the total purchase price of Rs. .... (Rupees .... thousand only) by cheques No. 4 and 5 on Y Bank Ltd.

WITNESS: ASSIGNOR

Notice of Purchase of Ownership Flat

To

Dear Sir

Re: Flat No. .... on .... floor in building as .... Plot No. .... Road, Mumbai.

Please note that I have this day purchased from .... all his/her right, title and interest whatsoever in respect of the aforesaid flat under an Agreement dated .... made between the said .... and myself *inter alia* on the terms and conditions contained in the Agreement dated .... made BETWEEN you and the said .... A copy of the Agreement dated .... is sent herewith. The said .... has also addressed to you by a separate letter dated .... in this connection.

I confirm that I have agreed and undertaken to abide by all the terms and conditions of the said Agreement dated .... between yourselves and the said .... in respect of the said flat and that I am and shall at all times hereafter remain liable to you all for arrears of the municipal taxes, water charge and lease money and other outgoings, if any, payable to you by my VENDOR aforesaid in respect of the said flat up to date and I shall punctually pay to you and/or the society that has been or is to be formed under the said Agreement dated .... all such outgoings and charges as above-mentioned that will hereafter be due and payable to you by me.

Kindly transfer the said flat to my name and oblige.

Thanking you

Yours faithfully

Deed of Sale of Office Space

THIS INDENTURE IS MADE this 10th day of September 2000 BETWEEN AB Co. P. Ltd. an existing company within the meaning of the Companies Act 1956 and having its Registered Office at .... in the town of .... hereinafter referred to as the VENDOR (which term shall unless contrary or repugnant to the context mean and include its successors and assigns) of the One Part and Mr. XY residing at .... hereinafter referred to as the PURCHASER (which term shall unless contrary or repugnant to the context mean and include his heirs, legal representatives, executors, administrators and assigns) of the Other Part.

WHEREAS by a conveyance dated 10th September 1999 registered in Book No. 1, Volume 2, Pages 10 to 20, being No. 5 for the year 1999 at the Office of the Registrar of Assurances, ... made between Mr. AB of .... the seller of the One Part and AB Co. P. Ltd. the PURCHASER of the Other Part the said AB Co. P. Ltd. purchased all that piece or parcel or plot of land containing by measurement an area of 10 cottahs be the same a little more or less together with 3-storeyed brick-built building, messuages, tenements, dwelling-house, heriditaments, premises, godowns, shops and other structures whatsoever lying at and being municipal premises No. .... in Holding No. .... Block No. .... in the town of Calcutta more fully described in the First Schedule hereunder written, hereinafter referred to as the said premises.

AND WHEREAS the said AB Co. P. Ltd. is seized and possessed of or otherwise well and sufficiently entitled to the said premises free from all encumbrances whatsoever.

AND WHEREAS the said AB Co. P. Ltd. having duly demolished all the buildings, godowns, shops and other structures whatsoever then lying erected thereon commenced the construction of a new multi-storeyed building comprising of several office rooms, shops, showrooms and other structures in or upon the land comprised in the said premises hereinafter called the said building.

AND WHEREAS the PURCHASER having inspected the original Title Deeds, documents and papers as also sanctioned Plan duly satisfied himself with regard to the right, title and interest of the VENDOR as also with regard to the areas, dimensions, measurements and other details of the said building.

AND WHEREAS by an agreement dated 5th June 2000 the purchaser herein agreed to acquire all that an office space bearing No. ...... on the 2nd floor of the said building more fully described in the Second Schedule hereunder written hereinafter referred to as the said office space for the consideration and on the terms and conditions therein contained.

AND WHEREAS the VENDOR from time to time entered into several similar agreements with various other persons or parties for transfer of the several other office spaces, shops, showrooms, parking spaces and other spaces of the said building.

AND WHEREAS in pursuance of the said Agreement dated 5th June 2000 the VENDOR herein duly completed the construction of the said building as also the said office space in accordance with the sanctioned plan.

AND WHEREAS in pursuance of the said Agreement as hereinbefore recited, the purchaser from time to time duly paid to VENDOR the entire agreed consideration money for acquiring the *said office space* as mentioned in the said Agreement whereupon the PURCHASER was duly put in vacant and peaceful possession of the *said office space*.

AND WHEREAS the PURCHASER herein having paid the entire agreed consideration money and also having been put in vacant and peaceful possession of the *said office space* as per the said Agreement as hereinbefore stated, has been occupying possessing using and enjoying the same.

AND WHEREAS the VENDOR being approached and requested by the PURCHASER, has agreed to complete the transfer by executing and registering these presents in respect of the *said office space* for the consideration and on the terms and conditions hereinafter appearing.

NOW THIS INDENTURE WITNESSETH that in pursuance of the said Agreement and in consideration of the said sum of Rs. 2,00,000 (Rupees two lakhs) only paid by the PURCHASER to the VENDOR as per the said Agreement the receipt whereof the VENDOR doth hereby admits and acknowledges and of and from the same and every part thereof acquits, releases, exonerates and discharges the PURCHASER as also the *said office space* intended to be transferred and/or assigned the VENDOR doth hereby grant transfer convey assign and assure unto and in favour of the PURCHASER ALL THAT the undivided half share of the office space No. 6 on the 2nd floor containing a super built up area of 500 sq. ft. be the same a little more or less situated lying at

.... more fully and particularly described in the Second Schedule hereunder written, hereinafter referred to as the *said office space* free from all encumbrances WHATSOEVER TOGETHER WITH all easements or quasi-easements or other stipulations or provisions for the beneficial use and enjoyment of the *said office space* as mentioned in the Third Schedule hereunder written TOGETHER WITH the right to use the common areas facilities and installations at the said Building, more fully described in the Fourth Schedule hereunder written, in common with the VENDORS as also the other owners and/or occupiers of other office spaces, shops, showrooms and other spaces of the said building for the purpose of uninterrupted ingress to and egress from the *said office space*.

OR HOWSOEVER OTHERWISE the *said office space* or any part thereof now are or is or heretofore were or was situated tenanted butted bounded called known numbered described as distinguished.

TO HAVE AND TO HOLD the *said office space* more fully described in the Second Schedule hereunder written together with all easements or quasi-easements or other stipulations or provisions for the beneficial use and enjoyment of the *said office space* as mentioned in the Third Schedule hereunder written AND TOGETHER WITH the right to use the common areas facilities and installations at the said building, more fully described in the Fourth Schedule hereunder written in common with the VENDOR and the owners and/or occupiers of the other spaces in the building excepting and reserving unto the vendor the easement or quasi-easement rights and privileges mentioned in the Fifth Schedule hereunder written AND FURTHER subject to the several restrictions mentioned in the Sixth Schedule hereunder written AND ALSO subject to the PURCHASER regularly and punctually paying proportionately the maintenance costs and other expenses as mentioned in the Seventh Schedule hereunder written.

THE VENDOR doth hereby covenant with the PURCHASER as follows:

(*a*) The interest in the *said office space* which the vendor does hereby profess to transfer subsists AND THAT the VENDOR has good rightful power and absolute authority to grant, convey, transfer, assign and assure the *said office space* in favour of the PURCHASER in the manner as aforesaid.

(*b*) It shall be lawful for the PURCHASER from time to time and at all times hereafter to enter into and upon and hold and enjoy the *said office space* AND ALSO to receive the rents issues and profits thereof without any interruption, disturbances, claims or demands from or by the VENDOR or any other person or persons claiming through or under or in trust for the VENDOR subject to the terms, conditions, covenants and restrictions as are herein contained.

(c) The *said office space* hereby transferred and conveyed are freed and discharged from and against all manner of encumbrances, charge, liens, trusts and attachments whatsoever save and except the terms, conditions, covenants and restrictions as are herein contained.

(d) The VENDOR shall from time to time and at all times hereafter at the requests and costs of the PURCHASER make do acknowledge execute and perfect all such further lawful and reasonable acts deeds matters and things whatsoever for further better and more perfectly assuring the *said office space* unto the PURCHASER in the manner aforesaid.

AND THE PURCHASER to the end and intent that his obligations covenants and restrictions herein contained, shall at all times hereafter run with the *said office space* hereby transferred, do hereby covenant with the VENDOR as follows:

(a) The PURCHASER so as to bind the owner and/or occupier for the time being of the said "office space" and so that this covenant shall be for the benefit of the said building as also the Owners and Occupiers of the different portions thereof hereby covenant with the vendor as also with the owners and/or occupiers of several other office spaces, showrooms and other spaces of the said building that the purchaser and all other persons deriving title under him will at all times hereafter observe the restrictions set forth in the Sixth Schedule hereunder written.

(b) The PURCHASER shall at all times hereafter regularly and punctually make payment of all Municipal taxes, Municipal surcharge, multi-storeyed building taxes and all other rates taxes, cess, imposition and outgoings whatsoever which may from time to time be imposed or become payable in respect of the *said office space*.

(c) The PURCHASER shall within six months from the date of execution of these presents apply for and get his name mutated as owner in respect of the *said office space* in the records of the Calcutta Municipal Corporation and shall also obtain separate assessment of the *said office space*.

(d) So long as the *said office space* is not separately assessed by the Calcutta Municipal authorities, the PURCHASER shall regularly and punctually pay the proportionate share of the assessed Municipal taxes, multi-storeyed building taxes and other outgoings, taxes, impositions whatsoever as may be assessed or found payable in respect of the *said office space.*

(*e*) The PURCHASER shall regularly and punctually contribute and pay month by month and every month the proportionate share of the costs expenses and outgoings including the maintenance and service charges as mentioned in the Seventh Schedule hereunder written. The apportionment of such costs and expenses shall be made by the VENDOR and the same shall be conclusive final and binding on the PURCHASER.

(*f*) The PURCHASER shall permit the VENDOR and its surveyors or agents with or without workmen and others at all reasonable times on prior appointment to enter into and upon the *said office space* for the purpose of repairing, making, reinstating, re-building, cleaning, lighting and keeping in order and good conditions, the sewers, drain-pipes, cables, water courses, wire structures or other conveniences belonging to or serving or used for the building and also for the purpose of laying down, maintaining, repairing, restoring, testing, drainage, gas, pipes, water pipes, electrical wires and cables and for such other similar purpose.

(*g*) The PURCHASER shall keep the *said office space* in good, substantial repair and condition so as to support and protect the other parts of the said building as they now enjoy.

(*h*) The PURCHASER shall at his own costs and expenses keep the *said office space* duly insured against fire and other risks and shall regularly and punctually pay premium in respect of such Insurance. In case of there being any damage to the said office space/said building due to fire or other accident, the amount of compensation as may be received and/or realised from the Insurance Company shall exclusively be utilised for the purpose of repairing of the *said office space* and the said building.

(*i*) The PURCHASER shall keep all sewers, drains, pipes, passages, stairs, main entrances, serving the said office space in good condition.

AND it is hereby mutually agreed by and between the VENDOR and the PURCHASER as follows:

(*a*) The parties hereto shall abide by the Agreement dated the 5th day of June 1999 with regard to the supply of electricity by the VENDOR from its own high-tension connection. The PURCHASER hereby agrees that in case of delay and/or default on the part of the PURCHASER in observing and performing the terms, conditions, stipulations and covenants contained in the said Agreement dated the 5th June 1999 and/or in case of delay and/or default in payment of electricity charges and other amounts by the PURCHASER to the VENDOR, then and in that event, the VENDOR shall be entitled to disconnect the electricity supply.

(*b*) The PURCHASER agrees to be a member of the Association or Syndicate or Company if any formed by the VENDOR for the administration and maintenance of the common areas and facilities at the said building and further agrees to sign and execute all papers, documents and applications, bye-laws, rules and regulations as may be necessary or required for formation and/or registration of such Association or Syndicate or Company and further agrees to be bound by the rules, regulations and bye-laws of such Association or Society or Company to be formed by the VENDOR as aforesaid. The purchaser also agrees that in case of default on the Part of the Purchaser, the VENDOR herein shall be entitled as Constituted Attorney on behalf of the PURCHASER to sign and execute all papers documents, applications, rules, regulations and bye-laws and this power and authority in favour of the VENDOR shall remain irrevocable and shall cease to have any effect immediately upon the formation of the proposed Association or Syndicate or Company.

(*c*) The PURCHASER shall render his best co-operation and assistance to the VENDOR in the formation of Association, Syndicate or Company for the maintenance and administration of the common areas and facilities as also the common service at the said building and also agrees with the rules regulations and bye-laws of such Syndicate or Association or Company as may be formed by the VENDOR in its absolute discretion shall be final and binding.

(*d*) The PURCHASER hereby agrees that the VENDOR herein shall at all times be entitled to erect and/or construct one or more floors or other structures on the roof or other vacant spaces of the said building and that such new floor or floors or other structures as may be erected by the VENDOR shall be entitled to all the existing sewers, drains, water connections as also to use and enjoy all common areas facilities described in the fourth schedule hereunder written, without any objection or obstruction by or at the instance of the PURCHASER or any person or party claiming under the PURCHASER. In this regard, the PURCHASER shall not be entitled to any compensation or damages whatsoever.

(*e*) The PURCHASER hereby agrees and confirms that nothing contained in these presents shall be construed to confer upon the PURCHASER any right title or interest of any kind whatsoever into and over the said premises and/or the land comprised therein and/or the said building except in respect of the *said office space* hereby transferred and conveyed subject to the terms, conditions, covenants, stipulations and restrictions as herein specifically stated.

The First Schedule above referred to

ALL THAT piece or parcel of land containing by measurement an area of 10 cottahs be the same a little more or less together with the building and structures whatsoever erected thereon situate lying at and being Municipal premises .... in Holding No. .... in Block .... in the North Division of the town of Calcutta and in respect whereof the Government revenue is payable at the rate of Rs. 10 and butted and bounded in the manner as follows:

On the North ... by ....

On the South ... by Premises No. ....

On the East ... by Premises No. ....

On the West ... by Premises No. ....

The Second Schedule above referred to

ALL THAT undivided half share of an office space containing the super built up area of 500 sq. ft. be the same a little more or less being office space No. .... situated on the 2nd floor of the said building at .... The said super built up area has been calculated by adding to the carpet area, the areas of pillars, inner walls and space covered by the outer-walls thereof and also the proportionate area of the spaces covered by the staircase, landings, lift, and other common areas on the said floor.

The Third Schedule above referred to

(*a*) The PURCHASER shall be entitled to all rights, privileges, vertical and lateral supports, easements, quasi-easements and appurtenances whatsoever belonging or in any way appertaining to the said office space or therewith usually held used occupied or enjoyed or reputed or known as part or parcel thereof or appertaining thereto which are hereinafter more fully specified, excepting and reserving unto the VENDOR the rights of easements quasi-easements, privileges and appurtenances hereinafter more particularly set forth in the Fifth Schedule hereunder written.

(*b*) The rights of access in common with the VENDOR and the other occupiers of the building at all times and for all normal business purposes connected with the use and enjoyment of the staircases.

(*c*) The right of way in common as aforesaid at all times and for all purposes connected with the reasonable use and enjoyment of the *said office space* over and along with the pathways comprised in the said building, PROVIDED ALWAYS and it is hereby declared that nothing herein contained shall permit the PURCHASER or any person deriving title under the PURCHASER or the servants agents employees and invitees of the PURCHASER to obstruct in any way by vehicles or deposit of materials, rubbish or otherwise the free passage of other person or persons including the vendor along such pathways as aforesaid.

(*d*) The right of protection of the SAID OFFICE SPACE by or from all parts of the building so far they now protect the same.

(*e*) The right of passage in common as aforesaid of Electricity, Telephone and Telex from and to the *said office space* through the cables already layed by the VENDOR for the said purpose and so far as may be reasonably necessary for the beneficial occupation of the said office space for all purposes whatsoever.

(*f*) The right with or without workmen and necessary materials for the PURCHASER to enter from time to time upon the other common parts of the said building for the purpose of repairing so far as may be necessary the Telephone and Telex wires, cables and conduits aforesaid.

The Fourth Schedule above referred to

The common areas and facilities mentioned in this Indenture shall include:

(*a*) The foundation columns, girders, beams supports, main walls, corridors, lobbies, stairs, stairways, lift pit in the basement, lift-well, lift machine room, entrance to and exits from the building and intended for common use.

(*b*) Installation of common services such as water, sewerage, etc.

(*c*) Lift, pump, motor, pipes, ducts and all apparatus and installations in the said building for common use.

(*d*) Toilets, water closets (w.c.) and urinals with all fittings and fixtures erected on all the floors of the said building.

The Fifth Schedule above referred to

The undermentioned rights easements and quasi-easements privileges and appurtenances are reserved exclusively for the VENDOR.

(*a*) The right in common with the PURCHASER and/or other person or persons entitled to the other part or parts of the building as aforesaid for the ownership of common part or parts of the building including its installations, staircases, open and covered spaces and other passages.

(*b*) The right of passage of electricity water and air and to any part other than the *said office space* or parts of the said building through pipes, drains, wires, conduits lying or being in under through or over the said office space so far as may be reasonably necessary for the beneficial use and occupation of the other portion or portions of the building for all purposes whatsoever.

(*c*) The exclusive right to erect and/or construct one or more floors and other structures in or upon the roof and/or other vacant spaces of the said building and further to permit all such additional floors and other structures and/or the owners and/or occupiers thereof to use and enjoy the all supplies, facilities, services including the common areas, installations and the essential and public utility services now existing or as may hereafter be available at the said building.

(*d*) The right of protection for other portion or portions of the building by all parts of the said office space as far as they now protect become vested in the purchaser by means of structural alterations to the *said office space* or otherwise in any manner to lessen or diminish the support at present enjoyed by other part of parts of the said building.

(*e*) The right of the VENDOR in common with the PURCHASER and other owners or occupiers of different parts of the building for the purpose of ingress and egress to and from such any part or parts of the building, to use and enjoy the front entrance, staircase, electrical installations upon and covered space and other common passages or parts of the said building.

(*f*) The right of the VENDOR with or without workmen and necessary materials to enter from time to time upon the *said office space* for the purpose of repairing so far as may be necessary for such pipes, drains, wires and conduits as aforesaid PROVIDED ALWAYS the VENDOR and other person or persons shall give to the PURCHASER 48 hours prior notice in writing of their intention for such entry as aforesaid.

(*g*) The exclusive right to use, occupy, possess and enjoy as also to sell, transfer, convey or otherwise let out, lease out or dispose the roof and/or other vacant spaces of the said building and/or the new floor or floors as may be erected by the VENDOR on the roof of the building, without any objection or hindrance by or at the instance of the PURCHASER or any other person or party claiming under the PURCHASER. In case of construction of one or more floors or other structures over the roof of the said building by the VENDOR, the such new floor or floors or other structures, the owners and/or occupiers thereof shall be entitled to use and enjoy all rights and privileges described in the Third Schedule above-written and further be entitled to use and enjoy the common areas and facilities described in the Fourth Schedule above-written.

The Sixth Schedule above referred to

(*a*) Not to use the *said office space* for any purpose other than for the purpose for which it be constructed *e.g.* the office space shall not be used for any purpose whatsoever except as an office.

(*b*) Not to use the *said office space* or any portion thereof in such manner, which may or is likely to cause nuisance or annoyance to the occupiers of the other portions in the said building or to the owners or occupiers of the neighbouring properties nor shall use the same for any illegal or immoral purposes.

(*c*) Not to carry on or permit to be carried on upon the *said office space* or any part thereof, any offensive or unlawful business whatsoever nor to do or permit to be done anything in the *said office space* which may be illegal or forbidden under any law for the time being in force.

(*d*) Not to demolish or cause to be demolished or damaged *said office space* or any part thereof nor to make or cause to be made any additions or alterations of whatsoever nature at or upon the *said office space* or any part thereof.

(*e*) Not to do or cause or permit to be done any act, deed or thing which may render void or voidable any Insurance of any office or other spaces in any part of the said building or cause any increased premium to be payable in respect thereof.

(*f*) Not to do or cause or permit to be done any act, deed, matter or thing which may cause obstruction or hindrance in the erecting and/or making one or more floors or other structures in or upon the roof of and/or other vacant spaces of the said building.

(*g*) Not to put or affix or install any signboard or neon sign nor display any advertisement on the outer walls of the *said office space.*

(*h*) Not to decorate the exterior of the *said office space* otherwise than in the manner as may be agreed in writing with the VENDOR and that the PURCHASER shall maintain the decor of the exterior of the *said office space* in the same manner in which the same was decorated at the time of delivering possession of the same by the VENDOR to the PURCHASER.

(*i*) Not to throw or accumulate any dirt, filth or other refuse or permit the same to be thrown or accumulated in his *said office space* or in any portion of the building.

The Seventh Schedule above referred to

Costs, expenses and outgoings and obligations for which all purchasers are to contribute proportionately:

(*a*) The expenses of maintaining, repairing, re-decorating and renewing the main structure and in particular the drainage system, sewerage, rain water discharge arrangement, water supply system, supply of electricity to all common areas, mentioned in the Fourth Schedule hereto.

(*b*) The expenses of repairing, maintaining, white-washing and colour washing the main structure of the building including the exterior of the building and also the common area of the building described in the Fourth Schedule above-written.

(*c*) The costs of cleaning and lighting the entrance of the building, the passage and spaces around the building, lobby corridors, staircases, lift and other common areas.

(*d*) Costs of maintaining lift.

(*e*) Costs of decorating the exterior of the premises.

(*f*) Salary, wages, fees and remuneration of durwans, lift-man, sweepers, plumbers, electricians, caretakers or any other person whose appointment may be considered necessary for maintenance and protection of the said premises and administration and management of the affairs thereof.

(*g*) The Municipal taxes, commercial surcharges, multi-storeyed building taxes, urban land taxes, watertaxes and other rates and taxes whatsoever as may be found payable on account of the said building.

(*h*) All expenses of common services and in common with common areas and facilities.

(*i*) Such expenses as are necessary for or incidental to the maintenance and upkeeping of the premises and of the common areas facilities and amenities.

IN WITNESSES WHEREOF the parties hereto have hereunto set and subscribed their respective hands and seals the day, month and year first above-written.

Signed, sealed and delivered by Mr. AD
pursuant to Board Resolution of 2nd
February 2000 of AB Co. P. Ltd.

For AB Co. P. Ltd.
Director

Signed, sealed and delivered by the
PURCHASER above-named at Calcutta in
the presence of:

Mr. XY
Signature

Received of and from the above-named PURCHASER the within mentioned sum as consideration as per the Memo of Consideration hereunder ... Rs. 2,00,000

MEMO OF CONSIDERATION

By A/c. Payee Cheques as well as cash from time to time paid by the purchaser to the vendor amounting to	...	Rs.	2,00,000
Total	...	Rs.	2,00,000

For AB Co. P. Ltd.
Sd/
Director

Deed of Sale

THIS INDENTURE MADE this 15th day of December 2000 BETWEEN X & Co., a Partnership Firm, having its Registered Office at .... represented by Mr. MN one of the Partners in his capacity as the "Partner" and a constituted Attorney of all the other Partners of the said Firm, hereinafter referred to as the VENDORS (which expression shall unless excluded by or there be something repugnant to the subject or context be deemed to mean and include the firm and its partners for the time being and each of their respective heirs, executors, administrators and legal representatives) of the one part and AB, son of CD by faith Hindu, by occupation business, residing at .... (hereinafter referred to as the PURCHASER, which expression shall unless excluded by or there be something repugnant to the subject or context be deemed to mean and include his heirs, executors, administrators, legal representatives and assigns) of the other part.

WHEREAS by a Deed of Conveyance dated 15th September 1966 registered with the Registrar of Assurance at Calcutta in Book No. 1, Volume No. 2, being No. 3 at pages 4 to 10 for the year 1966 the Vendors herein purchased from PQ and others all that Premises No. .... comprising an area of 10 bighas and for the consideration money therein mentioned.

AND WHEREAS three of the Partners of the VENDORS herein namely, OP (since deceased), QR (since deceased) and MN by a Deed of Conveyance dated 18th January 1972 registered with Registrar of Assurances at Calcutta in Book No. 2, Volume No. 3, at pages 4 to 10, being No. 11 for the year 1972 purchased from XY and ANOTHER ALL THAT piece and parcel of land being Premises No. .... containing an area of 3 bighas for the consideration money therein mentioned.

AND WHEREAS the total consideration money for the said property purchased by the Late OP, Late QR and MN was paid out of the till of the partnership firm namely the Vendors and the said Premises was treated as part of the assets of Vendors Firm and the VENDORS had all along been and still are in possession of the same as Owners thereof.

AND WHEREAS by a Deed of Declaration dated 7th February 1993 duly registered with the Registrar of Assurances at Calcutta in Book No. 3, Volume 4, being No. 5, pages 15 to 20 for the year 1993 by the heirs and legal representatives of the Late OP declared and confirmed that the said property belonged to the VENDORS.

AND WHEREAS by a Deed of Declaration dated 5th day of February 1993 duly registered with the Registrar of Assurances at Calcutta in Book No. 3, Volume 4, being No. 5, pages 21 to 30 for the year 1993 the heirs of the late A. Das declared and confirmed that the said property exclusively belonged to the VENDORS.

AND WHEREAS by a Deed of Declaration dated 5th March 1993 duly registered by MN with the Sub-Registrar of Assurances at Alipore in the State of West Bengal, in Book No. 5, Volume 13, being No. 14, pages 10 to 15 for the year 1993 it was declared and confirmed that the said property exclusively belonged to the VENDORS.

AND WHEREAS by virtue of the said two separate Deeds of Conveyance dated 15th September 1966 and 18th January 1972 and the said three Deeds of Declaration the VENDORS herein became the sole and absolute owners of ALL THAT the portion of the premises No. .... of ...., now known as .... and the portion of the premises No. .... now known as .... containing a total area of land measuring 13 bighas be the same a little more or less together with buildings and structures standing thereon and more fully described and set out in Parts I, II and III of the First Schedule hereunder.

AND WHEREAS after the purchase of the said land the VENDORS herein had constructed several Sheds, Godowns, Offices, Buildings, Staff Quarters and other essential parts for running of their factory smoothly with prior permission of the authorities concerned.

AND WHEREAS by an Order dated 5th December 1992 made by a competent authority under the Urban Land (Ceiling and Regulations) Act 1976, it was recorded that the said Premises No. .... and No. .... of .... have no excess vacant land.

AND WHEREAS the Partners of the Vendors Firm decided and framed a scheme amalgamating the said two premises for development and laid the necessary roads and passages for ingress in and egress out of the said plots as shown in the MASTER PLAN kept in the office of the VENDORS and to sell the said plots to the Buyers. The said amalgamated premises is hereinafter referred to as the SAID PREMISES.

AND WHEREAS (1) MN, (2) EF (3) GH and (4) JK are the present partners of the Vendors Firm.

AND WHEREAS by a Power of Attorney dated 14th December 1992 all the Partners of the Vendors Firm have jointly authorised MN one of the Partners to sign and execute and register the Conveyance and/or the Conveyances in favour of the PURCHASER and/or the PURCHASERS of the plot of land with or without structures and to receive consideration money.

AND WHEREAS the PURCHASER had offered to purchase 4 cottahs of land with structures standing thereon being a portion of Premises No. .... and .... being Plot No. E5 and shown with Red Borders in the Master Plan free from all encumbrances whatsoever and for the sake of brevity the said Plot No. E4 with the land and structures standing thereon is hereinafter referred to as the *demised premises.*

AND WHEREAS the VENDORS have accepted the offer made by the PURCHASER and agreed to sell the same to the PURCHASER.

AND WHEREAS the PURCHASER had inspected the original Title Deeds and documents in respect of the properties a list whereof are set out in the fourth Schedule hereunder written and fully satisfied about the Title of the demised premises and agreed not to raise any objection or question on the title or dispute the same in future and also inspected the Master Plan of the entire land and satisfied about the said plot, and common passages and roads for ingress in and egress out of the said plot which is more fully set out and described in the Third Schedule hereunder written.

AND WHEREAS the VENDORS have obtained the Clearance Certificate under section 230A of the Income Tax Act 1961 and the purchaser has taken inspection thereof.

AND WHEREAS the PURCHASER agreed to purchase and the VENDORS agreed to sell the said plot No. E5 with land and the structures standing thereon for a sum of Rs. 2,50,000 (Rupees two lakhs fifty thousand only) towards payment of the agreed consideration money.

AND WHEREAS a Master Plan prepared by the VENDORS is annexed hereto showing the said land with structures standing thereon and shown with red borders and the common areas and passages and roads to be used in common by the PURCHASER with the VENDORS and *other owners of the other plots* in respect of the use and occupation of the said plot of land with structures standing thereon and more fully described and mentioned in the Second Schedule hereunder written, and the said common areas and common passages are more fully set out and described in the Third Schedule hereunder written and shown with green and yellow colours on Master Plan annexed hereto.

AND WHEREAS the PURCHASER has now requested the VENDORS to complete the sale by executing and registering the Sale Deed in respect of the said plot of land with the building and structures standing thereon against payment of the full consideration money and agrees to observe and perform and comply with the obligations which are set out in the Fifth Schedule hereunder written.

NOW THIS INDENTURE WITNESSETH that in consideration of the agreement arrived at between the VENDORS and the PURCHASER and in consideration of the payment of a sum of Rs. 2,50,000 (Rupees two lakhs fifty thousand only) by the PURCHASER to the VENDORS being the full agreed consideration money (receipt whereof the VENDORS do hereby admit and acknowledge and of and from the same and every part thereof do hereby acquit, release and discharge the same and every part thereof and the said plot of land with structures standing thereon being demarcated portion of the said Premises No......... and .... containing an area of 4 cottahs intended to be conveyed herein as also the PURCHASER) they the VENDORS do hereby grant, transfer, sell, convey, assign and assure unto the purchaser all that the 4 cottahs of land with the pucca structures standing thereon being the demarcated portion of the premises Nos. .... and .... comprised in the plot No. E5 and shown within the "red" borders in the Master Plan more fully set out and described in the Second Schedule hereunder written and for the sake of brevity hereinafter referred to as the said land and/or the demised premises TO HAVE AND TO HOLD the same and every part thereof and the inheritance thereof in fee simple in possession unto and to the use of the PURCHASER absolutely and for ever together with all structures whatsoever belonging thereto or held and enjoyed therewith and all the estate, right, title, interest, claim and demand whatsoever of the VENDORS into and upon or in respect of the said portion of plot of land hereditaments AND PREMISES AND EVERY PART THEREOF AND XEROX COPIES OF ALL deeds pattahs writings muniments and evidences of title relating thereto or any part thereof which now are or may hereafter be in possession or custody of the VENDORS or any person or persons from whom the VENDORS may procure the same without any action either at law or in equity AND THAT NOTWITHSTANDING any act deed or thing done by the VENDORS or any of its predecessors in title to the contrary the VENDORS have good right full power and absolute authority to grant, convey, confer or transfer the said land hereditaments and premises unto the Purchaser in the manner aforesaid AND THAT the PURCHASER shall and may at all times hereafter peaceably and quietly possess and enjoy the same and every part thereof without any lawful eviction interruption claim or demand whatsoever from or by the VENDORS or through any person or persons having or lawfully claiming from under or in trust for the VENDORS or any of its predecessors in title AND THAT free from all encumbrances made or suffered by the VENDORS or any of its predecessors in title or any person having or lawfully claiming as aforesaid AND FURTHER THAT they the VENDORS and all persons having or lawfully claiming any estate or interest in the said land hereditaments and premises or any part thereof from under or in trust for the VENDORS shall and will at all times hereafter at the request and cost of the PURCHASER do and execute or cause to be done and executed all such acts deeds and things whatsoever for further better and more perfectly assuring the said land hereditaments and premises and every part thereof unto the PURCHASER as may be reasonably required AND ALSO THAT the VENDORS shall and will at all times hereafter at the request and cost of the PURCHASER produce to him or as he shall direct the deeds and writings specified in the Fourth Schedule hereunder written for evidencing the title to the said land hereditaments and premises and also furnish to the PURCHASER copies of or extracts from the said deeds and writings and shall and will in the meanwhile keep the same safe, unobliterated, damage by fire or other inevitable accident excepted AND THAT the VENDORS shall have exclusive right of ownership of all other areas which belong to them and shown on the Master Plan annexed hereto and which is comprised in the said Premises being No. .... and .... with full liberty to the Vendors to sell the other plot or plots shown on the *Master Plan* to any person or persons AND THAT the PURCHASER shall have no right of ownership over and in respect of any other plot or plots or other areas of land comprised in the said premises AND FURTHER THAT the VENDORS hereby covenant with the PURCHASER that the PURCHASER shall for ingress in and egress out of the said land have the right of use of the common passage/roads/facilities set out and described in the Third Schedule hereunder written and shown within Green and Yellow colours on the Master Plan annexed hereto without in any way obstructing the VENDORS or any other person or persons who may be PURCHASER or PURCHASERS or occupiers of other plots or areas and their employees agents and visitors nor the PURCHASER will cause any obstruction thereon by storing any materials and/or by construction of any permanent or temporary structure in whatsoever manner thereon or on any part thereof and/or by parking any vehicles, carts, etc. in the said common roads/passages/areas AND the PURCHASER hereby agrees undertakes and covenants with the VENDORS to become a Member of the Society or Association to be formed by the VENDORS at the cost of the PURCHASER and buyers of other plots for the purpose of maintenance of the common passages and roads and electric posts, lights on the passage, transformers, water pump, common toilets or any other purpose AND the PURCHASER hereby agrees and covenants that he will abide by and observe the terms and conditions rules and regulations of such Society or Association to be so formed by the VENDORS and pay to the VENDORS the maintenance charges, electricity charges and/or any other charges as will be fixed from time to time by the VENDORS so long the Society or the Association is not formed for the purpose of utilising common facilities, electricity etc. without raising any objection whatsoever and in default of payment of any one monthly Bill for the same the VENDORS shall have the full and absolute right to disconnect and discontinue any such facilities/electric connection till the amount of Bill is not paid AND the PURCHASER further agrees and covenants with the VENDORS that so long the Municipal rates and taxes and other levies are not being assessed separately by the authority concerned in respect of the said land and premises the PURCHASER will pay the proportionate rates, taxes charges and all outgoings as will be fixed by the VENDORS without raising any objection whatsoever and in default of payment of any two monthly Bills within seven days from the date of the Bill the VENDORS shall have the unfettered right to disconnect and discontinue the facilities which have been agreed to be given by the VENDORS to the PURCHASER without giving any further Notice to the PURCHASER and the PURCHASER covenants and agrees to observe perform and comply with the terms and conditions set out and mentioned in various clauses of the Fifth Schedule hereunder written AND THAT the VENDORS shall and will at all times hereafter at the request and costs of the PURCHASER produce to him or as he shall direct the deeds and writings specified in the Fourth Schedule hereunder written for evidencing the title to the said Land hereditaments and premises and also furnish to the PURCHASER copies of or extracts from the said deeds and writings and shall and will in the meanwhile keep the same safe, damage by fire or other accident excepted.

The First Schedule above referred to

Part I

ALL THOSE pieces or parcels of lands hereditaments and premises No. .... (formerly known as .... and prior thereto known as .... of ....) containing by measurement an area of 10 bighas be the same a little or less situate and lying in Mouza Malipanchghora within Police Station Bally and the District Howrah under Khatian and Dag. Nos. as follows:

Sl. No.	*Dag No.*	*Khatian No.*	*Touzi No.*	*J.L. No.*	*K.S. No.*	*Area in acre*
1.	54	53	77	15	1985	35
2.	55	70	82	15	1985	37
3.	56	93	...	...	...	380
4.	57	93	...	...	...	100
5.	58	40	82	15	1985	200
6.	59	40	20	15	1985	583
7.	60	70	39	15	1985	770
8.	61	13	87	15	1985	100

(Hooghly)

and butted and bounded as follows:

On the North by Vendors' Boundary Wall
On the East by Vendors' Boundary Wall
On the South by Vendors' Boundary Wall
On the West by Vendors' Boundary Wall

MOREFULLY delineated and shown in the Map or Plan annexed with the part recited Deed of Conveyance dated 15th day of September 1966.

Part II

ALL THAT piece or parcel of land and hereditaments TOGETHER WITH the structures and sheds standing thereon measuring an area of 2 bighas be the same a little more or less, being premises No. .... of .... an delineated and shown in the Map and Plan annexed hereto and registered on 15th day of January 1972 between X and Y and butted and bounded on the North by the land of M; on the East by passage; on the South by remaining portion of premises No. 5 G.T. Road and on the West by Roy Street. The property is recorded on the Settlement Record comprised in Touza No. 398 (Hooghly) Parganas Khalore Bora and Dharsu and Khatian Nos. 203, 358 and 175 jointly with LN and others.

Part III

ALL THAT piece or parcel of land and hereditaments TOGETHER WITH building, dwelling quarters, staff quarters, security office shed and structure standing thereon containing an area of 1 bigha and now amalgamated and aggregated to the total area of 13 bighas be the same a little more or less and now known as Municipal Holding

No. ...., Khatian No. ...., J.L. No .... Dag No. ...., a Total rent of Rs. .... (Rupees ....) only is at present payable to the State of West Bengal in respect of the said entire property, butted and bounded in the manner following:

On the North by Vendors' Boundary Wall

On the South by Vendors' Boundary Wall

On the East by Vendors' Boundary Wall

On the West by Vendors' Boundary Wall

OR HOWSOEVER the same was/is or may be butted and bounded called known numbered described and distinguished.

The Second Schedule above referred to

ALL THAT the piece and parcel of land measuring 4 cottahs be the same a little more or less TOGETHER WITH the structures and shed standing thereon being the demarcated portions of Premises No. .... and .... of .... being Plot No. E5 and shown in the *Master Plan* annexed hereto within .... butted and bounded in the manner following that is to say:

On the North by Plot No. E7

On the South partly by plot No. D5

On the East by Municipal drain; and

On the West by Common Road

and is delineated on the *Master Plan* annexed hereto and thereon bordered "Red" and the common passage and Roads coloured Yellow.

The Third Schedule above referred to

Common Passage as shown in the Map or Plan annexed hereto and thereon coloured Yellow.

Common area as shown in the Map or Plan annexed hereto and thereon coloured Green such as Transformer Room, Power House, Toilets, Security Office Room, Pump House, Association Office Room, Main Gates.

The Fourth Schedule above referred to

(1) Bengali Deed of Sale dated 10th June 1931 made between K and L.

(2) Bengali Deed of Sale dated 10th July 1945 made between M and N.

(3) Deed of Conveyance dated 15th September 1966 between O and P.

(4) Certified copy of the Partition Decree dated 25th June 1937 made in the High Court at Calcutta in Suit No. 1010 of 1943. (P-vs-Q)

(5) Deed of Conveyance dated 18th January 1972 between R and S registered with the Registrar of Assurances at Calcutta in Book No. 2, Volume No. 3, pages 100 to 108 being No. 4 for the year 1972.

(6) Deed of Declaration dated 7th February 1993 between T and U registered with the Registrar of Assurances at Calcutta in Book No. 3, Volume No. 4 being No. 5 for the year 1993.

(7) Deed of Declaration dated 5th day of February 1997 by V registered with the Registrar of Assurances at Calcutta in Book No. 3, Volume No. 4 being No. 5 for the year 1993.

(8) Deed of Declaration dated 5th March 1993 by W registered with the Sub-Registrar of Assurances at Alipore, District 24-Parganas in Book No. 5, Volume No. 13 being No. 14, pages 10 to 15 for the year 1993.

(9)(*i*) Deed of Partnership dated 3rd January 1997 between MN and EF.

(*ii*) Deed of Partnership dated 30th April 1997 between MN, EF and OP.

(*iii*) Deed of Partnership dated 10th June 1998 between MN, EF, OP and JK.

(*iv*) Deed of Partnership dated 15th May 1999 between MN, EF, UV and JK.

(10) General Power of Attorney by all the partners in favour of MN dated 15th June 1999.

The Fifth Schedule above referred to

(1) The rates, taxes and all other outgoings of whatsoever nature due and payable in respect of the said plot of land shall be borne and paid by the VENDORS upto the date of sale or delivery of possession whichever is earlier and thereafter the PURCHASER shall be taken to pay all rates, taxes and impositions and all other outgoings of whatsoever nature in respect of the said plot of land to the VENDORS.

(2) That the PURCHASER will pay the proportionate share of all Municipal rates and taxes, duties and levies to the VENDORS for his plot of land till the said plot is separately assessed and mutated in the name of the PURCHASER. The PURCHASER will upon registration of these presents apply for mutation of his name to the appropriate authorities.

(3) The PURCHASER may be allowed by the VENDORS to consume electricity energy out of the Vendor's Transformer to such extent as may be decided by the VENDORS for which the separate sub-meters will be installed by the VENDORS or by their authorised contractor at the cost of the PURCHASER.

(4) That the PURCHASER may be allowed to take the electric connection from the Vendors' Electric Transformer and shall erect, instal the said electric line only from the Junction Box as may be instructed permitted by the VENDORS either through authorised electrical contractor or directly and shall pay and shall bear all costs expenses installation charges of the same subject to regular payment for consumption of electricity. The PURCHASER shall have the right to take electric connection directly from the CESC. Ltd. and in that event connections taken from the Vendors Transformer shall be disconnected.

(5) The Electric Bill will be made for consumption of electricity on the electricity consumed as per sub-meter reading at the current rates charged by the C.E.S.C. Ltd. plus 5% of actual proportionate surcharge on account of leakage and loss of energy during transmission and supply from the Vendors' Transformer to the PURCHASER.

(6) That the PURCHASER will pay electricity charges within 7 days from the date of each English Calendar month and will obtain the Bill and in default of the payment of the same VENDORS shall have the full and absolute right to disconnect the electric line of the premises or plot of the PURCHASER without giving any further notice.

(7) That the PURCHASER will be liable to pay the proportionate maintenance charges, Municipal rates, taxes, Land revenues and other levies in respect of his plot and in respect of the common passages, roads and areas, to the VENDORS or to the authorised agents of the VENDORS or to the Society/Association as and when formed by the VENDORS. The PURCHASER agrees to become the Member of the Society or Association to whom the VENDORS may entrust the observance and performance of the various matters and items mentioned and set out in the Third Schedule hereinabove written in this Deed.

(8) That the proportionate Municipal rates and taxes of the Common Passages/Common Areas shall be borne by and paid by the Purchaser in respect of the said Plot as will be fixed by the Vendors or the Association/ Society from time to time.

(9) That the PURCHASER will pay such proportionate maintenance charges as will be fixed from time to time by the Vendors or Association formed by the VENDORS for providing expenses for common lights, salaries of watch and Ward Staff, Clerks, Accountants, Bill Collectors, Electrical Mechanics, and/or Engineers, Contractors, Plumbers, etc. the repairing and overhauling or replacement charges for the passages, water pumps, electric cables, transformers etc. and as also proportionate rates and taxes, Land Revenues of the demised Premises and in default of such payment of any monthly Bill raised by the VENDORS upon the Purchaser herein the PURCHASER shall be liable to pay an interest @ 24% p.a. to the VENDORS for such delayed payment.

(10) That the PURCHASER will keep a sum of Rs. 500 per cottah or portion thereof as interest free Security Deposit with the VENDORS for due payment of Services and Maintenance charges/proportionate taxes, duties, land revenues etc. interest free Security Deposit for due payment of electric charges shall be made at the rate of Rs. 1,000 per Horse Power.

(11) That the PURCHASER shall not put any obstruction to the use of the common passages and roads coloured green and common areas coloured green in the Map or Plan prepared by the VENDORS nor will store any materials on the same nor will allow any vehicles to be parked nor will be entitled to raise any structure and/or any projection whether permanent or temporary on or over the said common passages, roads and areas nor will at any time obstruct the use of the said common passages, roads and areas by the other lawful occupiers or by the VENDORS, their servants, customers, employees and invitees.

(12) That the PURCHASER may take drinking water at his/her own cost from the available water facilities and shall be entitled to sink his own tube-well in his own plot or take direct connection from the Municipality at his/her own costs, charges and expenses.

(13) That the PURCHASER shall not use the Plot purchased by him/her for doing any illegal trade or business or activity nor will commit any nuisance or cause any annoyance nor will keep or store any explosive/ hazardous articles or combustible articles except those required in usual course of business and if any licence is required it will be taken by the PURCHASER.

(14) That the PURCHASER will not have any right in respect of any other areas in the said property or in respect of any other plots made out by the VENDORS and as are shown in the Master Plan and hereby gives up his/her right, if any, to claim any right of pre-emption in respect thereof.

(15) That the PURCHASER and other lawful occupiers of the said land by prior written permission of the VENDORS shall be entitled to have right of laying down underground water pipe line, sewerage lines, electric and own costs and expenses to restore the surface of the said common passage in its original state and condition immediately without disturbing the right of use of the same by the other lawful occupiers, VENDORS and owners of other plots in the said premises.

(16) That the PURCHASER shall not disturb the boundary wall shown in the Master Plan by opening any door, entrance or window or by reducing the length or width thereof or otherwise.

IN WITNESS WHEREOF the VENDORS and the PURCHASER hereto have executed these Presents on the day, month and year first above-written.

Signed and delivered by the X & Co. the VENDORS through the Authorised Partner at Calcutta in the presence of:	MN and Partner of X & Co.
Signed and accepted and CONFIRMED by the PURCHASER at Calcutta in the presence of:	AB

RECEIVED of and from the within-named PURCHASER the within-mentioned sum of Rupees two lakhs fifty thousand only being the consideration money in full payable under these presents as per memo written hereinbelow:

MEMO OF CONSIDERATION

By Cheque No. 366931 dated 15th December 1999 Rs. 2,50,000 on Our Bank Ltd., Calcutta

WITNESSES: MN for X & Co.

Signature

Agreement to Sell

(Involving Life-interest)

THIS AGREEMENT made this 5th day of September One Thousand Nine Hundred Ninety Nine BETWEEN Sri GS son of Late PS by faith Hindu, by occupation Service, residing at 15, Anna Salai, Chennai 600 001 and Smt. LS wife of Late BS, by faith Hindu, by occupation housewife, residing at 15 Anna Salai, Chennai 600 001 (hereinafter referred to as the VENDORS which expression shall unless excluded by or repugnant to the subject or context be deemed to mean and include their heirs, executors, administrators, legal representatives and assigns) represented by their Constituted Attorney Sri RS son of Late M.S residing at 7A, India Exchange Place, Calcutta 700 001 of the one part and Sri PD son of Sri KD by faith Hindu, by occupation service, residing at BC 164, Salt Lake, Calcutta 700 064 hereinafter referred to as the PURCHASER (which expression shall unless excluded by or repugnant to the subject or context be deemed to mean and include his heirs, executors, administrators, legal representatives and assigns) of the other part:

WHEREAS:

1. Sri GS is the owner of premises No. .... of .... subject to life-interest of Smt. LS.

2. The said Smt. LS released her life-interest in favour of Sri GS but such release was not registered.

3. The VENDORS are now absolutely seized and possessed of or otherwise well and sufficiently entitled to ALL THAT the entire first floor measuring an area of 600 square feet be the same a little more or less together with the exclusive right to enjoy the roof of premises No. .... of .... having undivided proportionate share or interest in the land of the said premises which contains a total area of 2 cottahs be the same a little more or less whereupon one old two-storeyed brick built building is situated more fully and particularly described in the Schedule hereunder written (hereinafter referred to as the said PROPERTY) and delineated in the Map or Plan annexed hereto and bordered RED thereon free from all encumbrances charges, liens, *lis pendens* whatsoever or howsoever nature.

4. The VENDORS have agreed to sell and the PURCHASER has agreed to purchase the said property at or for the price of Rs. .... (Rupees ....) only free from all encumbrances (hereinafter referred to as the said PROPERTY) on the terms and conditions hereinafter appearing.

NOW THIS AGREEMENT WITNESSETH as follows:

A. The VENDORS hereby represent and assure the PURCHASER as follows:

(*a*) That the VENDORS are absolutely seized and possessed of or otherwise well and sufficiently entitled to ALL THAT the said property free from all encumbrances, charges, liens, lispendens, whatsoever or howsoever nature and have a good marketable title in respect of the said property more fully and particularly described in the Schedule hereunder written.

(*b*) That there is no legal or equitable bar or impediment on the part of the VENDORS to enter into this Agreement with the PURCHASER.

(*c*) That the VENDORS have not entered into any other Agreement for sale, development, to let out, lease out etc. in respect of the aforesaid property with any Third Party prior to entering into this Agreement.

(*d*) That there is no outstanding dues in respect of the said property to the Calcutta Municipal Corporation or to any other Authority.

(*e*) That no notice has been served on the VENDORS by the Calcutta Municipal Corporation on account of non-payment of tax and no proceedings are pending on account of the same.

(*f*) That no notice has been served upon the VENDORS by the Department of the Income-tax in regard to the said property.

(*g*) That the VENDORS have already sold the entire ground floor together with the proportionate share or interest in the land of the said premises to one KPS by an Indenture of Conveyance dated the ....

B. Relying on the aforesaid representations and assurances on the part of the VENDORS the PURCHASER has agreed to enter into this Agreement for purchase of the said property from the VENDORS on the terms and conditions hereinafter appearing:

(1) The PURCHASER shall pay to the VENDORS a sum of Rs. 10,000 out of Rs. .... as Earnest Money and/or part-payment of the total consideration money and the balance shall be paid by the PURCHASER to the VENDORS on or before the execution and Registration of the Deed of Conveyance or Conveyances either in favour of the PURCHASER or his nominee or nominees.

(2) That the VENDORS shall arrange for inspection of all the relevant and material documents of title relating to the said property for the purpose of investigation of title.

(3) That one of the VENDORS Smt. LS must be present before the registration office personally and shall sign in the Deed of Conveyance for conveying the said property.

(4) That the VENDORS shall make out a good and marketable title in respect of the said property and make the same free from all encumbrances, pre-emption rights, whatsoever.

(5) That the VENDORS shall answer all requisition on title that might be delivered to the VENDORS by the PURCHASER and/or his Advocate.

(6) The sale and purchase shall be completed within 6 months from the date of delivery of peaceful vacant khas possession of the said property by the VENDORS to the PURCHASER.

(7) The VENDORS shall execute and register the Deed of Conveyance in favour of the PURCHASER or his nominee or nominees against the payment of balance of consideration money. The Stamp Duty and registration cost and other incidental costs thereto shall be borne and paid by the PURCHASER.

(8) If the PURCHASER fails or neglects to complete the transaction in the manner and within the time aforesaid on payment of the balance of the consideration money then the VENDORS shall be entitled to either forfeit the said sum of Rs. 10,000 which has been paid by the PURCHASER to the VENDORS as earnest money and the PURCHASER should vacate the property or the VENDORS may sue the PURCHASER for specific performance of contract as per terms of this agreement.

(9) The VENDORS shall pay all arrears of Municipal taxes and other outgoings charges in respect of the said property before the execution of the Deed of Conveyance in favour of the PURCHASER or his nominee or nominees.

(10) Upon making out a good and marketable title and readiness of the PURCHASER to complete the transaction on payment of the balance of the consideration money if the VENDORS fail to complete the transaction in the manner aforesaid the PURCHASER shall be entitled to get back the entire earnest money with interest at 22% per annum and to sue the VENDORS for specific performance of contract and get the deal completed with compensation which is pre-estimated at Rs. 50,000.

(11) The VENDORS have further agreed and covenanted with the PURCHASER as follows:

(*a*) That during the continuance of this Agreement not to sell, transfer, let, further encumber or otherwise part with possession of the said property or any part thereof.

(*b*) Not to induct any person either as a tenant or otherwise into the said property or any part thereof.

(*c*) To pay and discharge all municipal rates and other taxes, levies, impositions and other outgoings payable in respect of the said property upto the date of execution of these presents.

(*d*) To cause all necessary parties to join in the Deed of Conveyance at their own cost.

(*e*) The VENDORS shall obtain the Income-tax clearance certificate under s. 230A of the Income-tax Act 1961 for transferring the said property at the costs of the VENDORS, if required.

Schedule

ALL THAT the entire first floor measuring super built up area of 600 sq. feet be the same a little more or less together with roof on the first floor along with the undivided proportionate share or interest in the land of the said premises which contains an area of 2 cottahs be the same a little more or less whereupon one old two-storeyed brick built building standing thereon or on part thereof situate lying at and being Premises No. .... within the limits of the.................................. and butted and bounded as follows:

On the North:

On the South:

On the East:

On the West:

A Map or Plan annexed hereto and bordered RED thereon.

IN WITNESS WHEREOF the Parties hereto hereunto set and subscribe their respective hands and seals on the day, month and year first above-written.

Signed, sealed and delivered by the VENDOR GS at Chennai in the presence of:

1. ....

2. ....

Signed, sealed and delivered by the VENDOR Smt. LS at Calcutta in the presence of:

1. ....

2. ....

Signed, sealed and delivered by the Sri RS Attorney of the VENDOR at Calcutta in the presence of:

1. ....

2. ....

Signed, sealed and delivered by the PURCHASER Sri PD at Calcutta in the presence of:

1. ....

2. ....

Received of and from the within-named Purchaser the within mentioned sum of Rs. 10,000 (Rupees ten thousand only) being the Earnest Money or part-payment of the consideration Money as per Memo below:

MEMO OF CONSIDERATION

By A/c. Payee cheque No.........................
dated .... Drawn on X Bank
Ltd., Calcutta Branch in favour of the
Vendors ... ... Rs. 10,000

(Rupees Ten thousand only)

1. Received

2. Signatures

WITNESSES:

GS

LS

18

Disclaimer

A proposed or named beneficiary may renounce his interest under the Trust by a Disclaimer addressed to the Trustee.[1] The intended Trustee may within a reasonable period disclaim it. Such disclaimer shall prevent the trust property from being vested in him. A disclaimer by one of two or more Co-trustees vests the trust property in other or others and makes the other or others the sole trustee or trustees from the date of creation of the trust.[2]

A person who has been appointed Trustee may disclaim the trust before acceptance of office but not afterwards. Such disclaimer must be before he does any act with reference to the trust estate. A person may have consented to act as trustee during the Testator's lifetime but after the death of the Testator he may disclaim the trust and refuse to act as a Trustee. Such disclaimer must be within a reasonable time and before the appointed trustee takes any step in the matter. The disclaimer need not be in any particular form, it may be by a deed or by mere writing or by conduct. The intention must be clear. The disclaimer may be in the form of release or even by conveyance in favour of other trustees or in some other form of writing or by conduct.

A Disclaimer must be total, it cannot be partial. A Disclaimer has the effect of vesting the trust estate in co-trustees. Mere appointment of a trustee does not vest the property in the trustee until he accepts it. A person after disclaiming the position of a trustee cannot act as a trustee thereafter even though he changes his mind by persuasion or otherwise.

The term Disclaimer has been used in the Law of Trusts, Law of Patents, Law of Landlord and Tenant and in the Law of Bankruptcy.

1 Section 9 of the Indian Trusts Act 1882.
2 Section 10 of the Indian Trusts Act 1882.

The term Disclaimer refers to the renunciation, by amendment of the specification, of a portion of an inventor's claim to protection. It means repudiation of landlord and tenant relationship by some act on the part of a tenant. Disclaimer means renunciation by a tenant of his character as such by setting up a title in a third person or by claiming title in himself. In Bankruptcy the term Disclaimer refers to the surrender by the Trustee of property belonging to a bankrupt, which is of an onerous character.

Disclaimer signifies utterly to renounce. It is an express denial or complete renouncing of a thing.

FORMS

Disclaimer of Benami Property

THIS INDENTURE is made this .... day of ...... 2000 BETWEEN .... son of .... by caste .... by occupation .... residing at .... hereinafter called the RELEASOR, which expression shall, where the subject or context allows or admits of, be deemed to include his heirs, executors, administrators and representatives of the ONE PART and .... son of.............. deceased by caste .... by occupation .... residing .... hereinafter called the RELEASEE which expression shall, where the subject or context allows or admits of, be deemed to include his heirs, executors, administrators, representatives and assigns of the OTHER PART.

AND WHEREAS the RELEASOR is the son of the RELEASEE AND WHEREAS the property fully mentioned and described in the schedule hereto was in fact and truth acquired by the RELEASEE under conveyance dated .... executed by .... and registered in Book I, vol. .... page .... to .... being No. .... of the office .... of Sub-registrar of .... with his own moneys and was at all material times owned, possessed and enjoyed by the RELEASEE for his use and benefit though in the name of the RELEASOR but not intending to make a gift or otherwise settle or to confer any estate or benefit thereof upon the RELEASOR under any circumstances AND WHEREAS in the circumstances the RELEASOR was a mere *benamdar* and/or name-lender or alias for the RELEASEE AND WHEREAS ever since the date of the said purchase and notwithstanding the fact of the name of the RELEASOR as the owner mentioned therein the RELEASOR never asserted nor claimed any ownership in respect of the same. And whereas the RELEASEE was at all material times and is still in lawful possession, control and enjoyment of the said property and every part thereof AND WHEREAS all the documents of title of the said property were at all material times and are also still in the possession and custody of the RELEASEE and all its outstandings and liabilities such as ground rent, municipal taxes, etc., are paid, discharged and satisfied by the RELEASEE without any aid or contribution of the RELEASOR AND WHEREAS in the circumstances and in the absence of any evidence as to advancement or gift by the RELEASEE in his favour the RELEASOR had never, nor presently has any right, title, interest or claim whatsoever in the said property or in any portion thereof—he being a benamdar and/or pretended trustee for the RELEASEE which the RELEASOR doth hereby admit and acknowledge AND WHEREAS by reason of the fact of the purchase of the property being in the name of the RELEASOR and in view of the relationship between the parties, it may be alleged or contended on any occasion that the RELEASOR had or has or the releasee intended or pretended to settle or confer upon the releasor any right, title or interest in the said property or any part thereof the RELEASOR has agreed to disclaim the said property and to execute and register a declaration and conveyance thereof in terms herein mentioned AND WHEREAS such declaration and conveyance is also necessary and/or expedient so as to remove in future the possibility of all doubts, disputes, differences on the question of the title of the releasee in, to, upon and concerning the said property and with a view to enabling the RELEASEE to enjoy better and deal with the same in any manner which he may deem fit and proper without any concurrence of the RELEASOR or any impediment whatsoever by the heirs, executors, administrators and representatives of the RELEASOR after his death NOW THIS INDENTURE WITNESSTH that in the circumstances hereinbefore stated and for good reasons and considerations as aforesaid, it is hereby agreed and declared by and between the parties as follows:

The RELEASOR doth hereby and hereunder absolutely disclaim, disown and relinquish and for ever discharge all and every such pretended right, title, interest, claim or demand or cause of action which may now or hereafter be alleged or contended or construed in his favour because of the said conveyance and/or the said property and otherwise relating thereto or concerning the same or any part thereof by virtue of the conveyance thereof having been made in the name of the releasor as hereinbefore stated or his relationship with the Releasee as aforesaid.

The RELEASOR doth hereby and hereunder further agree, declare, confirm and acknowledge the good right, full power and absolute authority and indefeasible title of the RELEASEE to grant, convey, sell and transfer the said property or to make a gift thereof or otherwise to deal with the corpus or income thereof in any manner and on any terms as the RELEASEE shall or may think fit and proper and even without the consent or concurrence of or any reference to the RELEASOR or his heirs, executors, administrators or representatives under any circumstances AND the RELEASOR doth hereby covenant with the RELEASEE that the RELEASOR had not done, executed, performed, nor been party or privy to any act, deed or thing whereby or whereunder or by reason or means whereof the said property or any part thereof may be in any manner charged, encumbered or otherwise affected or prejudiced in title or estate or the RELEASOR may be hindered or prevented from transferring the said property unto and to the use of the RELEASEE in the manner hereinbefore indicated.

The estimated value of the property is Rs. ....

The Schedule above referred to

IN WITNESS WHEREOF the RELEASOR hath hereunto set and subscribed his hand and seal the day, month and year first above-written.

Signed, sealed and delivered by
the RELEASOR within named at in
the presence of:

Executed by the RELEASEE in the
presence of:

N.B.: It was held by the Supreme Court in *Controller of Estate Duty* v *Aloke Mitra*[3] that a benamdar has no interest in the property. He is not even a mere trustee unless he is in possession of the property.

Disclaimer by Trustee Appointed under a Will

TO ALL WHOM THESE MAY CONCERN

KNOW ALL MEN by these presents I, AB son of CD do hereby and hereunder make known and declare as follows:

1. I for personal reasons and considerations disclaim all my office as trustee appointed under and by virtue of the will dated .... of CD son of MN of No. .... of which probate was granted to EF of No. .... by the court of ....

2. I also disclaim all estate interest, claims, profits and benefits thereof intended to be devised and powers provided under and by virtue of the said will in my favour.

I declare that I never assented to nor otherwise agreed expressly or impliedly nor did in any manner act deed or thing or participate in the execution or management of the trust or affairs ancillary or incidental thereto nor exercise any of those powers.

IN WITNESS WHEREOF I have set and subscribed my hand and seal this.......... day of .... 2000.

Signed, sealed and delivered

3 AIR 1981 SC 102.

Disclaimer by Trustee Appointed under a Deed of Trust

TO WHOM IT MAY CONCERN

WHEREAS by a deed of trust dated .... made between (*names, address and description of the parties*) the following properties appear to have been conveyed unto and in favour of AB, *viz*. myself TO HAVE AND TO HOLD the same in trust *inter alia* for the objects and purposes mentioned therein, AND WHEREAS for reasons of health and other good reasons and considerations I, the said AB, am unable to take upon myself the responsibility of execution of the trust and carry out the objects to which I never gave my consent.

Now know ye ALL I, the said AB, do hereby declare and confirm that I have all along disclaimed and do hereby also disclaim the office of the trustee under the said deed of trust and all estate and interest in the properties intended to be conferred upon me which did never in fact or truth vested in me.

I further declare that I shall not at any time hereafter claim the said office nor any of the powers.

IN WITNESS WHEREOF I have hereunto set and subscribed my hand and seal this 2nd day of June 2000.

Schedule of properties

Signed, sealed and delivered AB

19

Distributorship

A manufacturing concern normally appoints a dealer or distributor to sell the manufactured goods. A distributor is an agent who distributes the goods of manufacturer to the consumers. The distributor acts for and on behalf of the manufacturer. The transactions between them are not generally transactions of sale as a principal to principal. The distributor acts for the principal and earns a commission. He is not a buyer of goods from the manufacturer in his own account, he does not himself pay the price of the goods before the property in the goods passes to the consumers. However, a distributor by a special agreement may purchase the goods on payment of the commercial price to the manufacturer and then sell the same to the consumers or retailers. In such a case he is really a wholesale buyer and the property in the goods passes to him.

If a manufacturing concern after appointing a sole distributor for its products for a specified region for a specified period prematurely terminates the agreement then the manufacturing concern may have to pay compensation to the distributor. However, the relationship between the manufacturer and the distributor and their rights and obligations would be governed by the agreement appointing the distributor.

FORMS

Appointment of Overseas Distributors with Exclusive Rights

THIS AGREEMENT IS MADE on this 10th day of June 2000 BETWEEN AB Ltd., a company registered under the Companies Act 1956 and having its registered office at .... (hereinafter called the

COMPANY which expression shall unless repugnant to the context include its successors and assigns) of the One Part and CD Co. Ltd., a company registered under the appropriate laws of South Africa and carrying on business as distributor of diverse goods at .... South Africa (hereinafter called the DISTRIBUTOR which expression shall unless repugnant to the context include its permitted assigns).

WHEREAS the COMPANY manufactures diverse kinds of electronic goods under its trade name and the DISTRIBUTOR carries on business as wholesaler and retailer through its several outlets in South Africa and has approached to be appointed as the sole distributor of the COMPANY'S products in South Africa to which the COMPANY has agreed.

NOW THESE PRESENTS WITNESSTH and parties hereby agree as follows:

1. The COMPANY hereby grants to the DISTRIBUTOR the exclusive right during the continuance of this agreement to purchase for resale in the territory of South Africa the COMPANY'S products subject to the terms and conditions hereinafter appearing.

2. This agreement shall be in force for 5 years from 10th June 1999 and thereafter renewal for 5 years at a time on terms and conditions to be mutually agreed upon.

3. Orders for the products shall be placed by the DISTRIBUTOR on the COMPANY and the COMPANY shall sell the products to the DISTRIBUTOR at such prices as the COMPANY shall from time to time fix. The COMPANY shall execute orders of the DISTRIBUTORS for the products with all reasonable dispatch but shall not be liable for any loss of trade or profit, damages or expenses in the event of non-delivery of the products in time or at all due to labour trouble, strike, riots, lockouts, trade disputes, acts or restraints of governments, the imposition of restrictions on exportation or from any other cause not within the control of the COMPANY.

4. The title to the products shall pass to the DISTRIBUTOR when the invoiced products are placed on board the vessel at any Indian port and payment therefor shall become due from and payable by the DISTRIBUTOR in Indian Currency on receipt of shipping documents or on negotiation of shipping documents against Letter of Credit and/or on terms for payment as may from time to time be agreed upon by the parties.

5. The DISTRIBUTOR agrees and undertakes that it will at all times during the continuance of this agreement observe and perform the terms and conditions set out in this agreement.

6. The DISTRIBUTOR shall use at all times its best endeavours to promote sales of the products throughout the South Africa to all potential purchasers thereof and work diligently to obtain orders therefor by means of personal visits to and by correspondence with such purchasers, by advertising and

by the distribution of printed matter in the approved form, manner, extent and wording of such advertising and such distributed matter shall be at the costs and expenses of the DISTRIBUTOR.

7. The DISTRIBUTOR covenants that it will not without the previous consent in writing of the COMPANY be concerned or interested directly or indirectly in the manufacture, production, importation, sale or advertisement of any goods in South Africa which are similar to or which either alone or in conjunction with some other product perform or are designed to perform the same or a similar function to or which might otherwise compete or interfere with the sale of any of the COMPANY'S products.

8. The DISTRIBUTOR agrees and undertakes that it will not either directly or through any agent sell any of the products outside South Africa or knowingly allow to be resold the products to any person within South Africa with a view to their resale outside South Africa.

9. The DISTRIBUTOR shall in all correspondence and other dealings relating to the sale or disposition of the products clearly indicate that it is acting as principal.

10. The DISTRIBUTOR shall not incur any liability on behalf of the COMPANY or in any way pledge or purport to pledge the COMPANY'S credit or accept any order or make any contract sought to be binding on the COMPANY without prior written consent of the COMPANY.

11. The DISTRIBUTOR shall not sell the products at any price other than that for the time being fixed by the COMPANY for the sale of the products in South Africa without the previous consent in writing of the COMPANY.

12. The DISTRIBUTOR shall bring to the attention of the COMPANY any improper or wrongful use of the COMPANY'S patents, trade marks, emblems, designs, models or other similar industrial or commercial rights which comes to its notice and take all steps to safeguard the property rights and interests of the COMPANY and will assist the COMPANY in taking all steps to defend the rights of the COMPANY.

13. The DISTRIBUTOR shall keep proper and up-to-date books of account and records showing clearly all inquiries, transactions and proceedings relating to the distributorship and will allow the authorised officers of the COMPANY to have access to the said books and records and to take such copies thereof as they may require.

14. The DISTRIBUTOR shall from time to time upon the request of the COMPANY supply to the COMPANY reports, returns and other information relating to the distributorship and market conditions.

15. The DISTRIBUTOR shall not assign, transfer, charge or in any manner make over this agreement or their rights hereunder or any part thereof without the written consent of the COMPANY.

16. The DISTRIBUTOR shall be bound by the COMPANY'S conditions of sale that may from time to time be in force and in selling the products enforce similar terms and conditions and shall not make any promises, representations, give warranties or guarantees with reference to the products except such as are consistent with those conditions or as are expressly authorised by the COMPANY in writing.

17. The DISTRIBUTOR shall not alter, remove, conceal or otherwise interfere with any markings or nameplates or other indication of the source or origin of the goods which may be placed by the COMPANY on its products.

18. The COMPANY hereby agrees with the DISTRIBUTOR that it will not during the continuance of the agreement sell any of the products to any person in South Africa other than to the DISTRIBUTOR or to any person outside the South Africa with a view to the resale thereof within the territory of South Africa save as provided in this agreement.

19. The COMPANY shall at its own expense supply the DISTRIBUTOR with such amount of samples and patterns, instructions, books, technical pamphlets, catalogues and advertising material as it considers reasonably sufficient to promote sales of the products within the territory of South Africa.

20. The COMPANY shall use its best endeavour to safeguard the sole and exclusive rights hereby granted to the DISTRIBUTOR including the taking of such steps as may be available to it to prevent the infringement of those rights by other distributors or agents of the COMPANY and to prevent the infringement of its patents, trade marks, emblems, designs and other similar industrial or commercial monopoly rights within the territory of South Africa.

21. The COMPANY reserves to itself the right to supply the products to customers within the territory of South Africa in pursuance of firm orders placed with the COMPANY before the commencement of this agreement or in pursuance of orders resulting from negotiations pending at that date and no right to any payment shall accrue to the distributor in respect thereof provided that information relating to all such orders and negotiations shall be given to the DISTRIBUTOR within 7 days of the commencement of this agreement and in the event any products are sold by the COMPANY with knowledge that they are for use in the said territory the DISTRIBUTOR shall be entitled to be paid a commission of 20% on the net price f.o.b. (before carriage, freight, insurance or duty have been added) Indian port in consideration of the DISTRIBUTOR assisting the COMPANY to obtain business from the territory as and when requested and on receipt by the COMPANY of payment in full for the products.

22. It is agreed that (*a*) the DISTRIBUTOR shall not be entitled to commission on any sale in respect of which it has failed to render such assistance as was required of them; (*b*) the DISTRIBUTOR shall be entitled to such commission

as the COMPANY may in its absolute discretion determine on any sale direct by the Company to any Government Department or Agency, State-owned public utility or industry in the territory; (*c*) the Company may decline to submit a tender on any inquiry or to accept any order from the DISTRIBUTOR and by so declining shall not incur any obligation to the DISTRIBUTOR.

23. The COMPANY may vary the first schedule hereto defining the products either by withdrawing therefrom a class or classes of products named therein in the event of the company ceasing to manufacture that class or classes of products or by the addition thereto after consultation with the DISTRIBUTOR of further classes of products of the COMPANY.

24. If in the opinion of the COMPANY the DISTRIBUTOR becomes unable to effect adequate sales coverage throughout the whole of the territory without prejudice to any other rights the COMPANY may vary the First Schedule hereto so as to exclude from this agreement such part or parts of the territory therein defined as it thinks fit or to vary the Second Schedule hereto so as to exclude from this agreement such one or more of the products herein defined as it thinks fit or to take both these courses of action save that neither such course of action shall be taken under this clause without prior consultation with the DISTRIBUTOR.

25. The COMPANY shall be entitled to take such steps as may seem necessary or expedient including and without prejudice to the generality of the reserved right to appoint a representative in the said territory of South Africa and to notify the DISTRIBUTOR of any person, firm or body-corporate carrying on business in the territory who might appear to the COMPANY to be potential purchaser of its products.

26. The DISTRIBUTOR undertakes that they will not at any time divulge any information in relation to the COMPANY'S affairs or business or method of carrying on business.

27. The COMPANY shall have the right at any time by giving notice in writing to the DISTRIBUTOR to terminate the agreement forthwith (*a*) if the DISTRIBUTOR commits any breach of any terms or conditions of this agreement; (*b*) goes into compulsorily or voluntarily liquidation or compounds with its creditors or a receiver is appointed.

28. Before the expiration of the original term of agreement either party shall have the right to determine this agreement by giving one calendar month's notice in writing to the other party.

29. Upon the termination of this agreement from any cause or at any time previous to such termination at the request of the COMPANY the DISTRIBUTOR shall promptly return to the COMPANY or otherwise dispose of as the COMPANY may instruct all samples, patterns, instruction books, technical pamphlets, catalogues, advertising materials, specifications and other materials, goods documents and papers whatsoever sent to the

DISTRIBUTOR and relating to the business of the COMPANY at the cost of the DISTRIBUTOR.

30. Nothing in this agreement shall constitute or be deemed to constitute a partnership between the parties hereto or constitute or be deemed to constitute the DISTRIBUTOR as agent of the COMPANY for any purpose whatsoever. The DISTRIBUTOR shall have no authority or power to bind the COMPANY or to enter into contract in the name of the COMPANY or create any liability against the COMPANY in any way for any purpose.

31. Any dispute, difference or question which may arise at any time hereafter between the COMPANY and the DISTRIBUTOR touching the true construction of this agreement or the rights and liabilities of the parties hereto shall be referred to the decision of a single arbitrator to be agreed upon between the parties or in default of agreement to be appointed at the request of either party in accordance with and subject to the provisions of the Arbitration and Conciliation Act 1996 or any statutory modification or re-enactment thereof for the time being in force.

32. This agreement shall be deemed to have been made in India and the construction, validity and performance of this agreement shall be governed in all respects by the laws of India, arbitration shall be held in India and the Courts in India shall have the jurisdiction over any dispute and the Indian law shall govern this agreement.

First Schedule

The Territory

South Africa

Second Schedule

All kinds of Electronic Products

IN WITNESS WHEREOF the parties hereto have executed these presents at Calcutta on the day, month and year first above-written.

Signed, sealed and delivered by Mr. MN pursuant to Board Resolution dated 1st June 2000 of AB Ltd., in the presence of:

Signed, sealed and delivered by Mr. .... pursuant to Board Resolution dated 2nd June 2000 of CD Co. Ltd. at .... in the presence of:

Distributorship Agreement

THIS AGREEMENT OF DISTRIBUTORSHIP is made on this 16th day of December 2000 BETWEEN X Co. Ltd. a company registered under the English Companies Act, and carrying on business at ...., hereinafter called the MANUFACTURER (which term shall include its successors and assigns) of the one part and DC Co. Ltd. a company registered under the Companies Act 1956 and carrying on business at ...., hereinafter referred to as the DISTRIBUTOR (which term shall unless excluded by or repugnant to the context shall include its successors and permitted nominees and assigns) of the other part.

WHEREAS the MANUFACTURER is manufacturing Tele-communications Instruments, Computers, Softwares and Hardwares and exporting and marketing them in India and abroad.

AND WHEREAS the MANUFACTURER intends to strengthen its distribution machinery in the backward areas in India and in unexplored areas in the East Asian markets.

AND WHEREAS the DISTRIBUTOR approached the manufacturer for having the distributorship of the manufacturer's products in backward areas in India and unexplored areas in the East Asian and foreign markets.

AND WHEREAS the MANUFACTURER has agreed to the proposals of the distributor on certain terms and conditions.

NOW THESE PRESENTS WITNESSETH and the parties hereby agree as follows:

1. The MANUFACTURER hereby appoints and the DISTRIBUTOR accepts such appointment as the SOLE DISTRIBUTOR of the products of the MANUFACTURER in respect of its products and the areas mentioned in the Schedule hereunder.

2. The DISTRIBUTOR will have to deposit by way of Security Money free from interest a sum of Rs. 5 lakhs before the MANUFACTURER delivers any goods to the DISTRIBUTOR. The DISTRIBUTOR agrees and undertakes to lift the products of the MANUFACTURER and store them in the DISTRIBUTOR'S godown for ultimate distribution to the wholesalers or retailers as the case may be.

3. The DISTRIBUTOR agrees to lift such products of the MANUFACTURER not less than worth Rs. 5 lakhs at a time and always store in its godown goods worth not less than Rs. 4 lakhs.

4. The DISTRIBUTOR hereby agrees and undertakes not to deal with similar products of any other MANUFACTURER in respect of the scheduled areas for which the DISTRIBUTOR has been offered the distributorship of the MANUFACTURER'S products.

5. The DISTRIBUTOR shall ensure that the products are sold to the consumers at the prices marked on the commodities or on the packing.

6. The MANUFACTURER will pay to the DISTRIBUTOR a commission of 30% on the prices marked on the commodities and the DISTRIBUTOR, in turn, may grant a commission not more than 10% on the prices marked on the commodities or its packing to the wholesalers or retailers as the case may be.

7. The DISTRIBUTOR shall advertise the products and popularise the same and the actual expenses incurred will be reimbursed by the MANUFACTURER.

8. The DISTRIBUTOR shall lift the goods from the factory or godown of the MANUFACTURER and the entire costs of transport will be borne by the DISTRIBUTOR.

9. The DISTRIBUTOR shall submit quarterly reports to the MANUFACTURER about the efforts made to popularise the products of the MANUFACTURER. The DISTRIBUTOR shall submit quarterly statements of accounts of the goods lifted from the MANUFACTURER and distributed or sold by the DISTRIBUTOR. The DISTRIBUTOR shall also submit every quarter a market survey report in relation to the products of the MANUFACTURER and also available information regarding similar products of other manufacturers.

10. The DISTRIBUTOR shall at its own cost keep the products of MANUFACTURER fully insured against all insurable risks of such products from the time of lifting of the products from the premises of the MANUFACTURER till these are sold by the DISTRIBUTOR. The insurance policy to be taken will be in the joint names of the MANUFACTURER and the DISTRIBUTOR and the insurance policy when received and the receipt for premium paid will be forwarded to the MANUFACTURER within 7 days of the receipt thereof.

11. The DISTRIBUTOR shall inform the MANUFACTURER of any infringement of the brand name, trade mark or patent rights of the MANUFACTURER in any of the products in respect of which the agreement has been entered into and executed with the MANUFACTURER and take and permit to be taken all such actions as will be necessary to protect the right, title and interest of the MANUFACTURER in the aforesaid products.

12. The DISTRIBUTOR shall pay for the products lifted by it every quarter and if there be any delay in payment for goods lifted, interest at 15% shall be charged on the outstanding amount with quarterly rests.

13. This agreement is subject to the compliances by both parties of all rules, regulations and laws applicable to the agreement and the transactions as may be entered into by the MANUFACTURER and/or the DISTRIBUTOR.

14. This agreement is terminable by giving three months' notice by either side.

15. It is agreed and the DISTRIBUTOR covenants that in respect of products lifted by it from the MANUFACTURER if not paid for will remain the property of the MANUFACTURER and no right, title or interest will pass to the DISTRIBUTOR until full payment has been made for such products.

16. All disputes and differences that might arise in relation to or touching the agreement or the transactions between the parties or claims, liabilities and rights of the parties shall be referred to Mr. MN, Advocate of Old Post Office Street, Calcutta for adjudication by Arbitration in accordance with the provisions of the Arbitration and Conciliation Act 1996 including any modifications thereof for the time being in force.

The Schedule

(Particulars of the products and the areas for which the distributorship is obtained).

IN WITNESS WHEREOF the parties herein executed these presents on the day month and year first above-written.

Signed, sealed and delivered by
Mr. .... pursuant to
Board Resolution dated ....
of the Manufacturer in Calcutta
in presence of:

Signed, sealed and delivered by
Mr. .... pursuant to
Board Resolution dated ....
of the Distributor in Calcutta in
presence of:

Agreement of Bottling Beverages

THIS AGREEMENT IS MADE on this 10th day of October 2000 BETWEEN AB Co. Ltd., registered under the appropriate laws of Scotland and carrying on business at ...., Scotland hereinafter referred to as the PRINCIPAL (which term shall unless excluded by or repugnant to the context include its successors and assigns) of the one part and the CD Ltd., a company registered under the Companies Act 1956 and having its registered office at ...., hereinafter referred to as the BOTTLER (which term shall unless excluded by or repugnant to the context include its successors and permitted nominees and assigns) of the other part.

WHEREAS the PRINCIPAL is carrying on business as manufacturer of and dealer in Beverages under the trade name SCOTCH.

AND WHEREAS the PRINCIPAL intends to extend its business to India and South-East Asia but the cost of setting up a new manufacturing unit would not be economical and transportation of beverages from Scotland to the distant areas will not be commercially viable.

AND WHEREAS the BOTTLER has a plant for bottling aerated waters and the same has been recently modernised and is suitable for bottling the beverages manufactured by the PRINCIPAL.

AND WHEREAS the BOTTLER has approached the PRINCIPAL for arrangement of obtaining concentrates for the PRINCIPAL'S beverages for the purpose of bottling the same in India and selling it under the trade name of the PRINCIPAL on certain terms and conditions to which the PRINCIPAL has agreed.

NOW THESE PRESENTS WITNESSETH and the parties hereto hereunder agree as follows:

1. The PRINCIPAL appoints the BOTTLER as its Sole Bottling Agent in India for a period of 5 years which is renewable for another 5 years at a time on mutually agreed terms and conditions.

2. The BOTTLER shall maintain its Bottling Plant in good condition and repair at its own cost subject to periodical inspection by the representative of the PRINCIPAL. The BOTTLER shall use the water available from the Corporation of Calcutta or from the tubewell sunk by it and the same be filtered through a machine to be supplied by the PRINCIPAL free of cost.

3. The water so purified will be tested by a named organisation as to its purety and fitness for using for beverages and human consumption.

4. The PRINCIPAL shall supply the concentrates to be used with water and other permissible ingredients for the purpose of bottling the mixed liquid. After the concentrates converted into liquid is bottled, the same will be properly capped and labelled. All these are to be untouched by hand and to be done automatically by the plant.

5. The finished product in the bottles will be branded as SCOTCH and sold as soft drink at a price to be fixed by the PRINCIPAL.

6. The BOTTLER shall have arrangements for distribution to the retailers of the said Scotch Beverages and to be sold in retail at a price to be fixed from time to time by the PRINCIPAL.

7. The Bottles to be manufactured for the purpose of the said Scotch Beverages would be according to the specifications and designs of the PRINCIPAL and the cost whereof shall be reimbursed by the PRINCIPAL.

8. All breakages of bottles and missing bottles will be replaced by the BOTTLER at its own costs.

9. The PRINCIPAL will allow the BOTTLER for the said bottling and distribution a commission of 50% on the retail sale price of the Scotch bottles of beverages.

10. The BOTTLER shall publicise and popularise the said Scotch Beverages by advertisement in newspapers, posters, journals and otherwise, the

costs whereof will be borne in equal proportions by the PRINCIPAL and the BOTTLER.

11. The composition of the concentrate is a secret and the BOTTLER shall not make any effort to find out the composition thereof or discuss with anybody or furnish any sample of the concentrate to anybody so that composition of the concentrate remains a secret.

12. The said beverage Scotch is the registered trade mark of the PRINCIPAL and the BOTTLER shall inform the PRINCIPAL immediately on coming to know of any alleged infringement or passing off of the product and take immediate steps to protect the interests of the PRINCIPAL the expenses whereof will be reimbursed by the PRINCIPAL.

13. The plant of the BOTTLER shall be maintained in perfect condition subject to the supervision of the Engineer of the PRINCIPAL and such plants should not be used for bottling any other product except the Scotch Beverage.

14. The BOTTLER shall be responsible for complying with all local laws and paying all taxes, rates, cesses and other levies in connection with the said plant, maintenance thereof, manufacturing of the said beverage and selling the same through retail outlets.

15. In consideration of the PRINCIPAL granting the bottling rights of the Scotch Beverage to the BOTTLER, the BOTTLER will keep in deposit with the PRINCIPAL Rs. 10 lakhs free of interest which will be adjusted on the expiry or termination of this Agreement.

16. The BOTTLER shall render quarterly accounts of the concentrates supplied, the bottling made and the Scotch Beverage sold through retail outlets or otherwise and pay the sale proceeds of the Scotch Beverages after deducting the commission of the BOTTLER.

17. The BOTTLER shall submit statements of accounts and other expenses every quarter and on such accounts being furnished, the same would be settled by adjustment or payment.

18. In default of the BOTTLER in complying with any of the terms and conditions of this agreement, the PRINCIPAL will have the liberty to terminate this agreement by giving 3 months notice.

19. In default of payment of any money due from the BOTTLER, interest would be charged at 15% per annum with quarterly rests by way of compensation for withholding the payment.

20. The BOTTLER shall ensure proper customer satisfaction and from time to time make a market research to ascertain the customer reaction to the Scotch Beverage, nature of storing the bottles and the cooling arrangement therein as also suitability of retail outlets.

21. The BOTTLER shall on market research ascertain whether any plastic crates should be supplied free of cost to specified retailers for storage of the Scotch Beverages and also to supply to limited retailers Ice Box or Mini Refrigerators for the cooling arrangement of the Scotch Beverages. The cost of crates and Mini Refrigerators will be borne by the BOTTLER but for which the PRINCIPAL would make advances to be adjusted against the commission payable by the PRINCIPAL to the BOTTLER inasmuch as such an arrangement will directly benefit the BOTTLER in increasing the sales in competition with other market products.

22. The BOTTLER shall after manufacture of every lot of bottles of Scotch Beverages make random chemical tests by a competent person as to the suitability thereof for human consumption and should ensure that the same is free from any bacteria or harmful elements. The BOTTLER shall be solely responsible for any claims, proceedings, losses or damages due to any defect in the Scotch Beverages and the BOTTLER hereby undertakes and covenants to keep the PRINCIPAL harmless from and indemnified against all claims, proceedings, costs charges and expenses in relation to the Scotch Beverages manufactured, sold and distributed through outlets of the BOTTLER.

23. The BOTTLER shall be free to sell Scotch Beverages bottled by it in India or outside India without any restrictions.

24. All disputes and differences arising out of this agreement or in relation thereto or touching it or in relation to any transactions covered by this agreement or otherwise affecting the relationship of the PRINCIPAL and the BOTTLER shall be referred to the Bengal Chamber of Commerce for adjudication under its rules and/or the provisions of the Arbitration and Conciliation Act 1996 or any statutory modifications thereof for the time being in force.

IN WITNESS WHEREOF the parties hereto have executed these presents on the day, month and year first above-written.

Signed, sealed and delivered by
Mr. .... Power-of-Attorney
Holder from the AB Co. Ltd., and
authorised representative in
Calcutta in the presence of:

Signed, sealed and delivered by
Mr. .... pursuant to the
Board Resolution of the CD Co.
Ltd. dated .... in Calcutta
in the presence of:

Agreement for Distributorship

THIS AGREEMENT IS MADE on the 10th day of October 2000 BETWEEN AB Co. Ltd., a company registered under the Companies Act 1956 and having its registered office and carrying on business at .... (hereinafter called the COMPANY) and CD Ltd., a Company registeted under the Companies Act 1956 and carrying on business at .... (hereinafter called the DISTRIBUTOR).

WHEREAS the COMPANY carries on business as publisher and seller of books on legal and allied subjects.

AND WHEREAS the DISTRIBUTOR has a book shop at Bangalore with spare capacity with sales outlets.

AND WHEREAS the DISTRIBUTOR has approached the COMPANY for being appointed as the sole distributor of the COMPANY'S publications in Bangalore and within a radius of 5 miles thereof to which the COMPANY has agreed.

NOW THESE PRESENTS WITNESSETH and the parties agree as follows:

1. The COMPANY hereby appoints the DISTRIBUTOR to be its sole DISTRIBUTOR and the DISTRIBUTOR agrees to act as such to establish, promote and extend the sale of publications of the company in Bangalore and within a radius of 5 miles thereof (hereinafter called the said TERRITORY).

2. The agreement shall commence on the 10th day of October 2000 and shall continue for a period of 5 years and thereafter will stand extended from year to year until terminated by 6 months' notice in writing given by either party to the other.

3. The DISTRIBUTOR shall not engage in selling or otherwise being concerned in the sale of books competing with or in the same class as the publications of the COMPANY.

4. The COMPANY shall not sell the publications to any other person in the territory or outside the territory who the company knows or has reason to believe intends to resell the publications within the territory. The COMPANY further agrees to refer all inquiries for its publications reaching it from the territory to the DISTRIBUTOR.

5. The DISTRIBUTOR agrees to pay for all publications of the COMPANY ordered and accepted by it within 30 days of delivery.

6. All publications shall be dispatched by road transport or by goods train carriage paid or by such other means as may be agreed.

7. The COMPANY shall allow the distributor a discount or rebate of 30 per cent on the quoted price and shall allow a further discount/rebate of 10 per cent on the net value of all publications which the DISTRIBUTOR takes delivery of and pays for in any period of twelve calendar months in excess of the amount of Rs. 2 lakhs.

8. The DISTRIBUTOR shall at all times during the continuance of this agreement offer for sale and sell the publications without giving any warranty of any sort. The DISTRIBUTOR shall at all times during the continuance of this agreement maintain a stock of all the publications for display purposes. The DISTRIBUTOR shall have no right of action against the COMPANY in respect of any loss occurring to it by reason of any delay in delivery occasioned by shortage of stock or delays in transit or delays caused by accidents or strikes or for reasons beyond the control of the COMPANY. The DISTRIBUTOR shall not assign the benefit of this agreement without the prior written consent of the COMPANY.

9. The COMPANY reserves the right to grant licences for the printing of the Company's Publications within the territory and itself to establish shops for the sale or distribution of the products within the territory without being liable in any way to remunerate the DISTRIBUTOR in respect of sales of the products thereafter printed within the territory.

10. The DISTRIBUTOR shall submit its scheme for publicity for approval of the COMPANY at intervals and 3 months ahead of the date from which it is proposed that it should commence and the COMPANY agrees to reimburse the DISTRIBUTOR to the extent of 50% of its publicity costs provided that the liability of the COMPANY shall not exceed 3% of the value of the product ordered by the DISTRIBUTOR.

11. The DISTRIBUTOR shall report to the COMPANY from time to time upon the development of business and generally upon trade conditions in the territory.

12. This agreement shall not be construed as a partnership between the parties hereto or constitute or be deemed to constitute the DISTRIBUTOR an agent of the COMPANY for any purpose whatever and the DISTRIBUTOR shall have no authority or power to bind the COMPANY or to contract in the name of and create any liability against the COMPANY in any way or for any purpose.

13. The COMPANY shall have the right at any time by giving notice in writing to the distributor to terminate the agreement forthwith if the DISTRIBUTOR commits a breach of any term or condition of this agreement or winding up proceedings are initiated.

14. Any dispute, difference or question which may arise at any time hereafter between the COMPANY and the DISTRIBUTOR touching the true construction of this agreement or the rights and liabilities of the parties hereto shall be referred to the decision of a single arbitrator to be agreed upon between the parties or in default of agreement to be appointed at the request of either party in accordance with and subject to the provisions of the Arbitration and Conciliation Act 1996 or any statutory modification or re-enactment thereof for the time being in force.

IN WITNESS WHEREOF the parties herein have executed these presents on the day, month and year first above-written.

Signed, sealed and delivered by Mr. XY pursuant to Board Resolution of 2nd October 2000 of AB Co. Ltd. in the presence of:

Signed, sealed and delivered by Mr. MN pursuant to the Board Resolution of 3rd October 2000 of CD Ltd. in the presence of:

Petrol Station Agreement

THIS AGREEMENT IS MADE on the 15th day of December 2000 BETWEEN AB Co. Ltd., a company registered under the Companies Act 1956 and carrying on business at .... (hereinafter called the COMPANY) of the one part and ML carrying on business under the name and style of Auto Fil at .... (hereinafter called the AUTO FIL) of the other part.

WHEREAS ML owns a plot of land being premises No. .... and is desirous of setting up of a Petrol Station there and approached the COMPANY for dealership.

AND WHEREAS the COMPANY has supplied at the cost of AUTO FIL equipment for the installation of a petrol pump at .... and the installation is almost complete.

AND WHEREAS the AUTO FIL has assured the COMPANY that it will store the petrol and petroleum products of the COMPANY for the purpose of sale.

NOW THIS AGREEMENT WITNESSES and the parties hereby agree as follows:

1. The COMPANY shall supply as much petrol as it conveniently can do to AUTO FIL for storage in the tank installed underneath the petrol pump station and petroleum products in its rooms on the said premises .... being the AUTO FIL.

2. AUTO FIL shall maintain the equipment and the construction of the said petrol pump in good state of repair so as to keep it free from leakage, theft, fire and other like hazards.

3. AUTO FIL shall not store or handle petrol supplied by another person, firm or company or State.

4. AUTO FIL shall sell the petrol and petroleum products at the rate fixed by the COMPANY.

5. AUTO FIL shall not encumber or dispose of the installation or the equipment in any manner whatsoever or do or suffer anything to be done whereby the said petrol pump or any part thereof may be seized or possessed by any other person or authority.

6. AUTO FIL shall submit weekly accounts of the receipt and disposal of the petrol and petroleum products supplied to it and pay the price thereof forthwith along with the said accounts. The COMPANY shall be entitled to check, inspect, measure and investigate into the conditions, state, quantity of the petrol, petroleum products and the equipment as well as the installation and to verify any fact mentioned in the said accounts or otherwise at its discretion.

7. This agreement shall continue for a period of 5 years from the date hereof unless sooner terminated by service of 30 days notice on either side.

8. If AUTO FIL should commit any breach of the agreement the COMPANY shall be entitled to terminate this agreement by 7 days notice. On the expiry of the period so fixed in the notice the agreement so far as the rights of AUTO FIL are concerned shall be deemed to have come to an end but it shall be bound by the obligations undertaken hereunder.

9. AUTO FIL shall be entitled to receive from the COMPANY commission of 5% on the sale of petrol and petroleum products. AUTO FIL will be liable for and shall furnish a Bank Guarantee for payment of the price of petrol and petroleum products supplied to it. No commission shall be payable unless the price of petrol and petroleum products has actually been paid to the COMPANY.

10. AUTO FIL shall keep a sum of Rs. 5 lakhs interest-free deposit with the COMPANY as security for the due performance of the conditions of the agreement in addition to the Bank Guarantee. This is without prejudice to the terms and conditions mentioned above in respect of termination of this agreement.

11. On termination of this agreement after adjustments of the COMPANY'S claims against AUTO FIL the security deposit would be returned.

IN WITNESS WHEREOF the parties herein have executed these presents on the day, month and year first above-written.

Signed, sealed and delivered by Mr. .... pursuant to Board Resolution dated 10th December 2000 of AB Co. Ltd. in the presence of:

Signed, sealed and delivered by Mr. ML proprietor of AUTO FIL in the presence of:

20

Divorce—Nullity of Marriage and Judicial Separation

Marriage is a social institution which is known all over the world and common to all people. Every country, however, has its own laws and customs with regard to it.

Professor Edwin S. Bundell said: Marriage is the best insurance in the world—insurance against (*a*) crime, (*b*) insanity, (*c*) poverty and (*d*) premature death.[1]

Any two persons of opposite sex, who are desirous of marrying each other, may do so with the exception of (*a*) minors under certain ages according to the laws by which they are governed, (*b*) persons within the prohibited degrees of relationship, (*c*) persons who are already married to a living spouse, and (*d*) persons mentally deficient of contracting marriage.[2] The Hindu and Mahomedan marriages were and are still in many aspects regulated not by any legislation but governed by the personal law of the communities and customs. The idea behind those marriages is essentially different *inter se* from the background behind a Christian marriage—a contract between the parties. The Hindu Law permitted polygamy until the Hindu Marriage Act 1955, was enacted[3] and amended in 1964 (Act 44 of 1964). Although monogamy was the general rule, polygamy, though an exception, existed side by side. The Muslim Law permits marriages up to four wives.[4] Marriages contracted under the Special Marriage Act[5] are monogamous.

1 Mital: *Law of Marriage*, Preface.
2 Grant: *Marriage, Divorce and Separation*, p. 11.
3 Section 5 of the Hindu Marriage Act.
4 Baillie 30, 154; Ameer Ali: *Mahommedan Law*, 5th Ed., vol. 2, p. 280; Kader: *Muslim Law of Marriage & Succession in India*, 1st Ed. (1998), p. 79.
5 Section 4 of the Special Marriage Act 1954.

Breach of promise to marry. An engagement between a man and a woman imposes an obligation on both to marry each other in due course. This obligation is irrevocably binding unless (*a*) the parties at any time before marriage mutually agree to release each other from their mutual promises to marry, or (*b*) one of them breaks off the engagement for any reason which the law considers justifiable.[6] Law allows recovery of damages in certain cases.[7]

Husband and wife. Marriage imposes a duty upon both the spouses to live together and to cohabit with each other as husband and wife. Even in days gone by, a husband could enforce his wife's obligation of staying with him. If any of the parties without just cause refuses him or her the society of the other, the court will by judicial process restitute the conjugal rights.[8] A decree in all such suits can be enforced under Or. 21, rr. 32, 33 of Code of Civil Procedure.

The Statutory Law of Marriage in India, e.g. Indian Divorce Act 1869, Hindu Marriage Act 1955 as amended by the Hindu Marriage (Amendment) Act 1964; Parsi Marriage and Divorce Act 1936 and Special Marriage Act 1954 provides four types of remedies to parties to the marriage: (*i*) Divorce, (*ii*) judicial separation, (*iii*) nullity of marriage, (*iv*) restitution of conjugal rights and (*v*) mutual divorce. A judicially separated wife is considered a *fame sole*. Hindu law did not allow divorce except when the same was permitted by customs. Hindu Woman's Right to Separate Residence and Maintenance Act 1946, was repealed by s. 29 of the Hindu Adoptions and Maintenance Act 1956. Under s. 19 of the latter Act, a Hindu wife is entitled to live separately without forfeiting her claim as to maintenance in case of desertion, cruelty, change of religion on the part of the husband and other good causes. The Hindu Marriage Act 1955, as amended by Act 44 of 1964 is an overriding statute.[9] So all previous customs, usages, etc., have been repealed by the said Act. See also the Marriage Laws (Amendment) Act 1976.

Mahomedan law recognises marriage as a contract of the nature of contract of service and so the husband enjoyed the one-sided liberty of divorce which he could avail of by paying the wages in full,[10] whereas the wife had very limited power in that behalf until the enactment of Dissolution of Muslim Marriage Act 1939.[11]

6 Section 73 of the Indian Contract Act.
7 Desai's *Contract Act*, 7th Ed., p. 268.
8 Section 9 of the Hindu Marriage Act, s. 32 of the Indian Divorce Act, s. 36 of the Parsi Marriage and Divorce Act.
9 Section 4 of the Hindu Marriage Act.
10 Manchand's *Law and Practice of Divorce*, 2nd Ed., p. 435.
11 Section 2 of the Dissolution of Muslim Marriage Act.

Principles of res judicata. Under s. 45 of the Indian Divorce Act, the principles of *res judicata* as laid down in the Code of Civil Procedure applies to proceedings under the Indian Divorce Act.

Dissolution of Marriage

It is now a creature of statute. The law relating to marriage, divorce and other matrimonial causes is not uniform. Matrimonial causes between persons professing Christian religion are governed by the Indian Divorce Act 1869[12] or if the marriage had been solemnized under the Special Marriage Act 1954, by the latter Act.[13] In regard to Hindu marriages, matrimonial causes are governed by the Hindu Marriage Act 1955.

A Hindu marriage does not *ipso facto* stand dissolved by reason of the conversion of one party into some other religion but such conversion is one of the grounds for divorce.[14]

Matrimonial causes in regard to Muslim marriages are governed by the Mahomedan law and the Dissolution of Muslim Marriage Act 1939.[15] Divorce by a Muslim husband is outside the scope of the said Act. A Mahomedan husband has always the sanction of the *Koran* to give his wife *Talak*. Section 28 of the Special Marriage Act 1954 further provides for divorce by mutual consent.

When husband or wife can petition for dissolution of marriage. Under s. 10 of the Indian Divorce Act, any husband can present a petition to the District Court, or to the High Court, praying that his marriage may be dissolved on the ground that his wife has, since the solemnization thereof, been guilty of adultery.

Any wife can also present a petition to the District Court, or to the High Court, praying that her marriage may be dissolved, on the ground that, since the solemnization thereof, her husband has exchanged his profession of Christianity for the profession of some other religion, and gone through a form of marriage with another woman;

or has been guilty of incestuous adultery,

or of bigamy with adultery,

or of marriage with another woman with adultery,

or of rape,

or, sodomy or bestiality,

12 Section 10 of the Indian Divorce Act.
13 Section 13 of the Indian Divorce Act.
14 Section 13(*i*) and 13(*ii*) of the Hindu Marriage Act.
15 Section 2 of the Dissolution of Muslim Marriage Act.

or of adultery coupled with such cruelty as, without adultery, would have entitled her to a divorce a *mensa et toro*,

or of adultery coupled with desertion, without reasonable excuse for two years or upwards.

A husband may present a petition for divorce against his wife on the simple ground of adultery, but the wife in order to get divorce must establish certain other facts.

Extent of court's power to grant relief.[16] No court is authorised to grant any relief under the Indian Divorce Act, except in cases where the petitioner (or respondent) professes the Christian religion.

Or to make decrees of dissolution of marriage except where the parties to the marriage are domiciled in India at the time of the presentation of the petition.

Or to make decrees of nullity of marriage except where the marriage has been solemnized in India, and the petitioner is resident in India at the time of presenting the petition.

Or to grant any relief under this Act, other than a decree for dissolution of marriage or of nullity of marriage, except where the petitioner resides in India at the time of presenting the petition.

Contents of petition. Every petition for dissolution of marriage must distinctly state the grounds or facts upon which the petitioner seeks the relief. Every petition for dissolution of marriage must state, as distinctly as the nature of the case permits, the facts on which the claim to have such marriage dissolved is founded.

Upon such petition presented by a husband, the petitioner must make the alleged adulterer a co-respondent to the said petition, unless he is excused from so doing on one of the following grounds, to be allowed by the court:

(*i*) that the respondent is leading the life of a prostitute, and that the petitioner knows of no person with whom the adultery has been committed;

(*ii*) that the name of the alleged adulterer is unknown to the petitioner, although he has made due efforts to discover it;

(*iii*) that the alleged adulterer is dead.[17]

Decrees for dissolution will be nisi—confirmation of decrees. Every decree for a dissolution of marriage made by a High Court, not being a confirmation of a decree of a District Court, will, in the first instance, be a decree *nisi*, not to be made absolute till after the expiration of such time, not less than six

16 Section 2 of the Indian Divorce Act.

17 Section 11 of the Indian Divorce Act.

months from the pronouncing thereof, as the High Court, by general or specified order, from time to time directs.

Every decree for nullity of marriage made by the District Judge or by a Judge of the City Civil Court or of the Family Court is subject to confirmation by the High Court.[18] If the petitioner fails to apply to make the decree absolute, the other party may apply for rescission of the decree.[19] The effect of the rescission of the decree is dismissal of the suit.

Nullity of Marriages

Petition for nullity of marriage.[20] Any husband or wife can present a petition to the District Court or to the High Court praying that his or her marriage may be declared null and void. Such decree will be made on any of the following grounds:

(*i*) that the respondent was impotent at the time of the marriage and at the time of the institution of the suit;

(*ii*) that the parties are within the prohibited degrees of consanguinity (whether natural or legal) or affinity;

(*iii*) that either party was a lunatic or idiot at the time of the marriage;

(*iv*) that the former husband or wife of either party was living at the time of the marriage with such former husband or wife was then in force.

Nothing will affect the jurisdiction of the High Court to make decrees of nullity of marriage on the ground that the consent of either party was obtained by force or fraud. It will be interesting to note here that it is not necessary that the domicile of the parties should be Indian in order to present a petition for nullity of marriage as required in the case of divorce.

Every decree of nullity of marriage made by a District Judge or by a Judge of the City Civil Court or of the Family Court is subject to confirmation by the High Court.[1]

Children of annulled marriage. When a marriage is annulled on the ground that a former husband or wife was living and it is adjudged that the subsequent marriage was contracted in good faith and with the full belief of the parties that the former husband or wife was dead, or when a marriage is annulled on the ground of insanity, children begotten before the decree is made will be specified in the decree and will be entitled to succeed, in the

18 Section 20 of the Indian Divorce Act.
19 Manchand's *Law and Practice of Divorce*, 2nd Ed., p. 162.
20 Sections 18 and 19 of the Indian Divorce Act.
1 Section 20 of the Indian Divorce Act.

same manner as legitimate children, to the estate of the parent who, at the time of the marriage, was competent to contract.[2]

Judicial Separation

Application for judicial separation. Application for judicial separation on the ground of adultery or cruelty, or desertion without reasonable excuse for two years or upwards, can be made by either husband or wife by petition to the District Court or the High Court. The decree obtained will have the effect of a divorce a *mensa et thoro* under the existing law.[3]

Separated wife deemed spinster. In every case of judicial separation, the wife is, from the date of the decree and whilst the separation continues, considered as unmarried with respect to property of every description which she may acquire, or which may come to, or devolve upon, her. Such property can be disposed of by her in all respects as an unmarried woman, and, on her decease, the same will, in case she dies intestate, go as the same would have gone if her husband had been then dead:

Provided that, if any such wife again cohabits with her husband, all such property, as she may be entitled to when such cohabitation takes place, will be held to her separate use, subject, however, to any agreement in writing made between herself and her husband whilst separate.[4]

In every case of judicial separation, the wife will, whilst so separated, be considered as an unmarried woman for the purposes of contract, and wrongs and injuries, and suing and being sued in any civil proceeding, and her husband will not be liable in respect of any contract, act, or costs entered into, done, omitted, or incurred by her during the separation:

Provided that, where, upon such judicial separation alimony has been decreed or ordered to be paid to the wife, and the same is not duly paid by the husband, he will be liable for necessaries for her use:

Provided also that nothing will prevent the wife from joining, at any time during such separation, in the exercise of any joint power given to herself and her husband.[5]

Alimony, Damages and Costs

Alimony pendente lite. In any suit under the Divorce Act, whether it be instituted by a husband or a wife, and whether or not she has obtained an order of protection, the wife can present a petition for alimony pending the suit. Provided that alimony pending the suit will in no case exceed one-fifth of the husband's average net income for the three years next

2 Section 21 of the Indian Divorce Act.
3 Sections 22 and 23 of the Indian Divorce Act.
4 Section 24 of the Indian Divorce Act.
5 Section 25 of the Indian Divorce Act.

preceding the date of the order, and will continue, in case of a decree for dissolution of marriage or of nullity of marriage, until the decree is made absolute or is confirmed, as the case may be.[6]

Claim of damages from adulterer. Any husband can either in a petition for dissolution of marriage or for judicial separation, or in a petition to the District Court or the High Court limited to such object only, claim damages from any person on the ground of his having committed adultery with the wife of such petitioner.

Such petition must be served on the alleged adulterer and the wife unless the court dispenses with such service, or directs some other service to be substituted.[7]

Power to order adulterer to pay costs. Wherever in any petition presented by a husband, the alleged adulterer has been made a co-respondent, and the adultery has been established, the court can order the co-respondent to pay the whole or any part of the costs of the proceedings.

Provided that the co-respondent will not be ordered to pay the petitioner's costs—

(*i*) if the respondent was, at the time of the adultery, living apart from her husband, and leading the life of a prostitute, or

(*ii*) if the co-respondent had not, at the time of the adultery, reason to believe the respondent to be a married woman.[8]

Dissolution of Hindu Marriage

Law as to Hindu marriage. Law as to Hindu marriage has been revolutionized by the Hindu Marriage Act 1955 as amended by Act 68 of 1976. The Act applies to any person who is a Hindu, Buddhist, Jain or Sikh by religion.[9]

Conditions for a Hindu marriage. A marriage between any two Hindus may be solemnized if the following conditions are fulfilled, namely—

(*i*) neither party has a spouse living at the time of the marriage;

(*ii*) at the time of the marriage, neither party—

(*a*) is incapable of giving a valid consent to it in consequence of unsoundness of mind; or

(*b*) though capable of giving a valid consent has been suffering from mental disorder of such a kind or to such an extent as to be unfit for marriage and the procreation of children; or

(*c*) has been subject to recurrent attacks of insanity;

6 Section 36 of the Indian Divorce Act.
7 Section 34 of the Indian Divorce Act.
8 Section 35 of the Indian Divorce Act.
9 Section 2 of the Hindu Marriage Act.

(*iii*) the bridegroom has completed the age of 21 years and the bride the age of 18 years at the time of the marriage;

(*iv*) the parties are not within the degrees of prohibited relationship, unless the custom or usage governing each of them permits of a marriage between the two;

(*v*) the parties are not *sapindas* of each other, unless the custom or usage governing each of the permits of a marriage between the two.[10]

Judicial separation. (1) Either party to a marriage, whether solemnized before or after the commencement of this Act, may present a petition praying for a decree for judicial separation on any of the grounds specified in sub-sec. (1) of s. 13, and in the case of a wife also on any of the grounds specified in sub-sec. (2) thereof, as grounds on which a petition for divorce might have been presented.

(2) Where a decree for judicial separation has been passed, it shall no longer be obligatory for the petitioner to cohabit with the respondent, but the court may, on the application by petition of either party and on being satisfied of the truth of the statements made in such petition, rescind the decree if it considers it just and reasonable to do so.[11]

Void marriages. Any marriage solemnized after the commencement of Hindu Marriage Act shall be null and void and may, on a petition presented by either party thereto, be so declared by a decree of nullity if it contravenes any one of the conditions specified in cls. (*i*), (*iv*) and (*v*) of s. 5.[12]

Voidable marriages. (1) Any marriage solemnized, whether before or after the commencement of Hindu Marriage Act, shall be voidable and may be annulled by a decree of nullity on any of the following grounds, namely:

(*a*) that the marriage has not been consummated owing to the impotence of the respondent; or

(*b*) that the marriage is in contravention of the condition in cl. (*ii*) of s. 5; or

(*c*) that the consent of the petitioner or where the consent of the guardian in marriage of the petitioner is required under s. 5, as it stood immediately before the commencement of the Child Marriage Restraint (Amendment) Act 1978, the consent of such guardian was obtained by force or by fraud as to the nature of the ceremony or as to any material facts or circumstances concerning the respondent;

10 Section 5 of the Hindu Marriage Act 1955.
11 Section 10 of the Hindu Marriage Act.
12 Section 11 of the Hindu Marriage Act.

(*d*) that the respondent was at the time of the marriage pregnant by some person other than the petitioner.

(2) Notwithstanding anything contained in sub-sec. (1) no petition for annulling a marriage—

(*a*) on the ground specified in cl. (*c*) of sub-sec. (1) shall be entertained if—

(*i*) the petition is presented more than one year after the force had ceased to operate or, as the case may be, the fraud had been discovered; or

(*ii*) the petitioner has, with his or her full consent, lived with the other party to the marriage as husband or wife after the force had ceased to operate or, as the case may be, the fraud had been discovered;

(*b*) on the ground specified in cl. (*d*) of sub-sec. (1) shall be entertained unless the court is satisfied—

(*i*) that the petitioner was at the time of the marriage ignorant of the facts alleged;

(*ii*) that the proceedings have been instituted in the case of a marriage solemnized before the commencement of this Act within one year of such commencement and in the case of marriages solemnized after such commencement within one year from the date of the marriage; and

(*iii*) that marital intercourse with the consent of the petitioner has not taken place since the discovery by the petitioner of the existence of the said ground.[13]

13. *Divorce*. (1) Any marriage solemnized, whether before or after the commencement of this Act, may, on a petition presented by either the husband or the wife, be dissolved by a decree of divorce on the ground that the other party—

(*i*) has, after the solemnization of the marriage, voluntary sexual intercourse with any person other than his or her spouse; or

(*ia*) has, after the solemnization of the marriage, treated the petitioner with cruelty; or

(*ib*) has deserted the petitioner for a continuous period of not less than two years immediately preceding the presentation of the petition; or

(*ii*) has ceased to be a Hindu by conversion to another religion; or

13 Section 12 of the Hindu Marriage Act.

(*iii*) has been incurably of unsound mind, or has been suffering continuously or intermittently from mental disorder of such a kind and to such an extent that the petitioner cannot reasonably be expected to live with the respondent.

Explanation. In this clause,—

(*a*) the expression "mental disorder" means mental illness, arrested or incomplete development of mind, psychopathic disorder or any other disorder or disability of mind and includes schizophrenia;

(*b*) the expression "psychopathic disorder" means a persistent disorder or disability of mind (whether or not including sub-normality of intelligence) which results in abnormally aggressive or seriously irresponsible conduct on the part of the other party, and whether or not it requires or is susceptible to medical treatment; or

(*iv*) has been suffering from a virulent and incurable form of leprosy; or

(*v*) has been suffering from venereal diseases in a communicable form; or

(*vi*) has renounced the world by entering any religious order; or

(*vii*) has not been heard of as being alive for a period of seven years or more by those persons who would naturally have heard of it and that party been alive.

Explanation. In this sub-section, the expression "desertion" means the desertion of the petitioner by the other party to the marriage without reasonable cause and without the consent or against the wish of such party, and includes the wilful neglect of the petitioner by the other party to the marriage, and its grammatical variations and cognate expressions shall be construed accordingly.

(1A) Either party to a marriage, whether solemnized before or after the commencement of this Act, may also present a petition for the dissolution of the marriage by a decree of divorce on the ground—

(*i*) that there has been no resumption of cohabitation as between the parties to the marriage for a period of one year or upwards after the passing of a decree for judicial separation in a proceeding to which they were parties; or

(*ii*) that there has been no restitution of conjugal rights as between the parties to the marriage for a period of one year or upwards after the passing of a decree for restitution of conjugal rights in a proceeding to which they were parties.

(2) A wife may also present a petition for the dissolution of her marriage by a decree of divorce on the ground,—

(*i*) in the case of any marriage solemnized before the commencement of this Act, that the husband had married again before such commencement or that any other wife of the husband married before such commencement was alive at the time of the solemnization of the marriage of the petitioner:

Provided that in either case the other wife is alive at the time of the presentation of the petition; or

(*ii*) that the husband has, since the solemnization of the marriage, been guilty of rape, sodomy or bestiality; or

(*iii*) that in a suit under section 18 of the Hindu Adoptions and Maintenance Act 1956, or in a proceeding under section 125 of the Code of Criminal Procedure 1973 (or under the corresponding section 488 of the Code of Criminal Procedure 1898), a decree or order, as the case may be, has been passed against the husband awarding maintenance to the wife notwithstanding that she was living apart and that since the passing of such decree or order, cohabitation between the parties has not been resumed for one year or upwards; or

(*iv*) that her marriage (whether consummated or not) was solemnized before she attained the age of 15 years and she has repudiated the marriage after attaining that age but before attaining the age of 18 years.

Explanation. This clause applies whether the marriage was solemnized before or after the commencement of the Marriage Laws (Amendment) Act 1976.

13A. *Alternate relief in divorce proceedings.* In any proceeding under this Act, on a petition for dissolution of marriage by a decree of divorce, except in so far as the petition is founded on the grounds mentioned in clauses (*ii*), (*vi*) and (*vii*) of sub-section (1) of section 13, the court may, if it considers it just so to do having regard to the circumstances of the case, pass instead of a decree, for judicial separation.

13B. *Divorce by mutual consent.* (1) Subject to the provisions of this Act a petition for dissolution of marriage by a decree of divorce may be presented to the District Court by both the parties to a marriage together, whether such marriage was solemnized before or after the commencement of the Marriage Laws (Amendment) Act 1976, on the ground that they have been living separately for a period of one year or more, that they have not been able to live together and that they have mutually agreed that the marriage should be dissolved.

(2) On the motion of both the parties made not earlier than six months after the date of the presentation of the petition referred to in sub-section (1) and not later than 18 months after the said date, if the petition is not

withdrawn in the meantime, the court shall, on being satisfied, after hearing the parties and after making such inquiry, as it thinks fit, that a marriage has been solemnized and that the averments in the petition are true, pass a decree of divorce declaring the marriage to be dissolved with effect from the date of the decree.[14]

Jurisdiction and procedure. Every petition under the Hindu Marriage Act shall be presented to the District Court within the local limits of whose ordinary civil jurisdiction (*i*) the marriage was solemnized; (*ii*) the respondent at the time of presentation of the petition resides, or (*iii*) the parties to the marriage last resided together, or (*iv*) the petitioner is residing at the time of presentation of the petition in a case when the respondent is at that time, residing outside the territories to which the Act extends or has not been heard of as being alive for a period of seven years or more by those persons who would naturally have heard of him if he were alive.[15]

Every such petition shall state distinctly the facts on which the claim to relief is founded and shall also state that there is no collusion between the petitioner and the other party to the marriage.[16] The statements in such petition shall be verified just as a plaint. Before passing a decree the court must be satisfied that the petition is not presented or prosecuted in collusion with the respondent and that there has not been any unnecessary or improper delay in instituting the proceeding and that there is no other legal ground why relief should not be granted. Before granting any relief, the court should make every endeavour to bring about a reconciliation between the parties.

Where any party to such proceeding has no independent income sufficient for his or her support and maintenance and the necessary expense of the proceeding, the court may order the respondent to pay to the petitioner the expenses of the proceeding and such monthly sum during the proceeding as may seem to the court reasonable. At the time of passing the decree or subsequent thereto, the court may order the respondent to pay, while the applicant remains unmarried, such monthly or periodical sum as may seem to the court just and the court may also secure such payment by a charge on the immovable property of the respondent.

Present Forum. The Family Courts Act 1984 has conferred jurisdiction of District Courts and subordinate Courts on the Family Court by section 7. It shall exercise jurisdiction of Magistrate under Cr PC for ordering payment of maintenance. The Forms given hereunder give only indications which should be adapted according to Rules and practices of the concerned Forum.

14 Sections 13, 13A and 13B of the Hindu Marriage Act.
15 Section 19 of the Hindu Marriage Act.
16 Section 20 of the Hindu Marriage Act.

Petition under the Indian Divorce Act

FORMS

Petition by Husband for a Dissolution of Marriage with Damages against Co-respondent by Reason of Adultery

In the High Court of ....

To the Hon'ble Mr. Justice ....
(or to the Judge of..............)

AB .... *Petitioner*

versus

CB .... *Respondent*

XY .... *Co-respondent*

The humble petition of AB of (full name and address)

SHEWETH:

1. That the parties to the petition were and are domiciled in India and Christian by faith and religion.

2. That on the .... day of .... your petitioner was lawfully married to CB, then CD, a spinster aged about .... years at .... and the said marriage is still subsisting.

3. That ever since his said marriage, your petitioner lived and cohabited with his said wife from time to time at various places, viz. .... and lastly at .... in or about .... and that your petitioner and his said wife have had several issues of their said marriage, viz., ... children named .... who are aged respectively .... and .... years, the respective dates of their birth being .... day of .... and .... day of ....

4. That during the .... years immediately preceding the day of ...., XY was constantly, with few exceptions, residing in the house of your petitioner at .... aforesaid and that on diverse occasions during the said period, the dates of which are unknown to your petitioner, the said CB in your petitioner's said house committed adultery with the said XY.

State briefly the circumstances from which the petitioner came to the conclusion as to adultery.[17]

17 If the marriage was solemnised out of India, the adultery must be shown to have been committed in India.

5. That there was never nor is at present any collusion or connivance between the petitioner and his said wife for the purpose of obtaining a dissolution of their said marriage or for any other purpose.

6. That your petitioner has not condoned any of the acts of adultery on the part of the respondent.

Your petitioner, therefore, prays that this (Hon'ble) Court might be pleased to pass a decree for dissolution of the said marriage and that the said XY do pay the sum of Rupees .... as damages by reason of his having committed adultery with your petitioner's said wife, such damages to be paid to your petitioner, or otherwise paid or applied as to this (Hon'ble) Court seems fit.

Signed AB

Verification

I, AB, son of .... aged .... by occupation service residing at .... do hereby solemnly affirm and say as follows.

I am the petitioner above-named and I know the facts and circumstances of the case.

The statements in paragraphs 1, 2, 3, 4, 5 and 6 of the petition are true to my knowledge and belief and that I have not suppressed any material fact.

I sign this verification this .... day of .... at .... the Court House at ....

Before me Signature

Notary Advocate

Petition of Wife for Decree of Nullity of Marriage

(*See* sections 18 and 19)

In the High Court of ....

AB .... *Petitioner*

versus

CD .... *Respondent*

To the Hon'ble Justice .... or
to the Judge of ....

The humble petition of AB of (full name, occupation and address)

SHEWETH:

1. That at all material times the parties of these proceedings were and are at present Christian by faith and religion.

2. That on the .... day of .... your petitioner, then a spinster, aged about .... years went through a form of pretended marriage with the respondent (*at some place in India, state the place*) and was thereby and since that date known as married in fact, though not in law, to CD, then a bachelor of about 30 years of age.

3. That ever since the said marriage on the .... day of .... and until the .... day of .... your petitioner and the respondent lived and cohabited with each other at various places such as .... and lastly at ....

4. That the said CD has never consummated the said pretended marriage by carnal copulation.

5. That at the time of the celebration of your petitioner's said pretended marriage, the said CD was and still is by reason of his impotency or malformation, legally incompetent to enter into the contract of marriage.

(State other grounds if applicable, *e.g.*, prohibited degree, lunacy, idiocy, etc.)

6. That there is no collusion or connivance between the parties with respect to the subject of these proceedings.

Your petitioner therefore prays that this (Hon'ble) Court might be pleased to declare the said marriage as null and void.

Signed AB

Verification

I, AB daughter of .... aged .... by occupation service residing at .... do hereby solemnly affirm and say as follows:

I am the petitioner above-named and I know the facts and circumstances of this case.

The statements made in paragraphs Nos. 1 to 6 of the petition are true to my knowledge and belief and that I have not suppressed any material fact.

I sign this verification on this .... day of .... at the Court House at ....

AB

Before me Signature

Notary Advocate

Petition by Wife for Judicial Separation on the Grounds of her Husband's Adultery

(*See* section 22)

In the High Court of ....

CB .... *Petitioner*

versus

AB .... *Respondent*

To the Hon'ble Mr. Justice ....
(or to the Judge of ....)

The humble petition of CB of No. ....
the wife of AB residing at ....

SHEWETH:

1. That on the .... day of .... your petitioner, then CD (maiden name) was lawfully married to the respondent AB lived and cohabited at .... and .... and the said marriage is still subsisting.

2. That ever since the said marriage, your petitioner and the respondent AB lived and cohabited at .... and they have the following issue living of their said marriage.[18]

3. That on diverse occasions between the month of .... and the month of .... the respondent AB while staying at .... committed adultery with one EF who was then in the service of the said AB and your petitioner at their said residence aforesaid against the wishes of and in spite of protest from your petitioner.

4. That your petitioner has not condoned any of the acts of adultery on the part of the respondent.

5. That there is no collusion or connivance between your .... petitioner and the said AB with respect to the subject of the present suit. Your petitioner therefore prays that this (Hon'ble) Court might be pleased to pass a decree of a judicial separation of your petitioner from her said husband by reason of his aforesaid act of adultery.

Signed CB

Verification

I, CB wife of AB daughter of XY aged about .... years residing at .... do hereby solemnly affirm and say as follows:

18 State the respective ages of the children.

I am the petitioner above-named and I know and I have made myself acquainted with the facts and circumstances of this case.

The statements made in paragraphs 1 to 5 are true to my knowledge and belief.

I sign this verification on this .... day of .... at the Court House at ....

Signature of CB

Before me

Signature of Advocate

Notary

Petition for Protection Order

(*See* section 27)

In the High Court of ....

CB .... *Petitioner*

versus

AB .... *Respondent*

To the Hon'ble Mr. Justice ....
(or To the Judge of ....)

The humble petition of CB of .... the wife of AB residing at ....

SHEWETH:

1. That on the .... day of .... your petitioner was lawfully married to the respondent AB at .... according to the Christian rites.

2. That ever since the marriage your petitioner lived and cohabited with the said AB for .... years together at .... and thereafter also at .... and has had .... children, being issues of her said marriage of whom one is now living with your petitioner and wholly dependent upon her earnings.

(Dates of birth to be given)

3. That on or about the .... day of .... the said AB suddenly and without any reasonable cause withdrew himself from the society, left and deserted your petitioner and has ever since remained and is still remaining separate and apart from her without any reason whatsoever.

4. That since the desertion by her said husband your petitioner has maintained and is still maintaining herself by her own labour and industry

(or on her own property, as the case may be) and has also acquired certain other property consisting of (here state generally the nature of the property).

5. That the said AB is a man of most extravagant habits and always goes beyond his means and very often incurs debts in the market beyond his capacity to repay.

Your petitioner prays an order for the protection of her earnings and property acquired since the said .... day of .... from the said AB and from all creditors and persons claiming under him.

Verification

I, CB wife of AB .... aged .... years by occupation service residing at .... do hereby solemnly affirm and say as follows:

I am the petitioner above-named and I know the facts and circumstances of the case.

The statements made in paragraphs Nos. 1, 2, 3, 4, and 5 of the petition are true to my knowledge and belief and that I have not suppressed any material fact.

I sign this verification this .... day at the Court House at ....

Before me
Notary

Signature of CB
Signature of Advocate

Petition for Alimony Pending the Suit

(*See* section 36)

In the High Court of ....

Cause Title

To the Hon'ble Mr. Justice ....
.... (or To the Judge of ....)

The humble petition of CB, the lawful wife of AB

SHEWETH:

1. That on the .... day of .... the above suit was instituted by your petitioner against the respondent (state briefly the nature of relief asked for and the position of the suit).

2. That the said AB is in most affluent circumstances for some years past by reason of the business (state briefly the nature of the business)

carried on by him at .... under the name and style of .... and he alone receives the net annual income of Rs. .... or thereabout from such business every year. The said business is prospering year after year and yielding good returns.

3. That over and above the said business, he has other resources and incomes, *e.g.*, the house property at No. .... which alone fetches an income of Rs. .... per month and various shares and securities (state briefly the particulars) all of which he acquired in the right of your petitioner as his wife or purchased with money received through her, of the aggregated value of Rs. ....

4. That the said AB is entitled, under the will of his father, subject to the life interest of his mother therein, to property of the value of Rs. ....

Your petitioner, therefore, prays that this (Hon'ble) Court will order for payment of such sum or sums of money by way of alimony, pending the suit, as this (Hon'ble) Court may deem fit.

Verification

I, CD, wife of AB and daughter of XY aged about .... years by occupation housewife residing at .... do hereby solemnly affirm and say as follows:

I am the petitioner above-named and I know and I have made myself acquainted with the facts and circumstances of this case.

The statements in paragraphs 1 to 4 of the petition hereinabove are true to my knowledge and belief.

I sign this verification on this .... day of .... at the Court House at ....

Signature of CD

Before me
Signature of Advocate

Notary

Petition for a Judicial Separation by Reason of Cruelty

(*See* section 22)

In the High Court of ....

To the Hon'ble Mr. Justice ....
(or To the Judge of ....)

The humble petition of AB (wife of CB)
of ....

SHEWETH:

1. That at all material times the parties to the above proceedings were Christian by birth and religion and domiciled in India.

2. That on the .... day of .... your petitioner, then AD (spinster), was lawfully married to CB according to law governing them and the said marriage is still subsisting.

3. That there is no issue of the said marriage.

4. That ever since her said marriage, your petitioner lived and resided with her said husband all along except short stays outside at .... within the jurisdiction of this court until the .... day of .... when your petitioner's said husband wrongfully separated from and deserted her as hereinafter more particularly mentioned.

5. That the married life of your petitioner was most unhappy ever since and throughout the marriage as the said CB forced her to do all sorts of menial work in the house against her wish and desire and on failure or refusal thereof he insulted her, behaved roughly, habitually misconducted himself towards her and treated your petitioner with great harshness, negligence and cruelty, frequently abusing her in the coarsest and most insulting language and beating her at times violently with kicks and blows, sometimes with a cane, or with some other weapon.

6. That some particulars of harshness, neglect and cruelty are *inter alia* as follows:

(*a*) Throughout their married life and without any exception the said CD by words and deeds made it quite clear that he had no heart nor any love and affection for her but married simply for enriching himself with the wealth of her parents.

(*b*) That one evening in or about the month of .... the said CD tried to kick her out of the house in which your petitioner and the said CB were then residing at .... aforesaid, but was only prevented from so doing by the interference of FD, your petitioner's brother.

(*c*) That subsequently on the following evening, the said CB in his said house at .... aforesaid, struck your petitioner with a violent blow on her face.

(*d*) That on one night in the month of May 2000 the said CB in .... without provocation threw a knife at your petitioner thereby inflicting a severe wound on her right hand.

7. That in the afternoon of the .... day of .... the cruel behaviour and mental torture of the respondent reached such a climax that

your petitioner had no other alternative but to withdraw herself from and leave the house, and by reason of the continued cruelty practised on her she had to come also to the house of her father at .... and since then your petitioner has lived separate and apart from her husband and has never returned to his house or had cohabitation with him.

8. That your petitioner never condoned any of the acts of cruelty of the respondent and in any event even if there was any condonation (which is denied) each subsequent matrimonial offence or misconduct would revive all acts of cruelty.

9. That there is no collusion or connivance between your petitioner and her husband with respect to the subject of the present suit.

10. (State previous proceedings if any).

Your petitioner, therefore, prays that this (Hon'ble) Court might be pleased to pass a decree of judicial separation between your petitioner and the said CB and also order that the said CB do pay the costs of and incidental to the proceedings.

Signed AB

Verification

I, AB, wife of CB aged about .... years by occupation service residing at .... do hereby solemnly affirm and say as follows:

I am the petitioner above-named and I know and I have made myself acquainted with the facts and circumstances of this case.

The statements in paragraphs 1 to 10 are true to my knowledge and belief.

I sign this verification on this .... day of .... at the Court House at ....

Signature of AB

Before me Signature of Advocate

Notary

Petition for Reversal of Decree of Separation

(*See* section 26)

No. of suit and cause title

In the High Court of ....

To the Hon'ble Mr. Justice ......
.... (or To the Judge
of ....)

The petition of AB of ....

SHEWETH:

1. That your petitioner was on the .... day of .... lawfully married to .... and such marriage is still subsisting.

2. That on the .... day of .... this (Hon'ble) Court on the petition of .... pronounced a purported decree affecting the petitioner to the effect following, to wit,—

(*Here set out the decree*)

3. That such decree was obtained in the absence of and by practice of fraud on your petitioner, who was then residing at .... and thus kept completely ignorant of the same. (State facts tending to show how the petitioner came to know of the proceedings; and, further, that had he known. He might have offered a sufficient defence).

Or

That there were nor are any reasonable grounds for your petitioner leaving his said wife, for that his said wife .... (here state any legal grounds justifying the petitioner's separation from his wife).

Your petitioner, therefore, prays that this (Hon'ble) Court might be pleased to reverse the said decree.

Signed AB

Verification

I, AB, son of .... aged about .... years by occupation service residing at .... do hereby solemnly affirm and say as follows:

I am the petitioner above-named and I know and I have made myself acquainted with the facts and circumstances of this case.

The statements in paragraphs 1 to 3 of the petition are true to my knowledge and belief.

I sign this verification on this .... day of .... at the Court House at ....

Signature of AB

Before me
Commissioner

Signature of Advocate

Matrimonial Causes under Hindu Marriage Act 1955

Petition of Divorce

In the Court of .... at ....

Matrimonial Jurisdiction

In the matter of s. 13 of the Hindu Marriage Act 1955

In the matter of ....
AB ....*Petitioner*

versus

CD ....*Respondent*
EF ....*Co-respondent*

The humble petition of ....(full name and address)

MOST RESPECTFULLY SHEWETH:

1. That at all material times the parties to proceedings were and are Hindus governed by the Hindu Marriage Act 1955.

2. That on the .... day of .... your petitioner was duly married to CD at etc., ... and the said marriage was solemnised according to Hindu rites and customs. (An extract from the Marriage Register or an affidavit duly attested to be filed.)

3. That ever since the said marriage your petitioner and the said CD lived together as husband and wife at .... until the .... day of .... (state reasons of separation).

4. That the following are the issues of the said marriage (state name, address, date of birth, age and sex).

5. That on diverse occasions between .... and .... the respondent committed adultery with .... at .... against the wish of your petitioner and in spite of her protests.

6. That your petitioner has come to know of the same on .... and since then she has not in any manner been accessory to or connived at or condoned such adultery.

7. (When the applicant is the wife.) That the said CD had married on the .... day of .... Sm. .... and she is now living at ....

Or

That the said CD has, since the solemnization of the marriage, been guilty of rape (or sodomy or bestiality) on ....

8. That there is no collusion or connivance between the parties with respect to the subject-matter of the present petition.

9. That there were no previous proceedings between the parties relating to their marriage.

10. The marriage was celebrated at .... or the parties last lived and resided at .... within the jurisdiction of this Court.

Your petitioner therefore prays that the court might be pleased to pass a decree dissolving the marriage of your petitioner with CD.

Signed AB

Verification

I, AB, wife of CD aged about .... years by occupation service residing at .... do hereby solemnly affirm and say as follows:

I am the petitioner above-named and I know and I have made myself acquainted with the facts and circumstances of this case.

The statements in paragraphs 1 to 10 are true to my knowledge and belief.

I sign this verification on this .... day of .... at the Court House at ....

Signature of AB

Before me Signature of Advocate

Notary

Petition for Judicial Separation

In the Court of .... at ....

Matrimonial Jurisdiction

In the matter of s. 10 of the Hindu Marriage Act 1955, and in the matter of:

AB .... *Petitioner*

versus

CD .... *Respondent*

The humble petition of .... of No. .... (full name and address)

MOST RESPECTFULLY SHEWETH:

1. That at all material times and at present the parties to the proceedings were and are Hindu and so governed by the Hindu Marriage Act 1955.

2. That on the .... day of .... the applicant was duly married to CD at .... and the said marriage was solemnised according to Hindu rites. (An extract from the Marriage Registrar or an affidavit duly attested to be filed).

3. That the following are the issues of the said marriage (name, date of birth, age and sex).

4. That ever since the said marriage and until the ....,.... day of .... the applicant and the said CD lived and cohabited as husband and wife at etc. .... when he withdrew himself from the society of the applicant without any reasonable or probable cause and thereby deserted her to all intents and purposes.

5. That from and shortly after the marriage the said CD habitually and with very few exceptions conducted himself towards the applicant with severe harshness and cruelty and at times abused her in most filthy language (state particulars of cruelty).

6. That the applicant has not in any manner been accessory to or connived at or condoned any of the said acts of CD.

7. That the said CD further falsely, maliciously charged the applicant as having committed adultery, abused the applicant in various ways and treated the applicant with such cruelty as to cause a reasonable apprehension in the mind of the applicant that it will be most harmful or injurious for the petitioner to live further with the said CD.

8. That there were no previous proceedings between the parties and there is no collusion between the applicant and CD with respect to the subject-matter of the present petition.

9. That the applicant has come to court with the greatest promptitude and least delay (in case of delay the same must be explained).

10. That this court has jurisdiction to entertain this application as the marriage was celebrated at (*the parties reside* or *last resided within the jurisdiction of this court*).

The applicant therefore prays for a decree for judicial separation between the applicant and the said CD.

Signed AB

Verification

I, AB, daughter of XY and wife of CB aged about .... years by occupation service residing at .... do hereby solemnly affirm and say as follows:

I am the petitioner above-named and I know and I have made myself acquainted with the facts and circumstances of this case.

The statements in paragraphs 1 to 10 are true to my knowledge and belief.

I sign this verification on this .... day of .... at the Court House at ....

Signature of AB

Before me   Signature of Advocate

Notary

Petition for Decree of Nullity of Marriage

(*Title as in the previous precedents*)

In the matter of nullity of marriage under s. 11 of the Hindu Marriage Act 1955.

AB .... *Petitioner*
(Full name and address)

versus

CD .... *Respondent*
(Full name and address)

The humble petition of AB

MOST RESPECTFULLY SHEWETH:

1. That at all material times the parties to the petition were and are Hindu governed by the Hindu Marriage Act 1955 (Act 25 of 1955).

2. That a pretended marriage was however on the .... day of .... celebrated at .... between the applicant then a spinster aged .... with the respondent then known as .... aged .... declared as a bachelor under the purported Hindu rites and customs (an extract from the Marriage Register or an affidavit duly attested to be filed).

3. That the purported marriage was a fraud practised by the respondent upon the petitioner and is void *ab initio* inasmuch as the respondent had already a married wife named .... then and this fact was suppresed from the petition and she is still now alive.

4. That since the said marriage with CD, the applicant lived and cohabited with CD at etc., without having any issue of such purported marriage until the .... day of ....

Or

That the applicant and the said CD are within the prohibited degrees of relationship, the applicant being the first cousin sister of the said CD.

Or

That the said CD was impotent at the time of such marriage and continued to be so until the institution of the present proceeding (if this ground is alleged then omit the words "and cohabited" in para 4).

5. That the applicant is entitled to get the sum of Rs. .... per month from the said CD for her maintenance and support until she is married.

6. That there is no collusion between the applicant and the said CD in making this application.

7. That there were no previous proceedings with regard to the marriage in question by or on behalf of any party.

8. That this court has jurisdiction to entertain this application as the marriage was celebrated within the jurisdiction or the parties live and reside or last lived and resided within the jurisdiction.

The applicant therefore prays that the court may be pleased to declare that the said marriage between the applicant and CD is null and void and the said CD be ordered to pay to the applicant for her support and maintenance a sum of Rs. .... per month or such other monthly sum as the court thinks fit as long as the applicant remains unmarried.

Verification

I, AB, daughter of XY and wife of CD aged about .... years by occupation service residing at .... do hereby solemnly affirm and say as follows:

I am the petitioner above-named and I know and I have made myself acquainted with the facts and circumstances of this case.

The statements in paragraphs 1 to 8 are true to my knowledge and belief.

I sign this verification on this .... day of .... at the Court House at ....

Signature of AB

Before me — Signature of Advocate

Notary

Petition for Maintenance and Expenses of Proceedings

(*Title as in previous precedents*)

In the matter of maintenance *pendente lite* and expenses of proceedings under s. 24 of the Hindu Marriage Act 1955

The applicant above-named respectfully states as follows:

1. That on .... the applicant was married to the respondent according to the Hindu rites and customs and the said marriage is subsisting.

2. That the above suit is for divorce (or judicial separation or nullity of marriage) instituted by the applicant against the respondent (state briefly the grounds and the position of the suit).

3. That the applicant has no independent source of income sufficient for her maintenance and support as well as to meet the necessary expenses of the proceedings brought by her. The applicant and her two children are now dependent on the applicant's father Sri ....

4. That the respondent is an employee of Messrs .... drawing a salary and allowance of Rs. .... per month.

5. That the respondent has a house and considerable landed properties at .... wherefrom he gets Rs. .... per month as rent.

6. That the respondent has inherited from his father G.P. Notes and other securities and shares of the face value of Rs. .... The respondent gets Rs. .... per year as interest, dividend etc.

7. That the applicant requires Rs. .... per month for maintenance for herself and her two children.

8. That the applicant requires a sum of Rs. .... for expenses of the above proceedings.

The applicant therefore prays that this Hon'ble Court would order the respondent to pay to your petitioner the said sum of Rs. .... for expenses of the above proceedings and Rs. .... per month during the proceedings for maintenance or such sum as may seem to the court to be reasonable.

Verification

I, AB, wife of CB daughter of XY aged about .... years by occupation housewife do hereby solemnly affirm and say as follows:

I am the petitioner above-named and I know and I have made myself acquainted with the facts and circumstances of this case.

The statements in paragraphs 1 to 8 are true to my knowledge and belief.

I sign this verification on this .... day of .... at the Court House at ....

Signature of AB

Before me Signature of Advocate

Notary

Form of Petition for Restitution of Conjugal Rights under s. 9 of the Hindu Marriage Act 1955

In the District Court ....

AB .... *Petitioner*
(full name and address)

versus

WB .... *Respondent*
(full name and address)

The humble petition of Sri AB of ....

1. That a marriage was solemnised between the parties on .... at ....

(An extract from the Hindu Marriage Register is filed herewith. An affidavit, duly attested as the case may be).

2. That the status and place of residence of the parties to the marriage before the marriage and at the time of filing the petition were and are as follows:

	Husband		*Wife*	
	Status	*Place of residence*	*Status*	*Place of residence*
(*i*) Before marriage				
(*ii*) At the time of filing the petition				

(Whether a party is a Hindu by religion or not is a part of his or her status)

3. (In this paragraph particulars and places of cohabitation of the parties as husband and wife and the children from the marriage, if any, should be given. The date and place of birth and name and sex of each child and the fact whether he/she/they/is/are alive/dead should also be stated).

4. That on day of .... the respondent, without reasonable excuse and with a view to break the matrimonial home withdrew from the society of the petitioner .... (cause of the estrangement as known to the petitioner may be stated).

5. That this petition is not presented in collusion with the respondent.

6. There has not been any unnecessary or improper delay in filing this petition.

7. There is no legal ground why relief should not be granted.

8. There has not been any previous proceeding with regard to the marriage by or on behalf of any party.

Or

There have been the following previous proceedings with regard to the marriage by or on behalf of the parties but the bar of *res judicata* does not apply.

Serial No.	*Name of parties*	*Nature of proceedings with section of the Act*	*Number and year of the case*	*Name and the location of Court*	*Result*
(*i*)					
(*ii*)					
(*iii*)					
(*iv*)					

9. The marriage was solemnised at .... on ....The husband and wife live at .... The husband and wife last resided together within the local limits of the ordinary original civil jurisdiction of this court.

10. The petitioner prays for a decree for restitution of conjugal rights against the respondent.

Sd/- Petitioner

Verification

I, AB son of .... aged about .... years residing at .... do hereby solemnly affirm and say as follows:

I am the petitioner above-named and I know and I have made myself acquainted with the facts and circumstances of this case.

The statements in paragraphs 1 to 10 are true to my knowledge and belief.

I sign this verification on this .... day of .... at the Court House at ....

Signature of AB

Before me

Signature of Advocate

Notary

Petition for Divorce by Mutual Consent

In the Court of the ....

MC. No. .... of 1983

BETWEEN:

WB .... *First Petitioner*

And

AB .... *Second Petitioner*

Application under section 13B of the Hindu Marriage Act of 1955

The petitioners above-named beg to state as follows:

1. The address of the petitioners for the service of all notices and process is that of their advocates .... and Mr. ....

2. The first petitioner and the second petitioner are wife and husband respectively having been married at .... on the .... and the said marriage is still subsisting. The marriage was performed in accordance with Hindu Vedic Rites. A copy of the marriage invitation is filed herewith and marked 'A'. There are no children by the marriage.

3. The first petitioner and the second petitioner after the marriage lived and resided at .... and elsewhere and finally at .... at the address of the petitioner given above, whence they separated on the ....

4. Soon after the marriage owing to differences in temperament, habits, tastes, thoughts, and increasing incompatibility, the relationship between the first petitioner and the second petitioner deteriorated. Frequent quarrels resulted as between them with several reconciliations which did not, however, last for any length of time. Finally, after a very serious quarrel and in order to avoid further deterioration in relationship which might reflect on their families and friends, the first petitioner and the second petitioner out of free will and accord separated on the .... never to return to each other. The petitioners, therefore, finally separated owing to irreconcilable differences in habits and temperament on the .... within the jurisdiction of this Hon'ble Court.

5. Further efforts and attempts were made by mutual friends and acquaintances to effect a reconciliation and for a resumption of the marital relationship but it has not been possible owing to the vital differences in temperament and total incompatibility giving rise to invincible repugnance which had rendered normal married life impracticable and impossible and fraught with dangerous adverse physical and mental consequences.

6. The first petitioner states that she and the second petitioner have been separated and living apart for more than two years and the duration of cohabitation prior thereto was not in any case for much more than a year.

7. In the circumstances the first petitioner and second petitioner have mutually agreed and decided that there is no point for the continuance of the marital relationship and have further agreed upon the dissolution of the marriage tie by a decree of divorce.

8. The petitioners state and submit that in the circumstances aforesaid it is therefore desirable and necessary that the marriage should be dissolved in the mutual interests of the parties, there being no chance of reconciliation.

9. The cause of action for this petition arose on the .... when the first and the second petitioner were married and on the .... within the jurisdiction of this Hon'ble Court when the first petitioner and the second petitioner finally agreed to separate with the departure of the second petitioner.

10. A court-fee of Rs. .... is paid under .... of the ....

11. Both the first and the second petitioner state that there is no impediment to the dissolution of the marriage and the decision to separate and apply for a divorce has been arrived at after such consideration and after having given the utmost importance to all aspects of the case.

12. The first and the second petitioner therefore pray that this Hon'ble Court be pleased to pass a decree declaring the marriage solemnised between the first and the second petitioner under the Hindu Vedic Rites on .... be dissolved and for such other reliefs as this Hon'ble Court may deem fit.

First Petitioner

Second Petitioner

Verification

I, WB wife of AB aged about .... years residing at .... do hereby solemnly affirm and say as follows:

I am the petitioner above-named and I know and I have made myself acquainted with the facts and circumstances of this case.

The statements in paragraphs 1 to 13 are true to my knowledge and belief.

I sign this verification on this .... day of .... at the Court House at ....

Signature of WB

Before me

Signature of Advocate

Notary

I, AB son of XY aged about .... years residing at .... do hereby solemnly affirm and say as follows:

I am the petitioner above-named and I know and I have made myself acquainted with the facts and circumstances of this case.

The statements in paragraphs 1 to 13 are true to my knowledge and belief.

I sign this verification on this .... day of .... at the Court House at ....

Signature of AB

Before me Signature of Advocate

Notary

Petition of Divorce by Mutual Consent

(ANOTHER FORM)

In the City Civil Court at Calcutta

Matrimonial Suit No. .... of 2000

In the matter of Hindu Marriage Act 1955 (Act 25 of 1955)

And

In the matter of section 13B of the said Act

And

In the matter of .... son of .... of .... Husband

And

Sm. .... wife of the said .... and daughter of .... of ....

Petition for a decree for dissolution of marriage by mutual consent under section 13B of the Hindu Marriage Act (Act 25 of 1955).

The humble petition of the said ....

MOST RESPECTFULLY SHEWETH:

1. That the parties to this present petition are both by faith and religion Hindus and they were married according to Hindu rites and customs at

.... on .... and the said marriage is still subsisting. They are of age above 21 years.

2. That the status and place of residence of the parties to the marriage before the marriage and at the time of filing the petition were and are as follows:

	Husband		*Wife*	
	Status	*Place of residence*	*Status*	*Place of residence*
	Bachelor		Spinster	
At the time of presenting this petition	Married		Married	

3. The parties ever since the marriage did not pull on together being of different ideas, habits, tastes, and thoughts and so being completely of different temperament and nature did not and could never adjust themselves even for a few days and so had no heart nor love for each other and there is no chance of reconciliation between them in future.

4. That the parties last lived and cohabited at No. .... within the jurisdiction of this court when your petitioner .... for reasons of her own and out of free will and accord broke the matrimonial home and withdrew herself from the society of the said .... with all her personal belongings and since then she has been living and residing at her father's place and has no desire nor any wish for any union with the husband.

5. That save as hereunder mentioned there was no other proceedings between the parties particulars whereof are given below:

Number and year of the case	*Name of the parties*	*Date of decision*	*Remarks*

6. That the above petition is *bona fide* and not presented in collusion between the parties.

7. That there has not been any unnecessary or improper delay presenting this petition.

8. That there is no legal grounds why the relief should not be granted.

Your petitioners therefore pray for a Decree of dissolution of marriage by mutual consent under section 13B of the Hindu Marriage Act 1955 and further and other Orders be made as to this Learned Court may deem fit and proper. And your petitioners as in duty bound shall ever pray.

Verification

I, AB, son of .... aged about .... years residing at .... do hereby solemnly affirm and say as follows:

I am the petitioner No. 1 above-named and I know and I have made myself acquainted with the facts and circumstances of this case.

The statements in paragraphs 1 to 8 are true to my knowledge and belief.

I sign this verification on this .... day of .... at the Court House at ....

Signature of AB

Signature of Advocate

Before me

Notary

Verification

I, CD, wife of AB daughter of X, aged about .... years by occupation housewife residing at .... do hereby solemnly affirm and say as follows:

I am the petitioner No. 2 above-named. I know and I have made myself acquainted with the facts and circumstances of this case.

The statements in paragraphs 1 to 8 of the petition hereinabove are true to my knowledge and belief.

I sign this verification on this .... day of .... at the Court House at ....

Signature of CD

Signature of Advocate

Before me

Notary

21

Endowment

The word "Endowment" means that it is a deed settled on any person or institution. It is an act of settling a fund, a permanent provision for the performance of a public institution, charity, hospital, college etc. and it may consist of property set apart for the worship of some particular deity or for the establishment or maintenance of a religious or Charitable institution or for the benefit of public or some section of the public in the advancement of religion commerce, health, safety or any other object beneficial to mankind.

FORM

Deed of Endowment for Beds in a Hospital

THIS DEED OF ENDOWMENT is made on this 4th day of July 2000 BETWEEN Mr. D of .... (hereinafter called the DONOR) of the one part and Mr. AB and Mr. CD of .... (hereinafter called the TRUSTEES which expression unless the context otherwise requires shall include the Trustee or Trustees for the time being) of the other part.

WHEREAS the DONOR is the Owner of certain stocks, shares and securities and investments particulars whereof are given in a Schedule hereunder.

AND WHEREAS the DONOR is desirous of establishing an Endowment Fund for three paying beds in the Charitable Hospital (hereinafter called the HOSPITAL) and the maintenance of the same for persons who may be unable to pay the charges and expenses of the Hospital as a private patient.

AND WHEREAS the DONOR is about to transfer to the said TRUSTEES the Donor's stocks, shares, fund, securities and investments mentioned in the

Schedule hereunder (hereinafter called the FUNDS) whose present value is Rs. 30 lakhs and the monthly income is Rs. 30,000.

AND WHEREAS the DONOR is desirous of declaring such Trust funds as the D Trust (hereinafter called the TRUST) and shall be governed by the rules set out in the Second Schedule hereunder which rules have been approved by the Management Committee of the HOSPITAL. The present income of the Trust Funds and estimated future income will be sufficient for the maintenance of three beds occupied 365 days a year and there is every possibility of the income being increased to support the treatment of four patients for 4 beds in the HOSPITAL at any point of time.

AND WHEREAS the Management Committee of the HOSPITAL has agreed to appropriate and set apart for the TRUST three beds named D Ward in the HOSPITAL to be maintained out of the income of the Trust Funds which in all reasonable probability will be sufficient to maintain even 4 beds in the HOSPITAL.

NOW THIS DEED OF ENDOWMENT witnesseth as follows:

1. I, the DONOR do hereby convey in TRUST into the TRUSTEES the said FUNDS and the TRUSTEES shall be in possession of the Trust Fund and shall hold the same upon the TRUST for the purposes of maintaining the said Trust pay-beds in the said HOSPITAL.

2. The TRUSTEES shall be entitled to alter the investments at their sole discretion for the benefit of the said TRUST.

3. The TRUSTEES shall pay or apply the income of the Trust Fund in paying all costs, charges and expenses of the TRUSTEES in relation to the administration of the Trust Fund and shall pay or apply the net income of the Trust Funds in accordance with the rules of the TRUST set out in the Second Schedule hereto or the rules of the TRUST that might be in force for the time being.

4. The TRUSTEES shall hold meetings at least once a year. A special meeting may be called by any of the TRUSTEES by giving seven days' notice in writing mentioning the business to be transacted or discussed at such meetings. The Senior Trustee shall preside over the meetings and all decisions shall be of the meeting, but if at the said meeting both the TRUSTEES cannot agree, the presiding TRUSTEE shall have a second or casting vote.

5. The TRUSTEE may appoint an Honorary Secretary who shall cause the Minute Books and proper books of accounts to be maintained.

6. The TRUSTEES may from time to time make rules as regards meetings, conduct of business and management of the TRUST.

First Schedule

(Particulars of shares, stocks, investments,
securities and assets transferred to the TRUSTEES)

The Second Schedule

(Rules of the Trust)

7. The TRUST shall be called "D Trust". In these rules the "D Trust" shall be referred as the TRUST. HOSPITAL means the "Charitable Hospital". The TRUSTEES means the Trustees or the TRUSTEE for the time being of the Trust. The Council means a "Council of Management" for the time being constituted by these rules. Hospital Committee means the "Management Committee of the Hospital" for the time being. "Endowment Beds" means the three pay-beds. "Trust Funds" means shares, stocks, investments and other assets for the time being subject to the Trust. Beds subject to these rules shall be Beds for the time being appropriated by the hospital Committee with the concurrence of the Trustees to be managed wholly out of the income of the Trust.

8. The Endowed Beds shall be for persons male, female, child who are in the opinion of the Council unable to pay the usual fees and charges as private patients in the HOSPITAL.

9. The power of nominating patients for reception in the Endowed Beds shall be vested in the Council of Management which shall consist of 3 members namely the TRUSTEES for the time being and a member to be appointed from time to time by the Council.

10. A member of the Council who is absent from all meetings of the Council for a period of 3 months or who becomes insolvent or incapacitated from acting or absent from India for 3 months or who resigns from Office shall thereupon cease to be a member of the Council.

11. The Council may from time to time make such rules as to its meetings and conducting business. A quorum at the meeting of the Council shall be 2 members present. The Council shall act upon a majority decision and in case of equality the Presiding Officer shall have second or casting vote. In the event the number of members is reduced to one then the sole member may appoint another person as a member of the Council to carry on the transactions of the TRUST.

12. The Council may nominate a person for reception of the patients in the Endowed Beds.

13. The Council shall from time to time communicate with the Committee of the Hospital the names of the members of the Council who are entitled to nominate for the Endowed Beds.

14. The nomination of patients for the Endowed Beds shall be signed by the persons nominating for this purpose or by two members of the Council.

15. The Council shall maintain the books of accounts and Minutes Books of the meetings.

16. The Endowed Beds shall be for use of patients nominated by the Council or a member on whom the power has been delegated. Three Beds shall be reserved for that purpose. It will be at the sole discretion of the Council to judge whether the patient is in a position to pay the charges of the Hospital or he is eligible to its Endowed Beds.

17. In the event the other beds of the HOSPITAL are full and the Council has not nominated anybody for the Endowed Beds, the same may be used by the HOSPITAL for other patients who are likely to be discharged within a short period.

18. All patients nominated for the Endowed Beds shall be subject to the rules and regulations of the HOSPITAL.

19. The net income of the TRUST shall from time to time be paid by the TRUSTEES to the Hospital Committee for applying the same in the maintenance of the Endowed Beds in the HOSPITAL called "D Beds" intended to be reserved for the persons nominated by the Council.

20. If the Council is of the opinion that the HOSPITAL has refused to accept the nominated patient or discharged a patient prematurely, the Council shall make a report to the TRUSTEES who may suspend either wholly or in part payments to the Hospital Committee and make alternative arrangement with some other hospital.

21. The TRUSTEES may from time to time with the consent of the Hospital Committee or the Management revoke and/or amend or alter the rules and make such new rules as they may think fit, provided that any such rules so made shall provide for the application of the net income of the TRUST for the maintenance of the three beds in the said hospital or if circumstances so require in another hospital.

22. IN WITNESS WHEREOF the DONOR has executed these presents and the TRUSTEES have accepted the TRUST and agreed to act as the TRUSTEES and have also hereby put their signatures hereon on the day, month and year first above-written.

Signed and delivered by Mr. D
in the presence of: Signature

Signed and delivered by Mr. AB
in the presence of: Signature

Signed and delivered by Mr. CD
in the presence of: Signature

22

Exchange

Exchange. It is a sort of barter where two persons mutually transfer the ownership of one thing for the ownership of another; neither thing or both things being money only, the transaction is called an exchange.[1]

In addition to the transfer of property there may be payment of money by one party to equalise the exchange and such payment will not make the exchange lose its character as such. Under s. 119 of the Transfer of Property Act, if any party to an exchange or any person claiming through or under him is by reason of any defect in title of the other party is deprived of the thing or any part thereof then in the absence of a contrary intention appearing from the terms of the exchange such other party shall compensate for the loss or return of the thing transferred if still in his possession or in the possession of his legal representative or a transferee from him without consideration. On an exchange of money each party warrants the genuineness of the money.[2]

Rights and liabilities of parties. Each party has the right, and is subject to the liabilities of a seller as to that which he gives, and has the right and is subject to the liabilities of a buyer as to that which he takes.[3] On exchange of money, each party warrants the genuineness of money given by him.

Exchange, how made. A transfer of property in completion of an exchange can be made only in a manner provided for the transfer of such property by sale, and registration will or will not be compulsory according to the nature and the value of the properties involved. In a transaction of exchange, money can be added to the property or goods to equalize the consideration.

1 Section 118 of the Transfer of Property Act.
2 Section 121 of the Transfer of Property Act.
3 Section 120 of the Transfer of Property Act.

Part performance. The doctrine of part performance applies in the case of the exchange. So, if the parties have taken possession without registered conveyance, each party will be entitled to defend his title and continue in possession under s. 53A of the Transfer of Property Act. Covenant as to title was implied in exchange[4] before the Transfer of Property Act. Section 119 of the Act, which was introduced by the Amending Act (20 of 1929), gave the right to return of the property in cases where the same is in possession of the other party or his heirs and legal representative. This, however, is subject to the terms of the deed itself. The English Common Law contained a similar right of re-entry on eviction in an exchange of real properties, but the position was altered by the Real Property Act 1845.[5] So there is no remedy in case of defect in title in English law except on the ground of fraud or covenant as to good title.

The Rule of Estoppel enacted under s. 43 of the Transfer of Property Act is applicable[6] in the case of exchange.

FORMS

Deed of Exchange of Properties

THIS DEED OF EXCHANGE is made this .... day of .... 1999 BETWEEN AB, son of .... residing at .... of the one part and CD, son of .... residing at .... of the other part.

WHEREAS the said AB is the sole and absolute owner in possession of the property comprised in Schedule "A" hereto AND WHEREAS the said CD is the sole and absolute owner in possession of the property comprised in Schedule "B" AND whereas the parties have agreed to mutually exchange and transfer of the ownership of the said properties as between them, viz., that the said AB shall convey the property in Schedule A to CD who will convey in lieu thereof the property in Schedule B to AB.

NOW THIS DEED WITNESSES that in pursuance of the aforesaid agreement, and in consideration of the transfer effected by CD as hereunder appearing, the said AB as beneficial owner do hereby grant, convey, transfer, assign and assure unto and in favour of the said CD, free from encumbrances, the house and premises, etc., comprised in Schedule A to HAVE AND TO HOLD the

4 *Balusu* v *Bopana* (1916)31 Mad LJ 380.

5 8 & 9 Vict C 106, section 4 now replaced by section 59 of the Law of Property Act 1925.

6 *Bhairab* v *Jiban* (1921)33 CLJ 184; 60 IC 819.

same absolutely and forever in exchange for what is hereunder transferred by the said CD in favour of AB. AND THAT the said CD in further pursuance of the said agreement and in consideration of the transfer effected by AB as beneficial owner do hereby grant, convey, transfer, assign and assure unto and in favour of the said AB, free from encumbrances, the land, etc., comprised in Schedule B hereto TO HAVE AND TO HOLD the same absolutely and forever in exchange for the transfer as aforesaid effected by AB in favour of CD as aforesaid.

IT IS HEREBY AGREED AND DECLARED that each party hereto has good right, full power, absolute authority and indefeasible title to give, grant, transfer and convey the property exchanged by this deed: AND that each party shall at all times hereafter peaceably and quietly hold, possess and enjoy the same without any claim, demand or interruption by the other and will, at the request and costs of the other, execute every such assurance or assurances and further do execute and perform every such act, deed or thing as shall reasonably be required by the other for further and more perfectly assuring to the other the property hereby conveyed to him.

IT IS HEREBY FURTHER DECLARED that the value of the property specified in each of the schedules is equal and the same is Rs. .... only.

Schedule A above referred to

Schedule B above referred to

IN WITNESS WHEREOF the parties hereto have executed these presents on the day, month and year first above-written.

Signed, sealed and delivered by AB
in the presence of:

Signed, sealed and delivered by CD
in the presence of:

Deed of Exchange of Properties where Money is Paid to Equalize

THIS DEED OF EXCHANGE, made the .... day of .... BETWEEN AB of, etc., of the one part, and CD of, etc., of the other part whereas AB is the sole and absolute owner in possession of the property described in Schedule A hereto AND whereas CD is the sole and absolute owner in possession of the property described in Schedule B and whereas the parties hereto have agreed as to mutual exchange of their said respective properties, *viz.*, that the said AB shall grant, transfer and convey to the said CD the property in Schedule A and that said CD shall in lieu thereof grant, transfer and convey to AB the property in Schedule B. And whereas the property in Schedule A being of greater value the said CD shall pay a sum of Rs. ....

to AB for equality of exchange. Now this Deed WITNESSES that in pursuance of the said agreement and in consideration of the conveyance of the property described in Schedule B as hereunder effected by the said CD and of the sum of Rupees .... paid to the said AB by the said CD on (*or* before) the execution of this deed for equality of exchange (the receipt whereof the said AB do hereby admit, acknowledge and confirm) the said AB as beneficial owner do hereby grant, transfer and convey unto and to the use of the said CD, free from encumbrances, ALL THAT etc. (*describe the property*): TO HAVE AND TO HOLD the same absolutely and forever in lieu of and in exchange of the property effected by him in favour of the said AB as hereunder appearing AND THIS DEED ALSO WITNESSES that in consideration of the conveyance of the property in Schedule A by the said AB hereinbefore effected, the said CD as beneficial owner do hereby grant, transfer and convey to the said AB free from encumbrances ALL THAT, etc. (*describe the property*): TO HAVE AND TO HOLD the same to the said AB absolutely and forever in lieu of and in exchange for the property transferred by him as hereinbefore appearing.

IT IS HEREBY AGREED and declared that each party hereto has good right full power absolute authority and indefeasible title to give grant transfer and convey the property exchanged by this Deed AND that each party shall at all times hereafter peaceably and quietly hold possess and enjoy the same without any claim demand or interruption by the other and will at the request and cost of the other execute every such assurance and further would execute and perform every such act deed or thing as shall reasonably be required by the other for further and more perfectly assuring to the other the property hereby conveyed to him.

Schedule A containing description of
AB's property transferred to CD and its value

Schedule B description of property
of CD transferred to AB and its value

IN WITNESS WHEREOF the parties hereto have executed these presents on the day, month and year first above-written.

Signed, sealed and delivered by AB
in the presence of:

Signed, sealed and delivered by CD
in the presence of:

Deed of Exchange of Properties by separate Mutual Conveyances

THIS INDENTURE MADE the .... day of .... BETWEEN CD of, etc., of the one part, and AB of, etc., of the other part.

WHEREAS the said AB was the sole and absolute owner of the property described in Schedule A hereto and whereas the said CD was and presently is the sole and absolute owner of the property comprised in Schedule B hereto AND whereas the parties are in uninterrupted possession and enjoyment of their respective properties AND whereas the parties having agreed as to mutual transfer by way of exchange of their said respective properties and in part performance thereof by a deed bearing even date with these presents and made between the said AB of the one part and the said CD of the other part, the property comprised in Schedule A hereto has been granted, transferred and conveyed by the said AB unto and to the use of the said CD absolutely and forever TO HAVE AND TO HOLD in exchange for the property hereunder transferred and conveyed by the said CD in favour of AB. Now THIS INDENTURE WITNESSES that in further pursuance of the aforesaid agreement and in consideration of the premises, the said CD as beneficial owner do hereby grant, transfer and convey to the said AB free from encumbrances the property comprised in Schedule B hereto: TO HAVE AND TO HOLD the same unto and to the said AB, his heirs, executors, administrators or assigns absolutely and forever in exchange of the property transferred and conveyed by the said AB unto and in favour of CD as hereinbefore recited.

IT IS HEREBY AGREED that the said CD will, at the request and costs of the said AB, execute every such assurance and do every such act, deed or thing as shall reasonably be required by the said AB for further or more perfectly assuring to the said AB the property hereby conveyed to him.

IT IS HEREBY DECLARED that the value of the property hereby conveyed is Rs. ....

Schedule A—Description of the property conveyed to CD

Schedule B—Description of the property conveyed to AB

IN WITNESS WHEREOF the parties hereto have executed these presents on the day, month and year first above-written.

Signed, sealed and delivered by CD
in the presence of:

Signed, sealed and delivered by AB
in the presence of:

Deed of Exchange of Properties Adjusting Boundary

THIS EXCHANGE IS MADE the .... day of .... BETWEEN AB of, etc., of the one part, and CD of, etc., of the other part.

WHEREAS the said AB is the sole owner in possession, free from encumbrances, of the property situate at, etc., which is more particularly delineated in the plan annexed hereto and therein coloured pink and yellow, and the said CD is also the sole owner in possession, free from encumbrances, of the adjoining land and property which is more particularly delineated in the plan annexed hereto and therein coloured blue and green AND WHEREAS the said AB and CD have agreed to adjust, settle and demarcate the boundaries in respect of their respective properties by making conveyances of lands as hereinafter appearing, and by fixing and providing for a new boundary as hereinafter mentioned: NOW THIS DEED WITNESSES as follows:

1. In pursuance of the said agreement and in consideration of the conveyance by and agreement on the part of the said CD hereinafter contained, the said AB as beneficial owner do hereby grant, convey and transfer unto and to the use of the said CD ALL the several pieces or parcels of land situate at, etc. aforesaid and containing respectively .... and .... square feet approximately which several pieces or parcels of land are more particularly described in Schedule A hereunder and delineated in the plan annexed hereto and therein coloured yellow: TO HOLD the same to the said CD absolutely.

2. In further pursuance of the said agreement and consideration of the conveyance by the said AB hereinbefore contained, the said CD as beneficial owner hereby conveys and transfers unto and to the use of the said AB ALL THAT piece or parcel of land situate at, etc., aforesaid and containing .... square feet approximately, which piece or parcel of land is more particularly described in Schedule B hereunder and the delineated in the plan annexed hereto and thereon coloured green: TO HOLD the same to the said AB absolutely.

3. IT IS HEREBY AGREED AND DECLARED that henceforth the boundary between the said adjoining lands and properties of the said AB and CD between the points marked "A" and "B" in the said plan annexed hereto, shall henceforth be treated as demarcated and delineated, in the said plan by a red line drawn between the said points.

4. It is hereby declared that the value of the property described in each of the Schedules is Rs. ....

Schedule A above referred to

Schedule B above referred to

THE PLAN

IN WITNESS WHEREOF the parties hereto have executed these presents on the day, month and year first above-written.

Signed, sealed and delivered by AB
in the presence of:

Signed, sealed and delivered by CD
in the presence of:

23

Foreign Collaboration and Joint Venture

Some foreign individuals, firms and companies have adequate investible funds, modern technologies and know-how for manufacturing goods and rendering services and registered Trade Marks, patents and designs to market their products. In some sectors Indian business houses may work in association with such foreign business concerns. This association may be general collaboration almost like partnership or it may be mainly financial or technical or a combination thereof.

Such association or collaboration with a foreign entity involves the foreigner in acquiring shares in Indian companies, acquiring immovable properties, establishing offices, appointing agents in India and repatriation of royalties, dividends, interests, rents and other incomes derived from transactions in India.

The Indian laws have put certain restrictions on such activities of the foreigner with a view to protect Indian trade and industries and to have a control over outflow of foreign exchange.

For association or collaboration with a foreign business concern the prior permission or sanction of Reserve Bank of India and/or Government of India is necessary. Any foreign Collaboration Agreement should be got sanctioned by the Government Authority or Reserve Bank of India.

The guidelines for foreign collaboration are however changing from time to time.

Prior approvals of collaboration agreement. Foreign companies and foreign nationals are required to obtain prior permission of the Reserve Bank of India for accepting payment as agent in India of any person or company in its trading and commercial transactions or to carry on in India any activities of a trading, commercial or industrial nature or to establish in India a branch, an office or other place of business. Such permission is also required by foreign companies intending to set up a liaison office in India or to post a representative for liaison activity or to set up any office for promotion of exports from India. Whenever a foreigner wants the facilities of repatriation of dividends, royalties, technical fees and other monetary receipts out of investments or services rendered in India permission of Reserve Bank is necessary.

All proposals for foreign collaboration with or without equity participation are subject to approval of Reserve Bank of India and/or Government of India. The applications have to be made to the authorities concerned, namely, the Secretariat for Industrial Assistance (SIA) Department of Industrial Development, Ministry of Industry, Government of India, New Delhi or the Foreign Investment Promotion Board (FIPB) or Development Commissioner of the Export Processing Zone concerned, as the case may be. In relation to the dealings in immovable property by a foreigner, permission has to be obtained from the Central Office of Reserve Bank of India and Foreign Investment Division.

Prior approvals for remittances. (*a*) For remittance from India of profits, dividends, royalties, technical and other fees, generally the application is to be made to the bank which is a foreign exchange dealer in the prescribed form; (*b*) Royalty upto 15% of the published price of the reprint of foreign books in India can be repatriated through bank; Royalty up to 30% of the published price of Software produced from overseas Copyright-holder may be remitted; (*c*) In excess of 30% specific permission of Department of Electronics, Government of India is necessary; (*d*) Payment for Royalty and technical know-how fees through a foreign exchange dealer (Bank) designated for the purpose can be made if the technical collaboration agreement had been approved by Government of India or Reserve Bank of India. Generally Royalty at 5% of the domestic sales and 8% of the export sales is permitted to be repatriated subject to Indian Income-tax; (*e*) Foreign investment in India in equity shares upto 51% is permitted in priority industries and in trading companies primarily engaged in export activities; (*f*) Other foreign investments are subject to approval by the Secretariat for Industrial Approvals, Ministry of Industry, Government of India or the Foreign Investments Promotion Board, Government of India, New Delhi.

Foreign Institutional Investors (FII) may invest in shares, debentures, bonds and other securities in primary and secondary markets. Special incentives, concessions and facilities are given to non-residents of Indian origin and Overseas Corporate Bodies (OCB) mainly owned by NRIs to invest in India with or without repatriation benefits.

In respect of foreign investment in Consumer Goods Industries the outflow of foreign exchange should not exceed the inflow of foreign exchange from export earnings. This applies to Consumer Goods Industries and limited for a period of 7 years from the date of commercial production of each unit.

Forms

Foreign Collaboration Agreement

THIS AGREEMENT IS MADE at Calcutta this .... day of .... 2000 BETWEEN AMCO INC incorporated under the appropriate laws of the United States of America having its office at 3 Broadway, New York (hereinafter referred as AMCO) of the one part and CALCO LTD. a company registered under the Companies Act 1956 and carrying on business at 100 Netaji Subhas Road, Calcutta 700 001 (hereinafter referred to as CALCO) of the other part.

WHEREAS AMCO is carrying on business as manufacturer of and dealer in and exporter of Computers, Computer Hardwares and Softwares and intends to further expand its business in India and other East Asian countries.

WHEREAS CALCO is now carrying on business in a small way in manufacturing and exporting Computers, Computer Hardwares and Softwares and intends to improve its products and marketing and all-round development with the technical assistance from AMCO.

WHEREAS AMCO and CALCO have agreed to co-operate and collaborate in developing, manufacturing and marketing of Computers, computer Hardwares and Softwares and accessories in relation thereto for mutual benefit.

NOW THESE PRESENTS WITNESSETH and the parties herein agree as follows:

1. AMCO will supply to CALCO plant, machinery and equipments for the purpose of improving and adding to the existing factory and instal the same for manufacture of Computers, Computer Hardwares and Softwares and all related accessories.

2. AMCO will supply the necessary Designs, Lay-out, Drawings and other forms of technical know-how for the successful operation of the plant of CALCO so as to enable it to manufacture quality goods capable of competing with world players in world markets.

3. AMCO will render assistance by deputing experts and technicians for improvement in and development of the manufacturing processes, quality control, marketing and after-sales servicing.

4. AMCO will give appropriate training to selected employees of CALCO in Calcutta so that CALCO can operate more efficiently its plant, market its products and export the same to the best advantage possible.

5. AMCO will give advice on any new developments in technology or marketing or in any of the aspects of the business so that CALCO may successfully compete with global manufacturers in global markets.

6. The consideration for rendering these services will be 10% of the net profit of CALCO to be paid to AMCO, according to the Balance Sheet and Profit and Loss accounts finalised, approved by General Meeting and filed with the Registrar of Companies, West Bengal.

7. AMCO will by mutual agreement allow its Trade Marks, Patent Rights and other rights in relation to its products to be used by CALCO.

8. This agreement will be for a period of five years, renewable for another five years by mutual agreement and on terms and conditions mutually agreed upon.

9. During the subsistence of this agreement AMCO will not enter into any other agreement of any nature with any other company, partnership or concern in India or set up its branch or subsidiary in India or do anything which might adversely affect the business and profitability of CALCO.

10. This agreement is entered into subject to obtaining the necessary approvals from Government of India and other authorities concerned.

11. Any differences or disputes that might arise in relation to this agreement, performance or non-performance thereof or breach thereof or in relation to any other matter covered by this agreement, will be referred to Indian Chamber of Commerce for Arbitration and their decision shall be final and binding on both the parties herein.

12. IN WITNESS WHEREOF the parties hereto have signed, sealed and delivered these presents on the day, month and year first above-written.

Signed, sealed and delivered by
Mr. ....
pursuant to the Board Resolution
dated .... of AMCO INC. Signature

In the presence of:
1. ....
2. ....

Signed, sealed and delivered by
Mr. ....
pursuant to the Board Resolution
dated .... of CALCO LTD. Signature

In the presence of:

1. ....

2. ....

Collaboration Agreement

THIS AGREEMENT IS MADE at Calcutta on this 15th day of July 1999 BETWEEN Delco Limited, a company registered under the Companies Act 1956 and carrying on business at 5 Indra Prastha Marg, New Delhi 110 002, India (hereinafter referred to as the DELCO which term shall include, unless the context otherwise requires, its successors and assigns) of the one part and Japan Co. Ltd., a company registered under the appropriate laws of Japan and carrying on business at Cobe Road, Japan (hereinafter referred to as the JAPCO which expression shall, unless its context otherwise requires, include its successors and assigns) of the other part.

WHEREAS DELCO is carrying on business as manufacturer of, dealer in and exporter of electronic goods and has considerable technical knowledge regarding the manufacture of electronic products and information about the marketing possibilities of such products.

AND WHEREAS JAPCO is also carrying on business as manufacturer and exporter of electronic goods and has considerable know-how in this regard and intends to expand its business in collaboration with DELCO.

AND WHEREAS a joint team of DELCO and JAPCO made a detailed study of possibilities of setting-up of a Joint-manufacturing and exporting unit in India availing of the local infrastructure advantages and the expertise of DELCO and JAPCO to the mutual benefits of the parties herein.

AND WHEREAS the parties have agreed to procure formation and incorporation in West Bengal of a company with the main object of manufacturing electronic goods for exports.

AND WHEREAS the parties have agreed to assist each other and the said company to be incorporated by making available to the new company latest plant, machinery and the technical know-how, technical services, technical assistance and arranging for buy-back and exporting the products of the new company.

AND WHEREAS JAPCO has agreed to make a feasibility study and supply to the new company the latest plant, machinery, furnish latest technical know-how, information, assistance and trained personnel in the manufacture of electronic products by the said new company and to render financial assistance by subscribing to the shares of new company that may be issued to the extent of 49% and also in supplying on credit plant, machinery, technical know-how information and assistance which will be liquidated gradually by the new company within 10 years.

AND WHEREAS the parties have agreed that this collaboration will be subject to obtaining all necessary approvals, licences, permissions, authorisations and consent of the concerned authorities and that the said consents, approval or authorisations will be applied for and obtained by both parties jointly and/or severally assisted by the other.

NOW THIS AGREEMENT WITNESSETH and it is hereby agreed by and between the parties hereto as follows:

1. The new company to be formed shall be a public limited company to be incorporated under the Companies Act 1956 in accordance with the terms of this agreement having its registered office at .... under the name and style of "Joint Co. Ltd." (hereinafter referred to as the "JOINT CO.").

2. The JOINT CO. will have as its principal objects the manufacturing of all kinds of electronic products, machinery, consumer goods and all sorts of articles for sale in the domestic market as also export to other countries.

3. The JOINT CO. would have an authorised share capital of Rs. 1,000 crores divided into 100 crores Equity shares of Rs. 10 each. The initial issued, subscribed and paid-up capital would be Rs. 800 crores.

4. The Memorandum of Association and Articles of Association of the JOINT CO. proposed to be registered with the Registrar of Companies have to be approved by the Board of Directors of DELCO and JAPCO.

5. DELCO, Financial Institutions and members of the public shall be offered for subscription 51% of shares proposed to be issued for subscription by the JOINT CO.

6. JAPCO shall subscribe to and pay for the shares of JOINT CO. to the extent of 49% of the proposed issue of shares and pay for the same either in cash or kind.

7. The JOINT CO. shall have directors not less than five and not more than eleven.

8. DELCO and JAPCO shall exercise their voting rights at the General Meetings or Board Meetings in accordance with the terms and spirit of these presents.

9. The parties herein shall not without consent of each other in writing cause or allow any increase in or reorganisation of the share capital or alter the provisions of Memorandum of Association or the Articles of Association contrary to the rights and obligations of the parties herein.

10. The parties herein will have access to the books of accounts and other records of the JOINT CO. through their authorised representatives.

11. The JOINT CO. after incorporation shall ratify, consent, adopt and agree to be bound by the provisions of these presents.

12. In the event of impossibility of carrying on business of JOINT CO. in collaboration between the parties each party would be entitled to buy the shares of the other party at the valuation to be made by appointing an Auditor to be approved by the parties. In the event of such an arrangement

failing then the party, intending to going out of the Collaboration Agreement may dispose of its shares in the JOINT CO. in the manner it thinks best.

13. DELCO agrees to procure suitable land for the purpose of settingup of a factory for the JOINT CO. DELCO agrees to take up the work of construction of the factory premises in accordance with the plan and design to be prepared by the parties herein jointly.

14. The cost of land and the cost of construction will be reimbursed by the JOINT CO. either by payment of cash or by the allotment of shares.

15. It is agreed that JAPCO shall make the feasibility study of the proposed project, market survey, profitability, cash-flow projections and prepare comprehensive project report, provide manufacturing technology, assist in manufacture and development of electronic goods, assist in research and quality control of raw materials and finished products and explore the possibilities of obtaining local substitutes acceptable to customers, advice proper marketing, selling and distribution techniques, advice production planning to achieve optimum capacity utilisation of plant and machinery, assist in settingup infrastructure, including ancillary small and medium-scale industries for the growth and development of the business of JOINT CO. and generally to assist and advise to adapt to the changed situation in technology demand pattern of all markets.

16. JAPCO guarantees that the plant proposed to be set up by import of plant machinery and other articles from JAPCO would be capable of producing electronic goods in the required quantities and of the world standard of quality.

17. JAPCO shall furnish and/or provide to the JOINT CO. (*a*) detailed plans, blue prints, specifications, information and other data to enable the contractors to construct and make arrangement for production facilities at the factory site, capable of utilising the optimum capacity of the plant and machinery to be supplied and installed for production and for additions and expansions;

(*b*) technical information data and render all assistance necessary to ensure effective operation and maintenance of the machinery and equipment, supply spare parts, maintenance manuals, operating instructions, manuals relating to the construction and assembly of each plant, machinery and equipment and instructions regarding start up and shut down and shall depute a technical personnel to explain and train the employees of JOINT CO. in proper maintenance of the whole unit;

(*c*) all technical assistance and advice for operation for the plant including scheduling of material, specifications and ordering, production techniques, production planning, quality control, recommended safety procedures and methods and other industrial engineering activities in connection with the organisation, planning and development and operating tactics to obtain most efficient use of production facilities and on all aspects of plant operation and training of the personnel of JOINT CO. in giving effect to the aforesaid;

(*d*) all technical information and assistance as shall be necessary to keep the JOINT CO. abreast with the latest advancement in technology and utilise the same in its manufacture, sale and export of electronic goods;

(*e*) training and technical assistance to five operating employees of JOINT CO. for at least 3 months each for which the JOINT CO. shall bear and pay only for the transport expenses and salaries of such trainees and all other expenses and costs of these trainees shall be borne by JAPCO. JAPCO shall make arrangements for compliance with all formalities for such trainees for entering into and staying in Japan and obtaining training in the factory of JAPCO;

(*f*) qualified personnel for assembly and installation of plant and equipment supplied by JAPCO and JOINT CO. Such qualified personnel shall be responsible for start up production and continue to remain with the JOINT CO. till the commercial production starts;

(*g*) a competent personnel to plan and organise to procure raw materials, production in the factory of JOINT CO., marketing and exporting electronic goods to the world markets. JOINT CO. will bear and pay for all expenses of the personnel that JAPCO may depute at the factory of the JOINT CO. but their salaries shall be paid by JAPCO.

18. JAPCO shall assign to the JOINT CO. all the JAPCO's right, title and interest in all its present and future Patents, Trade Marks and Trade Names in relation to electronic goods.

19. JAPCO shall grant to JOINT CO. the right of an exclusive Licensee for the whole world for all Patents in relation to electronic goods for their production, manufacture, use, sale and export anywhere in the world.

20. JAPCO shall assign its right, title and interest in all licences held by it for production, manufacture, use and export of electronic goods.

21. The right, title and interest in or to the use of technical data which JAPCO at any point of time is entitled to use shall be assigned to JOINT CO. for production, sale, marketing the export of electronic goods.

22. JAPCO agrees to execute all such documents as JOINT CO. may require to give effect, perfect, confirm, record assignments and transfers to the JOINT CO. all the JAPCO'S Patents, Licences, Sub-licences and technical data.

23. JAPCO will be responsible for maintaining standards and quality of the products of JOINT CO. and for making available all technical know-how and other assistance to JOINT CO. for making the venture a success.

24. JAPCO will depute its trained personnel both technical and managerial every half year to inspect and examine the operation of plant and machinery,

product quality, marketing and export and suggest improvement in production techniques, marketing and exporting the products to enable JOINT CO. to remain efficient and competitive compared to similar industries in the world. Cost and expenses of such personnel other than salaries and remuneration shall be borne and paid by the JOINT CO.

25. JAPCO will not charge any Royalty or fees for rendering the services or furnishing know-how or deputing technical hands or assisting in production, improvement thereon and export of the same but would be entitled to reimbursement of actual extra costs incurred for rendering these services. JOINT CO. will reimburse the expenses of the technical personnel while stationed in West Bengal.

26. JAPCO will purchase from JOINT CO. at least 80% of its products on cost plus 30% profit basis and assist in exporting the balance quantity of products of the JOINT CO. to the World market.

27. It is hereby agreed and declared that all feasibility study report and reports of the project, market survey, profitability, drawings, specifications, advises and all other documents of DELCO, JAPCO and JOINT CO. shall be held in strict confidence and secrecy and shall not be disclosed by any of the parties herein or the JOINT CO. or any of the employees of any of these three companies without obtaining prior written permission from all these three companies.

28. It is agreed and understood that this agreement shall be subject to prior approvals being obtained by DELCO from the authorities concerned in India, JAPCO from the appropriate authorities in India and Japan and compliance of the provisions of law by JOINT CO. If the requisite approvals cannot be obtained within 36 months from the execution hereof then, unless the parties otherwise agree, this Agreement shall stand terminated.

29. It is agreed that no party to this agreement shall be responsible for any failure or delay on its part in performing any of its obligations or for any loss or damage, costs, charges and expenses incurred or suffered by the other party by reason of such failure or default or delay caused due to any *force majeure* conditions, acts of God, laws and regulations of the Government, strikes, lock-outs, riots, violence, war or any other cause beyond its control.

30. The parties hereby agree that this agreement as also the rights and obligations of the parties herein and in the JOINT CO. shall be governed by the laws of India.

31. Any dispute or difference or claim arising out of or in relation to this agreement shall be referred to the Bengal Chamber of Commerce for settlement in accordance with the Arbitration and Conciliation Act 1996

and the Award of the Bengal Chamber of Commerce shall be final and binding on both the parties to this agreement.

IN WITNESS WHEREOF the parties hereto have executed these presents on the day, month and year first above-written.

Signed, sealed and delivered by
Mr. ....
pursuant to a Board Resolution
dated .... of Delco Ltd.,
at Calcutta in the presence of: Signature

Signed, sealed and delivered by
Mr. ....
pursuant to a Board Resolution
dated .... of Japan Co. Ltd.
Calcutta in the presence of: Signature

Collaboration Agreement

THIS AGREEMENT IS MADE on this .... day of .... 1999 BETWEEN AMCO INC incorporated under the appropriate laws of America having its office at 5 Broad Street, New York (hereinafter referred to as AMCO) of the one part and INDCO LIMITED, a company registered under the Companies Act 1956 having its office at 99 Chowringhee Road, Calcutta 700 071 (hereinafter referred to as INDCO) of the other part.

WHEREAS AMCO carries on business as manufacturer of, dealer in and exporter of Computers, Computer Hardwares and Computer Softwares and has worldwide market and intends to extend its presence in Asian Countries.

AND WHEREAS INDCO is carrying on business as manufacturer of Computers, Computer Hardwares and Computer Softwares and intends to develop its industrial unit by adopting modern technology and technical skill and expertise in the field of manufacturing Computers, Computer Hardwares and Computer Softwares and Accessories in relation thereto with the assistance of technical services from AMCO.

AND WHEREAS AMCO has agreed to render comprehensive technical services including preparation of development project, feasibility study, market survey and a comprehensive report in relation to production, sales, exports and after-sales service. The technical assistance would also include manufacturing and engineering technology in relation to design, production methods, manufacturing and testing, adaptation of local technology and expertise and assisting INDCO in regular research, quality control of raw materials and finished products and to explore the possibilities of substitutes.

It would include exploration of marketing, selling and distribution techniques tendering advices regarding procurement of appropriate raw materials and to explore import substitutes and optimum utilisation of the production capacity of the existing plant and machinery. The technical services would also include advices and measures to be adopted against piracy and prevention of any mischief being done in the line of production or use of Computers, Hardwares and Softwares.

AND WHEREAS AMCO has agreed to render technical services as also to depute technical personnel to the factory of INDCO for a consideration mentioned hereinafter.

NOW THESE PRESENTS WITNESSETH and the parties hereby agree as follows:

1. AMCO will render technical services to INDCO with the object of improving and developing the manufacturing, production, sales and exports of Computers, Computer Hardwares, Computer Softwares, Computer Accessories and other things and articles in relation to Computers for a consideration of Rs. 1,00,000 per month and 10% of the net profit after tax of INDCO.

2. AMCO will depute technical personnel at least for 3 months every year to have thorough inspection of the method of production and giving suggestions for improvement and to train technical personnel of INDCO in its factory.

3. The technical personnel of AMCO will test the working of the plant and machinery and the products and suggest and assist to improve the quality of the products.

4. AMCO will every 6 months submit a report regarding market survey and suggest the prospective markets for exports of INDCO'S products.

5. AMCO will be paid in consideration of the aforesaid services of the technical personnel a sum of Rs. 1,00,000 per month and all expenses of board and lodging of the technical personnel including their air-fare for the entire journey.

6. AMCO shall purchase 60% of the entire products of INDCO at the prevailing market price and/or INDCO'S cost price plus 40% thereof.

7. This agreement will remain in force for 5 years from the date of execution of the agreement with option to extend the period by another 5 years on terms and conditions to be mutually agreed upon.

8. This agreement is subject to obtaining sanctions, approvals and permissions from the Government of India and other concerned authorities.

9. AMCO with a view to facilitate the development of marketing and exporting of INDCO'S products allow its Trade name or patent rights to be utilised by INDCO during subsistence of the agreement.

10. Any addition or alteration to the terms and conditions mutually agreed upon can be made by execution of a supplemental agreement.

11. All differences and disputes arising in relation to this agreement, its construction, validity, performance, breach or any other question arising in relation thereto shall be referred to the Indian Chamber of Commerce for settlement by arbitration or conciliation in Calcutta and the decision of the Arbitral Tribunal shall be final and binding on both the parties.

IN WITNESS WHEREOF the parties hereto have signed, sealed and delivered these presents on the day, month and year first above-written.

Signed, sealed and delivered by
Mr. .... pursuant
to Board Resolution dated.........
of AMCO INC at Calcutta
in the presence of: Signature
1. ....
2. ....

Signed, sealed and delivered by
Mr. .... pursuant to
Board Resolution dated .... of
INDCO LIMITED in the presence of: Signature
1. ....
2. ....

Joint Venture Agreement—Financial

THIS AGREEMENT IS MADE this .... day of .... 2000 BETWEEN AMCO INC incorporated under appropriate laws of the United States of America having its office at 3 Broadway, New York (hereinafter referred to as AMCO) of the One Part and Indco Ltd. a company registered under the Companies Act 1956 and carrying on business at 100 Netaji Subhas Road, Calcutta 700 001 (hereinafter referred to as the INDCO) of the Other Part.

WHEREAS the parties herein have agreed to carry on business of manufacturing of and dealing in Computers, its accessories, Softwares and Hardwares in collaboration with each other.

AND WHEREAS the parties have agreed that for better organisational, financial and marketing of the said goods the parties herein would float or incorporate a new company to which the parties herein would give all financial assistance along with technical know-how to make the venture a success.

NOW THEREFORE THIS AGREEMENT WITNESSETH and the parties hereby agree as follows:

1. The new company will be incorporated in India with the name CALCO LTD. or any modification thereof.

2. The Memorandum and Articles of Association of the new company would be prepared and filed with the Registrar of Companies West Bengal and would be registered subject to the modifications the Registrar of Companies might suggest.

3. The new company will have an Authorised Share Capital of Rs. 100 lakhs divided into one lakh equity shares of Rs. 100 each.

4. AMCO will subscribe to 49% of the shares in the new company and INDCO will subscribe to the extent of 51% of the shares in the new company.

5. The shares would be issued as fully paid-up.

6. The consideration for issue of 49% of the shares of new company to AMCO will he mainly in cash and partly by way of supply of plant, machinery, equipments, know-how and technical services to be rendered by AMCO to the said new company.

7. The management of the new company would be governed by the provisions in the Memorandum and Articles of Association of new company.

8. AMCO will render, *inter alia,* following assistance to the new company:

(*a*) it will make available know-how of manufacturing and sourcing of raw materials, marketing finished products including exporting the same to Global markets;

(*b*) it will depute technicians to study the operations of said company's plant and machinery, production and sales mechanism and train Indian personnel of the new company in all the phases of acquiring raw materials, manufacturing products, marketing the same and exporting to foreign countries;

(*c*) it will allow use of its patent rights, Trade Marks, and other exclusive rights so that the products of new company can be sold and compete in the world market.

9. AMCO will buy from new company its products to the extent of 60% at the cost plus 40% basis or the market price whichever is higher.

10. INDCO shall make available to the new company its own know-how, business contacts, sources of raw materials and equipments, financing from Banks, Financial Institutions and other sources, personnel recruitment, rendering administrative, fiscal and legal services and obtaining factory sites, and office premises for the new company.

11. The pre-incorporation expenses in promotion of the new company will be shared by AMCO and INDCO in the proportion of 49% and 51% respectively.

12. The pre-incorporation expenses so borne will be paid and recovered from the new company and the new company when incorporated will ratify and consent to such payment.

13. This agreement is subject to obtaining all necessary permissions, approvals and consent of Government of India and other authorities.

14. This agreement shall be governed by the laws of India.

15. All disputes and differences in relation to this agreement will be decided by the Indian Chamber of Commerce of Arbitral proceedings to be held in Calcutta and its decision shall be final and binding on both parties to the agreement.

IN WITNESS WHEREOF the parties hereto have signed, sealed and delivered these Presents on the day, month and year first above-written.

Signed, sealed and delivered by
Mr. .... pursuant
to Board Resolution of AMCO INC.
dated .... in Calcutta
in the presence of: Signature

1. ....

2. ....

Signed, sealed and delivered
by Mr. ....
pursuant to Board Resolution
of INDCO LTD. dated ....
in the presence of: Signature

1. ....

2. ....

Joint Venture with Foreign Company

THIS AGREEMENT IS MADE on this .... day of .... 2000 BETWEEN AMCO INC. incorporated under the appropriate laws of the United States of America having its office at 5 Seventh Street, New York of the ONE PART and INCO LTD. a company registered under the Companies Act 1956 having its office at 99 Chowringhee Road, Calcutta 700 071 of the OTHER PART.

WHEREAS AMCO INC. (hereinafter referred to as AMCO) carries on business as manufacturer of and dealer and exporter in Computers, Computer

Hardwares and Softwares and has worldwide market and intends to extend its market here in India and elsewhere.

WHEREAS Inco Ltd. (hereinafter referred to as INCO) carries on business as manufacturer of, dealer in and exporter of Computer Softwares and intends to expand its business in India and abroad.

WHEREAS AMCO and INCO intend to co-operate in manufacturing, dealing in and exporting Computers, Hardwares and Softwares in India and abroad for mutual benefit by setting up a new company.

NOW THESE PRESENTS WITNESSETH and the parties hereby agree as follows:

1. A Joint-stock company would be formed under the name and style of INDO-AMERICAN COMPANY PVT. LTD. under the Companies Act 1956 having its Registered Office at 99 Chowringhee Road, Calcutta 700 071.

2. AMCO and three of its nominees and INCO and three of its nominees would be the subscribers to the Memorandum and Articles of Association of the said company to be incorporated.

3. The shareholding in the Share Capital of the said company to be incorporated would be in equal proportions between AMCO and INCO.

4. The Memorandum and Articles of Association of the company proposed to be incorporated would be settled in mutual consultation and the same would govern the rights and obligations of AMCO and INCO in relation to the said proposed company.

5. AMCO will be allotted shares in the said new company partly in cash and partly towards the cost of plant, machinery and equipment to be supplied by AMCO to the new company and in consideration for assignments by AMCO of its Patent Rights, Trade Marks, Trade Names and Licences in favour of the new company to be incorporated. The consideration for allotment of shares to AMCO would also include the supply and transfer of technical formula, new inventions, secret processes, technical information concerning the production, manufacturing, testing, specifications, instructions and information as to the manufacture of, development, use and servicing, maintenance and improvement of quality of Computers, Hardwares and Softwares and generally in connection with the successful carrying on of the said business by the said new company to be incorporated.

6. AMCO will furnish necessary technical assistance and expertise to the new company for assembling, installation, start-up and for smooth running of the manufacturing and selling processes as might be required by the new company from time to time.

7. AMCO will furnish to the new company all other technical assistance and advice in relation to the operation of the plant and machinery, repairs thereof, testing facilities, training facilities and Research & Development

facilities should be arranged for, provided and continued for successful running of the business of the new company.

8. The shares that would be allotted by the new company should not be transferred by either AMCO or INCO within a period of five years from the date of allotment and thereafter if any of the parties intends to transfer any share then the same shall be offered first to the other party at a price to be determined by a Valuer to be appointed by mutual agreement and in absence by application to the Indian Chamber of Commerce.

9. The new company will manufacture Computers, Hardwares and Softwares and allied accessories and products and the same would be marketed in India and exported to other countries under the Trade name or Brand name made available by AMCO and by any other name and shall obtain new Trade Mark and obtain Patents for further and better manufacturing, selling and exporting the new company's products.

10. AMCO will buy 75% of the products of new company for exporting to other countries through its own organisations or outlets at a remunerative price not below the price at which the products are sold in India.

11. Neither party shall carry on their own business in a manner which will directly adversely affect the business and profitability of the new company.

12. The expenses for the setting up and promotion of the new company would be shared equally by AMCO and INCO.

13. The consideration for allotment of shares of the new company to INCO shall be paid in cash and in kind such as by transfer of immovable properties for the setting up of factory and making arrangement for the office accommodation of the new company. The valuation of such immovable properties including office accommodation would be decided by mutual agreement between AMCO and INCO.

14. Any disputes or differences arising in relation to this agreement, its construction, validity, performance, breach or any other question shall be referred to the Indian Chamber of Commerce for settlement by Arbitration or Conciliation in Calcutta and the decision of the said Arbitrator shall be final and binding on both the parties.

15. This agreement is made subject to obtaining approvals of the Indian Government and other concerned authorities.

16. In the event certain additions or alterations are required under this agreement due to imposition of certain terms and conditions by Government of India or appropriate authority granting the approval shall be incorporated in this agreement by way of a supplemental agreement and if required the Memorandum and Articles of Association of the new company would also be

in conformity with such directions or approvals of the appropriate authorities.

17. IN WITNESS WHEREOF the parties hereto have signed, sealed and delivered these presents on the day, month and year first above-written.

Signed, sealed and delivered by
Mr. ....
Pursuant to the Board Resolution — Signature
dated .... of AMCO INC.
in Calcutta in the presence of:
1. ....
2. ....

Signed, sealed and delivered by
Mr. ....
pursuant to the Board Resolution — Signature
dated .... of INCO LTD.
in the presence of:
1. ....
2. ....

Foreign Collaboration Agreement (Financial)

THIS AGREEMENT MADE this 15th day of December 2000 BETWEEN US Company Ltd., a company registered under the appropriate laws of the USA and carrying on business at San Francisco, USA hereinafter referred to as the FOREIGN COMPANY (which term shall unless excluded by or repugnant to the context include its successors and assigns) of the ONE PART and Ind Co. Ltd., a company registered under the Companies Act 1956 and having its Registered Office at ....Calcutta hereinafter referred to as the INDIAN COMPANY (which term shall unless excluded by or repugnant to the context include its successors and assigns) of the OTHER PART.

WHEREAS the parties herein have agreed subject to all necessary approvals, consents, validations, permissions and licences to procure the formation and incorporation in the State of West Bengal an INDIAN COMPANY with a Memorandum of Association as its principal objects, *inter alia*, of manufacturing and marketing and exporting Computers, setting up of infrastructures and to do acts incidental thereto.

AND WHEREAS the parties hereto have agreed to assist each other on certain matters to ensure the success of the operation of the INDIAN COMPANY.

NOW THEREFORE THESE PRESENTS WITNESSETH and the parties hereto hereby agree as follows:

1. The INDIAN COMPANY shall be the new Public Limited Company to be incorporated on terms of this Agreement in India with the name "New Company Ltd." (hereinafter referred to as the NEW COMPANY).

2. "Shares" shall mean Equity Shares of the NEW COMPANY to be subscribed by the Foreign Company and INDIAN COMPANY upon the terms hereof:

(*a*) the company will be incorporated with the name New Company Limited;

(*b*) Memorandum of Association of the New Company Ltd. will have as its principal objects manufacturing and marketing of Computers and Softwares and rendering services in relation thereto both in India and abroad and to engage in infrastructure and associated activities;

(*c*) the authorised share capital of the NEW COMPANY will be Rs. 50 crores, divided into 50 lakhs equity shares of Rs. 100 each out of which issued subscribed and paid-up capital shall be Rs. 40 crores divided into 40 lakhs Equity shares of Rs. 100 each;

(*d*) The Memorandum and Articles of Association of the new company shall be approved by the Foreign Company and the Indian Company.

3. The FOREIGN COMPANY shall subscribe to and pay for the shares of NEW COMPANY in the manner as the Board of Directors of the NEW COMPANY may decide. The FOREIGN COMPANY shall subscribe at any point of time 51% of total shares issued by the NEW COMPANY. The balance 49% of the issued shares of the NEW COMPANY shall be subscribed by the INDIAN COMPANY and its associates, promoters, their friends and relations.

4. The number of directors of the NEW COMPANY shall be minimum five and maximum eleven. The FOREIGN COMPANY and the INDIAN COMPANY shall have equal number of directors in the Board but the Chairman of the Board of Directors as also at the General Meeting shall be one of the directors representing the INDIAN COMPANY. The FOREIGN COMPANY and the INDIAN COMPANY shall exercise their rights as shareholders in accordance with the law and in terms of the present Agreement.

5. The NEW COMPANY shall not without the written consent of the Indian Company increase or reorganise its capital, alter its Memorandum and Articles of Association, sell, release, transfer, mortgage or otherwise dispose of all or substantial portion of its business or assets or take any steps for merger or amalgamation of the NEW COMPANY with another company or for liquidation of the NEW COMPANY. Without the written consent of the INDIAN COMPANY the NEW COMPANY shall not create, acquire or control any subsidiary

or make any substantial investment in any other company or venture or give loans or stand guarantee or extend credit to any person, firm or company except to its customers in the usual course of business.

6. The NEW COMPANY shall maintain proper books of accounts and records as required by law and the FOREIGN COMPANY and the INDIAN COMPANY shall have the right to inspect the books of accounts and records and correspondence of the NEW COMPANY and take copies thereof at its own costs.

7. The FOREIGN COMPANY and the INDIAN COMPANY shall give all requisite assistance to the NEW COMPANY to make the NEW COMPANY a success. The FOREIGN COMPANY shall make available to the NEW COMPANY the know-how required to achieve its objectives, give access to the NEW COMPANY all processes of know-how, requisite financial assistance apart from shareholding, marketing assistance and facilities, advantage of services of the International Network of the FOREIGN COMPANY and the use as Licencee or otherwise the Trade Marks, Patent Rights and goodwill of the FOREIGN COMPANY for the purpose of production, sale and export of the products of the NEW COMPANY.

8. The INDIAN COMPANY shall furnish to the NEW COMPANY with its know-how, technology, technical assistance including the management in the production and marketing of the products of the NEW COMPANY, the business connections of the INDIAN COMPANY, access to Indian know-how, assistance in procurement of raw materials, financial assistance, assistance in the recruitment of personnel and running the administrative, fiscal and legal services. INDIAN COMPANY shall also promote the name and goodwill of the NEW COMPANY and its products.

9. The FOREIGN COMPANY and the INDIAN COMPANY both shall from time to time make available to the NEW COMPANY their qualified employees for providing suitable services so that the NEW COMPANY can achieve its objectives.

10. The parties hereto agree that upon its incorporation the NEW COMPANY shall ratify, adopt, consent and agree to be bound by the terms of these presents. The FOREIGN COMPANY and the INDIAN COMPANY shall in equal proportion pay preliminary expenses for forming the NEW COMPANY and all such expenses shall be reimbursed by the NEW COMPANY within a year from the time it goes into commercial production.

11. In case of breach of any of the terms of this Agreement by a party the other party may give two months notice to rectify the breach in default its intention to terminate the agreement. In the event the breach is not remedied then the other party shall give a second notice that it would terminate the agreement with effect from 30 days from receipt of the said notice.

12. In case of such notice for termination or there being a stalemate in the management of the affairs of the NEW COMPANY, either party may offer to the other to sell its shareholdings at a valuation to be made by the NEW COMPANY'S Auditor and by a second independent Auditor. If the valuation

differs, then the value of shares will be taken as the average of the two valuations. If the offer is not accepted, then the shares shall be sold to outsiders. In the event the FOREIGN COMPANY or INDIAN COMPANY goes into liquidation the other company may buy the shares of the NEW COMPANY at the book value of shares held by the company in liquidation.

13. The agreement shall be governed by the laws of India and the courts in India shall have jurisdiction to entertain any legal proceedings in relation to any dispute in relation to the agreement. In the event any of the clauses or part of the agreement be held to be invalid, that will not affect the other part or clauses which valid portion shall be enforceable.

14. All notices are to be served in the manner permissible under the law at the addresses recorded in the books and records of the NEW COMPANY.

15. The FOREIGN COMPANY shall obtain all necessary permissions and consents of the Government of the FOREIGN COMPANY for entering into this Agreement and carrying on business of the NEW COMPANY in India. The parties hereto shall obtain the necessary sanctions, permissions, authorisations etc. of the Reserve Bank of India, Government of India and other concerned authorities in respect of the present agreement as also for the NEW COMPANY for its incorporation and carrying on its business. In the event necessary approvals, licences, permissions and authorisations are not available, then this agreement shall become void.

16. All disputes and differences between the parties or any claims by any of the parties arising out of or in relation to this agreement including its construction, validity, compliance or breach which the parties have tried to but could not settle shall be referred to the Bengal Chamber of Commerce for settlement by arbitration proceedings in accordance with the law in India in force and the Award of the said Chamber of Commerce shall be final and binding on the parties to this agreement.

IN WITNESS WHEREOF the parties hereto have executed THESE PRESENTS on the day, month and year first above-written.

Signed, sealed and delivered by
the said Mr. ....
pursuant to the Board Resolution
of the Foreign Company
dated .... at Calcutta
in the presence of: Signature

1. ....
2. ....

Signed, sealed and delivered by
Mr. ....
pursuant to the Board Resolution
of the Indian Company
dated .... at Calcutta
in the presence of:

Signature

1. ....

2. ....

Technical Foreign Collaboration

THIS AGREEMENT IS MADE at Calcutta this .... day of .... 2000 BETWEEN Amco Inc., incorporated under the appropriate laws of the United States of America having its office at 3 Broadway, New York (hereinafter referred to as AMCO) of the one part and Calco Ltd., a company registered under the Companies Act 1956 and carrying on business at 100 Netaji Subhas Road, Calcutta 700 001 (hereinafter referred to as CALCO) of the other part.

WHEREAS AMCO is the manufacturer, dealer and exporter of Computers Hardwares, Softwares and accessories (hereinafter referred to as the PRODUCTS) and has highly developed technical know-how, secret techniques, technical information and skilled technical personnel concerning the manufacture and marketing of Computers, Hardwares and Softwares and accessories (hereinafter referred to as the TECHNOLOGY).

AND WHEREAS AMCO has agreed at the request of CALCO to provide and render technical assistance and advice for setting up at the factory of CALCO a manufacturing unit for manufacturing, distribution, sale and export of the said products and to allow the use of AMCO'S Trade Marks, Patents, Licences and other rights in relation to the said products and CALCO has agreed to accept the same.

NOW THIS AGREEMENT WITNESSETH and the parties hereby agree as follows:

1. AMCO will provide, furnish and make available to CALCO latest technology including engineering and manufacturing information, designs, production methods, plant, future innovations, improvements relating to designs, production methods, manufacture, testing, processes of the said products and engineering blue-prints, plant lay-out, drawings, information and documents relating to manufacturing processes of the said products and all other related information and particulars for successful installation, running of and production in the said unit.

2. AMCO shall provide and depute technical personnel for the preparation of the factory site, installation of plant and machinery supplied or selected by AMCO, start up operation and selection and procurement of raw materials either from AMCO or from other sources till the commercial production of the unit is commenced.

3. AMCO will train at the factory of CALCO its personnel so that they may be able to run the unit smoothly and be abreast with all the technical know-how.

4. AMCO will ensure production of quality products at the CALCO'S unit with full capacity, marketing and export of the products.

5. AMCO will allow the use of its Trade Marks and Patent Rights and secret formula for the manufacture, sale and export of CALCO'S PRODUCTS.

6. AMCO will buy 60% of the PRODUCTS of the said unit of CALCO for sale or export to places or markets outside India and without impairing the sale of balance 40% of the products of CALCO.

7. AMCO will keep CALCO indemnified against and harmless from any claim or action in relation to the manufacturing, selling or exporting products of CALCO or for any alleged breach of the Trade Marks or Patent Rights.

8. AMCO will pay for the PRODUCTS 60% whereof it would buy from CALCO at the cost price plus 40% thereon and the account would be settled every third month.

9. In consideration of AMCO rendering the aforesaid services, supplying the technology, technical know-how, deputing technical personnel, training the personnel of CALCO and allowing CALCO the use of secret formula, Trade Marks and Patent Rights and miscellaneous other services and assisting export of CALCO'S PRODUCTS, CALCO will pay to AMCO the cost and expenses in relation to the technical personnel to be deputed from time to time by AMCO to the factory of CALCO and all actual expenses incurred in India in relation to the business of CALCO and 20% of the net profits after tax. In the event the profits so calculated does not permit any payment then CALCO would pay a minimum of Rs. 5 lakhs per year to AMCO in full and final satisfaction of its claims for imparting the technology, technical know-how and other services rendered.

10. This agreement will remain valid for a period of 5 years with option to renew the same for another 5 years.

11. This agreement is made subject to obtaining the necessary approvals of the Government of India and other concerned authorities, and subject to Indian laws.

12. Any additions or alterations to this agreement may be made by mutual consent by a Supplemental agreement.

13. All differences and disputes arising out of, in relation to or in connection with this agreement shall be referred to the Indian Chamber of Commerce in Calcutta for settlement by arbitration proceedings and the decision of the Arbitral Tribunal shall be final and binding on the parties.

14. This agreement will be governed by Indian law and the arbitration will be held in Calcutta unless the parties agree to hold the sittings of the Arbitral Tribunal at some other place convenient to the parties and the Arbitral Tribunal but within India.

15. IN WITNESS WHEREOF the parties hereto have signed, sealed and delivered these presents, the day, month and year first above-written.

Signed, sealed and delivered by
Mr. ....
pursuant to Board Resolution of
AMCO INC. dated ...... in Calcutta Signature

In the presence of:
1. ....
2. ....

Signed, sealed and delivered by
Mr. ....
pursuant to Board Resolution of
CALCO LTD. dated .... Signature

In the presence of:
1. ....
2. ....

24

Franchising

In commercial and business sense the word "Franchise" means a permission granted by a manufacturer to a distributor or retailer to sell its products within a specified territory. A franchise can be equated with a licence. A franchise may include a contract whereby the owner of a business grants to another person permission to carry on a particular business using the grantor's know-how and trade mark as the grantee's own business. The grantor may exercise continuing control over the management of the grantee's business and give all possible support in carrying on the said business. This is done for a consideration agreed upon by the parties. The grantor of such licence is in modern terminology called "Franchisor" and the grantee as "Franchisee". In some cases the Franchisee can carry on his existing business and take on the franchised business and both can be run at the same premises by the Franchisee. If required a Franchisee has to set up a factory and install plant and machinery to carry on the franchised business. By such franchise the Franchisor does not control his business but finds an additional outlet for sale of his products. The Franchise Agreement may require the Franchisee to deal exclusively with the franchised articles subject to any statute relating to Monopoly and Restrictive Trade Practices.

Franchising can be done within the same country by division of geographical area or Franchisor appointing the Franchisee in another country to expand its market share of the product.

Franchising can be in respect of an existing business or a new business. Franchising agreement may be in respect of construction business, automobile parts and services, petroleum products, business aids and services, education services, soft drinks, fast foods, restaurants, health, medical, beauty care, commercial and other miscellaneous matters.

A Franchisor appoints a Franchisee to sell his products in a new geographical area in a new market to increase his sales and income. To capture markets in other countries franchising is one of the methods, the other method may be establishing a subsidiary company or a joint venture or a new company in collaboration with the Franchisee company. It is a pure commercial matter and profit motive is the main criteria for the Franchisor and the Franchisee.

The advantages of a Franchise Agreement is that the Franchisor expands markets of his products and earns more profit and the advantage of the Franchisee is that it deals with a product already having a goodwill and reputation on its own right and thereby expecting a good turnover and consequently substantial profit. The Franchisee gets almost an assured share of the market for the product and as such he runs less risk of operating loss or loss of capital that he may invest for the franchised goods.

The Franchisor to protect his own interest must see that the Franchisee does not act for another franchisor and proper accounts are maintained and royalties and other payments are made regularly to the Franchisor by the Franchisee for use of the franchised items including goodwill. The Franchisor to protect its interest may try to control and regulate to some extent the business of the Franchisee. The Franchisee to earn this extra income by using the goodwill of the Franchisor has to surrender a portion of his liberty and is to carry on his business in consultation with the Franchisor and make utmost efforts to pay royalties and fees in time. Franchisor has an advantage over ordinary distributorship inasmuch as in normal circumstances the owner of the goods do not have sufficient control over the distributor and the distributor may not have any shop or outlet except his own godown. For the purpose of business profits and development a Franchising Agreement is more beneficial for both the manufacturer and the seller.

Before entering into the Franchising Agreement the Franchisee must satisfy himself that the Franchisor has in fact a goodwill and that his goods will be sold at a profit without much efforts. The Franchisor would see that the Franchisee has enough capital to invest and has a good set up to carry on the business of the franchised goods efficiently and profitably, the capital adequacy of the Franchisee and the know-how about the business or matter to be franchised. The Franchisee may be given some training so that he may make himself fully acquainted with the product of the Franchisor and become competent to deal with the customers and give satisfactory services to them. The Franchisor after giving the franchise will pass on the up-to-date technology to the Franchisee so that the products and services of the Franchisor may stand the competition of the market.

The Franchisor is to make sure that he will get payment by way of royalties and/or fees for the goods, services and/or technology transferred to enable the Franchisee to carry on the business in the franchised goods or services. The Franchisor may demand a lump sum payment in the beginning and thereafter royalties on the sale proceeds or on any other basis depending upon the nature of the transaction. If the Franchisee has no funds the Franchisor may help the Franchisee in raising loans from the Financial Institutions or by issue of shares. The Franchisor may take shares in lieu of lump sum, royalty and services thereby to some extent solving the cash flow difficulty of the Franchisee.

So long the parties are reasonably honest the Franchising Agreement will remain effective and both parties would gain but if one of the parties try to deprive the other of his legitimate dues the Agreement would fail and both will suffer. Therefore good faith and honesty of purpose will be essential in such an arrangement.

The requirement of capital in the business of Franchisee and the extent of control by the Franchisor over the business will depend upon the nature of the subject matter of the franchise. The Franchisor has to supervise to some extent the working of the Franchisee's business and to see that the Franchising Agreement works to the advantage of both the Franchisor and the Franchisee. Unless it is profitable for both the parties the agreement cannot work. There must be also provisions making it difficult for either party to deprive the other of his legitimate dues and/or expectations.

Before entering into the agreement both the Franchisor and the Franchisee should obtain all required information in respect of each other and consider whether in the particular type of business the arrangements would work profitably for both the parties.

The Franchise Agreement may contain all possible safeguards to avoid any misunderstanding at a later date. Both parties must see that the franchising business develops and remains prosperous. Unless the business is running well the Franchisee will not be able to pay the royalties or service charges and the Franchisor will not be able to recover its dues by way of royalties and service charges. Any litigation will damage the image of both the parties. A businessman will be reluctant to enter into any agreement with a Franchisor or a Franchisee who was involved in litigation in respect of its business transaction.

The quantum of lump sum initial payment, the rate of royalty and other payments to be made by the Franchisee are to be calculated taking into consideration the probable turnover in the business of the Franchisee, his capital structure, his access to market, his management efficiency as also capacity. In other words the financial solvency, technical ability, a fund of goodwill and good faith are required from both the parties to make the Franchise Agreement a success.

For foreign investment in India Reserve Bank of India permission will be required. Foreign companies and Nationals will require prior permission of RBI to carry on in India any activity of a trading, commercial or industrial nature or to set up a project or an office or a place of business for carrying on such activity. For the purpose of execution of any specific project or contract if the foreigner wants to obtain a temporary office then prior permission of RBI will be required. Foreign Franchisor intending to set up any office in India or to post a representative for liaison activity will require prior permission of RBI.

A foreign national or company with the permission of RBI may accept an appointment as an agent in India of a foreign Principal in his trading or commercial transaction. If the foreigner takes up employment in India or acts as an Advisor in India on non-repatriable basis then RBI permission will not be necessary.

Franchise Agreement that provides professional, technical, accountancy or consultancy services being a self-financing unit within India will require RBI approval if any remittance to foreign country is involved.

If a technician of a foreign Franchisor is on a short visit to train or supervise the staff or operation of the Franchisee, the Franchisee can pay for the air-fare and expenses in India of the foreign technician in Indian rupees. General permission of RBI is required to import or export Indian Currency.

Permission of RBI is necessary for giving a Guarantee in respect of debts, obligations or liabilities in favour of a person resident outside India. A Franchisee for opening a Performance Guarantee or for issuing a Letter of Credit in favour of the foreign Franchisor will have to obtain prior permission of RBI.

A Franchisee who seeks to obtain technical know-how must obtain the approval of RBI, for technical know-how or the collaboration agreement with the foreign Franchisor, the Franchisee has to obtain RBI permission for lump sum payment, remittance for royalty or technical fees. In approving such agreement RBI designates the branch of the authorised dealer preferably a Bank through whom remittances of the fees and royalty are to be made. In granting such permission RBI may modify the agreement in relation to payment. The authorised bank is under obligation to strictly follow RBI terms and conditions of remittances and of the Franchise agreement. The bank is required to maintain separate records for remittances under the Franchise Agreement till 5 years after termination of the agreement.

The Franchisee has to submit a return by 15th of January every year showing payments made under the agreement during the proceeding year. The Franchisee gives a guarantee to the Income Tax Authorities on behalf of the foreign Franchisor for payment of tax or to deduct tax at source at the applicable rates and deposit the same to the account of Income Tax Authorities. A No Objection Certificate or tax clearance certificate is required from the Income Tax Authorities before any remittance can be made to the foreign Franchisor.

A Franchisee may engage the services of a foreign national on a short term assignment not exceeding 3 months at a time without the approval of

RBI. All payments made in connection with the foreign personnel including payments made locally in rupee towards their travel, living expenses, etc. are liable to a cess at 5% under the Research and Development Cess Act 1996. For employment of a foreign national for technical assistance for more than 3 months Home Ministry's permission has to be obtained. Foreign nationals who are in regular employment with a Franchisee on monthly salary are permitted to make recurring remittances for family maintenance up to 75% of net salary after deduction of Provident Fund contribution and Indian Income Tax. A Franchisor having a branch in India has to obtain permission from RBI for remittance of profits.

Dividend, interest and other income on shares and securities and sale proceeds thereof originally acquired out of the remittance in foreign exchange may be repatriated after obtaining permission of RBI subject to deduction of Indian Income Tax. A Franchisee intending to remit dividends to its non-resident shareholders has to obtain permission of RBI.

In respect of foreign investments in about 22 Consumer Goods Industries, RBI has stipulated remittance of dividend on a balancing system rendering thereby that the amount of foreign exchange outflow by way of dividend should be balanced with similar amount of inflow of foreign exchange by way of export earnings.

A foreign Franchisor or a foreigner requiring permission of RBI to acquire, hold, transfer or dispose of by sale, mortgage, lease, gift, settlement or otherwise any immovable property in India excepting a lease not exceeding 5 years has to apply to Central Office of RBI, Foreign Investment Department in Mumbai.

By a notification dated 26th April 1993 RBI has granted general permission to foreign companies to acquire or hold any immovable property which is necessary for or incidental to any activity permitted by the RBI. On obtaining such permission the company has to submit a declaration to RBI within 90 days of such acquisition.

Foreign citizens, foreign companies, foreign trusts, societies and associations will be permitted to acquire immovable property by RBI provided the immovable property is acquired for consideration and is paid out of the foreign exchange remitted from abroad in convertible currency through normal banking channel and any income or proceeds of the property are to be credited only to the non-resident Rupee account and will not be allowed to be repatriated.

By a notification of 26th May 1993 RBI has granted permission to the foreign citizens of Indian origin who are resident in India or not to acquire or dispose of immovable property other than agricultural land, farm house and plantation property subject to fulfilment of certain conditions.

Foreign Franchisor cannot acquire any business in India as of right. The right of a foreign Franchisor under any Franchise Agreement will be subject to permission of RBI. RBI permission is necessary for acquiring the whole or part of any industry in India in trade and industry.

Provisions should be made to resolve the disputes between the Franchisor and the Franchisee in relation to their transactions. Both parties must consider whether arbitration in a foreign country would be feasible both from economic point of view and conducting proceeding in a foreign country involving huge foreign exchange. Provisions may be made to buy out the business of one party by the other in respect of which Franchise Agreement was entered into in the event of any such dispute.

FORMS

Agreement of Franchise—Gold and Jewellery

THIS AGREEMENT IS MADE on this 5th day of May 2000 BETWEEN AB Limited, a company registered under the applicable laws of South Africa having its office at 5 S.F. Road, Transvaal (hereinafter called the FRANCHISOR which term shall include its successors and assigns) of the first part and Ashok Jewellers Limited, a company registered under the Companies Act 1956 and carrying on business at 56 Ganesh Chandra Avenue, Calcutta (hereinafter called the FRANCHISEE which term shall include its successors and permitted assigns) of the second part.

WHEREAS the FRANCHISOR is engaged in mining and manufacturing Gold Jewellery and trading in gold and gold jewellery in Transvaal, South Africa and has acquired a reputation for supplying high quality ingots and jewellery under the registered Trade Marks in Transvaal for the last 10 years and having all the requisite licences and permission from the appropriate authorities for export and sale thereof through *inter alia* FRANCHISEES in other countries.

AND WHEREAS the FRANCHISOR has a paid up capital equivalent to Rs. 99,000 crores and has assets worth Rs. 10,00,000 crores and has been making regular profits commensurate to its investment.

AND WHEREAS the FRANCHISOR has acquired a reputation for its brand names TRANSVAAL and RAND and goodwill for quality of its gold and jewellery.

AND WHEREAS the FRANCHISEE is a company registered under the Companies Act 1956 with a paid-up capital of Rs. 10 crores carrying on business as a Jeweller having the requisite technical and administrative personnel and turnover of Rs. 20 crores per year with a profit of Rs. 2 crores per year.

AND WHEREAS the FRANCHISEE has several buildings in good localities where existing outlets are situate and where other outlets can be obtained for sale of jewellery.

AND WHEREAS the FRANCHISEE has inspected the relevant Title Deeds, Licences, Balance Sheets and other documents of the Franchisor and satisfied itself about the goodwill, credit-worthiness and ability to keep its commitments, render technical services and maintain good trade relations for mutual benefit.

AND WHEREAS the FRANCHISOR has made local enquiries about the FRANCHISEE, inspected its Title Deeds, Licences, Balance Sheets and other relevant documents and inspected the Works site and had discussions with the technical personnel and satisfied itself about the competence and ability of the FRANCHISEE to promote the sales of the FRANCHISOR'S gold, gold products and jewellery from the FRANCHISEE'S present outlets and its ability to honour its commitments as to the payment of Royalty and other obligations including the improvement and development of the FRANCHISEE company.

AND WHEREAS the FRANCHISOR has given the lists of FRANCHISEE in other countries and in India of the said FRANCHISOR.

AND WHEREAS the FRANCHISOR has been given list of companies of other FRANCHISORS for which the FRANCHISEE is acting in India and the Trade Marks and service marks under which the FRANCHISEE is carrying on business.

AND WHEREAS the FRANCHISOR has agreed to give the FRANCHISEE the right to use the FRANCHISOR'S Trade Marks, service marks, business systems, operation manual and to impart initial and ongoing training to the standard necessary to operate the proposed unit successfully and to give access to the FRANCHISOR'S know-how, technology, development and improvement in relation to the manufacture and sale of jewellery.

AND WHEREAS the parties have agreed to act in good faith towards each other and prevent any damage to the interests of the FRANCHISOR or FRANCHISEE and continuously work to develop and improve the system of manufacture and sale of jewellery under the existing Trade Marks or new Trade Marks or service marks and to protect the reputation and business of the parties herein.

AND WHEREAS the parties on enquiries made by themselves are satisfied about the information obtained from each other and nothing has been suppressed or concealed by any of the parties and they have agreed to enter into a Franchise Agreement for mutual benefit.

NOW THESE PRESENTS WITNESSETH and the parties hereby agree as follows:

1. This Agreement will remain in force till either party by giving three month's notice in writing terminates the same.

2. In consideration of the FRANCHISEE paying a lump sum of Rs. 2 crores and agreeing to pay 10% of the FRANCHISEE'S gross turn over of "Rand" gold, gold products and jewellery the FRANCHISOR hereby gives to the FRANCHISEE the licence to manufacture and sell the gold and gold jewellery and other ornaments under the FRANCHISOR'S Trade name RAND which Trade Mark is registered in South Africa. All necessary steps shall be taken by parties herein to get protection of and protect the said Trade Mark under the Indian law.

3. The FRANCHISOR agrees to give practical and theoretical training for six weeks in South Africa to the staff of the FRANCHISEE every year. The costs of travel and accommodation shall be shared equally by the parties herein.

4. The FRANCHISOR shall from time to time make available to the FRANCHISEE technical, administrative and operational know-how free of cost. The Copyrights in all the manuals and other materials shall remain vested in the FRANCHISOR. Such Trade Marks and know-how should be used exclusively for carrying on the business under the Trade Name RAND at the FRANCHISEE'S stores and shops and should not be allowed to be used by any other person.

5. The FRANCHISOR shall take necessary steps to protect its trade name RAND in India by complying with the applicable laws as also of any other territory where the products may be sold. In the event the FRANCHISEE comes to know of any infringement of the Trade Mark or any right of the FRANCHISOR, the FRANCHISEE should immediately inform the FRANCHISOR of the same and take immediate steps to prevent the continuance of such infringement. In any legal proceedings the parties herein shall cooperate and should be agreeable to being impleaded as parties therein.

6. The FRANCHISOR shall obtain necessary permission from South African Governmental authorities for export of gold and jewellery to India on account of FRANCHISEE and get the present agreement duly approved by the concerned authorities.

7. The FRANCHISOR shall have the right to send its representatives to inspect the shops and manufacturing processes of the FRANCHISEE and suggest improvements thereon with a view to maximise the sale of gold, gold products and jewellery under the Trade name RAND.

8. The FRANCHISEE shall sell the products of the FRANCHISOR from the Franchisee's shops and stores and the FRANCHISOR shall send its representatives to make proper arrangement in such shops, stores and arrange for proper display of the products and the Trade Name.

9. The FRANCHISEE should sell the product under the trade name in the whole of territory in India and will export to any other countries the gold jewellery and other products under the trade name RAND as it may think suitable under the market conditions.

10. In the event of termination of this agreement howsoever occurring the licence of the FRANCHISEE shall immediately cease and the FRANCHISEE shall perform such acts and execute such documents as would be required in order to ensure that the sole and exclusive right to use the Trade Marks remain vested in the FRANCHISOR.

11. The FRANCHISEE shall get the present agreement approved by the Indian Governmental authorities including the Reserve Bank of India for importation of gold and gold products including jewellery, sale thereof in India and export outside India.

12. The FRANCHISEE shall get necessary permission and approval of the authorities concerned for import of gold, gold products and jewellery from South Africa and to use the gold for manufacture of jewellery and other items under the trade mark RAND in the local market and also to export the same to other countries and to remit moneys in terms of the present agreement to the FRANCHISOR.

13. The FRANCHISEE shall have the right to carry on its existing business in the usual manner as also to import gold, gold products and jewellery from the Franchisor and manufacture articles and jewellery from the imported gold under the trade name RAND and sell the same in India and abroad.

14. The FRANCHISEE shall by the first week of every month place an order for gold, gold products and jewellery on the FRANCHISOR and the FRANCHISOR shall arrange to deliver the ordered goods through its representative personally at the shop of the FRANCHISEE at the costs and expenses of the FRANCHISOR.

15. The FRANCHISEE will sell the gold, gold products and jewellery under the trade mark RAND at a price which will get for the FRANCHISEE a gross margin of 30% and out of which the Franchisee will pay one-third to the Franchisor as the fee for the licence. Such payment is in addition to the costs of the goods sold and delivered to the Franchisee.

16. To ascertain the exact entitlement of the FRANCHISOR, namely, 10% of the total turnover of the goods sold under the brand name RAND the FRANCHISOR'S representative will have the right to inspect and take copies of the accounts maintained by the Franchisee.

17. The FRANCHISEE shall make payment of the price of the goods delivered within 24 hours and will make payment of licence fee up to 10% of the turnover by the first week of a month in respect of sales during the preceding month. The FRANCHISEE shall pay and bear all expenses incurred in India in connection with the present agreement entered into and the FRANCHISOR will pay and bear all the expenses that may be incurred in South Africa.

18. The FRANCHISEE shall not do anything which will cause injury to the trade name or reputation of the FRANCHISOR and that the FRANCHISEE agrees

to indemnify and keep the FRANCHISOR indemnified against all liabilities, claims, damages or injury of every description which may occur or affect the FRANCHISOR from any failure by the FRANCHISEE to perform its obligations under this agreement or from any act or omission whatsoever on the part of the FRANCHISEE or its servants or agents.

19. In the event the FRANCHISEE finds the goods delivered are not according to the standard specifications the FRANCHISEE shall immediately report the same with particulars of defects and the FRANCHISOR shall give appropriate credit to the FRANCHISEE for such defective goods.

20. Upon termination of this agreement, the FRANCHISEE will be entitled to sell the existing stocks under the brand name RAND or otherwise and that the FRANCHISOR shall take no responsibility of taking back the goods or pay for it.

21. It is agreed and declared that both the FRANCHISOR and the FRANCHISEE shall comply with all laws rules and regulations governing the transactions covered by the present agreement and that this agreement is entered into subject to obtaining the necessary approval of the authorities concerned.

22. If any term or any provision of the present agreement is declared by the court or by any governmental authority to be in conflict with the laws or any term is unenforceable that will not affect the validity and enforceability of the remainder of this agreement and in that event the offending part shall be deemed not to be part of this agreement and the resulting consequential amendment shall be deemed to have been incorporated therein.

23. This agreement shall not constitute the FRANCHISEE as the agent of the FRANCHISOR or a Partner or a representative or *vice versa* and that no act of the FRANCHISOR will affect the FRANCHISEE and no act of FRANCHISEE shall affect the FRANCHISOR.

24. No forbearance, delay or indulgence by either party in confirming any of the terms and conditions of this agreement shall prejudice its rights and remedies under this agreement or under the laws of their respective countries nor shall any waiver or any breach of any of the terms hereof shall operate as a waiver of any subsequent breach of the agreement. Any waiver or variation of any of the terms or conditions of the agreement shall not be valid unless the same is in writing and signed by the authorised officer of the FRANCHISOR and/or the FRANCHISEE, as the case may be.

25. Neither party shall disclose to any third party any information as to the methods of manufacture, operation, publicity, financial plans, present or future plans or the policy of the other which information is not in public domain and is not compulsorily disclosable under any Statute.

26. The FRANCHISOR and the FRANCHISEE shall take necessary steps for registration of the agreement in their respective countries for continuance

and validity of the agreement and each one will bear the costs therefor as also all rates, taxes, cesses, levies and other impositions in their respective countries.

27. Both the FRANCHISOR and the FRANCHISEE shall jointly act whenever necessary to obtain any permission from the governmental or other authorities in connection with the business under the agreement including payment of the licence fees, registration charges and expenses to be incurred by the representatives of the FRANCHISOR residing in India or the FRANCHISEE residing in South Africa.

28. No liability would lie on any of the parties for any breach of the agreement if caused by force majeure circumstances beyond its control.

29. This agreement is not assignable either by the FRANCHISOR or the FRANCHISEE without prior written approval.

30. All notices and reports are to be sent at the addresses given herein either by speed post or by telex or by courier service.

31. This agreement shall be governed by and construed in accordance with the Indian law and both parties agree to submit to the jurisdiction of Indian Courts.

32. All payments and transactions are to be expressed in Indian Rupees having no connection with the exchange rate of South Africa or any other Currency.

IN WITNESS WHEREOF the parties herein have executed THESE PRESENTS on the day, month and year first above-written.

Signed, sealed and delivered by
Mr. .... Director
pursuant to Board Resolution
dated .... of AB Ltd. in
Calcutta in presence of: Signature

Signed, sealed and delivered by
Mr. .... Director
pursuant to the Board Resolution
dated .... of Ashok
Jewellers Ltd. in presence of: Signature

Franchise Agreement—Washing Machines

THIS FRANCHISE AGREEMENT is made on this 10th day of May 1999 BETWEEN ELH Limited, 56 G.C. Avenue, Kobe, Japan (hereinafter referred to as the FRANCHISOR which term unless excluded by or repugnant to the context shall include its successors and assigns) of the one part and Sales Limited, a Company registered under the Companies Act 1956 having its registered office at 5 N.K. Road, Chennai, India (hereinafter referred to as the FRANCHISEE which term shall unless excluded by or repugnant to the context include its successors and permitted assigns) of the other part.

WHEREAS the FRANCHISOR is carrying on business as a manufacturer of and dealer in different kinds of Washing Machines and has established a reputation and demand for its high quality Washing Machines and after-sales-service.

AND WHEREAS the FRANCHISOR through its exclusive research and practical business experience has developed secret, substantial and identified know-how which forms a system for appropriate operation of business in the selling and servicing of washing machines and which is contained in the Franchisor's Operational Manual, which is the FRANCHISISOR'S sole property.

AND WHEREAS the said washing machine has been patented under the name and style of "EL" Washing Machines.

AND WHEREAS the FRANCHISOR has a package of non-selected practical information resulting from experience and testing by the FRANCHISOR which is the secret, substantial and identified and hereinafter called KNOW-HOW.

AND WHEREAS the FRANCHISOR'S KNOW-HOW in the body or in the precise configuration and assembly of its components is not generally known or easily accessible and not limited in the narrow sense the individual component of know-how should be totally unknown or unobtainable outside the FRANCHISOR'S business and such KNOW-HOW is "secret" to the FRANCHISOR.

AND WHEREAS the KNOW-HOW includes the information which is of importance for sale of washing machines and its components and spares with the provision of service to the consumers end-users and in particular for the presentation of washing machines for sale, the processing of components in connection with the provision of services, methods of dealing with customers, administration and financial management, the KNOW-HOW is useful for the FRANCHISEE by being capable at the date of conclusion of the agreement, of improving the competitive position of the Franchisee, *inter alia,* by improving its performance and helping it to enter a new market. All these are termed as "substantial KNOW-HOW".

AND WHEREAS the KNOW-HOW is described in a sufficiently comprehensive manner so as to make it possible to verify that it will fulfil the criteria of secrecy and substantiality are termed as "identified".

AND WHEREAS the FRANCHISOR has developed a System by virtue of having acquired the knowledge, experience in the field of electrical and manual operations of the washing machines, replacement or repair of its parts, oiling and cleaning of the related parts and to keep the machines in working condition.

AND WHEREAS the FRANCHISOR now intends to open sales and Service Centres in Chennai and in the neighbouring States.

AND WHEREAS the FRANCHISOR owns the Registered Trade Marks used in relation to the said Washing Machines and after-sales-service. In addition, the FRANCHISOR owns the valuable good-will in slogans of distinctive Marks which Markings are other identifying characteristics.

AND WHEREAS stocks of washing machines of the FRANCHISOR in Kobe (JAPAN) or surrounding areas depends among other things, upon the provisions by the FRANCHISOR of a prompt, efficient satisfactory and courteous service to the consumers using the washing machines being the subject-matter of the Franchise including the accessories and spare parts and upon the vigorous cultivation and extension of the market for the washing machines.

AND WHEREAS the FRANCHISEE has assured that it will develop the business of sales and service of washing machines in Chennai and neighbouring areas.

AND WHEREAS the FRANCHISOR has made enquiries about the financial soundness of the FRANCHISEE, the technical knowledge of the Managing Director of the FRANCHISEE, its sales personnel, accommodation and title to the said sales office and its total accommodation for storing and exhibiting the FRANCHISOR'S washing machines as also washing machines that might require repairing and servicing at the premises of the FRANCHISEE.

AND WHEREAS the FRANCHISEE has made enquiries into the title of premises from which the FRANCHISOR is carrying on manufacturing and selling business, the capital outlay, the personnel employed for running the business and its past dealings with other Franchisees and has satisfied itself about the adequacy of the same and ability of the FRANCHISOR to discharge its obligations under the present agreement.

AND WHEREAS the FRANCHISEE has made enquiries about the FRANCHISOR'S patent and other rights, the steps taken for building good-will and reputation and test reports and the correspondence with consumers in relation to the purchase by the Users of the machines and the FRANCHISEE has satisfied itself about the financial stability, good-will, reputation, technical competence and adequacy of trained personnel to carry on the said business of manufacturing and selling the washing machines in an expansive market and to render satisfactory services to the consumers.

The FRANCHISOR and the FRANCHISEE have made themselves acquainted with the rules, regulations and laws relating to the manufacture of washing machines, its operation, sales and servicing and have satisfied themselves that it is satisfactory and in accordance with the provisions of law to manufacture, assemble and/or deal with the said washing machines throughout India and also for exports to foreign countries.

NOW THESE PRESENTS WITNESSETH and the parties hereby agree as follows:

1. In consideration of the FRANCHISEE making payment as hereinafter provided the Franchisor hereby grants licence to the Franchisee to assemble and sell the FRANCHISOR'S washing machines under its Trade Mark inaccordance with the provisions of this Agreement.

2. The FRANCHISOR shall arrange for training for four weeks the FRANCHISEE'S two senior staff in the factory of the FRANCHISEE in the technicalities of manufacture and operation and repairs of the washing machines, its sales and after-sales-service. The travel and accommodation expenses of the two staff shall be paid and borne by the parties equally. The FRANCHISOR agrees that the FRANCHISEE may at its own expenses arrange for any of its employees at any time to visit the FRANCHISOR'S factory, office premises and other outlets to study the methods and to make notes and schedules relating thereto provided that in any year there should be only one visit by the employees of the FRANCHISEE and the duration of their stay with the FRANCHISOR shall not exceed two weeks and all their expenses would be borne equally by the parties.

3. The FRANCHISOR shall from time to time make available to the FRANCHISEE all technical, administrative, operational, after-sales-service know-how. The FRANCHISOR shall also provide the Franchisee with the training manual, display manual, operation manual, after-sales-service manual and all updating and replacement materials and manuals prepared by the FRANCHISOR, the copyrights whereof shall remain vested in the FRANCHISOR and the FRANCHISEE shall not make use of those matters other than for the purpose of this agreement and for sales and service of the FRANCHISOR'S "EL" Brand Washing machines.

4. The FRANCHISOR shall be under no obligation to continue to supply the EL washing machines if it discontinued selling in its own outlets in Kobe (JAPAN) and it shall have the right for good cause not to supply a particular type of EL washing machine which it considers to be unsuitable for sale in India.

5. The FRANCHISOR shall be entitled to require the FRANCHISEE to stop selling any EL washing machines which the FRANCHISOR had withdrawn from the market as being defective and such stock would be bought back by the FRANCHISOR at the price at which they were sold.

6. The FRANCHISOR undertakes to make every endeavour to assist the FRANCHISEE to obtain licences for the sole and exclusive use in India the said EL washing machine Trade Marks.

7. In the event of any infringement or threat of any infringement of the EL Trade Mark by a third party in India or any claim being made against the FRANCHISEE alleging the FRANCHISOR'S use of the Trade Mark EL infringes any Trade Mark or other industrial property belonging to third parties the FRANCHISEE shall forthwith notify to the FRANCHISOR and take such steps as

the FRANCHISOR may reasonably request to prevent any such infringement or to defend and protect against any such claim in accordance with the FRANCHISOR'S reasonable instructions without prejudice to the FRANCHISOR'S right to take action or conduct any court proceedings whether in its own name or in the name of the FRANCHISEE and any costs incurred shall be shared equally by the parties herein.

8. The FRANCHISEE undertakes not to use any name or mark other than the "EL" in connection with the sale of the washing machines. The FRANCHISEE shall not use any name or mark liable to be confused with "EL". The FRANCHISEE shall use the Trade Mark "EL" only in relation to the sale of the FRANCHISOR'S washing machines and any such forms, types, designs and colours as may from time to time be authorised by the FRANCHISOR in writing.

9. During the continuance of this agreement or after termination of this agreement, the FRANCHISEE shall not use the "EL" Trade Mark as part of the FRANCHISEE'S corporate name and on termination of this agreement shall perform such acts and execute such documents as shall be required in order to ensure that the sole and exclusive right to use "EL" Trade Mark in India shall remain vested in the FRANCHISOR.

10. The FRANCHISEE shall use its outlets for the sale of "EL" washing machines along with the type of machines that it sells at present from its outlets and of no other brand or type of washing machines.

11. The FRANCHISEE shall ensure that the retail business is conducted at the stores and outlets conform with the high standards associated with the FRANCHISOR and shall comply with all reasonable arrangements and requests of the FRANCHISOR regarding operation of the said business including after-sales-service.

12. The FRANCHISEE shall use in the stores and outlets, the display signs, packaging materials, display items and other presentational items as are consistent with the FRANCHISOR'S standards and image and for this purpose the FRANCHISE may order from the FRANCHISOR supplies of such items.

13. The FRANCHISEE shall in all its letters, stationery and other conspicuous spaces indicate in a manner approved by the FRANCHISOR that it is carrying on its business as FRANCHISEE of the FRANCHISOR of EL washing machines.

14. The FRANCHISEE shall carry on the business at each store or outlet on its own account and risk in an efficient and courteous manner giving complete satisfaction to its customers and shall not do anything to bring the name and reputation of the FRANCHISOR into disrepute.

15. The FRANCHISEE shall always promptly attend to any complaint in the functioning of the washing machine and rectify the same, replace any spare parts, if necessary, and to make it workable as quickly as possible

and perform all its contractual and legal obligations to its customers so that they need not go for legal action and shall indemnify the FRANCHISOR against all liabilities arising from any failure to do so.

16. The FRANCHISEE shall keep its stores open and appropriately staffed during normal shopping hours in the vicinity of its stores or shop outlets and make available its technical staff for receiving complaints and attending to the same and whenever required to repair the "EL" washing machines at the premises of the customers during the evening hours and on Saturdays and Sundays and Holidays by special arrangement. The Franchisor shall send its technical staff to conduct a formal pre-arranged inspection of received stores and meet some of the disgruntled workers and customers of the Franchisee and to meet their demands.

17. The FRANCHISEE shall sell "EL" washing machines at a competitive price but keeping a margin of at least 15% on the purchase price paid by the Franchisee for these washing machines.

18. The parties hereby agree that each one will assist the other in obtaining the necessary permission or compliance with the laws of Japan and India for the purpose of giving effect to the present agreement and complying with all the rules and regulations in relation to the business, the FRANCHISOR paying for and meeting all rates, taxes, fees and cesses payable in relation to this agreement in Japan and the FRANCHISEE shall pay and bear all Indian rates, taxes, cesses, levies fees and other expenses in relation to the present agreement in India.

19. This Agreement is made subject to compliance with the provisions of law in Japan and in India and wherever required by law the agreement will be suitably modified.

20. The FRANCHISOR shall deliver the EL washing machines and spare parts on receipt of the Order from the FRANCHISEE at the ruling price and supplies to be effected within six weeks plus the time required for transportation. All the expenses, costs, duties, etc. for delivery of the machines at the stores of the FRANCHISEE shall be borne by the FRANCHISOR and be added to the sale price of the machines. However, the FRANCHISOR shall not be liable for any delay in supplying the washing machines and spares ordered from the FRANCHISOR. In view of the apprehended delay in reaching supplies to the FRANCHISEE in time, sufficient supplies of spare parts for repairs to be stored by the FRANCHISEE at its every stores outlets.

21. The price payable by the FRANCHISEE for "EL" washing machines supplied by the FRANCHISOR shall be the current retail price at the FRANCHISOR'S shop plus the cost of delivery including the transport, insurance and other expenses. The FRANCHISEE shall make payment on delivery of its machines inclusive of all expenses of carriage, insurance and delivery charges.

22. All payments by the FRANCHISEE shall be in Indian Currency and the FRANCHISEE shall render all assistance in getting the same repatriated if the Reserve Bank of India and other authorities permit. The FRANCHISEE shall furnish a Bank Guarantee for the due payment of the price of the washing machines that might be delivered to the FRANCHISEE.

23. The FRANCHISOR shall not actively market or sell any "EL" washing machines in India nor permit any other FRANCHISEE or distributor to do so but such other FRANCHISEE or distributor may accept orders from the members of the public and pass on the same to the FRANCHISEE for delivery of machines ordered. The FRANCHISEE agrees to indemnify and keep the FRANCHISOR indemnified against all liabilities, claims, damages, actions or injury of every description which may occur or affect the FRANCHISOR for any failure of the FRANCHISEE to perform its obligations under this agreement or from any act or omission whatsoever on part of the FRANCHISEE and its staff.

24. The FRANCHISOR may withdraw from the market any of its "EL" brand washing machines which has been found defective and the FRANCHISEE shall ensure that if such machine has been sold to be replaced with a new one and if the defective machine has not already been delivered, the same shall be kept back by the FRANCHISEE and be kept in the custody of the FRANCHISEE to be replaced by the FRANCHISOR at no extra cost to the FRANCHISEE.

25. The parties herein may terminate the agreement by giving six months notice in writing to the other setting out the reasons for such termination and upon such termination the FRANCHISEE shall not sell "EL" brand washing machines except those are already in stock. The FRANCHISOR shall continue to be liable to supply the spare parts if required for the repair and service of EL washing machines already sold by the FRANCHISOR to the FRANCHISEE and suitable pre-estimate should be made for the possible requirements of spare parts and the FRANCHISOR shall supply these spare parts in terms of the agreement even though the agreement stands terminated.

26. The termination of this agreement shall not prejudice any right or claim of either party prior to the termination or obligation of either party under this agreement.

27. Upon termination of the agreement howsoever occurring the FRANCHISEE shall not order further washing machines from the FRANCHISOR but shall be entitled to continue to sell "EL" brand washing machines which are already in stock with the FRANCHISEE and to render the after-sales-service and for this purpose if required, the FRANCHISOR shall render all possible assistance to the FRANCHISEE.

28. The obligations contained under this agreement which expressly or by implication apply after termination of this agreement shall after such termination constitute a separate agreement and be enforceable notwithstanding termination of this agreement.

29. If any part or term or provision of this agreement herein is declared by any Court of Law to be invalid or be accepted by the parties as being in conflict with the law or unenforceable, then the validity and enforceability of the remaining portion of this agreement shall not be affected. In such a case the offending part or term or provision shall be deemed not to be part of this agreement.

30. This agreement does not constitute the FRANCHISEE an agent or legal representative or partner of the FRANCHISOR for any purpose whatsoever or *vice versa* save and except when it is expressly provided confirmed or otherwise agreed in writing. Neither party is in any way authorised to make any contract or agreement, or give any warranty or make any representation on behalf of the other nor to create any obligation expressed or implicit on behalf of the other.

31. No forbearance, delay or indulgence by either party in enforcing any of the terms and conditions of this agreement shall prejudice or affect the rights and remedies hereunder nor shall any waiver of any breach thereof operate as a waiver of any subsequent breach and no waiver or variation of any of the terms or conditions of this agreement shall be valid or have any effect unless the same be made in writing and signed by an authorised officer of the party concerned.

32. The parties hereby agree that they shall not disclose to a third party excepting to the Auditors, Professional Advisors and bankers and they shall not make any unauthorised use of any information as to the methods of operation, technicality, financial affairs, present or future plan or policies of the other party information which do not come under the public domain.

33. Each party shall be responsible for obtaining all necessary work-permits and permission in respect of all representatives of the parties for visiting the other for the purposes of this agreement and all costs and expenses to be borne and shared equally by the parties.

34. Neither party shall be liable for any breach of this agreement to the extent that it is caused by Force Majeure circumstances for which it is not responsible.

35. The benefit of this agreement may not be assigned by the FRANCHISEE without prior written consent of the FRANCHISOR and on such terms and conditions as the FRANCHISOR may impose.

36. All communications, notices, orders, or other matters between the parties under this agreement may be by fax, or telex or by the usual notices sent by Speed Post or Courier service. Such notices, reports and other matters shall be given at the address mentioned hereinabove of the parties.

37. This Agreement shall be governed by the laws of India and any proceedings arising out of this Agreement shall be in the appropriate Indian Court and all orders and decrees would be expressed in Indian Currency.

In witness whereof the parties herein executed these presents on the day, month and year first above-written.

Signed, sealed and delivered by
Mr. .... Director
of AB Ltd. pursuant to Board
Resolution dated .... in
Calcutta in presence of: Signature

Signed, sealed and delivered by
Mr. .... Director
of Sales Ltd. pursuant to Board
Resolution dated ....
in the presence of: Signature

25

Gift

Introductory observations. A gift is, as defined under s. 122 of the Transfer of Property Act, a voluntary transfer of a property in consideration of natural love and affection to a living person. An endowment though stamped as a gift is not a transfer to a living person it being transfer to God a living spirit but juristic person capable of holding property. A gift requires acceptance. All transfers for inadequate consideration, a release, discharge or even a surrender are also treated as gifts. It must be free, voluntary absolute and unconditional except in cases where any property is given for any particular purpose, *e.g.* gift of land or building to be used for educational purpose such as for a school, college or institute or for any religious object, *viz.* for building a mosque or temple or establishment of any hospital. In those cases, the property reverts to the donor when the object fails with all improvements made thereon[1] the condition of revocation being some event not depending on the will and pleasure of the donor. A gift with a condition that the donee shall not alienate the property is not revocable.[2] So also in cases where the donee does not fulfil the condition as to maintenance of the donor.[3] A gift of a property intended for the residence or maintenance of the donee is valid under ss. 28 and 31 of the Transfer of Property Act which correspond with s. 131 of the Indian Succession Act 1925, inasmuch as those gifts are of the nature of settlement and the property will revert to the donor after the death of the donee. A gift of the property to the wife on condition that, in case she dies without issue the property will vest in some other person alive at the date of the gift is valid.[4] The above decision is now questionable in view of an important decision by the Calcutta High Court in

1 Section 126 of the Transfer of Property Act.
2 *M.T. Brijlal Devi* v *Shivanand* AIR 1939 All 221.
3 *Tila Bewa* v *Muna Bewa* AIR 1962 Ori 130.
4 *Gobindraja* v *Mangadam* AIR 1933 Mad 80.

Lalit Mohon Mondal v *Prafulla Kumar Mondal,*[5] where the testator intended to confer an absolute estate without any restriction as regards the power of alienation of the legatee so the subsequent clauses as to succession to the property after her death were held as inoperative.

Gifts to women under the Hindu law is subject to special rules of construction—whether the gift passes an absolute estate or a limited estate depends upon the terms of the grant. It was held by the Privy Council that it depended upon the expressions used in the terms of the grant.[6] This concept of law has now been changed. It was held by the Supreme Court[7] where the property is acquired without any pre-existing right, *e.g.* under a will, gift, decree etc., or award her estate depends upon the terms of the instrument, but in cases, *e.g.* partition or in lieu of maintenance, etc., she acquires an absolute estate.[8] Where, however, a limited interest is conferred on a widow by a will in lieu of maintenance and in recognition of her pre-existing right the said right transformed into an absolute right and she is competent to make a gift of that property to her daughter[9] and the gift deed is valid. A Hindu, whether belonging to the Mitakshara or Dayabhaga School, can make a gift of his separate as also self-acquired estate subject, however, to the claims of those entitled under the Hindu Adoptions and Maintenance Act[10] (*vide* ss. 18 to 22, *e.g.* wife, widowed daughter-in-law, minor legitimate or illegitimate children, aged parents and others). A gift is completed as soon as the donor relinquishes his rights in the property followed by delivery of possession and acceptance by the donee.[11] The right of a wife or widow for maintenance attaches to her status so she can pursue the property even in the hands of a stranger acquiring the same with notice of her claim.[12] Before the abolition of the zamindary system, there were several types of grants in West Bengal, *e.g.*, brahmattar, devattur, lakhraj, mahatran Aymas. They were not gifts but grants of which the kharij or revenue was reduced to a nominal figure or exempted by special contracts; so they were liable for road cess and public work cess.

A gift is made by one party and accepted by the other. So without acceptance the gift is not valid.[13] So the best and safest course is to make

5 86 CWN 398.
6 *Shaliq Ram* v *Charanjit* (1930)57 IA 282; 128 IC 265.
7 *Vaddeboyina* v *Vaddeboyina* AIR 1977 SC 1944.
8 Section 14(1) and (2) of the Hindu Succession Act 1956.
9 *Beni Bai* v *Raghubir* AIR 1999 SC 1147.
10 Act 78 of 1956, which came into effect from 21st December 1956.
11 *Vide* judgment of Sir Ashutosh Mukherjee in *Bhupatinath* v *Ramlal* 10 CLJ 355 at p. 375; ILR 37 Cal 128.
12 *Radhabai* v *Gopal* AIR 1944 Bom 50; 45 BLR 950.
13 Section 122 of the Transfer of Property Act.

the acceptor a party to the deed of gift. A gift to two or more donees, of whom one does not accept, is void to the extent of the proposed interest of the non-acceptor.[14] The acceptance must be made during the life-time of the donor and while he is still capable of giving. In case the donee dies before the acceptance the gift is void.[15] Acceptance may be implied where a deed of gift executed and attested is handed over to the donee who accepts the same; it constitutes a sufficient acceptance of the gift.[16] A gift may be burdened by an obligation when it is called an onerous gift. The donee gets nothing by the gift unless he accepts it fully.[17] An universal donee, *i.e.* donee in respect of the entire estate of the donor, is liable for all debts due and liabilities of the donor as on the date of the gift to the extent of the property comprised therein;[18] such a gift is also liable to be challenged as a fraudulent transfer under s. 53 of the said Act.

Dedication to Churches and God. Section 123 of the Transfer of Property Act contemplates gifts between living persons. It is an endowment rather than a gift made through the equitable machinery of trust and not a transfer within the meaning of s. 5 of the Transfer of Property Act. It may be made orally. No acceptance is necessary. The tests are (*i*) *intention* (sole test); (*ii*) *sankalpa*; and (*iii*) *utsarga*.[19] No writing registered or unregistered is absolutely necessary.[20] It was also held by the Supreme Court in *Dasaratha* v *Subha Rao*,[1] that dedication to charity must not necessarily be by an instrument or grant.

A gift of any immovable property must be made by a registered deed irrespective of its value.[2] Further, the same requires attestation by two persons. The doctrine of part performance as contemplated under s. 53A of the Transfer of Property Act has no application in the case of gift. That section does not apply to the Mahomedans as such gifts can be made orally.[3] A gift of movable property may be made either by a registered document or by delivery of possession. A fixed deposit in a bank is an actionable claim and so requires a writing for the purpose of gift and not simply delivery of possession.[4] The essential features of all gifts are: (*i*) it must be free and

14 Section 125 of the Transfer of Property Act.
15 Section 122 of the Transfer of Property Act.
16 *Kalyana Sundaram* v *Karuppa* AIR 1927 PC 42.
17 Section 127 of the Transfer of Property Act.
18 Section 128 of the Transfer of Property Act.
19 Hon'ble Mr. Justice B.K. Mukherjea: *Hindu Law of Religious and Charitable Trust*, 4th Ed., p. 106.
20 *Ramtunga Chetty* v *Shiva Chidam* ILR 42 Mad 440.
1 AIR 1951 SC 1122.
2 Section 123 of the Transfer of Property Act.
3 Section 129 of the Transfer of Property Act 1882.
4 *Maiyandas* v *Sri Mohan* AIR 1945 All 409.

voluntary; (*ii*) absolute and unconditional except where made for a specific purpose; and (*iii*) irrevocable except where the condition not dependent upon the will and pleasure of the donor is broken in cases of a gift for any specific purpose or in cases where there is a specific contract to the effect.[5] A gift or assignment of an Insurance Policy subject to the condition that in the event of the assignee predeceasing the assignor before the maturity of the policy the assignor shall be entitled to the proceeds of the policy is valid under this section.

Where there is no proof of attestation by two witnesses in respect of a deed of gift such deed is invalid. Again the document would be vitiated by undue influence if person having no right of over the suit property getting right of residence therein and facts showed that the person concerned had obtained undue advantage the document would be vitiated by undue influence.[6]

A gift in contemplation of death is called *donatio mortis causa*—such a gift stands revoked on recovery of the donor.[7] Only movable properties, such as G.P. Notes, Cash Certificates, Insurance Policy, Savings Bank Pass Book, Bank Notes, etc., may form the subject of such a gift. A cheque payable to the donor or order and given by the donor is a valid *donatio mortis causa*.[8] There must be actual delivery of the thing to the donee.

Section 122 of the Transfer of Property Act corresponds to s. 191 of the Indian Succession Act.

Suspension or revocation of gift. The donor and the donee may agree that on the happening of any specified event, which does not depend on the will of the donor, a gift shall be suspended or revoked. A gift which is made revocable wholly or in part at the will of the donor is void wholly or in part as the case may be. A gift may be revoked on the grounds on which a contract may be rescinded except for want or failure of consideration.[9]

Gifts under Hindu and Mahomedan laws. The rule of Mahomedan law about gifts is not affected by the Transfer of Property Act.[10] No writing is necessary in respect of any gift of either movable or immovable property, (*i*) declaration, (*ii*) acceptance and (*iii*) delivery of possession are the three essential conditions of gift, registration of a deed does not cure the defect of want of delivery of possession. Section 129 of the Transfer of Property Act is

5 Section 126 of the Transfer of Property Act.
6 *Marci Celine D'Souza* v *Renie Fernandez* AIR 1998 Ker 280.
7 Section 191 of the Indian Succession Act 1925.
8 Williame on *Executors,* 12th Ed., p. 484.
9 Section 126 of the Transfer of Property Act.
10 Section 129 of the Transfer of Property Act.

not hit by Art. 14 of the Constitution of India.[11] This point was discussed by Sri Rameshwar B. Pandit, Advocate in his article under constitutional validity of oral gift under the Mahomedan law.[12] He even discussed the combined effect of Arts. 13, 14 and 15 of the Constitution of India and came to the conclusion that in view of the express provisions of s. 129 of the Transfer of Property Act, those principles cannot be ignored. It will not be out of place to say a few words about *hiba* in respect of an undivided share in a property. It was observed by R.K. Wilson in his *Digest of Anglo-Mahomedan Law* (page 329, s. 208) that the gift of an undivided share in a property capable of division is invalid except when made among the co-sharers, or for religious purposes. But Mulla's *Principles of Mahomedan Law*[13] says that such a gift may at the utmost be irregular but not void and so may be perfected by subsequent act.[14] It is, however, doubtful when any particular statute, *viz.* s. 12 of the Bihar Tenancy Act 1885 and s. 5(1) of the West Bengal Land Reforms Act (West Bengal Act X of 1956) requires the transfer of the holding to be done in writing whether any oral transfer shall be valid in law or not. The Hindu law, where delivery of possession was enough to complete a gift, is abrogated by s. 123 of the Transfer of Property Act, but the restrictions on powers to make gifts under the personal law still remain. A gift is different from a surrender by a Hindu widow having a limited interest in the property where she does not in fact or in law purport to transfer any interest in the property surrendered. The widow simply withdraws herself from the estate and the reversioner steps into the inheritance as a matter of law.[15] But in a case of transfer of the whole estate, the reversioner takes the same subject to the liability for her maintenance.[16] So in the case of relinquishment, the reversioner remains responsible for her debts.[17]

FORMS

Deed of Gift of Property in Consideration of Natural Love

THIS DEED OF GIFT made this .... day of .... 1999 BETWEEN AB of, etc. (hereinafter called the DONOR), of the one part, and CD of etc. (hereinafter

11 *Bebi Maniran* v *Mohd. Ishaque* AIR 1963 AP 229.
12 AIR 1981 Journal, pp. 161-163.
13 19th Ed., p. 121.
14 *Hayatuddin* v *Abdul Gani* AIR 1976 Bom 23; *Sk. Aftab* v *Smt. Yayabba* AIR 1973 All 54.
15 *Karunamoyee* v *Maya Moyi* AIR 1948 Cal 84.
16 *Narbadabai* v *Mahadeo* (1880)5 Bom 99.
17 *Sudhamoyee* v *Bhujendra Nath* (1937) AC 226.

called the DONEE), of the other part, WITNESSES, that in consideration of the natural love and affection which the DONOR had and still has for the donee, the latter being his daughter, the DONOR doeth hereby grant, convey, transfer, give and assure unto and to the use of the DONEE, freely and voluntarily, the property mentioned and described in the schedule hereto and hereinafter referred to as the said property and delivered possession of the same unto and in favour of the DONEE TO HAVE AND TO HOLD the same for her sole use and benefit absolutely and unconditionally forever. *Usual covenants as in a sale-deed* AND THAT the DONEE *accepts* the gift of the said property hereunder made as testified by her being a party hereto and executing these presents. The estimated value of the property is Rs. ....

The Schedule above referred to

IN WITNESS WHEREOF the DONOR has executed these presents and the DONEE has accepted the gift on the day, month and year first above-written.

Signed, sealed and delivered by AB
the DONOR in the presence of:

Signed, sealed and delivered by CD
the DONEE accepting the said gift.

Deed of Gift of Property for Particular Purpose

THIS DEED OF GIFT is made this the .... day of ...... 2000 BETWEEN AB of, etc. (hereinafter called the DONOR), of the one part, and CD of, etc. (hereinafter called the DONEE), of the other part.

WHEREAS the DONEE intends to start a school in his village .... for the education of girls AND whereas the DONOR is desirous of donating the land fully mentioned and described in the schedule hereto to be used as a site for the said school.

Now This Deed witnesseth that in pursuance of the said pious wish and desire and as a patron of the proposed school to be started by the DONEE, the DONOR doeth hereby and hereunder freely and voluntarily grant, convey, transfer, give, assign and assure unto and to the use of the DONEE and his successor ALL THAT, etc., etc., to be used solely and exclusively for the purpose of a site for construction and accommodation of the proposed girls' school TO HAVE AND TO HOLD the same so long as the same shall be used and occupied as a site and/or building of the school AND THAT the DONEE accepts the gift of the said property hereunder made solely and exclusively for the purpose hereinbefore indicated subject to the condition hereunder provided.

This deed further witnesseth that it is expressly agreed and understood by and between the parties that this gift of land will stand *ipso facto* revoked in the event the land hereunder given is not used for the purpose of the intended school for which the same is given within a period of one year from the date of these presents or in the alternative the said school is abolished or shifted elsewhere or amalgamated with some other institution when and in all or any such event or events the land with all buildings and structures, if any erected thereon, shall revert to and revest in the DONOR or his heirs, executors, administrators and representatives and shall form part of his former estate as if this deed of gift was never executed nor intended. And it is further agreed by and between the parties that in case the land is acquired by the Government, the DONEE or his successors, including any person or persons managing the school, shall invest the compensation money to be awarded in purchase of another land or building to be used solely and exclusively for the school unless otherwise directed by any court of competent jurisdiction. The estimated value of the property is Rs. ....

The Schedule

IN WITNESS WHEREOF the DONOR has executed this Deed of Gift and delivered the same to the DONEE who has also executed the same in token of acceptance thereof the day, month and year first above-written.

Signed, sealed and delivered by AB the DONOR in the presence of:

Signed, sealed and delivered by CD the DONEE in token of acceptance of the Gift.

Deed of Gift of Land in Trust to Charity

THIS DEED OF GIFT is made this .... day of .... 2000 BETWEEN AB son of .... residing at .... (hereinafter called the DONOR) of the one part and CD son of............ residing at .... and EF son of .... residing at .... (hereinafter called the TRUSTEES) of the other part.

WHEREAS it is proposed to erect a *serai* for the use of travellers, and a committee has been constituted to raise subscriptions for construction of the building and creation of the endowment AND WHEREAS the trustees are members of such committee: have approached the DONEE for help AND WHEREAS the DONOR has agreed to contribute the piece of land hereinafter described in the schedule below as a site for such *serai*: NOW THIS DEED WITNESSES that in pursuance of such pious wish and desire and as a patron for the proposed *serai*, the said AB does hereby freely, voluntarily and absolutely and subject to the condition hereunder imposed grant, convey, transfer and give unto and to the use of the said CD and EF and their successors in office as trustees as aforesaid ALL THAT, etc., (*describe the property*) and valued at Rs. .... TO HAVE AND TO HOLD the same as trustees upon trust hereinafter mentioned. And it is hereby AGREED AND DECLARED by and between the parties hereto that the trustees and their successors in office shall from time to time and at all times hereafter stand possessed of the land hereby conveyed and the building or buildings to be erected thereon IN TRUST to be used solely and exclusively as a *serai* for food and shelter of the travellers all through the year free of any charge or other contribution. AND it is hereby further agreed and declared that in case the object of the gift fails; or in the event *serai* is closed or shifted anywhere or used for any purpose contrary to law or against religion or if the object of the gift is frustrated otherwise for any reason whatsoever—this gift will stand *ipso facto* revoked and the property shall in that event revert to and revest in the DONOR or his descendants as may remain alive with all improvements thereon free from any claim on that account as if the gift was never made nor intended unless otherwise directed in an appropriate action by a court of competent jurisdiction.

The Schedule above referred to

IN WITNESS WHEREOF the parties hereto have executed these presents on the day, month and year first above-written.

Signed, sealed and delivered by
AB the DONOR

Signed and sealed by CD and EF
as Trustees in token of acceptance
of gifts and the Office of TRUSTEES

Memorandum of Gift of Movables

BE IT KNOWN TO ALL CONCERNED that the undersigned .... son of .... by caste .... by occupation .... residing at .... (the DONOR) do hereby declare and confirm that the donor on the .... day of .... 20......... in consideration of the natural love and affection which the DONOR had and bears for .... son of .... residing at .... by caste .... by occupation (the DONEE) intended for and actually gave by words of mouth and also expressed himself to give unto and to the use of the DONEE freely and voluntarily, absolutely and forever the several properties mentioned in the Schedule below with all beneficial interest therein and delivered possession thereof simultaneously with a view to divest himself of all ownership therein and pass title thereof unto and in favour of and/or otherwise vest them in the DONEE to all intents and purposes AND THAT the

DONEE doth hereby declare that the DONEE did at the same time accept the gift as aforesaid and took into possession and control of the same.

The Schedule above referred to

Serial No.	*Description*	*Valuation*	*Remarks, if any*

IN WITNESS WHEREOF the parties to these presents have hereunto set and subscribed their respective hands and seals this .... day of .... 2000.

Signed, sealed and delivered by
the within-named DONOR at ....
in the presence of:

Executed by the DONEE at ....
in the presence of:

Gift of Business Goodwill

THIS DEED OF GIFT OF BUSINESS GOODWILL is made this .... day of .... 1999 BETWEEN AB son of .... residing at .... (hereinafter called the DONOR) of the one part and CD and EF sons of .... residing at .... (hereinafter called the DONEES) of the other part.

WHEREAS:

1. The DONOR has for many years past carried on the trade or business of .... at .... (hereinafter called the DONOR'S business) and in connection therewith is the registered proprietor of the trade marks relevant particulars of which are set out in the first schedule hereto.

2. The DONOR is the inventor and patentee of the invention described in the second schedule hereto (hereinafter called the invention) the patent in respect of which was granted and trade mark registered ...... under number .... of ....

3. By articles of partnership bearing even date with and executed immediately before this deed and made between the donees respectively the DONEES agreed to carry on in co-partnership the trade or business of .... (hereinafter referred to as the PARTNERSHIP BUSINESS) subject to the stipulations therein contained for a term of .... years from the date thereof.

4. With a view to setting up the DONEES in the partnership business the DONOR is desirous of assigning the goodwill of his business and the said trade marks to the DONEES and granting to them the licence hereinafter contained.

NOW THIS DEED WITNESSETH as follows:

1. In consideration of his natural love and affection for the DONEES the DONOR hereby assigns unto the DONEES all that the goodwill of the DONOR in his business and also all those the trade marks specified in the first schedule hereto and all the rights and privileges incidental thereto to hold the same unto the DONEES absolutely as joint tenants as the property of the partnership business subject to the provisions and stipulations contained in the said articles of partnership.

2. For the consideration aforesaid the DONOR hereby grants unto the DONEES and the survivor of them personally rights so that this licence shall not be assignable but to have the sole and exclusive licence to make use, exercise and send the invention in all parts of India during the residue of the term of the said letters patent and any renewal or extension of such term if the DONEES or such survivor shall so long continue to carry on the partnership business subject to the DONEES or the survivor of them at their or his own cost keeping up the said letters patent and with power to the DONEES or the survivor of them to take in the name of the DONOR all necessary legal proceedings for effectively protecting or defending the same against infringement.

The First Schedule

The Second Schedule

IN WITNESS WHEREOF the DONOR, AB, has executed this deed of Gift which has been accepted on behalf of DONEES, CD and EF on the day, month and year first above-written.

Signed, sealed and delivered by
AB the DONOR in the presence of:

Signed and sealed by CD and EF
the DONEES as token of acceptance
of the gift

26

Guarantees and Indemnities

Introductory observations. A bond is defined under s. 2(5) of the Indian Stamp Act 1899, and also under s. 2(*d*) of the Limitation Act of 1963 (Act 36 of 1963). One is to look into the real intention of the parties to ascertain whether the writing in question is a bond or not.[1]

It is a deed poll whereby one or more persons bind himself or themselves under a seal to another to pay him certain sum of money from which he is to be relieved only on the happening of certain event or fulfilment of some specific condition. The distinction between a bond and a covenant is that in a bond the obligor *prima facie* binds himself to the obligee for payment of a certain sum of money or to compensate him against certain loss, injury or damages. The real object is that the obligation shall be void if the act or acts or performance or prevention is done or left undone as provided therein. A covenant is a stipulation in a deed *inter-parties* which expresses the real obligation intended to be created whether it be for payment of money or doing or not doing some act and further in the event of breach it stipulates payment of a sum as penalty or liquidated damages.

A special type of agreement with a penal clause is distinguished from a bond. Penalty is the primary part in a bond, the performance of the condition which grants relief against penalty is subsidiary. It is just the reverse in the case of agreement with a penal clause. Here the agreement is the primary part to which the penalty on default is subsidiary of a contingency which may never arise. The distinction is well explained in the leading case of *Gisborne & Co.* v *Subal Bowri*.[2]

Guarantees. (a) *"Contract of guarantee", "surety", "principal debtor", "creditor", "continuing guarantee".* *A contract of guarantee* is a contract to

1 *Radhaswamy* v *Raj Narain* AIR 1943 All 218.
2 (1881)8 Cal 284; 10 CLJ 219.

perform the promise, or discharge the liability, of a third person in case of his default.[3]

The person who gives the guarantee is called the *surety*; the person in respect of whose default the guarantee is given is called the *principal debtor*; and the person to whom the guarantee is given is called the *creditor*.

A guarantee which extends to a series of transactions is called a *continuing guarantee*.[4]

A contract of guarantee is a special promise to answer for a debt, default or miscarriage of another person.

(*b*) *Revocation of continuing guarantee.* A continuing guarantee can at any time be revoked by the surety as to future transactions by notice to the creditor.[5] The death of the surety operates, in the absence of any contract to the contrary, as a revocation of a continuing guarantee so far as regards future transactions.[6]

It stands also revoked by material variations of the terms of the contract,[7] also by changes in the constitution of the firm[8] and also by showing accommodation to the debtor.[9]

The discharge of the surety in all the cases referred to above is operative only with regard to future transactions. This is the principle laid down in *Lloyds* v *Harpar*.[10] It was held that the guarantor may terminate guarantee but remains answerable for past liabilities.

(*c*) *Rights, liabilities and discharge of surety.* Where a guaranteed debt has become due, or default of the principal debtor to perform a guaranteed duty has taken place, the surety, upon payment or performance of all that he is liable for, is invested with all rights which the creditor had against the principal debtor.[11] Section 145 of the Indian Contract Act protects the surety against the original debtor.[12]

3 Section 126 of the Indian Contract Act 1872.
4 Section 129 of the Indian Contract Act 1872.
5 Section 130 of the Indian Contract Act 1872.
6 Section 131 of the Indian Contract Act 1872.
7 Section 133 of the Indian Contract Act 1872.
8 Section 38 of the Indian Partnership Act 1932.
9 Section 135 of the Indian Contract Act 1872.
10 (1880)16 Ch D 290.
11 Section 140 of the Indian Contract Act 1872.
12 The surety by performance of the contract steps into the shoes of the creditor and so he is clothed with all the rights which the creditor had against the debtor. He is entitled to indemnity or contribution—a common law action of quasi-contractual nature. Anson's *English Law of Contract*, 22nd Ed., p. 571.

The liability of the surety is co-extensive with that of the principal debtor unless it is otherwise provided by the contract.[13]

Any variance, made without the surety's consent, in the terms of the contract between the principal debtor and the creditor discharges the surety as to transactions subsequent to the variance. The surety is discharged by any contract between the creditor and the principal debtor, by which the principal debtor is released[14] or by any act or omission of the creditor, the legal consequence of which is the discharge of the principal debtor. A contract between the creditor and the principal debtor, by which the creditor makes a composition with, or promises to give time to, or not to sue, the principal debtor, discharges the surety, unless the surety assents to such contract.[15]

Provided that—

Where a contract to give time to the principal debtor is made by the creditor with a third person, and not with the principal debtor, the surety is not discharged.[16]

A mere forbearance on the part of the creditor to sue the principal debtor, or to enforce any other remedy against him, does not, in the absence of any provisions in the guarantee to the contrary, discharge the surety.[17]

Where there are co-sureties, a release by the creditor of one of them does not discharge the other; neither does it free the surety so released from his responsibility to the other sureties.[18]

(*d*) *Invalid guarantee.* Any guarantee which has been obtained by fraud or means of misrepresentation made by the creditor or with his knowledge and assent, concerning a material part of the transaction, is invalid; and any guarantee which the creditor has obtained by means of keeping silent as to material circumstances is also invalid.[19]

(*e*) *Implied promise to indemnify surety.* In every contract of guarantee there is an implied promise by the principal debtor to indemnify the surety; and the surety is entitled to recover from the principal debtor whatever sum he has rightfully paid under the guarantee, but no sums which he has paid wrongfully.

(*f*) *Liability of co-sureties for contribution.* When two or more persons are co-sureties for the same debt or duty, either jointly or severally, and whether

13 Section 128 of the Indian Contract Act 1872.
14 Section 134 of the Indian Contract Act 1872.
15 Section 135 of the Indian Contract Act 1872.
16 Section 136 of the Indian Contract Act 1872.
17 Section 137 of the Indian Contract Act 1872.
18 Section 138 of the Indian Contract Act 1872.
19 Section 142 of the Indian Contract Act 1872.

under the same or different contracts, and whether with or without the knowledge of each other, the co-sureties, in the absence of any contract to the contrary, are liable, as between themselves, to pay each an equal share of the whole debt, or of that part of it which remains unpaid by the principal debtor.

Bank guarantee. A bank guarantee is an autonomous contract and imposes an absolute obligation on the bank to fulfil the terms and the payment in the bank guarantee becomes due on the happening of a contingency on the occurrence of which the guarantee becomes enforceable.[20]

Encashment of a bank guarantee can be restrained by an injunction (*a*) where the petitioner puts forward a case which shows that the bank guarantee was procured after practising fraud on the bank; (*b*) where the petitioner makes out a case and shows that in case an injunction is not granted then he is likely to suffer an irretrievable injustice; and (*c*) where the petitioner shows a case of special equity in his favour.[1] The right to recover the amount under the running bills has no relevance to the liability of the bank under the guarantee.[2] Where there is default in delivery of certain quantity out of the entire bulk the bank guarantee can be enforced only to the extent of the value of the undelivered portion and not for the entire sum.[3] In a contract for construction work the contractor executed bank guarantee against mobilisation advance and the contractor received advance. In the absence of any fraud or irretrievable injustice the bank guarantee was invokable though the work had been stopped.[4]

Where the bank has unconditionally and irrevocably agreed and undertaken to pay the party concerned on demand the sums specified therein and that the amount should be paid without demur and without requiring the creditor to invoke legal remedy and it is further provided that the said party will be the sole judge as to and whether the other party to the contract has committed any breach and the extent of the loss and damages and that his decision as to the outstanding amount will be final and binding the court cannot restrain the beneficiary from enforcing the guarantee.[5] Disputes relating to the liability to indemnify the owner in respect of the contribution can be adjudicated in a properly framed suit. If the contractor is ultimately found not to be liable for contribution then it could be recovered from the owner. Even if the contractor suffers any injury it could be compensated in appropriate proceeding and as such that cannot be any reason to restrain invocation of bank guarantee by injunction.[6]

20 *Syndicate Bank* v *Vijay Kumar* AIR 1992 SC 1066.
1 *GET* v *Punj Seris* AIR 1991 SC 1994.
2 *GET,* ibid; see also *National Textile* v *T.N. Co-op.* AIR 1998 SC 2658.
3 *G.M.* v *Dy. Registrar* AIR 1998 Kant 354.
4 *State of Bihar* v *Hindustan Construction* AIR 1998 Bom 331.
5 *H.S. Workers* v *G.S. Atwal* AIR 1996 SC 131.
6 *Geo Tech. Construction* v *Hindustan Steel* AIR 1999 Ker 72.

Indemnities. The statutory law on the subject is contained in ss. 124, 125 of the Indian Contract Act 1872. Although it is a well-settled principle of law that an obligor (person liable to indemnify) is entitled to avail himself of all legal ways and means by which the person indemnified might have protected or reimbursed himself against the loss, there is no statutory recognition of the right. The Law of Indemnity is thus based on natural equity. A contract of insurance is a contract of indemnity.

Sections 222, 223 and 224 of the Indian Contract Act deal with the liability of the principal to indemnify the agent.

(*a*) *"Contract of indemnity"*. A contract by which one party promises to save the other from loss caused to him by the conduct of the promisor himself, or by the conduct of any other person is called a *contract of indemnity*. A conveyance for sale of any immovable property contains amongst others a covenant as to indemnity by the vendor.[7] So when the vendor cannot produce title deeds he executes an indemnity bond in favour of the purchaser.

(*b*) *Rights of indemnity-holder.* The promisee, in a contract of indemnity, acting within the scope of his authority, is entitled to recover from the promisor:

(*i*) all damages which he may be compelled to pay in any suit in respect of any matter to which the promise to indemnity applies;

(*ii*) all costs which he may be compelled to pay in any suit if, in bringing or defending it, he did not contravene the orders of a promisor, and acted as it would have been prudent for him to act in the absence of any contract of indemnity, or if the promisor authorised him to bring or defend the suit; and

(*iii*) all sums which he may have paid under the terms of any compromise of any such suit, if the compromise was not contrary to the orders of the promisor, and was one which it would have been prudent for the promisee to make in the absence of any contract of indemnity or if the promisor authorised him to compromise the suit.

Agreement in restraint of legal proceedings or shortening limitation period void. In *National Insurance Company Limited* v *A.G. Nair & Co.*[8] the Supreme Court upheld a term in Insurance Policy whereby it limited the time within which the assured could enforce his right as also the term that on expiry of a particular period the Insurance Company shall cease to have any liability on the Policy. In some guarantees such clauses are incorporated.

Indian Contract (Amendment) Act 1996 with effect from 8th January 1997 has amended s. 28 of the Indian Contract Act 1872 whereby any

7 Section 55 of the Transfer of Property Act (Act IV of 1882).
8 AIR 1997 SC 2049.

restraint in enforcing a person's right under a contract by usual legal proceedings in the Ordinary Tribunal or limiting the time for enforcement of his rights has been made illegal. Similarly, a clause in a contract which extinguishes the rights of any party or discharges any party from any liability on the expiry of a specified period shorter than limitation period is void. Section 28 as amended reads as follows:

28. *Agreement in restraint of legal proceedings void.* Every agreement—

(*a*) by which any party is restricted absolutely from enforcing his rights under or in respect of any Contract, by the usual legal proceedings in the Ordinary Tribunal, or which limits the time within which he may thus enforce his rights; or

(*b*) which extinguishes the rights of any party thereto, or discharges any party thereto from any liability, under or in respect of any Contract on the expiry of a specified period so as to restrict any party from enforcing his rights, is void to that extent.

Explanation 1. This section shall not render illegal a Contract by which two or more persons agree that any dispute which may arise between them in respect of any subject or class of subjects shall be referred to arbitration and that only the amount awarded in such arbitration shall be recoverable in respect of the dispute so referred.

Explanation 2. Nor shall this section render illegal any Contract in writing by which two or more persons agree to refer to arbitration any question between them which has already arisen or affect any provision of any law in force for the time being as to reference to arbitration.

If two Civil Courts at different places have jurisdictions over a dispute the parties may agree that the dispute between them shall be tried in one of such Courts. Such an agreement is valid.[9]

FORMS

Guarantee for Payment of Debt

To
CD of, etc. (CREDITOR)

In consideration of your having this day lent and advanced the sum of Rs. .... to EF, of (PRINCIPAL DEBTOR), at my request, I, the undersigned, do

9 See *Hakam Singh* v *Gammon (India) Ltd.* AIR 1971 SC 740; *Patel Roadways Limited* v *Tropical Agro Systems P. Ltd.* AIR 1992 SC 1514 (1519).

hereby agree to be and shall, at all times hereafter until repayment of loans remain responsible to you for and guarantee payment of the said sum of Rs. ...... in case of his default together with interest thereon at the rate of .... per cent per annum, such interest to be calculated with effect from the date of service of the registered notice of demand on me. This guarantee shall not be affected by your granting any time or any other concession or indulgence to the said EF or by his death or insolvency. This guarantee is given without prejudice to all my rights of reimbursement as against the said EF or his estate as surety for him for all sums to be paid to you and costs, charges and expenses incurred in connection therewith.

(Date) AB

Guarantee to Pay for Goods Supplied

To
CD and Co. of, etc. (CREDITORS)

In consideration of your having had recently agreed at my request and on my assurance to keep and maintain regular supply to EF, of, etc. (PRINCIPAL DEBTOR), with articles of trade such as ...., etc., up to the value of Rs. .... on credit, I, the undersigned AB of, etc. (SURETY) do hereby promise and agree to remain liable for and guarantee payment of the sum as may be due and payable as the balance of amount to you by the said EF on demand. This guarantee shall not be construed as a continuing guarantee and shall not extend as against me to supply of any goods in excess of the value aforesaid. It shall not be at all necessary for you to institute any suit or other proceedings against the said EF before demanding of me such payment. This guarantee shall not stand determined by any change in the constitution of your firm, or by any concession or other indulgence being given, shown or granted by you to the said EF at any time.

(Date) AB

Continuing Guarantee to Pay for Goods Supplied

THIS AGREEMENT is made this .... day of ....BETWEEN AB of, etc. (SURETY), of the one part, and CD of, etc. (CREDITOR), of the other part.

WHEREAS the said CD has, at the request and assurance of the said AB, agreed to supply EF of, etc. (PRINCIPAL DEBTOR), from time to time in the course of his trade, with articles of trade such as............. on credit: NOW IT IS HEREBY AGREED AND DECLARED BY AND BETWEEN THE PARTIES as follows:

1. The said AB shall at all times hereafter so long as this guarantee shall continue remain responsible for payment and will pay or cause to be

paid to the said CD all such sum or sums of money as shall become due and payable to the said CD from the said EF for articles supplied or to be so supplied as aforesaid and not paid for by the said EF or otherwise adjusted not exceeding however Rs. .... at any time without confirmation from the said AB first had and obtained the same being the limit prescribed and subject thereto, this guarantee shall be a guarantee for the whole of such sum or sums.

2. The guarantee hereby given shall be a continuing guarantee and so cover all trade deals between CD and EF subject to the limit hereunder prescribed, but nevertheless the said CD shall, in case of any delay or default on the part of the said EF in making payment, give at least a fortnight's notice in writing to the said AB before taking any steps for enforcement of the guarantee hereunder given by the said AB.

3. PROVIDED ALWAYS THAT in the event of any adjudication order, whether voluntary or compulsory, being made against the said EF or his entering or attempting to enter into a scheme of composition with other creditors or any attachment effected or charging order made or Receiver being appointed over his business, even then the guarantee hereunder given shall not stand revoked, but the said CD shall nevertheless first proceed against the said EF or his estate to recover as much as possible before requiring any payment on that account to be made by the said AB under and by virtue of the guarantee hereunder given.

4. The said CD will, at any time during the continuance of this guarantee, give to the said AB, if and when requested in writing so to do, full and accurate information as to the amount of the indebtedness for the time being of the said EF to the said CD.

5. Any extension of time granted, concession or indulgence shown on the part of the said CD towards EF shall not prejudice the rights and obligations of the parties under these presents.

6. This guarantee may be determined at any time by the said AB by payment to the said CD of the amount for the time being owing by the said EF up to the limit specified in cl. 1 hereof, or as to subsequent transactions only, by .... calendar months' notice in writing given by the said AB to the said CD.

7. Notwithstanding anything hereinbefore stated, this guarantee shall stand determined on the death of the said AB absolutely.

IN WITNESS, etc.

AB

Signed, sealed and delivered CD

Bank Guarantee

Reference No. .... of
Suit No. .... of 2000

In the Court of ....

.... *Plaintiff*

versus

.... *Defendant*

Bank Guarantee of ....

KNOW ALL MEN BY THESE PRESENTS that I/we .... son of .... by occupation .... residing at No. .... Calcutta (hereinafter called the DEFENDANT and Bank of .... a body corporated and constituted incorporated under the Banking Companies (Acquisition and Transfer of Undertakings) Act of 1970 and carrying on banking business amongst other places at .... and having its registered office .... outside the jurisdiction of this court (hereinafter called the BANK) are jointly and severally held and firmly bounded unto Sri .... the District Judge/Registrar of the .... Court at .... his successor or successors-in-office and assigns in the sum of Rs. .... (Rupees ....) only of good and lawful money of the Union of India to be paid to the said Sri .... (hereinafter called the District Judge/Registrar) his successor or successors-in-office and assigns as the case may be for which payment well and truly to be made I/we the .... and we the Bank for ourselves and our respective successors and assigns do hereby jointly and severally bind and oblige ourselves and each and every one of us and them for the whole of the said amount unto the District Judge/Registrar, his successor or successors-in-office and assigns firmly by these presents. We the bank do hereby covenant with the District Judge/Registrar his successor or successors-in-office and assigns that under the Memorandum and Articles of Association we are authorised to stand as guarantor and to execute the necessary bond therefor, and I/we the .... and the BANK and our respective successors and assigns do hereby further covenant with the District Judge/Registrar, his successor or successors-in-office and assigns that we shall from time to time and at all times hereafter during the continuance of this security at our or their own costs and expenses execute in favour of the District Judge/Registrar his successor or successors-in-office and assigns such further and other assurance as may be required for the purpose of more fully and effectually securing the due payment of the said sum of Rs. .... (Rupees ....) only secured by this bond in accordance with the true intent and meaning thereof And I/we the .... and we the BANK do hereby submit ourselves to the jurisdiction of this court and appoint premises No.................... and C/o. .... Advocate as our respective addresses for service on us of all writs, proceedings and notices that may be issued, taken or given to us with reference to the condition of this bond or in respect of our liabilities hereunder.

Dated this .... day of .... 20.........

WHEREAS by an order dated .... 20 .... and made by the said High Court/District Judge in the above suit, it was *inter alia* directed that upon the DEFENDANTS furnishing security to the satisfaction of the District Judge/Registrar to the extent of Rs. .... (Rupees ....) only on or before the .... day of .... 20 .... the DEFENDANTS would be at liberty to withdraw the sum of Rs. .... lying in deposit in court And That the DEFENDANT would furnish such security by way of bank guarantee in favour of the District Judge/Registrar.

AND WHEREAS at a reference held before the District Judge/Registrar of the said court the DEFENDANTS proposed the Bank of Baroda as their guarantor for the said sum of Rs. .... (Rupees ....) only.

AND WHEREAS the bank expressed it willingness to stand as guarantor for the DEFENDANTS for the said sum of Rs. .... (Rupees.............) only.

AND WHEREAS the District Judge/Registrar has accepted the said BANK as the guarantor for the DEFENDANTS subject to the said bank along with the DEFENDANTS executing a bond in favour of the District Judge/Registrar of this court for the sum of Rs. .... (Rupees ....) only initially for a period of one year upon the undertaking of the said DEFENDANTS to have the bank guarantee renewed from year to year at least 14 days before the date of its expiry until final disposal of the said suit or until further order of this court.

NOW THE CONDITIONS of the above written Bond of Obligation are such that this bond shall remain in full force and virtue until final disposal of the above suit or until further order of this court PROVIDED FURTHER that in so far as the BANK is concerned its liability under this bond is restricted to the sum of Rs. .... (Rupees ....) only and the guarantee under this bond shall remain in full force and virtue for a period of one year from the date of this bond, *i.e.,* till the .... day of .... 19 .... PROVIDED FURTHER that if the said........... fails and/or neglects to renew this bond 14 days before the date of its expiry or within such time before the date of expiry of any subsequent renewal thereof, then and in such an event the BANK shall forthwith and of its own accord deposit with the District Judge/ Registrar the said sum of Rs. .... (Rupees ....) only being the amount secured under this bond together with a further sum of Rs. .... (Rupees ....) only being the amount of commission payable on the said sum of Rs. .... (Rupees ....) only to the Registrar under the rules of this court the total being Rs. ....

IN WITNESS WHEREOF I/We the said.......... and we the said BANK .... have signed the day, month and year above-written.

Signed, sealed and delivered
by Bank .... at
in the presence of:

Dated this............... day of .... 19...........

Renewal of Bank Guarantee

To
The Registrar High Court ......
District Judge ....

Dear Sir

Cause, title of the matter

Subject: Bank Guarantee dated 1999
for Rs. .... (Rupees............) only

With reference to the above Bank Guarantee we hereby agree that our guarantee for Rs. .... (Rupees ....) will further remain in force until .... day of .... 2000 with effect from the............ day of .... 1999 unless a demand or claim is lodged on us in writing on or before.......... day of......... 2000 when we shall stand discharged from all liabilities under the guarantee thereafter.

Save as aforesaid all other terms and conditions of the aforesaid guarantee remain unchanged and in force and effect.

This endorsement shall be attached to the original of the aforesaid guarantee and shall form an integral part of the guarantee dated .... day of 1999

Notwithstanding what has been stated above our liability under the guarantee is restricted to Rs........... only and we shall stand discharged from the same earlier in the event as aforesaid.

Thanking you,

Yours faithfully

Signature of the Bank

Deed of Guarantee by a Bank on behalf of a Company for the Performance of a Contract

THIS DEED OF GUARANTEE MADE THIS .... day of .... 1999 BETWEEN the Bank of .... (hereinafter called the BANK) of the one part and the

Governor of .... (hereinafter called the PURCHASER) of the other part;

WHEREAS .... a company registered under the Companies Act 1956 (hereinafter called the CONTRACTOR) have by a Deed of Agreement made on the .... agreed with the purchaser to supply those plants, machinery and equipment in accordance with the terms, specifications and conditions therein contained;

AND WHEREAS in accordance with the terms and conditions of the aforesaid agreement the purchaser has to make to the contractor an advance payment of .... Rs. .... (Rupees............ only) being equivalent to ....% of the total F.O.B. Value of the contract price, and such payment is to be secured by a Bank guarantee;

AND WHEREAS the BANK has at the request of the CONTRACTOR agreed to guarantee the refund of the said advance in case the plants, machinery and equipment of the value...... aforesaid are not delivered to the State Government in accordance with the terms and conditions of the said agreement, and the Governor has agreed to make the said advance on such security:

NOW THIS DEED WITNESSES AS FOLLOWS:

1. In consideration of the PURCHASER having agreed to advance a sum of.......... to the CONTRACTOR, through the BANK, the BANK doth hereby guarantee that if the contractor shall fail to supply to the PURCHASER the plants machinery and equipment of the value of .... in accordance with the specifications and conditions contained in the Deed of Agreement dated the .... and/or any amendments or modifications in the aforesaid agreement made between the PURCHASER and the CONTRACTOR ...., the BANK shall repay to the Governor such amount or amounts as the bank may be called upon to pay subject to the maximum aggregate of ....

PROVIDED FIRST that the liability of the BANK under this deed shall not at any time exceed the said advance of ....

AND PROVIDED SECONDLY that the guarantee hereunder furnished shall be released and stand discharged as soon as the CONTRACTOR has supplied to the PURCHASER the plants machinery and equipment of the value of........... in accordance with the aforesaid Deed of Agreement.

2. This guarantee of the bank will come into force immediately upon payment of the sum of........... being received by the BANK for and on behalf of the CONTRACTOR from the State Government and shall continue in force till the supply of plants, machinery and equipment of the value of.......... aforesaid is effected as testified by documents and invoices.

3. The guarantee hereinbefore contained shall not be affected by any change in the constitution of the BANK or of the CONTRACTOR.

4. Any account settled between the State Government and the contractor shall be the conclusive evidence against the BANK of the amount due and shall not be questioned by the BANK.

5. The neglect or forbearance of the Governor in enforcement of payment of any moneys the payment whereof is intended to be hereby secured or the giving of time by the State Government for the repayment thereof shall in no way relieve the BANK of their liability under this deed.

6. The expressions the BANK and the PURCHASER hereinbefore used shall include their respective successors and assigns.

IN WITNESS WHEREOF .... etc. FOR AND ON BEHALF OF THE BANK AND SECRETARY, DEPARTMENT for and on behalf of the Governor have signed this deed on the day and year first above written.

For and on behalf of the BANK

For and on behalf of the Governor

WITNESS: 1 ....

WITNESS: 2 ....

Counter Guarantee in favour of a Bank

.... BANK

IN CONSIDERATION of .... Bank having at our request stood as surety for and guaranteed payment of a sum of Rs. .... to the Registrar of .... Court in terms of guarantee dated this .... day of .... 1999 executed by the bank in his favour in Suit No. .... of (Cause title) in the circumstances mentioned in the said bond we GB and AB of .... do hereby covenant and agree by way of counter guarantee that we shall always remain jointly and severally liable to pay and reimburse the Bank or its successor in business to the extent of Rs. .... and or any other sum or sums as may be due and owing to the bank or its successor in business on that account inclusive of interest and costs, charges and expenses incurred and to indemnify and keep the bank indemnified against all such payments and all costs, charges and expenses which the bank shall incur or otherwise suffer by reason thereof.

We further declare that this guarantee unless we are otherwise relieved from its performance or non-performance by Statute or adjudication of any court of competent jurisdiction shall be a continuing guarantee and shall not be deemed to have been satisfied until payment or realisation of the amount as hereunder contemplated; Further we declare that the character of this guarantee shall not be affected by death or insolvency of any one or more of us and furthermore that we shall execute and register all further or other deeds and writings as may be required for securing or enforcing the counter guarantee and have all questions or disputes as to the extent of our liability to the bank adjudicated by reference to two arbitrators one to be appointed by the bank and we shall not be discharged by any compromise between the parties in the said suit unless the bank is discharged from its liability by adjudication of the said court.

IN WITNESS WHEREOF etc.

Dated this .... day of .... GB
AB

Agreement of Guarantee

THIS AGREEMENT OF GUARANTEE is made at Calcutta this .... day of .... 2000 BETWEEN AB, son of......................, residing at................ and CD, son of ...., residing at.................. (hereinafter called the GUARANTORS which term shall unless the context otherwise requires include their heirs, successors, legal representatives and assigns) of the first part and EF BANK constituted under the Banking Companies (Acquisition and Transfer of Undertakings) Act 1980 carrying on business, *inter alia*, at.......... (hereinafter called the BANK which term shall unless the context otherwise requires include its successors and assigns) of the second part.

In consideration of the BANK having agreed to grant, granting and/or continuing to grant credit facilities with limits which could be varied from time to time to the Borrower, X Company Limited, a company registered under the Companies Act 1956 and carrying on business at .... at our request in, *inter alia*,

Overdraft in Current Account
Clean Cash Credit Account
Cash Credit Hypothecation Account
Cash Credit Pledge Account
Letter of Credit Account
Letter of Guarantee Account
Deferred Payment Guarantee Account, or
In any other Account

from the BANK'S one or more branches on terms and conditions agreed upon or that might be agreed upon from time to time between the BANK and the borrower the GUARANTORS hereby agree and covenant with the BANK as follows:

1. The GUARANTORS hereby guarantee jointly and severally to the BANK the due performance of all present and future obligations by the borrower towards the BANK and payment of all moneys due or that might become due from the borrower to the BANK in the said or other Accounts with interest at the rate chargeable by the BANK from time to time in the said Accounts with all costs, charges and expenses in default of the borrower remedying the breach or making payment after being demanded by the bank.

2. The GUARANTORS declare and agree that this guarantee shall be a continuing guarantee and shall not be considered as cancelled or in any way affected by the fact that at any time the borrower may not have any liability on any of the said Accounts or the borrower may have even a credit balance in the Account but shall continue to be a guarantee and remain in operation in respect of all subsequent transactions.

3. The GUARANTORS hereby agree that the BANK shall be at liberty to vary the terms and conditions of granting credit facilities to the borrower as also vary the securities, take new securities or release existing securities without any consent of the GUARANTORS.

4. The GUARANTORS agree that as between the BANK and the GUARANTORS, the GUARANTORS are debtors and the BANK will be at liberty to proceed against the GUARANTORS without any obligation to exhaust its remedies against the borrower company. The GUARANTORS hereby declare and agree with the BANK that they shall not be entitled to and shall not claim any rights conferred on GUARANTORS by sections 133, 134, 135, 139 and 141 of the Indian Contract Act 1872.

5. The GUARANTORS agree that the BANK shall be entitled to obtain from the borrower company renewal documents or fresh documents and to open new Accounts and take new securities or consolidate or combine Accounts and/or securities and notwithstanding this the GUARANTORS shall continue to remain liable to the BANK for payment of all indebtedness and liabilities of the borrower both present and future including interest, cost and charges.

6. The GUARANTORS declare and agree that without first paying the claims of the BANK against the borrower they shall not claim or enforce any right against any assets of the borrower company or any Dividend or monies payable to or in relation to the borrower.

7. The GUARANTORS hereby agree that any Account settled between the BANK and the borrower or any acknowledgment made by the borrower or any Balance Confirmation or Acknowledgment of Debts and Securities executed by the borrower shall be binding on the GUARANTORS and for this purpose the borrower shall be deemed to be the agent duly authorised by the GUARANTORS herein.

8. The GUARANTORS hereby agree that their liability shall be joint and several and their respective heirs, successors, administrators and legal

representatives shall be liable to pay the claims of the BANK in relation to the said credit facilities to the borrower.

9. In the event the BANK in breach of its undertaking fails to grant credit facilities and as a consequence whereof the borrower ceases to carry on business or suffers substantial loss or is wound up then and in that event the GUARANTORS shall stand discharged from these presents and from all indebtedness and liabilities and obligations whatsoever towards the Bank.

10. The GUARANTORS agree that the BANK may enforce its rights as a pledgee or right of a lien on all goods, assets, properties and all moneys standing to the credit of the GUARANTORS for payment of BANK'S debts against the borrower and/or GUARANTORS.

11. The death, insanity or insolvency of the GUARANTORS shall not affect the transactions or loans given by the BANK to the borrower till the happening of such event. Any notice to determine the guarantee or death, insanity or insolvency of the GUARANTORS will terminate the guarantee only in respect of future transactions. In any such event the Clayton's Rule shall apply in respect of future transactions.

12. No infirmity or irregularity in the power of the borrower to borrow from the BANK or in the exercise of the borrowing power shall affect the validity of these presents or the obligations and liability of the guarantors to the BANK.

13. The GUARANTORS agree to accept as binding on them and as conclusive evidence of the moneys payable by the GUARANTORS to the BANK statements of Accounts duly certified under the Banker's Books Evidence Act furnished to the GUARANTORS.

14. Any notice to be served by any of the parties herein shall be deemed to have been duly served if sent by registered post at the address given herein unless some other address is specially communicated by a party herein.

15. The BANK agrees to act with due dispatch and in businessmanlike in all transactions with the borrower without any undue delay or arbitrariness and in the interest of trade and business without, however, jeopardising the public money and the prospect of recycling its funds.

IN WITNESS WHEREOF the GUARANTORS and the Bank have signed these presents on the day, month and year first above-written.

Signed and delivered by AB and CD,
the GUARANTORS in the presence of:

Signed on behalf of EF BANK by
Mr. .... the Manager,
authorised signatory and Power of
Attorney holder in the presence of:

Government Guarantee

THIS AGREEMENT IS MADE this 5th day of June 2000 BETWEEN the Governor of Arunachal Pradesh hereinafter called the GOVERNMENT (which expression shall unless excluded by or repugnant to the subject or context include his successors in Office) of the first part, Arbind Paper Mills Limited, a company incorporated under the Companies Act 1956 and having its registered office at Park Plaza, Calcutta 700 016 hereinafter called the COMPANY (which expression shall unless excluded by or repugnant to the subject or context include its successors and assigns) of the second part and ELH Bank, a body corporate constituted under the Banking Companies (Acquisition and Transfer of Undertakings) Act 1970 and having its Head Office at 3 Old Court House Street, Calcutta 700 069 hereinafter called the BANK (which expression shall unless excluded by or repugnant to the subject or context include its successors and assigns) of the third part.

WHEREAS the COMPANY is a borrower of the BANK and is indebted to the BANK for more than Rs. 2 crores.

AND WHEREAS for expansion of the business the company needs further advances of about Rs. 3 crores but is not in a position to give adequate security to the BANK.

AND WHEREAS the BANK has agreed to grant such advances if the GOVERNMENT guarantees repayment of said advances with applicable interest.

AND WHEREAS in the interest of the development of the State the Government has agreed to guarantee to the BANK payment of the company's present and future indebtedness to the BANK and has requested the BANK to grant such advances to the COMPANY.

NOW THEREFORE THESE PRESENTS WITNESSETH and the parties agree as follows:

1. In consideration of the BANK agreeing at the request of the GOVERNMENT to grant advances to the COMPANYupto Rs. 3 crores the GOVERNMENT hereby guarantees to the BANK the payment of all present and future indebtedness and liabilities of the company to the BANK. The Government shall hereafter indemnify and keep the BANK fully indemnified from and against all losses of principal and/or interest, charges and expenses which the BANK may incur or be put to on account of default of the COMPANY and in demanding, enforcing or obtaining payment of all or any such moneys either from the Company or the Government or howsoever otherwise.

2. The BANK shall have the fullest liberty without affecting this guarantee to postpone for any time or from time to time the exercise of any of the rights powers or remedies available to the BANK against the COMPANY or any other person or persons and/or any other security and the GOVERNMENT shall not be released from the liability under this guarantee by any exercise by the BANK of its liberty with reference to the matters aforesaid or any of them or by reason of time being given to the COMPANY or any other person as

aforesaid or any forbearance, act or omission on the part of the BANK or any other indulgence given to or composition by the BANK with the COMPANY or any other person or by any other matters or things whatsoever which under the law relating to the sureties would but for this provision have the effect of releasing the Government from such liability.

3. The guarantee herein shall be in addition to and without prejudice to all other securities if any that the BANK may now or hereafter at any time have from the COMPANY or any other person for all or any moneys covered by this guarantee and this guarantee shall be enforceable against the GOVERNMENT notwithstanding that all or any such securities held by the BANK shall at any time when demand is made from or proceedings taken against the GOVERNMENT hereunder be outstanding or unreleased.

4. This guarantee shall be a continuing guarantee for all principals and interests from time to time and at any time remaining due or unpaid by the COMPANY to the BANK in respect of the sum of Rs. 3 crores and interest thereon payable by it to the BANK and that all compositions and payments received by the BANK from the COMPANY or from any other person or persons for or on its account should be regarded for all purposes as payment in gross and the BANK shall be entitled to prove against the COMPANY before the Liquidator should it go into liquidation in respect of the whole of its indebtedness to the BANK without any right on the part of the GOVERNMENT to stand in BANK'S place in respect of or to claim the benefit until the BANK has received the full amount of the BANK'S claim against the COMPANY and that this guarantee shall apply to and secure all moneys now or at any time hereafter or ultimately remaining due from or unpaid by the COMPANY.

5. This guarantee shall not be affected by the BANK'S taking or varying or giving up any securities or rights if any held by or available to it from or against the COMPANY or any other person in respect of all or any moneys covered by this guarantee and this guarantee shall not be determined or in any way affected by the winding up of the Company or the amalgamation thereof with any other COMPANY or HOWSOEVER OTHERWISE.

6. All entries in the BANK'S Books kept by it and made in the ordinary course of its banking business as may be adduced by it shall be conclusive against the GOVERNMENT of the amounts from time to time thereby appearing due from the COMPANY to the BANK and the same shall not be disputed or questioned by the GOVERNMENT.

7. Any money or moneys covered by this Guarantee shall be due and payable to the BANK on demand after requiring payment of the same shall have been delivered or sent through the post by registered letters addressed to the Secretary, Ministry of Industries, Arunachal Government.

8. This guarantee shall be a continuing guarantee irrespective of any sum or sums which may be paid into any of the account or accounts of the COMPANY with the BANK at any time during the continuance of the guarantee

and this guarantee shall remain in force until all principal and interest payable by the COMPANY to the BANK are fully paid and satisfied.

9. The GOVERNMENT hereby expressly declare that this guarantee and the powers and provisions herein contained are in addition to and not by way of limitation of or substitution of any former or other guarantee or guarantees if any heretofore given to the BANK by the GOVERNMENT and now existing uncancelled and this guarantee is not intended to and shall not revoke or limit such other guarantee or guarantees and that this guarantee shall be in addition and without prejudice to any other securities, if any, negotiable or otherwise which the BANK may now or hereafter possess from the COMPANY or any other person or persons in respect of all or any moneys secured or intended so to be and the BANK shall be under no obligation whatsoever to marshall in favour of the GOVERNMENT any such securities or any of the funds or assets that the BANK may be entitled to receive or have a claim upon and the BANK may at its own absolute discretion vary exchange renew release modify or discharge or assign all or any of such securities or instruments negotiable or otherwise and whether satisfied by payment in full or in part or not.

10. This guarantee shall bind the GOVERNMENT and its successors and shall be available to and enforceable by the BANK and its successors and assigns including any other body corporate or Company or concern by or with which the BANK may become amalgamated or absorbed and that nothing done or omitted by the BANK in pursuance of any of the powers provisions authorities or permissions contained in this guarantee shall in any way affect or discharge the GOVERNMENT'S liability under it.

11. Notwithstanding anything hereinbefore contained the GOVERNMENT'S liability under this guarantee shall not at any time exceed the sum of Rs. 3 crores and interest thereon payable by the COMPANY to the BANK and all costs and other moneys, for which the GOVERNMENT shall or may become liable to the BANK and this Guarantee shall be irrevocable and the GOVERNMENT undertakes not to revoke the same or purport to do so at any time before the BANK has received payment of all moneys hereby guaranteed as aforesaid.

IN WITNESS WHEREOF THIS guarantee has been executed for and on behalf of the Governor of Arunachal Pradesh State by Mr. V. Venkateswaran, Secretary, Industries Department this 5th day of September 2000.

For and on behalf of and under Order of
Governor of Arunachal Pradesh

Sd/- 5.9.2000

Secretary, Department of Industries,
Arunachal Pradesh

Bank Guarantee in favour of Government

THIS AGREEMENT IS MADE on this............... day of .... 2000 BETWEEN the Governor of Tamil Nadu (hereinafter called the GOVERNMENT) of the one part and TN Bank Ltd. a banking company registered under the Companies Act 1956 and carrying on business, *inter alia*, at Tamil Nadu hereinafter called the BANK (which expression shall unless the context otherwise requires include its successors) of the second part and Builders Ltd. a company registered under the Companies Act 1956 and carrying on business at P.T. Road, Chennai hereinafter called the CONTRACTOR (which term shall include unless repugnant to the context its successors).

WHEREAS Builders Ltd. has been awarded a contract for construction of a housing complex at Green Avenue, Chennai for Rs. 350 lakhs and is required to deposit security money for Rs. 35 lakhs.

AND WHEREAS in consideration of the Government having agreed to exempt the CONTRACTOR from depositing the security deposit of Rs. 35 lakhs under the terms and conditions of the Contract entered into between the GOVERNMENT and the CONTRACTOR on the contractor furnishing a Bank Guarantee for security deposit amount in favour of the GOVERNMENT for the due fulfilment by the CONTRACTOR of the terms and conditions of the agreement with the Government.

AND WHEREAS the CONTRACTOR has approached the BANK for issue of such a guarantee in favour of the GOVERNMENT on behalf of the CONTRACTOR for the performance and discharge of the obligations of the CONTRACTOR under the said contract entered into by and between the GOVERNMENT and the CONTRACTOR.

AND WHEREAS the CONTRACTOR has approached the BANK for issue of such a Bank Guarantee in favour of the GOVERNMENT and is agreeable to deposit the requisite margin money as also to execute a Counter Guarantee in favour of the BANK.

AND WHEREAS the GOVERNMENT has forwarded a draft copy of the Bank Guarantee which the CONTRACTOR has scrutinised and approved and directed the BANK to issue a Bank Guarantee in favour of the GOVERNMENT in accordance with the terms contained in the draft Bank Guarantee forwarded by the GOVERNMENT.

NOW THEREFORE THESE PRESENTS witnesseth and the parties hereby agree as follows:

1. The BANK hereby undertakes to pay to the GOVERNMENT upto Rs. 35 lakhs as may be due and payable under this Guarantee on the first demand being made without any demur irrespective of any dispute between the CONTRACTOR and the GOVERNMENT in respect of any amount of claim against the CONTRACTOR as being due by way of loss or damage caused to and suffered by the GOVERNMENT without any question as to the factum or quantum thereof provided that the liability of the BANK shall be restricted to an amount not exceeding Rs. 35 lakhs covered by the guarantee.

2. The Bank Guarantee contained herein shall remain in full force and effect for a period of 12 months from the execution hereof and that it shall continue to be enforceable by the GOVERNMENT till all the dues thereunder or by virtue of the said agreement have been duly paid and the claim will be satisfied or discharged or that the said agreement is fully carried out by the said CONTRACTOR.

3. The BANK agrees and declares that the GOVERNMENT shall have the fullest liberty without the written consent or prior approval and without affecting anything in any manner any obligation hereunder to vary any of the terms and conditions of the said agreement or to extend the time of performance by the CONTRACTOR from time to time or to postpone at any time or from time to time any of the powers exercisable by the GOVERNMENT against the CONTRACTOR and to forbear to enforce any of the terms and conditions relating to the said agreement and it is declared that notwithstanding any such variation or extension or forbearance, act, omission or indulgence on the part of the GOVERNMENT in favour of the contractor, the guarantor shall not be released of its liability by reason of any such variation, extension or acts of forbearance.

4. The BANK hereby undertakes not to revoke the guarantee during its currency except with the previous consent in writing of the GOVERNMENT.

5. Any claim for breach of the contract by the contractor or for any loss or damages suffered by the GOVERNMENT should be made by invocation of the Bank Guarantee within the validity period of the said guarantee. No claim under the guarantee shall be entertained after the expiry of the Bank Guarantee period.

6. The BANK further undertakes not to revoke the guarantee during the currency of the guarantee except with the previous consent in writing of the GOVERNMENT in case of any dispute between the CONTRACTOR and the GOVERNMENT in relation to their contract. On invocation of the Bank Guarantee the BANK would pay to the GOVERNMENT without any question as to any breach of the agreement or loss sustained or otherwise and the invocation in terms of the guarantee will be taken as final and conclusive.

IN WITNESS WHEREOF the parties herein executed these presents on the 10th day of June 2000 at Calcutta.

Signed, sealed and delivered by
TN Bank Ltd. by its authorised
agent Mr. ....
in the presence of: Signature

Government Guarantee

Guarantee by the Governor of Welfare State to Industrial Bank Ltd. for payment of the value of the debentures of X Co. Ltd.

... ...

WHEREAS the Rehabilitation Scheme for X Co. Ltd. (hereinafter called the COMPANY) submitted *inter alia* by the Government of Welfare State was accepted by the Hon'ble High Court.

AND WHEREAS in pursuance of the Rehabilitation Scheme dues of Rs. 2 crores are to be paid by the company to the Industrial Bank Ltd. (hereinafter called the BANK) by issue of debentures to the BANK for the amount carrying 12% interest per annum.

AND WHEREAS these debentures will be convertible into equity capital as soon as the first dividend is declared by the COMPANY.

AND WHEREAS the BANK expressed difficulty in accepting the terms of issue of debentures by the COMPANY unless guaranteed by the Governor of Welfare State (hereinafter called the GOVERNMENT) and the GOVERNMENT agreed to give such guarantee.

NOW THEREFORE the GOVERNMENT hereby guarantee to the BANK the payment of the debentures issued to the BANK by the COMPANY for the sum of Rs. 2 crores carrying interest at 12% per annum on the conditions as follows:

1. At any time after the COMPANY shall have made default for more than 30 days in the payment of the said principal sum or any interest GOVERNMENT shall on demand pay the same to the BANK the holder of the debentures.

2. The debenture-holder, without exonerating the GOVERNMENT may grant time or any other indulgence to the COMPANY and may assent to modification of its rights and may accept or make any composition or arrangement with the COMPANY.

3. In order to give full effect to this guarantee the debenture-holder shall be entitled to act and treat as if the GOVERNMENT was the principal debtor to the debenture holder in respect of the moneys hereby guaranteed and the GOVERNMENT hereby waives all its suretyship or other rights, if any, which are inconsistent with any of the provisions of this guarantee.

4. Under no circumstances it shall be necessary for the debenture-holder to take any steps or proceedings for enforcing its rights against the COMPANY before enforcing this guarantee against the GOVERNMENT.

5. The principal sum or any interest covered by this guarantee shall be due and payable by the GOVERNMENT to the debenture-holder on demand after notice/s requiring payment of the same shall have been delivered or sent through the post by registered letter addressed to the Secretary to the Government, Ministry of Industries.

IN WITNESS WHEREOF this guarantee has been executed for and on behalf of the Governor of Welfare State by Mr. ...., Secretary Industries Department this 5th day of July 2000.

For and on behalf of the Governor of Welfare State

Sd/- ....

Secretary, Ministry of Industries

Government of Welfare State

27

Guardianship

Introductory observation. This branch of Hindu Law was not much developed in ancient India. The Hindu sages differed in opinion as to the age of minority. The foundation of the Rule is the text of Narada.[1] In Bengal, it was held that the age of majority is the end of 15 years,[2] but the Madras High Court held that a boy or a girl is *sui juris* when he or she completes the age of 16 years.[3] This difference is now academic as under the Indian Majority Act 1875, which applies to all persons domiciled in India and to all matters except marriage, dower, divorce and adoption, a person becomes major on completion of 18 years except a ward of court and in case of appointment of statutory guardian when he or she attains the age of 21 years.[4] In England, an infant attains majority on completion of 21 years and there is some distinction between a minor and an infant for the purpose of proceedings such as divorce, probate and admiralty.[5]

The law as prevailing in ancient India vested the guardianship of minor in the sovereign as *parens patriae.*[6] This was delegated to his parents as a sacred trust. This corresponds with the law of England where the King was the protector of all infants and he used to exercise his jurisdiction through the Lord Chancellor now vested in the Chancery division of the High Court.[7] The function of the King in England as to protection of the minor's estate is exercised in India by the District Judge under the provisions of the Guardians and Wards Act 1890, as representing the State, the universal guardian of all

1 *Manu* VIII 27.
2 *Cally Churn* v *Bhuggabutty* (1873)10 BLR 231 (FB).
3 *Reade* v *Krishna* 9 Mad 391 (397).
4 The Indian Majority Act 1875, s. 3.
5 Simpson's *Law of Infants,* 4th Ed., p. 1.
6 *Manu* VIII 27, IX 146, 190, 191.
7 Halsbury's *Laws of England*, Ed. 1935, vol. 7, p. 585.

minors.[8] The said Act also provides for appointment of the Collector of the district or other local area as guardian (*vide* s. 8 of the Act). Under the principles of ancient Hindu Law, a natural guardian had very wide powers in relation to the management of estate of the minor. No relations except the parents were as a matter of right entitled to guardianship. The Bengal Minor's Act 1858, and the Bombay Minor's Act 1864 which required a certificate of administration before instituting or defending any suit by or against the minor did not intend to alter the principles but conferred certain jurisdiction on persons who chose to avail themselves. As held by the Privy Council in *Hanuman Persad Pandey* v *Massamat Babooee*[8] the power of natural and even *de facto* guardians under the Hindu Law is limited and qualified. It can be rightly exercised in the case of legal necessity and for the benefit of a minor taking into account the pressure on the estate, the danger to be averted and the benefit to be conferred upon it and the transferee should, after reasonable enquiry be satisfied as to the existence of the legal necessity in relation to the transaction. This was followed in *Jiban Krishna Dutt* v *Sailendra Nath.*[9] The proposition of law laid down by the Federal Court in *Kundamudi* v *Meyani*[10] is as follows: A natural or *de facto* guardian has no authority to impose a personal obligation on the minor or his estate but he can borrow money for the protection or for the benefit of the estate of the minor.[11] The Privy Council held in *Subramanyam* v *Subba Rao*[11] as follows: A natural guardian could, however, sell any movable in danger of deterioration, compromise any debt or claim on behalf of the minor, enter into a valid contract for sale of the minor's property but not for purchase. If possession of the property is delivered to the purchaser and no sale deed is executed, he is protected under s. 53A of the Transfer of Property Act. A natural guardian could acknowledge a debt or pay interest so as to keep the same alive for the protection or benefit of a minor's property.[12] The Guardians and Wards Act 1890, which is the first statute applicable throughout India, did not and still does not interfere with the personal laws of the parties. The legislation did not intend to sweep away all ancient laws and customs. Although the Act does not purport to preserve all the rights of the natural guardian under the Hindu Law in their original form, nevertheless it did not and till now does not make it obligatory to obtain certificate of guardianship or any order of the court to deal with the property of a minor. It saves the right of a Hindu father to appoint a testamentary guardian and the right of the husband and the father to be appointed or declared statutory guardian if otherwise fit. No other rights of the father and none of the mother are saved in the sense that the court shall give effect to it as appointment under the Act has the effect

8 (1856)6 MIA 395.
9 50 CWN 129; AIR 1946 Cal 272.
10 (1949)11 FCR 65.
11 75 IA 115.
12 Section 21(1) of the Limitation Act 1908 or s. 20 of the Limitation Act 1963.

of supersession of all powers of the natural and *de facto* guardian and they are not revived by reason of the death or removal of the statutory guardian.

A natural guardian could, therefore, deal with the property of a minor until 25th August 1956, when the Hindu Minority and Guardianship Act 1956, received the assent of the President and was put on the Statute Book. This Act is an overriding statute[13] on all texts, rule, interpretation, customs, usages and laws in so far as they are inconsistent with its provisions but supplemental to Act VIII of 1890 except in the case of repugnancy between the two when the former shall prevail. The Guardians and Wards Act applies in respect of all applications under s. 8(5) of the other Act. The principal changes effected under this statute are of three kinds: It has crystallised in statutory form as to who are only the persons authorised to act as the natural guardians[14] and testamentary guardians.[15] The mother, under certain circumstances, is competent to act as natural guardian of a son even though the father is alive.[16] It imposes restrictions on the power of the natural guardian to sell, mortgage, exchange, give lease exceeding five years or beyond one year after attainment of majority.[17] Nevertheless, even under that section a natural guardian has still power to do all acts which are necessary or reasonable for realisation, protection or benefit of the minor's estate, but never to bind the minor by a personal covenant. Further, a natural guardian can purchase any property, carry on trade, contract loans to execute necessary repairs to the property of the minor without charging the estate and also refer any dispute to arbitration.[18]

De facto guardian. A *de facto* guardian is now almost a forgotten chapter in Hindu Law as regards the property of a minor. Although his office is not abolished but his power as against the estate of the minor is almost nil. He has no right to recover debts due to a minor nor to grant any receipt or keep alive any debt by acknowledgement. Section 11 of the Hindu Minority and Guardianship Act has completely done away with all his powers to dispose of or deal with the property of a minor even for necessities or for the benefit of the minor or his estate which he could exercise under the original texts of Hindu Law. Even prior to this Act eminent jurists expressed doubt about his authority as regards sale of the minor's property. It was held by the Privy Council in *Mata Din* v *Ahmad Ali*[19] that such a guardian cannot clothe himself

13 Section 5 of Hindu Minority and Guardianship Act 1956.
14 Section 5 of Hindu Minority and Guardianship Act 1956; only parents and husbands.
15 Section 9 of Hindu Minority and Guardianship Act 1956; only those appointed by parents.
16 *Gita Hariharan* v *Reserve Bank of India* AIR 1999 SC 1149.
17 Section 8 of the Hindu Minority and Guardianship Act 1956.
18 Chaudhuri's *Hindu Minority and Guardianship Act*, Notes under s. 8, pp. 100-4.
19 (1912)39 IA 49, 55; 14 Bom LR 192.

with legal power to sell the property of a minor. Nevertheless, if he incurs debts for necessaries, the estate of the minor is liable to repay the same on principles embodied under s. 68 of the Indian Contract Act.

Testamentary guardian. Under s. 9 of the Hindu Minority and Guardianship Act 1956, the testamentary guardian is empowered with all the rights of a natural guardian and subject to all restrictions on his powers as are specified in the said Act or the will.

Guardianship for marriage. Only persons referred to in s. 6 of the Hindu Marriage Act are competent to act as such guardians.

Mahomedan law. According to Islamic law, the minority terminates on attainment of puberty which is presumed on completion of 15 years. After the passing of the Indian Majority Act, the minority continues until completion of 18 years in all matters except marriage, dower and divorce.[20] A mother has preferential right and she, under the Sunni law, is entitled to the custody of a female child until she attains puberty and of the male child until he completes the age of seven years. She is therefore the guardian of the persons of her children in that sense until they complete the required age and thereafter the father is entitled to their custody, except however in the case of her remarriage, with a stranger, immoral life, neglect of the child and other good causes[21] which disqualifies her for the sacred office. In Shia law, the period of guardianship is only two years in the case of a male child and for a female child until she attains majority. A father is also entitled to the custody of children on failure of other female relations, *e.g.*, mother's mother, full sister, full sister's daughter and others when they are under-aged, as above; he is nevertheless the legal guardian of the property of the minor although he has no power to sell except—

(*a*) when the sale fetches double the value, or
(*b*) necessary for the maintenance of the minor, or
(*c*) required to pay the debts and legacies of the deceased, or
(*d*) property falling in decay, or
(*e*) expenses exceed the income and for other good causes.[1]

A mother has no right to sell any property belonging to a minor. A *de facto* guardian has no such right and, therefore, any transfer effected by him is not only voidable but also void.[2]

Residence of the proposed guardian. Although there is no prohibition in the Act as against the appointment of a non-resident applicant except by implication as under s. 39(*b*) nevertheless the court may not approve of his appointment.[2]

20 Mulla's *Mahomedan Law,* 19th Ed., p. 285.
21 *Imambadi v Mutsuddi* (1918)45 IA 73; 45 Cal 878.
1 Baille 687, 688; Macnaghten p. 64, s. 14, pp. 305-6.
2 *Asghar Ali v Anima Begum* 36 All 280; 12 ALJ 392.

Guardianship of minors. In jurisprudence minors are described as abnormal persons. They as a rule are capable of holding and receiving property and liable for wrongful acts but incapable of entering into valid contract but not incapacitated from entering into any contract of marriage unless under the age of consent which differs in different countries.[3] The exception to rule is contract for necessities. There is no remedy in law against an infant in the case of fraudulent misrepresentation about his age, but equity requires him to restore all his ill-gotten gains.[4] The case of mortgage stands on a different footing because of his incapacity to create a mortgage.[5]

(a) *Guardian, Minor and Ward. Guardian* means a person having the care of the person of a minor or of his property, or both his person and property. *Minor* means a person who, under the provision of the Indian Majority Act, is to be deemed not to have attained his majority. *Ward* means a minor for whose person or property, or both, there is a guardian. In England, the term generally used is 'infant', but there is some difference between the terms *minor* and *infant* in certain proceedings, *viz.* probate, divorce and admiralty, the former being under 21 years and the latter under seven years.[6]

(b) *Power of testamentary guardian.*[7] Formerly where a guardian has been appointed by will or other instrument, his power to mortgage or charge, or transfer by sale, gift, exchange or otherwise, immovable property belonging to his ward, is subject to any restriction which may be imposed by the instrument, unless he has been declared guardian by the court, and the court permits him, by an order in writing, notwithstanding the restriction, to dispose of any immovable property specified in the order in a manner permitted by the order. The Hindu Minority and Guardianship Act empowers him with all the authorities of a natural guardian, subject however to all restrictions on his powers.[8] So his powers are very much restricted.

(c) *Restriction of powers of, and obligations on guardian appointed by court.* Where a person, other than a Collector or a guardian appointed by will or other instrument, has been appointed or declared by the court to be the guardian of the property of a ward, he cannot, without the previous permission of the court—

(*i*) mortgage or charge, or transfer by sale, gift, exchange, or otherwise, any part of his immovable property of his ward, or

3 Holland's *Elements of Jurisprudence (Contracts of Minors),* p. 341.

4 *R. Leslie Ltd.* v *Shiell* (1914)3 KB 607, p. 618; also see s. 65 of the Indian Contract Act.

5 *Mohori Bibi* v *Dharmadas* (1903)30 Cal 539 (PC).

6 Halsbury's *Laws of England*, Ed. 1935, vol. 17, p. 582.

7 Section 28 of the Guardians and Wards Act.

8 Section 8 of the Hindu Minority and Guardianship Act.

(*ii*) lease any part of that property for a term exceeding five years or for any term extending more than one year beyond the date on which the ward will cease to be a minor.

Permission to the guardian to do any of the above acts will not be granted by the court except in case of necessity, or for an evident advantage of the ward.[9]

Where a guardian of the property of a ward has been appointed or declared by the court, and such guardian is not the Collector, he must under s. 34 of the said Act—

(*i*) if so required by the court, give a bond, as nearly as can be, in the prescribed form to the Judge of the court to enure for the benefit of the Judge for the time being, with or without sureties, engaging duly to account for what he may receive in respect of the property of the ward;

(*ii*) if required by the court, deliver to the court, within six months from the date of his appointment or declaration, or within such other time as the court directs, a statement of the immovable property belonging to the ward, of the money and other movable property which he has received on behalf of the ward up to the date of delivery of the statement, and of the debts due on that date to or from the ward;

(*iii*) if so required by the court, exhibit his accounts in the court at such time and in such form as the court from time to time directs;

(*iv*) if so required by the court, pay to the court, at such time as the court directs, the balance due from him on those accounts, or so much thereof as the court directs; and

(*v*) apply for maintenance, education and advancement of the ward, and of such persons as are dependent on him, and for other necessities of the ward and of such persons as are dependent on him, such portion of the income of the property of the ward as the court from time to time directs, and if the court so directs, the whole or any part of the property.[10]

(d) *Removal of guardian*.[11] The court can, on the application of any person interested, or on its own motion, remove a guardian appointed or declared by the court, or a guardian appointed by will or other instrument, for any of the following causes:

(*i*) For abuse of his trust;

(*ii*) for continued failure to perform the duties of his trust;

9 Section 29 of the Guardians and Wards Act.
10 Section 34 of the Guardians and Wards Act.
11 Section 39 of the Guardians and Wards Act.

(*iii*) for incapacity to perform the duties of his trust;

(*iv*) for ill-treatment, or neglect to take proper care, of his ward;

(*v*) for contumacious disregard of any provision of the Guardians and Wards Act, or of any order of the court;

(*vi*) for conviction of an offence implying, in the opinion of the court, a defect of character which unfits him to be the guardian of his ward;

(*vii*) for having an interest adverse to the faithful performance of his duties;

(*viii*) for ceasing to reside within the local limits of the jurisdiction of the court;

(*ix*) in the case of a guardian of the property, for bankruptcy or insolvency;

(*x*) by reason of the guardianship of the guardian ceasing, or being liable to cease, under the law to which the minor is subject:

Provided that the guardian, appointed by will or other instrument, will not be removed—

(1) for the cause mentioned in cl. (*vii*), unless the adverse interest accrued after the death of the person who appointed him or it is shown that that person made and maintained the appointment in ignorance of the existence of the adverse interest, or

(2) for the cause mentioned in cl. (*viii*), unless such guardian has taken up such a residence as, in the opinion of the court, renders it impracticable for him to discharge the functions of a guardian.

(e) *Cessation of guardian's authority.*[12] The powers of a guardian of a minor cease:

(*i*) by his death, removal, or discharge;

(*ii*) by the Court of Wards assuming superintendence of the person and property of the minor;

(*iii*) by the ward ceasing to be a minor;

(*iv*) in the case of a female ward, by her marriage to a husband who is not unfit to be her guardian;

(*v*) in the case of a ward whose father was unfit to be the guardian of the minor, by the father ceasing to be so.

(*f*) *Penalties.*[13] The following are the penalties to which the guardians are liable:

(*i*) if, for the purpose or with the effect of preventing the court from exercising its jurisdiction with respect of a ward, a guardian

12 Section 41 of the Guardians and Wards Act.

13 Sections 44 and 45 of the Guardians and Wards Act.

appointed or declared by the court removes the ward from the limits of the jurisdiction of the court, he will be liable to fine not exceeding Rs. 1,000 or to imprisonment in the civil jail for a term not exceeding six months;

(*ii*) if a person having the custody of a minor fails to produce him or cause him to be produced when required by the court to do so, or

(*iii*) if a guardian appointed or declared by the court fails to deliver to the court when required to do so by the court a statement of the immovable property money and other movable property of, and the debts due to or owing from, the ward, or to exhibit accounts, or to pay into the court the balance due from him on those accounts, or

(*iv*) if a person who has ceased to be a guardian fails to deliver any property or accounts of the court,

the person or guardian will be liable to fine not exceeding Rs. 100, and in case of recurrency, to a further fine not exceeding Rs. 10 for each day of default, and not exceeding Rs. 500 in all, and to detention in civil jail until he undertakes to obey the order of the court.

(g) *When minor attains majority.* In order to specify the age of majority, the Indian Majority Act 1875 has since been amended by the Indian Majority (Amendment) Act 1999[14] which received the assent of the President on 16th December 1999. By the amendment ss. 3 and 4 of the 1875 Act have been substituted by the following section:

"3. *Age of majority of persons domiciled in India.* (1) Every person domiciled in India shall attain the age of majority on his completing the age of eighteen years and not before.

(2) In computing the age of any person, the day on which he was born is to be included as a whole day and he shall be deemed to have attained majority at the beginning of the eighteenth anniversary of that day".

A minor is incompetent to act as guardian of any minor except his own wife or child, or, where he is the managing member of an undivided Hindu family, the wife or child of another minor member of that family.

Where a minor girl child after death of her mother lived with her maternal grandfather and its father as well as the maternal grandfather married for the second time, for the purpose of custody of the child step mother is to be preferred to step grandmother. As regards ill-treatment by step mother and the father having better means to support the family and give education to the child and to look after the interest and welfare of the child, custody cannot be denied to the father.[15] Where a child's mother committed suicide

14 Act 33 of 1999.

15 *N. Palaniswami* v *A. Palaniswamy* AIR 1998 Mad 264.

as its father developed illicit connexion with the maidservant and left a letter about it suggested giving custody of the child to a colleague of her instead of the father, the court respected the last wish of the mother and custody was denied to the father.[16]

A mother had two children both being minor. She left the house of her husband taking with her the younger son. Later she left that son in the custody of another person when she went outstation. The husband throughout looked after the elder son properly—and he was gainfully employed. The wife had no independent income and considering her conduct, custody of the younger son was given to the husband.[17] When a couple obtains divorce by mutual consent and under a mutual agreement the mother takes custody of the child with a periodic stay with father it is not proper to disturb that mutual arrangement on the mere allegation by the wife that the father had ill-treated the child and seek interim custody of the child.[18] The paramount consideration being the welfare of the minor, the fixed deposit money in the name of the minor should be allowed to continue till he attains majority.[19] Unless it is proved that the father is guilty of cruelty or of immorality he cannot be removed from the guardianship of his minor child more so because he is the natural guardian of the minor.[20] When divorce proceeding is pending between the parties arrangement of the child remaining with the mother and the father visiting the child once in a week is reasonable and should not be disturbed by giving over the custody of the child to the father.[21]

(h) *Right of guardian to custody of wards.* If a ward leaves or is removed from the custody of a guardian of his person, the court, if it is of opinion that it will be for the welfare of the ward to return to the custody of his guardian, can make an order for his return, and, for the purpose of enforcing the order, can cause the ward to be arrested and to be delivered into the custody of the guardian. For the purpose of arresting the ward, the court can now exercise the power conferred on any District Magistrate, Sub-Divisional Magistrate or a first class Magistrate under s. 100 of the Code of Criminal Procedure (Act 2 of 1974) which came into force from 1st April 1974. The residence of a ward against the will of his guardian with a person who is not his guardian does not, of itself, terminate the guardianship. In case of the guardian appointed or declared by the court, it has very wide power under s. 25 of the Guardians and Wards Act (Act VII of 1890) to recover the custody of the ward.

16 *S. Thirumavalavan* v *Natarajan* AIR 1998 Mad 281.
17 *Narbada* v *Sita Ram* AIR 1998 Raj 113.
18 *Shyam Sunder* v *Sunita* AIR 1998 Del 153.
19 *Prahallad* v *Anadi* AIR 1997 Ori 201.
20 *Pravat* v *Dilip* AIR 1997 Cal 326.
21 *Tara Devi* v *Mahaveer Singh* AIR 1997 Raj 87.

Where the father, though in sound financial position, never attempted to meet the child and befriend him since the wife left him with the child the father is not entitled to the custody of the child even though the wife was living as a concubine of another person.[22]

FORMS

Petition for Guardianship of a Minor

(Section 10 of the Guardians and Wards Act)

Act VIII of 1890 Case No. ...... of ....

In the matter of the Guardians and Wards Act 1890

And

In the matter of appointment of the guardian of GH minor residing at .... Application under s. 10 of the Guardians and Wards Act

The humble petition of .... (state full name and address)

MOST RESPECTFULLY SHEWETH:

The above-named applicant respectfully begs to state as follows:

(*a*) The name, sex, religion, date of birth and ordinary residence of the minor;

(*b*) where the minor is a female, whether she is married and if so, the name and age of her husband;

(*c*) the nature, situation and approximate value of the property, if any, of the minor;

(*d*) the name and residence of the person having the custody or possession of the person or property of the minor;

(*e*) what near relations the minor has, and where they reside;

(*f*) whether a guardian of the person or property or both of the minor has been appointed by any person entitled, or claiming to be entitled, by the law, to which the minor is subject, to make such appointment;

(*g*) whether an application has at any time been made to the court, or to any other court with respect to the guardianship of the person or property or both of the minor and, if so, when, to what court, and with what result;

22 *Jacob Mathew* v *Maya Philip* AIR 1999 Ker 192.

(*h*) whether the application is for the appointment or declaration of a guardian of the person of the minor, or of his property, or of both;

(*i*) where the application is to appoint a guardian, the qualifications of the proposed guardian;

(*j*) where the application is to declare a person to be a guardian, the ground on which that person claims;

(*k*) the causes which led to the making of the application; and

(*l*) such other particulars, if any, as may be prescribed, or as the nature of the application renders it necessary to state.

Verification as in Plaint

DECLARATION

I, AB, the above-named applicant, declare that I am ready willing to act as the guardian of the person and property of the minor.

ATTESTING WITNESSES: 1. AB
2. CD

N.B. As to Rule of Verification see Code of Civil Procedure, Or. VI, r. 15. The application must be supported by an independent affidavit. *Sarala Sundari* v *Hazari* (1915)42 Cal 953. The law giving right to apply must be quoted in the heading of the application (in the matter of *Govind Prasad* 50 All 709).

Petition for Permission to Sell Minor's Property under the Guardians and Wards Act

Act VIII of 1890 Case No. ....

In the Court of the District Judge .... at ....

In the matter of the Guardians and Wards Act VIII of 1890

And

In the matter of s. 29 of the said Act

And

In the matter of AB, a minor resident at ....

And

In the matter of permission to sell the said minor's property.

The humble petition of CD, the certificated guardian of the said minor

The applicant above-named states as follows:

1. That by an order made the .... day of .... your petitioner was appointed guardian of the person and properties of the minor CD. The said order is still in force and virtue and your petitioner is administering the estate of the said minor as his statutory guardian. Your petitioner has kept proper account of the said estate up to date and filed the same in court from which it will appear that the funds in the hands of your petitioner is Rs. .... only.

2. That at the date of appointment the estate of the minor which consists of *inter alia* one-fourth share in premises No. ...... was indebted to one XY of No. .... to the extent of Rs. .... being, his proportionate share of liability under a mortgage dated .... executed by the father of the minor which now comes to Rs. .... inclusive of interest calculated up till ....

3. That the said XY who instituted a suit being Title Suit No. .... of .... in the court of .... for enforcement of the said mortgage and obtained the preliminary decree for Rs. .... on the .... day of .... is now threatening to apply for final decree for sale of the property.

4. That in the circumstances aforesaid and in the best interest and for the benefit of the said minor, your petitioner and other co-sharers of the said minor who are liable to pay three-fourths share of the said debt, have agreed to sell the property for the sum of Rs. .... privately which would leave a margin of Rs. .... in their hands after satisfaction of the mortgage debt out of which a sum of Rs. .... will come in the hands of your petitioner being the proportionate share of the said minor in the surplus sale proceeds. An affidavit by the intending purchaser of the property for Rs. .... is filed herewith.

5. That the residential house of the said minor, *viz.*, premises No. .... is in urgent need of repairs without which the same will be unfit for habitation and unless certain urgent repairs are immediately executed a portion thereof may also collapse very shortly. The estimated costs of such repairs are Rs. .... as will appear from the certificate of the engineer hereunto annexed and marked A. The minor has no resources to execute the said repairs at present as appearing from the account filed as aforesaid.

6. That the market value of the property intended to be sold would be Rs. .... as will appear from the certificate of the valuer hereunto annexed and marked B, and the same at present fetches no income.

7. That this application is made *bona fide* and in the interest of and for the benefit of the minor.

Your petitioner therefore prays:

(*i*) Leave be granted to your petitioner to sell the undivided one-fourth share of the minor in the property described in Schedule A to .... or any other person or persons at a price not less than Rs. .... and to execute and register the necessary conveyance.

(*ii*) Your petitioner be at liberty to redeem the proportionate mortgage debt of the minor in respect of the said premises out of the proceeds of such sale and apply the balance towards the costs of repairs to the residential house of the said minor.

(*iii*) Further order or orders be made and directions given, as may appear just and proper and your petitioner as in duty bound shall ever pray.

THE SCHEDULE

Verification

I, AB, son of .... aged about .... years residing at .... by occupation service do hereby solemnly affirm and say as follows:

I am the petitioner above-named. I know and I have made myself acquainted with the facts and circumstances of this case and I am able to depose thereto.

The statements in paragraphs 1 to 7 and the Schedule hereinabove of the petition are true to my knowledge based on information derived from records in my possession, proceedings before this Learned Court. Orders and Valuation Report and believed by me to be true and that I have not suppressed any material fact.

The statements hereinabove are true to my knowledge.

I sign this verification on this .... day of .... 1999.

Before me Signature of AB

Notary Signature of Advocate

N.B. There shall be two affidavits from two independent persons as to what is the estimated value of the property and the benefit and advantage of the intended sale.

Application for Permission under the Hindu Minority and Guardianship Act

IN THE COURT of the District Judge of ....

Misc. Application No. .... of ....

Re: AB minor, aged ...., residing at .... by his natural/ testamentary guardian ....

XY Age .... Profession .... residing at .... *Applicant*

In the matter of an application for permission for sale/mortgage/lease of the immovable property of the said minor under s. 8 of the Hindu Minority Act (32 of 1956).

The humble petition of XY residing at No. ....

Most Respectfully Sheweth:

1. AB (State the name, sex, religion, date of birth and ordinary residence of the minor).

2. That the minor being a Hindu governed by the .... School of Hindu Law is governed by the Hindu Minority and Guardianship Act (XXXII of 1956).

3. That your petitioner is the natural guardian of the minor, according to s. 6 of the said Act, being related to the minor as his/her (state relationship, *i.e.*, legitimate or illegitimate son or daughter or husband, or adopted son).

Or

That your petitioner is the testamentary guardian of the minor, appointed under the will of the minor's father or mother named .... dated .... and produced herewith (state whether the probate has been granted or not).

A copy of the said will is herewith annexed and marked A.

4. That your petitioner is still fully competent to act as the natural (or testamentary) guardian of the minor, under the said Act or any other provisions of law.

5. No court has appointed or declared any other person as the guardian of the minor's person or property under the Guardians and Wards Act.

6. That the following are the near relations of the said minor:

(State names, addresses and relationship).

7. The applicant seeks permission for the disposal of the minor's immovable property by way of (state sale, mortgage, lease, etc.) described below:

(Give description of the property).

8. (State the necessity for the transaction).

(*a*) Where the sale or mortgage or lease is intended for the discharge of the debts (the particulars of each debt and the nature of the supporting documents should be separately specified).

(*b*) If the amount is needed to meet the present and future expenses, *e.g.*, education costs, maintenance, marriage expenses, payment of income-tax, Corporation rates and taxes, repair of any building, full particulars shall be given.

9. (State how the transaction is for the benefit and advantage of the minor or his or her estate).

10. (Where the natural guardian entered into an agreement of the sale of the property, mention that fact and state that the copy of the agreement is attached herewith).

11. (State the estimated market value of the property for the disposal of which the permission is sought. Report of the valuer to be annexed).

12. That in the circumstances aforesaid and in the ends of justice your petitioner submits that the court might be pleased to grant permission for the disposal (state the nature of disposal required) of the above immovable property of the minor which is situated within the jurisdiction of the court.

13. That the application is made *bona fide* and in the interest and for the benefit of the minor.

Your petitioner prays for (*i*) an order for sale/mortgage/lease of the said property stating the necessity or advantage of the transaction, (*ii*) such further order/s be made and direction/s given as may appear just and proper.

And your petitioner as in duty bound shall ever pray.

Verification

I, XY .... guardian of the minor AB, the applicant herein, do hereby declare and state that the statements contained in paragraphs I to II of the above petition are true to my knowledge and those contained in paragraphs 12 and 13 are my submissions before this court.

Signed at .... on the .... day of 1999

Attested by us   Sd. XY

N.B. It is always better that the petition shall be accompanied by two affidavits from independent persons stating what in his opinion is the value of the property proposed to be dealt with and the best manner of disposal thereof in the interest of minor and also the circumstances of the minor and the necessity and advantage of the disposition—Ghosh: *Rules of the Calcutta High Court,* 5th Ed., Ch. XXX, p. 199. An affidavit from a valuer approved by the court with his report annexed is most helpful.

Petition for Appointment of Guardian

In the Court of Civil Judge (Senior Division)

At Alipore

Guardianship Case No. .... of 1999

In the matter of:

MB, a minor under the age of 18 years residing at 1 Construction Road, Calcutta

And

In the matter of:

PN residing at ....
.... *Petitioner*

Versus

1. RS, residing at ....

2. RT, residing at ....
.... *Respondents*

Application under s. 10 of the Guardians and Wards Act 1890 for appointment of a Guardian of the Minor

The humble petition of the petitioner above-named most respectfully

SHEWETH:

1. MB above-named is the son of PQ. The said PQ was a businessman and was residing at .... The said PQ died on 15th June 1999 at his residence at .... The mother of MB predeceased PQ. Your petitioner was a close friend of the deceased.

2. The said MB is a minor born on 1st May 1989. He is now approximately 10 years of age.

3. The said minor is residing with his distant relative at ....
....

4. The said minor is entitled to, in his own right, several assets and properties, namely, moneys covered by two Life Insurance Policies No. 1 and 2 for Rs. 10,000 and Rs. 20,000 respectively in the name of his deceased father and in respect of which the minor is the nominee. There are two Fixed Deposits with X Bank Ltd. for Rs. 50,000 and Rs. 80,000 and the said Receipts are in the joint names of the said deceased and the minor and the moneys thereunder are payable to "either or survivor". The premises No. ....also belongs to the minor by inheritance.

5. The said minor is governed by the Hindu Law.

6. The other relatives of the said minor are the following:

(*a*) RS brother of the said deceased, residing at ....;

(*b*) QT, the brother's son of the deceased residing at ....

7. The guardian of the person or property of the said minor has not been appointed either by Will of the said PQ or by court. In fact, the said PQ has died intestate.

8. GP the proposed Guardian is a serviceholder and is the maternal uncle of the minor. He is married and is at present residing at .... The said GP is financially well-off having a monthly income of

Rs. 5,000. He is of a good character and habits. He is a fit and proper person to be appointed the guardian of the person and property of the said minor.

9. There is no person quite fit or in a position to look after the welfare of the minor or to protect and preserve the assets and properties of the minor.

10. The moneys receivable under the deceased's Life Insurance Policies and the Fixed Deposit Receipts are to be collected and properly invested. The minor in his own right is entitled to a property being premises No. .... which is tenanted. This property has to be repaired and the rents have to be collected. There is some urgency in the matter.

11. The minor has to be properly educated and for that purpose admitted to a good school. At present there is nobody suitable to look after his education and welfare, assets and properties. The maternal uncle is a teacher and can devote time and energy for the welfare of the minor.

12. In view of the aforesaid the present application is being made for the benefit of and in the interest of the minor.

13. Unless Orders are made as prayed for herein, the minor will be seriously prejudiced.

14. This application is being made *bona fide* and in the interest of Justice.

Your petitioner therefore humbly prays Your Honour for the following Orders:

(*a*) Mr. GP or some other fit and proper person be appointed as the Guardian of the person and properties of the said minor MB;

(*b*) Security to be furnished by said GP or the guardian may be fixed at Rs. 1 lakh and Mr. X and Mr. Y be accepted as Sureties for the said GP;

(*c*) A sum of Rs. 3,000 a month be fixed for the maintenance and education expenses of the minor;

(*d*) Rs. 500 per month be allowed to the said GP as the remuneration in respect of collection of rents, moneys and assets of the minor and investments thereof and for looking after the minor;

(*e*) The said guardian to be appointed herein be given liberty to invest the moneys of the minor in an appropriate safe manner;

(*f*) The said GP be given liberty to carry out the repairs of the tenanted premises and to take proper steps for realisation of arrear and current rents;

(*g*) The costs of this application be directed to be paid out of the income of the minor;

(*h*) Further Orders be made and directions be given as to this Learned Court may deem fit and proper to afford complete relief to the petitioner.

And your petitioner as in duty bound, shall ever pray.

Verification

I, PN, son of NP aged about 30 years and the petitioner above-named know the facts and circumstances of this case and I am able to depose thereto. The statements contained in paragraphs No. 1 to 14 hereinabove are true to my knowledge based on information derived from the documents shown to me and also the information derived from the mother of the minor and from my personal association with the deceased and I believe them to be true.

Place: Calcutta

Date .... Signature of the Petitioner

Identified by Advocate for the petitioner

DECLARATION OF GP

I, the undersigned GP, the Maternal Uncle of the minor residing at .... do hereby agree to accept the office of the Guardian of the person and property of the minor MB son of PQ of ...., in case this Learned Court shall think fit to appoint me as the Guardian of the minor.

Signature of the GP

Identified by Advocate

28

Hire-Purchase

A contract of hire falls within bailment governed by s. 148 of the Contract Act and subsequent sections in Chapter IX of the said Act. Hire-purchase contract is a form of hire contract where the hire is payable by instalments and the hirer has the option to purchase the goods or become the owner of the goods on making certain payments. As the very name indicates, it is a process of purchasing or acquiring title to the goods through a hiring contract. Exchange in the form of barter was the most primitive type of deal in commodities which afterwards became sale and purchase with the introduction of money as the medium of exchange. This single transaction in course of time broke itself up piecemeal and took the form of hire-purchase. In England, Parliament passed the Hire-Purchase Act 1938 (Statutes 1 and 2 Geo 6c 53). This was followed by the Hire-Purchase Act 1965. There was no such Act in India uptil 1972. A Bill modelled with necessary modifications on the Hire-Purchase Act 1965 in England was introduced in the Parliament. The Hire-Purchase Act XXVI of 1972 passed by the Parliament received the assent of the President on June 1972 and was to have come in force on 1st September 1973.

A hire-purchase agreement has two elements (*i*) element of bailment, and (*ii*) element of sale in the sense that it contemplates an eventual sale when the intending purchaser fulfils the terms of sale. So it is different from a sale in which the price is to be paid later by instalments. In case of such a sale, the property passes as soon as the sale is made. In case of hire-purchase agreement, the property in the goods does not pass when the agreement is made but only when the option is finally exercised.[1]

Although under the common law contractual rights are not assignable, the hirer under a hire-purchase agreement can lawfully assign his interest in

1 *K.L. Johar & Co.* v *Deputy Commercial Tax Officer* AIR 1965 SC 1082.

Equity, the vendee taking the interest subject to the terms and stipulation of the agreement.[2]

A hire-purchase agreement is drafted in the form settled in *Helby* v *Mathews*[3] like a hire contract with a special clause about the option to purchase. It is the leading case on the subject. About the special condition it should be noted that it is an agreement to hire, but it gives the hirer an option to purchase. It should be clearly stipulated that the property shall not pass till all the instalments are paid. The "hire" is therefore a fiction only and the purchase is the test. As observed by Lord Denning in *Bredge* v *Compell Discount Co. Ltd.*,[4] it is in effect, though not in law, a mortgage of the goods. Maitland in his *Lectures on Equity*[5] observed it as the worst type of mortgage deed.

It is usual to insert a minimum clause providing that in the event of determination of the agreement, the hirer shall be liable to pay 50 per cent of the price after deduction of the instalments already paid.

FORMS

Hire-Purchase Agreement

AN AGREEMENT made this .... day of .... BETWEEN AB etc. (hereinafter called the OWNER), of the one part and CD etc. (hereinafter called the HIRER), of the other part, WHEREAS IT IS AGREED as follows:

1. The OWNER will let and the HIRER will take on hire the goods and effects mentioned and comprised in schedule hereto annexed, for the term of .... months (or years) from the date hereof, at a rent of Rs. .... to be paid by instalments in the manner hereunder stated subject nevertheless the termination clause hereunder contained.

2. The HIRER has already paid to the OWNER the sum of Rs. .... being the first month's rent (the receipt of which sum the OWNER hereby acknowledges), and the HIRER shall continue to pay to the OWNER a further sum of Rs. .... per month, as instalment of such rent on the .... day of each succeeding month during the said term, the next payment to be made on the .... day of ....

2 *Standard Credit Corporation* v *Subramanian* (1966)1 MLJ 457.
3 (1895) AC 771.
4 (1962)1 All ER 385.
5 2nd Edition 1949 at p. 182.

3. The HIRER shall, until and unless all instalments of rent are paid keep and maintain all the said goods and effects in good order and condition and preserve them against loss or injury by theft etc. (reasonable wear and tear only excepted), and make good all damages whether accidental or otherwise, and at all times allow the OWNER, his agents or servants to inspect the same whenever demanded. In the event of the goods being damaged or destroyed beyond repairs or replacement or lost by fire, theft or any other cause, the hirer shall nevertheless remain liable for and pay the OWNER all remaining instalments due on the goods.

4. The HIRER shall not, without the owner's previous written consent, remove or permit removal of the said goods and effects from the above address of the HIRER; such consent shall not be unreasonably withheld.

5. The HIRER shall not—until and unless he becomes the full owner—sell, assign nor encumber or subject the goods or suffer any decree or order of any court whereby the goods or any portion thereof may be attached or charged, encumbered or otherwise seized or taken in execution nor commit any act of insolvency nor enter into any scheme or composition with his creditors.

6. The HIRER shall punctually and regularly pay or cause to be paid the rates and taxes payable by him in respect of the premises, where the said goods and effects may for the time being be kept, and if any such rates and taxes shall not be paid on the exact day whereon the same shall become due, this agreement shall thereupon and thereby stand terminated even without notice or demand.

7. If the HIRER fails and/or neglects to carry out any of the terms of this agreement, the OWNER may (without prejudice to his right to recover any arrears of rent and damages for breach of this agreement) terminate the hiring and retake possession of the said goods and effects, whether the same shall be in the possession of the HIRER or of any other person, and for that purpose the hirer hereby gives the OWNER, his agents or servants all facilities to enter in or upon any premises occupied by the HIRER, to search for, seize and retake possession of all the said goods and effects without being liable in any way for any action for trespass or otherwise or at all.

8. Notwithstanding anything hereinbefore contained, the HIRER may terminate this agreement at any time by surrender and return of the said goods and effects to the owner but nevertheless he shall remain liable for the balance of instalments still to be paid.

9. The HIRER may, at any time during the term of hiring, become the absolute OWNER of the goods and effects hereby hired by paying to the OWNER all arrears of rent (if any) and all rents which would become due on this agreement during the said term without any discount or deduction *or*, subject to a discount of .... per cent, on all payments stipulated.

10. The HIRER shall keep the goods insured against fire, theft, injury, accident and also third party risks in the name of the OWNER *or* in their joint

names and regularly and punctually pay each premium as and when the same shall become due.

11. Any time concession or indulgence granted or shown on the part of the OWNER will not prejudice his rights under this agreement.

12. (*To be added in case of guarantee to the performance of the hire*). In consideration of the delivery of the goods to the hirer I, EF, son of etc., stand surety for the hirer for due performance of the terms and conditions of this agreement and shall remain liable to the OWNER for payment of all sums as and when shall be due and payable by the HIRER as rent, damages, costs, charges and expenses or on any other account under and by virtue of this agreement.

AND I FURTHER DECLARE THAT any time indulgence, forbearance, waiver or variation of the terms of this agreement shall not operate as a discharge of my liability as surety under these presents.

IN WITNESS HEREOF the parties hereto have executed these presents on the day, month and year first above-written.

Signed, sealed and delivered by AB

Signed, sealed and delivered by CD

Signed, sealed and delivered by EF

WITNESS:

Hire-Purchase of Printing Machinery

THIS AGREEMENT of Hire-Purchase is made this .... day of .... BETWEEN X Co. Ltd. registered under the Companies Act 1956 having its registered office at .... (hereinafter called the COMPANY which term shall include its successors) of the one part and CD son of .... residing at .... carries on business under the name and style of CD & Co. (hereinafter called the HIRER) of the other part.

WITNESSETH:

1. That the COMPANY hereby agrees to let to the HIRER and the HIRER hereby agrees to take on hire from the COMPANY the (*description of the printing machinery*) (referred to as the MACHINERY) for the purpose of carrying on the HIRER'S business of printers at (*place*) for .... months from the date of delivery of the same upon the terms and conditions herein contained.

2. That the HIRER shall pay to the company as hire charges of the MACHINERY the sum of Rs. .... as follows: *viz*., the sum of Rs. .... to be paid on the execution of this agreement and the balance of Rs. .... to be paid in .... equal monthly instalments of Rs. .... each, the first of

such instalments to be paid on the......... day of........... 1999 and the remaining instalments on the 10th day of every succeeding calendar month thereafter.

3. That if the HIRER shall fail to pay any of the said stipulated instalments on the respective dates on which the same should be paid as hereinbefore mentioned then the HIRER shall pay, interest on the amount in arrears until payment thereof at the rate of .... per cent per annum.

4. That the HIRER shall, on the execution of this agreement, execute and deliver to the COMPANY promissory notes or bills of exchange for the respective amounts of the said instalments payable hereunder and such notes or bills shall respectively be made payable on the dates on which such instalments are respectively payable under this agreement and shall bear interest at the said rate of .... per cent per annum after the due dates. The said bills shall be deemed to be collateral security for the payment of the said instalments and shall not suspend or affect any other remedy or remedies of the company hereunder.

5. That the HIRER shall not, during the continuance of this agreement, in any way sell, assign, sublet or otherwise part with the possession of the MACHINERY or any part or parts thereof or remove the same from one building to another or attempt so to do or part with possession of their interest in the premises where the MACHINERY is kept, without first informing the company of such intended removal and receiving its consent in writing to do so. The machinery shall at all times be at the risk of the HIRER who shall bear any loss arising from destruction, loss thereof or damage thereto howsoever caused and who shall take all reasonable care thereof so long as the agreement for hiring remains in force and shall permit the COMPANY or its agents at all reasonable times to inspect the same; and if at any such inspection any part or parts of the MACHINERY shall be found broken, damaged or destroyed, the HIRER shall forthwith at his own expenses, and to the satisfaction of the COMPANY, replace and repair the parts so broken, damaged or destroyed. The HIRER shall not at any time during the said period purchase any parts as may be required to be used with or in connection with the MACHINERY except from the COMPANY, who shall from time to time supply the same at their ordinary prices current in (*name of place*) at the respective dates when such parts are required.

6. That the HIRER shall punctually pay all rents, rates and taxes payable in respect of the premises wherein the MACHINERY or any part thereof is kept and shall, upon demand, produce to the COMPANY or its agents the receipts for the said rents, rates and taxes and in the event of the same being in arrears, the company is hereby empowered to pay the same together with any expenses necessary for the purpose and the HIRER shall on demand repay the COMPANY any sums so paid.

7. That the HIRER shall at all times during the continuance of the hiring keep in a conspicuous position on the MACHINERY such plate or plates as the COMPANY may approve of for denoting that the machinery is the property of

the COMPANY and the HIRER shall not remove or obliterate any such plates or allow the same to be removed or obliterated.

8. That the COMPANY/HIRER shall insure the MACHINERY against fire in a recognised fire insurance office in the sum of Rs. .... and shall if required produce to the ...... for his or its inspection the policy of insurance and the receipts of the premiums paid (and the HIRER shall on demand repay to the COMPANY the premiums paid by it).

9. That if any of the instalments of hire or any part thereof shall be in arrear and unpaid for one calendar month after the same shall have become due, or if the HIRER shall at any time fail or neglect to perform or observe any of the stipulations or provisions herein contained and on his part to be performed and observed, or if a warrant of attachment or seizure shall be issued or executed against any of the property of the HIRER, or if a receiver shall be appointed of any of the assets of the HIRER, then and in any such case the COMPANY may even without notice to the HIRER terminate the agreement of hiring hereby made and may by its servants or agents, without any previous notice to the HIRER, enter upon and into any premises or building where the MACHINERY or any part or parts thereof may be and seize and take possession of and remove the same to such place as the COMPANY may think fit notwithstanding any payments previously made by the HIRER; and for that purpose leave and licence are hereby given to the COMPANY, its agents and servants or any other person employed by it, to break open and enter any building, premises or place where the said MACHINERY may be or be supposed to be and take possession of the same without being liable to any suit, action or other proceeding by the HIRER or any other person claiming under him.

10. That if the agreement of hiring shall be determined under the preceding clause hereof, the COMPANY shall not be liable to any claim or demand at the instance of any person whosoever in respect of any payments previously made by the HIRER, all of which shall in every such case as aforesaid be absolutely forfeited to the COMPANY and the COMPANY shall further be entitled to recover from the HIRER or his estate all such instalments (*if any*) or hire aforesaid as may then be in arrears with interest thereon as aforesaid and also the instalment payable during the month in which the determination shall take place and in addition thereto such sum (*if any*) as shall be required with the money so to be paid for hire (exclusive of interest) and the sum previously paid for hire (exclusive of interest) to make up a sum equal to 60 per cent of the said amount of Rs. .... payable as hire under clause 2 hereof and the COMPANY shall also be entitled to recover from the HIRER or his estate all costs and expenses incurred in or about the entry, seizure and removal as hereinbefore provided under this agreement and the HIRER shall not nor any person claiming through him, commence or maintain any action or proceeding against the COMPANY, its servants or agents by reason of the COMPANY taking possession of the MACHINERY or the temporary possession of the premises where the MACHINERY or any part thereof may then be for such time as may be reasonably required in the removal of the same.

11. That the HIRER may determine the agreement of hiring hereby made upon giving to the COMPANY one calendar month's previous notice in writing of his intention so to do specifying the date on which the hiring is to terminate and upon delivering up at his own cost the MACHINERY to the COMPANY on or before that date in good repair at the godown of the COMPANY at (*place*); provided that the HIRER shall at the same time pay to the COMPANY all moneys payable hereunder up to that date and in addition such sum (*if any*) as with the sums then and previously paid for hire (exclusive of interest) shall be required to make up a sum equal to 60 per cent of the total amount of Rs. .... payable as hire under clause 9 hereof.

12. That if the hiring hereby constituted shall be determined under clause 2 or clause 11 hereof, the COMPANY shall, upon payment by the HIRER of all sums payable under clause 10 or 11 hereof, as the case may be, return to the HIRER duly cancelled such of the notes and bills mentioned in clause 4 hereof as shall not at the time of such payment have fallen due.

13. That upon payment by the HIRER to the COMPANY of the full sum of Rs. .... and interest (*if any*) payable hereunder on the days and in manner aforesaid, the hiring shall cease and determine and the MACHINERY shall thenceforth be and become the sole and absolute property of the HIRER; but until such payment the MACHINERY shall remain the sole and absolute property of the COMPANY but let on hire to the HIRER.

Signed by the said .... (COMPANY) by and through .... duly authorised in that behalf under a power-of-attorney/resolution (date and description of the power-of-attorney or the resolution) in the presence of:

1. ....
2. ....

Signed by the said ....
(HIRER) in the presence of:

1. ....
2. ....

Hire-Purchase Agreement for Machinery for the Garden

THIS INDENTURE IS MADE this 30th day of September 2000 BETWEEN AB Ltd., a company registered under the Companies Act 1956 and having its office at .... in the town of .... hereinafter called the OWNER (which term shall unless excluded by or repugnant to the subject or context be deemed to include its successors) of the one part, Darjeeling Tea Ltd., a company registered under the Companies Act 1956 having its Registered Office at .... in the town of .... being the OWNER of a Tea Garden/Tea Factory in the District of Darjeeling hereinafter called the HIRER (which term shall unless excluded by or repugnant to the subject or context be deemed to include its successors) of the other part.

WHEREAS the OWNER carries on business of Hire-Purchase and lets out plants and machinery required by particular business organisation.

AND WHEREAS the HIRER is the owner of a Tea Garden/Tea Factory known as Darjeeling Tea Estate.

AND WHEREAS the HIRER with a view to improving the production of tea in its garden is desirous of installing machinery and equipment in its garden/ factory but does not have the necessary funds with which to purchase the same.

AND WHEREAS the HIRER has applied to the OWNER for obtaining the plants and machinery on Hire-Purchase basis.

AND WHEREAS the OWNER has agreed to supply the HIRER the requisite plant and machinery on Hire-Purchase on terms and conditions mentioned herein.

NOW THIS INDENTURE WITNESSETH and it is hereby agreed and declared by and between the parties as follows:

1. The OWNER shall purchase the specified plant, machinery and equipment described in the Schedule hereunder written (hereinafter called the MACHINERY) at such time in such manner and on such terms and conditions as the OWNER thinks fit. The HIRER has agreed to the description and specifications of the MACHINERY. The estimated total cost of the said machinery is Rs. 5,20,000. To the said amount shall be added estimated amount of all charges, expenses, freight, insurance charges, customs duty, sales tax including central sales tax, if payable, bank charges, charges for technical supervision of installation of the MACHINERY by the Suppliers/ Manufacturers or Engineers nominated by them and cost and expenses of installation in the case of driers, withering equipment, C.T.C. machine, roller equipment, dust extraction plant, oil burning equipment and steam engines and all other usual charges and expenses and interest on all moneys spent by the owner as hereinafter mentioned.

2. The OWNER shall let to the HIRER and the HIRER shall take on hire from the OWNER the said machinery or such of them as may be available after the purchase aforesaid.

3. The HIRER has paid as earnest money to the OWNER on the 20th day of September 2000 a sum of Rs. 60,000 (Rupees sixty thousand only) being approximately 10% of the estimated amounts of charges, expenses, etc. mentioned in clause 1 hereof.

4. The HIRER shall also pay to the OWNER the further sum of Rs. 60,000 (Rupees sixty thousand only) being 10% of the cost of MACHINERY and of charges, expenses, etc. mentioned in clause 1 hereof immediately on completion of installation of all the MACHINERY which are available in the opinion of the OWNER such opinion being final and binding on the parties provided however that payment of the said further sum of Rs. 60,000 (Rupees sixty thousand) shall in any event be made within 9 months from

the date of completion of delivery. In the case of loss or destruction of MACHINERY or any part thereof after delivery as mentioned in clause 6 hereof but prior to installation the time taken in obtaining MACHINERY or parts for replacing those lost or destroyed shall not be taken into account for the purpose of calculating time for completion of delivery of MACHINERY.

5. Immediately on receipt of advice from the suppliers the OWNER will send intimation to the HIRER that the machinery or equipment are ready for inspection and the HIRER shall send a representative to accompany the Owner's Engineer when the latter goes to inspect the machinery or equipment. The inspection should normally be carried out in Calcutta within three days from the date of advice that the equipment is ready. Should the representative of the HIRER fail to attend the inspection, such inspection will be held by the Engineer of the OWNER and his report will be final and binding on the HIRER. Immediately after such inspection a copy of the specification and inspection certificate will be sent to the HIRER.

6. Each MACHINERY or equipment or part thereof shall be deemed to be delivered to the HIRER as soon as each Railway Receipt, Bill of Lading or Air Consignment in respect thereof is delivered to it by or on behalf of the OWNER and delivery shall be completed or deemed to be completed as soon as the Railway Receipt, Bill of Lading or Air Consignment note in respect of the last machinery or equipment which in the opinion of the OWNER is available, is delivered to the HIRER.

7. The HIRER shall pay the OWNER without demand during each year the sum of Rs. 50,000 (Rupees fifty thousand only) (being approximately $^1/_8$th of the balance of the amount, charges etc. mentioned in clause 1 hereof) by way of hire rent for the said MACHINERY, the first of such payment to be made after one year from the date the payment of 10% under clause 4 hereof becomes due and payable and every subsequent payment during the next 7 years to be made on the like day of each and every succeeding year provided further that in the event of one-eighth of the total cost of the MACHINERY together with all charges, expenses, freight, insurance charges, customs duty, sales tax, central sales tax, if any, bank charges, costs and expenses of installation and all other usual charges and expenses and interest being less than or exceeding the said sum of Rs. 50,000 (Rupees fifty thousand only) the amount of yearly payment shall be proportionately reduced or increased.

8. In arriving at the amount of balance payable, interest has been calculated on the amount spent by the OWNER (after deducting the amount received by the OWNER under clause 3 hereof) from the date the same has been incurred at the rate of 12% (twelve percent only) per annum and such interest has been added to each of the yearly amounts hereinbefore mentioned and calculated upto the date of each payment. In the event of non-payment of any yearly amount on the respective due date the HIRER shall be bound to pay the additional interest on the amount which is in default at the rate of 2% per month or part thereof but without prejudice to

the right of the OWNER to enforce all other rights and power under this agreement or under law.

9. The OWNER hereby agrees that so long as the HIRER shall perform its obligations under this agreement and this agreement shall be subsisting the HIRER shall on payment of the full amount paid by the OWNER for purchasing the MACHINERY and all charges, expenses, freight, insurance charges, customs duty, State sales tax, Central sales tax, bank charges and all other expenses incurred by the OWNER in respect of the said machinery plus a margin of 20% have the option of purchasing all the MACHINERY at any time before the entire amount due to the OWNER has been fully paid. If the HIRER shall exercise such option the OWNER will give the HIRER credit against such purchase price to the extent of all payments which have been made by the HIRER under the provisions of clauses 3, 4 and 7 hereof, but until such price and expenses and the charges herein mentioned shall have been paid in full, the MACHINERY shall remain absolutely the property of the OWNER. The HIRER shall in addition pay all sales tax that may be payable for such sale and all other amounts due under this clause.

10. The HIRER shall at its own expenses transport each machinery equipment or part thereof immediately on arrival thereof at the railway station, steamer ghat, or air port of destination from the said railway station, steamer ghat or air port to its tea garden where the MACHINERY are to be installed and shall within 3 days of each such arrival at railway station, steamer ghat or air port, send intimation in writing by registered post to the OWNER of such arrival and of the arrangement made by it for such transport. The HIRER shall after receipt of the Railway Receipt, Bill of Lading or Air Consignment note in respect of such machinery send written intimation at least once every week as to whether the MACHINERY has reached the railway station, steamer ghat or air port of the destination or not.

11. Within 20 days from the date of receipt of the MACHINERY or any part thereof in the tea garden of the HIRER where they are to be installed the HIRER shall deliver by registered post a report to the OWNER about the condition thereof and shall point out therein any defect in the condition thereof. If the HIRER fails to deliver such report within 20 days from the date of receipt of each machinery or any part thereof it shall be presumed that the MACHINERY and every part thereof is in good condition and no complaint about the condition of the MACHINERY or any part thereof shall be entertained after the said period of 20 days and the HIRER shall be deemed to have waived all objections regarding the MACHINERY and the condition thereof.

12. The manufacturers of all machinery and equipment normally guarantee their products against faulty materials and/or workmanship for a period of six months except in the case of scientific instruments which must be tested immediately on arrival at destination. The guarantee operates from the date of arrival of the MACHINERY or equipment at destination. Items

of proprietary manufacture such as electric motors, switch gear, control gear, etc. are guaranteed only by the makers of the equipments. The OWNER does not give any guarantee whatsoever in respect of the MACHINERY or equipment but the HIRER shall be entitled to the benefit of the guarantees given by the manufacturers or makers and to enforce the same.

13. All machinery or equipment shall be insured by the supplier in their own name against the following risks *viz*. theft, pilferage, non-delivery, rain or fresh water damage, breakages and denting, strikes, riot or civil commotion, the cover to begin from the time of despatch and to continue until delivered at final destination. The HIRER shall not have any claim against the OWNER for any loss of or damage to the MACHINERY or equipment.

14. Each machinery after arrival at the tea garden shall be installed therein with reasonable speed and the HIRER shall once in every fortnight from the date of such arrival send intimation to the OWNER about the progress of installation of each machinery until completion of such installation. Erection of driers, withering equipment C.T.C. machine, roller equipment, steam engines, etc. shall be carried out by the manufacturers or suppliers otherwise their guarantee will be voidable.

15. A brass plate showing that the said machinery belongs to the OWNER company shall be affixed on each machine, the cost, if any, of such plate being borne by the OWNER and the plate shall not be removed by the HIRER so long as the said machinery remain the property of the OWNER.

16. It shall be lawful for the OWNER and all persons authorised by it at all times to enter upon the said tea garden/tea factory or any other place where the said machinery may be or believed to be for the purpose of examining the same.

17. The HIRER hereby agrees with the OWNER that until payment of the entire amount due to the OWNER in the manner herein provided:

(*a*) The MACHINERY shall be kept in good and serviceable order and condition and the HIRER shall maintain and protect the same from loss and damage by fire or accident, inundation, pilferage or any other cause whatsoever. The said machinery shall at all times remain at the risk of the HIRER and it shall be liable for all losses and damages thereto howsoever caused.

(*b*) The said machinery and each and every one of them shall be kept in the possession of the HIRER at the said Tea Garden/Tea Factory or at such other address as the HIRER may by writing authorise free from distress, execution or other legal process whatsoever and the HIRER shall on no occasion sell, mortgage, pledge, assign, let or otherwise deal with nor shall the HIRER part with possession thereof or any portion thereof.

(*c*) All rents, rates, taxes and other outgoings payable by the HIRER in respect of the said tea garden/tea factory shall be fully and punctually paid and discharged by the HIRER and the current receipt therefor shall be produced before the OWNER by the HIRER on demand.

(*d*) The MACHINERY shall be used for the purpose of production and manufacture of tea only and for no other purpose whatsoever save with the previous consent of the OWNER in writing.

18. The MACHINERY and equipment imported from outside India have been obtained by the OWNER under an Actual Users Licence and it is a condition of this agreement that the HIRER shall observe and perform all the terms and conditions of the Actual Users Licence not only so long as the OWNER remains the OWNER of the said imported MACHINERY and equipment but also after the HIRER becomes the owner on full payment of the purchase money and the HIRER shall even after becoming the OWNER use the MACHINERY and equipment solely for the purposes for which the same were purchased and no portion thereof shall be sold or used or permitted to be used by any other person or for any other purpose.

19. It is hereby declared that the OWNER has entered into this Agreement upon the express declaration by the HIRER and HIRER hereby expressly warrants that the said tea garden/tea factory in which the said MACHINERY are to be located are free from mortgage, encumbrances, *lis pendens* and other charges whatsoever except in favour of its Bankers for cash credit facilities.

20. The HIRER shall not so long as any money remains due and payable to the OWNER under the provisions hereof create or purport or agree to create any mortgage or charge on the said tea garden/tea factory or any of the lands and buildings thereof without previous consent in writing of the OWNER.

21. The HIRER shall keep the MACHINERY insured from the date of arrival at destination against damages or loss by fire, accident, pilferage, riot, civil commotion or such of them as the OWNER from time to time require, in the sum of Rs. 6,00,000 (Rupees six lakhs only) or such less sum as the OWNER may direct with some insurance office of repute to be approved by the OWNER in the joint names of the HIRER and the OWNER. The HIRER shall duly and punctually pay all premia for such policies of insurance at least 20 days before the same becomes due and shall produce to the OWNER or to its representatives all receipts for such premia paid on such policies of insurance at least 10 days before the same becomes due.

22. If any MACHINERY or any portion thereof be lost or damaged all moneys received or receivable in respect of the MACHINERY from the Insurance shall be received by the OWNER who may apply the same either in making good the damage done and/or in replacing the said MACHINERY by other articles of similar description and value and such substituted articles shall become subject to the provisions of these presents in the same manner as the MACHINERY for which they have been substituted. The OWNER may instead if

it so desires apply the money in whole or in part in payment of the amounts payable by the HIRER under the provisions of clause 7 hereof whether it has fallen due or not.

23. If the HIRER shall make default in punctual payment of any instalment payable under the provisions of clause 7 hereof or any interest due thereunder or goes into liquidation or be wound up or a petition for its winding up is filed or the HIRER amalgamates with any company or enters into any composition or a scheme or arrangement with its creditors or any distress or execution is levied or a Receiver is appointed on any of its properties or assets or if the HIRER fails to observe or perform any of the terms and conditions herein contained and on its part to be observed and performed then and in any of such cases it shall be lawful for the owner in addition to its other rights and powers hereunder forthwith to terminate this agreement and to forfeit all payments made by the HIRER to the OWNER if any and also to enter upon the said tea garden/tea factory or any other places where the said machinery might be located or believed by the OWNER or its officer to be located and if necessary to break open any door or locks and to take possession of the MACHINERY and to remove the same without being liable to any action for trespass or otherwise whatsoever. All costs of taking possession and of removal thereof shall be paid by the HIRER to the OWNER.

24. The OWNER may at its option extend the due date for the payment of any instalment under clause 7 hereof but such extension shall not in any event exceed six months from the date fixed under the said clause. Such extension shall be subject to such terms and conditions as the OWNER may in its absolute discretion determine, including payment of additional interest at the rate of 2% per month or part thereof for the period of the extension.

25. If the OWNER shall grant to the HIRER any time or indulgence the same shall not affect or prejudice any of the rights or powers of the OWNER hereunder.

26. In the event of the OWNER terminating this agreement and taking possession of the machinery for any cause whatsoever the OWNER shall be entitled to sell the MACHINERY by private treaty or public auction or by any other means at its discretion, and if the net resale proceeds of the MACHINERY fall short of the balance outstanding on the HIRER'S account the resultant loss shall be made good by the HIRER.

27. All rights and powers of the OWNER hereunder may be exercised by a Director or any other officer thereof authorised by the Managing Director from time to time.

The Schedule

One Kirloskar 50 KW, 72 KVA, 400/230 Volts, 3 phase, 50 cycles, 4 wire, 8 power factor, self-regulating diesel alternator set complete with Model JH 6, tank-cooled, six cylinder in line, vertical cold starting, etc. etc. complete in all respects.

IN WITNESS WHEREOF the parties herein have executed these presents on the day, month and year first above-written.

Signed, sealed and delivered by
Mr. .... pursuant to
Board Resolution dated ....
of AB Ltd. in the presence of: Signature

Signed, sealed and delivered by
Mr. .... pursuant to
Board Resolution of Darjeeling
Tea Ltd. in the presence of: Signature

Hire-Purchase Agreement for Transport Vehicles

THIS INDENTURE MADE THIS 18th day of September 2000 BETWEEN ELH Ltd., a company registered under the Companies Act 1956 and having its registered office at .... hereinafter called the OWNER (which term shall unless excluded by or repugnant to the subject or context be deemed to include its successors) of the first part, AND Transport Co. Ltd., a company incorporated under the Companies Act 1956 and having its registered office at .... being the OWNER of a fleet of vehicles carrying on Transport business hereinafter called the HIRER (which term shall unless excluded by or repugnant to the subject or context be deemed to include its successors) of the second part; AND Mr. XY of .... hereinafter called the GUARANTOR (which expression shall unless repugnant to the context be deemed to include his heirs, executors, administrators and legal representatives) of the third part.

WHEREAS the HIRER is the owner of a fleet of Transport vehicles AND WHEREAS the HIRER with a view to facilitate its transportation business has applied for hire purchase of a Jeep described in the Schedule hereunder and the GUARANTOR has requested the OWNER to supply the same to the HIRER on a hire purchase agreement being these presents and on the terms and conditions herein contained.

AND WHEREAS the OWNER at the request of the HIRER and the GUARANTOR has agreed to supply on hire purchase the Jeep described in the Schedule hereunder written on the terms herein contained.

NOW THIS INDENTURE WITNESSETH and it is hereby agreed and declared by and between the parties to these presents as follows:

1. The OWNER of the Jeep with fittings, tools and accessories spare parts more particularly described in the Schedule hereto which are of the value of

Rs. 2,55,000 (Rupees two lakhs fifty five thousand only) and hereinafter collectively called the VEHICLE agree to let and the HIRER agrees to hire the vehicle from the date of taking delivery, subject to the terms and conditions herein contained.

2. The HIRER has paid as earnest money to the OWNER on the 5th day of September 1999 the sum of Rs. 51,000 (Rupees fiftyone thousand only) which sum shall on the signing of this agreement become the absolute property of the OWNER.

3. The balance of the value of the Jeep mentioned in clause 1 hereof after deducting the amount already paid as indicated in clause 2 above (hereinafter called the principal amount) shall be paid by the HIRER in five equal annual instalments, the first of such instalments to be paid on the first anniversary of the date of delivery of the vehicle and the subsequent instalments on the like day in each subsequent year. Provided however the OWNER may at its absolute discretion extend the due date for payment of any instalment but such extension shall not in any event exceed 3 months and such extension shall be subject to such terms and conditions as the OWNER may determine including payment of additional interest for the period of extension.

4. Besides the instalment mentioned in clause 3 above, the HIRER shall also pay commencing from the date of delivery of the vehicle interest at the rate of 15% per annum on the balance sum of Rs. 2,04,000 payable yearly, the first of such payment to be made on the First Anniversary of the date of taking delivery and the subsequent payments on the like day of each and every year. If the HIRER shall pay to the OWNER interest on the principal amount (after deducting the earnest money) or so much thereof that may remain outstanding from time to time regularly on or before the date on which interest is made payable under these presents and perform and observe all the covenants and conditions herein contained, and on the part of the HIRER to be observed and performed and the balance of the said amount shall not have been called in by the OWNER then in that case the OWNER shall at the time of receipt of interest on the principal amount for the time being due and owing at the rate of 15% per annum grant to the HIRER a rebate of 0.5 per cent per annum for the year in which interest is regularly and punctually paid as aforesaid on the said amount or the balance thereof. In the event of nonpayment of any yearly amount on any of the respective due dates the HIRER shall pay additional interest on the amount which is in default at the rate of 1% per month or part thereof but without prejudice to the right of the owner to enforce all other rights and powers under this agreement or under law.

5. If the HIRER shall duly perform and observe all the terms and condition contained in this Agreement and on his part to be performed and observed and shall in the manner aforesaid pay the principal amount to the OWNER by yearly instalments as aforesaid and shall also pay to the OWNER interest as herein mentioned and all other sums of money which may become payable

to it by the HIRER under this Agreement the hiring shall come to an end and the vehicle shall at the option of the HIRER become his property and the OWNER will assign and make over all its right, title and interest in the vehicle to the HIRER, but until such payments as aforesaid have been made the vehicle shall remain the absolute property of the OWNER.

6. If the OWNER shall grant to the HIRER any time or indulgence the same shall not affect or prejudice any of the rights or powers of the OWNER hereunder.

7. The GUARANTOR in consideration of the OWNER agreeing to let the vehicle to the HIRER, hereby guarantees the due performance and observance by the HIRER of the terms and conditions of this Agreement and agrees to pay on demand any money due or which may become payable under this Agreement (and not paid by the HIRER) either by way of debt or damages, costs or expenses and further agrees that any time granted to the HIRER or any indulgence given in respect of the terms and conditions herein either in the shape of releasing or regiving the vehicle after seizure to the HIRER or in any other manner, shall not prejudice the OWNER'S rights nor relieve the GUARANTOR from his Guarantee and that it shall not be necessary upon the HIRER being granted any such concession or indulgence as aforesaid for the OWNER to give any notice to the GUARANTOR in respect thereof. The GUARANTOR further agrees that the OWNER'S rights on the vehicle or right to seize the same shall not be destroyed by reason of any judgment, decree or order obtained against the HIRER or himself or both.

8. The HIRER agrees with the OWNER as follows:

(*a*) To keep the vehicle in thorough working order and good condition and to make no alteration thereon or addition thereto without the written consent of the owner first had and obtained. The cost of body-building or extended chasis made with such permission of the OWNER shall be done by the HIRER at his own cost after taking delivery of the same. And it is agreed that in the event of this Agreement being terminated by the OWNER such additions or alterations as aforesaid shall be deemed to be the absolute property of the OWNER provided always that the HIRER shall not have or be deemed to have any authority to pledge the credit of the OWNER for repairs, alterations and additions.

(*b*) To indemnify the OWNER against loss by reason of damage to or destruction or loss of the vehicle from any causes whatsoever or by reason of claims by third parties in respect of the same.

(*c*) To keep the OWNER notified with his address and the address of the premises where the vehicle is kept and any change of the same as soon as made.

(*d*) To allow the OWNER'S representatives free access at all reasonable time to inspect the vehicle or to take possession of the same as hereinafter mentioned.

(*e*) To have the vehicle registered in the joint names of the owner and the HIRER in the State of West Bengal and not to sell, mortgage, pledge hypothecate hire or otherwise deal with the vehicle, not to part with possession of vehicle, not to remove it out of the State of West Bengal without the express written permission of the OWNER previously obtained also not to use the vehicle for any purpose other than that declared in the original application. The HIRER shall not use or allow it to be used for carrying any prohibited goods or smuggled goods.

(*f*) To pay all fees and taxes, payable in respect of the vehicle as and when the same becomes due.

(*g*) To keep the vehicle properly insured covering all sorts of risks under a comprehensive Policy of Insurance with an Insurance Company as would be approved by the OWNER in writing in the joint names of the OWNER and HIRER and in case of any accident to the vehicle the HIRER shall make his own arrangements for getting the vehicle repaired and shall duly claim the charges from the Insurer. In any case, the OWNER should not be made liable for payment of any damage/compensation due to any accident committed by the vehicle to any third party.

(*h*) To pay all expenses, premia for Insurance etc. in case the OWNER insures the vehicle in default of so doing by the HIRER.

(*i*) To return to the OWNER the permit, the Registration Certificate and all other certificates granted by Registering or any Controlling Authority in respect of the vehicle in the event of termination of the hire.

(*j*) To declare to the Registering Authority that the vehicle is subject to this Agreement and to have necessary endorsement to the effect made by the said Authority, but this in no way will affect or prejudice the OWNER'S rights under this Agreement.

9. The HIRER agrees to pay to the OWNER all sums due for taxes, fees, repairs and to suppliers which may be due from HIRER to the OWNER in respect of the vehicle but the provisions shall not in any way affect or prejudice the right of the OWNER as provided herein to recover possession of the vehicle and to determine this agreement on default of payment of any of the hire payments. It is further agreed that the payment of hire monies and other sums due under this Agreement is not subject to suspension or delay by reason of the vehicle requiring or undergoing repairs or being suspended by any traffic authority or by reason of delay in registration of the vehicle or its non-registration, or by reason of delay or non-receipt of the permit by the HIRER or of the pendency of an insurance claim or by any cause or reason whatsoever.

10. The HIRER acknowledges that he holds the vehicles as a bailee of the OWNER and shall not have any proprietary right or interest as purchaser

therein until he shall have paid the whole amount due under this agreement or under any term thereof and exercised his option of purchase as herein provided.

11. The OWNER may terminate, with or without notice, the contract of hiring and forthwith retake and recover the possession of the vehicle:

(*a*) If any annual hire amount or part thereof or any interest thereon or part thereof is in arrear and left unpaid for a period of seven days after the date fixed for its payment for any reason whatsoever and particularly notwithstanding any claim which the HIRER may have in respect of insurance.

(*b*) If the HIRER fails to keep the vehicle insured as herein provided.

(*c*) If the HIRER commits or suffers any other breach to the conditions and obligations herein stipulated to be observed and performed by him or does anything or suffers any act to be done which in the opinion of the OWNER may prejudice its title to the vehicle.

(*d*) If the HIRER omits to inform the owner within 48 hours of any accident which causes either damage to the vehicle, bodily injury to any third party or damage to any other vehicle or property.

(*e*) If the HIRER goes into liquidation or is wound up, allows the vehicle to be seized in distress or execution or under any other process of law.

Any such termination shall be without prejudice to the claims the OWNER may have in respect of any terms or conditions of this Agreement and it is further agreed that if the hiring is terminated by the OWNER or by the hirer in the manner herein provided all hire (and damages for the breach of this Agreement) upto the date of such termination shall be paid by the HIRER to the OWNER and no payment, credit or allowance, in respect of payment previously made shall be made or allowed to the HIRER. All costs of taking possession of the vehicle shall be paid by the HIRER to the OWNER.

12. The OWNER shall have the right to dispose of the vehicle after re-possession in any manner it thinks fit by private sale or re-hire without any notice to the HIRER and at any price that the OWNER may think fit. If on such sale the net amount realised is less than the balance of principal amount and interest due from the HIRER, the HIRER shall pay the short fall.

13. This agreement shall be treated as revised in case the vehicle after re-possession by the OWNER for any breach committed in respect of this agreement by the HIRER, is returned to the HIRER at his request in writing.

14. If the vehicle supplied by the OWNER is insured by the OWNER then the HIRER will, if he is not in default with his payment be granted such benefits as the OWNER may derive from the insurance in respect of claims. Such insurance shall not absolve the HIRER from his liability under

condition 11(*b*) hereof provided always that in the event of the vehicle being destroyed or being so extensively damaged as to be in the opinion of the Insurance Company a total loss, then and in that case the amount recoverable under the Insurance Policy shall be applied in the first place in paying all monies due by way of arrears of hire and thereafter if the same received by the OWNER under such policy shall exceed the balance of the amount due after deducting all sums previously paid by the HIRER for the hire including the amount paid under clause 2 of the Agreement then such excess shall be paid by the OWNER to the HIRER.

15. The HIRER shall pay on demand all expenses incurred by the OWNER in collecting or attempting to take possession of the vehicle from the HIRER or any other person using or possessing the same.

16. The grant of any time, or indulgence to the HIRER as provided in this agreement or otherwise including the acceptance of any payments after the due dates thereof shall not operate to affect or prejudice the OWNER'S rights against the HIRER or the GUARANTOR under this Agreement.

17. The HIRER has examined or caused to be examined the vehicle and satisfied himself thoroughly about the same. The delivery receipt passed by him regarding the vehicle has been accepted by him as duly fitted, equipped and according to contract. No claim on part of the HIRER shall be admissible and no warranty on the part of the OWNER as to quality or state of vehicle or the model of the vehicle or the accessories or spare parts supplied thereto or as to their fitness for any purpose shall be deemed to have been made or implied.

18. The HIRER and the GUARANTOR hereby declare that the statements made by them in the application with respect to their means, property and other assets are absolutely true and correct and that it is by these statements that they have induced the OWNER to enter into this Agreement.

Schedule

One Mahindra CJ 4A /4 WD Jeep

Universal fitted with petrol engine with
six Ply tyres and standard equipments.

IN WITNESS WHEREOF the parties herein have executed these presents on the day, month and year first above-written.

Signed, sealed and delivered by
Mr. .... a director of
The Transport Co. Ltd. pursuant
to Board Resolution dated 5th
September 2000 in the presence of: Signature

1. ....
2. ....

Signed and delivered by Mr. XY the said GUARANTOR in the presence of: Signature

1. ....
2. ....

Signed, sealed and delivered by Mr. .... a Director of ELH Ltd. pursuant to the Board Resolution dated 6th September 1999 in the presence of: Signature

1. ....
2. ....

29

Insolvency

In India, the law of insolvency is contained in two enactments, *viz.*, the Presidency Towns Insolvency Act 1909, which applies to the Presidency Towns (Bombay, Calcutta and Madras) and the Provincial Insolvency Act 1920, which applies to the mofussil, *i.e.*, the whole of the rest of India except Part B States and the schedule districts. Over and above these two statutes certain rules made by various High Courts under the rule-making power granted them by s. 112 of the Presidency Towns Insolvency Act and s. 70 of the Provincial Insolvency Act supplement the law of insolvency in India. These rules contain important provisions with regard to practice and procedure in insolvency. Both the Presidency Towns Insolvency Act and the Provincial Insolvency Act are based on the English Bankruptcy Law inasmuch as many of the provisions of the latter are incorporated in each of former statutes. The decisions on the English Bankruptcy Acts are considered whenever necessary in constructing the provisions of the Indian statutes.

Difference between Indian and English Bankruptcy Laws. In India the insolvency law differs from the law in England in two respects. In England, bankruptcy procedure is divided in two stages.

The court in England generally issues a 'receiving order' on a bankruptcy petition being filed. In the result all the property and assets of the debtor vest in the official receiver. The object of a 'receiving order' is to give the creditors an opportunity to decide as to whether their debts should be liquidated in bankruptcy as against the property of the debtor or, in the alternative, whether a scheme or composition is feasible under the circumstances of the case. If the creditors choose to accept the second alternative, the receiving order stands vacated. If, however, the creditors decide the other way, then and in such an event the court would pass the usual adjudication order.

The other noteworthy distinction between the two systems of law is that in England, bankruptcy administration is entrusted to two officers, *viz.*, the official receiver and the trustee in bankruptcy. The duty of the former is to collect, realise and distribute the property of the bankrupt, and the latter officer is to investigate the conduct of the debtor and report the same to the court. This bifurcation of functions is extremely useful. It helps the court to concentrate more attention on the conduct and dealings of the bankrupt with regard to his property prior to bankruptcy. This is a problem in India by reason of combining both the above functions in one officer only, *viz.* the Official Assignee.

"Insolvent" debtor, when debtor can petition—contents of petition. A person is insolvent who has ceased to pay his debts in the usual course of business, or who is incapable of paying them.

A debtor is not entitled to present an insolvency petition unless he is unable to pay his debts and—

(*i*) his debts amount to five hundred rupees; or

(*ii*) he is under arrest or imprisonment in execution of the decree of any court for the payment of money; or

(*iii*) an order of attachment in execution of such a decree has been made, and is subsisting, against his property.

A debtor in respect of whom an order of adjudication made under the Provincial Insolvency Act has been annulled, owing to his failure to apply, or to prosecute an application for the discharge, is not entitled to present an insolvency petition without the leave of the court by which the order of adjudication was annulled. Such court will not grant leave unless it is satisfied either that the debtor was prevented by any reasonable cause from presenting or prosecuting his application, as the case may be, or that the petition is founded on facts substantially different from those contained in the petition on which the order of adjudication was made.

Every insolvency petition under ss. 10 and 13 of the Provincial Insolvency Act which corresponds to ss. 14 and 15 of the Presidency Towns Insolvency Act and the Insolvency Rules of the High Courts presented by the debtor must *inter alia* state—

(*i*) that the debtor is unable to pay his debts;

(*ii*) the place where he ordinarily resides or carries on business or personally works for gain, or if he has been arrested or imprisoned, the place where he is in custody;

(*iii*) the court (if any) by whose order he has been arrested or imprisoned, or by which an order has been made for the attachment of his property; together with particulars of the decree in respect of which any such order has been made;

(*iv*) the amount and particulars of all pecuniary claims against him, together with the names and residences of his creditors so far as they are known to or can by the exercise of reasonable care and diligence be ascertained by him;

(*v*) the amount and particulars of all his property, together with—

(1) a specification of the value of all such property consisting of money;

(2) the place or places at which any such property is to be found; and

(3) a declaration of his willingness to place at the disposal of the court all such property save in so far as it includes such particulars (not being his books of account) as are exempted by the Civil Procedure Code, or by any other enactment from liability to attachment and sale in execution of a decree;

(*vi*) a statement whether the debtor has on any previous occasion filed a petition to be adjudged an insolvent, and (where such a petition has been filed)—

(1) if petition has been dismissed, the reasons for such dismissal, or

(2) if the debtor has been adjudged an insolvent, concise particulars of the insolvency, including a statement whether any previous adjudication has been annulled and, if so, the grounds therefor.

Who can present insolvency petition—Acts of insolvency. If a debtor commits an act of insolvency, an insolvency petition can be presented either by a creditor or by the debtor, and the court can make on such petition an order of adjudication adjudging him insolvent.

A debtor commits acts of insolvency in each of the following cases:

(*i*) if, in India or elsewhere, he makes a transfer of all or substantially all his property to a third person for the benefit of his creditors generally;

(*ii*) if, in India or elsewhere, he makes a transfer of his property, or of any part thereof, with intent to defeat or delay his creditors;

(*iii*) if, in India or elsewhere, he makes any transfer of his property, or of any part thereof, which would, under the insolvency law or any other law for the time being in force, be void as a fraudulent preference if he were adjudged an insolvent;

(*iv*) if, with intent to defeat or delay his creditors—

(1) he departs or remains out of India;

(2) he departs from his dwelling-house or usual place of business or otherwise absents himself;

(3) he secludes himself so as to deprive his creditors of the means of communicating with him;

(*v*) if any of his property has been sold in execution of the decree of any court for the payment of money;

(*vi*) if he petitions to be adjudged an insolvent under the provisions of the insolvency law;

(*vii*) if he gives notice to any of his creditors that he has suspended, or that he is about to suspend payment of his debts; or

(*viii*) if he is imprisoned in the execution of the decree of any court for the payment of money.

For the purpose of acts of insolvency, the act of an agent may be the act of the principal.

When creditor can petition[1]—secured creditor's option. A creditor will not be entitled to present an insolvency petition against a debtor unless—

(*i*) the debt owing by the debtor to the creditor, or, if two or more creditors join in the petition, the aggregate amount of debts owing to such creditors amounts to five hundred rupees, and

(*ii*) the debt is a liquidated sum payable either immediately or at some future time, and

(*iii*) the act of insolvency on which the petition is grounded has occurred within three months before the presentation of the petition.

No insolvency petition can be presented against any corporation or against any association or company registered under any law for the time being in force. Every insolvency petition presented by a creditor or creditors must set forth the place where the debtor ordinarily resides, or carries on business or personally works for gain, and if he is arrested or imprisoned, the place where he is in custody,[2] and must also specify—

(*i*) the act of insolvency committed by such debtor together with the date of its commission; and

(*ii*) the amount and particulars of his or their pecuniary claim or claims against such debtor.

If the petitioning creditor is a secured creditor, he must in his petition either state that he is willing to relinquish security for the benefit of the creditors in the event of the debtor being adjudged insolvent, or give an

1 *See* section 12 of the Presidency Towns Insolvency Act.

2 *See* section 3 of the Presidency Towns Insolvency Act which applies only to High Court and section 3 of the Provincial Insolvency Act which applies only to District Court and subordinate courts expressly invested with insolvency jurisdiction.

estimate of the value of the security. In the latter case, he can be admitted as a petitioning creditor to the extent of the balance of the debt due to him after deducting the value so estimated in the same way as if he were an unsecured creditor.

When insolvent's property vests in court.[3] On the making of an order of adjudication, the whole of the property of the insolvent debtor vests in the court or in a receiver, and becomes divisible among the creditors, with the exception of some property allotted by the court for his maintenance and the maintenance of his family.

Discharge, refusal of absolute discharge.[4] A debtor can, at any time after the order of adjudication, and must, within the period specified by the court, apply to the court for an order of discharge, and the court will, after considering the objections of any creditor and, where a receiver has been appointed, the report of the receiver—

(*i*) grant or refuse an absolute order of discharge; or

(*ii*) suspend the operation of the order for specified time; or

(*iii*) grant an order of discharge subject to any conditions with respect to any earnings or income which may afterwards become due to the insolvent, or with respect to his after-acquired property.

The court will refuse to grant an absolute order of discharge on proof of any of the following facts:

(*i*) that the insolvent's assets are not of a value equal to eight annas in the rupee on the amount of his unsecured liabilities, unless he satisfies the court that the fact that the assets are not of a value equal to eight annas in the rupee on the amount of his unsecured liabilities has arisen from circumstances for which he cannot justly be held responsible;

(*ii*) that the insolvent has omitted to keep such books of account as are usual and proper in the business carried on by him, and as sufficiently disclose his business transactions and financial position within the three years immediately preceding his insolvency;

(*iii*) that the insolvent has continued to trade after knowing himself to be insolvent;

(*iv*) that the insolvent has contracted any debt provable under the Provincial Insolvency Act without having at the time of contracting

3 *See* section 17 of the Presidency Towns Insolvency Act and section 28(2) of the Provincial Insolvency Act.

4 *See* section 41(2) of the Provincial Insolvency Act and section 38(2) of the Presidency Towns Insolvency Act.

any reasonable or probable ground of expectation that he would be able to pay it;

(*v*) that the insolvent has failed to account satisfactorily for any loss of assets or for any deficiency of assets to meet his liabilities;

(*vi*) that the insolvent has brought on, or contributed to, his insolvency by rash hazardous speculations, or by unjustifiable extravagance in living, or by gambling or by culpable neglect of his business affairs;

(*vii*) that the insolvent has, within three months preceding the date of the presentation of the petition, when unable to pay his debts as they became due, given an undue preference to any of his creditors;

(*viii*) that the insolvent has on any previous occasion been adjudged an insolvent or made a composition or arrangement with his creditors;

(*ix*) that the insolvent has concealed or removed his property or any part thereof, or has been guilty of any other fraud or fraudulent breach of trust.

Effect of order of discharge.[5] An order of discharge releases the insolvent from all debts provable under the Insolvency Act, except from the following:

(*i*) any debt due to the Crown;

(*ii*) any debt or liability incurred by means of any fraud or fraudulent breach of trust to which he was a party;

(*iii*) any debt or liability in respect of which he has obtained forbearance by any fraud to which he was a party; or

(*iv*) any liability under an order for maintenance made under the Code of Criminal Procedure.

An order of discharge will not release any person who, at the date of the presentation of the petition was a partner or co-trustee with the insolvent, or was jointly bound or had made any joint contract with him or any person who was surety for him.

Avoidance of voluntary transfer.[6] Any transfer of property not being a transfer made before and in consideration of marriage or made in favour of a purchaser or encumbrancer in good faith and for valuable consideration is, if the transferor is adjudged insolvent on a petition presented within two

5 *See* section 45 of the Presidency Towns Insolvency Act and section 44 of the Provincial Insolvency Act.

6 *See* section 55 of the Presidency Towns Insolvency Act and section 53 of the Provincial Insolvency Act.

years after the date of the transfer, voidable as against the receiver and can be annulled by the court.

Annulment of adjudication of insolvency.[7] Where in the opinion of the court, a debtor ought not to have been adjudged insolvent, or where it is proved to the satisfaction of the court that the debts of the insolvent have been paid in full, the court will, on the application of the debtor or of any other person interested, by an order in writing, annul the adjudication.

Schedule of creditors. When an order of adjudication has been made, all persons alleging themselves to be creditors of the insolvent in respect of debts provable under the Provincial Insolvency Act must tender proof of their respective debts by producing evidence of the amount and particulars thereof, and the court will, by order, determine the persons who have proved themselves to be creditors of the insolvent in respect of such debts and the amount of such debts, respectively, and will frame a schedule of such persons and debts. Provided that if, in the opinion of the court, the value of any debt is incapable of being fairly estimated, the court can make an order to that effect, and thereupon the debt will not be included in the schedule.

Any creditor of the insolvent can, at any time before the discharge of the insolvent, tender proof of his debt and apply to the court for an order directing his name to be entered in the schedule as a creditor.

Penalties. If a debtor, whether before or after the making of an order of adjudication—

(*i*) wilfully fails to perform the duties imposed on him of producing all books of account, giving such inventories of his property, and such lists of his creditors and debtors and of the debts due to him from them respectively, submitting to such examination in respect of his property or his creditors attending at such times before the court or receiver, executing such instruments, and generally doing all such acts and things in relation to his property, as may be required by the court or receiver, or to deliver up possession of any property of his which is divisible among his creditors, and which is for the time being in his possession or under his control, to the court or to any person authorized by the court to take possession of it, or

(*ii*) fraudulently with intent to conceal the state of his affairs or to defeat the object of the law of insolvency—

(1) has destroyed or otherwise wilfully prevented or purposely withheld the production of any document relating to such of

7 *See* sections 21, 22, 30(1), 41 of the Presidency Towns Insolvency Act and sections 35, 36, 39, 43(1) of the Provincial Insolvency Act.

his affairs as are subject to investigation under the Provincial Insolvency Act,

(2) has kept or caused to be kept false books, or

(3) has made false entries in or withheld entries from or wilfully altered or falsified any documents relating to such of his affairs as are subject to investigation under the Provincial Insolvency Act, or

(*iii*) fraudulently with intent to diminish the sum to be divided among his creditors or to give an undue preference to any of his creditors,—

(1) has discharged or concealed any debt due to or from him, or

(2) has made away with, mortgaged or concealed any part of his property

he is punishable on conviction by the court with imprisonment which may extend to one year.

An undischarged insolvent obtaining credit to the extent of fifty rupees or upwards from any person without informing such person that he is an undischarged insolvent is liable, on conviction by a first class Magistrate, to be punished with six months' imprisonment, or with fine or with both.

Disqualification of insolvent.[8] Whether a debtor is adjudged or re-adjudged insolvent, he is disqualified from—

(*i*) being appointed or acting as a Magistrate;

(*ii*) being elected to any office of any local authority where the appointment to such office is by election, or holding or exercising any such office to which no salary is attached; and

(*iii*) being elected or sitting or voting as member of any local authority:

Provided that the disqualifications, which an insolvent is subject to as above-mentioned, will be removed and will cease if—

(1) the order of adjudication is annulled, or

(2) he obtains from the court an order of discharge, whether absolute or conditional, with a certificate that his insolvency was caused by misfortune without any misconduct on his part.

Court-fee. The court-fee on a petition for insolvency is the same as on a petition to the Civil Court.

8 *See* sections 38-45 of the Presidency Towns Insolvency Act and sections 41-44 of the Provincial Insolvency Act.

Forms

Petition by Debtor to be Adjudged an Insolvent

In the Court of District Judge of ....

Insolvency Case No. .... of ....

Ex parte—The debtor

In the matter of debtor's petition for insolvency, under s. 13(1) of the Provincial Insolvency Act

The humble petition of AB residing at .... and lately of .... (give address where debts were incurred)

MOST RESPECTFULLY SHEWETH:

1. That the applicant, who is ordinarily living and residing (*or* carrying on business, *or* personally working for gain, *or* in custody) at .... having been unable to pay his debts exceeding Rs. 500 prays for an order of adjudication against him in the circumstances hereunder mentioned.

2. That on or about the .... day of .... the applicant was arrested and committed to prison at .... in execution of a decree for Rs. .... dated .... made in suit No. .... of .... (............... v ....) under order dated .... made by .... or (as the case may be) the movable and immovable property of the applicant such as (give short particulars) have been attached and the said attachment is still subsisting.

3. The amount and particulars of all pecuniary claims against the applicant, together with the names and residences of his creditors, are as follows:

4. The following are the particulars of debts and claims outstanding against the applicant.

Names, addresses and occupation of the creditors, particulars of the amounts due and securities.

5. The following are the particulars of the property belonging to the applicant and their respective values.

(1) Household furniture, utensils, etc., all worth about ....

(2) One house at .... worth about ....

The whole of the above property, which is situate at, etc., has been truly described, and the applicant is willing to surrender and put them entirely at the disposal of this court.

The applicant prays that the court may be pleased to adjudge him insolvent.

Verification

I, AB son of .... aged about .... years by occupation service residing at .... do hereby solemnly affirm and say as follows:

I am the petitioner No. 1 above-named and I know and I have made myself acquainted with the facts and circumstances of this case.

The statements in paragraphs 1 to 5 are true to my knowledge and belief.

I sign this verification on this .... day of .... at the Court House at ....

Before me Signature of AB

Notary Signature of Advocate

Petition by Creditor to Adjudge Debtor Insolvent

In the Court of the District Judge of .... at .... Insolvency Case No. .... *ex parte* AB the creditor

In re: CD Name and address of the debtor

In the matter of the adjudication for insolvency of the debtor under s. 13(2) of the Provincial Insolvency Act

MOST RESPECTFULLY SHEWETH:

1. That the above-named debtor CD who ordinarily resides at .... (*or* carries on business or personally works for gain at ....) is truly and justly indebted to the applicant to the extent of Rs. .... for principal and Rs. .... for interest due on a pronote executed by CD in favour of the applicant on the .... day of ....

2. That on the .... day of .... when the applicant called at the said premises and demanded payment of the amount due under the promissory note, the said CD gave notice to the applicant that the said CD has suspended payment of his debts.

3. That the said debtor has, within three months before the date of presentation of this petition, committed *inter alia* the following acts of insolvency (state briefly the acts of insolvency), *e.g.*

(*i*) The said debtor has departed from his usual place of business/ residence at .... and/or absented or kept himself secluded therefrom with intent to deprive his creditor of all means of communications.

(*ii*) Set out other acts of insolvency, if any.

The applicant therefore prays that this court may be pleased to adjudge CD an insolvent and order the realisation of all his assets and distribution of the same amongst all his creditors.

Verification

I, AB, son of .... aged .... years by occupation business residing at .... do hereby solemnly affirm and say as follows:

I am the petitioner above-named. I know the facts and circumstances of this case and I am able to depose thereto.

The statements in paragraphs 1, 2 and 3 hereinabove are true to my knowledge and believed by me to be true and that I have not suppressed any material fact.

I sign this Verification on this .... day of .... 1999 at the Court premises at Alipore.

Before me
Notary

Signature of AB
Signature of the Advocate

Petition for Discharge

CAUSE TITLE

In the matter of debtor's petition of absolute discharge under s. 41 of the Provincial Insolvency Act

The applicant above-named states as follows:

1. That on the .... day of .... by an order of this court the applicant was adjudged insolvent and he was to apply for discharge within the .... day of ....

2. That the receiver appointed in the above case has realised all the assets of the applicant and has declared a dividend of .... paise in the rupee and he has some more money in his hand (or the applicant having no realisable assets nothing has been paid to the creditors).

3. That on account of circumstances for which the applicant cannot justly be held responsible the applicant's assets are not of a value equal to fifty paise in the rupee on the amount of his unsecured liabilities.

4. That the applicant has kept all the usual or proper books of account of his business (or the applicant having had no business, no books of account have been kept by him).

5. That the applicant has not continued to trade after knowing himself to be insolvent and has not contracted any debt without having any reasonable or probable ground of expectation that he would be able to pay it nor has the applicant failed to account satisfactorily for any loss or deficiency of assets.

6. That the applicant has not brought on or contributed to his insolvency by rash or hazardous speculations or by unjustifiable extravagance in living or by gambling or by culpable neglect of his business affairs.

7. That the applicant has not given any undue preference to any of his creditors.

8. That the applicant has not concealed or removed his property or any part thereof nor has he been guilty of any other fraud or fraudulent breach of trust.

The applicant therefore prays for an order of absolute discharge.

Verification

I, CD son of .... aged .... years by occupation business residing at .... do hereby solemnly affirm and say as follows:

I am the applicant above-named. I know the facts and circumstances of this case and I am able to depose thereto.

The statements made in the paragraphs 1 to 8 in the above-mentioned application are true to my knowledge and belief and that I have not suppressed any material fact.

I sign this Verification on this .... day of .... 1999 at the Court Premises at Alipore.

Before me — Signature of CD
Notary — Signature of Advocate

Agreement for Composition with Creditors with Surety

THIS AGREEMENT is made this .... day of .... BETWEEN AB residing at .... (hereinafter called the DEBTOR) of the first part, CD and EF sons of .... residing at .... (hereinafter called the SURETIES) of the second part and the several persons being Creditors of the DEBTOR whose names and addresses are entered in the Schedule hereunder (hereinafter called the CREDITORS) of the third part; WHEREBY IT IS AGREED as follows:

1. In consideration of the DEBTOR having procured the guarantee of the above-mentioned SURETIES, the CREDITORS of the DEBTOR of the amounts and extents set out as against their respective names in the schedule below do hereby and hereunder jointly and severally agree with the DEBTOR to accept in full discharge of their respective original debts irrespective of the amounts particulars of which are set opposite to their respective names in the said schedule, a composition of .... paise in the rupee to be paid as hereunder mentioned.

2. The said composition shall be paid by .... instalments, the first of .... paise in the rupee in .... calendar months from the date hereof, the second of .... paise in the rupee in .... calendar months from the date hereof, and the third instalment of .... paise in the rupee in .... calendar months from the date hereof.

3. The said several instalments shall be secured by promissory notes to be executed by the SURETIES jointly with the DEBTOR for the respective amounts of the instalments or by bonds to the effect that the DEBTOR and the SURETIES will jointly and severally bind themselves unto the CREDITORS that they, the DEBTOR and the SURETIES, shall remain liable to and shall duly and punctually pay to the CREDITORS the said several instalments in the manner and at the times aforesaid.

4. Upon payment of the said respective amounts by the instalments and in manner aforesaid, the CREDITORS and each of them shall accept the same in full and final settlement and satisfaction of their respective claims and at the request and costs of the DEBTOR release and discharge the DEBTOR from the said debts and from all claims, demands and remedies in respect thereof.

5. This agreement shall operate as a bar to any action hereafter by any of the CREDITORS against the DEBTOR in respect of the said several debts or any of them so long he shall pay or cause to be paid the instalments hereunder provided in the manner hereinbefore indicated without any delay or default except, however, in case if the DEBTOR is adjudicated insolvent when and in such an event it will stand revoked.

6. If a default shall be made in the payment of the said instalments or any one of them, the CREDITORS shall then and in such a case be at liberty to enforce payment of the balance due to them under the composition, or to claim payment of their respective original dues after giving credit to the DEBTOR for all sums actually received by them hereunder respectively.

The Schedule above referred to giving the names and addresses of the creditors, short particulars of the debts and instalments payable

Serial No.	*Name and address of the creditor*	*Particulars of the debts*	*Security if any*	*Remarks*

IN WITNESS WHEREOF the parties have executed these presents on the day, month and year first above-written.

Signed, sealed and delivered by
AB

Signed, sealed and delivered by
CD and EF

Signed, sealed and delivered by the
CREDITORS named in the Schedule
in the presence of:

30

Labour Laws

The labour laws in the country enacted for the benefit and protection of labour have imposed certain obligations on employers and set up tribunals, labour courts and authorities which can be easily approached by aggrieved labour or on their behalf by Trade Unions or some authorised persons under the law for quick remedy without incurring heavy costs as required in litigations before ordinary civil courts. The special statutes have prescribed forms in which applications shall be made generally. As regards amendments, etc., the general principles about pleadings in court have been applied.

FORMS

Application for Permission under s. 33 of the Industrial Disputes Act (XIV of 1947)

Before (mention here the Conciliation Officer, Board or Tribunal).

In re: .... Ref. No. .... of .... A .... (Name and address) Applicant B. .... (Name and address) Opposite party/ies.

The above-mentioned applicant begs to state as follows:

(Set here all the relevant facts and circumstances of the case and in particular the grounds on which the permission is sought for).

The applicant, therefore, prays that the express permission may be granted to him to take *inter alia* the following action/s, namely:

[Mention here the action/s specified in cl. (*a*) or (*b*) of s. 33 of the Act.]

Dated this .... day of ....

Signature of the applicant

Date of verification .... Signature of the person verifying

Place of verification ....

NOTE: Section 33 of the Industrial Disputes Act 1947:
Condition of service, etc. to remain unchanged during the pendency of the proceedings. During the pendency of any conciliation proceeding/s before a tribunal in respect of any industrial dispute, no employer shall—

(*a*) alter to the prejudice of the workmen concerned in such dispute, the conditions of service applicable to them immediately before the commencement of such proceedings; or

(*b*) discharge or punish, whether by dismissal or otherwise, any workmen concerned in such dispute, save with the express permission in writing of the conciliation officer, board or tribunal, as the case may be.

Complaint under s. 33A of the Industrial Disputes Act 1947

A .... (full name, description and address) Complaint/s; and

B .... (full name, description and address) Opposite party/ies

The petitioner/s begs/beg to complain that the opposite party/ies has/have been guilty of wilful contravention of the provisions of s. 33 of the Industrial Disputes Act (XIV of 1947) as will appear from the particulars set out below:

(Here set out briefly the particulars showing the manner in which the alleged contravention has taken place and also the grounds on which the order or act of the management is challenged.)

(The complaint/s accordingly pray/s that the tribunal may be pleased to decide the complaint set out above and pass such orders thereon as it may deem fit and proper.)

The number of copies of the complaint and its annexures required by r. 59 of the Industrial Disputes (Central) Rules 1957, are submitted herewith.

Dated this .... day of ....

Signature or thumb impression
of complaint/s

Verification

I do solemnly declare that what is stated in paragraphs .... above is true to my knowledge and that what is stated in paragraphs .... above is stated upon information received and/believed by me to be true. Verification is signed by me at .... on .... day of ....

Signature or thumb impression
of the person verifying

Form of Application by an Employee under section 20(2) of the Minimum Wages Act 1948

In the Court of the Authority appointed under the Minimum Wages Act 1948 for .... Area.

Application No. .... of 19.........

(1) ....

(2) .... *Applicant/s*

(3) ....

through .... a legal practitioner .... Official of .... Union which is a registered Trade Union.

Address ....

versus

(1) ....

(2) .... *Opponents*

(3) ....

The applicant/s above-named beg/s respectfully to submit as follows:

1. That ....
2. That ....

The applicant/s has/have been paid wages at less than the minimum rate of wages.

The applicant/s estimate/s the value of the relief sought by him/them at the sum of Rs. ....

The applicant/s pray/s that a direction may be issued under sub-sec. (3) of s. 28 for—

(*a*) payment of the difference between the wages due according to the minimum rate of wages fixed by the Government and wages actually paid, and

(*b*) compensation amounting to Rs. ....

The applicant/s beg/s leave to amend or add to or make alterations in the application, if any, and when necessary.

Date ....

Signature or thumb impression of the employee/s or legal practitioner or official of a registered trade union duly authorised

Application by an Inspector or Person Acting with the Permission of the Authority under section 20(2) of the Minimum Wages Act 1948

In the Court of the Authority appointed under the Minimum Wages Act 1948, for .... area

Application No. .... of 19......

(1) ....

Address .... *Applicant*

versus

(2) ....

Address .... *Opponent*

The applicant above-named begs respectfully to submit as follows:

1. That ....
2. That ....

The opponent is bound to pay wages at the minimum rate of wages fixed by the Government, but he has paid less wages to the following employees:

(1) ....
(2) ....
(3) ....

The applicant estimates the value of the relief sought for the employees at the sum of Rs. ....

The applicant prays that a direction may be issued under sub-sec. (3) of s. 20 for—

(*a*) payment of the difference between the wages due according to the minimum rate of wages fixed by the Government and wages actually paid and

(*b*) compensation amounting to Rs. ....

The applicant begs leave to amend or add to or make alterations in the application if and when necessary.

Date .... Signature ....

The applicant does solemnly declare that what is stated above is true to the best of his knowledge, belief and information. The verification is signed at .... on .... day of .... 19....

Individual Application

[*See* sub-sec. (2) of s. 15 of the Payment of Wages Act]

In the Court of the Authority appointed under the Payment of Wages Act (IV of 1936) for .... area.

Application No. .... of .... 19.........

Between ABC ....

(through a legal practitioner) *Applicant*

an official of .... which is a registered trade union And XYZ .... *Opposite Party*

1. ABC is a person employed in/or the ....

Factory

Railway entitled .... and

industrial establishment resides at ....

The address of the applicant for the service of all notices and processes is:

2. XYZ, the opposite party, is the person responsible for the payment of his wages under s. 3 of the Act and his address for the service of all notices and processes is:

3. (1) The applicant's wages have not been paid for the following wage period(s) (give date). Or

A sum of Rs. .... has been unlawfully deducted from his wages of (amount) for the wage period(s) which ended on [give date(s)].

(2) Here give any further claim or explanation.

4. The applicant estimates the value of the relief sought by him at the sum of Rupees ....

5. The applicant prays that a direction may be issued under sub-sec. (3) of s. 15 for—

(*a*) Payment of his delayed wages as estimated or such greater or lesser amount as the authority may find to be due. Or

Refund of the amount illegally deducted.

(*b*) Compensation amounting to ....

The applicant certifies that the statement of facts contained in this application is to the best of his knowledge and belief accurate.

Signature or thumb impression of the employed person, or legal practitioner or official of a registered trade union duly authorised

Group Application

[*See* sub-sec. (2) of ss. 15 and 16 of the Payment of Wages Act 1936]

In the Court of the Authority appointed under the Payment of Wages Act (IV of 1936) for .... area.

Application No. .... of 19...........

Between ABC and state the number .... others ....

Applicants

(Through a *Legal Practitioner*)
an official of .... which is a
registered trade union And XYZ .... *Opposite party*

The applicants state as follows:

1. The applicants whose names appear in the attached schedule are persons employed in the *factory*.

on *Railway* entitled ....
Industrial establishment

The addresses of the applicants for service of all notices and processes are:

2. XYZ, the opposite party, is the person responsible for the payment of wages under s. 3 of the Act, and his address for the service of all notices and processes is:

3. The applicants' wages have not been paid for the following wage period(s).

4. The applicants estimate the value of the relief sought by them at the sum of Rupees ....

5. The applicants pray that a direction may be issued under sub-sec. (3) of s. 15 for—

(*a*) Payment of the applicants' delayed wages as estimated .... or such greater or lesser amount as the authority may find to be due.

(*b*) Compensation amounting to ....

The applicants certify that the statement of facts contained in this application is to the best of their knowledge and belief accurate.

Signature or thumb impression of two of the applicants or legal practitioner/an official of a registered trade union duly authorised

Schedule

Name of applicants

(1) ....

(2) ....

(3) ....

(4) ....

Application by an Inspector or Person Permitted by the Authority or Authorised to Act

[*See* sub-sec. (2) of ss. 15 and 16 of the Payment of Wages Act]

In the Court of the Authority appointed under the Payment of Wages Act, for .... area.

Application No. .... of 19...........

Between ABC (designation .... an Inspector under the Payment of Wages Act).

(or a person $\frac{\text{permitted by the authority}}{\text{authorised}}$ to act under sub-sec. (2) of s. 15) ....

Applicant

And XYZ, the opposite party, is the person responsible under the Act for payment of wages to the following person(s):

(1) ....

(2) ....

(3) ....

*

*

*

2. His address for the service of all notice and processes is:

3. The wage of the said person(s) due in respect of the following wage period(s) $\frac{\text{have not been paid}}{\text{have been subjected to the following illegal deductions}}$

4. The applicant estimates the value of the relief sought for the person(s) employed at the sum of Rs. ....

5. The applicant prays that a direction may be issued under sub-sec. (3) of s. 15 for—

(*a*) Payment of the delayed wages as estimated or such greater or lesser amount as the Authority may find to be due:

Or

Refund of the amount illegally deducted.

(*b*) Compensation amounting to ....

The applicant certifies that the statement of facts contained in this application is to the best of his knowledge and belief accurate.

Signature

Application under Workmen's Compensation Act for Compensation by Workmen

To the Commissioner for Workmen's Compensation ....
residing at .... *Applicant*

versus

residing at .... *Opposite party*

It is hereby submitted that—

1. The applicant, a workman employed by (a contractor with) the opposite party on the .... day of .... 19........, received personal injury by accident arising out of and in the course of his employment.

The cause of the injury was (here insert briefly in ordinary language the cause of injury) ....

---

2. The applicant sustained the following injuries, namely:

---

3. The monthly wages of the applicant amount to Rs. ....

The applicant $\frac{\text{is over}}{\text{under}}$ the age of 15 years.

4. (*a*) Notice of the accident was not served on the .... day of ....

(*b*) Notice was served as soon as practicable.

(*c*) Notice of the accident was not served (in due time) by reason of ....

The applicant is accordingly entitled to receive—

(*a*) half-monthly payment of Rs. .... from the .... day of .... 1999 to ....

(*b*) a lump sum payment of Rs. ....

5. The applicant has taken the following steps to secure a settlement by agreement, namely—

but it has proved impossible to settle the questions in dispute because ....

You are, therefore, requested to determine the following questions in dispute, namely—

(*a*) whether the applicant is a workman within the meaning of the Act;

(*b*) whether the accident arose out of or in the course of the applicant's employment;

(*c*) whether the amount of compensation claimed is due, or any part of that amount;

(*d*) whether the opposite party is liable to pay such compensation as is due;

(*e*) etc. (as required).

Dated .... 19 ...... *Applicant*

Application under Workmen's Compensation Act for Order to Deposit Compensation

It is hereby submitted that—

1. ....a workman employed by (a contractor with) the opposite party on the .... day of .... 19........ received personal injury by accident arising out of and in the course of his employment resulting in his death on the .... day of .... 19......... The cause of the injury was (here insert briefly in ordinary language the cause of the injury) ....

2. The applicant(s) $\frac{\text{is a}}{\text{are}}$ dependant(s) of the deceased workman being his ....

3. The monthly wages of the deceased amount to Rs. ....

4. The deceased was $\frac{\text{over}}{\text{under}}$ the age of 15 years at the time of his death.

5. (*a*) Notice of the accident was served on the .... day of ....

(*b*) Notice was served as soon as practicable.

(*c*) Notice of the accident was not served (in due time) by reason .... of ....

6. The deceased before his death received as compensation the total sum of Rs. ....

The applicant(s) $\frac{\text{is}}{\text{are}}$ accordingly entitled to receive a lump sum payment of Rs. ....

You are, therefore, requested to award to the applicant(s) the said compensation or any other compensation to which he may be entitled.

Dated .... Applicant(s)

Dated the .... day of .... 19 ......

Application for Registration of a Trade Union

1. We hereby apply for the registration of a trade union under the name of ....

2. The address of the head office of the union is ....

3. The union came into existence on the .... day of .... 19...... and has on its roll on the date of this application .... members.

4. The union is a union of employees/workers engaged in the .... industry (or profession).

5. The particulars required by s. 5(1)(*c*) of the Indian Trade Unions Act 1926, are given in Schedule I.

6. The particulars given in Schedule II show the provisions made in the rules for the matters detailed in s. 6 of the Indian Trade Unions Act 1926.

7. (To be struck out in the case of unions which have not been in existence for one year before the date of application). The particulars required by s. 5(2) of the Indian Trade Unions Act 1926, are given in Schedule III.

8. We have been duly authorised to make this application by ....

9. Written declaration from the officers of the trade union that they had given their consent to their being elected as such officers is given in Schedule IV.

	Signature	*Occupation*	*Address*
Signed 1.			
2.			
3.			
4.			
5			
6.			

To

The Registrar of Trade Unions, West Bengal

Schedule I

List of Officers

Title	*Name*	*Age*	*Address*	*Occupation*

NOTE: Enter in this schedule the names of all members of the executive including all honorary or temporary members of the union shown in column 1, the names of any posts held by the (*e.g.*, President, Secretary, Treasurer, etc.) in addition to their offices as members of the executive.

Schedule II

Reference to Rules

The number of the rules making provision for the several matters detailed in column are given in column 2 below:

1 *Matter*	*2* *Number of rules*
Name of Union .... The whole of the objects for which the union has been established .... The whole of the purposes for which the general funds of the union shall be applicable. The maintenance of a list of members .... The facilities provided for the inspection of the list of members by officers and members .... The admission of ordinary members .... The admission of honorary or temporary members	
The conditions under which members are entitled to benefits assured by the rules .... The conditions under which fines or forfeitures can be imposed or varied .... The manner in which the rules shall be amended, varied or rescinded .... The manner in which the members of the executive and the other officers of the union shall be appointed and removed .... The safe custody of the fund .... The annual audit of the accounts ....The facilities for the inspection of account books by officers and members .... The manner in which the union may be dissolved	

Schedule III

(This need not be filled in if the union came into existence less than one year before the date of application for registration). Statement of Liabilities and Assets on the .... day of .... 19..........

Liabilities	*Rs. p.*	*Assets*	*Rs. p.*
Amount of general fund		Cash—	
Amount of political fund		In hands of Treasurer	
Loans from:		In hands of Secretary	
....		In hands of	
....		In the .... Bank	
....		Securities as per list below,	
		unpaid subscriptions due	
Debts due to—		Loans to—	
....		....	
....		....	
		....	
Other liabilities (to be specified)—		Immovable property	
		Goods and furniture	
....		Other assets (to be specified)	
....			
....		....	
		....	
Loans from:			
Total Liabilities		Total Assets	

List of Securities

Particulars	*Nominal value*	*Market value*	*In hands of*
Signed 1.			
2.			
3.			
4.			
5.			

Schedule IV

We hereby declare having consent to our being elected as officers of the .... (name of the trade union):

	Signature	Designation
Signed:		
1		
2		
3		
4		
5		
6		
7		
8		
9		
10		
11		
12		
13		
14		
15		

Sickness or Temporary Disablement Benefit Claim for Benefit

I .... s/w/d of .... Insurance No. .... hereby state that I was certified sick/ temporarily disabled from .... a.m./p.m. on the .... day of .... 19......... and I have not been at work since .... a.m./p.m. on the day of .... 19......... .

I no longer claim to be sick/temporarily disabled from .... day of .... 19......... and I shall/did not take up any work for remuneration before that day.*

I claim benefit accordingly. I desire payment in cash at local office/by money order present/last employer .... Department .... Occupation .... shift (if any) .... present address ....

Signature or thumb impression

Local Office ....

* Strike out if not applicable, and then, before resuming work, a final certificate must be obtained.

Accident Case Only

Date, time and place of accident .... If a notice of the accident had not been given to the employer, state briefly on a separate paper how the accident happened.

Signature or thumb impression

Sickness or Temporary Disablement Benefit Claim for Benefit

I, ..., s/w/d of .... Insurance No. .... declare that because of sickness/temporary disablement, I have not been at work since the date of last/first certificate sent to you.

I claim benefit accordingly. I desire payment in cash at local office/by money order.

Signature or thumb impression

Date ....
Local office ....

Present Address ....

Claim for Permanent Disablement Benefit

I, ..., s/w/d of .... Insurance No. ....having been declared as permanently disabled by the Medical Board/Appeal Tribunal claim permanent disablement benefit accordingly for the period from .... to ....

The amount due may be paid to me by money order/in cash at local office.

Date ....
Signature or thumb impression

Present Address ....

ANOTHER FORM

I, ... s/w/d of .... Insurance No. .... declare that, because of sickness/temporary disablement, I have not been at work since the date of last/first certificate sent to you.

I no longer claim to be sick/temporarily disabled .... from .... day of .... 19........... and I shall/did not take up any work for remuneration before that day, I claim benefit accordingly. I desire payment in cash at local office/by money order.

Signature or thumb impression

Date ....
Local office ....

Present Address ....

Dependants' Benefit

CLAIM FORM

Claim arising from the death on .... of (insured person) .... s/w/d of .... having Insurance No. .... and that employed as .... by ....

I/We, the following, being dependants of the deceased insured person, whose particulars are given above, apply for dependants' benefit in respect of his/her death.

Nature of the dependants	*Date of birth or age*	*Relationship with the deceased*	*Sex*	*Marital status*	*Name of the guardian in case of a minor*
1	2	3	4	5	6

So far as I/we know, the following are the only other dependants who may be entitled to dependants' benefit in respect of the death of the above-named insured person.

Names and addresses of the dependants	*Date of birth or age*	*Relationship with the deceased*	*Sex*	*Marital status*	*Name of the guardian in case of a minor*
1	2	3	4	5	6

I/We declare that the particulars given above are true to the best of my/our knowledge and belief.

Signatures	Present Addresses
1.	....
2.	....
3.	....
4.	....

†Certified that the declarations made above are true to the best of my knowledge and belief.

Rubber stamp or seal of
the attesting authority

Signature ....

Designation ....

IMPORTANT: Any person who makes a false statement or representation for the purpose of obtaining benefit, whether for himself or for some other persons, renders himself liable to prosecution.

† This certificate is to be given by (*i*) an officer of the Revenue, Judicial or Magisterial Departments of Government; or (*ii*) a Municipal Commissioner; or (*iii*) a Workmen's Compensation Commissioner; or (*iv*) the Head of the Gram Panchayat under the official seal of the Panchayat; or (*v*) any other authority approved by the appropriate Regional Office.

Maternity Benefit

CLAIM FORM

I .... Insurance No. ....wife of/daughter of .... here claim maternity benefit with effect from the .... day of .... 19......... I hereby declare that I have ceased/shall cease to work for remuneration with effect from that date.

Present/last employer ....

Department, shift and occupation ....

Present address ....

Date ....

Signature or thumb impression

31

Leases

Introductory observations. "Lease", "Lessor", "Lessee", "Premium" and "Rent"—As defined in Bacon's *Abridgement*[1] a lease is a contract between the lessor and the lessee for possession and enjoyment of the profits of the land on one side and recompense by rent or other consideration on the other. The lessor must be a person competent to contract and also having title or authority to create the grant. Similarly the lessee must be a person also competent to accept contract on the date of the lease and shall further accept the demise of the estate. So neither an infant nor his guardian is competent to enter into a lease agreement, as a lessee.[2] Such an agreement vests the lessee with certain rights. It is an exception to the common law rule that contracts are personal. A lease is a transfer of an estate of inheritance and does not *ipso facto* terminate on the death of any one of the parties but passes on to their respective heirs and legal representatives. A lease of immovable property is, therefore, not mere contract, but it operates as a conveyance or transfer of the right to enjoy such property, made for a certain time, express or implied, or in perpetuity in consideration of a price paid or promised, or of money, a share of crops, service or any other thing of value, to be rendered periodically or on specified occasions, to the transferor by the transferee who accepts such transfer on terms.[3] The essential elements of a lease are (1) Parties; (2) Property; (3) Demise; (4) Terms and Conditions; and (5) Consideration.

Such transferor is called the lessor, the transferee is called the lessee, the price is called the premium, and the money, share, service or other things to be so rendered is called the rent. A lease creates a right *in rem*. Agreement to lease is an executory contract binding the parties. An agreement

1 Mulla's *Transfer of Property Act,* 8th Ed., p. 767.
2 Woodfall's *Landlord and Tenant*, 28th Ed., vol. 1, para 1-0138, p. 60.
3 Section 105 of the Transfer of Property Act.

to lease not creating a present demise is not a lease and does not require writing or registration.[4] It is drafted as an ordinary agreement but the property to be leased, period of lease, the date of commencement of the lease, rent and other terms and conditions agreed upon are mentioned. It was held by the Privy Council in *Giribala* v *Kalidas*[5] that a suit for specific performance cannot be decreed in the absence of a definite date as to commencement of the lease. Whether a document operates as a lease or agreement is a matter of construction and intention of the contracting parties. Words of present demise are generally conclusive of a lease. An intending lessee taking possession under an agreement for lease is not an actual lessee under an executed and registered deed of lease. The equity in *Walsh* v *Lonsdale*[6] does not apply in India as held by the Privy Council in *Arif* v *Jadunath*.[7] His possession can nevertheless be defended under s. 53A of the Transfer of Property Act. The powers of an executor or administrator to grant a lease are regulated by s. 307 of the Indian Succession Act (Act 39 of 1925). Under s. 29(*b*) of the Guardian and Wards Act, a statutory guardian can even without authority from the court grant lease for a period not exceeding five years; so also a natural guardian under s. 8 of the Hindu Minority and Guardianship Act (Act XXXII of 1956). The *de facto* guardian is not at all competent to grant any lease of the properties of a minor.

Lease of a debutter property. The *shebaits* of a deity who are in charge of the management and administration of the estate can grant a lease of the property of the deity for legal necessities in the interest of and for the benefit of the deity and its estate.[8] It is the settled law that the power of a *shebait* in charge of a *Math* to alienate the debutter property is analogous to that of the manager of an infant as observed by Judicial Committee in *Hanuman Persaud* v *Massamat Babooee*.[9] Following this principle the Judicial Committee held in the case of *Prosonnya Kumar Debya* v *Golap Chand*[10] that such a power is limited to case of legal necessities unavoidable.

In the case of *Konwar Doorganath* v *Ramchandra*[11] a makarari patta was supported on the ground that the same was granted in consideration of a lump sum money urgently required for repairs and construction of the temple inasmuch as the estate had no other resources. There shall be special circumstances to justify a grant beyond the lifetime of the grantor.

4 46 IA 240.
5 AIR 1921 PC 71.
6 (1882)21 Ch D 9.
7 58 IA 91.
8 Mulla's *Hindu Law*, 17th Ed., para 415, pp. 624-627.
9 (1856)6 MIA 393.
10 (1875)2 IA 145.
11 (1874)2 Cal 141; 4 IA 52.

Construction of a pucca building for the shelter of the devotees was held to be a legal necessity.[12]

Duration of lease. In the absence of a contract or local law or usage to the contrary, a lease of immovable property for agricultural or manufacturing purposes shall be deemed to be a lease from year to year terminable, on the part of either lessor or lessee, by six months' notice expiring with the end of the year of the tenancy; and a lease of immovable property for any other purpose shall be deemed to be a lease from month to month terminable, on the part of either lessor or lessee, by 15 days' notice expiring with the end of the month of the tenancy.[13]

Generally, leases are made to commence from the first day of a month or year according to the nature of the tenancy, but sometimes a lease is made to begin on any other date in which case, the special month or year of the tenancy, at the expiry of which the lease is to be terminated, is to be reckoned from that date; and sometimes it also happens that the date of the commencement of a lease is not known; in which case, the time of the expiry of the notice to be given either by the landlord or the tenant may be expressed in the following form:

> "At the end of the month (or year) of your (or my) tenancy which will expire next after the end of half a month (or half a year) from the date of the service of this notice".[14]

Requisites of notice. Every such notice as above must be in writing signed by or on behalf of the person giving it, and either be sent by registered post to the party who is intended to be bound by it or be tendered or delivered personally to such party or to one of the adult members of his family at his residence, or (if such tender or delivery is not practicable) affixed to a conspicuous part of the property. It shall be specific as regards the grounds of eviction and the property. It shall contain a demand for possession and also a threat to file a suit in default of compliance as required by such laws as the West Bengal Premises Tenancy Act 1997.

Creation of a lease.[15] Although the section provides that a lease of an immovable property can be created by two methods, (*i*) registered instrument in cases where the lease is from year to year or exceeding one year or reserving yearly rent, (*ii*) oral agreement followed by delivery of possession in other cases; nevertheless, it was held by the Privy Council in the case of *Ariff* v *Jodunath*,[16] that the theory in *Walsh* v *Lonsdale*[17] has no application

12 *Neladri Sahu* v *Mohini Chaturbunj* 53 IA 253 (267); 98 IC 576.
13 Section 106 of the Transfer of Property Act.
14 Section 106 of the Transfer of Property Act.
15 Section 107 of the Transfer of Property Act.
16 (1931)58 IA 91; 58 Cal 1235.
17 (1882)21 Ch D 9.

to India, there being no distinction between "legal estate" and "equitable estate" in India. Section 53A of the Transfer of Property Act, however, protects the lessee in defending his right of possession. This section was enacted in 1929 by the Transfer of Property (Amendment) Act 1929, and imports in India a theory about equity of part performance as developed in England in *Middleson* v *Alduson*,[18] The amending Act reinforced the position by amending the Indian Registration Act and the Specific Relief Act[19] The intending lessee can institute a suit for specific performance of the agreement for lease if not time-barred.

A lease can be created under a decree or order of the court, but the same must contain the terms 'clearly necessary particulars of the property' and shall be duly registered.[20]

Unregistered deed of lease executed by both landlord and tenant can be looked into and considered in order to determine whether lease was granted for residential or non-residential purpose or any other similar collateral purpose.[1] Where a registered deed of lease shows only the signature of one of the parties it is not enough to conclude that the non-signing party had not joined in the execution of the instrument.[2]

Rights and liabilities of lessor.[3] In the absence of a contract or local usage to the contrary, the lessor possesses the rights and is subject to liabilities as follows:

(*i*) The lessor is bound to disclose to the lessee any material defect in the property, with reference to its intended use, of which the former is, and the latter is not, aware, and which the latter could not with ordinary care discover. The obligation of the lessor as to the disclosure of the material defects in the property is limited to defects which are known to the lessor, *i.e.* patent defects but not to latent defects. The consequence of the breach is that before execution of the lease agreement, the lessee may refuse execution of the same; but if afterwards he may repudiate the same on grounds of fraud etc.[4] This is what is known as the law against letting out a tumble down house. There is no such law as in England under the Housing Act 1936, except implied covenant of fitness in the case of letting out a furnished house.[5]

18 (1883)8 App Cas 467.
19 Section 40 and section 27A.
20 Section 17(2)(*vi*) of the Indian Registration Act.
1 *Rai Chand* v *Chandra Kanta* AIR 1991 SC 744.
2 *Rajendra* v *Rameswar* AIR 1999 SC 37.
3 Section 108(A) of the Transfer of Property Act.
4 *Auqel* v *Joy* (1911)1 KB 666.
5 *Lakhmichand* v *Ratnabai* 51 Bom 274.

(*ii*) The lessor is bound, on the lessee's request, to put him in possession of the property; otherwise he is not entitled to any rent.[6] In England delivery of *seisin* is necessary to complete the title of the Lessee. This common law doctrine does not apply to India.[7] This Lessee can maintain an action against the Lessor for *mesne profits* though he has not received possession (see Notes under doctrine of suspension of rent).

(*iii*) The lessor will be deemed to contract with the lessee that if the latter pays the rent reserved by the lease and performs the contract binding on him the lessee may hold the property during the time limited by lease without interruption. If the lessee loses possession of any portion of the property owing to any act or default on the part of the lessor, the lessee can suspend payment of rent till restoration of possession. This is based on the rule of English law—"Eviction of the lessee from part of the demised premises justifies suspension of the entire rent."[8] This privilege is not available to the lessee in other cases where the lessor fails to perform his part of the contract.

The benefit of such contract will be annexed to and pass with the lessee's interest as such and may be enforced by every person in whom that interest is for the whole or any part thereof from time to time vested.

Lessee's rights and liabilities.[9] In the absence of a contract or local usage to the contrary, the lessee possesses the rights and is subject to the liabilities as follows:

(*i*) if, during the continuance of the lease, any accession is made to the property, such accession (subject to the law relating to alluvion for the time being in force) will be deemed to be comprised in the lease;

(*ii*) if by fire, tempest or flood, or violence of an army or of a mob, or other irresistible forces, any material part of the property be wholly destroyed or rendered substantially and permanently unfit for the purposes for which it was let out, the lease will, at the option of the lessee, be void. This is the example of partial application of the doctrine of frustration in India:

Provided that, if the injury be occasioned by any wrongful act or default of the lessee, he will not be entitled to avail himself of the benefit of this provision;

(*iii*) if the lessor neglects to make, within a reasonable time after notice, any repairs which he is bound to make to the property, the lessee can make

6 *Uday Chand* v *Narain* (1920)58 IC 186.
7 *Regia Begum* v *Mahomed Daud* AIR 1926 Pat 508.
8 *Nilkantha Pati* v *Khitish Chandra* AIR 1951 Cal 338.
9 Section 108(B) of the Transfer of Property Act.

the same himself and deduct the expense incurred for such repairs with interest from the rent, or otherwise recover it from the lessor;

(*iv*) if the lessor neglects to make any payment which he is bound to make, and which, if not made by him, is recoverable from the lessor or against the property, the lessee can make such payment himself, and deduct it with interest from the rent or otherwise recover it from the lessor;

(*v*) the lessee may, even after the determination of the lease, remove, at any time whilst he is in possession of the property leased but not afterwards, all things which he has attached to the earth, provided he leaves the property in the state in which he received it;

(*vi*) when a lease of uncertain duration determines by any means except for the fault of the lessee, he or his legal representative is entitled to all the crops planted or sown by the lessee and growing upon the property when the lease determines, and to free ingress and egress to gather and carry them;

(*vii*) the lessee may, in the absence of any restriction in the lease itself, transfer absolutely, or by way of mortgage or sub-lease, the whole or any part of his interest in the property, and any transferee of such interest or part thereof can again transfer it. The lessee cannot, by reason only of such transfer, cease to be subject to any of the liabilities attaching to the lease.

Nothing in this clause will be deemed to authorize a tenant having non-transferable right of occupancy, or the farmer of an estate in respect of which default has been made in paying revenue, or the lessee of an estate under the management of a Court of Wards, to assign his interest as such tenant, farmer or lessee;

(*viii*) the lessee is bound to disclose to the lessor any fact as to the nature or extent of the interest which the lessee is about to take, of which lessee is, and the lessor is not, aware, and which materially increases the value of such interest;

(*ix*) the lessee is bound to pay or tender, at the proper time and place, the premium or rent to the lessor or his agent in this behalf;

(*x*) the lessee is bound to keep, and on the termination of the lease, to restore the property in as good a condition as it was at the time when he was put in possession, subject only to the changes caused by reasonable wear and tear or irresistible forces, and to allow the lessor and his agents, at all reasonable times during the term, to enter upon the property, and inspect the condition thereof and give or leave notice of any defect found in such condition; and when such defect has been caused by any act or default on the part of the lessee, his servants or agents, he is bound to make it good within three months after such notice has been given or left;

(*xi*) if the lessee becomes aware of any proceeding to recover the property or any part thereof, or of any encroachment made upon, or any interference with, the lessor's rights concerning such property, he is bound to give, with reasonable diligence, notice thereof to the lessor;

(*xii*) the lessee may use the property and its products (if any) as a person of ordinary prudence would use them if they were his own; but he must not use, or permit another to use, the property for a purpose other than that for which it was leased, or fell or sell timber, pull down or damage buildings belonging to the lessor, or work mines or quarries not open when the lease was granted, or commit any other act which is destructive or permanently injurious thereto:

(*xiii*) the lessee must not, without the lessor's consent in writing, erect on the property any permanent structure except for agricultural purposes;

(*xiv*) on the determination of the lease, the lessee is bound to put the lessor in possession of the property.

Determination of leases.[10] A lease of immovable property determines:

(*i*) by efflux of the time limited thereby (Term lease);

(*ii*) where such time is limited conditionally on the happening of some event, by the happening of such event, *e.g.*, lease for the duration of a war, lease for the term of the life of the lessee.

(*iii*) where the interest of the lessor in the property terminates on, or his power to dispose of the same extends only to, the happening of any event—by the happening of such event. A lease by the mortgagee in possession stands determined on redemption of the mortgage where the mortgagor exercises his right in that behalf, *e.g.*, lease by a Hindu widow of her widow's estate unless justified by legal necessity, except in cases where she acquired an absolute estate by the operation of s. 14 of the Hindu Succession Act (Act XXX of 1956);

(*iv*) in case the interest of the lessee and the lessor in the whole of the property becomes vested at the same time in one person in the same right, *e.g.*, merger of both the interests. The lease in such a case sinks into the reversion. This is a rule of intention not applicable in case there are encumbrances on the property,[11] *i.e.* intervening estate or estates;

(*v*) by express surrender, that is to say, in case the lessee yields up his interest under the lease to the lessor by mutual consent and agreement between them; surrender being a voluntary act of the lessee operates as the disclaimer of the trustee in bankruptcy subject to the rights of the sub-lessee except as regards the amount of rent.[12]

(*vi*) by implied surrender;

(*vii*) by forfeiture, that is to say (1) in case the lessee breaks any condition of the lease which gives the lessor the right of re-entry in the property;

10 Section 111 of the Transfer of Property Act.
11 Section 101 of the Transfer of Property Act.
12 Section 115 of the Transfer of Property Act.

(2) in case the lessee renounces his character as such by setting up a title in favour of a third person, or by claiming title in himself; or (3) in the event the lessee is adjudicated an insolvent and the lease provides that the lessor may re-enter on happening of such event; provided that in any of these cases the lessor or his transferee gives notice in writing to the lessee of his clear intention to determine the lease; the date on which the lease shall stand determined such notice shall also contain a threat of legal action for eviction in default of compliance;

(*viii*) on the expiration of a notice to determine the lease, or to quit, or of intention to quit, the property duly given by one party to the other in the absence of any contrary provisions in the lease itself.

Sub-lease. In England, it was held in *Bryant* v *Wilson*,[13] that a sub-lease for the whole residue of the lessee's term operates as an absolute assignment of the lease. The Privy Council pointed out the *Hunsrati* v *Bejoylal Seal*,[14] that in India a sub-lease is not an absolute assignment and it was further held in *Akshoy Kumar* v *Akman Molla*[15] that there is no privity of estate as between the lessors and the sub-lessee, who does not step into the shoes of the lessee. A sub-lessee is not prejudiced by the surrender of the head lease (s. 115 of Transfer of Property Act)[16] but the position is different in the case of forfeiture which annuls all sub-leases except in case of fraud as between the lessor and lessee. A sub-lessee is entitled to relief against forfeiture under s. 114 of the Transfer of Property Act 1882, which is applicable only in the case of non-payment of rent—No relief is open to the sub-lessee in case of transfer in breach of covenant in restraint of transfer.

Implied surrender. Under illustration to cl. (*f*) of s. 111 of the Transfer of Property Act there would be an implied surrender in favour of lessor if a lessee accepts from his lessor a new lease of the property leased to take effect during the continuance of the existing lease. The said illustration is, however, not exhaustive of the cases in which there may be an implied surrender. Just as under the English law, there can be an implied surrender under the law of transfer of property in India, if the lessor grants a new lease to a third person with the assent of the lessee under the existing lease who delivers the possession to such person or where the lessee directs his sub-tenant to pay the rent directly to a lessor. Clause in assignment deed that the lessee-assignor would not object to payment of rent by assignee amounts to implied surrender of leasehold rights by lessee in favour of the assignee.[17]

13 (1868)1 QB 716.
14 (1930)57 Cal 1176; 57 IA 110.
15 (1915)19 CWN 1197; 27 IC 307
16 *Bhupatrai* v *Chunilal* 70 CWN 62.
17 *P.M.C. Kunhiraman* v *C.R. Naganatha* AIR 1993 SC 307.

Surrender of a part of the lease does not amount to implied surrender of the entire tenancy and the part of the tenancy remains untouched. Acceptance of a new lease of part only of the demised premises operates as a surrender of the part and no more.[18] Again, a mere increase or reduction of rent will not necessarily import a surrender of an existing lease and the grant of a new tenancy.[19]

Saving of agricultural leases. The provisions of the Transfer of Property Act on leases are not applicable to leases for agricultural purposes, but the State Government can declare all of such provisions to be so applicable in the case of all or any of such leases, together with, or subject to, those of the local law for the time being in force.[20] As regards restrictions on letting out the whole or any part of rayati holding see s. 4 of the West Bengal Land Reforms Act 1955.

Leases how made. A lease of immovable property from year to year, or for any term exceeding one year, or reserving a yearly rent, can be made only by a registered instrument.

All other leases of immovable property can be made either by a registered instrument or by oral agreement accompanied by delivery of possession.

Where a lease of immovable property is made by a registered instrument, such instrument must be executed by both the lessor and the lessee.[21] If a kabuliyat is followed by acceptance of rent, a tenancy is created.[1]

Surrender of leases. Surrender of lease is not a transfer but mere yielding up by the lessee of his interest under the lease to the lessor by mutual agreement. It is in effect merger of the estate of the lessee into the reversion. It is not a transfer or an assignment of any right or estate within the meaning of s. 5 of the Transfer of Property Act.[2] The person who surrenders is called the surrenderer and the person to whom surrender is made is called the surrenderee. A surrender must be made with clear intention to yield up as mere non-payment of rent for years together or abandonment of the site does not amount to surrender.[3] A Requisition Order by the Government does not amount to any surrender.[4] It may be express, or implied. Except in

18 *Bhagyashree Combines* v *Dist. Magistrate* AIR 1998 Kant 328; see also *Uttamchand* v *S.M. Lalwani* AIR 1965 SC 716; *Dwarka* v *Dwarka* AIR 1975 SC 1758.

19 *Krishna Kumar* v *Grindlays Bank* AIR 1991 SC 899; *N.M. Ponniah* v *Kamalakshmi* AIR 1989 SC 467.

20 Section 117 of the Transfer of Property Act.

21 Section 107 of the Transfer of Property Act.

1 *Asram* v *Ramkali* AIR 1958 SC 183.

2 *Makhanlal* v *Nagendranath* (1933)60 Cal 379; 37 CWN 119.

3 *Misri Lal* v *Durga Narain* AIR 1940 All 317; 189 IC 623.

4 *Torabai* v *Padan Chand* 62 CWN 176.

a case of some special kinds of leases as required by special Act, no writing or registration is necessary. A surrender may be oral, if accompanied by delivery of possession.

But in case where any writing is executed, it comes under s. 17 of the Indian Registration Act.

Holding over. The lessee remaining in possession after expiry of the term of the lease is said to hold over the lease.[5]

This section operates in the absence of an agreement to the contrary which determines the duration and the term of the renewed lease. The rights and liabilities of the lessees holding over on the strength of special statute like West Bengal Premises Tenancy Act are governed by such statute.

Renewal of lease. Renewal of a lease is creation of a fresh lease and it must be by a registered document. But where no such fresh lease is created in term of the renewal clause no question of registering it arises. If in such a case the lessee continues in possession in exercise of his option as per renewal clause over the leased property after the initial period is over, his continuance in possession would be deemed to be under the original lease deed. The further period is to be treated as part of the original deed of lease. The right to enjoy for further period gets conveyed to the lessee under the original registered deed. This continuance in possession would not be holding over under s. 116 of the T.P. Act and his tenancy would not be governed by the Premises Tenancy Act. Extension of a lease is not creation of a fresh lease but prolongation or extension of the old lease. Extension ordinarily implies the continued existence or something to be extended. In case of extension the same lease continues in force during the additional period by the performance of the stipulated act.[6]

Indian and English laws. In England, a transfer of property by lease is termed a demise. In England, a lease for more than three years can be created by a deed for the tenant to acquire legal estate in the property.[7] When the lease is in writing and not by a deed, it creates an equitable estate according to the doctrine of *Walsh* v *Lonsdale*.[8] But if there are acts of performance, it can be enforced in equity. This is based on the two equitable doctrine: (*a*) "Equity looks at the intention of the parties and not the form"; and (*b*) "Equity considers as done what ought to have been done." The equity of *Walsh* v *Lonsdale* has no application in India;[9] the statutory law here, *e.g.* Transfer of Property Act or the Registration Act makes no distinction between the legal estate and equitable estate. The right of a person under an agreement

5 Section 116 of the Transfer of Property Act.
6 *Ranjit Kumar* v *Tapan Kumar* AIR 1997 Cal 278.
7 Law of Property Act, sections 149 and 205.
8 (1882)21 Ch D 9.
9 *Ariff* v *Jadunath* (1931)58 IA 91; 58 Cal 1235.

for lease is a personal right and not an equitable estate.[9] Nevertheless, when the intending lessee is in possession of the property, he can resist an action for eviction against him under s. 53A of the Transfer of Property Act which gives him the right to retain possession. So the right conferred by this section is available only as a defence. Section 53A of the Transfer of Property Act does not however create any title nor dispense with the necessity of a registered document which the law requires to effect transfer of property. As observed by Lord Atkin, that that section does not operate to create any legal right. It operates as estoppel as between the proposed transferor and transferee and so is of no protection against third parties not claiming under or through them.[10] The Supreme Court approved of this principle.[11] A perpetual lease is treated in England as a grant of the fee simple subject to a rent charge.[12] The Common Law now recognises two types of estate—(*a*) freehold; and (*b*) leasehold for a term of years. In India, such a lease is recognised under s. 105 of the Transfer of Property Act. The three types of leases recognised under that section are (*a*) term lease; (*b*) periodic lease; and (*c*) permanent lease. In England, there is no law against the letting of a tumbled-down house except implied covenant of fitness in case of furnished house imposed under the Housing Act 1936 (26 Geo 5 and Edw 8 C5J), now re-enacted as Housing Act 1957 (5 and 6 Eliz 2, C56). Here the lessor warrants them to be fit for habitation at the commencement of the tenancy. In other cases, the tenant must take the property as it is and where it is. There is no such enactment in India except what are provided under s. 108(*a*) of the Transfer of Property Act as to disclosure of material defects in the property.

If the defect is patent, there is no duty nor any occasion for disclosure. Section 34 of the West Bengal Premises Tenancy Act 1956,[12a] makes it obligatory on the part of the landlord to execute repairs required for maintenance and essential supplies, *e.g.*, water, gases, electricity, sanitation, etc.

Under the English law, the lessee takes the premises subject to events which may in future depreciate its value. So in the absence of any express covenant, the tenant is not exonerated from payment of rent even if the premises is destroyed by fire or taken by enemy.[13] It is, therefore, doubtful whether the doctrine of frustration applies to put an end to a lease in England. This doctrine has been somewhat shaken of late by the observation of

10 *S.N. Banerjee* v *Kutchwar Lime and Stone Co. Ltd.* (1941)21 Pat 24; 40 CWN 374.

11 *Ram Gopal* v *Custodian* (1966)3 SCR 214; (1966)2 SCJ 782.

12 *Seven Oaks Maid Stone Tunbridge Railway Co.* v *London Chatham & Dover Ry Co.* (1879)11 Ch 625.

12a Section 35 of the W.B.P.T. Act 1997.

13 *Stocker* v *Planet Building Society* (1879)27 WR 877 (CA).

Viscount Simon L.C. and Lord Wright in *Cricklewood Property and Investment Trust Ltd.* v *Leighton's Investment Trust Ltd.*[14] It was however held by the Supreme Court in *Raja Dhruv Deb* v *Raja Harmohinder Singh*,[15] that inasmuch as the doctrine of frustration applies to all executory contract, but not to a completed conveyance the lessee cannot avoid the lease on the ground of the property having been rendered unfit for use. The doctrine, however, applies in cases where property is rendered substantially and permanently unfit and not merely damaged which can be repaired.

In English livery *seisin* is necessary to complete the title of the lessee and he is not recognised as a tenant before actual entry. The doctrine of English Common Law does not apply in India, nevertheless non-delivery of possession is a good defence to a suit for rent.[16] If the lessee has obtained possession of a portion he is bound to pay rent in proportion.[17]

In India if by fire or tempest or other causes as provided under s. 108(*e*) of the Transfer of Property Act the property is destroyed the lease shall, at the option of the lessee, become void. This clause therefore partially accepts the doctrine of frustration in its application to India.

Lease and licence. A licence is quite different from a lease. As defined in s. 52 of the Indian Easements Act, it is a right to do or continue to do something in relation to some immovable property. A licensee does not acquire any interest in the property. The test that is applied to ascertain whether any particular document creates any licence or a lease is (*a*) intention of the parties;[18] (*b*) whether any interest in the property is created; (*c*) who has the control of the property, exclusive possession generally implies a lease; and (*d*) to rely on the substance of the document, in preference to the forms.[19] Section 53A of the Transfer of Property Act does not apply to licences.[20]

Use of lease property. Premises taken on lease for doing business of a specific nature cannot be put to use for a different kind of business in violation of the conditions of the lease and hence tenant is liable to be evicted on that ground.[1]

Composite lease. Sections 105 to 117 of Transfer of Property Act deal with the lease of immovable properties. The hiring of equipments is governed by the terms of the agreement. There is no law prohibiting a composite lease of building along with the equipments or lease of a Mill which includes building and machinery or lease of a factory similarly which includes lease

14 (1945) AC 221.
15 AIR 1968 SC 1024.
16 *Meenakshi* v *Chidam Baram* 15 IC 711.
17 *Surendra* v *Bhudhar* AIR 1938 Cal 690.
18 *Associated Hotels* v *R.K. Kapoor* AIR 1956 SC 1262.
19 *O.C. Ganguly* v *Kamalapat Singh* 51 CWN 208.
20 *Traders and Miners Ltd.* v *Dhirendra* ILR 23 Pat 115; AIR 1944 Pat 261.
1 *Dashrath* v *Kashinath* AIR 1993 SC 2646.

of a building along with machinery and other equipments. A composite lease of a cinema business along with its equipments is equally valid.[2]

Doctrine of suspension of rent. This is an English rule based on the theory that the entire rent is due for the entire land to be demised.[3] This is the nature of penalty and so not enforced unless the eviction or loss of possession is a deliberate act, default or negligence on the part of the landlord or in a case where the lessor knew right from the very beginning that a portion of the property was in the possession of a third party and the lessor will not be able to give him possession.[4] The liability for rent is not finally determined and is revived as soon as the lessee is restored to possession. It is, therefore, not remission of rent but mere suspension unless full possession is restored the reason being that the landlord is not entitled to apportion his own wrong. If the premises are let out for one rent and the tenant is evicted from a portion he can nevertheless suspend payment. This is based upon the theory that the landlords being the defenders and protectors of tenants should not be encouraged to disturb them. But if the rent is divisible the doctrine has no application and the entire rent should not be suspended as observed by Rankin, CJ. in *Sajjad* v *Trailakshya*.[5] Further the doctrine has no application when the dispossession is not due to any deliberate and intentional act on the part of the landlord or by any title paramount. It was however held by the Privy Council in *Ramlal* v *Dhirendra*[6] on appeal from *Dhirendra* v *Ramlal*,[7] that in Bengal the doctrine of suspension of rent should not be applied to cases where the lessor fails to give possession to the lessee of part of the tenure for relief by specific performance, by damages by abatement of rent etc. is obtainable in the courts but non-delivery of possession is a good defence in a suit for rent.[8] It was held by Supreme Court in *Surendra* v *Stephen Court Ltd*,[9] that the doctrine of suspension of rent will not be applicable to all cases as an inflexible rule. It will be inequitable for a tenant not to pay any rent when he enjoys a substantial portion of the property without much inconvenience.[10]

Apportionment of rent. Sections 36 and 37 of the Transfer of Property Act deal with apportionment of rent. It means proportionate payment according to the period of liability or accrual of title on transfer or otherwise.

2 *Bhagyashree Combines* v *Dist. Magistrate* AIR 1998 Kant 328. See also *Uttam Chand* v *S.M. Lalwani* AIR 1965 SC 716; *Dwarka* v *Dwarka* AIR 1975 SC 1758.
3 *Sajjad Ahmad* v *Trailakshya* (1927-28)32 CWN 472; 55 Cal 464.
4 *Rameswharlal* v *Butta Kristo* (1934)13 Pat 396; AIR 1934 Pat 653.
5 (1928)55 Cal 464.
6 AIR 1943 PC 24.
7 42 CWN 1030.
8 Section 108 of the Transfer of Property Act.
9 AIR 1966 SC 1361.
10 See also *Pranab Ganguli* v *Shanbaza Land and Estate Ltd*. 86 CWN 40 at p. 43.

The Essentials of a lease are—

(*i*) Parties must be of full age.

(*ii*) Date of commencement.

(*iii*) Rent, salami etc.

(*iv*) Purpose of the demise.

(*v*) Duration—Proviso for earlier determination.

(*vi*) Covenant for renewal as may be agreed.

Drafting of a lease. A lease is usually drafted by the lessor's Advocate. The following special points may be noted:

(a) *Generally recitals* are not necessary and material facts are mentioned in the operative part.

(b) *Consideration*. Reserved rent is mentioned in the beginning of the Testatum. The entire consideration, including premium, etc. should be mentioned.

(c) *Operative part*. It should show clearly the lessor divesting himself of possession and the lessee coming into possession, *e.g.* by the use of such words as "The lessor hereby lets, or demises or grants a lease of, etc., etc with effect from the .... day of ....

(d) *Habendum*. The nature of the lease, commencement and duration of the term are specified here.

(e) *Reddendum*. This is peculiar to a deed of lease. Here is mentioned the mode and time fixed for payment. It begins with the word rendering or paying with reference to the reserved rent. Rent is payable during the term of the lease. Place where payable and instalments are mentioned. If there is apportionment of rent that is also mentioned.

(f) *Covenants*. Terms and conditions are mentioned in several paragraphs. The usual covenants are to be found in s. 108 of the Transfer of Property Act; other important covenants generally refer to payment of taxes, repairs, insurance, subletting, purpose of the lease, *e.g.*, residential purpose, renewal, forfeiture.

Covenant running with the land. This is an expression borrowed from English law relating to real property and is an exception to the general rule that all covenants are personal. A covenant may run with the land in law or in equity. A covenant is said to run with the land where not only its benefits pass on to the assignee of the covenantee but also the burden passes on to the assignee of the covenantor and independently of notice in all cases. Instances of such covenants are (*i*) covenant to pay rent; (*ii*) covenant to repair; (*iii*) covenant not to build but to keep open portion of the property; (*iv*) covenant not to assign without the consent of the lessor; (*v*) covenant to pay rates and taxes; and (*vi*) covenant for renewal; (*vii*) covenant given to the lessee, *i.e.* option to purchase the property.

Doctrine of Frustration of a Lease

(*Limited Application to India*)

This is a departure from the English law on the subject.

English law. Under English law the lessee takes the premises subject to all events which may depreciate the value. This is more so because the law is reluctant to imply covenants.[11]

Nevertheless under the English law the doctrine of frustration based upon the old theory of impossibility of performance, discharges a contract where the subject-matter is destroyed. The object of the doctrine was to give effect to the demands of justice, to achive a just and reasonable result to do what is reasonable and fair, as an expedient to escape from injustice where such would result from enforcement of a contract in its literal terms after a significant change in circumstances.[12]

Indian law. In India the application of the doctrine of frustration is very limited and the provisions of s. 56 of the Contract Act codify the law on the subject, which become impossible of performance, because of change of circumstances when the obligations of the respective parties stand discharged. This was observed by the Supreme Court in *Ganga Saran* v *Ram Charan Ram Gopal*.[13] Secondly the doctrine could at best apply to executory contracts and not executed contracts, *e.g.* contract for the sale of lands as such contracts do not in India create any interest in land and also to an agreement to grant a lease.[14]

Nevertheless under s. 108E of the Transfer of Property Act this doctrine applied in the limited sense when the property which is the subject-matter of the lease becomes destroyed by fire, violence of army or mob etc. then and in such an event the lessee by notice in writing may repudiate the lease.

Thus it was been held that where part or even the whole of the demised premises have been requisitioned there is no frustration of the lease as the same is of a temporary character.[15] It was however held in *Magneeram* v *Satyabrata*[16] that such an order has the effect of frustration of an agreement for sale but the same was reversed on appeal.[17]

11 Mulla's *Transfer of Property Act*, 8th Ed., p. 857.
12 Anson: *Law of Contract*, 27th Ed., p. 503.
13 1952 SCR 86; AIR 1952 SC 9.
14 *Dhirendra Dev Chand* v *Raja Har Mohindar Singh* AIR 1968 SC 1024; *Sushila Devi* v *Hari Singh* AIR 1971 SC 1756.
15 *Tarabar* v *Late Padam Chand* AIR 1950 Bom 89.
16 AIR 1951 Cal 352; 51 CWN 226.
17 1954 SCA 187; 1954 SCR 310.

FORMS

Contract for Leases

THIS AGREEMENT FOR LEASE made this .... day of .... 2000 BETWEEN AB residing at .... (hereinafter referred to as the INTENDED LESSOR) of the one part and CD residing at .... (hereinafter referred to as the INTENDED LESSEE) of the other part.

WHEREAS the INTENDED LESSOR is seized and possessed of premises No. .... described in the schedule hereunder and intends to lease out the same.

AND WHEREAS the INTENDED LESSEE has approached the said INTENDED LESSOR for taking the said premises on lease.

NOW THESE PRESENTS WITNESSETH and the parties hereby agree as follows:

(1) The said AB will demise to CD and CD will accept a lease of the house, fully mentioned and described in the Schedule for a term of .... years with effect from 1999 subject to a rent of Rs. .... per month, year and other conditions hereunder stated.

(2) The said rent shall be paid on the 15th day of every following month without any delay or default.

(3) The lease shall contain *inter alia* the following covenants and conditions to be observed and performed on the part of the lessee, namely: (*a*) to pay the rent on the day and in the manner aforesaid; (*b*) further to pay all existing and future taxes (except the house tax), rates, assessments and outgoings of every description for the time being payable in respect of the said premises; and (*c*) to keep the premises in wind and watertight condition and good and substantial repairs during the term of the lease and furthermore in such condition and repair to deliver up the same on the expiration or sooner determination of the lease.

(4) The said lease also shall contain further covenants on the part of the lessee, *e.g.* (*a*) not to carry on any offensive trade or prohibited business; (*b*) not to store any combustible or explosive substance except kerosene or petrol in small quantity required for domestic consumption in the premises; and (*c*) not to assign, or underlet, or part with the possession of the premises or any portion thereof without the consent in writing of the lessor AND furthermore a proviso for forfeiture of the lease and re-entry on the part of the lessor if and when any part of the rent shall remain at any time in arrear for 21 days or more whether demanded or not or there shall be a breach of any of the lessee's conditions AND the usual qualified agreement by the lessor for quiet enjoyment by the lessee upon regular payment of rent and performance of the covenants and conditions of the lease.

The Schedule above referred to

IN WITNESS WHEREOF the parties hereto have executed these presents on the day, month and year first above-written.

Signed, sealed and delivered by AB, the INTENDED LESSOR, in the presence of:

Signed, sealed and delivered by CD, the INTENDED LESSEE, in the presence of:

Deed of Lease of Dwelling-House

THIS DEED OF LEASE made the .... day of ...., BETWEEN AB of, etc. (hereinafter called the LESSOR) of the one part and CD of, etc., (hereinafter called the LESSEE), of the other part, WITNESSES, that in consideration of the rent reserved and of the lessee's covenants and the conditions to be observed and performed by him as hereinafter contained, the LESSOR doeth hereby grant, convey and transfer by way of lease to the LESSEE ALL THOSE premises, with compound, out-houses, appurtenance whatsoever, etc., bearing No. .... and situate at, etc.: TO HAVE AND TO HOLD the same to the LESSEE for the term of .... year (or years), with effect from the .... day of ...., at a monthly rent of Rupees ...., SUBJECT to the following terms and conditions:

1. THE LESSEE hereby agrees with the LESSOR as follows:

(*a*) To pay the said rent, free and clear of all deductions, on the .... day of every current month in advance during the term of the lease; such payment shall be made at the address of the lessor as aforesaid.

(*b*) To pay for and discharge and satisfy all rates, taxes, assessments and impositions (except the owner's share of the house tax) which are now or during the said term be hereafter imposed or assessed on the said premises, or the LESSOR or the LESSEE in respect thereof, by the authority of Government or otherwise.

(*c*) At all times during the term of the lease to keep and maintain the premises clean, tidy, healthy, wind and watertight in all seasons and further in good and substantial repair, reasonable wear and tear and damage by fire or storm excepted.

(*d*) To replace all broken fittings and fixtures by equally good or better substitutes and not to make any structural additions or alterations to the demised premises without the consent of the LESSOR first had and obtained in writing.

(e) To permit the LESSOR, his servants and agents at all reasonable hours to enter into the property to inspect the condition or to leave notice of all defects to be repaired.

(f) At all times during the said term to use and occupy the demised property as a private dwelling house for himself and the members of the family and not to keep any paying guests or share accommodation with outsiders nor to carry on or permit to be carried on any offensive or prohibited trade or business in the said premises.

(g) Without the consent in writing of the LESSOR, not to assign or part with his leasehold estate or interest in the said premises created under these presents nor sublet the same or any part thereof to any person or persons whomsoever, or make any structural addition or alteration therein.

(h) On the expiration or earlier determination of the lease to yield and deliver peaceful vacant possession of the premises in its entirety together with all improvements, if any, done thereto without any claim for compensation on that account.

2. THE LESSOR hereby agrees with the LESSEE as follows:

(a) At all times during the said term, to pay the owner's share of house tax of the premises whenever the same falls due and his income-tax and other personal taxes as and when assessed.

(b) That the LESSEE, paying the rent hereby reserved and observing and performing the conditions and covenants herein contained, shall quietly and peaceably hold, possess and enjoy the said premises during the said term without any interruption and disturbance by the LESSOR or any person claiming under or in trust for him: PROVIDED, however, and it is expressly agreed and declared by and between the parties hereto that, in case of non-payment of rent for any month beyond 2 days or in the event of breach of any of the conditions and covenants to be observed and performed by the lessee, the lease may at the option of the LESSOR stand determined when and in such an event the LESSOR shall be entitled to re-enter into the property and re-possess the same as his former estate without prejudice to his right to recover all arrears of rent and any damages for breach of such conditions and covenants.

The Schedule of property

IN WITNESS WHEREOF the parties hereto have executed these presents on the day, month and year first above-written.

Signed, sealed and delivered by AB,
the LESSOR, in the presence of:

Signed, sealed and delivered by
CD, the LESSEE, in the presence of:

Tenancy Agreement for Letting Furnished House

THIS TENANCY AGREEMENT IS MADE this .... day of .... 2000 BETWEEN AB residing at .... (hereinafter called the LANDLORD which term shall include, unless the context otherwise requires, his heirs, successors, legal representatives and assigns) of the one part and CD residing at .... (hereinafter called the TENANT) of the other part.

WHEREAS the LANDLORD is seized and possessed of a furnished house being premises No. .... described in the Schedule hereunder.

AND WHEREAS the TENANT has approached to take on rent the said furnished house to which the LANDLORD has agreed.

NOW THESE PRESENTS WITNESSETH and the parties hereby agree as follows:

The LANDLORD agrees to let and the TENANT agrees to take all that furnished house with fittings, fixtures and appurtenances together with the furniture and effects more fully described in the schedule hereto for the term of 5 years to be computed from the .... day of .... 1999 at the rent of Rs. 3,000 for the premises and Rs. 2,000 for the furniture per month respectively such rents to be payable by the 10th day of every following month.

(1) The TENANT agrees to pay the rents regularly and punctually without the least delay or single default.

(2) The TENANT shall at all times during the continuance of the tenancy keep and maintain the house with all fittings, fixtures and furniture clean, tidy and healthy, free from moth and dust and insured against whiteants, paint all wood works once in every three years and whitewash and colour wash the walls once in every two years.

(3) The TENANT shall keep all the furniture duly insured against fire, theft and other risks and replace all damaged, broken and worn-out parts of the furniture and fittings including sanitary fittings by equally good or better substitutes.

(4) The TENANT shall pay all rates, taxes and impositions which are now or during the said term be hereafter imposed or assessed on the said premises by the Government, Municipal Corporation or any other authority.

(5) To permit the LANDLORD his servants and Agents at all reasonable hours to enter into the property, inspect the condition or to leave notice of all defects to be repaired.

(6) The TENANT shall during the said term use and occupy the said premises as a private dwelling house for himself and the members of the family and not to keep any paying guest or share accommodation with outsiders and licensee or otherwise, not to carry on, or permit to be carried on any business or to store any inflammable or explosive articles or thing in the said premises.

(7) Without the consent in writing of the LANDLORD the TENANT shall not sublet or assign or part with possession of the said premises.

(8) The TENANT shall on the expiry or earlier determination of the lease yield and deliver to the LANDLORD peaceful and vacant possession of the premises in its entirety.

(9) Without the consent in writing of the LANDLORD the TENANT shall not assign or part with the tenanted premises or sub-let the same or give any licence to anybody to occupy the tenanted premises or any part thereof or make any structural additions or alterations therein.

(10) On the determination of the tenancy the TENANT shall give to the LANDLORD peaceful vacant possession of the tenanted premises.

The Schedule above referred to

IN WITNESS WHEREOF the parties hereto have executed these presents on the day, month and year first above-written.

Signed and delivered by the said AB
the LANDLORD in the presence of:

Signed and delivered by the said CD
the TENANT in the presence of:

Deed of Sub-Lease

THIS DEED OF SUB-LEASE is made this .... day of .... 2000 BETWEEN AB son of .... residing at .... (hereinafter called the SUB-LESSOR which term shall include his heirs, successors and assigns) of the one part and CD son of .... residing at .... (hereinafter referred to as the SUB-LESSEE which term shall unless inconsistent with the context include his heirs, successors and assigns) of the other part.

WHEREAS by a lease (hereinafter referred to as "the ORIGINAL LEASE) dated .... the day of .... and made between XY as owner and AB as lessee and registered in Book I, Vol. .... pages .... to .... being No. .... for the year .... in the Office of the Sub-Registrar of .... etc., the premises (or, etc.) described in the ORIGINAL LEASE were demised to the said original lessee for a period of .... years with effect from the .... day of .... on a yearly rent and subject to the covenants and conditions to be performed and observed as therein contained AND WHEREAS the original lessee has agreed to grant and the SUB-LESSEE has agreed to accept a sub-lease of the premises (or, etc.) hereinafter described upon the conditions hereinafter contained.

NOW THIS DEED WITNESSES that in consideration of the rent hereinafter reserved and the covenants by the sub-lessee hereinafter contained, the

ORIGINAL LESSEE doeth hereby grant to the SUB-LESSEE a lease of ALL THAT premises (or, etc.) known by the name of, etc., and situate at, etc., together with the appurtenances: TO HOLD the same unto and to use of the SUB-LESSEE for the period of .... years, commencing with effect from the .... day of ...., at the monthly rent of Rupees ...., SUBJECT to the following conditions:

1. The SUB-LESSEE hereby agrees with and covenants with its lessor, *viz.* the lessee as follows:

(*a*) To pay the said rent, clear of all deductions, on the ...... day of ...... every current month in advance during the term of the lease.

(*b*) To pay all taxes and outgoings now payable or hereafter to become payable in respect of the leased premises (or, etc.).

(*c*) To keep the said premises (or, etc.) in good and tenantable repair, and not to make any alteration therein without the written consent of the landlord.

(*d*) To perform all the covenants, conditions and stipulations contained in the ORIGINAL LEASE affecting the property hereby leased and to be observed and performed by the original lessee except payment of rent and not to do, execute or perform any act, deed or thing or suffer anything to the contrary whereby or by reason or means whereof the original lease may be avoided or forfeited and to allow the ORIGINAL LESSEE to enter upon the leased premises (or, etc.) for the purpose of inspection of the premises and performing any of such terms of agreement contained in the original lease, which may be necessary to prevent its forfeiture.

(*e*) To keep the ORIGINAL LESSEE indemnified against all actions, claims, demands and expenses on account of performance or non-performance by the sub-lessee (of any of the terms, conditions and stipulations of this agreement).

2. The ORIGINAL LESSEE does agree and covenant with the SUB-LESSEE as follows:

(*a*) That upon the SUB-LESSEE paying the rent hereby reserved and observing and performing the conditions and covenants herein contained, shall, quietly and peaceably, possess and enjoy the property, hereby leased during the said term without any interruption and disturbance by the original lessee or any person claiming under or in trust for him, provided that in case of any breach of any of the conditions and covenants to be observed and performed by the SUB-LESSEE the lease shall at the option of the ORIGINAL LESSEE stand determined who shall be entitled to repossess the property as his former estate without prejudice to his right to recover all arrears of rent and/or any damages for breach of such conditions or covenants.

(*b*) The ORIGINAL LESSEE shall duly and punctually pay the rent reserved, observe and perform all the covenants and conditions contained in the ORIGINAL LEASE, and keep the same alive and in full force and virtue and further will at all times keep the SUB-LESSEE and his estate indemnified against all actions, claims, proceedings and demands on account of any breach of any of the conditions and covenants contained in the ORIGINAL LEASE.

(*c*) The ORIGINAL LESSEE acknowledges the right of the SUB-LESSEE as to production of the ORIGINAL LEASE and to delivery of copies thereof and undertakes for the safe custody thereof.

3. It is further agreed that the terms the ORIGINAL LESSEE and SUB-LESSEE used herein shall, unless inconsistent with the context, include as well their respective successors and assigns.

The Schedule above referred to

IN WITNESS WHEREOF the parties hereto have executed these presents on the day, month and year first above-written.

Signed, sealed and delivered by AB,
the SUB-LESSOR in the presence of:

Signed, sealed and delivered by CD,
the SUB-LESSEE in the presence of:

Deed of Lease

(LONG FORM)

THIS DEED OF LEASE is made this .... day of .... 2000 BETWEEN AB and MN residing at .... (hereinafter called the LESSORS which term shall include their heirs, successors, executors, administrators and assign) of the one part and CD residing at .... (hereinafter called the LESSEE which term shall include his successors, heirs, administrators and executors) of the second part.

WHEREAS the LESSORS are the exclusive owners of .... an estate comprising land measuring .... known as .... and bounded as follows:

East ....
West ....
North ....
South ....

AND WHEREAS the LESSEE has agreed to take a lease of the said land from the LESSORS for a period of .... years upon terms and conditions hereinafter mentioned and has further undertaken to build a cinema hall to be named as .... according to the plan annexed hereto and to the specifications attached therewith.

Now this lease witnesseth as follows:

1. In consideration of a monthly rent of Rs. .... and the LESSEE'S covenants hereinafter mentioned and contained the LESSORS hereby demise and lease unto the LESSEE and the LESSEE hereby takes on rent the plot of land measuring .... or thereabout and comprised in .... for a period of .... years from the date hereof.

2. Immediately on the execution of these presents or as soon thereafter as possible, the LESSEE shall commence and complete with all possible expedition a suitable building or buildings and other structures on the land hereby demised according to and in conformity with the map or plans hereto annexed which have already been sanctioned by the Municipal Committee of .... so that such buildings and structures are completed and are ready for use for the purposes hereinafter mentioned within a period of one year from the date hereof. It is hereby declared that such buildings and structures shall at all times remain the property of the lessee during the term of the tenancy hereby created but immediately on the expiry of such term or on sooner determination thereof and in any event on the expiry of .... years from the date hereof the same shall vest in and become the absolute property of the LESSORS who shall then be entitled to enter upon and to take possession of the same and shall in the meantime have and possess a vested interest therein, it being agreed that during the continuance of the tenancy hereby created the LESSEE shall not sell or mortgage or otherwise alienate the buildings and/or the structures or the materials thereof.

3. All taxes which are now payable by the LESSORS, such as land revenue, property tax as well as all insurance premia on the buildings to be constructed on the land hereby demised, shall be paid by the LESSORS but all other taxes which may hereafter be levied by any authority whatsoever as payable in respect of the said land or buildings thereon by the LESSORS or by the lessee or the occupier thereof shall be paid by the lessee.

4. The rent payable hereunder shall be paid in advance every month by the LESSEE to the LESSORS on or before the 10th day of each calendar month and the receipt of any one of the lessors shall be a complete discharge in respect of the same on behalf of all the LESSORS.

5. If default is made in the payment of the rent for any three months, then on each such default it shall be lawful for the LESSORS, in addition to or in the alternative to any other remedy that may be available to them at their discretion, to eject the lessee from the land hereby demised and from the buildings and structures that may have been erected thereon and to take possession thereof as full and absolute owner thereof provided that a notice in writing shall be given by the LESSORS to the LESSEE of their intention to take possession of the same but if the arrears of the rent are paid within

seven days from the service of such notice then the LESSORS shall not be entitled to take possession of the said land and buildings.

PROVIDED FURTHER THAT if the LESSORS nevertheless exercise their right to take possession of the said land and buildings as provided herein then the LESSEE shall not be liable to pay to the LESSORS the full rent hereby agreed to be paid for the whole of the remaining term of the tenancy hereby granted, subject, however, to the right of the LESSEE to claim refund of the rent, if any, that the LESSOR may recover during such remaining term from the LESSEE.

6. The LESSORS shall whitewash the buildings erected on the said land once every year and shall renew the oil-painting thereof every three years and in the event of their failure to do so the LESSEE shall be entitled to do the same after a week's notice in writing to the LESSORS of his intention to do so and to deduct the expenses incurred by him in that behalf from the rent hereunder payable by him to the LESSORS.

7. The LESSORS (*the* LESSEE) shall insure and shall at all times during the continuance of this lease keep insured all the buildings that may be erected on the said demised land against loss or damages by fire with an insurance company approved in writing by the LESSEE (*the* LESSORS) for an amount which shall not be less than Rs. .... unless otherwise agreed to in writing between the parties.

8. In the event of loss by fire of the aforesaid buildings or part thereof, the insurance money received from the insurance company shall be applied in rebuilding or restoring the buildings as in their previous condition unless otherwise agreed to in writing between the LESSORS and the LESSEE and till the completion of such rebuilding or restoration, the rent hereby agreed or a proportionate part thereof shall remain suspended unless the fire was intentionally or wilfully caused by the LESSEE or his servants or agent and the period of the lease hereby granted shall be extended by the time occupied in such rebuilding or restoration. In the event of the insurance company refusing to pay the claim arising out of the loss aforesaid on the ground that the fire was intentionally or wilfully caused by the LESSEE or his servants or agent, the LESSEE shall be liable for and compensate the LESSORS on account of the loss or damage caused to the said buildings.

9. The LESSEE will be liable to keep the building or buildings and the structures erected on the said demised land in a good state of repair and wind and watertight condition and shall repair any damage or injury caused thereto except such damage as may be caused by ordinary and reasonable wear and tear.

10. The LESSEE shall permit the LESSORS or their duly authorised agent or agents to enter the premises at all convenient times for periodical inspection of the same except when any show or function is being held therein.

11. The LESSEE shall not, except with the permission of the lessors in writing first had and obtained, use the premises for any purpose other than

the following, namely, the exhibition of motion pictures, theatrical performances, concerts, public lectures, skating-rinks, refreshment rooms and other purposes subsidiary or connected therewith. In case of a breach of this condition the tenancy shall be deemed to have been terminated with all the consequences hereinbefore mentioned.

12. Subject to fulfilment of the terms and conditions of these presents, the LESSEE will have the option to extend the lease of the said land and buildings and structures erected thereon for a further period of 10 years on the expiry of the lease hereby granted provided he gives a notice to the effect in writing by registered post to the LESSORS of his intention to do so at least three calendar months before the termination of the present lease.

PROVIDED ALSO THAT with such notice the lessee shall deposit with the LESSORS the sum of Rs. .... as security for the regular payment by him of the rent during such extended term as hereinafter mentioned and for the due performance of the terms of the tenancy.

PROVIDED FURTHER THAT the rent payable by the LESSEE to the LESSORS during the extended term of the lease shall be Rs. .... per month which will include the rent of the land hereby demised as well as of the buildings constructed thereon which, on the expiry of the tenancy created hereby, shall vest in and be the absolute property of the LESSORS as hereinbefore mentioned. After the expiry of the said fresh term of 10 years the LESSEE shall not be entitled to exercise a further option of renewal of the tenancy and shall hand over and deliver the land and the buildings and structures to the LESSORS in a good condition as hereinbefore provided.

13. The LESSEE shall be entitled to proceed with the construction of the buildings and/or structures on the land hereby demised immediately after the registration hereof and the LESSORS shall allow the LESSEE all facilities in that behalf and on their failure to do so pay to the LESSEE compensation at the rate of Rs. 25 (Rupees twenty-five only) per day for such period as the LESSEE is unable to commence the construction owing to the fault of the LESSOR.

14. The LESSEE has deposited a sum of Rs. .... with the LESSORS as security for the due performance of the conditions hereof; this amount the LESSORS shall return without interest to the LESSEE on the termination of the tenancy created hereby subject, however, to any lawful deductions that they may be entitled to make hereunder.

IN WITNESS WHEREOF the said LESSORS and the said LESSEE have put their respective signatures hereunder the day, month and year first above-written.

Schedule of the property

1. WITNESSES:	Signature of LESSORS
	1.
2. WITNESSES:	2.
	Signature of LESSEE

Lease of a Calcutta Property

(*Proper changes may be made in the provisions in view of special Tenancy Laws in the State*)

THIS DEED OF LEASE is made this .... day of .... 2000 BETWEEN AB residing at .... (hereinafter referred to as the LANDLORD which term shall unless excluded by or repugnant to the context include his heirs, successors, representatives, executors, administrators, and assigns) of the one part and CD residing at .... (hereinafter referred to as the TENANT which expression shall unless excluded by or repugnant to the context include his heirs, successors, representatives, executors, administrators and assigns) of the other part.

WITNESSETH that the LANDLORD doeth hereby demise unto the TENANT ALL THAT premises together with the yards, compounds, buildings and ground held therewith and appurtenance TO HOLD the said premises unto the TENANT for the term of .... years from the .... day of .... 1999 yielding therefor during the said term a monthly rent of Rupees .... clear of all deductions, by equal monthly payments on the .... date of each and every current month the first of such payments to be made on the .... day of .... next and the last of such payment to be made in advance on the .... day of .... 2015 AND the TENANT doth hereby covenant with the LANDLORD that he the TENANT during the said term will pay the monthly rent hereinbefore reserved on the day and in the manner aforesaid and will pay all rates, taxes and outgoings now payable or hereafter to become payable, by the TENANT or occupiers in respect of the said premises and will, during the said term, keep the interior of the said premises in good and tenantable condition and will comply with all the requisitions of the municipality and will do, execute and perform at his own expense and cost all petty repairs that from time to time may be required or necessary to be done to the said premises and will make no alteration in the said premises except such as the LANDLORD shall previously approve of in writing and not at any time during the said term carry on or permit to be carried on or committed on the said premises any offensive business or occupation or nuisance and will use the same as a private dwelling-house or as an office and business premises only and at the expiration or sooner determination of the said term will peaceably and quietly yield up possession of the said premises to the said LANDLORD in as good a condition as the same now are and will not assign or underlet the said premises or any part thereof without the previous written consent of the LANDLORD nor keep any heavy articles on the roofs or the upper floors of the said premises, nor keep in or upon any part of the said premises any combustible or injurious articles such as gunpowder, dynamite, saltpetre, jute, cotton, spirit, sulphur, acid, hides or the other articles likely to injure the said premises or any part thereof nor remove any fixture now existing or that may hereafter be put up in the said premises nor do or commit or cause to be done or committed any act, matter or thing to the prejudice or injury of the premises, and will repair and restore at the TENANTS' own cost and expense any damage or injury the said premises may thereby sustain during the said term and also it shall be lawful for the LANDLORD his heirs, executors, administrators and assigns or his agents from time to time and upon reasonable notice with or without workmen and others to enter the said premises to view the state of repair and condition of the same and of all defects and want of repair then and there found and which the TENANT shall be liable to make good under the covenants hereinbefore contained to give or leave notice in writing to the TENANT and that the TENANT will within the period of one month after such notice or sooner carry out the requisite repair and make good the same according to such notice and the covenant in that behalf hereinbefore contained.

PROVIDED ALWAYS THAT if at any time any one or more of the said monthly rents or any part thereof shall remain unpaid for 21 days after the dates whereon they respectively are made payable as aforesaid whether the same shall have been legally demanded or not or in case the TENANT shall apply for or be adjudged an insolvent or bankrupt or enter into a composition with his creditors or in case of breach of the covenants or conditions by the TENANT herein contained and on his part to be observed and performed, it shall or may be lawful for the LANDLORD to re-enter, possess and enjoy the said premises and immediately thereupon the said term shall absolutely determine, provided always that if the TENANT during the said term without the previous consent in writing of the LANDLORD shall vacate the said premises it shall be lawful for the LANDLORD to take possession of the said premises for their protection without in any manner prejudicing this demise or the rights of the LANDLORD thereunder and without subjecting him to any action for trespass or otherwise howsoever and it shall be lawful for the LANDLORD to relet the said premises at any rent that he may reasonably obtain for the same and if such rent should fall short of the rent hereby reserved, the TENANT shall pay the difference without any objection whatsoever and the LANDLORD hereby covenants with the said TENANT and the TENANT performing and observing all the covenants and conditions by the tenant herein contained may quietly hold and enjoy the said premises during the said term without any interruption by the landlord or any person claiming through him and that he the LANDLORD will pay or cause to be paid all rates, taxes and outgoings now payable, or hereafter to become payable by the owner of the said premises and will keep the said premises wind and watertight and remove and change all beams and burgahs that may, during the said term, become decayed and require to be changed. And in case the property be taken up under the Land Acquisition Act or be destroyed by earthquake or other natural cause, the lease shall determine.

The Schedule

IN WITNESS WHEREOF the parties herein executed these presents on the day, month and year first above-written.

Signed, sealed and delivered by AB,
the LANDLORD in the presence of:

Signed, sealed and delivered by CD,
the TENANT in the presence of:

Deed of Lease of Land with Forfeiture Clause and Covenant for Renewal

THIS DEED OF LEASE is made on this .... day of .... 2000 BETWEEN AB son of .... residing at ....) hereinafter referred to as the LESSOR which term shall unless the context otherwise requires include his heirs, successors, executors, administrators and assigns) of the one part and CD son of .... residing at .... (hereinafter called the LESSEE which term shall unless excluded by or repugnant to the context include his heirs, representatives, executors, administrators and assigns) of the other part.

WHEREAS the LESSOR is seized and possessed of premises described in the Schedule hereunder and has good rightful power and absolute authority to grant a lease of the scheduled premises in the manner hereunder mentioned.

NOW THIS DEED WITNESSETH and the parties hereto agree as follows:

1. In consideration of the rent hereinafter reserved and the covenants and conditions hereinafter contained to be observed and performed on the part of the LESSEE the LESSOR does hereby grant, transfer, demise by way of lease to the LESSEE all that piece or parcel or parcels of land described in the schedule below TO HAVE AND TO HOLD the same unto and to the use of the LESSEE for the term of .... years commencing from the .... day of .... 1999 at the annual rent of Rupees ....

2. The LESSOR hereby covenants with the LESSEE as follows:

   (*a*) The LESSOR shall put the LESSEE in possession of the said land on the said .... day of .... 2000.

   (*b*) Upon the LESSEE paying the rent hereby and hereunder reserved and observing and performing the covenants and conditions, herein contained the LESSEE shall quietly and peaceably hold, possess and enjoy the said land during the said term without any claim, interruption or disturbance by the LESSOR or any person claiming under or in trust for him.

3. The LESSEE hereby covenants with the lessor as follows:

(*a*) The LESSEE shall pay the said rent without abatement or deductions on or before the .... day of ...., every year and the first of such payments shall be made on the .... day of .... 2000.

(*b*) The LESSEE shall bear and pay all rates, taxes and other assessments and outgoings which are now or may hereafter be imposed or assessed on the said land except those which are payable in law by the LESSOR.

(*c*) The LESSEE shall not use and occupy the said land for any purpose other than private residence for himself and the members of his family by construction of temporary structures according to the plan approved by the Municipal Authority.

(*d*) The LESSEE shall not, except with the consent in writing of the LESSOR first had and obtained assign, underlet or part with the possession of the said land or any portion thereof or of the structures to be constructed thereon or any portion thereof which consent the LESSOR may at his absolute discretion withhold.

(*e*) That if the LESSEE shall pay the rent punctually and regularly and duly observe and perform the conditions and covenants herein contained and apply in writing to the landlord not less than .... months prior to the expiration of the term herein reserved for renewal of the lease, the LESSOR shall then and in such an event grant to the lessee a new lease of the said land for a further period of .... years on the same terms and conditions as are herein contained except the covenant for renewal and subject to such variations as may be mutually agreed.

(*f*) On the determination of the lease, the lessee shall deliver peaceful vacant possession of the land hereby demised as also the structures to be erected by the LESSEE without claiming any compensation or value thereof.

The Schedule above referred to

IN WITNESS WHEREOF the parties herein have signed and executed these presents on the day, month and year first above-written.

Signed, sealed and delivered by
AB the LESSOR in the presence of:

Signed, sealed and delivered by
CD the LESSEE in the presence of:

Deed of Surrender of Lease

THIS DEED OF SURRENDER of LEASE is made this .... day of .... 2000 BETWEEN AB son of .... residing at .... (hereinafter called the LESSEE) of the one part and CD son of .... residing at .... (hereinafter called the LESSOR) of the other part.

WHEREAS by an indenture dated .... made between the parties hereto and registered in .... it was witnessed that the said CD, did in consideration of the rent thereby and thereunder reserved and of the covenants and conditions to be observed and performed on the part of the said AB as therein contained granted and demised by way of lease the property fully mentioned and described in the schedule hereto for a term of .... years AND WHEREAS such lease is in full force and virtue and all rents and conditions reserved by and contained thereunder on the part of the LESSEE to be paid, observed and performed, have been duly paid, observed and performed by the said AB up to the date of these presents AND WHEREAS the LESSEE was at all material times and is presently in possession of the property since the execution of the lease. AND WHEREAS for personal reasons and consideration the said AB having desired to be relieved from any further payment of such rent and performance of the covenants and conditions approached the said CD for a surrender of the said lease and delivery of the possession of the property AND WHEREAS the said CD has agreed to accept from the said AB a surrender of the aforesaid lease of the said premises: NOW THIS DEED WITNESSES that in pursuance of the said agreement and in consideration of a sum of Rs. .... being the token consideration paid by the said CD to AB, the said AB as beneficial user of the said property do hereby give up and relinquish all his leasehold estate and interest in and surrender and deliver possession to the said CD of the premises (*or*, etc.) comprised in and by the said deed of lease TO HOLD the same as before execution of the lease by the said CD TO THE INTENT and object that the same shall stand determined to all intents and purposes and that the residue of the said term of .... years created by the said deed of lease, and all other rights and interests of the said AB in the said premises (*or*, etc.) under or by virtue of the said deed shall stand extinguished and merged in the reversion freehold and inheritance of the premises with immediate effect as if the said lease was never granted nor intended.

AND THIS INDENTURE further witnesses that in consideration of the surrender of the lease which is accepted by the LESSOR he the said CD doeth hereby release and discharge the LESSEE AB, his successor and estate from all claims, demands and liabilities on account of future rent and/or arising out of performance or non-performance of the covenants, conditions provided under the hereinbefore recited Indenture of lease.

The Schedule

IN WITNESS WHEREOF the parties hereto have executed these presents on the day, month and year first above-written.

Signed, sealed and delivered by
CD the LESSEE in the presence of:

Signed, sealed and delivered by
AB the LESSOR in the presence of:

Deed Altering Conditions in a Lease

THIS DEED OF MODIFICATION of lease is made this .... day of .... 2001 BETWEEN AB son of .... residing at .... (hereinafter called the LESSOR) of the one part and CD son of .... residing at .... (hereinafter called the LESSEE) of the other part.

WHEREAS by a lease (hereinafter called the PRINCIPAL DEED) dated the .... day of .... and made between the parties hereto and registered at .... Registration office in Book No. .... Volume No. .... pages .... to .... Being No. .... for the year .... the said AB granted and demised to CD the house (*or*, etc.) situate at, etc. AND WHEREAS the parties hereto have agreed to alter and modify the terms and conditions of the principal deed in the following manner: NOW THIS DEED WITNESSES as follows:

1. Sub-clause (*e*) of clause 2 (*or*, etc.) of the principal deed shall be omitted and shall cease to have any effect.

2. Sub-clause (*e*) of clause 3 of the PRINCIPAL DEED shall be substituted by the following clause:

That if the LESSEE shall pay the rent punctually and regularly and duly complied with and performed the conditions and covenants herein contained for renewal of the lease agreeing to pay 20% enhanced rent, the LESSOR shall then and in such an event grant to the LESSEE a new LEASE of the said premises for a further period of 5 years on the same terms and conditions as are contained in the Principal Agreement except the covenant for renewal and subject to variation as may be mutually agreed.

3. That as altered and modified as aforesaid the PRINCIPAL DEED shall remain in full force and effect.

IN WITNESS WHEREOF the parties hereto have executed these presents on the day, month and year first above-written.

Signed, sealed and delivered by
AB the LESSOR in the presence of:

Signed, sealed and delivered by
CD the LESSEE in the presence of:

Tenancy Agreement of a Flat for a Fixed Period

From ....

To ....

Re: Tenancy of ....
in the ....

This is to place on record that at my request you have allowed me the use and occupation of the above flat on the 7th floor of the above premises No. .... consisting of one bed room, bath, kitchen, balcony, dining space etc. with right of ingress thereto and case and the facilities of the lift services with effect from .... with all care, maintenance and services thereof until .... day of .... on *inter alia* the following terms:

(1) I shall pay you a sum of Rs. .... as rent or occupation charges inclusive of proportionate taxes payable to CORPORATION OF CALCUTTA on that account and such payment shall always be made in advance on or before the 7th of every current month without any delay or default under any circumstances. I shall keep with you a sum of Rs. .... as security to be adjusted and/or paid at the end of my tenancy under you.

(2) I shall keep and maintain the flat with all its fittings and fixtures clean and tidy free from dust, moth, white ants and rust and paint the wooden works and inside walls whenever necessary, if so desired, during the period of my stay there at my costs for which I shall have no claim nor any right of re-imbursement or set-off against rent against you under any circumstances. I shall replace all broken parts, if any, by equally good or better substitutes whenever necessary.

(3) I shall not make any construction or constructions nor addition or additions or alterations thereto except inside removable wooden partitions by way of adjustments without your prior consent in writing which are all to be removed by me at the termination or earlier determination of my tenancy at my own cost and expenses without causing any mischief or damage to the buildings, such consent may be refused at your absolute discretion.

(4) I shall use and occupy the flat exclusively as my residence with the members of my family and shall never sublet the same or any portion thereof without your prior consent in writing nor share accommodation with any other person or persons nor keep any paying guests or use the same as a boarding or lodging house or for the purpose of any business nor store any combustible or inflammable goods except kerosene oil in small quantity for domestic consumption nor carry any illegal or prohibited trade.

(5) I shall leave and vacate the flat on expiry of my contractual period of tenancy as aforesaid or earlier determination thereof as hereunder provided and deliver peaceful and vacant possession thereof to you in good condition and order and in case of any delay or default on my part I shall be liable to

pay you damages for wrongful use and occupation thereof at the rate of Rs. 100 per day. I shall also leave and vacate the flat whenever required by you for your own use and occupation.

(6) In the event I fail and/or neglect to pay the rent for any two months whether demanded or not, or violate any of the terms hereunder provided or in law, commit any nuisance or annoyance to you or other occupiers of the property, you will be entitled to terminate my tenancy earlier upon a fortnight's notice notwithstanding the fact that the contractual period has not then expired when I shall leave and vacate the said flat and deliver the peaceful vacant possession to you with all improvements or constructions if any made therein with your approval and without any claim on that account.

(7) I shall pay all bills for electricity consumed by me and also telephone charges, if any, subscribed by me in the said flat, I agree and accept.

Dated .... Yours faithfully

Lease of Debuttar Property

THIS DEED OF LEASE is made this .... day of .... 2000 BETWEEN SHREE SHREE ISHWARJI, consecrated and established at premises No. .... Calcutta (hereinafter referred to as the DEITY) of the first part and AB son of .... by religion Hindu, by occupation priest, residing at .... (hereinafter referred to as the SHEBAIT the LESSOR which expression shall where the subject or context allows or admits of be deemed to include his successors in office) of the second part and CD, son of ...., residing at ...., by religion Hindu, by occupation priest, residing at .... (hereinafter referred to as the LESSEE which term shall where the subject or context allows or admits of include his heirs, executors, administrators, representatives and assigns) of the third part.

WHEREAS the party of the second part is at present shebait of the deity and so is fully in charge of management and administration of the estate of the deity which consist of *inter alia* property mentioned and described in SCHEDULE "A". AND WHEREAS the temple that is place of the said deity which is now lying in a most dilapidated condition for want of necessary repairs and maintenance for a long time AND WHEREAS the income of the estate of the deity that is the rent which is collected from other properties belonging to deity is hardly a sum of Rs. .... per month is Rs. .... per year out of which the following disbursements are to be made, *viz.*

(*a*) Amount paid to the priest for performance for daily *seva* and *puja* of the deity at the rate of Rs. .... per month Rs. .... per year.

(*b*) Amount paid to the milkman for supply of milk to the deity at the rate of Rs. .... per month that is Rs. .... for the year.

(*c*) Amount paid to he maid-servant for the cleaning of the temple of the deity and utensils Rs. ...... per month that is Rs. ...... per year.

(*d*) Amount paid as costs of fruit and sweets of the deity every day Rs. .... per month that is Rs. .... per year.

(*e*) Amount spent for kerosene oil for one Harricane lamp kept burning at night at the temple of the deity Rs. .... per month, *i.e.* Rs. .... per year.

(*f*) Miscellaneous and contingent expenses Rs. .... per year.

(*g*) Taxes payable to the Municipality per quarter Rs. .... per year.

Total: __________

AND WHEREAS in the circumstances there is no such surplus fund for the maintenance and repair of the temple and for essential services to the deity AND WHEREAS the said temple which is out of repair for a long time is liable to collapse before the ensuing monsoon unless urgent repairs are immediately executed the costs whereof are estimated at sum of Rs. ....

AND WHEREAS THE ESTATE of the DEITY have no funds or other resources or income to carry out the repairs to the estate of the DEITY the party of the second part contracted to grant a lease or demise the scheduled properties which is not yielding income on terms hereunder contained.

AND WHEREAS the party of the third part has offered to pay Rs. .... per month for leasing out the scheduled property and which offer is the highest among others received after advertisement in newspapers on two occasions AND WHEREAS the said LESSEE is also satisfied about the *bona fides* of such demise and has agreed to accept the same NOW THIS INDENTURE WITNESSES THAT in consideration of the sum of Rs. .... to be paid to the party of the first part as premium immediately on execution of these presents and a further sum of Rs. .... to be paid per month on account of rent and the covenants and conditions to be observed and performed on the part of the LESSEE and in the circumstances aforesaid and for legal necessities and justifying causes the party of the second part as shebait for and representing the DEITY and as such as LESSOR and in exercises of all powers authorities and liberties vested in him as such shebait doeth hereby and hereunder grant transfer demise and assure as and by way of lease unto and to the use of the party of the third part the property fully mentioned and described in SCHEDULE "A" TO HAVE AND TO HOLD the same on lease for a term of .... years as hereunder contained, *i.e.* until .... day of .... 2010 AND THAT the LESSEE doeth covenant and agree with the LESSOR as follows:

(*a*) To pay the said rent and all enhancements thereof from time to time free and clear of all deductions, on the .... day of every current month in advance during the term of the lease;

such payment shall be made at the address of the LESSOR as aforesaid.

Such rent shall be increased progressively every year at the rate of .... per cent of the last year's rent.

(*b*) To pay for and discharge and satisfy all Municipal rates, taxes, assessments and imposition (except the owner's share of the house tax) which are now or during the said term and other liabilities and outgoings as may be hereafter imposed or assessed on the said premises, or on the lessee in respect thereof, by any public or statutory body or authority and keep the LESSOR indemnified against all loss damages etc. suffered or costs charges and expenses incurred on that account.

(*c*) At all times during the term of the lease to keep and maintain the premises clean, tidy, healthy, free from moth and white ants, wind and water-tight in all seasons and further in good and substantial repair, reasonable wear and tear and damage by fire or storm excepted.

(*d*) To construct a building on the demised property at a cost not below Rs. .... according to the sanctioned plan of the authorities within a period of two years from date hereof which will vest in and be the property of the deity on termination or earlier determination of the lease hereunder created without any claim by LESSEE on that account.

(*e*) To pay a sum equivalent to 20% of the amount of rent in case the building when constructed is let out to tenants or of the estimated rent if the building is used and occupied by the LESSEE as royalty every month. Such payment shall be made along with the rent every month.

(*f*) To replace all broken fittings and fixtures by equally good or better substitutes and not to make any structural additions or alterations to the demised premises without the consent of the LESSOR first had and obtained in writing except interior alterations by way of adjustments.

(*g*) To permit the LESSOR, his servants and agents at all reasonable hours to enter into the property to inspect the condition or to leave notice of all defects to be repaired which will be executed within a fortnight thereafter.

(*h*) At all times during the said term to use and occupy the demised property as office premises or commercial or residential dwelling house for himself and the members of his family and the tenants and not to keep any paying guests or share accommodation with outsiders and not to carry on nor allow nor permit others to carry on any trade or business or publicity thereof in the said premises nor use nor permit others to use the same or any part thereof for any illegal purpose.

(*i*) Without the consent in writing of the LESSOR, not to create any sublease nor assign or part with his leasehold estate or interest in the said premises created under these presents nor sublet the same or any part thereof to any person or persons whomsoever, or make any structural addition or alteration therein.

(*j*) On the expiration or earlier determination of the lease to yield and deliver peaceful vacant possession of the premises in its entirety together with all improvements, if any, done thereto without any claim for compensation or otherwise on any account whatsoever.

And the LESSOR doeth hereby covenant and agree with the LESSEE as follows:

(*a*) To use the premium solely and exclusively for the purpose of repairs to the temple as hereunder contemplated.

(*b*) At all times during the said term, to pay the owner's share of house tax of the premises whenever the same falls due and his income-tax and other personal taxes as and when assessed.

(*c*) Upon the LESSEE paying the rent hereby reserved and observing and performing the conditions and covenants herein contained, the LESSEE shall quietly and peaceably hold, possess and enjoy the said premises during the said term without any interruption and disturbance by the LESSOR or any person claiming under or in trust for him.

Provided, however, and it is expressly agreed and declared by and between the parties hereto that, in case of non-payment of rent for any month beyond 3 days or in the event of breach of any of the conditions and covenants to be observed and performed by the LESSEE, the lease shall at the option of the LESSOR stand determined notwithstanding any waiver or condonation of the breach or any intermediate negotiations to the contrary when and in such an event the LESSOR shall be entitled to re-enter into the property and repossess the same as his former estate with all improvements done thereto and without prejudice in any case to his right to recover all arrears of rent and any damages for breach of such conditions and covenants.

AND THAT the party of the 2nd part doeth hereby further covenant and agree with the party of the 3rd part that the said property is free from encumbrances except the charge for the maintenance and *seva* and *puja* of the deity and that the same is not otherwise prejudiced in title or estate and that the party of the 2nd part has not done executed or performed anything whereby he is hindered or prevented from granting and/or transferring the same or lease in the manner hereinbefore indicated. AND THAT the LESSEE shall bear and pay all costs of and incidental to this lease, including stamp and registration charges.

The Schedule above referred to

SCHEDULE A

Description of property which is the subject-matter of the lease hereunder created:

IN WITNESS WHEREOF the parties hereto have set and subscribed their respective hands and seals the day, month and year first above-written.

For self and shebait for and representing the deity Sd/-

Signature of the LESSOR Sd/-

Signature of the LESSEE Sd/-

MEMO OF CONSIDERATION

Received of and from the within-mentioned LESSEE the sum of Rs. .... being the premium payable under the within-mentioned Deed by a Bank Draft No. 11 dated .... issued by X Bank Ltd. payable in Calcutta.

Received

Signature of the SHEBAIT for self and the DEITY

WITNESSES:

Signature of the LESSOR

Deed Modifying Terms of Lease

THIS DEED IS MADE this .... day of .... BETWEEN AB of, etc. (hereinafter called "the LESSOR") of the one part and CD of, etc., (hereafter called "the LESSEE") of the other part being supplemental to the deed of lease (hereinafter called "the PRINCIPAL DEED") dated the .... day of .... and made between the same parties being a lease of a house (*or*, etc.) situate at etc. WITNESSES as follows:

1. The LESSOR shall forthwith erect and construct and will complete on or before the .... day of ...... to the reasonable satisfaction of the LESSEE, a room (*or*, etc.) and other additions to the premises leased under the PRINCIPAL DEED, in accordance with the plans and specifications, copies whereof have for the purpose of identification been signed by the LESSOR and the LESSEE.

2. In consideration of the premises, the LESSEE hereby agrees with the LESSOR that as from the .... day of .... he, the LESSEE will pay to the LESSOR during the residue of the term granted by the lease under the PRINCIPAL DEED, the additional yearly rent of Rs. .... such additional rent to be paid by equal monthly payments on the same days and in the

same manner as are provided by the PRINCIPAL DEED for the payment of rent thereby reserved, the first of such payment to be made on the .... day of .... and that all the rights and remedies of the LESSOR shall be applicable to the said additional rent.

3. From and after the completion of the said additions and works to be erected and constructed by the LESSOR as aforesaid the agreements and conditions contained in the PRINCIPAL DEED shall apply thereto in the same manner as if the said additions and works had been completed prior to the grant of the lease by the Principal Deed.

IN WITNESS etc.

Signed, sealed and delivered CD

AB

The Plans, etc., above referred to

Licence for use of a House Property to a Company for Office Accommodation

AN AGREEMENT IS MADE this .... day of .... 1999 BETWEEN AB son of .... by faith .... by occupation .... (hereinafter referred to as the OWNER) of the one part and X & CO. Ltd. represented .... by its secretary being signatory to this agreement having its principal office at present at No. .... (hereinafter referred to as OCCUPIERS) of the other part.

WHEREAS the OCCUPIERS approached the OWNER for permission for using a portion of his property, *viz.* premises No. .... fully mentioned and described in the Schedule hereto for temporary accommodation and/or location of their offices for a period not exceeding eleven months only from the date of signing of this agreement which the owner has agreed to grant reserving for himself the care, maintenance and services to property and on the basis of leave and licence only (which will stand *ipso facto* revoked on the expiry of the said term). Now, it is hereby expressly agreed and declared by and between the parties as follows:

1. This writing shall never be construed as any tenancy agreement or lease nor otherwise creating any other right or interest in the property in favour of the OCCUPIERS which is not at all the intention of the parties but on the contrary merely a temporary agreement or arrangement simply to allow the occupiers to use and occupy portion of the premises for their office accommodation under the control and supervision of the owner for which purpose the OWNER shall retain .... rooms, *viz.* one in the ground floor and another in the first floor. The owner shall have his own staff in the said rooms for the care and supervision and maintenance of and services to the property.

2. The OCCUPIERS shall, in consideration of such accommodation as hereunder provided, pay to the OWNER a fixed sum of Rs. .... as charges for such temporary occupation for the period of .... months which sum will be paid at the rate of .... per month on the .... of every current month without delay or default and a further sum of Rs. .... per month on account of maintenance to the property over and above of the payments. He shall further pay a sum of Rs. .... for service charges and also use of fittings and fixtures making thus a sum total of Rs. .... per month. The two last-mentioned amounts shall also be paid on the .... of every current month.

3. The OCCUPIERS shall also pay to the OWNER on account of Corporation of Calcutta all existing and future occupier's share of rate and taxes of the property and also the enhancement in the owner's share, if any, during the period of their occupation and shall otherwise keep the OWNER and his estate indemnified as against any loss if any arising out of such non-payment or non-observance of any of the covenants herein contained.

4. The OCCUPIERS have as security deposit for such payments and observance of the covenants hereunder contained kept with the OWNER a sum of Rs. .... to be repaid without interest on revocation of licence and surrender and delivery of possession of the said portion of the property subject to such deductions as the OWNER shall be entitled as against the OCCUPIERS, *e.g.*, arrears of charges provided in clause 2, unpaid taxes, electric bills, etc., as hereunder provided or otherwise permitted in law.

5. The OCCUPIERS shall on expiry of the period of .... and licence hereunder granted or earlier revocation thereof surrender the property and deliver the same to the OWNER when and in such an event he will be entitled to the refund of Rs. .... subject to deductions provided in clause 4 hereof.

6. Provided, however, and notwithstanding anything hereinbefore contained, it is hereby expressly agreed by and between the parties hereto that in default of any payment on the dates hereinbefore referred to above to the OWNER or the Corporation of Calcutta or other appropriate authorities the OWNER shall be entitled to and shall have always the power to revoke the licence hereunder granted at his absolute discretion and reoccupy the said portion of the property without subjecting himself to any liability on that account and notwithstanding any intermediate negotiations or waiver of breach thereof when and in such an event the OCCUPIERS shall surrender the occupied portion of the property as hereunder contemplated.

7. The OCCUPIERS shall have no right to make any addition or alteration to the property except removable of wooden partitions by way of adjustments but shall be entitled to make interior decorations only by temporary wooden partitions which they shall remove at their own costs at the time of surrender of the said portion of the property on expiry of the term of the licence hereby granted or earlier revocation thereof and repair all the damages if any caused to the property.

IN WITNESS WHEREOF the parties have executed this Agreement this .... day of .... 1999.

Signed, sealed and delivered by AB at Calcutta in the presence of:

Signed, sealed and delivered by .... on behalf of X & Co. Ltd. pursuant of Board Resolution of .... in the presence of:

Deed of Licence

THIS DEED OF LICENCE is made this .... day of .... 2000 BETWEEN AB, son of .... residing at .... (hereinafter called the LICENSOR) of the one part and CD, son of .... residing at .... (hereinafter called the LICENSEE) of the other part.

WHEREAS the said CD has applied to AB for the use of the eastern outside wall of his building being premises No. .... for the purposes of utilising the same for publicity and advertisement of his goods a specimen copy whereof with type and design shall be delivered to the LICENSOR for a period of two years: AND WHEREAS the said AB has agreed to grant the licence.

NOW THESE PRESENTS WITNESSES and the parties hereby agree as follows:

1. That the said CD shall be entitled to use the said outer wall of premises No. .... for the purpose of advertisement of his goods by coloured signs, marks, letters or other representations for two years from the date in dimensions measuring .... and not contrary to any regulation of the Municipality or other public body or authority.

2. That the said CD shall pay Rs. .... as such advertisement charges per month in advance within the 5th day of every current month.

3. That in the event the said outer wall or the plaster thereof is damaged on account of any act, default or negligence or omission on the part of CD, he shall forthwith execute all the necessary repairs thereto or in the alternative pay adequate compensation to AB on that account.

4. That the said CD shall pay for all taxes and impositions on account of such advertisements.

5. That the said AB shall be entitled to revoke this licence within the said period of two years only on failure to pay regularly the fees or taxes or impositions as aforesaid.

6. That the said CD shall not be entitled to affix on the said wall any representation of other goods nor have any interest in the said wall and further shall indemnify the said AB against any damage suffered in case

such display or advertisement is found to be in breach of statutory rules or orders of any Authority.

IN WITNESS WHEREOF the parties have signed these presents on the day, month and year first above-written.

Signed, sealed and delivered by
AB the LICENSOR in the presence of:

Signed, sealed and delivered by
CD the LICENSEE in the presence of:

Agreement for Alternative Accommodation in the case of Demolition of the Premises

THIS AGREEMENT IS MADE on .... 1999 BETWEEN Shri AB son of .... residing at premises No. .... Calcutta, (hereinafter called and referred to as the LANDLORD) of the one part and Shri CD son of .... residing at .... (hereinafter called and referred to as the TENANT) of the other part:

WHEREAS the LANDLORD has decided to demolish the entire Premises No. .... which includes the shop room at present occupied by the TENANT in the ground floor facing north measuring .... sq. ft. more or less at a monthly rental of Rs. .... (Rupees ....) only payable to the said LANDLORD according to English calendar month and WHEREAS the LANDLORD intends to construct a new building in the place of the existing one, which is to be completely demolished and has agreed to provide the said TENANT with suitable alternative accommodation more or less approximately of the same area and similar in advantages and road frontage in the new building at the same rent immediately after its construction and as soon as possible.

NOW THIS AGREEMENT WITNESSETH as follows:

1. That the LANDLORD will immediately after execution of this agreement arrange for and provide the TENANT with temporary accommodation in a shop room in the said premises for the time being pending construction of the new building.

2. That the TENANT will thereupon leave and vacate the portion of the building now in his occupation and hand over vacant possession of the same to the LANDLORD by .... and shift his business to the newly arranged temporary room.

3. That the LANDLORD will immediately after the construction work in respect of the portion of the building which was under the possession of the TENANT be completed, provide the TENANT with the shop room more clearly shown in red colour on the map or plan annexed with this agreement.

4. That the TENANT shall continue in the portion given to him for the time pending the construction work of the building and shall be liable to go back to his own originally occupied portion or any portion similar in advantageous area and road frontage given to him by the LANDLORD.

5. That the TENANT shall so long he shall continue in the room temporarily provided for him pay its rent to the LANDLORD @ Rs. 3 (Rupees three) only per sq. ft. per month.

6. That the TENANT shall deposit a sum equivalent to three months' rent with the LANDLORD initially and that the said three months' rent shall all along be treated as 'DEPOSIT'.

7. That the new room to be made over to the TENANT shall be fitted with doors, windows and electric lines and fittings, flooring and ceiling and plastered and whitewashed walls, with a rolling shutter gate together with all facilities enjoyed in respect of the old room.

8. That the LANDLORD shall make over the new shop room to the TENANT in the newly constructed building two months after the date when the TENANT shall vacate the old shop room in the existing building.

IN WITNESS WHEREOF the parties hereto have set and subscribed their respective hands and seals the day, month and year above written.

Signed, sealed and delivered by AB and CD at Calcutta in the presence of:

1. .... AB
2. .... CD
3. ....

Lease of Jute Mill

THIS LEASE IS MADE BETWEEN XY Jute Mill Co. Ltd., a company registered under the Companies Act 1956 having its registered office at .... (hereinafter called the LANDLORD which expression shall where the context so admits include its successors and assigns) of the First Part and AB Co. Ltd., a company registered under the Companies Act 1956 having its registered office at .... (hereinafter called the TENANT which expression shall where the context so admits include the Tenant's successors and permitted assigns) of the Second Part and EF Co. Ltd., a company registered under the Companies Act 1956 and carrying on business at .... (hereinafter referred to as the SURETY which expression shall include its successors) of the Third Part.

WHEREAS the LANDLORD is carrying on business as manufacturer of and dealer and exporter in jute goods at .... for the last 30 years.

AND WHEREAS the LANDLORD is seized and possessed of the said XY Jute Mill along with the land in which the Mill is situate and has a good Title thereto.

AND WHEREAS the main promoter of the said XY Jute Mill Co. Ltd. intends to concentrate on his business in England and desires to leave India as soon as circumstances permit.

AND WHEREAS there are no other competent person at the moment to look after and run the XY Jute Mill in the absence of the main promoter.

AND WHEREAS the TENANT is carrying on business as manufacturer of and dealer in and exporter of jute goods in its own Mill and can conveniently utilise the capacity of XY Jute Mill Co. Ltd.

AND WHEREAS there have been discussions and negotiations between the LANDLORD and TENANT whereby the LANDLORD has agreed to let out the Mill premises along with the Mill comprising of plant, machinery, fittings and fixtures on monthly rental basis and the TENANT has agreed to take on rent the said Mill as a going concern and to run the Mill and keep the plant and machinery in working condition.

AND WHEREAS the parties intend that if the TENANT can run the Mill successfully the LANDLORD will ultimately sell the same to the TENANT.

AND WHEREAS the LANDLORD has agreed to meet the liabilities of the said XY Jute Mill Co. Ltd. from the rent that might be paid by the TENANT and that the TENANT will have no responsibility to the creditors and bankers of the LANDLORD.

AND WHEREAS it has been agreed between the LANDLORD and its creditors including bankers that they will not proceed against the assets of the Jute Mill and will get their payments out of the rents receivable by the LANDLORD and that they will not disturb the running of the Mill by the TENANT so long as the TENANT goes on paying the rent regularly fixed herein.

AND WHEREAS the SURETY has guaranteed the timely payment of the rent by the TENANT which the SURETY under its Memorandum of Association and Resolution of the General Meeting is authorised to do.

NOW THESE PRESENTS WITNESSETH and the parties hereby agree as follows:

1. The LANDLORD hereby demises unto the TENANT all those premises described in the First Schedule hereunder being premises No. .... being the Jute Mill with all structures, sheds, plant, machinery, fittings, fixtures, furniture, privileges appurtenant thereto (hereinafter called the "DEMISED PREMISES") with all permits, licences, consents and rights set out in the Schedule except those reserved and mentioned in the Schedule to hold unto the TENANT for a term of 15 years from January 1999 paying therefor in advance by monthly instalments on the first day of every month Rs. 1 lakh the first payment to be made on the execution hereof and thereafter by the first day of every month and also paying by way of additional rent a sum representing the interest @ 15% per annum or the

prevailing commercial bank rate whichever is higher on the due date for rent payment on the arrears of rent by more than 7 days from the date on which the payment fell due until payment is made in full. Such rent shall be enhanced by 10% every 3 years and such increased rent shall be payable by the Tenant as aforesaid.

2. The TENANT hereby agrees and covenants with the LANDLORD as follows:

(*a*) To pay such rent at the time and in the manner aforesaid;

(*b*) To pay all rates, taxes, assessments and outgoings of a periodically recurring and non-capital nature payable in respect of the DEMISED PREMISES during the term of the tenancy except, however, the outgoings as the owner is by law bound to pay notwithstanding any contract to the contrary.

(*c*) To pay all charges for gas, electric current and telephone services including rent supplied to or used on the DEMISED PREMISES during the tenancy. The metre readings at the commencement of the tenancy are electric current 1001 and gas 501.

(*d*) To keep the whole and every part of the DEMISED PREMISES the Jute Mill with all plant, machinery fittings and fixtures in good substantial repair and condition and properly operative and productive throughout the said term.

(*e*) To obtain and keep renewed in force all Licences, permits, entitlements, as are in force and that might be required by any law and observe all formalities and statutory requirements so that the Mill may run smoothly.

(*f*) To permit the LANDLORD and its agents at all reasonable hours in the day time to enter upon and inspect the condition of the DEMISED PREMISES and to give notice in writing to the TENANT of all defects found which the TENANT is liable to make good under the covenants hereinbefore contained and if the TENANT does not proceed diligently within 60 days of such notice to repair and to make good all defects, then to permit the LANDLORD to enter the demised premises with labourers to execute such repairs, the cost of so doing to be payable by the tenant on demand and if not so paid the amount to be recoverable as if the same were rent in arrears.

(*g*) To permit the LANDLORD and its agents with all necessary workmen and equipment at all reasonable times to enter the demised premises for the purposes of carrying out the repairs to the adjoining property of the LANDLORD provided that except in case of emergency the LANDLORD shall give not less than 48 hours notice of his intention to exercise such right and shall make good all damage caused by such entry.

(*h*) To pay on demand a proportionate part of cost of repairing, maintaining, cleansing and replacing all roadways, sewers, drains, gutters, pipes, wires, and cables and electrical, water and other services and things which serve the DEMISED PREMISES jointly with other property of the LANDLORD.

(*i*) To keep such parts of the DEMISED PREMISES as are not built upon in a proper and neat order and condition and not to store anything on them.

(*j*) To insure and keep insured the DEMISED PREMISES to their full reinstatement value thereof with an Insurance Company approved in writing by the LANDLORD in the joint-names of the LANDLORD and the TENANT against loss or damage by fire, explosion, storm, flood and earthquake including the surveyor's fees and loss of two years' rent and such other risks as may from time to time be required in writing by the LANDLORD and upon the request of LANDLORD to produce the Policy and the receipt for the last premium and cause all sums received to be forthwith laid out and expended in rebuilding or repairing or otherwise reinstating the demised premises in accordance with the building plan or otherwise as may be approved in writing by the Landlord and to make up any deficiency in the Insurance money out of Tenant's own funds.

(*k*) To deliver to the LANDLORD a copy of every notice relating to the demised premises served on the TENANT by any competent authority and comply with the requirements thereof.

(*l*) To execute or cause to be executed or done all such works and things as under any law directed or necessary to be done or executed and not to do or permit or suffer to be done any such act, matter or thing as contravenes such law and at all times to keep the LANDLORD indemnified against all claims, proceedings, demands and liability in connection therewith.

(*m*) To keep in force all licences, permits, sanctions, quotas, export rights and entitlements of the Mill and preserve unobstructed all rights of light and other easement appertaining to the DEMISED PREMISES in any way and at all times to afford to the LANDLORD such facilities and assistance as may enable the LANDLORD to prevent the acquisition by anyone of any right of light or other easement over the DEMISED PREMISES.

(*n*) Without prior written permission of the LANDLORD not to assign, underlet or otherwise part with possession of the DEMISED PREMISES or any part thereof.

(*o*) When Landlord's consent has been obtained the TENANT to give notice to the LANDLORD in writing setting forth the name, address and description of the assignee or person in whose favour the devolution has taken place and to produce the Instrument of Assignment or Devolution.

(*p*) Without the consent of the LANDLORD the TENANT shall not erect or permit to be erected on the DEMISED PREMISES any building or erection, boundary walls or fences and not to make or allow to be made any alterations or additions in the DEMISED PREMISES.

(*q*) Except within the DEMISED PREMISES the TENANT shall not part or permit the parking of any cars, bicycles or vehicles by its servants, visitors or agents or customers not to deposit any materials on or otherwise obstruct any roadway adjoining to or forming a part of the Landlord's adjoining property nor permit any loading or unloading to be carried on therefrom.

(*r*) Not to discharge any noxious matter or trade waste or effluent from any building or drain on the DEMISED PREMISES into the sewers of the LANDLORD which has or may have an injurious effect on the sewage therein or the said sewers or the local sewerage disposal works or the water flowing through the said sewers.

(*s*) Not to store or bring upon the DEMISED PREMISES articles which are combustible inflammable or of dangerous nature and not to do or permit or suffer anything to be done by reason of which any insurance on the building or the adjoining property may be rendered void or voidable or whereby the rate of premium thereon may be increased.

(*t*) To ensure that none of water, electricity, gas, telephone and other services serving all or any of the DEMISED PREMISES and the Landlord's other adjoining property are obstructed, terminated, diverted or interfered with in any manner.

(*u*) Not to use or permit to be used the DEMISED PREMISES or any part thereof for any trade or business other than the existing business.

(*v*) Not to do or suffer to be done on the DEMISED PREMISES anything which might be a nuisance or annoyance to the LANDLORD or to its TENANTS or other owners or occupiers of the adjoining lands thereof and not to use nor permit to be used the demised premises for any illegal, immoral or improper purposes.

(*w*) Without prior written approval of the LANDLORD the TENANT shall not affix or display or permit on the DEMISED PREMISES fixing or displaying any advertising sign or notice.

(*x*) To indemnify the LANDLORD against all proceedings, costs, claims and demands in respect of any injury or death of any person and any damage to any property or destruction of any right, easements or privileges that might arise directly or indirectly from the condition of the DEMISED PREMISES.

(*y*) To bear and pay all costs and expenses incurred or that might be incurred by the LANDLORD in connection with or incidental to the preparation of the lease and the counterpart thereof and any application for any approval or consent to any authority concerned whether or not any right of re-entry or forfeiture has been waived by the LANDLORD.

(*z*) On the expiry or sooner determination of the said term, the TENANT to yield to the LANDLORD the demised premises with all the buildings and additions made thereto in the meantime and all plant, machinery, fixtures in such good and substantial repairs and condition including any additions thereto.

3. The LANDLORD hereby covenants that the TENANT paying the said rent and observing and performing all obligations statutory and under this agreement may quietly enjoy and run the Mill, the demised premises, without any interruption by the LANDLORD.

4. The parties hereby agree and declare that:

(*a*) Whenever the said rent or any part thereof is in arrear for two months, whether demanded or not, or if the TENANT becomes insolvent or makes any arrangement with its creditors or commits any breach of any of the provisions herein contained then the LANDLORD may re-enter upon the DEMISED PREMISES with benefit of all licences, permits, entitlements, quotas and rights relating to the Mill and thereupon the tenancy hereby created shall stand determined but without prejudice to any remedy for any antecedent breach by the TENANT of any of the provisions hereof.

(*b*) In the event the DEMISED PREMISES or any part thereof are destroyed or damaged by any cause other than the act or default of the TENANT or his visitors or servants and are not re-built or restored within twelve months after the happening of such destruction or damage, then the rent hereinbefore reserved or a fair and just proportion thereof according to the nature and extent of damage shall be suspended during the period the demised premises or the destroyed or damaged part thereof remain unfit for use by reason of such damage or destruction.

(*c*) The TENANT shall not become entitled to any easement or right which would restrict or interfere with the free use of any adjoining property of the LANDLORD by the LANDLORD or any person deriving title under the LANDLORD for building or for any other purposes.

5. The SURETY hereby covenants with the LANDLORD that the TENANT shall pay the rent hereby reserved on the days and in the manner aforesaid and shall perform and observe all the Tenant's covenants hereinbefore contained and that in the case of default in payment of such rent or the performance and observance of such covenants as aforesaid, the SURETY shall pay and

make good to the LANDLORD on demand all losses, damages, expenses and costs arising or incurred by the LANDLORD, provided always and it is hereby agreed that any neglect or forbearance of the LANDLORD in endeavouring to obtain the payment of rent when the said becomes payable or entitled to the performance of the several stipulations herein on the tenant's part contained or any time which may be given to the tenant by the LANDLORD shall not release or exonerate or in any way affect the liability of the SURETY under this covenant.

6. It is further agreed as follows:

(*a*) if the TENANT is desirous of purchasing remainder of the rights of the LANDLORD, the TENANT shall give six months' notice to the LANDLORD before expiry of the term of the lease hereby granted then the LANDLORD shall on the expiry of the notice and upon payment of a sum to be mutually agreed convey the demised premises to the TENANT or as it directs free from all encumbrances;

(*b*) the TENANT has already investigated the title of the landlord to the demised premises and accepted by him;

(*c*) the sale shall be made in all other respects as might be mutually agreed to.

IN WITNESS WHEREOF the parties hereof put their signatures and seals and execute these presents on this 5th day of November 1999.

First Schedule

Second Schedule

Signed, sealed and delivered by Mr. .... pursuant to a Board Resolution of XY Jute Mill Co. Ltd. dated 10th January 1999 in the presence of: Signature

Signed, sealed and delivered by Mr. .... pursuant to Board Resolution dated 7th January 1999 of AB Co. Ltd. in the presence of: Signature

Signed, sealed and delivered by Mr. .... pursuant to the Board Resolution dated 10th January 1999 of EF Co. Ltd. in the presence of: Signature

32
Lease Financing of Equipment

Lease financing of equipment is in fact a lease of "equipment" in which the LESSOR retains the ownership of the equipment and the LESSEE is entitled to possession and use of the equipment at specified rentals. The rentals are to be paid over a period of years which will cover depreciation and overhead expenses. The rentals will include interest on capital investment and some margin of profit for the LESSOR. The lease financing is a method of financing the acquisition or use of plant, equipment and other durable assets by the manufacturing unit without investing substantial amount but on payment of initial amount, service charges and rentals.

The advantages of taking the equipment or durables under the Lease Financing System are that the lessee does not have to make huge capital investment for the assets, it pays monthly rent from its current earnings. Such rental payments are business revenue expenses and is deductible in computing the profits of the lessee for Income-tax purposes. The rent payable on the plants and equipment or durable goods is generally lower than the interest payable on the capital required to be borrowed for purchasing such plants, equipment or durables. Moreover such borrowings may not be available if the lessee cannot furnish adequate security to the lending institution. When the plant and equipment become obsolete, the lessee need not have to invest huge sums for replacing the same. The lessee may again take on lease the required new plants and equipment on rentals.

The lease of equipment is governed by the Indian Contract Act and in case of lease of motor vehicles also by the Motor Vehicles Act. The rights and obligations of the leasing company and the lessee are governed by the agreement between them.

FORMS

Lease Finance Agreement (Equipment)

THIS LEASE AGREEMENT MADE the 5th day of November 2000 BETWEEN AB Limited, a company incorporated under the Companies Act 1956 and having its registered office at 5 T.N. Road, Chennai hereinafter called the LESSOR (which expression shall unless excluded by or repugnant to the context include its successors and assigns) of the First Part, CD Co. Ltd. and a company incorporated under the Companies Act 1956 having its registered office at 6 G.K. Street, Calcutta hereinafter called the LESSEE (which expression shall unless excluded by or repugnant to the context include its successors) of the Second Part and Mr. MN, son of PQ, residing at 3 L.K. Street, Calcutta hereinunder called the GUARANTOR (which expression shall unless excluded by or repugnant to the context include his heirs, executors, administrators and legal representatives) of the Third Part.

WHEREAS the LESSEE has approached the LESSOR and has requested the LESSOR to purchase and/or acquire plants and machinery and equipment and thereafter to lease the same to the LESSEE subject to the terms, conditions and covenants herein contained and subject to payment of charges and Lease Rentals contained in the Schedule hereunder.

AND WHEREAS the LESSEE has agreed to pay to the LESSOR a one time fee called *Lease Management Fee* amounting to Rs. 1 lakh only simultaneously with the execution of this agreement which fee will be non-refundable and non-adjustable and shall not in any way constitute an obligation on the part of the LESSOR to provide the lease-assistance to the LESSEE which assistance shall always be at the sole discretion of the LESSOR and the LESSEE agrees to be bound by any such decision of the LESSOR.

AND WHEREAS the GUARANTOR in consideration of the LESSOR entering into this Agreement with the LESSEE and granting the equipment on lease to the LESSEE has agreed to guarantee the due payment and the performance and observance of all the terms, covenants and conditions herein contained and on the part of the LESSEE to be paid, observed and performed.

AND WHEREAS the Parties hereto have agreed to enter into this Agreement and record the terms and conditions.

NOW THIS AGREEMENT WITNESSETH and it is hereby agreed and declared by and between and among the Parties hereto as follows:

1. Lease of equipment. The LESSOR hereby leases out to the LESSEE and the LESSEE takes on lease from the LESSOR the equipments/plants and machinery and/or vehicles more particularly specified in Schedule I hereunder written and hereinafter called "the EQUIPMENTS" for the period and subject to the due and punctual payment of the lease-rentals as specified in Schedule I hereunder written and upon and subject to the terms, covenants, conditions and stipulations herein contained and on the part of the LESSEE to be paid observed and performed. Subject to the payment of the said lease-rentals and observance and performance of the terms, covenants, conditions and stipulations herein contained the LESSOR hereby grants unto the LESSEE the right to use by way of lease the said equipments.

2. Period. (*a*) The lease hereby created under this Agreement is for a period of 10 years commencing from the date of the Agreement; and if the LESSEE exercises the option to renew and the LESSOR agrees to such renewal, the lease-period shall run for a further period of five years commencing from the date of expiry of the 10 years.

(*b*) The lease for the first period is non-cancellable but at the end of the first period, the LESSEE shall have an option to terminate this Agreement by giving a notice of not less than 15 days before the end of the first period and in that event, the LESSEE shall at its own cost deliver the equipment to the LESSOR at the place to be indicated in good repair, order and condition.

3. Lease rent and payment. (*a*) The LESSEE shall during the said terms punctually pay to the LESSOR free of any deduction or abatement whatsoever the sum of money specified in Schedule I hereunder as rent for the equipment. All rent shall be paid at the address of the LESSOR shown above or as otherwise directed by the LESSOR in writing. The LESSEE further agrees that the obligations to pay the rentals shall remain absolute in all circumstances and is without any reference to the state, description, use or performance of the equipment leased out.

(*b*) The LESSEE either at the inception of the lease shall give to the LESSOR cheques, promissory notes or any other acceptable instrument for all or any sums payable under this Agreement. Such cheques or notes or other instruments shall be deemed to have been given for adequate consideration already received by the LESSEE and shall not absolve the LESSEE from his liability to pay the said sums hereunder until the cheques, notes or other instruments are duly realised.

(*c*) The LESSOR shall be entitled to appropriate at its absolute discretion any money received from the LESSEE first towards the costs, charges and expenses incurred by the LESSOR for receipts or recovery of such sums, secondly towards overdue charges and other money demanded but unpaid, thirdly towards the lease rentals due and payable and lastly towards the dues owed by the LESSEE under any other Agreement.

(*d*) It is recorded that the LESSEE has paid the sum mentioned in Schedule 1 as and by way of Security Deposit for the due observance and performance by the LESSEE of the terms and conditions of this Agreement. The said deposit is to be held by the LESSOR without any liability to pay interest thereon and with the right to the LESSOR to adjust the said deposit against all amounts due and payable by the LESSEE to the LESSOR. The LESSOR shall refund to the LESSEE the said deposit after necessary adjustments on the expiry of the lease of the equipment and on the return of the equipment to the LESSOR in accordance with the terms of the Agreement. From the amount to be so refunded, the LESSOR shall be entitled to deduct:

(*i*) any sum, which has become due to be paid by the LESSEE to the LESSOR as per this Agreement;

(*ii*) if any sum has become payable by the LESSEE to the LESSOR the exact quantum whereof is not ascertainable an estimated amount on account thereof, including overdue charges;

(*iii*) if it is likely that any liability of the LESSEE shall arise in future, the LESSOR may retain such part of the deposit as it thinks necessary to take care of such liability, and continue paying interest, if any, on the sum so retained as per Schedule I hereunder. The part so retained shall be adjustable against the liability of the LESSEE to the extent the same remains unsatisfied and the balance, if any, shall be refundable to the LESSEE.

PROVIDED that the LESSOR shall not be entitled to retain any sum in pursuance of this Clause if the LESSEE shall furnish a guarantee from a bank acceptable to the LESSOR for reimbursement of the apprehended or contingent liability or otherwise secures such reimbursement in a manner acceptable to the LESSOR.

4. Additional equipments and rents. (*a*) If further equipment is required by the LESSEE and the LESSOR agrees to lease out such further equipment the said further equipment as may be specified in Schedule IA attached and/or to be attached hereto shall be granted on lease on the same terms and conditions as herein contained save and except as to the respective commencement dates and the lease rentals as specified in Schedule IA hereunder written.

(*b*) It is agreed that the LESSEE shall abide by the draw down period as mentioned in Schedule I hereunder written and in no event the acquisition costs of the equipment shall exceed the sanctioned amount as mentioned in the Schedule. In the event of any part of the sanctioned amount being not utilised by the LESSEE within the draw down period, the unutilised amount shall lapse and the LESSEE shall thereafter not be entitled to claim the said unutilised amount.

5. Delivery, commencement and disbursement. (*a*) The equipment shall be delivered to the LESSEE and/or installed by the Supplier/Manufacturer at the factory of the LESSEE and the entire risk cost or any outgoing pertaining to the said delivery and installation shall be to the account of the LESSEE. If any advance payment is made by the LESSOR to the Manufacturer/Supplier, pending the commencement of the Lease it shall be deemed to have been advanced on the LESSEE's behalf and at his request as an accommodation to the LESSEE and the amount shall carry additional financial costs at the rate of Re. 1 per Rs. 1,000 per day with monthly rests on such advanced amount. The LESSEE must ensure that the equipment is delivered by the supplier within such time as may be stipulated by the LESSOR. For this purpose, time is essence of this Agreement. Any failure on the part of the LESSEE in ensuring such delivery shall entitle the LESSOR to treat the Agreement of the lease revoked and recover from the LESSEE the amount advanced to the supplier together with the financial costs and shall have a full and paramount lien over all unencumbered assets belonging to the LESSEE and/or lying at its place for the purpose of recovery of the amount advanced and the financial costs.

(*b*) It is explicitly agreed notwithstanding anything contained herein in case of any misstatement or any other material adverse change including any change in the Government policies taking place after execution of this Agreement but before commencement date or complete draw down of the Lease assistance as a result of which, in the opinion of the LESSOR, the LESSEE ceases to be an acceptable risk then any further draw down may be discontinued by the LESSOR and the LESSOR shall have the option to exercise his right to terminate the Lease in respect of equipment already delivered.

(*c*) If delivery on or before the date of commencement of the rentals is not effected by the manufacturer/supplier, the LESSOR shall not be liable for any loss suffered by the LESSEE thereby. Lease rentals shall be deemed to commence from the date of the commencement of the rentals as specified in Schedule II. In the event that the LESSEE causes cancellation of or instructs the LESSOR to cancel the purchasee order/contract with the supplier of the equipment or the LESSEE shall refuse or be unable for any reason to accept delivery, the LESSOR shall be entitled to terminate the lease of the equipment and the LESSEE shall pay to the LESSOR on demand all costs, charges, expenses, damages incurred by the LESSOR as a consequence thereof.

(*d*) The purchase order for individual item of equipment under this Agreement shall be placed forthwith by the LESSOR at the instance of the LESSEE. In the event of undue delay on receiving such instructions for placement of orders beyond 60 days from the date of this Agreement the LESSOR shall reserve the right to review this Agreement.

(*e*) Taking delivery of and using the equipment shall be deemed to have been found the same complete, in proper order and condition and entirely fit for its purpose and the LESSEE does not and will not at any time have any claim against the LESSOR in respect of or arising out of such equipment.

(*f*) The LESSOR shall not be responsible for any direct, indirect or consequential loss to the LESSEE or third party arising from any delay in delivery and/or installation of or damage to the equipment either by the action of the manufacturer or otherwise.

(*g*) The sole responsibility for obtaining timely delivery of the equipment and the necessary clearances, statutory or otherwise, required for obtaining such delivery shall be of the LESSEE.

(*h*) The LESSEE has selected the equipment and notified itself that it is of the required size, capacity and manufacture, suitable for its purpose.

(*i*) The LESSOR agrees that the LESSEE shall be entitled to the benefits of the warranties provided by the manufacturer/supplier of the equipment. Any performance guarantee provided by the supplier shall be in the joint names of the LESSOR and the LESSEE and shall be enforceable by the LESSOR or the LESSEE or both of them. For this purpose, the LESSOR if so requested by the LESSEE, shall authorise the LESSEE for enforcing the performance by the supplier of the equipment for any warranties or performance guarantees relating to the equipment.

6. Ownership. (*a*) The sole and exclusive ownership of the equipment shall remain with the LESSOR and the LESSEE shall have no right, title or interest therein except as a LESSEE.

(*b*) No attempt shall be made by the LESSEE to capitalise the leased assets in the LESSEE'S Balance Sheet since the ownership of the asset undisputably rests with the LESSOR. The LESSEE shall not claim any relief by way of reduction, losses or grant available to the LESSOR as the owner of the equipment under the Income Tax Act 1961 or any other statute, rules, etc. that are issued by the Government of India or any statutory authority or not to do or be done any act, deed or thing whereby the LESSOR is deprived, either wholly or partly of any such relief by way of reduction, allowance or grants. The LESSEE shall at the end of each accounting year of the LESSOR provide to the LESSOR such information as it may require to claim relief by way of deduction, allowance or grant as the owner of the equipment under the Income Tax Act 1961 and comply with and observe all the terms and conditions to be complied with in the use and operation of the equipment so as to entitle the LESSOR to obtain such a relief.

7. Location. The LESSEE shall keep the equipment at all times in the LESSEE'S possession and control at the location as stated in Schedule I and shall not be removed therefrom without the LESSOR'S written consent PROVIDED THAT in the case of the equipment being a motor vehicle within the meaning of the Motor Vehicles Act, the operation of the equipment may be in such State or area as the LESSOR may from time to time approve in writing.

8. Imported equipment. In the event of any equipment being an Imported Equipment, the LESSEE warrants that without prejudice to the generality of the provisions contained in this Agreement, the following provisions shall apply:

(*a*) The LESSEE shall not contravene any provision of Import Control, Regulations, Foreign Exchange Regulations or any other Statute, rule and regulation to which the equipment and/or the LESSEE is subjected.

(*b*) The LESSEE shall obtain all consent, Import Licence or other licences, Reserve Bank approval or any other approvals and permission as are necessary for or in connection with the acquisition or Import of the Equipment, clearances from the relevant authorities, for execution, validity and enforceability of the Agreement and for the storage, installation use and operation of the equipment and undertakes to keep them effective and in force during the period of this Agreement and till the equipment is delivered back to the LESSOR in good order and condition.

(*c*) The LESSEE agrees and undertakes that in the event of the acquisition of the imported equipment being financed out of the foreign currency lines of credit or foreign currency loans (hereinafter referred to as FCLC) availed of by LESSOR for this purpose, it shall:

(*i*) bear the entire exchange risk on the foreign currency funds utilised by the LESSOR out of the FCLCs;

(*ii*) reimburse the LESSOR with all such expenses, charges as are required to be paid by the LESSOR in respect of FCLCs to the Foreign Bank/Institution concerned;

(*iii*) observe and meticulously follow all the covenants in respect of such FCLCs as may be advised by the LESSOR;

(*iv*) Execute all such documents, deeds, undertakings, etc. as may be required under the covenants of the FCLC.

(*d*) It will be the obligation of the LESSEE to comply with all the terms, conditions and obligations of the Import Licence, including submission of reports and other requirements in that behalf to such authorities as may be required and shall also provide to the LESSOR all such informations as may be required to be furnished by the LESSOR to such authorities and as may be required in terms of the licence for the equipment. In default thereof the LESSEE shall indemnify the LESSOR for all claims and demands made upon the LESSOR by reason of such default.

9. Additional conditions in case of motor vehicles. The Clauses mentioned in this Agreement shall apply to the lease of a vehicle *mutatis mutandis* and to the extent they are not repugnant to the clauses herein and the following further clauses shall apply to the vehicle.

(*a*) The vehicle shall be registered as required under the Motor Vehicles Act 1988 in the name of the LESSEE as owner of the vehicle and the LESSOR's name shall be registered therein as the financier making the LESSEE fully liable and responsible for all the obligations, liabilities and duties as provided under the said Act or under any other law or instrument pertaining to the ownership, use or maintenance of the vehicle.

(*b*) The LESSEE shall deliver as soon as may be after the registration of the vehicle certified copies of the registration papers, Insurance receipts, tax tokens and all other papers connected with the vehicle and continue to provide to the LESSOR certified copies thereof.

(*c*) In the event of the termination of the lease, or the LESSOR taking repossession of the vehicle, the LESSEE shall sign, execute, and deliver all such instruments, forms, applications and writings and shall do all such other acts, deeds and things as may be required by the LESSOR and for this purpose the LESSEE hereby irrevocably and unconditionally authorises the LESSOR that in the event of the LESSEE refusing or being unable to or failing to sign and deliver any of the aforesaid instruments, application forms or other writings as may be required by the LESSOR, the LESSOR shall be entitled without being obliged to do so to sign such instruments, forms, applications papers and writings for and on behalf of the LESSEE as a duly constituted attorney of the LESSEE.

(*d*) The LESSEE shall operate the vehicle only in the areas specified in the schedule or in such other place or places previously approved in writing by the LESSOR and only for lawful purposes and in a lawful manner.

(*e*) The LESSEE shall keep the vehicle in good repair and working condition and replace all such parts, accessories, tyres, tubes or other annexures as becomes obsolete, get damaged or unusable parts replaced.

(*f*) The LESSOR may make reasonable use of force to possess the vehicle in any of the events of defaults and the LESSOR may possess the vehicle wherever the vehicle may be or is believed to be whether with or without whatever is in or on the vehicle and the LESSOR hereby disclaims and the LESSEE hereby assumes the liability on account of loss or damage caused to any person or property because of such repossession.

10. Operation and maintenance. The LESSEE shall at all times keep and maintain at its cost the equipment in good operation condition and working order and repair the same whenever necessary and shall dutifully follow the equipment's manufacturer's recommendations as to use, service and maintenance thereof.

11. Markings. (*a*) On the equipment there should be maker's names, marks plates and identifications and identification to show that the equipment is under lease from the LESSOR which shall not be removed or defaced in any manner whatsoever.

(*b*) The LESSOR's Banker/Financial Institution or any other financier has rights to inspect the aforesaid equipment, to seize the equipment and to appoint receiver thereon. The LESSEE shall not do or cause to be done anything during the currency of the Agreement which will impede the exercise of such rights.

12. Insurance. (*a*) The equipment shall be kept fully insured by the LESSEE at its own cost for an amount equal to its full insurable value with an insurance company approved by the LESSOR and in the name of the LESSOR against all insurable risks and shall keep such insurance in full force and effect during the terms of this Lease Agreement. The name of the respective Bank/financial institution/any other financier/creditor as specified by the

LESSOR shall be mentioned in the Insurance Policy as the hypothecatee of the equipment.

(*b*) Further, the LESSEE shall purchase and pay for policy under Public Liability Insurance Act 1991 and insure and keep insured all substances which have been declared to be hazardous under the notification issued from time to time under the Act or any rule framed thereunder or under any notification, clarification, modification or addendum thereto and which sustances are employed at or used in any of the LESSEE's undertakings whether or not connected with the operations of the equipments. The Insurance Policy should be taken out in the name and for the benefit of the LESSOR and the bankers of the LESSOR or such other names as the LESSOR may advise in this regard. The LESSEE shall indemnify and keep indemnified the LESSOR from any suits, proceedings, actions, claims, demands and/or prosecution and/or the costs, charges and expenses in relation to the liability and obligation suffered by the LESSOR on account of any such hazardous substance or on account of failure of the LESSEE to purchase the Insurance Policy as aforesaid as also pay any cost or expenses related to the LESSOR's defending any suit/proceeding action/claim/prosecution brought or launched against the LESSOR.

(*c*) If for any reason, the amount paid by the Insurance Company on a claim is less than the full insurance value of the equipment, then the LESSEE shall be liable to pay to the LESSOR the difference between the actual loss and the amount paid by the Insurance Company.

(*d*) (*i*) In case of a motor vehicle, the LESSEE shall have and keep at its own cost the same duly registered and have and keep the same insured against comprehensive risks including strike, riots and civil commotion, liability against passenger risks by a policy enuring to the benefit of both parties hereto;

(*ii*) The LESSOR agrees to permit the LESSEE to have the Registration under the Motor Vehicles Act 1988, any of the equipment in his own name provided that the LESSEE shall transfer the registration in the name of the LESSOR when the lease Agreement comes to an end or whenever required to do so by the LESSOR and especially when the LESSEE commits a breach of any of the conditions of this Agreement stated herein and the LESSOR is entitled to retake possession of the equipment.

(*e*) The LESSEE shall hand over to the LESSOR all Registration Certificates and policies of insurance or xerox copies thereof and pay promptly all premiums and stamp duty in respect thereof and promptly forward to the LESSOR all receipts evidencing payments thereof.

(*f*) In the event of any claim arising under the insurance hereunder the LESSEE shall give the LESSOR immediate written notice thereof and comply with all instructions of the LESSOR in connection therewith and the LESSOR shall be entitled to receive and retain to the exclusion of the LESSEE and without thereby divesting itself of the equipment or in the salvage thereof all moneys payable with respect to such claims.

(*g*) In the event the equipment is damaged and in the opinion of the LESSOR it is economic that such damage be made good, all insurance moneys payable under the said insurance may, if the LESSOR agrees, be applied in making good the said damage. If the equipment be destroyed or damaged to such an extent as to be in the opinion of the LESSOR incapable of economic repair then at the LESSOR's sole discretion the insurance moneys payable under the said insurance shall be applied so far as possible in replacing the equipment with another equipment of similar type and quality. In such an event, the fresh equipment shall be deemed to have been leased out by the LESSOR under this Agreement and the LESSEE shall hold the same on lease subject to the terms and conditions as are contained in the Agreement. The lease of the equipment so sold, lost or destroyed will be deemed to have been terminated except in the case where the LESSOR elects to exercise its option as stated above. Without prejudice to the aforesaid right of the LESSOR in the event of such termination, the LESSOR shall also be entitled to recover from the LESSEE all sums as payable under this Agreement.

(*h*) The LESSEE shall insure the equipment against the usual risks during transportation of the equipment from the place of manufacture/delivery to the place of installation and any other transportation during the currency of the lease period.

(*i*) Any failure to recover the insurance money shall not relieve the LESSEE from its responsibility under this lease Agreement.

(*j*) On the LESSEE failing to furnish evidence of insurance within a period of seven days from the date of installation of the equipment the LESSOR may in its absolute discretion arrange an insurance cover as may be needed, and the cost of such insurance shall be forthwith reimbursed by the LESSEE.

13. Loss or damage. The entire risk of loss and damage to the equipment from any cause whatsoever shall be borne by the LESSEE. In the event of any such loss or damage the LESSEE shall at the option of the LESSOR replace at the LESSEE'S cost the equipment which is in the opinion of the LESSOR comparable. Such equipment shall, for all purposes thereafter, be the equipment hereunder and be the property of the LESSOR. Any moneys received in respect of insurance against loss and/or damage to the equipment shall, if the LESSOR so requires, be applied in or towards discharge of obligations of the LESSEE.

14. Inspection. The LESSOR and the Bank, Financial Institution or any other financier to whom the assets covered by this Agreement are hypothecated by the LESSOR shall have the right at all reasonable times to enter upon any premises where the equipment is believed to be and inspect and/or test the equipment and/or observe its use.

15. Fees. The LESSEE will comply with all relevant Acts, Rules, Regulations and Bye-Laws relating to the registration or licensing of the equipment relating to it or its use and will pay promptly all requisite fees and charges.

16. Payments by lessor. On failure by the LESSEE to pay any sum payable, the LESSOR may pay the same and recover such amount with compensation for overdue period at the same rate as failure to make any payment of rent hereunder.

17. Covenants. The parties agree and covenant that:

(*a*) the equipment is of a size, design, capacity and manufacture selected by the LESSEE;

(*b*) the LESSEE is satisfied that the equipment is suitable for its purpose;

(*c*) after inspection of the equipment the LESSEE has signed this Agreement relying entirely on its own judgment and not on any statement made by the LESSOR or the agents or servants of the supplier and no warranty of fitness or that the equipment is merchantable shall apply to the contract;

(*d*) the equipment is accepted by the LESSEE with all faults and defects;

(*e*) the LESSOR has not made and does not hereby make any representation or give any warranty with respect to the merchantability, condition, quality, durability or suitability of the equipment in any respect;

(*f*) the LESSEE has obtained all consents, licences, approvals as are necessary for or in connection with the execution, validity and enforcement of the Agreement and for the import, storage, installation, use and operation of the equipment and undertakes to keep them effective and in force during the period of this Agreement and carry out all such tests or inspection as may be required statutorily or otherwise till the equipment is delivered back to the LESSOR in good order and condition;

(*g*) the LESSEE undertakes to abide by all the conditions of any licence, permit or other rule applicable to the LESSEE'S business or the equipment;

(*h*) the LESSEE has satisfied itself about the LESSOR'S right to enter into the lease hereunder;

(*i*) the LESSOR and the LESSEE hereby confirm that their intent is that the equipment shall at all times remain the property of the LESSOR. The LESSEE shall not sell, assign, sublet, pledge, hypothecate, or otherwise encumber or suffer a lien upon or against the equipment or remove the equipment from the Factory or office or site as originally put to use or located, without the prior consent of the LESSOR in writing which consent the LESSOR agrees will not be unreasonably withheld;

(*j*) the LESSEE shall not sell, mortgage, charge, demise, sublet or otherwise dispose of any land or building on or in which the equipment is stored, used or operated or enter into any Agreement or arrangement to do any of the aforesaid acts without prior approval in writing of the LESSOR. The LESSEE shall in any event ensure by giving such notices that may be necessary and by obtaining confirmations in writing that such sale, mortgage, charge, demise, sub-letting or other dispositions, as the case may be, is subject to the rights of the LESSOR as the owner of the equipment to repossess the equipment at any time whether or not the same or any part thereof shall have become affixed to the said land or building and for that purpose to enter upon such land or building and reclaim and repossess the equipment lying thereat. The LESSEE shall obtain declaration and undertaking containing 'no lien charge' over the equipment and recognition of the right of access of the LESSOR to the equipment from such transferees;

(*k*) the LESSOR shall not be liable to the LESSEE for any liability, claim, loss, damage or expenses of any kind or nature;

(*i*) caused directly or indirectly by the equipment or any inadequacy thereof for any purpose, or any defect therein or by the use thereof; or

(*ii*) arising out of or in relation to any repairs, servicing, maintenance or adjustments thereto or to any delay in providing or failure to provide the same, or in relation to any interruption or loss of use thereof or any loss of business or any damage whatsoever and however caused.

(*l*) the LESSOR shall not be under any liability with respect to any statements regarding the LESSEE'S right or position in respect to any law relating to taxation or any other matter; and

(*m*) the LESSEE shall pay lease rent as specified in Schedule I during the lease period irrespective of whether the equipment is under repair or otherwise not working.

18. Indemnity. The LESSEE shall indemnify and keep indemnified the LESSOR at all times against and in respect of the following:

(*a*) Any loss by seizure of the equipment under distress, execution or other legal process or loss or destruction or damage to the equipment by fire, accident or any other cause, any claim or demand arising out of the import, storage, installation, use or operation of the equipment or any risk or liability for death or loss of life or limb for any person whether employee of the LESSEE or of third party or not or injury or damage to any property of the LESSEE, or of any third party and hold the LESSOR harmless against all losses, damages, claims, penalties, expenses, suits or proceeding of whatsoever nature made, suffered or incurred consequent thereupon and for this purpose take out such workmen's compensation/third party insurance cover as may be necessary, customary or in practice in the business carried out by the LESSEE or as may be directed by the LESSOR in that behalf. The LESSEE undertakes not to do or omit to do any such act which may result in seizure and/or confiscation of the equipment by the Central or State Government or local authority or any public officer or authority under any law for the time being in force and in the event of seizure or confiscation of other equipments belonging to the LESSEE and coming in the process of such seizure or confiscation to keep the leased equipment separate from the block or similar or other assets belonging to the LESSEE.

(*b*) Any claim arising out of the use, operation or keeping of the equipment and depletion in value as a result of excessive use; and

(*c*) Any liability or additional liabilities the LESSOR may incur under the Income-tax Act or under any other law by reason of use of the equipment by the LESSEE for any purpose other than that stated by the LESSEE to the LESSOR.

(*d*) Any liability arising out of any and all Sales Tax payable on lease rentals as and when applicable to the lease.

(*e*) The LESSEE will be liable for all violation of statutory requirements all risks and liability for the equipment, for the use, operation and storage thereof and for injuries to or death of persons and damage to property howsoever arising from or incidental to such use, operation or storage whether such injury or death of persons be of agents or employees of the LESSEE or LESSOR or of third parties and such damage in property be of the LESSEE or of others. The LESSEE will save and hold the LESSOR harmless against all losses, damages, claims, penalties, liabilities and expenses including legal costs howsoever arising or incurred because of or incidental to the equipment or the use, operation or storage or alleged use operation or storage thereof.

19. Assignment. During the lease period the LESSEE shall not agree, attempt, offer or purport to sell, assign, pledge, charge suffer attachment, mortgage, lend or let on hire or otherwise part with or attempt to part with the possession of the equipment or its interest therein.

20. Automatic time related upward revision of amounts due. (*a*) Where any sums payable by the LESSEE hereunder is payable on the specified date and is paid by the LESSEE after such date, the difference between the date of payment and the specified date shall be taken as *the overdue period.*

(*b*) Where any sum payable by the LESSEE hereunder is payable on demand by the LESSOR and is paid by the LESSEE after three days from the date of demand the difference between the date of payment and the date three days after the date of demand shall be taken as *the overdue period.*

(*c*) Where any sum payable by the LESSEE hereunder does not fall under cls. (*a*) and (*b*) above and is payable without demand by the LESSOR and is paid by the LESSEE after three days from the date on which the such liability arises, the difference between the date of such payment and the date three days after the date on which the LESSEE first becomes aware of such a liability shall be taken as *the overdue period*.

(*d*) All sums paid by the LESSEE having an overdue period shall automatically stand increased by rupee one per thousand per day with monthly rests and the LESSEE shall pay such sums as increased hereunder and any sum payable hereunder but paid without overdue charge shall be deemed to be unpaid to the extent of the automatic increase provided hereunder.

(*e*) The LESSEE understands and affirms that the provisions for automatic increase of any sum paid with an overdue period:

(*i*) is an essential part of the sums payable hereunder and its non-payment shall be taken as a breach of an essential condition of the lease;

(*ii*) is a genuine pre-estimate of the commercial loss of opportunity and other damages suffered by the LESSOR on account of untimely payment of sums payable hereunder;

(*iii*) is capable of variation by a written notification by the LESSOR in case of a continuing recurring or persistent default in payment of sums hereunder and the LESSEE agrees not to call in question LESSOR's discretion in treating the LESSEE'S default as falling under this clause.

21. Fixture to immovable property. Plants and machineries have often to be fixed to the earth.

22. Warranty. The LESSEE warrants and represents that every statement made and every particulars given by it in relation to the transaction effected by the lease is true and correct.

23. Events of default and termination. On the occurrence of any of the events specified below, the LESSOR shall be entitled, without prejudice to any other right or remedy which the LESSOR may have under this agreement or otherwise in law and notwithstanding any subsequent acceptance of rental or indulgence shown to the LESSEE, to terminate this lease:

(*a*) If the LESSEE fails to pay the rentals on the dates and in the manner stipulated in the respective schedule(s) or other monies payable hereunder within 14 days of their becoming due, whether demanded or not or if a cheque, bill, promissory note or other instrument issued, made, drawn or accepted by the LESSEE for discharge of the lease rentals is returned unpaid for any reason whatsoever when presented for payment.

(*b*) If the LESSEE fails or neglects to observe or perform or commits or allows to be committed a breach of any of the terms, conditions, provisions or stipulations of this agreement on its part to be observed and performed (other than failure to pay any sum hereunder when due and payable) and if such breach is remediable, fails to remedy the same within 14 days of notice by the LESSOR specifying such default and requiring such default to be remedied.

(*c*) If the LESSEE fails or neglects to observe or perform or commits or allows to be committed breach of any of the terms, conditions or regulations in respect of the use, operation or keeping of the equipment imposed by any authority or by the manufacturer.

(*d*) If the LESSEE passes any resolution for its winding up or a petition for winding up be presented against it by any of its members or creditors or otherwise or if a receiver is appointed for the whole or part of the assets, properties or undertakings of the LESSEE or enters into any composition with its creditors.

(*e*) The following changes shall be regarded as material changes with reference to the financial year immediately preceding the one in which this agreement commences which will entitle the LESSOR to terminate the agreement and take possession of the equipment:

   (*i*) decrease in net worth, that is, the aggregate of paid up capital and the reserves (including credit balance in P and L Account and premium but excluding unrealised revaluation reserves) by 40% or more;

   (*ii*) decrease in return on investment, that is profits before tax, interest and lease rentals, to long term funds including assets financed under finance lease to the extent not repaid consecutively for two financial years, by 40% or more;

   (*iii*) decrease in turnover excluding stock adjustments and excluding extraordinary or non-recurring items consecutively for two financial years by 40% or more;

   (*iv*) decrease in debt (including obligations under finance lease) service coverage ratio by or more than 20% consecutively for two financial years of the LESSEE.

(*f*) On failure of the LESSEE to provide to the LESSOR cheques, promissory notes or other instruments as required by the LESSOR, whether post dated or otherwise for discharge of the LESSEE'S obligations hereunder, or having provided to the LESSOR any such instrument the LESSEE, by any act or omissions on its part impedes the possibility of such instrument being honoured when presented for payment.

24. Remedies. On the occurrence of any event of default and at any time thereafter, the LESSOR shall declare all sums due and to become due hereunder for the full term of the lease including any renewal thereof immediately due and payable and on failure of the LESSEE to make payment of the sum due within 14 days thereof the LESSOR may in its sole discretion do any one or more of the following:

(*a*) upon notice to the LESSEE terminate the Agreement;

(*b*) demand that the LESSEE return all equipment to the LESSOR at its own cost and upon failure of the LESSEE to do so within 14 days from the date of demand the LESSOR shall be entitled to remove or repossess the equipment by itself, its servants or agents, enter upon the land, building or premises where the equipment is situated or is reasonably believed by the LESSOR to be situated for the time being and for such entry, the LESSEE hereby gives to the LESSOR an irrevocable licence, and detach and dismantle and take away the same;

(*c*) sell the equipment by public auction or private sale with or without notice to LESSEE or otherwise dispose of, hold, use, operate, lease to others such equipment;

(*d*) without prejudice to and in addition to the LESSOR's right provided herein the LESSOR shall also be entitled to recover from the LESSEE:

(*i*) the entire amount of the rental already fallen due and in arrears together with any charges due;

(*ii*) the entire amount of lease rentals for the unexpired period of lease;

(*iii*) all other sums which may have become due along with overdue charges and other sums that may become due;

(*iv*) the cost of all repair and maintenance of the equipment and all expenses incurred by the LESSOR in repossessing the equipment and in enforcing its remedies;

(*v*) a default premium equal to 10% of the amount mentioned in cls. (*i*) and (*ii*) above.

PROVIDED that the estimated market value and in case the equipment is sold by the LESSOR then its net sale proceeds shall be allowed as a deduction from the aggregate amount calculated under this clause.

The parties hereto agree and record that amounts to be paid by the LESSEE to the LESSOR as aforesaid have been *bona fide* and satisfactorily estimated to be the proper and reasonable amount that may be suffered by the LESSOR as and by way of liquidated damages and are not as deterrent or *in terrorem*.

All rentals or other sums paid by the LESSEE herein shall be deemed to have been appropriated against the liabilities of the LESSEE hereunder immediately upon payment thereof.

In addition the LESSEE shall be liable to all legal fees costs and other expenses resulting from the foregoing defaults or the exercise of the LESSOR's remedies including repossession of any equipment. No remedy referred to herein above is intended to be exclusive but each shall be in addition to any other remedy available to the LESSOR at law.

25. Inability to retake possession. If the LESSOR upon the termination of the lease be unable to recover possession of the equipment then without prejudice to the other amounts payable by the LESSEE hereunder, the LESSEE shall be liable to pay and pay to the LESSOR by way of liquidated and ascertained damages a sum equal to 25% of the cost of the equipment and shall continue to pay every month to the LESSOR during the unexpired portion of the lease twice the monthly rent payable as per Schedule I till such time as the LESSOR is able to get possession of the equipment.

26. Residual value. Having regard to LESSEE'S use of equipment under these presents, the residual value hereof at the expiration of the terms of the lease hereby granted shall not be less than Rs. 55,000.

27. Collateral security. On execution of these presents the LESSEE shall place the documents/certificates mentioned in Schedule II hereunder as and by way of collateral security with the LESSOR to ensure due compliance with the terms and conditions of the lease including the return of the equipment at the end of the lease period and thereupon, the LESSOR shall be deemed to be holding beneficial interest in the properties represented by the documents/certificate lodged with the LESSOR which the LESSOR shall hold, until complete satisfaction of the lease terms.

28. Prepayment. The LESSEE may pay and the LESSOR shall accept any payment hereunder before they are due and allow in respect thereof such concession on account of advance payment as the LESSOR may think fit. The LESSEE may foreclose the lease before the expiry of the term of the lease by paying to the LESSOR all the sums referred to above, and delivering the equipment to the LESSOR in good working order and condition, reasonable wear and tear excepted.

29. Imposts, taxes and other charges. The LESSEE shall during the period of this agreement and till the equipment is delivered back to the LESSOR in good working order and condition, bear all imposts, charges, taxes and penalties as may be levied from time to time by the Government or any other authority pertaining to or in respect of this equipment (including purchase tax or differential tax or other sums in case the LESSOR has concessional rate of tax), any incremental duty or other tax payable with reference to the purchase or acquisition of the equipment or this transaction. The LESSEE shall reimburse to the LESSOR all taxes (including sales tax), duties or other sums imposed now or hereafter may be imposed on the equipment or on this transaction or on the rentals hereunder.

30. Time. Time shall be of the essence of this contract in so far as it relates to performance of obligations.

31. Lessor's right to assign the receivables, etc. (*a*) The LESSOR may transfer, assign, hypothecate or create any lien upon or in any other manner deal with or encumber the equipment covered under this lease or any interest therein in favour of the LESSEE's Bank(s)/Financial Institution(s) or any other financier or may assign, transfer to any person any right or any interest in the lease or any part thereof on notice to the LESSEE and the consent of the LESSEE to such assignment, hypothecation, encumbrance or transfer, if any, is hereby given and any notice to the LESSEE is hereby waived by the LESSEE.

(*b*) In case the LESSOR has obtained finance against the equipment from any bank(s) the LESSEE does hereby agree to:

(*i*) assignment by LESSOR all or any part of the lease rental in favour of the bank(s) and to make payment of such lease rentals strictly to the bank(s) if so desired by the LESSOR;

(*ii*) to allow the LESSOR's Banker to cause any inspection of the equipment to be made at any time and from time to time during reasonable hours on any day during the continuance of the Agreement on prior notice;

(*e*) The LESSOR may on notice to the LESSEE transfer, hypothecate or mortgage the equipment and the rights attached thereto under the Agreement whether in whole or in part and the LESSEE shall have no right to raise any objection thereto.

32. Disruption of work to be notified. The LESSEE will inform the LESSOR promptly in the event of disruption of work/go-slow in its organisation of a continuous period exceeding 15 days due to whatsoever reasons.

33. Modification of rental payments. In the event of the Bank lending rates chargeable to the LESSOR by its Banker(s) and/or Financial Institution and other financier is increased the lease rentals reserved hereunder are liable to upward variation. The lease rentals will stand increased by Rupee one per month for every Rs. 1,000 of lease rental for every percentage of increase in the said bank lending rate. A letter from any of the LESSOR's Banker/Financial Institution indicating the revised rate of interest consequent to any announcement of increase in interest rates shall be final and conclusive evidence of the extent and the date of such increase.

The lease rentals hereunder are based on the assumption that the LESSOR shall be entitled to claim depreciation based on the acquisition cost of the equipment at the rate specified in respective Schedule for the whole of the period of the lease. Should the LESSOR not be able to claim the said benefit on account of any change in law, or rules or for any act or omission of the LESSEE or for any other reason whatsoever either for the whole or any part of the lease period and at all those rates, the lease rental specified in the respective schedule shall stand altered so as to compensate the LESSOR for the loss in the tax benefits thereby and maintain the post-tax implicit rate of return to the LESSOR as would have been available to the LESSOR had the depreciation allowance been granted as stipulated in the respective schedules, all factors other than the depreciation allowance being kept constant for that purpose.

34. Consequence of the breach of contract. If the LESSEE commits a breach of any of the terms and conditions of this Agreement, the LESSOR shall be entitled to claim damages/repossession of the equipment and/or any other appropriate remedy.

35. Warranties. The LESSEE shall be entitled to the benefit of the warranties provided by the manufacturer/supplier of the equipment. Any performance guarantee provided by the supplier shall be in the joint names of the LESSOR and the LESSEE and shall be enforceable by the LESSOR or the lESSEE or both of them.

36. Sale and lease back. (*a*) The LESSOR has bought the equipment on specific requisition from the LESSEE and the actual cost of the equipment has been negotiated and ascertained by the LESSEE which the LESSOR has paid/shall pay at the LESSEE'S instructions.

PROVIDED that where the LESSEE himself is the supplier/manufacturer, the cost of the equipment to the LESSOR shall be the fair market price of the equipment in an arms length transaction. If the cost transpires to be more than fair market value of the equipment the LESSOR may, at his sole discretion, have either of the following recourses against the LESSEE:

(*b*) If the fair value of the equipment or part thereof supplied by the LESSEE is substantially less than the cost of the equipment the LESSOR may treat this agreement as having been entered into with a basic mistake of fact and on misrepresentation by the LESSEE, and may treat the lease as terminated and forthwith demand upon the LESSEE to pay up all the sums as stated in the agreement hereof, along with any other or further damages that the LESSOR might have suffered as a result of such a misrepresentation, including any loss of the benefits and all the consequences arising therefrom; or

(*c*) The LESSOR may treat the lease to have been terminated to the extent the cost of the equipment or the part thereof supplied by the LESSEE exceeds the fair value of asset so established, and ask the LESSEE to immediately pay up the lease rentals proportionate to such excess along with any other or further damages that the LESSOR might have suffered as a result of such a misrepresentation, including any loss of tax benefits and all the consequences arising therefrom; or

(*d*) The LESSOR may claim appropriate damages, by revision of rentals or otherwise and/or security deposit to cover himself to the extent of such excess and continue the lease in the status *quo ante.*

37. Waiver—must be express. The rights and powers of the LESSOR under this Agreement shall remain in full force notwithstanding any indulgence given forbearance or neglect or delay in the enforcement thereof by the LESSOR. The LESSOR shall not be deemed to have waived any of the LESSOR'S rights or any provisions of this Agreement or any notice given hereunder unless such waiver be in writing signed by the LESSOR and no waiver by the

LESSOR of any breach by the LESSEE of this Agreement shall be deemed a waiver of any continuing or recurring breach.

38. Indulgence is not waiver. The failure of the LESSOR to insist upon the punctual performance of any of the obligations of the LESSEE hereunder or to exercise of any right or remedy available to the LESSOR, under this Agreement or to require payment from or by the LESSEE, when due or any sum owing hereunder or any extension of credit or any forbearance on the part of the LESSOR shall not constitute a waiver by the LESSOR of any subsequent or continuing default by the LESSEE hereunder nor shall the same prejudice affect or restrict the rights and powers of the LESSOR hereunder.

39. Renewal of lease. Subject to the LESSEE punctually observing and performing the terms covenants and conditions of this Agreement and unless the LESSEE is in default the LESSEE shall at the discretion of the LESSOR have an option to renew the lease after expiry of the present agreement by efflux of time for such further period on such rental and such other terms as would be decided mutually by the LESSOR and the LESSEE.

40. Affirmation as to statement made by parties. The parties herein declare and represent that every statement and representation made and every particular given in relation to this transaction are true and correct and by execution hereof, the respective signatories hereby certify that they have read this agreement including the Schedules hereto and that they are duly authorised to execute the agreement on behalf of the respective parties.

41. Service of notices. Any notice by one party to the other shall be in writing and posted to the party's address first above-written. Any change in the address of any party shall be notified to the other by Registered Post.

42. Financial Information. The LESSEE shall furnish the LESSOR during the continuance of this Agreement its latest audited Balance Sheet and Profit and Loss Account together with all notes and reports attached to the same, as and when they are ready and such other statements of accounts and financial statements as may be requested by the LESSOR from time to time.

43. Guarantee. In consideration of LESSOR agreeing at the requests of the guarantor to lease out the equipment to the LESSEE, the guarantor guarantees to the LESSOR the due observance and performance of all obligations of the LESSEE and to pay on demand any money due under this Agreement and not paid by the LESSEE either by way of lease rent, residual charges, collection expenses, expenses on repossession, garage rentals, costs of repairs and replacement, compensation charges for the late payments, costs of legal proceedings, damages and any other charges. The guarantor agrees that any time granted to LESSEE or any indulgence shown to it in respect of this Agreement either in the shape of releasing to the LESSEE the equipment after detention, seizure, or in any other manner, shall not prejudice the LESSOR's rights or release the guarantor from his guarantee which shall be continuing guarantee and his liability will be co-extensive with that of the LESSEE and that it shall not be necessary for the LESSOR to give notice to the guarantor for any defaults committed by the LESSEE or any concession or indulgence shown to the LESSEE by the LESSOR. The obligation of the guarantor under this guarantee shall be continuing and irrevocable.

The GUARANTOR declares that no charge has been created on the lease equipment by the LESSEE for giving of this guarantee and the GUARANTOR agrees that he will not so long any moneys remain outstanding take any such security in respect of the guarantor's liability hereunder.

44. Variation. This Agreement represents the entire agreement of lease between the parties hereto and shall be capable of variation only if agreed upon in writing by a note of amendment signed by and on behalf of the LESSOR and the LESSEE.

45. Place for payment. All monies due and payable by the LESSEE to the LESSOR under these presents shall be paid only at the corporate office of the LESSOR or such other place as the LESSOR may designate by cheque or bank draft drawn in favour of the LESSOR on a scheduled bank and shall be so paid as to enable the LESSOR to realise at par on or before the due date. Credit for all payments by cheque/bank draft will be given only on the realisation thereof.

46. Arbitration. Any dispute or difference arising out of or in connection with the agreement between the parties including any dispute or difference relating to the interpretation of the agreement or any clause thereof shall be referred to the sole arbitration of Mr. XY with summary powers and the provisions of the Arbitration and Conciliation Act 1996 and rules framed thereunder and any amendment thereto from time to time shall apply. No objection shall be taken on the ground that the arbitrator so appointed is an employee of the LESSOR or is in any way associated with the LESSOR. It is made clear that the venue of Arbitration Proceedings will be the sole discretion of the Arbitrator and no objection shall be entertained from any party in this regard. The award of the Arbitrator shall be final, conclusive and binding on all the parties. The Arbitrator shall be competent to decide whether any matter of dispute or difference referred to him falls within the purview of arbitration as provided for above and/or any matter relating to arbitration comes under the Arbitration and Conciliation Act 1996.

The award shall be made in writing within four months after entering upon the reference or within such extended time as agreed upon by the parties.

The Arbitrator shall be entitled to proceed summarily and in a summary manner.

The Arbitrator shall have power to order and direct either of the parties to abide by, observe and perform all such directions as the Arbitrator may think fit having regard to the matter in dispute before him. The Arbitrator shall have all necessary powers and may take such evidence oral and/or documentary, as the arbitrator in his absolute discretion thinks fit and shall be entitled to exercise all powers under the Arbitration and Conciliation Act 1996 including admission of any affidavit as evidence concerning the matter in dispute before him.

The Arbitrator shall be at liberty to appoint, if necessary, any accountant or engineer or other technical person to assist him, and to act on the basis of the opinion, if any, taken.

The parties hereby agree that the Courts in Calcutta shall have jurisdiction to entertain any application or other proceedings in respect of anything arising under this Agreement and any award made by the sole Arbitrator hereunder shall be filed in the concerned court in the city of Calcutta only.

PROVIDED however that if the LESSOR apprehends that the LESSEE may allocate or charge or dispose of the equipment or may cause damage to the equipment, the LESSOR is at liberty to seek redress in a Court of Law under the said Act.

47. Court of jurisdiction. (*a*) This Agreement and the terms, covenants and conditions herein contained have been negotiated by and between the Parties hereto at the LESSEE'S Office at 6 G.K. Street, Calcutta and the Lease Agreement has been concluded at the lessee's said office and executed by the LESSOR, LESSEE and the GUARANTOR at 6 G.K. Street, Calcutta.

(*b*) Subject to the arbitration as aforesaid it is agreed between the Parties that Courts in Calcutta shall have jurisdiction in respect of any matter, claim or dispute arising out of or in any way relating to this Agreement.

Signed, sealed and delivered by the
LESSOR at Calcutta in the presence of:

....
.... Calcutta

Signed, sealed and delivered by the
LESSEE in the presence of:

....
.... Calcutta

Signed, sealed and delivered by the
GUARANTOR in the presence of:

....
.... Calcutta

Schedule I

To Lease Agreement Dated ....

1. Fixed non-cancellable period	:	....months from the commencement date of the lease
2. Renewal	:	As may be opted by the LESSEE
3. Lease management fee	:	..................% of the asset cost/ Rs. ....
4. Contingency deposit/Sales tax	:	At applicable rates (to be borne by LESSEE) .... (included as part of rentals as on actuals)
5. Security deposit	:	....
6. Interest on security deposit	:	..................% p.a. ....
7. Collateral security	:	....
8. Depreciation allowance as per I.T. Act	:	....
9. Assured residual value at the end of the primary lease period	:	....
10. Sanctioned amount	:	Rs. ....
11. Drawdown periods	:	....

Sd. Sd. Sd.

Schedule I (contd.)

12. Particulars of Equipment

Type of Equipment	*Manufacturer's Suppliers Name & Address*	*Quantity*	*Location of the Equipment*	*Date of delivery of the Equipment*	*Acquisition cost of the Equipment*	*Commencement date of the Lease*	*Any other special terms*
(a)	(b)	(c)	(d)	(e)	(f)	(g)	(h)

Sd. Sd. Sd.

Schedule I (contd.)

13. Lease Rental

(*a*) Due Date :

(*b*) Payment Terms : All Lease Rental are payable .... in advance/arrear at par.

	January	February	March	April	May	June	July	August	September	October	November	December
1999												
2000												
2001												
2002												
2003												
2004												
2005												
2006												
2007												
2008												

Schedule II

Sd. Sd. Sd.

Leasing of Plants and Machinery

THIS AGREEMENT IS MADE this 6th day of June 2000 BETWEEN AB Financial Services Ltd., a company registered under the Companies Act 1956 and carrying on business at .... (hereinafter referred to as the LESSOR which term shall include its successors and assigns) of the One Part and CD Ltd., a company registered under the Companies Act 1956 and carrying on business at .... (hereinafter called the LESSEE which term shall include its successors and assigns) of the Other Part.

WHEREAS the LESSOR carries on business as Lease Financing and leasing-out equipment and the LESSEE carries on business as manufacturer of and dealer in Hosiery goods and intends to take on lease certain plant and machinery from the LESSOR.

AND WHEREAS the LESSOR has agreed to give on lease such plant and machinery that may be required by the LESSEE.

AND WHEREAS the LESSEE has selected the plant and machinery from the manufacturer and seller thereof.

NOW THESE PRESENTS WITNESSETH and the parties hereby agree as follows:

1. The LESSEE hereby agrees to lease out to the LESSEE and the LESSEE agrees to take on lease from the LESSOR the plant and machinery described in Schedule I hereunder.

2. The LESSEE hereby admits that the LESSOR has paid for the plant and machinery mentioned in Schedule I hereunder to the supplier thereof and the said plant and machinery have been installed in the factory of the LESSEE and are working satisfactorily. The LESSEE admits that the LESSOR is the sole owner of said plant and machinery.

3. The lease of the said plant and machinery shall be for a period of three years which may be renewed for another three years by mutual agreement.

4. The LESSEE agrees to pay the lease rentals at the rates specified in Schedule II hereunder. The lease rentals would be paid by LESSEE within 10 days of the same becoming due and payable.

5. In default of payment on due date, interest at 3% per month on each instalment due would be charged on the outstanding amount. The time for payment of the instalment is understood by the parties to be of the essence of the Lease Agreement.

6. The LESSEE expressly declares that the LESSEE has made the selection of plant and machinery based upon its own judgment and has not relied upon any statement or representation of the LESSOR.

7. The LESSEE undertakes to be responsible for all repairs, service defects and smooth running of the plant and machinery. The LESSEE will, however,

be entitled to the benefits of the manufacturer's warranties in respect of the plant and machinery.

8. No right, title or interest in the plant and machinery shall pass to the LESSEE by virtue of these presents and the leased-out plant and machinery mentioned in Schedule I hereunder shall remain the property of the LESSOR and the LESSEE undertakes not to sell, assign, sub-let, sub-lease, pledge or hypothecate or otherwise encumber or suffer lien upon or against any interest in the leased-out plant and machinery or in this agreement. The LESSEE further undertakes not to remove except for purposes of repairs the leased-out plant and machinery from the factory where they have been installed except with the prior written consent of the LESSOR and further undertakes not to allow any third person to use as the licensee or otherwise the said plant and machinery without the written consent of the LESSOR.

9. The LESSEE agrees and undertakes to comply with all laws and regulations and orders relating to the possession of, operation and use of leased-out plant and machinery and assumes all risks, responsibilities and liabilities arising from or pertaining to the possession, operation or use of the leased-out plant and machinery. The LESSEE hereby agrees and undertakes to keep the LESSOR fully indemnified against and harmless from any claims, costs, expenses damages and liabilities, whether civil, criminal or of any other nature whatsoever arising from or pertaining to the use, possession, operation or transportation of the leased-out plant and machinery.

10. The LESSEE undertakes to pay all fees, taxes, levies or other lawful charges and in default if the LESSOR has to pay the same, the LESSEE undertakes to reimburse the LESSOR of such payment. The Indemnity hereby granted by the LESSEE to the LESSOR shall operate in respect of all risks, or liabilities arising from possession, use, operation or storage of the plant and machinery and for injuries or deaths of persons or damages to property arising from possession, use or anything to do with the leased-out plant and machinery. Such indemnity shall survive the termination of this agreement.

11. The LESSEE will cause the leased-out plant and machinery to be operated in accordance with manufacturer's Manuals and Instructions by competent and duly qualified personnel and in accordance with the applicable government regulations and for the LESSEE's business purposes only.

12. During the term of the lease, the LESSEE shall at its own cost and expense keep the plant and machinery in good repair and working condition.

13. The LESSEE shall keep the plant and machinery fully insured and in case of loss, theft or damages beyond repair, the LESSEE shall pay the balance lease rentals forthwith and the LESSOR shall transfer its right title or interest in plant and machinery to the LESSEE so that the LESSEE could recover the insurance money. The LESSEE undertakes to keep the plant and machinery

fully insured for the value thereof plus 10% and regularly pay the renewal premium.

14. During the term of this Agreement, the LESSEE shall furnish to the LESSOR Annual Audited Accounts duly reflecting the said plant and machinery taken on lease and the lease rentals payable for same.

15. The LESSEE agrees to bear and pay all extra or additional or new taxes or levies in relation to plant and machinery on leasing out the same to the LESSEE.

16. Upon expiry of the lease period or in case of default on termination of the lease by the LESSOR, the LESSEE undertakes to deliver up possession of plant and machinery to the LESSOR at specified storage space intimated by the LESSOR at the cost and expense of the LESSEE and in good and working condition.

17. In the event the LESSEE fails to pay the stipulated lease rent on the due dates in respect of two instalments or fails to perform or observe any covenant, condition or undertaking contained herein or becomes commercially insolvent or winding-up petition is filed against the LESSEE, the LESSOR shall be at liberty to terminate the agreement and declare the outstanding lease rentals, the late payment charges and quantum of interest at 30% per annum and future rentals payable by the LESSEE, and the LESSEE shall have option to pay the entire amounts due discounted at the rate of 12% per annum within 30 days of receipt of such declaration. If the LESSEE does not pay the outstanding amount due so discounted at 12% per annum within 30 days then the LESSOR will have the liberty to take action for recovery of the outstanding dues as liquidated damages for loss of bargain and not as penalty of the said total amount together with interest at 36% per annum.

18. On any default in payment of any lease rental or breach of any of the terms and conditions hereof the LESSOR would be entitled to take possession of plant and machinery mentioned in Schedule I hereunder and take such action as are permissible in law for recovery of the dues.

19. The waiver of any particular default or breach of the LESSEE by the LESSOR shall not be treated as waiver of any other default or breach of the terms and conditions of this agreement.

20. Any notice of demand required to be given shall be given by post or by hand-delivery to the addresses of the parties given hereinabove.

21. The LESSEE agrees and undertakes that its obligations to pay all lease-rentals and any other amount owing hereunder shall be absolute and unconditional. The LESSEE shall not be entitled to cancel or terminate this agreement without paying the entire lease-rentals.

22. All disputes and differences claims and questions whatsoever which could arise either during the subsistence of this agreement or afterwards between the parties and/or their respective representatives touching these

Presents or any clause or thing herein contained or otherwise in any way relating to or arising from these Presents shall be referred to Arbitration of Mr. PQ of .... and shall be subject to the jurisdiction of the .... High Court. Such Arbitration shall be in accordance with and subject to the provisions of the Arbitration and Conciliation Act 1996 or any statutory modification thereof for the time being in force.

Schedule I

20 Automatic Vests Knitting Machines, Colour Motif, colour-in-colour, floating pattern, mesh pattern, plating horizontal and vertical stripes, etc.

AND other particulars.

Schedule II

Total worth of rentals payable by the LESSEE ... Rs. 51,78,800

AND other particulars.

Lease rentals and due date

Rs. 5,56,980 payable quarterly beginning from 10th June 2000 and thereafter on 10th of every third month and the entire amount would be paid by 10th March 2003.

The Lease Rentals is in addition to the Lease Management fee of Rs. 51,788 payable at the time of signing of the agreement.

IN WITNESS WHEREOF the parties herein have signed, sealed and delivered these presents on the day, month and year first above-written.

Signed, sealed and delivered by
Mr. ....
pursuant to Board Resolution
of 1st June 2000 of CD Ltd. in
in presence of: Signature

1.

2.

Signed, sealed and delivered by
Mr. ....
pursuant to Board Resolution of
2nd June 2000 of AB Financial
Services Ltd. in the presence of: Signature

1.

2.

Tripartite Agreement for Leasing Finance

THIS AGREEMENT IS MADE this 10th day of June 2000 BETWEEN AB Financial Services Limited, a company registered under the Companies Act 1956 and carrying on business at .... (hereinafter referred to as the LESSOR which term shall include its successors and assigns) of the First Part, CD Limited, a company registered under the Companies Act 1956 and carrying on business at .... (hereinafter called the LESSEE which term shall include its successors and assigns) of the Second Part and Lease Financing Bank Limited, a Banking Company within the meaning of the Companies Act 1956 and carrying on business at .... (hereinafter referred to as the BANK which term shall include its successors and assigns) of the Third Part.

WHEREAS under an Agreement of Hypothecation dated 6th June 2000 executed by the LESSOR in favour of the BANK, the BANK granted to the LESSOR advance of a sum of Rs. 40 lakhs in Cash Credit Account to enable the LESSOR to purchase 20 Automatic Knitting Machines for the purpose of leasing out the same to the LESSEE against hypothecation of the said plant and machinery and on terms and conditions contained in the said agreement.

AND WHEREAS the LESSOR has entered into an Agreement of Lease with the LESSEE on 6th June 2000 leasing out the said plant and machinery subject to payment of lease rent and on terms and conditions contained in the said Lease Agreement.

AND WHEREAS the terms of sanction of the said loan of Rs. 40 lakhs by the BANK to the LESSOR provided that the plant and machinery purchased by the LESSOR would be leased-out to the LESSEE subject to the bank's hypothecation and that the LESSEE should undertake that it would not assign or transfer in any manner its rights as a LESSEE in the said plant and machinery and that the LESSEE would undertake to pay the lease rentals directly to the BANK, if so required, and that the moneys realised under any Insurance Policy would belong and be paid to the BANK.

NOW THESE PRESENTS WITNESSETH and it is hereby agreed by the parties as follows:

1. The LESSEE hereby confirms that the plant and machinery taken on lease from the LESSOR remain hypothecated to the BANK.

2. The LESSEE undertakes not to deal with the said plant and machinery in a manner prejudicial to the interest of the BANK as a hypothecatee.

3. The Insurance moneys that may be recovered for loss or damage to the said plant and machinery would be paid to the BANK if demanded.

4. The LESSEE would pay the lease rentals to the BANK as hypothecatee if so demanded by the BANK.

5. In case of any dispute or differences between the LESSOR and the LESSEE the LESSEE undertakes to make direct payment to the BANK of all lease rentals according to the Agreement of Lease dated 6th June 2000.

6. If the LESSEE makes default in payment of any lease rentals or commits any breach of any of the terms contained herein or in the Lease Agreement dated 6th June 2000 the BANK will have the liberty to take appropriate action for enforcement of its hypothecation for recovery of its claim in respect of the said advance of Rs. 40 lakhs made to the LESSOR and will be at liberty to take possession of the said leased out plant and machinery.

7. The LESSEE undertakes to affix a board on the plant and machinery indicating that the same are remaining hypothecated to the BANK.

8. The LESSOR agrees that in default of repayment of the said loan of Rs. 40 lakhs with interest in terms of the Hypothecation Agreement the BANK would be at liberty to ask the LESSEE to pay the lease rentals in respect of the said plant and machinery directly to the BANK.

9. The LESSOR shall from time to time keep the BANK informed as to the lease rentals paid by the LESSEE or realised by the LESSOR under the said Lease Agreement.

10. The parties herein agree and declare that the terms and conditions contained herein will prevail over the provisions made in the said Lease Agreement and the said Hypothecation Agreement in case there is any conflict among them.

IN WITNESS WHEREOF the parties hereto have executed these presents on the day, month and year first above-written.

Signed, sealed and delivered by
Mr. .... pursuant
to Board Resolution of AB
Financial Service Limited dated
5th June 2000 in the presence of: Signature

1.
2.

Signed, sealed and delivered by
Mr. ....
pursuant to Board Resolution
of 5th June 2000 of CD Limited
in the presence of : Signature

1.
2.

Signed, sealed and delivered by
Mr. ....
pursuant to Board Resolution of
Lease Financing Bank Limited
dated 5th June 2000 in the
presence of: Signature

1.

2.

Lease Agreement (Equipments)

THIS AGREEMENT OF LEASE made this .... day of .... BETWEEN AB Co. Limited, a company incorporated under the Companies Act 1956 with its Registered Office at ...., hereinafter called the LESSOR (which expression shall, unless repugnant to the subject or context thereof include its successors and assigns) of the One Part, CD Co. Ltd., a company registered under the Companies Act 1956 and having its registered office at .... hereinafter called the LESSEE (which expression shall unless repugnant to the subject or context include its successors and permitted nominees) of the Second Part, EF Co. Ltd., a company registered under the Companies Act 1956 and carrying on business at .... hereinafter called a CO-LESSEE (which term shall include its successors, nominees and assigns) of the Third Part and (1) MN, working for gain at .... and (2) PQ, working for gain at .... both of them jointly and severally are referred to as the GUARANTORS (which expression shall, unless repugnant to the subject or context shall include their heirs and successors) of the Fourth Part.

WHEREAS the LESSEE is desirous of installing and utilising the equipments referred to in the Schedule I attached hereto has approached the LESSOR and has requested the LESSOR to acquire the said equipments and/or such other equipments which may from time to time be specified in Schedule I to be executed by and between the LESSOR and the LESSEE and thereafter to lease-out the same to the LESSEE.

AND WHEREAS in consideration of the LESSOR entering into this agreement with the LESSEE at the request of the guarantors, the guarantors have guaranteed the due performance of all the terms and conditions herein agreed to by the LESSEE and to pay the LESSOR all indebtedness and liabilities of the LESSEE to the LESSOR.

AND WHEREAS the LESSEE has agreed to pay to the LESSOR a one time non-adjustable and non-refundable fee to be called the "Lease-Management Fee" of Rs. .... (Rupees ....) immediately on execution of this Agreement.

AND WHEREAS the parties hereto have decided to enter into this agreement for the purpose of recording the terms and conditions of lease of the said equipments and also enable the parties by mutual consent to make and attach, from time to time, Schedule to this agreement, containing relevant particulars and specific terms and conditions, if any.

NOW THEREFORE THESE PRESENTS witnesseth and the parties herein agree as follows:

1. Definitions. In this agreement, unless the context requires otherwise the following expressions shall have the following meanings, *viz.*,

(a) *Commencement date for lease.* The commencement date shall be such date as may be specified in the Schedule hereunder written. There may be different dates of commencement of lease in respect of different equipments described in the Schedule attached from time to time and made an integral part of these presents.

(b) *Equipments.* The equipment described in Schedule to the Agreement acquired/purchased/imported by the LESSOR at the request of the LESSEE from the supplier named in the Schedule and leased to the LESSEE and includes all individual items comprised in the equipment or any item or part thereof during the period of this Agreement, and until the equipment is returned to the LESSOR in pursuance hereof.

(c) *Fixed period.* The fixed period of the lease as stated in Schedule which is non-cancellable by the LESSEE and/or the LESSOR except as provided herein.

(d) *Lease rentals.* Lease rentals shall mean the lease rent to be paid by the LESSEE to the LESSOR and shall include any increase in the rentals as provided herein.

(e) *Person* includes any person (natural or juridical) and shall include any form of association of persons.

(f) *Schedule.* The Schedule or Schedules which may now or from time to time be incorporated hereunder as an integral part of this Agreement.

(g) *Acquisition cost.* Acquisition cost shall mean the aggregate of the sums paid/incurred/to be paid/incurred by the LESSOR on account of or in relation to the acquisition of the equipment, irrespective of when such sum is paid or incurred and where the amount referred to in Schedule is lesser than such aggregate, such aggregate shall be deemed to have substituted the amount mentioned in Schedule effective from the commencement date.

2. Terms of lease. (a) The LESSOR hereby gives on lease and the LESSEE hereby takes on lease the equipments for the fixed period from the respective commencement dates as specified in the Schedule subject to the terms, conditions, covenants and stipulations contained herein and in schedules hereunder written. The LESSEE shall have an option to renew the lease as provided hereinafter at the time of its determination. The LESSOR hereby agrees to transfer unto the LESSEE the right to use by way of lease the equipments specified in the Schedule or such other Schedules attached hereto and/or to be attached from time to time to this agreement on and from the respective commencement dates specified in respect of the individual items in the said Schedules and the LESSEE hereby agrees to take on lease the equipments for the fixed period subject to the terms, conditions, covenants and stipulations contained herein and/or the individual Schedules signed by the parties pursuant to this agreement.

(b) *Lease rentals.* The LESSEE shall pay to the LESSOR during the continuance of this agreement lease rentals and other charges as are specified in the Schedule subject to the provisions for variation of the lease rentals as hereinafter provided. The said lease rentals shall be paid punctually on their due dates to the LESSOR by the LESSEE whether demanded or not and without any deduction or abatement. The LESSOR at his option may recover from the LESSEE in a lump sum at the beginning of the lease or at the time of their incurrence, as the case may be, the expenses incurred by the LESSOR to the extent the same are not included in the said acquisition cost.

(c) *Obligation to pay rentals is absolute.* The LESSEE shall pay the instalments of rentals regularly and punctually without any deduction or abatement and without any reference to the state, description, use or performance of the equipment.

(d) *Increase in lease rentals.* Without affecting the LESSEE's obligation to pay the rental for the fixed period on the respective due dates and without prejudice to the right of the LESSOR, any arrear of rentals payable hereunder shall be increased by the sum relatable to the overdue period.

(e) *Payment of rentals.* The LESSOR may require the LESSEE either at the inception of the lease or at any time thereafter to give to the LESSOR any cheques, promissory notes or any other acceptable instrument for all or any sums payable under this Agreement, immediately or in future, and such cheques or notes or other instruments shall be deemed to have been given for adequate consideration already received by the LESSEE and shall not absolve the LESSEE from his liability to pay the said sum hereunder until the cheque, note or other instrument is duly realised.

(f) *Dishonour of negotiable instruments.* In the event of any cheque, note or other instrument given by the LESSEE in payment of any of the sums payable hereunder being returned unpaid or dishonoured the cheques, notes or other instrument, the LESSOR shall be entitled to levy on the LESSEE a sum of Rs. 1,000 for each such return, without prejudice to its right to taking such other actions against the LESSEE as may be available under the law.

3. Payment of security deposit. The LESSEE shall pay to and keep deposited with the LESSOR, at the inception of the lease, the sum as mentioned in

Schedule as and by way of Security Deposit to ensure due compliance by the LESSEE of the terms and conditions of the lease including the redelivery of the equipment. The said deposit shall be refundable at the end of the latest lease tenure without interest as mentioned in Schedule provided the LESSEE is not in default under any of the terms and conditions of this lease. From the amount to be so refunded, the LESSOR shall be entitled to make the following deductions:

(*a*) where any sum, which is ascertainable at the time of such refund and has become due to be paid by the LESSEE to the LESSOR as per this Agreement, including any sum deemed to be unpaid;

(*b*) where any sum has become payable by the LESSEE to the LESSOR the exact quantum whereof is not ascertainable at the time of such refund, an estimated amount thereof, including interest, if any;

(*c*) where, in view of the continuing indemnities provided by the LESSEE hereunder or for any other reason, it is likely that any liability on the lease hereunder shall arise in future, the LESSOR may retain such part of the deposit as it things is necessary to take care of such liability. The part so retained shall be adjustable against the liability of the LESSEE to the extent the same remains unsatisfied, and the balance, if any, shall be refundable to the LESSEE after all such apprehended liabilities have been fully settled;

PROVIDED that the LESSOR shall not be entitled to retain any sum in pursuance of this clause, if the LESSEE shall furnish a guarantee from a bank acceptable to the LESSOR, for reimbursement of the apprehended liability, or otherwise secures such reimbursement in a manner acceptable to the LESSOR.

4. Redelivery of the equipment by the lessee on termination

(*a*) Upon termination of this Agreement either by efflux of time or otherwise under this Agreement, the LESSEE shall, on its own volition and without any demand from the LESSOR deliver the equipment at such time and place as may be directed by the LESSOR in good repair, order and workable condition (subject to normal wear and tear).

(*b*) In the event of the LESSEE not so returning the equipment within a period of 15 days from the date of termination, the LESSEE shall be deemed to be in unauthorised possession of the equipment, and if it continues to so retain the equipment even after a period of 15 days of a written demand raised by the LESSOR to peacefully return the equipments the LESSOR shall be entitled to take such criminal and/or civil action as it may be advised:

PROVIDED that nothing contained in the aforesaid clause shall be deemed to have been taken any effect and force in the event of the LESSEE opting to take the equipment on lease during the secondary lease period.

5. Payment of consideration to be pre-requisite for use. It is expressly understood by the LESSEE that the payment of the consideration hereunder to the LESSOR is a necessary pre-requisite under all circumstances for obtaining any right of possession or use of the equipment.

6. Lessor's right to assign the receivables, etc. The LESSOR may assign, hypothecate or create any lien upon or in any other manner deal with or encumber the equipment covered under this lease or any interest therein in favour of the LESSOR'S Bank(s)/financial institution(s) or any other financier or creditor, or may assign, transfer to any person, receivables or any interest in the lease or any part thereof, and the consent of the LESSEE to such assignment, hypothecation, encumbrance or transfer, if any, is hereby given and any notice to the LESSEE is hereby waived by the LESSEE. In case the LESSOR has obtained finance against the equipment from any Bank(s), the LESSEE does hereby agree to:

(*a*) assign all or any part of the lease rentals in favour of the Bank(s), and to make payment of such lease rentals directly to the Bank(s), if so desired by the LESSOR;

(*b*) comply with such other terms and conditions as the LESSOR may agree with the Bank, including the power of the bank to cause an inspection of the equipment to be made at any time and from time to time during reasonable hours on any day during the continuance of the Agreement.

7. Rights of the lessor during the period before delivery of the equipment. (*a*) The equipment shall be delivered by the supplier/manufacturer to the LESSEE or to the LESSOR or to any agent or either of them, as the case may be, and as may be instructed by the LESSOR, and it is hereby agreed that the entire risk, cost or any outgoing pertaining to the said delivery shall be at the cost and risk of the defaulting party. The LESSOR makes no representation as to the time to be spent in delivery of the equipment, and the LESSEE must ensure that the equipment is delivered by the supplier within such time as may be stipulated by the LESSOR. Any failure on the part of the LESSEE in ensuring such delivery shall entitle the LESSOR to treat the agreement of the lease revoked and recover from the LESSEE the amount advanced to the supplier together with the financial costs referred to above. In case of revocation of the agreement of lease under this clause, the LESSOR shall have a full and paramount lien over all unencumbered assets belonging to the LESSEE and/or lying at its place for the purpose of recovery of the amount of advance and the financial costs referred to above.

(*b*) Notwithstanding anything to the contrary contained in any provisions of the agreement it is explicitly agreed by and between the parties that in the event of any misstatement, or any material adverse change in circumstances including any change in the Government policies taking place after execution of this agreement but before complete draw down of the lease assistance as a result of which, in the opinion of the LESSOR, the LESSEE ceases to be an acceptable risk then any further draw down may be discontinued by the LESSOR and the LESSOR shall have the option to exercise its right to terminate the lease in respect of equipment already delivered and so far as possible the parties shall be restored to their original position.

8. Revocation of agreement. Notwithstanding anything contained hereinabove and without any prejudice to such further or other conditions in the letter sanctioning lease finance, the agreement of the LESSOR to lease the equipment to the lessee shall, at the option of the LESSOR exercised at any time before the commencement of the lease, be revocable, in the following circumstances:

(*a*) if the LESSEE makes any material misstatement in furnishing or causing to furnish any information to the LESSOR that might have been used by the LESSOR for any purpose pertaining to this agreement to lease, whether such misstatement formed the basis of this agreement or not;

(*b*) if the cost of the equipment to be acquired by the LESSOR for lease is higher than the comparable other equipment by the same or other supplier, delivered at the same place;

(c) if the equipment to be acquired by the LESSOR for lease does not comply with generally acceptable quality standards;

(*d*) if the LESSEE'S financial position as known at the time of the execution of this agreement undergoes adverse material change or any other material change takes place of the corporate character or financial position of the LESSEE, or any material change occurs in the assessment of the LESSEE'S credit quality, or the value and quality of the asset undergoes adverse change.

9. No claim against the lessor. It is agreed that no claim of any nature whatsoever shall lie against the LESSOR in the event of any *bona fide* revocation of the agreement on grounds mentioned herein.

10. Lessor's rights and lessee's obligation. In the event of such revocation, the LESSOR may, at his discretion, acquire the equipment and deal with it in such a manner as the LESSOR may choose, or the LESSOR may cancel the order for acquisition, and claim the refund of any advances made on the LESSEE'S behalf from the supplier, and in either event, claim from the LESSEE the whole of the loss and all costs suffered.

11. Collateral security. The LESSEE shall after inception of the lease place the documents/properties/certificates mentioned in Schedule hereunder as and by way of collateral security with the terms and conditions of the lease including the return of the equipment at the end of the lease period and thereupon the LESSOR shall be deemed to be holding beneficial interest in the properties represented by the documents/certificates with the LESSOR, which the LESSOR shall hold until complete satisfaction of the LESSOR'S claims under the lease. During the terms of the lease, the LESSEE shall not transfer, encumber or in any way affect the LESSOR'S beneficial interest in the properties referred to herein.

12. Lessee's initial covenants purchase/acquisition for the purpose of the lease. The LESSOR affirms and declares that the LESSOR has bought/acquired/shall buy/acquire the equipment for the purpose of its lease hereunder only to the LESSEE and subject to the compliance by the LESSEE of the initial covenants contained herein and/or the Schedules and unless the LESSEE refuses or fails or omits to take the equipment on lease, the LESSOR shall not, after purchase or acquisition of the equipment, divert the equipment for any other purpose.

PROVIDED that nothing in this clause shall apply in case of termination of the lease under this Agreement.

13. Consents given by the lessee. (*a*) The LESSEE affirms and declares that he has requested the LESSOR to purchase/acquire the equipments for effective and *bona fide* use by the LESSEE itself and the LESSEE further covenants that;

(*b*) the execution of this Agreement and the use and the operation of the equipment by the LESSEE will not;

(*c*) contravene any provision of any statute, rule and regulations which the LESSEE is subject to and to the lessee's Memorandum and Articles of Association;

(*d*) result in any breach of any agreement or arrangement to which the LESSEE is a party;

(*e*) affect any right of LESSOR in any manner whatsoever in respect of the subject equipment;

(*f*) the LESSEE has obtained all consents, licences, approval, etc. as are necessary for or in connection with the execution, validity and enforceability of the agreement and for the import, storage, installation, use and operation of the equipment and undertakes to keep them effective and in force during the period of this Agreement and carry out all such tests or inspections as may be required statutorily or otherwise till the equipment is delivered back to the LESSOR in good order and condition;

(*g*) the LESSEE undertakes to abide by all the conditions of any licence, permit or other rule applicable to the LESSEE'S business or to the equipment;

(*h*) the LESSEE affirms that the LESSEE has satisfied itself about the LESSOR'S right to enter into the lease hereunder;

(*i*) the LESSEE affirms that, save as otherwise provided in this Agreement, no right, title or interest, in the equipment shall pass to the LESSEE by virtue of these presents. The LESSEE shall at no time contest or challenge the LESSOR'S sole and exclusive right, title and interest in the equipment. The LESSOR and the LESSEE hereby confirm that their intent is that the equipment shall at all times remain as the property of the LESSOR. The LESSEE also agrees and undertakes not to sell, assign, sublet, pledge, hypothecate or otherwise encumber or suffer a lien upon or against the equipment or remove the equipment from the factory or office or site where originally put to use or located, without the prior consent of the LESSOR in writing, which consent the LESSOR agrees will not be unreasonably withheld.

(*j*) Though the LESSOR will request the manufacturer/supplier to effect delivery on or before the date of commencement of the rentals, yet, if for whatsoever reason the delivery is not effected by the manufacturer/supplier by that date, the LESSOR shall not be liable for any loss suffered by the LESSEE thereby. Lease rentals shall be deemed to commence from the date of commencement of the rentals as specified in Schedule. This will be accepted as a constructive delivery of the equipment to the LESSEE. In the event that the LESSEE causes cancellation of or instructs the LESSOR to cancel the purchase order/contract with the supplier of the equipment or the LESSEE shall refuse or be unable for any reason to accept delivery, the LESSEE shall be entitled to terminate the lease of the equipment and the LESSEE shall pay to the LESSOR on demand all costs, charges, expenses, damages incurred by the LESSOR arising out of such an action of the LESSEE.

(*k*) The LESSEE hereby expressly agrees that the purchase order for individual items of equipment under this agreement shall be placed forthwith by the LESSOR at the instance of the LESSEE. In the event of undue delay on receiving such instructions for placement of orders beyond 45 days from the date of this agreement the LESSOR shall reserve the right to review this agreement.

(*l*) The LESSEE agrees to provide annual certificates regarding the depreciation eligibility of the equipment and that the equipment is in good working order and condition and also that the equipment is in physical possession of the LESSEE.

(*m*) The LESSEE hereby covenants that subject to any hypothecation or any sort of security created and/or to be created by the LESSOR in favour of its bankers for any loan or other financial facilities granted or to be granted to the LESSOR by such bankers the equipment will remain the absolute property of the LESSOR and undertakes not to sell, transfer the same to any party or encumber the same in any manner without the prior written consent of the LESSOR.

(*n*) The LESSEE affirms that the LESSEE has satisfied itself about the LESSOR'S right to enter into the lease agreement.

14. Rights and obligations of the co-lessee. All references in this Agreement to the LESSEE shall be deemed to refer to the CO-LESSEE as well. The CO-LESSEE shall have all the rights of LESSEE and CO-LESSEE shall at all times be jointly and severally liable for the performance of the obligations and duties of the LESSEE under this Agreement.

15. Lessee's continuing covenants. During the tenure of this lease and till the equipment is delivered back to the LESSOR in good order and proper condition, subject to normal wear and tear, the LESSEE shall discharge the obligations mentioned hereunder.

16. Lessee's obligations under Public Liability Insurance Act 1981. (*a*) LESSEE will keep insured all substances which have been declared to be of hazardous substances under the notification issued from time to time under the Public Liability Insurance Act 1981 or any rule framed thereunder or under any notification or clarification issued by the appropriate authority, or under modification or addendum thereto in accordance with the said Act, and which are employed at or used in any of the LESSEE'S undertakings, whether or not connected with the operations of the equipments.

(*b*) LESSEE will pay the premium to be paid under the insurance policy to be taken out by the LESSEE in respect of such "hazardous" substances in accordance with the said Act. The LESSEE shall produce for the inspection of the LESSOR or his authorised representative at the LESSOR'S office the original showing the payment of premium in respect of the said insurance immediately after the payment has been effected and furnish a xerox copy thereof to the LESSOR within seven days from the date of obtaining such a receipt.

(*c*) LESSEE will take out Insurance Policy in the name and for benefit of the LESSOR and the bankers of the LESSOR or such other names as the LESSOR may advise in this regard.

(*d*) LESSEE will reimburse to LESSOR the amount spent by LESSOR, in the event of the LESSEE failing and/or neglecting to purchase the Insurance Policy under the said Act and/or keeping the same renewed for the benefit of the LESSOR and/or his banker, without prejudice to the rights of the LESSOR to terminate the agreement in such an event.

(*e*) LESSEE will permit LESSOR to appropriate the amount paid by LESSOR as aforesaid from out of the security deposit lying with and further replenish the amount by which the security deposit falls short of the required quantum.

(*f*) LESSEE will keep indemnified the LESSOR from any suit, proceedings, actions, claims, demands and/or prosecutions and/or the costs, charges and expenses in relation to the liability and obligation, suffered by the LESSOR on account of any such hazardous substance or on account of failure of the LESSEE to purchase the Insurance Policy, as aforesaid, as also to pay any cost or expenses related to the LESSOR'S defending any suit/proceeding/action/claim/prosecution brought or launched against the LESSOR.

(*g*) *Lessee to affix name plate.* LESSEE will keep affixed nameplate or other mark on the equipment identifying the sole and exclusive ownership thereof of the LESSOR by putting the following in block letters *viz.* under lease from LESSOR, Leasing Company Ltd. and not allow or permit the same to be removed or defaced during the continuance of this agreement.

17. Lessee not to part with possession. LESSEE will keep the equipment in its possession and control of its plant or premises specified in the Schedule(s) and not to remove the same therefrom without the prior written permission of the LESSOR.

18. Lessee not to convert the property. LESSEE will not affix permanently the equipment to any immovable property nor in any way impair the identifiability, ascertainability, severability and redeliverability of the equipment, nor to adversely affect the value of the equipment when severed for redelivery to LESSOR.

19. Lessee not to have any right in equipment except as bailee. LESSEE will hold the equipment as bailee of LESSOR and not claim any right, title or interest in the equipment other than that of a LESSEE or contest the LESSOR'S sole and exclusive ownership thereof.

20. Lessee to make proper use of the equipment. LESSEE will use the equipment carefully in the same way as would have been the case with the LESSEE'S own equipment, and in accordance with the supplier's instructions/ guidelines, if any, and maintain the same in good working condition and repair at its own cost and expenses and comply with all statutory and other requirements of law, rules, regulations and directions applicable to the storage or installation or governing use and operation of the equipment and not to do or allow to be done any act or thing by which the warranties and performance guarantees given by the manufacturer would be invalidated or become unenforceable, wholly or partly, and not to do any act nor omit to do anything whereby the value of the equipment be reduced or depleted. The LESSEE will also not sub-lease/hire out the equipment nor will deal with the equipment in any manner except as a LESSEE, on the terms and conditions herein contained without prior written consent of the LESSOR.

21. Lessee to pay outgoings pertaining to the equipment. LESSEE will duly pay or cause to be paid all rates, taxes, licence fees, surcharges, registration charges and other outgoings payable in respect of the equipment or the storage, installation, use or operation thereof or of the premises where the same is kept or used and on demand produce to the LESSOR all receipts and other evidences of such payment.

22. Lessee to insure the equipment. It is agreed by and between the parties hereto that the LESSEE shall, for and on behalf of the LESSOR:

(*a*) take out insurance policy on the equipment against loss in transit, erection and installation risks, maritime risks, wherever necessary prior to the despatch of the equipment, or alternatively to ensure that the insurance on the equipment in respect of the said risks is effected by the manufacture/supplier before delivery of the equipment. Such insurance policy will be in the name of the LESSOR to be described therein as the owner and as the loss payee;

(*b*) immediately after the delivery of the equipment, insure the equipment and keep the same insured throughout the term of this

Agreement against loss or damage by accident, lightning, fire, flood, storm, earthquake, tempest, falling aircraft, malicious damage, riot, strike, civil commotion, explosion, implosion, accidental, mechanical, electrical breakdown of the equipment etc. and where necessary against third party claims in respect of equipment used in hazardous industries and those requiring environmental protection as also for other risks usually covered by insurance in the type of business for which the equipment is for the time being used to the satisfaction of the LESSOR upto the full replacement value thereof under a Comprehensive Policy of Insurance in joint names of the LESSOR and the LESSEE with an endorsement showing the LESSOR as the owner and as the loss payee;

(*c*) punctually pay all premia payable under such insurance and send the policy and the receipts (or photostat copies thereof) for such payments to the LESSOR and do everything necessary to maintain the said insurance in full effect and not to do any thing whereby the said insurance will or may be vitiated, failure of the LESSEE to handover such Insurance Policy and premium receipt (or photostat copy thereof) to the LESSOR within seven days from (*a*) the date of delivery of the equipment in the case of an original policy or (*b*) the due date for renewal of the policy in case of renewal of the policy, shall constitute failure to insure the equipments. In such an event, the LESSOR without prejudice to its rights under the Agreement and without any notice to the LESSEE, may effect the insurance, as aforesaid, and the LESSEE shall reimburse to the LESSOR the amount of premium paid and the cost incurred therefor;

(*d*) where the equipment or any part thereof is lost, destroyed, stolen or damaged by the negligence or act of a third party, the LESSEE shall immediately notify the LESSOR the same and shall not compromise any claim without the consent of the LESSOR and shall, unless the LESSOR in its sole discretion directs otherwise, take over the conduct of all negotiations and shall also at its own expense and risk take such proceedings as the LESSOR shall direct. The LESSEE shall hold, all sums recovered inclusive of any claims under the Insurance taken, in trust for the LESSOR and hand over the same to the LESSOR immediately upon receipt thereof without claiming any part thereof on any account whatsoever and shall apply the same or such part thereof as the LESSOR directs. In no case shall such claim/sum of money be adjusted or set off against any sum payable by the LESSEE to the LESSOR hereunder;

(*e*) if the equipment be damaged during the continuance of this Agreement and in the opinion of the LESSOR it is economic that such damage be made good, all insurance moneys payable under the said Insurance may, if the LESSEE agrees, be applied in making good the said damage;

(*f*) if the equipment be destroyed or damaged to such an extent as to be, in the opinion of the LESSOR, incapable of economic repair then at the LESSOR'S sole discretion the Insurance moneys payable under the said Insurance shall, at the option of the LESSOR be applied so far as possible in replacing the equipment with another equipment of similar type and quality, in which event the fresh equipment shall be deemed to have been leased by the LESSOR under this Agreement and the LESSEE shall hold the same on lease subject to the terms and conditions as are contained in this Agreement;

(*g*) the lease of the equipment so lost/destroyed will be deemed to have been terminated except in the case where the LESSOR elects to exercise its option under cl. (*f*) above;

(*h*) without prejudice to the aforesaid right of the LESSOR in the event of such termination, the LESSOR shall also be entitled to recover from the LESSEE who shall be liable to pay to the LESSOR all sums payable hereunder.

23. Lessee not to transfer of dispose of equipment or interest in the lease. Unless otherwise agreed to by the LESSOR in writing the LESSEE will not transfer, assign or otherwise dispose of or purport to transfer, assign or dispose of the LESSEE'S right or obligations or interest hereunder by way of mortgage, charge, sub-lease, sale or other assignment, hypothecation, pledge, hire, encumbrance, conducting arrangement, licence or otherwise in any manner or part with the possession of the equipment or any part thereof or allow or purport to allow or create any lien, charge, attachment or other claim of whatever nature on the equipment or any part thereof. The LESSEE shall also not without the prior written consent of the LESSOR change the location of the equipment or in case of mobile equipment where it is normally parked when not in use.

24. Lessee not to make alterations in the equipment—additions to belong to the lessor. Not to make any alteration, addition or improvement to the equipment or change the condition thereof without the prior written consent of the LESSOR and all additions, improvements and attachment of any nature whatsoever, including any spares, accessories or other materials added by the LESSEE when made to the equipment by the LESSEE (whether at its own cost or not and whether with or without the approval of the LESSOR) shall belong to the LESSOR and be deemed to be part of the equipment and shall be subject to the terms and conditions of this Agreement.

25. Lessee to indemnify lessor for loss or distress. Indemnify and keep indemnified the LESSOR at all times, against any loss or seizure of the equipment under distress execution or other legal process or loss or destruction or damage to the equipment by fire, accident or any other cause, from any claim or demand arising out of the import, storage, installation, use or operation of the equipment or any risk or liability for death or loss of life or limb of any person whether employee of the LESSEE or of third party or not or injury or damage to any property of the LESSEE or of any third party and hold the LESSOR harmless against all losses, damages, claims, penalties, expenses, suits or proceeding of whatsoever nature made, suffered or incurred consequent thereupon and for this purpose take out such workmen's compensation/third party insurance cover as may be necessary, customary or in practice in the business carried on by the LESSEE or as may be directed by the LESSOR in that behalf.

26. Lessee not to alienate the premises where equipment is kept. Not to sell, mortgage, charge, demise, sub-let or otherwise dispose of any land or building on or in which the equipment is stored, installed, used or operated or enter into any agreement or arrangement to do any of the aforesaid acts without prior approval in writing of the LESSOR. The LESSEE shall in any event ensure by giving such notices as may be necessary that such sale, mortgage, charge, demise, sub-letting or other disposition, as the case may be, is subject to the rights of the LESSOR as the owner of the equipment to repossess the equipment at any time (whether or not the same or any part thereof shall have become affixed to the said land or buildings) and for that purpose to enter upon such land or building and reclaim and repossess the equipment lying thereat. The LESSEE shall obtain declaration/ undertaking containing *no lien / charge* over the equipment and recognising the right and access of the LESSOR to the equipment, from such transferees.

27. Lessee to reimburse lessor's incremental costs. On demand pay to the LESSOR all costs, charges and expenses incurred by the LESSOR in connection with the equipment or the preservation, protection or enforcement of the LESSOR'S rights or of retaking or repossessing of the equipment or any other expense incurred by the LESSOR on the understanding that the parties have agreed to keep the LESSOR free from all costs except financial costs on the purchase of the equipment.

28. Lessee to regularly furnish lessee's financial statements. Furnish to the LESSOR its audited Balance Sheet and Profit and Loss Account simultaneously with the issuance thereof to the shareholders of the LESSEE and such other information as may be required by the LESSOR from time to time including certificates as to the state of the equipment or its manner of accounting, upkeep or use by the LESSEE.

29. Variation of lease rentals based on bank lending rates. The LESSEE irrevocably agrees and undertakes that in the event of the bank lending rates chargeable to the LESSOR by its banker(s)/financial institutions is increased/ decreased the lease rentals reserved hereunder are liable to upward or downward variation, as the case may be, in the manner described hereinafter. In such an event, the lease rentals will stand increased/decreased, as the case may be, by Rs. 0.50 paise per month for every Rs. 1,000 of lease finance for every percentage of increase/decrease in the said bank lending rate. However, in case the bank lending rate falls below 16% p.a. no further reduction in lease rentals will be made. The LESSEE agrees that such lease rentals corresponding to the bank lending rate of 16% p.a. will be the bare minimum rentals which the LESSEE has agreed and undertaken to pay to the LESSOR. The LESSEE further agrees that a letter from any of the LESSOR'S Bankers indicating revised rate of interest consequent to any announcement of increase/decrease in interest rates shall be the final and conclusive evidence of the extent and the date of such increase/decrease.

30. Variation of lease rentals based on adverse variation in depreciation allowance and increased sales tax, customs and excise duties, etc. (*a*) The LESSEE further agrees that the lease rentals hereunder are based on the assumption that the LESSOR shall be entitled to claim depreciation based on the acquisition cost of the equipment at the rate specified in respective Schedule for the whole of the period of the lease starting from the year of commencement of the lease. Should the LESSOR not be able to claim the said benefit on account of any change in law or rules or for any act or omission of the LESSEE or for any other reason whatsoever either for the whole or any part of the lease period and at those rates, the lease rentals specified in the respective Schedules shall stand altered so as to compensate the LESSOR for the loss in the tax benefits thereby and maintain the post tax implicit rate of return to the LESSOR as would have been available to the LESSOR had the depreciation allowance been granted as stipulated in the respective Schedules, all factors other than the depreciation allowance being kept constant for that purpose.

(*b*) The LESSEE guarantees that the equipment shall be maintained in such a position and its use shall be so monitored as to ensure to the LESSOR that the equipment has at the end of the lease period a minimum residual value as mentioned in the respective Schedules.

(*c*) *Seizure and / or confiscation of the equipment.* The LESSEE undertakes not to do or omit to do any such act which may result in seizure and/or confiscation of the equipment by the Central or State Government or local authority or any public officer or authority under any law for the time being in force and in the event of seizure or confiscation of other equipments belonging to the LESSEE and coming in the process of such a seizure or confiscation to keep the leased equipment separate from the block of similar or other assets belonging to the LESSEE.

(*d*) *Not to claim any relief, allowances, etc.* The LESSEE undertakes not to claim any relief by way of reduction, losses or grant available to the LESSOR as the owner of the equipment under the Income Tax Act 1961 or any other statute, rules, etc. that are issued or may be issued by the Government of India or any statutory authority or not to do or allow to be done any act, deed or thing whereby the LESSOR is deprived, either wholly or partly, of any such relief by way of reduction, allowances or grants. The LESSEE shall at the end of each accounting year of the LESSOR provide to the LESSOR such information as it may require to claim relief by way of any deduction, allowance or grant as the owner of the equipment under the Income Tax Act 1961 and the LESSEE undertakes to comply with and observe at all times all the terms and conditions to be complied with in the use and operation of the equipment so as to entitle the LESSOR to obtain such a relief.

(*e*) The LESSEE hereby expressly covenants with the LESSOR that: As between the LESSOR and the LESSEE and their respective successors in title, the equipments hereby given on lease or agreed to be given on lease shall remain the exclusive property of the LESSOR and shall continue to remain in the ownership of the LESSOR notwithstanding that the same may have been affixed to any land or building and the LESSEE shall not have any right, title or interest thereon otherwise than as a bailee. The LESSEE shall be responsible for any damage caused to any such land or building by affixing the equipment thereto or the removal, if any, effected by the LESSOR or the LESSEE and shall indemnify the LESSOR against any claim made against it in respect of such a damage. To allow the LESSOR, notwithstanding any instructions issued to the contrary by the LESSEE, to appropriate at its absolute discretion any money received from the LESSEE as follows:

Firstly, towards the costs, charges and expenses incurred by the LESSOR for receipts or recovery of such sums;

Secondly, towards overdue charges and other money demanded but unpaid;

Thirdly, towards the lease rentals due and payable; and

Lastly, towards the dues owed by the LESSEE under any other agreement entered into with the LESSOR.

31. Additional covenants in respect of imported equipments. (*a*) The LESSEE warrants that without prejudice to the generality of provisions contained in other clauses hereof the execution of the Agreement and the use and operation of the equipment by the LESSEE will not contravene any provision of Import Control Regulations, Foreign Exchange Regulations, Customs Act or any other statute, rule and regulation to which the equipment and/or the LESSEE is subjected;

(*b*) The LESSEE further warrants that:

The LESSEE has obtained all consents, import licence or other licences, Reserve Bank approvals or any other approvals and permissions as are necessary for or in connection with the acquisition by import of the equipment, clearances from the relevant authorities, for execution, validity and enforceability of this Agreement and for the storage, installation, use and operation of the equipment and undertakes to keep them effective and in force during the period of this Agreement and till the equipment is delivered back to the LESSOR in good order and condition.

Under the applicable provisions of the Import Export Policy and the rules made thereunder and the other relevant rules prevailing for the time being the LESSEE is entitled to import the equipment if the LESSEE had bought the equipment and was using and operating the same as the owner thereof;

(*c*) The LESSEE agrees and undertakes that, in the event of the acquisition of the imported equipment being financed out of the foreign currency lines of credit or foreign currency loans (hereinafter referred to as FCLC) availed by LESSOR for this purposes, it shall;

(*d*) bear the entire exchange risk on the foreign currency funds utilised by the LESSOR out of the FCLCs;

(*e*) reimburse LESSOR with all such expenses, charges as are required to be paid by the LESSOR in respect of FCLCs to the Foreign Bank/Institution concerned;

(*f*) observe and meticulously follow all the covenants in respect of such FCLCs as may be advised by the LESSOR;

(*g*) execute all such documents, deeds, undertakings, etc. as may be required under the covenants of the FCLC;

(*h*) The LESSEE agrees and undertakes that it shall comply with all the terms, conditions and obligations of the import licence, including submission of reports and other requirements in that behalf to such authorities as may be required and shall also provide to the LESSOR all such informations as may be required to be furnished by the LESSOR to such authorities and as may be required in terms of the import licence for the equipment, in default thereof the LESSEE agrees to indemnify the LESSOR for all claims and demands made upon the LESSOR by reason of such default by the LESSEE.

32. Additional conditions in case of a motor vehicle. In case the equipment be a motor vehicle within the meaning of the Motor Vehicles Act 1988, the LESSEE shall comply/ensure compliance with the further conditions mentioned in Schedule hereunder.

33. Lessee's guaranteed residual value. The LESSEE guarantees that the equipment shall be maintained in such a position and its use shall be so monitored so as to ensure to the LESSOR that the equipment has at the end of the lease periods a minimum residual value as mentioned in Schedule.

34. Acceptance of the equipment—acceptance of delivery by the lessee and lessor's disclaimer on account of quality or fitness of the equipment. (*a*) By accepting the delivery of the equipment (deemed or actual) the LESSEE shall be deemed to have examined the equipment and to have found it complete, in proper order and condition and entirely fit for its purpose and the LESSEE does not and will not, at any time, have any claim against the LESSOR in respect of or arising out of the equipment.

(*b*) The LESSOR shall not be responsible for any direct, indirect or consequential loss to the LESSEE or third party, arising from any delay in delivery and/or installation of the equipment either by the action of the manufacturer or otherwise howsoever. The LESSOR will not be liable or responsible for any damage to the equipment either before or in the process of the delivery.

35. Lessee's confirmation of cost, quality, etc. The LESSEE acknowledges, represents, declares, agrees and confirms that:

(a) *Lessee to obtain timely delivery.* The LESSEE alone, as an agent of the LESSOR, shall be responsible for obtaining timely delivery of the equipment and also for obtaining all the necessary clearances, statutory or otherwise, required for obtaining such delivery.

(b) *Lessee's confirmation as to quality, etc.* The equipment is of the required size, design, capacity and manufacture, suitable for its purpose and is selected by the LESSEE relying entirely on its own judgment and not on any statement or representations made by the LESSOR or its agent or servants.

36. Antecedent negotiations made by the lessee, specific clauses in case of a sale and lease back. (*a*) The LESSOR has bought the equipment on a specific requisition from the LESSEE and for the purpose of lease to the LESSEE, and for no other purpose, and the actual cost of the equipment has been negotiated and ascertained by the LESSEE, which the LESSOR has paid/shall pay at the LESSEE'S instructions. It is expressly understood by and agreed between the parties that the equipments shall be ordered by the LESSOR or LESSEE as the agent of the LESSOR on the specifications given by the LESSEE and the choice of the supplier is exclusively of the LESSEE.

PROVIDED that where for the whole or any part of the equipment, the LESSEE himself is the supplier/manufacturer, the LESSEE affirms that the cost of the equipment to the LESSOR is the fair market price of the equipment in an arms length transactions and that in the event of it being established at any time in future that the cost to the LESSOR is more than such fair market value, the LESSOR may, at his sole discretion, have either of the following recourses against the LESSEE;

(*b*) If the fair value of the equipment or part thereof supplied by the LESSEE is substantially less than the cost of the equipment to the LESSOR, the LESSOR may treat this agreement as having been entered into with a basic mistake of fact and on misrepresentation by the LESSEE, and may proceed to treat the lease as terminated, and forthwith demand upon the LESSEE to pay up all the sums referred to herein, along with any other or further damages that the LESSOR might have suffered as a result of such a misrepresentation, including any loss of tax benefits and all the consequences arising therefrom; or

(*c*) the LESSOR may treat the lease to have been terminated to the extent the cost of the equipment or the part thereof supplied by the LESSEE exceeds the fair value of asset so established, and ask the LESSEE to immediately pay up the lease rentals proportionate to such excess discounted at the rate mentioned herein, along with any other or further charges that the LESSOR might have suffered as a result of such a misrepresentation, including any loss to tax benefits and all the consequences arising therefrom; or

(*d*) the LESSOR may claim appropriate damages, by revision of rentals or otherwise and/or security deposit to cover himself to the extent of such excess, and continue the lease in its *status quo* ante.

37. Selection of the equipment by the lessee. It is clearly understood by the LESSEE that the LESSOR is not the manufacturer or dealer of the equipment. The equipment so purchased/acquired by the LESSOR has been selected and approved by the LESSEE.

The LESSOR has not at any time made nor does it hereby make any representation of warranty whatsoever with respect to the merchantability, quality, conditions, durability, suitability or fitness for the purpose of use, operation or performance of the equipment.

38. Disclaimer of any liability by the lessor regarding quality, etc. The LESSOR hereby disclaims any liability on any account pertaining to the quality, fitness or suitability of the equipment to the LESSEE and in order to give effect to the warranties, indemnities, guaranties or other facilities provided by the manufacturer, the LESSOR hereby appoints the LESSEE as its agent but the LESSEE shall not have any claim against the LESSOR in the event of the manufacturer not providing to the LESSEE the benefit of any such warranty, indemnity, guarantee or other facility.

39. All Indemnities to survive the agreement. All indemnities contained under this agreement shall survive the termination of the agreement or on expiry of the respective leases hereunder sought to be created as the case may be.

40. Imposts, taxes and other charges. The LESSEE shall during the period of this agreement and till the equipment is delivered back to the LESSOR in good working order and condition, bear all imposts, charges and other duties, taxes and penalties as may be levied from time to time by the Government or any other authority pertaining to or in respect of this equipment and/or agreement, the acquisition of the equipment (including purchase tax or differential tax or other sums in case the LESSOR has concessional rate of tax), any incremental duty or other tax payable with reference to the purchase or acquisition of the equipment or this transaction. Further, the LESSEE shall reimburse to the LESSOR all taxes (including sales tax), duties or other sums imposed now or hereafter, on the equipment or on this transaction or on the rentals hereunder, and where the LESSOR has not paid the same under an honest belief formed under competent advice that the same is not payable, the LESSEE shall also reimburse to the LESSOR the interest or penalty payable in respect of the same. The LESSEE agrees to pay immediately on demand these sums whether the same are ascertained during or after the termination of this lease.

41. Termination. On the occurrence of any events specified in cls. 43 to 52 below, the LESSOR shall be entitled, without prejudice to any other right or remedy which the LESSOR may have under this agreement or otherwise in law and notwithstanding any subsequent acceptance of rentals or indulgence shown to the LESSEE, to terminate this lease, without any notice at any time after the occurrence of such events.

42. Failure to pay rentals or dishonour of cheques, etc. If the LESSEE fails to pay the rentals on the dates and in the manner stipulated in the respective schedule(s), or other monies payable hereunder within 15 days of their becoming due, whether demanded or not, or if a cheque, bill, promissory note or other instrument issued, made, drawn or accepted by the LESSEE for discharge of the lease rentals is returned unpaid, for any reason whatsoever, when presented for payment, the LESSOR shall be entitled to terminate this lease.

43. Breach of any other terms of the lease. If the LESSEE fails or neglects to observe or perform or commits or allows to be committed a breach of any of the terms, conditions, provisions or stipulations, of this agreement on its part to be observed and performed (other than failure to pay any sum hereunder when due and payable) and if such breach is remediable, fails to remedy the same within fourteen days of notice by the LESSOR specifying such default and requiring such default to be remedied the LESSOR may terminate the lease.

44. Breach of mandatory conditions. If the LESSEE fails or neglects to observe or perform or commits or allows to be committed breach of any of the terms, conditions, or regulations in respect of the use, storage, operation or keeping of the equipment imposed by any authority or by the manufacturer, the LESSOR may terminate the lease.

45. Misrepresentation, etc. by the lessee. If any representation or warranty whether precedent or subsequent made or deemed to be made by the LESSEE in or in relation to this agreement is or proves to have been incorrect in any material respect or the particulars supplied by the LESSEE about itself or about the supplier or the equipments are found to be incorrect, the LESSOR.

46. Resolution of winding up, etc. If the LESSEE passes any resolution for its winding up or a petition for winding up be presented against it by any of its members or creditors or otherwise or if a receiver is appointed for the whole or part of the assets, properties or undertakings of the LESSEE or enters into any composition with its creditors, the LESSOR may terminate the lease.

47. Distress of the equipment, etc. If the LESSEE does or suffers any act or thing or omits to do or suffers any act or thing whereby or in consequence of which the equipment may be or is likely to be distressed, endangered, attached or taken in execution under any legal process or by public authority, the LESSOR may terminate the lease.

48. Apprehended default. If the LESSEE by any act or omission gives to the LESSOR reasonable grounds to consider that its rights may be prejudiced or be in jeopardy, the LESSOR may terminate the lease.

49. Default under other agreements. If the LESSEE commits any default under any other agreement of lease or other financing arrangement between the LESSOR and the LESSEE, the LESSOR may terminate the lease.

50. Adverse material changes. If there takes place any material change in the financial or corporate position of the LESSEE as a result of which it becomes reasonably apprehensible that the lease rentals hereunder may not be paid as due or there may be any other default under this agreement or that the LESSOR'S rights and entitlements hereunder may be endangered, or if the LESSEE'S business or management is taken over, the LESSOR may terminate the lease.

PROVIDED that it is agreed, without affecting the generality of the foregoing, that the following changes shall be regarded as material changes, with reference to the financial year immediately preceding the one in which this agreement commences:

(*a*) decrease in net worth, that is, the aggregate of paid up capital and free reserves (including credit balance in P&L account and premium, but excluding unrealised revaluation reserves) by 40% or more;

(*b*) decrease in return on investment, that is, profits before tax, interest and lease rentals, to long term funds including assets financed under finance lease to the extent not repaid, consecutively for two financial years, by 40% or more;

(*c*) decrease in turnover excluding stock adjustments and excluding extraordinary or non-recurring liens consecutively for two financial years by 40% or more;

(*d*) decrease in debt (including obligations under finance leases), service coverage ratio by or more than 20% consecutively for the last two financial years of the LESSEE.

51. Offence pertaining to negotiable instruments. If the LESSEE fails to provide to the LESSOR cheques, promissory notes, or other instruments as required by the LESSOR, whether post-dated or otherwise, for discharge of the LESSEE'S obligations hereunder, or having provided to the LESSOR any such instrument the LESSEE, by any act or omission on the part of the LESSEE impedes the possibility of such instrument being honoured when presented for payment, the LESSOR may terminate the lease.

52. Lessor's rights and lessee's obligations on termination. On the termination of this agreement pursuant to provisions contained in this agreement the LESSOR may terminate the lease and take steps mentioned hereunder.

53. Repossession of the equipment by the lessor and his rights for that purpose. The LESSOR, shall, without any notice or permission, be entitled to remove or repossess the equipment and for that purpose by itself, its servants or agents, enter upon any land, buildings or premises where the equipment is situated or is reasonably believed by the LESSOR to be situated for the time being and for such entry, the LESSEE hereby gives to the LESSOR an irrevocable license, and detach and dismantle the same and the LESSOR shall not be responsible for any damage which may be caused by any such detachment or removal of the equipment. It is hereby clarified that the LESSOR may make use of reasonable force for the purposes of repossession of the equipment and repossess the equipment with anything that is in or in it, or attached, fastened, bolted, or in any other manner affixed to it, and remove, if necessary by dismantling all obstructions in the way of repossession of the equipment, and generally do all such things as a reasonable man would do on being unlawfully deprived of his personal property to reinstate himself in possession of his property expediently and with least damage to his property.

54. Recovery of defaulted amounts and costs. Without prejudice to and in addition to the LESSOR'S right provided hereinabove, the LESSOR shall also be entitled to recover from the LESSEE and the LESSEE shall be bound to pay to the LESSOR the following amounts, *viz.*

(*a*) the entire amount of the rental already fallen due and in arrears together with interest as provided hereunder;

(*b*) the entire amount of lease rentals for the unexpired period of lease discounted at the then prevailing prime lending rate of commercial banks;

(*c*) all other sums payable hereunder which may have become due along with interest from the date on which due and all such other sums that may become due or may be estimated to become due in view of the events or defaults already having occurred;

(*d*) the cost of all repair and maintenance of the equipment to render and maintain it in good working order and condition and all cost, charges and expenses incurred by the LESSOR pursuant to the agreement and in repossessing the equipment and in enforcing its remedies however occasioned.

PROVIDED that in case the equipment is sold by the LESSOR then its net sale proceeds, or otherwise its market value as may be estimated by the LESSOR shall be allowed as a deduction from the aggregate amount calculated under this clause.

The parties hereto agree and record that the amounts to be paid by the LESSEE to the LESSOR as aforesaid have been *bona fide* and satisfactorily estimated to be the proper and reasonable amount that may be suffered by the LESSOR as and by way of liquidated damages and are not deterrent or in terrorem.

55. Appropriation of rentals. All rentals or other sums paid by the LESSEE herein shall be deemed to have been appropriated against the liabilities of the LESSEE hereunder immediately upon payment thereof.

56. Sale etc. of the equipment by the lessor, sale through the agency of the lessee and the lessee's rewards. In the event of termination of the lease the LESSOR shall also be entitled to sell, realise or otherwise dispose of the equipment in such a manner as the LESSOR may think fit and the LESSOR shall not be bound to account to the LESSEE in any manner whatsoever, nor to give any preemptive right to the LESSEE.

PROVIDED that where in case of termination of lease by efflux of time or premature termination as provided herein the LESSOR may, in case he wants to dispose of the equipments, organise open market bids for the proposed sale of the equipment, and may appoint the LESSEE or any other person to organise such sale, and in case the sale proceeds exceed the minimum guaranteed value mentioned in Schedule hereunder, the LESSOR may pass on such excess to the LESSEE after deducting therefrom the expenses in organising such sale, and as a reward for good maintenance of the asset by the LESSEE.

PROVIDED that the LESSOR shall allow the LESSEE an opportunity of participating in such an open market sale.

57. Premature termination, advance payment, etc. The LESSOR may, but shall not be obliged to, accept any payments hereunder before they are due and allow in respect thereof such concessions on account of advance payment as the LESSOR may think fit, and such concession shall not vest in the LESSEE any right to similar concession in future.

58. Premature termination. (*a*) The LESSOR may, but shall not be obliged to, allow the LESSEE to foreclose the lease before the expiry of the terms of the lease, and in that case the LESSEE shall:

(*b*) Pay to the LESSOR all the sums referred to in clauses hereinabove after deducting the sum mentioned in the proviso to that clause.

(*c*) Deliver the equipment to the LESSOR in good working order and condition, reasonable wear and tear excepted.

59. General conditions—time related upward revision of amounts due. (*a*) Where any sum payable by the LESSEE hereunder is payable on the specified date, and is paid by the LESSEE after such date, the difference between the date of payment and the specified date shall be taken as *the overdue period.*

(*b*) Where any sum payable by the LESSEE hereunder is payable on demand by the LESSOR, and is paid by the LESSEE after three days, from the date of demand, the difference between the date of payment and the date three days after the date of demand shall be taken as *the overdue period.*

(*c*) Where any sum payable by the LESSEE hereunder does not fall under cls. (*a*) and (*b*) above and is payable without demand raised by the LESSOR, and is paid by the LESSEE after three days from the date on which the LESSEE first becomes aware of such liability, the difference between the date of such payment and the date three days after the date on which the LESSEE first becomes aware of such a liability shall be taken as *the overdue period*.

(*d*) All sums paid by the LESSEE having an overdue period shall automatically stand increased by Rupee one per thousand per week and the LESSEE shall pay such sums as increased hereunder and any sum payable hereunder but paid without over due charge shall be deemed to be unpaid to the extent of the automatic increase provided hereunder.

(*e*) The LESSEE undertakes and affirms that the provision for automatic increase of any sum paid with an overdue period:

(*i*) is an essential part of the sums payable hereunder and its non-payment shall be taken as a breach of an essential condition by the LESSEE;

(*ii*) is a genuine estimate of the commercial loss of opportunity and other damages suffered by the LESSOR on account of untimely payment of sums payable hereunder;

(*iii*) is capable of variation by a written notification by the LESSOR in case of a continuing, recurring or persistent default in payment of sums hereunder by the LESSEE, and the LESSEE agrees not to call in question LESSOR'S discretion in treating the LESSEE'S default as failing under this clause.

60. Payments to be clear of deductions. All payments to be made by the LESSEE to the LESSOR hereunder shall be made free from and clear of, any payment or deduction on any account.

61. Place for payment. All monies due and payable by the LESSEE to the LESSOR pursuant to the agreement shall be paid by telegraphic, telex or mail transfer to the account of the LESSOR at .... or such other place as the LESSOR may designate or by cheque or bank draft drawn in favour of the LESSOR on a scheduled bank and shall be so paid as to enable the LESSOR to realise at par, the amount sought to be paid on or before the due date to which the payment relates. Credit for all payments by cheque/ bank draft will be given only on the realisation thereof by the LESSOR or on the due date to which the payment relates, whichever is later.

62. Service of notices. Any notice to the LESSEE by the LESSOR shall be in writing and posted to the LESSEE'S address first above written and for proving service by the LESSOR it shall be sufficient to show that the communication was complete from the LESSOR. Any notice required to be given by the LESSEE to the LESSOR shall be in writing and be sent to the LESSOR'S address first above written. Any change in the address of the LESSEE shall be notified to the LESSOR by Registered Post in order to make the same cognizable for the purpose of this clause.

63. Time to be of essence. Time shall be of the essence in this agreement in so far as it relates to the observance or performance by the LESSEE of all or any of the obligations including payment of any sum hereunder.

64. Warranties. The LESSOR agrees that the LESSEE shall be entitled to the benefits of the warranties provided by the manufacturer/suppliers of the equipment. Any performance guarantee provided by the supplier shall be in the joint names of the LESSOR and the LESSEE and shall be enforceable by the LESSOR or the LESSEE or both of them. For this purpose, the LESSOR, if so requested by the LESSEE, shall authorise the LESSEE for enforcing the performance by the supplier of the equipment for any warranties or performance guarantees relating to the equipment.

65. Waiver or remission not to have precedent value—demands or notices waived. The failure of the LESSOR to insist upon the punctual performance of any of the obligations of the LESSEE hereunder, or the failure of the LESSOR to exercise any right or remedy available to the LESSOR under this agreement or any failure of the LESSOR to require payment from or by the LESSEE when due of any sum owing hereunder, or any extension of credit or any forbearance on the part of the LESSOR shall not constitute waiver by the LESSOR of any subsequent or continuing default by the LESSEE hereunder nor shall the same prejudice, affect or restrict the rights and powers of the LESSOR hereunder. All demands for payments and performance and all notices of non-payment or other default hereunder, are hereby waived by the LESSEE.

66. Option to renew. Unless the LESSEE is in default under this Agreement at the relevant time the LESSEE shall have an option to renew the lease after expiry of the present agreement by efflux of time for a further period on such rental and other terms as would be mutually agreed upon between the parties.

67. Affirmation as to statements made by the lessee. The LESSEE declares and represents that every statement and representation made and every particular given by it in relation to this transaction are true and correct. By execution hereof, the respective signatories hereby certifies that he/they has/have read this agreement including the Schedules hereto and that he/they is/are duly authorised to execute this agreement on behalf of the respective parties.

68. Agreement to be sole and exclusive. This agreement represents the entire agreement of lease between the parties hereto and shall be capable of variation in writing by a note of amendment signed by and on behalf of the LESSOR the LESSEE and guarantors.

69. Interpretation of words. Words importing the plural shall, except where the context otherwise requires, include the singular and *vice versa.* Clause heading shall not control clear meaning of the text, but may be used to clarify the intention in case the same is not clear.

70. Arbitration. Except where it has been provided otherwise, any dispute or difference arising out of or in connection with the agreement between the parties including any dispute or difference relating to the interpretation of the agreement or any clause thereof shall be referred to the sole arbitration of Mr. XY or of a person nominated by Mr. XY (with summery powers) and the provisions of the Arbitration and Conciliation Act 1996 and rules framed thereunder and any amendment thereto, from time to time, shall apply. No objection shall be taken on the ground that the arbitrator so appointed is an employee of the LESSOR or is in any way associated with the LESSOR. It is made clear that the venue of Arbitration proceedings will be the sole discretion of the Arbitrator and no objection shall be entertained from any party in this regard. The award of the arbitrator shall be final, conclusive and binding on all the parties. The arbitrator shall be competent to decide whether any matter of dispute or difference referred to him falls within purview of arbitration as provided for above and/or any matter relates to arbitration under the Arbitration and Conciliation Act 1996.

71. Jurisdiction. For all disputes arising out of this contract the jurisdiction shall be with the High Court at Calcutta.

IN WITNESS WHEREOF the parties hereto have caused these presents to be executed in duplicate on the day, month and year first herein above-written.

(1) Signed and delivered by the within named LESSOR under the hand of its authorised signatory Mr. .... at ....

(2) Signed and delivered by the within named LESSEE under the hand of its authorised signatory Mr. .... and Mr. .... in pursuance of a resolution passed by its Board of Directors/Authorisation by the partners dated .... at ....

(3) Signed and delivered by the within named CO-LESSEE under the hand of its authorised signatory(ies) Mr. .... and Mr. .... in pursuance of a resolution passed by its Board of Directors dated .... at ....

(4) Guarantors

(5) Witness

In the presence of:

(*a*) ....

(*b*) ....

Schedule I

To Lease Agreement Dated ....

1.	Fixed non-cancellable period	:	.... months from the date of commencement of the lease.
2.	Renewal	:	As may be opted by the LESSEE.
3.	Lease Management Fee	:	........% of the asset cost/ Rs. ....
4.	Lease rentals	:	As per Schedule 1(1) below.
5.	Contingency Deposit/Sales Tax	:	At applicable rates (to be borne by lessee) .... (included as part of rentals as on actuals).
6.	Security Deposit	:	....
7.	Interest of Security Deposit	:	....
8.	Collateral Security	:	....
9.	Assumption for Depreciation Allowance	:	....
10.	Depreciation as per I.T. Act	:	....
11.	Assured residual value at the end of the primary lease period	:	........% of the acquisition cost/ Rs. ....
12.	Sanctioned Amount	:	....
13.	Draw down Period	:	....

Lessor Lessee Guarantor/s

14. Particulars of Equipments

Type of Equipment	*Manufacturer's/ Suppliers Name & Address*	*Quantity*	*Location of the Equipment*	*Date of Delivery of the Equipment*	*Acquisition cost of the Equipment*	*Commencements date of the Lease*	*Any other Special Terms*
(a)	(b)	(c)	(d)	(e)	(f)	(g)	(h)

Schedule 1(1)

(*a*) Due date : ....

(*b*) Payment Terms : All rentals are payable .... in advance/arrear at par at Calcutta.

	April	May	June	July	August	September	October	November	December	January	February	March
1999												
2000												
2001												
2002												
2003												
2004												
2005												
2006												
2007												
2008												

Sd/-

LESSOR, LESSEE

CO-LESSEE, GUARANTORS

Schedule II

Special Provision Applicable to the equipment being a Motor Vehicle.

1. If the equipment given in lease is a motor vehicle (in this clause referred to as the vehicle) within the meaning of the Motor Vehicles Act 1988 then the clauses abovementioned shall apply to the lease of the vehicle *mutatis mutandis* and to the extent they are not repugnant to the clauses mentioned below or to the nature of the vehicle being leased and the following further clauses shall apply to the vehicle.
2. The vehicle shall be registered as required under the said Motor Vehicles Act in the name of the LESSEE as owner of the Motor Vehicle and the LESSOR'S name shall be registered therein as the financier under the Agreement but that shall not in any way affect the absolute ownership of the LESSOR of the vehicle or confer upon the LESSEE any right other than of the LESSEE as provided herein, while at the time making the lease fully liable and responsible for all the obligations, liabilities and duties as provided under the said Act or under any other law or instrument pertaining to the ownership, use or maintenance of the vehicle.
3. The LESSEE shall deliver as soon as may be after the registration of the vehicle certified copies of the registration papers, insurance receipts, tax tokens and all other papers connected with the vehicle and continue to provide to the LESSOR such papers in original or by way of certified copies as the LESSOR may require.
4. In the event of the termination of the lease, for any reason whatsoever or in the event of the LESSOR taking repossession of the vehicle, the LESSEE hereby unconditionally and irrevocably undertakes to and agrees with the LESSOR that the LESSEE shall sign, execute and deliver all such instruments, forms, applications and writings and shall do all such other acts, deeds and things as may be required by the LESSOR and for this purpose the LESSEE hereby irrevocably and unconditionally authorizes the LESSOR that in the event of the LESSEE refusing or being unable to or failing to sign and deliver any of the aforesaid instruments, application forms or other writings as may be required by the LESSOR, the LESSOR shall be entitled without being obliged to do so to sign such instruments, forms, applications papers and writing for and on behalf of the LESSEE as a duly constituted attorney of the LESSEE.
5. The LESSEE shall during the subsistence of this lease and till the vehicle is delivered back to the LESSOR in good order and condition, operate the vehicle only in the areas specified in the schedule or

in such other place or places previously approved in writing by the LESSOR and only for lawful purposes and in a lawful manner.

6. The LESSEE shall keep the vehicle in good repair and working condition and replace all such parts, accessories, tyres, tubes or other annexures as becomes obsolete, get damaged or unusable or in other way uneconomical, and all such replaced parts, accessories, tyres or other annexures shall become the property of the LESSOR.
7. The LESSOR may make reasonable use of force to retake the possession of the vehicle in any of the events of defaults and the LESSOR may retake the possession of the vehicle wherever the vehicle be or is believed to be, whether with or without whatever is in or on the vehicle and the LESSOR hereby disclaims and the LESSEE hereby assumes the liability on account of loss or damage caused to any person or property because of such repossession including the loss or damage due to the repossession of the vehicle with whatever might be contained in or on it.

The Schedule

Sd/-
LESSOR
LESSEE
CO-LESSEE
GUARANTORS

33

Leave & Licence and Easement

Licence. Where one person grants to another or to a definite number of other persons, a right to do, or continue to do in or upon the immovable property of the grantor, something which would, in the absence of such right, be unlawful and such right does not amount to an easement or an interest in the property, the right is called a license.[1] License is a permission to do something on an immovable property such as occupation or enjoying benefit thereon or using it for some other purpose. The intention of a license is that the licensee will have a personal privilege but no interest in the property. A license is a personal right, the licensee cannot transfer the license or exercise it through an agent. The exception is a place of public entertainment. As the license is of personal nature when the licensor transfers the property, the license comes to an end.[2]

Revocation. A license is revocable unless the licensee has acted upon the license and executed work of a permanent nature incurring expenses or the license is coupled with transfer of property. Revocation may be expressed or implied.[3] A license stands revoked when the licensor ceases to have any interest in the property or the licensee releases the license or the period or specific act for which the license was granted is over or the subject-matter of the license is destroyed or altered or the purpose of the license becomes impracticable or is abandoned or the employment, office or character for which the license was given ceases to exist, or for more than 20 years the licensee ceased to use the property.[4]

License or lease A license does not create an interest in the property but a lease creates an interest thereon. One of the tests of a lease is exclusive

1 Section 52 of the Indian Easements Act 1882.
2 Section 59 of the Indian Easements Act 1882.
3 Sections 60 and 61 of the Indian Easements Act 1882.
4 Section 62 of the Indian Easements Act 1882.

possession of property. Whether an agreement creates relationship of the landlord and tenant or the licensor and licensee, the intention of the parties is decisive.[5]

License coupled with interest. Section 60 of the Act provides that a license is revocable by the creator unless it is coupled with transfer of property and such transfer is in force and the licensee acting upon the license has executed a work of a *permanent nature* and incurred expenses. "Transfer of Property" in the present context means transfer of right to do something in or upon the property of a permanent nature and is equivalent to "grant" but not amounting to transfer of any right in the property. A bare license can be terminated at any time even if it was granted for a consideration or for a fixed period.[6]

A license which gives the licensee the right to "profits a prendre" or to excavate earth or to draw water is a license coupled with transfer of the property.[7] If a licensee constructs any permanent structure with the knowledge and consent of the licensor the license cannot be revoked.[8] The important thing is that the construction should be made by the licensor in pursuance of the license granted to him.[9]

The court will interpret the agreement of license taking into consideration all the facts and surrounding circumstances to come to a conclusion as to whether it is a license or lease. Therefore, the Leave and License Agreement may not be the exclusive of relationship between the parties to the agreement but the wordings of the Agreement are most important.

FORMS

Leave and License Agreement

THIS AGREEMENT IS MADE this 10th day of August 1999 BETWEEN Mr. AB residing at .... (hereinafter referred to as the LICENSOR which term shall include his successors and assigns) of the one part and Mr. CD residing at .... (hereinafter referred

5 *Associated Hotels of India Ltd.* v *R.N. Kapoor* AIR 1959 SC 1262; *M.N. Clubwalla* v *Eida Hussain Saheb* AIR 1965 SC 610; *Rajkumar Rajindra Singh* v *State of Himachal Pradesh* AIR 1990 SC 1833.

6 *Dominion of India* v *Sohanlal* AIR 1950 East Punjab 40.

7 *Ghissu* v *Hashim Ali* AIR 1954 All 683.

8 *Gopalan Nair* v *Thevi Amma* AIR 1969 Ker 23; *Fazal Haq* v *Data Ram* AIR 1975 All 373.

9 *Ayyappan* v *Dharmodayan* AIR 1966 SC 1017.

to as the LICENSEE which term shall include his heirs and successors) of the other part.

WHEREAS the LICENSOR is owner of land and building situate at......... .... consisting of 5 floors, partly occupied by the tenants and the LICENSOR and partly vacant.

WHEREAS the LICENSEE has requested the LICENSOR to allow the LICENSEE to occupy and use temporarily about 1000 sq. ft. floor area on the ground floor on the South Eastern corner of the building on leave and license basis for carrying on his business till the LICENSEE gets an alternative accommodation for his business.

AND WHEREAS the LICENSOR has agreed to allow on leave and license basis the LICENSEE to occupy and use the said ground floor portion of the said building on temporary basis.

NOW THESE PRESENTS WITNESSETH and the parties hereby agree as follows:

1. The LICENSOR hereby allows the LICENSEE on leave and license basis to use the said 1000 sq. ft. area on the South-East corner of the ground floor of the said premises No. .... of .... belonging to the LICENSOR and where the LICENSOR maintains an office for correspondence and will continue to maintain (hereinafter referred to as the said LICENSED PORTION) for a period of six months from the date of execution hereof in the first instance.

2. The LICENSOR and his stenographer shall have the right to use the office at any time and to enter upon the licensed portion at any time during working hours to inspect the premises.

3. The LICENSOR shall be responsible for all sorts of repairs and paintings to be carried out not more than once a year.

4. The LICENSEE agrees to vacate the said premises on the expiry of six months or earlier if the LICENSEE secureds an alternative accommodation.

5. The LICENSEE shall pay to the LICENSOR Rs. 50 per month per sq. ft. of the area given to the LICENSEE as license fee payable in advance by the 10th of each month.

6. The LICENSEE shall not be responsible for any repairs or payment of any rates, taxes or levies in respect of the said licensed portion.

7. The LICENSEE shall pay 98% of the electric charges and water charges on the basis of actual consumption by the LICENSEE and for this purpose a separate Electric and Water Meter would be provided in the said licensed portion and the LICENSOR would pay the balance 2% of such charges apportionable to his office in the said licensed portion.

8. The LICENSEE shall not use the licensed portion except for carrying on its business.

9. The license is given on a personal basis and the LICENSEE will not be entitled to transfer the benefit of this agreement or give sub-license to anybody else.

10. The LICENSEE agrees that the LICENSOR would lock up the entrances to the entire building including the licensed portion at midnight and thereafter the ingress to or egress from the licensed premises would not be permissible or possible till 6 A.M. in the morning except in case of emergency when the LICENSOR's Durwan or Night Watchman will be available for opening the doors.

11. The LICENSEE undertakes not to cause any damage or defacement of the ceiling, walls or floors of the licensed portion.

12. The LICENSEE shall not carry out any structural repairs, additions or alterations and shall not cause any nuisance or annoyance to the neighbours or store any hazardous goods or do anything which would damage the premises or jeopardise others.

13. On any breach of any of the terms of the agreement the LICENSOR will be entitled to terminate the license on giving seven days' notice.

14. On termination of the LICENSE or on expiry of period of the license the LICENSEE shall make over vacant and peaceful possession of the licensed portion to the LICENSOR in good condition.

IN WITNESS WHEREOF the parties hereto have executed these presents on the day, month and year first above-written.

Signed and delivered by Mr. AB
the LICENSOR in the presence of: Signature

1.

2.

Signed and delivered by Mr. CD
the LICENSEE in the presence of: Signature

1.

2.

Leave and License Agreement for Company's Officers

THIS AGREEMENT IS MADE this .... 2000 BETWEEN Mr. AB having his office at .... (hereinafter referred to as the LICENSOR which term shall include his successors and assigns) of the one part and CD Co. Limited, a company registered under the Companies Act 1956 and carrying on business at.. (hereinafter referred to as the LICENSEE which term shall include its successors and permitted assignees) of the other part.

WHEREAS the LICENSOR is the owner of the premises No. ...... of .... wherein he resides on the ground floor and has an office on the first floor.

AND WHEREAS the LICENSEE approached the LICENSOR for a temporary accommodation for its officers on the first floor of the said premises and is agreeable to take on leave and licence basis the first floor flat excluding office portion therein.

AND WHEREAS the LICENSOR has agreed to grant on leave and license basis use of the first floor flat having an area of 1000 sq. ft. floor area excluding the area occupied by the office of the LICENSOR.

AND WHEREAS the LICENSEE has inspected the said flat complete with all amenities and has satisfied itself as to its suitability for the occupation of its officers for a temporary accommodation.

NOW THESE PRESENTS WITNESSETH and the parties hereby agree as follows:

1. The LICENSOR hereby allows on leave and license basis the use of the first floor flat by officers of the LICENSEE for a period of two years for residential purpose.

2. The LICENSEE agrees that at a time not more than one of its officers with family members may occupy or reside in the said flat.

3. The LICENSEE shall pay to the LICENSOR a sum of Rs. 5,000 per month as license fee or compensation for occupation of the said flat payable in advance by the 10th of each month.

4. The LICENSOR will continue to have his office on the first floor as usual and shall have a duplicate key of the main door of the first floor for free ingress to and egress from the said office on first floor.

5. All municipal taxes, rates and other levies in respect of the said flat would be paid by the LICENSOR.

6. All internal and external repairs shall be carried out by the LICENSOR once a year.

7. There will be separate electric meters and water meters for the first floor and the LICENSEE would pay electric charges and water charges consumed by the LICENSEE.

8. The LICENSOR would pay electric charges for the electricity consumed by him for his office on the first floor.

9. The LICENSEE shall not be entitled to transfer the license to any other person or allow any person to occupy the said flat except by an officer of the LICENSEE.

10. The LICENSOR shall have the right to enter into and inspect the portion of the first floor flat given to LICENSEE on leave and license basis.

11. The LICENSEE shall not cause any damage to the premises or cause any nuisance or annoyance to the neighbouring people or store any hazardous goods or do anything which would jeopardise safety of premises or people.

12. On breach of any of the terms of this agreement the LICENSOR will be entitled to terminate this license by giving 10 days' notice.

13. The LICENSEE undertakes to vacate the licensed premises on expiry of two years or earlier determination of the license.

14. The LICENSEE undertakes that if the services of the officer occupying the licensed premises is terminated then the LICENSEE should get the flat vacated by the officer immediately.

15. It is agreed that by these presents the LICENSEE does not acquire any right, title or interest in the said first floor flat in any manner whatsoever and would occupy the said flat during the currency of this agreement as a mere LICENSEE.

IN WITNESS WHEREOF the parties have executed these presents on the day, month and year first above-written.

Signed, sealed and delivered by
Mr. ....
pursuant to Board Resolution
dated .... of CD Co. Limited
in the presence of: Signature

1.
2.

Signed and delivered by Mr. AB
in the presence of: Signature

1.
2.

Easements

Easement is a right which the owner or occupier of a land possesses over adjoining land for the beneficial enjoyment of the former. It is a privilege without profit which the owner of a land or building has over another land or building.[1]

1 Section 4 of the Indian Easements Act 1882.

An easement may be a right of way over another's land or a right to air and light through particular apertures which the neighbours cannot obstruct and such right may be by grant or acquired by long user by prescription. Grants of easement may be a right to construct or right of support, the right to surface and underground water, right to flow of stream of water, the right to drainage and sewage and the right to use water of a stream running over somebody else's land for consumption or irrigation.

The land which claims a right either in law or under contract over another land is called the dominant land and the other land which suffers such right is called the servient land. The owners are called the dominant owner and the servient owner. Easement rights can be enjoyed only by the dominant owner for enjoyment of the dominant land or building. Such enjoyment should not be a burden on the servient land. The dominant owner shall not cause any inconvenience to the servient owner except as is essential.[2]

An easement cannot be transferred apart from the dominant land. When a property is transferred the easement right attached to the property is also transferred along with the property.[3] However, an easement can be created, modified or extinguished by agreement.

An agreement granting or modifying or extinguishing an easement touches the immovable property and it requires registration under s. 17 of the Registration Act. Stamp duty on such an agreement would be under Art. 5 of the Indian Stamp Act treating it as an agreement. However, the Registration Office may contend that the document is a grant of a right in relation to immovable property and is a conveyance and the Stamp Duty has to be paid on the consideration *ad valorem*.

Read also ss. 25 and 26 of the Limitation Act 1963.

FORMS

Agreement of Easement of Right of Way

THIS AGREEMENT IS MADE on this .... day of .... 1999 BETWEEN Mr. AB, ... (hereinafter referred to as the DOMINANT OWNER which term shall include his successors and transferees) of the one part and Mr. CD of .... (hereinafter referred to as the SERVIENT OWNER which term shall include his successors and transferees) of the other part.

2 Sections 20-31 of the Indian Easements Act 1882.

3 Sections 6 and 8 of the Transfer of Property Act.

WHEREAS the DOMINANT OWNER is the owner of 3 cottahs of land being premises No. .... of .... surrounded on all sides by lands of other persons and has no opening to the main road.

AND WHEREAS the SERVIENT OWNER owns the land in front of the DOMINANT OWNER'S land being premises No. ...... of .... and is situate facing the road with wide front.

AND WHEREAS the DOMINANT OWNER proposes to construct a three-storied building on his land for residential purpose and requires a direct passage to the road through the land of the SERVIENT OWNER.

AND WHEREAS the DOMINANT OWNER has approached the SERVIENT OWNER for granting easement right for ingress to and egress from the DOMINANT OWNER'S premises through and over the land of the SERVIENT OWNER and on being approached the SERVIENT OWNER has agreed to grant such right of way over his land.

NOW THESE PRESENTS WITNESSETH and the parties hereby agree as follows:

1. In consideration of the DOMINANT OWNER paying Rs. 5 lakhs to the SERVIENT OWNER, the receipt whereof is acknowledged hereby, the SERVIENT OWNER hereby grants to the DOMINANT OWNER the right of passage through the South-Eastern portion of premises No. ...... of ....

2. The passage will be 10 ft. wide running from North to South connecting the DOMINANT OWNER'S land with the main road.

3. The said passage will be used by the occupiers of premises No. ...... of .... and also by the occupiers of premises No. .... of ......

4. The said common passage shall be maintained by the DOMINANT OWNER and the expenses thereof would be shared equally by the DOMINANT OWNER and the SERVIENT OWNER.

5. The right of way will attach to the dominant land over the servient land and such right will run with the land.

6. The common passage can be used for all purposes of entering into and coming out of the dominant land with men, material, animals, vehicles and all other things which may enter the passage without damaging the land or structure thereon or causing annoyance or jeopardising the occupiers of the servient land and buildings.

7. The said common passage is to be kept open to the sky and unobstructed in any manner whatsoever.

8. If the DOMINANT OWNER fails to make repairs or keep the passage repaired then the SERVIENT OWNER may for the time being cause the repair to be done and recover 50% of such costs from the DOMINANT OWNER or the occupiers of the dominant land.

IN WITNESS WHEREOF the parties have executed these presents on the day, month and year first above-written.

Signed and delivered by Mr. AB the
DOMINANT OWNER in the presence of: Signature

1. ....
2. ....

Signed and delivered by Mr. CD the
SERVIENT OWNER in the presence of: Signature

1. ....
2. ....

Easement of Drainage and Sewage

THIS AGREEMENT IS MADE on this 10th day of August 1999 BETWEEN Mr. AB, residing at .... (hereinafter referred to as the DOMINANT OWNER which term shall include his successors, heirs and transferees) of the one part and Mr. CD residing at .... (hereinafter referred to as the SERVIENT OWNER which term shall include his successors, heirs and transferees) of the other part.

WHEREAS the DOMINANT OWNER owns the landed property being premises No. .... of ....

AND WHEREAS the SERVIENT OWNER owns the plot of land being premises No. ...... of .... which is situated on and facing the .... Road and in front of ....

AND WHEREAS premises No. .... of .... has no separate arrangement for the outlet of rain water or any used water or sewage.

AND WHEREAS the premises No. ...... of .... has the modern drainage system and sewage system directly connected with the Municipal Corporation drainage system and the sewage system running underground the main road.

AND WHEREAS the DOMINANT OWNER approached the SERVIENT OWNER for granting facilities for drainage of water and sewage under the land of the SERVIENT OWNER for connection with the main drainage and sewages systems of the Municipal Corporation and the SERVIENT OWNER has agreed to grant such right to the DOMINANT OWNER.

NOW THESE PRESENTS WITNESSETH and the parties hereby agree as follows:

1. In consideration of the DOMINANT OWNER paying to the SERVIENT OWNER a sum of Rs. 2 lakhs the receipt of which the SERVIENT OWNER hereby acknowledges the SERVIENT OWNER hereby grants to DOMINANT OWNER the

right of easement of laying down sewage and drainage pipes underneath the said land of the SERVIENT OWNER so as to connect them from the land of DOMINANT OWNER through the land of SERVIENT OWNER to the Municipal Corporation's main sewage and drainage system on the main road known as .... Road.

2. The said pipes would be laid by the DOMINANT OWNER under the land of SERVIENT OWNER in accordance with the plan to be sanctioned by the Municipal Corporation.

3. The DOMINANT OWNER while laying the drainage and sewage pipes shall not cause any damage to the existing structures of the SERVIENT OWNER and such pipes should be laid down on one side of the land generally used for passage for ingress to and egress from the premises of SERVIENT OWNER.

4. The said pipes should be laid in a manner which would permit periodical cleaning possible and it should be free from possibility of any leakage.

5. The DOMINANT OWNER should keep the said sewage and drainage pipes in good repairs.

6. In the event the DOMINANT OWNER fails to carry out any urgent repairs the SERVIENT OWNER will get it done and recover the costs and expenses of such repair works including replacement of the pipes and all expenses in relation thereto from the DOMINANT OWNER and such cost and expenses should be a first charge on the land of the DOMINANT OWNER.

7. The easement right created herein will run and remain attached to the land of DOMINANT OWNER over the servient land and shall be attached thereto and run with the same and shall be binding on the owners for the time being of the said two premises.

IN WITNESS WHEREOF the parties have executed these presents on the day, month and year first above-written.

Signed and delivered by Mr. AB the
DOMINANT OWNER in the presence of: Signature

1.

2.

Signed and delivered by Mr. CD the
SERVIENT OWNER in the presence of: Signature

1.

2.

Easement of Support

THIS AGREEMENT IS MADE on this .... day of .... 2000 BETWEEN Mr. AB of .... (hereinafter referred to as the DOMINANT OWNER which term shall include his successors and transferees) of the one part and Mr. CD of .... (hereinafter referred to as the SERVIENT OWNER which term shall include his successors and transferees) of the other part.

WHEREAS the DOMINANT OWNER owns the land being premises No. ...... of ....

AND WHEREAS the SERVIENT OWNER owns the land and construction thereon being premises No. ...... of ....

AND WHEREAS the DOMINANT OWNER proposes to construct a multi-storeyed building on his land and requires the support of sub-soil and foundation under the surface of the soil of the land of the SERVIENT OWNER.

AND WHEREAS the DOMINANT OWNER has approached the SERVIENT OWNER for granting easements for support of said sub-soil and foundation of servient land and the SERVIENT OWNER has agreed to grant such easement right to the DOMINANT OWNER.

NOW THESE PRESENTS WITNESSETH and the parties hereby agree as follows:

1. The SERVIENT OWNER grants to the DOMINANT OWNER the right to have all necessary support on the sub-soil and foundation underneath the surface of the servient land in accordance with the plan to be sanctioned by the Municipal Corporation for construction of a multi-storeyed building on the dominant land.

2. It is recorded that in consideration of the DOMINANT OWNER paying Rupees Two lakhs to the SERVIENT OWNER receipt whereof the SERVIENT OWNER hereby acknowledges the SERVIENT OWNER has and is granting to DOMINANT OWNER the said right of easement.

3. The DOMINANT OWNER will be at liberty to dig and excavate the land of SERVIENT OWNER as might be essential for the support for constructing the said multi-storeyed building but without causing any damage to the existing building of SERVIENT OWNER.

4. The DOMINANT OWNER hereby undertakes not to make any construction which would damage the existing building of the SERVIENT OWNER and undertakes to compensate the SERVIENT OWNER for any damage that might be discovered in future because of the said construction and/or the said support for the said construction of the said multi-storeyed building.

5. This agreement shall be treated as the easement right available to the DOMINANT LAND over the SERVIENT LAND for beneficial enjoyment of

DOMINANT LAND and shall be binding on the owners for the time being of the said DOMINANT LAND and SERVIENT LAND.

IN WITNESS WHEREOF the parties hereto have executed these presents on the day, month and year first above-written.

Signed and delivered by Mr. AB the
DOMINANT OWNER in the presence of: Signature

1. ....

2. ....

Signed and delivered by Mr. CD the
SERVIENT OWNER in the presence of: Signature

1. ....

2. ....

34

Mentally ill Persons

The Lunacy Act of 1912 has been repealed. It has been replaced by the Mental Health Act 1987, some of the broad features of the new Act are given below:

Under the new Act a mentally ill person has been defined as one who is in need of treatment by reason of any mental disorder other than mental retardation. He is to be treated in any psychiatric hospital or psychiatric nursing home established or maintained either by the Government or by any private person under licence issued under the Act.

For admission to such institution any person feeling that he is mentally ill may voluntarily get himself admitted there and in case of a minor person somebody on his behalf may get the minor admitted as a voluntary patient after approaching the medical officer-in-charge.

The husband, the wife, or any other relative of a mentally ill person may make an application to the Magistrate within whose jurisdiction the hospital or nursing home is situated for detention of the mentally ill person under a reception order. Such application should be supported by medical certificate as to the condition of the patient and the Magistrate will make enquiry and after he is satisfied that the person concerned is so mentally ill and that his detention in the hospital or nursing home is necessary the Magistrate will pass a reception order.

Similarly the officer-in-charge of the police station believing a person within his jurisdiction to be mentally ill or upon receipt of an information that there was a mentally ill person and is not under proper care and control or is neglected by any relative shall report to the Magistrate who on getting a report about such a person may cause him to be produced before him and after necessary investigation admit him in the hospital or nursing home.

D: Convey–55

Provisions have been made for holding inquisition by the District Court which means the Court of the District Judge in a District or the City Civil Court where such Courts have been established.

Provisions have also been made for appointment of a guardian or manager in respect of the properties of in-patient and for providing maintenance to him or collecting his pension, if he is a pensioner and for transfer of stock, security or shares belonging to such in-patient. Provisions have also been made for providing legal aid to mentally ill person at state expense in certain cases.

So far as discharge of an in-patient is concerned where a patient was admitted on application there must be an application for discharge. In other cases the patient may be discharged on the recommendation of two medical practitioners one of whom shall preferably be a psychiatric; there is a third category of cases where a patient detained in pursuance of an order under this Act may be discharged, if he feels that he has recovered from his mental illness but in that case he must make an application to the Magistrate for his discharge supported by a medical certificate and the Magistrate will pass an order of discharge after making due enquiry. But a person who is dangerous and unfit to be at large cannot be discharged.

A person of unsound mind or a mentally ill person is incompetent to enter into any contract. Matters relating to such persons are now governed by the Mental Health Act 1987 replacing the Indian Lunacy Act 1912. The provisions of s. 68 of the Indian Contract Act apply only in case of necessaries supplied, but the statutory reliefs under s. 33 of the Specific Relief Act 1963, are available as against the lunatic[1] in the case of cancellation of any transfer.

Section 12 of the Indian Contract Act lays down the test as to what is sound mind for the purpose of contract, *i.e.* capacity of understanding and forming a rational judgment as to the effect thereof on his interest. A contract by a person of unsound mind is void but when it is for necessaries supplied he will be compelled to fulfil his obligation.[2] Under s. 31 of the Indian Lunacy Act 1912, since repealed, the court may order performance by the manager in case of pre-lunacy contracts.

Lunatic. A lunatic means an idiot or person of unsound mind. *Lunacy or insanity* is a defect of reason, consisting either in its total or partial absence or in its perturbance.[3]

1 *Monosse* v *Shapurji* 10 Bom LR 1004 (1007).
2 *Amina Bibi* v *Saiyd Yusuf* (1922)44 All 748; 79 IC 955.
3 Section 3(5) of the Indian Lunacy Act 1912 defines a lunatic as an idiot or person of unsound mind.

Application by whom to be presented. The petition must be presented by the husband or wife of the person concerned or, if there is no husband or wife, or the husband or wife is prevented by some reason from making the presentation, by the nearest relative of the person.

When reception order can be made. No reception order can be made save in the case of a mentally ill person who is dangerous and unfit to be at large, unless—

(*i*) the Magistrate who passes the order is satisfied that the person in charge of an asylum is willing to receive the lunatic, and

(*ii*) the petitioner or some other person is engaged in writing to the satisfaction of the Magistrate to pay the cost of maintenance of the lunatic.

Order of discharge on relative's undertaking. When any relative or friend of the mentally ill person detained under the Act applies for his discharge he shall be delivered over to his care and custody, the authority, if it thinks fit, in consultation with the person in charge of the Hospital or nursing home and the relative or friend entering into a bond (*Precedent*—Chapter on BONDS) with or without sureties for such sum of money as the said authority thinks fit, on condition that such person shall be properly taken care of and shall be prevented from doing injury to himself or to others, can make an order for the discharge and such mentally ill person will thereupon be discharged.

The inquiry will, as far as may be, be conducted in the same manner as is prescribed for an inquisition into the unsoundness of mind of an alleged lunatic, and if it is found that the unsoundness of mind has ceased, the court will order all proceedings in the lunacy to cease or to be set aside on such terms and conditions as to the court may seem fit.

Guardian of lunatic and manager of estate. An application for inquisition as to the mental condition of a lunatic is to be made to the High Court within whose Original Jurisdiction he resides. If the lunatic resides beyond such jurisdiction, the application is to be made to the District Judge within whose jurisdiction he resides. The application may be made by any relative of the lunatic. After notices are served on the lunatic and his relations, the court makes an inquisition as to the mental condition of the alleged lunatic. If upon enquiry the court is satisfied as to the unsoundness of mind, it can appoint a manager of his estate and a guardian of his person. The legal heirs of a lunatic shall not be appointed guardian of the person of such lunatic unless the court for reasons to be recorded in writing considers that such appointment is for the benefit of the lunatic. The court may require the manager of a lunatic's estate to furnish such security as it thinks fit.

FORMS

Petition for Order of Reception of Mentally ill Person

To
The Metropolitan Magistrate/
Sub-divisional Magistrate/
Magistrate empowered under
Act 14 of 1987

In the matter of AB of .... etc., a person alleged to be a mentally ill person under s. 2(*m*) of the Mental Health Act 1987

The petition of CD (full name, address and relationship) as follows:

1. I, the applicant, an .... years of age.

2. I desire to obtain an order for the reception of AB of, etc., as a mentally ill person in the Psychiatric Hospital/Nursing home at etc. etc.

3. I last saw AB at, etc., on the .... day of ....

4. I am the .... (relationship) of the said AB.

The circumstances under which this petition is presented by the applicant are as follows, etc.

(*Or, if the applicant is not a relative*—That the applicant is not a relative of the said AB. The reasons why this petition is not presented by a relative are as follows, etc.)

5. The persons signing the medical certificates which accompany the application are, etc.

6. A statement of particulars relating to the said AB accompanies this petition.

7. An application for an enquiry into the mental capacity of the said AB was made to the, etc., on the .... day of ...., and a certified copy of the order made on the said application is annexed hereto.

(*Or*—No application for an enquiry into the mental capacity of the said AB has been made previous to this application).

I therefore pray that a reception order may be made in accordance with the foregoing statement.

(Date)

CD

The statement contained or referred to in paragraphs are true to my knowledge; the other statements are true to my information and belief.

(Date)

EF

The statement of particulars above referred to

The following is a statement of particulars relating to the said AB:

Name of patient in full.—

Sex and age.—

Married, single or widower.—

Previous occupation.—

Caste and religion.—

Residence at the time of the application.—

Names of any near relative to the patient who are alive.—

Whether this is first attack of mental illness.—

Age on first attack.—

Supposed cause.—

Whether the patient is subject to epilepsy.—

Whether suicidal.—

Whether the patient is known to be suffering from any form of tubercular disease.—

Whether dangerous to others and in what way.—

Whether any near relative (stating the relationship) has been afflicted with insanity.—

Whether the patient is addicted to alcohol or the use of opium, ganja, charas, bhang, cocaine or other intoxicant.—

(*If any of the particulars in the above statement be not known, the fact to be so stated*).

Petition for Appointment of Guardian of a Mentally ill Person and Manager of his Estate

In the Court of the District Judge of ....

Case No.................. of ....

Applicant—

AB (*add description and residence*)

In the matter of the Mental Health Act (Act 14 of 1987)

And

In the matter of inquisition as to CD, a lunatic and appointment of guardian of his person and manager of his estate

MOST RESPECTFULLY SHEWETH:

1. That the aforesaid CD is a Hindu by faith and nationality and is at present aged.............. years having been born on the day of ....

2. That the said CD lives and resides at .... with the applicant who is his .... (state the relationship) under his care and protection.

3. That the said CD has the following near relatives, *viz.*

Name	*Address*	*Relationship*
(a)		
(b)		

4. That for some time past and since the .... day of .... or thereabout, the said CD has developed signs of insanity and is at present completely of unsound mind and has become incapable of managing himself and his properties and of taking proper care of his person. Two medical certificates as to mental condition of the said CD are attached herewith.

5. That the said CD is seized and possessed of the following properties, the nature, description, value and approximate income are given in the Schedule below.

6. That the appointments hereunder prayed for are necessary for proper care and custody of the person of CD as also for management of his properties.

The applicant, therefore, prays that this court may be pleased to direct an inquisition as to the mental condition of CD and appoint the applicant guardian of the person and manager of the estate of CD.

Schedule above referred to

Verification

I, AB, son of .... aged above .... years by occupation business residing at .... do hereby solemnly affirm and say as follows:

I am the petitioner above-named and I know the facts and circumstances of this case and I am able to depose thereto.

The statements in paragraphs 1 to 6 hereinabove are true to my knowledge and belief and I have not suppressed any material fact.

I sign this Verification on this .... day of .... 1999 at the Court Premises at Alipore.

Signature of AB

Before me

Signature of Advocate

Notary

(In the absence of Prescribed Forms)

Application for Admission of Mentally ill Person under s. 19 of the Mental Health Act 1987

To
The Medical Officer-in-Charge
Psychiatric Hospital

Sir

I submit that Sree ...., aged .... years, my nephew has been suffering from mental illness for the last two months and, I have been looking after him as both of his parents are dead. On his behalf, therefore, I request you to admit him as an in-patient in your hospital for his necessary treatment. Medical Certificates from two medical practitioners including one from a medical practitioners in Government service regarding the condition of the patient are enclosed.

Yours faithfully

Application for Discharge of the In-patient

To
The Medical Officer-in-Charge etc.

Sir

I beg to state that my nephew .... was admitted in your hospital as an in-patient on .... He now appears to be cured of his illness. I request that he may now be discharged and made over to me.

Yours faithfully

Application for Reception Order under s. 20 of the Mental Health Act 1987

To
The Sub-divisional Judicial Magistrate

Sir

I beg to submit that my wife Smt. .... aged .... and mother of two children, has become a mentally ill person for the last several months. She has been treated by local physicians but there appears to be no improvement in her condition. It is necessary for the patient to be admitted in a psychiatric hospital or nursing home for observation and proper treatment. Medical certificates from two physicians one, of whom is a medical practitioner in the service of the Government, testifying to the mental condition of the said patient Smt. .... are enclosed.

It may be noted that no previous application had been made either for enquiry into the condition of the patient or for her admission to any hospital.

The statements made above are true to my knowledge.

Yours faithfully

35

Maintenance

Section 125 of the Code of Criminal Procedure 1973 provides that a person having sufficient means if neglects or refuses to maintain his wife, minor child (legitimate of illegitimate) or a major child (other than married daughter) who is physically or mentally abnormal or injured or father or mother unable to maintain, he or she is entitled to claim maintenance. The application is to be made to the Magistrate of the First Class by the wife or the minor son or daughter of the father or mother unable to maintain himself or herself. On being satisfied about the genuineness of the complaint the Magistrate may order the accused to pay a monthly maintenance of not more than Rs. 500 for each complainant. The West Bengal Legislature has amended the section and has provided for payment of monthly allowance of Rs. 1,500 instead of Rs. 500 per month. Section 125 applies to all persons of all communities. A divorced Muslim woman is governed by the Muslim Women (Protection of Rights on Divorce) Act 1986. However, a Muslim woman who is still a "legally married wife" can claim maintenance under section 125, Cr PC.

The right of the child for maintenance is independent of mother's right.[1] Even if the marriage has not been solemnised with the mother, the child, born outside wedlock is entitled to maintenance.[2] Even if the mother has separate income the father cannot deny maintenance to the child.[3] A Muslim divorced wife may not apply under s. 125, Cr PC for her maintenance but the child living with her after divorce can, through mother, apply for maintenance under s. 125, Cr PC and Muslim Women (Protection of Rights on Divorce) Act 1986 is no bar.[4]

1 *Mohd. Muneruddin* v *Rakshma* 1978 Cr LJ NOC 4 (AP).
2 *Punnakal* v *Vellai Padmini* 1992 Cr LJ 3562 (Ker).
3 *C.M. Mani* v *Esther* 1981 Cr LJ NOC 76 (Ker).
4 *G.M. Jeelani* v *Shanswar* 1994 Cr LJ 271 (AP).

An application under s. 125, Cr PC may be filed by a wife against her husband when he having sufficient means neglects or refuses to maintain her provided the wife is unable to maintain herself. A wife whose marriage is void on the ground that her husband has a spouse living cannot be treated as legally married wife and cannot claim maintenance under this section.[5] A divorced wife until she remarries is entitled to apply under s. 125 for maintenance. Since the passing of Muslim Women (Protection of Rights on Divorce) Act 1986 a Muslim divorced wife can apply for maintenance under this section. A parent can apply under this section for maintenance from his or her son or daughter. However, if a wife is living separately from her husband without a just cause she cannot claim maintenance. When the husband subjects the wife to cruelty she has a right to live separately and can claim maintenance.[6] When the husband remarries or keeps a mistress the wife can live separately and can claim maintenance.[7] Where the wife is living separately with mutual consent she cannot claim maintenance.[8] If she is living in adultery, she is not generally entitled to get maintenance.[9] Against a petition for maintenance the husband may take various pleas. He can dispute the marriage. When marriage is disputed, the petitioner has to prove valid marriage with the opposite party in order to claim maintenance. He can take the plea that the wife had no just cause to live separately. He can take the plea which disentitles wife to claim maintenance as laid down in s. 125(4), Cr PC.

The wife has to apply under s. 128, Cr PC for recovery of maintenance if the husband refused to pay the maintenance in terms of the order of the court. Arrears of maintenance for one year prior to filing of application can be recovered by attachment and sale of property of husband under s. 421, Cr PC. If the recovery proceeding fails the husband can be imprisoned.[10] When the warrant of attachment and sale of property could not be executed as the husband did not have any property an order sentencing the husband to imprisonment is justified.[11] The distress warrant may not be issued if the court is satisfied that this would be futile.[12] One month's imprisonment for default of one month should be ordered.[13]

5 *Vimala* v *Veeraswamy* (1991)2 SCC 375.
6 *Gitanjali* v *Fanindra* 1992 Cr LJ 4046 (Ori).
7 *Subanu* v *Abdul* AIR 1987 SC 1103; *Narayan* v *Sushama* 1992 Cr LJ 2912 (Ori).
8 *M. Rama Krishna* v *T. Jayamma* 1992 Cr LJ 1368; *Ramesh* v *Veen* AIR 1978 SC 1807.
9 *Bilawati* v *B. Phukan* 1988 Cr LJ NOC 30 (Gau).
10 *Iftekhar* v *Hameeda* 1980 Cr LJ 1212 (All).
11 *Om Prakash* v *Vidya Devi* 1992 Cr LJ 658 (P&H).
12 *Rajendra* v *Pramila* 1993 Cr LJ 3813 (Ori).
13 *P. Brahmaniah* v *P. Padma* 1991 Cr LJ 607 (AP).

Read also the relevant provisions in the Hindu Adoptions & Maintenance Act 1956. There can be maintenance which has been fixed by the parties themselves to bring peace and harmony into the family. The consideration such type of settlement is love and affection, peace and harmony and satisfaction to flow therefrom. It is not hit by s. 25 of the Contract Act.[14]

FORMS

Maintenance Agreement between Husband and Wife not being a Separation Agreement

(A SHORT FORM)

THIS AGREEMENT IS MADE this .... day of .... BETWEEN AB son of .... residing at .... (hereinafter called the HUSBAND) of the one part and CD, daughter of .... residing at .... and wife of AB (hereinafter called the WIFE) of the other part.

HEREBY it is agreed between the parties hereto as follows:

1. The HUSBAND will pay to the WIFE for her support and maintenance (and for the support and maintenance of their children hereinafter mentioned) a monthly sum of Rs. .... during the joint lives of the parties hereto so long as the WIFE shall lead a chaste life the first payment hereunder to be made on ....

2. The WIFE will out of the said sum support and maintain herself (and the said children) and will indemnify the HUSBAND against all debts if incurred by her (and against all liability whatsoever in respect of the said children) and will not in any way at any time hereafter pledge the husband's credit.

3. The WIFE while living separate from the husband shall have the custody and control of the minor children of the marriage. The right of the wife to such custody and control shall cease upon the children respectively attaining the age of eighteen years.

4. Upon the failure of the HUSBAND to make the said payments as and when the same become due the WIFE shall be at full liberty to pursue all and every remedy in this regard either by enforcement of the provisions hereof or as if this agreement had not been made.

14 *Manali Singhal* v *Ravi Singhal* AIR 1999 Del 156.

IN WITNESS WHEREOF the parties hereto have signed these presents on the day, month and year first above-written.

Signed and delivered by AB the HUSBAND in presence of:

Signed and delivered by CD the WIFE in the presence of:

Separation Agreement between Husband and Wife

THIS AGREEMENT IS MADE the .... day of .... BETWEEN AB of etc. (hereinafter called the HUSBAND) of the one part and CD, of, etc. the wife of the said AB (hereinafter called the WIFE) of the other part.

WHEREAS unhappy differences and disputes having arisen between the parties hereto, as a result whereof the marriage between them has broken down and they are now living separate and apart from each other and intend to so live hereafter unless there is any reconciliation and for which purpose they have agreed to enter into such arrangement as is hereinafter contained: NOW IT IS HEREBY AGREED as follows:

1. The parties hereto shall further live and continue to live separate and apart from each other and neither of them shall have the right to the society of the other or shall molest, annoy or interfere with each other.

2. The HUSBAND shall, during the joint lives of himself and the WIFE pay to the WIFE, during her life for the maintenance of herself a monthly sum of Rs. .... commencing from.

3. The WIFE shall have the custody and control as also guardianship of the children of the marriage, EF and GS now aged .... years and .... years respectively, and shall, out of the said sum of Rs. .... maintain and educate the said children until they shall respectively attain the age of .... years, and shall keep the husband and his estate indemnified from and against all claims and demands on that account.

4. The WIFE shall be at liberty to remove forthwith from .... aforesaid all her wearing apparel, jewellery and other personal effects, and also such of the furniture and other household goods and effects at .... aforesaid as belong to her as her separate property.

5. The WIFE shall pay for and discharge all debts incurred by her after the date hereof, whether for maintenance, support or otherwise and keep the HUSBAND and his estate indemnified therefrom and against all actions, claims and demands in connection therewith; otherwise the HUSBAND shall have the right to set off all sums so paid as against the WIFE out of the moneys payable by him to her as aforesaid.

6. The HUSBAND shall have access to the children under arrangements to be made between them from time to time.

7. The HUSBAND may see and have the sole society of the said EF and GH at .... every Saturday, (*or* etc.), between the hours of .... and ...... p.m.

PROVIDED ALWAYS AND IT IS HEREBY AGREED that in case the HUSBAND and the WIFE shall at any time hereafter with their mutual consent live together as man and WIFE, then and in such case the said sums shall be no longer payable, and all the agreements hereinbefore contained shall become void and ineffective.

PROVIDED ALSO, that this deed shall stand revoked by the death of either party.

IN WITNESS WHEREOF the parties hereto have executed these presents on the day, month and year first above-written.

Signed, sealed and delivered by AB
the HUSBAND in the presence of:

Signed, sealed and delivered by
CD the WIFE in presence of:

Agreement for Maintenance of Wife and Daughter

THIS AGREEMENT IS MADE this .... day of .... BETWEEN AB son of .... residing at .... (hereinafter called the HUSBAND) of the one part and CD wife of AB and daughter of .... residing at .... (hereinafter called the WIFE) of the other part.

WHEREAS unhappy differences and disputes having arisen between the parties hereto, who are HUSBAND and WIFE and could not be adjusted by the intervention of friends and well-wishers, they by mutual consent and agreement are now living separate and apart from each other and for that purpose they have agreed to the arrangement as hereunder mentioned:

NOW IT IS HEREBY AGREED as follows:

1. The HUSBAND shall pay or cause to be paid regularly for the WIFE so long as she will live separate a maintenance allowance of Rs......... per month, and a further sum of Rs...................... per month for the daughter EF, on that account as long as their daughter EF lives with and is maintained by the WIFE and is not married.

2. In consideration of such payment or payments as aforesaid, the WIFE shall not incur any debt or liabilities against the credits of the HUSBAND nor otherwise pledge nor institute any action or proceedings against the husband on account of her maintenance and support or that of the daughter but shall pay for and discharge all her debts and liabilities and keep the HUSBAND and his estate indemnified against all actions and proceedings in relation thereto.

3. Provided, however, and it is hereby agreed that notwithstanding anything hereinbefore contained no monthly allowances as hereunder agreed shall be payable for the period during which the WIFE shall live and reside with the HUSBAND and be maintained by him.

IN WITNESS WHEREOF the parties hereto have executed these presents on the day, month and year first above-written.

Signed, sealed and delivered by AB
the husband in the presence of: AB

Signed, sealed and delivered by CD
the wife of AB in the presence of: CD

NOTE: The authority of the wife to pledge the credits of her husband is a delegated and not an inherent authority. If she binds him she can do only as agent. This is a well established doctrine.[15] It is applicable to things which are really necessary for person in the position of life of the couple in cases where she is turned away without justification or the husband refuses to supply necessities or the means of obtaining the same. The Hindu Adoptions and Maintenance Act 1956 (Act 78 of 1956) is the codified law on the subject of maintenance of Hindu wives. It protects the right of maintenance against the properties of the husband in the hands of alienees (s. 39 of the Act) with notice.

Separation Agreement between Husband and Wife

(A SHORT FORM)

AN AGREEMENT IS MADE the................ day of................1999 BETWEEN AB of etc. (hereinafter called the HUSBAND) of the one part and CD of etc. his wife (hereinafter called the WIFE) of the other part.

WHEREAS unhappy disputes and differences have arisen between the HUSBAND and WIFE and they are now living separate and apart from each other.

NOW IT IS HEREBY AGREED as follows:

1. The HUSBAND and the WIFE shall continue to live separate and apart from each other and neither of them shall molest, annoy or interfere with the other.

2. The HUSBAND shall pay to the WIFE during her life for the maintenance of herself and her children hereinafter named the monthly sum of Rs. .... first of such payments to be made on the .... day of ....

15 2 Sm IC 417 *vide* Dutt on *Contract*, 5th Ed., p. 665.

3. The WIFE shall have the custody of the children namely, DB, EB and FB, now aged seven, five and four years respectively and shall out of the said sum maintain herself and also maintain (and educate) the said children until they shall respectively attain the age of (eighteen) years and shall keep the HUSBAND indemnified from and against all claims and demands in respect of such children.

4. The WIFE shall be at liberty forthwith to remove from.......... all her wearing apparel, jewellery and personal effects and also such of the furniture and other household goods and effects at .... aforesaid as belong to her as her separate property upon which the husband shall have no claim hereafter.

5. The WIFE shall pay and discharge all debts and liabilities incurred by her after the date hereof and keep the HUSBAND indemnified therefrom and the HUSBAND may deduct from the said sum any amount paid by him for debts or liabilities incurred by the WIFE after the date hereof for which the HUSBAND may be held liable and any sums paid by him to any authority for the maintenance of the WIFE or for the maintenance (and education) of the said children until the said children shall respectively attain the age aforesaid.

IN WITNESS WHEREOF the parties hereto have executed these presents on the day, month and year first above-written.

Signed and delivered by AB in the presence of:

Signed and delivered by CD the wife of AB in the presence of:

Petition seeking Order for Maintenance of a Minor

Before the Learned Metropolitan Magistrate, Calcutta

Case No. .... of 1999

Application under section 125 of the Code of Criminal Procedure 1973

And

In the matter of:

Shri X, a minor under the age of 18 years, son of Shri Y, residing at .... Police Station ...., District .... through his next friend Shri Z, son of Shri M, residing at .... being the maternal uncle of X, Police Station ...., District ....

.... *Applicant*

versus

Shri Y, son of Shri B residing at ...., Police Station ...., District ....

.... *Opposite Party*

To

The Hon'ble Magistrate of the
Aforesaid Court

The humble application of the applicant above-named most respectfully

SHEWETH:

1. The opposite party is the father of Shri X a minor on whose behalf the present application is being made.

2. That Smt. AB the mother of the applicant X was married to the opposite party in 1992 and out of the said marriage the applicant Sri. X was born on .... day of 1994.

3. At present the applicant is 5 years old, a minor and therefore, the present application is being filed through the next friend of the minor applicant, he being his maternal uncle.

4. That on .... the opposite party threw out Smt. AB and the applicant of his house and thereafter refused to maintain and support the applicant and his mother.

5. That ever since .... the applicant was living along with his mother at the house of his aforesaid maternal uncle who was taking care of both the applicant and his mother.

6. On ...., Smt. AB the mother of the applicant suddenly died on account of heart attack.

7. Since the last several months the financial position of the maternal uncle of the said minor Sri X has considerably deteriorated and he is unable to maintain the applicant minor.

8. Several requests were made by the maternal uncle of the applicant to Shri Y the opposite party for some allowances for maintenance of his minor son but he has refused to do so.

9. The opposite party has an income of more than Rs. 8000 per month and is a man of good standing. Further he owns a two-storeyed house which is fully tenanted from which he receives monthly rent of Rs. 5000.

10. The opposite party is legally and morally bound to support and maintain his minor son the applicant herein who has no means of supporting himself.

11. In the premises the applicant states that suitable Order for maintenance be made against the opposite party and in favour of the minor applicant.

12. This application is made *bona fide* and in the interest of justice.

The applicant therefore humbly prays Your Honour that the Opposite Party be directed to pay a sum of Rs. 2500 per month to the applicant as his maintenance allowance. And the applicant as in duty bound shall ever pray.

Place .... Court
Calcutta

Date ....

Signature of applicant
by the pen of maternal uncle

Identified by
Applicant's Advocate

Maintenance Charge Deed

THIS DEED OF CHARGE is made at Calcutta this .... day of .... 2000 BETWEEN Mr. Y of ...., hereinafter referred to as the first party and Smt. AB residing at .... hereinafter referred to as the second party.

WHEREAS the first party is the husband of the SECOND PARTY and that both of them are living separate.

AND WHEREAS the first party as husband is liable to pay and has agreed to pay the second party by way of maintenance a sum of Rs. 1500 per month in advance on or before the 5th day of each month hereafter.

AND WHEREAS the parties have agreed that such payment of monthly maintenance would be a charge on the immovable property being a two-storeyed building at ...., Calcutta belonging to the first party.

NOW THIS DEED WITNESSTH and it is agreed by and between the parties as follows:

1. The first party would pay to the second party month by month and every month the sum of Rs. 1500 by the 5th of each month in advance for the upkeep and maintenance of the second party.

2. That such payment of the maintenance shall be a charge on the said property of the first party being premises No. ...... of .... and the first party hereby charges the said land and premises being No. ...... of ....with the payment of the said sum of Rs. 1500 per month by way of maintenance to the second party.

3. It is further agreed that in the event the first party fails to pay any two monthly instalments of the said maintenance to the second party then in that event the second party will be entitled to enforce the charge hereby created on the premises by bringing the said land and premises to sale through any competent Court of Law and to realise and receive the amount due out of the nett sale proceeds thereof.

4. Such charge is created without prejudice to other rights and remedies of the second party to realise and enforce payment of the said maintenance allowance in accordance with law.

IN WITNESS WHEREOF the parties hereto have executed these presents on the day, month and year first above-written.

Signed and delivered by Mr. Y the within-named first party in the presence of: Signature

Accepted by and signed by the within-mentioned second party Mrs. AB in the presence of: Signature

Petition Claiming Payment of Maintenance

Before the Learned Chief Metropolitan Magistrate, Calcutta

Case No. .... of 2000

In the matter of:

An application under section 126 of the Criminal Procedure Code 1973, claiming payment of Maintenance

And

In the matter of:

Smt. AB, daughter of Mr. X residing at ...., Police Station: ......, ... District: ....

.... *Applicant*

versus

Sri. Z, son of ML residing at ....
............, Police Station ....,
District: ....

.... *Opposite Party*

To

The Learned Chief Metropolitan
Magistrate, Calcutta

The humble petition of Smt. AB, the applicant abovenamed most respectfully

SHEWETH:

1. The applicant and the opposite party are Hindus and are governed by Dayabhaga School of Hindu Law.

2. The applicant is a legally married wife of the opposite party. The applicant's marriage with the opposite party was solemnised on ....
....

3. Soon after the marriage of the applicant the opposite party and his parents and sisters started harassing the applicant for not bringing sufficient dowry. The applicant was constantly pressurised to bring further moneys from her parents.

4. The applicant's father is a small earner and working as a clerk in a Government Office having no other source of income. His total salary is Rs. 2000 nett. The applicant's father is unable to satisfy the unreasonable demands of further moneys by way of dowry made by the opposite party, his parents and sisters.

5. The applicant repeatedly expressed her father's inability to pay further sums as dowry as he had no other source of income or any assets out of which such further dowry could be paid.

6. With a view to put further pressure and to extort money from the applicant's father on ...., the opposite party, his mother and two sisters assaulted the applicant and threw her out of the matrimonial house on the threat of not to come again without sufficient dowry.

7. The applicant with great humiliation with a heavy heart and with difficulty could manage to reach her parental house.

8. Thereafter the applicant made several requests to the opposite party to take her back home and not to demand any further dowry. This the opposite party has refused to do.

9. The applicant thereafter requested the opposite party to pay her something for her maintenance and upkeep. The opposite party knew

that the applicant had no other source of income and yet the request was ignored.

10. The opposite party is an officer in the Excise Department and draws a salary of Rs. 10,000 per month. He has a house property from which he gets rent of Rs. 2000 per month. His father is also earning. The opposite party has no dependant member or any other known liability.

11. The applicant has no means to support her while as stated above the opposite party has sufficient means to maintain the applicant.

The applicant, therefore, humbly prays this Learned Court for a direction on the opposite party to pay Rs. 1500 per month to the applicant towards her maintenance.

Place: Calcutta Signature of the applicant

Date:

Signature of Advocate for applicant

Petition by a Guardian of Minor Child for Maintenance against Father under section 125, Cr PC

In the Court of................ Magistrate

Case No. ...... of 2000

Petitioner (minor M through his next friend U) maternal uncle		*Opposite Party* F
Son of	*versus*	Son of ....
Village		Village ....
Thana		Thana ....

In the matter of maintenance of minor M, son of opposite party F under s. 125, Cr PC.

The humble petition of the minor M through his maternal uncle U

MOST RESPECTFULLY SHEWETH:

1. That the opposite party F lawfully married the petitioner's mother according to the Hindu rites in the year .... Your petitioner is the son of the opposite party born of that marriage on ....

2. Your petitioner's mother died on .... Since his mother's death the petitioner has been living under the care and protection of his maternal uncle.

3. The opposite party, although a man of means, took no notice of the petitioner since his mother's death except by casual enquiries. Your petitioner's maternal uncle went out of job last year and it is somewhat difficult for him now to maintain his family. Your petitioner, the minor son of the opposite party, is now .... years old and is already in school.

4. Your petitioner's maternal uncle requested the opposite party several times to come forward with some help every month for the education and upbringing of his son, the petitioner.

5. The opposite party has been avoiding his liability to pay for maintenance and education of his child and has not so far paid any sum in spite of repeated requests.

6. The opposite party has a monthly income of Rs. 5000 from salary and house rent and is capable of maintaining his child.

Your petitoner prays that the court may be pleased to issue notice on the opposite party and after taking necessary evidence be pleased to order the opposite party to pay a monthly allowance of Rs. 500 for the maintenance and education of the petitioner, his child.

And your petitioner, as in duty bound, shall ever pray.

Verification

I, U, son of MN, residing at .... do hereby solemnly affirm and say as follows:

1. I am the uncle of the petitioner, M. The petitioner is living with me for the last several years since the death of his mother. I know my sister's husband F since his marriage to my sister, since deceased. I am able to depose to the facts of the case. I am affirming this affidavit for self as also as representative and on behalf of M.
2. The statements in paragraphs 1 to 6 of the foregoing petition are true to my knowledge.

Solemnly affirmed by the said U
on this .... of 2000
at the Court House in Calcutta Signature

Before me
Commissioner/Magistrate
Notary

Petition by Wife under section 125, Cr PC for Maintenance

In the Court of .... Judicial Magistrate 1st Class
Case No. .... under s. 125, Cr PC

Petitioner W (wife)		*Opposite Party* H (husband)
Daughter of	*versus*	Son of ....
Village		Village ....
Thana		Thana ....
Occupation		Occupation ....

In the matter of petition for maintenance of petitioner W from the husband H under s. 125, Cr PC

The humble petition of W (wife), the petitioner above-named

MOST RESPECTFULLY SHEWETH:

1. Your petitioner W is the married wife of the opposite party. The marriage between them was solemnised according to the Hindu rites on ....

2. The opposite party H is a clerk on the staff of AB & Co. Ltd. holding a responsible position and drawing salary of Rs. 8000 per month.

3. The opposite party severely assaulted the petitioner on .... and drove her away from the matrimonial house on .... in presence of several gentlemen of the locality.

4. That the opposite party leads a life of drunkenness and debauchery. He is besides a man of uncertain temperament and would fly into rage in season and out of season without any reason whatsoever. He has lost all sense of decorum and would use extremely filthy language.

5. Your petitioner after being driven out of the house by the opposite party, came over to her father's place on the same day and has been staying at father's house with his family members.

6. The opposite party was served with a pleader's notice to send your petitioner Rs. 900 every month for her maintenance but with no result. Having regard to the violent temper of H and his inhuman way of beating your petitioner she does not venture to go back to the place of the opposite party.

Your petitioner, therefore, prays that Your Honour may be pleased to issue notice on the opposite party and after taking evidence of both sides be pleased to order the opposite party to pay the petitioner maintenance at the rate of Rs. 900 per month.

And your petitioner, as in duty bound, shall ever pray.

Verification

I, W, daughter of MN residing at .... do hereby solemnly affirm and say as follows:

1. I am the petitioner above-named and I know the facts and circumstances of the case and I am able to depose thereto.
2. The statements in the paragraphs 1, 2, 3, 4, 5 and 6 of the foregoing petition are true to my knowledge and that I have not suppressed any material fact.

Solemnly affirmed by the said
Mrs. W on the .... day of ....
2000 in the Court House at Calcutta

Before me
Notary

Petition by Wife for Enforcing Maintenance Allowance Ordered by Court under section 128, Cr PC

In the Court of.............. Judicial Magistrate of ....

Petitioner (wife) W .... *Opposite Party* (husband) H

versus

Daughter of .... Son of ....
Village .... Village ....
Thana .... Thana ....

In the matter of petition by the wife for enforcing the order as to the payment of maintenance

The humble petition of petitioner (wife) W

MOST RESPECTFULLY SHEWETH:

1. That the opposite party was ordered by Your Honour by Order No. ...... dated .... passed in Case No. 365 to pay a monthly allowance of Rs. 850 to his wife, the petitioner.

2. That since the order the opposite party has not paid any money to the petitioner in terms of the aforesaid order or otherwise. A copy of the order which was furnished to the petitioner by the Learned Court is attached hereto.

Your petitioner prays that after issuing notice to the opposite party Your Honour may be pleased to enquire into the statements made in the petition and on being satisfied that they are true may be pleased to attach the properties of the opposite party mentioned in the Schedule hereunder for enforcing payment or in the alternative the Learned Court may be pleased to issue a warrant for the arrest of the opposite party and put him into prison for such a period as the Learned Court may deem proper.

And your petitioner, as in duty bound, shall ever pray.

The Schedule

All that pieces and parcels of land measuring 5 cottahs with two-storeyed building thereon being premises No. .... of ....

Verification

I, W, daughter of MN and wife of H residing at .... do hereby solemnly affirm and say as follows:

1. I am the petitioner above-named. I know the facts and circumstances of this case and I am able to depose thereto.
2. The statements in the foregoing petition are true to my knowledge and I have not suppressed any material fact.

Solemnly affirmed by the said W
on .... at the Court House
at Calcutta

Before me
Notary/Proper Officer

Deed of Separation between Husband and Wife

THIS DEED OF SEPARATION is made on the .... day of .... 2000 BETWEEN AB, son of DC, aged 40 years residing at .... (hereinafter called the HUSBAND) of the one part and BW, wife of AB and daughter of MN, aged about 30 years residing at .... (hereinafter called the WIFE) of the other part.

WHEREAS differences have arisen between the HUSBAND and the WIFE and they have mutually agreed to live apart from each other and to enter into an arrangement to that effect.

AND WHEREAS the HUSBAND has by the wife four children, namely EF, GH, JK and LM.

NOW THIS DEED WITNESSES and the parties hereby agree as follows:

1. The WIFE may at all times hereafter live separate and apart from the HUSBAND in all respects and neither the HUSBAND nor the WIFE shall interfere with the living of the other.

2. The WIFE shall have the sole custody and control of the aforesaid children and the responsibility of their education and upbringing during their minority but shall allow the husband at all convenient and reasonable times free access and communication with them.

3. The HUSBAND shall pay to the WIFE during her life and so long as she shall continue to live a life of chastity, shall not engage herself in any gainful employment or profession and perform and observe the conditions and terms herein contained, the monthly allowance of Rs. 5000 for her maintenance on the first day of each month in advance commencing from 1st January 2001.

4. The HUSBAND shall pay to the wife in addition to the monthly payments stipulated in cl. 3 above a further monthly sum of Rs. 4000 for the maintenance and education of each of the said children until he or she attains the age of 18 years and the WIFE shall, out of such sum, maintain and educate the said children and shall also keep the HUSBAND indemnified from and against all claims and demands in respect of the maintenance and education of such children.

PROVIDED that if any of the said children before attaining the said age of 18 years dies or is settled in life and begins to earn his or her own livelihood or in the case of female child EF marrying, proportionate allowance herein stipulated to be paid for his or her maintenance shall cease to be payable.

5. The WIFE shall be at liberty to forthwith remove from the husband's house all her wearing apparel, jewellery and personal effects and also such of the further and other household goods and effects at the said house as belong to her as her separate property/stridhan along with children's clothes, dolls, playing or sports goods.

6. The WIFE shall pay and discharge all debts and liabilities incurred by her after the date hereof and keep the HUSBAND, his heirs, executors and administrators indemnified therefrom and if the HUSBAND has to pay any such debt or liability, he will be at liberty to deduct the same from the maintenance allowance of the WIFE.

7. In case the WIFE dies during the lifetime of the HUSBAND, all her separate estates, movables as well as immovable, which remain undisposed of in her lifetime or by will shall go to the person or persons who would become entitled to it if the husband died in her lifetime and the husband shall permit her will to be proved or administration to her estate to be taken out by the person entitled to.

8. If the parties shall reconcile and return to cohabitation or if their marriage shall be dissolved or they shall be judicially separated by reason

of any misconduct of the WIFE or the husband occurring after the date hereof, then and in any such case, all the covenants and provisions herein contained shall become void but without prejudice to the right of any party to take proceedings in respect of any antecedent breach of any such covenant or provisions.

9. This deed shall not stand revoked by the death of the WIFE or the HUSBAND or of any child till the children attain majority and become capable of earning their livelihood. The estate of the HUSBAND shall remain charged with the payment of the said maintenance.

IN WITNESS WHEREOF these presents are executed by the parties on the day, month and year first above-written.

Signed and delivered by AB in the
presence of:

Signed and delivered by BW in the
presence of:

36

Mortgages and Pledges

Mortgages

HISTORICAL BACKGROUND

Mortgages in India. A very early form of mortgage among Hindus and Mahomedans was the one which took the form of a conditional conveyance. Among Muslims, it was developed as a device for evading the Koranic injunctions against usury. The transaction was called a bye-bil-wafa (sale with a promise). The mortgagee enjoyed the usufruct in lieu of interest and became the absolute owner if the debt was not paid. This form of mortgage is common among the Hindus also and is known variously—in Bengal as *Khatkabala*, in Madras as *Avadhi Vikrayam* or *Muddata Kriyam*, and in Bombay as *Gahan Lahan*. This type of security bore a close resemblance to the Roman 'fiducia'. Corresponding to the Roman Pignus there are the usufructuary mortgagees of Indian law. The usufructuary mortgage is called in Madras *Bhogyam* or *Swadhina Ayakam*. In Malabar, it is known as *Kanom* or *Otti*. The Roman hypotheca is also reproduced in the latter developments of the mortgage in India. The simple mortgage of India which corresponds to the 'hypotheca' is known in the vernacular of the Madras Presidency as *Dhrista Bhandaka* or *Chupudu-Ayakam, Tanaka* or *Adaimana Patram*. The Transfer of Property Act of 1882 codified *inter alia* the law relating to mortgagees.

DOCTRINE OF EQUITY OF REDEMPTION

Meaning of equity of redemption. The mortgagor's right to redeem the mortgage is jealously guarded by the courts. If the mortgagor stipulates with the mortgagee to redeem the property within a specified time and to forfeit the property in the event of default, he will not be held to his contract in a Court of Equity. For the reason even when the time for exercising the contractual right to redeem has gone by, the mortgagor can still in equity claim to redeem the property. This right of the mortgagor is called the Equity of Redemption, Lord Bramwell defines it in *Salt* v *Marquess of Northampton*[1] Act thus:

> "An equity of redemption is a right not given by the terms of the agreement between the parties to it, but contrary to them to have back securities given by a borrower to a lender on payment of principal and interest at a day after that appointed for payment, when by the terms of the agreement between the parties the securities were to be the absolute property of the creditor. This is now a legal right of the debtor."

The doctrine of equity of redemption is expressed in the maxim 'once a mortgage, always a mortgage.' As explained by Lord Davey in *Noakes & Company* v *Rice*,[2] the maxim means "that a mortgage cannot be made irredeemable and that a provision to that effect is void."

Meanings of the expression—equity of redemption. The residue of interest left in the mortgagor after he has mortgaged the property is also called the equity of redemption. This must not be confused with the equitable right to redeem also designated the equity of redemption. As Lord Parker observes in *Kreglinger's* case.[3]

> "The equity to redeem which arises on failure to exercise the contractual right of redemption must be carefully distinguished from the equitable estate which, from the first, remains in the mortgagor and is sometimes referred to as an Equity of Redemption."

Under the Transfer of Property Act—recognition of the doctrine of equity of redemption. The statutory interference suggested by the Privy Council in *Thumbuswami's case* was effected by the enactment of the Transfer of Property Act in 1882. By s. 60 of the Act the right of redemption was conferred. This right can be claimed when the principal money of the mortgage becomes due and subsists until put an end to in due course of law. It is noteworthy that s. 60 is not subject to a contract to the contrary. This makes it clear that the equitable right to redeem subsists until the mortgagor's interest is effectually extinguished by due process of law.

This is a new legal right to the debtor not provided for under the terms of contract, but contrary thereto, to have back the securities against payment of mortgage debt even after the appointed date. The other doctrine that followed is 'once a mortgage always a mortgage'. As explained by

1 (1892) AC 1.
2 (1902) AC 24.
3 (1914) AC 25.

Lord Davey in *Noakes & Co.* v *Rice,*[4] the maxim means—"A mortgage cannot be made irredeemable and a provision to that effect is void." Formerly a mortgagor in English law had no power to grant any lease of the property in the absence of express authority provided for in the mortgage deed. Section 18 of the Conveyancing Act of 1881 as re-enacted by s. 99 of the Law of Property Act 1925 remedied the anomaly by conferring such a power to grant agricultural lease for 21 years and building lease for 99 years.[5] The law in India on the subject is contained in s. 65A of the Transfer of Property Act 1882 as amended by Transfer of Property Amendment Act (XX of 1929) which permits a lease of the mortgaged property subject to certain reservations in the absence of contrary provisions in the deed of mortgage. The leading case on the subject is *Madan Mohan* v *Raj Kishore*.[6]

It is well-settled that when a person enters into possession of immovable property not in the assertion of any absolute title but on the basis of unregistered mortgage deed in his favour and remains in possession for more than 12 years, he acquires the status of a mortgagee by the doctrine of prescription and even though unregistered mortgage deed is not a valid transaction for want of registration, the mortgagor is entitled to redeem the property. Such an unregistered mortgage deed cannot be treated as an agreement to enter into a mortgage deed in future.[7]

The Law of Property Act 1925 [*vide* s. 85(2)] has completely amended the law—a legal mortgage is no longer a conveyance of the property.[8]

The Act, however, gives the mortgagee a power of sale of the property,[9] also to have a Receiver appointed (*vide* s. 101) to take possession of the property, also the right of foreclosure which the court may in its discretion refuse and direct sale of the property (s. 91 of the Act). The law in India on this subject is contained in ss. 67, 69, 69A of the Transfer of Property Act.

Although a deed of mortgage, in particular a simple mortgage, may not contain any covenant as to title, etc., as in the case of sale under s. 55(2) of the Transfer of Property Act, nevertheless under s. 65 the mortgagor shall be deemed to contract with the mortgagee as to his title and power to mortgage. He is also deemed to have covenanted with the mortgagee as to defend his title and payment of all public charges. In the case of leasehold estate, he is to keep alive the lease by payment of rent and performance of all other covenants and conditions of the lease. In default on his part the

4 (1902) AC 24.

5 Venkatasubba Rao's *Principles of Equity*, p. 163; Topham's *Real Property*, 11th Ed., p. 205.

6 21 CWN 88.

7 *Vora Aminbai* v *Vora Taherali* AIR 1998 Guj 31.

8 Topham's *Real Property*, 11th Ed., pp. 194-195.

9 Section 103 of the Law of Property Act 1925.

mortgagee under s. 72 of the said Act can meet all the expenses at the first instance and all such amounts will be added to his claim.

Equitable mortgage. The court of equity recognised two types of other mortgages known as equitable mortgage. This is based upon the maxim—"Equity looks at the intention of the parties rather than the form", *e.g.* (1) mortgage by equitable owners of their equitable rights, and (2) creation by legal owners of equitable rights by way of security. Such a mortgage can be created by deposit of original title deeds[10] without word of mouth, and even without writing provided the mortgagor intended to create a security on the properties relating thereto. It may or may not be accompanied by a memorandum. It differs from an English mortgagee in this sense that the mortgagee acquires no legal estate in the property. All that he can claim is at least an equitable charge. So he has no right of foreclosure. He has no right of possession; so he cannot enter into possession and collect the rents and profits of the mortgaged property.

In India, such a mortgage can be created only in Presidency Towns. The deposit of title deeds must in any event be made within the said towns.

Since the introduction of the new s. 96 of the Transfer of Property Act in consequence of the amending Act 20 of 1929, such a mortgage has been placed by far on a better footing, *viz.* that of a mortgage by a deed under s. 58(*f*) of the Act.[11] The Privy Council in *Imperial Bank of India* v *Rai Gyawthu*[12] observed that the requisites of such a mortgage are (*a*) debt, (*b*) deposit, and (*c*) intention to create security. Order XXXIV, r. 15 of the CPC as amended in 1976, makes all the provisions of the order relating to simple mortgage applicable to mortgage by deposit of title deeds and also to charges as contemplated under ss. 58 and 100 of the Transfer of Property Act, respectively.

As regards *raiyati* holdings, s. 7 of the West Bengal Land Reforms Act 1955, has imposed certain restrictions on the general power to mortgage under the Transfer of Property Act. A mortgage by a *raiyat* of his holding or any share thereof other than a simple mortgage or an usufructuary mortgage not exceeding 15 years shall be void.

This section came into force from 1st March 1965; *vide* Calcutta Gazette Notification No. 2798 L/Ref. of 22nd February 1965.

Mortgage and charge. A mortgage as defined in s. 58 of the Transfer of Property Act is the transfer of an interest in specific immovable property for the purpose of securing payment of money advanced or to be advanced by

10 Topham's *Real Property*, 11th Ed., p. 208.
11 B.B. Mitra on *Transfer of Property Act*, 12th Ed., p. 849.
12 76 IC 910; 50 IA 283.

way of loan, an existing or future debt, or the performance of any contract or engagement which may give rise to a pecuniary liability.

It is distinguishable from a charge as defined under s. 100 of the Transfer of Property Act in which there is no transfer of any property or any right therein, *e.g.* security bond. A charge is at best the creation of a right of payment out of any particular property without any transfer of any interest or fund therein. A mortgage is in essence a transfer of some interest in some specific immovable property.[13] Under Or. XXXIV, r. 15(2) of the CPC as amended in 1976, a decree ordering payment of money charged on some immovable property can be realised by its sale in execution.[1] It cannot be enforced against a *bona fide* purchaser for value except when the same is created under a decree or order of the court which can be enforced by sale of the property in execution.[2]

A charge may be created by operation of law, *e.g.* arrears of land revenue, arrears of rent under s. 65 of the Bengal Tenancy Act, arrears of consolidated rates and taxes under the Calcutta Municipal Act. They are enforceable against the property.

The transferor in case of the mortgage is called the *mortgagor*, the transferee the *mortgagee*, the principal money and interest of which payment is secured for the time being are called the *mortgage money*, and the instrument of transfer, a *mortgage deed*.

Mortgagor, mortgagee and mortgaged properties. Any person, company, association or body of individuals not otherwise disqualified can be the mortgagor. In the case of a company or association, such a mortgage must be authorized by the Memorandum and approved by a Resolution of the Board of Directors or the governing body as the case may be. Under s. 292 of the Companies Act 1956, it is the Board of Directors who can borrow money on mortgage and the same shall be done by resolutions passed at the Board and general Meetings. A minor or a lunatic cannot create any mortgage in respect of their properties.[3] A mortgage by a lunatic is void under s. 11 read with s. 12 of the Indian Contract Act. A partner has no implied authority to mortgage any immovable property belonging to the firm.[4] A person whose property is being managed by the Collector cannot create nor submit his property to any mortgage.[5]

13 *Shiva Prosad* v *Benimadhab* AIR 1929 Pat 529.
1 *Shiva Prosad* v *Benimadhab* AIR 1922 Pat 520.
2 *Seethalakshmi* v *Srinivaso* AIR 1958 Mad 23.
3 *Mohori Bibi* v *Dharmadas Ghosh* 30 IA 114.
4 Section 19(2)(g) of the Indian Partnership Act.
5 Mulla's *Code of Civil Procedure*, 12th Ed., p. 1382.

A Karta of a Mitakshara joint family cannot create a mortgage except for legal necessities and for the benefit of the estate. An executor in the absence of any restriction can mortgage any property belonging to the estate of the deceased for the purpose of administration.[6] A minor is not disqualified to be a mortgagee in India and also under the English law in respect of a legal estate.[7] A trustee cannot be the mortgagee of a trust property. A guardian of a minor is in the same position as that of a trustee. A specific immovable property of description sufficient to identify it within the meaning of ss. 21 and 22 of the Registration Act can be mortgaged, but the position is different in case of floating charge created by a company unless the same is crystallised.[8]

The following are the different kinds of mortgage:

(i) *Simple mortgage*. In a simple mortgage, in this sense that the *mortgagor*, without delivering possession of the mortgaged property, binds himself personally to pay the *mortgage money*, and agrees, expressly or impliedly, that in case he fails to pay according to his contract, the property will be sold and the proceeds to be applied in payment of the mortgage money.[9]

(ii) *Mortgage by conditional sale*. In a *mortgage by conditional sale*, the *mortgagor* ostensibly sells the mortgaged property on condition that in default of payment of the *mortgage money* on a certain date the sale shall become absolute, or on condition that on such payment being made the sale shall become void and the buyer shall transfer the property to the seller, provided that no such transaction shall be deemed to be a mortgage unless the condition is embodied in the document which effects or purports to effect the sale.[10] Where clauses of deed consistent with express intention of making the transaction a conditional sale with option to repurchase, the Supreme Court held that the document was not a mortgage by conditional sale.[11]

(iii) *Usufructuary mortgage*. It is a transfer of a right to possession of the mortgaged property and the right to receive the rents and profits accruing from such property. Where the lessor of a leased property creates a usufructuary mortgage in respect of such property what he transfers under s. 109 of the Transfer of Property Act as a mortgagor in favour of the usufructuary mortgagee includes his right to possession of such property and the right to receive the rents and profits accruing from it. Section 109 entitles the usufructuary mortgagee from the lessor as against the lessee, for all rights which the lessor had against such lessee.[12]

6 *Sunil* v *Sisir* (1969)67 IA 102.
7 *Raghava* v *Srenivasa* ILR 40 Mad 308.
8 *I.P. Jones & Co.* v *Ranjit* AIR 1927 Cal 682.
9 Section 58(*b*) of the Transfer of Property Act.
10 Section 58(*c*) of the Transfer of Property Act.
11 *Tamboli* v *Ghanchi* AIR 1992 SC 1236.
12 *Narpatchand* v *Shantilal* AIR 1993 SC 1712.

In a usufructuary mortgage, the mortgagee delivers possession of the mortgaged property or expressly or by implication the *mortgagor* binds himself to deliver its possession to the *mortgagee,* and authorizes him to retain such possession until payment of the mortgage money and to receive the rents and profits accruing from the property, or any part of such rents and profits, and to appropriate the same in lieu of interest or in payment of the *mortgage money*, or partly in payment of the *mortgage money*, or partly in lieu of interest.[13]

(iv) *English mortgage*. It is out and out conveyance subject to proviso for redemption. In an *English mortgage*, the mortgagor binds himself to repay the *mortgage money* on a certain date, and transfers the mortgaged property absolutely to the *mortgagee*, subject to a proviso that he will re-transfer it to the *mortgagor* upon payment of the *mortgage money* as agreed. This right of redemption is provided under s. 60 of the Transfer of Property Act 1882. An *English mortgage* usually provides for appointment of a Receiver to take charge of the mortgaged property and to collect the rents, issues and profits.[14]

(v) *Mortgage by deposit of title-deed*. Within the towns of Calcutta, Madras, Bombay or any other town specified by any State Government, a mortgage by deposit of title-deeds is effected by the mortgagor delivering to the creditor, or his authorised agent, documents of title to immovable property, with intent to create a security thereon.[15] It was held that a mortgage by deposit of title-deeds can be created even in the case of a barred debt. No written acknowledgement is necessary.[16] It is however always prudent to have a record of transaction as already effected to avoid the difficulty to establish the creation of the mortgage. In any event the original title deeds are to be deposited or with the intention to create security some documents or copies of documents relating to the property.[17] Section 96 of the Transfer of Property Act inserted by the Amending Act XX of 1929 has put such a mortgage on the same footing as a mortgage by a deed under s. 58. The corresponding amendment in adjective law is Or. 34, r. 15 of the CPC now Or. 34, r. 15(1) by the amendment of the CPC 1976.

Delivery of document of title alone is sufficient to create an equitable mortgage. There is no necessity to execute any document. In case, a document was executed for the purpose of creating a mortgage under s. 58(*f*) of the Transfer of Property Act no doubt it requires registration. A

13 Section 58(*d*) of the Transfer of Property Act.
14 Section 58(*e*) of the Transfer of Property Act.
15 Section 58(*f*) of the Transfer of Property Act.
16 *Monoj Kumar Saha* v *Nabadwip Chandra Poddar* 82 CWN 166.
17 *Punjab and Sindh Bank Ltd.* v *Ganes Das* AIR 1935 Lah 721; *State Bank of Mysore* v *Official Liquidator* 58 Comp Cas 609; *C. Asiamma* v *State Bank of Mysore* AIR 1990 Ker 157; *Amulya Gopal Majumdar* v *United Industrial Bank* AIR 1981 Cal 404.

letter or a memorandum executed after delivery of the documents and only endorsing the earlier deposit of title deeds which already had created the mortgage does not require registration. The law as settled is that where a document is executed simultaneously with the delivery of title deeds, the intention of the parties being to create a separate mortgage in the document in question for securing the money advanced under a promissory note such document requires registration.[18]

(vi) *Anomalous mortgage.* An anomalous mortgage is the combination of any of the above forms of mortgage, or any other mortgage which is not one of them.[19]

Mortgage how effected? When the principal money secured is one hundred rupees or upwards, a mortgage, other than a mortgage by deposit of title deeds, can be effected only by a registered instrument signed by the mortgagor and *attested by at least two witnesses.*[20]

Mortgagor's rights.[1] At any time after the principal money has become due, the mortgagor has a right, on payment or tender, at a proper time and place, of the mortgage money, to require the mortgagee (*i*) to deliver to the mortgagor the mortgage deed and all documents relating to the mortgaged property which are in the possession or power of the mortgagee, (*ii*) where the mortgagee is in possession of the mortgaged property, to deliver possession thereof to the mortgagor; and (*iii*) at the cost of the mortgagor either to re-transfer the mortgaged property to him, or to such third person as he may direct, or to execute and (where the mortgage has been effected by a registered instrument) to have registered an acknowledgement in writing that any right in derogation of his interest transferred to the mortgagee has been extinguished.[2] The mortgage money may be deposited in court.[3]

Provided that the right conferred as above has not been extinguished by act of the parties, or by decree of a court, or operation of law.

This right of the mortgagor is called a right *to redeem, and a suit* to enforce it is called *suit for redemption*.[4] Such a right can under no circumstances be negatived though the mortgagor may be precluded from exercising the same for a short period.[5] So a stipulation in the mortgage deed giving the mortgagee option to purchase the equity of redemption at a

18 *Hubert Peyali* v *Santhavilasathu* AIR 1998 Ker 344.
19 Section 58(g) of the Transfer of Property Act.
20 Section 59 of the Transfer of Property Act.
1 Section 60 of the Transfer of Property Act.
2 Section 60 of the Transfer of Property Act as amended by Act XX of 1929.
3 Section 83 of the Transfer of Property Act.
4 Order XXXIV, Rule 7 of Code of Civil Procedure.
5 *Jeevan* v *Smith* (1882)20 Ch D 727 (729).

specified price is invalid.[6] Nevertheless, it is quite lawful to make a *bona fide* conveyance with option to repurchase.[7] Where a mortgagee having the power under the deed of mortgage enters into an agreement in that behalf the mortgagor can nevertheless redeem the property.[8]

Where the previous owner has mortgaged the property during his lifetime which is subsisting at the time of his death, then after his death his heirs only inherit the mortgagor's interest in the property. By discharging the mortgage debt his heir who has inherited the property acquires the interest of the mortgagee in the property. As a result of such payment made for the purpose of clearing of the mortgage the interest of the mortgagee in the property has been acquired by the heir.[9]

In a usufructuary mortgage if for some default in payment of rent or rent decree is obtained and the mortgagee pays off the same even then the mortgage in question is liable to be redeemed at the option of the mortgagor. The mortgagee cannot escape from his obligation by bringing the equity of redemption to sale in execution of a decree on the personal covenant. By virtue of purchase of the property by the mortgagee in court sale, no merger takes place between the two rights nor the mortgage stands extinguished.[10]

A mortgagor interested in a share only of the mortgaged property cannot redeem his own share only, on payment of a proportionate part of the amount remaining due on the mortgage, except only where a mortgagee, or, if there are more mortgagees than one, all such mortgagees, has or have acquired, in whole or in part, the share of a mortgagor. This is known as the principle of indivisibility of mortgage.[11]

In the case of a usufructuary mortgage, the mortgagor has a right to recover possession of the mortgaged property, together with the mortgage deed and all documents relating to the mortgaged property which are in the possession or power of the mortgagee—

(*i*) where the mortgagee is authorized to pay himself the mortgage money from the rents and profits of the property—when such money is paid;

(*ii*) where the mortgagee is authorized to pay himself, from such rents and profits or any part thereof, a part only of the mortgage money—when the term (if any) prescribed for the payment of the mortgage money has expired, and the mortgagor pays or tenders to the

6 *Globe Finance Corporation* v *Montgomery* 18 TLR 661.

7 *Barton* v *Bank of South Wales* (1890)15 App Cas 379.

8 *Mansoor* v *Usman* AIR 1944 Bom 156.

9 *R.M. Arunachalam* v *I.T. Commr.* AIR 1997 SC 2905.

10 *Parichhan Mistry* v *Acchiabar Mistry* AIR 1997 SC 456.

11 Section 60 of the Transfer of Property Act.

mortgagee the mortgage money or the balance thereof or deposits it in court.

The Code of Civil Procedure as amended in 1976, Or. XXXIV, r. 10 gives the mortgagor relief against costs in case where he deposits the amount or an amount not substantially deficient at the time of institution of the suit.

Implied contracts by mortgagor.[12] In the absence of a contract to the contrary, the mortgagor is deemed to contract with the mortgagee—

(*i*) that the interest which the mortgagor professes to transfer to the mortgagee subsists, and that the mortgagor has power to transfer the same;

(*ii*) that the mortgagor will defend, or if the mortgagee be in possession of the mortgaged property, enable him to defend, the mortgagor's title thereto;

(*iii*) that the mortgagor will, so long as the mortgagee is not in possession of the mortgaged property, pay all public charges accruing due in respect of the property.

Mortgagee's rights. In the absence of a contract to the contrary, the mortgagee has, at any time after the mortgage money has become due to him, and before a decree has been made for the redemption of the mortgaged property or the mortgage money has been paid or deposited, a right to obtain from the court a decree that the mortgagor shall be absolutely debarred of his right to redeem the property, or a decree that the property be sold.[13]

The mortgagee has under s. 68 of the Transfer of Property Act a right to sue for the mortgage-money in the following cases only—

(*a*) where the mortgagor binds himself to repay the same, *i.e.* in cases where the mortgage contains a personal covenant, *i.e.* English mortgage and simple mortgage;

(*b*) where, by any cause other than the wrongful act or default of the mortgagor or mortgagee, the mortgaged property is wholly or partially destroyed or the security is rendered insufficient, and the mortgagee has given the mortgagor a reasonable opportunity of providing further security enough to render the whole security sufficient, and the mortgagor has failed to do so; *vide* also s. 66 of the Transfer of Property Act—Impairment of the security;

(*c*) where the mortgagee is deprived of the whole or part of his security by or in consequence of the wrongful act or default of the mortgagor; and

12 Section 65 of the Transfer of Property Act.

13 Section 67 of the Transfer of Property Act.

(*d*) where, the mortgagee being entitled to possession of the mortgaged property, the mortgagor fails to deliver the same to him or to secure the possession thereof to him without disturbance by the mortgagor or any person claiming under a title superior to that of the mortgagor.

Provided that, in the case referred to in cl. (*i*), a transferee from the mortgagor or from his legal representative will not be liable to be sued for the mortgage-money.

Where a suit is brought under cl. (*i*) or cl. (*ii*), the court can, at its discretion, stay the suit and all proceedings therein, notwithstanding any contract to the contrary, until the mortgagee has exhausted all his available remedies against the mortgaged property or, what remains of it, unless the mortgagee abandons his security and, if necessary, re-transfers the mortgaged property.[14]

Further charges. *Further charge or advance* is a second or subsequent loan of money to a mortgagor by the mortgagee either upon the same security or an additional one. Further charge includes all cases in which the same parties to the original deed desire to increase the liability to which the land is already subject.

A deed of further charge is a deed of further mortgage, requiring therefore to be executed, attested and registered as a mortgage deed.

Reconveyance of mortgaged property. In an English mortgage and in a mortgage by conditional sale, the mortgagor makes a conveyance of his property to the mortgagee. If the mortgagee receives the mortgage-money, the mortgaged property has to be reconveyed to the mortgagor. It was held by the Privy Council in *Pattabhiramier* v *Vencatrow*[15] that the time fixed in a mortgage deed is not the essence of contract. A reconveyance should be made by a separate deed, executed, attested and registered as a mortgage deed. Reconveyance of the mortgaged property to the mortgagor is not, however, absolutely necessary to effect redemption of other mortgages as, if the mortgage money is fully paid, there is no debt left and its security is automatically extinguished. The payment of the mortgage money is usually endorsed on the mortgage deed which is returned to the mortgagor. This procedure is regarded as sufficient.[16] The position is different in the case of English mortgage which is a conveyance, *i.e.* absolute transfer of the property, subject to the proviso for redemption and the deed itself provides for reconveyance of the property. The remedy is sale and not foreclosure.[17] An agreement of mortgage does not create any right and cannot be specifically

14 Section 68 of the Transfer of Property Act.
15 (1871)13 MIA 560.
16 *Kunja Bihare* v *Bisheswar* (1934) 148 IC 68; AIR 1934 Oudh 98.
17 Section 67 of the Transfer of Property Act.

enforced.[18] But when the mortgagee has advanced the money and the mortgagor refuses to execute the mortgage the former can bring a suit to compel *execution* of the mortgage.[19]

Mortgage of future crops. A *mortgage of future crops* is valid provided that the *mortgagor* has a potential interest in that out of which the property may arise.

PLEDGES

Pledge, pawnor and pawnee. The bailment of goods as security for payment of a debt or performance of a promise is called a *pledge*. The bailor is called the *pawnor* and the bailee is called the *pawnee*.[20] A pledge is different from a mortgage as a pledgee only acquires the right to sell the pledged articles in case of default. The leading English case on the subject of bailment is *Coggs* v *Bernard*.[1] It was held that a bailment is a pledge when goods are delivered as security for money borrowed.

Pledge how made. A pledge can only be made effective by transfer of possession of the goods pledged, and therefore a mere licence to take, or a contract to give, possession although it may operate as a hypothecation, cannot constitute a pledge; but if, in pursuance of such contract under which an advance is made, the goods are afterwards delivered, there is complete pledge, and it is no objection that the advance and delivery of goods were not contemporaneous, nor is a pledge necessarily determined by the return of goods to the owner, for they may be delivered to him as agent of the pledgee or for temporary purpose or on trust.

Pawnee's right. The pawnee can retain goods pledged, not only for payment of the debt or the performance of the promise, but for the interest of the debt, and all necessary expenses incurred by him in respect of the possession or for the preservation of the goods pledged.[2]

The pawnee cannot, in the absence of a contract to that effect, retain the goods pledged for any debt or promise other than the debt or promise for which they are pledged, but such contract, in the absence of anything to the contrary, will be presumed in regard to subsequent advances made by the pawnee.[3]

If the pawnor makes default in payment of the debt, or performance at the stipulated time of the promise in respect of which the goods were

18 *S.K. Golim* v *Sadarjan Bibi* 43 Cal 59.
19 Ghosh's *Law of Mortgage,* 5th Ed., pp. 74-75.
20 Section 172 of the Indian Contract Act.
1 (1704)1 Sm LC (12th Ed.) 191.
2 Section 173 of the Indian Contract Act.
3 Section 174 of the Indian Contract Act.

pledged, the pawnee can bring a suit against the pawnor upon the debt or promise, and retain the goods pledged as a collateral security; or he can sell the thing pledged on giving the pawnor reasonable notice of the sale.[4]

If the proceeds of such sale are less than the amount due in respect of the debt or promise, the pawnor is still liable to pay the balance. If the proceeds of the sale are greater than the amount so due, the pawnee must pay over the surplus to the pawnor.

Defaulting pawnor's right to redeem. If the pawnor makes default in payment of the debt or performance of the promise, for which the pledge is made, at the stipulated time, he can redeem the goods pledged at any subsequent time before the actual sale of them; but he must, in that case, pay in addition any expenses which have arisen from his default.[5]

Duties of solicitor or advocate acting for the mortgagee. Same as in the case of conveyance, *e.g.*, preparation of abstract on title searches, production and inspection of title deeds, requisitions on title, preparation of draft mortgage, execution and registration of the mortgage. He must also see that the mortgagor does not take advantage of the Moneylenders Act. He should advise his client to take the requisite licence under the said Act, specify the object of the loan in the deed of mortgage, get a solemn declaration from the borrower as to the object of borrowing. Further, he should insist upon entry of the loan amount in the books of the debtor and keep a copy thereof duly certified by the debtor.

REQUIREMENTS OF A DEED OF MORTGAGE

(1) A thorough investigation of title up to 60 years and preparation of an abstract on title and a thorough search in all the places as required in the case of sale.

(2) Parties to the deed. *Mortgagor* first and thereafter the *mortgagee*.

(3) Recitals. A short history of the property right up to its vesting in the *mortgagor* and the object of the loan—Amount and rate of interest.

(4) Operative words. In the case of a simple mortgage, the property is charged and assured as security for repayment of the mortgage debt. In case of *English mortgage*, it is out and out sale to the mortgagee subject to the covenant as to reconveyance upon repayment of the debt with interest.[6]

(5) Possession. An English mortgagee has the right to take possession of the property. Such a mortgage should contain a clause as to the appointment of a Receiver who may be a nominee of the mortgagee.[7]

4 Section 176 of the Indian Contract Act.
5 Section 177 of the Indian Contract Act.
6 Section 58(e) of the Transfer of Property Act.
7 Section 69A of the Transfer of Property Act.

(6) Redemption. Period is fixed by agreement between the parties. Under Act. 61 of the Limitation Act of 1963 a suit for redemption may be brought within 30 years from when the right to redeem accrues according to the agreement. In case where the property has been transferred by the mortgagee for valuable consideration the period of limitation is 12 years from the date of knowledge.

(7) Execution and attestation. Attestation is compulsory to every mortgage. In case where the mortgagor does not know the language, the deed must be explained to him by some competent person.

(8) Registration. Compulsory in case of mortgage of value above Rs. 100, and in all cases under the West Bengal Land Reforms Act (*vide* s. 7).

(9) Delivery of title deeds. A mortgagee is entitled to all the title deeds of the mortgaged property. If for any reason they are left with the mortgagor through inadvertence or negligence, he can manipulate a prior equitable mortgage by depositing the same elsewhere.

FORMS

Deed of Simple Mortgage

THIS DEED OF MORTGAGE made the .... day of .... BETWEEN AB of, etc. (hereinafter called the MORTGAGOR), of the one part and CD of etc., (hereinafter called the MORTGAGEE), of the other part, WITNESSES, that in consideration of a sum of Rs. .... lent and advanced to the MORTGAGOR by the MORTGAGEE the receipt whereof the MORTGAGOR does hereby and also by the receipt hereunder admit, acknowledge and confirm, he, the said AB does hereby and hereunder transfer and mortgage, as and by way of simple mortgage, unto and in favour of the said CD, his heirs, executors, administrators or assigns, ALL THAT property specifically described in the schedule hereunder, and charge and assure the same by way of security for the repayment of the said sum of Rs. .... together with interest thereon at the rate of .... per cent per annum: AND the MORTGAGOR does hereby agree and covenant with the MORTGAGEE that he will pay or cause to be paid to the MORTGAGEE the principal sum aforesaid, together with the interest then due, on or before the .... day of .... without delay or default AND THIS DEED further witnesseth and it is hereby agreed and declared by and between the parties that in case the said sum of Rs. .... with interest thereon at the stipulated rate is not paid within the time and in the manner as aforesaid, it shall be lawful for the MORTGAGEE to enforce this mortgage and to cause the property or any portion thereof to be sold and appropriate the proceeds towards satisfaction of the mortgage debt provided, however, that in the event of any shortfall or deficiency, *i.e.* should the claim be not then satisfied, the MORTGAGEE shall be entitled to recover the balance personally as against the MORTGAGOR who shall be entitled to redeem the said mortgage at his option by payment of the amount of mortgage debt inclusive of interest at any time before the............ day of........... AND THIS DEED further witnesseth that the MORTGAGOR does hereby covenant with the MORTGAGEE that notwithstanding any act, deed or thing herebefore done, executed, performed or suffered to the contrary, the MORTGAGOR has good title, full power and absolute authority to charge, assure and mortgage the said property in the manner hereunder effected and that the same is free from all encumbrances and attachments.

The Schedule above referred to

IN WITNESS WHEREOF the parties herein have executed these presents on the day, month and year first above-written.

Signed, sealed and delivered by the withinmentioned MORTGAGOR AB in the presence of:

Signed, sealed and delivered by the withinmentioned MORTGAGEE CD in the presence of:

MEMO OF CONSIDERATION

Received a Cheque No. .... dated .... for Rs. .... on B Bank etc.

Received payments
Sd/. CD

Deed of Mortgage by Conditional Sale

THIS DEED OF MORTGAGE made this .... day of .... 2000 BETWEEN AB son of.................................. residing at........................ hereinafter called the MORTGAGOR (which term shall include his heirs, successors, executors, administrators and assigns) of the one part and CD son of................ residing at............ hereinafter called the MORTGAGEE (which term shall include his heirs, successors, executors, administrators and assigns) of the other part WITNESSES that in consideration of the sum of Rs. .... paid to the MORTGAGOR by the MORTGAGEE (the receipt whereof the MORTGAGOR hereby acknowledges) the MORTGAGOR does hereby grant, transfer, convey, assign and assure to the MORTGAGEE ALL THAT etc. To Have and to Hold the same absolutely and for ever subject to the condition hereby expressly declared, namely, that if and when the MORTGAGOR shall repay or cause to be repaid the said sum of Rs. .... with interest thereon at the rate of .... per cent per annum on or before .... day of .... time for which purpose shall be deemed as essence of contract then and in such an event the sale hereby effected shall stand void and shall be of no effect to all intents and purposes and the MORTGAGEE shall at the costs of the MORTGAGOR reconvey and retransfer the said property and every part thereof as then existing to the MORTGAGOR provided, however, that if the MORTGAGOR shall fail and/or neglect to repay the said sum with interest at the said rate on or before the said date, or any portion thereof the sale hereby effected shall become absolute and the MORTGAGEE shall be entitled to foreclose the mortgage when and in such an event the MORTGAGEE shall be the absolute owner of the property freed and discharged from all right of equity of redemption of the MORTGAGOR, AND IT IS HEREBY further AGREED AND DECLARED that notwithstanding anything hereinbefore contained the MORTGAGOR shall remain in possession of the said property and pay all rents, cess, taxes, rates and other impositions which are now or may hereafter be imposed on the said property and in case the MORTGAGOR fails and/or neglects to make such payments on or before the due date of payments therefor, the MORTGAGEE shall be at liberty to pay the same and add such sum or sums to the principal money hereby secured which shall carry interest at the aforesaid rate. And that the MORTGAGOR does hereby covenant with the MORTGAGEE that he has good title to the property and absolute authority and power to transfer the same in the manner hereinbefore indicated and that the property is free from all encumbrances and attachments whatsoever.

The Schedule above referred to

IN WITNESS WHEREOF the parties hereto have executed these presents on the day, month and year first above-written.

Signed, sealed and delivered by AB
the MORTGAGOR in the presence of:

Signed, sealed and delivered by CD
the MORTGAGEE in the presence of:

MEMO OF CONSIDERATION

Received of and from the withinmentioned MORTGAGEE the sum of Rs. .... being the consideration withinmentioned by Bank Draft No. .... dated .... for Rs. .... issued by X Bank Ltd. payable in Calcutta.

WITNESSES: Received

Signature of the MORTGAGOR

Deed of Usufructuary Mortgage

THIS DEED OF MORTGAGE made this .... day of .... 2000 BETWEEN AB son of .... residing at .... hereinafter called the MORTGAGOR (which term shall include his heirs, successors, executors, administrators and assigns) of the one part and CD son of .... residing at .... hereinafter called the MORTGAGEE (which term shall include his heirs, successors, executors, administrators and assigns) of the other part, WITNESSES that in consideration of the sum of Rs. .... paid by the MORTGAGEE to the MORTGAGOR at the time of the execution of this deed (the receipt of which sum the MORTGAGOR hereby acknowledges), the MORTGAGOR does hereby convey as and by way of usufructuary mortgage to the MORTGAGEE ALL THAT etc. To Have and To Hold the same and posses as security until the repayment of the said sum with interest thereon at the rate of Rs. .... per cent per annum.

AND THIS INDENTURE further witnesseth and it is agreed and declared that the MORTGAGOR hereby delivers possession of the said property to the MORTGAGEE who shall retain such possession until payment of the said sum with interest as aforesaid and shall receive the rent, issues and profits accruing from the said property and pay all rents, cesses, taxes and other impositions and appropriate the balance firstly, in payment of the interest due and then in reduction or payment of the principal sum advanced and that on such payment and satisfaction of the whole of the principal sum and interest thereon the MORTGAGOR shall be entitled to get back possession of the said property.

AND it is further agreed and declared that the MORTGAGEE shall at all times hereafter until satisfaction of the mortgage debt take care of, manage and preserve the said property as a person of ordinary prudence would manage it if it were his own and use his best endeavours to collect the rents and profits thereof and make necessary arrangements for maintenance, preservation and repair of the said property and keep clear, full and accurate accounts of all sums received and spent by him as MORTGAGEE and furnish the MORTGAGOR at his cost true copies of such accounts and of the receipts and vouchers by which they are supported.

AND it is furthermore agreed that in any event after expiry of................ years the mortgage debt shall be deemed as satisfied and extinguished out of the usufruct of the property and the MORTGAGEE shall unconditionally reconvey the property to the MORTGAGOR at his costs and expenses.

The Schedule above referred to

IN WITNESS WHEREOF the parties hereto have executed these presents on the day, month and year first above-written.

Signed, sealed and delivered by AB
the MORTGAGOR in the presence of:

Signed, sealed and delivered by CD
the MORTGAGEE in the presence of:

MEMO OF CONSIDERATION

Received of and from the withinmentioned Mortgagee the sum of Rs........... being the consideration withinmentioned by Bank Draft No......... dated .... for Rs. .... issued by X Bank Ltd. payable in Calcutta.

WITNESSES: Received

Signature of the MORTGAGOR

Deed of Usufructuary Mortgage by Conditional Sale (Anomalous Mortgage)

THIS DEED OF MORTGAGE made this .... day of .... 2000 BETWEEN AB son of .... residing at .... hereinafter called the MORTGAGOR (which term shall include his heirs, successors, executors, administrators and assigns) of the one part and CD son of .... residing at .... hereinafter called the MORTGAGEE (which term shall include his heirs, successors, executors, administrators and assigns) of the other part WITNESSES that on consideration of the sum of Rs. .... now paid to the MORTGAGOR by the MORTGAGEE (the receipt whereof the MORTGAGOR does hereby acknowledge), the said AB hereby conveys to the said CD. ALL THAT, etc. (*describe the property*): from this day AND THAT the MORTGAGEE shall be in possession of the mortgaged property under the terms of the deed for securing payment on the................ day of............ of the principal sum secured, with the interest thereon at Rs. .... per cent per annum, which mortgage-money will be set off against the usufruct of the mortgaged property, and the MORTGAGEE does hereby promise to keep clear accounts thereof.

The MORTGAGOR hereby agrees that the MORTGAGEE shall retain possession of the mortgaged property until the principal sum together with the interest due be paid off out of the proceeds of the property and on payment of the aforesaid sum, the MORTGAGEE shall execute and register a release of the mortgaged property in favour of the MORTGAGOR, AND THAT the MORTGAGEE shall not do, execute, perform, nor suffer to the contrary any act, deed or thing whereby or by reason or means whereof the value of the said property in his possession may be diminished or the same may otherwise be prejudiced in title or estate.

The MORTGAGOR does also agree to pay the Government revenue and the municipal taxes of the said property regularly, and in case he fails to make such payment, the MORTGAGEE shall be at liberty to pay such revenue and taxes, and such sum paid shall be considered an additional principal sum advanced to the MORTGAGOR, and shall carry interest at the rate stipulated above AND LASTLY, the MORTGAGOR also agrees that if he, the MORTGAGOR, does not pay the principal sum with the interest then due on the stipulated date, this conveyance will become absolute and the MORTGAGEE will be entitled to foreclose the mortgaged property, and thereafter the MORTGAGOR, his heirs, executors, administrators or assigns shall be absolutely debarred of all the rights to redeem the same.

The Schedule above referred to

IN WITNESS WHEREOF the parties hereto have executed these presents on the day, month and year first above-written.

Signed, sealed and delivered by AB
the MORTGAGOR in the presence of:

Signed, sealed and delivered by CD
the MORTGAGEE in the presence of:

MEMO OF CONSIDERATION

Received of and from the withinmentioned Mortgagee the sum of Rs. .... being the consideration withinmentioned by Bank Draft No. .... dated .... for Rs. .... issued by X Bank Ltd. payable in Calcutta.

WITNESSES: Received

Signature of the MORTGAGOR

Deed of English Mortgages

THIS DEED OF MORTGAGE made this .... day of .... 2000 BETWEEN AB son of .... residing at .... hereinafter called the MORTGAGOR (which term shall include his heirs, successors, executors, administrators and assigns) of the one part and CD son of .... residing at .... hereinafter called the MORTGAGEE (which term shall include his heirs, successors, executors, administrators and assigns) of the other part. WHEREAS the MORTGAGOR is absolutely seized and possessed or is otherwise well and sufficiently entitled to an absolute estate of inheritance or an estate equivalent thereto free from encumbrances to the lands, hereditaments .... fully mentioned and described in the Schedule hereto AND whereas the MORTGAGOR intending to borrow a sum of Rs. .... approached the MORTGAGEE which the MORTGAGEE has agreed to lend and advance on having repayment thereof with interest at ....% per annum and secured by a conveyance by way of mortgage of the said property. NOW THIS DEED witnesseth that in consideration of the sum of Rs. .... this day paid to the said AB by the said CD (the receipt whereof the said AB hereby acknowledges), the MORTGAGOR hereby agrees with and covenants to pay to the MORTGAGEE on the .... day of .... the sum of Rs. ...., with interest thereon in the meantime at the rate of .... per cent per annum computed from the date of this deed such interest to be paid monthly and every month on the 15th of every current month AND THIS DEED also WITNESSES that for the consideration aforesaid the said AB, as the beneficial owner, does hereby grant, transfer, convey unto and to the use of the said CD ALL THAT etc. (*describe the property*): TO HAVE AND TO HOLD the same absolutely and for ever PROVIDED ALWAYS that if the MORTGAGOR shall pay or cause to be paid the sum of Rs. .... with interest thereon, on the .... day of ...., according to the foregoing agreement in that behalf, the MORTGAGEE, shall, at the request and costs of the MORTGAGOR, reconvey to him or them as he or they shall direct, the said property. AND THAT the MORTGAGOR does hereby covenant unto the MORTGAGEE that the MORTGAGOR has absolute title to the land, hereditaments, messuages and premises hereby granted and conveyed and that the MORTGAGOR has good right, full power, absolute authority and indefeasible title to grant, convey, transfer, assign and assure the same unto and to the use of the MORTGAGEE in the manner hereinbefore indicated and further the MORTGAGOR and all persons having lawfully or equitably any estate or interest in the same shall at all times hereafter during the continuance of the security does execute or perform or cause to be done, executed and performed all such further or other acts, deeds and things as may be reasonably required for further and more perfectly assuring the same unto and in favour of the MORTGAGEE.

PROVIDED, HOWEVER, and it is further agreed by and between the parties that if the MORTGAGOR commits any default in payment of the principal amount on the due date or any three instalments of interest, whether they have been demanded or not it shall be lawful for the MORTGAGEE to institute a suit for sale and to have a Receiver appointed over the mortgaged property.

The Schedule above referred to

IN WITNESS WHEREOF the parties to this Mortgage Deed have executed these presents on the day, month and year first above-written.

Signed, sealed and delivered by AB
the MORTGAGOR in the presence of:

Signed, sealed and delivered by CD
the MORTGAGEE in the presence of:

MEMO OF CONSIDERATION

Received of and from CD the sum of Rs. .... being the loan amount for the said Mortgage.

WITNESS: I say received

Signature

Mortgage of Land and Building to be erected thereon to Secure Present and Future Advances

THIS DEED OF SIMPLE MORTGAGE made this .... day of .... 2000 BETWEEN AB son of .... residing at .... hereinafter called the MORTGAGOR (which term shall include his heirs, successors, representatives and assigns) of the one part and CD Company Ltd. registered under the Companies Act 1956 having its registered office at .... hereinafter referred to as the CD Company, the MORTGAGEE (which term shall include its successors and assigns) of the other part.

WHEREAS AB is the sole owner and in possession in his own right of the open lands measuring .... square feet affronting .... Road in the city of .... and numbered as Plots Nos. 2, 3 and 4 in the .... Housing Scheme of the Improvement Trust free from all encumbrances fully mentioned and described in the Schedule hereto and hereinafter referred to as the said property.

AND WHEREAS the said AB intends to erect a two-storeyed building thereon having five shops on the ground floor and residential quarters on the first floor.

AND WHEREAS the plans of the said building have been approved and sanctioned on the .... day of .... 20....... by the requisite Municipal Corporation.

AND WHEREAS the said AB has approached the said CD Company for a loan or financial accommodation up to Rs. .... (Rupees .... only) immediately against security of the said property and for such further or other sum or sums of money not exceeding Rs. .... (Rupees .... only) in any event and against such security as aforesaid as and when required during the period of construction of the building of the said premises AND whereas the said CD Company has agreed to do so on the assurance of the said AB for repayment of the said sum and all further sums to be advanced to the said AB with interest in all cases at the rate of............ and in the manner hereinafter appearing.

NOW THIS DEED WITNESSES that in pursuance of the said agreement and in consideration of the sum of Rs. .... (Rupees ....) only now paid by the said CD to the said AB which said sum the said AB hereby admits and acknowledges as having received AND ALSO in consideration of the further sum or sums hereinafter to be advanced the said MORTGAGOR hereby covenants with the MORTGAGEE to pay to it within a period of .... years the sum of Rs. .... with interest on the same at the rate of ....% per annum AND ALSO such sum or sums as may hereafter be advanced by the said CD to the said AB with interest thereon at the rate aforesaid calculated from the time or respective times of advancing the same AND it is hereby declared and agreed that the said CD shall upon the requests of AB advance the further sum or sums of money not exceeding limit of Rs. .... (Rupees .... only) as aforesaid.

AND THIS DEED ALSO WITNESSES that in further pursuance of the said agreement and for the consideration aforesaid, the said AB as the beneficial owner hereby charges and assures by way of first mortgage unto the said CD ALL THAT open land comprising Plots Nos. 2, 3 and 4 on the .... Road in the city of .... (*full description*).

AND ALSO ALL THAT the building consisting of five shops and residential quarters now in the course of construction upon the said three plots of land by the said AB with all fittings and fixtures TO HAVE AND TO HOLD the same with all the rights of a simple MORTGAGEE under the Transfer of Property Act. The charge hereunder created shall extend to the building as and when gradually constructed and when completed to the entirety of the same.

PROVIDED ALWAYS that if the said principal sum or sums of money hereinbefore covenanted to be paid with interest at the rate and within the period stipulated shall not be duly paid or if the MORTGAGOR fails and/ or neglects to complete the building or delays in so doing, the MORTGAGEE may at its discretion refuse to make any further advance or advances and shall have the right to enforce the security hereunder created and to sell the property and/or such of the buildings which might then be complete and realise out of the proceeds of such sale all sums due to it together with principal and interest after paying the costs and expenses of such sale and if the mortgage debt be still unsatisfied the MORTGAGEE may enforce the loan against the person or other property of the MORTGAGOR and in case of there being a surplus, the same shall be refunded to the MORTGAGOR.

PROVIDED HOWEVER and it is further agreed by and between the parties that if the MORTGAGOR commits any default in payment of the principal amount on the due date or any three instalments of interest whether they have been demanded or not it shall be lawful for the MORTGAGEE to institute a suit for sale and to have a Receiver appointed over the mortgaged property.

The Schedule above referred to

IN WITNESS WHEREOF the parties hereto have executed these presents on the day, month and year first above-written.

Signed, sealed and delivered by AB
the MORTGAGOR in the presence of:

Signed, sealed and delivered by CD
the MORTGAGEE in the presence of:

MEMO OF CONSIDERATION

Received of and from CD the Mortgagee the sum of Rs. .... (Rupees ....) being the loan amount for the mortgage of the property mentioned above.

WITNESS: I say received

Signature

Deed of English Mortgage to Secure Existing Debt and Future Advances

THIS DEED OF MORTGAGE is made this .... day of .... 2000 BETWEEN AB son of .... residing at .... (hereinafter referred to as the MORTGAGOR which term shall include his heirs, representatives and assigns) of the one part and CD son of .... residing at .... (hereinafter referred to as the MORTGAGEE which term shall include his heirs, successors and assigns) of the other part.

WHEREAS the said AB is the sole and absolute owner of the property intended to be hereby mortgaged: AND WHEREAS the said AB is indebted to the said CD in the sum of Rs. ...., and he has agreed to secure repayment thereof, and of any further or other sum or sums of money up to Rs. .... which may hereafter be advanced to him by the said CD with interest for the same, in the manner hereinafter expressed; NOW THIS INDENTURE WITNESSES that in consideration of the sum of Rs. .... already due and payable by the said AB to the said CD which the said AB does hereby admit, acknowledge and confirm and further advance of Rs. .... to be hereafter made at the reasonable satisfaction of CD making thus a sum total of Rs. .... upon having repayment thereof with interest at ....% per annum and secured by a conveyance of the property hereunder fully described, the said AB hereby agrees with the said CD that he shall pay him, on the .... day of .... the sum of Rs. .... with interest for the same at the rate of .... per cent per annum, computed from the date of this deed: AND ALSO to pay the said CD such sum or sums of money as may hereafter be advanced by the said CD to the said AB with interest thereon at the rate aforesaid, computed from the time or respective times of advancing the same: AND ALSO, so long as any principal money hereinbefore agreed to be paid shall remain unpaid after the day hereby appointed for payment thereof, to pay to the said CD interest thereon at the rate aforesaid on the. .... day of ...., and the .... day of .... AND THIS DEED ALSO WITNESSES that in consideration of the premises the said AB as the beneficial owner hereby grants, transfers, conveys to the said CD ALL THAT, etc. (*describe the property*): TO HAVE AND TO HOLD the same to the said CD absolutely and for ever: PROVIDED ALWAYS that if the principal sum or sums of money hereinbefore agreed to be paid, with interest thereon, shall be duly paid at the time or times hereinbefore appointed for payment thereof, then and in such case the said mortgaged property shall, at the request and costs of the said AB, be reconveyed to him absolutely.

AND THAT the MORTGAGOR doth hereby covenant unto the MORTGAGEE that the MORTGAGOR has absolute title to the land, hereditaments, messuages and premises hereby granted and conveyed and that the MORTGAGOR has good right, full power absolute authority and indefeasible title to grant convey transfer assign and assure the same unto and to the use of the MORTGAGEE in the manner hereinbefore indicated and further the MORTGAGOR and all persons having lawfully or equitably any estate or interest in the same shall at all time hereafter during the continuance of the security do execute perform or cause to be done executed and performed all such further or other acts, deeds and things as may be reasonably required for further and more perfectly assuring the same unto and in favour of MORTGAGEE.

The Schedule above referred to

IN WITNESS WHEREOF the parties hereto have executed these presents on the day, month and year first above-written.

Signed, sealed and delivered by AB
the MORTGAGOR in the presence of:

Signed, sealed and delivered by CD
the MORTGAGEE in the presence of:

Endorsements to be made on the above Deed on the Occasion of a further Advance

I HEREBY ACKNOWLEDGE to have this day received from the within-named CD the sum of Rs. ...., being a further sum advanced on the within-mentioned security in terms of the mortgage Deed.

(Date) AB

Deed of Further Charge on Mortgaged Property

THIS DEED OF FURTHER charge made this .... day of .... 2000 BETWEEN AB son of .... residing at .... hereinafter called the MORTGAGOR (which term shall include his heirs, successors, executors, administrators and assigns) of the one part and CD son of .... residing at .... hereinafter called the MORTGAGEE (which term shall include his heirs, successors, executors, administrators and assigns) of the other part, and supplemental to a deed of mortgage (hereinafter called the PRINCIPAL DEED), dated the. .... day of .... and made between the same parties, and registered in Book I, Vol. ....

pages .... etc. etc., for securing the sum of Rs. .... and interest at the rate of .... per cent per annum, on the property at, etc. WITNESSES, that in consideration of a further sum of Rs. .... now paid to the MORTGAGOR by the MORTGAGEE (the receipt of which sum the MORTGAGOR hereby acknowledges), the MORTGAGOR hereby agrees with the MORTGAGEE to pay or cause to be paid to him on the .... day of .... the said sum of Rs. ...., with interest thereon in the meantime at the rate of Rs. .... per cent per annum; AND ALSO as long thereafter as any principal money remains due under this further charge, to pay to him interest thereon at the same rate by equal half-yearly instalments on the half-yearly days as mentioned in the Principal Deed for payment of interest.

For the same consideration, the MORTGAGOR HEREBY FURTHER AGREES with the MORTGAGEE that the entire property as comprised in the PRINCIPAL DEED fully mentioned and described in the Schedule hereto shall remain charged also for the payment to the MORTGAGEE of the said further sum of Rs. .... and the interest thereon hereunder agreed to be paid, as well as the sum of Rs. .... and interest secured by the PRINCIPAL DEED, AND that all the provisions of the PRINCIPAL DEED shall *mutatis mutandis* apply as if the principal sum (Rs. ....) and the interest thereon had been originally secured by the PRINCIPAL DEED.

The Schedule above referred to

IN WITNESS WHEREOF the parties hereto have executed these presents on the day, month and year first above-written.

Signed, sealed and delivered by AB
the MORTGAGOR in the presence of:

Signed, sealed and delivered by CD
the MORTGAGEE in the presence of:

MEMO OF CONSIDERATION

Deed of the Reconveyance of Mortgaged Property

THIS DEED OF RECONVEYANCE made this .... day of .... 2000 BETWEEN CD son of .... residing at .... hereinafter called the MORTGAGEE (which term shall include his heirs, successors, legal representatives and assigns) of the one part and AB son of .... residing at .... hereinafter called the MORTGAGOR (which term shall include his heirs, successors, legal representatives and assigns) of the other part WHEREAS by an Indenture of Mortgage dated .... made BETWEEN the parties hereto and registered in Book I, vol. ...., page .... to .... being No. .... of the office of Sub-Registrar of .... of .... it was witnessed that for the consideration mentioned therein the property fully mentioned and described in the schedule hereto and hereinafter referred to as the said property was granted, transferred, assigned and assured unto and to the use of the MORTGAGEE subject to the proviso for redemption thereunder contained AND whereas the MORTGAGOR has paid up, satisfied and discharged the entirety of the mortgage debt inclusive of all interest due thereon and also all costs due and payable to the MORTGAGEE on that account AND WHEREAS the MORTGAGEE has delivered back to the mortgagor all the title deeds in respect of the said property including the deeds of mortgage with full satisfaction endorsed thereon. Now this Indenture witnesses that in consideration of all principal money, interest and costs due under the hereinbefore recited Indenture of Mortgage having been paid, satisfied and discharged which the MORTGAGEE hereby admits, acknowledges and confirms the said CD hereby release the said AB from all his liability and obligation under the deed of mortgage hereinbefore recited and also the mortgaged property and does hereby grant, transfer and reconvey the same unto and to the use of the said AB ALL THAT property mentioned in the schedule TO HAVE AND TO HOLD the same absolutely, and forever freed and discharged from all principal moneys, interest and costs secured by and from all claims and demands and the security on that account created under the hereinbefore recited Indenture of Mortgage AND that said CD does hereby covenant with the said AB that he has not done, executed or suffered to the contrary any act, deed or thing whereby or reason or means whereof the mortgaged property or any part thereof may be affected or prejudiced in title or estate or he, the said CD, may be hindered or prevented from reconveying the same in the manner hereinbefore indicated.

The Schedule above referred to

IN WITNESS WHEREOF the parties hereto have executed these presents on the day, month and year first above-written.

Signed, sealed and delivered by AB
the MORTGAGOR in the presence of:

Signed, sealed and delivered by CD
the MORTGAGEE in the presence of:

MEMO OF CONSIDERATION

Deed of Release of Mortgaged Property

THIS DEED OF RELEASE made this .... day of .... 2000 BETWEEN CD son of .... residing at .... hereinafter called the RELEASOR of the one part and AB son of .... residing at .... hereinafter called the RELEASEE of the other part.

WHEREAS by a deed of simple mortgage dated the .... day of .... made BETWEEN the parties hereto and registered in the office of Sub-Registrar of .... in Book I, vol. ...., page .... to .... being No. .... for the year................ the properties described in the Schedule hereto were mortgaged by AB to CD to secure the repayment of the sum of Rs. .... lent and advanced by CD to AB with interest thereon at the rate of .... per cent per annum AND WHEREAS the said AB has paid to the said CD a sum of Rs. .... in full satisfaction of all the dues of the said CD under the said deed inclusive of interest and costs. *Now this deed of release* witnesses that in consideration of the sum of Rs. .... being the principal sum, interest and costs due under the said deed having been paid by AB to CD (the receipt whereof the said CD does hereby admit, acknowledge and confirm the said CD does hereby release, discharge and reassure the properties described in the Schedule hereto from all principal moneys, interest, costs, claims and demands secured by the said deed of mortgage AND the said CD hereby covenants with the said AB that the said CD has not done, executed or performed or knowing suffered to the contrary or been a party or privy to any act, deed or thing whereby or by reason or means whereof the said properties or any one or part thereof is, are or may be affected or prejudiced in title or estate in any way whatsoever or that the said CD may be hindered or prevented from releasing and reassuring the same in the manner hereinbefore indicated.

The Schedule above referred to

IN WITNESS WHEREOF the parties herein have executed these presents on the day, month and year first above-written.

Signed, sealed and delivered by CD
the RELEASOR in the presence of:

Signed, sealed and delivered by AB
the RELEASEE in the presence of:

MEMO OF CONSIDERATION

Memorandum of Mortgage by Deposit of Title-deeds

(SHORT FORM)

MEMORANDUM that this .... day of ...., AB of, etc. (THE MORTGAGOR), as beneficial owner, has deposited with CD of etc. (THE MORTGAGEE), the original title-deeds comprised in the Schedule A hereto, relating to the premises belonging to the said AB and situate at .... etc., described in Schedule B with intent to create security thereon for repayment to the said CD of the sum of Rs. .... this day lent and advanced by the said CD to the said AB on demand with interest for the same from this date at the rate of Rs. .... per cent per annum.

The said AB does hereby undertake as and when required by the said CD to execute and register at the costs of the said AB a legal mortgage in such form and containing such covenants and provisions as he may reasonably require.

The Schedule A above-referred to

Description of the Title Deeds deposited

The Schedule B above-referred to

Description of the property

Signature of the MORTGAGOR

Deed of Sub-mortgage

THIS DEED OF SUB-MORTGAGE made this .... day of ....2000 BETWEEN AB son of .... residing at .... hereinafter called the SUB-MORTGAGOR (which term shall include his heirs, successors, legal representatives and assigns) of the one part and CD son of .... residing at .... hereinafter called the SUB-MORTGAGEE (which term shall include his heirs, successors, legal representatives and assigns) of the other part.

WHEREAS by a deed of mortgage deed dated the .... day of .... and registered in Book I, vol. ...., pages .... to. .... being No. .... in the office of............. the properties described in the Schedule hereto were mortgaged by XY to the SUB-MORTGAGOR AB as security for repayment of the sum of Rs. .... lent and advanced by the SUB-MORTGAGOR AB to XY with interest thereon at the rate of .... per cent per annum .... subject to the terms and conditions thereunder contained AND WHEREAS the said XY has paid from time to time an aggregated sum of Rs. .... in part payment of interest due on such mortgage AND WHEREAS a sum of Rs. .... as principal and a further sum of Rs. .... as interest are still due and owing to the said AB by the said XY upon the said mortgage AND WHEREAS the SUB-MORTGAGEE has agreed to lend and advance to the SUB-MORTGAGOR a sum of Rs. .... upon the security of the amount due under and by virtue of the said mortgage and against sub-mortgage of the said properties NOW THIS DEED OF SUB-MORTGAGE WITNESSES that in pursuance of the said agreement and in consideration of the sum of Rs. .... lent and advanced by the SUB-MORTGAGEE to the SUB-MORTGAGOR (the receipt whereof the SUB-MORTGAGOR hereby acknowledges) the SUB-MORTGAGOR does hereby covenant with and agree to repay the SUB-MORTGAGEE the said sum of Rs. .... with interest thereon at the rate of Rs. ....per cent per annum on or before the .... day of .... and as security for the same hereby transfers all the debt secured by the aforesaid mortgage deed and benefits of the charge of and all securities thereunder created on all properties mortgaged as also all rights, remedies and benefits expressly or impliedly conferred upon the SUB-MORTGAGOR under and by virtue of the said mortgage-deed or otherwise by law or in equity.

The Schedule above referred to

IN WITNESS WHEREOF the parties hereto have executed these presents on the day, month and year first above-written.

Signed, sealed and delivered by AB
the SUB-MORTGAGOR in the presence of:

Signed, sealed and delivered by CD
the SUB-MORTGAGEE in the presence of:

MEMO OF CONSIDERATION

Mortgage-deed in favour of Bank to Secure Indebtedness on Loan Account

THIS INDENTURE made the .... day of .... 2000 BETWEEN AB of .... (hereinafter called the MORTGAGOR which expression shall be deemed to include his heirs, executors, administrators and assigns) of the one part AND the ELH Bank Limited, a Joint Stock Company incorporated under the Indian Companies Act and having its registered office at .... (hereinafter called the BANK which expression shall include its assigns) of the other part.

WHEREAS the MORTGAGOR is the owner and the Proprietor of the messuages, lands, hereditaments and premises described in the Schedule hereto and intended to be hereby mortgaged free from encumbrances and whereas the BANK has agreed to lend to the MORTGAGOR the sum of Rs. .... only on having the repayment thereof with interest secured in the manner hereinafter appearing.

NOW THIS INDENTURE WITNESSETH as follows:

1. In pursuance of the said agreement and in consideration of the sum of Rs. .... paid on or before the execution of these presents by the BANK to the MORTGAGOR (the receipt whereof the MORTGAGOR hereby acknowledges) the MORTGAGOR hereby covenants with the BANK as follows:

(*a*) That the MORTGAGOR will pay to the BANK the said principal sum of .... by equal half-yearly instalments of Rs. .... on the first day of .... and the first day of .... each year, commencing from ...., and any interest due thereon so that the whole debt is paid in full on or before the ....

(*b*) That the MORTGAGOR shall in addition pay interest on the principal sum secured by these presents at the rate of .... per cent per annum.

(*c*) That the MORTGAGOR shall pay to the BANK interest at the rate stipulated in cl. (2) with half yearly rests on the .... and .... up to date of realisation in case the BANK has to institute a suit for recovery of the principal and interest or any portion thereof that may be due to the BANK. And if at any time six months' interest payable under these presents shall remain owing and unpaid then the interest so in arrears shall be converted into principal and until paid off shall carry interest at the aforesaid rate of .... per cent per annum with half-yearly rests.

(*d*) That the MORTGAGOR shall and will during the subsistence of this security at his own costs and charges and expense keep and maintain the said premises hereby mortgaged in good repair and tenantable condition.

(*e*) It is hereby agreed and declared that in case any of the instalments of principal or interest payable under these presents be not satisfied on the dates hereinbefore appointed for the payments of such instalments of principal or interest then the whole amount of principal remaining unpaid together with interest due shall at once become payable to the BANK and the BANK may forthwith enforce at once any of the remedies to which a holder of a simple mortgage is entitled under the Transfer of Property Act.

(*f*) That the MORTGAGOR will within one month from the date of these presents insure and keep insured the building and such other part of the mortgaged premises as are of an insurable nature or any part or parts thereof from loss or damage by fire in the full value thereof in some insurance office to be approved of by the BANK in the joint names of the MORTGAGOR and the BANK as mortgagee (the relative policy to contain the agreed BANK clause of the Fire Insurance Association) and will duly pay all premiums and sums of money payable for that purpose and will deliver to the BANK the policy for such insurance and the receipt for every such payment within seven days after it shall become due and in case the MORTGAGOR shall neglect or refuse to keep the said premises insured to the amount aforesaid or to deliver such policy and receipts as aforesaid then and in every such case it shall be lawful for the BANK to insure the same to the amount aforesaid or any less amount and all sums of money expended by the Bank in or about such insurance as aforesaid with interest for the same at the rate of Rs. .... per cent per annum (with half-yearly rests) computed from the time or respective times of advancing the same shall be repaid by the MORTGAGOR to the BANK on demand and in the meantime shall be a charge on the premises hereby mortgaged in addition to the principal sum and interest thereon.

(*g*) That the MORTGAGOR agrees that all sums of money awarded as compensation for any compulsory acquisition of any portion of the mortgaged property by any Government, municipal or railway or district board authority shall be receivable by the BANK direct on behalf of the MORTGAGOR and that such money as well as moneys received under and by virtue of any such insurance as aforesaid shall at the option of the BANK either be forthwith applied in or towards substantially rebuilding, re-instating or repairing the said premises or in or towards payment of the principal money, interest and costs for the time being remaining due on the security of these presents.

2. For the consideration aforesaid and in further pursuance of the said agreement the MORTGAGOR hereby grants and transfers by way of simple mortgage unto the BANK all the property described in the Schedule hereto together with all rights, easements and appurtenances thereto and all his rights, title and interest in and to the said premises to the intent that all the said premises hereby mortgaged shall remain and be charged by way of simple mortgage and free from all encumbrances as security for the payment to the Bank of the said principal money, interest and costs in accordance with the covenants hereinbefore contained.

3. That the MORTGAGOR shall allow the BANK, its servants, agents and surveyors at all reasonable times to enter the said premises and view and examine the state and condition thereof.

4. Provided always that the MORTGAGOR may at any time after giving the BANK thirty days' notice pay the BANK the whole of the principal sum and interest and costs that may be due to the BANK.

The Schedule above referred to

IN WITNESS WHEREOF the parties hereto have executed these presents on the day, month and year first above-written.

Signed, sealed and delivered by AB
the MORTGAGOR in the presence of:

Signed, sealed and delivered by
Mr. .... pursuant to
Board Resolution of ....
of ELH Bank Ltd. in the presence
of:

MEMO OF CONSIDERATION

Memorandum of Pledge of Movables

To

CD of, etc. (the PLEDGEE)

The articles specified in the annexed schedule which I, the undersigned AB of, etc (THE PLEDGOR) have this day deposited with you, are to be held as a security for the repayment to you, within .... months from this date, of the sum of Rs. .... which you have this day lent and advanced to me, together with interest at the rate of Rs. .... per cent. per annum. And I hereby authorize and empower you, in the event of non-payment thereof within that period, to sell the same or cause the same to be sold at any time in any way you may think proper, at my risk and on my account and out of the proceeds of such sale, after paying all costs, charges and expenses of and incidental to the same, to retain, appropriate the said sum of Rs. .... and interest, and to pay the balance (if any) to me. You would not be liable for any loss or damage of or to the said articles unless caused by your own wilful negligence or default. In case of any shortfall I shall remain personally responsible to pay for the same to you with interest at the aforesaid rate.

Signed, sealed and delivered

AB

The Schedule above-referred to

Mortgage-deed with Guarantors

THIS DEED OF MORTGAGE is made this .... day of .... 2000 BETWEEN X Ltd. an existing company within the meaning of the Companies Act 1956 having its registered office at .... (hereinafter referred to as the MORTGAGORS which term shall include its successors and assigns) of the first part and Friendly Society Ltd. registered under the West Bengal Societies Registration Act and having its principal office at .... (hereinafter referred to as the MORTGAGEES which term shall include its successors and assigns) of the second part and AB and CD, sons of EF residing at .... (hereinafter called the GUARANTORS which term shall include their heirs, executors and administrators) of the third part. WHEREAS the MORTGAGORS have, by the Indenture dated ...., acquired from the Improvement Trust a Plot No. .... situated in .... measuring .... acres in area or thereabout (and more particularly described in the Schedule hereunder) on lease with option to purchase all the said land together with all rights, easements and appurtenances to the same except mines, and mineral products, buried treasures, petrol oil and quarries whatsoever in, under or within the said land as mentioned in the said Indenture, for a consideration of Rs. ....

payable in seven instalments as therein described, out of which the said MORTGAGORS have paid to the said Improvement Trust, first .... instalment with interest amounting to Rs. .... in addition to a sum of Rs. .... deposited as earnest money to be adjusted against the last instalment, and now only the remaining .... instalments of Rs. .... each (which shall fall due on .... and .... respectively) remain to be paid out of which Rs. .... earnest money as aforesaid shall be adjusted against the last instalment. A sum of Rs. .... therefore remains to be paid to the said Lessor in respect of the aforesaid plot of land; AND WHEREAS the MORTGAGORS have on the said plot of land erected a building at the cost of about Rs. .... and have besides machinery installed thereon worth about Rs. .... AND WHEREAS the MORTGAGORS are under their Memorandum and Articles of Association empowered to raise money and secure the payment thereof by mortgage or otherwise of all those assets; AND WHEREAS in exercise of the said powers, the Board of Directors have by their Resolution No. .... dated .... authorized Shree .... ; and Shree .... two of the directors of the Company, to sign and execute relevant mortgage-deed in favour of the MORTGAGEES and to comply with all other formalities (including registration, etc.) in respect thereof.

NOW THIS INDENTURE WITNESSETH as follows:

1. That in consideration of Rs. .... to be paid by the said MORTGAGEES to the MORTGAGORS by their cheque No. .... dated .... on .... Bank Ltd., at the time of registration before the Sub-Registrar, the said MORTGAGORS, as beneficial owners thereof, do hereby charge and assure unto the said MORTGAGEES, all the rights and interests in the said plot of land, building and the machinery aforesaid and more particularly described in the Schedule hereunder to have and to hold the same unto and to the use of the said MORTGAGEES subject, however, to the terms of the Indenture of Lease dated .... except that the amount of Rs. .... still unpaid to the said Lessor shall be paid by the MORTGAGORS as and when it becomes payable under the terms of the said Indenture of Lease. Provided always that if the said MORTGAGOR shall pay to the said MORTGAGEES on or before the expiry of two years from the date of these presents the mortgage money including interest, if any, as may be then accruing thereon, then and in such an event the MORTGAGEES, will at any time thereafter upon the request and at the cost of the said MORTGAGORS release and retransfer the said property unto the said MORTGAGORS or as they shall direct.

2. That the MORTGAGORS hereby covenant with the MORTGAGEES that they shall pay or cause to be paid to the said MORTGAGEES by way of interest on the aforesaid principal amount of Rs. .... calculated at the rate of .... per cent. in the meantime.

3. That the MORTGAGORS further covenant with the MORTGAGEES that notwithstanding the period of two years stipulated in cl. (1) hereof, the

MORTGAGEES shall be entitled to recover the mortgage money together with interest then accruing thereon, if any, after giving three months' clear notice to MORTGAGORS.

4. That the Guarantors in consideration of the MORTGAGEES having advanced the sum of Rs. .... to the MORTGAGORS as aforesaid, do hereby agree and covenant with the MORTGAGEES that if for any reason the MORTGAGORS wind up or suspend their business or are unable to pay this debt or the Lessor forfeits the lease of the plot of land aforesaid in default of the observance of the terms of the Indenture of lease aforesaid or any one or more of them or if there is a shortfall or deficiency in the sale proceeds of the mortgaged property, so that the mortgaged money is not fully recovered therefrom then and in such events, they will be jointly and severally liable for the payment of the mortgage money to the MORTGAGEES or such part thereof as might the remain unrecovered at that time, which can in that case be recovered from their respective persons and properties.

5. Nothing herein contained shall in any way prejudice any of the remedies available to the MORTGAGEES under the law. Nor shall the liability of the GUARANTORS be in any wise affected by any concession or indulgence shown by the MORTGAGEES to the MORTGAGORS or by any extension of time granted by the former to the latter beyond that specified in cl. (3) hereof or otherwise.

6. And it is hereby declared that the expression MORTGAGORS and MORTGAGEES and the GUARANTORS where the context allows, includes all persons deriving title under them respectively.

The Schedule above referred to

IN WITNESS WHEREOF the parties hereto have executed these presents on the day, month and year first above-written.

Signed, sealed and delivered by X Ltd. through Mr. .... pursuant to Board Resolution dated .... in the presence of:

Signed, sealed and delivered by Mr. .... pursuant to Resolution of Friendly Society Ltd. dated .... in the presence of:

Signed, sealed and delivered by AB and CD Guarantors in the presence of:

MEMO OF CONSIDERATION

Deed of English Mortgage
Where part of the Consideration Money of a Sale is Unpaid

THIS MORTGAGE DEED is made this .... day of .... 2000 BETWEEN AB son of .... residing at .... (hereinafter called the MORTGAGOR which term shall where the subject or context admits of include his heirs, executors, administrators, representatives and assigns) of the first part and CD son of .... residing at .... (hereinafter called the MORTGAGEE which term shall unless the context otherwise requires include his heirs, executors, administrators, representative and assigns) of the second part.

WHEREAS the MORTGAGEE was the sole and absolute owner of Premises No. .... fully mentioned and described in the Schedule hereto and hereafter referred to as the said property AND WHEREAS by an Indenture of Conveyance executed this day immediately prior to these presents the MORTGAGEE has granted, conveyed, sold, transferred, assigned and assured the said property unto and in favour of the MORTGAGOR for the sum of Rs. .... absolutely and forever.

AND whereas at the treaty for the sale it was finally agreed by and BETWEEN the parties hereto that the MORTGAGOR shall pay a sum of Rs. .... and secure the balance at Rs. .... by execution of an English Mortgagee on the said property on terms hereunder contained AND WHEREAS the MORTGAGOR is by virtue of the said conveyance absolutely seized and possessed or is otherwise well and sufficiently entitled to an absolute estate of inheritance or an estate equivalent thereto free from encumbrances to the said property. Now this Indenture witnesseth that in consideration of the sum of Rs. .... being the unpaid balance of the consideration money in respect of the sale and in consideration of the terms and conditions finally agreed to and decided between the parties and in consideration of the possession of the property having been delivered to the MORTGAGOR in pursuance of the said conveyance, the MORTGAGOR does hereby agree with and covenant to pay to the MORTGAGEE on or before the .... day of .... in the manner hereunder indicated the said sum of Rs. .... with interest thereon in the meantime at the rate of .... per cent per annum computed from the date of these presents such interest to be paid monthly every month on the .... of every current month without any delay or a single default and the MORTGAGOR as beneficial owner does hereby grant, transfer, convey, assign and assure unto and to the use of the MORTGAGEE the said property with all building, yards, courtyards, areas, drains, sewers, rights, liberties, easements, privileges, appendages, appurtenance whatsoever and all deeds, attaches, muniments, writings and evidences of title which in any way relate to the said promises TO HAVE AND TO HOLD the same absolutely and for ever subject to the proviso for redemption hereunder contained, that is, if the MORTGAGOR shall pay or cause to be paid the sum of Rs. .... with interest thereon at 10% per annum for the debt hereof on or before the .... day of .... according to the agreement in that behalf, the MORTGAGEE, his heirs, representatives or assigns shall, at the request and costs of the MORTGAGOR, his heirs, representatives or assigns reconvey to him or them as he or they shall direct the said property. And that the MORTGAGOR does hereby covenant unto the MORTGAGEE that the MORTGAGOR has absolute title to the land, hereditaments, messuages and premises hereby granted and conveyed and that the mortgagor has good right, full power, absolute authority and indefeasible title to grant, convey, transfer, assign and assure the same unto and to the use of the MORTGAGEE in the manner hereinbefore indicated and further the MORTGAGOR and all persons having lawfully or equitably an estate or interest in the same shall at all times hereafter during the continuance of the security would execute or perform or cause to be done, executed and performed all such further or other acts, deeds and things as may be reasonably required for further and more perfectly assuring the same unto and in favour of the MORTGAGEE.

PROVIDED, however, and it is further agreed by and between the parties that if the MORTGAGOR defaults in payment of any instalments of the principal amount on the due dates or any two instalments of interest or commits any breach of the covenants, conditions and stipulations hereunder contained to be observed and performed on his or their part the entire mortgage money shall become at once due and payable and it shall be lawful for the MORTGAGEE to institute a suit for enforcement of the mortgage and sale and to have a Receiver appointed over the mortgaged property notwithstanding the fact that the period of redemption hereunder provided shall not have then expired.

And that the MORTGAGOR, his heirs, executors, administrators, representatives and assigns to the intent that he shall personally remain responsible for performance of all covenants on his part covenant and agree with the MORTGAGEE as follows that the mortgagor shall, after appointment of such Receiver, shall not receive or collect any payment in respect of the mortgaged premises and shall forthwith deliver possession and attorn all tenancies to the Receiver so appointed without any objection of any kind whatsoever, and that the MORTGAGEE shall be entitled to apply for such direction or directions on the Receiver as in law he may be entitled to do so.

And also in case the MORTGAGOR fails and/or neglects to pay the mortgage money as hereunder provided, the MORTGAGEE shall be entitled to cause the property to be sold, and in that event he shall, out of the proceeds of such sale at the first instance, be entitled to repayment of the mortgage money with all interest at the rate aforesaid payable till the date of payment or realization through court and in the event of any deficiency, the MORTGAGOR and also the confirming party shall remain personally liable for the same and submit to a personal decree on that account.

And that the MORTGAGOR shall at all times during the continuity of the security hereunder created keep the property with all buildings, erections, fixtures, etc. in good repair and condition and shall not cause nor suffer, any loss, damage or mischief thereto until the said sum of Rs..... with all interest and the costs, charges and expenses of the MORTGAGEE, if any, is fully paid and also free from encumbrances and attachment and duly insured against fire and other insurable risks during the subsistence of this mortgage and shall not deliver possession of the property to any person or persons. And that the MORTGAGOR shall not suffer any decree or attachment affecting the property and that the MORTGAGEE shall be entitled to have property insured unless the mortgaged premises already insured by the MORTGAGOR who shall give timely information thereof to the MORTGAGEE and any expenses incurred by the MORTGAGEE in that behalf shall be added to his claim and shall bear interest thereon at the rate mentioned above.

And that the MORTGAGOR shall not grant any lease or leases of the property or any portion thereof not let out the same except on monthly tenancy basis nor erect any temple or other place of religious worship, nor create any trust or debutter or settlement or endowment except with the consent and permission in writing of the MORTGAGEE who shall be entitled to refuse in all such cases at his absolute discretion without assigning any reasons. The MORTGAGOR shall, in the event of any such lease or leases granted with the permission of the MORTGAGEE, keep the mortgagee apprised of the terms and conditions under which the MORTGAGOR shall propose to give the mortgaged premises or portion thereof on lease and shall give sufficient notice thereof prior to the grant of any such lease and shall also make the entire premium if any available to the MORTGAGEE who shall credit and adjust the same against the mortgage debt.

And that MORTGAGOR shall, during the subsistence of this security, pay all his income-tax and other personal taxes and all public charges, *e.g.* rates and other assessments, impositions and outgoings in respect of the property and produce for inspection of the MORTGAGEE all paid up bills and challans as and when demanded nor submit to nor suffer any attachment or charge on the mortgaged property.

And that in case the MORTGAGOR sells any portion of the property, he shall obtain prior permission in writing from the MORTGAGEE and has to make the entire consideration money available to the MORTGAGEE who shall adjust the sum or sums so received *in pro tanto* satisfaction of the mortgage debt due to him.

And that on payment of the mortgage money and all expenses and charges that may have accrued due to the MORTGAGEE from the MORTGAGOR up till the date of redemption, the MORTGAGEE shall reconvey the mortgaged premises to the MORTGAGOR at the costs and expenses of the MORTGAGOR free from all encumbrances, if any, created by the MORTGAGEE in respect of the mortgaged premises and return all documents of title or other necessary documents, which may be in possession of the MORTGAGEE, having been delivered to him by the MORTGAGOR or his representative in interest at any time prior to such redemption.

And that the MORTGAGEE shall have the right to assign the mortgage debt together with the security or nominate any person or persons to receive the mortgage money as shall remain outstanding from time to time and receipts of such person or persons shall be a complete discharge to the MORTGAGOR who shall have no liability to see the application of the money. And that MORTGAGOR shall keep the MORTGAGEE informed of all proceedings if any, for compulsory acquisition of the mortgaged property and developments from time to time and shall consent to the payment of the claim of the MORTGAGEE in full at the first instance together with all costs, charges and expenses ancillary or incidental thereto notwithstanding the period of redemption hereunder provided shall not have expired.

And that these presents shall at all times he construed as an English MORTGAGEE within the meaning of Transfer of Property Act and the MORTGAGEE shall have and be entitled to all powers, authorities, rights, remedies and reliefs open to the MORTGAGEE of the same description and that all notices, letters, etc. addressed to the MORTGAGOR shall be deemed to have been sufficiently served if sent at his residence or hereinbefore mentioned under certificate of posting.

The Schedule

IN WITNESS WHEREOF the parties hereto have executed these presents on the day, month and year first above-written.

Signed, sealed and delivered by AB
the MORTGAGOR in the presence of:

Signed, sealed and delivered by CD
the MORTGAGEE in the presence of:

Deed of Floating Charge

THIS INDENTURE MADE this .... day of .... 2000 BETWEEN X Ltd. a Company registered under the Companies Act 1956 having its registered office at .... (hereinafter referred to as the MORTGAGOR which term shall unless the context requires otherwise include his successors and assigns) of the one part and CD son of .... residing at .... (hereinafter referred to as the MORTGAGEE which term shall include unless the context otherwise requires his heirs, executors, legal representatives and assigns) of the other part.

WHEREAS the MORTGAGOR is in urgent need of capital for the purpose of its business.

WHEREAS at a meeting of the Board of Directors of the MORTGAGOR, held at its registered office on .... day of .... it was resolved that a sum of Rs. .... be raised as the loan on security of all the assets of the MORTGAGOR by creating floating charge thereon. And whereas the MORTGAGEE has agreed to lend and advance the same sum of Rs. .... upon the security of the entire undertaking of the MORTGAGOR as hereunder created. Now this Indenture witnesses that in pursuance of the said agreement and in consideration of the loan of Rs. .... advanced by the MORTGAGEE to the MORTGAGOR simultaneously with the execution of these presents, the MORTGAGOR doeth hereby covenant with the MORTGAGEE to repay the same on the.......... day of .... 2005 and shall meanwhile until such repayment pay interest thereon at the rate of .... per cent per annum.

And this Indenture further witnesseth that in pursuance of the said agreements and the consideration aforesaid the mortgagor doeth hereby grant, convey, transfer, assure, assign and confirm unto the MORTGAGEE free from all encumbrances all the furniture, materials for manufacture, stores, stocks whether in process or otherwise, manufactured goods, machinery, fixtures, fittings, tools, implements, goods, chattels and effects which now or hereafter may belong to or be used or acquired by the MORTGAGOR in its said business whether mentioned in the said Schedules hereunder written or not with all accessories, additions, substitutes, replacements and the assets and book debts the particulars whereof are entered in the books of account of the said business of the MORTGAGOR and all moneys receivable by the MORTGAGOR by sale of their shares and/or by way of calls on shares or otherwise in connection with the said business of the MORTGAGOR and all securities for money and the benefit of all existing contracts and orders for the supply of articles and things manufactured by them in their said business and all goods, chattels and things which now are or may hereafter during the continuance of this security be placed or brought into or manufactured for the purposes of the said business of the MORTGAGOR whether in substitution of the goods, chattels and things mentioned in the said schedules or otherwise ALSO all the debts, securities, moneys, properties, freehold or leasehold and assets which now belong or hereafter may belong to the MORTGAGOR together with all the sheds, structures and factories as belong to the MORTGAGOR and as shown in the map or plan annexed hereto AND ALL the estate, right, title, interest, claim, demand whatsoever both at law and in equity of the MORTGAGOR in the properties hereinbefore mentioned and hereby transferred, assigned and assured and all deeds, documents and other evidence of title which in any wise relate or may relate hereafter to the said properties transferred and assigned (all the said properties transferred, assured and assigned by these presents being collectively hereafter referred to them as the mortgaged property) subject to the proviso that if the MORTGAGOR shall pay on or before the .... day of .... the said sum of Rs. .... with interest thereon at the rate of .... per annum and all other sums of money due and payable to the MORTGAGEE under these presents, then and in such an event the MORTGAGEE shall, at the costs of the MORTGAGOR, reconvey and reassure the mortgaged property unto and to the use of the MORTGAGOR at the costs and expenses of the MORTGAGOR. The charge hereunder created shall be a floating charge on all assets of the MORTGAGOR from time to time as a going concern. It will attach on the subject and the undertaking of the company all properties, present and future, as changing from time to time in the varying condition in which the same will happen and shall crystallise only on liquidation unless the same is for the purpose of reconstruction or in the event the interest or capital hereunder advanced falling in arrear.

The MORTGAGOR shall, during the subsistence of the security created by these presents, regularly and punctually pay from its business or otherwise all income-tax, sales tax, all such rates, taxes, assessments and impositions which now is or are or may hereafter be payable in respect of the said business and the premises where the said business are now or may hereafter be carried on and/or the mortgaged property or any portion thereof may be kept, stored or stocked as and when the same shall from time to time become due and payable and produce the receipts or other papers showing such payments to the MORTGAGEE for its inspection and in default of payment as aforesaid of the same by the MORTGAGOR the MORTGAGEE may in its discretion pay the same and add the same to its claim and further that the MORTGAGOR shall neither terminate nor accept the termination of its tenancy nor its surrender which it now have or may hereafter have, nor give up possession of the premises where the said business of the mortgagor is now or may hereafter be carried on or where the mortgaged property are now or may hereafter be situate, stored or kept without the consent in writing first had and obtained by the MORTGAGOR from the MORTGAGEE.

1. That these presents shall be a continuing security and the charge shall float on all properties, assets and credits of the mortgagor from time to time for all loans and advances made and to be made by the MORTGAGEE to the MORTGAGOR on the footing of these presents until the MORTGAGOR shall redeem the security hereby created.

2. It shall be lawful for the MORTGAGEE on the execution of these presents at all times upon 24 hours notice during the continuance of this security to enter into or upon the premises where the business of the MORTGAGOR are or may be carried on or wherein the mortgaged property or any part thereof may be kept to view the state of the conditions thereof and to take inventories and/or inspect accounts and other books of the company and to take copies or abstracts thereof.

3. It shall further be lawful for the MORTGAGEE, its servants or agents to take possession of all or any part or portion of the mortgaged property hereby charged and either to remove the same or to remain in possession thereof without removing the same and at its option to carry on the said business of the MORTGAGOR through the MORTGAGOR without being answerable for any loss on the account and for the benefit of the MORTGAGEE or allow the

MORTGAGOR to carry on the same subject to such superintendence and control as the MORTGAGEE may think fit to exercise and also relinguish possession of the mortgaged property and again to retake and retain possession thereof without invalidating the securities hereby created and without being answerable for any loss which may happen in or about the exercise or execution of any of the powers conferred on the MORTGAGEE by these presents or by any statute or for any loss which may happen by reason of any involuntary mistake whether of law or fact or by reason of circumstances over which the MORTGAGEE has no control and all moneys expended by the MORTGAGEE in that behalf shall be added to moneys hereby secured and bear interest at the rate of 12 per cent. per annum as aforesaid and after the moneys secured by these presents have become due and payable under these presents all moneys received by the MORTGAGEE by the sale of the mortgaged property and/or all or any assets, properties or goods, whether or not seized or taken possession of, shall be appropriated towards the claim of the MORTGAGEE notwithstanding any thing herein contained.

4. It shall be lawful for the MORTGAGEE after the moneys secured by these presents shall become due and payable under the provisions of these presents to sell the mortgaged properties or any of them either in one lot as a going concern or in separate lots pursuant to the powers of sale conferred on bailees or pledgees by the Indian Contract Act or under any other law in force and thereafter to appropriate the sale proceeds towards the claim of the MORTGAGEE and any notice addressed to the MORTGAGOR at its registered office under registered cover shall be sufficient for the purpose of the said Act and shall be deemed to have been served when in the usual course such registered cover should have been received by the MORTGAGOR if properly addressed at the registered office and put into post office.

5. That the MORTGAGOR shall give all necessary and effective authority and power under the Articles of Association of the MORTGAGOR to enable the MORTGAGEE to make call for the uncalled money due on the shares allotted or to be allotted.

6. That the MORTGAGOR shall, during the continuance of the security created by these presents at all times, keep the mortgaged property of the same value as they are now and shall also keep the mortgaged property insured against loss or damage by fire or theft or burglary for the full value thereof in the joint names of the MORTGAGOR and the MORTGAGEE and shall duly and punctually pay from its business or otherwise all premiums and moneys payable to keep up the said insurance and shall on demand produce to the MORTGAGEE the policy or policies of insurance and the receipts for every such payment of premium and that in default of effecting or keeping up such an insurance, it shall be lawful for the MORTGAGEE to insure and keep insured the mortgaged property or any part thereof for such sum as it may think fit and add to its claim under these presents all costs, charges and expenses in connection with the insurance unless these costs, charges

and expenses are repaid on demand by the MORTGAGOR which the MORTGAGOR hereby covenants to repay on demand and that all moneys which may be received in respect of the said insurance policies or any of them shall either be applied in making good the loss or damage or towards the discharge of the moneys that may be due and owing to the MORTGAGEE by virtue of these presents.

7. The MORTGAGOR shall, so long as it shall carry on the said business keep and submit to the MORTGAGEE and when required statement of stocks and goods comprised in the mortgaged property and accounts and any other information which the MORTGAGEE may require duly certified by the auditors and two directors.

8. That the MORTGAGEE shall not be bound to exercise all or any of the powers hereby conferred on it and the exercise of any of the said powers shall not prejudice or affect the rights of the MORTGAGEE under these presents for the recovery of the moneys hereby secured and/or for the realisation of the bills and properties hereby charged by a suit or otherwise.

9. That the MORTGAGEE shall be at liberty to have a Receiver appointed of the mortgaged property in case it may have to file a suit in respect of any matter arising under these presents and the MORTGAGOR shall not object to the appointment of such Receiver on sufficient security and usual remuneration.

10. The MORTGAGOR shall always keep the MORTGAGEE duly informed as to the whereabouts of the mortgaged property and every portion thereof and the MORTGAGOR covenants and declares that the mortgaged properties are not subject to any lien, attachment, encumbrances or *lis pendens* that the value of the mortgaged properties is not less than Rs. .... estimated and calculated at the present market rate.

And that the MORTGAGOR has authority to grant transfer, assure, assign and confirm the mortgaged property hereby granted, transferred, assured and assigned and confirmed or expressed or intended so to be unto the use of the MORTGAGEE in the manner aforesaid and the MORTGAGOR further covenants that the security created by these presents will attach to the mortgaged property and continue during the subsistence of this security although the mortgaged property or any portion thereof may be removed from the premises where they are now and attached to or embedded in some other premises and that the MORTGAGOR further covenants that it shall *at its own cost* and at the request of the MORTGAGEE do and execute or cause to be done or executed all such acts, deeds and things as may at any time hereafter or from time to time be reasonably required by the MORTGAGEE for further and more perfectly transferring, assuring and assigning and confirming the mortgaged property and every part thereof so as to protect and preserve the security created by these presents unto and to the use of the MORTGAGEE in the manner aforesaid.

The Schedule above referred to

The above Schedule is not exhaustive but illustrative; all properties, assets and credits of the MORTGAGOR as belonging from time to time stand charged as security in favour of the MORTGAGEE.

IN WITNESS WHEREOF the parties herein have executed these presents on the day, month and year first above-written.

Signed, sealed and delivered by
Mr. .... pursuant to Board
Resolution dated.......... of X Co.
Ltd. in the presence of:

Signed, sealed and delivered by CD
the MORTGAGEE in the presence of:

Pari Passu Charge Agreement

TRIPARTITE AGREEMENT

THIS TRIPARTITE AGREEMENT IS made this 5th day of June 1999 BETWEEN Castings Ltd., a company registered under the Companies Act 1956 having its Registered Office at 1 Netaji Subhash Road, Calcutta 700 001 (hereinafter referred to as the MORTGAGOR, which term shall unless repugnant to the context or meaning include its successors and assigns) of the first part, X Bank Ltd., a Banking Company within the meaning of the Companies Act 1956, having its Head Office and carrying on business at 14 Netaji Subhash Road, Calcutta 700 001 (hereinafter called the BANK which expression shall unless repugnant to the subject or context include its successors and assigns) of the second part and ELH Financial Corporation Ltd. a Company within the meaning of the Companies Act 1956 and having its Head Office and carrying on business at 9 Netaji Subhash Road, Calcutta 700 001 (hereinafter referred to as the CORPORATION, which term shall unless repugnant to the subject or context shall include its successors and assigns) of the third part.

WHEREAS the MORTGAGOR is seized and possessed of land measuring about 10 acres, situated at 1 Netaji Subhash Road, Calcutta 700 001 with structures, factory sheds, plant, machinery, furniture and fixtures and carrying on business as manufacturer of and dealer in all kinds of castings of machine parts.

AND WHEREAS by a Deed of Mortgage dated 5th January 1998 made BETWEEN the MORTGAGOR and the BANK, the MORTGAGOR borrowed Rs. 10 lacs from the BANK and the MORTGAGOR in consideration thereof conveyed assigned, granted and assured unto the BANK all those pieces and parcels of land, being the Premises No. 1 Netaji Subhash Road, Calcutta 700 001 and described in the First Schedule hereunder with all buildings, structures and sheds created or constructed or to be created or constructed on the said land and all and singular plant, machinery, motors, electric and other installations, implements, equipments, spares, accessories, stores and other block assets but excluding raw materials, semifinished and finished products of the MORTGAGOR then being or which shall at any time hereafter during the continuance of the said security be brought in or affixed, installed or erected upon the said lands and buildings or kept anywhere else by the MORTGAGOR or which may belong to the MORTGAGOR or are capable of being transferred by the MORTGAGOR (all of which assets are collectively referred to as the PLANTS AND MACHINERY.

TO HAVE AND TO HOLD the said land, PLANTS AND MACHINERY unto the BANK absolutely but subject to the proviso for redemption of securities therein contained.

AND WHEREAS the MORTGAGOR being in further need of money has requested the Corporation to lend and advance to the MORTGAGOR a sum of Rs. 10 lakhs which the CORPORATION has agreed to do on certain terms and conditions and on the MORTGAGOR creating, *inter alia*, a mortgage by deposit of the Title Deeds of all lands, buildings and fixed machinery and on executing an Agreement of Hypothecation in respect of the PLANT AND MACHINERY of the MORTGAGOR in favour of the CORPORATION to secure such advance.

AND WHEREAS one of the terms and conditions of the said agreement with the Corporation is that the MORTGAGOR shall create a mortgage by deposit of Title Deeds and execute an Agreement of Hypothecation in favour of the CORPORATION and shall cause the BANK to enter into a Tripartite Agreement whereby the BANK mortgage shall be modified so that the mortgage by deposit of Title Deeds and Agreement of Hypothecation of the PLANT AND MACHINERY in favour of the CORPORATION shall rank *pari passu* in point of security and in all other respects with the Bank's mortgage and Hypothecation.

AND WHEREAS the BANK has agreed to the modification of its mortgage and Hypothecation so as to concede *pari passu*, charge on the BANK mortgage in favour of CORPORATION.

AND WHEREAS it is now necessary to record such an arrangement among the parties in a Tripartite Agreement.

NOW THIS AGREEMENT WITNESSETH and it is hereby agreed and declared by and among the parties hereto as follows:

1. The BANK shall whenever required by the CORPORATION make the Title Deeds available to the MORTGAGOR for the express purpose of being deposited with the CORPORATION with the intent to create in favour of the CORPORATION a Mortgage by deposit of the Title Deeds within the meaning of section 58(*f*) of Transfer of Property Act as security for payment of all moneys to be advanced by CORPORATION to the MORTGAGOR.

2. Notwithstanding anything to the contrary contained in the BANK Mortgage and the Corporation Mortgage, the rights of the BANK and CORPORATION in respect of the securities to be created by the Corporation Mortgage shall rank *pari passu* for all purposes and to all intents without preference and priority of one over the other.

3. During the subsistence of the securities mentioned in the immediately preceding paragraph all insurance policies in respect of the mortgaged premises shall be taken by the mortgagor in the name of the MORTGAGOR as Mortgagor and the BANK and the CORPORATION as mortgagees and shall be held by the CORPORATION and in case of moneys becoming due under such insurance the amount realised from the insurance company or companies shall be received in the first instance by the CORPORATION and shall subject to the mutual consent of the BANK and the CORPORATION be applied to the repairs and reinstatement of the mortgaged premises so damaged or destroyed and towards the payment of the dues of the Bank and the Corporation on *pro rata* basis.

4. The BANK or the CORPORATION or any of them shall be entitiled to bring suits or proceedings for enforcement of the securities created in their respective favour or otherwise for realisation of the respective dues from the MORTGAGOR and in the event of the suit or proceeding by any of the parties it shall join the other as party to such suit or proceeding.

5. Notwithstanding anything contained in the Bank Mortgage or the Corporation mortgage the following provisions shall apply as between the BANK and the CORPORATION in relation to the mortgaged premises:

(*i*) If the BANK, the CORPORATION or any of them shall enforce their respective securities created by the Bank mortgage or the Corporation mortgage all monies realised from the enforcement of such securities or the amount realised from the insurance company or companies as mentioned in paragraph 3 above or any compensation money for acquisition or requisition of the mortgaged premises or any of them or any part thereof or any other realisation from the securities by enforcement or otherwise shall be applied in the manner hereinafter appearing:

(*a*) Firstly there shall be paid out of the said moneys all costs, charges and expenses incurred by the Bank or the Corporation or by both of them of and incidental to the enforcement of the securities or realisation or receipt of such moneys.

(*b*) In the event of the moneys available for distribution to the BANK and the CORPORATION being sufficient to pay to them the full amount of the moneys due under the Bank mortgage and the Corporation mortgage the same shall be applied simultaneously in payment of the BANK and the CORPORATION of the full amount respectively due under the said securities and the surplus, if any, out of the said moneys shall be paid to the person or persons entitled thereto.

(*c*) In the event of the moneys available for distribution to the BANK and the CORPORATION not being sufficient to pay to them the full amount of the moneys due under the Bank mortgage and the Corporation mortgage the same shall be applied *pari passu* as nearly as practicable towards payment to the BANK and the CORPORATION in proportion to the amounts due to them under the said Bank mortgage and the Corporation mortgage without any preference or priority whatsoever and shall be applied towards repayment of the dues of the BANK and the CORPORATION in proportion ratio with the total amount then due (including interest, costs, charges and expenses) by the MORTGAGOR to the BANK and the Corporation respectively bears to the amount available for distribution.

6. All the title deeds in respect of the mortgaged premises shall remain in the custody of the CORPORATION and the CORPORATION shall make the same available to the BANK as and when required by the BANK at the cost of the MORTGAGOR. Without the consent of the BANK the CORPORATION shall not part with the title deeds in favour of any one including the MORTGAGOR and after all dues of the CORPORATION under the Corporation Mortgage are fully satisfied the CORPORATION will make over the title deeds to the BANK instead of to the MORTGAGOR against proper receipt provided the Bank mortgage be then subsisting.

7. Prior to taking any action for the enforcement of the aforesaid securities the BANK and the CORPORATION shall duly inform the other of the same and each of them shall consult the other in respect of all matters pertaining to the securities aforesaid so far as the same is practicable without affecting its own right and each of them at all times keep the other informed of all serious and important matters coming to its knowledge relating to the mortgaged premises or any part or portion thereof or otherwise relating to the MORTGAGOR.

The First Schedule above referred to

ALL THOSE PIECES AND PARCELS OF LAND, containing an area of 10 acres, in Mouza............, Parganas ...., Thana ...., sub-Registrar's office ...., J.L. No. .... Plot and Khatian Nos. .... are as given below:

Particulars of Building existing or proposed

The Second Schedule above referred to

(Details of plant and machinery existing or proposed to be acquired)

IN WITNESS WHEREOF the parties have executed these presents on the day, month and year first above-written.

Signed, sealed and delivered by Mr. .... pursuant to the Board Resolution dated .... of Castings Ltd. in the presence of:

For Castings Ltd.
Sd/-
Managing Director

Executed for and on behalf of X Bank Ltd. by its Constituted Attorney Mr. ...., at Calcutta in the presence of:

For X. Bank Ltd.
Sd/-
Constituted Attorney

Signed, sealed and delivered by Mr. .... pursuant to a Board Resolution dated .... of ELH Financial Corporation Ltd. in the presence of:

For ELH Financial Corporation Ltd.
Sd/-
Managing Director

Stamp Paper No. .... sold to .... Advocate of the Mortgagor of 1 Old Post Office Street, Calcutta .... at the Court Building at Calcutta.

Presented for Registration at 11.00 A.M. on ...... day of .... 1999 at his residence by Mr. .... one of the executants.

Signature of Registrar of Assurances, Calcutta, dated ....

Signature of Executant

Execution is admitted by Mr. .... Managing Director of ELH Financial Corporation Ltd. of 3 Garia Road, Calcutta

For ELH Financial Corpn. Ltd.
Sd/-
Managing Director

Execution is admitted by Mr. .... Managing Director of Castings Ltd., Calcutta

For Castings Ltd.
Sd/-
Managing Director

Thumb impression of the Executants are dispensed with, Identified by Mr. .... son of .... residing at 6 Garia Road, Calcutta, by Religion–Hindu by occupation–service

Signed by Mr. ...,............
of 6 Garia Road, Calcutta

Signature of
Registrar of Assurances, Calcutta

Dated ....

Having visited the residence and/ or offices of Mr. .... and Mr. .... both of X. Bank Ltd., 2 Garia Road, Calcutta

I have this day examined the said Mr. .... and Mr. .... who have been identified to my satisfaction by Mr. .... son of .... of 7 Garia Road, Calcutta, by religion–Hindu, by occupation service and the said officer of the Bank as Constituted Attorney admitted execution of this document.

Signature of
Registrar of Assurances
Calcutta

Dated ....

Transfer of Mortgage and Creation of Further Charge for Further Loan

THIS DEED IS MADE at Calcutta on this 20th day of December 1999 BETWEEN Mr. X of .... and Mr. Y of .... hereinafter referred to as the TRANSFERORS of the first part and Mr. PL of .... hereinafter referred to as the MORTGAGOR of the second part and Mr. T. of .... and Mr. U of ...., hereinafter referred to as the TRANSFEREES of the third part.

WHEREAS the MORTGAGOR is absolutely seized and possessed of or otherwise well and sufficiently entitled to the land and premises at .... and more particularly described in the Schedule hereunder written.

AND WHEREAS by a Deed of Mortgage dated 1st March 1998 and made BETWEEN the MORTGAGOR and the TRANSFERORS (therein referred to as the

MORTGAGEES) the MORTGAGOR in consideration of sum of Rs. 4 lakhs lent and advanced by TRANSFERORS to the MORTGAGOR and agreed to grant and convey and assure unto the TRANSFERORS all the said piece and parcel of land together with buildings and structures standing thereon being Premises No. .... and more particularly described in the Schedule to the said Deed of Mortgage subject to covenant for redemption therein contained.

AND WHEREAS there is still owing by MORTGAGOR to the said TRANSFERORS the said principal sum of Rs. 4 lakhs, all interest on the principal having been paid uptodate.

AND WHEREAS the MORTGAGOR has requested the TRANSFEREES to lend and advance to him a sum of Rs. 4 lakhs with a view to pay off the said mortgage debt to the TRANSFERORS and also a further sum or Rs. 1 lakh to meet certain liabilities of the Mortgagor thus aggregating to Rs. 5 lakhs.

AND WHEREAS the TRANSFEREES have agreed to lend and advance the said sum of Rs. 4 lakhs and Rs. 1 lakh upon the TRANSFERORS and the MORTGAGOR executing these presents.

AND WHEREAS at the request of the MORTGAGOR the TRANSFERORS have also agreed to execute these presents with a view to transfer the said mortgage debt and the security therefor to the TRANSFEREES upon payment of the said sum of Rs. 4 lakhs to the TRANSFERORS.

NOW THIS DEED WITNESSETH and the parties hereby agree as follows:

1. In consideration of the sum of Rs. 4 lakhs paid by the TRANSFEREES to the TRANSFERORS on behalf of and at the request of the MORTGAGOR on or before the execution of these presents (the receipt whereof the TRANSFERORS hereby admit and acknowledge) the TRANSFERORS do and each of them doth hereby assign and the MORTGAGOR hereby confirms unto the TRANSFEREES all that the said sum of Rs. 4 lakhs secured by the said Deed of Mortgage dated 1st March 1998 and all interest and costs henceforth to become due in respect thereof and the full benefit of the covenants power of sale and other powers and provisions contained in the said Deed of Mortgage for securing the payment of the said sum and interest together with the full power to demand sue for recover and give effectual receipts and discharge for the same respectively and all the right, title interest property claim and demand of the TRANSFERORS in the said moneys and premises to have receive and take the said sum of Rs. 4 lakhs and interest and costs and the premises hereby assign or expressed so to be unto the TRANSFEREES absolutely.

2. TRANSFERORS do and each of them doth hereby grant and transfer unto the transferees and the MORTGAGOR doth hereby grant and confirm unto the TRANSFREES all and singular the land and the premises more particularly described in the Schedule in the said Deed being the same as described in the Schedule hereunder written comprised in and granted or otherwise assured by the said Deed of Mortgage and all their rights title interest and claims therein to have and to hold the land and the premises

hereby granted unto and to the use of the TRANSFEREES subject to such right or equity of redemption as is now subsisting in the said premises under or by virtue of the said Deed of Mortgage.

3. In pursuance of the said Agreement and in consideration of the said sum of Rs. 4 lakhs paid by the TRANSFREES to the TRANSFERORS at the request and by the direction of the MORTGAGOR, as aforesaid, and in further consideration of the sum of Rs. 1 lakh lent and advanced by the TRANSFEREES to the MORTGAGOR on the execution of these presents (receipt whereof the MORTGAGOR doth hereby admit) making a total of Rs. 5 lakhs the MORTGAGOR doth hereby covenant with the TRANSFEREES that the MORTGAGOR will pay to the TRANSFEREES in 5 instalments of Rs. 1 lakh each year on 5th day of December the said sum of Rs. 5 lakhs with interest at the rate of twelve per cent per annum payable every month from the date of these presents and the first of such payment to be made on or before 1st March 2000 and the next and subsequent payments to be made on the 1st day of each and every succeeding month so long as the said sum of Rs. 5 lakhs or any part thereof shall remain unpaid to the TRANSFEREES with compound interest with monthly rests.

4. That all and singular the land and the premises hereby granted or conveyed shall stand charged with and remain security for the payment to the TRANSFEREES the said sum of Rs. 4 lakhs secured by the said Deed of Mortgage and interest thereon and other moneys due and payable thereunder but also of the said further sum of Rs. 1 lakh and interest thereon pursuant to the covenant in that behalf hereinbefore contained and shall not be redeemed or redeemable until the said aggregate sum of Rs. 5 lakhs and interest thereon shall be fully paid and satisfied.

5. The MORTGAGOR agrees and covenants that the power of sale and all provisions ancillary thereto other powers and provisions and the Mortgagor's covenants available to the TRANSFERORS for securing the payment of the principal and interest and all other moneys payable by the MORTGAGOR and contained in the Deed of Mortgage shall be available to the TRANSFEREES and shall extend and be applicable so as to be security for repayment of the said sum of Rs. 5 lakhs and interest at 12% per annum and all costs incurred in relation to the above security realisation of all moneys due by the MORTGAGOR under the said Mortgage.

6. IT IS HEREBY AGREED between the MORTGAGOR and the TRANSFEREES that the covenants and provisions in reference to the insurance of the mortgaged premises against fire, in the said Deed of Mortgage shall extend to and be applicable to the security hereby created by substitution of Rs. 12 lakhs in lieu of Rs. 10 lakhs under the said Deed of Mortgage and that in the event the TRANSFEREES becoming entitled to appoint a Receiver of the income of the said land and premises under the Transfer of Property Act 1882 the TRANSFEREES shall be entitled to appoint Mr. R as such Receiver instead of the person named in the said Deed of Mortgage and the due date referred in

the said Deed of Mortgage will be deemed to be extended to the date of 20th day of January 2008 and that if the MORTGAGOR fails to pay the mortgage amount on the due date or to pay any instalment of interest as herein provided on the date fixed for the payment thereof or commits breach of any other term of these presents and/or the Deed of Mortgage the TRANSFEREES shall have the option to claim the whole amount even though the due date has not expired.

AND IT IS HEREBY agreed and declared among the parties hereto that nothing in these presents contained shall be deemed to impose or continue any liability on the TRANSFERORS or any of them for the title to the property or render the TRANSFERORS or any of them liable for or in respect of the mortgaged debt hereby assigned or any part thereof or for the sufficiency of the security in any manner whatsoever and howsoever.

IN WITNESS WHEREOF the parties herein have executed these presents on the day, month and year first above-written.

The Schedule above referred to

ALL THAT PIECE and parcel of land measuring about 5 cottahs with structures thereon being Premises No. .... registered in the Registration Office at .... in Book No. 1, Being No. 2, pages 10 to 20.

Signed and delivered by Mr. X and
Mr. Y the TRANSFERORS in the presence of: Signature

Signed and delivered by Mr. PL the
MORTGAGOR in the presence of: Signature

Signed and delivered by Mr. T and
Mr. U the TRANSFEREES in the presence of: Signature

MEMO OF CONSIDERATION

Received by Cheque No. .... dated .... for Rs. 4 lakhs on X Bank Ltd.

Received payments
Sd/. X & Y

Received by Cash Rs. 1,00,000.

Received payment
Sd/. PL

37

Negotiable Instruments

History of the origin of Negotiable Instruments. In India, the Negotiable Instruments Act 1881, is the statutory law on the subject as the Bills of Exchange Act 1882, in England.

In ancient England, people used to keep their savings deposited with goldsmiths who in return issued a receipt or receipts known as "goldsmiths notes". They were equivalents to our present system of currency notes or bank notes payable on demand to the bearers;[1] cheques are later developments although it originated out of the system of banking as then controlled by goldsmiths as whenever any such depositor wanted to make any payment out of his deposit, he used to send a written order known as "Drawn Note" on the goldsmith. Cheques were later on invented out of "Drawn Notes."

Thus, the negotiable instrument came to be largely employed by merchants as an effective substitute for money.

In India, the banking business is of most ancient origin but was the monopoly of a class of people called *Subarnabanik* (goldsmith) and thereafter conducted by Shroffs, Seths and Poddars, particularly during the Moghul period. Nevertheless, instruments of exchange were in use from early times. In ancient society, every village had its Shroff who used to do not only the job of money-exchangers but also acted as bankers in remitting moneys and issuing letters of exchange.

The system of banking by Shroffs, Seths and Poddars continued till the days of the East India Company when the currency was unified and joint stock banks were established. In fact, the word 'hundi', a term used to denote instruments of exchange in vernacular, is derived from its Sanskrit

1 Davar's *English Banking History and Development*, 5th Ed., p. 5.

root "hund" meaning "to collect" and well expresses the purpose for which such instruments were utilised in their origin. It dates back to the days of the *Mahabharata*.[2] The ancient banking business in India was confined to the issue and discount of bills of exchange, money-lending and money changing. Before passing of the Act of 1881, the law of negotiable instruments was prevalent in England, *viz.*, Statute 9 of William III C 17 relating to inland Bill of Exchange and 3 and 4 Anne C 8 relating to promissory notes was applied by the courts[3] in India when any question relating to such instruments arose between the Europeans. When the parties were Hindus or Muhammedans, the courts applied their personal law to their respective cases. The customs prevailing among the merchants of the respective community were recognised by the courts and applied to the transactions among them. There is no doubt that by the time the Act was passed in 1881, there had developed in the country a strong body of usage relating to hundies, which even the legislature could not ignore without hardship to native bankers and merchants.

NEGOTIABLE INSTRUMENTS

Negotiable instruments—negotiation. A *negotiable instrument* means an instrument assignable by delivery or assignment. It may be either a promissory note, or a bill of exchange or a cheque payable either to order or to bearer.[4]

(*a*) A promissory note, bill of exchange or cheque, is payable to order which is expressed to be so payable or which is expressed to be payable to a particular person, and does not contain words prohibiting transfer or indicating an intention that it shall not be transferable.

(*b*) A promissory note, bill of exchange or cheque is payable to bearer which is to be so payable or on which the only or last endorsement is an endorsement in blank.

(*c*) Where a promissory note, bill of exchange or cheque, either originally or by endorsements, is expressed to be payable to the order of the specific person, and not to him or his order, it is nevertheless payable to him or his order at his option.

(*d*) A negotiable instrument may be made payable to two or more payees jointly, or it may be made payable in the alternative to one or two, or one or more of several payees.

2 Tanan's *Banking Law and Practice in India*, 19th Ed., p. 10.
3 *Brojo Lal Shaha Banikya* v *Budhilal & Co.* 55 Cal 551.
4 Section 13 of the Negotiable Instruments Act 1881.

(e) When a promissory note, bill of exchange or cheque is transferred to any person so as to constitute that person the holder thereof, the instrument is said to be *negotiated*.[5]

Inland and foreign instrument: "at sight" and "on presentment": "after sight". A promissory note, bill of exchange or cheque drawn or made in India, and made payable in, or drawn upon any person resident in India is deemed to be an *inland instrument;* and any such instrument not so drawn, made or made payable, is deemed to be a *foreign instrument*.[6]

In a promissory note or bill of exchange, the expressions *at sight* and *on presentment* mean 'on demand'. A promissory note or bill of exchange, in which no time for payment is specified, and a cheque are payable on demand.

The expression *after sight* means in a promissory note after presentment for sight, and in a bill of exchange, after acceptance or noting for non-acceptance, or protest for non-acceptance.

Bills or notes to bearer on demand illegal. Promissory notes and bills of exchange cannot be made payable to bearer on demand; provided that cheques, or drafts payable to bearer on demand or otherwise, can be drawn on bankers, shroffs, or agents by their customs or constituents, in respect of deposits of money in the hands of such bankers, shroffs or agents, and held by at the credit and disposal of the person drawing such cheques or drafts.

Holder: holder in due course: payment in due course. The *holder* of a promissory note, bill of exchange or cheque means any person entitled in his own name to the possession thereof, and to receive or recover the amount due thereon from the parties thereto.[7]

Holder in due course means any person who for consideration becomes the possessor of a promissory note, bill of exchange or cheque, if payable to bearer, or to the payee or endorsee thereof, if payable to order, before the amount mentioned in it became payable, and without having sufficient cause to believe that any defect existed in the title of the person from whom he derived this title.

Payment in due course means payment in accordance with the apparent tenor of the instrument in good faith and without negligence to the person in possession thereof.

"Endorsement": "endorser: endorsee". When the maker or holder of any negotiable instrument signs the same, otherwise than as such maker, for the purpose of negotiation, on the back or face thereof, or on a slip of paper

5 Section 14 of the Negotiable Instruments Act 1881.
6 Sections 11 & 12 of the Negotiable Instruments Act 1881 also s. 21.
7 Section 10 of the Negotiable Instruments Act 1881.

annexed thereto or so signs for the same purpose a stamped paper intended to be completed as a negotiable instrument, he is said to *endorse* the same and is called the *endorser*.[8]

If the endorser signs his name only, the endorsement is said to be *in blank,* and if he adds a direction to pay the amount mentioned in the instrument to, or to the order of, a specified person, the endorsement is said to be in *full;* and the person so specified is called the *endorsee* of the instrument.

Subject to the provisions as to crossed cheques, a negotiable instrument endorsed in blank is payable to the bearer thereof even although originally payable to order.

Liability of endorser. In the absence of a contract to the contrary, whoever endorses and delivers a negotiable instrument before maturity without, in such endorsement, expressly excluding or making conditional his own liability, is bound thereby to every subsequent holder, in case of dishonour by the drawee, acceptor, or maker, to compensate such holder for any loss or damage caused to him by such dishonour, provided due notice of dishonour has been given to, or received by, such endorser.

Every endorser after dishonour is liable as upon an instrument payable on demand.[9]

Maker, drawer and acceptor liable as principals. The maker of a promissory note or cheque, the drawer of a bill of exchange until acceptance, and the acceptor are, in the absence of a contract to the contrary, respectively liable thereon as principal debtors, and the other parties thereto are liable thereon as sureties for the maker, drawer or acceptor as the case may be.

"Maturity": day of maturity on public holiday: The maturity of a promissory note or bill of exchange is the date at which it falls due.

When the day on which a promissory note or bill of exchange is on maturity is a public holiday, the instrument will be deemed to be due on the next preceding business day.[10]

"Day of Grace". Every promissory note or bill of exchange, which is not expressed to be payable on demand, at sight, or on presentment, is at maturity on the third day after the day on which it is expressed to be payable.[11]

"Dishonour by non-payment": notice of dishonour. A promissory note, bill of exchange or cheque is said to be *dishonoured* by *non-payment*, when the

8 Section 15 of the Negotiable Instruments Act 1881.
9 Section 35 of the Negotiable Instruments Act 1881.
10 Section 22 of the Negotiable Instruments Act 1881.
11 Section 22 of the Negotiable Instruments Act 1881.

maker of the note, acceptor of the bill, or drawee of the cheque, makes default in payment upon being duly required to pay the same. As regards the dishonour by non-acceptance of a bill of exchange,[12] when a promissory note, bill of exchange or cheque is dishonoured by non-acceptance or non-payment, the holder thereof, or some party thereto who remains liable thereon, must give oral or written notice that the instrument has been so dishonoured, to all other parties whom the holder seeks to make severally liable thereon, and to someone of several parties whom he seeks to make jointly liable thereon; but it is not necessary to give notice to the maker of the dishonoured promissory note, or the drawee or acceptor of the dishonoured bill of exchange or cheque.

No notice of dishonour is necessary—

(*i*) when it is dispensed with by the party entitled thereto;

(*ii*) in order to charge the drawer when he has countermanded payment;

(*iii*) when the party charged could not suffer damage for want of notice;

(*iv*) when the party entitled to notice cannot after due search be found; or the party bound to give notice is, for any other reason, unable, without any fault of his own, to give it:

(*v*) to charge the drawer, when the acceptor is also a drawer;

(*vi*) in the case of a promissory note which is not negotiable; and

(*vii*) when the party entitled to notice, knowing the facts, promises unconditionally to pay the amount due on the instrument.[13] It has been laid down by the Supreme Court,[14] that a bill of exchange requires presentment for acceptance under s. 61 of the Negotiable Instruments Act and s. 62 of the Act deals with presentment for payment, s. 7 of the Act provides that a drawee becomes acceptor when he has signed his assent upon the bill. This is the analogy underlying the principle behind a cheque marked "good for payment" by any banker; nevertheless it was held by the Privy Council[15] that such marking is not acceptance within the meaning of the English Act, Indian Act or Common Law. Apart from mercantable usage, there cannot be oral acceptance by conduct or possession. Section 30 of the Act lays down liability in case of dishonour by the drawee or the acceptor, under s. 31 of the Act

12 Section 93 of the Negotiable Instruments Act 1881.

13 Section 97 of the Negotiable Instruments Act 1881.

14 *Jagivan* v *Ranchhoddas* AIR 1954 SC 544.

15 *Bank of Baroda Ltd.* v *Punjab National Bank Ltd.* 1944 AC 176 (PC).

> the drawee is liable on the cheque if funds are there to the credit of the drawer to honour the cheque. The liability of a banker in respect of damages by reason of dishonour of a cheque is governed by this section. Section 32 lays down the liability of an acceptor of a bill of exchange in case of a bill is payable after sight, presentation for acceptance must precede presentation for payment, when a bill is payable on demand or at sight both stages may synchronise, when it is not paid or dishonoured it is really dishonoured for non-acceptance. Under s. 78 the holder of the instrument is entitled to payment and he is the person entitled to present a hundi for acceptance.

It must be remembered that acceptance is not necessary in the case of a cheque as in the case of a bill of exchange where acceptance only establishes the privity on the instrument between the drawee and the payee. Acceptance by endorsement of certificate for the purpose of clearance is not an acceptance to create negotiability.

"Noting": "protest". When a promissory note or bill of exchange has been dishonoured by non-acceptance or non-payment, the holder can cause such dishonour to be noted by a Notary Public upon the instrument, or upon a paper attached thereto, or partly upon each. Such note must be made within a reasonable time after dishonour, and must specify the date of dishonour, the reason, if any, assigned for such dishonour, or if the instrument has not been expressly dishonoured, the reason why the holder treats it as dishonoured.[16]

When such dishonour has been noted and certified by the Notary Public, such certificate is called a protest.

Capacity to make, etc., negotiable instruments.[17] Every person capable of contracting, according to the law to which he is subject, can bind himself and be bound by the making, drawing, acceptance, endorsement, delivery, and negotiation of a promissory note, bill of exchange, or cheque.[1]

An alien cannot draw a promissory note on the principle that all contracts with the alien are void[2] unless he lives here by the permission of the Government.

16 Section 99 of the Negotiable Instruments Act 1881.

17 A promissory note made by a minor is wholly void. He is not even precluded under s. 120 of the Act to deny its validity. Srinivasan's *Negotiable Instruments Act,* p. 1711.

1 Section 26 of the Negotiable Instruments Act 1881.

2 Re, *Helbert Wagg & Co. Ltd.* (1956)1 All ER 129 at p. 143.

Interest. An agreement to pay interest can be entered in a promissory note or bill of exchange, and if no rate of interest is specified in the instrument, interest on the amount due thereon will be calculated at the rate of 18 per cent per annum, from the date at which the same ought to have been paid by the party charged, until tender or realization of the amount due thereon.[3]

Negotiable instruments, not duly stamped, or their adhesive stamps not cancelled. The effect of the negotiable instruments not being duly stamped, or of the non-cancellation of their adhesive stamps is that the same is inadmissible in evidence.

PROMISSORY NOTES

"Promissory note". A *promissory note* is an instrument in writing (not being a bank note or a currency note) containing an unconditional undertaking signed by the maker, to pay a certain sum of money only to, or to the order of, a certain person, or to the bearer of the instrument. The essentials of a promissory note are, according to *Shri Bal Mukand* v *Munna Lal Ramji*[4] as follows:

The test is that it must be a promissory note in form and in intent. Even the absence of the words "I promise to pay" does not make any difference.

Section 4 of the Negotiable Instruments Act 1881, is complied with if the amount is specific, and the writing contains an unconditional undertaking to pay on demand and is signed by the debtor.

Effect of attested promissory note. A promissory note, not payable to order or bearer, should not be attested as, if attested, it will be construed to be a bond and, as such, will be liable for the stamp duty provided for a bond[5] and like any other unstamped or insufficiently stamped instrument, except an instrument chargeable with duty or a promissory note or bill of exchange, will be admitted in evidence on payment of the duty with which the same is chargeable, or, in the case of an instrument insufficiently stamped, of the amount required to make up such duty, together with a penalty of five rupees, or, when ten times the amount of the proper duty or deficient portion thereof exceeds five rupees, of a sum equal to ten times such duty or portion.[6]

3 Section 80 of the Negotiable Instruments Act 1881.
4 AIR 1970 Punj 516.
5 Section 2(5)(*b*) of the Indian Stamp Act 1880. See also *Barisal Rindan* v *Situl Chander* 34 CWN 911.
6 Section 35A of the Indian Stamp Act.

Bills of Exchange

Bill of exchange. *A bill of exchange* is an instrument in writing containing an unconditional order, signed by the maker, directing a certain person to pay a certain sum of money only to, or to the order of, a certain person, or to the bearer of the instrument.

"Cheque": crossed cheque: payment of cheques. A *cheque* is a bill of exchange drawn on a specified banker and not expressed to be payable otherwise than on demand.

Where a cheque bears across its face an addition of the words "and company" or any abbreviation thereof, between two parallel transverse lines or of two parallel transverse lines simply, either with or without the words "not negotiable", that addition will be deemed a crossing, and the cheque will be deemed to be crossed *generally*; and where a cheque bears across its face an addition of the name of a banker, either with or without the words "not negotiable", that addition will be deemed a crossing, and the cheque will be deemed to be *crossed specially*, and to be crossed to that banker.

Where a cheque is crossed generally, the banker on whom it is drawn will not pay it otherwise than to a banker; and where a cheque is crossed specially, the banker on whom it is drawn will not pay it otherwise than to the banker to whom it is crossed, or his agent, for collection.

Cheque marked "Account payee" means that it can be encashed through the account of the particular payee only but an ordinary crossed cheque can be endorsed in favour of any person who, however, has to collect it through his banking account.

Sets of bills: holder of first acquired part: stamps for parts of bills. Bills of exchange can be drawn in parts, each part being numbered and containing a provision that it shall continue payable so long as the others remain unpaid. All the parts together make a set; but the whole set constitutes only one bill, and is extinguished when one of the parts, if a separate bill, would be extinguished; except that when a person accepts or endorses different parts of the bill in favour of different persons, he and the subsequent endorsers of each part are liable on such part as if it were a separate bill.

As between holders in due curse of different parts of the same set, he who first acquired title to his part is entitled to the other parts and the money represented by the bill.

Adhesive stamps cannot be used for parts of bills of exchange, not payable on demand and drawn in sets.

"Drawer", "drawee", and "payee": section 7 of the Negotiable Instruments Act: "drawee in case of need". The maker of a bill of exchange or cheque is called the *drawer*; the person thereby directed to pay is called the *drawee;*

and the person named in the instrument to whom or to whose order the money is by the instrument directed to be paid, is called the payee.

When in the bill or in any endorsement thereon the name of any person is given in addition to the drawee to be resorted to in case of need, such person is called *a drawee in case of need.*

"Acceptor" and "acceptance": "acceptance for honour". After the drawee of a bill of exchange has signed his assent upon the bill, or upon one part of the bill and delivered the same, or given notice of such signing to its holder, he is called the *acceptor*, and his act of doing so is *acceptance*.

When a bill of exchange has been noted or protested for non-acceptance, or for better security, any person, not being a party already liable thereon, can, with the consent of the holder by writing on the bill, *accept* the same *for the honour* of any party thereto.

Liability of drawee of cheque. The drawee of a cheque having sufficient funds of the drawer in his hand properly applicable to the payment of such cheque must pay the cheque when duly required so to do, and, in default of such payment, must compensate the drawer for any loss or damage caused by such default.

Liability of drawer. The drawer of a bill of exchange or cheque is bound, in case of dishonour by the drawee or acceptance thereof, to compensate the holder, provided due notice of dishonour has been given to, or received by, the drawer.

Section 138 of the Negotiable Instruments Act 1881 is a penal provision. When a cheque is returned by the Bank unpaid and so dishonoured on account of insufficient funds or the amount of the cheque exceeds the amount agreed or arranged to be paid from that account or to 'stop payment' order issued by the drawer in spite of his remaining liable to pay the amount in discharge of a debt, the drawer of the cheque comes within the mischief of s. 138 and is liable to punishment.[7]

Dishonour by non-acceptance. A bill of exchange is said to be dishonoured by non-acceptance when the drawee or one or several drawees, not being partners, makes defaults in acceptance upon being duly required to accept the bill, or where presentment is excused, and the bill is not accepted.

7 *Modi Cements* v *Kuchil Kumar* Cal LT 1998(2) SC 41; *Electronics Trade* v *Indian Technologists* JT 1996(1) SC 643; *K.K. Sidharthan* v *T.P. Praveena* JT 1996(9) SC 191; *R. Janardhana Rao* v *G. Lingappa* AIR 1999 SC 780.

FORMS

Promissory Note Payable on Demand

Rs. .... Date

ON DEMAND (or at sight, *or, on presentation*), I promise to pay to AB (*or*, to AB or order) the sum of Rupees .... (Rs. ....) only, with interest at the rate of 18 per cent per annum until payment, for value received.

CD (*Debtor*)

Joint Promissory Note Payable on Demand

Rs. .... Date

ON DEMAND (*or*, at sight, *or*, on presentment), we jointly and severally promise to pay to AB (*or*, to AB or order), at Delhi, the sum of Rupees .... (Rs. ....) only, with interest at the rate of 18 per cent per annum until payment, for value received.

EF
CE (*Debtor*)

Joint Promissory Note Payable After Date or Sight

Rs. .... Date

THREE MONTHS AFTER DATE (*or*, after sight), we jointly and severally promise to pay to AB (*or,* to AB *or* order) the sum of Rupees .... (Rs. ....) only, with interest at the rate of 18 per cent per annum from the date hereof until payment, for value received.

EF
CD (*Debtors*)

Joint Promissory Note Payable in Instalments

Rs. .... Date

WE JOINTLY and severally promise to pay to AB (*or*, to AB *or* order) the sum of Rupees .... (Rs. ....) only (for value received), by instalments of Rs. .... per month with interest on each instalment at 18 per cent per annum from the date hereof until payment, the first instalment with interest thereon to be paid on the .... day of .... next, and each succeeding instalment with interest thereon to be paid on the......... day of each following month at ...., until the whole of the said sum of Rs. .... be repaid; any one instalment being in arrear for seven days, the balance of the said sum of Rs. .... remaining owing shall become immediately payable, with interest thereon until payment.

EF
CD (*Debtors*)

Inland Bill of Exchange Payable on Demand

Rs. .... Date

ON DEMAND (*or*, at sight, *or*, on presentation), pay to EF (*or*, to EF *or* order *or*, to myself *or* my order) the sum of Rupees .... (Rs. ....) only, for value received.

CD (*Drawer*)

To

AB (*Drawee*) *or* CD (*Drawer himself*)

Inland Bill of Exchange Payable After Date or Sight

Rs. .... Due .... 19........ Date

Three months after date (or after sight) pay to EF or order (or to EF or order) or to bearer the sum of Rupees .... (Rs.) only for value received.

To AB (*Drawee*) CD (*Drawer*)

In case of need apply to GH or, etc. (*Drawee in case of need*).

Cheque

No. ....

To AB etc. (Bank).

Pay to EF, or bearer/order Rupees ....
Rs. .... only

CD (*Drawer*)

Foreign Bill of Exchange in Sets

No. .... Exchange for £ ....

Calcutta, 1st January 2000

Six months after sight of this first of Exchange (second and third unpaid), pay to the order of AB .... pounds for value received, and charge the same to account of Messrs. CD & Co. against your letter of credit No. ....

EF (*Drawer*)

To GH, London (*Drawee*)

Foreign Bill of Exchange in Sets

No. ....

London, 1st February 20.........

At sixty days after sight of this first of Exchange (second and third unpaid), pay to the order of AB & Co. .... rupees, which place to account shipment of ...., etc. (*name of goods*), per s.s. "........", etc. (*name of ship*).

CD (*Drawer*)

EF, Calcutta (*Drawee*)

To

Foreign Bill of Exchange (French)

Paris le. ......

B.P. 1,000 fr.

A deux dois de vue vous plaira payer per cette seule de change a lordre de M. ...... le somme de mille francs, valeur en merchandises (*ou* en Compte, *ou* en agrent, etc.), sans autre avis de.

Votre serviteur

AB (*Drawer*)

....

A Messieurs CD & Cie,
Ah Havre (*Drawee*)

Date

PAY ORDER

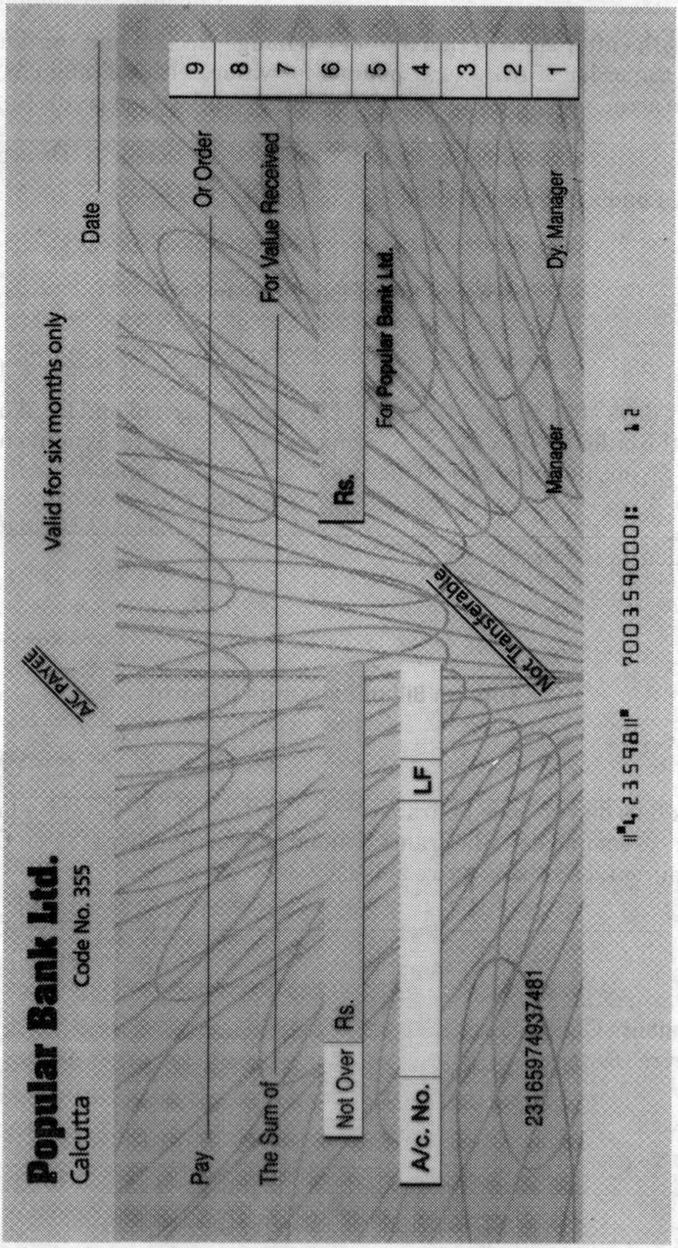

Popular Bank Ltd.
Calcutta Code No. 355

A/C PAYEE

Valid for six months only

Date ______

Pay ______ Or Order

The Sum of ______ For Value Received

Not Over Rs. | Rs.

For Popular Bank Ltd.

A/c. No. | LF

Not Transferable

Manager Dy. Manager

23165974937481

1 2 3 4 5 6 7 8 9

DEMAND DRAFT

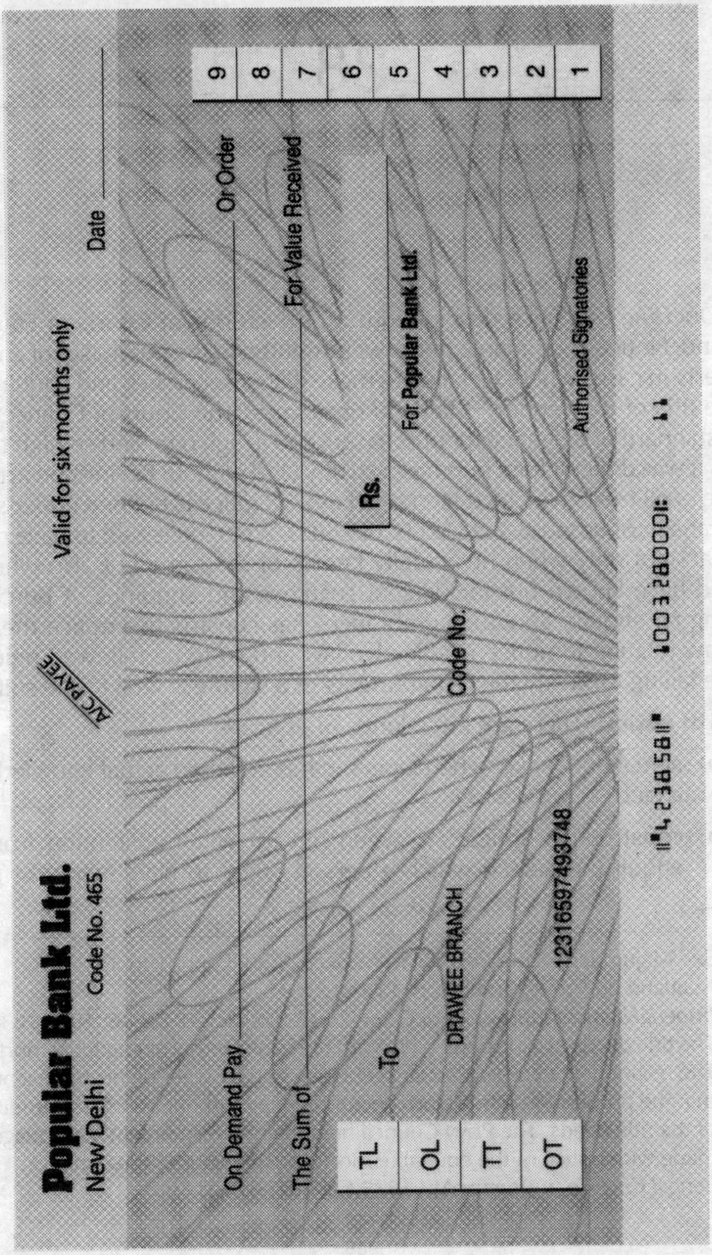

Popular Bank Ltd.

New Delhi   Code No. 465

Valid for six months only   Date ________

A/C PAYEE

On Demand Pay ________________ Or Order

The Sum of ________________ For Value Received

Rs. ________

For Popular Bank Ltd.

To

DRAWEE BRANCH   Code No.

12316597493748

Authorised Signatories

TL	OL	TT	OT

9	8	7	6	5	4	3	2	1

⑈423858⑈ 100328000⑆ 11

38

Notice

The Doctrine of Notice developed out of decisions of Courts in Equity in England. Notice of equitable rights was imputed to the purchaser of any real property in cases where he failed to make diligent searches and enquiries as to the title of the vendor.[1] Maitland observes: "The Court of Chancery set up a standard of diligence for purchasers and a high one, and so high that at times it was difficult for a purchaser to buy land without having constructive notice of all trusts which concern the land."[2] Notice is defined under s. 3 of the Transfer of Property Act (Act IV of 1882): A person is said to have notice of a fact not only when he actually knows of the same but also when he should have known but for diligent searches and enquiries. A purchaser making no enquiry about encumbrances has constructive notice thereof.[3] The law relating to notice is adjective law and so to be followed rigidly. A notice failing to satisfy the requirements of a statute is fatal to the suit.[4]

Kinds of notice. There are three kinds of notice—

(*a*) actual notice, *i.e.* when a person has acquired actual knowledge of a fact;

(*b*) constructive notice, *i.e.* when but for wilful abstention from an enquiry or search which a person ought to have made, or gross

1 See Majumder's *Laws Relating to Notices*, 6th Ed., pp. 1 to 3.

2 Maitland on *Equity*, 2nd Ed., p. 117.

3 *Imperial Bank of India* v *U. Rai Gyaw, Thu & Co. Ltd.* 51 Cal 86; 50 IA 283 (PC). The title deeds of a property were with the bank by way of equitable mortgage. The respondent company advanced a loan to the owner on his representation that the property was free from encumbrances without asking for production of the title deeds. The Privy Council held that the respondent's mortgage was made with notice of the equitable mortgage in favour of the bank.

4 *Bengal Coal Co.* v *Sitaram* AIR 1935 Cal 667; 61 CLJ 560.

negligence, he would have known it, *e.g.* solicitor entrusted with preparation of a conveyance not doing any searches nor making an enquiry as to the claim of the dependants under the Hindu Adoptions and Maintenance Act 1956.

(*c*) notice to the agent, *i.e.* information received by or given to the agent in the course of his ordinary duties, whether he communicates it to his principal or not. Notice to active partner has the effect of notice to the firm in the absence of fraud.[5]

Requisites and service of notice. A notice is an announcement or intimation and, in some cases, caution. So except notices prescribed under the Code of Civil Procedure and certain public notices used at the Government level, there is no hard and fast rule about forms. An actual notice to be valid must be clear and certain so as to bind the party who gives it and to enable the opposite party to act upon it and the information given by a person interested in the matter, in respect of which the notice is issued, must be definite.

Where a notice is required to be given by any statute, e.g., s. 80 of the Code of Civil Procedure; s. 106 of the Indian Railways Act 1989; s. 106 of the Transfer of Property Act 1882; s. 10 of the Carriers Act 1865; s. 54(2) of the Indian Sale of Goods Act 1930; s. 3 of the Arbitration and Conciliation Act 1996; s. 41 of the Presidency Small Causes Court Act; Art. 226 of the Constitution of India, it must comply with the requirements of law as regards addressee, contents of the notice and service thereof.[6] Where no mode of service is provided by law, it is usual to send the notice by registered post with acknowledgement due; where service by post is required by any Act or Rule, then unless a different intention appears the service shall be deemed to have been effected by properly addressing, pre-paying and posting by registered post a letter containing the document and to the correct address unless the contrary is proved, to have been effected at the time at which the letter would be delivered in the ordinary post.[7] Refusal by the addressee to accept the notice after it was tendered to him by the peon raises a presumption of due service. Again, if the notice properly addressed is proved to have been put into the Post Office, it is presumed that it reached its destination at the proper time and was received by the addressee.[8] That

5 Section 24 of the Indian Partnership Act.

6 Meaning of "service"—Delivery with announcement of the contents to the person affected vide *Oxford Dictionary*.

7 Section 27 of the General Clauses Act 1897; see also s. 28 of the Bengal General Clauses Act 1899.

8 Presumption of service *re* notice sent by registered post—section 114, illustration (*f*) of the Evidence Act. See also *Amulya Charan* v *Corporation of Calcutta* AIR 1950 Cal 256.

presumption will apply with greater force to registered letters. Such presumptions are, however, rebuttable.[9] As to effect of endorsement 'not claimed' and 'left', see the decision in *H.K. Das* v *Hahnemann Co.*[10]

Out of the aforesaid notices, those under s. 80 of CPC, s. 106 of the Indian Railways Act 1989,[11] s. 10 of the Carriers Act[12] and, lastly, under s. 54(2) of the Indian Sale of Goods Act[13] are mandatory notices. A suit without any such notice must fail.

Some notices are also statutory but not mandatory, *e.g.* notice of allotment under s. 109 of the Transfer of Property Act, notice of transfer of actionable claim under s. 131 of the Transfer of Property Act and notice of revocation of agency.[14]

The above list is illustrative but not exhaustive.

Registration, possession and notice to agent as notice to principal are cases of constructive notices. The leading case on the subject, *Tilakdharilal's* cases,[15] laid down that it was obligatory on the part of all purchasers to examine title as recorded in the register and the omission to search attributed to gross negligence. The rule that registration operates as a notice has been adopted in England by s. 198 of the Law of Property Act and in India by Explanation I to s. 3 of the Transfer of Property Act 1872.

Possession in certain circumstances operates as constructive notice. This principle is enacted in Explanation II to s. 3 of the Transfer of Property Act and is also illustrated under s. 27(*b*) of the Specific Relief Act 1877, which is equivalent to illustration under s. 19 of the Specific Relief Act of 1963 (Act 47 of 1963). Lastly, under s. 229 of the Contract Act, notice to the agent is notice to the principal.

Special provisions. Where there are provisions in particular statutes about the requirement of notice and the manner of service of notice, the special provisions must be complied with for validity of the notice. The prescribed modes shall be the only valid mode of service for purposes of the particular statute. A notice under s. 106 of the Transfer of Property Act, *i.e.* notice to quit, must be in writing signed by or on behalf of the person giving it, either sent by post to the party or tendered or delivered personally to him or to one of his family members or servants at his residence or, if such tender or delivery is not practicable affixed to a conspicuous part of the property.

9 *Saibalini Saha* v *Snehalata Bose* 65 CWN 690.
10 70 CWN 262.
11 *Amar Nath Dogra* v *Union of India* AIR 1963 SC 424.
12 *British & Foreign Marine Insurance* v *Indo-General Steam Navigation* ILR 38 Cal 50.
13 *Naraindas* v *Kunjilal* AIR 1924 Nag 162.
14 Section 206 of the Indian Contract Act.
15 *Tilakdharilal* v *Khedanlal* (1920)47 IA 239; 48 Cal 1.

Besides notice between private parties, there are special provisions for service on private persons by a public officer, *e.g.* a notice by a Controller or Appellate Officer under the West Bengal Premises Tenancy Act.[16]

There are important provisions in the Indian Railways Act prescribing service of notice on the Railway Administration or by the Railway Administration.[17]

There is a special provision in s. 194 of the Indian Railways Act 1989 where notice is served by post, similar to the provisions in the General Clauses Act and the Evidence Act.

It should further be noted that special statutes require specific grounds to be mentioned in the notice. They must be incorporated, *e.g.*, notice under the Transfer of Property Act between landlord and tenant should be supplemented by the provisions of the West Bengal Premises Tenancy Act. Similarly, the notice of suit under s. 407 of the West Bengal Municipal Act 1993 must contain the particulars therein.

Notices are also required to be served on some public offices about certain facts, *e.g.* notice of accident under the Factories Act 1948, and the Workmen's Compensation Act 1923. Those statutes also prescribe the mode and form of notice.

Notice of arbitration. A notice of arbitration under the Arbitration and Conciliation Act 1996 should contain the following matters so long as no specific Rules are framed under the Act:

(1) A demand that the dispute be referred to arbitration.

(2) The names and addresses of the parties.

(3) A reference to arbitration clause.

(4) A reference to contract out of or in relation to which the dispute arises.

(5) The general nature of the claim and an indication of the amount involved.

(6) The relief or remedy sought.

(7) A proposal as to the number of arbitrators which must not be of an even number.

(8) The proposal for the appointment of a sole arbitrator and an appointing authority.

(9) The notification of appointment of arbitrator(s).

(10) The statement of claim.[18]

16 Rules 12 and 25 of the West Bengal Premises Tenancy Rules 1956.

17 Sections 192 and 193 of the Indian Railways Act 1989.

18 Roy Chowdhury & Saharay: *Law of Arbitration and Conciliation*, 4th Ed., p. 287.

FORMS

Notice by Landlord to Quit[19]

(Combined Notice under s. 106 of T.P. Act and s. 13 of W.B. Premises Tenancy Act)

To
AB (*Tenant*)

Re: Premises No. ....

Dear Sir

I, the undersigned, your landlord and owner/lessor of the above premises, do hereby give you notice to quit, vacate and deliver peaceful vacant possession of the demised premises No. .... (or land, or farm, No. .... etc.) to me of which you now a monthly tenant under the English calender at a rent of Rs. .... per month on the expiry of the month (.........) of .... (or, the ......day of......... being the date of expiry of the month of your tenancy as you have failed and/or neglected to pay the said rent for .... months and thereby made yourself liable to eviction even on that ground alone. Please note that your tenancy in respect of the demised premises and all your relationship with me as between landlord and tenant shall stand determined with effect from the said date. So if you fail and/or neglect to comply with this notice, I shall institute proceedings for recovery of possession against you, making liable also for *mesne profits*, damages and costs.

Particulars of the demised premises.

Dated this .... day of ....

Yours faithfully
CD (*Landlord*)

Notice Demanding Possession after Expiry of Lease[20]

To
AB *(Ex-tenant)*

Re: Premises No. ....

Dear Sir

I, the undersigned, owner of the house and premises (or land) situate at, etc., and your ex-landlord, do hereby give you notice that the lease dated

19 See *Surya Properties Pvt. Ltd.* v *Bimalendu Nath Sarkar* AIR 1964 Cal 1; 67 CWN 977. A combined notice or both the notices are necessary to proceed with a suit for ejectment. The decision in *Muralidhar's* case AIR 1961 Cal 175 was dissented from.

20 It should be noted that in cases governed by the West Bengal Premises Tenancy Act or Non-Agricultural Tenancy Act the special grounds for eviction under those Acts should be mentioned.

the .... day of ...... and made between you, of the one part, and myself, of the other part, has expired by efflux of time on the .... day of .... I have not agreed to any renewal or extension thereof nor otherwise permitted you to continue in occupation of the property in any way. So I hereby give you notice demanding delivery of possession of the said house and premises (or land) on or before the .... day of .... 2000 failing compliance, I shall institute a suit against you for recovery of possession and you will be held responsible for all damages and *mesne profits* that I may be entitled to in law as against you.

Particulars of the demised premises.

Yours faithfully

Date CD *(Owner)*

Notice to Determine Tenancy for Breach of Covenants in a Lease

To

AB *(Tenant)* *Date* ....

Re: Premises No. ....

Dear Sir

I hereby give you notice that the indenture of lease dated the .... day of .... made .... between you of the one part and me of the other part contained *inter alia* the following covenant/s to be observed and performed on your part, *viz.,* ...... The said lease also provides for forfeiture of your tenancy interest in the said property and my consequential right of re-entry in the property on violation *inter alia* of any such covenant. As you have without my knowledge or consent (state the nature of breach or breaches) thereby violated and is still now continuously violating the terms of the lease (which are not at all waived or condoned by me) I hereby give notice of determination of the lease and call upon you to deliver possession of the property to me within .... days of the receipt of this notice, failing which I shall exercise my right of re-entry and bring a suit for ejectment against you also claiming *mesne profits*, damages and costs.

Schedule of the property

Yours faithfully

CD *(Landlord)*

Notice by Tenant to Determine Lease

To

CD *(Landlord)* Date ....

Re: Premises No. ....

Dear Sir

This is to write to you that, in pursuance of the power, authority and liberty for this purpose reserved in my favour under and by virtue of the deed of lease dated the .... day of .... 2000 and made between you, of the one part, and myself, of the other part, I hereby give you notice and determine the lease with effect from the .... day of .... 2000, when I shall quit, vacate and deliver up possession of the house and premises (or, etc.) as comprised in the said deed. Please take further notice that all our relationship also as lessor and lessee shall come to an end on that day and I shall no further remain responsible for performance or non-performance of any of the covenants, conditions and stipulations thereunder contained.

Yours faithfully

AB *(Tenant)*

Notice by Landlord's Advocate to Quit

To

AB (*Tenant*)

Re: Premises No. ....

Client ....

Dear Sir

Under instructions from my client, CD of etc., I hereby give you notice to leave and vacate the house and premises (or, etc.) which you now hold, possess and occupy under my said client as a monthly tenant under the English calendar (or from year to year) on the expiry of the current month of tenancy and deliver peaceful vacant possession thereof to my said client as (state the grounds of eviction). Please note also that on and from the said date, the lease heretobefore subsisting shall cease and stand determined. So the relationship of landlord and tenant as between you and my client shall also cease. Therefore, on your failure to deliver peaceful vacant possession as herein demanded, my client shall bring a suit for ejectment against you making you liable also for *mesne profits*, damages and costs which please note.

Yours faithfully

Date EF Advocate for CD

Notice by Landlord to Repair Dilapidations

To

AB (*Tenant*)

Re: Premises No. ....

Dear Sir

Please take notice that in pursuance of the covenant contained in a deed of lease dated the .... day of .... 2000 and made between you, of the one part, and myself, of the other part [or, of cl. (*m*)] of s. 108 of the Transfer of Property Act (in the absence of any such agreement) I hereby give you notice to keep and maintain the above premises wind and watertight and in good and substantial repair and condition and in particular to execute the several repairs mentioned in the schedule hereto. You have violated the said covenant by not having the said repairs done so far.

Please take further notice that if you continue to make default or fail to remedy such breach of conditions in the manner above-mentioned within .... days, I shall exercise my right of re-entry into the said premises in accordance with the said covenant and execute the said works at your costs and expenses as therein provided.

Schedule above referred to

Yours faithfully

Date CD (*Landlord*)

Notice by Tenant for Renewal of Lease

To

CD (*Landlord*)

Re: Premises No. ....

Dear Sir

I, the undersigned AB your tenant state that, in pursuance of the agreement for renewal contained in the deed of lease dated the .... day of .... 2000, and made between yourself, of the one part, and myself, of the other part, I hereby give notice of my intention to have a renewed lease of the property comprised in the said deed of lease for a further term of .... years; I therefore hereby request you to grant me a renewed lease on the terms and conditions specified in the said deed of lease and send me the draft thereof for approval.

Yours faithfully

Date AB (*Tenant*)

Notice to Tenant to Attorn

To

AB (*Tenant*)

Re: Premises No. ....

Dear Sir

I, the undersigned CD, hereby authorise and request you, the above-named AB, forthwith to attorn to and become a direct tenant of EF of etc. (the purchaser or mortgagee, etc.) in respect of the above-mentioned house which you hold under me as my tenant; I further authorise and request you to pay to the said EF, his heirs, executors, administrators or assigns, all such rent as (now is and) hereafter shall from time to time become due by you for or in respect of the said premises (or, etc.); and for so doing, this shall be to you a sufficient warrant and authority.

Signed at ...., this .... day of 2000

Yours faithfully

CD (*Landlord*)

Notice to Debtor

To

AB (*Debtor*)

Dear Sir

I hereby demand of you payment of the sum of Rs. ...., due on account of the loan taken by you on the .... day of ...., with interest at the rate of .... per cent. per annum, and request you to be good enough to pay or cause to be paid the said amount by the .... day of .... failing which legal proceedings will be taken for the recovery of the amount due with costs and interest without any further reference which please note.

Yours faithfully

CD (*Creditor*)

Notice by Lawyer to Debtor

To

AB (*Debtor*)

Re: Client CD

Dear Sir

I am instructed by my above client, CD of, etc., to demand of you payment of the sum of Rs. .... due by you to my client as per account below, by the .... day of ...., failing which my client shall institute a suit against you for recovery of the amount due, with costs and further interest up to the full realization of the debt which please note.

The account above referred to

Date Yours faithfully

Notice of Dishonour (or Protest) of Bill of Exchange to Drawer

(Section 93 of the Negotiable Instruments Act 1881)

To
CD (*Drawer*)

Dear Sir

Take notice that a bill of exchange for Rs. .... drawn by you under date etc., on AB (drawee) and payable to me or order .... days after date etc., has been dishonoured by non-payment (or non-acceptance) which has been noted and protested (*in case of a foreign bill*), and that you are held responsible therefor.

Yours faithfully
Date EF (*Payee*)

Notice of Dishonour (or Protest) of Bill of Exchange to Endorser

To
EF (*Endorser*)

Dear Sir

Take notice that a bill of exchange for Rs. .... drawn by CD under date the, etc., on AB and payable at, etc., and which bears your endorsement, has been dishonoured by non-acceptance (or non-payment) and noted and protested and that you are held responsible therefor.

CD (*Endorsee*)

Notice of Dishonour of Cheque

(Section 93 of the Negotiable Instruments Act 1881)

To
AB (*Drawer*)

Dear Sir

Please take notice that a cheque No. ...... dated the ...... day of ...., drawn by you on the .... Bank for Rs. ...., payable to CD of etc. or order (when required, add and endorsed by the said CD to EF of etc.), has been dishonoured by non-payment, and that you are held responsible therefor.

(Date)

Yours faithfully

CD (or EF)

Notice by Partner to Determine Partnership

[Section 43(1) of the Indian Partnership Act 1932]

To
CD (*Partner*) Date ....

Dear Sir

By virtue of the power for this purpose contained in clause .... of the deed of partnership, dated the .... day of .... 2000 and made or expressed to be made between yourself of the one part, and myself of the other part [or under s. 43 of the Partnership Act (if the partnership is "at will")] I hereby give you notice that the partnership now subsisting between us under the said deed shall stand dissolved with effect from the .... day of .... 2000 (or immediately on receipt of this notice).

Yours faithfully

AB (*Other Partner*)

Notice of Expulsion of Partner

(Section 33 of the Indian Partnership Act 1932)

To
AB (*Partner*) Date ....

Please note that in *bona fide* exercise of the power and authority vested in us by virtue of clause .... of the articles of partnership, dated the .... day of ...., we, the undersigned being the majority of the partners, hereby determine the partnership heretofore subsisting between us and yourself as from the .... day of .... 2000, so far as you are concerned, and expel you therefrom on grounds that, etc., (state the grounds for expulsion).

Yours faithfully

CD
EF
(*Other Partners*)

Notice by Vendor to a Pre-emptor

To

AB Date ....

Re: Premises ....

Please note that I intend to sell my one-third share in the property described in the Schedule hereto to CD of etc. for the price of Rs. .... As you have a prior right to purchase the same under Act ...... of .... or by virtue of the provisions of the Deed of Partition (or Agreement or Lease dated .... made between you and me) or under the prevailing customs in the locality, you are requested to signify your acceptance thereof at the aforesaid price within .... days. In case I do not hear from you about your acceptance of the offer within the time aforesaid I shall complete the sale with the said CD without reference to or regard for such right which shall be deemed as extinguished for ever.

Schedule of the Property

Yours faithfully

ANOTHER FORM

To

AB

Re: Premises No. ....

Notice is hereby given pursuant to clause .... of the deed of partition dated .... executed between you and others of the one part and the undersigned of the other part, whereby each allottee covenanted not to sell his divided share to any outsider without first offering the same to the others. The undersigned is desirous of selling his share in the above property for which he has already received an offer for Rs. ....

Please take notice that pursuant to the said pre-emption clause you are given the first choice to complete the sale of the said share of the said property at the aforesaid price within a fortnight of the receipt of this. On your failure to do so within the aforesaid period the undersigned shall close the sale with the party offering the said price of Rs. ....

Dated the .... day of .... 2000.

Yours faithfully

CD

Notice by a Vendor to Complete a Purchase

To

AB (*Purchaser*) Date ....

Re: Premises No. ....

Dear Sir

Please refer to the agreement for sale dated .... At all material times I was and am still now ready and willing to complete the sale of the above property in terms of the aforesaid agreement, but the same was not done for reasons of your own. You are, therefore, guilty of delay and laches in the matter. I hereby call upon you to have the conveyance executed by me against payment of the balance of the consideration money on or before the .... day of ...... failing which that agreement will stand cancelled and the earnest money paid by you forfeited. This, however, is without prejudice to other rights and remedies available to me by reason of the breach of agreement on your part as aforesaid.

Yours faithfully

CD (*Vendor*)

Notice by Purchaser to Complete a Sale

To

CD (*Vendor*)

Re: Premises No. ....

Dear Sir

Please refer to the contract dated the .... day of .... 2000, made between you, as vendor of the one part, and myself as purchaser of the other part, by which you agreed to sell to me the, etc., situate at, etc., for the sum of Rs. .... I was at all material times and till now am ready and willing to complete the purchase subject to your performing your part of the said agreement. So I hereby give you notice that if you still fail and/or neglect to carry out your part of the said contract within .... days from this date, I shall institute a suit for specific performance of the said agreement with damages and costs as against you.

Yours faithfully

AB (*Purchaser*)

Date

Notice of Re-sale of Goods on Buyer's Default

[Section 54, clauses (2) and (4) of the Sale of Goods Act 1930][1]

To
AB (*Purchaser*)

Dear Sir

I write to you demanding payment of a sum of Rs. .... due by you to me on account of sale and purchase of goods as per account stated below on or before the .... day of .... 2000 I hereby also give you notice that the goods purchased by you are lying at your risk at .... So if you fail and/or neglect to make the said payment on or before the said date I shall proceed with the re-sale of the goods by public auction on the day of ....at .... p.m. and hold you liable for the shortfall, if any, on that account as also for all costs, charges and expenses incidental thereto and all losses and damages suffered by me.

Account of the goods purchased above referred to

Yours faithfully
CD (*Seller*)

Date

Notice to Determine Guarantee for Faithful Service

(Section 127 of the Indian Contract Act 1872)

To
EF (*Employer*)

Dear Sir

I hereby give you notice that the guarantee dated the .... day of ...., which I executed in your favour for true and faithful service of AB of, etc., as, etc., and also for the payment of any sum that may become due to you on account of any loss or damage sustained by you by reason of any act, breach of trust, mismanagement, neglect, default or dereliction of duty on the part of the said AB while in due course of employment, is hereby revoked and determined the same being without consideration and so void. I therefore give you notice that I shall not be liable for any such loss or damage, if any, sustained by you hereafter.

Yours faithfully

Date CD (*Surety*)

1 The above section is based upon s. 48 of the English Act and under ss. 151,152 and 161 of the Indian Contract Act 1872.

Notice to Determine Continuing Guarantee

(Section 130 of the Indian Contract Act 1872)

To
EF (*Creditor*)

Dear Sir

I hereby give you notice that the guarantee dated the .... day of ...., which I executed in your favour for payment of all moneys which were then or at any time thereafter may be due to you from AB of, etc., on the balance of his account, is hereby revoked and determined; and I give you further notice that if you make any further advances or payments, or give further credit to the said AB, you would do so on your own and the same shall have nothing to do whatsoever with the said guarantee which stands hereby revoked.

Yours faithfully

Date CD (*Surety*)

Notice of Transfer of Mortgage

To
AB (*Mortgagor*)

Re: Premises No. ....

Dear Sir

Please take notice that, by a registered deed of assignment dated the .... day of ...., and made between CD of, etc., of the one part and myself of other part all that principal sum of Rs. .... and interest thereon due by you to the said CD under and secured by a deed of mortgage dated the .... day of ...., made between you of the one part, and the said CD of the other part, were for good and valuable consideration mentioned therein assigned unto and in my favour absolutely, together with the benefit of the security and all the premises (or, etc.) comprised in the said deed were granted, conveyed, transferred, assured and assigned to me, subject to the equity of redemption subsisting thereunder in your favour.

Please take further notice that all payments of principal and interest thereon shall therefore be made to me, and not to the said CD.

Yours faithfully

Date EF of, etc. (*Transferee*)

Notice claiming Mortgage Money

To
AB (*Mortgagor*)

Re: Premises No. ....

Dear Sir

Please refer to the deed of mortgage dated the .... day of .... and made between yourself, of the one part, and myself, of the other part and note that the entire principal amount together with all interest has been due and repayable on the .... day of ...., I therefore do hereby give you notice that if you fail and/or neglect to pay the said principal sum and interest within ...... days after the service of this notice, I shall immediately thereafter institute a suit for enforcement of the said mortgage for the sale (or foreclosure) of the mortgaged property.

Yours faithfully
Date CD (*Mortgagee*)

Notice for Production of Documents

To
AB

In pursuance of your covenant contained in a conveyance (or, etc.) dated the ...... day of ......, and made between yourself, of the one part, and myself (or etc.), of the other part, I hereby give you notice to produce before me at, etc., on the .... day of ...., all the documents mentioned in the said deed, for which I shall bear all the costs, charges and expenses. List of documents to be produced is given below.

List of documents

Yours faithfully
Date CD

Notice of Sale of Pledged Articles

(Section 176 of the Indian Contract Act 1872)

To
AB (*Pledgor*)

Dear Sir

I hereby demand of you payment of the sum of Rs. .... long overdue by you to me as per account below, request you to be good enough to pay or cause to be paid the said amount by the .... day of ....; in default, the articles pledged shall be sold by public auction to the highest bidder at the, etc., at .... o'clock, on the .... day of .... Nevertheless you shall remain responsible for shortfall or deficiency, if any, which will be recovered from you after appropriation of the proceeds of such sale, first, towards the costs and expenses of such sale; secondly, all interest due until the date of sale; and, thirdly, the principal amount, all to be deducted therefrom. Be that so, I would ask you to attend such sale personally and exert yourself for the best price or prices which they may fetch.

Account and the list of the articles above referred to

Yours faithfully

(Date) (*Pledgee*)

Notice of Assignment by Assignor

To
EF (*Debtor*)

Date ....

Dear Sir

I, the undersigned AB (*creditor assignor*), do hereby give you notice that, by an instrument in writing bearing date, etc., and made between me and CD of etc., I, the said AB, have for valuable consideration transferred and assigned unto and in favour of the said CD the bond (or etc.), executed by you and bearing date, etc., whereby you became bound to me in the sum of Rs. .... together with all arrears of interest thereon due and payable (or, etc.). I hereby give you further notice henceforth to pay the said sum or sums to the said CD, his heirs, executors, administrators or assigns, for his or their own use and benefit.

Yours faithfully
AB

Notice of Assignment by Assignee

To
EF (*Debtor*)

Date ....

Dear Sir

I, the undersigned CD of etc., hereby give you notice that, by an instrument in writing bearing date, etc., and made between myself and AB of, etc. (*creditor assignor*), a certain bond (or, etc.) executed by you and bearing date, etc., whereby you became bound to the said AB in the sum of Rs. .... (or, etc.), has in consideration of the sum of Rs. .... been assigned by him, the said AB to me; and, as the said AB has refused to give you notice. I hereby give you further notice to pay the said sum of Rs. .... and all interests to become due upon or in respect thereof from the said .... day of .... (the date of assignment), to me, my heirs, executors, administrators or assigns, or as I or they shall direct.

Yours faithfully
CD (*Assignee*)

Notice of Assignment of Policy of Life Insurance

[Section 38(2) of the Insurance Act 1938]

To
The Zonal Manager   Date ....
.... Life Insurance Corporation of India

Re: Policy No. ....

Dear Sir

I, the undersigned AB etc., do hereby give you notice that, pursuant to s. 38 of the Insurance Act (Act IV of 1938) and by a deed dated the .... day of ...., and made between myself of the one part and CD of, etc., of the other part, the policy of insurance effected by me with .... Co. on my life for the sum of Rs. ...., dated the .... day of ...., and numbered ...., and all moneys assured by me or to become payable under the said policy, were assigned by me unto and in favour of the said CD absolutely, and I request you to acknowledge receipt of this notice and register his name as the assignee of the said policy for value. The policy is annexed hereto for your making the endorsement thereon.

Yours faithfully
Encl: Policy No. ....   AB (*Assignee*)

Notice of Assignment of Lease

(Section 109 of the Transfer of Property Act)

To
AB (*Lessor*)   Date ....

Re: Premises No. ....

Dear Sir

I hereby give you notice that, by a deed of assignment dated the .... day of ...., and made between CD of, etc., of the one part, and myself of the other part, the leasehold interest in the property known as, etc., comprised in a lease dated the .... day of ...., and made between yourself of the one part, and CD of the other part, was assigned by the said CD unto and in my favour for the residue of the term of .... years as provided therein subject nevertheless to the payment of the rent and to the performance and observance of the covenants on the part of the lessee, and the conditions of the said lease.

Yours faithfully
EF (*Assignee*)

Notice for Removal of Nuisance and Obstruction

To
AB

Dear Sir

Please take notice that you are hereby required to remove forthwith the nuisance and/or obstruction arising from, etc., (describe the cause of nuisance) at, etc., which is causing injury to my personal comforts and health. In default, I shall be under painful necessity to take legal steps for securing abatement discontinuance and removal thereof without further reference to you.

This notice is given without prejudice to any right of action for damages, which I have already sustained and may sustain by reason of the continuity of the nuisance and obstruction.

Yours faithfully
CD

Date

Notice of Suit against Municipality

(Under s. 407 of West Bengal Municipal Act 1993)

To
....
.... Municipality

Re: Premises No. ....

Dear Sir

I hereby give you this notice that unless you withdraw the notice dated .... served by you on me for demolition of the building (or for filling up of the tank) in the above premises and unless proper and satisfactory amends are made in the meantime, I will, on the expiry of one month from the date of service of this notice, institute in a proper court a suit on the cause of action and for the reliefs set forth in the draft plaint sent herewith which is made a part of this notice.

Encl: A draft plaint.

Yours faithfully

AB

Date

PUBLIC NOTICES

Notice of Termination of Agent's Authority

(Section 208 of the Indian Contract Act 1872)

NOTICE is hereby given that the power-of-attorney given by the undersigned AB of etc. to CD of etc. has been revoked (or, that CD of etc. has ceased to be an attorney or agent of the undersigned AB of etc.) as from the .... day of ....

The agency of the said CD having been thus terminated, he has no authority whatever to transact any business or to act in any way on behalf of the said AB; so any person transacting any business with him will do so at his own risk as to consequences.

Yours faithfully

AB

Date

Notice of Wife's Leaving Husband's Protection

NOTICE is hereby given that my wife, CD having left my care and protection on her own as from the .... day of ...., I am not at present nor shall in future be responsible for any debt or liability incurred or to be hereafter incurred by her on any account whatsoever and further she has no authority to pledge my credit.

AB

Address ....

Date

Notice to Creditors to Deceased's Estate

Re: Estate of AB deceased

NOTICE is hereby given that all persons having any claim as against the estate of the late AB who died at etc., on the .... day of ...., are hereby requested to send full particulars thereof in writing together with the proof to the undersigned CD the executor named in the will (or, the administrator of the estate) of the deceased, at etc., within one month from the date hereof, after which date no claim will be entertained.

Notice by Attorney to Creditors and Debtors to Deceased's Estate

Re: Estate of AB deceased

NOTICE is hereby given that all persons having any claim or claims as against the estate of the late AB of, etc., who died at, etc., on the .... day of ...., and probate of whose will (or, letters of administration to whose estate) having effect throughout the whole of India (or throughout the State, ...), was (or were), granted by the High Court of Judicature at .... (or by the Court of etc.), on the .... day of ...., to CD of, etc., the executor named in the said will (or the administrator of the estate) of the said deceased, are required to send full particulars thereof together with proof within one month from the date hereof to the undersigned attorney for the said executor (or administrator) at his office at, etc., after which time the executor (or administrator) will proceed to administer the assets having regard only to the claims of which he shall then have received notice, and no claim sent subsequently will be recognised.

And all persons indebted to or holding any securities or property belonging to the said deceased are hereby required forthwith to pay the amounts owing by them, or to deliver up the said securities or the property, as the case may be, to the said executor (or administrator) at the office of the said attorney, EF at his address aforesaid.

Date

EF

Attorney for the Executor (or Administrator)

Notice of Dissolution of Partnership

[Section 45(2) of the Indian Partnership Act 1932]

NOTICE is hereby given that the partnership heretofore subsisting between the undersigned AB of, etc., and CD of, etc., carrying on business of (or, as) etc., at, etc., under the firm name of, etc., has been dissolved by mutual consent (or by effluxion of time, or, by the death of the said CD) as from the .... day of ...... (if the business is to be continued, add) so far as the same concerns the said CD who has thus ceased to have any interest in the said business.

All debts due to or by the said firm will be received and paid respectively by the said AB who will continue to carry on the said business on his sole responsibility under the same old firm name (or under the new firm name of, etc.).

Date AB

Notice of Suit to a Common Carrier for Damages for Loss of Goods

(Section 10 of the Carriers Act 1865)

Dated the 2000

To
The ....
....
Sir

Under instructions from my client Sri .... (*name, description and address*) I call upon you to pay to my said client, within 30 days, from the date of receipt of this notice, a sum of Rs. .... detailed in the Schedule below, as compensation for the loss of .... bags of (name the material) which were entrusted to you at your office at Calcutta (etc.) on .... by M/s. .... for carriage for reward through your transport service (state the nature of service) to etc., the consignee being self (or, my client as the case may be), under Con. Note/Despatch Receipt No. .... dated .... 2000.

The above loss is due to the misconduct and gross negligence on the part of the aforesaid (name the carrier) and/or their agents and/or employees in due course of employment.

Please take notice that in default of your compliance with this notice a suit will be brought against (name the carrier) for recovery of the said sum of Rs. .... together with all incidental costs after the expiry of the period hereinabove allowed.

Yours faithfully

Schedule of claim

NOTE: A common carrier is a person other than a Government engaged in the business of transporting for hire property from one place to another by land or inland navigation for all persons indiscriminately but did not include the Railway under sub-sec. (1) of s. 64 of the Indian Railways Act 1989 which made the Railway Administration liable as bailees as under ss. 151, 152 and 161 of the Indian Contract Act 1872.

RAILWAY CLAIM NOTICES

Notice to the General Manager of a Railway Administration claiming Compensation for Short Delivery, Non-delivery or Delivery in Damaged Condition

Notice by party (simple form)

Regd. with A/D

Dated ....

Subject: Notice under s. 106 of the Indian Railways Act 1989

To
The General Manager .... Railway, ...
(name the Railway with address)

Details of consignment short delivered or lost or delivered in damaged condition.

Ex .... on .... Rly. .... to .... on ....

Rly. Invoice No. .... P.W.B./B.R. No. .... dated ....

Sender/Consignor ....

Consignee ....

Endorsed to .... for valuable consideration

Contents .... bags/bales/tins, etc. of .... each bag/bale weighing (or containing) ....

Date of delivery at the destination ....

Condition in which the consignment was delivered ....
(state here shortage, or deterioration, etc.)

In case of total loss an averment to effect ....

Short (or damage) certificate issued by .... on ....

Dear Sir

In serving you with the notice under s. 106 of the Indian Railways Act 1989, I hereby call upon the Railway to pay to me within .... days from the date of receipt of this notice a sum of Rs. .... as compensation assessed on account of shortage (or loss/deterioration) of goods in the above consignment. Please note that unless the said sum is paid within the aforesaid time I shall file a claim before the Railways Claims Tribunal for recovery of the said sum with interest and costs.

Yours faithfully

Notice to the General Manager, Railway claiming Compensation for Non-delivery, Short Delivery/Deterioration, etc.

ANOTHER FORM

Regd. with A/D

Dated ....

To
The General Manager ....
Railway, ...

Dear Sir

Subject: Notice under s. 106 of the Indian Railways Act 1989

Under instruction from my client Sri .... of .... I hereby give you this notice claiming a sum of Rs. .... as compensation for the loss of goods suffered by my above client for reasons of non-delivery/shortage (in case of short delivery)/destruction/deterioration (as the case is) as stated below:

The consignment of goods consisting of .... bags/packets/tins, etc. of .... each bag etc. weighing .... kg. of .... was/were booked by my client from .... on .... Rly. under R.R. No. .... dated .... for carriage forward to .... a station on .... Rly., the consignor/sender being .... and the consignee being .... (or self) which was endorsed to my said client for valuable consideration.

At the time of taking delivery of the consignment on .... at .... (state here the condition in which the consignment is received) my client discovered a shortage and/or loss of .... goods in the said consignment (or the entirety or portion thereof completely damaged) for which a certificate to that effect was issued by the .... Rly. station on .... etc.

(Or, the said consignment having been lost or misdirected elsewhere in course of transit and so not reached the destination as yet, the Railway Administration failed to deliver the same to my aforesaid client in spite of repeated demands).

These being the circumstances, I am instructed by my client to demand of the Railways to pay to me or to my said client, within .... days from the date of receipt of his notice, a sum of Rs. .... as loss and damages suffered by reason of loss, deterioration or wrongful conversion of goods as aforesaid.

Schedule of claim

1. Loss for shortage of ....
at Rs. .... per qtt.
as per Bijuk/market rate .... Rs. ....
2. For proportionate Rly. freight
(in case of partial delivery) paid ...... Rs. ....
3. Other costs (packing cost, etc.) .... Rs. ....
4. Costs of notices etc. .... Rs. ....

Total Rs. ....

Yours faithfully

Notice to General Manager of a Railway Claiming Refund of Overcharge

Dated ....

To

The General Manager, ... Railway, ...
(Name the Railway with address)

Dear Sir

Subject: Notice under s. 106 of the Indian Railways Act 1989

Under instructions from my client .... (name, description and address) I hereby give you a notice calling upon the Railways for refund to my said client, within .... days from the date of receipt of this notice, a sum of Rs. .... which the Railways wrongfully and/or illegally charged, in excess of actual legitimate and really payable freight which my client had to pay under Money Receipt No. .... dated .... to Railways, for the carriage and delivery of the consignment from .... a station on the .... Rly. to .... a station on the .... Railway under R/R PWB No. .... dated .... the consignor being (name and address) and the consignee being (name and address) endorsed to my client for valuable consideration.

Please note that in default of payment within the time aforesaid my client shall file a claim before the Railways Claims Tribunal against the Railways for recovery of the said sum with costs and interests.

Yours faithfully

Notice to a Railway claiming Damages for Liabilities in Tort of a Railway Administration (case of Physical Injury)

Dated ....

Regd. with A/D

To
The General Manager, ... Railway, ...
(Name the Railway with address)

Dear Sir

Subject: Notice under s. 106 of the Indian Railways Act 1989

Under instructions from my client (state here name, description and address) I hereby give you a notice claiming damages of Rs. .... on account of personal injuries suffered by him as hereunder stated.

My said client was a qualified surgeon of good repute.

My said client had on (date) .... purchased a 1st class ticket at .... Rly. station on the .... Railway for a journey from .... to .... by .... (......................, etc., name the train) and availed himself of a reserved seat in a 1st class compartment of the train. On .... at about .... hours the train while driven carelessly and negligently by the workmen of the Railway met with a serious accident after it had collided with another train waiting in a station of the same Railway. In the result my client who was thrown off his seat lost both of his arms and became permanently disabled and unfit for carrying on his livelihood as a surgeon.

My client is entitled to recover from the Railways a sum of Rs. .... as per account below.

Please take notice that unless the said Railway pay to my client the said sum of Rs. .... within 60 days from the date of receipt of this notice, my client shall file a claim petition before the Railways Claims Tribunal.

Particulars of claim

(*a*) Medical expenses incurred for treatment	Rs. ....
(*b*) Physical and mental agony caused by injury	Rs. ....
(*c*) Loss of future earning as a surgeon because of the loss of arms	Rs. ....
Total	Rs. ....

Yours faithfully

A Combined Notice under section 106 of the Indian Railways Act 1989 and under section 80 of the Code of Civil Procedure 1908

Regd. with A/D

The General Manager, ... Railway Dated ....
(Address) ....

Dear Sir

Please take notice that my client (name, description) of .... (address) will institute a suit against the Union of India, owning and administering the aforesaid Railway in a court of competent jurisdiction after expiry of two months after service of this combined notice of claim under s. 106 of the Indian Railways Act and s. 80 of the Code of Civil Procedure for reliefs hereunder claimed unless they are all granted to my client by the said Railway within the said period of two months.

The relevant facts justifying my client's claim and constituting cause of action of the proposed suit and relief thereunder will appear hereinbelow:

(*a*) On or about the .... day of .... my said client made over to the said Railway a consignment of .... bags .... each bag .... weighing .... kg. .... of .... for carriage for reward from .... a station on the said Railway to .... a station on the same Railway under P.W.B. No. .... dated .... consignor being M/s. .... and the consignee being self-endorsed to my client for valuable consideration. The said consignment has not reached as yet so far the said destination and so was not delivered to my client uptill now in spite of repeated demands.

(*b*) The loss and consequent non-delivery of the consignment is due to wilful act, default, misconduct, carelessness and gross negligence of the aforesaid Railway Administration, its agents and/or employees concerned. My client is at this stage unable to give full particulars of the same until after full disclosure of facts and evidences by the Railway as to how they have dealt with the consignment during the period the same was in possession and control of the Railway.

(*c*) My client hereby claims a sum of Rs. .... as damages suffered on account of the loss or non-delivery of the consignment and is entitled to recover the same as against the Railway.

The following are particulars of the claim:

(*i*) Loss for shortage of at
Rs. ....
(as per Bijuk/market rate) Rs. ....

(*ii*) For proportionate railway freight
(in case of partial delivery) paid Rs. ....

(*iii*) Other costs (packing costs, etc.) Rs. ....

(*iv*) Costs of notices etc. Rs. ....

Total Rs. ....

The cause of action arose on the .... day of on account of wrongful loss caused to my client because of the non-delivery of goods without any just or sufficient cause.

(*d*) The names, addresses and description of the plaintiff and the defendant, nature of cause of action and relief claimed as required to be stated in the notice under s. 80 of CPC are contained in the particulars hereinbefore given.

Yours faithfully

STATUTORY NOTICE UNDER CODE OF CIVIL PROCEDURE 1908

Notice of Suit of General Manger of different Railways under section 80, CPC, claiming Compensation for Short Delivery

Regd. with A/D

Address ....

Dated ....

To

1. The General Manager, ... Railway, ...
2. The General Manager, ... Railway, ...
3. The General Manager, ... Railway, ...

Dear Sirs

Subject: Notice under s. 80 of the Code of Civil Procedure

Please take notice that my client (state here name, description and address) will institute a suit against the Union of India, owning and administering the aforesaid Railways in a court of competent jurisdiction, after expiry of two months after service of this notice unless reliefs claimed hereinbelow are granted to my client within the said period of two months. The relevant facts constituting the cause of action and reliefs claimed are as follows:

1. That on or about the .... day of .... my said client made over to the said Railway a consignment of .... bags of .... each bag containing .... of .... for carriage for reward, from .... a station on the .... Railway under Invoice No. .... R/R, P.W.B. No. .... dated .... to a station on the .... Railway, the sender/consignor being .... and the consignee being .... endorsed to .... At the time of delivery of the said consignment on the .... day of .... bags were not

found and so short delivered (or ...... bags were received badly torn etc.) resulting thus in a shortage for which usual short certificate was given by the station concerned.

2. My client thus suffered a loss of Rs. .... full particulars whereof are given in the schedule below due to default and/or negligence and/or misconduct on the part of the aforesaid Railway, their agents and/or employees concerned. My client cannot at this stage give full particulars of the said default and/or negligence and/or misconduct until full disclosure of the conduct of the agent and employees of the Railways as to how they dealt with the consignment during the period while the same was in their possession, custody or control.

3. My client (name the client ....) has already served the Railway a notice dated .... under s. 106 of the Indian Railways Act demanding the Railway payment of the said sum Rs........... within 30 days from the date of receipt of the said notice but to no effect.

4. The following are particulars of the claim:

(*a*)	Loss for shortage of .... at Rs. .... per qt. as per Bijuk/ market rate	Rs. ....
(*b*)	For proportionate Rly. freight (in case of partial delivery) paid	Rs. ....
(*c*)	Other costs (packing cost, etc.)	Rs. ....
(*d*)	Costs of notices etc.	Rs. ....
	Total	Rs. ....

5. The particulars required under s. 80 of the Code of Civil Procedure are as follows:

(*a*)	Name, address and description of the plaintiff	CD residing at ....
(*b*)	Name, address and description of the defendant	Union of India representing the .... Railway.
(*c*)	Cause of action	Damages suffered due to short delivery or non-delivery of goods.
(*d*)	Relief claimed	Decree for Rs. .... being the loss caused by short delivery or non-delivery of goods.

Yours faithfully

SECTION 80 OF CODE OF CIVIL PROCEDURE 1908

NOTICE. (1) Save as otherwise provided in sub-section (2), no suit shall be instituted against the Government (including the Government of the State of Jammu and Kashmir) or against a public officer in respect of any act purporting to be done by such public officer in his official capacity, until the expiration of two months next after notice in writing has been delivered to, or left at the office of—

(*a*) in the case of a suit against the Central Government, except where it relates to a railway, a Secretary to that Government;

(*b*) in the case of a suit against the Central Government where it relates to a railway, the General Manager of that railway;

(*bb*) in the case of a suit against the Government of the State of Jammu and Kashmir, the Chief Secretary to that Government or any other office authorised by that Government in this behalf;

(*c*) in the case of a suit against any other State Government, a Secretary to that Government or the Collector of the district;

and, in the case of a public officer, delivered to him or left at his office, stating the cause of action, the name, description and place of residence of the plaintiff and the relief which he claims; and the plaint shall contain a statement that such notice has been so delivered or left.

(2) A suit to obtain an urgent or immediate relief against the Government (including the Government of the State of Jammu and Kashmir) or any public officer in respect of any act purporting to be done by such public officer in his official capacity, may be instituted, with the leave of the court, without serving any notice as required by sub-section (1); but the court shall not grant relief in the suit, whether interim or otherwise, except after giving to the Government or public officer, as the case may be, a reasonable opportunity of showing cause in respect of the relief prayed for in the suit:

Provided that the court shall, if it is satisfied, after hearing the parties, that no urgent or immediate relief need be granted in the suit, return the plaint for presentation to it after complying with the requirements of sub-section (1).

(3) No suit instituted against the Government or against a public officer in respect of any act purporting to be done by such public officer in his official capacity shall be dismissed merely by reason of any error or defect in the notice referred to in sub-section (1), if in such notice—

(*a*) the name, description and the residence of the plaintiff had been so given as to enable the appropriate authority or the public officer to identify the person serving the notice and such notice had been delivered or left at the office of the appropriate authority specified in sub-section (1), and (*b*) the cause of action and the relief claimed by the plaintiff had been substantially indicated.

Notice of Election by the Minor Concerning Partnership

[Section 30(5) of the Indian Partnership Act 1932]

NOTICE is hereby given that the undersigned AB, who was admitted to the benefits of the partnership subsisting between CD and EF (or etc.), carrying on the business of (or as), etc., at etc., under the firm name of etc., having attained majority on the .... day of .... (if necessary), add .... and on the ...... day of ......, having obtained knowledge of the fact that he had been admitted to the benefits of the said partnership, does hereby elect to become (or, not to become) a partner in the said partnership.

Date AB

Notice by Purchaser's Solicitor Previous to Purchase of Property

NOTICE is hereby given that AB, of etc., having contracted on the day of .... to sell the undermentioned property to my client, CD, of etc., any person or persons claiming any interest on the said property, or any part thereof, by way of sale, exchange, mortgage, gift, trust, inheritance, bequest, possession, lease, lien, easement or otherwise, is hereby required to communicate the same to the undersigned at his office at, etc., within .... days from the date hereof, as otherwise the said sale will be completed without any reference or regard to any such purported claim or interest, which shall be deemed to have been waived to all intents and purposes.

The description of the property.

Date EF, Solicitor for CD

Notice of Sale of Business

NOTICE is hereby given that the business of etc., heretofore carried on by the undersigned AB at, ... as its sole proprietor .... was sold, transferred and assigned on the .... day of .... unto and to use of CD of, etc., who will nevertheless remain responsible for and to pay up, discharge and satisfy all its debts and liabilities up to and inclusive of the date of such transfer but not for any debts, performance or non-performance of any contract or contracts or other liabilities incurred, made or entered into by the said CD or any other person whatsoever in connection with the said business next after the said .... day of ....

Date AB

39

Partnership

Introductory observations. The relationship between partners arises not out of status but from contract.

Partnership is the relation which subsists between persons carrying on a business in common with a view to profit.[1] Partnership is a contract between two or more persons to invest their money and effects and to utilise their labour and skill or some or all of them in lawful commerce or industry and to divide the profits and share the loss in certain proportions.

The word 'partnership' is defined in s. 4 of the Partnership Act (Act X of 1932) as a relation between persons who have agreed to share profits of business carried on by all or any one of them acting for all. As observed by the Bombay High Court,[2] partnership requires three elements—(*a*) an agreement entered into by all persons concerned; (*b*) distribution of the profits of the business; and (*c*) management of the business by all or any one or more of them acting for all, *i.e.*, mutual agency. One partner is not only an agent of the firm but also of the other partners and, if so, can bind another which falls within the scope of partnership subject to limitation under s. 20 of the Act as regards the implied authority of the firm, Societies and clubs whose object is not to acquire profits are not partnership; so the members are as such not liable for each other's debts.[3]

Out of these three, the third element, *i.e.* the element of mutual agency is most essential and it distinguishes partnership from other type of contractual relationship between the parties. If this element is absent the partnership fails.

1 Lindley on *Partnership*, 15th Ed., p. 11.
2 *Chimanram Motilal* v *Jayantilal Chhaganlal* (1939)41 Bom LR 899; AIR 1939 Bom 410 (DB).
3 8 Ex 898.

A partnership is distinguishable from associations, *e.g.* clubs, societies, co-operative bodies and incorporated companies. So societies and clubs, the object of which is not to acquire profit, are not partnership.[4] The tests of partnership was as laid down by the House of Lords in the case of *Cox* v *Hickman*,[5] the real intention and conduct of the parties appearing from the (*a*) written agreement, or (*b*) verbal agreement together with surrounding circumstances. So a partnership is possible between owners of a building or co-owners of a mine if they deal with the same in such a way as to amount to carrying on business[5] and satisfy the essential requirement of partnership. It is the question of agency and authority, in other words, the existence of the relationship as between the principal and the agent. Although people enjoy freedom of contract, nevertheless certain types of partnership are still considered illegal, *e.g.* (*a*) partnership from carrying on banking business with more than 10 persons (s. 4 of the Companies Act) or any partnership consisting of more than 20 persons; (*b*) for objects forbidden by law (see Akbari and Excise Act),[6] partnership for running a lottery,[7] for selling smuggled goods,[8] when the licence is worked by a third party; (*c*) when opposed to public policy *e.g.* traffic in public office;[9] and (*d*) partnership with alien enemy[10] or formed for the purpose of profits from some illegal venture, a criminal *e.g.* smuggling, theft, robbery etc.[11]

War puts an end to all contracts of partnership as between citizens of the Enemy States.[12] All contracts entered into before the outbreak of the hostility are abrogated if they enure to the aid of the alien enemy or involve any dealing with the alien enemy.

Partnership—partner—firm and firm name. Partnership is the relation between persons who have agreed to share the profits of a business carried on by all or any of them acting for all.

Persons who have entered into partnership with one another are called individually *partners* and collectively a *firm*, and the name under which their business is carried on is called the *firm name*.[13]

It is a voluntary contract as between people to place their capital, labour and skill in lawful commerce or business.[14] A valid partnership is possible

4 Lindley on *Partnership*, 15th Ed., p. 13.
5 (1860)8 HLC 268.
6 *Marudamuthu* v *Rangasami* (1901)24 Mad 401.
7 *Dorabji Tata* v *Lance* (1918)42 Bom 676.
8 *Briggs* v *Lawrence* (1789)2 Term Rep 456.
9 *Ledu Coachman* v *Hiralal* (1916)43 Cal 115.
10 *Marshall & Co.* v *Naginchand* (1918)42 Bom 473. Also see *Porter* v *Freudenberg* (1915)1 KB 857.
11 *Briggs* v *Lawrence* 3 TR 454.
12 Section 41(*b*) of the Indian Partnership Act.
13 Section 4 of the Indian Partnership Act.
14 Story on *Partnership*, s. 21.

between persons even though one is a *benamdar* for another and the existence of such a partnership cannot be questioned by a third party.[15] A firm must be registered under s. 58 of the Partnership Act or otherwise a suit filed whether as between partners or against a third party will not be maintainable. Section 69 is mandatory. Partnership Deed may contain no fixed period as its duration and no provisions for dissolution. Such a partnership is known as Partnership at Will.

Multiple partnership. The Partnership Act permits a person to become a partner with another person in a particular adventure or undertaking (s. 3). The same partners may enter into an agreement for the creation of two or more partnerships. The firm name is only a collective name for each of the partners but each partnership is a distinct relationship. Partners may agree to carry on a business and share its profits followed by separate agreement between the same partners to carry on another business and share profits therein. The intention will have to be ascertained by the terms of the agreement and the surrounding circumstances including evidence as to interlacing or interlocking of management, finance and other incidents of the respective business.[16]

Partnership at will. Where partners contemplated that the management would be carried on the rotation between them in four-yearly periods and the heirs of the partners would also carry on the management in rotation, the partnership could not be brought to an end by notice by either partner. The intention obviously was to have a partnership of some duration though duration was not expressly fixed in the agreement. Partnership will not be one at will if the duration can be implied.[17] But where duration is not only uncertain but the same depends upon an event which may happen *i.e.* grant of a permanent licence for running the particular business, the partnership will be at will.[18] Where a licence was granted to a proprietorship concern but the licensee entered into partnership with others he cannot institute suit for settlement of accounts on the basis of such illegal and forbidden partnership agreement.[19]

Rights, duties and liabilities of partners. Partners are bound to carry on the business of the firm to the greatest common advantage, to be just and faithful to each other, and to render true accounts and full information of all things affecting the firm to any partner or his legal representative.[20]

15 *Narul Hasan* v *Amir Hasan* AIR 1962 Cal 569.
16 *Dy. Commr.* v *K. Kelukutty* AIR 1985 SC 1143.
17 *K. Thiagarajan* v *E.M. Muthappa* AIR 1961 SC 1225.
18 *Gobardhan* v *Abani Mohan* AIR 1991 Cal 195.
19 *Gobardhan*, ibid.
20 Sections 9, 12 and 13 of the Indian Partnership Act.

Every partner must indemnify the firm for any loss caused to it by his fraud in the conduct of the business of the firm. Every partner is liable, jointly or severally, for all acts of the firm done while he is a partner.[21]

Partner is an agent—what a partner is not empowered to do. A partnership business is the business of all partners and the power of management is co-extensive.[1] Each partner is in contemplation of law the general agent of the partnership. He may buy and sell goods on account of partnership, contract debts, pay debts, draw, make, endorse bills of exchange, cheque, etc. He can bind the firm by all acts done by him which are not in the nature beyond the scope of partnership. But there are statutory restrictions on his power.[2]

Limitations of implied authority. In the absence of an usage or custom of trade to the contrary, the implied authority of a partner does not empower him to—

(*i*) submit a dispute relating to the business of the firm to arbitration;

(*ii*) open a banking account on behalf of the firm in his own name;

(*iii*) compromise or relinquish any claim or portion of a claim of the firm;

(*iv*) withdraw a suit or proceeding filed on behalf of the firm;

(*v*) admit any liability in a suit or proceeding against the firm;

(*vi*) acquire immovable property on behalf of the firm; or

(*vii*) enter into partnership with another on behalf of the firm.

Consequence of notice given to the partner. Notice to any partners who habitually acts in the partnership business of any matter relating to partnership affairs operates as notice to the firm, except in the case of a fraud on the firm committed by or with the consent of the partner.[3]

It is absurd to hold that the firm has notice of everything done by all its members.

Consequences of partner being adjudicated an insolvent. Where a partner in a firm is adjudicated an insolvent, he ceases to be a partner on the date on which the order of adjudication is made, whether or not the firm is thereby dissolved.[4]

21 Section 10 of the Indian Partnership Act.
1 *Donaldson* v *Williams* (1833)2 LJ Ex 173.
2 Section 19 of the Indian Partnership Act.
3 Lindley on *Partnership*, 15th Ed., pp. 291-292 and see s. 24 of the Indian Partnership Act.
4 Section 41 of the Indian Partnership Act 1932.

It is well settled in England, as also in India, that a minor partner, *i.e.* partner admitted to the benefits of partnership, cannot be adjudged as insolvent, but in any case the entire property of the firm including the minors shall vest in the official assignee or Receiver in insolvency.[5]

Non-liability of deceased partner's estate.[6] Where under a contract between the partners, the firm is not dissolved by the death of a partner, the estate of a deceased partner is not liable for any act of the firm done after his death.

Minors admitted to benefits of partnership. The law regarding minors who have been admitted to the benefits of partnership is as follows:

1. Any person, who is a minor according to the law to which he is subject, may not be a partner in a firm, but with the consent of all the partners for the time being, he can be admitted to the benefits of partnership.[7]

2. Such minor has a right to such share of the property and of the profits of the firm as may be agreed upon, and he can have access to inspect and copy any of the accounts of the firm.[8]

3. Such minor's share is liable for the acts of the firm, but the minor is not personally liable for any such act.[9]

4. Such minor may not sue the partners for an account or payment of his share of the property or profits of the firm save when severing his connection with the firm, and in such a case the amount of his share will be determined by a valuation made as far as possible in accordance with the rules regarding the mode of settlement of accounts between parties; provided that all the partners acting together, or any partner entitled to dissolve the firm upon notice to other partners, may elect in such suit to dissolve the firm, and thereupon the court will proceed with the suit as one for dissolution and for settling accounts between the partners, and the amount of the share of the minor shall be determined along with the shares of the partners.[10]

5. At any time within six months of his attaining majority, or of his obtaining knowledge that he had been admitted to the benefits of the partnership, whichever date is later, such person may give public notice that he has elected to become, or that he has elected not to become a partner in the firm and such notice shall determine his position as regards

5 *Sanyashi Charan Mondal* v *Krishnadone Banerjee* (1922)49 Cal 560 (570); AIR 1922 PC 237.

6 The Supreme Court summarised the incidents and true nature of benefits of a minor in the case of *Commissioner of Income-tax* v *Shah Mohandas Sadhram* AIR 1966 SC 15 (17) held—A guardian can do all that is necessary to effectuate the confirment and receipts of the benefits of partnership.

7 Section 30(1) of the Indian Partnership Act.

8 Section 30(2) of the Indian Partnership Act.

9 Section 30(3) of the Indian Partnership Act.

10 Section 30(4) of the Indian Partnership Act.

the firm; provided that, if he fails to give such notice, he shall become a partner in the firm on the expiry of the said six months.[11]

6. Where such person becomes a partner—

(*i*) his rights and liabilities as a minor continue up to the date on which he becomes a partner, but he also becomes personally liable to third parties for all acts of the firm done since he was admitted to the benefits of the partnership;[12]

(*ii*) his share in the property and profits of the firm shall be the share to which he was entitled as a minor.[13]

7. Where such person elects not to become a partner—

(*i*) his rights and liabilities will continue to be those of a minor under the law up to the date on which he gives public notice;

(*ii*) his share will not be liable for any acts of the firm done after the date of the notice; and

(*iii*) he will be entitled to sue the partners for his share of the property and profits in accordance with what is provided in cl. (4).[14]

Dissolution of partnership. The dissolution of partnership between all the partners of a firm is called the dissolution of the firm.[15]

The firm is dissolved—

(*i*) by the adjudication of all partners, or of all the partners but one, as insolvent; or

(*ii*) by the happening of an event which makes it unlawful for the business of the firm to be carried on, or for the partners to carry on partnership; e.g. partnership with alien enemy or one partner *e.g.* dentist is struck off the roll,[16] provided that, where more than one separate adventure or undertaking is carried on by the firm the illegality of one or more shall not, by itself, cause the dissolution of the firm in respect of its lawful adventures and undertakings.

Subject to contract between the partners, a firm is dissolved—

(*i*) if constituted for a fixed term, by the expiry of that term;

(*ii*) if constituted to carry out one or more adventures or undertakings by the completion thereof;

11 Section 30(5) of the Indian Partnership Act.
12 Section 30(7)(*a*) of the Indian Partnership Act.
13 Section 30(7)(*b*) of the Indian Partnership Act.
14 Sections 30(8)(*a*) and 30(8)(*b*) of the Indian Partnership Act.
15 Sections 41 and 42 of the Indian Partnership Act.
16 *Clifford* v *Timms* (1908) AC 12.

(*iii*) by the death of a partner; and

(*iv*) by the adjudication of a partner as an insolvent.

Law of insolvency and partnership. Under the English Law, no order of adjudication can be made against a firm but it can be made against the partners individually[17] but such an order may be made under the Indian Law.[18]

Common partners. A firm in England cannot bring an action against another firm in which there is a common partner. This is based on the common law principle that a suit between one house of trade against another house of trade having a common partner is not maintainable. The Judicature Acts being a rule of procedure do not create a cause of action which does not exist in common law.[19]

The only relief the plaintiff is entitled to is an account of the dealings and transactions of the partners.[1] Otherwise no justice could be done to the parties.

In India, however, the Civil Procedure Code under Or. XXX, r. 9, which corresponds with Or. 48(A), r. 10 of the Rules of the Supreme Court in England authorises such firms to litigate as against another under two circumstances, (*i*) the firm must carry on business in India; and (*ii*) all the partners must not be common.[2]

The rule does not alter the substantive law but qualifies the same.[3]

Nomination of successor. Introduction of a new partner is a matter of agreement between the partners.[4]

It is not uncommon in partnership agreements to find a clause as to nomination of a successor who has the right to be declared and admitted as partner in the event of death or retirement of a partner. It was, however, held by the Supreme Court that the nomination is not effective in case of partnership firm consisting of two partners only[5] as it stands dissolved on the death of a partner; nevertheless, in view of the rights and obligations of a person to be nominated as under s. 31 of the Act, the same principle in case of agreement between two persons[6] is applicable in case of partnership

17 Ex parte *Blain* 1879.

18 Section 99 of the Presidency Town Insolvency Act.

19 Lindley on *Partnership*, 15th Ed., p. 49.

1 *Meyer and Co.* v *Faber (No. 2)* (1923)2 Ch D 421 (435, 439).

2 Ghosh on *Law of Pleadings*, Ed. 1966, p. 196.

3 *Rustomji* v *Purushattam* (1901)25 Bom 606 (612); Mulla on *Code of Civil Procedure*, 12th Ed., p. 1031.

4 Section 31 of the Partnership Act 1932. See also s. 42 of the said Act.

5 *Commissioner of Income-tax* v *Govindram Sugar Mills* AIR 1966 SC 24 (27).

6 Desai on *Partnership*, 4th Ed., p. 203.

between two partners. The nomination must be specific. It may be made by will as specific legacy.[7]

Registration of firms. The registration of a firm can be effected under s. 58 of the Partnership Act at any time by sending by post or delivering to the Registrar of the area, in which any place of business of the firm is situated or proposed to be situated, a statement in the prescribed form and accompanied by the requisite fee, stating—

(*i*) the firm name;

(*ii*) the place or principal place of business of the firm;

(*iii*) the names of other places where the firm carries on business;

(*iv*) the date when each partner joined the firm;

(*v*) the names in full and permanent address of the partners; and

(*vi*) the duration of the firm.

The statement shall be signed and verified by all the partners or by their agents especially authorised in this behalf. The effect of non-registration under s. 69 of the Act is that it bars the right of suing by and on behalf of the firm.

Execution and attestation—registration. A deed of partnership, or of dissolution of partnership, must be executed and attested as a bond, and its registration is not compulsory; but where a deed of dissolution of a firm involves transfer of immovable property worth Rs. 100 or upwards, the deed is compulsorily registrable.

FORMS

Partnership among Solicitors or Advocates

THIS INDENTURE IS MADE this .... day of ....2000 BETWEEN (*i*) AB son of .... etc., hereinafter referred to as the first partner of the first part, (*ii*) CD son of etc., hereinafter referred to as the second partner of the second part and EF son of ...., etc., hereinafter referred to as the third partner of etc., of the third part Witnesseth that the said first partner, second partner and third partner hereby mutually covenant and agree to be partners in the profession of solicitors on terms as follows:

1. The said partners will carry on the profession of solicitors in partnership at .... under the name and style of .... as from the .... day of ....

7 *Bachubhai* v *Shamji* (1885)9 Bom 536.

2. The partnership shall continue for the term of .... years with effect from the said .... day of .... unless previously determined as hereinafter provided. The death, withdrawal or retirement (or bankruptcy) of any partner shall not determine the partnership as to the other partners.

3. The first party shall have .... shares in the said partnership business and the second party .... shares and the third party .... shares and they shall be entitled to the net profits accordingly.

4. The capital requisite for carrying on the partnership business at present is Rs. .... which shall be contributed by the partners in proportion to their respective shares immediately on execution of these presents. Any further capital required from time to time shall be contributed by the partners in the shares in which they are for the time being entitled to the net profits of the said business and such capital shall carry interest at the rate of .... per cent per annum payable on the .... day of .... in each year before any division of profits.

5. Subject to the provisions of these presents, the goodwill of the partnership business shall belong to the said FIRST PARTNER and SECOND PARTNER in equal shares.

6. The staff to be maintained shall consist of one managing clerk, one court clerk, two typists, one bill clerk and two peons. All appointments and dismissals, fixation of salaries, bonus, retirement benefits, etc. shall be done by the party of the first part.

7. Proper books of account *e.g.*, day book, cash book, ledger, law ledger and diaries, counsels' memo files shall be kept by the partners at the business premises and the same at all times be available for inspection by all the parties.

8. Each partner shall duly punctually make full and proper entries of all business transacted by him on account of the partnership and check up the bill or bills for all such matters but none except the first party shall have any right to settle any bill by forgoing any amount.

9. Each partner shall be entitled to draw a sum of Rs. .... each month and the balance on account of his share in the partnership property twice a year once on 2nd January and another on 2nd July after adjustment of all accounts of the firm; such account shall be prepared containing the details of the assets and liabilities of the firm, amount of capital contributed, amount due to each partner about his share of profits and shall be kept signed by the partners.

10. Each partner shall be just and faithful to one another, devote his whole time and attention to the partnership business and no partner shall, without the consent of the other partner or partners, engage in any other business or hold any office of profits or appointment nor do any professional work outside the office except free and voluntary service to his friends and

relations provided that each of them, the said FIRST PARTNER and SECOND PARTNER shall be at liberty to hold any office in the company and such honorary offices as he or they may think fit. Provided also that (save as aforesaid) all offices and appointments held by any partner during the partnership shall be held for the benefit of the partnership.

11. No partner shall pledge the credit of partnership except in the usual and regular course of the business or give credit to and conduct any business for any person, company or firm (other than such persons as are mentioned in the next following clause hereof) after being required in writing not to do so by the other partner or partners.

12. Upon the death of any partner and upon any person ceasing to be a partner, the share of the deceased or outgoing partner, including capital stock-in-trade and other assets shall be purchased by and belong to the remaining partners who shall take upon themselves all debts and liabilities when and in such an event, all deeds, papers and writings belonging to the firm shall be handed over to and retained by the surviving partners.

13. If, during the continuance of the partnership or at any time thereafter, any difference or disputes shall arise between the partners or their respective legal representatives or any other person or persons under these articles as to the meaning or construction on the rights and liabilities or matter or things done or to be done in pursuance hereof, such disputes and differences shall be referred to arbitration and award of the President of the Incorporated Law Society and his decision and award shall be final and binding upon the parties.

In witness whereof the parties have hereunto set and subscribed their respective hands and seal the day, month and year first above-written.

Signed, sealed and delivered AB
etc. CD
EF

Deed of Admission of Partner

ARTICLES OF PARTNERSHIP MADE this .... day of .... 2000 BETWEEN AB son of etc. .... of the one part and CD son of etc. of the other part to the following effect. WHEREAS the said AB has been carrying on the business in .... as its sole proprietor under the name and style of .... at .... AND WHEREAS, for development of the said business by mutual assistance and co-operation the said AB has agreed to admit CD as a working partner and in consideration of the service to be rendered to pay him a sum equivalent to .... % share of the net profits. NOW THIS DEED WITNESSETH and it is hereby agreed and declared as follows:

1. The said CD is hereby admitted as a working partner of the said AB in his said trade with effect from the date of execution of these presents in

consideration of good, faithful and efficient service to be rendered for development of the trade but shall have no claim to the assets or goodwill.

2. The said CD shall not have to contribute any sum towards the capital and shall have accordingly no claim or interest in the stock-in-trade and other assets or in the goodwill of the trade which shall all remain the exclusive property of AB as before but shall be entitled only to a sum representing .... % of the net profits in exchange of good and faithful service to the said AB as hereunder stipulated.

3. The said CD shall serve the said AB truly and faithfully in all respects, carry out all his orders to the best of his knowledge, skill and power, observe all rules of the establishment, maintain and preserve all its trade secrets and shall do, execute and perform ungrudgingly all work entrusted to him by the said AB but shall have no right to interfere with the management.

4. The partnership hereunder created shall continue until such time when the same is dissolved by the said AB upon giving one month's notice in writing to the said CD provided, however, that in case of fraud, misconduct or dereliction of duty on the part of the said CD the same may be dissolved with immediate effect.

5. The said CD shall have no power to raise any loan or loans nor to pledge the credits of the firm under any circumstances.

6. The said CD shall not, during the continuance of this partnership directly or indirectly, serve anywhere in any capacity but shall devote his whole time and whole-hearted attention to the said trade and never make himself absent except casually without leave of absence and after dissolution shall not directly engage himself in any concern carrying on similar trade or business within a radius of ...... miles from its present place.

IN WITNESS WHEREOF the parties hereto have executed these presents on the day, month and year first above-written.

Signed, sealed and delivered
by AB in the presence of:

Signed, sealed and delivered
by CD in the presence of:

Deed of Partnership between Two Partners

THIS DEED OF PARTNERSHIP is made this .... day of ...... 1999 BETWEEN AB son of .... residing at .... of the one part and CD son of .... residing at .... of the other part.

THIS DEED WITNESSETH and the parties hereby agree as follows:

1. The parties hereto shall carry on business in co-partnership as manufacturer and trader of jute goods under the name and style of CD Brothers at .... with effect from .... until the expiration of 3 months' notice in writing to determine the partnership left by either party for the other at the place of business of the firm, at any time after the .... day of .... subject to the terms and conditions hereunder contained and subject to such change in the constitution of the firm, if any, hereafter effected by addition, withdrawal, retirement or expulsion of partner or partners.

2. Within .... days from the commencement of the business, the firm shall be registered both under the Indian Partnership Act as also under the Income Tax Act and the rules prescribed under both the statutes shall be applicable to the firm.

3. The name of the firm shall be "Eastern Law House" and the same may be changed hereafter into some other name as desired by the partners.

4. The business of the firm shall at present be carried on at ...., etc., or such other place or places as the partners may hereafter from time to time determine.

5. The capital of the firm shall presently consist of a sum of Rs. .... to be contributed by the partners in equal shares, and shall be paid soon after the execution of these presents. Each partner shall be entitled to interest at the rate of .... % per annum on the capital standing to his credit in the books of the firm to be paid at the first instance out of the gross profits except when the firm suffers any loss, such interest being cumulative the deficiency for one year will be made up out of the profits for the succeeding year or years.

6. If any partner is made to advance any further money or moneys over and above the proportion of capital agreed to be contributed by him to meet emergent expenses on behalf of the firm or shall choose to leave his share of net profits undrawn at any annual general accounting, he will also be entitled to interest thereon at the rate of .... % per annum unless required by the other partner or partners to withdraw the same in which event the interest shall cease to accrue.

7. All outgoings and expenses of the firm shall be paid out of the capital and profits of the business and, in case of deficiency, by the partners in equal shares.

8. The bankers of the firm shall be Messrs. ...., etc., or such other bankers as the partners shall from time to time mutually agree upon, and all moneys, cheques and other securities belonging to the firm, except those required for current expenses, shall be paid into or deposited with the said bank.

9. All cheques drawn for amounts exceeding Rs. .... bills and other documents for the purposes of the firm shall be signed by both the partners;

each partner shall have the authority to sign all other cheques individually in the name of the firm.

10. The profits and losses shall belong to and be borne by the partners in equal shares.

11. In the event of any increase in the capital agreed upon by the majority or unanimously by the partners such additional capital unless otherwise agreed, shall be contributed by equal shares.

12. Partners may draw out in advance such sum or sums not exceeding Rs. .... in each month as may be agreed but, if on taking general accounts in any year, it appears that either partner has drawn more than his share of profits for that year, he shall refund the excess at once.

13. Both the partners shall attend diligently to the business of the partnership and carry on the same for the greatest advantage of the partners; and neither of them shall be, directly or indirectly, engaged or interested in any trade or business except that of the partnership.

14. Partners shall punctually pay and discharge their separate debts and liabilities, and shall indemnify and keep indemnified the firm effectually against the same.

15. No partner shall, without the consent in writing of the other partner or partners for the time being, release or compound any claim or debt due or owing to the firm or otherwise compound or settle the same or diminish any security without receiving the full amount thereof, or lend any money or deliver on credit goods belonging to, or otherwise give credit on behalf of, the firm other than in the usual course of the business of the firm, or contract debts and liabilities exceeding Rs. .... or institute suits or proceedings or make himself liable as surety for any person, or sell, transfer or assign or otherwise deal with either absolutely or by way of mortgage or declaration of trust, his share or interest in the firm, or the profits and/or benefits thereof except in favour of another partner or do, execute or perform or suffer to the contrary any act, deed or thing whereby the property of the firm may be exposed to the danger of being seized, attached or taken in execution, when and in such an event he shall be liable to be expelled from the partnership, if so decided by the then majority of partners, who may in the alternative file a suit for dissolution of the firm with all consequential reliefs.

16. The partners shall keep and maintain proper books of account. The books of account securities, vouchers, etc. shall be kept at the place of the business and be open to the inspection of each partner or his agent at all reasonable times with power to take copies.

17. On the .... day of .... and on that day of every succeeding year, during the continuance of the partnership, a general account of the preceding year shall be taken and a just valuation made of all the assets and liabilities of the firm; such general account shall be audited by such registered accountant as the partners shall from time to time mutually

appoint, and shall be entered in a book and signed by both the partners, and when so signed, the entries in such book shall be binding on both, provided that, if within—months from the date of the signing of the book any manifest error shall be found therein, such error, shall be rectified. All profits (after setting apart an amount equivalent to .... % thereof as Reserve Fund to meet emergent expenses) and loss shall be divided as aforesaid after such signature.

18. The firm shall not stand dissolved upon the death, retirement or insolvency of any partner, but upon dissolution in other cases it shall be wound up and the assets and liabilities dealt with in accordance with the provisions of the Indian Partnership Act.

19. If any partner infringes any one of the clauses hereunder or becomes insane, or is adjudicated an insolvent, the other partner may forthwith determine the partnership by notice in writing, and may thenceforth continue the business alone and may publish notice of the dissolution in the local Official Gazette and in local vernacular newspaper, and also inform the Registrar of Firms in writing.

20. Upon the dissolution of the firm either by death of a partner or by notice under cl. (19) the other partner may purchase his shares in the effects at a valuation to be made by arbitrators or their umpire as hereinafter mentioned. The price, when ascertained, shall be paid by three (*or* etc.) equal instalments at the end of four, eight and twelve calendar months (*or*, etc.), from such date of the award by the continuing partner or purchaser, who shall also execute all deeds and things necessary for indemnifying the outgoing partner or his estate from all the liabilities of the firm; and the outgoing partner or his representatives shall execute all such deeds and documents and do all acts necessary for effectually vesting in the purchaser the share purchased, including the goodwill, and the outgoing partner shall not carry on, or be engaged in any business competing with or interfering with the business of the firm, within a radius of .... miles of, etc., during the remainder of the term of the said partnership term.

21. All notices required to be given to either partner hereunder shall be deemed to be duly served if addressed to such partner at the office of the firm and sent by registered post.

22. Any dispute or difference which may arise between the partners or their representatives, with regard to the construction, meaning and effect of this deed or any part thereof, or respecting the accounts, profits or losses of the business, or the rights and liabilities of the partners under this deed, or the dissolution or winding up of the business, or any other matter relating to the firm, shall be referred to arbitration and the decision of a sole arbitrator, if the parties in dispute so agree, otherwise to two or more arbitrators, according to the number of the partners of the firm one to be nominated by each party or his representative and in case of difference of

opinion between them, by the umpire selected by them at the commencement of the reference and this clause shall be deemed to be a submission within the meaning of the Arbitration and Conciliation Act 1996 including its statutory modification and re-enactment.

IN WITNESS WHEREOF the parties hereto have executed these presents on the day, month and year first above-written.

Signed, sealed and delivered
by AB in the presence of:

Signed, sealed and delivered
by CD in the presence of:

Deed of Partnership between more than Two Partners

THIS DEED OF PARTNERSHIP is made this .... day of .... 2000 BETWEEN AB son of .... residing at .... of the first part, CD son of residing at .... of the second part, EF son of .... residing at .... of the third part and GH son of .... residing at .... of the fourth part.

NOW THIS DEED WITNESSETH and the parties hereby agree as follows:

1. The parties hereto shall at present constitute and become partners of the firm .... subject to the terms hereunder contained subject to such modification in its constitution or object clauses as may hereafter be agreed.

2. The name of the firm shall, at present be, etc., and the objects of the partnership shall, etc., the partners shall enter into engagements on behalf of the firm in the firm's name only. The said name and the objects may be altered hereafter if so unanimously decided by all the partners then constituting the firm.

3. The business of the partnership shall be carried on at, etc., or at such other place or places as the partners shall from time to time determine.

4. The partners and their survivors will remain partners in the business, from the date of this deed, for a term of .... years, if they, or any two of them, shall so long live, but subject to the provision for determination hereinafter contained.

5. Any partner may retire from the partnership at the end of .... years, from the date of this deed, on giving to the other partners not less than— calendar months' previous notice in writing of his intention to do so, and at the expiration of such notice the partnership shall, as regards the partner giving such notice, stand dissolved; and the partner retiring during the continuance of the partnership shall not, during the remainder of the partnership term, carry on or be interested directly or indirectly in any other business competing or in way interfering with the business of the partnership, within a radius of .... miles from the site of the firm's premises.

6. The retirement or death or insolvency of any partner shall not have the effect of dissolving the partnership between the partners; and the share of such retiring or deceased partner shall be purchased by one or more of the remaining partners at a price to be arrived at by the Auditor of the firm on the basis of last Balance Sheet and the working result upto the date of retirement and such sum will be paid to the retiring partner or the heirs of the deceased partner in four half-yearly instalments.

7. Every partner shall have a right to sell or mortgage his share or interest, but such partner, before selling or mortgaging it to a stranger, shall make the offer by registered letter to the other partners who shall have the first option to purchase the share at a valuation to be made. The Auditor shall value the share of the partner concerned on the basis of the Balance Sheet of the firm and in the event the outgoing partner does not agree to such valuation then he may get the share valued and he should be paid the average of the two valuations and such payment would be made in four half yearly instalments.

8. Every partner shall attend diligently to the business of the partnership and carry on the same for the greatest advantage of the partners; and no partner shall be directly or indirectly engaged or interested in any other trade or business except that of the partnership (or when required, substitute the following clause):

The said AB (or, etc.) shall be the manager of the business of the partnership and shall devote his whole time and attention to the management of the said business, he shall receive a salary of Rs. .... per month for his service in the firm and shall not be directly or indirectly engaged or interested in any other trade or business except that of the partnership.

9. No partner shall without the written consent of the other partners do any of the following things, namely, dispose of, or encumber any of the assets of the firm, borrow any money or incur any liability on behalf of the firm or stop operation of any banking account or cancel any transaction entered into by the firm. No partner shall without the written consent of the other partners keep the business place closed or prevent any partner from entering the business premises of the firm. In these respects the decision of the majority of the partners will be treated as the consent of the partners and/or the firm.

10. Any partner may be expelled from the partnership after giving him opportunity to explain his conduct or allegations against him as regards fraudulent conduct misappropriation manipulation of accounts making secret profits or carrying on some other business competitive to the business of the firm or utilising the know-how and particulars of customers of the firm.

11. The capital of the partnership business shall be the sum of Rs. .... made up and raised as follows, namely, etc. and any further capital which

may be required hereafter shall be contributed by the partners in the proportions in which they shall for the time being be entitled to the net profits of the business.

12. Each partner shall be entitled to interest at the rate of .... per cent per annum on the amount of his capital for the time being in the business, and at the rate of .... per cent per annum for further advances.

13. The partners shall be entitled to share the net profit of the business as reflected by the audited accounts and shall share the losses reflected by the audited accounts of the firm in equal proportions irrespective of their capital contribution.

14. All outgoings and expenses of the partnership and all losses including interest and capital, shall be payable, first out of the profits, next, out of capital and in the case of further deficiency, by the partners in the proportion in which they are entitled to share in the net profits of the business.

15. An account of the partnership business shall be taken every six months, or at such times as the partners shall determine, and the net profits shall be divided between the partners.

16. All moneys and securities for money belonging to the partnership (except moneys required for current expenses) shall be paid into and deposited with K. Bank or such other bankers as the partners shall from time to time determine. Cheques drawn on partnership accounts shall be signed at least by two partners or by the authorised signatory.

17. The partners shall keep proper books of account which shall be kept at the place of business for the time being of the partnership, and each partner shall have access to and power to take copies of the same.

18. The partners shall get the accounts audited by a qualified auditor and such accounts to be finalised and copies of Profit and Loss Account and Balance Sheet to be furnished to each partner within six months of the closing of the Accounting Year which will end on 31st March every year.

19. If on the determination of the partnership by effluxion of time or otherwise than by death or retirement, there shall be two or more partners still living, an account shall be taken of the assets and the liabilities and transactions of the partnership and the assets as soon as they may be realized shall be applied first in the payment of the cost of realization, secondly in discharge of the liabilities of the firm; thirdly in payment of any unpaid profits or interest on capital due to any partner; fourthly in payment to each partner of the sums subscribed by each towards the capital; and lastly, the balance shall be divided among the partners for the time being in the shares, in which they shall then be entitled to the net profits of the partnership.

20. All the other matters, for which no provision is made in this deed, shall be decided by the majority of the partners.

21. All notices to be given either to partner or by a partner to the firm hereunder shall be deemed to be duly served if addressed to such firm or the partner at the address given hereinabove and sent by registered post.

22. Any dispute or difference which may arise between the partners or their heirs and representatives or between the firm and a partner with regard to the construction meaning and effect of this Deed or respecting accounts profits or losses of the business of the firm or the rights or liabilities of the partners hereunder or the dissolution or winding up of the business or any other matter relating to the firm shall be referred to arbitration of Mr. .... and this clause shall be deemed to be the submission and/or reference to the Arbitrator or the procedure for appointment of the Arbitrator within the meaning of the Arbitration and Conciliation Act 1996 including any statutory modification thereof. IN WITNESS WHEREOF the parties hereto have executed these presents on the day, month and year first above-written.

Signed, sealed and delivered by	AB
the said AB, CD, EF and GH	CD
respectively in the presence of:	EF
	GH

Deed of Dissolution of Partnership

THIS DISSOLUTION OF PARTNERSHIP is made on this .... day of .... BETWEEN AB of, etc., of the first part, CD of, etc. (hereinafter called "*the Surety*"), of the second part, and EF of, etc., of the third part. WHEREAS it has been agreed between the parties hereto of the first and third parts that the partnership subsisting between them in the business of, etc., carried on by them at, etc., in the firm name of, etc., under the provisions of a partnership deed dated, etc., and made, etc., shall be dissolved by mutual consent as from the date hereof: AND WHEREAS prior to the execution thereof the said EF has delivered to the said AB the whole of the partnership stock, effects and credits: NOW THIS DEED WITNESSES as follows:

1. It is hereby recorded that the said partnership stood dissolved by mutual consent as from the day of .... and the said business shall henceforth belong to exclusively and be carried on by the said AB as its sole proprietor.

2. In consideration of the sum of Rs. .... now paid (*or* agreed to be paid, hereafter) by the said AB and the surety to the said EF, the said EF, as beneficial owner, hereby assigns to the said AB, ALL his share and other right, title and interest in the said dissolved partnership, the goodwill, fixtures, fittings, book and other debts, benefits of contracts, and all effects thereof TO HAVE AND TO HOLD the same unto and to the use of the said AB absolutely and forever.

3. The said AB and the surety hereby jointly and severally agree with the said EF that they, or one of them, will pay or cause to be paid to the said EF the said sum of Rs. .... by instalments and the date following, namely (*state amounts and dates*), and shall further pay on all instalments in arrear interest at the rate of .... per cent per annum from the date appointed for payment until actual payment thereof.

4. The said AB shall alone have full right, liberty and authority to collect all the assets of the said late partnership with power to appropriate the same for his use and benefit and to ask, demand, sue for, recover and receive, and to sign and give full and effectual receipts and discharges for all the debts, estate and effects of, or due or owing or in anywise belonging to the said partnership, and to settle all accounts, reckonings, matters and things whatsoever relative to the said business with all and every or any person or persons whosoever, and to compound for or release all or any of the debts or claims belonging thereto, and to institute any actions or other proceedings for compelling payment or delivery thereof.

5. The said AB shall alone remain solely and exclusively liable for the debts and liabilities of the said late partnership and also all future rent of the partnership business premises to be paid and discharged by him who shall further indemnify and keep indemnified the said EF therefrom and from all actions, proceedings, costs, claims and demands in respect thereof.

6. Each of the parties hereto shall respectively sign, execute and do all such further documents, deeds, acts and things as the other party may reasonably require for completely effectuating this agreement, and each party shall pay his own costs in connection therewith.

7. All moneys payable by instalments at a future date under this agreement shall become payable immediately in the event of any act of insolvency being hereafter committed or suffered by the said AB.

8. The said EF shall not, for the period of .... years from the date hereof, carry on or be engaged or concerned in, either by himself or as partner with any person or persons, or as employee or director of any company, any business of, etc., within five miles of such business premises, but this clause shall cease to be of effect if three (or, etc.) of the before-mentioned instalments shall at any time be in arrear and unpaid.

9. For every breach of cl. 8 hereof, the said EF shall pay to the said AB the sum of Rs. .... as ascertained and liquidated damages.

IN WITNESS WHEREOF the parties hereto have executed these presents on the day, month and year first above-written.

Signed, sealed and delivered by
AB, CD and EF respectively in
the presence of:

40

Partition

Introductory observations. Partition means putting an end to joint ownership. It is effected by destruction of the unities, *i.e.* unity of ownership and unity of possession. It covers both, *viz.* division of title and division of possession. It is in effect surrender of a portion of the joint estate in exchange for absolute proprietory rights in a portion acquired from the co-sharers. In other words, it is the process by which the property held in common by joint tenants or tenants-in-common or coparceners is divided and each is allotted a defined share in severalty absolutely in lieu of his undivided share in the whole. It is effected by the process of mutual conveyance and release. It is a mixture of surrender and conveyance of rights in the property. It defines a fresh title and takes effect from the date mentioned in the deed.

In India, the Partition Act 1893 (Act IV of 1893), was enacted within a quarter of a century after the passing of the English Statute (English Partition Act, 31 Henry VIII C) which empowers courts in India to sell property under similar circumstances, even *suo motu* in cases where partition is difficult or unreasonable or will destroy the intrinsic value of the property.[1]

In India, there are three types of joint estate, *viz.* (*a*) joint tenancy; (*b*) tenancy in common; and (*c*) coparcenary. Mitakshara coparceners resemble in some respects joint tenancy of England and Dayabhaga co-sharers resemble tenants-in-common; nevertheless, on minute analysis there is not much difference between the two systems.

Joint tenancy. This is an English concept having very limited application in India. Section 106 of Indian Succession Act 1925 makes the principle applicable to a gift by Will of an Indian Christian, Parsee, and Muslim but not Hindu jointly to two or more persons whereby they take the property as joint tenants unless contrary intention is expressed. Joint tenants have unity

1 *Nitya Gopal* v *Pran Kristo* 57 CWN 439.

of (i) title, (ii) commencement of title, (iii) interest and (iv) possession. They have no defined interest in the property and none of them can transfer his share and on his death his interest in the property does not devolve on his heirs but goes to the other survivors.

Tenancy-in-common. When two or more persons get property by transfer or inheritance they become tenants-in-common having unity of commencement of title and unity of possession. The interest of a tenant in common is transferrable and on his death it devolves on his heir inasmuch as he has a definite share though undivided. A joint tenant has no defined share in the property.

Trustees, executors and administrators are like joint tenants although neither the Trust Act nor the Indian Succession Act says so in express terms. In the case of grant by the Government to two persons, even if they form a joint Hindu family, the judicial committee held that they take as tenants-in-common.[2] In Hindu law "partition does not mean simply division of the property into specific shares, it covers also division of title". So when in a Hindu coparcenary family a partition is effected, the same involves severance of the joint status as regards the separating members with all legal consequences resulting therefrom—a special feature quite distinct from *de facto* division of the property into specific shares.[3]

Section 6 of the Hindu Succession Act 1956, introduced an important change in the general rule of succession by survivorship in cases where a male Hindu dies leaving a female relative specified in class 1 of its schedule or a male relative specified in the class through such female. Formerly, under the Hindu law widows and daughters, except in Bombay (Mumbai), used to enjoy only the benefits of the estate left by their respective husbands and fathers in the absence of sons as joint tenants. The Hindu Succession Act 1956, is a charter of rights for the Hindu females giving them absolute estate with right of partition with some special provisions as regards dwelling-house under s. 23 of the said Act only when the male heirs decide to have the same partitioned. The Mahomedan Law does not recognise joint family system. Hence there is no presumption of jointness among them.

Partition—whether a transfer or not? A partition is not a transfer of property within the meaning of s. 5 of the Transfer of Property Act nor an exchange within the meaning of s. 118 of the said Act but a mixture of the surrender and conveyance of rights in the property. It was held by Privy Council that a partition does not give a co-sharer any title nor create any title in him. It enables him to obtain what is his own indefinite in specific forms. A deed of partition does not require any certificate under s. 230A of the Income Tax

2 *Mst. Badhu Rani* v *Thakur Rajendra Baksh* 60 IA 95; AIR 1933 PC 72.
3 *Girja Bai* v *Sadashiv* 43 Cal 1031 (1047, 1048) (PC).

Act 1961, for the purpose of registration. It is not even any exchange nor a conveyance.[4] Each co-sharer loses his right in the property or portion thereof allotted to the other.[5] All controversies to the contrary were settled by the Supreme Court in *V.N. Sarin* v *Ajit Kumar*.[6] The Supreme Court held it as a transfer of the joint enjoyment of the property by the coparceners into enjoyment in severalty. Section 10 of the Transfer of Property Act 1882, says that a transfer of property can be made without writing in cases where writing is not required by law, but if done by writing the provisions of the Stamp Act and the Registration Act are at once attracted.

Section 14 of the West Bengal Land Reforms Act 1955, excludes oral partition of holdings among co-sharer raiyats; such a partition can be effected under the court decree or by a registered instrument. A mere list, *i.e. chitta* of properties allotted or a memorandum of partition is not a deed of partition and so it does not require registration.[7] The basis of partition is equality, *i.e.* the parties shall have shares equal to the value of their undivided interest in the joint estate otherwise one will pay owelty money to another.

Partition when operates as a transfer. When the intention is fraudulent, *i.e.* to deprive creditors, it operates as a transfer under s. 53 of the Transfer of Property Act.[8]

Adverse possession by one co-owner. The Supreme Court held that the possession of a co-owner cannot be adverse unless such possession is hostile and in denial of the other's title to his knowledge and to the exclusion and ouster following thereon beyond the statutory period.[9] The same principle applies in the case of a transferee from a co-owner.[10]

Agreement not binding on heirs. Agreements made between coparceners that they would never effect severance of their interests may bind them if the same is a part of family arrangement for preservation of family peace. The Privy Council held that such an agreement might have bound the parties who agreed among themselves to abide by it,[11] but such agreements to the effect that neither the coparceners nor their heirs should ever effect any partition are not binding on the heirs on the principle that the same is a condition restrictive of enjoyment of an absolute estate. Unless the agreement

4 *Suhasini* v *Srinath* 49 CWN 769.
5 *Ramkrishna* v *Ganpat Mahadeo* 60 Bom 34; AIR 1936 Bom 10 at pp. 12, 17.
6 AIR 1966 SC 432; (1966)1 SCA 285.
7 *Kshetra Mohan* v *Tufani* 37 CWN 112, 114; AIR 1933 Cal 474.
8 *Woman* v *Ganpat* AIR 1936 Bom 10.
9 *Mahammad Baqqar* v *Nain-un-nisa* AIR 1956 SC 548. See also *Govinda* v *Upendra* 47 Cal 274.
10 *Dipnarain* v *Pundeo* AIR 1947 Pat 99.
11 *Jafri Begam* v *Ali Raza* 28 IA 111.

against partition between coparceners provided also against alienation, the alienee would be competent to seek partition. A direction in a will prohibiting partition is void.[12] A testator cannot restrain partition as it creates a perpetuity.[13]

The Partition Act provides that whenever in any suit for partition, in which a decree for partition might have been made, it appears to the court that a division of the property cannot conveniently be made and that a sale of the property subject to a reserve price and distribution of the proceeds would be more beneficial for all the shareholders, the court can, at the request of such shareholders interested to the extent of one moiety or upwards, direct a sale of the property and a distribution of the proceeds.[14]

Deeds of partition are executed and attested like bonds, and their registration is compulsory if the value of the immovable property comprised therein is Rs. 100 or upwards; but deeds of partition made by the W.B. Revenue Officer do not require registration. All partitions under s. 14 of the W.B. Land Reforms Act require registration irrespective of the value.

Partition of a dwelling-house.[15] The purchaser of a share of a dwelling-house simply acquires the right to have the property partitioned but no right to joint possession. This right is subject to s. 4 of the Partition Act which is a corollary to s. 44 of the Transfer of Property Act and applies equally to Hindus, Mahomedans and other communities living in India and under which the court may direct sale of his share to any willing co-sharer.

The word dwelling-house has almost the same meaning both under s. 44 of the Transfer of Property Act and s. 4 of the Partition Act. It does not mean the house itself only. It includes adjacent building, gardens, court-yards and all that is necessary for convenient use and occupation of the property.

Section 23 of the Hindu Succession Act (Act XXX of 1956) restricts the right of a female heir as to demand for partition in a dwelling-house of the deceased unless the male heirs decide on partition. It is submitted that s. 23 of the Hindu Succession Act offends against Art. 14 of the Constitution of India being a clog upon a female's absolute right to the dwelling-house. This question was considered by the Calcutta High Court in *Surje Kumar* v *Maya Dutt*,[16] where the claim of a daughter for partition was rejected.

12 Section 138 of the Indian Succession Act.

13 *Kalicharan* v *Kironbala* 29 CLJ 494; 51 IC 948; see s. 11 of the Transfer of Property Act which enacts the same principle based on public policy.

14 Section 2 of the Partition Act 1893; *Satya Bhusan* v *Jatindra Mohan* 49 CLJ 136; AIR 1929 Cal 269.

15 Section 44 of the Transfer of Property Act.

16 86 CWN 358.

Partial partition. Although partition of the entire estate is the rule to avoid multiplicity of proceedings nevertheless, partial partition is recognised in law under certain circumstances. This Rule is a rule of adjective law.

This may be both with regard to the property and also the status of the persons even among the coparceners governed by the Mitakshara School of Hindu Law. The purchaser of a co-owner's share in any property can file a suit for recovery of that share only.[17]

By express agreement among themselves, the members of a joint family can make a division and severance of interest in respect of the joint estate, but they will be presumed to hold the rest as tenants-in-common in the absence of clear intention to the contrary. Similarly, a coparcener separated from others may have his interest partitioned, and it is open to non-separating members to remain joint as regards the rest of the estate.[18] A mere declaration and definition of the share of the coparceners is not partition.[19] The Income-tax Act 1961, requires certain conditions to give effect to partition under s. 171 of the Act, mere severance of status is not partition. Income from properties capable of division but not divided is liable to be assessed as HUF.[1]

A suit for partition must, however, be in respect of the entire estate and the entire joint family must be represented expressly or by implication[2] except when a portion of the property, *viz.* land is situate outside the jurisdiction of the court or not available for partition, *e.g.* being in the possession of a mortgagee or held by the joint family along with a stranger or in the possession of a trespasser[3] or where the properties belong to some and not to all the co-sharers.

Partition and right of pre-emption. Section 22 of the Hindu Succession Act (Act XXX of 1956) drawn up on the lines of ss. 3 and 4 of the Partition Act is easily workable. No suit but simply an application is necessary and the right of pre-emption is not confined to the family dwelling-house but extends to any property of the intestate. The object of this section is to prevent family property or business from breaking up or going out of hands. A deed of partition usually provides for right of pre-emption among the co-sharers in the event of sale of any allotment.

17 Section 44 of the Transfer of Property Act.
18 *Bhagwati Prasad* v *Rameshwari Kuir* 1951 SCR 603; AIR 1952 SC 72.
19 *Sushil* v *Ramchandra* AIR 1982 All 129.
1 *Kalloomal* v *CIT, Kanpur* AIR 1982 SC 160.
2 Order 2, rr. 1 and 2 of the Code of Civil Procedure.
3 *Harey* v *Hari* 40 CWN 1237.

Essentials of deeds of partition. The draftsman of a deed of partition will bear in mind that the following are essentials in a deed of partition:

(*i*) recitals of the title of the parties;

(*ii*) recital of the agreement to effect partition;

(*iii*) accurate description of the allotments and their market values;

(*iv*) provisions of owelty moneys (*i.e.* money compensation) to be paid by one co-owner for properties of greater value allotted to him for equality of partition with another co-owner in case of allotments of unequal values;

(*v*) custody of the title deeds—*covenant as to production*;

(*vi*) right of first purchase among the allottees in case of sale of any allotment particularly when the property is a dwelling-house;

(*vii*) usual covenants as in a conveyance;

(*viii*) date on which the partition will be effective.

The person who gets the largest share is entitled to the custody of the title deeds subject to a covenant for production and also to the original deed.

It is often desirable to execute a partition deed in duplicates according to the number of the parties, one party keeping the original and others getting the copies.

Notional partition. Under s. 6 of the Hindu Succession Act (Act XXX of 1956) although the devolution of the interest of a Mitakshara coparcener in the HUF estate is by survivorship upon the rest, nevertheless in the event of his death leaving a female as specified in class 1 of the schedule or male relations specified thereunder claiming through such female a notional partition is presumed and the share which would have been allotted to him vests in all such persons. This principle applies only in the event of intestate succession.

Partition of shebait rights and debutter properties

Family idols and places of worship are not divisible.[4] In the absence of any dedication of any property but used for merely for the benefit of the deity the same is not excluded from partition.[5]

A Hindu deity is a juristic person capable of holding the dedicated property and of being taxed through the shebait. The Hon'ble Dr. B.K. Mukherjea in his book on *Hindu Law of Religious and Charitable Trust*,[6] observed as follows:

4 Manu, Chap. IX, Verse 219.

5 *Sachindra* v *Hemchandra* (1931)35 CWN 151; 132 IC 688.

6 5th Ed., pp. 242-244.

It is now the settled law on the subject ever since the decision of the Judicial Committee in *Ramanathan* v *Murugappa*[7] that when the management can without detriment to the trust be held by turns the shebaits can agree to do so in such order as they think proper on grounds of convenience in order to avoid any confusion. They can therefore agree to discharge their duties and functions by turns or in some other settled order. As regards the right of the shebaits as to partition of the shebaiti rights through court in the absence of any agreement as between themselves His Lordship after having considered the decision of the Allahabad High Court in *Raman Lalji* v *Gopal Lalji*[8] observed that unless the shebaits have any personal or pecuniary interest in the endowment or the income thereof, none can approach the court and ask for partition. This principle is also followed among the trustees and the above decision was followed in *Puranmal* v *Brijlal*.[9] In *Anandamoyee* v *Baikuntha*,[10] the Calcutta High Court held that the place of worship and place of sacrifice are indivisible. This question was considered by the Orissa High Court in the case of *Laksmidhar Patnaik* v *Rangapati*,[11] which held that the temple and its site were not partible; so also the house or rooms let out to tenants and the land leased out on rent as the shebaits had no emolument but nevertheless the land on which their residential houses were constructed which they were enjoying generation after generation without payment of any rent and thus acquired a personal interest therein, *i.e.* emolument in the management of the temple. The portion so held can be partitioned without detriment to the title of the deity.

A partition of the debutter property for the purpose of convenience of the user for the seva is not a violation of the trust; yet a thakurbati and not even a thakurdalan is partible.[12] But a chandimandap was treated as partible.[13] In *Mahamaya Dasi* v *Haridas Halder*,[14] the Hon'ble Justice Ashutosh Mukherjee upheld the custom of the transfer as also division of the pala of Kalighat Temple among the shebaits or in favour of a person standing in the line of succession and not disqualified by personal unfitness because of longstanding practice. Attachment and sale of such pala was held legal.[15] The interest of the shebait of the goddess Kali is saleable and divisible.

7 1916 LR 33 IA 119.
8 ILR 19 All 428.
9 ILR 39 All 651; AIR 1937 Ass 123.
10 8 WR 198.
11 AIR 1967 Ori 90 (93).
12 *Dharma Das* v *Gostha Behari* 16 CWN 29.
13 *Debendra* v *Haridas* 15 CWN 552.
14 ILR 42 Cal 480; 19 CWN 2081.
15 *Haridas* v *Charu* 37 CWN 978.

FORMS

Demand for Partition

By Registered Post with A/D

To
G.H. (*co-sharer*)

Re: Premises No. ....
Clients ....

Dear Sir

We are instructed by our client, AB of, etc., to write to you as follows:

Our client is a co-sharer with you in respect of the above property (or properties) which he desired to have partitioned by metes and bounds and approached you for that purposes on several occasions, but you put off the same on one pretext or another.

We, therefore, call upon you to have the said property (or properties) partitioned forthwith and on hearing from you we shall send you the draft deed of partition for your approval and return. Alternatively, if you so agree to have the same partitioned by arbitration you would nominate some person as arbitrator on your behalf and on hearing from you, our client would nominate and let you know the name of his arbitrator.

If you do not agree to any of the suggestions as aforesaid, our client shall on expiry of a fortnight from the date of receipt of this notice institute a suit against you for partition of the said property (*or* properties) with all consequential reliefs.

(Date) Yours faithfully
E.F. & Co. (*Attorneys*)
(*Advocates*)

Agreement for Partition

THIS AGREEMENT FOR PARTITION is made this .... day of ...... 2000 BETWEEN AB son of .... residing at .... one of the co-owners of the one part and CD son of .... residing at .... the other co-owner of the other part.

WHEREAS the parties hereto are the joint owners of the property comprised in the schedules hereto as absolute co-owners AND WHEREAS the parties have agreed to have the same partitioned and divided by metes and bounds for better enjoyment and effective control and dealings of their respective shares NOW IT IS HEREBY AGREED by and between the parties as follows:

1. AB shall accept in severalty absolutely as his defined and demarcated share in lieu of his undivided share in the entire property the portion comprised in the first schedule and the said CD shall likewise accept in severalty as his defined and demarcated share the portion comprised in the second schedule, and the said CD shall pay to the said AB the sum of Rs. .... as owelty money for equality of partition (*or*, and the said CD shall pay to the said AB for equality of partition such sum as shall be determined and awarded by EF etc., to whom the same shall be referred for arbitration).

2. The partition shall be effective as from the .... day of ...., when the mutual conveyances and releases shall be executed for completing and giving effect to the same, and the said sum (of Rs. ....) shall also be paid. In case the said sum shall not be paid on that day for any reason whatsoever, the same shall be a first charge on the allotment and will carry interest at the rate of .... per cent, per annum until payment or realisation.

3. The documents of title relating to the property shall be retained by the said AB, who shall enter into a covenant in favour of CD as to their production and delivery of copies thereof and an undertaking for safe custody.

4. The Deed of Partition shall be executed in duplicate and all the costs, charges and expenses of and incidental to this agreement and the partition to be made in pursuance hereof shall be borne and paid by the said AB and CD in equal shares.

The First Schedule

The Second Schedule

IN WITNESS WHEREOF the parties hereto have executed these presents in duplicate on the day, month and year first above-written.

Signed, sealed and delivered by AB
in the presence of:

Signed, sealed and delivered by CD
in the presence of:

Partition Deed

THIS DEED OF PARTITION is made this .... day of .... 1999 BETWEEN AB son of .... residing at .... of the first part, CD, son of .... residing at .... of the second part and EF son of .... residing at .... of the third part.

Whereas AB is entitled to an undivided half share of and in all the properties described in the First, Second and Third Schedules hereto and hereinafter referred to as the said properties AND WHEREAS CD and EF are each entitled to an undivided one-fourth share of and in the said properties AND WHEREAS for the purpose of partition and/or division of the said properties into separate lots in accordance with the respective shares of the parties as aforesaid and for more convenient and exclusive possession and better use occupation and enjoyment of the divided portions the said AB, CD and EF have mutually agreed and decided to have the said properties partitioned by metes and bounds in the manner hereinafter appearing, *viz.*, that the said AB shall accept the properties set out in the First Schedule, the said CD shall accept the properties in the Second Schedule and the said EF shall accept the properties mentioned in the Third Schedule hereto as their exclusive properties in lieu of their respective shares in the joint estate all questions as to accounts and mutual dealings having been waived AND WHEREAS the said properties were valued by Sri .... Engineer/ Surveyor AND WHEREAS on the basis of the report of the said Engineer/Surveyor the values of the properties in the Schedule are Rs. ...., Rs. .... and Rs. .... respectively AND WHEREAS for equality of the partition the said AB and EF shall each pay to the said CD a sum of Rs. .... as owelty money which shall be a first charge on their respective allotments.

NOW THIS DEED WITNESSETH AS FOLLOWS:

1. That in pursuance of the said agreement and in consideration of the absolute ownership acquired by the parties in respect of the allotments hereunder made under and by virtue of mutual transfers and releases hereunder effected, the said CD and EF hereby and hereunder grant, convey, transfer assure, assign, confirm and release unto the said AB ALL THAT the property (or properties) set forth in the First Schedule hereto together with all areas, sewers, drains, water, water courses, lights, liberties, easements, appendages and appurtenances whatsoever so as to constitute the said AB the sole and absolute owner of the property (or properties) comprised in the said First Schedule freed and discharged from all rights in common and all claims, demands whatsoever of the parties of the other parts concerning the same and TO HAVE AND TO HOLD the same absolutely and for ever in fee simple in severalty against the said CD and EF.

2. That in pursuance of the said agreement and in consideration of the absolute ownership acquired by the parties in respect of the allotments hereunder made by virtue of the mutual transfers and release hereunder contained, the said AB and EF do hereby and hereunder grant, convey, transfer, assure, assign, confirm and release unto the said CD ALL THAT the property (or properties) set forth in the Second Schedule hereto annexed together with all areas, sewers, drains, water, water courses, lights, liberties, easements, appendages and appurtenances whatsoever so as to constitute the said CD the sole and absolute owner of the property (or properties) comprised in the Second Schedule hereto freed and discharged from all rights in common and all claims and demands whatsoever of the other parties,

concerning the same TO HAVE AND TO HOLD the same absolutely and for ever in fee simple in severalty as against AB and EF.

3. That in pursuance of the said agreement and in consideration of the absolute ownership acquired by the parties in respect of the allotments hereunder made by virtue of mutual transfers and releases hereunder contained, the said AB and CD do hereby grant, convey, transfer, assign, assure and release unto the said EF ALL THAT the property set forth in the Third Schedule hereto together with all areas, sewers, drains, water and water courses, lights, liberties, easements, appendages and appurtenances whatsoever so as to constitute the said EF as the sole and absolute owner of the property (or properties) comprised in the Third Schedule hereto freed and discharged from all rights in common and all claims, demands whatsoever of the parties of the other parts concerning the same TO HAVE AND TO HOLD the same absolutely and for ever in fee simple in severalty as against the said AB and CD.

AND this deed furthermore witnesseth as follows:

(*a*) That the said AB shall have the custody and possession of all the documents of title as also the original of this deed and will at the request and costs of either CD or EF, his heirs, successors or assigns produce or cause to be produced all or any of them for inspection or as evidence on their behalf at all trials, examination or commission or otherwise as may be required by him or them and unless prevented by fire or any other inevitable accident keep them safe, unobliterated and uncancelled.

(*b*) That save and except the charge hereby created for owelty money, the properties set forth in the First, Second and Third Schedules hereto annexed are free from encumbrances.

(*c*) That no party shall be entitled to any easements or quasi-easements over the allotments made to the other parties which are all hereby extinguished.

(*d*) The parties shall enter upon their respective allotments and hold, possess and enjoy the same in severalty absolutely against each other without any claim, demand or interruption whatsoever.

(*e*) Each party shall, at the request and costs of the other parties, do execute and perform or cause to be done, executed and performed all and every such acts, deeds and things or writings whatsoever as may be required for further better and more perfectly assuring the allotments hereunder made or for rectification of any error or omission.

(*f*) That none of the parties shall be entitled to sell or otherwise transfer his allotment to a stranger unless he has first offered the same to the other party or parties and in cases only when they or each one of them have refused to take the same at the best available market price.

(*g*) This partition shall not be reopened nor challenged under any circumstances by reason of any error or omission whatsoever, but the parties shall execute and register such further deed or deeds or writings as may be necessary to rectify the error or errors or implement the omission or comissions.

The First Schedule above referred to

* * *

The Second Schedule above referred to

* * *

The Third Schedule above referred to

* * *

IN WITNESS WHEREOF the parties hereto have executed these presents in triplicate on the day, month and year first above-written.

Signed, sealed and delivered by AB
in the presence of:

Signed, sealed and delivered by CD
in the presence of:

Signed, sealed and delivered by EF
in the presence of:

Deed of Partition by Trustees

THIS DEED OF PARTITION by trustees made this .... day of .... 2000 BETWEEN AB son of .... residing at .... and XY son of .... residing at .... (hereinafter called the TRUSTEES) of the one Part and CD and EF sons of .... residing at .... (hereinafter called the BENEFICIARIES) of the other part.

WHEREAS GH son of Late .... residing at .... by his will dated .... appointed the TRUSTEES to be the executors and TRUSTEES thereof and among other provisions, directed the TRUSTEE to hold the properties and administer the same in trust in the manner indicated therein until the youngest of the BENEFICIARIES, *viz.* the said EF shall attain majority when and in such an event the TRUSTEES would partition the same into two equal shares and grant, convey and transfer them unto and to the use of the BENEFICIARIES separately AND WHEREAS the said will was duly proved in the court of .... and probate thereof was granted to the said AB and XY *viz.* to the trustees as executors appointed thereunder AND WHEREAS such probate is still in force and virtue AND WHEREAS the TRUSTEES as the executors have completed the administration of the estate of the deceased and filed the inventory and account AND WHEREAS the said EF has attained majority on the day of .... AND WHEREAS the trustees have already divided and demarcated the said properties into two lots, viz. lot A & lot B which are of equal value AND WHEREAS the said CD has agreed to accept lot A and the said EF has agreed to accept lot B as their defined and demarcated portions of the estate of the said GH. Now this Indenture witnesses that in exercise of the power and authority contained in the said will and all other powers enabling him the trustees as statutory owners do hereby grant, convey, transfer, assign and assure unto and to the use of the said CD the properties mentioned and described in Schedule A hereto TO HAVE AND TO HOLD the same absolutely as his own for his exclusive use and benefit freed and discharged from the trust created under the will and also all rights in common and in severalty as against EF.

AND this Indenture further witnesses that the TRUSTEES as statutory owners do hereby further likewise grant, convey, transfer, assign and assure the properties mentioned and described in Schedule B hereto unto and to the use of EF TO HAVE AND TO HOLD the same absolutely as his own for his exclusive use and benefit freed and discharged from the trust created under the will and also all rights in common and in severalty as against CD AND that the TRUSTEES do hereby covenant and agree with the said BENEFICIARIES that as TRUSTEES they have not done, executed and performed nor suffered to the contrary any act, deed or thing whereby or by reason or means whereof the trust estate may be prejudiced in title or estate or the trustees may be in any way hindered or prevented from granting, transferring and conveying them unto and to the use of the BENEFICIARIES in the manner hereinbefore indicated. And this Indenture furthermore witnesses that the BENEFICIARIES do hereby join with TRUSTEES and confirm and accept the partition of properties hereunder made to them respectively as testified by their being parties hereto and executing the same.

Schedule A

Schedule B

IN WITNESS WHEREOF the parties hereto have executed these presents in triplicate on the day, month and year first above-written.

Signed, sealed and delivered by AB and
XY the TRUSTEES in the presence of:

Signed, sealed and delivered by CD
the BENEFICIARY in the presence of:

Signed, sealed and delivered by EF
in the presence of:

Memorandum of Oral Partition

THIS MEMORANDUM OF ORAL partition is made this ……… day of ………… 2000 BETWEEN AB son of ……… residing at ……… of the First Part, CD, son of .... residing at .... of the Second Part and EF daughter of .... residing at .... of the Third Part.

WHEREAS one XY who was a Hindu governed by the Dayabhaga or Bengal School of Hindu Law died intestate on the .... day of .... leaving behind him surviving his two sons, *viz*. the said AB and CD and a daughter, the said EF as his heirs and legal representatives under the said School of Hindu Law and the movable and immovable properties described in Schedules A, B and C hereunder as part of his estate AND WHEREAS upon his death the said AB, CD and EF became entitled to the said properties absolutely and in equal shares by right of inheritance and succession AND WHEREAS for better use and enjoyment of the said properties the said AB, CD and EF had the same mutually partitioned and divided by metes and bounds in three equal lots, *viz*. the said AB agreed to and accepted the properties mentioned and described in Schedule A as his defined and demarcated share in the joint estate, similarly the said CD and EF have agreed to and accepted the properties mentioned and described in Schedules B and C respectively at a sitting held on .... at ...... in presence of some of the well-wishers of the family AND WHEREAS notwithstanding the fact that no formal deed of partition was then executed by the parties the estate of the said XY has in fact, truth, reality and substance been partitioned by metes and bounds among his said heirs and legal representatives by conduct of the parties AND WHEREAS the parties have given effect to and acted upon such partition by entering into their respective allotments and have recorded their respective individual names in the Municipal as also Revenue Records of the properties and collecting the rents, issues and profits thereof accordingly AND WHEREAS in the circumstances aforesaid the said AB has become the sole absolute and exclusive owner of the properties described in Schedule A hereunder and the said CD has become the sole, absolute and exclusive owner of the properties described in Schedule B hereunder and the said EF has become the sole absolute and exclusive owner of the properties described in Schedule C hereunder. AND WHEREAS the parties have accepted the said partition as fair, final, conclusive and binding on them.

Now by this Memorandum the parties place on record, declare and confirm the said partition as final, conclusive and binding on the parties to all intents and purposes.

Schedule A above referred to

* * *

Schedule B above referred to

* * *

Schedule C above referred to

* * *

IN WITNESS WHEREOF the parties hereto have executed these presents in triplicate on the day, month and year first above-written.

Signed, sealed and delivered by AB
in the presence of:

Signed, sealed and delivered by CD
in the presence of:

Signed, sealed and delivered by EF
in the presence of:

Deed of Partition of Mitakshara Coparcenary Estate where some Properties are Retained as HUF Estate

THIS DEED OF PARTITION made this .... day of .... BETWEEN (1) .... son of .... by caste Hindu, by occupation trader at present .... hereinafter referred to as party of the FIRST PART, (2) Sm. .... wife of the said .... by caste Hindu, by occupation trader and housewife at present of ...... hereinafter referred to as party of the SECOND PART, (3) .... son of........., by caste Hindu, by occupation trader of .... hereinafter referred to as party of the THIRD PART, (4) Sri .... by caste Hindu, by occupation trader at present of ...., hereinafter referred to as party of the FOURTH PART, (5) Sri .... son of .... by caste Hindu, by occupation trader at present of .... hereinafter referred to as party of the FIFTH PART, (6) .... son of .... by caste Hindu, by occupation trader at present of .... hereinafter, referred to as party of the SIXTH PART, and (7) .... son of .... by caste Hindu, by occupation .... at present of .... hereinafter referred to as party of the SEVENTH PART:

WHEREAS the parties hereto, *viz*. the parties of the first, third, fourth, fifth and sixth parts constitute a Mitakshara family joint in food worship and estate of which the party of the first part is the karta or head and the party of the second part his wife and the other parties are coparceners AND WHEREAS the HUF estate of the family consists mainly of the properties described in Schedule I hereto. AND WHEREAS for reasons and considerations best known to the parties and for better management, enjoyment, control and administration of their estate the parties hereto have agreed to have the same partitioned by metes and bounds in the manner hereunder appearing, *viz*. that the HUF shall henceforth continue and constitute the parties of the first, fourth, fifth and seventh parts who represent $^{4}/_{7}$th share in the HUF estate which is valued at Rs. .... by mutual agreement and consent as under s. 269(*q*) of the Income-tax Act 1961, and a stamp duty of Rs. .... has been paid on the value of the separated $^{3}/_{7}$th share.

WHEREAS under the Hindu law to which the parties are subject the party of the second part, *viz.* the said Sm. ...... being the wife of the karta is also entitled to a share in the said property in the event of partition and each of the other parties hereto is accordingly entitled to a $^1/_7$th share of the same.

WHEREAS the party hereto of the first part with the mutual consent of and agreement with the other coparceners divided the said HUF properties in four lots for the purpose of partition out of which one lot comprising the properties described in the Second Schedule hereto and representing approximately $^4/_7$th share of the entire HUF estate, including movables comprised in the First Schedule will continue as undivided and shall be retained by the said HUF as continuing and consisting of the parties hereto of the *first part, fourth part, fifth part and seventh part* and the second lot comprising the properties described in the Third Schedule hereto and representing the approximately $^1/_7$th share of the entire HUF estate shall be allotted to the party hereto of the second part as her separated share to which she is entitled to under the law in the event of the partition of the HUF estate as aforesaid and the third lot comprising the properties described in the Fourth Schedule hereto and representing approximately $^1/_7$th share of the entire estate shall be the allotted share of the party hereto of the third part as his separated share in lieu of his said undivided share and the fourth lot comprising the properties described in the Fifth Schedule hereto and representing approximately the $^1/_7$th share of the entire HUF estate shall be allotted to the party hereto of the sixth part as his separated share in lieu of his said undivided share in the joint family estate.

WHEREAS inasmuch as the value of the properties in the Second Schedule to be retained by the parties hereto of the first, fourth, fifth and seventh parts and to be continued as HUF properties including movables allotted as per books of account exceed $^4/_7$th share of the entire estates by Rs. .... they agreed to pay a sum of Rs. .... as an owelty money to the party of the third part for equality of partition (of which a sum of Rs. .... has already been paid on ....) and also to pay a further sum of Rs. .... to the party of the second part as an owelty money and such payment has already been made on .... and whereas the value of the property allotted to the party of the sixth part as described in Fourth Schedule exceeds the value of $^1/_7$th share of the entire estate by Rs. .... the party of the sixth part has agreed to pay a sum of Rs. .... as an owelty money to each of the parties of the first, fourth, fifth and the seventh parts and the said amounts have already been paid on .... (all such payments having been made by adjustment of entries in the books of account maintained by the said HUF in respect of its estate hereunder partitioned). WHEREAS in consideration of the absolute or sole ownership acquired by each party in respect of the allotment made out of the heretofore joint properties by mutual transfer and releases hereunder effected and in consideration of the covenants hereinafter mentioned and agreed to be observed and performed by all the aforesaid parties the said parties resolved to incorporate the terms of the partition in a deed of partition as follows:

NOW THIS INDENTURE WITNESSES that in pursuance of the said agreement and in consideration of partition and/or division of the shares of the parties in their ancestral properties and allotment thereof in severally and individually to them as hereunder made under and by virtue of these presents the parties of the second, third and sixth parts and each of them do hereby grant, convey, transfer, assign, assure, release and confirm unto and to have the use of the parties of the first, fourth, fifth and seventh parts all the properties described in Schedule II so as to enable them to hold possess and enjoy the same as the continuing HUF properties with the party of the first part as its karta freed and discharged from all rights in common and all claims, demands whatsoever by the parties of the other parts in, to, upon or concerning the same subject however to the rights of their respective male descendants and jointly as between themselves.

In pursuance of the said agreement and in consideration of the partition and/or division of shares of the parties in their ancestral properties by allotment of portions thereof as hereunder effected the parties of the first, third, fourth, fifth, sixth and seventh parts do hereby grant, convey, transfer, release, assign, assure and confirm unto and to the use of the party of the second part the properties described in Schedule III so as to constitute her as the sole and absolute owner thereof and to have hold, possess and enjoy the same as her own freed and discharged from all rights in common and claims and demands whatsoever of the other parties concerning the same.

In pursuance of the said agreement and in consideration of the partition and/or division of the shares of the parties in their ancestral properties as hereunder made by their respective allotments as hereunder effected by the parties of the first, second, fourth, fifth, sixth and seventh parts grant, convey, transfer, assign, assure, release and confirm unto and to the use of party of the third part all the properties described in Schedule IV so as to enable him to have hold, possess and enjoy the same as his own freed and discharged from all rights in common and claims and demands whatsoever of the parties of the other part in to upon or concerning the same, but subject to the rights of his male descendants.

In pursuance of the said agreement and in consideration of the absolute ownership acquired by the parties in respect of their respective allotments as hereunder effected, the parties of the first, second, third, fourth, fifth and seventh parts do hereby grant, convey, transfer, assign, assure, release and confirm the properties described in Schedule V unto and to the use of the party of the sixth part so as to constitute him the sole and absolute owners thereof and to have hold, possess and enjoy the same as his own freed and discharged from all rights in common and claims and demands whatsoever of the other parties in to upon or concerning the same but subject to the rights of his male descendants.

AND this Indenture furthermore witnesseth as follows:

1. All Income-tax, Wealth-tax and other capital and revenue liabilities of the estate as on this day shall be borne and paid by the parties proportionate to the shares in the joint family properties hereunder partitioned.

2. That the parties hereto shall henceforth be the separate owners of the shares allotted to each of them and shall hold and enjoy the shares so allotted in severalty and free and discharged from all claims and demands of the other parties hereto or anyone claiming through, under or in trust for them.

3. None of the parties shall be entitled to sell, mortgage or otherwise deal in his or her share hereby allotted to a stranger unless he or she has offered the same to the other parties.

4. That it has been further agreed that each party shall execute and get registered, if necessary, any other deed or deeds, document or documents or receipt which he/she or they may be required to do at the instance of any other party or parties to this deed at the latter's expenses, in order to more effectually assure or confirm any right or title conferred on him/her under these presents.

5. That the original Deed of Partition shall remain with the party hereto of the first part and a true copy thereof signed by all the parties hereto will be delivered to each of the other parties hereto who shall be entitled to require production of the original from the former before any court or public officer or arbitrator or bank or insurance company etc., if so desired.

6. It is hereby agreed that each party will be entitled to realise the arrears of rent including arrears if any outstanding in respect of the property allotted to him/her without any claim or objection from any of the other parties and to effect mutation of their respective names in all public records.

7. That all revenue taxes and other public charges in respect of any property shall be borne by the party to whomsoever the same has by virtue of this deed been allotted.

8. Parties shall bear and pay all costs, charges and expenses in connection with the preparation, execution and registration of this deed and also the stamp costs in equal shares.

AND THIS INDENTURE furthermore witnesses that the parties do hereby covenant agree and declare that all of them had and still have good title full power and absolute authority to have the properties partitioned in the manner hereinbefore indicated and none of them has charged nor encumbered the same or any part thereof nor otherwise dealt with, nor done, executed or performed any act, deed or thing or suffered anything to the contrary whereby or by reason or means whereof the same may be affected or prejudiced in title or estate or they may be hindered or prevented from having the same granting, conveying or having the same partitioned as effected by these presents AND THAT the respective allottees shall hold, possess, enjoy their respective allotments peaceably and quietly without any claim or demand or interruption whatsoever by any other parties AND THAT further the parties shall at the request and costs of any allottee or any person or persons claiming under or in trust from him do execute and perform all such acts, deeds and things for further better and most perfectly assuring the same according to the true intent and meaning of these presents.

Schedule I above referred to

* * *

Schedule II above referred to

* * *

Schedule III above referred to

* * *

Schedule IV above referred to

* * *

IN WITNESS WHEREOF the parties have executed these presents in quadroplicate on the day, month and year first above-written.

Signed, sealed and delivered at Calcutta in the presence of: Sd. All seven parties

Partition of a Debutter Estate

THIS DEED OF PARTITION made on this 5th day of October 2000 BETWEEN .... AB, son of .... by religion Hindu by occupation .... hereinafter referred to as party of the first part and CD, son of......... residing at .... by religion Hindu by occupation .... hereinafter referred to as party of the second part AND SREE SREE .... JEW a deity consecrated and established by late .... the grand father of the parties of the first and second parts at present located at the place of worship at premises No. .... which belongs absolutely to the deity, of the third part represented by the parties hereto as their present shebaits:

WHEREAS the estate of the said deity consists of the properties namely the said premises No. .... and other properties altogether mentioned and described in SCHEDULE A & B under an endowment created by the said .... many years ago AND WHEREAS the properties in SCHEDULE "B" are the parent estate of the deity which were expressly dedicated to be used as place of worship and sacrifice (which are inpartiable) AND WHEREAS the said late .... acted as shebait of the said deity ever since the endowment was created until his death which occurred on .... AND WHEREAS upon the death of the said .... the parties hereto who are his grandsons by a predeceased son became shebaits and have been as such jointly performing the daily seva puja and the periodical worships of the said deity AND WHEREAS the parties are also jointly in possession of the other properties belonging to the deity which they acquired out of the income of the debutter estate AND WHEREAS the parties also developed the properties out of their personal funds and resources which are all mentioned in Part I of SCHEDULE "A" by constructing two pucca buildings thereon of which they have let out the ground floor and live in the first floor with the members of their respective families AND WHEREAS the parties have thus acquired a personal or proprietary interest in the said properties.

AND WHEREAS disputes and differences having arisen between the parties as to performance and non-performance of the seva and puja of the deity, apportionment of the income of the debutter estate their rights, duties, obligation and responsibilities and to avoid confusion on the subject the parties have agreed to discharge the functions attached to their offices as shebaits severally and to worship the deity by turns, *i.e.* by palas on grounds of necessity and convenience and to manage and administer the debutter properties by partition or division thereof into two lots as hereunder appearing AND WHEREAS such partition being also necessary for the sake of convenience of the parties and benefit of the deity and its estate without any detriment to and in conformity with the trust or obligation attached thereto they have agreed to the sequence as follows, *viz.* that they should perform the daily seva and puja by turns, *viz.* by palas, *viz.* that the party of the first part shall do the same for the Bengali months of Baisakh, Ashar, Bhadra, Kartick, Pous and Falgoon and the party of the second part for the months of Jaistha, Sravan, Ashwin, Agrahan, Magh and Chaitra every year with effect from the beginning of the next Bengali year and the debutter estate shall be partitioned as hereunder provided.

NOW THIS INDENTURE of partition of debutter estate witnesseth that on and from the beginning of next Bengali year the parties shall perform the daily worship and periodical festivals of the deity according to their respective palas, *viz.* that the party of the first part shall perform the seva and puja alternatively for the months and the party of the second part for the months as hereinbefore stated and, further and without destroying the intrinsic value of the estate and for facilities for better enjoyment and administration of the estate of the deity the party of the first part as shebait of the deity do hereby grant, transfer, assign in favour of the party of the second part, the property fully mentioned and in Lot I of SCHEDULE "A" hereto to have and to hold and manage the same in severalty as shebait of the deity free from all rights in common without any detriment to the interest of the deity and subject to performance of the daily seva and periodical worships for the months hereinbefore mentioned which will be a first charge on the same AND THIS INDENTURE WITNESSETH THAT the party hereto of the second part do hereby and hereunder accordingly grant, transfer, assign unto and to the use of the party of the first part the property mentioned in SCHEDULE "B" hereto To Have and To Hold the same in severalty as shebait of the deity free from all rights in common without any detriment to the interest of the deity subject to performances of the daily seva and puja and periodical worships of the deity for the months hereinbefore mentioned which will be a first charge on the same AND THIS INDENTURE FURTHER WITNESSETH AND it is agreed by and between the parties that the properties, *viz*. the temple and thakurdalan and the place of sacrifice mentioned in SCHEDULE "B" shall remain as absolute debutter without any claim for partition by any of the parties or any other right thereto on any account under any circumstances subject to peaceful occupation and enjoyment and in all cases for the exclusive performance of the daily seva and periodical worships.

Schedule "A"

Lot I: Description of the property allotted to the party of the first part.

Schedule "B"

Lot II: Description of the property allotted to the party of the second part.

Schedule "C"

Properties which will remain in exclusive possession of the deity.

IN WITNESS WHEREOF the parties have hereunto set and subscribed their respective hands and seal the day, month and year first above-written.

Signed, sealed and delivered at
Calcutta in the presence of:

41

Patents and Trade Marks

The Patents Act 1970 amended and consolidated the law relating to Patents. 'Patent' means a Patent or exclusive right granted by the Government. Certain methods or processes of manufacture are patentable. Certain inventions have been made not patentable. A person claiming to be the true and first inventor may make an application for a Patent. An Assignee of the original inventor may also make an application for a Patent in respect of his rights. This application is to be made to the Controller of Patents and/or the appropriate Authority in the prescribed form.

A mere inventor of a process of manufacturing does not give the inventor any right for its exclusive use. He has to apply to the Government for grant of a Patent Right in respect of his specialised article or to his specialised process of manufacturing an article. Such article or process must have the utility, novelty and productivity. Whether the specialised article or process of manufacturing an article is patentable or not will be decided by the Controller of Patents or the Government on the application of the inventor and after hearing objections thereto of any member of the public or interested persons.

A Patent confers on the Owner of Patents (Patentee) the exclusive right to make, use, sale or distribute the patented article in India. If the Patent relates to a process of manufacturing then the Patentee shall have the exclusive right to the method or process of manufacturing the article or substance in India. An amendment introduced in 1999, effective from 1st January 1995, has the object of granting products patents in respect of medicine and drug and exclusive marketing rights to sell or distribute such products with certain restriction.

A Patent may be granted to two or more persons jointly. It is granted generally for 14 years. If the patent relates to manufacture of food or an article intended or capable of being used as food or medicine or drug, then the Patent is granted for 5 years. Such patent for a limited period is renewable.

A Patent or a share in Patent can be assigned or mortgaged or can be given on licence. Such transfer of interest in the Patent must be in writing containing the terms and conditions and it should be filed in the Office of the Patents for registration within 6 months or within further 6 months if permitted by the Controller. Normally the transferee makes an application in the prescribed form.

The Agreement of Assignment or transfer of the Patents should not contain monopolistic reservation of rights or imposition of obligations. Any such monopolistic reservation of rights or imposition of obligations either in the same contract of assignment or in a separate contract contrary to the provisions of the Patents Act shall be void. The Patentee on grant of the Patent has the exclusive right to manufacture or sale the patented article to the exclusion of all others and any infringement of this right is actionable. The Patentee can restrain such wrongful infringement and can also claim damages against the wrongdoer.

The Agreement relating to the transfer or assignment or licensing of the Patents or any rights therein attracts the Stamp Duty and it is required to be registered with the Patents Office. The Registration Act of 1908 is not generally attracted to such agreements.

FORMS

Agreement to Assign a Patent

THIS AGREEMENT IS MADE on this 10th day of September 2000 BETWEEN Mr. AB residing at .... (hereinafter referred to as the ASSIGNOR which term shall include his successors and assigns) of the one part and CD Co. Ltd. a company registered under the Companies Act 1956 and carrying on business at .... (hereinafter referred to as the ASSIGNEE which term shall include its successor and permitted assigns) of the other part.

WHEREAS the ASSIGNOR has invented a specialised process of manufacturing Pocket Airconditioner and on his application sanction has been given for the Patent to be registered as "PAC" under the Patents Act 1970.

AND WHEREAS the said patented process of manufacture of article require investment of Capital for its exploitation and marketing.

AND WHEREAS the ASSIGNEE has approached the ASSIGNOR for exploitation and marketing of the patented article and to invest the requisite capital for that purpose.

AND WHEREAS the ASSIGNOR has agreed to allow the ASSIGNEE to exploit the patented manufacturing process of the article.

NOW THIS AGREEMENT WITNESSETH and the parties hereby agree as follows:

1. The ASSIGNOR agrees to transfer and assign to the ASSIGNEE all the rights, title and interest of ASSIGNOR in the said Patent and the ASSIGNEE has agreed thereto.

2. In consideration of the said agreement to assign the right, title and interest of the ASSIGNOR in the said Patent, the ASSIGNEE agrees to pay to the ASSIGNOR Rs. 10 lakhs out of which Rs. 2 lakhs has been paid by the ASSIGNEE by way of Earnest Money receipt of which is acknowledged hereby and the Assignee agrees to pay the balance amount on or before execution of the Deed of Assignment.

3. The Deed of Assignment will be executed after the ASSIGNEE exploits the market and finds out the prospect of successfully marketing the patented article but if the Deed of Assignment be not executed within 6 years from the date of execution of these presents then the agreement to execute the Deed of Assignment will stand terminated.

4. Till the execution of the Deed of Assignment of the Patent or termination of these Presents the ASSIGNEE will be at liberty to exploit and use the patent and/or patented manufacturing process and article and sell the patented article and for sale of each article the patentee shall pay a royalty of Rs. 95 per article to the ASSIGNOR. Such payment should be made every six months commencing from June 2000 and thereafter by the last day of every 6th month.

5. The ASSIGNEE shall not be entitled to sub-assign or give licence for manufacture or sale of the patented article.

6. The ASSIGNEE shall maintain proper books of accounts in respect of manufacture and sale of the patented article and such record should be made available to the ASSIGNOR and his representative for inspection and to take copies thereof.

7. The ASSIGNEE shall not do anything which may result in cancellation of the registration of the Patent.

8. The ASSIGNEE shall exploit the Patent by manufacturing and selling the patented article to the full extent and would invest the requisite capital required for full exploitation of and use of the patented article.

9. The ASSIGNOR shall maintain registration of patents by getting it renewed from time to time. But he does not warranty or guarantee the continued validity or registration of the said patent or that the manufacture or sale of the patented article will not infringe any other patent or other rights of other persons.

10. The ASSIGNOR however agrees that in any action taken by the ASSIGNEE or against the assignee the ASSIGNOR will assist the ASSIGNEE in protecting

his right, title or interest in relation to the manufacture and sale of the patented article.

11. All disputes and differences arising between the parties herein in relation to the meaning, scope and effect or validity of this Agreement or the right, title or interest of the parties herein and matters in relation to or arising out of this Agreement shall be referred to the arbitration of the Bengal Chamber of Commerce whose decision shall be final and binding on the parties.

IN WITNESS WHEREOF the parties have signed sealed and delivered these presents on the day, month and year first above-written.

Signed and delivered by the said Mr. AB the ASSIGNOR in presence of:

1. .... Signature

2. ....

Signed, sealed and delivered by Mr. XY pursuant to Board Resolution dated .... of CD Co. Ltd. in the presence of:

1. .... Signature

2. ....

Agreement of Assignment of Patents

THIS AGREEMENT IS MADE on this 5th day of September 2000 BETWEEN Mr. AB residing at .... (hereinafter referred to as the ASSIGNOR which term shall include his successors and assigns) of the one part and CD Co. Ltd. a company registered under the Companies Act 1956 and carrying on business at .... (hereinafter referred to as the ASSIGNEE which term shall include its successors and assigns) of the other part.

WHEREAS the ASSIGNOR is the owner of Patent 'PAC' for manufacture and sale of Pocket Airconditioner and the said Patent was registered and continues to be registered under the Patents Act 1970.

AND WHEREAS the ASSIGNOR has been exploiting and using the said Patent under an agreement to assign dated 10th September 1999 providing for ultimate assignment of the said Patent in favour of the ASSIGNEE.

AND WHEREAS the ASSIGNEE has duly performed its obligations under the said Agreement to assign the patent and has requested the ASSIGNOR to execute the Deed of Assignment of the Patent to which the ASSIGNOR has agreed.

NOW THIS DEED OF assignment witnesseth and the parties herein agree as follows:

1. In consideration of payment of Rs. 20 lakhs by the ASSIGNEE to the ASSIGNOR receipt whereof is acknowledged hereto, the ASSIGNOR transfers and assigns all rights, title and interest in the said Patent 'PAC' in favour of the ASSIGNEE.

2. The ASSIGNEE has satisfied itself by making enquiries and taking inspection of the relevant documents that the ASSIGNOR has the right and authority to assign the said Patent and the said Patent is still valid and continues to be registered.

3. The ASSIGNEE has satisfied itself that the Patent is free from all encumbrances and claims of any kind.

4. The ASSIGNEE shall be entitled to as the holder and owner of the said Patent to use the said Patent in any manner permissible under law peaceably without any interruption or objections from or on behalf of the ASSIGNOR.

5. The ASSIGNOR agrees to execute any further documents or Deeds as may be required for further and more perfectly assigning the ownership and use of the said Patent by the ASSIGNEE.

6. The ASSIGNEE hereby declares and agrees that by execution of these presents the ASSIGNOR will have no liability in respect of any claims proceedings, costs and expenses and that the ASSIGNEE undertakes to keep the ASSIGNOR fully indemnified against and harmless from all such actions, claims, proceedings, costs and expenses in relation to the said Patent, assigned herein or manufacture and sale of the said product or use of the Patent or in relation to the same.

IN WITNESS WHEREOF the parties herein have executed these presents on the day, month and year first herein above-written.

Signed and delivered by the said Mr. AB, the ASSIGNOR in the presence of:

1. .... Signature

2. ....

Signed, sealed and delivered by Mr. .... pursuant to a Board Resolution dated .... of CD Co. Ltd. the ASSIGNEE in the presence of:

1. .... Signature

2. ....

Licence to Use a Patent

THIS AGREEMENT IS MADE on this 20th day of January 2000 BETWEEN Mr. AB residing at .... (hereinafter referred to as the LICENSOR which term shall include his successors and assigns) of the one part and CD Co. Ltd. a company registered under the Companies Act 1956 and carrying on business at .... (hereinafter referred to as the LICENSEE which term shall include its successors and permitted assigns) of the other part.

WHEREAS the LICENSOR has invented a specialised process of manufacturing Pocket Air-conditioners and on his application sanction has been given for Patent to be registered as 'PAC' under the Patents Act 1970.

AND WHEREAS the LICENSOR has been granted the said Patent for the process of manufacture of the said article and sale thereof under the Brand name 'PAC'.

AND WHEREAS the LICENSEE has approached the LICENSOR for exploitation and marketing of the said Patent under a Licence from the LICENSOR.

AND WHEREAS the LICENSOR has agreed to permit the LICENSEE to use the said Patent.

NOW THIS AGREEMENT WITNESSETH and the parties hereby agree as follows:

1. In consideration of the LICENSEE agreeing to pay a licence fee of Rs. 2 lakhs per year the LICENSOR hereby grants the LICENSEE permission or a licence to use the specialised manufacturing process or manufacturing the Pocket Air-conditioners to market and sell such air-conditioners under the Patent name 'PAC'.

2. The licence hereby granted will be valid for 10 years after which the Licence would be renewed or not would be decided by mutual agreement.

3. In addition to the said licence fee the LICENSEE shall pay to the LICENSOR a Royalty of Rs. 100 for each PAC sold. The LICENSEE shall maintain and furnish regular accounts of the manufacture and sale of the said Patented article. Such accounts would be open to inspection through representative of the LICENSOR.

4. The LICENSEE shall not assign the licence or allow anybody else to use the said Patent.

5. The LICENSEE shall take immediate action for any infringement of the said Patent making the LICENSOR a party to the such proceedings.

6. The LICENSEE shall keep the LICENSOR fully indemnified against and harmless from all proceedings, claims, costs and expenses in relation to the manufacture and sale or use of the said Patented article or in relation thereto.

7. The LICENSEE has made enquiries and inspected the relevant documents and has satisfied itself about the right, title or interest of the LICENSOR in the said Patent.

8. The LICENSOR does not give any warranty or undertaking about its right, title or interest in the said Patent or about any litigation in relation thereto.

9. The LICENSEE shall submit accounts and make payment of the Royalties, the first of such statement of accounts and payment of Royalty would be by end of April 2000 and thereafter by the end of each third month.

IN WITNESS WHEREOF the parties hereto have executed these presents on the day, month and year first above-written.

Signed and delivered by the said Mr. AB, the LICENSOR in the presence of:

1. .... Signature

2. ....

Signed, sealed and delivered by Mr. XY pursuant to a Board Resolution dated .... of CD Co. Ltd. the LICENSEE in the presence of:

1. .... Signature

2. ....

Assignment of Design

THIS DEED OF ASSIGNMENT is made at .... this 30th day of September 2000 BETWEEN Mr. AB residing at .... (hereinafter referred to as the ASSIGNOR) of the one part and CD Company Pvt. Ltd., a company registered under the Companies Act 1956 and having its Registered Office at .... (hereinafter referred to as the ASSIGNEE) of the other part.

WHEREAS the ASSIGNOR has invented and made a new design of a Computer and the same has been registered under the Designs Act 1911 being No. 1140 in the name of the ASSIGNOR as the Proprietor thereof and the particulars whereof with a photocopy of the Design are given in the Schedule hereunder.

AND WHEREAS the ASSIGNEE has approached the ASSIGNOR for the use of the said Design for manufacturing computers and has requested the ASSIGNOR to assign the said Design to the ASSIGNEE to enable it to manufacture the Computers of the said Design and the ASSIGNOR has agreed to assign the said Design to the ASSIGNEE.

NOW THESE PRESENTS WITNESSETH and the parties hereby agrees as follows:

1. In consideration of the ASSIGNEE making payment of Rs. 5 lakhs to the ASSIGNOR on the execution of these presents the receipt whereof the ASSIGNOR hereby admits the ASSIGNOR doth hereby assign unto the ASSIGNEE all the Assignor's right, title and interest in the said Registered Design to hold the same unto and to the use of ASSIGNEE absolutely for the validity period of the said design including extensions thereof.

2. The ASSIGNOR hereby covenants with the ASSIGNEE that the ASSIGNOR shall whenever requested by the ASSIGNEE execute all documents and do all acts and things as may be required by the ASSIGNEE.

3. The ASSIGNOR hereby declares that he is the sole proprietor of the said Design and he has the absolute right, title and interest therein to assign the same in favour of the ASSIGNEE.

4. The ASSIGNOR hereby declares that he has not encumbered the said Design in any manner and has not given any Licence to anybody to use the same.

5. The ASSIGNOR hereby agrees and undertakes to execute all and further documents that may be required to vest in the ASSIGNEE more completely the right, title and interest of the ASSIGNOR in the said Design and to transfer the name of the ASSIGNEE in the register maintained by the Controller under the Designs Act 1911 and also register the said Design in any country where such rights subsist.

6. The ASSIGNOR agrees and undertakes to render all assistance to the ASSIGNEE to prevent infringement of the Design by anybody.

7. The ASSIGNEE undertakes to keep the ASSIGNOR fully indemnified against and harmless from all claims, proceedings, costs, charges and expenses in relation to the use of the Design, the execution of any documents or any proceedings before any Court of Law or authority or Arbitrator or Tribunal.

IN WITNESS WHEREOF the parties herein have executed these presents on the day, month and year first above-written.

Signed and delivered by Mr. AB
in the presence of:

1. .... Signature

2. ....

Signed, sealed and delivered by Mr. XY pursuant to a Board Resolution dated 28th September 2000 of CD Company Pvt. Ltd. in the presence of:

1. .... Signature

2. ....

Licence to use Trade Mark

THIS DEED OF LICENCE IS MADE on this 11th day of November 2000 BETWEEN RP Co. Ltd., a company registered under the appropriate laws of the USA and carrying on business at San Francisco, USA, hereinafter called the LICENSOR (which term shall unless excluded by or repugnant to the context include its successors and assigns) of the one part and AB Co. Ltd. a company registered under the Companies Act 1956 and carrying on business at .... hereinafter referred to as the LICENSEE (which term shall unless excluded by or repugnant to the context include its permitted nominees) of the other part.

WHEREAS the LICENSOR is the manufacturer of and dealer in Computers for office purposes and hold the registered Trade Mark COMOF being Trade Mark No. 5 in Class No. I in respect of Computers for office purposes.

AND WHEREAS the LICENSOR intends to expand its business and sell its products under its Trade Mark in India and Eastern Asia.

AND WHEREAS the LICENSEE in India has a manufacturing Unit to manufacture Computers.

AND WHEREAS the LICENSEE has approached the LICENSOR to grant licence to use the Licensor's Trade Mark COMOF for sale of the products manufactured by the LICENSEE.

AND WHEREAS the LICENSOR has agreed to allow the LICENSEE to use its said Trade Mark COMOF to sell the Licensee's products on certain terms and conditions.

NOW THEREFORE THESE PRESENTS witnesseth and the parties hereby agree as follows:

1. The LICENSOR hereby doth grant to the LICENSEE non-exclusive right to use the Licensor's Trade Mark COMOF in India and Eastern Asia for sale of its computers, components and parts under the Trade Name COMOF.

2. The use of the Trade Mark by the LICENSEE shall be confined only to the items that might be manufactured by the LICENSEE at its own factory.

3. The LICENSEE shall pay half-yearly to the LICENSOR licence fee at the rate of 10% on the turnover of business of the LICENSEE and such payment to be made by 30th June and 31st December every year.

4. The LICENSEE shall comply with the requirements and provisions of all laws rules and regulations in relation to manufacture and sale of computers and its components under the said Trade Mark of the LICENSOR.

5. The LICENSEE shall manufacture and sell computers under the said Trade Mark COMOF in accordance with the specifications, make-up, brand and packing that the LICENSOR may from time to time intimate to the LICENSEE.

6. The LICENSOR shall have access to the manufacturing unit of the Licensee and to inspect the Licensee's books of accounts and other records at all reasonable times on giving prior notice.

7. The LICENSEE agrees, declares and covenants not to use the said Trade Mark or advertise or publish in newspapers and journals or in labels or in any other documents or packages or do anything having the effect of diluting the distinctiveness of the trade mark of the LICENSOR and the LICENSEE shall give indications either visually or phonetically to the purchasing public that the LICENSEE is using the Trade Mark COMOF as the LICENSEE of the LICENSOR.

8. The LICENSEE undertakes to compensate the LICENSOR and keep the LICENSOR harmless from and indemnified against all claims, proceedings, losses, costs and expenses for any wilful or negligent conduct of the LICENSEE in relation to the use of the Trade Mark of the LICENSOR.

9. The LICENSEE shall not acquire any right of registration of the Trade Mark by virtue of the LICENSEE manufacturing and selling computers as user of the Trade Mark COMOF for any number of years or after termination of the licence or otherwise.

10. The LICENSEE shall inform the LICENSOR any infringement of the Licensor's Trade Mark COMOF with particulars of the infringement or passing off and the names and addresses of the offenders.

11. The LICENSOR shall take and/or permit the LICENSEE to take all possible legal steps for the protection and preservation of the Trade Mark and prevention of its infringement or passing off by any person.

12. This agreement is terminable by giving 3 months notice from either side.

13. In any legal proceedings or in any action against the infringement or passing off in relation to the Trade Mark of the goods covered by the Licence the LICENSEE will take appropriate steps to protect the interests of the LICENSOR and allow the LICENSOR to take any legal action or steps and to join the LICENSEE as a party therein.

The Schedule

IN WITNESS WHEREOF the parties herein have executed these presents on the day, month and year first above-written.

Signed, sealed and delivered by
Mr. .... the Constituted
Attorney of RP Co. Ltd. in the
presence of:

1. .... Signature

2. ....

Signed, sealed and delivered by
Mr. .... pursuant to a
Board Resolution dated ....
of AB Co. Ltd. in the presence of:

1. .... Signature

2. ....

Agreement of Registered User of Trade Mark

THIS AGREEMENT IS MADE on this 5th day of October 2000 BETWEEN RP Co. Ltd., a company registered under the appropriate laws of the U.S.A. and carrying on business at San Francisco, U.S.A. hereinafter called the REGISTERED PROPRIETOR (which term shall include unless excluded by or repugnant to the context its successors and assigns) of the one part and AB Co. Ltd., a company registered under the Companies Act 1956 and carrying on business at .... hereinafter referred to as the USER (which term shall include unless excluded by or repugnant to the context its permitted nominees) of the other part.

WHEREAS the REGISTERED PROPRIETOR is the manufacturer of and dealer in Computers for office purposes and holds the registered Trade Mark COMOF No. 5 in Class No. I in respect of Computers for office purposes.

AND WHEREAS the REGISTERED PROPRIETOR intends to expand its business and sell its products or similar products under its Trade Name in India and Eastern Asia.

AND WHEREAS the USER in India has a manufacturing unit for manufacture Computers.

AND WHEREAS the USER has approached the REGISTERED PROPRIETOR to sell its products using the registered proprietor's said Trade Mark.

AND WHEREAS the REGISTERED PROPRIETOR has agreed to allow the USER to sell its products under the Trade Mark as the REGISTERED PROPRIETOR on certain terms and conditions:

NOW THEREFORE THESE PRESENTS witnesseth and the parties hereby agree as follows:

1. The REGISTERED PROPRIETOR hereby doth grant to the USER the non-exclusive right to use the said Registered Proprietor's Trade Mark COMOF in respect of the USER'S computers for office purposes.

2. The USER shall pay to the REGISTERED PROPRIETOR a Royalty at 10% of the sale price of each computer and parts and components thereof.

3. The said royalty will be paid every six months on the basis of total sales effected irrespective of the collection of bills or receipt of payment for the said sale of computers by the USER.

4. In default of payment of any two half-yearly payments the REGISTERED PROPRIETOR would be entitled to terminate this agreement.

5. The USER shall manufacture and sell the computers in accordance with the specifications, make-up, brand and packing requirement of the REGISTERED PROPRIETOR.

6. The REGISTERED PROPRIETOR shall have access to the manufacturing unit of the USER and to inspect the USER'S books of accounts and records at all reasonable times on giving prior notice.

7. The USER agrees, declares and covenants not to use the said mark or advertise or publish in journals, labels or on any other documents or on packings anything having the effect of diluting the distinctiveness of the Trade Mark of the REGISTERED PROPRIETOR and to give indications either visually or phonetically to the purchasing public that the USER is using the Mark on the licence of the REGISTERED PROPRIETOR.

8. The USER will make an application to the Registrar of Trade Marks for recording the present agreement and the fact that the USER has been permitted to use the said Trade Mark of the REGISTERED PROPRIETOR in India.

9. The USER shall inform the REGISTERED PROPRIETOR about any infringement of the said Trade Mark and take appropriate legal proceedings to protect the interest of the REGISTERED PROPRIETOR and all costs in relation thereto shall be borne by the USER.

10. The USER shall use the said Trade Mark so long as it manufactures computers itself in accordance with the terms and specifications of the REGISTERED PROPRIETOR.

11. This agreement is determinable by giving 3 months notice by the REGISTERED PROPRIETOR or by the USER by showing any valid grounds therefor.

12. The USER hereby undertakes to make necessary application and comply with the rules and regulations in relation to the User Agreement as also in connection with the manufacture and sale of computers for office purposes under the said Trade Mark.

The Schedule

(Particulars of goods covered by Trade Mark)

IN WITNESS WHEREOF the parties hereto have executed these presents on the day, month and year first above-written.

Signed, sealed and delivered by
Mr. .... at Calcutta
pursuant to Board Resolution
dated .... of RP Co. Ltd. in
the presence of:

1. .... Signature
2. ....

Signed, sealed and delivered by
Mr. .... at Calcutta
pursuant to Board Resolution
dated .... of AB Co. Ltd. in the
presence of:

1. .... Signature
2. ....

Affidavit of Constituted Attorney of Registered Proprietor

In the Matter of The Trade and Merchandise Marks Act 1958

And

In the Matter of an application to register AB Co. Ltd. as the Registered User of the Registered Trade Mark No. 5 in Class 1 now standing in the name of RP Co. Ltd.

Affidavit

I, ..., aged.......... years, son of.............. residing at............... by occupation service do hereby solemnly affirm and say as follows:

1. I am a citizen of India. I am a Director of RP Co. Ltd. having its registered office in San Francisco, U.S.A. hereinafter referred to as the REGISTERED PROPRIETOR of Trade Mark COMOF and I have been serving with the REGISTERED PROPRIETOR for the last several years.

2. The said Trade Mark COMOF has been registered having Trade Mark No. 5 Class 1. The said Trade Mark is registered in India since the last 5 years.

3. AB Co. Ltd. is registered under the Companies Act 1956 in India and it has been manufacturing computers for office purpose. For mutual advantage it has been agreed between the parties that AB Co. Ltd. will manufacture computers in accordance with specifications of the REGISTERED PROPRIETOR and sell the same on certain terms and conditions.

4. An agreement has been entered into between the REGISTERED PROPRIETOR and AB Co. Ltd. on .... to use the Registered Trade Mark COMOF in respect of all computers to be manufactured and sold by AB Co. Ltd. By such agreement, AB Co. Ltd. has been given a non-exclusive right to use the Trade Mark COMOF without any limitation of period subject to termination of the agreement on prior 3 months' notice from either side.

5. The REGISTERED PROPRIETOR is carrying on business as the manufacturer of and dealer in Computers for office purpose for the last ten years and for expansion of business AB Co. Ltd. has been formed as a subsidiary of the REGISTERED PROPRIETOR.

6. The REGISTERED PROPRIETOR has not entered into any agreement or allowed the use of the said Registered Trade Mark to any person prior to the present agreement. The REGISTERED PROPRIETOR acquired the ownership or proprietorship of the said Trade Mark COMOF by use and registration and not by any other means.

7. The REGISTERED PROPRIETOR will exercise control over the use of Trade Mark by AB Co. Ltd., and keep a check as to the compliance by the latter of the terms and conditions of the said user agreement. The annual expenses likely to be incurred by the REGISTERED PROPRIETOR for such supervision and control cannot be reasonably estimated.

8. The permitted use of the said Trade Mark by AB Co. Ltd. is intended for sale of Computers in India and for export to other countries.

9. I know and I have made myself acquainted with the business activities of the REGISTERED PROPRIETOR and also of AB Co. Ltd. I have read and understood the contents of the User Agreement between the Registered User and AB Co. Ltd. The statements contained in the said agreement are true and correct and the same are incorporated herein as a part of this affidavit.

10. The statements contained in paragraphs 1 to 9 are partly on personal knowledge and partly based on information derived from records maintained by the REGISTERED PROPRIETOR which I believe to be true.

Signature

Solemnly affirmed by the said Mr. ...., pursuant to the Power of Attorney dated .... executed by RP Co. Ltd., at Calcutta on this .... day of October 1999.

Before me

Notary

Application for Registration of User of Trade Mark

To
The Registrar of Trade Marks
15/1 Chowringhee Road
Calcutta 700 071

Date ....

Dear Sir

Re: Trade and Merchandise Act 1958 (S. 49, R. 82)
Application for Registration of Registered User.

An application is hereby made by RP Co. Ltd., an American Company, the Registered Proprietor of Trade Mark COMOF Trade Mark No. 5 Class I in respect of Computers for office use and by AB Co. Ltd.

The AB Co. Ltd. the Indian company may be registered as the Registered User of the above-named Trade Mark in respect of computers for office use subject to the following conditions but without a time-limit.

(*a*) The Registered User will manufacture computers in its factory in accordance with the specifications to be supplied by the REGISTERED PROPRIETOR;

(*b*) The REGISTERED PROPRIETOR will have the right to inspect the factory premises, office premises, books of accounts and other records of AB Co. Ltd.;

(*c*) The technical knowhow, designs, data and other particulars that will be furnished by the Registered Proprietor shall be subject to periodical review;

(*d*) The Registered User agreement is without any limitation of period but subject to the terms and conditions contained in the agreement.

(*e*) Copies of the Registered User Agreement and affidavit of the Constituted Attorney of the Registered Proprietor are annexed hereto.

Yours faithfully

Signature of the authorised Officer of Registered User AB Co. Ltd. at	Signature of the Power of Attorney Holder of the Registered Proprietor RP Co. Ltd. residing at ....

ENCLO: As above

Assignment of Trade Mark

THIS DEED OF ASSIGNMENT IS MADE on this .... day of .... 1999 BETWEEN RP Co. Ltd., a company registered under the appropriate laws of the U.S.A. and carrying on business at San Francisco, U.S.A. hereinafter called the ASSIGNOR (which term shall include unless excluded by or repugnant to the context its successors) of the one part and AB Co. Ltd. a company registered under the Companies Act 1956 hereinafter referred to as the ASSIGNEE (which term shall include unless excluded by or repugnant to the context its successors and assigns) of the other part.

WHEREAS the ASSIGNOR is manufacturer of and dealer in Computers for office purposes and holds the Registered Trade Mark COMOF, Trade Mark No. 5 in Class I in respect of the Computers for office purposes.

AND WHEREAS the ASSIGNOR intends to assign its Trade Mark COMOF in respect of the computer products.

And WHEREAS the ASSIGNEE has agreed to take an assignment of the said Trade Mark COMOF on certain terms and conditions to which the Assignor has agreed.

NOW THEREFORE THESE PRESENTS witnesseth and the parties hereby agree as follows:

1. The ASSIGNOR hereby doth assign its Trade Mark COMOF to the ASSIGNEE together with the goodwill of business in the goods for which the said Trade Mark is registered.

2. The ASSIGNEE to hold the said Trade Mark absolutely.

3. In consideration of such assignment the ASSIGNEE shall pay to the ASSIGNOR a sum of Rs. .... of which a sum of Rs. .... has already been

paid by the ASSIGNEE receipt whereof is herein acknowledged by the ASSIGNOR. The balance sum of Rs. .... shall be paid to the ASSIGNOR by six half-yearly instalments payable by the 30th June and 31st December every year, in equal proportion.

4. The assignee hereby declares and undertakes to keep the Assignor fully indemnified against and harmless from any claims, proceedings, losses, damages and expenses that may be incurred by ASSIGNOR in relation to the said assigned Trade Mark COMOF.

5. The ASSIGNEE declares and undertakes that it shall take all necessary steps to comply with all provisions of law, rules and regulations, in relation to the said Trade Mark COMOF.

The Schedule

IN WITNESS WHEREOF the parties hereto have executed these presents on the day, month and year first above-written.

Signed, sealed and delivered by
Mr. .... the Constituted
Attorney of the RP Co. Ltd.
in presence of: Signature

Signed, sealed and delivered by
Mr. .... pursuant to a
Board Resolution dated............ of
AB Co. Ltd. in the presence of: Signature

Notice regarding Infringement and/or Passing off the Trade Mark

Date ....

To
XY Co. Ltd.
3 White Road
Calcutta

Dear Sirs

Our Client: RP Co. Ltd., USA

Re: Infringement of Trade Mark COMOF.

Under instructions from our above client we address you as follows:

Our client carries on business as manufacturer of and dealer in Computers for office purposes under the Trade Mark COMOF No. 5 in Class I for Computers and its components.

The said Trade Mark COMOF has been advertised in the Newspapers and particularly in the Trade Marks Journal Issue No. 5 dated 5th July 1991.

Our client has been using the said Trade Mark COMOF since 1991 which has acquired a distinctive feature in respect of the goods of our client by such continued and extensive use of the said Trade Mark and advertisements thereof. The high standard of the performance of the Computers COMOF has come to be exclusively associated in the minds of the public with our client's goods. Our client is an established manufacturer of and dealer in computers for office purposes.

It has come to our client's knowledge that you have been manufacturing and selling computers for office use under a Mark COMFO. The get-up, packing and mark of your computers are deceptively similar to that of the our client's computers, both in look and phonetically.

You were aware of our client's said COMOF computers for office purposes at the time of your initial business enquiries, market research and setting up of your factory and marketing the products. In spite of such knowledge of our client's products and Trade Mark the manufacturing and marketing of your computers with the Mark COMFO have been with the *mala fide* intention to trade over our client's goodwill and reputation which our client has built up by spending huge amounts apart from expenditure for the research and development of our client's computers.

Your product under the Mark COMFO in the market and our client's Trade Mark COMOF have given rise to confusion and deception in the public mind and specially the intended user of the computers.

By your wrongful use of the Mark COMFO for marketing the computers for office use knowing fully well our client's established Trade Mark COMOF for computers for office use, you have made yourself liable to legal proceedings both Civil and Criminal under the Trade and Merchandise Marks Act 1958.

In the premises, we call upon you to cease and desist forthwith from using the Mark COMFO and agree in writing to destroy all your dies, blocks, labels and cartons and printed or packing materials and give an undertaking to our client's satisfaction.

If we do not hear from you within a period of two weeks from the date of receipt of this notice we have instructions to take appropriate legal proceedings against you without further notice and in that event you will be held solely responsible for all costs and consequences thereof.

Yours faithfully

Advocate

for RP Co. Ltd.

Trade Mark – Passing Off Suit

Suit No. .... of ......
In the High Court at Calcutta
Ordinary Original Civil Jurisdiction

XY Company Ltd., a company registered under the Companies Act 1956 having its registered office at .... Calcutta within the said jurisdiction

.... *Plaintiff*

versus

MB Company Limited, a company registered under the Companies Act 1956 and carrying on business at .... Mumbai outside the said jurisdiction

.... *Defendant*

The plaintiff states:

1. The plaintiff carries on business as the manufacturer of and dealer in Electronic goods in Calcutta. The plaintiff has agents in various places in India for sale of its products. The plaintiff's products have acquired good reputation and its products have distinctive features on the shape, size, layout marking as also the packaging.

2. The plaintiff uses its Trade Mark XY on all its products. The sale of the plaintiff's products are quite substantial both in India and abroad.

3. The plaintiff has advertised its products under its said Mark extensively since the last six years and spent a minimum sum of Rs. 6 lakhs on account thereof.

4. By reason of such extensive advertisement and sale of the products, the public associated the said mark XY to the plaintiff and with the plaintiff's products. As such the plaintiff enjoys good reputation abroad and throughout India including Calcutta within the jurisdiction of this Hon'ble Court.

5. The goods of the plaintiff are manufactured in Calcutta and sold in domestic market and exported abroad. Particulars of the sales for the last 5 years are given in a Schedule annexed hereto marked 'A'. Copies of some newspaper cuttings of advertisements are annexed hereto collectively marked 'B'. Particulars of advertisement costs yearwise are given in a Schedule annexed hereto marked 'C'.

6. The plaintiff complied with all the necessary formalities and provisions of law for the registration of its products under the Trade Mark XY. The plaintiff's Trade Mark XY was registered with the Registrar of Trade Marks, Chowringhee Road, Calcutta being Trade Mark No. 1 in Class I in respect of the electronic goods and computers both hardware and software. The Office of the Registrar of Trade Marks, the Register concerned and the Record Containing registration of the plaintiff's said products are all within the jurisdiction of this Hon'ble Court. Certified copies of the application as also of the Certificate of Registration are annexed hereto collectively marked 'D'.

7. The said mark XY became very popular among the purchasers of the plaintiff's products and the Mark XY became very much associated with the plaintiff's products.

8. On or about 10th September 1999 it was brought to the plaintiff's knowledge by the Trade Marks Registry, Calcutta that the respondent has applied for registration of the alleged Trade Mark XZ for similar goods as that of the plaintiff. A copy of the Letter of Registrar of Trade Marks, Calcutta is annexed hereto marked 'E' informing the plaintiff of the said application of the defendant.

9. The defendant has been wrongfully selling the electronic goods and computers software and hardware through its sale outlets in Calcutta with the said Trade Mark XZ within the jurisdiction of this Hon'ble Court. Copies of certain cash memos showing the dealer's name, address, articles and the Trade Mark used thereon are annexed hereto collectively marked 'F'.

10. The plaintiff states that the sale of the said products by the defendant under the Trade Mark XZ has amounted to passing off of the plaintiff's goods as the goods of similar description under a deceptively similar Mark. The defendant has therefore infringed the plaintiff's said Trade Mark inasmuch as the articles marked XZ is deceptively similar to that of the plaintiff's Trade Mark XY and the goods are similar and of the same description.

11. The defendant's Trade Mark has been so much similar to the plaintiff's Trade Mark that the defendant has been passing off its goods as those of the plaintiff's goods and/or the defendant is enabling the others to do so and thus the defendant is deriving the ultimate benefit out of the reputation and goodwill of the plaintiff which the plaintiff was enjoying during the last several years. Such goodwill and reputation were created at a huge cost of the plaintiff.

12. The plaintiff states that the conduct of the defendant in respect of sale and advertisement of its products has been fraudulent and deceptive in nature inasmuch as the same are calculated to deceive the purchasers of the plaintiff's goods into believing that the products of the defendant are very much similar to and very much connected with the plaintiff. Thus the

public have been made to wonder about the source or origin of the products which are very much the same and/or of similar description.

13. The defendant is by reason of such sales and advertisements causing great loss and injury to the public and to the plaintiff. The plaintiff has suffered and is still suffering and will continue to suffer substantial loss and injury if the defendant continues with its wrongful acts. Until full discovery is made about the sales of the products of the defendant the plaintiff is unable to quantify the total amount of financial loss suffered by it and is likely to be suffered by the plaintiff due to the wrongful acts of the defendant.

14. The financial loss or injury caused to the plaintiff by the wrongful acts and conduct of the defendant cannot be ascertained and as such the compensation in money cannot be adequate and sufficient relief for the damages and loss suffered and/or likely to be suffered by the plaintiff.

15. The plaintiff claims delivery up of the infringing dies, blocks, labels etc. for cancellation and destruction. The plaintiff states that the defendant is not entitled to sell its products or advertise the same in the market under the Trade Mark XZ and as such the defendant should be restrained from selling its products under the Mark XZ or giving any publicity in respect thereof.

16. The plaintiff's cause of action for the suit is arising day-to-day inasmuch as the defendant is passing off its products as the products of plaintiff, *inter alia*, in Mumbai and Chennai outside the said jurisdiction and in Calcutta within the jurisdiction of this Hon'ble Court day to day and every day till date and intends to continue to do so.

17. The plaintiff's substantial cause of action arose in Calcutta where the defendant sold its products wrongly under the Trade Mark XZ similar to the mark of plaintiff deceiving the general public into believing that they have been purchasing the goods of the plaintiff. The office of the Trade Marks Registry is situated at Chowringhee Road, Calcutta, within the jurisdiction of this Hon'ble Court where the plaintiff's said Trade Mark XY is registered. As the said passing off took place both outside and within the said jurisdiction the plaintiff prays for leave under cl. 12 of the Letters Patent to institute this suit in this Hon'ble Court inasmuch as part of the cause of action arose within the jurisdiction of the Hon'ble Court and part of the cause of action arose in Chennai where the defendant is manufacturing the goods and packing the same with the deceptive Mark XZ and selling the same with the object of passing off the same as goods of the plaintiff outside the jurisdiction of this Hon'ble Court.

18. The plaintiff has other causes of action and also other claims for the continuing infringement of the plaintiff's Trade Mark and passing off the products of the defendant as the product of the plaintiff and as such the plaintiff has other claims which cannot be ascertained now and prays for

leave under Or. 2, r. 2 of the Code of Civil Procedure 1908 to take further and appropriate legal proceedings in such Forum as the plaintiff may be advised.

19. For the purposes of jurisdiction and court fees the suit is valued at Rs......... on which court fees in stamps have been paid and as such this Hon'ble Court has the jurisdiction to entertain, try and determine this suit.

The plaintiff therefore prays for leave under Clause 12 of the Letters Patent under Or. 2, r. 2 of the Code of Civil Procedure 1908 and claims:

(*a*) Permanent Injunction restraining the defendant, its agents, servants and representatives from wrongfully selling the products or offering for sale or otherwise dealing in any goods similar to the goods of the plaintiff under the Trade Mark XZ or any other Mark deceptively similar to plaintiff's Trade Mark XY;

(*b*) A Decree for accounts of the profits earned by the defendant by wrongful use of the mark XZ similar to the mark of the plaintiff's Trade Mark XY and a decree for such amount in favour of the plaintiff against the defendant as may be found due on taking the accounts;

(*c*) An enquiry into the damages suffered by the plaintiff due to the wrongful acts of the defendant and a decree against the defendant for the sum found due on such enquiry;

(*d*) Decree for delivery up of the infringing dies, blocks, labels, etc. including the packing and advertising materials and destruction thereof;

(*e*) Receiver;

(*f*) Attachment;

(*g*) Injunction;

(*h*) Costs;

(*i*) Further and other reliefs as the plaintiff is entitled to in law and in equity.

Name and address of the
plaintiff's Advocate

Signature of the plaintiff

Verification

I, ... son of .... by occupation service residing at .... do hereby solemnly affirm and say as follows:

1. I am a principal officer and the Constituted Attorney of the plaintiff and as such I am competent to sign this plaint and all petitions, Vakalatnamas and affirm affidavits on behalf of the plaintiff.
2. I know and I have made myself acquainted with the facts and circumstances of this case and I am able to depose thereto.
3. The statements contained in the paragraphs 1 to 16 of the foregoing plaint including the cause title thereof are true to my knowledge based on records maintained by the plaintiff and believed by me to be true and those mentioned in paragraphs 17 to 19 are my humble submissions before this Hon'ble Court.

Solemnly affirmed by the said
Mr. .... at the Court
House in Calcutta on this .... day
of .... 1999.

Sd/.

Before me
Commissioner

Application for Rectification of Trade Mark Registry

Matter No. .... of 1999

In the High Court at Calcutta

Ordinary Original Civil Jurisdiction

In the Matter of Trade and Merchandise Marks Act 1958

And

In the Matter of an Application under Sections 56 and 57 of the said Act for rectification of Register of Trade Marks.

And

In the Matter of Registered Trade Mark No. 567 in Class 1 of AB Co. Ltd.

And

In the Matter of:

XY Co. Ltd. a company registered under the Companies Act 1956 and having its registered office at 5 White Road, Calcutta

.... *Petitioner*

versus

1. AB Co. Ltd., a company registered under the Companies Act 1956 having its registered office at 3 A.K. Avenue, Mumbai

2. RC Co. Ltd., a company registered under the Companies Act 1956 having its registered office at 4 B.K. Avenue, Calcutta

3. Registrar of Trade Marks having his office at 15/1 Chowringhee Square, Calcutta

.... *Respondents*

To

The Hon'ble Mr. ....
Chief Justice and His Companion
Justices of the said Hon'ble Court

The humble petition of the petitioner above-named most respectfully

SHEWETH:

1. Your petitioner is an aggrieved person by reasons of entries made in the Register maintained by respondent No. 3 without sufficient cause as also by an entry wrongfully remaining in the Register.

2. Your petitioner carries on business as a manufacturer of, dealer in and exporter of Electronic goods and Computer articles both hardware and software.

3. The first respondent is the registered proprietor of Trade Mark No. 10 in Class I in respect of Computer and Electronic articles.

4. The second respondent purports to be the licensee and permitted user of the Registered Trade Mark UTILITY (hereinafter referred to as the MARK) which is registered in the name of the first respondent.

5. The third respondent is the Registrar of Trade Marks having his address as mentioned above within the jurisdiction of this Hon'ble Court.

6. Your petitioner in the year 1991 adopted the Trade Mark UNITY hereinafter referred to as the petitioner's mark and the said adoption of the

said mark was without any knowledge of the first respondent's said mark and has since been selling its products with the said mark UNITY.

7. Your petitioner's said mark has been used continuously and exclusively in India and outside India since 1991 and has been widely advertised in the newspapers, journals and other publicity media and thereby it has acquired the distinction of being the goods manufactured by your petitioner. Particulars of the newspapers, journals and other media in which the said advertisements appeared and the corresponding expenses incurred during the last several years to popularise the products of your petitioner under the said mark are given in a schedule annexed hereto marked 'A'. A statement of sales and the turnover of your petitioner's goods under the said mark are annexed hereto marked 'B'.

8. Your petitioner made an application for registration of the said mark in respect of the electronic goods described therein to the Trade Marks Registry at Calcutta, the respondent No. 3. The said application was made on 5th March 1996. The application was classified in Class I and was numbered as 5. The application is pending registration at the Trade Marks Registry, Calcutta. A copy of the said application with connected papers are annexed hereto collectively marked as 'C'.

9. Your petitioner was surprised to receive a cease and desist notice dated 2nd October 1997 from the Trade Mark lawyer of the first respondent calling upon your petitioner to discontinue use of the Trade Mark UNITY and to give an undertaking not to use the mark or any deceptively similar mark thereto in future. Your petitioner through its Advocate's letter dated 20th October 1997 informed the first respondent as also the Trade Mark Lawyer of the first respondent that the petitioner has been using the trade mark since last six years and that there has been a substantial expenditure in making the petitioner's mark known to the general public by advertisement and publicity. It was also stated that there was no confusion in mind of the public during the said period during which your petitioner used its mark in the open market. It was further stated that the petitioner was using the said mark honestly and *bona fide* and that there was no *mala fide* intention for utilising or trading on the goodwill or reputation, if any, of the respondent Nos. 1 and 2. Your petitioner also specifically denied the other allegations contained in the said notice.

10. Without replying to the said letter of your petitioner, respondent Nos. 1 and 2 filled a suit in the Madras High Court alleging infringement of first respondent's said purported Trade Mark. The suit has been numbered as 259 of 1997 and the suit is still pending before the said Hon'ble High Court. A copy of the plaint filed in the Hon'ble Madras High Court is annexed hereto marked 'D'.

11. Your petitioner denies each and every allegation contained in the plaint filed in the said suit at Madras. Your petitioner states that the goods sold by the respondents Nos. 1 and 2 under the first respondent's said mark were different in look and description from those of the petitioner's goods. Further your petitioner honestly adopted and has been openly using the said mark UNITY for the last six years and thereby your petitioner has acquired the right of concurrent registration of the mark UNITY under s. 12(3) of the Trade and Merchandise Marks Act 1958.

12. The first respondent's registration of the mark in the records of the Registry is in respect of a variety of goods. Many of such goods have not been marketed or sold or used in the Indian market for the last six years. The first respondent's said mark is liable to be rectified by expunging or deleting from the specification of the items covered by your petitioner's said mark UNITY in accordance with the provisions of s. 16 of the said Act.

13. Your petitioner as stated above is a person aggrieved within the meaning of s. 16 of the Trade and Merchandise Marks Act 1958 inasmuch as your petitioner's said mark is pending registration at the Trade Marks Registry. The first respondent has caused to be issued cease and desist notice and also filed in the Hon'ble High Court at Madras the said suit wrongly alleging infringement of the first respondent's said mark UTILITY.

14. Your petitioner states that the first respondent's said mark was registered without any *bona fide* intention to use the same in respect of the first respondent's goods for which the mark was registered. As a matter of fact, there was no *bona fide* use of the said mark by the first respondent in selling the goods upto a date of one month prior to the making of the present application.

15. Prior to the date of this application for a continuous period of six years there was no *bona fide* use of the first respondent's mark in relation to the goods sold by your petitioner under the mark UNITY.

16. The second respondent the alleged user of the said mark of the first respondent has also not used the said mark for any of the goods sold by the petitioner under the mark UNITY. The second respondent is a Licensee and not registered proprietor of the said mark of the first respondent. The use of the mark UTILITY as alleged by second respondent cannot be the use of respondent No. 1 within the meaning of s. 48(2) of the said Act. During the last six years after registration of the mark of the first respondent the said mark has not been used for any goods manufactured by the first respondent.

17. In view of the aforesaid your petitioner states that the first respondent obtained registration of the said mark UTILITY without any intention to use it, either by itself or through respondent No. 2. Your petitioner states that the first respondent's said mark is, therefore, liable to be and be removed from the Register under s. 18 of the said Act.

18. Your petitioner states that by reasons of the aforesaid the registration of the first respondent's said mark and the entry made in the Register by respondent No. 3 have been without sufficient cause and the same are unlawfully remaining on the Register. By reasons thereof the first respondent's name and the said mark should be removed from the Register and the Register should be suitably rectified.

19. The Trade Mark Registry of Calcutta is situated at the address given in the Cause Title where all the records in relation to the first respondent's Trade Marks are situated and are being maintained and as such this Hon'ble Court has the jurisdiction to entertain, try and determine this petition.

20. Your petitioner is a person aggrieved by the entry made in the Register of Trade Marks without sufficient cause as also by such entry wrongfully remaining in the Register. Your petitioner states that the Register be rectified by cancelling the first respondent's said mark or deleting from the said mark of first respondent the goods dealt with by your petitioner.

21. Unless orders are made as prayed for herein your petitioner will suffer irreparable loss and injury.

22. This petition is made *bona fide* and in the interest of justice.

Your petitioner, therefore, humbly prays Your Lordships for the following orders:

(*a*) Direction on respondent No. 3 to rectify the Register of Trade Marks by expunging or cancelling the first respondent's registered trade mark UTILITY being No. 10 in Class I from the Register;

(*b*) Alternatively, directions on respondent No. 3 to amend and/or remove by deletion from the Register of the goods covered by your petitioner's mark and goods of similar and same description from the specification of the goods included in the entry in respect of the first respondent's Trade Mark No. 10 in Class I;

(*c*) Alternatively direction on respondent No. 3 to correct by deletion or striking out the goods covered by the petitioner's mark UNITY and the goods of similar description from the entry in respect of the first respondent's Trade Mark No. 10 in Class I;

(*d*) Costs of this application be paid by respondents Nos. 1 and 2 to the petitioner;

(*e*) Further orders be made and directions be given as to this Hon'ble Court may deem fit and proper to afford complete relief to your petitioner.

And your petitioner as in duty bound shall ever pray.

Name and address of the Advocate Signature of Petitioner

Verification

I, ... son of .... by occupation service, residing at .... do hereby solemnly affirm and say as follows:

I am the Constituted Attorney and a principal officer of the petitioner above-named. I know and I have made myself fully acquainted with the facts and circumstances of the case and am able to depose thereto. I have due authority and competence to sign and verify this petition. I do declare and say that the statements made in paragraphs 1 to 19 of the foregoing petition are true to my knowledge based on information derived from records maintained by the petitioner which I believe to be true and those mentioned in paragraphs 20 and 22 hereinabove are my humble submissions to this Hon'ble Court.

I sign this Verification at Court House in Calcutta on this 7th day of November 1999.

Signed

Before me Identified by...........

Commissioner Clerk of Advocate

Complaint for Infringement of Trade Mark

In the Court of Chief Presidency Magistrate

..............., Calcutta

In the Matter of:

A complaint in relation to offence under Sections 2(1)(*f*), 77, 78 and 79 of the Trade & Merchandise Marks Act 1958 read with section 420 of the Indian Penal Code

And

In the Matter of:

RP Co. Ltd. a company registered under the laws of U.S.A. and carrying on business at San Francisco and a Branch Office at .... through its Constituted Attorney Mr. XY son of Mr. Z.

.... *Complainant*

versus

Infringing Co. Ltd. a company registered under the Companies Act 1956 and having its Registered Office at 3 White Road, Calcutta, P.S. Hare Street

.... *Accused opposite party*

The humble petition of the Complainant above-mentioned most respectfully

SHEWETH:

1. RP Co. Ltd. is a manufacturer of and dealer in Computers for office purposes having its registered office in San Francisco, U.S.A. and a Branch at No. 1 White Road, Calcutta, Police Station Hare Street.

2. The complainant is the Registered Proprietor of the Trade Mark COMOF in respect of the computer for office purposes and its components being Registered Trade Mark No. 5 in Class I in respect of Computers for office purposes and its components. A certified copy of the registration of the said Trade Mark which is subsisting is annexed hereto marked 'A'.

3. The complainant made application for registration of the said Trade Mark at the Trade Mark Registry, 15/1 Jawaharlal Nehru Road, Calcutta within the jurisdiction of this Learned Court. The said application was advertised in Trade Marks Journal No. 6 dated .... at page 10. A xerox copy of the said advertisement as appearing in the said Journal in relation to the said Trade Mark is annexed hereto marked 'B'.

4. The said Trade Mark is valid and subsisting and will remain to be so for another three years.

5. The complainant is the Registered Proprietor of the said Trade Mark and has been using the same in India and abroad since last several years.

6. The complainant has spent huge sums of money for advertisement in respect of the said Trade Mark. Particulars of expenses are given in a Schedule annexed hereto marked 'C'.

7. The sale of the computers under the said Trade Mark both in Indian market and in foreign markets for the last 10 years are given in a schedule annexed hereto marked 'D'.

8. The complainant has been spending huge sums of moneys in carrying out the sales promotion and publicity of its products under the said Trade Mark and built up high reputation about the goods, goodwill and utility of its products and the name has been associated in the minds of the purchasing public with the name of the complainant and no one else and

the said Trade Mark and no other Trade Mark. Such reputation and goodwill are still enjoyed by the complainant in Calcutta and elsewhere in India and abroad.

9. The complainant has recently come to know that the accused opposite party is using an identical Trade Mark in respect of computers for office use with similar description to those of the complainant and selling the same in the market in Calcutta. The accused opposite party has also issued advertisements and leaflets and packing materials/cash memos which will show that the name of the complainant has been falsely used by the accused opposite party. Copies of certain cash memos, advertisement materials and cartons and labels are annexed hereto collectively marked 'E'.

10. The accused opposite party made deceptive sales of and deceptive advertisements in Calcutta within the police station Hare Street and within the jurisdiction of this Learned Court. The office of the accused opposite party is also situated within the Police Station Hare Street, Calcutta and the advertisements of the complainant's Trade Mark also appeared in the newspapers appearing in places within the Police Station Hare Street, Calcutta within the jurisdiction of this Learned Court.

11. The complainant is the Registered Proprietor of the said Trade Mark and is using the same and the said Trade Mark has acquired high reputation as will be evident from the documents annexed hereto as also the fact of deceptive use of the identical mark in respect of the computers for office purposes and/or of similar description by the accused opposite party and "false trade description" within the meaning of s. 2(1)(*f*) of Trade and Merchandise Marks Act 1958. The accused opposite party has falsified the said Trade Mark of the complainant inasmuch as the accused has used the Trade Mark without the assent of the complainant, the Registered Proprietor of the Trade Mark, and has made and used that Trade Mark as deceptively similar Mark. The accused opposite party has thus committed offence under s. 57(1) of the Trade and Merchandise Marks Act 1958.

12. The accused opposite party has falsely applied the complainant's Trade Mark to the accused's own goods on packages and cartons containing those goods, namely, computers for office purposes without the assent of the complainant being the Registered Proprietor of the said Trade Mark COMOF. The accused opposite party has thus committed offence under s. 77(2) of the Trade and Merchandise Marks Act 1958.

13. The accused opposite party has packed, wrapped and put in cartons sub-standard products for sale to the unwary purchaser falsifying the complainant's said Trade Mark COMOF thereon and thus the accused has also committed an offence under s. 420 of the Indian Penal Code.

14. The accused opposite party has committed offences under the said Trade and Merchandise Marks Act 1958 under ss. 78 and 79 thereof and also under the Indian Penal Code and is thus liable to be punished accordingly.

15. The complainant submits that cognizance should be taken of the offences committed by the accused opposite party and processes issued and the accused be tried and punished in accordance with the provisions of law.

16. The said offences have been committed, *inter alia*, at places within the Police Station Hare Street, Calcutta and the accused also carried on business and/or is situated at a place within the Police Station Hare Street, Calcutta within the jurisdiction of this Learned Court.

Your petitioner therefore prays Your Honour to issue process against the accused opposite party for offence committed under ss. 77, 78 and 79 of the Trade and Merchandise Marks Act 1958 and under s. 420 of the Indian Penal Code and to try and punish him in accordance with law.

Verification

I, ... son of .... by occupation service working for gain at 1 White Road, Calcutta do hereby solemnly affirm and say as follows:

1. I am the Constituted Attorney and a principal officer of the RP Co. Ltd. at its Calcutta Office. I know and I have made myself acquainted with the facts and circumstances of this case and I am able to depose thereto. I am duly authorised and competent to make the present complaint and also sign the verification. I do make verify the complaint for and on behalf of RP Co. Ltd.
2. The statements in paragraphs Nos. 1 to 14 above are true to my knowledge based on information derived from record maintained by RP Co. Ltd. at its Calcutta Office and believed by me to be true and those in paragraph Nos. 15 and 16 hereof are my humble submissions to this Learned Court.

Solemnly affirmed by the said
Mr. .... at Court House
at Bankshall Street, Calcutta on
this 15th day of November 1999.

Before me
Magistrate

42

Power-of-Attorney

Power-of-Attorney. A power-of-attorney is a deed poll. It requires authentication as provided under s. 85 of the Indian Evidence Act 1872 which reads as follows:

> "The court shall presume that every document purporting to be a power-of-attorney, and to have been executed before, and authenticated by, a Notary Public, or any court, Judge, Magistrate, (Indian) Consul or Vice-Consul or representative of the Central Government, was so executed and authenticated."

So, ordinarily it does not require registration except where it creates any interest in any immovable property, *e.g.* charge in favour of the donee[1] or authority of donee to recover rent of any property for his benefit or when it gives the creditor the right to sell any property and appropriate and proceeds towards satisfaction of the debt due to the constituted attorney.

It will not be out of place to mention here that a power-of-attorney authenticated in the manner prescribed under s. 85 of the Indian Evidence Act serves many purposes; nevertheless for the purpose of presenting any document of registration only a power-of-attorney is to be executed sometimes before and authenticated by a Registrar, *e.g.* if the executant lives at the time of execution at a place where the Indian Registration Act 1908, is in force, otherwise, *e.g.* Kashmir and Jammu where the said Act is not in force before Magistrate and in case of foreign document, *i.e.* execution outside India before the Notary Public, any court, judge, magistrate and others.[2]

1 *Indre Bibi* v *Jain Sardar Aheri* 35 Cal 845 (848).
2 Section 33 of the Indian Registration Act 1908.

Revocation of power-of-attorney. A power-of-attorney authenticated before a Registrar may be revoked by an application on a paper without any court fee.[3] If registered then by a deed of cancellation.

A power-of-attorney is in general revocable in its nature but in cases where the same as part of a security for any debt, it is irrevocable notwithstanding the death of the debtor until the debt is repaid.[4] The bankruptcy of the principal operates as revocation of the authority of the agent except however things done without notice.[5]

(a) *Power-of-attorney—agent and principal.* The authority of an agent is discussed under Chapter X of the Indian Contract Act. A power-of-attorney is an instrument empowering a specified person or persons to act for, and in the name of, the person executing it. It is always kept by the attorney. If made generally for certain acts it is called General.

An agent is a person employed to do any act for another, or to represent another in dealings with third persons. The person for whom an act is done, or who is so represented, is called the principal.[6] The essential list about agent's position is his authority to make the principal answerable to third parties. A person does not become an agent by advising another in relation to the latter's business.[7] It includes all the necessary and usual means of executing it or normally done in conducting the business.

(b) *Who can give power-of-attorney—who can be agent.* Any person competent to contract can appoint an agent. At common law there is some difference between the Government and individuals in so far as delegation of authority is concerned. The Government is liable only to the extent of its power actually delegated, whereas individuals are liable to the extent they have apparently given.[8] Although, generally speaking, it can be executed by a person capable of entering into a contract, but under s. 5 of the Power of Attorney Act 1882, a married woman, whether major or minor, can execute the same.

As between the principal and third persons, any person can become an agent; but no person who is not of the age of majority and of sound mind can become an agent so as to be responsible to his principal according to the provisions of the Indian Contract Act.

3 Clause 148 of the Bengal Registration Manual 1928. Also see *Kala Chand* v *Gopal* (1869)12 WR 163.
4 Section 127 of the Law of Property Act 1925.
5 Re, *Snowball* LR 7 Ch 534.
6 Section 182 of the Indian Contract Act 1872.
7 *Mohesh* v *Radha Kishore* 12 CWN 28.
8 *Secretary of State* v *Kasture Raddi* 26 Mad 268.

No consideration is necessary to create an agency.[9]

(c) *Extent of agent's authority.* (Express or implied s. 186 of the Indian Contract Act 1872). Ratification of agent's acts. An agent can, if authorized, do every lawful thing which is necessary in order to do such act. An agent having an authority to carry on a business, has authority to do every lawful thing necessary for the purpose, or usually done in the course, of conducting such business.[10]

Where acts are done by one person on behalf of another, but without his knowledge or authority, he may elect to ratify or to disown such acts. If he ratifies them, the same effects will follow as if they had been performed by his authority.[11] In order to constitute a binding adoption of acts *a priori* unauthorised the conditions to be filled are: (*a*) It must be done for and in the name of the supposed principal; and (*b*) full knowledge of what the acts were or unqualified adoption.[12]

A power of attorney would remain operative when the principal is in a position to make an authorisation and continues to exercise his or her authority so that the agent binds the principal. He cannot go beyond the principal. When the principal becomes old, feeble, weak and mentally infirm and not in a position to think independently the power of attorney, though executed with a conscious and alert mind, becomes worthless. If an agent knowing that the principal is mentally unsound, weak and suffers from mental incapacity having no legal capacity to authorise, still continues to act it would be acting on a power of attorney of a dead man. The agent's action in such a situation would be fraught with fraud, misappropriation and cheating and criminal breach of trust. The principal in that mental state and health neither can take accounts from the agent nor the agent can render accounts to him. The court will declare such a power of attorney as null and void and cancel it and intimate the Sub-Registrar concerned accordingly, if the power-of-attorney has been registered.[13]

(d) *Agent's duty.* An agent shall always act honestly and *bona fide* in the best interest of his principal. He is bound to conduct the business of his principal according to the instructions given by the principal, or, in the absence thereof, according to the usages and customs of the trade. When the agent acts otherwise, if any loss be sustained, he must make it good to his principal and, if any profit accrues, he must account for it. An agent is subject to the well-established rule that he cannot appropriate any illegitimate profits.[14]

9 Section 185 of the Indian Contract Act 1872.
10 Section 188 of the Indian Contract Act 1872.
11 Section 196 of the Indian Contract Act 1872.
12 *Surendra* v *Kedar* AIR 1936 Cal 87.
13 *Mahendra* v *Padam Kumari* AIR 1993 All 143.
14 *Parkar* v *McKenna* 10 Ch App 96.

An agent is bound to keep and maintain proper accounts and submit the same to his principal on demand.[15]

(e) *Agent's right of retainer and lien.* Agent to be indemnified. An agent can retain, out of any sum received on account of the principal in the business of the agency, all moneys due to himself in respect of advances made or expenses properly incurred by him in conducting such business, and also such remuneration as may be payable to him for acting as agent. In the absence of any contract to the contrary, an agent is entitled to retain goods, papers, and other property, whether movable or immovable, of the principal received by him, until the amount due to himself for commission, disbursements and services in respect of the same has been paid or accounted for to him.[16] The lien is not affected by the bankruptcy of the principal or action barred by limitation.[17]

An Advocate is not entitled to act in a professional capacity as well as a constituted attorney of a party in the same matter or cause. An Advocate cannot combine the two roles. If a firm of Advocates is appointed as Advocates by a suitor, none of the partners of the Advocates' firm can act as a recognised agent in pursuance of a power of attorney concerning the same cause.[18]

The employer of an agent is bound to indemnify him against the consequences of all lawful acts done by such agent in exercise of the authority conferred upon him.

(f) *Enforcement of agent's contracts.* Effect of notice given to agent. Contracts entered into through an agent, and obligations arising from acts done by an agent, may be enforced in the same manner, and will have the same legal consequences, as if the contracts had been entered into and the acts done by the principal in person.[19]

Any notice given to, or information obtained by the agent, provided it be given or obtained in due course of the business transacted by him for the principal, has, as between the principal and third parties, the same legal consequences as if it had been given to or obtained by the principal.[20] The

15 Section 213 of the Indian Contract Act 1872.

16 Section 217 of the Indian Contract Act 1872. Special privileges of a solicitor—He can ask the court to call upon the opposite party to pay him his costs when he has got judgment for his client and the court will not allow parties to deprive him of the benefit by compromise without his knowledge. Ex parte, *Marison* LR 4 QB 153. Also see *Cullanji* v *Raghawji* (1906)30 Bom 27.

17 *Ex parte Beall* 24 Ch D 408.

18 *Oil and Natural Gas* v *Offshore Enterprises* AIR 1993 Bom 217.

19 Section 226 of the Indian Contract Act 1872.

20 Section 229 of the Indian Contract Act 1872.

underlying principle is that the agent is identified with the principal and, as such, the principal is bound by the notice unless the agent withholds the notice acting in fraud or conspiracy with a third party.[1]

(g) *Misrepresentation or frauds by agents.* Misrepresentations made, or frauds committed, by agents acting in the course of their business for their principals, have the same effect on agreements made by such agents as if such misrepresentations or frauds had been made or committed by the principals; but misrepresentations made, or frauds committed, by agents, in matters which do not fall within their authority, do not affect their principals.[2]

(h) *Termination of agency and its effect.* An agency is terminated by the principal revoking his authority; or by the agent renouncing the business of the agent; or by the business of the agency being complete; or by either the principal or agent dying or becoming of unsound mind; or by the principal being adjudicated an insolvent under he law of insolvency. Reasonable notice must always be given of such revocation or renunciation; otherwise the damage thereby resulting to the principal or the agent, as the case may be, must be made good to the one by the other.[3] In the case of a company, the power-of-attorney executed by the directors ceases to be operative as soon as an order for winding-up is made as the directors cease to function.[4]

The termination of the authority of an agent does not, so far as regards the agent, take effect before it becomes known to him, or, so far as regards third persons, before it becomes known to them.[5] Registration of a document by an agent even after revocation of his authority is not invalid unless such revocation is, in fact, known either to the grantee of the document or to the Registrar.[6]

(i) *Construction of a power-of-attorney*. Powers-of-attorney are strictly construed.[7] Persons dealing with others acting under powers should enquire into the authenticity of the documents.

Where an act done under a power-of-attorney is challenged as being in excess of the authority conferred by the power, it is necessary to show that on a fair construction of the whole instrument the authority in question is to be found within the four corners of the instrument either in express terms

1 *Kettle Wall* v *Watson* 21 Ch D 706; *Hormasji* v *Mankuvarbai* 12 Bom 262 (HC); *Cave* v *Cave* 15 Ch D 630.
2 Section 238 of the Indian Contract Act 1872. *Lloyds* v *Grace Smith & Co.* (1912) AC 716 reversing (1911)2 KB 489.
3 Section 3 of Power of Attorney Act 1882.
4 *Fowler* v *Broade P.N. Light & Co.* (1893)1 Ch 724.
5 Section 208 of the Indian Contract Act 1872.
6 *Maung Lu* v *U.P.O. Hlaing* AIR 1934 Rang 104.
7 Palmer's *Company Law* 24th Ed., para 20-19, p. 238.

or by necessary implication. The general words used in subsequent clauses of a power-of-attorney must be read with the special power given in earlier clauses and cannot be construed so as to enlarge the restricted power therein mentioned. A power "to pay" is not the same thing as "promise to pay". A power "to endorse and accept" to an employee of a bank does not include power to bank bills on its behalf.[8]

A power-of-attorney to negotiate, make sale, dispose of, assign and transfer Government promissory notes does not include power to pledge.[9] The operative part of a deed is controlled by recitals; the general words following to do particular acts are limited to the purposes for which the authority is given. The special powers are enlarged by general words only when necessary for the particular purpose. A power-of-attorney is construed to include all medium powers for its effective execution.[10] A power-of-attorney should be strictly construed. A power-of-attorney for execution of deed authorizes the execution of an agreement for it in the absence of fraud or dishonesty on the part of the agent.[11]

(j) *Power-of-attorney by a company.* In England, under s. 31 of the Companies Act 1929,[12] a company may by writing under the common seal empower either generally or in respect of any specified matter as its attorney to execute deeds on its behalf. Section 46 of the Indian Companies Act 1956, provides for execution of documents by the company under its common seal. In any event a power-of-attorney must be executed in conformity with the Articles of Association. See also Regulation 84 of Table A to Companies Act 1956.

(k) *Power-of-attorney executed in a foreign country.* The Notary Public is an institution of very ancient origin. It is of great utility and the Notary Public is an officer recognised by the whole commercial world and a certificate by him, competent to administer an oath to persons making declaration or affidavits, is sufficient evidence of the execution of the instrument to which it refers.[13] When a seal of the Notary is put on the document, s. 57 of the Evidence Act comes into play and a presumption can be raised regarding the seal of the said Notary, meaning thereby that the said document is presumed to have been attested by a competent Notary of that country. If

8 *Bank of Bengal v Ramanathan Chetty* AIR 1915 PC 121. See also AIR 1933 PC 78. (*Oapramar v Thomas Cook & Sons, Banker Ltd.*).
9 *Jonmenjoy Coondoo v George Alder Watson* 11 IA 94.
10 *Ananta v Rathnasabapathy* (1968)2 MLJ 574.
11 *Kumar Narendra Nath Mitra v Sm. Bimla Sundari* 42 CWN 718; *Thakur Prasad v Syed Yahya Hossain* (1911)16 CLJ 119 distinguished.
12 19 & 20 Geo. S.C. 23.
13 In re, *K.K. Ray (P) Ltd.* AIR 1967 Cal 636.

the first power of attorney is not duly authenticated a second power ratifying the earlier is valid.[14] An act of the agent, although shown to be unauthorised when the act was committed, yet the principal can subsequently execute a document ratifying the said act.[15]

FORMS

Proxy

I, AB of, etc., being a member of (or, subscriber to), etc., hereby appoint CD of, and failing him EF of etc., as my proxy to vote for me and on my behalf at the annual general, ordinary or extraordinary, etc., of the, etc., to be held on the .... day of ...., and at any adjournment thereof.

Signed, etc., AB

(*Voter*)

WITNESS:

NOTES ON PROXY. *Vide s.* 176 of the Companies Act 1956. Form is prescribed in Schedule IX. A proxy does not require any attestation unless so prescribed under Articles of Association.[16] When the Company concerned furnishes a prescribed form the same should be incorporating the necessary particulars.

Power-of-Attorney to Present Document for Registration

BY THIS POWER-OF-ATTORNEY I, AB of etc., do hereby appoint CD of, etc., my attorney, for me and on my behalf to appear for and represent me before the Sub-Registrar of, ... all times as may be necessary and to present before him for registration the .... deed dated the .... day of .... made between, etc., to admit my signature and execution of the said deed (*if necessary to admit the receipt of consideration*) to do any act, deed or thing as may be necessary to complete the registration of the said deed in the manner required by law and when it has been returned to him after being duly registered, to give proper receipt and discharge for the same.

14 *Rajesh Wadha* v *Sushma Govil* AIR 1989 Del 144.
15 *Jugraj Singh* v *Jaswant Singh* AIR 1971 SC 761.
16 *Harben* v *Philips* (1883)23 Ch D 14 at pp. 22 and 31.

And I, the said AB, do hereby agree and declare that all acts, deeds and things done, executed or performed by the said CD shall be valid and binding on me to all intents and purposes as if done by me personally which I undertake to ratify and confirm whenever required.

Signed, sealed and delivered

WITNESS: AB

Power-of-Attorney to Sell a Particular Property

BY THIS POWER-OF-ATTORNEY I, AB of, etc., hereby appoint CD of, etc., my attorney, in my name and on my behalf to do *inter alia* the following acts, deeds and things, *viz.*

1. To negotiate on terms for and to agree to and enter into and conclude any agreement of sale and sell my house No. .... (*or,* etc.) situate at, etc., fully mentioned and described in the schedule hereto to any purchaser or purchasers at such price which my said attorney, in his absolute discretion, thinks proper and/or to cancel and/or repudiate the same.

2. To receive from the intending purchaser or purchasers any earnest money and/or advance or advances and also the balance of purchase money, and to give good, valid receipt and discharge for the same which will protect the purchaser or purchasers without seeing the application of the money.

3. Upon such receipt as aforesaid in my name and as my act and deed, to sign, execute and deliver any conveyance or conveyances of the said property in favour of the said purchaser or his nominee or assignee.

4. To sign and execute all other deeds, instruments and assurances which he shall consider necessary and to enter into and/or agree to such covenants and conditions as may be required for fully and effectually conveying the said property as I could do myself, if personally present.

5. To present any such conveyance or conveyances for registration, to admit execution and receipt of consideration before the Sub-Registrar or Registrar having authority for and to have the said conveyance registered and to do all acts, deeds and things which my said attorney shall consider necessary for conveying the said property to the said purchaser or purchasers as fully and effectually in all respects as I could do the same myself.

And I hereby agree to ratify and confirm all and whatever other act or acts my said attorney shall lawfully do, execute or perform or cause to be done, executed or performed in connection with the sale of the said property under and by virtue of this deed notwithstanding no express power in that behalf is hereunder provided.

Schedule of the property to be sold

IN WITNESS WHEREOF, I, the said AB, have hereto signed (or, put my signature, or set my hand and seal at ...., this .... day of ....

Signed, sealed and delivered AB

Power-of-Attorney to Recover Debts

BY THIS POWER-OF-ATTORNEY I, AB of, etc., do hereby constitute and appoint CD of, etc., my attorney, for me, in my name and on my behalf to do *inter alia* all or any of the acts, deeds and things, *viz*.

(*i*) To ask or demand and receive from the person or persons named in the Schedule below the respective amounts mentioned against their respective names and all or any other debt or debts or claim or claims now or hereafter due.

(*ii*) To collect, receive and realise all such amount or amounts due and payable by them now or hereafter fully or partially, in lump sum or by instalments (which he is empowered to grant) or otherwise and to give and execute all necessary receipts and discharges for the same with power to accept security and grant time for payment.

(*iii*) To institute suits or other legal proceedings authorized by law for recovery of all or any of such debts or claims and to sign any plaint, petition or other pleadings, vakalatnama, warrant of attorney, to execute any decree or order.

(*iv*) To compromise any such debt or claim, withdraw any suit or other proceedings, to refer to arbitration any dispute or difference and to prosecute or defend any bankruptcy or insolvency proceedings.

(*v*) Generally to do all such acts, deeds and things as he shall think fit and proper as fully and effectually as I could do myself notwithstanding no express power or authority in that behalf is hereunder provided.

And I, the said AB, do hereby agree to ratify and confirm all and whatever my said attorney shall do, execute or perform or cause to be done, executed or performed in exercise of the power or authority hereunder conferred upon or otherwise expressed or intended.

The Schedule above referred to

Name and address of the debtor	*Amount due*	*Remarks*

IN WITNESS WHEREOF I, the said AB, has hereunto set and subscribed my hand and seal this .... day of ....

Signed, sealed and delivered AB

Accepted CD

Power-of-Attorney by a Firm

KNOW ALL MEN BY THESE presents that we .... all carrying on business at present in co-partnership under the name and style of .... (a firm duly registered under the Indian Partnership Act being No. ....) as Exporters in .... do hereby nominate, constitute and appoint Sri ...., son of .... by caste .... by occupation .... at present residing at .... as the Constituted Attorney for and on behalf of our said firm as the same is now or hereafter constituted from time to time to do *inter alia* the following acts, deeds and things:

1. To appear for and represent our above firm to all intents and purposes in or outside India in connection with its said business and all affairs ancillary or incidental thereto and to sign jointly and/or severally all contracts and orders and other documents, letters, receipts, papers and writings whatsoever and to conclude all bargains and deals, to accept all estimates, tenders, quotations, etc., to settle all disputes and differences in connection with its said trade or business and affairs ancillary or incidental thereto.

2. To ask for, demand, recover, receive and collect all moneys due and payable to the said firm in connection with its said business from any person or persons, company or association, including any statutory body or authority, Government or semi-Government concern or concerns including insurance, claims, compensation and damages against Railways, Airways, Roadways etc. etc. and to give good valid receipts and discharges therefor.

3. To appear for and represent the firm before all Municipal bodies, Corporation, Improvement Trust, Railways, Airways, Roadways, Travel Agents, Chamber of Commerce and Industry, Controller of Patents, in all Collectorate, Treasury, Revenue offices, Settlement offices, before any Magistrate and in all courts having civil, criminal, original or appellate, revisional or special jurisdiction, including jurisdiction of any High Court, under Art. 226 of the Constitution of India, before any tribunal of arbitration or other tribunal or judicial authority, Wealth Tax, Sales Tax and other authorities and in all other Government or semi-Government offices and departments.

4. To acquire, sell or dispose of goods and stock-in-trade for cash or on credit for the purpose of carrying on business of the firm.

5. To apply for, obtain and renew all licences, permits, etc. as may be necessary or requisite for the purpose of carrying on or developing the trade or business.

6. To prepare, sign and submit all returns and statements, *e.g.*, income-tax and sales tax returns, declarations and to verify the same by production of books and vouchers and other documentary evidence.

7. To appoint and dismiss or discharge any staff, agent, broker, menials, durwan and other menials and settle and pay their remuneration and fix up conditions of service.

8. To institute, defend and prosecute, enforce, or resist any suit or other actions and proceedings, appeals, in any court anywhere within or outside India including the International Court in its civil, criminal, revenue, revision or before any tribunal of arbitration or industrial court, income-tax and sales-tax authorities whether by and on behalf of the said firm or against it, to execute warrant of attorney, vakalatnama, and other authorities, to act and plead; to sign and verify plaints, written statements, petitions and other pleadings, including pleadings under Arts. 226 and 227 of the Constitution of India, and also to present any Memorandum of Appeal, tabular statement, accounts, inventories, to accept service of summons, notice and other legal processes, enforce judgment, execute any decree or order, to appoint and engage on behalf of the said firm pleaders, attorney, counsel and other legal agents as our said attorneys may think fit and proper and to adjust, settle all accounts, to refer to arbitration all disputes and differences, to compromise cases, to withdraw the same or to be non-suited and to receive delivery of documents or payments of any money or moneys from any court, office or opposite party either in execution of decree or order or otherwise as he shall think fit and proper and to do all acts, deeds and things that may be necessary or requisite in connection therewith.

9. To settle, compromise, or compound, any debt or claim whether in favour or against the firm.

To refer any dispute or differences arising out of the same to arbitration.

To appoint Arbitrator or Arbitrators, to file the statement of facts or counter-statement of facts, to proceed with or oppose arbitration proceedings and to apply for execution of award or to set aside the award.

10. To open any one or more banking account or accounts in the name and on behalf of the said firm in any or more bank or banks, to deposit and withdraw money and fully operate the same.

11. To accept bills and money order, cheques, bank drafts, payment orders or other securities for money drawn in favour of the said firm and to negotiate encash credit and collect the proceeds thereof through the said account or accounts.

12. To apply for and obtain overdraft or overdrafts on behalf of the firm from any such bank or banks against such security or securities of its said trade or business or estate as he shall think fit and proper subject to clause 16 hereunder.

13. To sell, purchase, pledge, raise money or convent into money or securities for money and transfer and/or exchange and/or otherwise deal in all shares, stocks and other securities, marketable or non-marketable, cheques, bills, drafts, hundis, and promissory notes and investments through authorised brokers or otherwise and to raise loan by pledge or hypothecation of the same.

14. To compound and accept in part in lieu of or satisfaction of the whole or compromise any debt or other claim and demand against any person, firm or company or any Government or semi-Government department or Government undertaking or Life Insurance Corporation of India, to grant any extension of time for payment or satisfaction thereof upon such terms and conditions with or without securities as the said attorney may think fit and proper.

15. And generally to do all acts, deeds and things as may be necessary on behalf of the said firm to all intents and purposes as the partners constituting the same for the time being could do in their own persons.

16. Provided always that the aforesaid power shall not extend to—

(*i*) any investment or advance out of the funds and assets of the said business nor to draw, accept, negotiate, retire, pay, discount or satisfy any hundi, cheque or cheques, Promissory Note, Bill of Exchange or other negotiable instrument or instruments;

(*ii*) winding up of the business or change of its place or places or abandonment or closure thereof without the express consent of the partners in writing obtained previously thereto; and/or

(*iii*) any sale, lease, pledge, charge, mortgage or hypothecation of any of its properties, assets, credits, or goodwill which rights are all expressly reserved for the partners and are not hereunder conferred upon or delegated or otherwise intended.

Provided always that the said constituted attorney shall always keep and maintain true and faithful accounts of all dealings and transactions in relation to the said business and affairs ancillary and incidental thereto and furnish the same to the partners at all reasonable times as and when demanded and account for all receipts and vouchers for all expenses and disbursements made by him as are usual or customary in business of like nature and pay the surplus amount lying with him to the partners on demand. The said attorney shall also prepare quarterly statements of profit and loss and the balance-sheet in respect of the said business and submit the same to the partners regularly.

17. And we, the undersigned partners, do hereby and at all times hereafter shall ratify and confirm all and whatsoever other act or acts our said attorney or attorneys shall lawfully and *bona fide* do or cause to be done by virtue of these presents.

This power-of-attorney shall remain valid notwithstanding any change in the constitution of the firm.

IN WITNESS WHEREOF we, the present partners of the said firm, have hereunto set and subscribed our respective hands and seals this .... day of ....

Signed, sealed and delivered
at .... in the presence
of:

Power-of-Attorney by Trustee

THIS POWER-OF-ATTORNEY is executed this .... day of .... by me, AB of, etc.

WHEREAS I am one of the present trustees under a deed of trust or settlement (or, etc.), dated the .... day of .... and made between, etc.; And whereas I am about to depart and intend to remain out of, etc., for a period exceeding (state approximate period) or more: Now this deed witnesses that I, the said AB, hereby nominate, constitute and appoint CD of, etc., to be my attorney, in my name and on my behalf to do, execute and perform and exercise during my temporary absence from etc., all or any of the trusts, powers, liberties, authorities and discretions vested in me as such trustee as aforesaid, and to carry out all my functions under the said trust or settlement to manage, control and administer all or any of the properties comprised thereunder, to sign and execute any deed or deeds, pay or receive any money or moneys either alone or jointly with any other person or persons: And I hereby agree and undertake to ratify and confirm all and whatsoever my said attorney shall lawfully do, execute or perform or cause to be done during my absence under and by virtue of the power, authority and liberty hereunder conferred upon him. Provided, however, that this power-of attorney shall not be construed as any delegation of my office as trustee under the deed of trust hereinbefore recited.

IN WITNESS, etc.

Signed, sealed and delivered AB

Power-of-Attorney to obtain Letters of Administration on behalf of Person Resident Abroad

BY THIS POWER-OF-ATTORNEY I, AB the undersigned, son of etc., state as follows:

Whereas (name of the deceased) died on .... day of .... leaving him surviving me as one of (state the relationship as one of the persons interested in his estate). And whereas I am at present residing at ....

Now by this power-of-attorney I do hereby irrevocably nominate, appoint and constitute CD, son of etc., as my true and lawful attorney to do *inter alia* the following acts, deeds and things:

1. To apply for and obtain letters of administration in respect of the estate of the said (deceased) from the court of competent jurisdiction for my use and benefit until when I shall apply for and obtain the same.

2. To file the account and inventory in respect of the said estate.

3. To appoint and engage any solicitor, counsel, advocate or other lawyer or lawyers, to sign and verify any petition for the grant, to affirm any affidavit or affidavits, enter or lodge any caveat or to apply for its discharge.

4. To do all other acts, deeds and things as may be necessary or requisite in connection with the grant as aforesaid.

And I, the said AB, do hereby agree and undertake to ratify and confirm all and whatsoever my said attorney shall lawfully do, execute, perform or cause to be done, executed or performed by virtue of the power or authority hereunder conferred upon.

IN WITNESS WHEREOF I the AB have executed this power-of-attorney on this .... day of ....

Signed, sealed and delivered AB

Power-of-Attorney to Agent for any particular Court Case

BY THIS POWER-OF-ATTORNEY I, AB of, etc., plaintiff (or, etc.), in suit (or Case) No. .... of 2000, in the court of, etc., do hereby nominate, constitute and appoint CD of, etc., as my attorney, for me, in my name and on my behalf:

1. To represent me before the said court to all intents and purposes in connection with the said suit (or Case No. .... of ....).

2. To appear for and prosecute and defend all actions and proceedings, to sign and verify all plaints, written statements and other pleadings, applications, petitions or documents to the court, to deposit, withdraw and receive documents and any money or moneys from the court or from the

opposite party, either in execution of the decree or otherwise and, on receipt of payment thereof, to sign and deliver for me proper receipts and discharges for the same.

3. To engage and appoint any solicitor, advocate or advocates or counsel to act and plead and otherwise conduct the said case whenever my said attorney thinks proper to do so.

4. To do all other lawful acts and things in connection with the case as effectually as I could do the same if I were personally present: And all and whatever my said attorney shall lawfully do, I do hereby agree to ratify and confirm.

In witness, etc.

Signed, sealed and delivered AB

Power-of-Attorney to Advocate for Court Case

In the Court of, etc.

Suit (or Case) No. .... of 2000

Plaintiff (or Applicant, or Complainant)—

AB, son of ...., of, etc.

versus

Defendant (or Non-applicant, or Accused),—

CD, son of ...., of, etc.

Claim for (or, in the matter of), etc.

By this power-of-attorney, I, CD, defendant (or, etc.), in the above suit (or case), do hereby nominate, constitute and appoint EF, advocate etc., my attorney, for me, in my name and on my behalf to appear, act and plead in the said case, to make or present written statements, applications or petitions to the court, to withdraw and receive documents and any money from the court or from the opposite party either in execution of the decree or otherwise, and on receipt thereof, to sign and deliver for me proper receipts and discharges for the same, and to do all other lawful acts, deeds and things in connection with the case as effectually as I could do the same, if I were personally present; to engage and appoint any other advocate or advocates whenever my said advocate thinks proper to do so.

Provided, however, that, if any part of the advocate's fee remains unpaid before the first hearing of the case (or, etc.), or if any hearing of the case be fixed beyond the limits of this town, then and in such an event my said advocate shall not be bound to appear before the court; PROVIDED ALSO that if the case be dismissed by default, or if it be proceeded *ex parte,* the said advocate shall not be held responsible for the same except in case of gross negligence, wilful default. And all whatever my said advocate shall lawfully do, I do hereby agree to and shall in future ratify and confirm.

Signed, sealed and delivered CD

Accepted, subject to the aforesaid conditions. EF, Advocate

General Power-of-Attorney to a Manager of Estate

KNOW ALL MEN BY this power-of-attorney I, AB of, etc., do hereby nominate, constitute and appoint CD of, etc. my true and lawful attorney, for me, in my name and on my behalf, to do and execute and perform or cause to be done, executed and performed all or any of the following acts, deeds and things:

1. To work, manage, control and supervise the management of all and administer properties now or hereafter belonging to me and to develop the same.

2. To cultivate all agricultural lands belonging to my estate, open and work quarries, mines and minerals and to enter into contract, covenant and arrangement of any kind whatsoever in relation thereto and to modify, revoke and cancel the same as he shall think fit and proper without making me liable for any loss on that account.

3. To let out and/or otherwise settle all and any land or building or any part or parts thereof belonging to my estate on rent, selami, premium, on monthly tenancy basis or lease and to realise all rents, issues and profits thereof and to accept, surrender of leases and tenancies and to evict all trespassers and other unauthorised occupiers.

4. To sign and give notice or notices to any tenant or tenants and other occupiers of the lands and buildings belonging to my estate, to quit and vacate or to repair any damage or to abate any nuisance or to remedy a breach of covenant or contract or for any other purpose or purposes whatsoever and to avail of and enforce all remedies open to me in respect thereof and to enter into any such property or properties with a view to inspecting the same or exercising any right vested in me.

5. To make, sign and verify all applications or objections to appropriate authorities for all and any licence, permission or consent, etc., required by law in connection with the management and development of my property or properties.

6. To accept and withdraw on my behalf any compensation payable to me for acquisition or compulsory purchase, requisition or hiring of any land or building belonging to my estate by the Government or any competent body or authority.

7. To appoint staff and workers and to settle their remuneration and other terms of office and to dismiss or suspend them.

8. To effect mutation or separation of holding in the Revenue and/or Municipal Records and sign all applications or objections.

9. To appear for and represent me before the Board of Revenue, Collector of any district, Sub-Divisional Officer, any Magistrate, Judge, Munsif and in all Government offices, Calcutta Corporation, Improvement Trust, Commissioners of any division in all matters and things relating to my estate or its affairs.

10. To appear for and represent me in all the courts, civil, criminal or revenue, including Labour Tribunals, original, revisional or appellate, in any Registration offices, and to sign, execute, verify and file plaints, written statements and petitions, and also to present appeals in any court, and to accept services of all summonses, notices and other processes of law.

11. To appoint, engage on my behalf pleaders, advocates or solicitors whenever my said attorney shall think proper to do so and to discharge and/or terminate his or their appointment.

12. To compromise, compound or withdraw cases, or be non-suited to refer to arbitration all disputes and differences.

13. To sign, verify and file applications for execution of decrees or orders of any court, and to purchase property at court auction sales in execution of decrees up to the amount of the decree.

14. To withdraw and receive documents or money from any court, office or opposite party, either in execution of decrees or otherwise, and to do all the acts that may be necessary in connection with any of such cases.

15. To invest with my approval all surplus moneys in his hands and to charge and/or vary such investment.

16. To receive and recover any debt due and owing to me by any person, company or association, and on receipt or payment of any money whatever due and payable to me, to give proper receipt and discharges for the same, and on non-payment thereof, to file suits or any other proceeding for recovering and compelling payment thereof.

Provided always that the powers hereby conferred shall not extend to—

(*a*) winding-up or closing or sale of any business;

(*b*) sale or mortgage of any property or granting of a lease for a term of over .... years, or reserving a yearly rent exceeding Rs. ....;

(*c*) granting of a lease of house property for a term of over .... years, or reserving a yearly rent exceeding Rs. ....;

(*d*) any investment or advance out of the funds and assets of the estate or to draw, accept, negotiate, retire, pay, discount any hundi, cheque or promissory note, bill of exchange or other negotiable instruments; and

Provided also that in every case my said attorneys shall always keep and maintain a true and correct account of all income and expenditure, which shall be rendered to me annually (or monthly), and shall pay me every month all balances of money in their hands.

And I do hereby agree to ratify and confirm whatever all acts, deeds and things lawfully and *bona fide* done by my attorney which shall be construed as acts, deeds and things done by me to all intents and purposes as if I was personally present.

IN WITNESS WHEREOF the parties herein have executed these presents on this .... day of ....

Signed, sealed and delivered by AB and CD

AB
CD

General Power-of-Attorney from Person going to Reside Abroad

KNOW ALL MEN BY THESE presents I, AB, son of etc. state as follows: whereas I intend to go abroad and stay outside for long. And whereas in the circumstances aforesaid it is necessary and also expedient for me to appoint an agent to look after all my affairs during my absence. Now know ye by these presents I, the said AB, do hereby and hereunder nominate, appoint and constitute CD of, etc., my true and lawful attorney, for me, in my name and on my behalf, either solely or jointly with some other person or persons, to do and execute all or any of the following acts, deeds and things, that is to say:

1. To demand, sue for, enforce payment of, recover, receive and give proper receipts and discharges for, all moneys, debts, goods, effects, securities for money, stocks, shares, or other property, now belonging or hereafter to belong to me which receipts and discharges will exonerate any or all persons so paying without seeing the application thereof and on non-payment or non-realisation thereof to institute suits or other appropriate proceedings for receiving or compelling payment or delivery thereof.

2. To institute, commence, prosecute, carry on or defend or resist all suits and other actions and proceedings or be added as a party or be non-suited or withdraw the same concerning my property or any part thereof, or concerning anything in which I may be a party in any court in civil, criminal, revenue or Revisional jurisdiction, including special jurisdiction of the High Court under Art. 226 of the Constitution of India, etc., before Income-tax, Sales-tax and Wealth-tax Authorities and to sign and verify all plaints, written statements, accounts, inventories, to accept service of all summonses, notices and other judicial processes to execute any judgment, decree or order and to appoint and engage any solicitor, pleader, counsel or advocate and to sign and execute any vakalatnama, warrant of attorney or other authority to act and plead.

3. To accept the transfer of any stocks, funds, shares, annuities and other securities which shall or may at any time hereafter be transferred to me by sale, gift or otherwise.

4. To settle, adjust, compound, compromise or submit to arbitration all actions, suits, accounts, claims and disputes, between me and any other person or persons to compound or compromise the same.

5. To invest with my approval any of my moneys in such manner, at such rate of interest and upon such securities as my said attorney shall in his discretion think fit and from time to time to alter and vary the said investments or any of them into any other investments, and in the meantime and pending such investments as aforesaid, to deposit the said moneys or any part thereof with any banker or bankers to whom my said attorney shall think fit to entrust the same.

6. To vote at the meetings of any company, or otherwise to act as my attorney or proxy in respect of any stocks, shares or other investments now held or which may hereafter be acquired by me in such company.

7. To execute, carry into effect and perform all agreements and contracts entered into by me with any other person or persons, as my own act and deed and/or to cancel and/or repudiate the same without making me liable for any loss or damage by reason thereof.

8. To draw, endorse and sign any cheques, drafts, pay orders, dividend or interest, warrants or other investments payable to me, and to sign my name and execute on my behalf all contracts, transfers, assignments, deeds and instruments whatsoever.

9. To concur in doing any one or more of the acts, deeds and things hereinbefore mentioned in conjunction with any other person or persons without making me liable for any loss or damage on that account under any circumstances.

10. To enter into any agreement for sale, to sell, exchange, surrender, lease or otherwise dispose of any of my property or properties or portion or

portions thereof and to transfer, release any mortgage or charge or also to execute or enforce any powers of sale or other powers under any such mortgages or charges, or otherwise to realize or obtain the benefit thereof in such manner as my said attorney shall think proper.

To execute and register any document or documents in that behalf.

11. To raise loan and/or borrow from time to time such sums of money or moneys on my account and upon such terms as my said attorney may think fit for my benefit only upon the security of any of my properties, whether movable or immovable, and for such purpose, to execute such mortgages, charges, pledges or other securities upon such agreements, terms, conditions as he may think proper.

12. To pay for and discharge any debt or debts, or any part of them, contracted by me or my said attorney, as my said attorney shall from time to time think proper to pay and discharge.

13. To purchase or take on lease or otherwise acquire for me and/or for my use and benefit any property whatever as my said attorney shall think proper.

14. To appoint and engage, transfer, suspend and remove at pleasure any employee or agent, staff workers, for or from permanent, temporary or special service and to settle the terms and conditions and also retirement benefits as he, my said attorney, shall think fit and to determine their powers and duties.

15. To delegate all or any of the powers, authorities and liberties hereunder vested and to appoint any substitute or substitutes limited to any one or more purpose or purposes as he shall from time to time desire in that behalf.

16. And generally to do, execute and perform any other act or acts, deed or deeds, matter or thing whatsoever which in the opinion of my said attorney ought to be done, executed and performed in relation to my property or my concern, engagements and business, or affairs ancillary or incidental thereto as fully and effectually as I myself could do the same if I were personally present.

And I hereby agree and undertake to ratify and confirm all and whatsoever my said attorney, under the power in that behalf hereinbefore contained, shall lawfully do, execute or perform in exercise of the power, authorities and liberties hereby conferred upon, under and by virtue of this deed.

IN WITNESS WHEREOF the parties herein have executed these presents on this .... day of ....

Signed, sealed and delivered by
AB and CD

Irrevocable Power-of-Attorney

THIS POWER-OF-ATTORNEY is made the .... day of .... by me, AB of, etc.

WHEREAS I have obtained this day from CD of, etc., the sum of Rs. .... as and by way of loan agreeing to repay the same with interest thereon at the rate of 18 per cent per annum: And whereas it has been agreed between me and the said CD that the said CD would be authorised by me to sell my house No. .... (or, etc.) situate at, etc., and out of the proceeds of such sale adjust, appropriate and pay himself and liquidate the debt due to him: Now this deed witnesses that for the consideration as aforesaid I hereby nominate, appoint and constitute CD my aforesaid attorney, in my name and on my behalf:

To enter into any agreement for sale, to sell, exchange, surrender, lease or otherwise dispose of any of my property or properties or portion thereof and to transfer realise and mortgage or charge or to execute or enforce any powers of sale or other power under any such mortgages or charges or otherwise to realise or obtain the benefits thereof in such manner as my said attorney shall think proper.

To adjust, appropriate and pay himself at the first instance out of the proceeds of such sale less all costs, charges and expenses the amount due to him and thereby to liquidate the debt payable by me to him and to pay the balance thereafter to me.

And I hereby agree to ratify and confirm all and whatsoever my said attorney shall lawfully do or cause to be done by virtue of this deed. This power-of-attorney is irrevocable provided however that the constituted attorney shall keep and maintain proper account of the sale and allow me inspection thereof as and when demanded.

Description of the property

IN WITNESS WHEREOF the parties hereto have executed these presents on the day, month and year first above-written.

Signed, sealed and delivered by AB in presence of: AB

Accepted by CD in the presence of: CD

Deed of Revocation of Power-of-Attorney

BE IT KNOWN TO ALL CONCERNED I, ... son of, etc., by a power executed on the .... day of .... and registered in Book .... Vol. .... Pages .... to .... being No. .... for the year .... in the office of .... appointed CD of, etc., my lawful attorney and agent for me, in my name and on my behalf to do, execute and perform all acts, deeds and things, therein recited: And whereas for personal reasons and consideration it has become necessary and/or expedient to revoke the power: Now know ye all that by this deed I cancel the said power-of-attorney and absolutely and completely revoke also all powers or authority thereby and thereunder given to him, either expressly or impliedly, to all intents and purposes provided that nothing herein contained shall render invalid or ineffective any act, deed or thing lawfully and *bona fide* done or caused to be done by the said attorney under and by virtue of the power given to him before the revocation thereof by these presents.

IN WITNESS WHEREOF, I, AB, have executed these presents on this .... day of .... 2000.

Signed, sealed and delivered by AB

AB
CD

WITNESS:

43

Promoters' Loan Agreement

Agreement for Loan by Promoters

THIS LOAN AGREEMENT IS MADE on this 10th day of May 1999 BETWEEN Mr. AB, by occupation business, residing at .... (hereinafter referred to as the BORROWER which term or expression shall unless excluded by or repugnant to the context mean and include his heirs, executors, administrators, legal representatives and assigns) of the one part and ELH Home Finance Ltd., a company registered under the Companies Act 1956 and having its registered office and carrying on business at .... (hereinafter referred to as the LENDER which expression shall unless excluded by or repugnant to the context include its successor and assigns) of the other part.

WHEREAS the BORROWER is seized and possessed of as the absolute owner of all that premises No............... of .... comprised of a total land area of 5 (five) Cottahs more fully and particularly described in the schedule hereunder was purchased by the Borrower under Deed No. .... dated .... registered with the Registrar of Assurances, Calcutta.

AND WHEREAS the BORROWER with a view to commercial exploitation of the said plot of land decided to develop the said property and got the appropriate Plan sanctioned by the Corporation of Calcutta which provided for construction of a four-storied building comprising 16 independent flats/units thereon and sale thereof to the intending buyers.

AND WHEREAS the BORROWER has already commenced the foundation work of the project out of his own resources and has completed construction upto the first floor level incurring expenses of about Rs. 18 lakhs.

AND WHEREAS the BORROWER is in urgent need of money to complete the project and has approached the LENDER for a loan of Rs. 40 lakhs with request to disburse the same in stages as detailed in schedule I hereto to meet his progressive financial requirements to complete the construction of the said four-storied building by June 2000 and proposed repayment of loan together with accrued interest thereon at 20% per annum from, *inter alia* the sale proceeds of the flats/units by thirty equated monthly instalments of Rs. .... each commencing from the first day of the month following the receipt of last instalment of loan till the liquidation of the entire dues with interest, costs and other charges within a maximum period of three years from the receipt of the last instalment of the loan. In the event the BORROWER failing to pay according to the repayment schedule the interest element will correspondingly be enhanced and also the total repayable amount.

AND WHEREAS the LENDER has agreed to accept the proposal of the BORROWER in sanctioning the loan of Rs. 30 lakhs as confirmed in the LENDER'S letter of 30th April 1999 addressed to the BORROWER subject to the observance of the usual terms and conditions applicable to such loans such as creation of mortgage of the property including the structure thereon, both present and future, by way of first charge by deposit of Title Deeds, payment of the specified rate of interest, observance of repayment terms, payment of additional interest in case of default, provision for assignment and creation of other collateral securities.

AND WHEREAS the BORROWER has deposited with the LENDER a sum of Rs. 25,000 to meet the costs of documentation in connection with the said loan.

NOW THIS AGREEMENT WITNESSETH and it is hereby agreed by and between the parties hereto as follows:

1. In pursuance of this agreement and in consideration of the payment of Rs. 25,000 as mentioned above the LENDER doth hereby agree to sanction a loan of Rs. 30 lakhs to the BORROWER payable by instalment as detailed in the Schedule II hereunder and confirmed in the LENDER'S letter of .... addressed to the BORROWER to enable the BORROWER to complete the project construction work of the four-storied residential building comprising 16 indenpendent self-contained flats/units/apartments at the said premises of which the BORROWER is the owner.

2. The LENDER upon completion of formalities and execution of documents has this day paid the first instalment of Rs. 10 lakhs to the BORROWER against creation of mortgage by deposit of Title Deeds of the said premises the receipt of which the BORROWER has already acknowledged.

3. The first instalment as also all the balance instalments shall be secured by Promissory Note to be executed by the BORROWER for the respective amounts of the instalments and further the repayment of the entire loan shall be guaranteed by a person of substance.

4. The construction work has commenced by the BORROWER with first class materials. The construction has to be completed in all respects latest by June 2000.

5. The subsequent instalment of Rs. 20 lakhs will be released to the BORROWER in accordance with the terms and conditions detailed in Annexure hereto on receipt of Certificate of satisfactory progress of detailed construction work by the attending Architect and in the event of any extension of time granted for completion of construction work beyond June 2000 the instalment of loan will be correspondingly deferred.

6. The BORROWER shall get the building properly insured comprehensively both during the construction and thereafter jointly in the name of Lender against riot, flood, collapse, malicious damage, fire and earthquake risks making the LENDER beneficiary thereof and shall get the Insurance Cover renewed every year till the entire loan is repaid in full with applicable interest. In default of the BORROWER taking out the Policy the Lender may get such insurance to be taken out and/or renewed in the joint names as above at the cost of the BORROWER and the amounts so spent will be treated as loan to the BORROWER repayable with interest at 18% per annum.

7. The BORROWER shall pay all existing and future rates, taxes, charges, assessments, levies, impositions, cesses payable by the BORROWER of the property.

8. The BORROWER shall produce a Certificate from the Architect engaged for the construction on completion of the work of construction certifying that the construction was done in accordance with the sanctioned Plan and specifications and that the same was safe and suitable for residential purpose. The BORROWER shall produce Occupancy Certificate from the Corporation of Calcutta.

9. Immediately upon disbursement of the first instalment of the proposed loan the BORROWER shall create a mortgage of the entire property with construction and proposed construction by deposit of Title Deeds with the LENDER at his office as a security for payment of the loan granted and the proposed loan to be granted by the LENDER to the BORROWER.

10. Upon completion of the building in accordance with the sanctioned Plan, the BORROWER shall deliver vacant possession of the building over which the LENDER shall have a lien till such time the entire dues against the loan disbursed to the BORROWER together with interest thereon are repaid. If the principal amount of the loan and interest thereon or any part thereof shall remain unrealised then the LENDER shall have the right and liberty to sell the said flat on behalf of the BORROWER and appropriate the proceeds thereof in *pro tanto* satisfaction of the outstanding amount of the said loan.

11. The BORROWER shall execute an Irrevocable Power of Attorney for this purpose.

12. In the event of failure on the part of the BORROWER to complete the construction within the specified time for any reason whatsoever the BORROWER hereby agrees and declares that in that event the LENDER will have the right and liberty to take over the possession of the unfinished

construction work and complete the same at the cost and expense of the BORROWER and sale the flats and/ or the building in the name and on behalf of the BORROWER for which the BORROWER hereby authorises the LENDER to act on his behalf. The BORROWER will be liable to all costs of recovery that might be incurred by the LENDER including all costs in connection with any suit for realisation of the LENDER'S claims.

13. BORROWER undertakes not to create any further mortgage of the land and building or any part thereof to any other person, Financial Institutions or Bank for raising any loan. The BORROWER hereby declares and confirms that the original Title Deeds executed in favour of the BORROWER is in possession of the BORROWER. The BORROWER declares that he has not obtained any loan from any other Home Finance Company, Bank, Life Insurance Corporation of India or any other similar Institution in connection with the cost of construction of the aforesaid building.

14. The BORROWER will be at liberty to sell the flats/units/apartments at the said premises with prior consent and approval of the LENDER on terms and conditions agreed or upon liquidation of all dues payable to the LENDER in relation to the construction of the said building.

15. The LENDER shall put up a board at the construction site that the premises is mortgaged with the LENDER and such board shall not be removed by the BORROWER till the loan is fully liquidated.

Schedule I

All that pieces and parcel of land measuring 5 Cottahs be the same a little more or less together with four-storied building under construction with all fittings and fixtures comprised in 16 self-contained flats/units/ apartments and common areas, pathways, pump house being premises No. .... Khatian No. .... Mouza .... butted and bounded

On the North by	..	R. S. Dag No. 5
On the South by	..	16 ft. wide common passage
On the East by	..	Part of Dag No. 5
On the West by	..	Part of Dag No. 5

Schedule II

(Sanctioning of loan and disbursement schedule with terms)

The loan is sanctioned for a sum of Rs. 30 lakhs to be secured by creation of first mortgage of the entire premises No. .... of .... Khatian No. .... with semi-finished construction and construction that will be made on the said land. The loan will be repayable in thirty equated monthly instalment of Rs. .... Each equated monthly instalment comprises of principal and interest calculated on the basis of annual rate at 20% per annum and is rounded up to the next rupee. The rate of interest is subject to revision to higher rate prevalent at the time of disbursement of the last instalment of loan without any further notice.

The loan amount will be disbursed in three instalments depending on the progress of work as under:

(*a*)	On completion of all formalities/execution of documents for the present loan	...	Rs. 10 lakhs
(*b*)	On completion of casting of roof of third floor		Rs. 15 lakhs
(*c*)	On fixation of doors, windows, grills and completion of floorings and plastering	...	Rs. 15 lakhs

The second and subsequent instalment will be released upon receipt of information about the progress of work duly certified by a qualified Engineer/Architect. It is understood that the entire construction work will be completed by June 2000. The BORROWER has paid to the Lender Service Charges at 2% of the sanction amount and technical fee all of which are non-refundable.

... Rs. ....

IN WITNESS WHEREOF the parties hereto have executed this agreement on the day, month and year first above-written.

Signed and delivered by the
BORROWER Mr. AB, at Calcutta
in the presence of:

(Signature)
Borrower

Signed, sealed and delivered by
Mr. .... pursuant to Board
Resolution dated .... of
ELH Home Finance Ltd. in the
presence of:

for and on behalf of
ELH Home Finance Ltd.
(Director)

Letter of Guarantee for the Promoter's Loan

Place: Calcutta
Date: 10th May 1999

To
ELF Home Finance Ltd.
56 G.C. Avenue
Calcutta

Dear Sirs

In consideration of your having agreed to grant Promoter's loan of Rs. 30 lakhs to Mr. AB of .... (hereinafter referred to as BORROWER) broadly on terms and conditions stated in the Promoter's Loan Agreement dated 10th May 1999. I, Mr. CD, by occupation business, residing at .... give you this Guarantee.

1. I hereby guarantee that the BORROWER will duly and punctually observe and perform each and every one of the obligations, to pay money whether for or towards principal, interest, other charges, expenses or otherwise howsoever on the BORROWER'S part to be performed under the said Promoter's Loan Agreement. I do hereby agree and undertake that in the event of default on the BORROWER'S part in making payment in discharge of such obligation I shall forthwith upon your notifying such default to make payment to you not only of the instalments due in respect of the defaulted instalments but also in the event of your having accelerated payment of the said amounts make payment to you of the entire loan without demur or protest on my part notwithstanding any objection from the BORROWER and I shall without prejudice to all your other rights indemnify you and keep you indemnified against all losses of principal, interest or other moneys due and payable to you in respect of the loan and all costs, charges and expenses whatsoever which you may incur by reason of any such default on the part of the BORROWER.

2. I hereby accord my consent to the terms of the said Promoter's Loan Agreement and/or any instruments that may hereafter be executed by the BORROWER in your favour varying or modifying the main agreement without requiring my consent or approval thereto and I agree that my liability under this Guarantee shall not in any manner be affected and/or reduced by such variation and modification and I expressly waive and relinquish my rights as a surety under the provisions of any law for the time being in force in that behalf.

3. You shall have the fullest liberty without in any way affecting this guarantee or discharging me from my liability hereunder to postpone for any time or from time to time the exercise of any power reserved to or conferred on you by the said Promoter's Loan Agreement or any other instrument that may hereafter be executed by the BORROWER in your favour and to exercise the same at any time and in any manner and either to enforce or forbear to enforce payment of the principal or interest or other moneys due and payable to you by the BORROWER or any of the remedies or securities available to you or to grant any indulgence or facility to the BORROWER and I shall not be released by any exercise by you of your liberty or by reasons of time being given to the BORROWER or any other forbearance, act or omission on your part or any other indulgence given by you to the BORROWER or by any other matter or thing whatsoever which under the law relating to sureties would but for this provision have the effect of releasing me. I hereby waive all those rights relating to the suretyship and other rights which I might otherwise be entitled to and in force howsoever but for this provision have the effect of releasing me.

4. This guarantee shall be enforceable against me notiwthstanding that the securities comprised in any instrument that may be executed by the borrower or any other person in your favour shall be at the time when the proceedings are taken against me hereunder are remaining unrealised.

5. In order to give effect to the guarantee you will be entitled to act as if I were a principal debtor to you for all payments guaranteed by me as aforesaid.

6. Without prejudice to anything stated in any other clause herein, and without in any way limiting or restricting the scope and operation of the guarantee herein contained all the obligations and liabilities would remain in full force and effect and I agree, assure and undertake that the BORROWER shall in terms of the said Promoter's Loan Agreement and/or any other Instrument or document that may be executed hereafter pay you every month during the period of loan a sum of Rs. .... as loan repayment by equated monthly instalments failing which I shall make good the deficit by full payment of the equated monthly instalments within seven days of notice of such default. I also undertake to pay forthwith without demur, protest or objection and notwithstanding any objections from BORROWER the amount demanded without being required to obtain any consent or confirmation from the BORROWER.

7. This Guarantee is a continuing one and shall be binding on me, my heirs, executors, successors, administrators, legal representatives and assigns for all amounts of the principal of the loan that may be advanced by you to the BORROWER under the said Promoter's Loan Agreement as also for all interest, additional interest, commitment charges, extra charges, service charges, cost and other moneys which may from time to time become due and remain unpaid to you by the BORROWER and shall remain in force until all such moneys shall be paid off in full with interest, costs and charges. Notwithstanding anything contained anywhere herein my liability towards the principal amount of the loan together with interest, additional interest, other charges, extra charges on arrears, service charges, costs or otherwise howsoever under the guarantee may not exceed Rs. 35 lakhs.

8. The benefit of this guarantee shall enure to your successors and assigns and shall be irrevocable until all obligations hereunder be discharged.

9. I assure that I am not under any disability or restriction to give you this guarantee and I undertake to make payment to you and discharge the pecuniary obligations of the BORROWER as set out in the Promoter's Loan Agreement.

10. I agree that this guarantee shall automatically come into force and become valid and binding on me immediately on disbursement being made under the Promoter's Loan Agreement executed between the BORROWER and yourself without requiring any further consent or approval from me.

11. You shall have the fullest liberty to increase the loan amount and vary the rate of interest and/or payment terms without any reference to me or prior consent from me. A certificate in writing signed by any of your duly authorised officers stating the amount at any particular time payable under the guarantee shall be conclusive evidence against me.

12. I further assure you that I have not applied for loan from you or any other bank or person or for myself or in respect of any person and I undertake not to apply for laon from you or any other Bank or person or give guarantee to any other company, Bank or person until this Guarantee has been cancelled by you on full repayment of your loan claims.

Signature of CD

Signature attested

Irrevocable Power-of-Attorney

KNOW ALL MEN BY these presents, I, Mr. AB, residing at ...., hereinafter referred to as the PRINCIPAL state as follows:

WHEREAS I am the owner of the land with partly constructed house on which further construction is in progress as mentioned in the Schedule hereunder.

AND WHEREAS for effective management of the property I wish to engage an Attorney so that from the income of the property or from the sale proceeds of the property, the said Attorney can liquidate any outstanding claim lying or occuring or arising against me with Messrs. ELH Home Finance Limited, in the event of my failure to settle the same.

NOW KNOW ALL MEN by these presents that I, Mr. AB, do hereby and hereunder irrevocably nominate, constitute and appoint the said ELH Home Finance Limited or any Principal Officer thereof and/or any other person who may be nominated by the said ELH Home Finance Limited, or its assigns from time to time in this behalf to be my true and lawful Attorney for me and in my behalf and in my name to represent me and do all acts, deeds, matters and things in connection with the sale of the Property/ Properties as per Schedule below that is to say:

1. To negotiate on terms for and sell my property, details whereof are mentioned in the schedule to any purchaser or purchasers at such price which my said Attorney in its absolute discretion think proper, to agree upon and to enter into any agreement or agreements for such sale and/or to cancel and/or repudiate the same.

2. To receive from the purchaser or purchasers any earnest money and also the balance of purchase-money and to give good valid receipt and discharge for the same which will protect the purchasers without being required to see the application of the money.

3. Upon such receipt as aforesaid in my name and on my behalf to sign and execute any conveyance or conveyances of the said property in favour of the said Purchasers or their nominee or assignees.

4. To sign and execute all other deeds, instruments and assurances which it shall consider necessary and to enter into such conveyance as may be required for fully and effectually conveying the said property and for that purpose to engage lawyers, file suits before appropriate Courts of Law and to execute decree as I could do myself.

5. To deliver possession of the aforesaid house, flats/apartments described in the schedule below, if necessary by evicting the occupants, irrespective of their legal status in the said property and for that purpose to engage lawyers, file suits before appropriate Courts of Law and to execute decree as I could do for myself.

6. To present any such conveyance or conveyances for registration, to admit execution and receipt of consideration before the Sub-Registrar or Registrar having authority for and to have the said conveyance registered and to do all acts deeds and things which my said Attorney shall consider necessary for conveying the said property to the said purchasers as fully and effectually in all respects as I could do the same myself.

7. And I hereby agree to ratify and confirm all and whatever other act or acts my said Attorney shall lawfully do execute or perform or cause to be done, executed or performed in connection with sale of the said property under and by virtue of this DEED NOT WITHSTANDING no express power in that behalf is herein provided.

8. This Power-of-Attorney shall remain in force and be irrevocable till all my dues with interest are liquidated finally with the said ELH Home Finance Limited and upon and full liquidation of my account with interest and costs the Power-of-Attorney shall be void automatically.

Schedule

All that pieces and parcel of land measuring 5 Cottahs be the same a little more or less together with under-construction four-storied building with all fittings and fixtures comprised in 16 self-contained flats/units/ apartments and common areas, pathways, pumphouse being premises No. .... Khatian No. .... Mouza .... butted and bounded.

On the North by	..	R. S. Dag No. 5
On the South by	..	16 ft. wide common passage
On the East by	..	Part of Dag No. 3
On the West by	..	Part of Dag No. 6

IN WITNESS WHEREOF I the said PRINCIPAL have hereunto sign and execute this Irrevocable Power-of-Attorney on this the .... day of .... 2000.

Signed, sealed and delivered by
the above principal in the presence
of witnesses:

1. ....

2. .... Principal

Agreement regarding Construction Loan with a Bank

Date 2000

The Agent
Bank of ....
(Address) ....

Dear Sir

I agree to grant to the Bank of Jaipur (hereinafter referred to as the BANK) a lease of my building bearing No..... situated in the main bazar owned by me and already in use of the bank for its branch.

2. I agree to carry out at my cost all the necessary additions and alterations to the premises by attaching further portion owned by me to the entire satisfaction of the BANK in accordance with the attached plan. The following covered accommodation would be available to the BANK after completion of the additions and alterations:

GROUND FLOOR:

(*a*) Banking hall

(*b*) Agent's room

(*c*) R.C.C. locker room (existing strong room)

(*d*) R.C.C. strong room (to be constructed)

(*e*) Passage

(*Steel flexible gates would be provided in the entrance doors*)

FIRST FLOOR:

(*a*) Staff lunch room

(*b*) Stationery room

(*c*) Record room

(*d*) Guard room

(*e*) Toilet

(*f*) Covered verandah

(***Skylight vents would be provided in the ceiling of banking hall for light and ventilation***)

3. I will commence the said work within 30 days and will carry out and complete the same within four months from the date hereof.

4. The BANK will grant me a construction loan of Rs. .... @ .... p.a. against a registered mortgage of the property, which will be repaid within five years by adjustment of Rs. .... per month out of the monthly rent payable by the BANK. The loan will be granted by the BANK in the following four instalments dependant on the basis of progress in construction work, as under:

(a) *1st instalment of Rs. ....*: To be allowed after the mortgage is registered in favour of the BANK and other prescribed documents /certificates produced to the branch and the construction work is taken up in hand.

(b) *2nd instalment of Rs. ....*: To be allowed when the construction of R.C.C. strong room is completed.

(c) *3rd instalment of Rs. ....*: To be allowed when the entire construction work of the ground floor is completed.

(d) *4th instalment of Rs. ....*: To be allowed when the construction jobs relating to 1st floor are completed and the building handed over to the bank complete in all respects with water connection/ sanitary and electric fittings, etc., and the prescribed lease deed is executed by me.

5. I shall arrange to get the building properly insured against fire and earthquake risk, and the insurance cover will be renewed every year till the entire loan is repaid in full. In the absence of my doing this, the BANK is fully authorised to get the insurance done at my cost.

6. I will, at my cost, do white washing/colour washing and painting/ varnishing on the wood work of the premises agreed to be demised to the BANK and deliver vacant possession of the same to the BANK not later than .... as soon as it is approved by the BANK.

7. The BANK will pay or cause to be paid to me a monthly rent of Rs. .... only payable on or before the fifth day of every month for the preceding month. The said monthly rent will be payable from the date the said premises are ready for occupation and are complete in all respects and vacant possession is delivered to the BANK. The part amount of monthly rent, *viz.*, Rs. .... shall, however, be deposited by the Agent direct

into my construction loan account towards its payment till the entire loan is liquidated with interest.

8. I will bear and pay and discharge all existing and future taxes, rates, charges and assessments payable by the owners of the said property. The BANK will pay only electricity, water and education taxes as per their actual consumption as shown in the meter/bills.

9. I will provide electic fittings, fixtures and sanitary equipment in accordance with a layout to be given by the BANK. I will also provide tap water facility in the building with an overhead tank.

10. I will construct a *pucca* strong room as per specifications supplied by the BANK. The work of construction of the *pucca* strong room will be done by me under the direct supervision of a P.W.D. official whose supervision and other charges will be borne by me. The strong room doors will, however, be provided by the BANK but affixed at my cost.

11. I will produce a certificate from the Executive Engineer, P.W.D., on completion of the work of construction of the *pucca* strong room to the effect that the strong room constructed in the premises is in accordance with the bank's standard specifications and plans. The Executive Engineer will certify that the strong room is duly reinforced with iron bars, cement and concrete from all sides including ceiling and floor, and it is fire and burglary-proof and quite safe and suitable for housing of currency chest and small coin depot.

12. The BANK shall be at liberty to remove at any time all materials employed by the bank in the construction of the strong room and all counters, strong room doors, safes, steel fittings, expanded metal apartments and temporary constructions which may have been brought in, fixed or erected by the BANK in the said premises during the continuance of the period of lease agreed to be granted by me to the BANK.

13. I will, during the terms of the lease, keep the said premises wind and watertight and will every year carry out white washing/colour washing and execute necessary repairs to the said premises as well as to any additions thereto, if any, erected and made by the BANK, at my cost. The oil painting/varnishing on wood work will be done every alternate year at my cost.

14. I will execute a deed of lease in favour of the BANK on the BANK'S standard form as per specimen enclosed for a period of five years with two options in favour of the BANK of renewing the said lease for a further period of five years each time, on the same terms and conditions. The cost of stamps for the lease deed and registration charges shall be borne by me and the BANK equally.

15. I will, in the event of my deciding to sell the said premises during the currency of the lease or at the expiration of the same, offer the same in the first instance to the BANK at the lowest price which I will be prepared to accept for myself and the BANK will, within one calendar month from the date of receipt of such offer, accept or reject such offer.

16. If I commit any breach of any of the terms and conditions herein to be observed and performed by me and if such breach is not remedied by me on a written requisition from the BANK within the time stipulated by the BANK in such written requisition, the BANK shall have an option to rescind this agreement and I shall be liable for payment of any loss or damage or compensation which the BANK may suffer either directly or indirectly or remotely as a result of such breach on my part.

Yours faithfully

(Owner)

44

Public Interest Litigation

Article 32 of the Constitution is designed for the enforcement of fundamental rights of a citizen by the Supreme Court. If anything endangers or impairs the quality of life in derogation of laws recourse may be had to Art. 32. It is maintainable at the instance of affected persons or even by a group of social workers or journalists, genuinely interested in the protection of society on behalf of the community. Public interest litigations cannot be invoked by a person or body of persons to satisfy his or its personal grudge and enmity. Public interest litigation contemplates legal proceedings for implementation or enforcement of fundamental rights of a group of persons or community which are not able to enforce their fundamental rights on account of their incapacity, poverty or ignorance of law.[1]

Conversion of a public park into a private nursing home even by the Government is illegal and petition by inhabitants of the locality is maintainable under Art. 226 of the Constitution as public interest litigation.[2] Merely because authorities constituted under a Statute failed in their effort to get interim order vacated is hardly any occasion for invoking jurisdiction under Art. 226 by way of public interest litigation. Besides, in such a petition the person may be honest and his grievance genuine yet the court may dismiss it for want of territorial jurisdiction or the petition may be defective as the person approaching may not be entitled to file it. Decision by High Court on the basis of subsequent events and not on facts existing as they were on the date of filing is also not proper.[3] Order of the court must be a speaking order after affording reasonable opportunities of hearing to the parties.[4]

1 *Subhas Kumar v State of Bihar* AIR 1991 SC 420; (1991)1 SCC 598; (1991)1 SCR 5; 1991 AIR SCW 121; see also, AIR 1984 SC 802; (1987)2 SCC 295; (1990)4 SCC 449.
2 *Bangalore Medical Trust v B.S. Muddappa* AIR 1991 SC 1902.
3 *T.N. Rugmani v C. Achutha Menon* AIR 1991 SC 983.
4 *Gram Panchayet v Collector* AIR 1991 SC 1082.

Health care of workmen and members of their families and education of the children as also the adults in exclusive locality should be of the employer even of the State where it is the employer. Their necessities include reasonable housing, supply of water, a provision store at hand, facility for a hospital recreational facilities and attention to the law and order. A welfare State has to cater to these requirements. A public interest litigation is maintainable for the purposes and the High Court is competent to give directions for enforcement of its order.[5] There can be a public interest litigation to undo any mischief done by Government official affecting the upkeep and maintenance of the temple and also for doing certain *sevas* of the deity.[6]

High Courts cannot, however, *suo moto* register a public interest litigation assuming judicial jurisdiction to probe into matters even of an administrative nature relating to High Court.[7]

The public interest litigation should not be a cloak for attaining private ends of third party or of the party bringing the action. The court must be careful to weigh conflicting public interests before intervening.[8] An Administrative Tribunal cannot entertain any public interest litigation at the instance of a total stranger.[9]

FORM

Specimen of a Writ Petition for Public Interest Litigation

District ....

In the High Court at Calcutta, Constitutional writ jurisdiction

Appellate Side

C.O./C.R. No. .... (W) of 1999

In the matter of:

An application under Article 226 of the Constitution of India

And

5 *Bandhna* v *Union of India* AIR 1992 SC 38.

6 *S. Sumitra* v *State* AIR 1993 Kant 108.

7 *Kumar Padma* v *Union of India* AIR 1992 SC 1213.

8 *Raunaq International* v *I.V.R. Construction* AIR 1999 SC 393.

9 *Duryodhan Sahu* v *Jitendra* AIR 1999 SC 114.

In the matter of:
Articles 14, 21, 48A and 51A(*g*) of the Constitution of India

And

In the matter of:
West Bengal Municipal Act 1993

And

In the matter of:
The Environment Protection Act 1986

And

In the matter of:
West Bengal Town and Country (Planning and Development) Act 1979

And

In the matter of:
Illegal attempt on the part of the Respondents (1) & (2) for raising a Cinema building by destroying one large water-body situated in the .... in violation of the draft outline/ Development Plan for the area concerned

And

In the matter of:
Shri .... son of ...., President of .... residing at ....

Petitioner

versus

1. ...., a company incorporated under the Companies Act 1956 having its registered office at ....

2. Mr. .... managing partner for Cinema, a partnership firm having its office.

3. The Chairman, ... Municipality ...., having its office at ....

4. State of West Bengal, Department or Urban Development .... having

its office at Writers Building, Calcutta through its Secretary

Respondent

To

Hon'ble Mr. .... The Chief Justice and His Companion Justices of the said Hon'ble Court

The humble petition of and on behalf of the petitioner above-named

MOST RESPECTFULLY SHEWETH:

1. The petitioner is a citizen of India and is also the President of .... an unincorporated Association of persons formed on .... by eminent citizens of .... at a general meeting held at .... with the object, *inter alia*, of protecting the ecology and environment of the country with particular emphasis on the preservation of national heritage buildings and architectures .... as well as for upholding the Constitutional and Legal Rights of the Citizens of India, particularly of the persons belonging to economically weaker section of the society and living within the municipal area of .... The petitioner craves leave to refer to and rely upon the aims and objects of the said .... at the time of hearing, if necessary.

2. The petitioner is also an Ecologist and having a specialised knowledge in ecology and environment.

3. The instant application is being filed by the petitioner for and on behalf of the .... as well as representing the weaker sections of the community residing within the municipal area of .... seeking a writ or order or direction in the nature of mandamus upon the Respondents Nos. 1 and 2 commanding them to forbear from changing or disturbing the environment and ecological pattern of the land in respect of one large water-body situated in .... under the jurisdiction of the .... for the ostensible purpose of construction of a cinema building at the instance of Respondent No. 2 to be financed by the Respondent No. 1 or for any other purpose which might cause any such disturbance of ecology and environment.

4. The petitioner submits that such constructions, if effected, would not only cause disaster to the ecology and environment of the municipal area and in particular the south western portion of the town, but it would be in violation of the draft outline of Development Plan of the Greater Calcutta prepared for the .... under the .... and the said plan prohibits *inter alia*, filling up of any water-body covering an area beyond 200 sq. m. the petitioner craves leave to refer to a copy of the said draft plan, at the time of hearing, if necessary.

5. The land on which such water-body is situated is owned by the Commissioners of .... Municipality for the purpose of converting the same into a green park and a swimming pool attached to it for the health and welfare of the residents and rate payers of the municipal area concerned but at present it is being used for pisciculture and which is being used by leasing out from time to time to different agencies for the purpose of pisciculture in order to accumulate the necessary finance for the ultimate object of laying the park and setting up the swimming pool and funds have been set apart for the same.

6. In course of time, almost the entire area round the said water-body has been built up by raising one school building besides residential complexes and a market place and the water-body in question is the only water-body in the area.

7. The petitioner has come to know that the Commissioners of the Municipality concerned are now devising various strategies to change the land use pattern of the said water-body by filling up the same as also by destroying the surroundings jeopardising the health and sanitation of the residents of the area in gross violation of the Constitutional Rights of the people of the area and the pupils of the educational institution close by as also in violation of the Town and Country (Planning and Development) Act 1979 and the Environment Protection Act 1986.

8. The Government has already taken steps for protection of wet-lands and in this regard has published an approach paper.

9. The State Government has also published a similar policy document for preservation of the wet-lands.

10. That the Respondent No. 1 is a company engaged in manufacturing iron rods having a Rolling Mill at Lilooah in the district of Howrah and it is a stranger to any cinema business but in order to augment its income has surreptitiously come to an understanding with the Respondent No. 2 to start a cinema business by providing the finance. The Respondent No. 2 is just a ghost firm set up by Respondent No. 1 to avoid the rigours of the Companies Act.

11. The wet-land described in the Schedule below serves the cause of environment in various ways which are indicated hereunder:

(*a*) Each water-body keeps the atmosphere cool by absorbing heat. Water vapours also keep the surrounding area cool. It absorbs carbon dioxide which are regularly discharged into the atmosphere.

(*b*) Wet-lands absorb dust particles discharged into the atmosphere by various sources and elements.

12. That the setting up of a cinema building so close to the school in the area will be dangerously affecting the education and health of the pupils and it is a co-educational institution.

13. Article 48A of the Constitution of India casts a duty upon the respondents to protect and improve the environment and to safeguard the forest and wild life of the country and they are also in duty bound to prevent any action which is likely to degrade the environment and affect the health and living conditions of the area and to prevent destruction of the aforesaid water-body.

14. The petitioner, therefore, begs to move this application as the President of .... and its members, and also on behalf the citizens/residents of said municipal area in order to protect their rights as enshrined under Article 21 read with Article 48A of the Constitution inasmuch as the persons likely to be prejudiced and affected by the aforesaid action of the Municipality of .... are so numerous and scattered and moreover the damage that is likely to be caused to them by the aforesaid action of the municipal authority will be slow and gradual before the same became manifest, it would not be possible for residents and tax payers to move this Hon'ble court individually. The petitioner and .... society and the member of .... are also duty bound under the provisions of Article 51A(*g*) of the Constitution to institute action for protection of environment since Article 51A(*g*) states that it will be the duty of every citizen of India to protect and improve the natural environment including various lakes and rivers and wild life to have combination for the living creatures, to initiate action for protection of the aforesaid water-body as the said municipal authority is bent upon destroying the water-body and has initiated urgent measures for the same, threats of destruction of the said water-body having become apparent and real and imminent the petitioner as the President of .... along with some eminent citizens of the Municipal area have already written several letters to the Chairman of the Municipality urging him not to, in any way diminish or destroy the water-body.

15. The concern shown by the petitioner as well as other eminent citizens of the area have failed to elicit any positive response from the Municipality and they appeared to be bent upon destroying the water-body by filling up the same in violation of statutory provisions and Government circulars and directions.

16. The petitioner states that the purported decision of the municipal authority if implemented would cause destruction and disturbance of the ecological and environmental equilibrium in the impugned areas by filling up of the aforesaid water-body and the impugned action is not only arbitrary but is also in violation of Article 14 of the Constitution.

17. Being aggrieved by and dissatisfied with the various actions and threats of the municipal authority the petitioner begs to move the instant application under Article 226 of the Constitution of India on the following amongst other.

GROUNDS

(I) For the purported decision of the municipal authority to fill up the aforesaid water-body is to cause great injuries to the ecology/

environment of the town and consequently would infringe the right of the residents of the area to a clean environment as impliedly enshrined in Article 21 of the Constitution and would thus be violative of the fundamental rights of the life of the residents of the area as guaranteed in Article 21 of the Constitution.

(II) For that the setting up of the cinema hall close to the school and the residential area and denial of a green park and swimming pool to the residents would amount to creating educational and health problems for the pupils and the residents.

(III) For that ....

18. The petitioner states that the petitioner has not moved any other application on the self-same cause of action before the Hon'ble Court or any other Court of Law.

19. The petitioner states that it is apparent that the Municipal Authority is actively proceeding towards the filling up the aforesaid water-body and unless restrained by an order of injunction, the respondent Nos. 1 and 2 as agents of the Municipality would fill up the said water-body which will render the instant application infructuous.

20. The cause of action of this instant application arose outside the Ordinary Original Civil Jurisdiction of this Hon'ble Court.

21. The petitioner has no other efficacious and alternative remedy and the remedies prayed for hereunder would give full and final relief to the residents of the area concerned on whose behalf the instant application is being moved.

22. The petitioner has also made demand for justice vide Annexure .... to the petition, but justice has been denied.

23. As indicated hereinabove, the petitioner is moving this application in public good to protect the public interest and not intended to serve any interest of any individual and in case the orders, as prayed for hereunder, are not granted the residents of the area concerned would suffer irreparable loss and injury.

24. That this application is being moved *bona fide* and in the interest of justice.

In the premises, your petitioner humbly prays Your Lordships for the following orders:

(*a*) Writ in the nature of *mandamus* directing the respondent Nos. 1 and 2 not to change the land use pattern of the water-body known as .... situated in .... of the Municipality of;

(*b*) Writ in the nature of *mandamus* directing the respondent Nos. .... give suitable direction to the respondent Nos. 1 and 2 requiring them to maintain the water-body as mentioned above in its present nature and character.

(*c*) An order or direction upon the respondent Nos. .... and each of them and their subordinates agents restraining them from according any sanction or permission or to do any act or omission which would enable the respondent Nos. 1 and 2 to disturb/diminish the said water-body.

(*d*) An order or direction upon the respondent Nos. 1 and 2 directing them to bring into this Hon'ble Court all the records relating to any decision that might have been taken for construction of cinema building so that conscionable justice may be administered by quashing the same;

(*e*) Rule *nisi* in terms of prayers (*a*), (*b*), (*c*) and (*d*) above;

(*f*) Rule be made absolute;

(*g*) Interim order of injunction restraining the respondent Nos. 1 and 2 from taking any steps towards destroying and/or diminishing the water-body known as .... situated at .... in any manner whatsoever till the disposal of this application;

(*h*) *Ad interim* order in terms of prayer (*g*) above;

(*i*) And pass such other or further order or orders as to Your Lordships may seem fit and proper.

And your petitioner, as in duty bound, shall ever pray.

Affidavit

I, Shri .... son of .... aged about .... years, by religion .... by occupation .... residing at .... do hereby solemnly affirm and say as follows:

1. I am the petitioner in the instant application and am well acquainted with the facts and circumstances of the case. I am duly authorised by the society to affirm this affidavit and I am competent to affirm this affidavit on behalf of the society and for self.
2. That the statements made in paragraphs .... are true my knowledge and those made in paragraphs .... are my humble submissions before this Hon'ble Court.

Prepared in my office | The deponent is known to me

Advocate | Clerk to: Mr. ....

Solemnly affirmed before me on this .... day of .... 1999 | Advocate

Commissioner

45

Claims against Railways

Present position. For breach of contract, say, for supply of goods or construction of roads or bridges or laying of railway line or supplying provisions, a suit in the Civil Court is maintainable against the Railways. Notice under s. 80 of the Code of Civil Procedure 1908 will be necessary and Union of India will be a necessary party along with the Railways to the suit. Section 43 of the Railways Act 1989 does not bar such a suit.

The Railways have to carry out construction and maintenance works and in connection therewith may enter into lands belonging to others, alter the position of pipe, electric supply line, drain, sewer, etc., remove obstruction to repair or to prevent accident.[1] The person aggrieved by any such act of the Railways and claiming damages or loss cannot file a suit against the Railway Administration. The Railway Administration shall pay or tender such sum by way of damages or loss as it may think reasonable. Either party, if aggrieved, may make an application to District Judge having jurisdiction over the matter for a decision. The decision of the District Judge shall be treated as a decision of the Appeal Court and shall be treated as final.[2]

The Railway Administration makes and maintains crossings, bridges, culverts, tunnels, drains, etc. at its own cost for the benefit of the owner of the adjoining lands. Such works are termed as "accommodation works".[3] Any person aggrieved may make a claim against the Railways. Such claim is to be made within six months of the cause of action and any claim should be filed with the Railways Claims Tribunal. No suit is maintainable.

Notice. The notice under s. 78B of the Railways Act 1890 or s. 80 of the Code of Civil Procedure 1908 is not any more necessary. Section 106 of the

1 Sections 11 to 14 of the Railways Act 1989.
2 Section 15 of the Railways Act 1989.
3 Section 16 of the Railways Act 1989.

Railways Act 1989 is a substitute for both the sections. Within six months of the cause of action a notice has to be served to the Railway Administration concerned. Such notice is to be given under s. 106 of the Railways Act 1989 by a person claiming compensation against Railway Administration for the loss, destruction, damage, deterioration, non-delivery of goods to the Railway Administration to which the goods were entrusted for carriage or on whose Railway the destination lies or the loss, destruction, damage or deterioration occurred. This notice has to be given within six months from the date of "entrustment" of the goods. The entrustment is the cause of action. So far as claim for refund of an overcharge in respect of goods is concerned, the notice has to be served to the Railway Administration to which the overcharge has been paid. This notice has to be served within six months from the date of such payment or the date of delivery of such goods at the destination station whichever in later.[4]

Competent Tribunal. An application for compensation for loss, destruction, damage, deterioration or non-delivery of goods shall be filed before the Tribunal against the Railway Administration on whom the notice under s. 106 has been served.[5]

Mode of service. Any notice or other documents may be served on the General Manager of the Zonal Railway or on the Railway servant authorised by the General Manager. The notice is to be served by delivering it to the General Manager or his authorised servant or leaving the notice at his office or by registered post to his office address. In case of a Railway other than a Zonal Railway the notice is to be served on the owner or lessee of the Railway or the person working the Railway under an agreement.[6] Similar provisions have been made in s. 193 for serving of notice, etc. by the Railway Administration.[7]

Rules. Under s. 198 Central Government may make Rules for carrying out the purposes of the Railways Act 1989.

Tribunal. The Railway Claims Tribunal Act 1987 provides for the establishment of Tribunals for determining claims against Railway Administration for loss, destruction, damage, deterioration or non-delivery of animals or goods entrusted to it to be carried by Railway or for the refund of fares or freight or for compensation for death or injury to passengers occurring as a result of Railway accidents or untoward incidents and matters connected therewith or incidental thereto.

Rules. Central Government has made the Railway Claims Tribunal (Procedure) Rules 1989 providing, *inter alia*, the form in which applications to be made to the Tribunal, the fees to be paid and procedure for hearing of such applications.

4 Section 106 of the Railways Act 1989.
5 Section 107 of the Railways Act 1989.
6 Section 192 of the Railways Act 1989.
7 Section 193 of the Railways Act 1989.

Limitation. A suit for money claim for breach of contract will have to be filed within three years. A claim in Tort not covered by the Railways Act 1989 is to be filed within one year.

An application to the Railway Claims Tribunal for recovery of damages for carriage of goods or refund of excess payment of freight or fare the limitation is three years. For recovery of compensation arising out of accidents is one year.[8] From a final order of the Tribunal an appeal lies to the High Court within ninety days from the date of the order.[9]

Procedure. The Railway Claims Tribunal (Procedure) Rules 1989 framed under the Railway Claims Tribunal Act 1987 provides for the form of application, fees payable and proceedings before the Tribunal.

FORMS

Combined Notice under section 106 of the Railways Act 1989 and section 80 of the Code of Civil Procedure 1908

Regd. A/D.

Dated ....

General Manager
Eastern Railway
Koilaghat Street
Calcutta

Dear Sir

Re: Payment for goods sold and delivered.

Please take notice that my client AB residing at .... will institute a suit against the Union of India owning and administering the aforesaid Railway in a Court of competent jurisdiction after expiry of two months after service of this notice under section 106 of the Railways Act 1989 and section 80 of the Code of Civil Procedure for reliefs and on causes of action described in the draft plaint annexed hereto unless the reliefs claimed are granted to my client by the said Railway within the said period of two months.

The relevant facts justifying my client's claim and constituting cause of action of the proposed suit and reliefs thereunder are given in short hereinbelow.

8 Section 17 of the Railways Claims Tribunal Act 1987.
9 Section 23 of the Railways Claims Tribunal Act 1987.

On or about .... at your request my client sold and delivered to you 100 reams of foolscap paper, 100 bottles of black writing ink 1000 pieces of lead pencils and 100 boxes of carbon papers for a total sum of Rs. .... You have duly received the said goods and signed challans and appropriated the said goods. My clients raised bills which you received and you did not complain either about the goods or the said bills but delayed payment on some pretext or other.

In spite of several demands made by my client, you have not paid the said sum or any portion thereof though you promised from time to time to pay the same.

My client hereby demands the said sum of Rs. .... with interest at 15% per annum from the date of submission of the bills till payment by you to my client.

Please note that unless payment is received within a period of 65 days from date of receipt of this notice, I have instructions to file suit against you for recovery of the claim of my client without any further notice to you and in that event you shall be held responsible for costs and consequences thereof.

Yours faithfully

FORM I

Rule 5 of the Railway Claims Tribunal (Procedure) Rules 1989 and section 16 of the Railway Claims Tribunal Act 1987

Title of the Case : AB .... *Claimant*

And

General Manager ...... Railways
Respondent

Description of documents attached :
Signature of the applicant :
For use in Tribunal's Office :
Date of filing: :
Registration No. :
Registrar Signature

In the Railway Claims Tribunal
Before the .... Bench

AB, residing at .... *Applicant*

And

General Manager .... Railways *Respondent*

1. Particulars of the applicant
   Name: AB
   Address:
2. Particulars of the respondent: General Manager ....
3. Value of claim and details of application fee:
   (*a*) Value of claim: Rs. 5,00,000
   (*b*) Details of application fee: ....
4. (*i*) Name and address of the Bank on which the draft is drawn: X Bank Ltd.
   (*ii*) Demand Draft No. .... for Rs. .... payable at Calcutta Branch
5. Full booking particulars of the consignment:
   (*a*) Date of booking
   (*b*) R/R or parcel way bill
   (*c*) Station from .... to ....
   (*d*) description of consignment
   (*e*) value of consignment
   (*f*) any other particulars
6. Date on which notice served on Railway Administration under section 106 of the Railways Act 1989 (copy to be attached)
7. (*i*) Facts of the case
   (*ii*) (*a*) nature of the relief sought
   (*b*) grounds of relief
8. Matters not previously filed or pending with any other court.
9. Jurisdiction of the Bench:
10. List of enclosures

Verification

I, ... son of .... aged .... residing at .... do hereby verify that the contents of paragraphs .... to ....are true to my personal knowledge and paragraphs .... to .... are believed to be true to the best of my knowledge or the legal advice given to me and that I have not suppressed any material fact.

Signature of the applicant

Full address

Date:

Place:

To
The Registrar
Railway Claims Tribunal
.... Road, Calcutta

FORM II

Application for Compensation under section 16 of the Railway Claims Tribunal Act 1987 in respect of Claims for Compensation for Death Injury etc. in a Train Accident read with Rule 5 of the Railway Claims Tribunal (Procedure) Rules 1989

AB .... *Claimant*

And

General Manager, Railways *Respondent*

INDEX

Description of documents attached :
Signature of the applicant :
For use in Tribunal's Office :
Date of filing :
Registration No. :

Registrar Signature

In the Railway Claims Tribunal
Before the .... Bench

AB .... *Claimant*

And

CD/General Manager .... Railways

.... *Respondent*

I, ... son of .... residing at .... having been injured in Railway accident hereby apply for the grant of compensation for the injury sustained.

I, ... son of .... residing at ....hereby apply as dependant for the grant of compensation on account of injury sustained by Shri .... son of .... residing at .... who was injured in the railway accident referred to hereunder.

Necessary particulars in respect of the deceased/injured in the accident are given below:

1. Name and father's name of the person injured/dead and husband's name in case of married woman.
2. Full address of the person injured/dead.
3. Age of the person injured/dead.

4. Occupation of the person injured/dead.
5. Name and address of the employer of the deceased if any.
6. Brief particulars of the accident indicating the date and place of accident and the name of the train involved.
7. Class of travel, and ticket/pass No. to the extent known.
8. Nature of injuries sustained along with medical certificate.
9. Name and address of the medical officer/practitioner if any who attended on the injured/dead and period of treatment.
10. Disability for work if any caused.
11. Details of the loss of any luggage on account of the accident.
12. Has any claim been lodged with any other authority? If so, particulars thereof.
13. Name and permanent address of the applicant.
14. Local address of the applicant, if any.
15. Relationship with the deceased/injured.
16. Amount of compensation claimed.
17. Where the application is not made within one year of the occurrence of the accident the grounds thereof.
18. Any other information or documentary evidence that may be necessary or helpful in the disposal of the claim.
19. Mention the documents if any filed along with application.

I, ... solemnly declare that

(*a*) the particulars given above are true and correct to the best of my knowledge and

(*b*) I have not claimed or obtained any compensation in relation to the injury/death which is the subject-matter of this application.

Signature or left thumb
impression of the applicant

Date:
Place:

Name of witness & address in case of left thumb impression is put by the applicant

Verification

I, ... son of .... aged .... residing at .... do hereby verify that the contents of paragraphs .... to

.... are true to my personal knowledge and paragraphs .... to .... are believed to be true to the best of my knowledge or the legal advice given to me and I have not suppressed any material fact.

Signature of the applicant

Full address:

Date:

Place:

To

The Registrar

Railway Claims Tribunal

.... Road, Calcutta

FORM III

Application under section 16 of the Railway Claims Tribunal Act 1987 read with Rule 5 of the Railway Claims Tribunal (Procedure) Rules 1989 in respect of Claims for Refund of Fares or Part thereof or for Refund of any Freight Paid in respect of Animals or Goods entrusted to a Railway Administration to be Carried by Railway

In the Railway Claims Tribunal

Before the .... Bench

AB .... *Claimant*

And

General Manager .... Railways

.... *Respondent*

INDEX

Description of documents attached	:	
Signature of the applicant	:	
For use in Tribunal's Office	:	
Date of Filing	:	
Registration No.	:	
Registrar	:	Signature

In the Railway Claims Tribunal
Before the .... Bench

BETWEEN

AB .... *Claimant*

And

General Manager .... Railways
Respondent

1. Particulars of the applicant:
   Name: AB
   Address:
2. Particulars of the respondent:
3. Value of the claim and details of application fee.
   (*a*) value of claims: Rs. 5,00,000
   (*b*) details of application fee:
4. Particulars of Bank Draft/Postal Order in respect of application fee:
   (*i*) name and address of the Bank on which the draft is drawn. X Bank Ltd., Calcutta Branch.
   (*ii*) demand draft No. .... payable at Calcutta Branch.
5. Full particulars of payment of freight/fare:
   (*a*) Claim for refund of freight.
      (*i*) date of booking
      (*ii*) R/R/Parcel Way Bill
      (*iii*) Station from .... to ....
      (*iv*) description of consignment
      (*v*) freight paid
      (*vi*) amount of refund of claims
      (*vii*) Money Receipt/Credit Note or other payment particulars.
   (*b*) Claim for refund of fare:
      (*i*) Date of journey
      (*ii*) Train No.
      (*iii*) Class of travel
      (*iv*) Class actually travelled
      (*v*) ticket or ticket deposit receipt/excess fare ticket etc. guard's or conductor's certificate
      (*vi*) fare paid: Rs. ....
      (*vii*) refund claimed: Rs. ....
6. Date on which notice served on Railway administration under

section 106 of the Railways Act 1989 in respect of claims for refund of freight. (attach proof).

7. (*i*) Facts of the case.

(*ii*) (*a*) Nature of relief sought
(*b*) grounds of relief.

8. Matters not previously filed or pending with any other court (in case the applicant took any legal action give details and attach certified copy of the order).

9. Jurisdiction of the Bench.

10. List of enclosures.

Verification

I, ... son of .... aged .... residing at .... do hereby verify that the contents of paragraphs .... to .... are true to my personal knowledge and those of paragraphs .... to .... are believed to be true to the best of my knowledge or the legal advice given to me and that I have not suppressed any material fact.

Date: Signature of the applicant

Place: Full address:

To
The Registrar
Railway Claims Tribunal
.... Bench
.... Road
Calcutta

NOTE: Application fee: Rs. 314 for a claim of Rs. 5,000; Rs. 1,064 for claim of Rs. 20,000; Rs. 1,464 for a claim of Rs. 30,000; Rs. 1,664 for Rs. 40,000; Rs. 1,764 for claim of Rs. 50,000 and thereafter at half per cent subject to maximum application fee of Rs. 50,000.

46

Receipt and Acknowledgement

Receipt. It is defined in s. 2(23) of the Indian Stamp Act 1899 as under:

(23) Receipt includes a note, memorandum or writing—

(*a*) whereby any money or any bill of exchange, cheque or promissory note is acknowledged to have been received, or

(*b*) whereby any other movable property is acknowledged to have been received in satisfaction of a debt, or

(*c*) whereby any debt or demand, or any part of a debt or demand, is acknowledged to have been satisfied or discharged, or

(*d*) which signifies or imports any such acknowledgement, and whether the same is or is not signed with the name of any person.

Obligation to give receipt. Any person receiving any money exceeding Rs. 20, or any bill of exchange, cheque or promissory note for an amount exceeding Rs. 20 or receiving in satisfaction or part satisfaction of a debt any movable property exceeding Rs. 20 in value, shall, on demand by the person paying or delivering such money, bill, cheque, note or property, give a duly stamped receipt for the same.

Any person receiving or taking credit for any premium or consideration for any renewal or any contract of fire insurance, shall, within one month after securing or taking credit for such premium or consideration, give a duly stamped receipt for the same.[1]

The amount of stamp duty is prescribed by Art. 53, etc., of the Stamp Act. Section 65 of the Stamp Act prescribes punishment for refusal to give receipt. Section 25 of the West Bengal Premises Tenancy Act 1956, enjoins that a receipt for the rent paid shall be forthwith given to the tenant on payment of the rent.

1 Section 30 of the Indian Stamp Act 1899. This section refers to "stamped" receipt for money exceeding Rs. 20. However Art. 53 provides that stamp is payable only if the receipt is for more than Rs. 500.

Instruments not duly stamped inadmissible in evidence.[2] Section 2(11) of the Indian Stamp Act (Act 11 of 1899) defines the expression "Duly Stamped". It means that the instrument must bears an adhesive or impressed stamp of not less than the proper amount and that such stamp has been fixed or used in accordance with the law for the time being in force in India.[3] Receipts, promissory notes or a bill of exchange are not admissible in evidence if they are not duly stamped; provided that, where any person, from whom a stamped receipt could have been demanded, has given an unstamped receipt, and such receipt if stamped would be admissible in evidence against him, then such receipt shall be admitted in evidence against him on payment of a penalty by the person tendering it; and where any receipt chargeable with a duty tendered to produced before any officer unstamped in the course of the audit of any public account, such officer may, in his discretion, instead of impounding the document, require a duly stamped receipt to be substituted therefor.[4]

Cancellation of adhesive stamps. On any instrument bearing an adhesive stamp, the executant must cancel the stamp, so that it cannot be used again, by writing on or across its face his name or initials, or the name or initials of his firm with the true date of his so writing, or in any other effectual manner.[5]

Penalties.[6] If any person—

(*i*) receiving any money exceeding twenty rupees in amount, or any bill of exchange, cheque or promissory note for an amount exceeding twenty rupees, or receiving in satisfaction or part satisfaction of a debt any movable property exceeding twenty rupees in value, refuses or neglects to give a receipt, or

(*ii*) with intent to defraud the Government of any duty, upon a payment of money or delivery of property exceeding twenty rupees in amount or value give a receipt for an amount or value not exceeding twenty rupees, or separates or divides the money or property paid or delivered, or

(*iii*) required to cancel an adhesive stamp, fails to cancel such stamp according to law,

he shall be liable to be punished with fine not exceeding one hundred rupees.

It will not be out of place to point out here the responsibility of lawyers and professional deed writers engaged by parties for preparation of

2 Section 35 of the Indian Stamp Act 1899.
3 Section 2(11) of the Indian Stamp Act 1899.
4 Section 37 of the Indian Stamp Act 1899.
5 Section 12 of the Indian Stamp Act 1899.
6 See ss. 62 & 63 of the Indian Stamp Act 1899. In view of Art. 53 of the Schedule to the Act Rs. 20 should be read as exceeding Rs. 500.

documents. A solicitor, advocate, pleader and even their respective clerks are liable to prosecution if they, with a view to defraud the Revenue Authorities, omit to set forth all facts in a document, *i.e.* suppress material facts to keep down stamp duty.[7]

Instruments by or in favour of Government. Receipts, any other instrument, executed by, or on behalf of or in favour of, the Government, in cases where the Government would otherwise be liable to pay the duty chargeable in respect of such instrument, are not subject to stamp duty.

Registration. Registration of receipts is not compulsory; but if a receipt by itself creates an interest in immovable property of the value of Rs. 100 and upwards, its registration will be compulsory.

Exemptions. Under Art. 53 of the Indian Stamp Act, the following receipts are exempted from stamp duty—

(*i*) endorsed on or contained in any instrument duly stamped, or any instrument executed on behalf of the Government, or any cheque or bill of exchange payable on demand, acknowledging the receipt of the consideration money therein expressed or the receipt of any principal money, interest, annuity, or other periodical payment thereby secured;

(*ii*) for any payment of money without consideration;

(*iii*) for any payment of rent by a cultivator on account of land assessed to Government revenue, or (in the Presidencies of Fort St. George and Bombay) of inam lands;

(*iv*) for pay or allowances by non-commissioned or petty officers or soldiers, sailors or airmen of the Indian military, naval or air forces when serving in such capacity, or by mounted police constables;

(*v*) for pensions or allowances by persons receiving such pensions or allowances in respect of their services as such non-commissioned officers or soldiers, and not serving the Government in any other capacity;

(*vi*) given by the headman or lambardar for land revenue or taxes collected by him; and

(*vii*) given for money or securities for money deposited in the hands of any banker to be accounted for:

Provided that the same is not expressed to be received of, or by the hands of, any other than the person to whom the same is to be accounted for; provided also that this exemption is not extended to a receipt or acknowledgement for any sum paid or deposited for or upon a letter of allotment of a share, or in respect of a call upon any scrip or share in any

7 *Trimbuck Mahadeo* v *Emperor* (1936)166 LC 681.

incorporated company or other body corporate or such proposed or intended company or body, or in respect of a debenture being a marketable security.

Acknowledgements. Article 1 of the Stamp Act provides for stamp duty on acknowledgement of a debt exceeding Rs. 20 in amount or value written or signed on behalf of a debtor in order to supply evidence of the debt. If there is any promise to pay the debt or interest or any other property, it is an agreement and not an acknowledgement.

Section 18 of the Limitation Act 1963, states that an acknowledgement of liability before the expiry of the prescribed period of limitation for a suit or application starts a fresh period of limitation for a suit or application from the date of signing of the acknowledgement.

An unconditional acknowledgement has been held to imply a promise to pay and a suit on the basis of such acknowledgement has been held to be competent.[8] A deposition signed by a party as witness[9] or an admission in a written statement[10] may be a sufficient acknowledgement.

FORMS

Receipt in Full Discharge of Claims

RECEIVED on this .... day of ...., from AB the sum of Rupees .... (Rs. ....) only, being in full discharge of all claims and demands which I have against him up to date.

CD (*Creditor*)

Receipt of Account Due

RECEIVED on this .... day of ...., from AB through EF the sum of Rupees ...... (Rs. ......) only, being in full (*or* part) payment on his account of Rupees .... due to me (*or* us).

CD (*Creditor*)

Receipt for Bond Debt

I, the undersigned CD, hereby acknowledge to have this .... day of ...., received from AB the sum of Rupees ...... (Rs. ......) only, on account of the

8 *Hiralal* v *Budkulal* AIR 1953 SC 225.

9 *Venkata* v *Partha Sarathi* 16 Mad 220.

10 *Sriniwas* v *Narhar* 32 Bom 296.

principal sum and interest due to me under the bond dated the .... day of ...., and executed by the said AB.

CD (*Creditor*)

Receipt for Endorsement on Bond

RECEIVED on this .... day of ...., from the within-named (or above) AB the sum of Rupees......... (Rs. ......) only, being in full payment of the debt (or in part payment of the debt, or, being the instalment due, or, on account of interest due) under the within-written (or above) bond.

Sd.

Receipt for Loan

BORROWED AND RECEIVED on this .... day of ...., from CD the sum of Rupees .... (Rs. ......) only, to be repaid within .... years from this date, with interest at the rate of Rs. .... per cent per annum.

AB (*Debtor*)

Receipt for Price of Watch with Warranty

RECEIVED on this .... day of ...., from AB Rs. ...... being the price of a watch warranted by us to keep correct time within .... minutes per week, for ...... months from this date.

CD (*Watchmaker*)
for X & Co.

Receipt for Sale of a Business

RECEIVED on this .... day of ...... from Mr. .... of .... the sum of Rs. ...... being the price for the sale of the business in .... carried on by me under the name and style of .... at ...... including all assets, liabilities, furniture, fittings, stock-in-trade, benefits and obligations of all pending contracts, permits, licences and engagement in connection with the said business.

AB

Rent Receipt

RECEIVED from AB the sum of Rupees .... only, on account of the rent of the house No. ...., situate at, etc., inclusive of all taxes, for the month of .... 2000, Arrears ...... nil (or Rs. ......).

CD (*Landlord*)
(Date)

Rent Receipt in Bill Form

Bill No. .... Date ....

AB (*Tenant*) Dr. ....

To CD

INTEREST @ ....% p.a. will be charged if this bill is not settled within a month from the date of its presentation.

Particulars			*(Rs.)*
To the rent of the house .... situate at, etc. for the month of ...., 2000, at Rs. .... per month	...		...
To Municipal and other taxes	...		...
" Arrears	...		...
" Interest on arrears	...		....
		TOTAL	...

E. & O.E. Received Rs. ....
.... in full/part payment

WITNESS: CD (*Landlord*)

Receipt at the End of Agreement

RECEIVED on the day and year first above-written from the above-named AB the sum of Rupees .... (Rs. ......) only, being the deposit money (or, etc.), in terms of clause .... of the above agreement.

WITNESS: CD

Receipt for Mortgage Money (For Endorsement on Deed)

RECEIVED on this .... day of ...., from the within-named (or above-named) AB the sum of Rupees .... (Rs. ......) only, being the amount (or balance) of the principal and interest due to me under the within-written (or above-written) mortgage deed.

WITNESS: CD (*Mortgagor*)

Receipt of Title Deeds by Mortgagor

RECEIVED on this ...... day of ...., from CD all the title deeds relating to the house (or, etc.), which had been mortgaged by me to the said CD on the .... day of ....as that mortgage has this day been fully paid off.

WITNESS: AB (*Mortgagor*)

Receipt of Title Deeds on Mortgage by Deposit of Title Deeds

RECEIVED on this .... day of ...., from AB etc., the following documents of title deposited by him at .... as security for due repayment of the sum of Rs. .... advanced by me to him this day with interest thereon at the rate of .... per cent per annum.

List of documents deposited—
1. ....
2. .... CD

Receipt by Creditor for Composition of Debt

RECEIVED on this .... day of ...., from AB of, etc., a payment from CD of, etc., the sum of Rupees .... (Rs. ....) only, being a composition of .... in the rupee upon a debt of Rs. .... owing by the said AB to me, and which composition I accept in full satisfaction and discharge of the said debt, and I undertake to execute a formal release of the said debt at his request and expense.

WITNESS: EF (*Creditor*)

Receipt for Earnest Money

I, the undersigned AB, hereby acknowledge to have this day of ...., received from CD of etc. Rupees ...... (Rs. ......) only, as earnest money for the sale of my house (or, etc.), situate at, etc., free from all encumbrances which I have agreed to sell to him for Rs. ...., and execute the sale deed on or before the .... day of ...., on receipt of Rs. ...., being the balance of the purchase money.

WITNESS: AB (*Vendor*)

Receipt by Retiring Partner

I, the undersigned AB, of, etc., (*retiring partner*) hereby acknowledge to have this day received from CD of, etc., (*continuing partner*), the sum of Rupees .... (Rs. ....) only being the full amount of all moneys due or owing to me in respect of my share in the partnership business of etc., carried on under the firm name of, etc., by me in partnership with the said CD up to the .... day of ...., the date of my retirement from the said partnership.

Signed, etc.

WITNESS: AB

Receipt by Residuary Legatees

WE, the undersigned, hereby certify that we have respectively examined the foregoing accounts contained on this and the preceding .... sheets of paper and the vouchers in support thereof, and that the same are correct. And we hereby severally acknowledge to have this day received from CD (or, CD and etc.), the executor (or executors) of the will (or the administrator, or the administrators of the estate) of the said AB deceased, the sum of Rupees .... (Rs. ......) only each in payment of our respective shares of the residuary estate under the said will, and in full discharge of all our respective claims and demands under the said will as shown in the said accounts.

Signed, etc.

WITNESS:

EF

GH (*Residuary Legatees*)

FORMS OF ACKNOWLEDGEMENT

Acknowledgement to Save Limitation

Dated ....

I HAVE received your letter dated .... demanding Rs. .... due to you on account of a bond dated .... executed by me in favour of ....

I shall be much obliged if you will kindly wait for three months more within which time I hope to be able to pay the amount due.

Sd/- AB

Acknowledgement of Part Payment

Dated ....

I HEREBY acknowledge that I have this .... day of .... paid Rs. ...... in part payment of the debt of Rs. .... which I borrowed from .... on a pronote dated .... executed by me in his favour.

Sd/- AB

Acknowledgement of Liability

Dated ....

THIS is to acknowledge and place on record that a sum of Rs. ...... has been found due from me on the basis of account settled between us and I bind myself to pay off the some by ....

Sd/- AB

Declaration of Change of Surname

KNOW ALL MEN by these presents that I, the undersigned, do hereby absolutely renounce and abandon the use of my said *surname of* (*original surname)* and in lieu thereof assume and adopt the *surname of* (*assumed surname*) And for the purpose of evidencing such change of name I hereby declare that I shall at all times hereafter in all records, deeds, documents and other writings and in all actions, suits and proceedings, as well as in all dealings and transactions, matters and things whatsoever and upon all occasions use and subscribe the said name of (*assumed surname*) as my surname in lieu of the said surname of (*original surname*) so abandoned as aforesaid.

AND I therefore hereby expressly authorise and require all persons whomsoever at all times to designate, describe and address me and my heirs by such adopted surname of (*assumed surname*) only.

In witness whereof I have hereto subscribed my christened name of (*christened name*) and my adopted and substituted surname of (*assumed surname*) this .... day of ....

Signed, sealed and delivered by
the above-named ....
in the presence of:

Signature with original surname
Signature with assumed surname

47
Rectification and Modification of Deeds

Mistakes or errors in deeds arising from any accidental slip or omission should be corrected by a deed of rectification. It is an equitable relief granted by the Court of Equity on the doctrine of mistake. In order that rectification may be granted there must be mutual mistake and that the document does not represent the true intention between the parties[1] and the mistake relates to some facts and not of law.[2] A mistake of foreign law has the same force as mistake of facts.[3] When parties to a deed agree to modify or vary, add to or subtract from the terms of any previous deed, it is necessary that the intention of the parties should be expressed in a written instrument, as oral testimony of such agreement is not admissible in evidence. Such deeds require registration if the principal deed was registered. Relief action may be granted by the court even in case of fraud to carry out the real intention of the parties. This is entirely discretionary and when granted the order does not prejudice the rights acquired by third parties in good faith and for value.[4]

FORMS

Deed of Rectification of Mistakes in a Previous Deed

THIS DEED is made the .... day of .... BETWEEN AB of, etc., (hereinafter called the RELEASOR) of the one part and CD of, etc., (hereinafter called the RELEASEE) of the other part.

1 *Amanti Bibi* v *Lachman* 14 Cal 308.
2 Section 26 of the Specific Relief Act 1963.
3 Section 20 of the Indian Contract Act 1872.
4 Section 21 of the Indian Contract Act 1872.

WHEREAS by a deed of release dated the .... day of .... the said AB granted and released to the said CD the land described in the schedule hereunder and the said deed has been registered at .... Registration Office in Book No. 1, Volume No. ......, pages .... to .... being serial No. .... for the year .... (hereinafter called the PRINCIPAL DEED). AND WHEREAS certain mistakes and inaccuracies have accidentally and inadvertently crept in the principal deed which require rectification in the manner hereinafter appearing: NOW THIS DEED WITNESSES that the principal deed shall be rectified and corrected in the following manner, namely,—

(*a*) in the Schedule in the principal deed for the words "12 cottahs" the words "12 cottahs and 8 chittaks" should be substituted and read.

(*b*) In page .... line .... of the principal deed after the words "........." insert the words "..........".

That as rectified and modified as aforesaid the principal deed shall remain in full force and effect.

The Schedule

IN WITNESS, etc.

Signed, sealed and delivered AB

Deed of Rectification of Hire Purchase Agreement

THIS DEED OF CORRECTION made this 15th day of December 1999 BETWEEN ELH Ltd., Calcutta, the OWNER, Transport Co. Ltd., Calcutta the HIRER and Mr. XY the GUARANTOR.

WHEREAS by the within written Hire Purchase Agreement bearing dated the 18th September 1999 and made between the ELH Ltd. therein called the OWNER of the One Part and the Transport Co. Ltd., Calcutta therein called the HIRER of the Second Part and Mr. XY of Calcutta therein called the GUARANTOR of the Third Part it was *inter alia* agreed between the parties that the OWNER shall purchase the Jeep described in the First Schedule thereunder written and shall let to the HIRER and the HIRER shall take on hire the said Jeep as may be available after the purchase thereof AND in the First Schedule included.

One CJ 4A/4 WD. "Jeep Universal" with Petrol Engine, 6 Ply tyres.

AND WHEREAS the cost of the aforesaid item has been revised due to change in Machinery or increase in other charges it is necessary to rectify the said Agreement so as to include therein the revised figures in various clauses of the Agreement.

NOW IT IS AGREED between the Parties hereinabove:

(1) In cl. 1 of the said Hire Purchase Agreement bearing date the 18th September 1999 the amount of the total cost of the machinery, namely, Rs. 2,55,000 should be substituted by the total cost of Rs. 2,80,000 (Rupees two lakhs eighty thousand only) and similarly in cl. 2, the sum of Rs. 51,000 should be substituted by the sum of Rs. 60,000 (Rupees sixty thousand only) and shall be deemed always to have been substituted.

(2) Subject to the said modifications the within written Agreement bearing date the 18th September 1999 shall remain in full force and effect and shall be read and construed as the terms of these presents were inserted therein by way of substitution or rectification.

IN WITNESS WHEREOF these presents have been executed by the parties herein this the day of 15th December 1999.

Signed, sealed and delivered by
Mr. ....
pursuant to Board Resolution
dated ...... of Transport Co. Ltd.
in the presence of:

Signed, sealed and delivered
by Mr. XY, the GUARANTOR in the
presence of:

Signed, sealed and delivered by
Mr. ....
pursuant to Board Resolution
dated .... of ELH Ltd.
in the presence of:

48

Release

Introductory observations:

(a) *Release.* Release is an instrument whereby a person renounces a claim upon another or against any specified property which he has or may be entitled to enforce. It may be a deed poll or an indenture. It cannot, however, be a substitute for assignment of a claim or transfer of any property.

(b) *Execution and attestation—registration.* A release must be executed and its registration is compulsory if the amount or value of the claim affecting immovable property is Rs. 100 or upwards.[1]

A deed of release does not create title. A release may be drafted in the same form as a deed of transfer or simply as a deed poll or a deed to which both parties may join stating the circumstances under which the release is based. Either the monetary consideration or "the premises", *i.e.* facts in consideration of which the release is made shall be stated.

A disclaimer as distinguished from a release operates merely as an agreement.

A release or disclaimer is a deed of relinquishment by which one person renounces a claim against another person, or any property or office.[2] A release, however, presumes some right or claim of the releasor in the subject-matter of the deed of release.

It may be of personal obligation. It is not a substitute for any assignment or surrender of any right or rights. A tenant in common cannot by release extinguish his interest in the property in favour of the other inasmuch as he has a distinct interest in the property.[3] On this principle, Hindu widows and

1 Section 17(1)(*b*) of the Indian Registration Act.
2 Article 55 of the Schedule of the Stamp Act.
3 Wharton's *Law Lexicon*, p. 859.

daughters cannot by execution of release create or establish absolute title in the property in favour of other co-sharers as under the Hindu Succession Act 1956, they are entitled to distinct shares in the property. Before the enactment of the Hindu Succession Act 1956, a Mitakshara coparcener could execute a valid release in respect of his coparcenary interest in favour of the other members of the family,[4] but the position has since been changed as she has a distinct interest in the joint family properties of which she can even make a will though the same is subject to fluctuation.

A *benamdar* may execute a release in favour of the real owner, but it is prudent to have a declaration of trust from him.

A release is distinguishable from a deed of surrender by a Hindu widow inasmuch as an estate for life is extinguished so as to make the reversioner the full owner of the property. It operates at the death of the widow.[5] The widow withdraws herself from the estate and the next heir steps into the inheritance as a matter of law.[6]

Essentials of Release

(*i*) Full recitals of the origin of the claim, which form the most important part;

(*ii*) knowledge of the releasor about the claim, intended to be released;

(*iii*) words and expressions sufficiently clear to convey the intention of the releasor to discharge the right or the claim.[7]

FORMS

Mutual Release by Two Persons

THIS DEED OF RELEASE is made on the .... day of ...., BETWEEN AB of, etc., of the one part, and CD of, etc., of the other part.

WHEREAS the said AB and CD were lately carrying on the business under the name and style of, X &Co. in course of which several sums of money fell due mutually against each other as will appear from the books of account of the said business maintained by the said CD AND WHEREAS the said business has been closed with effect from the .... day of .... 1999 .... AND WHEREAS in consideration of the services rendered by the

4 *Chander Kishore* v *Danpat Kishore* 16 All 369.
5 *Jwala Bank* v *Sheobodh* AIR 1947 All 104.
6 *Karunamoyee* v *Maha Moyi* AIR 1948 Cal 84.
7 Davidson's *Precedents*, vol. 5, p. 618.

parties hereto to each other for development of the business and with a view to maintaining good feelings and relationship between them the parties have agreed to write off all such amounts and to execute a mutual release: NOW THIS DEED WITNESSES that in pursuance of the said agreement, and for the consideration as aforesaid the said AB does hereby release, discharge and exonerate the said CD, and also that the said CD does hereby release, discharge and exonerate the said AB from all sums of money, accounts, proceedings, claims and demands whatsoever which either of them had or has or may have in future against the other, in respect of or in relation to, the said business which will be deemed as written off and the parties relieved from all liabilities on account therefor to all intents and purposes.

IN WITNESS WHEREOF etc.

Signed, sealed and delivered AB
CD

Release by Creditors under Composition Scheme

THIS DEED OF RELEASE is made this .... day of .... 1999 BETWEEN AB son of .... CD residing at .... and EF residing at .... (hereinafter called the CREDITORS which term shall include their successors and assigns) of the One Part and XY son of .... residing at .... (hereinafter called the DEBTOR which term shall include his heirs successors and legal representatives of the Other Part.

WHEREAS the DEBTOR was and still is indebted to each of the CREDITORS, whose names, addresses and descriptions are given in the schedule hereto, in the several sums written opposite their names in the said schedule: AND WHEREAS the creditors have agreed with the debtor to accept a composition of .... in the rupee in full satisfaction and discharge of their respective claims and to forego, release and discharge the balance on terms and conditions hereinafter appearing. Now THIS DEED WITNESSES that in consideration of the mutual benefits between the parties under the scheme of composition as to payments of their respective dues the said creditors do and each of them doth hereby release and discharge the debtor and his heirs, executors, administrators and representatives from all their debts and claims other than the portion payable under the deed of composition on condition that the DEBTOR shall pay or cause to be paid to each of the CREDITORS on or before the .... day of ...., a composition of .... in the rupee on their debts:

PROVIDED, HOWEVER, AND, IT IS HEREBY AGREED THAT notwithstanding anything hereinbefore stated, this release shall stand *ipso facto* void and be of no effect, if the said payments or any one of them be not made on or before the above stipulated date or dates or if the DEBTOR be adjudged an insolvent before the said date of payment, PROVIDED ALSO that this release shall be without prejudice to the right of the CREDITORS to proceed against the sureties or guarantors or co-debtors of the DEBTOR for their debts specified in the schedule hereto.

The CREDITORS hereby agree with the DEBTOR that this release shall be effectual and binding on them, although some creditors other than those who have executed this deed do not agree with the scheme of composition and are not willing to give up their right to realize in full their debts or claims.

It is hereby declared that the amount or value of the claims hereby renounced is Rs. ....

The Schedule above referred to

Serial No.	*Name and address of the creditor*	*Amount of debt or claim*	*Date of payment*	*Remarks*
1				
2				
3				
4				
5				
6				
7				
8				
9				

IN WITNESS WHEREOF the parties herein have executed these presents on the day, month and year first above-written.

Signed, sealed and delivered by
AB, CD, EF the CREDITORS in the
presence of:

Signed, sealed and delivered by XY
the DEBTOR in the presence of:

Release by a Minor in favour of the Certified Guardian on Attaining Majority

THIS DEED OF RELEASE is made this .... day of ...... 1999 BETWEEN AB son of .... residing at .... by caste .... by occupation .... (hereinafter called the

RELEASOR which expression shall unless the context otherwise requires include his heirs, successors, and legal representatives) of the One Part and CD son of .... residing at .... by caste .... by occupation .... (hereinafter called the RELEASEE which term shall include his heirs, successors, legal representatives and assigns) of the Other Part.

WHEREAS by order dated the .... day of .... made by the District Judge of .... in Misc. Case No. .... of 1999 the said CD was appointed certificated guardian of the person and properties of the aforesaid AB who was then a minor under the age of .... years which properties are fully mentioned and described in the schedule hereto. And whereas the said order was in full force and virtue until the date hereunder mentioned.

AND WHEREAS in pursuance of the said order the said CD took charge of the management and control of the estate of the said AB and administered the same duly and faithfully and submitted accounts, which were passed by the said court.

AND WHEREAS the said AB having attained majority, on or about the .... day of .... his date of birth being .... day of .... and accepted the said accounts as true, correct, faithful and complete AND WHEREAS by an order dated the .... day of .... 1999 the said CD has been discharged from further acting as certificated guardian of the said AB.

AND WHEREAS the said CD has made over to the said AB all properties both movable and immovable of the said AB so long held by him as guardian and he the said AB has taken charge and possession of the same.

AND WHEREAS the said AB is fully satisfied that the aforesaid guardian CD did not commit any act of waste, negligence or misfeasance or malfeasance in respect of the properties or in management thereof or affairs ancillary and incidental thereto.

NOW THIS INDENTURE witnesseth that in the circumstances aforesaid the said AB does hereby release and discharge the said CD from all claims as to management and administration of the estate or affairs ancillary or incidental thereto as well as all questions as to account and dealings with the estate.

The Schedule above referred to

IN WITNESS WHEREOF the parties hereto have executed these presents on the day, month and year above-written.

Signed, sealed and delivered by AB
the RELEASOR in the presence of:

Signed, sealed and delivered by CD
the RELEASEE in the presence of:

Disclaimer by a Member of a Joint Family in respect of the Separate Property of a Member

TO ALL WHOM THIS MAY CONCERN

KNOW ALL MEN BY THIS DEED poll I, AB, son of etc. .... declare as follows: WHEREAS I, the said AB along with CD son of etc., both residing at .... constitute a Hindu undivided family joint in food, worship and estate AND WHEREAS by a conveyance dated .... executed by one EF in favour of the said CD it was witnessed that the said CD purchased the property fully mentioned and described in the Schedule thereto with his own moneys and without any aid or contribution from the said family or its estate AND WHEREAS in the circumstances aforesaid the said property belongs absolutely to the said CD as his separate property but nevertheless it is necessary and expedient to have a disclaimer from me in terms hereunder contained to avoid future disputes and differences in relation thereto, NOW KNOW YE ALL BY THIS DECLARATION I, the said AB, declare and confirm the said property as the personal property of CD and disclaim and release all my supposed right, title and interest claim in the said property and every part thereof absolutely and forever.

The Schedule above referred to

IN WITNESS WHEREOF etc.

Signed, sealed and delivered

Release of Property from Charge for Maintenance under a Will

THIS DEED OF RELEASE made the .... day of .... BETWEEN AB wife of .... residing at .... by caste .... by occupation .... etc. (hereinafter called the RELEASOR) of the one part and CD son of .... residing at .... by caste .... by occupation .... (hereinafter called the RELEASEE) of the other part.

WHEREAS one XY of .... who died on the .... day of .... left a will dated .... whereby and whereunder he appointed the said CD as the sole executor and bequeathed all his estate and effects thereof unto and to the use of the said CD subject to a payment of Rs. .... per month to his daughter, *viz*., the said AB for her maintenance for the term of her natural life to be paid out of his estate which was charged for the purpose of such payment AND WHEREAS the said will was duly proved in the court of the .... Judge and probate thereof was granted to the said CD on the .... day of .... AND WHEREAS the said CD has been regularly paying the said sum of Rs. .... to the said AB monthly and every month And Whereas the said CD has agreed to sell the properties now representing the estate (or one property *viz*. premises No. .... out of the estate) free from all encumbrances and charges, trust, lien whatsoever including the charge for maintenance in favour of the said AB as aforesaid And Whereas at the request of the said CD the said AB has agreed to accept a lump sum of Rs. .... being the amount equivalent to 12 years' maintenance and give up her claim for future maintenance (or other properties being sufficient security for her maintenance the said AB has agreed to give up her claim as to future maintenance) as against this property NOW THIS INDENTURE witnesseth in the circumstances aforesaid and that in consideration of the said sum of Rs. .... paid by the said CD to AB which the said AB doth hereby admit, acknowledge and confirm (or other properties being sufficient security for her maintenance) the said AB does hereby and hereunder release and discharge the said CD from all her claims as to future maintenance under and by virtue of the hereinbefore recited will and also the properties (or property) fully mentioned and described in the schedule hereto and also from all actions, claims and demands whatsoever on account therefor.

The Schedule above referred to

IN WITNESS WHEREOF the said Sm. AB has hereinto set and subscribed her hand and seal the day, month and year first above-written and that the said CD doth hereby accept the Release hereunder made as testified by his being a party hereto and executing these presents.

Signed, sealed and delivered
by Sm. AB in the presence of:

Signed, sealed and delivered
by CD as a token of acceptance
of Release in the presence of:

Disclaimer by a Benamdar

THIS INDENTURE MADE THIS .... day of .... BETWEEN AB .... son of XY .... by caste .... by occupation .... residing at .... hereinafter called the RELEASOR (which expression shall where the subject or context allows or admits of be deemed to include his heirs, executors, administrators and representatives) of the ONE PART AND CD .... son of EF .... deceased by caste .... by occupation .... residing at .... hereinafter called the RELEASEE (which expression shall where the subject or context allows or admits of be deemed to include his heirs, executors, administrators, representatives and assigns) of the OTHER PART.

WHEREAS it appears that by a conveyance dated the .... day of .... 1976 executed by MN .... in favour of the said AB ...... and registered in the office of .... in Book I, vol. .... page .... to .... being No. .... for the year, the RELEASOR, hereto he, the said MN, for the consideration mentioned therein purported to grant, convey, sell, transfer and assign in favour of the said AB .... the property fully mentioned and described in the schedule thereto and also particularly written in the schedule below:

AND WHEREAS the transaction having been a *benami* purchase the said property was in fact and truth, reality and substance acquired by the RELEASEE with his own moneys and for his use and benefit though in the name of the RELEASOR but not intending to make a gift or advancement or otherwise settle or to create or confer any title or benefit thereof upon the RELEASOR or to defraud any creditor(s), who thus having acquired no title nor any interest in the said property but was a mere name lender or *benamdar* and the RELEASEE was at all material times and still now is the lawful owner and in possession, enjoyment and control of the said property and every part thereof and has at all times and is still been administering the same to all intents and purposes. AND WHEREAS all the documents of title in relation to the said property were and are also still in the possession and custody of the RELEASEE and all outstanding and liabilities of the property such as ground rent, municipal taxes, etc., were and are still paid and satisfied by the RELEASEE.

AND WHEREAS for reasons and considerations hereunder mentioned the RELEASOR has in the circumstances aforesaid and to avoid any dispute or difference in future and to safeguard the future interest of the RELEASEE agreed to disclaim the said property and execute and register a declaration in respect thereof in terms herein mentioned AND NOW THIS INDENTURE WITNESSETH that in the circumstances hereinbefore stated and for good reasons and considerations as aforesaid it is hereby agreed and declared by and between the parties as follows:

1. The RELEASOR doth hereby and hereunder agree, declare and confirm that although the purported conveyance of the said property stands in the name of the RELEASOR as purchaser, the same was a *benami* transaction for the RELEASEE and, as such, the RELEASEE was at all times and is also at present the sole beneficial owner in possession and real proprietor of the said property and every part thereof and that the RELEASOR had not nor at present has nor shall in future claim any right, title or interest whatsoever in, to, upon or otherwise relating to the same or any portion thereof or otherwise concerning the same.

2. The RELEASOR doth hereby and hereunder absolutely disclaim, disown and relinquish and for ever discharge all and every such pretended right, title, interest, claim or demand or cause of action which may now or hereafter be alleged or contended or construed in his favour in respect of the said purchase and/or the said property and otherwise relating thereto or concerning the same or any part thereof by virtue of the hereinbefore recited conveyance the same having been made in the name of the RELEASOR as hereinbefore stated.

AND THIS INDENTURE FURTHER WITNESSETH that for the consideration hereinbefore stated the RELEASOR doth hereby and hereunder acquit, release, discharge, grant, convey, transfer and assure unto and to the use of the RELEASEE the said property and every part thereof absolutely and for ever in the manner hereunder indicated AND the RELEASOR doeth hereby covenant with the RELEASEE that the RELEASOR had not done, executed, performed nor been party or privy to any act, deed or thing whereby of whereunder or by reason or means whereof the said property or any part thereof may be in any manner charged, encumbered or otherwise affected or prejudiced in title or estate or the releasor may be hindered or prevented from transferring the said property unto and to the use of the RELEASEE in the manner hereinbefore indicated.

The estimated value of the property is Rs. ....

The Schedule above referred to

IN WITNESS WHEREOF the said AB has hereunto executed these presents on the day, month and year first above-written. And that the said CD doth hereby accept the Release hereunder made as testified by his being a party hereto and executing these presents.

Signed, sealed and delivered by AB
the RELEASOR in the presence of:

Signed, sealed and delivered by CD
the RELEASEE in the presence of:

N.B.— It was held by the Supreme Court in *Controller of Estate Duty* v *Aloke Mitter*.[5] A *benamdar* has no interest at all in the property. He is not a trustee unless he is in actual possession of the property.

Mutual Release between a Separated Member of the Mitakshara Family and the Old Branch

THIS DEED OF RELEASE made the .... day of .... 1999 BETWEEN AB, son of .... residing at .... etc. for himself and as Karta and representing the coparceners of a joint Hindu family consisting at present of himself and his sons and grandsons namely .... hereinafter referred to as the RELEASOR of the ONE PART and CD son of .... residing at .... etc. for self and as Karta of and representing the coparceners of a joint Mitakshara family consisting of his sons and grandsons hereinafter referred to as the RELEASEE of the OTHER PART.

5 AIR 1981 SC 102 at p. 103.

WHEREAS the said AB and his brother EF since deceased were joint in food, worship and estate and carried on a joint family business at various places, viz .... under the name and style of...........

AND WHEREAS the said EF died on the .... day of .... leaving a son, *viz.*, the said CD the RELEASEE hereto who did not have intention nor any inclination to remain joint with the said AB and/or to continue in the business of the family AND WHEREAS the said CD became thus completely separated from the joint family and its estate and the business thereof and started his own business independently at .... under the name and style of .... without any aid or contribution from the joint family funds or the estate AND WHEREAS the said CD having been in affluent circumstances independently of the joint family estate did never have nor at present claim any share or interest of the joint family estate nor in the profits or benefits thereof which he has renounced for ever.

AND WHEREAS it is nevertheless necessary and expedient to safeguard the future interest of the parties and their representatives after their demise and in order to end all possible claims or disputes and differences which the parties or their representatives may have or hereafter raise in respect of the separate properties of the said CD although such claim or claims do not in fact or reality exist;

NOW THIS DEED OF RELEASE WITNESSES in the circumstances aforesaid and for good reasons and considerations the said AB for self and representing all other persons who are jointly living with him doeth hereby release and discharge unto the RELEASEE and other members mentioned above as are joint with him absolutely and for ever, all the purported right, title, interest and claim which the said RELEASOR may have had or has in or against the property or properties of the said CD or his joint family now in existence fully mentioned and described in Schedule A hereto or which may hereafter be acquired by the RELEASEE or his family AND THIS INDENTURE FURTHER WITNESSETH that the said RELEASEE for himself and as Karta of and representing all persons constituting his joint family mentioned above doeth hereby release and for ever discharge the said RELEASOR and other persons as are joint with him as aforesaid from all right, title, interest, or claim which the said CD or the members of his joint family may have as against the RELEASOR or against his representative or their property or properties now existing fully mentioned and described in Schedule B or which he or they may hereafter acquire.

It is also mutually agreed that the value of the property for the purpose of stamp duty is Rs. ....

Schedule A

Schedule B

IN WITNESS WHEREOF the said AB and CD for themselves and as Kartas of their respective Joint Families have set and subscribed their respective hands and seals the day, month and year first above-written.

Signed, sealed and delivered by
AB for self and as Karta of Joint
Family in the presence of:

Signed, sealed and delivered by
CD for self and as Karta of Joint
Family in the presence of:

Release of Right of Way

THIS DEED OF RELEASE made the .... day of ...., BETWEEN AB of, etc. (the RELEASOR), of the one part, and CD of, etc. (the RELEASEE), of the other part.

WHEREAS by a conveyance dated the .... day of ...... 1999 and made BETWEEN the said AB of the one part, and YZ of, etc., of the other part, the land and property coloured blue and brown in the plan annexed thereto were conveyed to the said YZ absolutely, save and except and reserving nevertheless unto the said AB, his heirs, executors, administrators, representatives and assigns, and the owners and occupiers for the time being of the land and property coloured pink in the said plan and his and their sub-tenants and servants, and agents full and free right and liberty at all times thereafter and for all purposes to go, pass and repass over and upon the way or passage coloured brown in the said plan and described in the schedule hereunder: AND WHEREAS by a conveyance dated, etc., and made between the said YZ of the one part, and the said CD of the other part, the property coloured blue and brown was conveyed to the said CD absolutely, subject to the reservation of the right of way over the said way or passage, as excepted and reserved by the said conveyance of the .... day of .... 1999 AND WHEREAS the said AB has, for a token consideration of a sum of Rs. .... agreed to release unto the said CD the said right of way over the way or passage aforesaid: NOW THIS DEED WITNESSES that in consideration of the sum of Rs. ...., now paid by the said CD to the said AB (the receipt of which sum the said AB hereby acknowledges), the said AB, as the beneficial owner, hereby releases unto the said CD the said right of way over the said way or passage described in the schedule hereunder to the extent that the same shall henceforth cease and be extinguished, to all intents and purposes.

The Schedule above referred to

IN WITNESS WHEREOF the said AB and CD have executed these presents on the day, month and year first above-written.

Signed, sealed and delivered by AB the RELEASOR in the presence of:

Signed, sealed and delivered by CD the RELEASEE in the presence of:

Release by a Legatee in favour of an Executor

THIS DEED OF RELEASE is made this .... day of .... 1999 BETWEEN AB son of .... residing at .... (hereinafter called the LEGATEE) of the One Part and CD son of .... residing at .... (hereinafter called the EXECUTOR) of the Other Part.

WHEREAS XY died on the ...... day of ......1999 leaving a will dated .... whereby and whereunder he appointed the said CD as the EXECUTOR of his estate and left and bequeathed all his estate unto and in favour of the said AB absolutely and for ever AND WHEREAS the said will was duly proved in the court of the .... judge at .... and probate thereof was granted unto and in favour of the said CD on the .... day of .... AND WHEREAS the said CD has duly and faithfully administered the estate and filed the inventory and account and/or otherwise completed the administration thereof AND WHEREAS the said CD has duly assented to the LEGACY provided for in the said will unto and in favour of the said AB and has made over all properties fully mentioned and described in the schedule below so long held by him as EXECUTOR who has taken charge and possession thereof and thus relieved the said CD AND WHEREAS the said AB after having gone through the accounts and taking charge of the properties is fully satisfied that the said CD has not committed nor suffered any act of mismanagement, waste, misfeasance or malfeasance in course of administration thereof. Now THIS INDENTURE WITNESSETH that in the circumstances aforesaid the said AB does hereby release the said CD from all claims as to management or administration of the estate and affairs ancillary or incidental thereto as well as from all liabilities as to account and dealings with the properties.

The Schedule above referred to

IN WITNESS WHEREOF the parties hereto have executed these presents on the day, month and year first above-written.

Signed, sealed and delivered by AB the LEGATEE in the presence of:

Signed, sealed and delivered by CD the EXECUTOR in token of acceptance of the Release in the presence of:

Deed of Release of Mortgage

THIS DEED OF RELEASE made this 15th day of September 2000, BETWEEN Mr. X, son of .... residing at .... hereinafter called the RELEASOR (which expression shall include his heirs, legal representatives and successors) of the One Part and Mr. AB son of .... residing at .... hereinafter called the OWNER (which expression shall include his heirs, legal representatives and successors) of the Other Part.

WHEREAS the OWNER executed a Deed of Mortgage in favour of the RELEASOR mortgaging the premises No. .... (hereinafter referred as the said premises) as security for a loan of Rs. 4 lakhs bearing interest at 12% per annum with half-yearly rests on the 10th day of September 1992 and registered in the Book No. 1, vol. 1, page 1, being No. 1, for the year 1992 in the Registration Office at ....

AND WHEREAS the OWNER has this day paid to the RELEASOR a sum of Rs. 5 lakhs in full and final satisfaction of the Mortgage money and debt due under the aforesaid Mortgage, receipt whereof the Releasor hereby acknowledges.

NOW THESE PRESENTS WITNESSETH and the parties hereby agree as follows:

1. The RELEASOR admits and acknowledges the receipt of payments from time to time and a sum of Rs. 5 lakhs being the outstanding amount as on this day in respect of the mortgage money both by way of the principal and interest up-to-date and of and from the same and every part thereof acquits, releases, exonerates and discharges the owner as also the said premises intended to be and thereby releases the said premises and the said owner of all indebtedness and liabilities to the Releasor and in respect of the said premises.

2. The RELEASOR hereby declares that the said premises is free from any charge, encumbrance, rates, taxes and levies and liabilities of any sort.

3. The RELEASOR hereby declares and warrants that he has not made any transfer of the interest in the said premises and has not done anything to encumber the said premises and has not created any interest thereon in any way.

4. The RELEASOR hereby agrees and undertakes to the OWNER to indemnify against and keep him harmless from all claims, proceedings, costs charges and expenses in relation to the said premises suffered or incurred by the OWNER arising out of or in relation to any act, deed or omission on the part of the RELEASOR in relation to the said premises.

5. The RELEASOR hereby returns and makes over to the OWNER the original Title Deed No. 56 and the Mortgage Deed dated 10th September 1992 and the said OWNER hereby acknowledges receipt of the original Title Deed made over by the RELEASOR and also the original Mortgage Deed.

IN WITNESS WHEREOF the parties hereto doth hereby and hereunto put their signatures in this DEED OF RELEASE on the day, month and year first above-written.

Schedule of property

All those pieces and parcels of land measuring about 5 Cottahs with two-storied building thereon with fittings and fixtures, privileges and appurtenances thereto being the Premises No. .... and butted and bounded in the North by ...., in the East by Premises No. .... in the South by Canal and in the West by Premises No. .... and as described in the Title Deed.

Signature of RELEASOR

WITNESSES:

Signature of OWNER

1.

2.

49

Sales

Introductory observations. Section 54 of the Transfer of Property Act 1882 defines sale. It is a complete transfer of ownership of the property. No rights are left with the transferor.[1] Any property other than those prohibited under s. 6 of the said Act may be transferred. The Act imposes restriction as to transfer not only as to property but also as against persons who may be transferors and transferees, *viz.*, a minor, lunatic, insolvent, alien enemy, persons having their properties managed by the Court of Wards who are disqualified persons to effect any transfer of their properties.[2] A contract for sale to a minor is, however, valid, but the minor must be represented by an appropriate guardian acting *bona fide* in the interest of and for the benefit of the minor. But he cannot bind the minor by any personal covenant.[3] Section 136 of the Transfer of Property Act deals with other disqualified transferees. Persons under disability cannot even take a transfer where the same involves covenants;[4] so also persons in fiduciary relationship, e.g. guardian and ward, parent and children, solicitor and client inasmuch as one is in a position to dominate the will of the other;[5] so a presumption of undue influence arises in cases of transaction between them.

Sale—sale how made—contract for sale. Sale is a transfer of ownership of any property or properties in exchange for a price paid or promised, or part-paid and part-promised.[6]

1 Section 8 of the Transfer of Property Act which corresponds with s. 63 of the English Law of Property Act 1925.
2 Sections 6(*h*) and 7 of the Transfer of Property Act 1925.
3 Section 8 of the Hindu Minority and Guardianship Act 1956.
4 *Satya Devi* v *Trebani* 161 IC 579: AIR 1936 Pat 153.
5 *Plowright* v *Lambart* 52 LT 645.
6 Section 54 of the Transfer of Property Act.

Such transfer in the case of tangible immovable property of the value of one hundred rupees and upwards, or in the case of reversion or other intangible thing, can be made only by a registered instrument.[7] In the case of tangible immovable property of a value less than one hundred rupees such transfer can be made either by a registered instrument or by delivery of the property. Delivery of tangible immovable property takes place when the seller places the buyer or such person as he directs in possession of the property.

Passing of title and ownership. The execution of the conveyance and the payment of price are reciprocal.[8] Price is the essence of the contract for sale but its payment is not a *sine qua non* to passing of title and transfer of ownership. A contract fails and becomes void for want of consideration[9] but not a conveyance perfected by execution and registration. This was held by the Supreme Court in *State of Kerala* v *Cochin Chemical Refiners*.[10] A sale deed duly executed and registered and not tainted with any fraud passes the title notwithstanding non-payment of price.[11]

It always depends upon the intention of the parties as to when title to the property will pass unto and vest in the purchaser.[12] The vendor can prove that no consideration has in fact been paid notwithstanding an admission in the sale deed.[13] It was recently held by the Supreme Court in *Prosad* v *Govindaswami*[14] that if the sale deed is not supported by adequate consideration the transaction is void and so no relief will be granted to the parties.

Thus where the vendor retains possession of the property or the deed pending payment of price or where the deed expressly provides that it shall be void and of no effect unless the price, unpaid in whole or portion as the case may be, is paid within a fixed time, no right is acquired by the purchaser in such cases by the execution and registration of the deed. The intention of the parties being that the conveyance will take effect upon payment only. In other cases a sale is completed and perfected by execution and registration (when compulsory) of the conveyance, irrespective of the fact of non-payment of purchase money and it does not prevent the passing of the title of the property sold from the vendor to the purchaser; and the vendee, notwithstanding such non-payment, can maintain a suit for possession of

7 Section 54 of the Transfer of Property Act.

8 Section 51 of the Indian Contract Act and ss. 55(1)(*d*) and 55(5)(*b*) of the Transfer of Property Act.

9 Section 25 of the Indian Contract Act.

10 (1963)3 SCR 556.

11 *Chety Firm* v *Chety Firm* 34 IC 125.

12 *Raj Kumar* v *Uchit* AIR 1951 Pat 414.

13 *Sohlal* v *Indrojit* 22 All 370.

14 AIR 1982 SC 84.

the property except in cases of fraud.[15] It was held that a false assertion in the sale deed that money was paid will have the effect of invalidating the sale transaction.[16]

A contract for the sale of immovable property in view of s. 54 of the Transfer of Property Act 1882 does not of itself create any interest in or charge on the property. It creates a personal obligation as recognised in s. 10 of the Specific Relief Act of 1963 and s. 91 of the Trusts Acts and is described in s. 40 of the Transfer of Property Act—an obligation annexed to the ownership but not amounting to any easement or interest therein.[17] It was, however, held by the Hon'ble Mr. Justice G.N. Ray in *Jayanta Kumar Banerjee* v *State of West Bengal*[18] that an intending purchaser has the *locus standi* to challenge acquisition proceedings in respect of any property under Art. 226 of the Constitution of India inasmuch as the same may ultimately frustrate the contract. An agreement for sale of such property even after a decree for specific performance is made does not create any interest in the property.[19] Such a decree operates as an injunction but does not, by itself, create any interest in, or charge on such property; and it being a mere agreement to obtain another document,[20] unless it is an agreement under s. 5 of the West Bengal Apartment Ownership Act (Act XVII of 1972), its registration is not compulsory unless the earnest money forms a charge on it. A buyer does not acquire any right *in rem* in the property intended to be sold though he has paid its full value and obtained possession of the same. He can at best claim a charge on it under s. 55(6)(*b*) of the Transfer of Property Act and defend his possession under s. 53A of the Act. This is called equities of persons contracting to buy any property. A buyer, under such circumstances, is liable to take care of the property against physical destruction as a prudent man would have taken. The case of a sale of any property under agreement after attachment is discussed below. All these are old concepts of law about agreement. But in cases where the purchaser has been in possession of the property lawfully in the assumed character of the owner much of the period prescribed by the Statute of Limitation for creation of ownership and further peacefully exercising the ordinary rights of ownership he becomes its owner.[1] This case further held that such a purchaser can create a valid equitable mortgage by deposit of the title deeds of the property even though there is no conveyance in his favour.

15 *Somsundaram* v *Shwebwa* (1920)57 IC 948.
16 *Marni Veeranna* v *Kanumuri* AIR 1977 AP 405.
17 *Kartick Chandra Shaw* v *Ranjita Pul* AIR 1977 Cal 496.
18 AIR 1981 Cal 138.
19 *Enayatulla* v *Khaliullah* AIR 1938 All 432.
20 Section 17(2)(*v*) of the Indian Registration Act.
1 *Usha Rice Mills Co. Ltd.* v *United Bank of India* 82 CWN 92.

The English Rule of Law as it is under s. 40 of the Law of Property Act 1925, transfers an equitable estate to the purchaser. It does not apply to India, but the same was the law prior to the Transfer of Property Act and such an agreement required registration for its validity. So, in places where the Act is not in force, the English Rule still applies and an agreement for sale requires registration. The mode of transfer by sale under the Transfer of Property Act is twofold: (*a*) delivery of possession in cases of transfer of small value not exceeding Rs. 100; (*b*) registration.[2] There is no third method except as held in 82 CWN 92 as discussed above as the title to land cannot pass when the statute requires a deed.[3] Section 53A of the Transfer of Property Act though does not expressly confer any substantive right in the transferee, nevertheless protects him against any action for eviction by the transferor.[4] Mere delay in enforcing the agreement to sell is not sufficient to deny specific performance unless there is a waiver or abandonment of the rights.[5]

This section was first enacted in 1929 by the Transfer of Property (Amendment) Act 1929 which imported in India in modified form the equity of part performance as developed in *Maddison* v *Alderson*.[6] This amending Act reinforced the position by amending the Registration Act of 1908 and the Specific Relief Act 1881. Under s. 27A a suit for specific performance of a contract of lease could be filed. Section 27A was not, however, re-enacted in the Specific Relief Act 1963. It is based on the Doctrine of Part-performance. The rule in *Walsh* v *Lonsdale*[7] which laid down the principle—"Equity considers what ought to have been done as done"—is excluded from its operation by the statutory law in India. The requirement under s. 53A of the Transfer of Property Act is that the contract must be in writing and signed by the parties and further that the transferee shall take possession of the property. Section 53A therefore does not create any title. This is the distinguishing feature between the English law and Indian law of conveyancing. The other features are mentioned below. A word or two may be said here as to the rights and liabilities of the parties when any attachment is effected on any property after the agreement for sale. A contract for sale under s. 54 of the Transfer of Property Act 1882 does not create any interest in or charge in the property but nevertheless it creates a personal obligation as contemplated in s. 3 of the Specific Relief Act and s. 91 of the Trust Act—an obligation annexed to the ownership of the property of the nature of a trust, so a *bona fide* purchaser acquires good title in spite of attachment.[8] Under s. 64 of the

2 Section 17 of the Indian Registration Act.
3 *Fati Chand* v *Leelamber* 14 MLA 129.
4 *Mathura Mohan* v *Ramkumar Saha* (1916)43 Cal 720.
5 *K.M. Rajendran* v *Arul Prakasam* AIR 1998 Mad 336.
6 53 IC 205; (1833)8 App Cas 467.
7 (1882)21 Ch D 9.
8 *Purna* v *Daulat* 78 CWN 352.

Code of Civil Procedure, any private transfer of the property will be void as against the claim of the attaching creditor, but in the case of an agreement for sale, the contractual obligation will prevail.[9] The same result will be achieved if the purchaser institutes a suit for specific performance and the court enforces the conveyance.[10] In other words, s. 53A of the Transfer of Property Act creates a statutory right in favour of the transferee though derived from the English equitable doctrine of part performance. It cannot be whittled down on the concept of laches or implied limitation. The failure on the part of the transferee to sue for specific performance of the contract within the period of limitation under the Limitation Act 1963 does not lead to extinction of his statutory right created by s. 53A. In spite of limitation the right subsists and the contract remains valid and operative to exert his right to retain possession over the property in exercise of his statutory right under s. 53A by way of defence in a suit brought against him by his transferor for recovery of possession.[11]

Section 54 applies to Mahomedans as well; so in places where the Transfer of Property Act applies the rule in Mahomedan law that a sale becomes complete on payment of the price has become obsolete.

Rights and liabilities of the seller under s. 55 of the Transfer of Property Act 1882. In the absence of a contract to the contrary—

(1) the seller is bound—

(*i*) to disclose to the buyer any material defect in the property, or *in the seller's title thereto*, of which the seller is, and the buyer is not, aware, and which the buyer could not with ordinary care discover;

(*ii*) to produce to the buyer on his request for examination of all documents of title relating to the property which are in the seller's possession, control or power;

(*iii*) to answer to the best of his knowledge all relevant questions put to him by the buyer in respect to the property or the title thereto;

(*iv*) on payment or tender of the amount due in respect of the price, to execute a proper conveyance of the property when the buyer tenders it to him for execution at a proper time and place;

(*v*) between the date of the contract of sale and the delivery of the property, to take as much care of the property and all documents of title relating thereto which are in his possession as an owner of ordinary prudence would take of such property and also of the documents;

9 *Madan Mohon* v *Rebate* (1916)21 CWN 158.

10 *Laxan* v *Ramchandan* 139 IC 650.

11 *Narasimhasetty* v *Padmasetty* AIR 1998 Kant 389.

(*vi*) to give, on being so required, the buyer or such person as he directs, such possession of the property as its nature admits; and

(*vii*) to pay all public charges and rent accrued due in respect of the property up to the date of the sale, the interest on all encumbrances on such property due on such date, and except where the property is sold subject to encumbrances, to discharge all encumbrances on the property then existing.

(2) The seller will be deemed to contract with the buyer that the interest which the seller professes to transfer to the buyer subsists, and that he has power to transfer the same.

(3) Where the whole of the purchase money has been paid to the seller, he is also bound to deliver to the buyer all documents of title relating to the property which are in seller's possession and power.

When, however, the seller retains a portion of the property or where he sells the same in different lots to different purchasers, a question very often arises as to who shall have the title deeds. In the former case, the seller retains the title deeds and in the latter event the purchaser, who buys the largest share, is entitled to the custody of the title deeds, but in any case they are to enter into covenant for production.[12]

Although under s. 55(1)(*a*) of the Transfer of Property Act 1882, a seller is bound to disclose any material defect in the property, nevertheless it applies to latent defects which the buyer cannot discover even by diligent searches and enquiries.

In the absence of a contract to the contrary, the seller under s. 55(4)(*a*) & (*b*) of the Transfer of Property Act 1882 is entitled—

(*i*) to the rents and profits of the property till the ownership thereof passes to the buyers; and

(*ii*) where the ownership of the property has passed to the buyer before payment of the whole of the purchase money, to a charge upon the property in the hands of the buyer. Any transferee without consideration or any transferee with notice of non-payment, for the amount of the purchase money or any part thereof remaining unpaid and for interest on such amount or part, from the date on which possession has been delivered, takes the property subject to the charge.

Rights and liabilities of the buyer. In the absence of a contract to the contrary, the buyer, under ss. 55(5)(*a*) to (*d*) of the Transfer of Property Act, is bound—

(*i*) to disclose to the seller any fact as to the nature or extent of the seller's interest in the property, of which the buyer is aware, but of which he

12 Section 55(3) of the Transfer of Property Act.

has reason to believe that the seller is not aware and which materially increases the value of such interest;

(*ii*) to pay or tender at the time and place of completing the sale the purchase money to the seller or such person as he directs: Provided that, where the property is sold free from encumbrances, the buyer can retain, out of the purchase money, the amount of any encumbrances on the property existing at the date of the sale, and must pay the amount so retained to the persons entitled thereto;

(*iii*) where the ownership of the property has passed to the buyer, to bear any loss arising from the destruction, injury or decrease in value of the property not caused by the seller; and

(*iv*) where the ownership of the property has passed to the buyer, as between himself and the seller, to pay all public charges and rent which may become payable in respect of the property, the principal moneys due on any encumbrances, subject to which the property is sold, and the interest thereon afterwards accruing due.

Section 92 of the Evidence Act does not debar the party to contract from adducing evidence for purpose of contradicting recitals of facts mentioned in the documents. The bar imposed by s. 92, sub-clause (1) applies only when a party seeks to rely upon the document embodying the terms of the transaction.[13]

In the absence of a contract to the contrary, the buyer, under s. 55(6)(*a*)(*b*) of the Transfer of Property Act 1882 is entitled—

(*i*) where the ownership of the property has passed to him, to the benefit of any improvement in, or increase in value of, the property, and to the rents and profits thereof;

(*ii*) unless he has improperly declined to accept delivery of the property, to a charge on the property, as against the seller and all persons claiming under him, to the extent of the seller's interest in the property, for the amount of any purchase money properly paid by the buyer in anticipation of the delivery, and for interest on such amount; and, when he properly declines to accept the delivery, also for the earnest money (if any) and for the costs (if any) awarded to him of a suit to compel specific performance of the contract, or to obtain a decree for its rescission;

(*iii*) where two properties are subject to a common charge and one of the properties is sold, the buyer is, as against the seller, entitled to have the charge satisfied out of the other property, so far as such property will extend.

Contract for sale—effect of. A contract for sale creates a right to obtain a sale deed and does not require registration, unless the charge for the earnest

13 *K.M. Rajendran v Arul Prakasam* AIR 1998 Mad 336.

money is created thereby. In view of s. 54 of the Transfer of Property Act it does not create any interest in or charge on the property. Nevertheless, it creates an obligation as recognised in s. 3 of the Specific Relief Act and s. 91 of the Trust Act. The enforceable agreement for sale shifts the benefits of ownership from the vendor to the purchaser if he has paid the price and has taken possession on the agreement. He is not the owner although he is entitled to a statutory charge under s. 55(6)(*b*) of the Transfer of Property Act for the advance made against the property and is protected from dispossession on the strength of his rights under s. 53(*a*) of the said Act.

An agreement to sell immovable property is enforceable by a decree for specific performance.

Extension of time. The fixation of the period within which the contract has to be performed does not make the stipulation as to time the essence of the contract.[14] When a contract relates to sale of immovable property it will normally be presumed that the time is not the essence of the contract.[15] Later, the Supreme Court held that even if it is not of the essence of the contract the court may infer that it is to be performed in a reasonable time if the conditions are (*a*) from the express terms of the contract; (*b*) from the nature of the property; and (*c*) from the surrounding circumstances for example, the object of making the contract.[16] As the Madras High Court recently held even though the time is not the essence of the agreement or the contract that does not mean that the vendor has to go on extending the time eternally and must always be ready to receive the money and execute the sale deed after the lapse of any amount of time.[17] Keeping in view the developments of recent times the Supreme Court recently held that the rigour evolved by courts that time is not the essence of the contract in the case of immovable properties requires to be relaxed. The Apex Court further observed that the courts should bear in mind that when the parties prescribe certain time-limit for taking steps by one or the other party it must have some significance and the said time cannot be ignored altogether. Thus where there was delay or rather total inaction on the part of the plaintiff for $2^1/_2$ years in clear violation of the term of the agreement and this delay coupled with substantial rise in prices the plaintiff was disqualified to get the relief by way of specific performance.[1]

An agreement for sale besides mentioning the property, fixes a time for completion, payment of earnest money or part payment of purchase money. It provides for delivery of possession. It fixes time also for delivery of

14 *Govinda* v *Hari Dutt Shastri* (1977)2 SCC 539; AIR 1977 SC 1005.
15 *Gomalthinayagam* v *Pallaniswami* AIR 1967 SC 868; (1967)1 SCR 227.
16 *Chand Rani* v *Kamal Rani* AIR 1993 SC 1742.
17 *Devchand* v *P. Sivapragasa* AIR 1998 Mad 304.
1 *K.S. Vidyanadam* v *Vairavan* AIR 1997 SC 1751.

requisitions on title and answers thereto, preparation of draft conveyance and approval and return thereof. If any defect in title is discovered before the sale the purchaser is entitled to refund of the earnest money with damages and costs but in case of discovery after the sale he can file a suit for cancellation and refund of the consideration money etc.

Right of reconveyance. Where the operative portion of the sale deed records that all rights and privileges in and concerning the property either in presenti or accruing in future as vesting in the vendor, formed the subject- matter of the sale and that the vendor retained no right of any kind whatsoever, the Supreme Court held that the right of reconveyance under contract for sale was also transferred by the sale deed.[2]

Incidents of conveyancing

(i) *Abstract of title.* Drafting is more a science than an art. The careful draftsman should follow certain principles according to some well-established system to achieve the best result.

The first and foremost requisite, and also it is the duty of the lawyer to study the title deeds minutely and prepare an abstract of title which is a summary of the evidence of the ownership of the property in which all the title deeds are shortened and simplified. A solicitor or advocate may, in course of investigation, come across four types of title: (*a*) Absolute title, *i.e.* fee simple, (*b*) Qualified title *i.e.* freehold but subject to some defect mentioned in the register, (*c*) Possessory title *i.e.* a title acquired by virtue of long possession, (*d*) Good leasehold title.

In England, the common practice, where the title is not registered under the Land Registration Act 1925 is that the vendor's solicitor delivers an abstract of title to the purchaser's solicitor. In America, abstract of title are usually prepared by officials or professional abstractors. In India, the vendor's solicitor or advocate, as the case may be, makes the title deeds available to purchaser's solicitor or advocate for inspection and the latter prepares his own abstract of title.

An abstract of title starts from the document which is the root of the vendor's title to the property and indicates all intermediate transfers or change of ownership by acts *inter vivos* between the parties or operation of law, explains all links in the change of title. In England the root of title as fixed now by s. 44 the Law of Property Act 1925 has to cover 30 years. Originally it was 60 years under the Old Land Registration Act 1862 and thereafter reduced to 40 years by the Vendor and Purchaser Act 1874.[3] And to 30 years by s. 44 of Law of Property Act 1925. Although there is no such statutory limit in India and marketable title is the rule, nevertheless it is an obligation

2 *Khiria Devi* v *Rameshwar* AIR 1992 SC 1482.
3 37 & 38 Vic C 78, s. 1.

on the part of the vendor to establish a title free from any doubt.[4] See also *Duggan* v *Talyar Khan*.[5] A title by adverse possession is a marketable title as held in the above case if the property is acquired openly. The purchaser's solicitor or advocate shall see that at least a title of not less than 40 years is made out, although it is always prudent to investigate title up to 60 years; but if the root is from some Improvement Trust or Government or other statutory body or authority, no investigation of earlier title is necessary. Moreover, in England, under s. 45(6) of the Law of Property Act 1925, re-enacting s. 2 of the Vendor and Purchaser Act 1874 the purchaser cannot question the correctness of recitals of an abstracted deed more than 20 years old unless they are otherwise proved to be inaccurate. There is no such law in India except what are contained in s. 90 of the Evidence Act (1 of 1872).

A perfect abstract is one which contains the effect of all instruments which constitute the title of the vendor and shows that the vendor is the full owner and competent to dispose of the property free from encumbrances.

(ii) *Searches and Inquiries.* The doctrine of *caveat emptor* applies to sale of real estate as also to sale of goods in England, but in India, the same as embodied in s. 16 of the Sale of Goods Act is applicable to transactions as regards movables and purchase at the court sale but, nevertheless, the principle should not be ignored. The purchaser's solicitor or advocate, as the case may be, shall make a thorough search of the public index and map through some responsible person in the Municipal Office, local Registration Office, C.M.D.A., Collectorate, Court, Land Reform Office and Estate Acquisition, and Land Acquisition Office, M.T.P. Improvement Trust, if any, and Insolvency Court to ascertain who is the owner in the public records and other entries affecting the property in particular whether the property is subject to any encumbrance, attachment or other charges or any notice of acquisition or requisition. The Registrar of the Presidency town has jurisdiction to register any document in respect of any property situate anywhere in the Republic of India subject to payment of luxury fee. So it is always prudent to make searches there for a few years even in cases of transactions relating to properties outside the Presidency towns. A purchaser, who makes no enquiry as to encumbrances, is guilty of gross negligence and has constructive notice thereof.[6] Inspection of the Record of Rights is necessary in cases of Muffasil properties. If the party is a Mahomedan, a search is also necessary in the office of the Commissioner of Wakfs and Custodian of Enemy Properties. The Hindu Adoption and Maintenance Act of 1956 has codified the duties of the heirs of the deceased person to provide

4 *Hoje Mahomed* v *Musaji* 15 Bom 657.

5 AIR 1938 Bom 657; 173 IC 714.

6 *Bengal Coal Co.* v *Sitaram* AIR 1935 Cal 667; 61 CLJ 560.

for maintenance of the dependants, *e.g.* aged parents, widowed daughter-in-law, illegitimate children and others. A dependant's claim on that account, though not a charge under s. 27 of the Act but nevertheless the same, can be enforced against a transferee with notice or gratuitous transferee under s. 28 of the said Act. It is, therefore, the duty of the purchaser to make enquiry and be satisfied on this point also. As observed by Maitland (*Equity,* 2nd Ed., p. 117): "The Court of Equity set up a standard of diligence for the purchaser and a high one so high that it is difficult for the purchaser to buy land without having constructive notice of all trusts which concern the land". An enquiry shall be made also of the persons in occupation of the property and their rights also of the tenant or tenants as to the terms and conditions of tenancy[7] and to whom they have attorned their tenancy and also of the advance if any deposited by them, and the litigation, if any, with the owner. The nature of enquiry depends upon circumstances of each case.[8] Failing which he cannot get the benefit of s. 41 of the Transfer of Property Act much less of s. 50 of the said Act.

(iii) *Production of title deeds.* Sections 55(1)(*a*) & (*b*) of the Transfer of Property Act makes it obligatory on the part of the vendor to produce all title deeds which means and includes map paper receipts being evidence of title and answer all requisitions on title.[9] So if there is any link missing in the chain of title or any document is wanting, the purchaser's solicitor would call for an explanation for their absence. In case any title deed is lost or cannot be traced, it is prudent to advertise the loss in the newspaper and to get an inquiry from the vendor on that account.

All certificates about births and deaths of the predecessors in title or ancestors in interest shall be produced. It was held by the Privy Council in the case of *Imperial Bank of India* v *U. Rai Gyaw Thu & Co.*[10] that abstention from enquiry about the custody of the title deeds is an act of negligence and amounts to notice under s. 3 of the Transfer of Property Act.

(iv) *Requisition on title.* See s. 55(1)(*c*) of the Transfer of Property Act. This is prepared by the purchaser's solicitor and sent to the vendor's solicitor or advocate for answers. The answers should be signed by the vendor on all pages. The conditions in the agreement for sale may restrict the right of the buyer as regards requisition both in point of time and about facts to be assumed.[11]

7 *Hunt* v *Luck* (1902)1 Ch 428; 71 LJ Ch 239.

8 *Ram Kumar* v *Mc Queen* 18 WR 160 (PC).

9 See observation of Rankin, CJ. in *Jyotiprasad* v *H.W. Low & Co.* (1930)57 Cal 1189.

10 *Imperial Bank of India* v *U. Rai Gyam Thu and Co. Ltd.* 51 Cal 86; 50 IA 283 (PC); 71 IC 910.

11 Section 55(6)(*b*) of the Transfer of Property Act.

(v) *Marketable title*. It means a title must be free from any reasonable doubt.[12] Good title also means a title free from any reasonable doubt.[13] Under s. 17(*b*) of the Specific Relief Act 1963 a vendor cannot enforce specific performance in the absence of such a title made out by himself. Although every agreement for sale provides for approval of the title of the vendor by the purchaser's solicitor or advocate but such stipulation does not give absolute power to him to reject the title however much good the same may be. He must act reasonably and *bona fide*.[14] A purchaser is entitled to rescind a contract if his solicitor lawyer requisitions and the objections are proper, real and reasonable otherwise the agreement will be binding.[15]

(vi) *Preparation of draft conveyance.* After the vendor has made out a good and marketable title to the property intended to be sold and the same is also free from encumbrances, attachments and other defects and furthermore, there is no dispute about the possession of the vendor, the solicitor or advocate draws up the conveyance and sends the same to the vendor's solicitor or advocate for approval. In case of any doubt or dispute regarding the title of any property situate within the original jurisdiction of the High Court, he can take out an originating summons for the opinion of the court. Although no particular words are needed to validate a deed, the draftsman should nevertheless use such words and phrases as would make the intention of the executant amply clear and the sense is expressed in unequivocal language. The following are the component parts of a valid deed: (1) Date, (2) description of the deed, (3) names, addresses and descriptions of the parties, (4) introductory recitals about the history of the property and motive of the parties behind the proposed transaction, (5) testatum which runs as follows—"Now this Deed Witnesses" etc., (6) consideration and its acknowledgement, (7) operative portion, (8) description of the property by reference to its municipal number, boundaries, survey plots, police station, registration office, etc., (9) reservations and exceptions, if any, *e.g.*, underground rights, right of way, right to discharge water, etc. It begins with the words "Provided Always", (10) habendem which begins as "To Have and To Hold" etc., and (11) covenants—Purchaser's solicitor or advocate shall see that the essential parts of a deed are there in the draft prepared by him so as to make the same a perfect conveyance. In case of transfer by a person who is authorised under certain conditions, they shall form part of the recitals.

(vii) *Execution and registration.* These two things are further necessary for completion of the transaction. A deed is always executed against payment

12 *Oosman* v *Haroon* 47 Bom 369; AIR 1923 Bom 148.

13 *Mahomed* v *Musaji* 15 Bom 657; *Mahamed Ziaid* v *Calcutta Vyapar Prathisthan* AIR 1966 Cal 605.

14 *Clack* v *Wood* 9 QBD 276.

15 *Nusri* v *Netai* 58 CLJ 513.

of the price or the balance by the purchaser and registered particularly if the same comes under s. 17 of the Registration Act. Execution of the conveyance and payment of the consideration are reciprocal. The rule of English law that a contract under seal is valid even without consideration is not applicable in India. Be that so, mere non-payment of consideration does not prevent passing of title unless otherwise intended by the parties.[16] If the price is not paid the seller can sue for it but cannot have the sale set aside. The execution is done according to the English practice at the residence of the vendor or the office of his solicitor. The text of the document must be explained to the executant in cases where he is not familiar with its language or possess a meagre knowledge of the same, more so in the case of *purdanashin* lady and further she must have independent legal advice. All documents should be attested by independent witnesses and in particular mortgage, charge, gift, lease, settlement, bond and will where attestation is compulsory. The attestation means to bear witness to the fact of the execution.

Title under a sale deed passes on the date of the execution of the sale deed and even if the registration of the sale deed is completed on a later date, it must relate back to the date of sale.[17]

(viii) *Possession of the property.* It is to be taken simultaneously with the execution of the deed.[1] The section provides for delivery of possession as permitted by the nature of the property. So when any property is sold with all rights of the vendors and free from encumbrances, he must give vacant possession unless otherwise provided in the agreement. Possession was known as *seisin* in early English Law. Ownership was ignored when not accompanied by *seisin* which was equated with ownership. Such possession was recognised notwithstanding the fact that some other person or persons, even the public at large have a right of way and passage over the same. This is known as the Doctrine of seisin.[2]

Mutation of the name of the purchaser in the Municipal and Collectorate Records should be effected. Mutation does not confer title. The mutating authority cannot decide question of title.

Duties and liabilities of a solicitor in matters relating to conveyancing. Codery in his book on *Solicitors* has said as follows:

> "A solicitor is the trustee, guardian and adviser of his client in all work entrusted to him.[3] He should be extra cautious in transactions relating to trust or *benami* or the property of any minor, widow, lunatic and also when any of the parties is Mahomedan or governed by the

16 *Ghoto Behari* v *Rohini* 13 CWN 692.
17 *Kameshwar* v *State* AIR 1998 Pat 141.
1 Section 55(1)(*f*) of the Transfer of Property Act.
2 Salmond's *Jurisprudence*, 12th Ed., p. 200.
3 *Plowright* v *Lambart* (1885)52 LT 646.

Mitakshara School of Hindu law. It is customary, though not the Rule of Law, for a solicitor to give a certificate as to the good title of the property.""

A transferee acting in good faith and for adequate consideration is always protected in law. A settlement of property made in good faith and *bona fide* in favour of wife and children is not liable to be set aside even if it has the effect of defrauding creditors subsequently.[4] So the mere knowledge of some pending execution or financial embarrassment is not enough inasmuch as the transferee does not share the intention of the transferor to defraud creditors.[5]

A Court of Law does not however lend its support at all to a party when a transaction is tainted with fraud. In refusing its assistance the court acts on the principle of letting the estate lie where it falls. This principle is based upon the *maxim in pari delicto potior est conditio possedentis* (in equal fault the condition of the possessor is far more favourable.

A transferor cannot recover the property from the transferee's possession when fraud has been accomplished by reason of the *maxim in pari delicto*, so it is not necessary that the unlawful agreement should have been fully carried out. It is sufficient if there has been substantial performance of the same.[6]

Rights of a third party are not affected by the sale of the property. Section 53 of Transfer of Property Act 1882 new as: The new section runs as follows:

"53. *Fraudulent transfer.* (1) Every transfer of immovable property made with intent to defeat or delay the creditors of the transferor shall be voidable at the option of any creditor as defeated or delayed.

Nothing in this sub-section shall impair the rights of a transferee in good faith and for consideration.

Nothing in this sub-section shall affect any law for the time being in force relating to insolvency.........."

Fraudulent preferences of a creditor. In the leading case on the point *Musahar Sahu* v *Hakim Lal*[7] Lord Wrenbury observed:

"The transfer which defeats or delays creditors is not an instrument which prefers one creditor to another, but an instrument which removes property from the control of the creditors to the benefit of the debtor. The debtor must not retain a benefit for himself. He may pay one creditor and leave another unpaid.[8] As soon as it is found that the transfer impeached was

4 *Ibrahim* v *Fulbai* 26 Bom 577.
5 *Islan Chander* v *Bishu Sirder* 24 Cal 825.
6 *Mathu Raman Chetty* v *Krishna Pilai* 29 Mad 72.
7 43 IA 104; 43 Cal 52.
8 *Middleton* v *Pollock* 1876 Ch D 104.

made for adequate consideration in satisfaction of genuine debts and without reservation of any benefit to the debtor, no ground for impeaching it lies on the fact that the plaintiff was a loser by payment being made to be preferred creditor, there being no question of bankruptcy. Where, however, the transferor has a fraudulent motive or design, the transferee is protected only if (1) he has acted in good faith and (2) paid consideration for the transfer.[9] A transfer by operation of law or by execution of a decree of a court would be caused by s. 53 if the person who obtained the transfer of the property under an order of the court by practising fraud upon it.[10]

Fraudulent preference and insolvency law. A transfer which prefers one creditor is therefore not within the mischief of s. 53, but where the debtor is adjudged an insolvent, the transfer may be impeached under the law of insolvency as a fraudulent preference. So s. 53 expressly provides that nothing in sub-s. (1) shall affect any law for the time being in force relating to insolvency.

The Transfer of Property (Amendment) Act XX of 1929, in recasting the s. 53 of Transfer of Property Act 1882 has omitted the rule of presumption enacted by the old section and thus brought the Indian law into line with the English authorities.

Partition. Though partition is not a transfer. Instruments of Partition relating to joint family properties brought about with intent to defeat or delay the creditors of the family or of any of its members may be impugned under s. 53 as fraudulent.[11]

(*a*) Where the partition is unequal and the father has been allotted a smaller share that would be his due with intent to defeat his creditors, the latter can avoid the partition under s. 53 and proceed against what would be his proper share in the family properties in execution of the decree obtained against him, ignoring the allotment of the properties at the partition; (*b*) they cannot however proceed against the sons' shares in execution, as the division of status brought about by the partition will stand notwithstanding the avoidance of the partition as a fraudulent transfer; but (*c*) where the partition is fair and in accordance with the proper shares of the parties, it is not liable to be impeached under s. 53, although it was entered into with a view to prevent attachment of the sons' shares in execution of decrees obtained against the father after the partition and was in that sense *mala fide*; and (*d*) a mere colourable partition not meant to

9 Section 53 of the Transfer of Property Act.

10 *Ramanathan* v *Unnamalai* AIR 1942 Mad 632.

11 *Waman Ramkrishna* v *Ganpat* (1935)60 Bom 34; *Vinoyak Samara* v *Moreshwar* ILR (1944) Nag 342; AIR 1944 Nag 44 (FB); *Ratan Devi* v *Jagadhar* AIR 1956 Punj 46.

operate between the parties could be ignored and the creditor could enforce his remedies as if the parties still continued to be joint." Where in a partition no property was allotted to the father who was indebted the partition would be illusory though the sons were directed to pay the father's debts.[12]

Persons entitled to maintenance. Some persons have in law the right to maintenance out of the immovable property in the hands of another. A familiar instance of this is that of the widow in Hindu law to receive maintenance out of joint family property in the hands of her deceased husband's coparceners. As settled by the Supreme Court this right is the pre-existing right of the widow.

Section 39 of the Transfer of Property Act 1882 protects such rights providing that the claim to maintenance would prevail notwithstanding a transfer of the property made with the intention of defeating the right provided the transfer was gratuitous or the transferee took the property with notice of the transferor's fraudulent intention.

Transfer when third person is entitled to maintenance. According to s. 39 of the Transfer of Property Act where a third person has a right to receive maintenance or a provision for advancement or marriage from the profits of immovable property, and such property is transferred, the right may be enforced against the transferee, if he has notice or if the transfer is gratuitous; but not against a transferee for consideration and without notice of the right, nor against such property in his hands.

The Hindu Adoptions and Maintenance Act (Act 78 of 1956) provides for such right of maintenance for some persons, *viz.* wife (s. 18), widowed daughter-in-law (s.19), children including unmarried daughters and aged parents (s. 20) and other dependents, e.g. widow besides parents.

Maintenance whether a charge. The liability to maintenance is in some cases personal, in some cases dependent on possession of inherited property and in others on possession of joint family property. In none of these cases however is the right to receive maintenance a charge upon the assets of the person personally liable or upon the property in the hands of the heir or the manager. It is only enforceable like any other personal obligation until it is made a charge upon property either by virtue of a decree of a court or by agreement between the parties or by the terms of the will granting maintenance. In the absence of a charge, the claim to maintenance could prevail only where the property is alienated in fraud of the claim and the purchaser bought it with notice of such claim[13] and of the vendor's fraudulent intention, or the transfer is of all the property available for payment of

12 *Picha Moopanar* v *Velu Pillai* AIR 1947 Mad 203.

13 Section 39 of the Transfer of Property Act.

maintenance. The beneficiary is a necessary party to the deed of sale as otherwise the same is liable to be set aside.

In the event a wife has a right to maintenance not only from her husband personally but also out of his property, she can pursue the property even in the hands of a stranger who has purchased it with notice of her claim. Bare notice of the existence of the right would be sufficient to make it a burden on the property in the hands of the transferee.[14] It is therefore, prudent to make the wife a party to the deed of sale more so in a case where she is in possession of the property intended to be sold in lieu of maintenance.

Maintenance suit and s. 39, Transfer of Property Act 1882. In *Mst. Dan Kuer* v *Sarla Devi*[15] the property liable to maintenance was alienated on 5th August 1921, and the suit to enforce the maintenance claim was filed on 9th January 1933. Present s. 39 of the Transfer of Property Act was introduced by the Amending Act of 1929. The amended section under which notice of the right to receive maintenance would be enough was in operation at the date of the suit, 9th January 1933. It was held that s. 39 as amended was applicable to the case and that therefore the claimant need only prove that the purchaser had notice of the maintenance right.

Future Ownership

A property cannot remain without any owner:

Future estates fall broadly into two classes—(1) those vested in interest but not immediately in possession and enjoyment e.g. vested remainders and reversions and those contingent which takes effect at a future date on the happening of an uncertain event e.g. contingent remainders and contingent executory interests. A vested interest is the proprietary right acquired in a property except that the right of possession and enjoyment is deferred until the happening of a certain event. In contingent interest neither any proprietary right is acquired nor any right of enjoyment which is also deferred till the happening of a specified event, till such interest becomes vested and the future estate comes into existence there can be no owner or owners to convey the same. A transfer is not complete until happening of the stipulated event which is uncertain. So contingent estate is not transferable, but a vested interest is transferable and heritable. A vested interest is not defeated by the death of the transferor before he obtains possession. The present owner too cannot alienate the estate as contingent interest in discharge of such future interest. A restraint is thus imposed upon alienation although the future interest may never come into existence

14 *Radhabhai* v *Gopal Dhondo* AIR 1944 Bom 50.
15 40 Bom LR 123; AIR 1947 PC 8 at p. 13.

and the event contemplated may never occur.[16] The vested interest is also heritable on the death of the transferee.[17]

In other words a vested interest is not subject to any condition precedent and it takes effect on the happening of a certain event whereas the contingent depends upon happening of a most uncertain condition or event which may not happen at all.[18]

Perpetuity

English law. A perpetuity is an interest which will not vest till a remote period. The period for which vesting may lawfully be postponed is called the perpetuity period. The rule against perpetuity or the rule against remoteness of limitation, defines the perpetuity period and lays down the test of validity of future limitations.[19]

Indian law. Under the Hindu law as it stood before the Hindu Disposition Property Act (Act IV of 1916) a gift to an unborn person not in existence at the time of distribution of the assets was under the rule as laid down in *Tagore* v *Tagore*[1] was void. Since then the law has changed. Section 14 of the Transfer of Property Act is the statutory recognition of the rule— life or lives in existence on the date of transfer and the minority of an unborn person not then in existence but must come in existence at the expiration of that period and be of full age. A perpetuity in the sense of a present interest having a tendency of being indefinitely inalienable has always been held to be invalid. The leading case on the subject is *Sookhmoy Chunder Doss* v *Monohuri Dassi*.[2]

Granting successive life-estate is not permissible under Hindu Law. No one can create an estate unknown to Hindu Law.[3] The rule against perpetuity relates to any property, whatever be its nature and whether it is movable or immovable.[4]

Mahomedan law. The rule against perpetuity embodied in s. 14 of the Transfer of Property Act was once held as having no application to Mahomedans. Nevertheless under the Mahomedan law a gift to remote and unborn generations is invalid except in the case of a wakf. *i.e.* charitable trust.

16 Subba Rao: *Law of Property*, p. 335.
17 *Krishna Aiyar* v *Swanilnath* 47 IC 723.
18 William on *Executors*, 11th Ed., vol. 11, pp. 973-74. See also ss. 119 & 124 of the Indian Succession Act (Act XXXIX of 1925) and ss. 19, 20, 21 of the Transfer of Property Act (Act IV of 1882).
19 See. s. 14 of the Transfer of Property Act and s. 114 of the Indian Succession Act.
1 LR IA Supp vol. 47.
2 12 IA 103 (PC).
3 *Sitesh Kumar* v *Ramesh* AIR 1981 Pat 339.
4 *Cowanji* v *Rustomji* 20 Bom 511.

The scope of this rule was considered by the Privy Council in *Abdul Fata Mahomed* v *Russomoy*.[5] In that case a Mahomedan settled his property in perpetuity on his family with an ultimate gift to the poor was held as invalid. This decision caused great hardship to the Mahomedan community until the Mussalman Wakf Validating Acts 1913 and 1930 was passed providing that for remoteness a Wakf shall not be invalid (s. 4). The present law of Wakfs is governed by the Wakf Act 1995.

Hindu law. No transfer of property can operate to create an interest which is to take effect after the lifetime of one or more persons living at the date of such transfer and the minority of a person who shall be in existence at the time of death of last survivor-beneficiary. This applies to gift as also to bequest and to Private Trust. The rule against perpetuity does not apply to charitable or religious endowments. The rule is contained, *inter alia,* in s. 14 of the Transfer of Property Act 1882 and s. 114 of the Indian Succession Act 1925.

Distinction between the English and the Indian Rules against Perpetuity

The following points of distinction between the English and Indian rules against perpetuity may be noted:

(1) The perpetuity period is different. Under the English law the perpetuity period is a life, or any number of lives in existence when the instrument under which the interest arises takes effect, plus a term of 21 years. Under the Indian law it is a life or lives in being at the time of the grant plus the period of minority of the beneficiary taking under the grant.

(2) Under the English Rules the additional period of 21 years allowed after lives in being is a term in gross without reference to the infancy of any person. Under the Indian statutes the term is the period of minority of the person to whom if he attains full age the interest created is to belong.

(3) The period of gestation, where it actually exists may be added to the perpetuity period as above defined. In English law it admits of addition at both ends of the perpetuity period. But in Indian law it may be added only at its commencement.

(4) The Law of Property Act 1925, by s. 163 has validated certain remote gifts by allowing the substitution of the age of 21 years when the gift is to fail for remoteness on the ground that the ascertainment of the beneficiary or class of beneficiaries is made to depend on the attainment by the beneficiary or members of the class of an age exceeding 21 years. There is no corresponding provision under the Indian law.

5 22 Cal 619; 22 IA 76 (PC).

Pre-emption

History of origin. The law of pre-emption was introduced in this country by the Mahomedans. There is no indication of any such conception in the Hindu law and the subject has not been noticed or discussed either in the writings of the Smriti writers or in those of later commentators. Sir William Macnaghten in his *Principles and Precedents of Mahomedan Law* at page 14 has referred to a passage in the "Mahanirvana Tantra" which, according to the learned author, implies that pre-emption was recognised as a legal provision according to the notions of the Hindus. But the treatise itself is one on mythology, not on law. No value can be attached to a stray passage of this character, the authenticity of which is not beyond doubt.

Pre-emption. (1) Pre-emption is a right attached to the property. It arises from ownership. It protects against intrusion of strangers in the family property so as to check the same going out of family—judicial opinions in this aspect differed until recently on the point that is to say whether pre-emption is an incident of property or it was a mere personal right of repurchase. The Full Bench of Calcutta High Court in *Seikh Kudratullah* v *Mohirti Mohon*[6] held (Norman and Macpherson, JJ., dissenting) that it was a mere personal right. Whereas contrary views were however expressed in Allahabad, Patna and Bombay in *Govinda Dayal* v *Inayatullah*[7] *Achyutananda* v *Biki*,[8] *Dasharathilal* v *Bai Dhondu Bai*[9] which held the right of pre-emption as an incident of the property.

Immediately on payment of the purchase money on or before the specified date the title to the property would vest in the pre-emptor without any further documentation. Where the pre-emptor executed a document describing it as a deed of assignment he clearly transferred his interest in the pre-emptional land and such assignee shall have the same rights which had accrued to the executant decree-holder. It would not be a case of a transfer of a mere decree with the property remaining vested in title in the pre-emptor.[10]

(2) All the divergence of judicial opinion has been set at rest by *A.B. Singh* v *G. Jaipuria*[11] which disapproved the Calcutta view and affirmed the view taken in Allahabad, Patna and Bombay. In other words the Supreme Court held that it is a right attached to the property.

(3) Section 8 of the West Bengal Land Reforms Act (Bengal Act X of 1956) gives right of pre-emption first to co-sharers of the holding analogous

6 4 BLR 134.
7 ILR 7 All 775.
8 ILR 1 Pat 578.
9 AIR 1941 Bom 262 (FB).
10 *Bhoop* v *Matadin* AIR 1991 SC 373.
11 AIR 1954 SC 417; 1955 SCA 132.

to s. 26F, B.T. Act (repealed) and then to owners of adjoining property, *i.e.* right of pre-emption on the ground of vicinage—the owner having longest common boundary having preference. A bargader is also entitled to pre-empt under the Act.

(4) Right of pre-emption does not infringe Art. 19(1)(*f*) of the Constitution of India ensuring to a citizen the right to acquire, hold and dispose of property.[12]

(5) Although there was some confusion earlier about the constitutional validity of the provision relating to right of pre-emption on the ground of vicinage, the enactment having been under the Ninth Schedule of the Constitution by the Constitution (Thirty-fourth) Amendment Act 1974, it can no longer be challenged as violative of any right conferred by Part III of the Constitution.[13]

(6) Section 29A of the Kerala Land Reforms Act was struck down as violative of Art. 14, Constitution of India. The effect of the Kerala Act being included in the Ninth Schedule is that the provision is revived back from the date of the Act retrospectively.[14]

(7) Sale of entire plot cannot prevent pre-emption under the Bengal Act by a raiyat owning contiguous land if the transferor raiyat has other lands or holding anywhere in West Bengal.[15]

FORMS

Agreement for Sale

ENGLISH FORM

ARTICLES OF AGREEMENT made this .... day of ....1999 BETWEEN .... son of .... etc. residing at .... (hereinafter called the VENDOR) of the one part and Mr. .... son of .... etc. residing at .... (hereinafter called the PURCHASER) of the other part. Whereby it has been agreed and declared by and between the parties hereto as follows:

(1) The expressions VENDOR and PURCHASER shall include their respective heirs, executors, administrators, representatives and assigns.

12 *Atam Prakash* v *State of Haryana* AIR 1986 SC 859.

13 *Narayan Chandra Ghosh* v *Sanat Kumar* (1975)2 Cal LJ 79; *Satish Chandra* v *Kalipada Maity* (1977)2 Cal LJ 480.

14 *Koshy* v *State of Kerala* AIR 1976 Ker 108.

15 *Devendra* v *Rekha Pal* 90 CWN 22; (1986)1 Cal LJ 227; (1986)1 Cal HN 183.

(2) The VENDOR shall sell and the PURCHASER shall purchase the property particularly mentioned described in Schedule hereto and hereinafter referred to as the said property as an absolute estate in fee simple or an estate equivalent thereto free from encumbrances, attachments or other defects in title. The vendor shall at his own costs make all other necessary persons join with him in the conveyance whether as conveying parties, confirming parties or assuring parties as shall be required to pass and convey unto and to the use of the purchaser a clear title of the said property free from all doubts as hereunder contemplated.

(3) The price of the property is settled at Rs. .... to be paid by the purchaser as follows (that is to say) a sum of Rs. .... as earnest money immediately upon execution of this agreement and the balance thereof at the time of the completion of the purchase.

(4) Subject to the vendor's making out a good and marketable title to the said property to the reasonable satisfaction of the PURCHASER or his solicitor and performing the other terms of this Agreement as hereunder appearing, the purchase shall be completed on or before the 5th day of December 1999 and the relevant conveyance shall be executed at the office of the vendor's solicitor. Time for this purpose shall be deemed as Essence of Contract.

(5) Upon the PURCHASER paying the purchase money in full, he shall, as from the date fixed for completion, be entitled to possession of the property and shall as from that day pay all outgoings and liabilities in respect thereof; the outgoings and liabilities up to and inclusive of the date of completion being cleared by the vendor.

(6) (*a*) If the completion of the purchase is delayed beyond the date fixed for completion by reason of any act, default or negligence on the part of the PURCHASER in spite of the readiness and willingness on the part of the VENDOR, he shall be entitled to interest on the balance of the purchase money at the rate of 12 per cent per annum from the date fixed for completion of the purchase.

(*b*) No interest shall become payable by the PURCHASER if delay in completion is due to failure on the part of the VENDOR to establish a good and a marketable title to the property or performance or non-performance of any of the covenants, conditions or stipulations contained in this Agreement.

(7) The VENDOR or his solicitor shall on or before the .... day of .... deliver to the PURCHASER or his solicitor an abstract of title of the property intended to be sold and make all the title deeds and other papers and writings concerning the title thereto available for inspection for which he will deliver them to the purchaser's solicitor on accountable receipt.

(8) The PURCHASER shall within 14 days after the actual delivery of the abstract on title and the production of the documents send to the VENDOR or

his solicitor a statement in writing containing all the objections and requisitions (if any) to or on the title and the documents and all particulars and information relating to the same required by him and send back the title deeds and other papers and writings received by him to enable the vendor or his solicitor to answer them.

(9) Any answer to any objection or requisition shall be replied to in writing within 10 days after delivery thereof.

(10) (*a*) If notwithstanding a good and marketable title as hereunder contemplated is made out, the PURCHASER shall nevertheless make any objection or further requisition or requisitions, which the VENDOR is unable to comply with, and the PURCHASER shall not withdraw such objection or requisition within 10 days after being so required, in writing, the VENDOR may, in that event by notice in writing delivered to the PURCHASER or his solicitor cancel this agreement notwithstanding any intermediate negotiations to the contrary.

(*b*) If the contract is so rescinded, the VENDOR shall within three days after rescission, refund to the PURCHASER the entire earnest money but without interest and the purchaser shall return forthwith all title deeds, abstracts and other papers and writings in his possession belonging to the VENDOR and shall not make any claim on the vendor for costs, compensation or otherwise. Otherwise the vendor shall pay a sum of Rs. .... as the assessed costs of the PURCHASER for searches, investigation on title; preparation of the draft conveyance and other connected matters.

(11) (*a*) The conveyance(s) shall be prepared by the purchaser at his own costs and expenses and the draft thereof shall be delivered at the office of the Lawyer of the VENDOR at least 14 days before the date fixed for completion, for perusal and approval on behalf of the VENDOR.

(*b*) The conveyance(s) engrossed on stamped paper ready for execution by the VENDOR shall be left at the office of his Solicitor within four days next after the draft has been returned approved on behalf of the VENDOR.

(12) Upon payment of the purchase money at the time and in the manner aforesaid and tender of the sale deed, the VENDOR shall execute a conveyance of the said property with proper covenants for title, peaceful enjoyment, non-encumbrance and further assurance in favour of the purchaser or his nominee.

(13) The VENDOR shall hand over to the PURCHASER all documents of title relating to the property sold and deliver possession of the same simultaneously with the execution of the conveyance.

(14) (*a*) If the PURCHASER shall neglect or fail to perform his part of the contract, the vendor may give to the purchaser or to his lawyer at least 15 days' notice in writing specifying breach and requiring the PURCHASER to make good the default before the expiration of the notice.

(*b*) If the PURCHASER does not comply with the terms of such notice—

(*i*) The deposit money shall be forfeited to the VENDOR.

(*ii*) The VENDOR may resell the property without previously tendering a conveyance or instrument of transfer to the PURCHASER.

(*iii*) The resale may be made by auction or private contract at such time subject to such conditions and in such manner—generally as the VENDOR may think proper and the defaulting purchaser shall have no right to any part of the purchase money thereby arising.

(15) If in course of searches and investigation of title the property is found to be affected by any notice of acquisition or requisition by the Government or any statutory body or authority or injunction or prohibitory order from any court the PURCHASER shall be entitled to rescind this agreement in which event the VENDOR shall refund the earnest money.

(16) The VENDOR shall have his name recorded in the municipal and revenue records relating to the property as owner of the property unless the same has already been done as will appear from the title deeds.

(17) Notwithstanding anything hereinbefore contained, each party shall have the right to sue for specific performance with or without damages.

The intended sale includes all fittings and fixtures in the property sold as they are now and the VENDOR shall not remove nor cause any damage to any of them before the sale.

(18) Save and except what are hereinbefore provided, the rights and liabilities of the parties shall be governed by the law in force as between VENDOR and PURCHASER.

The Schedule above referred to

(Full description of the property intended to be sold)

IN WITNESS WHEREOF the parties hereto have set and subscribed their respective hands and seal the day, month and year first above-written.

Signed, sealed and delivered
at .... by VENDOR
in the presence of: Signature

Signed, sealed and delivered
at .... by PURCHASER
in the presence of: Signature

MEMO OF CONSIDERATION

RECEIVED from the within named PURCHASER the sum of Rupees .... as earnest money for within-mentioned Agreement for Sale.

WITNESS Signed by VENDOR

NOTE: An agreement as defined in s. 2(*f*) of the Contract Act is a promise and promise forming the consideration of each other. In other words it is the result of mutual assent of the parties. But before it becomes enforceable in law it must fulfil certain conditions (vide s. 10 of the Indian Contract Act), viz. (*i*) free consent of the parties, (*ii*) competency of the parties, (*iii*) lawful consideration. The English doctrine about solemnity of a contract in writing under seal was never applied in India. Although law permits the parties to make their own bargain but inadequacy of consideration raises presumption as to fraud, undue influence etc. vitiating a contract which weighs heavily with a court of Equity in deciding whether a contract shall be set aside or specific performance should be granted or refused under s. 53 of the Transfer of Property Act. Any transfer without consideration motivated by fraud is voidable. The amended section mentions no fraud as inadequacy of consideration unless established by evidence. See also s. 20 of the Specific Relief Act of 1963.

Agreement for Sale

INDIAN FORM

MEMORANDUM OF AGREEMENT made this .... day of .... 1999 BETWEEN .... son of .... by caste .... by occupation .... residing at .... hereinafter called the VENDOR (which expression shall unless excluded by or repugnant to the context be deemed to include his heirs, executors, administrators and representatives) of the one part and............... son of .... by caste .... by occupation .... residing at .... hereinafter called the PURCHASER (which expression shall unless excluded by or repugnant to the context be deemed to include his heirs, executors, administrators, representatives and assigns) of the other part: IT IS HEREBY AGREED by and between the parties as follows:

1. The VENDOR agrees to sell and the PURCHASER agrees to purchase the entirety of the premises No. .... comprising an area of .... cottahs .... chittacks .... sq. ft. particularly mentioned and described in the Schedule hereunder written and hereinafter referred to as the said premises as an absolute estate in fee simple or an estate equivalent thereto subject to a good and marketable title being made in respect thereof and the property being found free from all encumbrances, attachments, charges and other claims and demands at or for the price of Rs. .... subject to the terms and conditions hereunder contained.

2. The PURCHASER has this day paid to the VENDOR the sum of Rs. .... (Rupees ....) as and by way of earnest money and the balance of the purchase money amounting to Rs. .... shall be paid at the time of completion of the purchase. Simultaneously with the execution of this agreement, the VENDOR shall deliver to the purchaser's solicitor on his accountable receipt all title deeds and other papers and writings including the sanctioned building plan and municipal bills relating to the premises and the purchase shall be completed within .... days from the date hereof provided a good marketable title is made out and the VENDOR makes the property free from all encumbrances, claims and demands whatsoever and not subject to any scheme of acquisition or requisition. Time shall for this purpose be deemed to be the essence of contract.

3. The VENDOR doth hereby agrees to answer all reasonable requisitions on title to be made by the purchaser's solicitor.

4. If a good and marketable title is made out and the property is found to be free from all encumbrances, attachments and charges and other claims and demands and not affected by any notice or scheme of acquisition or requisition, the VENDOR will execute a proper conveyance or conveyances in favour of the PURCHASER or his nominee or nominees or assignee in which the VENDOR shall make such other person or persons, if any, join, if necessary, as conveyancing, confirming or assuring party or parties as the case may be to pass and convey an absolute title unto the PURCHASER or to redeem any charge or encumbrance. The VENDOR shall bear and pay all outgoings and liabilities of the property up to and inclusive of the date of sale.

5. The VENDOR shall deliver peaceful vacant possession of a portion of the said premises which is in his occupation and the rest by attornment of tenancy to the PURCHASER at the time of completion of the purchase. In case any other portion(s) now occupied by the tenants falls vacant, the VENDOR shall not induct any new tenant or tenants nor allow the same to be otherwise occupied and shall also deliver vacant possession thereof to the PURCHASER.

6. If a good and marketable title is not made out or the property is found to be subject to any encumbrances, attachments or charges or other claims or demands, the PURCHASER shall be at liberty to rescind this agreement and the VENDOR shall in that event and on demand by the PURCHASER refund the said earnest money with interest @ 15% per annum and shall pay to the PURCHASER a sum of Rs. .... only as settled costs of searches and investigation of the VENDOR'S title and of this agreement as between party and party.

7. If the VENDOR fails and/or neglects to complete the sale after the title being made out as aforesaid or otherwise to carry out any one or more of the obligations on his part as hereunder provided or otherwise required by law, the PURCHASER will be at liberty to enforce specific performance of agreement by institution of legal proceedings or, at his option, may sue the VENDOR for recovery of the earnest money with interest, costs and other reliefs.

8. If on the title being found good and marketable, the PURCHASER fails to complete the purchase within the time aforesaid, the earnest money shall be forfeited to the VENDOR or the VENDOR may at his option enforce specific performance of this agreement by the PURCHASER and the PURCHASER will also be liable to pay the costs and expenses of proceedings for specific performance.

9. The said premises or any portion thereof is not at present affected by any Notice or Scheme of the Municipality or any other local public authority or body corporate. If it be found to be so affected before the completion of the sale, it shall be optional on the part of the PURCHASER to rescind this agreement and in that event the VENDOR shall refund the earnest money to the PURCHASER and shall further pay to his said solicitor a sum of Rs. .... as aforesaid as settled costs of investigation of title and of this agreement.

10. The VENDOR shall procure the necessary certificate under s. 230A of the Income Tax Act 1961 and permission under s. 27 of the Urban Land Ceiling (Regulation and Control) Act 1976, if necessary and produce the same for inspection of the purchaser's solicitor.

The Schedule above referred to

IN WITNESS WHEREOF the parties hereto have set and subscribed their respective hands and seals on the day, month and year first above-written.

Signed, sealed and delivered by
the within-named VENDOR at
Calcutta in the presence of:

Executed by the within-named
PURCHASER at Calcutta in the
presence of:

MEMO OF CONSIDERATION

Received of and from the within-mentioned purchaser a sum of Rs. 1,50,000 as Earnest Money for the within-mentioned agreement for sale by bank draft No. 34, dated 15th December 1999 for Rs. 1,50,000 on X Bank Ltd. payable in Calcutta.

WITNESS: Received

Signature of the VENDOR

Agreement for the Sale of Assets of a Running Business to a Limited Company

AGREEMENT FOR SALE made this .... day of .... in the year 1999 BETWEEN Messrs .... hereinafter called the VENDORS (which expression shall, unless repugnant to the context, include the vendors, their successors and assigns) of the first part and MB Co. Ltd. a company duly registered under the Companies Act 1956 (Act 1 of 1956) having its registered office at .... hereinafter called the PURCHASER (which expression shall, unless repugnant to the context, include its successors in business and assigns) of the SECOND PART, WHEREAS the vendors who have been for some time past carrying on business as cabinet makers and dealers in furniture etc., at .... And whereas the VENDORS have agreed to sell to and the PURCHASER has agreed to purchase the entire stock-in-trade and other assets of their business and transfer the same as a going concern (excluding, however, the liabilities) as on this day for the consideration hereinafter mentioned.

Now IT IS HEREBY AGREED by and between the parties hereto as under:

1. The VENDORS shall sell and the PURCHASER shall purchase the entire stock-in-trade and other assets of the aforesaid business of the VENDORS consisting of lands, factory buildings, temporary constructions, structures, machinery, stock-in-trade, book-debts, benefit of all the subsisting contracts, formula, trade marks, patents, goodwill, rights, concessions, licences and other privileges, more particularly detailed in the schedule hereunder on or after the date when the PURCHASER company shall be entitled to commence business.

2. The consideration of the sale shall be a sum of Rs. .... which shall be satisfied by the allotment to the VENDORS of .... shares in the capital of the company as fully paid-up shares. In determining the amount of consideration referred to above, the machinery, furniture and stock-in-trade have been assessed at their book-value as per balance-sheet as on .... plus a sum of Rs. .... to be paid by the VENDORS to their predecessors in title Messrs .... when making over the business to the latter, while the book-debts (which have all along been considered good) have been taken into account at their full value and the land at its actual purchase price. The value of other assets has for the present been tentatively fixed at .... as correctly as the circumstances permit, subject however to such adjustments (by payment in cash by either side) as may later on be found necessary at the date of the sale.

3. The VENDORS shall make all necessary arrangements for delivering to the company all assets of the said business agreed to be transferred as fully detailed in the Schedule hereunder upon the allotment of the shares to the VENDORS as aforesaid.

4. The purchase shall be completed on the day the PURCHASER obtains the commencement certificates or as soon thereafter as possible, when the VENDORS shall, at the expenses of the PURCHASER company, execute and register a deed of sale as may be necessary for effectually vesting the said assets in the PURCHASER company.

5. That the PURCHASER company shall have no responsibility for the debts and liabilities of the vendors which the vendors shall pay for and discharge themselves.

6. The VENDORS shall at all times keep the PURCHASER company harmless from and indemnified against any or all claims by any person or persons whomsoever in respect of any or all of the assets agreed to be transferred to the PURCHASER company as detailed in the Schedule hereunder.

Schedule above referred to

IN WITNESS WHEREOF the parties hereto have set their respective hands and seals hereunto and to a duplicate hereof, on the day, month and year first hereinabove written.

Signed, sealed and delivered by the within-named VENDOR in the presence of:

Signed, sealed and delivered by the within-named PURCHASER in the presence of:

Model Form of Requisition on Title & Answers

Questions *Answers*

(1) Please produce paid-up Municipal rate bills or receipts for the last 12 years, showing that no taxes are in arrears.

(2) (*a*) Is the property vacant or in the occupation of anybody?

Any other person, if any, interested in the property who is in actual possession of the property (vide Exp. 11 of s. 3 of the Transfer of Property Act 1882).

(*b*) In the latter event, under what right is he in occupation thereof?

(*c*) If the property is held by virtue of a lease, please state all particulars of the lease and produce the rent receipts.

(*d*) Have all covenants and conditions of the lease been observed and performed? In case of any continuing breach necessary steps should be taken for its remedy.

(*e*) Any notice received from the landlords regarding any complaint in respect of the property.

(3) Is the property subject to or affected by any trust, mortgage, charge, lease, lien, lispendens maintenance, marriage expenses, attachment or any other encumbrance or any right of easement in favour of any person or persons?

Questions *Answers*

Any right of pre-emption in favour of any person?

(4) Is the property subject to any prescriptive rights of anybody?

(5) Is the property affected by—

(*i*) any scheme of acquisition of the Calcutta Improvement Trust, C.M.D.A. or Tube Railway?

(*ii*) any scheme of alignment of the Corporation of Calcutta or any other scheme under the Municipal Act?

(*iii*) any notice under the Land Acquisition Act?

(*iv*) Any notice under the Calcutta Metropolitan Planning Area (Use and Development) of Land Control Act (W.B. Act XIV of 1965)?[1]

(6) Are any requisitions of the Municipality or Corporation subsisting in respect of the property including notice re. unauthorized construction, demolition, encroachment, etc.?

(7) Are any impositions or outgoings other than the Municipal rates and taxes payable out of or in respect to the said property?

If so, please state the amount thereof and to whom they are payable and produce receipts, challans, dakhilas or other documentary evidence showing payment up to date.

(8) Is there any defect in the title which it is not possible for the purchaser to discover or ascertain by searches

---

1 Although named as the Calcutta Metropolitan Planning Area (Use and Development) of Land Control Act which received the assent of the Governor on 17th June 1965, the State Government, in exercise of the power conferred under sub-sec. (1) read with sub-sec. (2) of s. 4 may by Notification in the *Official Gazette*, extend its application to any area throughout the State of West Bengal except the Cantonment as declared under s. 3 of the Cantonments Act 1924. These areas are called "controlled areas" where no construction or development is permitted without the permission of the Controller. The Calcutta Metropolitan District extends to the west and east banks of the River Hooghly. The Act has now been extended to the District of Darjeeling which is now declared a controlled area (vide Notification No. 6259-T&C.P. 3a-1/6711 dated 22.10.75). In the result no construction shall be made and development undertaken without the written permission of the Controller who is the Deputy Commissioner of Darjeeling.

Questions	*Answers*

and enquiries but which is or may be within the vendor's knowledge or which the vendor may be in a position to ascertain?

(9) Was any agreement entered into by the vendor previously for sale of the said property to any other party and was any earnest money received? (See s. 91 of the Indian Trusts Act as to acquisition of the property with notice of an existing agreement. Also see s. 92).

(*i*) If so what is the present position with reference to such agreement?

(*ii*) If it was cancelled,

(*a*) on what grounds?

(*b*) was the earnest money refunded?

Please produce the cancelled agreement, if any.

NOTE: If the vendor sells all his properties without any exception the person entitled to maintenance will be deprived of their resources. So it is prudent to issue an advertisement inviting claims and objections to such a sale and to make the dependants particularly the wife of the vendor a party to the sale in case the vendor has no other property or properties.

(10) (*a*) Who are the persons entitled to maintenance against the property under the Hindu Adoption and Maintenance Act 1956?

(*b*) Any suit for maintenance touching or concerning the property. Any portion of the property occupied separately in lieu of maintenance.

(11) Please produce income-tax clearance under s. 230A of the Indian Income-tax Act.

(12) Who are the persons in actual possession of the property and under what rights?

(13) Are there any public rights, easements or any restrictive covenant affecting the property?

(14) Which title deeds and documents will be handed over to the purchaser on completion of sale?

(15) Did the property ever vest in Official Trustee or Official Assignee?

(16) Have all roads or streets abutting on or traversing the property been taken over by the local authority?

(17) Are there any outstanding charges for street works, sewers etc?

Questions *Answers*

(18) Official certificates about the deaths of persons concerned with the property.

(19) Whether any member of the family was given in adoption?

(20) Whether any widow is in possession of any portion of the property in lieu of maintenance?[2]

(21) Any execution proceeding pending against the vendor?

In view of the fact that the purchaser as well as his solicitor desire to complete the transaction with as much expedition as possible, these requisitions are sent before completing the necessary searches and enquires. The right to make further requisitions arising from the result thereof and from the answers to the above requisitions is therefore reserved.

Purchaser's Solicitors Vendor's Solicitors

Special Requisitions in Case of Sale of Agricultural Land

Questions *Answers*

(1) What is the total area of land in the possession of the vendor? Are they all in his khas possession and also under personal cultivation? Are they situated in irrigated or non-irrigated area? Are there any bhagchase in the property?

(2) In case the lands are held since before the acquisition of the interest of intermediaries under the Estate Acquisition Act 1953 have the vendor submitted return in terms of s. 6 of the said Act? Did the vendor file any return in Form No. 10 of the West Bengal Land Reforms Act 1955 (see r. 15A of the West Bengal Land Reforms Rules 1965)? If so, please produce a copy of the same for my inspection. Old rent receipts granted by zamindars are to be produced.

(3) Who are the person or persons actually cultivating the lands and the nature of products? Was there any proceeding or report to the Bhag Chase Board in connection with the land? Any person other than the owner cultivating the same not being a member of his

2 *Ram Kumar* v *Amar* 52 All 572.

Questions *Answers*

family. [*Vide* West Bengal Land Reforms (Amendment) Act 1977. Amended s. 21B of the Act].

(4) What is the total area of lands in possession of the members of the vendor's family? Did the same ever exceed the maximum ceiling limit permitted under the Estate Acquisition Act and its amendments from time to time. Are they also *benamdars* of the vendor or real owners?

(5) Are the lands subject to any levy? How much paddy is delivered by the vendor? Please produce the relevant papers in that connection.

Any proceedings in the High Court in connection with the levy under Art. 226 of the Constitution of India?

(6) Was the land ever subject to any proceeding under the Bengal Restoration of Alienated Land Act (Act XXIII of 1937) or the West Bengal Acquisition and Settlement of Homestead Land Act (W.B. Act XV of 1969)? If so give full particulars.

(7) Name of the Gram Panchayat and taxes if any payable.

(8) Mutation certificate of the J.L.R. rename of the vendor.

(9) Names of the co-sharers in the jama (they have right of pre-emption under s. 8 of the West Bengal Land Reforms Act 1955).

(10) What is the amount of rent and public charges *e.g.* road cess, education cess, etc. in respect of the lands?

Please produce receipts showing payments up to date.

(11) Corresponding C.S. Khatians are to be produced for inspection.

(12) In cases of transfer of land by a member of thc Scheduled Tribes, permission of the Revenue Officer. (Chapter IIA of the West Bengal Land Reforms Act 1955).

Form of Conveyance—English Precedent

THIS INDENTURE MADE THIS .... day of .... BETWEEN AB son of .... etc., hereinafter referred to as the VENDOR which expression shall where the subject or context allows etc. of the one part and CD son of etc. hereinafter referred to as the PURCHASER which expression shall where the subject or context allows, etc. etc. of the other part.

State the recitals concisely and precisely

WHEREAS the VENDOR .... as lawful owner is seized and possessed of or otherwise well and sufficiently entitled to the messuage, tenements, land, hereditaments and premises (hereby intended to be granted and conveyed and hereinafter referred to as the said property) as an absolute and indefeasible estate in fee simple or an estate equivalent thereto free from encumbrances AND WHEREAS the VENDOR has contracted with the PURCHASER for the absolute sale to him of the said property hereinafter more particularly mentioned and described free from encumbrances at or for the price of Rs. .... NOW THIS INDENTURE WITNESSETH that in pursuance of the said agreement and consideration of a sum of Rs. ....to the VENDOR paid by the PURCHASER at or immediately before the execution of these presents the receipt whereof the vendor doeth hereby admit and acknowledge and of and from the same and every part thereof acquit, release and discharge the PURCHASER, his heirs, executors, administrators, representatives and assigns and everyone of them and also the said property he the VENDOR as beneficial owner doeth by these presents indefeasibly grant, sell, convey and transfer, assign and assure unto the PURCHASER, his heirs, executors, administrators, representatives and assigns free from encumbrances, attachment and other defects in title ALL THAT the said premises No. .... fully mentioned and described in the schedule hereto or HOWSOEVER otherwise the said property now or heretofore were or was situate, butted, bounded, called, known, numbered, described and distinguished TOGETHER with the land or ground whereupon or on part whereof the same is erected and built together further with all houses, out-houses or other buildings, erections, fixtures, walls, yards, courtyards and benefit and advantages of ancient and other lights, liberties, easements privileges, appendages and appurtenances whatsoever to the said property or any part thereof belonging or in any wise appertaining to or with the same or any part thereof usually held, used, occupied or enjoyed or reputed to belong or be appurtenant thereto AND the reversion and reversions, remainder and remainders, rents, issues and profits thereof and of every part thereof together furthermore all the estate, right, title, inheritance, use, trust, property, claim and demand whatsoever both at law and in equity of the VENDOR into and upon the said property or every part thereof AND all deeds, pattas, muniments, writings and evidences of title which in any wise relate to the said property or any part or parcel thereof and which now are or hereafter shall or may be in the custody, power or possession of the VENDOR, his heirs, executors, administrators or representatives or any persons from whom he or they can or may procure the same without action or suit at law or in equity TO ENTER INTO AND HAVE HOLD, OWN, POSSESS AND ENJOY the said property and every part thereof hereby granted, sold, conveyed and transferred or expressed and intended so to be with their rights, members and appurtenances unto and to the use of the PURCHASER, his heirs, executors, administrators, representatives and assigns forever freed and discharged from or otherwise by the vendor well and sufficiently indemnified of and against all encumbrances, claims, liens etc. whatsoever created or suffered by the vendor from to these presents AND the VENDOR doeth hereby for himself, his heirs, executors, administrators and representatives, covenant with the PURCHASER, his heirs, executors, administrators, representatives and assigns, THAT notwithstanding any act, deed, or thing whatsoever, by the VENDOR or by any of his predecessors and ancestors in title, done or executed or knowingly suffered to the contrary he the VENDOR had at all material times heretofore and now has good right, full power, absolute authority and indefeasible title to grant, sell, convey, transfer, assign and assure the said property hereby granted, sold, conveyed and transferred or expressed or intended so to be, unto and to the use of the PURCHASER, his heirs, executors, administrators, representatives and assigns in the manner aforesaid AND THAT the PURCHASER, his heirs, executors, administrators, representatives and assigns shall and may at all times hereafter, peaceably and quietly enter into hold, possess and enjoy the said property and every part thereof and receive the rents, issues and profits thereof, without any lawful eviction, hinder and interruption, disturbance, claim or demand whatsoever from or by the VENDOR or any person or persons lawfully or equitably claiming any right or estate thereof from under or in trust for him or from or under any of his ancestors or predecessors in title AND THAT free and clear and freely and clearly absolutely acquitted, exonerated and released or otherwise by and at the costs and expenses of the VENDOR well and sufficiently save indemnified of from and against all and all manner of claims, charges, liens, debts, attachments and encumbrances whatsoever made or suffered by the VENDOR or any of his ancestors or predecessors in title or any person or persons lawfully or equitably claiming as aforesaid AND FURTHER THAT the vendor and all persons having or lawfully or equitably claiming any estate or interest whatsoever in the said property or any part thereof from under or in trust for him the vendor or from or under any of his predecessors or ancestors in title shall and will from time to time and at all times hereafter at the request and costs of the PURCHASER, his heirs, executors, administrators, representatives and assigns do and execute, or cause to be done and executed all such acts, deeds and things whatsoever for further better and more perfectly assuring the said property and every part thereof unto and to the use of the PURCHASER, his heirs, executors, administrators, representatives and assigns according to the true intent and meaning of these presents as shall or may be reasonably required AND FURTHERMORE THAT the VENDOR and all his heirs, executors and administrators shall at all times hereafter indemnify and keep indemnified the purchaser, his heirs and executors, administrators and assigns against loss, damages, costs, charges and expenses if any suffered by reason of any defect in the title of the vendor or any breach of the covenants hereinunder contained.

The Schedule above referred

IN WITNESS WHEREOF the VENDOR has hereunto set and subscribed his hand and seal by the day, month and year first above-written.

Signed, sealed and delivered at

Seal

MEMO OF CONSIDERATION

RECEIVED from the within-named PURCHASER the said sum of Rs. .... being the full amount of consideration as per memorandum below:

WITNESS: Signature of VENDOR

Deed of Sale of House Property

(SHORT FORM)

THIS DEED OF SALE is made this .... day of .... 1999 BETWEEN AB of .... hereinafter referred to as the VENDOR (which term shall unless the context otherwise requires include his heirs, administrators, successors and assigns) of the ONE PART and CD of .... hereinafter called the PURCHASER (which term shall unless the context otherwise requires include his heirs, successors, administrators and assigns) of the OTHER PART.

WHEREAS the VENDOR is lawfully seized and possessed of or is otherwise well and sufficiently entitled to the dwelling-house being premises No. .... in the town .... as its absolute owner in fee simple free from encumbrances which is fully mentioned and described in the schedule hereunder written and hereinafter referred to as the said property.

WHEREAS by an agreement dated the .... day of .... made between the parties hereto the vendor agreed with the PURCHASER for the absolute sale to him of the property on terms thereunder contained at and for the price of Rs. .... NOW THIS DEED WITNESSES that in pursuance of the said agreement and in consideration of the sum of Rupees .... paid by the PURCHASER to the VENDOR simultaneously with the execution of these presents (the receipt whereof the VENDOR hereby admits and acknowledges and of and from the same releases and discharges the PURCHASER and the said property the said AB as beneficial owner does hereby grant, convey, sell, transfer, assign and assure unto and to the use of the said CD free from encumbrances. ALL THAT dwelling-house with compound, outhouse, gardens, garage and appurtenances belonging thereto, commonly called or known premises No. .... situate at, etc. together with the land or ground whereupon or on part whereof the same is erected and built and bounded on the north by etc. (*boundaries on all sides*) containing land by measurement .... Bigha .... cottah .... chittaks .... square feet approximately, which dwelling-house and premises now is (or late) was in the occupation of, etc. as monthly (*or yearly*) tenant thereof, more particularly delineated and coloured red in the map or plan hereto annexed: TOGETHER WITH all buildings, trees, fences, hedges, ditches, ways, waters, watercourses, lights, liberties, privileges, easements and appurtenances whatsoever to the said dwelling-house and premises belonging or in any way appertaining or usually held or occupied therewith, or reputed to belong or be appurtenant thereto.

AND ALL the estate, right, title, interest, claim and demand whatsoever of the vendor into or upon the same and every part thereof in law and equity TO ENTER UPON AND TO HAVE HOLD OWN and possess the same unto and to the use of the PURCHASER, absolutely and for ever together with title deeds, writings, muniments and other evidences of title, AND THE VENDOR does hereby covenant with the PURCHASER, that notwithstanding any acts, deed or things heretofore done, executed or knowingly suffered to the contrary the vendor is now lawfully seized and possessed of the said property free from any encumbrances, attachments or defect in title whatsoever and that the vendor has full power and absolute authority to sell the said property in manner aforesaid. AND the purchaser shall hereafter peaceably and quietly hold, possess and enjoy the said property in khas or through tenants without any claim or demand whatsoever from the VENDOR or any person claiming through or under him. AND further that the VENDOR, covenants with the purchaser, to save harmless, indemnify and keep indemnified the PURCHASER, from or against all encumbrances, charges and equities whatsoever. AND the VENDOR, further covenants that he or they shall at the request and costs of the PURCHASER, his heirs, executors, administrators or assigns do or execute or cause to be done or executed all such lawful acts, deeds and things whatsoever for further and more perfectly conveying and assuring the said property and every part thereof in manner aforesaid according to the true intent and meaning of this deed.

The Schedule

IN WITNESS WHEREOF the said VENDOR and PURCHASER have hereunto set and subscribed their respective hands, the day, month and year first above-written.

Signed and delivered by the within-
named VENDOR in the presence of:

Signed and delivered by the within-
named PURCHASER in the presence of:

MEMO OF CONSIDERATION

RECEIVED of and from the within-named PURCHASER the within-mentioned sum of Rs. .... in full payable under these presents by Bank Draft No. 567891 dated. .... for Rs. .... drawn on PM Bank.

Signature of VENDOR

Deed of Assent from Executor

(SHORT FORM)

THIS DEED OF ASSENT made .... BETWEEN .... AB, son of .... residing .... service-holder executor to the estate of............ deceased under his will dated .... hereinafter referred to as the EXECUTOR to the estate of .... of .... the FIRST PART and CD, son of .... Hindu .... residing at .... and EF, wife of .... residing at............ Hindu .... hereinafter collectively referred to as the BENEFICIARIES of the second part: WHEREAS the parties hereto of the second part are amongst other legatees under the said will of the deceased .... which *inter alia* provides as follows:

* * * *

AND WHEREAS the said will was proved before................. and probate thereof was granted to the said............. out of and under the seal of the said court .... as its EXECUTOR .... AND WHEREAS the said grant is still in force and virtue AND WHEREAS the said AB .... as such EXECUTOR took possession of the estate in pursuance of the said probate, duly discharged all funeral and testamentary expenses and has completed administration of the immovable properties and filed the inventory and account thereof as provided under the grant, and whereas the parties hereto of the second part have requested the said EXECUTOR to assent to the legacy of the immovable property fully mentioned and described in the Schedule below pending realisation and distribution of the movables amongst the legatees in terms of the said will NOW THIS INDENTURE WITNESSETH that the said AB .... as such EXECUTOR as aforesaid doeth hereby and hereunder assent to the vesting of the legacy in respect of the said Premises No. .... in the party of the second part as the BENEFICIARY so as to make their title clear complete and perfect to the property bequeathed under the will of the deceased absolutely and for ever. And this DEED OF ASSENT FURTHER WITNESS that AB as such EXECUTOR doth hereby deliver possession of the said property to the beneficiaries and covenant with the BENEFICIARIES that the said EXECUTOR has not done, executed or performed or knowingly suffered to the contrary or been party or privy to any act, deed or thing whereby or by reason or means whereof the said premises No. .... particularly mentioned and described in the Schedule hereunder written are, is or can or may be in anywise affected or prejudiced in title or estate or he may be hindered and/or prevented from assenting to the legacy in respect of the same in the manner as aforesaid and further he does hereby acknowledge the right of CD as to production of the original probate and inspection to copy thereof or abstract thereof as may be desired. AND THAT the BENEFICIARIES do hereby accept the legacy as testified by their being parties hereto and executing the same.

The Schedule

IN WITNESS WHEREOF the said EXECUTOR and the BENEFICIARIES have hereunto set and subscribed their respective hands and seals the day, month and year first above-written.

Signed, sealed and delivered by	AB
the within-named EXECUTOR	CD
at .... and CD and EF	EF

Beneficiaries in the presence of:

Deed of Transfer from the Executor to the Beneficiary under a will

THIS INDENTURE MADE THIS................ day of.................. 2000 BETWEEN AB son of......... as Executor to the Estate of XY hereinafter referred to as the TRANSFEROR (which term shall unless the context otherwise requires include all persons representing the Estate of the said XY from time to time) of the one part and CD son of........... residing at........... hereinafter referred to as the TRANSFEREE (which expression shall unless the context otherwise requires include his heirs, executors, administrators, successors and assigns) of the other part.

WHEREAS the said XY who was a Hindu by faith and by nationality Indian died on the day of............ leaving *inter alia* the property mentioned and described in the schedule below as part of his estate AND whereas prior to his death the said XY made and published his last will and testament in English language and character whereby and whereunder he appointed the said AB as executor of his said will and trustee of his estate and left and bequeathed the same among the legatees mentioned therein AND whereas by his said will the said XY left and bequeathed the undermentioned property unto and to the use of the said CD, AND whereas the said will was duly proved before the court of......... and probate thereof was granted to the said AB out of and under the seal of the said court AND whereas the said probate is still in full force and virtue AND whereas the said AB has duly paid and/or discharged all the testamentary and general expenses and other debts and liabilities of the estate completed the administration thereof and filed the usual account and inventory thereof on the day of................ Now this Indenture witnesses that in pursuance of the said will and in order to give full and complete effect to the wish and desire of the said XY he the said AB does hereby and hereunder assent to the legacy in respect of the said property as provided under the said will with intent to divest himself from and vest the same in the said CD to all intents and purposes and for that purpose grant, transfer, convey, assign and assure the same unto and to the use of the said CD to have and to hold the same absolutely and forever.

And that the said AB does hereby covenant with the said CD that he, the said AB has not done, executed or performed nor suffered anything to the contrary whereby or by reason or means whereof the said property or any part thereof may be in any way affected or prejudiced in title or estate or that the said AB may be hindered or prevented from granting, transferring, conveying, assigning or assuring the same unto and to the use of the said CD in the manner hereinbefore indicated AND FURTHER THAT the said AB has had at no time heretofore given or made any assent or conveyance affecting the said property or any part thereof in favour of any other person or persons nor expressed or intended so. And furthermore he acknowledges the right of the beneficiary as to production of the original probate and inspection or copy thereof as may be desired.

The Schedule above referred to

IN WITNESS WHEREOF the parties hereto have put their signatures hereto the day, month and year first above-written.

Signed and delivered by the within-mentioned TRANSFEROR in the presence of:

Signed and delivered by the within-mentioned TRANSFEREE in the presence of:

Assignment of a Lease in the Absence of any Restriction on Assignment

THIS DEED OF ASSIGNMENT made this .... day of .... 2000 BETWEEN AB of, etc., (hereinafter called the ASSIGNOR) of the ONE PART and CD of, etc., (hereinafter called the ASSIGNEE) of the OTHER PART.

WHEREAS by an Indenture of lease dated the .... day of .... and made BETWEEN XY described therein as lessor and the said AB, namely, the ASSIGNOR to these presents described therein as lessee of the OTHER PART and registered in Book I, Vol. .... etc. it was witnessed that the property fully mentioned and described in the schedule hereto was granted, transferred, assigned and demised unto and use of the assignor on a lease for a term of .... years with effect from the .... day of .... subject to payment of such rent as thereby reserved and the covenants and conditions thereunder contained AND WHEREAS the said lease is still valid and subsisting and all its covenants and conditions have been observed and performed.

AND WHEREAS the ASSIGNOR has agreed with the said CD, *viz.*, the ASSIGNEE for sale of the said property as comprised in the said lease for the residue of the term thereof at and for the sum of Rs. .... being the consideration thereof. Now this Indenture witnesseth that in pursuance of the said agreement and in consideration of the said sum of Rs. .... paid by the assignee to the ASSIGNOR simultaneously with the execution of these presents the receipt whereof .... etc. (as in the case on conveyance) he the ASSIGNOR as the lessee does by these presents grants, convey, sell, transfer and assign all his leasehold estate or interest of the ASSIGNOR in the said property inclusive of land thereunder acquired under and by virtue of the hereinbefore lease together with all house, outhouses etc. (as in the case of a conveyance) TO ENTER INTO AND TO HAVE HOLD AND ENJOY the same for the unexpired term of the said lease together with all benefits and advantages thereof and subject to performance of the covenants, agreements and conditions provided therein.

AND THIS Indenture further witnesseth that the ASSIGNOR does hereby covenant with the assignee that the said lease is still valid and subsisting and that the ASSIGNOR has duly paid all rents due and payable thereunder and observed and performed all the covenants and conditions thereof AND the ASSIGNOR does hereby covenant with the ASSIGNEE that notwithstanding any acts, deeds, or things heretofore done, executed or knowingly suffered to the contrary the ASSIGNOR now lawfully is seized and possessed of said property free from all encumbrances attachments or defect in title whatsoever and that the ASSIGNOR has the full power and sole authority to assign the said property in the manner aforesaid and the ASSIGNEE shall hereafter peaceably and quietly hold, possess and enjoy the said property without any claim or demand whatsoever from the ASSIGNOR or any person claiming from or under him. AND further that the ASSIGNOR covenants with the ASSIGNEE to save him harmless, indemnify and keep indemnified the ASSIGNEE against all encumbranced charges and equities and the ASSIGNOR further covenants that he shall at the request of and cost of the ASSIGNEE do or execute or cause to be done or executed all such lawful acts, deeds and things whatsoever for further and more perfectly assigning the said property in the manner aforesaid according to the true intent and meaning of this deed of assignment.

AND this Indenture furthermore witnesses that the assignee does hereby agree and covenant with the ASSIGNOR that the assignee shall at all times regularly and punctually pay or cause to be paid the rent payable to the lessor under and by virtue of the lease and observe and perform all the covenants, conditions thereof to keep the lease alive with all its benefits and advantages and shall also indemnify and keep indemnified the ASSIGNOR and his estate against any act, default, negligence or error in judgment arising out of performance or non-performance thereof on his part.

Schedule above referred to

IN WITNESS WHEREOF the parties hereto have set and subscribed their respective hands and seals the day, month and year first above-written.

Signed, sealed and delivered by
the within-mentioned AB, the
ASSIGNOR in the presence of:

Signed, sealed and delivered by
the within-mentioned CD, the
ASSIGNEE in the presence of:

Deed of Sale by a Certificated Guardian of a Hindu Minor

THIS DEED OF SALE made the .... day of .... 1999 BETWEEN AB of, etc., (VENDOR) of the one part and CD of, etc. (PURCHASER) of the other part whereas by an order made by the District Judge of .... in Case No. .... of .... under Act VIII of 1890 (cause title) the said AB was appointed certificated guardian of XY who was then and is still now a minor under the age of 21 years AND whereas by an order dated .... the .... day of .... made by the District Judge of .... in Misc. Judicial Case No. .... of .... the said AB was authorised to sell the lands, hereditament and tenement belonging solely and exclusively to the said minor on terms thereunder contained which property is fully mentioned and described in the Schedule hereto AND whereas the said order is still in full force and virtue AND whereas in pursuance of the said order the said AB as such certificated guardian has contracted with the said CD for absolute sale of the said property at and for the sum of Rs. ....

NOW THIS Indenture witnesseth that for the consideration as aforesaid and in exercise of the powers, authorities and liberties conferred upon and vested under and by virtue of the hereinbefore recited order dated .... and all other powers and authorities enabling him in that behalf the said AB does hereby grant, convey, sell, transfer, assign and assure as certificated guardian of the said minor the said property and every part whereof unto and to the use of the said CD, TO HAVE AND TO HOLD the same absolutely and for ever.

AND THIS Indenture further witnesseth that the said AB does hereby covenant with the said CD that the said AB has not heretofore done, executed, performed or knowingly suffered to the contrary any act, deed or thing whereby or by reason or means whereof the said property or any part thereof may in any way be encumbered or prejudiced in title or estate or the said AB may be hindered or prevented from granting, transferring, conveying, selling, assigning or assuring the same in the manner hereinbefore indicated.

The Schedule above referred to

IN WITNESS WHEREOF the parties hereto have executed this Deed of Sale on the day, month and year first above-written.

Signed, sealed and delivered by the within-mentioned AB, the VENDOR in the presence of:

Signed, sealed and delivered by the within-mentioned CD, the PURCHASER in the presence of:

MEMO OF CONSIDERATION

Sale Deed of Agricultural Land

THIS DEED OF SALE made this............... day of........ 1999 BETWEEN AB, son of........... residing at............ hereinafter called the VENDOR (which term shall include his heirs, successors and assigns) of the one part and Mr. CD son of.......... residing at................ hereinafter called the PURCHASER (which term shall include his successors and nominees) of the other part.

AND WHEREAS the VENDOR is lawfully seized and possessed of or otherwise sufficiently entitled to the property described fully in the schedule below AND WHEREAS the VENDOR (or vendor's predecessor-in-interest exercised his option to retain the said property by submission of B form under the W.B. Estates Acquisition Act 1953 or whereas the property described in the schedule below stands retained by reason of the then raiyat not having agricultural lands beyond the ceiling of the predecessor-in-interest as the case may be. AND WHEREAS the land described in the schedule below has been recorded in the finally published khanda-khatian of the VENDOR or vendor's predecessor-in-interest as the case may be AND WHEREAS the land fully described in the schedule below stands retained by the vendor through operation of family ceiling as envisaged in Chapter IIB, W.B. Land Reforms Act.

AND WHEREAS the VENDOR has obtained previous permission in writing under s. 14C, W.B. Land Reforms Act by Revenue Office for transfer (this is necessary when the VENDOR is a member of Scheduled Tribe but vendee is not—it is appropriate to quote the number of the case through which the permission was obtained).

NOW THIS DEED WITNESSES THAT in consideration of a sum of Rs. .... paid by the vendee or promised to be paid by the vendee or a sum of Rs. .... paid by the vendee out of the total agreed sum of Rs. .... being agreed as the price of the property, and the receipt whereof is being acknowledged the VENDOR does hereby and hereunder grant, convey, sale, transfer, assign and assure all his estate and interest in the scheduled property with all appurtenances, together with all homestead, trees, tanks, hedges, ditches, ways, waters, watercourse, lights, liberties, privileges easements whatever to the land described in the Schedule, to the PURCHASER.

AND ALL the estates, right, title, interest, claim and demand whatsoever of the VENDOR into or upon the same and every part thereof: TO HAVE AND TO HOLD the same unto and to the use of the PURCHASER, his heirs, executors, administrators, assigns absolutely and forever together with title deeds, writings, muniments and other evidences of title AND the VENDOR does hereby covenant with the purchaser, his heirs, executors, administrators, representatives and assigns that notwithstanding any acts, deed or things hereto before done, executed or knowingly suffered to the contrary the VENDOR is now lawfully seized and possessed of the said property free from any encumbrances, attachments or defect in title whatsoever and that the VENDOR has full power and absolute authority to sell the said property in manner aforesaid AND the PURCHASER shall hereafter peaceably and quietly hold, possess and enjoy the said property in khas without any claim or demand whatsoever from the VENDOR or any person claiming through or under him. AND FURTHER THAT the VENDOR, his heirs, executors, administrators or assigns, covenant with the PURCHASER his heirs, executors, administrators and assigns to save harmless indemnify and keep indemnified the PURCHASER, his heirs, administrators or assigns from or against all encumbrances, charges and equities whatsoever. AND THE VENDOR, HIS HEIRS, ADMINISTRATORS OR ASSIGNS FURTHER COVENANT THAT HE OR THEY SHALL AT THE REQUEST AND COST OF the PURCHASER, his heirs, executors, administrators or assigns do or execute or cause to be done or executed all such lawful acts, deeds and things whatsoever for further and more perfectly conveying and assuring the said property and every part thereof in manner aforesaid according to the true intent and meaning of this deed.

Schedule of property

IN WITNESS WHEREOF the parties herein have executed these presents on the day, month and year first above-written.

Signed, sealed and delivered by the within-mentioned AB the VENDOR in the presence of:

Signed, sealed and delivered by the within-mentioned CD the PURCHASER in the presence of:

MEMO OF CONSIDERATION

Deed of Sale of Mortgaged Property, Mortgagee Joining

THIS INDENTURE IS MADE this .... day of ....1999 BETWEEN AB of etc., (VENDOR and MORTGAGOR), of the first part, CD of ...., etc. (MORTGAGEES), of the second part, and MN of, etc., etc., (PURCHASER) of the third part.

WHEREAS BY DEED OF MORTGAGE dated .... day of .... made BETWEEN the said AB described therein as MORTGAGOR of the one part and the said CD described therein as MORTGAGEE of the other part and registered in Book I, Vol. ..... pages .... to .... in the office of .... it was witnessed that the said AB did for the consideration mentioned therein grant, convey, sell, transfer, assign and assure unto and to the use of the said CD the property fully mentioned and described in the Schedule thereto and also particularly written in the Schedule below subject to the proviso for redemption as therein contained AND WHEREAS there is now due and payable to the said CD by the said AB a sum of Rs. .... as principal and a further sum of Rs. .... as interest making thus an aggregate of Rs. .... which sum the said AB has no resources to repay except by sale of the said property as hereunder mentioned AND whereas in the circumstances aforesaid the said AB has agreed with the said MN for sale of the said property at and for the sum of Rs. .... AND WHEREAS the said CD has agreed to join with the said AB in effecting such sale and assuring the same so as to pass an absolute title in the said property unto the said MN free from encumbrances. Now this Indenture witnesseth that in consideration of the said sum of Rs. .... out of which a sum of Rs. .... has been paid to the said CD in satisfaction and discharge of the mortgage debt and the balance retained by the said AB the receipts whereof they, *viz.* the said AB and CD do hereby and hereunder respectively admit, acknowledge and confirm he, the said AB doth hereby and hereunder grant, convey, sell, transfer, assign and assure and the said CD join with the said AB and convey, sell, transfer and release unto and to the use of the said MN the said property and every part thereof TO HAVE HOLD AND POSSESS the same absolutely and forever freed and released from the said mortgage and all moneys due and payable thereunder together with buildings etc.

And the VENDOR doeth hereby covenant with the PURCHASER that except the said mortgage the VENDOR is now lawfully seized and possessed of the said property free from all encumbrances attachments or defect in title whatsoever and that the VENDOR has full power and absolute authority to sell the said property in the manner aforesaid and the PURCHASER shall hereafter peaceably and quietly hold, possess and enjoy the said property without any claim or demand whatsoever from the VENDOR or any person claiming through or under him. And further the VENDOR covenants to save harmless and indemnify and keep indemnified the PURCHASER from or against all such acts, deeds and all encumbrances, charges and equities whatsoever and shall execute and do all such lawful acts, deeds and things for further and more perfectly conveying and assuring the said property and every part thereof in the manner aforesaid according to the true intent and meaning of this deed.

And that the said CD doeth hereby covenant with the said MN that he has not done any act, deed or thing, nor suffered anything to the contrary whereof or by reason or means whereof the said property or any part thereof may be in any way affected or prejudiced in title or estate. And that he has full power and absolute authority to grant, convey, sell, transfer, assign and release the same in the manner hereinbefore indicated.

Schedule above referred to

IN WITNESS WHEREOF the parties have executed these presents on the day, month and year first above-written.

Signed, sealed and delivered by the VENDOR in Calcutta in the presence of:

Signed, sealed and delivered by the PURCHASER in Calcutta in the presence of:

Signed, sealed and delivered by the MORTGAGEE in Calcutta in the presence of:

MEMO OF CONSIDERATION

Deed of Sale by Co-owners of Undivided Property

THIS DEED OF SALES IS MADE on .... day of .... 1999, BETWEEN AB, son of .... residing at .... and CD, son of .... residing at ...., hereinafter referred to as the VENDORS (which term shall include their heirs, successors and legal representatives) of the one part and EF, son of .... residing at .... hereinafter referred to as the PURCHASER (which term shall include his successors, nominees and assignees) of the other part.

WHEREAS one PQ late of, etc. who was a Hindu governed by the Dayabhaga or Bengal School of Hindu Law died on the .... day of .... intestate, leaving him surviving only two sons *viz*., the said AB and CD as his heirs and legal representatives under the said school and whereas the said PQ left *inter alia* the following property as part of his estate AND whereas the estate of the said PQ has been fully administered AND WHEREAS the said AB and CD are in joint possession and enjoyment of the property hereinafter described as co-owners in equal shares without effecting any partition or division thereof AND WHEREAS the said AB and CD have agreed to sell the said properties free from encumbrances, to the said EF for the sum of

Rs. ....*Now this deed witnesses* that in pursuance of the said agreement and in consideration of the sum of Rupees ...., paid to the said AB and CD by the said EF at or immediately before execution of these presents the receipt whereof the said AB and CD hereby admit, acknowledge and confirm, they, the said AB and CD and each as beneficial owner of one equal undivided moiety thereof do hereby and hereunder grant, convey, sell, transfer, assign and assure unto and to the use the said EF ALL THAT, etc. (*parcel etc., as in a conveyance*): TO HAVE AND TO HOLD the same unto and to the use of the said EF, his heirs, executors, administrators, representatives and assigns absolutely and forever.

AND THE VENDOR doth hereby covenant with the PURCHASER that notwithstanding any act, deed, matter or thing whatsoever by the VENDOR or any person lawfully or equitably claiming by, from, through, under or in trust for the VENDOR, made, done committed or omitted or knowingly suffered the contrary the VENDOR hath the rightful power and absolute authority to grant, convey and assure the said premises hereby convey and assure the said premises hereby and assure and intended so to be unto and the use of the PURCHASER in the manner aforesaid and it shall be lawful for the PURCHASER from time to time and at all times hereafter peaceably and quietly to enter upon possess and enjoy the said premises described in the Schedule hereunder written and to receive all rents issues and profits thereof and of every part thereof to and for the Purchaser's own use and benefit without any suit lawful eviction interruption claim or demand whatsoever for or by the VENDOR or any person lawfully or equitably claiming or to claim by, under or in trust for VENDOR and that free and clear and freely and clearly and absolutely acquitted exonerated and forever discharged or otherwise by the VENDOR well and sufficiently saved, defended and kept harmless and indemnified of from and against all former and other estates titles charges and encumbrances whatsoever had made executed occasioned or suffered by the VENDOR or any other person lawfully or equitably claiming or to claim by from under or in trust for VENDOR and further that the VENDOR and all persons having or lawfully or equitably claiming any estate or interest whatsoever in the said premises or any of them or any part thereof from under or in trust for the VENDOR shall and will from time to time and at all times hereafter at the request and costs of the PURCHASER do and execute or cause to be done and executed all such further and other lawful reasonable acts, deeds, things and assurances in the said land hereditaments and premises whatsoever for the better and more perfectly assuring the said premises described in the Schedule hereunder written and for every part thereof unto and to the PURCHASER in the manner aforesaid as by the PURCHASER shall be reasonably required.

The Schedule above referred to

IN WITNESS WHEREOF the parties herein have executed these presents on the day, month and year first above-written.

Signed, sealed and delivered by
the within-mentioned VENDOR
in the presence of:

Signed, sealed and delivered by
the within-mentioned PURCHASER
in the presence of:

MEMO OF CONSIDERATION

RECEIVED of and from the within-named PURCHASER the sum of Rs. .... (Rupees ....) being the full consideration mentioned above by Bank Draft No. .... dated .... for Rs. .... on X Bank Ltd., Calcutta Branch.

WITNESS Received

Signature

Deed of Sale of Joint Family Property for Legal Necessity

THIS DEED OF SALE made this............ day of........... 2000 BETWEEN AB for self and as karta of and representing all other coparceners, *viz*., his sons named .... all constituting a Hindu Mitakshara undivided family of, etc., (hereinafter called the VENDOR) which expression shall, where the subject or context allows, be deemed to include at all times hereafter all persons being from time to time the coparceners of the said family of the one part and CD of etc. (hereinafter called the PURCHASER) of the other part.

WHEREAS the said joint family for several years past owned and still owns and possesses *inter alia* the lands, hereditaments and premises described in Schedule A hereto as part of its estate AND WHEREAS the said joint family also carried on and still carries on business as dealers and suppliers of .... at No. .... under the name and style of .... which suffered a heavy loss of its capital and reserves estimated at Rs. .... in the year .... owing to outbreak of fire .... at its godown at No. .... on the day of .... AND WHEREAS the joint family could not also pay its income tax and other capital and revenue liabilities of the said business aggregating to Rs. .... for the years .... and also its business debts estimated at Rs. .... AND whereas the said joint family has at present no funds nor any other means or resources to make up the deficit as regards capital loss and to pay the liability of the family as regards the said income-tax except by sale of one of its properties AND WHEREAS in the circumstances aforesaid the said AB for self and as Karta of the said joint family has by an agreement in writing dated .... agreed with the said CD for sale of the property fully mentioned and described in the Schedule hereto at and for the sum of Rs. .... AND WHEREAS such sale is to the interest and for the benefit of the said joint family and its estate. And whereas the said CD after *bona fide* and independent enquiry is satisfied about the present financial condition of the family and in particular the debts and liabilities as aforesaid and the reasons for circumstances behind and the necessity for the sale. Now this Indenture witnesseth that in pursuance of the said agreement and in consideration of the sum of Rs. .... paid by the said CD to the said AB simultaneously with the execution of these presents he, the said AB both hereby and hereunder for self and as karta for and representing all other coparceners of the said joint family do hereby grant, sell, convey, transfer, assign and assure the said property together with all houses, buildings, fixtures etc. (as usual in a conveyance) unto and to the use of the said CD absolutely and forever.

AND THE VENDOR doth hereby covenant with the PURCHASER that notwithstanding any act, deed, matter or thing whatsoever by the VENDOR or any person lawfully or equitably claiming by, from, through, under or in trust for the VENDOR, made, done committed or omitted or knowingly suffered the contrary the VENDOR hath the rightful power and absolute authority to grant, convey and assure the said premises hereby and assure and intended so to be unto and the use of the PURCHASER in the manner aforesaid and it shall be lawful for the PURCHASER from time to time and at all times hereafter peaceably and quietly to enter upon possess and enjoy the said premises described in the Schedule hereunder written and to receive all rents issues and profits thereof and of every part thereof to and for the Purchaser's own use and benefit without any suit lawful eviction interruption claim for or demand whatsoever for or by the VENDOR or any person lawfully or equitably claiming or to claim by, under or in trust for VENDOR and that free and clear and freely and clearly and absolutely acquitted exonerated and forever discharged or otherwise by the VENDOR well and sufficiently saved defended and kept harmless and indemnified of from and against all former and other estates titles charges and encumbrances whatsoever had made executed occasioned or suffered by the VENDOR or any other person lawfully or equitably claiming or to claim by, from, under or in trust for VENDOR and further that the VENDOR and all persons having or lawfully or equitably claiming any estate or interest whatsoever in the said premises or any of then or any part thereof from under or in trust for the VENDOR shall and will from time to time and at all times hereafter at the request and costs of the PURCHASER do and execute or cause to be done and executed all such further and other lawful reasonable acts, deeds, things and assurances in the said land hereditaments and premises whatsoever for the better and more perfectly assuring the said premises described in the Schedule hereunder written and for every part thereof unto and to the PURCHASER in the manner aforesaid as by the PURCHASER shall be reasonably required.

The Schedule above referred to

IN WITNESS WHEREOF the parties herein have executed these presents on the day, month and year first above-written.

Signed, sealed and delivered by
the within-mentioned VENDOR
in the presence of:

Signed, sealed and delivered by
the within-mentioned PURCHASER
in the presence of:

MEMO OF CONSIDERATION

RECEIVED of and from the within-named PURCHASER the sum of Rs. .... (Rupees ....) being the full consideration mentioned above by Bank Draft No. .... dated .... for Rs. .... on X Bank Ltd., Calcutta Branch.

WITNESS

Received

Signature

Conveyance on Sale of Property by the Executor

THIS DEED OF SALE made this .... day of .... 2000 BETWEEN AB, son of, etc., as executor to the estate of XY (hereinafter called the VENDOR) which expression shall, where the subject or context allows or admits to be deemed to include person or persons being representing the said estate and all beneficiaries from time to time of the one part and EF Ltd., a public limited company whose registered office is at etc. (hereinafter called the PURCHASER) of the other part.

WHEREAS the said XY, late of, etc., died on the .... day of .... leaving a will dated, etc., whereby and whereunder he appointed the VENDOR to be the executor and trustee thereof, And whereas the said will was duly proved before the District Judge of .... in Probate Case No. .... of .... and probate thereof was granted to the said AB on the .... day of .... AND WHEREAS the said grant is still in full force and virtue And whereas by virtue of the grant of the probate the estate of the deceased was vested in the said AB for the purpose of representation and administration AND WHEREAS the said AB has paid all funeral and testamentary expenses and filed the inventory and account in the court AND WHEREAS and in order to complete administration of the estate it is now necessary to sell some portion of the estate for payment of certain debts and discharge of the legacies provided for in the will, specified in Schedule A hereunder written there having been no funds to the credit of the estate or any other available resources, the said AB has agreed with the said EF Ltd. to sell the property fully mentioned and described in Schedule B below at and for the price of Rs. .... the same being the highest offer received so far according to present conditions of the market, AND WHEREAS the intended sale is in due course of administration and for the benefit of the estate. Now this Deed of Sale witnesses that in pursuance of the said agreement and in consideration of the sum of Rupees .... now paid by the PURCHASERS to the VENDOR (the receipt of which sum the VENDOR do hereby acknowledge), the said AB as executor to the estate of the said XY doth hereby grant, convey, sell, transfer, assign and assure (description of the property) unto and to the use of the said EF Ltd. TO HAVE AND TO HOLD the same absolutely and forever.

And this Indenture further witnesses that the said CD do hereby join with the said AB and ratify and confirm these presents for enabling the said AB to grant, convey, sell, transfer, assign and assure unto and to the use of the said EF Ltd. the said property in the manner hereinbefore indicated.

AND the Deed of Sale further witnesses that the said AB doth hereby covenant with the said EF Ltd. that the said property is free from all encumbrances and attachments and further that the said AB has not at any time done, executed or performed or suffered to the contrary or been party or privy to any act, deed or thing whereby or by reason or means whereof the said property is or may be impeached, charged, encumbered or affected or whereby the said AB be prevented from transferring or conveying the said property in the manner aforesaid and furthermore that the said AB has not at any time heretofore assented to the vesting of the said property nor given nor made any conveyance or conveyances thereof in favour of any person or persons whomsoever.

IN WITNESS, etc.,

A

Schedule of the debts and legacies AB

CD

B

Schedule of the property sold

Signed, sealed and delivered

NOTE: It is prudent to have the deed attested by the adult coparceners with the endorsement as follows: "I attest this document with full knowledge of its contents".

NOTE: Section 307 of the Indian Succession Act—

An executor has power to sell any property of the deceased which vests in him under sec. 211 of the Act. He has no beneficial interest in the estate. So it is prudent to make the beneficiaries parties to the deed of sale.

Power of executor. The executors are vested with large powers as extensive as those enjoyed by executor in England before 1926.[3] The principle why executors are vested with such large powers was stated by Lord Thurlow in *Scott* v *Tyler*[4]: "IT is of great consequence that no rules should be laid down

3 *Gitarani* v *Narendra Krishna* 60 Cal 394; AIR 1933 Cal 429.
4 2 Dick 725.

here which may impede executors in their administration or render their disposition of the testator's effects unsafe or uncertain to the purchaser, his title is complete by sale and delivery what becomes of the price is of no concern to them."

The alienee from an executor who is acting as such has a right to infer that the latter is acting fairly. The fact that the alienation does not purport to be made for administrative purposes does not affect his title. The alienee is not bound to see to the application of the money. The immunity is however lost when the alienee has notice, actual or constructive, of the title of other persons and of the fact that the executor is acting in breach of trust, or the alienation is made for purposes which the executor has no power to do in the course of the administration.[5] This section does not mean that an executor must be clothed with a probate of the will before he can dispose of any property of the testator. The title of the executor is derived from the will and not from the probate, the definition of "executor" in s. 2(*c*) does not suggest that probate is any part of his title. Consequently it is impossible to hold that unless probate is obtained the executor has no power of disposal at all.[6] An alienation made by an executor before the grant of probate is validated if the probate is subsequently granted.[7]

Agreement for Sale of Stock-in-Trade, Furniture and Effects

THIS AGREEMENT IS MADE this .... day of ....1999 BETWEEN AB of etc. (hereinafter called the VENDOR), of the one part, and CD of etc. (hereinafter called the PURCHASER), of the other part:

NOW THIS AGREEMENT WITNESSES and the parties hereby agree as follows:

1. The VENDOR will sell and the PURCHASER will purchase, at the valuation and upon the terms hereinafter mentioned, all the stock, implements, trade utensils, household furniture, fixtures, fittings and effects fully mentioned and described in the Schedule hereunder now being in and about the, etc., premises, at present in occupation of the VENDOR.

2. The sale of the stock, implements, etc., shall be "as they are and where they are" and no complaint on any account shall be entertained after the sale.

3. The PURCHASER shall deposit with the VENDOR a sum of Rs. .... as earnest money and shall pay the balance immediately after the valuation is

5 *Adeline Maud Elenor* v *Sunderlal* 85 CLJ 256; AIR 1950 Cal 559 relied on the *Tincouri* v *Narayan* AIR 1957 Cal 364.

6 *Venkatasubbamma* v *Ramayya* 55 Mad 443 (PC); 62 MLJ 365; 36 CWN 441 (455); 136 IC 111; AIR 1962 PC 92.

7 *Khaivala Venkata Subamma* v *Katreddi Rammayya* 59 IA 112 (PC).

made unless the time for payment is extended by mutual consent when and in such event the goods shall be at the risk of the PURCHASER.

4. The valuation of the goods shall be made on or before the .... day of .... unless the date is extended by mutual consent when the PURCHASER shall make it convenient to attend at the sale and shall immediately upon completion thereof pay the balance to the VENDOR, who will thereupon deliver to the purchaser possession of the said movables and effects.

5. The said valuation will be made by two independent valuers, one to be chosen by each party, or by an umpire to be chosen by such valuers before entering upon such valuation, and such valuation shall be deemed to be, for all purposes, an arbitration within the meaning of the Arbitration and Conciliation Act 1996 and its statutory re-enactment or modification.

6. In the case the PURCHASER shall refuse or neglect to pay the balance amount on such valuation on the date thereof, he shall lose and forfeit the deposit and the goods shall be sold by auction and he shall further be liable for the shortfall, if any. If however, the VENDOR refuses or neglects to deliver up possession of the said movables and effects, then and in such an event he shall be liable to pay to the PURCHASER a sum of Rs. .... as liquidated damages, and this deed shall become void to all intents and purposes.

The Schedule of goods above referred to

IN WITNESS WHEREOF the parties hereto have executed these presents on the day, month and year first above-written.

Signed, sealed and delivered by the
said AB in presence of: AB

Signed, sealed and delivered by the
said CD in presence of: CD

Sale of Ownership Flats

THIS CONVEYANCE MADE this the. .... day of .... 1999, BETWEEN AB son of .... hereinafter referred to as the VENDOR which expression unless repugnant to the context shall mean and include the said vendor, his heirs, successors, executors, administrators and assigns of the ONE PART AND CD son of .... hereinafter referred to as the PURCHASER which expression unless repugnant to the context shall mean and include the said purchaser, his heirs, successors, executors, administrators and assigns of the OTHER PART witnesses as follows:

WHEREAS the VENDOR the sole and absolute owner of the multi-storeyed building consisting of .... floors divided into .... flats with all other houses, outhouses, garages, servants' quarters and other erections, fittings and fixtures together and with the piece or parcel of land or grounds thereunder whereupon or on part whereof the same is erected and built being premises No. .... fully mentioned and described in Schedule A hereto and hereinafter referred to as the said building AND WHEREAS the VENDOR offered sale of the said flats as ownership flats AND WHEREAS by an agreement dated .... made between the parties the VENDOR agreed to sell and the PURCHASER agreed to purchase and thereby own the flat in the front portion of the third floor of the building known as flat No. .... with sole exclusive transferable and irrevocable right to use the same together with undivided .... share of interest in the staircase and equipments other common parts services and of the building. NOW THE INDENTURE WITNESSES that in pursuance of the said agreement and in consideration of the sum .... paid by the PURCHASER to the VENDOR the receipt of which sum the VENDOR hereby acknowledges, the said VENDOR as beneficial owner does hereby grant, convey, transfer and assign, assure unto the said PURCHASER free from all encumbrances the flat on the front portion of the second storey of .... being the property described in Schedule B hereunder written with half the depth in all the joints above between its ceiling and the floor above and also between the floor and its ceiling of the flat below and with full ownership of all doors, windows, fittings, fixtures both sanitary and electrical, all external and internal walls with .... share or interest in the staircase, land below and all ways and passages, drains, water courses, together with the benefit of all ancient and other lights, liberties, easements, appendages and appurtenances and all estate right, title, interest, property claim, whatsoever of the VENDOR in the said flat free from encumbrances and attachments whatsoever to have and hold the property hereby conveyed to the PURCHASER absolutely.

AND THAT the VENDOR doth hereby covenant and agree with the PURCHASER that notwithstanding any acts, deeds or things heretofore done executed or knowingly suffered to the contrary the VENDOR is now lawfully seized and possessed of the said property free from any encumbrances attachments or defects in title whatsoever and that the VENDOR has full power and absolute authority to sell the said property in the manner aforesaid.

AND the PURCHASER shall hereafter peaceably and quietly hold, possess and enjoy the said property in khas or through tenant without any claim or demands whatsoever from the VENDOR or any person claiming through or under him.

AND FURTHER that the VENDOR covenants with the PURCHASER to save harmless from and indemnified against all encumbrances, charges and claims whatsoever.

AND the VENDOR further covenants that he shall at the request of and costs of the PURCHASER do and execute or cause to be done or executed all such lawful deeds and things whatsoever for further and more perfectly conveying and assuring the said property and every part thereof in the matter aforesaid according to the true intent and meaning of the Deed.

And it is further agreed and declared between the parties as follows:

(1) The PURCHASER shall be liable to pay directly to the authorities or contribute in proportion to the floor area of the flat and garage, if any, hereby conveyed to the PURCHASER towards payment of municipal taxes and other outgoings payable in respect of the property and in cases where the said payments are not made directly to any statutory authority then the same shall be made by the PURCHASER to the co-owners of the flats in the building represented by the co-operative of the purchasers of the flats in the building for the said purpose and the said co-owners as a body shall have right of attachment and sale of the purchaser's flat No. .... as security for the dues as aforesaid in case of non-payment.

(2) The PURCHASER shall have full and absolute proprietary rights such as the VENDOR derives from his title save and except that of demolishing or committing waste in respect of the property described in Schedule B in any manner so as to affect the VENDOR or other co-owners who have already purchased and acquired or may hereafter purchase or acquire similar property rights as covered by this conveyance.

(3) The PURCHASER shall also be entitled to sell, mortgage, lease or otherwise alienate the property hereby conveyed subject to the terms herein contained to any one without the consent of the VENDOR or any other co-owner who may have acquired before and who may hereafter acquire any right, title or interest similar to those acquired by the PURCHASER under the terms of this conveyance.

(4) The PURCHASER'S undivided interest in the soil as more fully described in Schedule C hereunder written shall remain joint for all times with the VENDOR and/or other co-owners who may thereafter or heretobefore have acquired right, title and interest in the land and in any flat/garage in the building, it being hereby declared that the interest in the soil is impartible.

(5) The PURCHASER shall have the right and ownership of the servants' quarters and the garage indicated in the map or plan hereunto annexed which are also hereunder conveyed and allotted for his separate use.

Schedule A

Description of the property

Schedule B

Schedule of property hereby conveyed

(*a*) Flat No. .... on .... floor in building named .... under Municipal No. .... comprising a floor area of .... sq. ft. with all doors, windows, fittings, fixtures, walls consisting of .... rooms .... bath .... kitchen.

(*b*) The VENDOR'S entire right, title and interest in all common parts and services the .... which shall be impartible together with the owners of the other flats in the said building.

Schedule C

Particulars of undivided interest in the soil

IN WITNESS WHEREOF the parties have put their signatures hereunto on the day, month and year first above-written.

Signed, sealed and delivered by the VENDOR in Calcutta in the presence of:

Signed, sealed and delivered by the PURCHASER in Calcutta in the presence of:

MEMO OF CONSIDERATION

RECEIVED of and from the within-mentioned PURCHASER a sum of Rs. .... being full consideration within-mentioned and payable by PURCHASER to the VENDOR by Bank Draft No. 6 dated .... for Rs. .... on X Bank Ltd. payable in Calcutta.

WITNESSES: Received

Signature of the VENDOR

Deed of Sale of a Business and Assignment of Goodwill

THIS INDENTURE MADE THIS.............. day of........... 1999 BETWEEN AB son of......... residing at........... hereinafter referred to as the VENDOR (which term shall unless inconsistent with the contexts include his heirs, administrators and assigns) of the one part and CD, son of............. residing at................ hereinafter referred to as the PURCHASER (which term shall unless inconsistent with the context shall include his heirs, successors, administrators, executors and assigns) of the other part.

WHEREAS the said AB has been carrying on the trade and business of, etc., etc., at premises No. ...... under the name and style of .... AND WHEREAS the said AB has contracted with the said CD for the sale to him of all his stock-in-trade and other assets and goodwill of the said trade of and the business in entirety as a going concern together with all book debts and other debts and all rights and benefits of all pending contracts, orders, securities, etc., full particulars whereof are contained in the books of the said business and all moneys due and payable to the said AB on account therefor whether adjusted or unadjusted subject however to all contracts, orders and engagements which are still to be executed or for which the said AB is otherwise liable; at and for the sum of Rs. .... upon the terms hereinafter mentioned: AND WHEREAS the said AB has delivered to the said CD the books of account and other books relating to the said business containing full particulars of the debts, respectively due and owing to and from the said AB and also the particulars of the contracts and engagements to which he is liable in respect of the said business: NOW THIS DEED OF SALE WITNESSES that in pursuance of the said agreement and in consideration of the sum of Rupees .... paid by the said CD to the said AB (the receipt whereof the said AB hereby admits and acknowledges), and also in consideration of the covenants and conditions hereunder contained to be observed and performed on the part of the said CD the said AB does hereby and hereunder grant, convey, sell, transfer, assign and assure unto and to the use of the said CD all that the trade or business carried under the name and style of .... at premises No. .... with ALL beneficial interest and goodwill of the said AB, in the said trade and business of, etc. so carried on by him as aforesaid, and also all the book and other debts now due and owing to him on account of the said trade and the business and all securities for the same, and also all contracts and engagements and benefits and advantages thereof which have been entered into with the said AB and also all the stock-in-trade goods, fixtures, articles and things which, at the date of this deed, belong to the said AB on account of the said trade and business, and all the right, title and interest of the said AB to and in the said premises: TO HAVE AND TO HOLD the same to the said CD absolutely.

AND THAT THE SAID AB does hereby covenant with the said CD that he, the said AB, will not at any time hereafter, either by himself or in collaboration with any other person or persons, or as a partner or as a director of any limited company carry on the said trade and business of, etc., within a radius of .... miles of, etc. AND that the amount and particulars of the debts respectively due and owing to and from the said AB on account of the said trade and business and the particulars of the contracts and engagements to which he is liable with respect to the said trade and business, are correctly stated in the books of account and other books delivered by the said AB to the said CD AND further that the said AB will pay or cause to be paid all and every sum to the said trade and business in excess of the amount or amounts which by the said books appear to be so due and owing AND furthermore that the said AB has good right, full power, absolute authority and title to grant, convey, sell, transfer, assign and assure the trade or business of "...." unto and to the use of the said CD in the manner hereunder indicated together with the benefit of the tenancy according to the nature and tenure of the contract. AND THIS INDENTURE also WITNESSES that in pursuance of the said agreement in this behalf and in consideration of the premises, the said CD does hereby agree with the said AB that he, the said CD, shall and will from time to time and at all times hereafter execute and perform all outstanding contracts and orders and engagements and/or otherwise save harmless, indemnify and keep indemnified the said AB and his estate and effects against all losses, claims, demands, costs, charges and expenses as against the several sums of money which by the said books appear to be due owing from the said AB in respect of the said trade and business, and also from and against the contracts and engagements to which by the said books the said AB appears to be now liable for performance or non-performance thereof.

AND this indenture also witnesses that the said AB does hereby irrevocably nominate, appoint and constitute the said CD as his attorney for him and in his name to do, execute and perform all acts, deeds and things as shall be necessary or requisite to carry on the said business as his successor and for that purpose to represent him before all appropriate authorities and in all courts of law and to sue for, recover, realise and to give good valid discharges for all moneys due and payable to him on account of or in connection with the said trade or business hereby assigned and appropriate the same for his use and purposes.

IN WITNESS WHEREOF the parties have executed these presents on the day, month and year first above-written.

Signed, sealed and delivered by the VENDOR in Calcutta in the presence of:

Signed, sealed and delivered by the PURCHASER in Calcutta in the presence of:

MEMO OF CONSIDERATION

Assignment of Decree

This deed of ASSIGNMENT made this .... day of ...... 1999 BETWEEN AB son of .... residing at .... hereinafter referred to as the ASSIGNOR (which term shall include his successors-in-interest and persons claiming under him) of the one part and CD son of .... residing at .... hereinafter referred to as the ASSIGNEE (which term shall include his heirs, successors and assigns) of the other part.

WHEREAS by a decree dated .... made in Suit No. .... of .... (cause title) of the court .... it was ordered and decreed that the said CD do pay to the said AB a sum of Rs. .... with interest at .... % and costs AND whereas there is now due and payable to the said AB a sum of Rs. .... inclusive of interest under the said decree AND whereas the said AB has agreed to assign and sell the said decree unto and in favour of the said CD at and for the sum of Rs. .... Now this Indenture witnesses that in pursuance of the said agreement and in consideration of the sum of Rs. .... paid by the said CD to the said AB the receipt whereof ...... he, the said AB, doth hereby and hereunder transfer, sell and assign unto the said CD all moneys now due or hereafter to be due and payable to the said AB by the said (Judgement-debtor) under and by virtue of the aforesaid decree inclusive of interest and costs and all benefits and advantages thereof including the right to execute the same in any manner prescribed by law to have the same unto and to the use of the said CD absolutely: AND the said AB doth hereby covenant with the said CD that the said sum of Rs. .... in entirety is due and payable to the said AB by the said judgment-debtor under the said decree AND further that he has not entered satisfaction of the decree nor into any compromise or arrangement with the judgment-debtor or otherwise written off the said debt or claim with a view to exonerate him from his liability on that account and that the said decree is in full force and virtue and fully executable AND that there is no cross-decree as against him and this Indenture furthermore witnesses that the said AB doth hereby and hereunder irrevocably nominate, appoint and constitute the said CD as his constituted attorney to execute the said decree, realise all moneys payable thereunder and appropriate the same for his own use and purpose to all intents and purposes.

IN WITNESS WHEREOF the parties hereto have executed these presents on the day, month and year first above-written.

Signed, sealed and delivered by
AB in the presence of:

Signed, sealed and delivered by
CD in the presence of:

Deed of Assignment of Mortgage, Mortgagor Joining

THIS TRANSFER OF MORTGAGE made this .... day of .... 1999 BETWEEN AB of, etc. (hereinafter called the MORTGAGEE) of the first part, CD of, etc. (hereinafter called the MORTGAGOR), of the second part, and EF of, etc. (hereinafter called the TRANSFEREE), of the third part, whereas by an Indenture dated .... made between the parties hereto of the first and second parts and registered in Book I, Vol. .... etc. it was witnessed that the said CD did for the consideration mentioned therein grant, convey, sell, transfer, assign and assure unto and to the use of the said AB the property fully mentioned and described in the schedule thereto and also particularly written in the schedule below absolutely and forever subject to the proviso for redemption thereunder contained AND whereas there is now due and payable to the said AB a sum of Rs. .... by the said CD under and by virtue of the hereinbefore recited mortgage all interest having been paid up till the date of these presents AND whereas the said AB has agreed to assign the said mortgage unto and to the use of the said EF at and for the sum of Rs. .... NOW THIS DEED OF transfer witnesseth as follows:

In consideration of the sum of Rupees .... now paid to the MORTGAGEE by the TRANSFEREE (the receipt of which sum the MORTGAGEE) hereby admits, acknowledges, and confirms the said AB as MORTGAGEE with the concurrence of CD the MORTGAGOR, doth hereby grant, transfer, assign and assure unto and to the said EF (1) All the said principal sum of Rs........ due and owing upon the principal deed and all interest to be hereafter due thereon and the benefit of all existing securities thereof: TO HAVE AND TO receive the same to the TRANSFEREE absolutely. (2) All that the mortgaged premises being Premises No. .... fully mentioned and described in the Schedule hereto and vested in the MORTGAGEE under and by virtue of the hereinbefore recited mortgage .... TO HAVE AND TO HOLD the same absolutely and forever subject to the proviso for redemption thereunder contained. AND THIS INDENTURE further witnesseth that the said AB doth hereby agree and declare that the said sum of Rs. .... is due and owing to him under and by virtue of the hereinbefore recited mortgage AND THAT the said AB has not done, executed or performed nor suffered anything to the contrary whereby or by reason or means whereof the mortgaged property or any part thereof may be in any way affected or prejudiced in title or estate or that the said AB may be prevented from transferring and assuring the same unto and to the use of the said EF in the manner hereinbefore indicated.

AND THIS Indenture furthermore witnesseth that the said CD doth hereby join with the said AB and concur with him in effectively transferring, assigning and assuring the said sum of Rs. .... together with the benefit of the security created on the property under and by virtue of the hereinbefore recited mortgage and further that the said CD doth hereby agree and confirm with the transferee to pay to him on or before the .... day of .... the said principal sum of Rs. ...... with interest thereon at the rate of .... per cent per annum. AND ALSO so long after that day as any principal money shall remain due interest at the same rate on the days mentioned in the principal deed. And further to observe and perform all the covenants and conditions and stipulations provided for in the deed of mortgage.

The Schedule above referred to

IN WITNESS WHEREOF the parties hereto have executed these presents on the day, month and year first above-written.

Signed, sealed and delivered by
AB in the presence of:

Signed, sealed and delivered by
CD and EF in the presence of:

MEMO OF CONSIDERATION

IN WITNESS WHEREOF the parties hereunto execute these presents on the day, month and the year first above-mentioned.

Signed, sealed and delivered by
AB in the presence of: AB

Signed, sealed and delivered by
CD in the presence of: CD

Sale by the Liquidator of a Company in Voluntary Liquidation

THIS SALE DEED MADE on this .... day of .... 1999 by X Co. Ltd. (in liquidation) having its registered office at .... (hereinafter called the COMPANY) and AB, son of .... residing at .... liquidator of the company, (hereinafter called the VENDOR) of the one part and ML Co. Ltd. a company registered under the Companies Act 1956 having its registered office at .... (hereinafter called the PURCHASER which term shall include its successors, nominees and assigns) of the other part.

WHEREAS by extraordinary resolution dated the .... day of .... 1999 the company resolved to go into voluntary liquidation:

AND WHEREAS the COMPANY in its extraordinary general meeting held on the. ...... day of .... 1999, appointed the said AB liquidator for the purpose of winding up the affairs of the company.

AND WHEREAS the premises hereinafter described were at the date of the said resolution and are still vested in the COMPANY absolutely and free from encumbrances:

AND WHEREAS the VENDOR has for and on behalf of the Company agreed to sell to the PURCHASER the premises hereinafter described for the sum of Rs. .... (in words, Rupees ....) absolutely and free from encumbrances:

NOW THIS Indenture witnesses that in consideration of the sum of Rs. .... (*in words* Rupees ....) now paid by the PURCHASER to the VENDOR as such liquidator as aforesaid (the receipt of which sum the vendor and the COMPANY hereby acknowledge), the COMPANY by the direction of the VENDOR as liquidator and the VENDOR doth hereby sell and convey to the PURCHASER all that premises (99 White Road, Calcutta) which is more particularly described in the Schedule hereto together with all rights, easements and appurtenances whatsoever to the said premises belonging or in any wise appertaining: To hold the same unto and to the use of the PURCHASER absolutely and forever.

The VENDOR as liquidator of the COMPANY and pursuant to authority given by the resolution passed by the shareholders and in due course of realisation of assets, debts and properties doth hereby and hereunder grant, convey, sell, transfer, assign and assure the said property and every part thereof unto and to the use of the PURCHASER to have and to hold the same as an absolute owner thereof forever. And that the VENDOR doth hereby covenant with the PURCHASER that the said property is free from all encumbrances to the best of his knowledge and further that he as liquidator has not done, executed, performed or suffered any act, deed or thing whereby or by reason or means thereof may be in any way affected or prejudiced in title or estate or he as liquidator may be prevented from granting, conveying, selling, transferring, assigning or assuring the same in the manner hereinbefore indicated. And furthermore that the said VENDOR has not at any time given or made any assent or conveyance affecting the said property or any part thereof in favour of any person whatsoever.

The Schedule above referred to

IN WITNESS WHEREOF the VENDOR as such liquidator as aforesaid has caused the common seal of the COMPANY to be affixed to these presents and the VENDOR has hereunto set his hand and seal the day and year first above-written.

Signed, sealed and delivered by
the said AB as liquidator of X Co.
Ltd. appointed under resolution
dated .... of the Company:

Signed, sealed and delivered by
Mr. .... pursuant to
Board Resolution of ML. Co. Ltd.
dated .... in presence of:

MEMO OF CONSIDERATION

RECEIVED of and from the within-mentioned Purchaser the sum of Rs. .... being the consideration payable by the Purchaser by Bank Draft No. 7 dated .... for Rs. .... on X Bank Ltd. payable at Calcutta.

Received, Signed by Vendor

WITNESSES:

Sale on behalf of a Mentally ill Person

THIS DEED OF SALE made on the .... BETWEEN AB, etc., a mentally ill person represented by and acting through XY etc., manager of his estate appointed by the court (hereinafter called the VENDOR) which expression shall, when the subject or context allows or admits of, be deemed to include all persons managing the estate and affairs of AB of the one part, etc., and CD son of etc. hereinafter referred to as the PURCHASER which expression shall etc., etc., his heirs, executors, administrators and representatives of the other part.

WHEREAS by an inquisition held before the District Judge of .... in Case No. .... of .... the VENDOR was declared to be and confirmed as mentally ill person and by order of the said Judge dated .... the said XY was appointed as the manager of his estate.

AND WHEREAS in pursuance of the said order the said XY took possession of the estate of AB and is now managing the same and all its affairs.

AND WHEREAS in course of such administration it having been necessary to raise a sum of Rs. .... in order to pay off certain debts of the VENDOR incurred for purchase of food, medicine and necessaries supplied aggregating to Rs. .... and also to pay for the necessary expenses for the maintenance and support of the VENDOR and his family relations, the estate having no other resources to meet those liabilities, the said XY as such manager submitted a report to that effect and applied before the said District Judge for permission to sell one of his properties AND WHEREAS such sale is to the interest and for the benefit of the vendor.

AND WHEREAS by an order dated the .... the said District Judge after full enquiry about the necessities for such sale authorised the said XY to raise the said sum of Rs. .... by sale certified such sale as beneficial to the lunatic and of property of the VENDOR fully mentioned and described in the Schedule hereto on terms contained therein.

AND WHEREAS by an agreement in writing dated .... the said XY has agreed to sell and the said CD has agreed to purchase the property fully mentioned and described in the schedule hereto at and for the sum of Rs. .... the same being the highest offer received so far according to the present conditions of the market.

NOW THIS INDENTURE WITNESSES as follows:

1. In pursuance of the said agreement and in exercise of the power, authority and liberty granted by the order dated .... as aforesaid and all other powers enabling him and in consideration of the sum of Rs. .... paid by the said CD the purchaser hereto to the said XY as such manager as aforesaid (the receipt of which the said XY doth hereby and hereunder admit, acknowledge and confirm) he the said AB represented by and acting through the said XY as such manager as aforesaid doth hereby grant, convey, sell, transfer, assign and assure unto and to the purchaser, *viz.*, the said CD the property fully mentioned and described in the schedule hereto and hereinafter referred to as the said property absolutely and forever AND THAT the said XY doth hereby covenant with the purchaser that the said order dated .... is still in force and virtue AND THAT the said XY has not encumbered the property in any way nor at any time heretofore done, executed, performed or suffered to the contrary any act, deed or thing whereby by reason or means whereof the said property of AB may be in any way prejudiced in title or estate or the said XY prevented from granting, transferring or conveying the said property in the manner hereinbefore indicated.

The Schedule above referred to

IN WITNESS WHEREOF the parties hereto have executed these presents on the day, month and year first above-written.

Signed, sealed and delivered by the said AB acting through and represented by said XY as Manager in the presence of:

Signed, sealed and delivered by the within-named PURCHASER CD in the presence of:

MEMO OF CONSIDERATION

Sale by a Hindu Widow[8] as Limited Owner for Legal Necessity

THIS DEED OF SALE made on the .... day of .... 1999 BETWEEN AB widow of XY of .... (VENDOR) of the one part and CD son of .... of (PURCHASER) of the other part.

WHEREAS the VENDOR is seized and possessed of and/or otherwise entitled to a limited estate in the properties fully mentioned in the schedule and has been in use and occupation thereof accordingly under and by virtue of the will left by XY of which the probate has been obtained from the Court of .... AND WHEREAS the said grant is in full force and virtue and which right has been created in her favour of the first time only.

AND WHEREAS the said AB has no funds nor any other resources to meet her necessary expenses for her maintenance and livelihood as provided in the said will.

AND WHEREAS in the circumstances aforesaid and under legal necessities and justifying causes the said AB has agreed to sell unto the said CD at and for the sum of Rs. ...... (in words, Rupees ....) the premises hereinafter described absolutely out of which a sum of Rs. .... shall be applied for satisfaction and discharge of the loan of Rs. .... already incurred from creditors namely, EF and GH, who are pressing for the same, there being

8 The latest concept of law about the estate of a Hindu widow is that under the Hindu Succession Act (Act XXX of 1956) which has improved her status and rights over the estate is that unless the property is given for the first time without any pre-existing right she will have an absolute estate—*Vaddboyina* v *Vaddboyina* AIR 1977 SC 1944. See also *Limba* v *Manikrao* AIR 1978 Bom 83. Possession in lien of maintenance created an absolute title. Her title to be ascertained in each individual case.

no other funds to liquidate the same, the loans having been incurred for repairs of the dwelling house and maintenance and the balance to be held as provisions for her maintenance for the time being AND WHEREAS the said CD has after *bona fide* and independent enquiries as to the existence of the necessity for the sale is satisfied as to the existence and validity of the debts and of the said necessity and emergency of the party as to the immediate sale of the said property.

NOW THIS DEED of sale witnesseth that in the circumstances aforesaid and in consideration of the sum of Rs. .... paid by the said CD to the said AB to be appropriated for the purposes hereinbefore indicated, the said AB doth hereby grant, convey, transfer, sell, assign and assure unto and to the use of the said CD the said property and every part thereof for the term of her natural life and the VENDOR covenants that the PURCHASER shall hereafter peaceably and quietly hold, possess and enjoy the said property without any claim or demand whatsoever from the VENDOR and the VENDOR shall keep the PURCHASER harmless and indemnified from or against all encumbrances, charges and equities whatsoever and the VENDOR further covenants that she at the request of and costs of the PURCHASER will execute and do all such lawful acts deeds and things for further and more perfectly conveying and assuring the said property in the manner and according to true intent and meaning of this DEED.

The Schedule

IN WITNESS WHEREOF the parties hereto have executed these presents on the day, month and year first above-written.

Signed, sealed and delivered
by the VENDOR in Calcutta in the
presence of:

Signed, sealed and delivered
by the PURCHASER in Calcutta in
the presence of:

MEMO OF CONSIDERATION

RECEIVED of and from the within-mentioned purchaser the sum of Rs. .... being the full consideration payable by the PURCHASER by Bank Draft No. 9 dated .... for .... Rs. .... issued by X Bank Ltd. payable in Calcutta.

WITNESS Received

Signature of VENDOR

Sale of Equity of Redemption of Simple Mortgage

THIS DEED OF SALE MADE THIS 15th day of December 1999 BETWEEN, AB son of .... aged .... residing at .... hereinafter referred to as the VENDOR (which term shall unless excluded by or repugnant to the context, include his heirs, successors, legal representatives and assigns) of the ONE PART and CD, son of .... aged .... residing at .... hereinafter referred to as the PURCHASER (which term shall unless excluded by or repugnant to the context include his heirs, legal representatives and assigns) of the other part.

WHEREAS by a Deed of Mortgage dated the .... day of .... 1999 made BETWEEN the said AB described therein as MORTGAGOR of the one part and XY son of .... of .... described therein as Mortgagee of the OTHER PART and registered in Book I, Vol. .... pages .... to .... being No. .... for .... in the office of .... it was witnessed that the premises hereinafter described in the Schedule hereto was charged and assured unto and in favour of the said XY as and by way of simple mortgage for securing the principal sum of Rs. .... (in words Rupees ....) with interest thereon at .... per cent per annum, subject to the proviso for redemption thereof on the .... day of .... as thereunder provided AND WHEREAS there is now due and payable to the said XY the said sum of Rs. .... as principal and a further sum of Rs. .... as interest thereon making thus a sum total of Rs. .... under and by virtue of the hereinbefore recited deed of mortgage AND WHEREAS the said AB has agreed to sell and the said CD has agreed to purchase the said property at and for the sum of Rs. .... free from all encumbrances except, however, the hereinbefore recited mortgage and subject to payment of all moneys due thereunder.

NOW THIS INDENTURE WITNESSES that in pursuance of the said agreement and in consideration of the sum of Rs. .... (in words Rupees ....) now paid by the said CD to the said AB (the receipt of which sum the said AB hereby acknowledges) the said AB doth hereby grant, convey, sell, transfer, assign and assure the said property and every part thereof (with the boundaries thereof more particularly described in the Schedule hereto): TO HAVE AND TO HOLD the same to the use of the said CD absolutely and forever, subject, nevertheless, to the payment of the debt secured by the said mortgage of the .... day of .... 1999 and observance and performance of all the covenants and conditions thereunder provided.

AND THE said CD for himself, his heirs, executors and administrators hereby covenants with the said AB, his heirs, executors and administrators that he, the said CD, his heirs, executors, administrators, representatives or assigns shall pay or cause to be paid to the said XY, his heirs, executors, administrators or assigns the entire debt payable under the said mortgage of the .... day of .... 1999 and observe and perform all the covenants and conditions thereunder contained on the part of the said AB and shall at all times indemnify and keep indemnified the said AB, his heirs, executors and administrators against all claims or demands, loss or damages, costs, charges and expenses, suits, proceedings, arising out of payment or non-payment of the said mortgage debt or performance or non-performance of the covenants and conditions to be observed and performed on the part of the said AB under the said deed of mortgage.

The Schedule

IN WITNESSES WHEREof the parties hereto have executed these presents on the day, month and year first above-written.

Signed, sealed and delivered
by the VENDOR in Calcutta in the
presence of:

Signed, sealed and delivered
by the PURCHASER in Calcutta in
the presence of:

MEMO OF CONSIDERATION

RECEIVED of and from the within-mentioned Purchaser the sum of Rs. .... being the full consideration payable by bank draft No. 10 dated .... issued by X Bank Ltd. payable in Calcutta.

WITNESS

Received

Signature of VENDOR

Sale by an Administrator under an Order of Court

THIS DEED OF SALE made this .... day of .... 2000 BETWEEN AB son of........... Administrator to the estate of .... deceased (hereinafter called the VENDOR which expression shall where the subject or context .... be deemed to include his successor or successors in office of the one part and CD son of .... of .... hereinafter called the PURCHASER which expression shall where the subject or context allows .... of the other part:

WHEREAS one W son of .... of .... died on .... leaving a will dated .... but without appointing any executor AND WHEREAS the said will was duly proved in the court of .... on the .... day of .... in Probate Case No. .... of .... and Letters of Administration with a copy thereof in respect of the properties and credits of the deceased was granted to the said AB on the .... day of .... AND WHEREAS the said grant is still in full force and virtue and the said AB is still now administering the estate AND

WHEREBY by an order dated .... made by the said .... in Misc. Case No. .... of .... the said AB was authorised to sell the property fully mentioned and described in the Schedule hereto subject to the terms contained therein AND WHEREAS the said AB has pursuant to the said order agreed to sell and CD, the PURCHASER, hereto has agreed to purchase the said property at and for the sum of Rs. ....

Now this deed of sale witnesses that in pursuance of the said agreement and in consideration of the sum of Rs. .... paid by the purchaser to the VENDOR the receipt whereof the vendor doth hereby admit, acknowledge and confirm and in exercise of the powers, authorities and liberties conferred upon, under and by virtue of the hereinbefore recited order and all other powers enabling him in that behalf he the said AB, *viz.*, the VENDOR as Administrator and in due course of administration doth hereby and hereunder grant, convey, sell, transfer, assign and assure the said property and every part thereof unto and to use of the said CD PURCHASER, hereto his heirs, executors, administrators, representatives and assigns to have and to hold the same as an absolute owner thereof forever. And that the said AB doth hereby covenant with the said CD that the said property is free from encumbrances to the best of his knowledge and further that he as administrator has not done, executed and performed or suffered to the contrary any act, deed or thing whereby or by reason or means whereof the said property or any part thereof may be in any way affected or prejudical in title or estate or he as administrator may be prevented from granting, conveying, selling, transferring, assigning or assuring the same in the manner hereinbefore indicated. And furthermore that the said AB has not at any time heretofore given or made any assent or conveyance or conveyances affecting the said property or any part thereof in favour of any person or persons whatsoever.

IN WITNESS WHEREOF the VENDOR and purchaser above-mentioned have hereunto set and subscribed their hands and seal the day, month and year first above-written:

The Schedule above referred to

Signed, sealed and delivered etc. AB

CD

MEMO OF CONSIDERATION

Sale of a Property by the Heirs of a Mohamedan

THIS DEED OF SALE made on this .... day of .... 1999 by AB, CD, EF sons of MN and KL, daughter of MN, all residing at .... (hereinafter called the VENDORS (which expression shall unless the context otherwise requires include their respective heirs, executors, administrators and representatives of the ONE PART and OP, son of XY, residing at .... hereinafter called the PURCHASER (which term shall where the subject or context allows or admits include his heirs, successors and assigns) of the other part:

WHEREAS the said MN who was a Mohamedan governed by .... School of Mohamedan Law died intestate on .... possessed of *inter alia* a building known as .... in the town of .... fully mentioned and described in the schedule hereto and hereinafter referred to as the said property.

AND WHEREAS by an agreement dated .... made between the parties, the VENDORS have for the consideration mentioned therein agreed to sell and the purchasers agreed to purchase the said property at and for the consideration mentioned therein on terms thereunder contained.

AND WHEREAS VENDORS have assured the PURCHASER that all expenditure incurred in respect of funeral and other expenses and death-bed charges as well as salaries and wages due to servants and others for services rendered to the deceased have been duly paid off out of other assets left by the deceased and further that the deceased left no will nor made any gift or wakf in respect of the aforesaid building nor was the same encumbered or charged in any way by the deceased during his lifetime or by the VENDORS after his death and furthermore that the VENDORS aforesaid are the only heirs of the deceased and as such are entitled to the proprietary as well as possessory interests in the said property.

NOW THIS DEED OF sale witnesses as follows:

In consideration of the sum of Rs. .... paid by the PURCHASER to the VENDORS on .... (the date of the agreement for sale mentioned above) and in consideration of a further payment of Rs. .... as the balance of price of Rs. .... (the receipt whereof the VENDORS hereby admit, acknowledge and confirm), the said VENDORS hereby grant, convey, sell, transfer, assign and assure unto and to the use of the said PURCHASER absolutely and forever all that building more particularly described in the Schedule hereto to have and to hold the same and forever enjoy without any claim, demand, interruption from the VENDORS or any other person or persons claiming under any one of them together further with all rights, interest, which the VENDORS heretofore enjoyed in respect of the said premises and with further covenants and indemnities which are hereby agreed to and/or assured unto the said PURCHASER.

AND THAT the VENDORS do hereby assure the purchaser and covenant as follows:

(*i*) That the VENDORS are the absolute owners of the said property and are lawfully entitled to convey the same unto the PURCHASER in the manner hereinbefore indicated:

(*ii*) that no right of easements of any kind is available to any other person or persons in respect of the use and enjoyment of the said property;

(*iii*) that the said property is free from all encumbrances, attachments and other charges and all rates and taxes due in respect thereof have been paid up to the date of sale and in the event of any encumbrance or public charges aforesaid are or is hereafter found to be due in respect of the same vendors shall forthwith pay the same to the appropriate authorities;

(*iv*) that the PURCHASER shall at all times, hereafter have peaceful and quiet possession and enjoyment of the said property free from any claim, demand, interference and disturbance whatsoever by the VENDORS or their heirs, executors, administrators and representatives or person or persons claiming under or in trust for them or any of them;

(*v*) that in the event the entirety of the property or any part or any share in the said property being lost to the PURCHASER on account of any claim made thereto by any other person or persons, the VENDORS and their heirs shall indemnify and keep indemnified the PURCHASER or his heirs against such loss together with all costs, charges and expenses which he or they may or shall incur to protect his or their title to the property or to defend the same;

(*vi*) that the VENDORS shall execute any further deed or assurance that may be necessary in order to perfect the title of the PURCHASER in respect of the said property or any portion thereof.

The Schedule above referred to

IN WITNESS WHEREOF the parties have set and subscribed their respective hands and seals the day, month and year first above-written.

Signed, sealed and delivered
by the said VENDORS AB, CD, EF
and KL in the presence of:

Signed, sealed and delivered
by the said PURCHASER OP in the
presence of:

MEMO OF CONSIDERATION

RECEIVED of and from the within-named Purchaser the sum of Rs. .... (Rupees ....) being the full consideration within-named was to be paid by the Purchaser to us.

WITNESSES We say received

AB, CD, EF, KL

Deed of Boundary Demarcation

THIS DEED OF BOUNDARY demarcation is made on this ...... day of ...... 1999 BETWEEN Mr. XY of .... (hereinafter referred to as the FIRST PARTY which expression shall unless the context otherwise requires include his heirs, legal representatives and successors) of the first part and Mr. MN of .... (hereinafter referred to as the SECOND PARTY which expression shall unless the context otherwise requires include his heirs, legal representatives and successors) of the other part.

WHEREAS Mr. Z was the owner of Premises No. ...... of ....

AND WHEREAS by a Deed of Sale dated 5th August 1999 Registration No. 124 in the year 1999 and recorded in Book No. 2, volume 3, pages 50 to 65, the FIRST PARTY purchased the eastern portion of the premises No. ......of .... and the same has been mutated in the records of the Municipal Corporation of Calcutta numbered as ....

AND WHEREAS the western portion of the said premises No. .... of .... has been purchased by the SECOND PARTY by a Deed dated ....1999 and bearing Registration No. 15 in the year 1999 recorded in Book No. 4, volume 2, pages 1 to 5 and the same was mutated in the records of the Calcutta Municipal Corporation and has been numbered as ....

AND WHEREAS there is a common wall between the eastern portion and the western portion of the said premises now known as ....

AND WHEREAS the FIRST PARTY commenced construction of additions, alterations within the premises .... in accordance with the sanctioned plan of the Calcutta Municipal Corporation and such reconstruction work is still going on though it is in the final stage.

AND WHEREAS the second party objected to such reconstruction, additions and alterations in so far as the same affected the premises No. ...... of .... and has also obstructed the natural flow of air and light in the premises No. ...... of ....

AND WHEREAS the parties had discussions and negotiations and ultimately have agreed to avoid further escalation of the dispute and amicably settled the disputes for ever in regard to the said premises.

NOW THESE PRESENTS WITNESSETH and the parties agree as follows:

1. On the ground floor only of the premises No. ...... of .... the first party shall demolish a portion of the western side of common wall near Column No. G5 as shown in the drawing annexed hereto in order to facilitate the widening by 2 ft. of the attached shop-room of second party in the premises No. ...... of ....

2. A fresh 5 inches thick brick partitions wall will be constructed shifting it towards the west as shown in the drawing enclosed hereto.

3. The parties will maintain the common wall at their own costs and expenses from their respective sides and each party will have the right to fix false ceilings, wall rack or other supports on this wall from their respective sides without putting undue weight on the common wall or structurally damaging the wall.

4. The said shifting of the wall in the premises No. ...... of .... shall be only for the ground floor without affecting the corresponding walls on the 1st, 2nd, 3rd and the 4th floors.

5. By virtue of the such shifting of the above, the 5 inch brick common wall towards the western side of the column G5 of premises No. .... of .... will now be within the western side line of premises No. ...... of ....

6. The second party undertakes and agrees not to do any structural damages by way of chiselling the said column No. G5 or do any other act which will weaken the structural strength and stability of premises No. ...... of .... and if any strengthening of the column G5 is required on the ground floor the second party will allow the first party to do the same from the side of first party and/or the second party and for this purpose allow the workers of the first party to enter the portion occupied by the second party.

7. As a result of shifting of wall towards western side, some structural modifications in the affected portion will be required with a view to protecting the ground floor roof of premises No. ...... of .... which will be done by the second party before demolition of the common wall of premises No. ...... of ....

8. On the western side of common wall of the premises No. ...... of .... there are four windows/openings for air and light. As the two premises that is ...... and ...... of .... are attached all the existing wall openings of premises No. ...... of ....are to be closed by brick work by the first party and it is agreed that in future neither of the parties will make any opening in the common wall on any floor of the buildings.

9. In the courtyard of premises No. ...... of .... on eastern side there is 5 inch thick brick-wall of approximately 16 feet length on the ground floor only. In the said attached/ common wall of premises No. ...... of .... the western side wall is only 5 inches thick on all floors. With a view to prevent percolation or seepage of rain-water through this brick wall a further 5 inches thick brick wall will be constructed from ground floor to the 4th floor in addition to the existing 5 inches thick brick-wall of premises No. ...... of .... Such brick wall to be constructed shall be finished with cement plastering. Such work has to be done from premises No. ...... of ....

10. It is recorded that during the negotiation and preparation of these presents and execution thereof, the aforesaid additions/alterations/ modifications have been executed by the first party at its own expenses and to the satisfaction of the second party.

11. The said demarcation property line on the common portion of premises Nos. ...... and ...... of .... will be treated as final as existing as on 15th September 1999. The eastern side wall of premises No. ...... of .... and the western side wall of the premises No. ...... of .... and as shown in the enclosed drawings and the existing demarcation of the common wall of the two premises shall supersede the demarcation shown in respect of the common wall or attached portion of the two premises in the respective Purchase Deeds and plans of premises Nos. .... and ...... of ....

12. The parties hereby agree that neither party will have any right to claim or any cause of action against the other regarding the boundary demarcation of the attached and/or common wall or the said premises Nos. .... and ...... of .... and all disputes in regard thereto are hereby finally settled.

IN WITNESS WHEREOF the parties hereto have executed these presents on the day, month and year first above-written.

Signed and delivered by Mr. XY
in the presence of: Signature

Signed and delivered by Mr. MN
in the presence of: Signature

50

Sole Selling Agency

An Agent is a person entitled to do an act for another or to represent another in dealings with third parties. The person who employs an agent is called the Principal.[1] The Agent is an intermediary who is authorised to create legal relationship between the Principal and the third party. He is like a conduit pipe connecting two parties. He may make the Principal responsible to the third party for his action. An agent is not however a servant of the Principal.

The authority of an agent may be expressed or implied. If a person has authority to act on behalf of another called the Principal and consents to so act then he is called an agent of the Principal. The relationship of Principal and agent arises out of a contract.

A sole selling agent is a person who is appointed to sell the goods or products of the Principal in a particular area to the exclusion of all others. The appointment of a sole selling agent by a company registered under the Companies Act is subject to the provisions of section 294-AA of the Companies Act 1956. Under the section the Central Government may prohibit the appointment of the sole selling agents by a company in certain cases mainly in respect of certain goods or products having adequate demand in the market.

A sole selling agent may be appointed by a written document or such agency may come into existence by operations of law or the Principal may ratify the act of the agent. An agency may be inferred from the conduct of the parties and the circumstances surrounding the transactions.

For creation of an agency no consideration is necessary but the fact that a person will act for another to their mutual benefit will itself be a consideration for the validity of the agreement.[2]

1 Section 182 of the Indian Contract Act 1872.
2 Section 185 of the Indian Contract Act 1872.

An agency may be terminated in accordance with the agreement. If there be any written agreement, the Principal has the right to revoke the authority of the agent at any time subject to compensating the agent where the agency is coupled with some interest.

An agent may be remunerated by a commission on the sale of goods effected by him or on the goods purchased by him from the Principal.

A sole selling agent is given the authority to sell the products of the Principal in a specified geographical area with the understanding that within that area for the same goods the Principal shall not appoint any other agent for selling the goods. Whether the unsold goods will be taken back or not will be governed by the agreement.

The main object of appointing a sole selling agent is that the Principal will be assured that the agreed quantity of goods would be sold and/or paid for by the agent. The agent is also benefited inasmuch as he gets the goods at a competitive price and has practically a monopoly right to sell the goods within the agreed geographical area. Such agreement is beneficial to both the Principal and the agent to expand business. The Principal is not required to carry huge stock or take on rent godowns or warehouses or set up selling outlets and its capital is not thereby blocked.

FORMS

Sole Selling Agency Agreement

THIS SOLE SELLING AGENCY Agreement is made on this ...... day of .... BETWEEN X Co. Ltd. a company registered under the English Companies Act and carrying on business at ...., England hereinafter referred to as the PRINCIPAL (which term shall unless excluded by or repugnant to the context shall include its successors and assigns) of the one part and S. Co. Ltd. a company registered under the Companies Act 1956 and having its registered office at ...., Calcutta hereinafter referred to as the AGENT (which term shall unless excluded by or repugnant to the context include its successors and permitted nominees and assigns) of the other part.

WHEREAS the PRINCIPAL is carrying on business as the manufacturer of and dealer in and exporter of Telecommunications and Computers and Hardwares and Softwares thereof.

AND WHEREAS the AGENT is carrying on business in diverse products of various manufacturers as selling agent and has acquired experience and obtained the infrastructure for dealing with these goods.

AND WHEREAS the AGENT has extra capacity for carrying on the business as the selling agent and has approached the PRINCIPAL for marketing the Principal's products in the backward areas of India and also in the foreign countries where the markets have not yet been fully exploited.

AND WHEREAS the PRINCIPAL has agreed to the proposal of the AGENT and intends to appoint the AGENT as the Sole Selling Agent in respect of certain areas in domestic markets as also in certain areas of the foreign markets.

NOW THESE PRESENTS WITNESSETH and the parties hereby agree as follows:

1. The AGENT is appointed as the Sole Selling Agent of the Principal's products in the domestic market and also in the foreign market particulars whereof are given in the Schedule hereunder.

2. The AGENT shall advertise and make popular the Principal's products in the scheduled areas by advertisement in newspapers, journals and through representatives who would visit the Consumers' offices and/or residences to popularise the quality and utility of the products of the PRINCIPAL.

3. The PRINCIPAL shall provide the AGENT literature and other documents explaining the products and would also supply certain samples for demonstration wherever possible.

4. The PRINCIPAL shall pay to the AGENT a commission of 30% on the published sale price of the products that would be supplied through the AGENT.

5. All expenses for transport upto the agent's godown shall be borne by the PRINCIPAL and further expenses for handling and selling the products and for advertisement and publicity shall be borne by the AGENT.

6. The AGENT shall maintain an efficient team of personnel for properly running the after-sales-service in respect of the Principal's products and for these services the PRINCIPAL would pay an additional 2% as service charges on the published price of the commodities sold by the AGENT.

7. The AGENT shall ensure that the after-sales-service is rendered promptly and no customer should have any grievance that the customer is not being properly attended to or the customer's instrument has not been properly repaired.

8. The AGENT shall ensure proper customer satisfaction by rendering the after-sales-service as also immediately returning the genuine manufacturing defective instrument to the PRINCIPAL for replacement.

9. The AGENT shall on receipt of any complaint inspect the machinery concerned at the customer's place and remedy the defect or replace the

part if required and immediately inform the PRINCIPAL with a report about the defects and the repairs done.

10. The AGENT shall submit a statement of receipts of the products and the sale thereof as also the number and nature of customers attended to by way of after-sales-service.

11. The AGENT shall keep a deposit of Rs. 2 lakhs free from interest with the PRINCIPAL by way of Security Money.

12. The AGENT shall render proper accounts every quarter and remit the sale proceeds less the commission and service charges along with a statement of accounts.

13. The AGENT will not be entitled to any commission but only its out-of-pocket expenses in attending a customer who has ultimately rejected the product of the PRINCIPAL on some ground or the other.

14. The AGENT undertakes and covenants not to sell in the scheduled areas any other products of any other manufacturer similar to or competitive with the products of the PRINCIPAL.

15. The AGENT shall keep all the products delivered to it insured against risks of fire, burglary, civil commotion rioting and loss by any other insurable risks in the joint names of the PRINCIPAL and the AGENT at the cost of the PRINCIPAL.

16. The AGENT shall inform the PRINCIPAL and take immediate action for any infringement of the Principal's Trade Mark or Patent Rights or passing off other manufacturer's products as those of the PRINCIPAL.

17. The AGENT hereby agrees and undertakes to take all possible steps and to execute and sign all plaint, petition, affidavit and other documents that may be necessary for successfully prosecuting any party for infringement of the said Trade Mark, Patent Rights or for passing off or committing other wrongful acts done to the Principal's products by any person and to protect the right, title and interest of the PRINCIPAL.

18. This Agreement is subject to obtaining the necessary permission or approvals of the authorities concerned.

19. This Agreement is terminable by giving three months' notice by either party on any breach of any of the terms mentioned hereinabove.

20. All disputes and differences arising out of this agreement or in relation to any transactions covered by the agreement or otherwise affecting the relationship of the PRINCIPAL with its AGENT shall be referred to Mr. MN, Advocate of Old Post Office Street, Calcutta for adjudication of such disputes in accordance with the provisions of the Arbitration and Conciliation Act 1996 or any statutory modifications thereof for the time being in force.

The Schedule

(Particulars of the commodities and areas given to the Sole Selling Agent under this agreement).

IN WITNESS WHEREOF the parties have executed these presents on the day, month and year first above-written.

Signed, sealed and delivered by
Mr. ....
pursuant to the Board Resolution
dated .... of the PRINCIPAL
in Calcutta in the presence of:

Signed, sealed and delivered by
Mr. ....
pursuant to Board Resolution
dated .... of the AGENT in
Calcutta in the presence of:

Appointment of Selling Agent for a District or Town

THIS AGREEMENT IS MADE on this 15th day of September 2000 BETWEEN AB Co. Ltd., a company registered under the Companies Act 1956 and carrying on business at .... (hereinafter called the PRINCIPAL) of the One Part and CD, a proprietorship concern of AP of .... (hereinafter called the AGENT) of the Other Part.

WHEREAS the PRINCIPAL is a manufacturer and dealer in Computers and is willing to appoint a suitable concern as the sole selling agent for the town of Chennai for its products.

AND WHEREAS the AGENT has approached the PRINCIPAL and has expressed his consent to act as the sole selling agent of the PRINCIPAL to which the principal has agreed.

NOW THIS AGREEMENT WITNESSES and the parties hereby agree as follows:

1. The PRINCIPAL hereby appoints the AGENT as the sole agent of the principal for the town of Chennai (hereinafter called the TERRITORY) for the purpose of making sales of the principal's goods for the term of 5 years from the date hereof on the terms and conditions herein contained.

2. The AGENT shall not while selling the principal's goods make any representation in the trade or give any warranty other than those contained in the principal's printed current price list.

3. The AGENT shall be entitled to deduct and retain with himself 20 per cent from the list price of all goods sold by him on behalf of the PRINCIPAL as his commission. The AGENT shall keep a record of all sales and shall remit to the PRINCIPAL regularly each week/each Monday all moneys/sale proceeds received by him in respect of such sale. All sales shall be made for cash against delivery of goods unless the principal's consent first obtained in writing to give credit to any particular purchaser and in case of such credit sales the PRINCIPAL may direct the agent to charge 20% more than the principal's price list.

4. The AGENT shall not make any purchase on behalf of nor in any manner pledge the credit of the PRINCIPAL without prior written consent of the principal.

5. The AGENT shall at his expense take on rent and occupy for the purpose of the agency suitable premises with prior approval of the PRINCIPAL and shall keep insured for the full value against all risks of all the goods entrusted to him under this agreement and on request by the PRINCIPAL shall produce to the PRINCIPAL receipts for the rent, rates and taxes of the said premises and for the premiums on insurance policies showing that the same have been paid on due dates.

6. The AGENT shall not sell nor allow anybody else in the trade to sell the principal's products outside the agency territory nor sell to the public below the listed price for the time being.

7. The AGENT shall in all his commercial dealings, documents, on name-plates or letter-heads describe himself as selling agent for the PRINCIPAL.

8. It is agreed that any breach of any term or condition of this agreement by the AGENT shall entitle the PRINCIPAL to put an end to this agreement forthwith and also to recover from the AGENT in addition to the listed price by way of liquidated damages 30% of the listed price for each such article sold in breach of such clause. The agent undertakes that all the purchasers to whom he may sell the principal's goods shall be duly entered into the books of the agent.

9. The PRINCIPAL shall keep with the agent a stock of its goods worth Rs. 50 lakhs at the principal's current price and the PRINCIPAL shall replenish such stock on the close of each month subject to availability of stock and exigencies such as delay in transit, accidents, strikes or other unavoidable occurrences.

10. The PRINCIPAL shall have the right to check the stock of the said goods and on any shortage or deficiency found on such stock-taking the agent shall on demand pay to the PRINCIPAL the listed price thereof less commission.

11. The AGENT shall not alter, remove or tamper with the marks or numbers on the principal's goods. He shall not sell the goods of the PRINCIPAL

at a price less than the listed price. However, he may allow a discount of 5 per cent on the listed price.

12. If any dispute arises between the AGENT and the PURCHASER of the principal's goods, the AGENT shall immediately inform the PRINCIPAL of the same and shall not without the principal's approval or consent in writing take any legal proceedings in respect of or compromise such dispute or grant a release to the purchaser.

13. This agreement may be terminated by either party at any time after the expiration of 5 years by giving to the other one month's notice in writing.

14. The benefits under this agreement shall not be assignable to any other person.

15. The PRINCIPAL shall redirect all inquiries or orders for principal's goods received by it from persons residing in the agency TERRITORY of the said agent and in the event where the PRINCIPAL supplies such purchasers directly it shall allow the AGENT the same commission or rebate as the agent would have been entitled to retain if he had done the transaction.

16. The agent undertakes to refer to the PRINCIPAL all enquiries or orders for the principal's goods from the persons residing outside the agency territory of the agent and similar enquiries or orders from persons residing in the agency TERRITORY for the purchase for re-sale outside the said TERRITORY and the AGENT shall be entitled to 2% commission in respect of any sale resulting from any such enquiries or orders.

17. The AGENT undertakes to devote his whole business, time and energy for pushing the sale of the principal's goods and shall in all such dealings act honestly and faithfully to the PRINCIPAL and shall carry out principal's orders and instructions and shall not engage himself or be interested either directly or indirectly as AGENT or servant in any other business or trade without the prior consent in writing of the PRINCIPAL.

18. On the termination of this agreement for any reason whatsoever the agent shall not for a period of one year solicit trade or orders from the persons who had been purchasers of the principal's goods any time within 5 years immediately preceding the date of such termination and the agent shall not for a period of one year engage or be interested as agent or servant in any business, firm or company manufacturing, selling or dealing in goods similar to those manufactured and/or dealt with by the PRINCIPAL.

19. Without prejudice to any other remedy the PRINCIPAL may have against the AGENT for any breach or non-performance of any term of this agreement the PRINCIPAL shall have the right summarily to terminate this agreement if the agent is found guilty of misconduct or negligence in discharge of his duties or absenting himself from his business duties for more than 15 days without sufficient cause, or the agent committing any act of bankruptcy.

20. The PRINCIPAL shall be entitled to terminate this agreement by giving one month's notice in writing to the agent in the event the PRINCIPAL ceases to carry on its business.

21. On the termination of this agreement for whatever reason the AGENT shall immediately return to the PRINCIPAL all unsold stock of goods and pay for the shortages in stock at the listed prices less commission. The agent shall deliver to the PRINCIPAL all books of account, document or securities he may have received during the normal course as a result of sales of the principal's goods and shall transfer, assign or negotiate in favour of the PRINCIPAL all such securities on demand.

22. In the event of any dispute arising out of or in relation to or touching the agreement the same shall be decided by arbitration in accordance with the provisions of the Arbitration and Conciliation Act 1996.

IN WITNESS WHEREOF the parties hereto have executed these presents on the day, month and year first above-written.

Signed, sealed and delivered by Mr. .... pursuant to Board Resolution dated .... of AB Co. Ltd. in the presence of:

Signed and delivered by Mr. AP the proprietor of CD in the presence of:

Appointment of Sole Selling Agent

THIS AGREEMENT IS MADE on this 11th day of October 2000 BETWEEN AB Co. Ltd., a company registered under the Companies Act 1956 and carrying business at ...., Calcutta (hereinafter referred to as the COMPANY) of the One Part and CD Co. Ltd., a company registered under the Companies Act 1956 and carrying business at ...., Kerala (hereinafter called AGENT) of the Other Part.

WHEREAS the COMPANY is engaged in the manufacture of cotton and textiles polyster fibre yarn suitings and shirtings.

AND WHEREAS the AGENT is the wholesale trader in suitings and shirtings and textile goods and materials in South India with headquarters at Ernakulam and has approached the COMPANY for being appointed as sole selling agent of the COMPANY in South India.

AND WHEREAS the COMPANY in its general meeting held on 15th September 2000 has decided to appoint CD Co. Ltd. as the sole selling agent for Southern

India for whole-sale business of the company's manufactured suitings and shirtings and the Central Government has also approved the appointment of the said sole-selling agent for the said goods.

NOW THIS AGREEMENT WITNESSES and the parties hereby agree as follows:

1. The COMPANY appoints CD Co. Ltd., Kerala as the sole selling agent for South India for the suitings and shirtings manufactured by the COMPANY and the said Agent will have the exclusive right and authority to sell whether in cash or on credit and procure the orders for sale of the said products of the COMPANY in any manner in the said territory.

2. The appointment shall take effect from 1st day of November 2000 and shall remain in force for five years from the said date without prejudice to the right of re-appointment but subject to the approval by the COMPANY in general meeting and also subject to the approval by the Central Government as required under section 294 of the Companies Act 1956 and rule 2 of the Companies (Appointment of Sole Agents) Rules 1975.

3. The AGENT shall have the right to operate in the entire territories of South India either directly or through their branch offices, associates or sub-agents for giving effect to this agreement.

4. The AGENT in consideration of its selling and procuring orders for the sale of the company's products shall be paid a commission of 25% on the total sales effected by it but on the amount actually collected by it and paid to the COMPANY.

5. The AGENT hereby covenants that it will exclusively engage in the sale of the company's products to the best of its ability and shall not engage in the sale of similar or identical products of other manufacturers and it will protect, preserve and maintain patents and trade mark of the company's products sold by it in all possible manner at its own cost and will never allow others to use the same unauthorisedly. The AGENT will keep and maintain full and complete accounts of the sale of the company's products, area-wise and region-wise and submit quarterly reports of sale, stock-in-hand, realisation of credit bills and any other information as may be desired by the COMPANY from time to time. It will not create any obligations involving payment either in cash or kind on behalf of the COMPANY and shall not assign any interest, right and obligation arising out of these presents to any third party. The AGENT shall keep the company well informed of the demands of the COMPANY'S products arising in the territories of its operation from time to time.

6. The COMPANY hereby covenants that it shall provide to the AGENT complete catalogues, instruction books, circulars for promoting sales of its products and publish advertisements in local and regional newspapers for promoting sales of the company's products. It shall execute orders placed

by the AGENT with all reasonable despatch and shall not entertain or execute direct orders from the territories assigned to the agent and in case any orders are received by it the same shall be passed on to the AGENT and it will be paid commission at 25% on such orders when executed.

7. The parties hereto hereby agree that nothing contained herein shall prejudice the rights of the COMPANY to appoint another selling agent in the same territory or to open its own retail shop where it is found necessary to promote public distribution system or to execute any special programme of the Government of India. However, the COMPANY shall obtain prior consent in writing of the AGENT in that behalf.

8. The retail price of the product shall always be determined by the COMPANY in consultation with the AGENT.

9. This agreement shall be renewable subject to mutual consent of the parties hereto on the expiry of five years.

10. The agreement may be terminated by either party on giving six months' notice in advance to the other party in writing.

11. Any dispute arising between the parties hereto shall be referred to the sole arbitrator Mr. MN whose decision/award shall be binding upon the parties hereto.

12. The Calcutta Courts will have the jurisdiction to decide the issues in dispute between the parties hereto.

IN WITNESS WHEREOF the parties herein execute these presents on the day, month and year first above-written.

Signed, sealed and delivered by Mr. .... pursuant to Board Resolution dated 30th September 2000 of AB Co. Ltd. in the presence of:

Signed, sealed and delivered by Mr. .... pursuant to Board Resolution dated 1st October 2000 of CD Co. Ltd. in the presence of:

51

Special Leave Petition to Appeal

According to the rules and forms available a Special Leave Petition to the Hon'ble Supreme Court of India is to be filed in a Paper Book form. The Paper Book will have the cover page an index with documents annexed, office report on limitation, synopsis of facts and circumstances of the case, a List of the relevant dates, a copy of the impugned Judgment decree or order appealed from, the main petition under Art. 136 of the Constitution of India, a Certificate and an affidavit.

Though special leave is granted the discretionary power which vested in the court at the stage of the Special Leave Petition continues to remain with the court even at the stage when the appeal comes up for hearing and when both sides are heard on merits in the appeal. Even when the Supreme Court is dealing with the appeal after grant of special leave, the court is not bound to go into merits and even if the court does so and declares the law or points out the error—still the court may not interfere if the justice of the case on facts does not require interference or if the court feels that the relief could be moulded in a different fashion.[1]

A form of hypothetical Paper Book is given below for a rough idea which form, however, is subject to changes that may be made from time to time by the Apex Court.

FORMS

Model Form of Special Leave Petition

In the Supreme Court of India

Civil Appellate Jurisdiction

Special Leave Petition (Civil) No. .... of 1999.

(From the Judgment and Final Order dated .... passed by the Hon'ble Calcutta High Court consisting of the Hon'ble Mr. Justice ....

1 *Taherakhatoon* v *Salambin* AIR 1999 SC 1106.

and the Hon'ble Mr. Justice .... in FMA No. .... of 1999) with interim relief.

Sri .... son of .... *Petitioner*

versus

Co-operative Housing Society Ltd. and Ors. *Respondents*

WITH

I.A. No. .... of 1999

(Paper Book)

(Index kindly see inside)

Advocate for the Petitioner

INDEX

Model Form of Special Leave Petition

In the Supreme Court of India
Civil Appellate Jurisdiction

Special Leave Petition (Civil) No. .... of 1999

(From the Judgment and Final Order dated .... passed by the Hon'ble Calcutta High Court consisting of the Hon'ble Mr. Justice .... and the Hon'ble Mr. Justice .... in FMA No. .... of 1999).

In the matter of Sri .... son of .... *Petitioner*

versus

Co-operative Housing Society Ltd. and Ors. *Respondents*

OFFICE REPORT ON LIMITATION

The above-mentioned matter is in time/time barred.

Dated .... Section Officer

Synopsis

AB, owner of a rent-free land at .... (hereinafter referred to as the VENDOR), entered into an agreement with the CD Housing Society Ltd. for sale thereof on which land the Society intended to construct apartment building. An Indenture was entered into between the said owner and the Society. The price was fixed and Earnest Money was paid by way of part payment of the total price.

Clause 5 of the said agreement provided that the Society will construct multistoried building on the said land and the VENDOR will have the right to purchase 8 flats in the said building in the name of himself or his nominees each flat containing a floor-area of not less than 1200 sq. ft. The purchase price will be at the same rate as might be payable by other purchasers of similar flat in the said building. The society shall not sell those 8 flats without first offering to the vendor by giving at least sixty days' notice in writing. On failure of the vendor to signify his willingness to purchase within the said period of sixty days the Society will be entitled to dispose of the flat to any other person.

By a letter the Society informed the VENDOR that the vendor's application for membership was accepted and a three bedroomed flat No. 2 has been allotted to him at Rs. .... and for a garage space another Rs. .... In default of making payment on due dates, the allotment of the flat would be liable to be cancelled, and that the right of the VENDOR in the Society will be governed by West Bengal Co-operative Societies Act, Rules and its Bye-laws.

The Society issued two Share Certificates for Rs. 100 each in favour of the VENDOR and flat No. 2 in the said building allotted to him and demanded payment of the consideration money. The VENDOR had paid a lump sum amount against six flats out of eight flats and intimated that the balance amount would be paid within two months.

The VENDOR surrendered two flats out of the three allotted to him in the first instance and requested the Society to adjust the amount paid on account of those two flats against the flats booked by his two daughters. The shortfall would be paid within a specified date.

Due to certain litigations involving the Society the Hon'ble High Court at Calcutta appointed Special Officer in which the VENDOR was not a party.

The VENDOR being the allottee of flat No. 2 and the two Share Certificates of the Society died. During his lifetime the Society did not make any demand in regard to any liability of the VENDOR in respect of the said flat No. 2. The vendor's son wrote to the Special Officer that he was taking steps under the West Bengal Co-operative Societies Act to get his father's flat and two shares of the Society transferred to one of the heirs of the VENDOR.

The Special Officer replied that the claim for transfer of interest was not made within the stipulated period and as such the flat had been allotted to somebody else.

Vendor's son filed a case under sections 95 and 96 of the West Bengal Co-operative Societies Act 1983 before the Registrar of Co-operative Societies praying for possession of flat No. 2, a declaration as null and void the allotment made by Special Officer and for other reliefs.

The son also filed a writ petition under Art. 226 of the Constitution of India praying for a writ of mandamus commanding the Special Officer to cancel the allotment of flat No. 2, delivery of possession of flat No. 2 to the petitioner and for other reliefs. The son stated in the writ petition that he was ready and willing to pay the balance amount, if any, in respect of the said flat.

Ultimately the matter came before the Division Bench which gave directions in respect of other flats and in respect of the flat No. 2 the Division Bench did decide the issue but observed that this was the subject-matter of a pending writ petition.

The said writ petition was disposed of by a Single Judge directing the transfer of flat No. 2 to the writ petitioner, the son of the VENDOR, on payment of arrears. Against this order of the Single Judge the Society preferred an appeal. This appeal was heard and disposed of by the Division Bench which allowed the appeal and held against the son, the writ-petitioner.

Being aggrieved by and dissatisfied with the Judgement and order passed by the Hon'ble Division Bench of the Hon'ble High Court at Calcutta on

.... in First Miscellaneous Appeal No. .... of .... your petitioner begs to move the instant Special Leave Petition.

LIST OF DATES

....	Agreement BETWEEN the VENDOR and CD HOUSING SOCIETY LTD. for the sale of land at ...., Calcutta. A copy of the agreement is annexed hereto marked 'P-1'.
....	The Deputy Registrar, Co-operative Societies (Housing) Calcutta Metropolitan Area granted permission to the CD HOUSING SOCIETY to admit eight persons as members. The SOCIETY mentioned the names of the VENDOR and his five daughters in the list of members.
....	The society applied to the Registrar, Co-operative Societies (Housing), Calcutta Metropolitan Area seeking permission to admit eight persons as members which permission was granted by letter a copy whereof is annexed hereto marked 'P-2'.
....	The VENDOR executed conveyance in favour of the SOCIETY, and advance payment was made for three flats to be given by the SOCIETY to the VENDOR. A copy of the Sale Deed is annexed hereto marked 'P-3'.
....	The SOCIETY allotted flat No. 2 and two shares to the VENDOR (owner).
....	The Share Certificates and allotment of flat was communicated to the owner and the owner was informed that the specified sum was outstanding in respect of allotment of the said flat.
....	The owner retained one flat in his own name and surrendered two flats which the SOCIETY accepted. A copy of the letter is annexed hereto marked 'P-4'.
....	Special Officer was appointed by the Hon'ble High Court at Calcutta in FMA No. .... of .... to complete the construction and to consider allotment of available flats. A copy of the order is annexed hereto marked 'P-5'.
....	VENDOR died leaving behind five married daughters and a married son.

.... The Deputy Registrar of the Co-operative Societies was informed of death of the VENDOR and that the legal heirs were considering about the allotment of his interest. A copy of the letter is annexed hereto marked 'P-6'.

.... Son of the VENDOR informed the society that they could not decide in whose favour the flat will be transferred and wanted some more time. A copy of the letter is annexed hereto marked 'P-7'.

.... SOCIETY informed the son that as no information as to transfer of interest was given within the stipulated period the flat was re-allotted to an outsider. A copy of the said letter is annexed hereto marked 'P-8'.

.... The moneys lying with the SOCIETY was not refunded. The legal heirs finally decided to transfer the interest of the VENDOR in flat No. 2 to his son.

.... The son filed a dispute case under sections 95 and 96 of the West Bengal Co-ooperative Societies Act, 1983 against the Society and Special Officer before the Registrar, Co-operative Society, West Bengal.

.... The son filed a writ petition against the SOCIETY and Special Officer.

.... The writ petition was allowed and the allotment of flat No. 2 to some other person was cancelled and it was directed that the flat be transferred in the name of the son and to hand over the possession on payment of the balance amount. A copy of the Judgement is annexed hereto marked 'P-9'.

.... The society preferred an appeal before the Division Bench of the Hon'ble High Court at Calcutta against the said Judgement and Order of the Single Judge.

.... The said appeal from the Order of the Single Judge was heard by the Hon'ble Division Bench and by a Judgment and Order the Hon'ble Division Bench has been pleased to hold that the writ petition was not maintainable and directed the society to refund the moneys lying with it to the legal heirs of the VENDOR with 12% interest from the date of filing of the writ application till payment.

.... Special Leave Petition is filed today.

In the High Court at Calcutta
Appellate/Revisional Civil Jurisdiction

Present:

The Hon'ble Mr. Justice ....
And
The Hon'ble Mr. Justice ....

FMA No. .... of 1999

Co-operative Housing Society Ltd.
versus
The son and others

For Appellant/Petitioner
For Respondent/Opposite Party
Heard on ....
Judgment on ....
.... , J
....

Sd/- .... J
Sd/- .... J

Special Leave Petition seeking Stay Order from Operation of Impounged Judgement

In the Supreme Court of India

[Order XVI Rule 4(1)(*a*)]

Civil Appellate Jurisdiction

Petition for Special Leave to Appeal (Civil) No. ...... of 1999 (under Article 136 of the Constitution of India).

BETWEEN	Position of the parties	
	In the Calcutta High Court	In this Court

Shri .... son of	*Respondent No. 1*	*Petitioner*
AND		
1. Cooperative Housing Society Ltd. of .... Calcutta	*Appellant*	*Respondent No. 1*
2. .... Calcutta	*Respondent No. 2*	*Respondent No. 2*
3. State of West Bengal Service through	*Respondent No. 3*	*Respondent No. 3*
4. Registrar of Cooperative Societies, West Bengal, Calcutta	*Respondent No. 4*	*Respondent No. 4*

To

The Hon'ble the Chief Justice of India,
and His Companion Justices of the
Hon'ble Supreme Court of India

The Special Leave Petition of the Petitioner above-named

MOST RESPECTFULLY SHEWETH:

1. That your petitioner desires to move the instant Special Leave petition before the Hon'ble Supreme Court of India against the judgment and order passed by the Hon'ble Division Bench of the Hon'ble Calcutta High Court dated .... in FMA No. .... of ....

2. *Questions of Law*

(*a*) Whether the right of the Ownership of an apartment in the multistoried building under the West Bengal Co-operative Societies Act 1983 is heritable and transferable?

(*b*) Whether in the event of death of a member the legal heirs of such deceased member are entitled to inherit and get allotment of the apartment which the deceased member was entitled to?

(*c*) Whether in the event of the member dies without nominating any person to inherit the apartment interest of the deceased member for such apartment could it be inherited by all the legal heirs or by one of the legal heirs or by one of the legal heirs in the event other legal heirs give up their rights in favour of such single legal heir?

(*d*) Whether the right and interest of the legal heirs of the deceased member could be forfeited in the event of time taken in nominating particular legal heir for the same exceeded 3 months from the date of the death of the member because of certain unavoidable circumstances as the legal heirs were not available immediately in giving their consent and giving up their rights in favour of the single legal heir in whose favour the property desired by all the legal heirs to be transferred. More so when the Co-operative Society was intimated well in advance seeking extension of time in providing particular name in whose favour the property the legal heirs desired to be transferred?

(*e*) Whether on the issue of transfer of share of the deceased member any consideration in respect of admission of a member is relevant?

(*f*) Whether the valid membership in favour of the deceased member could be cancelled only because the name of the nominee in whose favour the property was to be transferred had taken some time for selecting such nominee by all the legal heirs?

(*g*) Whether the Cooperative Society is competent to re-allot a valid allotment in favour of the deceased member even when all financial obligations are complied with and the allottee was not a defaulter?

(*h*) Whether the Cooperative Society can re-allot the duly allotted apartment of a valid member in the event of death to a stranger ignoring the rights of the legal heirs of such deceased member?

(*i*) Whether the question of re-allotment on expiry of 3 months could arise when admittedly the court was moved when allotment was made and in view of specific term of the Hon'ble High Court dated .... by which the Society was specifically directed not to allot the earmarked apartment being Flat No. 2 and could the Society ignoring such direction reallot the flat to a stranger?

3. *Declaration in terms of rule 4(2).* The Petitioner states that no other petition seeking leave to appeal has been filed by him against the impugned judgment and order.

4. *Declaration in terms of rule 6.* The Annexures produced alongwith the Special Leave Petition are true copies of the documents which formed part of the records of the Case in the Court below against whose order the leave to appeal is sought for in this petition.

5. *Grounds*

(*a*) For that s. 87 of the West Bengal Co-operative Societies Act 1983 (hereinafter referred to as the said Co-operative Societies Act) deals in member's right of ownership and sub-sec. 3 of the said section which makes it abundantly clear that a plot of land or a house or an apartment in a multistoried building (including the undivided interest in the common areas and facilities) shall constitute a heritable and transferable immovable property within the meaning of any law for the time being in force provided that notwithstanding anything contained in any other law for the time being in force such heritable and transferable immovable property shall not be partitioned or sub-divided for any purpose whatsoever.

In terms of West Bengal Co-operative Societies Act and Rules the heirs of a deceased person are, therefore, entitled to inherit the flat allotted to the deceased, as in the instant case. Admittedly the flat in question was allotted to the said vendor father of petitioner who died thereafter and as a consequence thereof the heirs of the said deceased became and would be entitled to succeed to the estate and as a result thereof to the said flat with proportionate interest in the land.

(*b*) For that s. 80 of the said Co-operative Societies Act deals with disposal of the deceased member's share or interest and cl. (*b*) of sub-sec. (1) speaks that if there is no nominee or if the existence or residence of the nominee cannot be ascertained by the Board or if, for any other cause, the transfer cannot be made without unreasonable delay to the person who (subject to the production by such person of probate or letter of administration or succession certificate) appears to the Board to be entitled, in accordance with rules, possession of such shares or interest as part of the estate of the deceased members, or sub-sec. (*c*) on the application of the person referred to in cl. (*b*) within 3 months from the date of death of member to such person as may be specified in the application, which clearly indicate that while disposing of deceased member's share or interest the preferential claim always goes to the heirs and legal representatives of the deceased member in absence of any nominee.

(*c*) For that s. 82 of the said Co-operative Societies Act is very specific that notwithstanding anything contained elsewhere in the Act or any other law for the time being in force when the membership of a member of a Co-operative Society referred to in cl. (*a*) terminates by reason of death or any other cause his possession of, or interest in land held by him under Co-operative Society shall vest in his heirs or in the person,, if any, nominated by him under s. 79, if such heir is willing to be admitted as a member of the Co-operative Society.

(*d*) For that on a careful reading of the said cl. (*c*) of s. 80 of the said Co-operative Societies Act, it is clear that on the death of the member of the Co-operative Society his share or interest in the Co-operative Society shall be transferred on the application of the person referred to in cl. (*b*) within three months from the date of death of the member to such person as may be specified in the application. Therefore transfer of share or interest can be made only by a Co-operative Society. It is an obligation of the Society to transfer the share or interest of the deceased member within the stipulated period referred to in s. 80 of the Act.

(*e*) For that while disposing of the appeal the Hon'ble Court of Appeal below gave much stress on sub-sec. (3) of s. 85 of the said Act as also sub-rule (5) of rule 135 taking the present case to be a case for admission of membership which is not in the present case. In the instant case the question of admission of membership becomes absolutely immaterial, the real question is of transfer or devolution of interest of a deceased member. The applicant/petitioner herein being one of the heirs of a deceased member was and still is entitled to succeed to the estate of the deceased member as per the mandatory provision of the statutes and that being so the right, title and interest of the deceased member in the apartment of the Co-operative Society devolves upon the heirs and in that background the aforesaid s. 85(3) and rules 135(5) neither have nor can have any application in the instant case because there cannot be any manner of doubt that on the death of a member of a Co-operative Society his share of interest in the Co-operative Society shall in the absence of a nominee be transferred to a person who appears to the Board to be entitled to in accordance with rules, possession of such interest as part of the estate of the deceased member and herein in the instant case the son who himself is admittedly not a member of the society in question or any other housing society became entitled to be considered for such allotment immediately he gave notice to the appropriate authority which too long before the alleged re-allotment was said to have been made.

(*f*) For that it was not only improper but also highly illegal, arbitrary, motivated and unconstitutional for the Special Officer to re-allot the flat to a stranger even after he had received letter regarding transfer of ownership in favour of legal heirs in .... long long before such alleged re-allotment, claimed to have been made in .... *i.e.* more than 16 months from receipt thereof, without giving any opportunity of being heard and without deciding the question as to who was entitled to the said flat in accordance with law.

(*g*) For that on proper construction of the statute that a member of a Co-operative Society shall cease to be such member if he dies and upon his death his share or interest, in absence of any nomination to that effect, may be transferred by the Board of the Society in favour of any person who presents in writing his or her claim for the said share or interest and in this background the alleged re-allotment of the apartment of the deceased member to a stranger not being the legal heirs of the deceased member is without jurisdiction, unconstitutional, and not maintainable in law and as such is liable to be set aside due to the reason that the Special

Officer in the instant case had taken the decision to re-allot the said apartment without considering the case of the legal heirs of the deceased member and without giving them any opportunity of hearing which decision manifestly appears to be contrary to the principle of natural justice.

(*h*) For that the Hon'ble Division Bench was wrong in dismissing the writ application holding *inter alia* that the petitioner thus having failed to show that any of the mandatory provisions of statute has been violated by the appellant society, the writ petition was not maintainable because the ground taken hereinabove show that most of the mandatory provisions of the statute had been violated by the said society and as such in that view of the matter the impugned judgement deserved to be set aside.

(*i*) For that the learned court below erred in law in dismissing the writ petition holding *inter alia.* In fact, the writ petition ought to have been dismissed also on the ground that the special officer rightly or wrongly had re-allotted the flat as far back as in the year .... in favour of a 3rd party. By reason of allowing the writ petition the right of the 3rd party would be affected but despite the same he had not been impleaded as a party therein.

In this view of the matter also the writ petition was not maintainable for non-impleading a necessary party.

It is not a case where the question of ownership was required to be considered *vis-a-vis* the right of a 3rd party without considering that on the date of filing of the said writ petition *i.e.* .... the writ petitioner was not aware of allotment of the flat in question to any 3rd party not a heir of the deceased member. The society revealed for the first time in their letter dated .... that they would submit to the Division Bench of their Lordships the Hon'ble Mr. Justice .... and the Hon'ble Mr. Justice .... (as their Lordships then were), a proposal for allotment of flat No. 2 that is the flat already allotted to late vendor on .... to Mr. Z. This letter was written to .... on .... a reapondent in FMA No. .... Moreover by their order dated .... Their Lordships gave the Special Officer of the Society liberty to deliver all other flats on the terms and conditions except the said flat No. 2. Therefore, the dismissal of the writ petition by the Division Bench on the ground of non-impleading the said allotee in the writ petition could not be held to be justified or made in accordance with law.

6. *Ground for interim relief*

(*i*) That the respondent No. 1 Society has informed that the allotment in favour of the deceased allottee stood cancelled because no appropriate person could be named as the legal heir of the deceased allottee in whose favour the respondent No. 1

Society was to make the allotment and as such the Society has been threatening of re-allotting flat No. 2 of the deceased allottee to a stranger ignoring the rights of the legal heirs. The petitioner understands till date no such allotment has been made and even if the some steps have been taken by the Society it will be wholly against the direction given by the Calcutta High Court as early as on .... by which the society was specifically directed not to allot the earmarked apartment No. 2 to any stranger and in such a position it is extremely essential for your petitioner to obtain appropriate order from this Hon'ble Court restraining the respondent No. 1 to make such irregular and illegal allotment.

(*ii*) Your petitioner submits that not only by the impugned judgement and order dated .... passed in FMA No. ...... the fundamental right of the heirs and legal representatives of the vendor since deceased, the erstwhile owner in respect of the flat No. 2 in the 5th floor of premises No. .... has been seriously prejudiced but also there has been grave miscarriage of justice because of the fact that the said right to property is right *in rem* as guaranteed under the Constitution of India and the said right to property has been denied by the impugned judgement for which the petitioner has been constrained to prefer the instant Special Leave Petition and petitioner prays that the Society respondent No. 1 should be restrained from taking any steps to reallot the earmarked apartment till the disposal of the petitioner's present appeal otherwise the petitioner will suffer irreparable loss and injury.

7. *Main Prayers.* Under the circumstances stated hereinabove your petitioner most humbly and respectfully prays that Your Lordships would graciously be pleased to grant Special Leave to your petitioner to Appeal under Art. 136 of the Constitution of India against the judgement and order passed by the Hon'ble Division Bench of Calcutta High Court in FMA No. .... of .... and/or to pass such other or further orders as to this Hon'ble Court may deem fit and proper.

8. *Interim Relief*

(*a*) Under the circumstances set forth above, it is therefore prayed that Your Lordships may graciously be pleased to pass an order staying operation of the impugned judgement and order dated .... in FMA No. .... thereby restraining the Co-operative Housing Society Ltd., respondent No. 1 herein, from making allotment of the Flat No. 2 to any stranger till the disposal of the petitioner's present appeal before this Hon'ble Court.

(*b*) pass such other order or orders as Your Lordships may deem fit and proper.

AND FOR THIS YOUR PETITIONER SHALL EVER PRAY.

Drawn by

Filed by
Advocate for the Petitioner

REQUISITE CERTIFICATE

Certified that the Special Leave Petition is confined only to the pleadings before the court whose order is challenged and the other documents relied upon in those proceedings. No additional facts, documents, or grounds have been taken therein or relied upon in the Special Leave Petition. It is further certified that the true copies of the documents have been annexured and/ or attached to the Special Leave Petition for consideration of this Hon'ble Court. This certificate is given on the basis of the instructions given by the petitioner whose affidavit is filed in support of the Special Leave Petition.

Filed by
Filed on: .... Advocate for the Petitioner

In the Supreme Court of India
Civil Appellate Jurisdiction

Special Leave Petition (Civil) No. .... of 1999

Sri .... son of .... *Petitioner*

.........Co-operative Housing Society Ltd. .... *Respondents* & Ors.

AFFIDAVIT

I, Sri .... son of .... aged about .... years residing at .... presently in New Delhi do hereby solemnly affirm and say as follows:

1. That I am the petitioner in the present Special Leave Petition and am fully conversant with the facts and circumstances of the present case and am fully competent to swear the present affidavit.

2. That the facts stated in the Synopsis, List of Dates and the petition for Special Leave are all true to my knowledge and the rest are all submissions before the Hon'ble Supreme Court of India.

3. That the Annexures filed with the Special Leave Petition are all true copies of their Originals and the same formed part of the records in the court below.

4. That the contents of this affidavit are true to my knowledge.

DEPONENT

Verified at New Delhi, this the
.... day of 1999

52

Surrender

A lease of immovable property may be determined by surrender, by yielding up the interest of the lessee under the lease to the lessor by mutual agreement.[1] The surrender of lease or tenancy takes effect like a contract by mutual consent, by surrender by tenant of the tenancy and acceptance of the surrender by the owner/lessor. The surrender must be to a person who is the immediate owner of the premises. If there are several lessees, one of them can surrender his interest in favour of the lessor. A Deed of Surrender without more is not compulsorily registrable. Registration is optional. Stamp Duty is payable generally under Art. 61 of the Stamp Act. If the intention to surrender is sufficiently expressed, no particular form is required. The surrender takes effect in the present. It is not made to take effect in future. However an agreement to surrender can be enforced by specific performance. In surrender delivery of possession is essential.

A Deed of Surrender of Lease or tenancy may be on market value of the property but that is not decisive or conclusive as the rights of surrender cannot be equated to the market value of the property. A Deed of Surrender of Lease is liable to Stamp Duty under Art. 61 of the Indian Stamp Act 1899. If surrender of tenancy is coupled with the transfer of any assets, then the stamp duty will be payable on the document as a Deed of Surrender as also as transfer of the assets.

FORMS

Deed of Surrender of Tenancy

THIS DEED OF SURRENDER of tenancy is made on this 10th day of June 2000 BETWEEN the X Co. Ltd., a company registered under the Companies Act

1 Section 111 of the Transfer of Property Act 1882.

1956 and having its Registered Office at and carrying on business, *inter alia*, at .... (hereinafter referred to as the TENANT) of the one part and Mr. .... residing at .... (hereinafter referred to as the OWNER) of the OTHER PART.

AND WHEREAS on 7th April 2000 an agreement was entered into by and between the TENANT and the OWNER whereby and whereunder the OWNER let out to the TENANT one ground-floor flat comprising of four rooms, one kitchen, two bathrooms, one car parking space, common use of servant-latrines and common passage around the flat with 5 ceiling fans and one Geyser at .... at a monthly rental of Rs. .... from 9th April 1998.

AND WHEREAS all rates, taxes, cesses and levies or impositions were agreed to be paid by the OWNER and that the TENANT would have no responsibility in respect thereof.

AND WHEREAS under the said agreement and pursuance thereof, the said OWNER gave occupation of the said flat to the TENANT and the Tenant has been in occupation thereof since then.

AND WHEREAS the OWNER approached the TENANT for vacating the said flat on various grounds including hardship to him and the TENANT then duly considered the same and with a view to avoid any possible litigation and expenses has agreed to surrender the said tenancy of the said flat.

NOW THEREFORE THIS DEED witnesseth and the parties agree as follows:

1. The said OWNER hereby admits confirms and acknowledges that on this day he has received peaceful vacant possession of the said ground floor flat comprising of four rooms, one kitchen, two bath rooms, one car parking space, common servant latrine and common passage around the flat with all fittings and furniture, water, drainage, sanitary fittings and electrical installations in the same good order and conditions as they were when the said flat was let out to the TENANT less normal wear and tear.

2. The TENANT declares that it has not created any encumbrance over the said flat and the same is free from all encumbrances.

3. The OWNER agrees and declares that the TENANT has paid all dues, including rent in respect of the said flat up to this day and nothing is due or payable by the TENANT to the OWNER in respect of the said flat.

4. The parties hereby agree that neither party has paid any money to the other by way of inducement for surrender of the tenancy.

5. The OWNER hereby agrees confirms and declares that he has received peaceful and vacant possession of the said flat from the TENANT free from all encumbrances and the OWNER has accepted the delivery of vacant possession of the said flat with all fittings and furniture and also the keys and he has no claim whatsoever against the tenant in relation to the said flat or otherwise.

6. The OWNER hereby confirms and declares that nothing is due from and payable by the TENANT in respect of the said rent or municipal charges,

water charges, electricity bills or any other charges or claims in respect of the said flat.

7. The OWNER hereby agrees and declares that he would keep the TENANT fully indemnified against and harmless from all proceedings, claims, actions, expenses, charges and costs thereof whatsoever in relation to the said flat for giving peaceful vacant possession of the said flat to the said OWNER.

8. It is recorded that neither party has any claim against the other in relation to the said flat or otherwise whatsoever.

9. It is recorded that the Security Deposit of Rs. .... has already been refunded on receiving peaceful vacant possession of the said flat the receipt thereof the tenant hereby admits.

IN WITNESS WHEREOF the parties hereto have executed this Deed on the day, month and year first above-written.

Signed, sealed and delivered by
Mr. .... duly authorised
by and holder of Power of Attorney
from X. Co. Ltd. on this 10th day
of June 2000 in the presence of:

Signed and delivered by Mr. ......
.... the OWNER in the
presence of:

Surrender of Lease

THIS DEED OF SURRENDER of lease is made on this 10th day of June 2000 BETWEEN X. Co. Ltd. having its Registered Office at and carrying on business, *inter alia*, at .... (hereinafter called the TENANT) of the one part and Smt. AB residing at .... (hereinafter called the OWNER) of the OTHER PART.

WHEREAS by registered lease dated .... Mr. CD demised unto the Tenant Flat No. 3 on the 5th Floor of the building at .... for 5 years commencing from .... at the rent of Rs. ...... per month, the owner paying all the rates, taxes and assessments payable or that might be imposed or assessed on the said premises by the Government or the Municipality or any other bodies and keep the Tenant indemnified therefrom and from all proceedings, costs, claims and demands in respect thereof and keep the tenanted premises in good repair.

AND WHEREAS the said premises was transferred by Mr. CD on .... to Smt. AB and the lease was extended from time to time and the last increase in rent was on .... to Rs. .... per month.

AND WHEREAS the OWNER approached the TENANT for vacating the said Flat No. 3 on the 5th Floor of .... on various grounds.

AND WHEREAS the TENANT has duly considered the request of the OWNER and has agreed to the request of the OWNER to avoid future complications and litigations.

NOW THEREFORE THIS deed witnesseth and the parties hereto agree as follows:

1. The said Smt. AB the owner hereby declares that she is the full owner of the said Flat No. 3 on the 5th floor, premises No. .... and is entitled to receive on surrender of the said flat by the TENANT possession thereof and give complete discharge to the TENANT from all obligations whatsoever in respect of the said flat.

2. The OWNER declares that there is no arrears of rent, electricity bills, or any other claim in respect of the said flat and all dues payable by the TENANT upto and including the .... have been received.

3. The OWNER hereby confirms and records that she has received quiet, peaceful and vacant possession of the said flat free from all encumbrances with all furniture and fixtures in the same good order and condition in which the same demised flat was let out to the TENANT.

4. The OWNER hereby records confirms and declares that neither party has paid to the other any money by way of compensation or otherwise and this is being executed on consideration of avoiding any future litigation and avoidable expenses.

5. The parties agree and declare that in consideration of the aforesaid, the TENANT has delivered peaceful and vacant possession of the said flat with all fittings and furniture and the OWNER has received delivery thereof including the keys of the said flat and taken vacant possession of the said flat together with all fittings and furniture in the same condition in which the said flat was demised to the TENANT after having removed all the articles and things belonging to the TENANT.

6. It is declared that neither party has any claim against the other in respect of the said flat No. 3 on the 5th Floor at the premises No. .... of ....

7. Each party hereby releases the other from all obligations arising under the said tenancy agreement including any security deposit.

8. The OWNER hereby declares and undertakes to keep the TENANT fully indemnified against and harmless from any action, proceedings, expenses, charges, costs and claims of whatsoever nature in relation to the said flat No. 3 on the 5th floor of premises No. .... of .... for delivering peaceful and vacant possession of the said flat to the OWNER for whatsoever reason or cause of action.

In witness whereof the parties hereto have executed this Deed on the day, month and year first above-written.

Signed, sealed and delivered by Mr. .... duly authorised by and the Power of Attorney Holder of X Co. Ltd. on this 10th day of June 2000 in the presence of:

Signed and delivered by Smt. AB whom the contents and effects hereof have been explained by her Advocate on this 10th day of June 2000 at Calcutta in the presence of:

Surrender of Tenanted Flat

This deed of surrender of tenancy is made on this 10th day of June 2000 between X. Co. Ltd. having its registered office at ...., Mumbai and carrying on business, *inter alia*, at ...., Calcutta (hereinafter called the tenant) of the one part and Mr. JK, residing at .... (hereinafter called the owner) of the other part.

Whereas by an agreement dated .... the owner demised unto the tenant a self-contained flat having carpet area of 1200 sq. ft. comprising of three bedrooms, one drawing room, one kitchen, two baths, balcony, corridor, garage space, meter room being flat No. ...... of .... commencing from .... as a monthly tenant at the rent of Rs. 3,850 per month and security deposit of Rs. 7,850 the owner paying all the rates, taxes and assessments payable or that might be imposed or assessed on the said premises by the Government or the Municipality or any other bodies and keep the tenant indemnified therefrom and from all proceedings, costs, claims and demands in respect thereof and keep the tenanted premises in good repair.

And whereas the owner approached the tenant for vacating the said flat on various grounds and a Writ Petition for vacation of the said flat on reasonable requirements is pending.

And whereas the tenant has fully considered the request of the owner and has agreed to the request of the owner to avoid further complications and litigations.

Now therefore this deed witnesseth and the parties hereby agree as follows:

1. The said owner hereby declares that he is still the full owner of the said flat and is entitled to receive on surrender of the said flat by the tenant possession thereof and give complete discharge to the tenant from all obligations whatsoever in respect of the said flat.

2. The OWNER declares that there is no arrears of rent, electricity bills or any other claims in respect of the said flat and all dues payable by the tenant up to and including the .... have been received and the security deposit has been refunded and adjusted.

3. The OWNER hereby confirms and records that he has received quiet, peaceful and vacant possession of the said flat free from all encumbrances with all furniture and fixtures in the same good order and condition in which the same demised flat was let out to the said TENANT.

4. The OWNER hereby records confirms and declares that neither party has paid to the other any money by way of compensation or otherwise and this is being executed in consideration of avoiding any further litigations and expenses.

5. The parties agree and declare that in consideration of the aforesaid the tenant has delivered peaceful and vacant possession of the said flat with all fittings and furnitures and the OWNER has received delivery thereof including the keys of the said flat and taken vacant possession of the said flat together with all fittings and furniture in the same good condition in which the said flat was demised to the tenant after having removed all the articles and things belonging to the TENANT.

6. It is declared that neither party has any claim against the other in respect of the said flat and the owner undertakes to withdraw the Writ Petition being Matter No. ...... of .... pending in the Hon'ble High Court at Calcutta.

7. The OWNER hereby releases in favour of the TENANT the entire security deposit of Rs. 7,850 by a Demand Draft being No. .... etc. the receipt of which the TENANT hereby acknowledges.

8. Each party hereby releases the other from all obligations arising under the said tenancy agreement and any extension and/or modifications thereof and/or in relation to the said flat.

9. The OWNER hereby declares and undertakes to keep the TENANT fully indemnified against and harmless from any action, proceedings, expenses, charges, costs and claims of whatsoever nature in relation to the said flat first above described for delivering peaceful and vacant possession of the said flat to the owner for whatsoever reason or cause of action.

IN WITNESS WHEREOF the parties hereto have executed this Deed on the day, month and year first above-written.

Signed, sealed and delivered by Mr. .... duly authorised by X Co. Ltd. on this 10th day of June 2000 in the presence of:

Signed and delivered by Mr. JK on this 10th day of June 2000 in the presence of:

53

Testamentary Matters*

Probate—Letters of Administration and Succession Certificates

Introductory observations. An executor may be appointed by the testator himself or he may ask another to make the appointment.[1] He only is entitled to probate of the will of a deceased person under s. 221 of the Indian Succession Act. He is the legal representative and all the property of the deceased vests in him for the purpose of representation and administration. Under s. 307 of the said Act, he has power to sell any such property in course of administration and in the absence of any contrary provisions in the will. This, however, does not mean that he becomes the absolute owner by virtue of his position as an executor. An executor has no beneficial interest in the property which vests in him under s. 211 of the said Act and he holds the same in trust for the administration of the estate of the deceased.[2] Therefore, s. 307 read with s. 211 makes his power to sell limited for the purpose of administration. The City Civil Court (Amendment) Act 1980 has taken away the jurisdiction of the High Court under the Indian Succession Act (Act 39 of 1925).

The property of the deceased vests in Executor on his acceptance of the office. He may institute a suit but must obtain the probate before the decree is made.[2] If he himself is a legatee then he must prove the will or otherwise manifest his intention to act as executor.[3] The High Court had special jurisdiction to grant probate of will in the common form. This is based upon the English practice where an affidavit of one of the attesting witnesses in

* *See* Chapter 56 on Will.

1 *Mosa Hagi* v *Hagi Abdul* 5 Bom LR 630.

2 *Bibhuti Bhusan* v *Nagendra Narayan* AIR 1951 Cal 228.

3 Section 141 of the Indian Succession Act.

compliance with s. 63 of the Indian Succession Act read with s. 68 of the Indian Evidence Act is considered as sufficient evidence as regards the proof of the will. A probate granted in common form could be easily revoked than when it is granted in solemn form. If the grant was made in the common form, it may even then be shown that the will is forged.[4] The difference in grant in solemn form and in common form was observed by the Privy Council in *Ramanandi* v *Mt. Kalawati.*[5] If after service of the citation there is no contest, the procedure corresponds to the English practice of probate in the common form. But where the grant is challenged also on the ground that the will is forged which fails on evidence, it could be revoked even though there was no citation on proper parties. Further, it had in its original jurisdiction power to grant probate or letters of administration concurrent with the District Court.[6] Moreover, it could, under s. 301 of the Act, remove any executor and give administrative directions under s. 302. It acts in pursuance of its testamentary and intestate jurisdiction under cl. (34) of the Letters Patent, but this section was not a substitute for a suit and did not mean adjudication of any substantive rights.[7] An executor must obtain probate of will before he can establish his right as executor.[8]

A probate court is a court of conscience. A probate when granted establishes the will from the death of the testator[9] and conclusive as regards execution according to the law of the country. It is no evidence as to the title of the testator in respect of the properties bequeathed. Nevertheless it is conclusive as to the appointment of the executor.[10] Its judgment nevertheless operates as the judgment *in rem*,[11] but the same does not operate as *res judicata*. So the decision of the probate court on the construction of the will for the purpose of the grant does not bar any action for construction of the will.[12] A grant of administration does not decide any question of title but merely the right to administer the estate.[13]

Persons standing in confidential relationship cannot take any benefits under a will unless he can establish that the testator had competent and independent legal advice. So, if a solicitor prepares a will of which he is also a beneficiary, he is to discharge the onus.[14] Similarly, a solicitor attesting a

4 *Priestman* v *Thomas* 53 LJP 109; 51 LT 843; 33 WR 842.
5 LR 55 IA 18.
6 Section 300 of the Indian Succession Act.
7 *Akshoy* v *Ghosh* AIR 1949 Cal 462.
8 Section 213 of the Indian Succession Act.
9 Section 227 of the Indian Succession Act.
10 Section 41 of the Indian Evidence Act.
11 Section 41 of the Indian Evidence Act.
12 *Arunmoyi* v *Mohendra* 20 Cal 888.
13 *Kamala Prasad* v *Murli* AIR 1926 Pat 356 at p. 358.
14 *Gangabhai* v *Bhagwandas* 32 IA 142.

will of which he is also a beneficiary loses his professional charges.[15] This section does not apply to Hindus, Buddhists etc. This is the legacy of the principle of old English law by which the testimony of persons interested in the transaction was not admissible in evidence.

Law contemplated other types of grant, *viz.*, certificate.

(*a*) Under s. 29 of the Administrator-General's Act (Act 45 of 1963) and in cases of small estates of values not exceeding Rs. 5,000 (excluding Government Savings Bank deposits and Provident Fund moneys). The said Act has no application in those cases. The Administrator-General of the State can issue a certificate to receive the assets mentioned therein. This is still granted.

(*b*) Under s. 12 of the Indian Securities Act 1920, read with s. 19 of the said Act, a District Magistrate could grant a certificate of heirship in case of Government promissory notes where the deceased was a member of a joint Mitakshara family and in the other cases when the face value does not exceed Rs. 5,000.[1] The laws as to Government securities have been consolidated by the Public Debt Act 1944 (Act XVIII of 1944), which came into force on 1st May 1946 (*vide* Gazette of India 1946, Part 1, page 575). Although under s. 7 of the said Act the executors or administrators of a deceased and the holder of a succession certificate are the only persons who may be recognised by the Reserve Bank, nevertheless it can in the case of the Mitakshara family, recognise the title of the next holder. The Reserve Bank can, on summary procedure on the death of the holder of G.P. Notes of the value not exceeding Rs. 5,000, adjudicate the title of the claimant (*Government Securities Manual*, 4th Ed., pp. 137-138). The functions of the Administrator-General are in no way less than those of the executor or of the administrator. He can be appointed as executor or administrator. He has also the power to take possession of any property under s. 10 of the Administrator-General's Act (Act 45 of 1963) in case of immediate danger of appropriation. He can, under s. 22 of the Act, accept transfer of assets from executors and administrators.

PROBATES OF WILL AND LETTERS OF ADMINISTRATION WITH WILL ANNEXED

(a) *Executor, Administrator, Probate, Letters of Administration.* 'Executor' is the nominee of the deceased. It means a person to whom the execution of the last will of a deceased person is, by the testator's appointment, confided [s. 2(c) of the Indian Succession Act]. The testator may himself appoint or ask somebody to appoint an executor.

15 *Re, Pooley* 40 Ch D 1; 60 LT 63.

1 See also s. 66 of the *Government Securities Manual*, 3rd Ed., p. 77.

'Administrator' means a person appointed by the court to administer the estate of the deceased in cases where there is no executor or where the executor has renounced probate or is incapable to act or dies before taking out the probate.[2] A creditor can apply for Letters of Administration under s. 218 in cases where no interested person come forward for the grant. No action lies against an executor named for delay in taking out the probate. Where letters of administration are granted to the Administrator-General, the estate of the deceased vest in him though the Administrator-General's Act does not contain any provisions to that effect.[3] No administration bond is required in case of the Administrator-General. Probate means proof of the will under the seal of a court of competent jurisdiction with a grant of administration to the estate of the testator. Probate of will can be granted only to an executor appointed by the will. The appointment may be expressed or by necessary implication.[4] Probate of a will when granted establishes the right of the executor with effect from the death of the testator, and renders valid all intermediate acts of the executor as such.[5]

'Letters of administration' mean the grant of administration by a court of competent jurisdiction to the estate of the testator or intestate. In case where the executor dies before completion of administration, a grant under s. 258 of the Indian Succession Act is issued in India which is called Letters of Administration *de bonis non*. The practice in England is different as the executor of the executor does the needful to complete the administration. He is called derivative executor.[6]

Powers of the Executor for Sale of the Property of the Testator before and after Probate is Obtained, and the Effect thereof

An executor derives his title under the will. All properties of the testator except the trust property and the coparcenary interest in the HUF estate unless the same comes under the amendment introduced by s. 6 of the Hindu Succession Act 1956 read with s. 30 of the said Act vest in him immediately on the death of the testator.

In what Cases an Alienation by an Executor or Administrator may be Impeached?

The general rule is that under s. 307 of the Indian Succession Act an executor or administrator has power to dispose of property of the deceased vested in him under s. 211 in such manner as he thinks fit and the assets so transferred cannot be followed in the hands of the transferee either by a creditor or by

2 Section 232 of the Indian Succession Act 1925.
3 *Alwar Chetti* v *Chidanbara* 38 Mad 1134.
4 Section 222 of the Indian Succession Act 1925.
5 Section 227 of the Indian Succession Act 1925.
6 *DeSouza* v *Secretary of State* 12 BLR OC 423.

a legatee. The other rule is that the transferee is not bound to see to the application of the moneys by the executor. The alienee from an executor who is acting as such has a right to infer that the executor is acting fairly. The fact that the alienation does not purport to be made for administrative purposes does not affect his title. But there is a well recognised exception to these rules. This immunity is lost if the alienee is privy to the breach of trust or has actual or constructive notice of the fact that the executor is acting in breach of trust or the alienation is made for purposes which the executor has no power to do in the course of administration or if the transaction of sale is in its nature incompatible with the legitimate alienation of the estate (*i*). Therefore, fraud and collusion will vitiate any transaction and if fraud is proved the transaction will be set aside. Generally an alienation will be set aside in the following cases:

(*a*) If the property is sold at a nominal price or at a fraudulent undervalue.[7]

(*b*) Where the alienation is made by the executor for the payment of his own debt.[8]

(*c*) Where the alienation is made by the executor for other private purposes of his own.

(*d*) If any specific property bequeathed, the sale of the Chattel by the executor will be set aside if it is proved that the purchaser had notice of the same and of the fact that there were no debts of the testator or that they have since been discharged.[9]

(*e*) If a great length of time has elapsed since the testator's death, it will be presumed that all the debts of the testator have been discharged, and that the alienation was for a purpose foreign to the administration of the deceased estate.[10]

Executor cannot delegate his authority to any person to sell any property. A power-of-attorney in so far as it confers on the authority of the agent to exercise his discretion is void.[11]

(b) *Right as executor or legatee when established.* No right as executor or legatee can be established in any court of justice unless a court of competent jurisdiction in India has granted probate of the will under which the right is claimed. Letters of administration with the will or with a copy of an authenticated copy of the will annexed.[12]

7 *Vertannes* v *Robinson* 23 Bom LR 1017 at p. 1024.
8 *Mlead* v *Drammend* 17 Ves 155.
9 *Ewer* v *Corbet* 2 PW 149.
10 Re: Verrell's *Contract* (1903)1 Ch 65.
11 *Jogendra Chunder* v *Apurba Dutt* 13 CWN 1190.
12 Section 213 of the Indian Succession Act.

This provision of law does not apply in the case of wills made by any Mahomedan.

(c) *Persons to whom probate or letters of administration cannot be granted.* Probate or letters of administration cannot be granted to any person who is a minor though letters of administration with the will annexed may be granted to his guardian pending minority or is of unsound mind, or to any association of individuals unless it is a company which satisfies the rules prescribed by the State Government[1] as now framed by the Governor-General in Council in this behalf under the amending Act XVII of 1931. The said rules were published at page 40 of Part I of the *Gazette of India* dated 17th January 1933.

(d) *Accrual of representation to surviving executor.* When probate has been granted to several executors, and one of them dies, the entire representation of the testators accrues to the surviving executor or executors.[2]

(e) *Effect and extent of probate or letters of administration.* Probate of a will or letters of administration entitle the executor or administrator to all rights belonging to the testator or intestate as effectually as if the administration had been granted at the moment after his death.[3] This is what is known as Doctrine of Relation Back in the case of the grant of letters of administration. Probate of will or letters of administration have effect over all the property of the estate, movable or immovable, of the deceased, throughout the State in which the same is or are granted, unless the same is or are for special purposes or with exception[4] and are conclusive as to the representative title against all debtors of the deceased, and all persons holding property which belongs to him, and will afford full indemnity to all debtors, paying their debts and all persons delivering up such property to the person to whom such probate or letters of administration have been granted.[5]

Provided that probates and letters of administration granted—

(*i*) by a High Court, or

(*ii*) by a District Judge, where the deceased at the time of his death had a fixed place of abode situate within the jurisdiction of such Judge, and such Judge certifies that the value of the property and estate affected beyond the limits of the State does not exceed ten thousand rupees, will, unless otherwise directed by the grant, have like effect throughout the whole of India.[6] Probate is conclusive as to the genuineness of the will but nevertheless it does not establish

1 Section 223 of the Indian Succession Act.
2 Section 226 of the Indian Succession Act.
3 Sections 220 and 227 of the Indian Succession Act.
4 Sections 248 and 256 of the Indian Succession Act.
5 Section 273 of the Indian Succession Act.
6 Section 273 of the Indian Succession Act.

the title of the testator to the property bequeathed.[7] It is not even *prima facie* evidence as to the death of the testator.[8]

Resealing of Probate of Will Executed by Hindus outside India and Probated there—Ancillary Probate is a Condition Precedent

In cases of Will executed by a Hindu outside India, in respect of which a foreign probate has also been obtained, an ancillary probate or what is termed in English law as the resealing of the probate is required under s. 213(1), of the Indian Succession Act as otherwise, the requirement of the *lex fori* enacted under s. 213(1) may not be satisfied more so, to enable parties claiming under such a Will with reference to properties situate in India, the procedure under s. 228 of the Act has been prescribed. If this is not so, then as the probate obtained in respect of a will executed in a foreign country would be operative only within that country and persons entitled to other properties under the will, which are situate outside the country where the will was executed will be left without any remedy, s. 228 is an enabling provision and when read with s. 270 permits an ancillary probate. Section 270 is enacted on the principle that the presence of personal property of the deceased would be sufficient foundation of jurisdiction for purposes of granting probate. If, therefore, s. 213 requires the production of a probate as a procedural requirement before recognition of the rights to property by court under a Will either as an executor or a legatee and s. 228 read with s. 270 further provide for ancillary probate in respect of wills executed and probated outside India for the purpose of enabling the executors and legatees to assert rights to the estate of a deceased in India, then the requirement as to the obtaining of a probate in such case in the shape of an ancillary probate cannot be stated to be unnecessary in view of s. 57(*a*) and (*b*) of the Act.[9]

(f) *When probate or letters may be granted by District Judge or delegate.* Probate of the will or letters of administration to the estate of a deceased person will be granted by a District Judge, if it appears by a petition verified by the person applying for the same that the testator or intestate, as the case may be, at the time of his death, had a fixed place of abode, or any property, movable or immovable, within the jurisdiction of the Judge.[10] Probate and letters of administration will, upon application for that purpose to any district delegate, be granted by him in any case in which there is no contest, if it appears by a petition verified that the testator or intestate, as the case may be, had, at the time of his death, a fixed place of abode within the jurisdiction of such delegate.[11]

7 In the goods of *Nanda Lal Sett* 58 CWN 568.
8 *Chettiyar* v *Kulsum Bibi* AIR 1936 Rang 103.
9 *Alagammal* v *Rakkammal* AIR 1982 Mad 354; see also AIR 1959 Mad 410.
10 Section 270 of the Indian Succession Act.
11 Section 272 of the Indian Succession Act.

(g) *Contents of the application for probate.*[12] (1) Application for probate or for letters of administration with the will annexed must be made by a petition, duly signed and verified by the petitioner, stating—

(*i*) the date of the testator's death, date of the will;

(*ii*) that the writing annexed is his last will and testament;

(*iii*) that it was duly executed and attested;

(*iv*) the amount of assets which are likely to come to the petitioner's hands; and

(*v*) when the application is for probate, that the petitioner is the executor named in the will.

(2) In addition to these particulars, the petition must further state—

(*i*) when the application is to the District Judge that the deceased at the time of his death had a fixed place of abode, or had some property, within the jurisdiction of the Judge;

(*ii*) when the application is to a district delegate, that the deceased at the time of his death had a fixed place of abode within the jurisdiction of such delegate; and

(*iii*) names, addresses and descriptions of persons who are his heirs and legal representatives under the Hindu Succession Act 1956.

(3) When the application is to the District Judge and any portion of the assets likely to come to the petitioner's hands is situate in another State, the petition must further state the amount of such assets in each State and District Judges within whose jurisdiction such assets are situate.[13]

(4) The application shall be signed and verified by the applicant as required under s. 280 of the said Act. Moreover, it requires the verification of one of the attesting witnesses in the manner prescribed under s. 281 of the said Act. A petition by the Administrator-General for Letters of Administration shall be deemed as sufficiently verified by his signature only.[14]

Sections 68 to 72 of the Indian Evidence Act (Act I of 1872) prescribed the mode for proof of a document which requires attestation. A will is not admissible in evidence unless at least one of the attesting witnesses comes and proves the same. But if the attesting witnesses are dead, or otherwise not available, an affidavit by a person in proof of the handwriting of the attesting witness may be accepted as a substitute for verification.[15]

(5) An affidavit as to valuation is to be filed along with the petition.

12 Section 276 of the Indian Succession Act.

13 Section 276 of the Indian Succession Act.

14 In the goods of *McComiskey* 20 Cal 879.

15 Section 69 read with s. 114 of the Indian Evidence Act—*Nooruddin* v *Md. Omer* AIR 1956 Bom 641.

(h) *Time for grant of probate and letters.* No probate of a will can be granted until after the expiration of seven clear days; no letters of administration can be granted until after the expiration of 14 clear days, from the date of the death of the testator or intestate.[16] There is, however, no time limit. An application for probate or letters of administration can be made any time before the assets have been administered, but the delay gives rise to suspicion.[17]

(i) *Liability of executor or administrator.* The executor or administrator, as the case may be, of a deceased person is his legal representative for all purposes and all the property of the deceased vest in him as such for the purpose of representation and administration of the estate.[18]

But when the deceased was a Hindu, Mahomedan, Buddhist, Sikh or Jain, or an exempted person, nothing herein contained will vest in an executor or administrator, any property of a deceased person which would otherwise have passed by survivorship to some other person or persons. In other words, a person governed by the Mitakshara School of Hindu Law had no right to make any will of his coparcenary interest in the joint family estate. The Hindu Succession Act 1956, has changed the law on this subject to the effect that under s. 6 read with s. 30 of the Act, such an interest can be disposed of under a will.

If a legacy is bequeathed to a person who is named and executor of the will, he cannot take the legacy unless he proves the will or otherwise manifests his intention to act as an executor.[19] If an executor renounces or fails to accept executorship within the time limited for the acceptance or refusal thereof, the will can be proved and letters of administration with a copy of the will annexed can be granted to the person who would be entitled to administration in case of intestacy. Where the legacy is attached to the office the executor loses all benefits even though prevented from obtaining probate for any sufficient cause.[20]

(j) *Minority of executor or residuary legatee.* When a minor is a sole executor or sole residuary legatee, letters of administration, with the will annexed, can be granted to the legal guardian of such minor or to such other person as the court may think fit, until the minor has attained his majority, at which period, and not before, probate of the will may be granted to him.[21]

16 Section 293 of the Indian Succession Act.
17 *General Accident, Fire and Life Assurance Company Ltd.* v *Janmohamad* (1941)1 MLJ 88 (PC).
18 Section 211 of the Indian Succession Act.
19 Section 141 of the Indian Succession Act—*Rajam* v *Pankajam* AIR 1944 Mad 337.
20 *Henbury* v *Spooner* 5 Beav 680.
21 Section 244 of the Indian Succession Act.

(k) *Administration to attorney of the executor.* When any executor is absent from the State in which application is made and there is no executor within the State willing to act, letters of administration with the will annexed can be granted to the attorney or agent of the absent executor for the use and benefit of his principal limited until he shall obtain probate or letters of administration granted to himself.[1]

(l) *Ad valorem duty.* The grant of probate or letters of administration is subject to *ad valorem* duty. In West Bengal the maximum duty is as in a suit, namely Rs. 10,000. The benefit of maximum court fee, where limited, is available in probate proceedings.[2] No duty is payable—

(*i*) where the value of the estate does not exceed Rs. 2,000;[3]

(*ii*) in respect of trust property;[4]

(*iii*) in cases of more than one grant or grants in respect of the same estate;[5]

(*iv*) on the property of any person subject to military law both army and navy killed or died of wounds suffered while on active service up to the value of Rs. 50,000 (revised notification under s. 35 of the Old Court Fees Act 1870, No. 23321 dated 4th March 1938 for Bengal only);[6]

(*v*) on the moneys which vest in the dependents under s. 3(2) of the Provident Funds Act 1923;[7] and

(*vi*) deposits in Government Savings Bank not exceeding Rs. 3,000.[8]

When the karta of a Mitakshara family dies leaving bank deposits and shares standing in his name alone, he is the owner of those assets *vis-a-vis* the bank and the companies. In other words, he was ostensible owner of those assets which he held as a trustee for the benefit of all members of the coparcenary. It was held that such a grant was exempted from duty,[9] but since the enactment of the Hindu Succession Act 1956, and in cases where the deceased left any female relations as referred to in s. 6 of the said Act, such grant is subject to duty only to the extent of the share of the deceased in the joint family assets.

(m) *Caveat against grant of probate or administration.* A caveat is a caution or warning entered in the testamentary court—a notice to the Registrar not

1 Section 241 of the Indian Succession Act.
2 *PMA Setty* v *State of Karnataka* AIR 1989 SC 100 (para 36).
3 Section 23(*ii*) of the West Bengal Court Fees Act 1970.
4 Section 27 of the West Bengal Court Fees Act 1970.
5 Section 26 of the West Bengal Court Fees Act 1970.
6 Repealed by W.B. Act X of 1970.
7 In the goods of *Maurice Saleh* 60 Cal 1016.
8 Section 8 of the Government Savings Bank Act.
9 In the goods of *Shewprasad Saraf* AIR 1954 Cal 444.

to issue any grant or to take any steps without notice to the caveator. A caveat remains valid for six months only unless it is renewed further if the caveator dies within the period the caveat may be discharged by an order on chambers summons. The caveator must have some interest in the estate of the deceased. The test laid down[10] is—"Does the grant displace any right to which the caveator would otherwise be entitled?"[11] A caveat against the grant of probate or administration can be lodged in the High Court or with the District Judge or a district delegate. No action can be taken on a petition for probate or letters of administration after a caveat against the grant thereof has been entered with the Judge or the district delegate to whom the application has been made or notice has been given of its entry with some other delegate until after such notice to the person by whom the same has been entered, as the court may think reasonable.[12]

Under s. 148A of Code of Civil Procedure 1908 a caveat may be filed before any proceeding has been taken. It remains valid for 90 days. Under s. 284 of Indian Succession Act 1925 caveat may be filed before or after making application for probate. If filed before application of probate then the caveat is likely to remain valid for 90 days under s. 148A, CPC.

LETTERS OF ADMINISTRATION WITHOUT WILL ANNEXED

(a) *Right to intestate's property.* No right to any part of the property of a person who has died intestate can be established in any court of justice unless letters of administration have first been granted by a court of competent jurisdiction. Letters of administration are absolutely necessary in case of intestacy among Europeans, East Indians, Armenians and Jews. This provision of law does not apply in the case of the intestacy of a Hindu, Mahomedan, Buddhist, Sikh, Jain or Indian Christian.[13]

(b) *Persons to whom letters of administration cannot be granted.* Under s. 298 of the said Act the court can refuse the grant in cases of Hindus not coming under s. 57 and Mahomedans at its discretion. Such grant is also refused in ship. Letters of administration are absolutely necessary in case of intestacy among the Europeans. East Indians, Armenians and Jews.

(c) *Grant of administration to the estate of Hindus, etc.* If the deceased has died intestate and was a Hindu, Mahomedan, Buddhist, Sikh or Jain or an exempted person, administration of his estate can be granted to any person who, according to the rules for the distribution of the estate applicable in

10 *Baggiammal* v *Rajagopala* AIR 1948 Mad 81.
11 *Pradip* v *Umarani* AIR 1954 Cal 277.
12 Section 285 of the Indian Succession Act.
13 Section 212 of the Indian Succession Act. In the goods of *Annapurna* (1949)2 Cal 287.

the case of such deceased, would be entitled to the whole or any part of such deceased's estate.[14]

When no such person applies, it can be granted to a creditor of the deceased.

(d) *Rules for distribution of intestate's property.* Chapters I and II, Part V of the Indian Succession Act, are not applicable to Hindus except those married under the Special Marriage Act or to Mahomedans, Buddhists, Sikhs or Jains. The whole of this part applies to Europeans, Indian Christians, Jews, Armenians and other persons professing Christian faith and domiciled in India. The following are the rules for the distribution of intestate's property under ss. 29 to 49 of the Indian Succession Act.

(*i*) Where the intestate has left a widow or widower and lineal descendants—

Two-thirds of his property will go to the surviving children in equal shares, but, in that case, if there be surviving grand-children through a deceased child, they will, along with the children, inherit *per stirps, i.e.*, will take in equal shares only the shares which their respective parents would have taken if living at the intestate's death. In the same manner the intestate's property will be equally divided among the surviving grandchildren, or more remote lineal descendants, in the event of surviving children, grandchildren, or more remote lineal descendants, respectively, being previously dead.

In any of the above cases, the remaining one-third of the property will go to surviving widow or widower.

(*ii*) Where the intestate has left a widow or widower but no lineal descendants—

If the net value of his property does not exceed five thousand rupees, the whole of his property will belong to the widow or widower; but, if the net value of the property exceeds five thousand rupees, the widow or widower will be entitled to five thousand rupees thereof, with interest thereon at the rate of four per cent per annum from the death of the intestate, provided that the provision for the widow or widower will not apply to the property of any Indian Christian, or of any child or grandchild of any male Indian Christian. After payment of the said sum of five thousand rupees with interest as aforesaid, one-half of the residue of the intestate's property will go to the father; if the father be dead, the surviving mother, brothers and sisters, or any of them, will inherit the moiety of the residue in equal shares, or the whole of such moiety, as the case may be, but, in that case, if there be surviving children of a deceased brother or sister, they will inherit *per stirps* along with the mother, brothers and sisters. In the absence of any surviving

14 Section 218 of the Indian Succession Act.

parent, brothers and sisters, one-half of such residue of intestate's property will be divided equally among those of intestate's surviving relations who are in the nearest degree of kindred to him.

In any of the above cases, the remaining one-half of the residue will go to the surviving widow or widower, who will inherit the whole of the property if there be no surviving kindred of the intestate.

(*iii*) Where the intestate has left no widow, the whole of his property will be inherited by his lineal descendants or kindred, according to the above rules. In the absence of either surviving lineal descendants or kindred, the property will go to the Crown.

For the purpose of succession, there is no distinction—

(*i*) between those who are related to a person deceased through his father and those who are related to him through his mother, or

(*ii*) between those related to him by the full blood and those related by the half blood, or

(*iii*) between those who are actually born in his lifetime and those who have been born after his death.

(e) *Grant of administration to other persons.* If the deceased has died intestate and was not a person belonging to any of the classes above referred to, those who are connected with him either by marriage or by consanguinity are entitled to obtain letters of administration of his estate and effects.

(f) *Effect of letters to attorney of absent person.* See corresponding note under Probate.

(g) *Grant of letters to attorney of absent person.* Where a person entitled to administration in case of intestacy is absent from the State, and no person equally entitled is willing to act, letters of administration do not render valid any intermediate acts of the absent person for the use and benefit of his principal limited until he will obtain letters of administration granted to himself.

When any person to whom if present letters of administration with the Will annexed might be granted is absent from the State, Letters of Administration with the Will annexed may be granted to his Attorney or Agent limited until a probate or Letter of Administration is granted to the said person.[15]

(h) *Time for grant of letters of administration.* No probate of a Will is granted before expiry of seven days and no Letter of Administration is granted until expiry of fourteen days from the death of the testator or of the intestate.[16]

15 Sections 241 and 242 of the Indian Succession Act.

16 Section 293 of the Indian Succession Act.

(i) *Acts not validated by letters of administration.* Letters of administration do not render valid any intermediate acts of the administrator tending to the diminution or damages of the intestate's estate.

(j) *When letters of administration can be granted by District Judge or Delegate.* The District Judge has jurisdiction to grant or revoke probate and Letters of Administration within his district. This applies to Calcutta, Mumbai, Chennai as also to the notified areas in case of the deceased being a Hindu Mohammedan, Buddhist, Sikh or Jaina or an exempted person.[17]

(k) *Contents of petition.* See s. 278 of the Indian Succession Act. Application for letters of administration must be made by a petition, duly signed and verified by the petitioner, stating—

(*i*) the time and place of the deceased's death;

(*ii*) the family or other relatives of the deceased, and their respective residences;

(*iii*) the right in which the petitioner claims;

(*iv*) the amount of assets which are likely to come to the petitioner's hands;

(*v*) when the application is to the District Judge, that the deceased at the time of his death had a fixed place of abode, or had some property, situate within the jurisdiction of the Judge; and

(*vi*) when the application is to a district delegate, that the deceased at the time of his death had a fixed place of abode within the jurisdiction of such delegate.

Where the application is to the District Judge and any portion of the assets likely to come to the petitioner's hands is situate in another State, the petition must further state the amount of such assets in each State and the District Judge within whose jurisdiction such assets are situate.

(l) *Administration bond, assignment of administration bond.* Every administrator, except such attorney or agent as mentioned in the above cl. (*g*), must give a bond to the District Judge, with one or more surety or sureties, engaging for the due collection, getting in and administering the estate of the deceased.[18]

The court can, on application made by petition and on being satisfied that the engagement of an administration bond has not been kept, and upon such terms as to security, or providing that the money received be paid into court, or otherwise, as the court may think fit, assign the bond to some person, his executors, or administrators who will thereupon be entitled to

17 Section 264 of the Indian Succession Act 1925.

18 Section 291(1) of the Indian Succession Act.

sue on the said bond in his or their own name or names as if the same had been originally given to him or them instead of the Judge of the court, and will be entitled to recover thereon, as trustees for all persons interested, the full amount recoverable in respect of any breach thereof.[1]

SUCCESSION ACT

(a) *Restriction on grant of succession certificate.* A succession certificate cannot be granted under s. 370(1) of the Indian Succession Act 1925 with respect to any debt or security to which a right is required to be established by probate or letters of administration as in the cases of Jews, Parsis, Armenians, Europeans and East Indians. A Succession Certificate can be granted to any person claiming to be entitled to the effect of a deceased Indian Christian or with respect to any debt or security. The fact that such right can be established by Letters of Administration will not prevent the issue of such Succession Certificate. Any Hindu including a Brahmas, Sikh, Jaina or Buddhist can apply for a Succession Certificate where there is no Will of the deceased. Even where there is a Will but right to any debt or security cannot be established by the Will a Succession Certificate can be granted.[2]

Provided that nothing will prevent the grant of a succession certificate to any person claiming entitled to the effects of a deceased Indian Christian, or any part thereto, with respect to any debt or security, by reason of the fact that the right thereto can be established by letters of administration. Table A of the Companies Act 1956 and Articles of Association of limited companies in many cases require probate or letters of administration for transmission of shares. So the Rules of companies having safe deposit lockers may require probate or Letters of Administration to establish the right of the claimants to open the same after the death of the person in whose name the same stands.

(b) *Security.* For the purpose of succession certificate. Security means—

(*i*) any promissory note, debenture, stock or other security of the Government of India or the State Government;

(*ii*) any bond, debenture or annuity charged by Act of Parliament on the revenues of India;

(*iii*) any stock or debenture of, or share in, a company or other incorporated institution;

(*iv*) any debenture or other security for money issued by or on behalf of a local authority;

(*v*) any other security which the Governor-General in Council may declare to be a security for the purposes of succession certificate.

1 Section 292 of the Indian Succession Act.
2 Sections 370-382 of the Indian Succession Act 1925.

(c) *Application for succession certificate.* Application for such certificate must be made under s. 372 of the Indian Succession Act to the District Judge by a petition signed and verified by the applicant, stating—

(*i*) the time and place of death of the deceased;

(*ii*) the ordinary residence of the deceased at the time of his death, and if such residence was not within the local limits of the jurisdiction of the Judge to whom the application is made, then the property of the deceased within these limits;

(*iii*) the family and other near relatives of the deceased, and their respective residences. In cases under the Hindu Succession Act (Act XXX of 1956) the names of the heirs under the said Act;

(*iv*) the right in which the petitioner claims;

(*v*) the absence of any impediment under s. 370(1) or under any other provision of the Indian Succession Act or any other enactment to the grant of the certificate or to the validity thereof if it were granted; and

(*vi*) the debts and securities in respect of which the certificate is applied for.

(d) *Extension of succession certificate.* The District Judge can, on the application of the holder of a succession certificate, extend the certificate to any debt or security not originally specified therein and every such extension will have the same effect as if the debt or security to which the certificate is extended had been originally specified therein.[3]

(e) *Local extent and effect of succession certificate.* A succession certificate has effect throughout the whole of India.[4] It is conclusive as against persons liable to whom full indemnity is afforded for payments made.[5]

(f) *Security, bond, assignment of security.* The District Judge must in any case in which he proposes to proceed when questions of law or fact which seem to him to be too intricate and difficult for determination in a summary proceeding, or when there are more applicants than one for a certificate, and it appears to the Judge that more than one of such applicants are interested in the estate of the deceased, and may, in any other case, require as a condition precedent to the granting of a certificate, that the person to whom he proposes to make the grant shall give to the Judge a bond with one or more surety or sureties or other sufficient security for rendering an account of debts and securities received by him and for indemnity of persons who may be entitled to the whole or any part of those debts and securities.

3 Section 376 of the Indian Succession Act 1925.
4 Section 380 of the Indian Succession Act 1925.
5 Sections 381 and 386 of the Indian Succession Act.

The Judge can, on application made by petition and on the cause shown to his satisfaction, and upon such terms as to security, of providing that the money received be paid into the court, or otherwise, as he thinks fit, assign the bond or other securities to some proper person, and that person will thereupon be entitled to sue thereon in his own name as if it had been originally given to him instead of to the Judge of the Court, and to recover, as trustee for all persons interested, such amount as may be recoverable thereunder.[6]

NOTE: The law as it now stands after the amendment of the Code of Civil Procedure in 1976 is that the liability of the surety is co-extensive with the principal debtor even for fulfilment of any condition imposed upon any person under any order of the court in any suit or other proceeding (s. 145 of CPC).

Effect of Certificate under s. 381 of the Indian Succession Act. The effect of the certificate is no adjudication of title of the deceased far less than that of the holder as regards the debts and securities covered thereunder, but simply to afford protection to the parties paying the debts. The question whether the debt belonged to the deceased is not a matter to be decided on an application for a Succession Certificate.[7] The grant of succession certificate is no proof of the debts far less an adjudication of the rights of the parties.

This section protects the debtors and affords full indemnity to the persons liable to pay the debts and in respect of the securities covered by the certificate as persons having the same paid in "good faith".[8] The expression "good faith" is defined in the General Clauses Act. Even if payment is made without due care and caution still it will be considered as honestly paid. It affords full indemnity to the banks. If any one refuses to pay the debts to the holder of the certificate, he will become liable to pay interest. It entitles to the holder to institute a suit to recover the debt.

In the case of securities a Succession Certificate enables the grantee to transfer the security.[9] Even so if the articles of association of the company provide that the executor or administrator of a deceased member shall be the only person to be recognised by the company, a transfer by a person to whom the Succession Certificate is granted is to be recognised as the legal representative of the deceased.

Nevertheless the certificate is only conclusive of the representative title of the holder thereof as against the debtors. A suit will not lie for the declaration that the holder of the certificate is not the legal representative of the deceased. Until the certificate is revoked under s. 383, it is good as

6 Section 375 of the Indian Succession Act.
7 *Srinivasa* v *Gopalan* 20 MLJ 865; 28 IC 424.
8 *Ganga Prasad* v *Mt. Saeedan* AIR 1952 All 801.
9 *Thenappa* v *Indian Overseas Bank* AIR 1943 Mad 743.

regards the representative title of the holder. Even in the case of a minor if the certificate is granted to the guardian of the minor it will afford indemnity to the debtor concerned and the certificate does not terminate on the minor attaining majority.

REVOCATION OF GRANTS
(Section 263 of the Indian Succession Act)

(a) *Just causes for revocation of grants.* A grant of probate of will or letters of administration can be revoked or annulled for just causes, *e.g.*

(*i*) that the proceedings to obtain the grant were materially defective in substance, *e.g.* want of jurisdiction, suppression of citation, etc.;

(*ii*) that the grant was obtained fraudulently by making a false suggestion, or by concealing from the court something material to the case, *e.g.* probate of a forged will, fraud on court, etc.;

(*iii*) that the grant was obtained by means of an untrue allegation of a fact essential in point of law to justify the grant, though such allegation was made in ignorance or inadvertently, *e.g.* probate of a will revoked.

(*iv*) that the grant has become useless and inoperative through circumstances, *e.g.* discovery of a subsequent will or codicil;

(*v*) that (*for grant of probate or letters of administration*) the person to whom the grant was made has wilfully and without reasonable cause omitted to exhibit an inventory or account in accordance with the provision of law, or has exhibited an inventory or account which is untrue in material respects, or (*for grant of a succession certificate*) that a decree or order made by a competent court in a suit or other proceeding with respect to effects comprising debts or securities specified in the certificate renders it proper that the certificate be revoked.

(b) *Effect of revocation.* The effect is not to revoke the entire proceedings *but to revoke the grant*. The will does not go off except when the probate is revoked on the ground of forgery of the will.

An important question arises as to the effect of revocation of probate or letters of administration as regards interim dealings in relation to the property of the deceased in particular when any property has been sold. The revocation does not make the grant void *ab initio*, so a *bona fide* purchaser acting in good faith for valuable consideration is always protected.[10] Under ss. 216 and 273 of the Indian Succession Act the grant is conclusive. So people dealing with the grantee in good faith and in due course of administration

10 *Akshoy Kumar* v *Nandalal* (1946)1 Cal 432.

are protected. The law is that every person shall give credit to probate. This was also the law in England and is now embodied in a statute.[11] A distinction is however drawn between grant which are voidable and those void *ab initio*. In the former event a purchaser acting *bona fide* is protected.[12] When the grant is void *ab initio,* such a purchaser is not protected unless the dealing was effected under compulsion and in the best interest of the estate. He can at best claim to be a creditor.[13]

FORMS

Caveat against Grant of Probate or Administration

In the Court of ....

In the goods of AB (full name and nationality). In the matter of grant of probate of the will (or letters of administration of the estate) of the said deceased.

Caveat on behalf of CD (full name and address and relationship).

Let nothing be done in respect of the application, particulars of which are given below without due notice to the above-named caveator.

Dated this .... day of .... 1999.

Yours faithfully
Advocate
Address

1.	Name of the caveator in full particulars.	1. ....
2.	Address of the caveator in full.	2. ....
3.	In case the caveator resides outside the jurisdiction of the court, address of the caveator for service of notice within the jurisdiction of this court.	3. ....
4.	Name of the applicant in respect of the application against which caveat is lodged.	4. ....
5.	Address of such applicant.	5. ....
6.	Number of the suit/proceeding and the cause title thereof if instituted.	6. ....

11 15 Geo Vict 23, s. 27 replacing 2 or 21 Vict C 71, 77, 78.

12 *Gopal Lal* v *Badridar* 33 Cal 657 also *Boxall* v *Boxal* 27 Ch D 220.

13 *Ellis* v *Ellis* (1905)1 Ch 613.

7. Name and address of intended parties to the suit/proceeding as far as the caveator is aware if the suit/proceedings have not been instituted. 7. ....
8. Nature of the proceedings. 8. ....

Petition for Probate or Letters of Administration with the Will Annexed

IN THE COURT OF THE DISTRICT DELEGATE (or District Judge) OF District ....

Original petition No. .... of .... under Indian Succession Act 1925 in the Matter of the Will of AB .... deceased

Petition of XY son of EF by caste .... by occupation .... resident of ....

MOST RESPECTFULLY SHEWETH:

(1) That the above-named AB hereinafter referred to as the said deceased who was a Hindu governed by the Hindu Succession Act (Act XXX of 1956) and died on the .... day of .... at .... within the jurisdiction of this court which was his fixed place of residence (or where he was temporarily residing, his fixed place of residence being at ...... within the jurisdiction of this court or leaving the property within the jurisdiction of this court as will appear from the affidavit of assets filed herewith.

(2) That prior to his death and on the .... day of .... the deceased made and published his last will and testament whereby he appointed your petitioner as the sole executor and left and bequeathed his estate and effects thereof as indicated therein.

(3) The said will is annexed to the affidavit of Sri ...., one of the attesting witnesses and it will appear from the said affidavit that the same was duly executed by the said deceased in the presence of the witnesses whose names appear at the foot thereof and was also attested by them.

(4) Your petitioner is the same person as XY, the executor named in the will and, as such, he is entitled to probate thereof (or where the application is for letters of administration with a copy of the will annexed—as the said testator did not appoint any executor of his said will, your petitioner being his eldest son and one of the persons entitled to a share of his estate in the event of intestacy—is entitled to and so claims administration of the property and credits of the said AB.

(5) That your petitioner has truly set forth in Annexure A to his affidavit of valuation filed herewith all the properties and credits which the deceased died possessed of or was otherwise entitled to at the time of his death which have come or are likely to come to the petitioner's hands and so far as your petitioner has been able to ascertain or is aware, there are no property and credits other than what are specified in the Annexure A of the said affidavit and in case of discovery of other assets your petitioner undertakes to pay the requisite court-fee on that account.

(6) That your petitioner has also truly set forth in Annexure B to his said affidavit all the items that by law he is allowed to deduct.

(7) The value of the assets which are likely to come to your petitioner's hands in the event of probate of the will or letters of administration with a copy annexed thereto being granted does not exceed the aggregated sum of Rs. .... and the net amount after deducting all items which he is by law allowed to deduct, is under the value of Rs. ....

(8) That the deceased was a Hindu governed by the Hindu Succession Act (Act 30 of 1956) and at the time of his death he left the following and no other relations who would have been his heirs in the event of intestacy under the said Act.

Name, address, age and relationship: remarks, if any
(full details)

(9) That your petitioner has duly paid the *ad valorem* duty payable in respect of the estate of the deceased.

(10) That no application has been made before any other court for probate of the said will or letters of administration with a copy annexed thereto and no suit or other proceedings are pending for administration of the estate.

(11) Your petitioner hereby undertakes to administer the property and credits of the said AB deceased and to make and file a full and true inventory thereof and exhibit the same in this court within six months from the date of grant of probate of the will (or letters of administration) to him, and also to render to this court a true account of the said property and credits within one year from the said date.

(12) That this application is made *bona fide.*

Your petitioner therefore prays:

(*a*) That probate of the said will (or letters of administration to the property and credits of the said deceased, with a copy of the said will annexed) with effect throughout the State of .... may be granted to him.

(*b*) For such other reliefs as this court may seem fit.

Prepared in my office:

Advocate for the petitioner

Verification of the Applicant

I, ..., the above-named petitioner, do declare and say that the statements contained in paragraphs 1, 2, 3, 4, 5, 6, 7, 8, 9, 10 and 11 of the above petition are true to my knowledge and those contained in paragraphs 12 and 13 thereof are my submissions.

I sign this verification at .... this .... day of ....

DECLARATION OF WITNESS

I, ..., one of the witnesses to the last will and testament of .... the testator mentioned in the above petition, do declare and say that I was present on the .... day of .... at .... and saw the testator affix his hand and signature or mark to the said will, marked A to the Affidavit of .... filed herewith (or that the said testator acknowledge the writing annexed to the above petition and marked A, to be his last will and testament in my presence).

Solemnly affirmed by the said
.... witness this ....
day of .... at Court House at
Calcutta

Sign

Before me

Commissioner/Magistrate
/Oath Officer

Petition for Probate to have Effect throughout India

In the court of the District Judge

Original Petition No. .... under Indian Succession Act 1925

In the Goods of AB late of No. ...... deceased

MOST RESPECTFULLY SHEWETH:

(1) That the above-named AB hereinafter referred to as the said deceased who was a Hindu governed by the Hindu Succession Act (Act XXX of 1956) died on the .... day of .... at .... within the jurisdiction of this court, which was his fixed place of residence.

(2) That at the time of his death the deceased left the following and no other persons who would have been his heirs under the said Act in case of intestacy (state name, address, age and relationship).

(3) That prior to his death and on the .... day of .... the said deceased made and published his last will and testament in English language and character whereby and whereunder he appointed your petitioner as the sole executor and left and bequeathed his estate and the effects thereof in the manner indicated therein.

(4) The said will is annexed to the affidavit of Sri ...., one of the attesting witnesses and marked with the letter A and it will appear from the said affidavit that the said will was duly executed by the deceased in the presence of witnesses whose names appear at the foot thereof and attested by them.

(5) Your petitioner is the same person named as CD, the executor appointed by the said will.

(6) That the petitioner has truly set forth in Annexure A to his affidavit of valuation filed herewith all the properties and credits which the deceased died possessed of or was otherwise entitled to at the time of his death which have come or are likely to come to the petitioner's hand and so far as the petitioner has been able to ascertain or is aware, there are no property and credits other than what are specified in the Annexure A of the said affidavit and in case of discovery of other assets your petitioner undertakes to pay the requisite court-fee on that account.

(7) That the petitioner has also truly set forth in Annexure B to his said affidavit all the items that by law he is allowed to deduct.

(8) It will appear from the said affidavit of assets that the value of the assets which are likely to come to your petitioner's hands in the event of the grant of probate of the said will in his favour does not exceed in the aggregate the sum of Rs. .... out of which assets of the value of Rs. .... are situate in the State of West Bengal, within the jurisdiction of this court and assets of the value of Rs. .... are situate in the State of Maharashtra, within the local limits of the jurisdiction of the High Court of Bombay.

The value of the assets of the said deceased beyond the limit of the State of West Bengal does not exceed Rs. 10,000.

(9) That to the best of your petitioner's knowledge, no application has been made to any High Court or other District Court for probate of the said will or for letters of administration of the said estate, intended to have effect throughout India, (or, on or about the .... day of .... application was made to the Court of the District Judge of .... by EF ..... of .... for a grant of probate of the said will to him, and the same was on the .... day of .... dismissed on the ground that the said EF was not appointed executor by the said will, or as the case may be).

(10) That your petitioner has paid the *ad valorem* duty payable for the grant of probate hereunder made and in case of discovery of any further assets, your petitioner undertakes to pay the deficit court-fees on that account.

(11) Your petitioner does hereby undertake to duly administer the property and credits of the said deceased and to make a full and true inventory thereof and exhibit the same in this court within six months from the date of grant of probate to him and also to render to this court a true account of the said property and credits within one year from the said date.

Your petitioner therefore prays:

(*a*) Probate of the will with effects throughout the Union of India may be granted to him.

(*b*) For such other relief as to the court may deem fit.

Verification of the Petitioner

I, ... the above-named petitioner do hereby declare and say that the statements contained in paragraphs 1 to 9 of the above petition are true to my knowledge and those contained in paragraphs 10 and 11 thereof are my humble submissions.

I sign this verification at Calcutta
this .... day of ....

DECLARATION OF WITNESS

I, ... one of the witnesses to the last Will and Testament of .... the Testator mentioned in the above petition do declare and say that I was present on the .... day of .... at .... and saw the Testator affix his hand and signature or mark to the said Will marked "A" to the affidavit of .... FILED HEREWITH (or that the said Testator acknowledged the writing annexed to the above petition and marked "A" to be his last Will and Testament in my presence.

Solemnly affirmed by the said ....
this .... day of .... at the Court
House at Calcutta Signature

Before me
Commissioner/Magistrate

Petition for Letters of Administration of Property and Credits as no Will was Made

IN THIS COURT OF THE DISTRICT JUDGE (OR DELEGATE) OF ..../...........
Original Petition No. .... of .... under Indian Succession Act 1925
in the Goods of AB late of No. .... deceased.

Petition of XY under s. 278 of the Indian Succession Act 1925 for Letters of Administration—

MOST RESPECTFULLY SHEWETH:

1. That the above-named deceased AB hereinafter referred to as the said deceased late of .... died on or about the .... day of .... at .... within the jurisdiction of this court, which was his fixed place of residence (or where he was temporarily resident, his fixed place of residence being at .... within the jurisdiction of this court) or leaving properties specified in the Annexure A to the affidavit of assets filed herewith within the jurisdiction of this court.

2. That the said deceased died intestate and although your petitioner made due and diligent search to ascertain whether the deceased left any will, none so has been found up till now.

3. That the said deceased was a Hindu governed by the Dayabhaga or Bengal School of Hindu Law and at the time of his death he left him surviving the following and no other person or persons as his heirs and legal representatives under the Hindu Succession Act (Act 30 of 1956).

(1) CD, your petitioner as eldest son—age and residence;

(2) EF of (residence, age and description) his youngest son;

(3) J. the wife of LM of etc. his daughter (residence and age);

(4) N of etc. his wife—residence and age;

(5) PQ of etc.—residence and age.

4. That the petitioner as the eldest son of the deceased is entitled to .... share of his estate and he claims Letters of Administration in respect of the estate of the deceased.

5. That the petitioner has truly set forth in Annexure A to his affidavit of valuation filed herewith all the properties and credits which the deceased died possessed of or was otherwise entitled to at the time of his death which have come or are likely to come to the petitioner's hands and so far as the petitioner has been able to ascertain or is aware, there are no property and credits other than what are specified in the Annexure A of the said affidavit and in case of discovery of other assets your petitioner undertakes to pay the requisite court-fee on that account.

6. That the petitioner has also truly set forth in Annexure B to his said affidavit all the items that by law he is allowed to deduct.

7. That the said assets exclusive of what the deceased may have been possessed of or was entitled to as a trustee for another and beneficiary or with power to confer a beneficial interest and also exclusive of the items mentioned in the said Annexure B but inclusive of all rents, interests and dividends and increased value since the date of his death are under the value of Rs. ....

8. That no application has been made to any District Court or delegate or to any High Court for probate of any will of the said deceased or letters of administration with or without the will annexed in respect of his property and credits.

9. That your petitioner has paid the *ad valorem* duty payable in respect of the estate of the deceased.

10. That your petitioner undertakes to duly administer the property and credits of the said AB deceased and to make a full and true inventory thereof and exhibit the same in this court within six months from the date of grant of letters of administration to him, and also to render to this court a true account of the said property and credits within one year from the said date.

11. That this application is made *bona fide*.

Your petitioner therefore prays:

(*a*) Letters of Administration be granted to him having effect throughout the State of West Bengal.

(*b*) For such other relief as this court may deem fit.

Verification

I, ... the petitioner above-named, do solemnly declare and say that what is stated in paragraphs 1, 2, 3, 4, 5, 6, 7, 8 and 9 of the above petition are true to my knowledge and that what is stated in the remaining paragraphs 10 and 11 are my submission before this court.

I sign this verification at No. .... this .... day of .... 2000.

Prepared in my office Sd/-
Advocate for the petitioner

Form of Valuation (to be used with such Modifications, if any) as may be Necessary

AFFIDAVIT OF ASSETS

In the Court of ....

Re.: Probate of the will of .... (or administration of the property and credits of ....) deceased.

Solemnly Affirm

I, ... make oath .... and say that I am the executor (or one of the executors, or one of the next-of-kin) of deceased and that I have truly set forth in Annexure A to this affidavit all the property and credits which the above-named deceased died possessed of or was entitled to at the time of his death, and which have come or are likely to come to my hands.

2. I further say that I have also truly set forth in Annexure B all the items I am by law allowed to deduct.

3. I further say that the said assets, exclusive only of such last-mentioned items, but inclusive of all rents, interests, dividends and increased values since the date of the death of the deceased or under the value of—

Annexure A

Properties of Deceased

Valuation of the movable and immovable property of deceased	Rs.	P.
Cash in the house and at banks, household goods, wearing apparel, books, plates, jewels, etc. Property in Government securities transferable at the public debt office		
Immovable property consisting of		
Leasehold property		
Property in public companies		
Policy of insurance upon life, money out on mortgage and other securities, such as bonds, mortgages, bills of exchange, notes and other securities for money		
(State the amount of the whole; also the interest separately, calculating it at the time of making the application)		
Book debts		
Stock in trade .... (estimated value, if any ....)		
Other property not comprised under the foregoing heads (state the estimated value, if any).		
Total		
Deduct amount shown in Annexure B not subject to duty.		
Net Total		

Annexure B

Schedule of Debts, etc.

	Rs.	P.
Amount of debts due and owing from deceased, payable by law out of the Estate		
Amount of funeral expenses		
Amount of mortgage encumbrances		
Property held in trust not beneficially or with general power to confer a beneficial interest.		
Other property not subject to duty		
Total		

4. The statements contained in paragraphs 1, 2 and 3 of the above affidavit are true to my knowledge.

Solemnly affirmed by the said ......
at the Court House on this ....
day of .... before me.

Commissioner

Petition for the Grant of Succession Certificate by Widow

In the Court of the District Delegate at ....

District ....

Indian Succession Act 1925, Case No. .... of 1999

In the Goods of (name, address, caste and nationality of the deceased)

And

In the matter of Succession Certificate in respect of the debts and securities of the estate of the deceased

The humble petition of .... sole widow of the deceased of No. ....

RESPECTFULLY SHEWETH:

1. That your petitioner is the sole widow of the deceased.

2. That the deceased above-named, hereinafter referred to as the 'said deceased' who had been during his lifetime and until his death permanently living and residing at the said premises .... within the jurisdiction of this court and was by faith and nationality a Hindu citizen of India governed by the Dayabhaga or Bengal School of Hindu Law, died intestate on the .... day of .... at his aforesaid place of residence.

3. The deceased, at the time of his death, left only his widow, the present applicant and none else as his heir under the Hindu Succession Act 1956.

4. That at the time of his death the deceased left no son or daughter or father or any grandson or granddaughter by any predeceased son or daughter or any great-grandson or any great-granddaughter by any predeceased grandson and granddaughter or any widow of any predeceased son or predeceased grandson or great-grandson or any other relation specified in class I and class II of the Schedule under s. 8 of the said Act.

5. That the deceased left at the time of the death *inter alia* assets for which succession certificate has been prayed for of the market value of Rs. ....

A full and complete schedule of the said assets is hereunto annexed and marked "A".

6. That strict and diligent searches were made by your petitioner to ascertain whether the deceased left any will or made other disposition in respect of the properties, assets, and credits but no such will has been discovered up till now. Your petitioner, therefore, believes and has reasons to believe that he died intestate. No letter of administration has been issued in respect of the estate of the deceased. No application for letter of administration or succession certificate is pending in this court or in any other court.

7. That your petitioner is the same and identical person described as the sole widow of the deceased and she is interested in the administration of the estate of the deceased.

8. That it is evident from the facts and circumstances hereinbefore stated that there is no impediment under s. 370 of the Indian Succession Act 1925 or any other provisions of the said Act or any other enactment against the grant of Succession Certificate hereunder prayed to your petitioner nor to the validity thereof when granted.

9. That your petitioner states and submits that in the circumstances aforesaid, she alone is entitled to the grant of Succession Certificate in respect of the said assets payable to the estate of the deceased.

10. That the *ad valorem* duty of Rs. .... payable in respect of the grant of Succession Certificate hereunder prayed for has been paid.

11. That this application is made *bona fide*.

Your petitioner, therefore, prays for an order in the following terms:

(*i*) Succession certificate may be granted to your petitioner in respect of the properties, assets and credits specified in Schedule "A" hereto with power to collect and/or receive and/or realise the same including all interests accrued thereon and to negotiate and/or sell and/or deal with the same without any restriction.

(*ii*) Your petitioner be exempted from furnishing any security on that account.

And your petitioner as in duty bound shall ever pay.

Schedule A, PART-I

Debts and Liabilities

Sl. No.	*Name of the debtors*	*Amount of debt including interest on the date of application*	*Description and date of the instrument, if any, by which the debt is secured*
1.	....	Rs.	....
2.	....	Rs.	....
3.	....	Rs.	....
4.	....	Rs.	....

PART-II

Securities

Sl. No.	*Distinguishing number and letter of security*	*Number, title or nature of security*	*Amount or par value*	*Market value on the date of application*
1.	....	....	....	....
2.	Unsecured dividend warrant No. ... in respect of the above shares.	....	....	....
3.	....	....	....	....

Verification

I, Sm. ...., sole widow of the .... above-named residing at No. ...., do hereby declare and say that the statements contained in paragraphs 1, 2, 3, 4, 5, 6, 7, 8 and 10 of the above petition and also the particulars contained in the Schedule .... including all figures, are true to my knowledge and those contained in paragraphs 9 and 11 hereof are my submission to this Learned Court.

I sign this verification at
No. .... this ....
day of 1999

Prepared in my Office
Advocate for the Petitioner

Petition for Grant of Succession Certificate

In the Court of .... in the goods of .... (state name, address and nationality)

In the matter of the grant of a succession certificate in respect of the debts, securities of the said deceased

The humble petition of AB (state address and relationship)

The above-named applicant respectfully begs to state as follows:

1. That the deceased GH of, etc., at etc., hereinafter referred to as the said deceased died intestate at No. .... on the .... day of ....

2. That prior to and at the time of his death the said deceased has had his fixed place of residence at No. .... within the jurisdiction of this court, where he ordinarily lived and resided and left also some property.

3. That the said deceased was governed by the Hindu Succession Act (or Indian Succession Act) etc., and the applicant being his legal heir under the said law is entitled to succession certificate in respect of the debts and securities hereunder mentioned.

4. That the said deceased left him surviving at the time of his death, only the following and no other relatives.

(*a*) CD son of, etc., of, etc.

(*b*) EF son of, etc., of, etc.

5. That as the said deceased left no will, no application was or could therefore be made in any court for the grant of probate thereof or of

administration of his estate, with a copy annexed thereto and there is no impediment to the grant of a certificate to the applicant.

6. That the particulars of the debts and securities in respect of which the certificate is prayed for are set forth in Annexure A.

The applicant prays that the court may be pleased to grant him the succession certificate for collection of the debts and securities with interest thereon mentioned in Annexure A below.

Annexure A

Debts

Sl. No.	*Name of debtor*	*Amount of debt, including interest on date of application for certificate (or extension)*	*Description and date of instrument, if any, by which the debt is secured*
1.	....	....	....
2.	....	....	....
3.	....	....	....
4.	....	....	....

Annexure B

Securities

Sl. No.	*Distinguishing number or letter of security*	*Name, title or class of security*	*Amount of par value of security*	*Market value of security on date of application for certificate (or extension)*
1.	....	....	....	....
2.	....	....	....	....
3.	....	....	....	....

Verification

I, ... residing at .... being the .... of the above-named .... do hereby declare and say that the statements contained in paragraphs 1 to 6 of the above petition and also the particulars contained in the Annexures 'A' and 'B' including all figures are true to my knowledge and the rest are my humble submissions to this Learned Court.

I sign this verification at .... this .... day of .... 2000.

Signature

Before me

Notary

Prepared in my Office

Advocate for the Petitioner

Petition for Extension of Succession Certificate

In the Court of etc.

In the goods of (state name, address and nationality)

In the matter of the grant of extension of Succession Certificate in respect of the debts and securities of the said deceased under s. 376 of the Indian Succession Act

The applicant above-named states as follows:

1. That CH of etc., hereinafter referred to as the said deceased died at etc., intestate on the .... day of .... 2000.

2. That the fixed place of residence of the said deceased at the time of his death was at etc. within the jurisdiction of this court, where he has left also some property.

3. That the said deceased was governed by the Hindu Succession Act (or Indian Succession Act) and the applicant, being his legal heir under the said law, was entitled to the grant of succession certificate already granted and so is entitled to the extension thereof hereunder prayed for.

4. That the said deceased left heirs surviving at the time of his death only the following relatives:

(*a*) CD, son of etc., of etc.

(*b*) EF, son of etc., of etc.—Address and age.

5. That the said deceased left no will and no application has been made to any court for the grant of probate or any letters of administration with a copy annexed thereto and there is no impediment to the grant of extension of certificate.

6. That the applicant obtained on the .... day of .... a succession certificate from this court in respect of some of the debts and securities of the said deceased. A copy of the said certificate is hereunto annexed and marked A.

7. That the applicant on the .... day of .... came to know that the said deceased also left behind several other debts and securities mentioned in Schedule hereunder.

The applicant, therefore, prays that this court may be pleased to grant him an extended certificate for collection of the debts and securities with interest thereon mentioned in Schedule hereunder on payment of additional duty, if necessary.

THE SCHEDULE

Verification

I, ... residing at .... being the .... of the above-named .... do hereby declare and say that the statements contained in paragraphs 1 to 7 of the above petition and also the particulars contained in Annexure "A" and the Schedule including all figures are true to my knowledge and the rest are my humble submissions to this Learned Court.

I sign this verification at .... this .... day of ....

Signature

Before me
Notary
Prepared in my Office
Advocate for the Petitioner

Petition for Revocation of Grant of Probate, Letters of Administration, Certificate

In the Court of ....

In the goods of .... (full name, address and nationality)

And

In the matter of revocation of the grant of probate of will *or* letters of administration of the estate, or, in of GH deceased

AB residing at .... *Petitioner*

versus

CD residing at .... *Respondent*

The humble petition of AB (state full name, address and nationality)

RESPECTFULLY SHEWETH:

1. That the deceased above-named who was a Hindu governed by the Dayabhaga or Bengal School of Hindu Law died intestate on the .... day of .... at ....

2. That the deceased was governed by the Hindu Succession Act 1956 and at the time of death he left the following and no other persons as heirs and legal representatives (state, name, address, age and relationship).

3. That your petitioner being a son of the deceased is entitled to .... share in the estate of the deceased.

4. That your petitioner was most surprised when he came to know on the day of .... that the Respondent No. .... has had on the .... day of .... obtained probate of a pretended will (which is completely a forged document manufactured by the said respondent) alleged to have been made and published by the deceased on the day of .... of which he never heard except for the first time as on the .... day of .... and of which he had no means of knowledge of the proceedings in relation thereto.

5. That your petitioner was not served with any citation or any other notice nor had any information in connection with the grant of probate of the said purported will.

6. That the said will is also hard and unkind inasmuch as it has left out all near relations, including your petitioner, and purports to give the entire estate unto and in favour of the respondent No. 1 and thereby deprive your petitioner and also the other heirs from their legitimate rights and shares in the estate.

7. That in the circumstances and in the ends of justice your petitioner is advised and he respectfully submits that this court might be pleased to revoke the grant of probate.

8. That this application is made *bona fide*.

Your petitioner therefore prays for an order revoking probate of the said will.

Verification

I, ... residing at .... being the .... of the above-named .... do hereby declare and say that the statements contained in the paragraphs 1 to 8 of the above petition and are true to my knowledge and the rest are my humble submissions to this Learned Court.

I sign this verification at .... this .... day of ...... 2000.

Signature

Before me
Notary

Prepared in my Office
Advocate for the Petitioner

Compromise in Probate Proceedings

THIS DEED OF SETTLEMENT made on .... day of ....1999 among AB and CD, sons of PQ, now deceased, of .... of the First Part (hereinafter called collectively the SONS) AND EF, wife of ...., CH, wife of .... and LM, wife of .... of the Second Part (hereinafter called the DAUGHTERS) Witnesses as under:

WHEREAS the said PQ of .... hereinafter referred to as the said deceased died on the .... day of .... And whereas the said PQ was at the time of death seized, possessed of properties and outstandings, more particularly detailed in the schedule hereunder written and hereinafter referred to as the said properties.

WHEREAS prior to his death and on the day of .... 1999 the said deceased made and published his last will whereby and whereunder he left and bequeathed all his estate and effects thereof unto and in favour of his SONS providing only certain annuities for his DAUGHTERS. And whereas the said SONS applied for probate of the said will in the court of .... on the .... day of .... whereupon citations were issued and served on the said DAUGHTERS who have all entered caveat and filed their respective affidavits in support thereof challenging *inter alia* the authenticity of the will and the testamentary capacity of the testator.

WHEREAS there are also various other disputes and differences between the parties as to the administration of the estate of the deceased, And whereas in order to avoid the costs of protracted litigation and for preservation of the honour, dignity and prestige of the family the said parties having consulted their respective lawyers and under advice from them have settled all disputes relating to the distribution or inheritance of the properties left by the said deceased in an amicable manner for all times in the manner hereunder appearing.

NOW THIS DEED OF SETTLEMENT WITNESSETH as follows:

(1) The DAUGHTERS shall withdraw the caveat filed by them and shall not contest probate of the will which the SONS shall obtain after proof of the will in the solemn form and manner required by law, without prejudice to their rights in the inheritance and distribution of the estate of the deceased as hereinafter appearing by virtue of the settlement hereunder made.

(2) In consideration of the settlement herein made, the sons and each of them shall divide and distribute the properties of the deceased and have the same partitioned into two lots and one lot, *viz.*, lot A consisting of premises No. .... and No. .... shall be transferred, assigned and delivered to the DAUGHTERS to have and to hold the same jointly and in equal shares and the other lot B consisting of the premises No. .... and premises No. .... shall be held possessed and enjoyed by the SONS absolutely free from all claims and demands of the DAUGHTERS. The DAUGHTERS will not press for any after-claim as to the other benefits provided

for them in the said will which are all hereby renounced. It is further agreed that the properties to be allotted to the DAUGHTERS shall be transferred to them after the SONS shall obtain probate of the will and prior thereto the SONS shall not charge, encumber or otherwise deal with the same.

IN WITNESS WHEREOF the parties aforementioned all together and each individually for himself and herself have set their respective hands on this final compromise in token of acceptance thereof.

Schedule of the properties: Lot A which will be allotted to the DAUGHTERS.

Lot B which will be absolutely held possessed and enjoyed by the SONS.

Sd/. Sons

Sd/. Daughters

Disclaimer by a Trustee of a Will

THIS DISCLAIMER IS MADE this 5th day of November 1999 by Mr. X of ....

WHEREAS Mr. Z late of .... since deceased (Testator), by his Will dated ...., appointed the said Mr. X and Mr. Y of .... to be the Executors thereof and thereby devised and bequeathed all his Real and personal Estate unto the said Mr. X and Mr. Y upon the Trusts and with and subject to the power and provisions declared therein.

AND WHEREAS the Testator died on .... and his said Will was duly probated on .... in the Court of the District Delegate at Alipore by the said Mr. Y the said Mr. X having renounced the Probate thereof.

AND WHEREAS the said Mr. X has in nowise acted and has declined to act as an Executor or Trustee of the said Will.

NOW THIS DEED of Disclaimer Witnesseth that the said Mr. X has from the death of the Testator disclaimed and by this Disclaimer does disclaim the office of Executor and Trustee and all Estate and interest in the movable assets and immovable properties of the Testator, and all Trusts and powers devised or bequeathed to or vested or reposed in him by or under or by virtue of the said Will of the Testator jointly with the said Mr. Y.

This Disclaimer shall not operate to disclaim or release any beneficial interest whether vested or contingent to which the said Mr. X now is or may hereafter become entitled to under the Trust or provisions of the said Will or any legacy thereby given to Mr. X for his own benefit.

IN WITNESS WHEREOF the said Mr. X has executed these presents on the day, month and year first above-written.

WITNESS: Signature

Disclaimer by Devisee of a Gift by Will

BY THIS DEED I , Mr. X of ...., the undersigned, hereby disclaim all benefits under the devise of land and building being Premises No. .... in my favour contained in the Will of Mr. MN dated .... and probated in the Court of the District Delegate, Alipore by Mr. MN the Executor named therein and also disclaim all Estate and interest in the subject-matter of the said Devise.

IN WITNESS WHEREOF I hereby execute these Presents on this day of 5th September 1999 at Calcutta.

WITNESS:

Signature

Deed of Disclaimer by a Person who is Entitled to an Interest in the Settled Property

THIS DEED OF DISCLAIMER is made on this .... by Mr. X of .... (the Disclaimant).

WHEREAS by a Deed of Settlement dated .... made BETWEEN Mr. MN (Settlor) of the ONE PART and Mr. AB and Mr. GH (Trustees) of the OTHER PART certain properties mentioned therein were transferred to the Trustees upon Trust for the family members of the Settlor as mentioned in the Settlement.

AND WHEREAS the Settlor died on .... leaving his family members as the beneficiaries under the said Settlement.

AND WHEREAS the Disclaimant is also one of the persons mentioned as the beneficiary of the Settlement and become entitled to an interest in the property comprised in the Settlement which he wishes to disclaim.

NOW THIS DEED WITNESSETH that the disclaimant hereby disclaims all interest and benefit in his favour in or under the Settlement and also disclaims all estate and interest in the property comprised in and subject of the Settlement.

IN WITNESS WHEREOF I have executed these Presents on the day, month and year first above-written.

WITNESS:

Signature

54

Trust

History of trust ownership. Modern trusts are successors of what was originally called Uses in England. A trust is an obligation attached to the ownership of the property out of confidence reposed in and accepted by the owner or declared and accepted by him for the benefit of another.[1] Although every person capable of holding property can be a trustee but not the Government of India.[2] A Government servant cannot be the trustee of a mosque, temple or other religious institution.[3]

In a trust there are more than one party to the instrument of trust but in fact there would at least be two main parties, namely, the settlor on the one hand and the trustees on the other and also there would be the beneficiaries who would be indirectly third parties to the instrument though not being direct parties thereto. Thus the settlor is one party to the trust who settles the property in trust for the benefit of others who become beneficiaries and the legal ownership of the property is transferred to the trustees. Accordingly, it would be almost a tripartite transaction.[4]

Legal and equitable trusts. The distinction between the "legal" and the "equitable estate" is the essential characteristic of the trust. Equitable estates in land had their origin out of the ancient practices in England of people putting their trusted friends and relations in possession of their lands in faith and confidence that they would deal with and/or dispose the same according to their wish and desire.[5] A trust ownership is different from other types of

1 Section 3 of the Indian Trusts Act 1882.
2 *Vizaramarju* v *Secretary of State* 8 Mad 525 (PC).
3 Section 22 of the Religious Endowment Act 1863.
4 *I.T. Commr.* v *Kamla Town Trust* AIR 1996 SC 620.
5 William's *Real Property,* 20th Ed., p. 165.

legal relationship, *e.g.* bailment, agency, mortgage, etc., which cannot pass a good title to the property even to a *bona fide* transferee for value without notice.[6]

A trustee cannot take advantage of the statute of limitation.[7] If a trustee wrongfully sells the trust property, the beneficiaries have the right to follow it so long as it can be traced notwithstanding any intermediate change or changes in its ownership except in the case of a *bona fide* sale for value and without notice of the trust.[8] In England, the evolution of the trust estate was by the method of double use. Thus, when *A* wanted to convey the legal estate of any particular property to *B* and the equitable estate to *C*, the following form was adopted—"To *A* in fee simple to the use of *B* in fee simple to the use of *C* in the fee simple". There were two *uses*. As the common law courts did not grant any relief in cases like this, the Chancellor stepped in and used to make an order upon *B* to hold the property for the benefit of *C* and the old form of double use was simplified and the following form was reproduced—"unto and to the use of *B* in trust for *C*". Trust was thus a posthumous legacy of the "medieval use". The Statute of Uses (27 Henry VIII C. 10) was enacted to abolish the distinction created between legal estate and equitable estate by the Chancellor's Court which has been repealed by the Law of Property Act 1925 as from 1st January 1926.

A trust may be created by the act of the parties or by operation of law. The former may be express or implied. The latter is either a resulting or a constructive trust except where the same defeats the policy of law.

Where a compromise decree provided that out of 50% of the sale proceeds of a property a land was to be purchased in the name of *A* and the latter was to convey it to *B* husband of *C* after his death without there being any statement in the compromise that it was for the benefit of *C*, it could not be said that there was conferred any equitable or legal interest on *C* and as such *A* was not a trustee for *C* and subsequent sale by *A* to a third party was not void.[9]

Permission for sale of trust property by the Trustees should be refused by the court where it was not disclosed that there was a higher offer by a person and at the same time pleading that in spite of best efforts they could not secure higher offer as this conduct amounts to practising fraud upon the court.[10]

Trusts among the Hindus. The Hindu law is based upon Hindu religion which is encyclopedic in character—not a particular form of faith but a

6 *Taylor* v *Plummer* (1815)3 M & S 575.
7 Section 10 of the Limitation Act.
8 *Taylor* v *Blackelock* (1885)32 Ch D 650 (see also s. 63 of the Indian Trusts Act).
9 *N.A. Mohammed* v *Sulochana* AIR 1995 SC 1624.
10 *Gowrishankar* v *Joshi Amba* AIR 1996 SC 2202.

commonwealth of faiths. The Hindu law did not recognise two estates in the same property, half by two different persons. So it made no provisions for trust analogous to English law but it recognises endowment under which the property vest straightway in the beneficiary. The Mahomedan law which is also based upon Islamic religion does not recognise trust in the English sense but it permits gifts through the medium of trust. A public wakf is however treated as a trust for the purpose of s. 92 of the Code of Civil Procedure.[11]

Doctrine of Advancement as applies in England in cases of purchase of any property in which the person providing for the purchase money is under some obligation to support or make provision for the person to whom the same was conveyed, *i.e.* where the former is the husband or father or stands in *loco parentis* in relation to the latter as observed by Lord Justice Baron Eyer.[1] The doctrine however has no application to India.[2] A *benamdar* has no interest in the property. He is not a trustee unless he is in possession of the property,[3] though as an ostensible owner he can sell same unless the purchaser has notice of his pretended title. Nevertheless, the relationship is a fact to be taken into account in determining whether the transaction is *benami* or not.[4] Although the Doctrine of Advancement has no application to India, nevertheless the presumption of *benami* is rebutted by evidence to the contrary. The doctrine is applicable where it is established by evidence that the husband intended to create a title in favour of or intended to make provisions for the wife.[5]

Endowment and trust. A deed of trust by itself creates no endowment of the property. The author must prove that he intended for and divested himself of the ownership in the property and caused the same vested in the deity. The mutation of the name of deity and production of account showing the application of the income for the benefit of the idol are evidence *aliunde* of the creation of the debutter.[6] The absence of any ceremony is an item of evidence but mere performance is not conclusive test.[7] It was held in *Sankar Raghunath* v *Ganeshgopal*,[8] that *sankalpa utsarga* followed by *samarpan* are

11 *Mahomed Kuzin* v *Syed Abi* 136 IC 417; AIR 1932 Pat 238.
1 *Dyer* v *Dyer* (1788)2 Cox Equity Case 92.
2 *Bhusan Mohini* v *Kumud Bala Dashi* AIR 1924 Cal 467 (see also s. 82 of the Indian Trusts Act); *CED* v *Aloke* AIR 1981 SC 102.
3 *Controller of Estate Duty* v *Aloke Mitter* AIR 1981 SC 102.
4 Sections 81 and 82 of the Indian Trusts Act 1882 are the statutory recognition of *benami* in India.
5 *Pritinarayani* v *Patit Paban* 60 CWN 890.
6 *Mohini Das* v *Pareshnath* AIR 1934 Ori 198.
7 *Manohari* v *Sambhunath* AIR 1933 All 622.
8 AIR 1982 NOC 7.

the ingredients of dedication. Intention to extinguish the rights of the owner and vest the same in the deity is the most important factor in an endowment.

Discretionary trust. In a discretionary trust which was to survive for 18 years and having two categories of beneficiaries. Neither category has a right but only on expectation to receive income and in that sense the Supreme Court held that members of the second category are as much beneficiaries as the members of the first category. The trustees are entitled to choose not to pay a pie out of the income to any one and invest the whole of it in their own concerns. They are under no obligation to disburse or distribute the income received in a year in that year or in the following year. Either category could receive income wholly to the exclusion of the other or both could receive it partly.[9]

Endowment for other. Trusts in the sense as understood in English law were unknown to Hindu law. It was observed by the Chief Justice Peacock: 'The Hindu law does not provide for trust'[1] in the sense of bifurcation of ownership by the creation of 'legal estate' and 'equitable estate'. Nevertheless, trust in the wider sense of the term was not unknown to old Hindu society and law. It was not very uncommon among the ancient Hindus to create endowment for the benefit of others, *e.g.*, dharamsalas, rest houses, sarai, etc., are living examples of religious and charitable trust of ancient societies. So also the dedication of tanks and trees intended for the benefit of the public. Further, the cases of religious and charitable endowments, gifts to idols, establishment of hospitals, were and still are most common in India since ancient days as clear evidences that trusts were never forbidden in Hindu law nor repugnant or inconsistent with their existence. The same court used to administer Law and Equity in India. Properties were dedicated for or subject to pious uses. All these facilitated the growth and development of trust in India. A Hindu who is of sound mind and not a minor may dedicate his property for religious and charitable purposes. It is not absolutely necessary that the same shall be done by a registered deed. All that is necessary is a clear intention on the part of the donor to divest himself of all ownership and control in the beneficiary and vest the same in the beneficiary. The dedication shall be for an object which is not vague or uncertain, *e.g.* a gift for advancement of religion, to Dharma or for social services without particulars or for good work without specification are void.

A gift to an idol to be consecrated and established after the death of the donor is valid.[2] The dedication is not invalid by reason of the fact that the members of the settler's family are nominated *shebaits* or given reasonable remuneration for services to the deity or was entitled to a share of the

9 *Gosar Family Trust v I.T. Commr.* AIR 1995 SC 1644.
1 *Kumar Asima Krishna Dev v Kumar Kristo Krishna Dev* (1869)2 BLR OC 11.
2 Vide *Bhupati Nath Smrititirtha's* case 37 Cal 128 (SB).

income.[3] It was also held that it is not necessary that the idol shall be in existence at the time of creation of the trust.[4]

The Indian Trusts Act 1882, does not affect the Mahomedan Law of Wakf or the mutual relations of the members of an undivided family as determined by the customary or general law of public or private religious or charitable endowments.

The Mahomedan law recognises gift with a condition in the nature of trust, e.g. a gift of a property without reserving any dominion over the corpus but with the stipulation for enjoyment of the income is valid.[5]

Public trust. A private trust is one intended for the benefit of an ascertained or ascertainable number of individuals. A public trust, on the other hand, is for the benefit of the public at large or of some considerable portion of it. It is synonymous with religious or charitable trust. (*i*) Relief to the poor; (*ii*) advancement of education; (*iii*) support of scholars; (*vi*) advancement of religion etc. are *inter alia* illustrations of religion or charitable objects.[6] Section 18 of the Transfer of Property Act dispense with the restrictions on transfers under ss. 14, 16 & 17 thereof in cases of transfer for religious or charitable objects. The Indian Trust Act deals only with Private Trusts. It has no application even to private or public endowments.[7] The Charitable and Religious Trusts Act (Act XIV of 1920) controls the administration of public trusts, *i.e.* charitable and religious trusts.

Although the court administers a public trust in theory under s. 92 of the Code of Civil Procedure yet some of the principles of the Indian Trusts Act 1882, apply also to public trusts.

A charitable trust cannot be implied from the fact that the owner used a part of the income of the property in charity. Where a temple was built on a plot of land by its proprietor and the Hindu community uses the temple for worship and maintenance of the temple for performance of religious ceremonies without any objection by anyone, the property may be regarded as a public trust. The principles embodied in ss. 44, 52, 62, 63 and 76 of the Indian Trusts Act are applicable to all kinds of trusts. In settling a scheme for the administration of a charitable trust involving the appointment of trustees or managers, the court is bound to secure persons whom it regards as suitable. Hence it cannot be contended that the court has no jurisdiction to remove a person nominated as the head of a Math by will by his

3 *Jadunath Singh* v *Silaramji* 44 IA 187.

4 *Ratan Sen* v *Suraj Bhan* AIR 1944 All 11; *Jagadish* v *Mt. Kausilla* AIR 1947 All 317.

5 Mulla on *Mahomedan Law*, 19th Ed., pp. 134-135.

6 See judgment of Lord Macnaghten in *Commissioner of Income-tax* v *Pemsel* (1891) AC 583. See also s. 118 of the Indian Succession Act 1925.

7 *Gopal* v *Sami* ILR 28 Mad 517.

predecessor when it is found as a fact that the person has by his conduct and/or dealings made himself unfit for such position. The existence of a trust for public or charitable purposes can be proved either by direct evidence of dedication or by user extending over a long period and the conduct of the parties concerned.

An order under s. 3 of the Charitable and Religious Trusts Act (Act XIV of 1920) which control the administration of religions and charitable trusts holding certain property to be a public charitable trust does not operate as *res judicata.* The use of the word "pratishtha" shows that the author has dedicated the property.

Doctrine of cy pres. If the donor declares his intention in favour of a defined object which happens to fail for whatever cause, yet if the general purpose is charity, such purpose will, notwithstanding the failure of its immediate object, be carried into effect with a substituted object.

In order that the Charitable and Religious Trusts Act of 1920 may apply, the trust must be substantially for public purpose. It is not sufficient if one of the purposes of the trust is public. A mere provision for the service of sadhus, occasional guests and way-farers in a dedication to an idol does not render the dedication substantially for public purposes.

The Act is intended to provide more effectual control over the administration of charitable and religious trusts and provision is made therein for obtaining an order calling on the trustee to give particulars of the object of the trust and, if the trust is denied, to file a suit. No such provision is made in the Mussalman Wakf Act of 1923.[8]

Trust and settlement. A trust is not always a settlement nor is a settlement always a trust. As defined in s. 2(24) of the Stamp Act, a settlement is a non-testamentary disposition of property either (*i*) in consideration of an intended marriage; (*ii*) for distribution of some property among persons intended to be provided for by way of partition or otherwise, *e.g.* a family settlement; or (*iii*) for religious and charitable purposes.

It was laid down by Lord Langdale in *Knight* v *Knight*[9] that a trust requires three certainties for its creation, *viz.* (*a*) certainty of words; (*b*) certainty of subject-matter; and (*c*) certainty of object. In other words (*a*) the declaration of trust shall be of imperative nature. (*b*) The property shall be specified and (*c*) the beneficiary must be clearly indicated. The legal title passes unto and the property vests in the trustee. So every instrument creating a trust must be executed by a competent person and shall contain express words of

8 AIR 1927 Pat 189. See also AIR 1936 Lah 695.

9 (1840)3 Beav 148 at p. 171.

transfer. There is, however, no uncertainty in case an alternative subject-matter is provided for where the property specified may not be available.

Salmond in his *Jurisprudence,* 7th Ed., at p. 286 says: "A trust is more than an obligation as to the use of one's property for the benefit of another or others. The beneficiary has more than a personal right as to performance of the duties and obligations of the trust. He, in other words, is in effect the owner of the property". Although Indian law does not recognise equitable estate or ownership in the same sense as in English law but for all practical purposes, there is very little or no difference between a beneficiary under the English law and beneficiary under the Indian Trust Act.

A trustee may, whether appointed under any will or deed of trust, disclaim his office before acceptance and within a reasonable time.[10]

Section 118 of the Indian Succession Act 1925, contains some illustrations of charitable objects, *e.g.* (*i*) relief of the poor; (*ii*) maintenance and support of the sick people; and (*iii*) education of the orphans. Section 4(3) of the Income-tax Act 1922, exempts income of such a trust from taxation.[11]

Creation of Wakf. A Mahomedan can make an oral Wakf of his property under the Mussalman Wakf Validating Acts 1913 and 1930. A Wakf may be also created by a will. If created by a deed, it is to be registered under s. 17 of the Indian Registration Act in cases where the value of the property is Rs. 100 or upwards. It is a permanent dedication of some property for any purpose recognised as pious, religious or charitable in Mahomedan law. The property vests in God. Trusts in the sense as understood in English jurisprudence, *e.g.*, legal and equitable ownership, is unknown to the principles of Mahomedan law.[12] A Sunni Mahomedan can create a valid wakf even though the gifts to charity are illusory. A wakf is something quite different from a trust. It is a dedication to God only for religious or charitable purposes. According the Muslim law, a valid wakf is completed by the declaration of the wakif intending thereby a dedication of the property in good faith for some pious or religious purposes. A wakf does not fail even if the objects are not at all specified or where the objects specified fail for impracticability or where the objects specified are partly valid and partly not valid.

By virtue of s. 92(3) of the Code of Civil Procedure, inserted by the amendment in 1976 the court may alter the original purposes of an express or constructive trust created for public purpose of a charitable or religious nature applying the doctrine of *cy pres* and frame a scheme. The rules requiring the objects of the trust specified with certainty as contained in s. 6 of the Indian Trusts Act do not apply to a wakf and its validity is tested

10 Section 10 of the Indian Trusts Act 1882.

11 Sections 11, 12 & 13 of the Income-tax Act 1961—*Commissioner of Income-tax* v *Pemsel* (1891) AC 581.

12 *Tagore* v *Tagore* 6 BLR 401.

according to Mahomedan law.[13] When a wakf commissioner holds certain properties to be wakf properties even wrongly interpreting documentary evidence such finding cannot be vitiated for lack of jurisdiction and cannot be challenged under Art. 226.[14]

Execution and attestation—registration. A deed of settlement is executed and attested as a bond, and its registration will be compulsory if the value of the immovable property involved be Rs. 100 or upwards.

Although the law relating to trust has been codified under the Indian Trusts Act 1882, nevertheless the Act does not apply to public or private religious endowments.

Section 18 of the Transfer of Property Act 1882, relaxes all restrictions provided under ss. 14, 16 and 17 in cases of transfers of any property for the benefit of the public, *e.g.*, advancement of knowledge, religion, commerce, health and other allied objects.

Nature of trust. A trust thus is an obligation annexed to the ownership of property arising out of confidence reposed in and accepted by the owner, or declared and accepted by him, for the benefit of another, or the owner.

The person who reposes or declares the confidence is called *the author of the trust;* the person who accepts the confidence is called the trustee.

"Trust property", "beneficial interest" and "instrument of trust"—"breach of trust". The subject-matter of the trust is called the *trust property or trust money.* The *beneficial interest or interests* of the beneficiary is his right against the trustee as owner of the trust property; and the instrument (if any) by which the trust is declared is called the *instrument of trust*. A breach of any duty imposed on a trustee, as such, by any law for the time being in force, is called a *breach of trust.*

Lawful purpose of trust. A trust as provided under s. 6 of the Indian Trusts Act 1882, may be created for any lawful purpose. The purpose of a trust is lawful unless it is (*i*) forbidden by law; or (*ii*) is of such a nature that, if permitted, it would defeat the provisions of any law; or (*iii*) is fraudulent; or (*iv*) involves or implies injury to the person or property of another; or (*v*) the court regards it as immoral or opposed to public policy. The following trusts were declared illegal, *e.g.* trust in restraint of marriage,[15] trust creating a perpetuity by settlement of properties intended for maintenance of persons born and to be born indefinitely,[16] trust to defraud creditor.[17]

13 *Haji Isak* v *Fauz Mahomed* AIR 1943 Sind 134.
14 *Board of Muslim Wakfs* v *Sm. Hadi Begum* AIR 1992 SC 1083.
15 *Allen* v *Jackson* (1875)1 Ch D 399.
16 *Ajit Kumar* v *Tarubala* ILR 63 Cal 209.
17 Re, *Great Berlin's Steam Boat Co.* 26 Ch D 616 (CA).

Every trust of which the purpose is unlawful is void.[18] It therefore follows that trust tying the property or income for any period longer than or offending against rule against perpetuity or intended to defeat the law relating to bankruptcy or to defraud creditors or for immoral purposes are all void. And where a trust is created for two purposes, of which one is lawful and the other unlawful, and the two purposes cannot be separated, the whole trust is void.

The expression "law" includes, where the trust property is immovable and situate in a foreign country, the law of such country.

Trust of immovable and movable property. No trust in relation to immovable property is valid unless the same is intended for and declared by a non-testamentary instrument in writing signed by the author of the trust or the trustee and registered, or by the will of the author of the trust or of the trustee.

No trust in relation to movable property is valid unless declared as aforesaid, or unless the ownership of the property is transferred to the trustee.[19] The above section corresponds with s. 53(1)(*b*) of the Law of Property Act 1925, replacing s. 7 of the Statute of Frauds.[1]

Creation of trust. A trust is created when the author of the trust indicates with reasonable certainty by any words or acts:

(*i*) an intention on his part to create thereby a trust;

(*ii*) the purpose of the trust is lawful;

(*iii*) the beneficiary;

(*iv*) the trust property, and (unless the trust is declared by will or the author of the trust is himself to be the trustee) the transfers the trust property to the trustee;[2] and

(*v*) the author of the trust, the trustees and the beneficiary all being competent powers (s. 8).

Agreement to create a trust if supported by consideration may be specifically enforced.

Reimbursement of expenses. Every trustee can reimburse himself, or pay or discharge out of the trust property, all expenses properly incurred in or about the execution of the trust, or the realisation, preservation, or benefit of the trust property, or the protection or support of the beneficiary.[3]

18 Section 4 of the Indian Trusts Act 1882.

19 Section 5 of the Indian Trusts Act 1882.

1 State 29 Car 11 C 3.

2 Section 6 of the Indian Trusts Act 1882—*Knight* v *Knight* (1846)3 Beav 148—three certainties of trust.

3 Section 32 of the Indian Trusts Act 1882.

Prohibition to buy beneficiary's interest. No trustee and no person, who has recently ceased to be a trustee, can without the permission of a principal Civil Court of original jurisdiction buy or become mortgagee or lessee of the trust property or any part thereof, and such permission is not given unless the proposed purchase, mortgage or lease is manifestly for the advantages of the beneficiary.[4]

When trustee can renounce. A trustee who has accepted the trust cannot afterwards renounce it except (*i*) with the permission of a principal Civil Court of original jurisdiction, or (*ii*) if the beneficiary is competent to contract, with his consent, or (*iii*) by virtue of special power in the instrument of trust.

Discharge of trustee. A trustee can be discharged from his office only as follows:

(*i*) by the extinction of the trust;

(*ii*) by the completion of his duties under the trust;

(*iii*) by such means as may be prescribed by the instrument of trust;

(*iv*) by appointment under the Indian Trusts Act of a new trustee in his place;

(*v*) by consent of himself and the beneficiary, or where there are more beneficiaries than one, all the beneficiaries being competent to contract, or

(*vi*) by the court to which a petition for his discharge is presented under the Indian Trusts Act.[5]

Trust how revoked. A trust created by will can be revoked at the pleasure of the testator.

A trust otherwise created can be revoked only—

(*i*) where all the beneficiaries are competent to contract by their consent;

(*ii*) where the trust has been declared by a non-testamentary instrument or by word of mouth—in exercise of power of revocation expressly reserved to the author of the trust; or

(*iii*) where the trust is for the payment of the debts of the author of the trust, and has not been communicated to the creditors—at the pleasure of the author of the trust;[6]

(*iv*) by a court of competent jurisdiction on sufficient grounds, *e.g.*, a trust for unlawful objects or created to defraud creditors.

4 Section 53 of the Indian Trusts Act 1882.

5 Section 71 of the Indian Trusts Act 1882.

6 Section 78 of the Indian Trusts Act 1882.

Extinction of trust. A trust is extinguished (*a*) when its purpose is completely fulfilled or (*b*) its purpose becomes unlawful or (*c*) when the fulfilment of its purpose becomes impossible by destruction of the trust property or otherwise or (*d*) where the trust, being revocable, is expressly revoked. A trust will, however, be not extinguished on the failure on the part of all trustees to administer the trust.[7] But a trust will come to end where the deed had provided for such termination on the death of the wife or son's attaining certain age whichever was later on the happening of that event[8] or where the purpose of a certain deposit was achieved.[9]

FORMS

Deed of Settlement by Father in Favour of Children

THIS DEED OF SETTLEMENT is made this .... day of .... 1999 BETWEEN AB son of .... residing at .... (hereinafter called the SETTLOR) of the one part and CD, son of .... residing at .... and EF son of .... residing at .... (hereinafter called the CHILDREN) represented by their mother XY residing at .... of the other part.

WHEREAS the SETTLOR has been hitherto paying allowance of Rs. .... a month freely and voluntarily to each of the CHILDREN and is desirous of placing the same on record and for that purpose to enter into an agreement as to the future payment of the same in the manner as hereinafter provided: NOW THIS DEED WITNESSES as follows:

In consideration of his natural love and affection which the SETTLOR had and still bears for the CHILDREN, the SETTLOR hereby agrees in writing and covenants with the said XY that he, the SETTLOR, will so long as the CHILDREN shall, all or any one of them remain alive, pay or cause to be paid to each of them through the said XY the sum of Rs. .... on the .... day of every month, for their maintenance and livelihood without any delay or default subject to such modification or release thereof as may be hereafter agreed between the said AB and XY or between the said AB and the CHILDREN on their becoming of full age.

If, however, any of the CHILDREN shall become insolvent or shall do or suffer anything whereby the monthly sum hereinbefore agreed to be paid to him (*or* her) is attached or any prohibitory order of injunction is made in

7 *Vadivelu* v *Kuppuswami* (1972)1 MLJ 265.
8 *Darshan Lal* v *Dalliwall* AIR 1952 All 825 (DB).
9 *Jugalkishore* v *Ambala* AIR 1953 Punj 98.

respect thereof or the official assignee or receiver-in-insolvency or any third party become entitled to collect the same, then and in such event this settlement shall be inoperative in so far as he or they is or are concerned but the cessation of the payment to any one or more of the CHILDREN of the said monthly sums under this provision shall not prejudice the payment of the said monthly sums to the others or other of the CHILDREN, but in the case of all on grounds hereinbefore stated this settlement shall stand revoked.

The Schedule above referred to

IN WITNESS WHEREOF AB the SETTLOR has executed these presents on the day, month and year first above-written.

Signed, sealed and delivered by AB
the SETTLOR in the presence of:

Signed, sealed and delivered by
XY mother of the children in the
presence of:

Settlement of Property for the Benefit of Minor Children

THIS DEED OF SETTLEMENT is made on this .... day of .... 2000 BETWEEN AB son of .... residing at .... (hereinafter called the SETTLOR) of the first part and CD son of .... residing at .... (hereinafter called the TRUSTEE which term shall unless the context otherwise requires include his heirs, successors legal representatives) of the second part and X, Y and Z all are sons of K represented by their mother and natural guardian (the said X, Y, Z are hereinafter referred to as the BENEFICIARIES which term shall unless excluded by or repugnant to the context shall include their heirs, successors, legal representatives) of the third part.

THIS DEED WITNESSETH as follows:

In consideration of natural love and affection which he, the SETTLOR, had and bears for X,Y,Z, the minor sons of K, and for other good reasons and considerations he, the SETTLOR, doth hereby and hereunder grant, convey, transfer, assign, assure unto and to the use of the said CD and settle the property belonging to the SETTLOR which is fully mentioned and described in the schedule below and deliver possession of the same TO HAVE AND TO HOLD the same in trust and for the use and benefit of the said BENEFICIARIES, *viz.*, the said X, Y, Z as aforesaid subject to the terms and conditions hereunder expressed and declared.

(1) The TRUSTEE shall assume charge, possession, control, supervision and management of the said property and administer and develop the same

either personally or through an agent to be employed by him in a manner as might be most profitable and beneficial to the interest of or otherwise most advantageous to the trust and also the BENEFICIARIES.

(2) The TRUSTEE shall, out of the rents, issues and profits, pay all municipal taxes and other capital and revenue liability of property, all costs, charges and expenses for maintenance and preservation and spend the surplus for the maintenance and education of the BENEFICIARIES and invest the balance, if any, in some securities approved by law. He shall have power to change such investment from time to time as he shall think fit and proper.

(3) The TRUSTEE shall have no power to sell, mortgage or otherwise deal in the said property or any part thereof except with the consent in writing of the SETTLOR first had and obtained, or in the alternative with the permission of the District Judge having jurisdiction over the subject-matter of the trust.

(4) The TRUSTEE shall keep and maintain proper accounts of all incomes and expenses which shall be open to the inspection of the SETTLOR and upon the youngest beneficiary attaining the age of 21 years grant, convey, transfer the said property unto and in their favour absolutely and for ever when and in such an event the trust executed hereunder shall come to an end.

PROVIDED, however, that in case the property or any portion thereof is acquired by the Government, the TRUSTEE shall invest the compensation money to be awarded in purchase of some other property to be held in trust on terms hereunder provided.

The estimated market value of the property is Rs. ....

The Schedule

IN WITNESS WHEREOF the said AB the SETTLOR has executed these presents on the day, month and year first above-written.

Signed, sealed and delivered by AB
the SETTLOR in the presence of:

Signed, sealed and delivered by
the mother and natural guardian
of the BENEFICIARIES.

Trust Deed

(Provident Fund)

THIS DEED OF TRUST is made this .... day of .... 2000 BETWEEN X Co. Ltd. having its registered office at .... (hereinafter called the COMPANY) of the one part and AB, CD and EF all are residing at .... and/or working for gain at .... (hereinafter called the TRUSTEES) of the other part.

WHEREAS THE COMPANY intends to create a Provident Fund for the benefit of the employees and whereas it is necessary to execute a declaration of trust in respect of the contribution of the company and of the contributories to the fund.

THIS DEED WITNESSES and it is hereby agreed and declared as follows:

1. That the above-named persons, *viz.*, (1) AB (2) CD and (3) EF are hereby appointed as the TRUSTEES for administering the Provident Fund of the COMPANY and the income thereof as provided in the rules in force for the time being.

2. That the TRUSTEES shall stand possessed of the existing fund as also all contributions made in future from time to time with all accumulations to the said fund upon trust for the benefit of the employees of the COMPANY according to the rules of the fund a copy whereof is attached hereto.

3. That this trust shall not be revocable except with the consent of all contributories to the fund.

4. That the money for the time being constituting the fund shall be invested by the TRUSTEES in any one or more of the following securities:

(*a*) In promissory notes, debentures, stock or other securities of any local Government or of the Government of India.

(*b*) In bonds, debentures and annuities charged on the revenues of India.

(*c*) In stock or debentures of, or shares in, Government and other companies the interest whereon shall have been guaranteed by the Government of India.

(*d*) In debentures or other securities for money issued, under the authority of any Central Act or Act of a Legislature established in the States of India, by or on behalf of any Municipal Body, Port Trust or City Improvement Trust in any Presidency town.

(*e*) On a first mortgage of immovable property situate in the States of India: Provided that the property is not a leasehold for a term of years and that the value of the property exceeds by one-third, or, if consisting of buildings, exceeds by one-half of the mortgage money.

5. Provided that in execution of the trust and in performance of his duties and powers hereunder conferred no trustee shall be made liable for any loss caused to the trust arising by reason of any improper investment made *bona fide* and in good faith or for the negligence or fraud of any agent employed by them or by reason of any error of judgment or act, default, mistake or omission done in good faith and under *bona fide* belief by any trustee or by reason of any other matter or thing except wilful and individual wrong or fraud on the part of the trustee who is sought to be made liable.

6. The TRUSTEES shall be appointed by the company, and shall administer the fund and the income thereof as provided in the rules for the time being in force.

The number of TRUSTEES shall be not less than three nor more than seven.

A trustee shall continue in office until he dies or becomes insolvent or is removed or withdrawn by the company, from the trust or resigns his office as trustee, and upon the happening of any such event the COMPANY may nominate and appoint a successor who shall thereupon be and become a trustee in the place of such trustee so ceasing to be a TRUSTEE. On the appointment of a new TRUSTEE or new TRUSTEES, the number of TRUSTEES may be increased notwithstanding that there shall be no vacancy. The COMPANY shall not be bound to fill a vacancy in the number of TRUSTEES provided that the number of TRUSTEES shall not be reduced to less than three. The COMPANY may, in its absolute discretion, appoint an additional TRUSTEE or TRUSTEES notwithstanding that no case for appointing a new TRUSTEE may exist to be a TRUSTEE or TRUSTEES of the fund jointly with the continuing TRUSTEES.

7. The TRUSTEES shall at each meeting of the TRUSTEES elect one of the TRUSTEES present to be Chairman of the meeting. Questions arising at meetings of TRUSTEES shall be decided by a majority of votes and, in case of an equality of votes, the Chairman of the meeting shall have a casting vote. Three of the TRUSTEES shall be a quorum. The TRUSTEES may from time to time by a resolution or resolutions under their signatures authorise any one or more of them to sign and endorse for transfer or for conversion or for payment, Government Promissory Notes, and Bonds, Treasury Bills and other securities issued by the Government of the India or any State Government or by any Municipality or Improvement Trust or other local authority or any other securities held by the TRUSTEES or to sign or endorse cheques, drafts, interest, warrants or receipts for interest.

8. The fund shall be exclusively managed and administered by the TRUSTEES in accordance with these rules, and the decision of the TRUSTEES upon any question relating to the fund or any rights or benefits in connection therewith or generally upon the interpretation of any provision of these rules shall be absolutely final and binding on all subscribers, their executors, administrators, representatives, widows or relatives and the employers.

The costs, charges and expenses of administering the fund and of the determination of any question arising under these rules or otherwise including expenses incurred by the TRUSTEES in the discharge of their duties shall be charged to the funds and may be properly paid therefrom from time to time.

Any decision of the TRUSTEES may be given under the hand of any one or more of them.

9. The TRUSTEES shall have power to employ any person or persons (including any one or more of their number) to do any secretarial, legal, accountancy or other work which they may consider necessary or expedient in connection with the management of the fund or the funds thereof and to pay in addition to all other proper disbursements all ordinary or reasonable charges out of the fund or the funds.

10. Every subscriber shall subscribe to the fund at the rate of 10 per cent. of his monthly salary or wages and such percentage shall be deducted from his salary at the time of payment thereof and shall, as soon as practicable, be paid to the TRUSTEES who shall credit the same to the account of the employee in the books of the fund.

The COMPANY may at any time on three months' notice to the subscribers increase the rate of subscription up to but not exceeding $12^1/_2$ per cent. of their monthly salaries and on similar notice the company may reduce the rate of subscription but not below $7^1/_2$ per cent. of such monthly salaries. Provided nevertheless that the subscriptions of an employee in any year shall be a definite proportion of his salary for that year.

11. Subject to the previous approval by the Commissioner of Income-tax, the TRUSTEES shall, with the approval of the Board of Directors, be competent to vary, alter, omit, modify or add to the rules of the provident fund.

12. In the event of any vacancy by reason of resignation, death or otherwise in the office of a trustee, the COMPANY shall appoint a new trustee in the vacancy so caused. But the surviving TRUSTEES shall, notwithstanding such vacancy, be competent to administer the fund.

IN WITNESS WHEREOF the parties above-named have hereunto affixed their seals and subscribed their names the day and the year first above-written.

Signed, sealed and delivered by
Mr. .... pursuant to
Board Resolution dated ....
of X Co. Ltd. in the presence of:

Signed, sealed and delivered by AB,
CD and EF the TRUSTEES as a token
of acceptance in the presence of:

Trust Deed Constituting Guarantee Fund
(As Security)

THIS DEED OF TRUST is made this .... day of .... 2000 BETWEEN X Bank Ltd., a banking company registered under the Companies Act 1956 and carrying on business at .... (hereinafter called the BANK which term shall include its successors) of the one part and AB son of .... residing at .... and CD son of .... residing at .... (hereinafter called the TRUSTEES) of the other part.

WHEREAS the BANK has determined to establish a guarantee fund for the purposes hereinafter appearing: AND WHEREAS the said AB and CD have agreed to act as TRUSTEES for the purposes of these presents.

Now, THEREFORE, IT IS AGREED as follows:

1. A fund, to be called 'the guarantee fund', shall be established and such fund shall be formed by contributions to be made by officers and clerks in the employment of the bank, who shall become subscribers to the said fund in the manner following:

2. Every officer or clerk who desires to become a subscriber to the said fund shall apply to the bank to fix the amount of his security and, when that has been fixed, shall sign and deliver to the BANK a letter as follows:

'To the X Bank Ltd.

'Gentlemen, ... My security having been fixed by you at Rs. ...., I beg to apply for liberty to become a subscriber to the guarantee fund in respect of a guarantee of Rs. ...., and I request your consent thereto, and in consideration thereof agree to be bound by the provisions of the trust deed constituting the said fund.

Yours, etc.,

3. It shall be for the BANK to determine whether an applicant as aforesaid shall or shall not be admitted to subscribe to the fund, and notice of such determination shall be given to such applicant.

4. A register of subscribers to the said fund shall be kept by the BANK, and in such register there shall be entered the name of each subscriber to the fund, and the amount of the guarantee in respect of which he subscribes, and the time from which he is a subscriber for that amount, and the time when he ceases to be a subscriber.

5. Every applicant, who is admitted to subscribe as aforesaid, shall be bound to contribute to the fund a premium of 5% per annum on the amount fixed as his security, and such contribution must be made by equal quarterly payments on the usual quarter days.

(Provision may be made for contributions by the company, *e.g.*, a sum equal to the yearly contributions of the subscribers until the fund amounts to a specified sum, and that when the fund amounts to that sum subscribers who have subscribed for 10 years shall not pay further subscriptions unless and until the fund is reduced to less than the specified amount. Sometimes it is provided that when the fund exceeds a specified sum, the surplus shall be carried to the superannuation fund).

6. If any subscriber makes default for more than seven days in paying any contribution due from him as aforesaid, the BANK may, by notice in writing, exclude such subscriber from the benefit of the fund and thenceforth he shall forfeit all interest in the fund, but the BANK, in its discretion, may annual any such forfeiture on such terms and conditions as it may think expedient.

7. The fund shall be treated as a security to the BANK against all defalcations and misfeasances by the subscribers thereto for the time being, but as regards each subscriber, such security shall be limited to the amount in respect of which he has been a subscriber.

8. Wherever the BANK certifies under its seal that any subscriber to the fund has been guilty of any defalcation or misfeasance, and the amount necessary to compensate the BANK therefor, then and in any and every such case the BANK may withdraw from the fund and appropriate a sum equal to the amount so certified, but not exceeding the amount of the security in respect of which such employee has been contributing.

9. In the event of any subscriber to the fund voluntarily retiring from the service of the bank, or dying, such subscriber, or his legal personal representatives, as the case may be, shall, provided such subscriber has not been guilty at any time of any defalcation or misfeasance in relation to the BANK, be entitled to payment out of the fund of a sum equal to one-half the amount of the premiums paid by him to the fund.

10. A subscriber to the fund, who is dismissed by the BANK from its service for any cause whatsoever, shall forfeit all interest in the fund.

11. All contributions to the fund shall be paid to the BANK, and the BANK shall keep a proper account thereof; but it shall not be bound to keep such contributions separate from the general assets of the BANK, or be regarded as a trustee of such fund.

12. The BANK may at any time by deed dissolve the fund, and in that case the fund shall be applied, first, in making good to the BANK all sums certified by the BANK under clause (8) hereof, and the surplus shall be applied, so far as the same may extend, in paying off to each subscriber who has not been guilty of any defalcation or misfeasance in relation to the BANK, one-half the amount of the premiums subscribed by him, and the residue shall belong to the BANK.

13. The BANK may at any time by deed alter all or any of the regulations and provisions herein contained, and may make new regulations and provisions to the exclusion of or in addition to all or any regulations and provisions herein contained, and any regulations and provisions so made by deed shall be deemed to be regulations and provisions of the same validity as if they had been originally contained in these presents and shall be subject in like manner to be altered or modified.

14. The BANK may at any time, and from time to time, appoint any of the officers of the BANK to act as a consultative committee for the purposes of these presents, and may from time to time define the duties and powers of such committee, and may modify or dissolve sZuch committee.

15. Nothing herein contained shall prevent the BANK from requiring or taking from any subscriber to the fund any additional or special security for his fidelity.

16. The personal liability of every subscriber to the fund to make good his defalcations and misfeasances shall remain and subsist in every respect as if the said guarantee fund had not been established and each subscriber shall enter into a bond for faithful service framed in accordance with the form approved by the BANK.

17. The statutory power of appointing new TRUSTEES hereof shall be vested in the BANK.

The Schedule above referred to

IN WITNESS WHEREOF the parties herein have executed these presents on the day, month and year first above-written.

Signed, sealed and delivered by
AB and CD the TRUSTEES in token
of their acceptance of Trusteeship
in the presence of:

Signed, sealed and delivered by
Mr. .... pursuant to Board
Resolution dated .... of
X Bank Ltd. in the presence of:

Trust Deed Constituting Superannuation Fund

THIS DEED made the .... day of .... 1999 BETWEEN X. Co. Ltd., (hereinafter called the COMPANY) of the one part, and S, of ...., secretary of the company, and N, of .... as nominee of the committee of the sick fund (hereinafter called the TRUSTEES) of the other part.

WHEREAS the COMPANY is desirous of establishing a superannuation fund for the benefit of its employees.

NOW THESE PRESENTS WITNESS and declare as follows:

1. In these presents, unless excluded by the subject or context, 'the trustees' means and includes the TRUSTEES for the time being. 'The fund' means the superannuation fund to be constituted as hereinafter provided.

2. A fund to be called the superannuation fund shall be constituted and established.

3. The superannuation fund shall consist, of the several investments specified in the schedule hereto, and there shall be added to the fund all contributions and additions which are to be carried to it as hereinafter provided, and the income of the fund and of the investments for the time being representing the same shall also be added to the fund.

4. The fund shall be vested in the present TRUSTEES and their successors in the trust.

5. The moneys from time to time in the hands of the TRUSTEES not presently required for making any payment pursuant hereto, shall, if and so far as the COMPANY shall be willing to accept the same, be advanced to the COMPANY by way of loan, repayable on demand, and carrying interest at 15 per cent per annum and the COMPANY may at any time pay off any moneys so advanced, and any moneys in the hands of the TRUSTEES upon the trusts hereof, which the COMPANY shall at any time be unwilling to accept on loan, may be invested in any investments by law permitted to TRUSTEES, and the investments thereof may at any time be varied as may seem expedient to the TRUSTEES, or may be placed on deposit with any bank as may seem expedient to the TRUSTEES.

6. The COMPANY may contribute each year to the fund the sum of Rs. ...., or such other sum as the COMPANY shall from time to time determine.

7. The fund is to be regarded as primarily established for the benefit of employees whose nature and length of service may, in the judgment of the TRUSTEES, entitle them to a claim on it, and, secondly, for the purpose of assisting survivors who may have been dependent on deceased employees, and whose circumstances may necessitate some help.

8. The establishment of the fund is not to be regarded as in any way relieving employees of their duty to make such provision for old age and those dependent upon them as their means will permit.

9. Any employee of the company who has been in the service of the company or its predecessors in business for at least 25 years, and has completed the 60 years of his age, may apply for a retiring allowance.

10. Except in cases where ill-health or special circumstances shall, in the opinion of the directors, justify it, no allowance shall be granted to an employee who is not 60 years of age and has not completed 20 years of service with the COMPANY or its predecessors in business.

11. Any employee who has been in the service of the COMPANY or its predecessors in business for at least 20 years, and has become mentally or physically incapacitated, may be granted an annual or other allowance subject to the provisions hereof.

12. Any employee under 60 years of age who shall be in receipt of a retiring allowance shall, when required by the trustees, be bound to satisfy

them, by medical certificate or otherwise, that there has been no material change in the circumstances in which the allowance was granted.

13. The TRUSTEES may withdraw or modify or determine any allowance when, in their opinion, the circumstances or conduct of the recipient shall justify them in so doing.

14. An allowance as aforesaid is to be regarded as strictly personal and cannot be assigned, charged, or alienated in any way, and any attempt to assign, charge, or alienate shall determine the allowance, but without prejudice to the trustees' discretion to continue the same if they think fit after an interval or otherwise.

15. In fixing the amount of each allowance and in making any modification therein, the TRUSTEES may exercise their discretion with reference to all the circumstances; but, without prejudice to such discretion, it is declared that the following is the retiring allowance which, it is contemplated, will be payable, that is to say:

(*a*) until such time as the fund shall have reached the sum of Rs. .... the retiring allowance per month after 20 years' service shall be one-third of the person's average monthly earnings for the last three years of his employment, but so that such allowance shall not exceed Rs. 500 per month.

(*b*) after the fund shall have reached the sum of Rs. .... and upwards, the retiring allowance per month after 20 years' service shall be one-half of the person's average monthly earnings for the last three years of his employment, but so that such allowance shall not exceed Rs. 600 per month.

16. Any employee, who shall be dismissed, or shall retire from the service of the COMPANY in consequence of misconduct, shall be disqualified from receiving any allowance hereunder.

17. The TRUSTEES may grant such temporary or other allowance to widows and other dependants of employees who may die in the service of the company, or shortly after leaving the service of the company, as in their absolute discretion they may think proper.

18. The TRUSTEES may meet together for the despatch of business, adjourn, and otherwise regulate their meetings as they think fit, and may determine the quorum necessary for the transaction of business. Until otherwise determined, three TRUSTEES shall form a quorum. A trustee may at any time convene a meeting of the trustees to be held at the office of the company. Questions arising at any meeting shall be decided by a majority of votes, and in case of an equality of votes the Chairman shall have a second or casting vote.

19. A meeting of the TRUSTEES for the time being at which a quorum is present shall be competent to exercise all or any of the authorities, powers, and discretions by these presents vested in the TRUSTEES generally.

20. The TRUSTEES shall cause proper minutes to be kept and entered in a book provided for the purpose, of all their resolutions and proceedings, and any such minutes of any meeting of the TRUSTEES, if purporting to be signed by the Chairman of such meeting, or by the Chairman of the next succeeding meeting, shall be receivable as *prima facie* evidence of the matters stated in such minutes.

21. A register shall be kept by the TRUSTEES in which shall be entered the names and addresses of the persons for the time being, and from time to time, who are in receipt of allowances hereunder, and of the trustees for the time being hereof.

22. For the purposes hereof any notice to any trustee, or to any person in receipt of any allowance hereunder, may be given by sending the same through the post, in a letter addressed to him at his registered place of address, and any notice so sent shall be deemed to be served on the day following that on which it is posted.

23. The COMPANY may from time to time, by instrument in writing under its common seal, with the assent in writing of the TRUSTEES, alter all or any of the regulations contained in these presents for the time being relating to the fund hereby constituted, and make new regulations to the exclusion of, or in addition to, all or any of the regulations for the time being relating to such fund; and the regulations so made and for the time being in force shall be deemed to be regulations, in relation to the fund, of the same validity as if they had been originally contained in these presents, and shall be subject in like manner to be altered or modified by any subsequent instrument in writing as aforesaid. For the purposes hereof, all the provisions herein contained shall be deemed to be regulations in relation to the fund.

24. The TRUSTEES, in the exercise of the authorities and discretions hereby vested in them, shall have an absolute and uncontrolled discretion, and may exercise the same from time to time, and at any time.

25. The TRUSTEES shall respectively be indemnified against all liabilities incurred by them in the execution of the trusts hereof, and shall have a lien on the fund for such indemnity.

26. The TRUSTEES of the fund shall always include two of the directors of the COMPANY, the secretary of the COMPANY, and one other person to be appointed by the majority for the time being of the committee of the sick fund which has been established in relation to the COMPANY. The said M and N are two of the present directors, the said S is the secretary, and the said T has been nominated by the committee of the sick fund.

27. The statutory power of appointing new TRUSTEES in the place of any trustee appointed in respect of his being the managing director or director or secretary of the COMPANY shall be vested in the COMPANY, and the statutory power of appointing a new trustee in the place of any trustee nominated by

the committee of the sick fund shall be vested in the majority of the committee of the sick fund.

28. Any trustee, who having been appointed as the managing director or a director or secretary of the COMPANY, vacates office as such, shall be deemed thereupon to desire to be discharged from the trusts hereof for the purposes of the exercise of the statutory power of appointing new TRUSTEES.

29. If the COMPANY shall at any time give to the trustees notice in writing stating that the COMPANY does not intend to make any further contributions to the fund, or an order shall be made or an effective resolution shall be passed for the winding-up of the COMPANY, the fund shall be realised and shall be distributed amongst the employees of the company in such proportions as shall be determined to be just and equitable by an arbitrator to be appointed as hereinafter provided, and accordingly such person shall forthwith be appointed an arbitrator as the COMPANY and the TRUSTEES hereof shall unanimously appoint, and if such appointment is not made within three months after such order or an effective resolution is made or passed, then the majority of the TRUSTEES hereof may request the President for the time being of the Incorporated Law Society of Calcutta to appoint such arbitrator, and such President shall have authority to appoint him accordingly.

30. The determination of the arbitrator appointed under the foregoing clause shall be absolute and final, and all the costs, charges and expenses of and incidental to the realisation and distribution of the fund, including the remuneration of the arbitrator, shall be payable out of the fund.

IN WITNESS, etc.

The Schedule above referred to

(Particulars of Investments)

Signed, sealed and delivered by S on behalf of X Co. Ltd. in presence of:	Sd. for X Co. Ltd.
Signed and delivered by the TRUSTEES in presence of:	Sd. TRUSTEES

Trust Deed Constituting Pension Fund

THIS DEED, MADE THE .... day of ....1999 BETWEEN AB, of ...., hereinafter called the FOUNDER of the one part, and C of ...., and D of .... of the other part.

WHEREAS the founder, who is largely interested in the N. Co. Ltd. (hereinafter called the COMPANY), is desirous of establishing a pension fund in relation to that company, and with a view thereto has transferred .... fully-paid shares of Rs. .... each in the company, numbered .... to .... inclusive, to the said C and D. Now IT IS AGREED AND DECLARED as follows:

1. The trustees, which expression in this deed means the said C and D, or other the trustees or trustee for the time being hereof, shall hold the said shares and the income thereof in trust for the purposes hereof.

2. The income of the trust fund shall be applied in paying the pensions from time to time payable hereunder, and if the income of any half-year or other period shall be insufficient to pay the said pensions, such pensions shall abate rateably.

3. The following persons shall be eligible as pensioners, that is to say—

(*a*) Persons who, having served the company for more than 10 years, have attained the age of 65.

(*b*) Widows and orphans of employees who have died in the service of the COMPANY.

4. During the life of the founder, it shall rest with the FOUNDER and after his death it shall rest with the COMPANY to elect pensioners and to determine the amount of the pensions payable to them respectively, and the time or times of payment, and to withdraw, reduce, or increase any pension.

5. A register of pensioners shall be kept by the COMPANY and there shall be entered therein the names and addresses of the pensioners and the amounts of their respective pensions and any other particulars relating thereto.

6. Any surplus income from time to time in the hands of the trustees may be invested by them in any investments authorised by law for the investment of trust funds, and the moneys so invested and the income thereof shall constitute a reserve fund and may be applied by the trustees or trustee at any time in augmentation of the income of any half-year which shall be insufficient to pay the subsisting pensions.

7. Pensioners shall be elected for one year only, but they may be re-elected.

8. The FOUNDER may at any time during his life by deed modify the provisions of this deed, and after his death the COMPANY may at any time by deed modify the provisions of this deed.

9. The statutory power of appointing new trustees hereof shall be vested in the founder during his life and after his death in the COMPANY.

10. Any notice to any pensioner may be given, etc.

11. Proviso for winding-up within legal limits as in clause (29) of form of the trust deed constituting superannuation fund.

IN WITNESS, etc.

Deed of Ante-nuptial Settlement

THIS SETTLEMENT IS MADE the .... day of .... 2000 BETWEEN AB of, etc. (INTENDED HUSBAND AND SETTLOR) of the first part, CD of, etc. (INTENDED WIFE), of the second part, and EF of, etc., and GH of, etc., hereinafter called the TRUSTEES of the third part.

WHEREAS a marriage is intended to be solemnized shortly BETWEEN the said AB and CD and upon the treaty of the said marriage it was agreed that the settlement hereinafter appearing shall be effected: AND WHEREAS with a view to effect such settlement the said AB has, with the consent and approbation of the said CD, agreed to transfer in the names of the trustees the property, hereinafter described: NOW THIS DEED WITNESSES as follows:

1. In pursuance of the said agreement and in consideration of the intended marriage, the said AB as the beneficial owner, with the approbation of the said CD do hereby grant, convey, transfer and assign unto and to the use of the trustees ALL THAT etc., (*describe the property*) TO HAVE AND TO HOLD the same IN TRUST for the said AB until the said intended marriage, and after the solemnization of the said marriage UPON TRUSTS hereinafter declared.

2. The TRUSTEES shall, after the solemnization of the said marriage, stand possessed of the said property (hereinafter referred to as the TRUST PROPERTY), UPON TRUST either to hold the same as at present situated (*or* invested) or, with the consent of in writing of the said AB and CD during their joint lives and the survivor during his or her life, to sell the same and invest the proceeds thereof in any investments which may for the time being be authorized by law for the investment of trust funds, and stand possessed thereof and of the investments from time to time representing the same UPON TRUST to paý the income thereof to the said AB during his life, and after his death to pay the same to the said CD during her life, and after the death of the survivor of them, the said AB and CD to stand possessed of the Trust Estate IN TRUST for such child, children or remoter issue of the said intended marriage in such shares (if more than one) and in such manner as the said AB and CD shall by deed or deeds jointly appoint, and in default of any such appointment, or so far as the same shall not extend IN TRUST for the child or all the children of the said marriage who, being sons, shall attain the age of 21 years or, being daughters, shall attain that age or marry under that age, in equal shares: BUT if there shall be no child of the said intended marriage who shall live to attain a vested interest in the Trust Funds, IN TRUST for such person or persons as under the law for the distribution of the estates of intestates would, on the death of the said CD, have been entitled, if she had died possessed thereof intestate and without having been married.

3. The TRUSTEES may, at any time or times, with the consent in writing of the said AB and CD during their joint lives, and of the survivor of them during his or her life, and after decease of such survivor at the sole discretion

of the trustees, raise any part of parts, not exceeding one-half, of the vested or presumptive share of any child or other issue of the said intended marriage, of and in the Trust Estate, and may pay or apply the same for his or her advancement or benefits as they shall think fit.

4. The said AB and CD during their joint lives, and the survivor of them, during his or her life, shall have power to appoint new trustee or trustees.

5. The said CD may, after the death of the said AB, grant either by deed or will a life interest in a moiety of the Trust Estate in favour of any future husband whom she may marry.

6. The TRUSTEES shall not be responsible for any *bona fide* act, default, omission or error in judgment on the part of the said AB about maintenance, preservation or repair of the said property or any part thereof or for any loss or damage occasioned thereto by the said AB.

7. Provided, however, and it is hereby expressly agreed by and between the parties that in case the said intended marriage breaks off this deed shall stand *ipso facto* cancelled and be void and of no effect and the said property hereby assigned shall be reassigned to the said AB or as he shall direct.

IN WITNESS WHEREOF the parties herein have signed these presents on the day, month and year above-written.

Signed, sealed and delivered by CD
the INTENDED WIFE in the presence of:

Signed, sealed and delivered by EF and
GH the TRUSTEES in the presence of:

Signed, and sealed and delivered by AB
the SETTLOR in the presence of:

Deed of Settlement of Family Disputes

THIS DEED OF FAMILY SETTLEMENT, made the 6th day of December 1999 BETWEEN AB of, etc., of the first part, and CD of etc., of the second part.

WHEREAS the business and undertaking described in Schedule A hereunder were started and carried on, organised and developed by AB by his own initiative and efforts in his own name and with his own capital AND WHEREAS the movable and immovable properties described in Schedule A hereunder have also been acquired by AB out of the moneys of the said business in his name and for his use and benefit AND WHEREAS the said CD, who is the son of the deceased elder brother of AB has been living with AB for some time past and was at all times treated as a member of his family under the care and patronage of AB as an assistant or helper in his said business for which he was paid a share of profits as his remuneration AND WHEREAS the said CD having thus contributed his labour and skill for the growth and development of the said business and rendered valuable services claims to be and has set up and asserted his right as an equal partner thereof and so also as moiety holder of said properties which right and claim are denied and disputed by the said AB AND WHEREAS in the circumstances aforesaid disputes and differences having thus arisen between the parties and with a view to save themselves from ruinous litigation and for the sake of peace and preservation of the honour and dignity of the family they have themselves settled and/or adjusted their said disputes and differences as follows:

1. That it is hereby agreed and declared by and between the parties as follows, *viz.* that the said AB shall at all times hereafter hold own, possess and enjoy as full and absolute owner the business and properties mentioned and described in Schedule B and that the said CD has at present no right nor any claim or interest therein which is hereby expressly relinquished by the said CD in favour of the said AB to all intents and purposes.

2. That it is further agreed and declared that the said CD shall likewise at all times hereafter own, possess and enjoy the properties mentioned in Schedule C without any claim or demand by the said AB on any account whatsoever for which purpose they are hereby expressly granted, conveyed, transferred, assigned and assured by the said AB unto and to the use of CD.

3. That it is further agreed and declared that all disputes and differences as between the parties as regards account and mutual dealings etc. in relation to said business and the properties have been fully and finally adjusted and settled and in any event neither party has any claim against the other on any account whatsoever and this deed of family settlement shall not be reopened on any ground whatsoever.

AND that the parties hereto in so far as it relates to their respective acts, deeds and things covenant with each other that they have not done, executed, performed nor suffered anything to the contrary whereby or by reason whereof the properties hereunder settled may be in any way affected or prejudiced in title or estate or they or any of them are or is hindered or prevented from settling the same in the manner hereinbefore indicated.

Schedule A

Schedule B

Schedule C

IN WITNESS WHEREOF the parties hereto have signed these presents on the day, month and year first above-written.

Signed, sealed and delivered by
AB in the presence of:

Signed, sealed and delivered by
CD in the presence of:

Private Trust for Management and Preservation of Property

THIS DEED OF TRUST is made on this .... day of .... 2000 by AB son of .... residing at .... (hereinafter referred to as the SETTLOR) of the one part and CD son of .... residing at .... EF son of .... residing at .... and GH son of .... residing at .... (hereinafter called the TRUSTEES which term shall include the Trustee or Trustees for the time being) of the other part.

WHEREAS the said AB owns and possesses all that property detailed and specified in the Schedule hereto which are his self-acquired property and over which he has full disposing power under the Hindu law.

AND WHEREAS the said AB has for some time past been keeping indifferent health and is unable to look after his affairs and manage the said properties and has lost all hopes of complete recovery.

AND WHEREAS his only son CD having long been subject to epileptic fits is now a man of weak intellect and of almost unsound mind totally incapable of managing the household and estate affairs.

AND WHEREAS for reasons and considerations as aforesaid and for the due management, protection and preservation of his estate, the said AB is desirous of creating a trust in respect of his aforesaid property in the manner hereinafter appearing.

AND WHEREAS the total value of the aforesaid property is estimated at Rs. .... as detailed in the Schedule hereto.

NOW THIS DEED WITNESSES as follows:

1. This said AB in pursuance of his wish and desire as aforesaid do hereby grant, convey and transfer ALL that property described in the Schedule hereto (hereinafter referred to as THE TRUST PROPERTY) unto and to the use of the TRUSTEES TO HAVE AND TO HOLD the same in trust for the said AB and after his death upon trust hereinafter declared concerning the same with and subject to such powers and limitations as are hereinafter specified.

2. The TRUSTEES shall by themselves or through an agent or agents employed by them manage and administer the trust property in such a

manner as might be most beneficial to the interest of the trust and shall realise the rent, dividend, interest and other income accruing from the trust property and the said AB shall make such formal endorsements and execute such document or documents and do every such thing as may be legally necessary to enable the trustees to realise such income:

PROVIDED that so long as the said AB or his wife shall remain alive and in full possession of his senses, the TRUSTEES shall have no power to sell, mortgage or otherwise transfer any portion of his residential house except with his express consent if he is alive and able to give consent or with the consent of his wife in the event he is dead or is unable to give his consent.

3. During the said AB's lifetime, the TRUSTEES shall spend the income of the trust property in such a manner as the said AB may direct and in case he is not able to give any directions the said income shall be spent for the maintenance of the said AB, his wife, his son, his son's wife and such other members of his family as may for the time being be in existence and dependent on him and on all religious, social and customary needs of the family.

4. After the death of the said AB, the income of the trust property shall be spent for the maintenance of his wife, his son, the said CD, the said CD's wife and such member or members of his family as may be in existence and on all such religious, social and customary needs of the family as aforesaid.

5. If at any time the TRUSTEES find that the income of the trust property is not sufficient for the objects of the trust as hereinbefore recited, they shall be at liberty to raise money by disposing of such stocks, shares or securities mentioned in the said schedule as they may think proper, provided that except in cases of sudden, urgent and unavoidable necessity they shall not be entitled to raise more than rupees ten thousand in any one year by disposing of such stocks, shares or securities.

6. If on account of death or other cause the office of a trustee falls vacant, and the said AB is alive and in proper senses and after his death or if he is not in his proper sense the remaining TRUSTEES shall appoint a new trustee or trustees if they so agree unanimously and in the event they cannot agree about the appointment of a new trustee or fail to appoint one within a reasonable time, the court may appoint a new trustee in accordance with the law for the time being in force in this behalf and, in making such appointment, the TRUSTEES or the court shall respect the wishes, if any, of the said AB's wife and the wife of the said CD expressed in this behalf.

Pending the appointment of a new trustee, the remaining trustee shall continue to administer the trust.

7. On the death of both the said AB and his son, the said CD, this trust shall cease and the trust property or such portion of it as may be in existence shall immediately vest in the heirs and legal representatives of the said CD.

8. The said AB hereby expressly reserves to himself the power to revoke or modify any time at his pleasure the trust hereby created, but such revocation or modification will not affect any act already done by the TRUSTEES in good faith in due execution of the trust.

The Schedule

IN WITNESS WHEREOF the parties have signed this Deed on the day, month and year first above-written.

Signed, sealed and delivered by
AB the SETTLOR in the presence of:

Signed, sealed and delivered by
CD, EF and CE the TRUSTEES in
the presence of:

Deed of Settlement for Establishing a Girls' School

THIS DEED OF SETTLEMENT is made on this .... day of .... 2000 BETWEEN AB son of .... residing at .... (hereinafter called the SETTLOR) of the One Part and CD son of .... residing at ...., EF son of .... residing at .... and GH son of .... residing at .... (hereinafter called the TRUSTEES which expression shall where the subject or context allows or admits of be deemed to include the survivor or survivors of them and the successors in office as also the Trustees or Trustee for the time being of the Trust hereby created) of the Other Part.

WHEREAS the SETTLOR is the sole and absolute owner of the immovable property fully mentioned and described in the First Schedule hereto as also of the securities mentioned in the Second Schedule hereto;

AND WHEREAS for good reasons and considerations and in order to perpetuate the memory of the settlor's father .... the SETTLOR is desirous of establishing a girls' high school at .... to be named after the said .... and settling the said property irrevocably for its maintenance.

AND WHEREAS the SETTLOR has also endorsed the securities mentioned and described in the Second Schedule hereto in favour of and delivered to the TRUSTEES to provide for the necessary capital for establishing such ....

AND WHEREAS the estimated value of the properties mentioned is Rs. ....

NOW THIS INDENTURE WITNESSES as follows:

1. In pursuance of the said wish and desire of the SETTLOR, the SETTLOR do hereby grant, convey, transfer, assign and assure to the TRUSTEES ALL

THAT property described in the First Schedule hereto AND DELIVER ALL the securities described in the Second Schedule hereto duly endorsed in favour of the TRUSTEES TO HAVE AND TO HOLD them all upon trust for the objects and with the intent and subject to the powers, provisions and agreements hereunder declared and expressed concerning the same.

2. The TRUSTEES or the TRUSTEE shall, not later than one year from the date of these presents, erect, build, construct on the land described in the First Schedule hereto a building suitable for a girl's school at a cost of not more than Rs. .... to be raised by sale of such of the securities mentioned in the Second Schedule hereto or portion thereof as the TRUSTEES may think proper.

3. The TRUSTEES or TRUSTEE shall immediately after such a sale establish a girls' high school in the said building with the sanction of the appropriate authorities and pay all initial costs in that connection out of the income of the property described in the First Schedule and the securities described in the Second Schedule hereto and in case of any deficiency shall make good the same out of the sale proceeds of such securities as the TRUSTEES may consider necessary to sell for the purpose.

4. The TRUSTEES shall manage and develop the said property and every part thereof as mentioned in the First Schedule hereto and after having paid Government revenue, cesses, taxes and all expenses of collection and management shall use the balance of the income as well as the income from such of the securities mentioned in the Second Schedule hereto as may remain unsold or of any other securities into which the same may hereafter be converted by them, for the recurring expenses of the girls' high school and any balance remaining after making such expenses shall be deposited in such bank and invested in such manner as the TRUSTEES may consider proper.

5. The TRUSTEES shall have power to convert such securities mentioned in the Second Schedule hereto as they think necessary into other securities or into money, but they shall have no power to sell, mortgage, otherwise transfer the said property described in the First Schedule hereto except with the permission of the District Judge having jurisdiction over the subject-matter of the trust.

6. In case of any vacancy amongst the TRUSTEES occasioned by death, resignation or incapacity of any trustee or otherwise, the SETTLOR shall have the power to fill up the vacancy and after his death, the remaining TRUSTEES shall make the appointment.

7. In case the land where the school building is to be created or erected is acquired by the Government, the trustee shall utilise the entire compensation money for purchase of another land or lands suitable for the purpose and erect a new building or buildings and restart the girls' school thereon.

The First Schedule

The Second Schedule

IN WITNESS WHEREOF the parties hereto have signed these presents on the day, month and year first above-written.

Signed, sealed and delivered by the said AB the SETTLOR in the presence of:

Signed, sealed and delivered by CD, EF and GH the TRUSTEES as a token of acceptance of the Office of TRUSTEES in the presence of:

Endowment for Building a Ward in a Hospital and Maintenance of Beds therein

THIS INDENTURE MADE THIS ....day of .... 2000 BETWEEN XY son of .... of .... (MAKER OF THE ENDOWMENT) of the one part and the said AB and CD son of .... of .... of .... (TRUSTEES) of the other part (which expression shall where the subject or context allows or admits of be deemed to include their successor or successors in office).

AND WHEREAS the said XY having been motivated by pious wishes and desire and benevolent consideration for relieving the suffering of the ailing poor and being desirous of creating an endowment for the maintenance of a ward in the hospital known as ELH Hospital located at premises No. .... to be named after his deceased parents as MN ward has set apart and kept earmarked a fund and constituted AB and CD as the first TRUSTEES NOW THIS INDENTURE WITNESSETH THAT in pursuance of the said wish and desire and for consideration as aforesaid the said XY hereby declare that the said AB and CD as joint TRUSTEES do hold and possess ALL AND SINGULAR the Promissory Notes, Stocks and Securities etc. of the aggregated value of Rs. .... of denominations and numbers described in the Schedule hereto TOGETHER WITH a cash sum of Rs. 10 lakhs hereinafter referred to as the trust fund as trustees for the endowment to be created for the purpose as aforesaid for ever, upon trust and subject to the terms, powers, provisions and declaration hereinafter mentioned:

AND IT IS HEREBY DECLARED THAT out of the sum of Rupees ten lakhs the said AB and CD shall construct and build a ward in the premises of the ELH HOSPITAL., according to the directions and specifications contained in the plan as approved by the Hospital Authority and shall from and out of the income, dividend etc. of the TRUST FUND accruing from the said Promissory

Notes, Stocks and Securities maintain 25 beds in the said ward upon the terms and conditions hereinafter appearing PROVIDED ALWAYS that the said number of beds may be increased or decreased according to the income of the trust fund accruing from time to time AND IT IS HEREBY FURTHER DECLARED THAT upon the death of any of the TRUSTEES or in the event any of them shall desire to retire or be discharged from or refuse to act or become unfit to continue as trustee by reason of any personal disqualification or become incapable to act as trustee as aforesaid, then, in every such case, it shall be lawful for the surviving or continuing trustee or TRUSTEES for the time being and if there be no surviving or continuing trustee it shall be lawful for the MAGISTRATE AND COLLECTOR of the place for the time being, by writing or writings to nominate and/or appoint any person or persons to be trustee or trustees in the place of the trustee or trustees so dying or desiring to be discharged or refusing or becoming unfit or personally incapable to act as aforesaid, and that upon such appointment the trust fund shall to all intents and purposes vest in the newly appointed trustee or trustees jointly with the continuing or surviving trustee. Provided however that in every such appointment the number of TRUSTEES may be increased or reduced, but the TRUSTEES OR TRUSTEE for the time being and every trustee so appointed shall act and assist in the execution of the said trust as fully and effectually as if he had been originally appointed a trustee by the said .... PROVIDED always that the number of TRUSTEES of the said trust shall never be less than two or more than five AND IT IS HEREBY FURTHER DECLARED as follows:

(*i*) Firstly, that the said ward shall be named after the deceased parents of the said AB and shall be called, known and distinguished as MN ward.

(*ii*) Secondly, that the said ward shall be a free ward and open to all the poor people irrespective of their caste religion faith or nationality. The trustee or TRUSTEES shall have the power to nominate two patients for admission at a time who shall have preferential right of admission over the patients.

(*iii*) Thirdly, subject to what are hereinbefore stated the right of admission of patients in the said ward shall be reserved and the same shall be exercised and controlled by the Chief Medical Officer of the said Hospital for the time being only in consultation with the said .... and .... or the TRUSTEES for the time being if so desired.

(*iv*) Fourthly, that the said .... and .... or the TRUSTEES for the time being, shall keep and maintain proper accounts of the income and expenditure of the said trust fund and get such accounts duly audited in every year by one qualified auditor to be appointed by them in that behalf.

(*v*) Fifthly, that the said .... and .... or the TRUSTEES for the time being, shall meet at least once in every six months for the purpose of transacting the business of the said trust and the decision of both the trustee, or of the majority of TRUSTEES shall regulate all such actions and proceedings in that behalf PROVIDED ALWAYS THAT it shall be open to the said TRUSTEES to make rules and regulations relative to such meetings and the conduct of their business.

(*VI*) Sixthly, that the said .... and .... or the TRUSTEES for the time being, may at any time break the trust fund sell the trust securities or any part hereof for the purpose of investing the sale proceeds on more profitable securities; Provided always that such securities shall in no case be other than those mentioned in s. 20 of the Indian Trusts Act 1882, PROVIDED also that permission of the Magistrate and Collector for the time being shall have been first obtained therefor in all cases of changes of investments.

The trustee or trustees for the time being shall have power to apply to court for such directions and order as they may be advised and if necessary for removal or discharge of any trustee or appointment of any new trustee or trustees.

In case the said hospital is closed or shifted elsewhere the trustee or TRUSTEES shall make the interest of the fund available for some similar object or purpose or for any other hospital for such ward or wards.

The Schedule above referred to

IN WITNESS WHEREOF the maker of the endowment and the TRUSTEES have set and subscribed their respective hands and seals the day, month and year first above written.

Signed, sealed and delivered at Calcutta in the presence of:

XY
AB
CD

Trust Deed Establishing a Scholarship

THIS INDENTURE IS MADE on the 2nd day of November 2000 BETWEEN AB, etc. (hereinafter called THE FOUNDER) of the One Part and CD, etc., EF etc., and GH etc. (hereinafter called THE TRUSTEES which expression shall where the subject or context allows or admits of, be deemed to include the survivor or survivors of them and also the successor or successors in office or the trustee or trustees for the time being of the trust) of the Other Part.

WHEREAS the FOUNDER has made over to the TRUSTEES a sum of Rs. 20 lakhs and/or put them in effective control over the same for investment thereof in some approved security and apply the income exclusively for the objects hereunder mentioned.

Now THIS INDENTURE WITNESSETH and it is hereby agreed and declared by and between the parties as follows:

1. The TRUSTEE or TRUSTEES shall invest and at all times keep the said sum of Rs. 20 lakhs invested in some approved security or securities prescribed under s. 20 of the Indian Trust Act and apply the income thereof in perpetuity for awarding a scholarship to be named after the FOUNDER to a most meritorious student who will secure the highest number of marks in Electronics every year in the MSc Examination of the University of .... tenable for two years at the rate of Rs.5,000 per month.

2. The TRUSTEES may at any time and from time to time vary such investment or investments for others of a like nature for the sake of better return but shall on no account change the character of the investment or investments.

3. The said sum of Rs. 20 lakhs and the investment or investments representing the same shall be known as *ELH Trust Fund* and is hereinafter referred to as the *Trust Fund*.

4. The TRUSTEE or TRUSTEES shall out of the income of the TRUST FUND pay at the first instance all costs, charges and expenses of or incidental to the maintenance and administration of the TRUST FUND and shall apply the balance for awarding the scholarship as aforesaid. In case of any surplus the same shall be invested in the same type of security. In case of any deficit the value of the award shall abate proportionately.

5. The award of the scholarship shall be subject to such terms and conditions as shall from time to time be prescribed by Statutes, Regulations, Ordinance of the said University and in case there is no candidate eligible for such scholarship in any particular year or years the TRUSTEES may utilise for any other purpose or purpose for advancement and promotion of education the entire amount thereof as may be desired by the University.

6. The TRUSTEES or TRUSTEE may at any time and from time to time set apart as and by way of sinking fund the whole or any part of the surplus income produced by the trust fund in any year not needed to meet the cost of the said scholarship and may invest any such sum or sums so set apart and the resulting income thereof in the manner aforesaid with power at any time to vary any such investment or investments.

7. The TRUSTEES or TRUSTEE may at any time sell any investment or investments representing the capital income of the sinking fund and apply the proceeds thereof or the capital or income of the sinking fund as if the same were income produced by the trust fund.

8. The TRUSTEE or TRUSTEES may at any time apply the income for the grant of any such other scholarship or scholarships and in such manner as the University may from time to time direct in so far as the same is permitted by the surplus income of the trust fund in any year as is not required for the aforesaid scholarship or sinking fund.

9. The TRUSTEES may, with the concurrence of the Vice-Chancellor of the said University, at any time wholly or partially vary any of the purposes for which the income of the TRUST FUND is to be applied and such income or part thereof shall then be applied to such other purpose provided that the same shall not be applied to any purpose unless the same is conducive to the promotion or encouragement of education at the said University.

10. In case of any vacancy amongst the TRUSTEES occurred by reason of death or bankruptcy or resignation of any trustee or for any other cause, the FOUNDER will have the right to appoint a new trustee or trustees and failing him and after the death of the founder the remaining trustees shall have power by a majority of votes to appoint a new trustee and in case of equality of votes or failing same the appointment shall be made by the Vice-Chancellor of the said University or by the court having jurisdiction in this behalf.

IN WITNESS WHEREOF the parties hereto have set and subscribed their respective hands and seals the day, month and year first above-written.

Signed, sealed and delivered by AB
the FOUNDER at Calcutta in the
presence of:

Signed, sealed and delivered by CD,
EF and GH indicating consent to
act as TRUSTEES in the presence of:

Deed of Trust for the Purpose of Paying Debts

THIS DEED OF TRUST made this .... day of .... 2000 BETWEEN AB son of .... (hereinafter called THE DEBTOR) of the First Part AND CD son of .... and EF son of .... (hereinafter called THE TRUSTEES) of the Second Part, GH son of .... (hereinafter called THE CREDITOR) of the Third Part.

WHEREAS the said AB is truly and justly indebted to the said CD in the sum of Rs. 5 lakhs only for which the latter has served the former with legal notice and intends to institute a suit for recovery of the said sum with costs and interest.

AND WHEREAS the said AB having at present no means nor any further resource to liquidate the said loan approached the said GH for time and accommodation to pay up the said debt by instalments which the said GH has agreed to grant only if adequate arrangement is forthwith made to secure regular payments of instalments and for preservation of the assets of the said AB as they are now until repayment of the entire debt.

THIS DEED OF TRUST WITNESSES that in pursuance of the said agreement and in consideration of the said GH refraining from taking any action against AB for immediate enforcing payment, the said AB doth hereby and hereunder grant, convey, transfer and assign all his property mentioned in the Schedule below UNTO the said TRUSTEES TO HAVE AND TO HOLD the same upon TRUST for the purpose hereinafter mentioned:

(*i*) That the said TRUSTEES shall exert themselves by all legitimate ways and means, exercise all the powers and authorities hithertofore exercised by AB, supervise, manage and develop all the properties of the said AB so as to yield much better income from all sources.

(*ii*) That the said TRUSTEES continue to hold, possess, manage and administer the said properties until full satisfaction and discharge of the debt of the said AB to the said GH and thereafter the said properties shall be retransferred to the said AB.

(*iii*) The TRUSTEES shall out of the income of the said properties as and when collected shall, after payment of the municipal taxes and other capital and revenue liabilities, pay or cause to be paid to the said AB an allowance of Rs. 2,000 per month regularly not later than the 7th of every current month subject to such increase or decrease thereof as may be necessitated by the rise or fall of the annual income of the trust properties.

(*iv*) The TRUSTEES shall divide the entire balance of the income of the properties hereby transferred in four parts, one part of which shall be kept deposited in an account in some bank approved by the said GH to meet such unforeseen or emergent expenses as may be necessary in the interest of and for the benefit of the trust. The TRUSTEES shall pay the remaining three parts to the said GH towards liquidation of the debt inclusive of interest until the entire debt is liquidated.

AND IT IS HEREBY furthermore agreed and declared by and between the parties that subject to aforesaid the said TRUSTEES shall stand possessed of the said properties hereby transferred in trust for the purpose aforesaid but shall have no power to sell, mortgage, charge or otherwise encumber the same except with the consent of the other parties first had and obtained or under order of a court of competent jurisdiction.

PROVIDED ALWAYS and it is hereby agreed and declared that in the event of the office of any of the trustee falling vacant the appointment of a new trustee or trustees shall only be made at a meeting called for the purpose to be presided over by the said GH and attended by the parties, and in case the trustees fail to carry out the object of the trust in the manner hereinunder provided, it shall always be lawful but not compulsory on the part of the said GH to institute a suit for recovery of the amount due to him and to have a Receiver appointed to take possession, control and management of the trust property.

The Schedule above referred to

The estimated value of the trust property is Rs. ....

IN WITNESS WHEREOF the parties hereto have set and subscribed their respective hands and seals the day, month and year first above-written.

Signed, sealed and delivered by
AB the DEBTOR in presence of:

Signed, sealed and delivered by CD
and EF accepting the TRUSTEESHIP
in presence of:

Signed, sealed and delivered by
GH the CREDITOR in presence of:

Deed for Public Charitable Trust

THIS INDENTURE IS MADE this 2nd day of November 2000 BETWEEN AB son of .... by faith .... by occupation .... residing at .... hereinafter called the SETTLOR (which expression shall unless excluded by or repugnant to the subject or context be deemed to include his heirs, executors, administrators, assigns, and representatives) of the one part and CD son of .... by faith and EF son of .... by feith .... both .... residing at .... hereinafter jointly called the TRUSTEES (which expression shall unless excluded by or repugnant to the subject and context be deemed to include the trustees for the time being of these presents and/ or Survivor or Survivors of any of them and their Successor or Successors in Office) of the other part:

WHEREAS

1. The SETTLOR is desirous of creating an endowment by setting apart and establishing a Fund for the Public Religious and Charitable objects and purposes in India hereinafter expressed.

2. The TRUSTEES have at the request of SETTLOER agreed to act as TRUSTEES of these presents upon the terms and provisions hereinafter contained.

NOW THIS INDENTURE WITNESSETH as follows:

1. In order to effectuate the said object of creating and establishing a Public Charitable Trust, the Settlor has delivered to and made over to the TRUSTEES a sum of Rs. 250 lakhs (Rupees two hundred fifty lakhs) only, with intent to part with all his right, title and interest claim therein and vest the same in the TRUSTEES to have and to hold the same and the investment or investments for the time being representing the same and all other properties

that may for the time being represent the trust estate together with all additions and accretions thereto and all accumulated income thereof and all other property or properties that may be acquired out of the same or otherwise may hereafter be subject to the trust (hereinafter referred to as the TRUST FUND) for the charitable objects and purposes and uses hereinafter expressed with the powers and on the terms and conditions herein contained of and concerning the same.

2. The name of the Trust shall be ELH CHARITABLE TRUST and the office of the trust shall be situated at No. ....which may be shifted from time to time to such other place or places as the trustees may deem fit and proper at their discretion.

3. The objects of the Trust shall be:

(*i*) to establish, promote, set-up, run, maintain, assist, finance support and/or aid to or help in the setting up and/or maintaining and/or running schools and other institutions orphanages, widow homes, lunatic asylums, poor houses or other establishments for relief and/or help to the poor, old and infirm people and/or destitutes.

(*ii*) To give, provide and/or render help and assistance in cash or kind to poor and/or destitute people widows, etc.

(*iii*) To give, provide and/or render help and assistance to and/or implement any scheme for providing livelihood and upliftment of the poor.

(*iv*) To give provide and or render food, medicine and other help and/ or assistance in any shape or form to the poor deserving and needy persons.

(*v*) To give, provide and/or render monetary and/or other help and assistance for the relief of persons and animals affected by natural and other calamities such as flood, fire, famine, cyclone, earth-quake, storm, accident, pestilence, drought, epidemic, unbearable cost of living and the like, to give donations, subscriptions or contributions to institutions, establishments, centres or persons doing relief work on such occasions.

(*vi*) To start, maintain and assist any relief measures in those parts which are or become subjected to natural calamities such as flood, fire, drought, famine, cyclone, earth-quake, epidemic, storm, accident, pestilence, etc.

(*vii*) To establish, maintain or grant aid for the establishment or maintenance of wells, tube-wells, tanks, water-reservoirs and trees and constructions of and repairs to paths, roads, bridges, etc. for the use of the public.

(*viii*) To give, provide, distribute *dhoties*, blankets, rugs, woollen clothings, quilts of cotton, woollen, silk, or other varieties of cloths or other articles of necessity and facilities for the poor.

(*ix*) To open, found, establish, promote, set-up, run, maintain, assist, finance, support and/or aid or help in the setting up and/or maintaining and/or running schools, colleges, lecture halls and other establishments or institutions for advancement of education and of knowledge in arts, science, literature, humanities and all other useful subjects in all their manifestations.

(*x*) To open, found, establish, promote, set-up, run maintain, assist, finance, support and/or aid or help in the setting up and/or maintaining and/or running hospitals, boarding houses, libraries, reading-rooms, gymnasium and other training and vocational institutes.

(*xi*) To promote, advance and encourage and/or aid in helping, promoting, advancing and encouraging primary, secondary and higher education including technical and medical education also physical training, training of handicrafts, fine art and other useful arts, crafts among the public including the establishment and maintenance of Shilpa-Shikshalayas, Kala-Kendras and other welfare centres for them.

(*xii*) To foster and encourage education and training in handicrafts, fine arts, among women folk in general and establish and found institutions imparting such education and to establish, maintain, support or help by monetary gifts or otherwise, centres and institutions for women and children and to provide social welfare works for women and children.

(*xiii*) To meet travelling, boarding and lodging expenses for students going abroad for higher commercial and technical education.

(*xiv*) To grant, pay or give scholarship, stipends, prizes, rewards, allowance and other financial assistance or help in cash or kind to students with a view to help them in prosecuting their studies in schools, colleges, educational institutions, technical institutions, art schools, institutions teaching commercial and other arts including teaching of cultural arts or other training, research or educational works in India or abroad.

(*xv*) To open, found, establish, promote, set-up, run, maintain, assist, finance, support and/or aid or help in the setting up and/or maintaining and/or running hospitals, charitable dispensaries, maternity homes, child welfare centres, convalescent homes, sanatoriums, hostels and other similar institutions or centres for rendering or providing medical relief and/or aid to the suffering humanities or for research centres and institutions for promotion of research and education for medical science including surgery.

(*xvi*) To open, found, establish, promote, set-up, run, maintain, assist, finance, support and/or aid or help in the setting up and/or maintaining and/or running by monetary gifts or otherwise, centres, stadium, playgrounds and parks for public use sports, and games and other social welfare works and/or activities in Calcutta and/or other places in India.

(*xvii*) To open found, establish, promote, set-up, run, maintain, assist, finance, support and/or aid or help in the setting up and/or maintaining and/or running institutions, centres, auditoriums and the like for the running of welfare and other services to the public and to provide meeting-room for socially useful activities and functions.

(*xviii*) To open, found, establish, promote, set-up, run, maintain, assist, finance, support and/or aid or help in the setting up establishment, maintenance and/or running dharamsalas, wells, deep tubewells, tanks, roads, etc.

(*xix*) To promote, organise, administer, establish, support, maintain, and/or grant aid to any person, institution or society or organisation whatsoever having for its objects of charitable purposes and to incur expenditure in connection therewith.

(*xx*) To renovate or repair any such temple, mosque, gurudwara, church or other places which is notified by the Central Government in the Official Gazette to be of historic, archaeological or artistic importance or to be a place of public worship of renown throughout any State or States.

(*xxi*) To promote, assist and/or maintain all activities by whosoever carried on or wherever carried on in India in conformity with the objects of the Trust and as are conducive to the well being and general welfare of the nation or are conducive for advancement of any object or objects of general public utility not involving/ carrying on any activity for profit.

(*xxii*) To help in the preservation of cattle and useful animals.

(*xxiii*) To publish and or publishing books, pamphlets, periodicals and newspapers in India or outside for the spread and advancement of education and culture.

4. If any one or more of the objects specified in clause (3) of these presents are held not to be objects of a public charitable nature, the TRUSTEES shall not carry out such object or objects as if the same are not incorporated in these present but the validity of the trust created by these presents as a trust for public charitable purposes shall not be affected in any manner.

5. The financial year of the trust shall end on 31st March, every year provided that the Board of Trustees shall be at liberty to change the same from time to time if they so deem it fit and proper. The first financial year of the trust shall close on 31st March 2001.

6. The TRUSTEES shall from time to time after meeting the expenses of and incidental to the management of the Trust Properties and of the Trust

decide the particular object or objects for which the income or corpus of the TRUST FUND or Properties for the time being available shall be applied.

7. The TRUSTEES may accept any donation or contribution in cash or in kind from any person, firm, company, corporation, associations, institution or trust (including the SETTLOR or the trustees or any of them) for the furtherance of the objects of the trust or for any one or more of them upon such terms and conditions as they may in their absolute discretion think fit and which are not inconsistent with the objects of the trust. The trustees may also take over the management of any other charitable or public institutions on such terms as they think fit and may manage such institutions.

8. Without affecting the generality of powers and functions of the TRUSTEES to manage and administer the trust, the Board of Trustees shall have the following functions.—

(*i*) To borrow if needed against the security of the assets of the trust by way of bank overdrafts, loan or otherwise, as may be necessary, for the benefit of the trust and for more effectively carrying out the objects of the trust provided however the trustees unanimously agree on such borrowing and limited to the terms of their decision or agreement and to authorise two or more of the trustees to execute such documents, deeds, papers, etc. as may be necessary in connection therewith.

(*ii*) To arrange for and/or authorise the signing or execution of any agreement, contract, instrument, document or any other paper or writing required to be signed or executed on behalf of the trustees by any two of the trustees to be nominated in this behalf by the Board of Trustees and to make the same effective and binding as if the said agreement, contract, instrument or document or paper or writing were signed by all the trustees.

(*iii*) To appoint or make provision for the appointment of a sub-committee of trustees and/or others to attend to or supervise or conduct specified jobs or functions or trust matters in such manner and subject to such rules and regulations as the trustees may prescribe.

(*iv*) To authorise any one or more trustees to hold any property or any fund or any investment of the trust subject however to the terms of these presents in such manner and subject to such terms and conditions, rules and regulations as the Board of Trustees may from time to time think fit and proper.

(*v*) To spend any portion of the corpus or the income of the trust fund for purchasing any land and or constructing any building or buildings for and in the name of the trust for the purpose of carrying out promoting and/or executing any or all of the objects of the trust.

9. The TRUSTEES shall cause true and accurate accounts to be kept of all moneys received and spent and of all matters in respect thereof in course of management of trust properties or in relation to the carrying out of the objects and purpose of the trust as well as of all the assets, credits and effects of the trust properties.

10. The TRUSTEES may invest the Trust Estate either in the purchase of immovable properties or of mortgage immovable properties, or in such manner as allowed by law as may be in force from time to time and to convert, alter, vary, dispose of or transfer such investments from time to time provided that such investments shall not be made which are directly or indirectly for the benefit of any person referred to in sub-section (3) of section 13 of the Income-tax Act 1961, or any subsequent amendments as may be made from time to time.

11. If the income from the trust property in a particular year is not fully utilised, the unexpended income subject to the applicable provisions of the Income-tax Act 1961, shall be carried over to the next year or years and spent in such subsequent year or years for the advancement of any of the objects of the trust.

12. The TRUSTEES shall be at liberty to sell such portion or portions of the movable or immovable properties forming part of the Trust Estate either by public auction or by private contract at such price or prices and on such terms and conditions relating to title or otherwise in all respects as they may in their absolute discretion think fit and to rescind or vary any contract for the sale thereof and to resell the same without being answerable for any loss occasioned thereby and to execute all conveyances or other assurances and to pass valid and effectual receipts and discharges for all moneys received by them.

13. The TRUSTEES shall keep an account or accounts with any bank or banks, to operate such account or accounts whether in debit or in credit and to give all appropriate instructions to the banker or bankers concerning the operation of such account or accounts and to authorise by appropriate resolution two or more of the trustees jointly with an agent appointed by the Board of Trustees in this behalf to operate such account or accounts.

14. The TRUSTEES may pay all charges and outgoings payable in respect of any immovable property for the time being forming part of the TRUST FUND and may carry out repairs required to be done to the same and keep the same insured against loss or damage by fire and may incur all other costs, charges, and expenses incidental to the administration and management of the Trust Estate and the properties for the time being belonging to the trust as they may in their absolute discretion think fit.

15. The TRUSTEES may manage or supervise the management of any lands, hereditaments, and premises for the time being comprised in the Trust Estate or any part thereof with power to erect, pull down, re-build, add to,

alter and repair houses and other buildings and to build drains and make roads and fences and otherwise to improve and develop and to cultivate or cause to be cultivated all or any of the said lands, hereditaments and premises and to insure houses and buildings against loss or damage by fire and/or other risks or to let, lease, make allowances to and arrangements with tenants, agriculturists and generally to deal with the said lands, hereditaments and premises as they may deem fit in their absolute discretion.

16. The TRUSTEES may appoint Secretaries, Managers, Lawyers, Solicitors, Auditors, Architects, Engineers, Surveyors, Gomastas or other employees for the purpose of management and supervision of the Trust Estate, for collection of rents, effects and profits, for keeping the accounts and records and for other purpose of the trust.

17. The TRUSTEES may establish their office at such place or places and may change such places from time to time as they may think fit.

18. The TRUSTEES may demise the immovable property or properties for the time being and from time to time belonging to the trust either from year to year or for any fixed term or for any term of years or on monthly tenancies at such rent and subject to such covenants and conditions as they may think proper and also accept surrenders of lease and tenancies and generally manage the same in such manner as they think proper.

19. The TRUSTEES shall have full power to compromise or compound all actions, suits, and other proceedings and settle differences and disputes touching the Trust Estate and/or the Trust Properties and to refer any such differences or disputes to arbitration and to adjust and settle all accounts relating to the Trust Estate and/or the Trust Properties and to do all other acts and things fully and effectually without being liable or answerable for any *bona fide* loss occasioned thereby.

20. The TRUSTEES may join, co-operate and amalgamate the trusts created by these presents or any portion thereof with any trust or institution having allied and or similar objects upon such terms as they may in their absolute discretion think fit.

21. The TRUSTEES may from time to time frame schemes and rules and regulations to carry out the objects of the trust and for managing the affairs of the trust and otherwise for giving effect to the objects and purposes of the trust and to vary the same from time to time as the trustees may in their discretion deem fit and proper.

22. The receipts granted by the TRUSTEES or any one or more of them for any moneys, stocks, funds, shares, securities or investments paid, delivered or transferred to them in exercise of the trust or powers hereof shall effectually release and discharge the person or persons paying, delivering or transferring the same therefrom and from seeing or from being bound to see the application thereof or being answerable for the loss or misapplication thereof.

23. The TRUSTEES shall be entitled at their discretion from time to time to start, discontinue, abolish and re-start any charity or charitable institution, to impose any condition or conditions to any subscription or donation made by them and to earmark any portion of the Trust Property or income for any particular object or objects.

24. The TRUSTEES may reimburse themselves and pay and discharge out of the TRUST FUND all expenses incurred by them in or about the execution of the trust or any of their duties under these presents including travelling expenses, but will not be entitled to any remuneration.

25. All the TRUSTEES unless they voluntarily resign or otherwise decide, shall continue to be the trustees during the term of their natural lives.

26. The number of trustees shall be not less than two and not more than nine.

27. Any trustee may retire at any time without assigning any reason and without being responsible for any costs occasioned by such retirement.

28. The surviving or continuing TRUSTEES may notwithstanding any vacancy in their board act as trustees PROVIDED HOWEVER that if the number of TRUSTEES shall fall below two the minimum fixed by these presents, the trustees shall not, except for the purpose of filling any vacancy, act so long as the number is below the said minimum.

29. Two TRUSTEES at a meeting shall form a quorum for any meeting of the TRUSTEES.

30. The TRUSTEES for the time being shall elect from amongst them one Chairman and he shall hold office for years, unless he resigns or refuses to act as Chairman or otherwise ceases to be trustee.

31. All proceedings and questions and matters arising at the meeting of the TRUSTEES shall be decided by a majority of votes and in case of equality of votes the Chairman shall have a second or casting vote PROVIDED HOWEVER that notwithstanding anything herein stated no question dealing with the disposal of the corpus of any of the trust properties and/or investment out of the trust corpus shall be decided except with the consent of the Chairman of the trust.

32. In case of difference of opinion between the TRUSTEES the opinion of the majority shall prevail and if the TRUSTEES are equally divided in any matter, the Chairman shall have a casting vote.

33. A resolution in writing circulated amongst all the TRUSTEES and signed by a majority of the trustees present in India shall be as valid and effectual as if it had been passed at a meeting of the TRUSTEES duly convened and held.

34. Notice of the meeting of the TRUSTEES and all communications may be sent to the TRUSTEES at their addresses registered for the time being in the records of the trust.

35. All meetings of the trust shall be held at such place and at such time as the Chairman of the trust shall decide from time to time.

36. A trustee who is unable to be present at a meeting of the TRUSTEES may send his views on the agenda in writing and such expression of opinion shall be taken to be his vote on the matter concerned.

37. The minutes of the proceedings of every meeting of the TRUSTEES shall be entered in a book to be kept for that purposes and signed by the Chairman of such meeting or of the following meeting when they are read over and shall when so entered and signed be conclusive evidence of the business and other matters transacted at such meeting.

38. No person being—

(*i*) an undischarged insolvent; or

(*ii*) convicted of an offence involving moral turpitude; or

(*iii*) of unsound mind; or

(*iv*) a minor;

shall be eligible to be a trustee.

39. The power to appoint new or additional TRUSTEES, but so as not to exceed the maximum number and to fill vacancies in the office of the trustees, shall vest in the continuing trustee or trustees.

40. A person shall cease to be a trustee in any of the following events:

(*a*) if he dies; or

(*b*) if he becomes bankrupt; or

(*c*) if he becomes insane or otherwise become incapable to act; or

(*d*) if he resigns his office.

41. On a new or additional trustee being appointed and on his signifying his acceptance in writing to the effect of his accepting the appointment, the Trust Property shall automatically vest in him along with the other TRUSTEES for the time being and he will be entitled to carry out all the duties and functions of a trustee without any other deed or writing.

42. The Board of Trustees shall be entitled to sue in the name of the trust and may similarly be sued in the name of the trust.

43. The Board of Trustees may, by a unanimous vote of all the TRUSTEES for the time being except the trustee proposed to be removed, remove any trustee, permanent or otherwise, from office after finding the trustee proposed to be removed guilty of serious misconduct in relation to or concerning the trust estate or trust affairs and after arriving at a definite conclusion that for the reasons to be recorded in writing the continuance of the trustee proposed to be removed as trustee or these presents was desirable keeping to the objects of the trust in view and other related or connected matters provided however that no conclusion of such guilt shall be arrived

at without giving to the trustee proposed to be removed a full and fair opportunity of explaining his conduct and/or the charges levelled against him for his removal. And the decision of the Board of TRUSTEES in this behalf shall be final and binding and shall not be called in question anywhere.

IN WITNESS WHEREOF the SETTLOR and the TRUSTEES have executed these presents on the day, month and year above-mentioned.

Signed and delivered by the SETTLOR
at Calcutta in the presence of:

Signed and delivered by the TRUSTEES at Calcutta in the presence of:

Deed of Trust when no Trustees are Appointed but Money is given Straight to the University Direct

THIS INDENTURE made this 10th day of December 1999 BY me AB etc.

WHEREAS I am desirous of establishing a scholarship at the .... University (to be known as .... SCHOLARSHIP) to be awarded to the student who would stand first in the first class in Political Science in the M.A. Examination every year at the rate of Rs. 900 per month for two years and for that purpose purchased with the approbation of the said University and in the name of the said University 9 per cent. Government Promissory Relief Bonds (or other security as may be described by the SETTLOR) of the face value of Rs. 2 lakhs yielding interest of Rs. .... per annum (*state particulars of the security*).

AND WHEREAS I have made over the said Government Promissory Relief Bonds (or other security) to the Registrar of the said University on the .... day of .... for the purpose as aforesaid.

NOW THIS INDENTURE WITNESSES and I the said AB do hereby declare that the University shall at all times hereafter hold and possess the said Relief Bond (or other security) upon trust hereunder created and with and subject to the powers and provisions hereinafter contained.

(*a*) The University shall collect the interest of the said Bonds (or other security) twice each year on due dates and after meeting therefrom the costs, charges and expenses for such collection including bank charges, if any, keep the amount earmarked for the purpose of awarding the scholarship after the final publication of the result of the said examination.

(*b*) In case there is no award of such SCHOLARSHIP for any particular year or years, none having passed in the first class in Political Science the University may, if so decided by the syndicate, award the said SCHOLARSHIP to the student who would stand first in the second class or alternatively the University may declare no award for that particular year. If, however, the particular student is not available for any reason whatsoever, the SCHOLARSHIP will go to the next best student for that year.

(*c*) The University shall have ordinarily no power to encash the said Bonds (or other security) but shall, on the contrary, hold the same for the trust hereunder created except upon its redemption whether on their maturity or earlier when it shall convert them and invest the proceeds in sum or other good security yielding an income of Rs. 18,000 per annum tax free or so.

IN WITNESS WHEREOF I the said AB have set and subscribed my hand and seal this 10th day of December 1999.

Signed, sealed and delivered by
AB Accepted and confirmed:

For and on behalf of the University:

Appointment of New Trustee by continuing Trustees in pursuance of a Power in a Deed of Charitable Trust

DEED OF APPOINTMENT MADE this 30th day of November 1999 BETWEEN AB son of .... of .... and CD son of .... of .... (CONTINUING TRUSTEE) of the first part, EF son of .... of .... (RETIRING TRUSTEE) of the second part AND GH son of .... of .... (NEW TRUSTEE) of the third part:

WHEREAS by a Deed of Trust dated the .... day of .... 1999 and made BETWEEN XY son of .... of .... of the One Part and the said AB, CD and EF of the Other Part, and registered in Book I, vol .... pages .... being No. .... for the year .... in the office of the Sub-Registrar of .... the said XY granted, transferred and assured unto and to the use of the said AB, CD and EF the lands, houses, securities and moneys described in the First Schedule hereto TO HAVE AND TO HOLD the same in trust for the objects thereunder indicated and whereas the said Deed of Trust is still in force and virtue.

AND WHEREAS it was provided in the said deed that in case of death of any of the said trustees or should any of them be unwilling to continue and/or desirous of being discharged or refuse to act or become unfit or physically incapable or mentally deficient to act as such trustee as aforesaid, then, and in such an event it shall be lawful for the surviving or CONTINUING TRUSTEES OR TRUSTEE for the time being to appoint any person or persons as the trustee or trustees in the place and stead of the trustee or trustees so dying or desiring to be discharged or refusing to act or becoming unfit or physically incapable or mentally deficient to act as such trustee or trustees in their place and stead.

AND WHEREAS it was further provided in the said deed that the number of trustees for the time being shall under no circumstances be less than three or more than five:

AND WHEREAS it was furthermore provided in the said Deed of Trust that all the trust estates and premises upon such appointment or appointments being made shall vest in the new trustees or trustee jointly with the surviving or CONTINUING TRUSTEES or trustee to all intents and purposes.

AND WHEREAS the said EF having been unwilling to act any longer as a trustee of the trusts as aforesaid is desirous of being discharged as testified by his being a party hereto and executing these presents.

AND WHEREAS the trust estates and premises now consist of the items described in the Second Schedule hereto:

NOW THIS INDENTURE WITNESSES that in exercise of all powers and authorities to that effect vested in them under and by virtue of the said Deed of Trust and of all other powers in that behalf enabling them, they the said AB and CD do hereby appoint the said GH as trustee of the said trust in the place and stead of EF to the intent that the said GH shall have the same powers, authorities and discretions and shall in all respects act as if he had been originally nominated a trustee under the said instrument: AND THIS INDENTURE further witnesses that in consideration of such appointment they the said AB, CD and EF do hereby grant, transfer, assign and assure to the said AB, CD and GH all and singular the trust estates and premises described in the Second Schedule hereto; TO HOLD the estate and premises hereby transferred, assigned and assured to the said AB, CD and GH for ever, upon trust and subject to the same powers, terms and provisos applicable thereto by virtue of the said instrument.

And this Indenture furthermore witnesseth that the said AB, CD and EF and each of them so far as it relates to his own acts and omissions doth hereby for himself, his heirs, executors and administrators covenant with the said GH, his heirs and assigns that they the said AB, CD and EF have not done or executed, performed or knowingly suffered to the contrary or been party or privy to any act or thing whereby or by reason or means whereof the estate and premises hereby transferred and assured or any part thereof are or is in any way encumbered or affected in any manner whatsoever or whereby the said AB, CD and EF respectively are in any way prevented from transferring and assuring the said premises or any part thereof in the manner aforesaid.

The First Schedule above referred to

The Second Schedule above referred to

IN WITNESS WHEREOF the parties hereto have hereunto set their respective hands and seals the day, year first above-written.

Signed, sealed and delivered by
AB, CD, GH, EF in presence of:

Appointment of a New Trustee on the Death of a Trustee, the Appointment being made by the Surviving Trustee in Exercise of Power of Appointment

This DEED OF APPOINTMENT MADE on the 11th day of December 1999 BETWEEN the within-named CD (SURVIVING TRUSTEE) of the one part and EF son of .... of .... (NEW TRUSTEE) of the other part. Whereas by a Deed of Trust dated .... made BETWEEN AB son of .... of the one part and CD son of .... and XY son of .... of the other part and registered in Book I vol....... pages .... to .... in the office of the Sub-registrar of .... the said AB granted, transferred and assured the lands, houses, etc., fully mentioned and described in the Schedule hereto and hereinafter referred to as the TRUST PROPERTY unto and to the said CD and XY TO HAVE AND TO HOLD the same in trust for the objects thereunder created. AND WHEREAS the said Deed of Trust is still in force and virtue AND WHEREAS it is expressly provided in the said deed that in the event of the death of any one of the trustees the SURVIVING TRUSTEE shall be entitled to appoint a NEW TRUSTEE in the place and stead of the deceased.

AND WHEREAS XY one of trustees appointed thereby died on or about the 4th day of November 1999.

Now this INDENTURE witnesses that in exercise of the power, authorities and liberties for that purpose vested in him under and by virtue of the aforesaid Deed of Trust and all other powers in that behalf in any way enabling him, he the said CD does hereby and hereunder appoint the said EF to be a trustee in the place of the said XY for the purposes of the said Deed of Trust dated .... jointly with him the said CD upon trust and subject to the same powers, terms, provisions, etc., applicable thereto by virtue of the said Deed of Trust dated .... and in the same manner as if the said EF had been originally appointed a trustee of the said Deed of Trust. AND THIS INDENTURE further witnesses that in consideration of the said appointment he the said CD doth hereby grant, transfer and assure the TRUST PROPERTY and every part thereof unto and to the use of the said CD and EF TO HAVE AND TO HOLD the same jointly as trustees for the purpose and subject to the terms and conditions of the said Deed of Trust.

Schedule of trust property

In witness whereof the parties hereto have hereunto set their hands and seals the day and year first above-written.

Signed, sealed and delivered   CD
in presence of: EF

Deed of Trust

THIS DEED OF TRUST is made the 2nd day of March 2000 BETWEEN AB etc. (hereinafter called the SETTLOR), of the one part and CD of, etc., and EF of, etc. (hereinafter called the TRUSTEES), of the other part.

WHEREAS the SETTLOR is desirous of creating a settlement or trust in respect of the properties described in the schedule hereto to the intents and purposes hereinafter appearing: NOW THIS INDENTURE WITNESSES that the SETTLOR does hereby grant, convey, transfer and assign and assure unto and to the TRUSTEES the properties described in the schedule hereto TO HAVE AND TO HOLD the same to the use of the TRUSTEES or any one or more of them subject to and upon the following trusts namely:

1. The TRUSTEES or the trustee for the time being shall, at the first instance, pay out of the rents, issues and profits thereof all Government revenue, cess, taxes, rates, and other impositions and outgoings in respect of the said properties.

2. Secondly, pay out of the balance of income the costs, charges and expenses for the maintenance, upkeep and repair of the said properties.

3. Thirdly, make the following payments available out of the residue thereof.

(*a*) A sum of Rs.8,000 monthly for the deity worship and periodical festivals of the deity located at ....

(*b*) A grant of Rs. 5,000 per month to MN as his maintenance allowance for the term of his natural life.

The TRUSTEES or TRUSTEE shall, out of the rest and residue of the income of the estate keep and maintain a sum equivalent to 20 % thereof as reserved to meet emergency expenses and pay the balance to the SETTLOR during the term of his natural life for his absolute use and enjoyment and after his death to his two sons X and Y and their natural heirs in equal shares.

The TRUSTEES or TRUSTEE hereby appointed or to be appointed in future as hereinafter provided shall have full power to sell, transfer, alienate or convert any one or more of the properties set forth in the schedule hereto with the permission of the court of the District Judge having jurisdiction over the subject-matter of the trust and to convert the proceeds thereof in other property or properties and/or securities as are prescribed by law.

In case of death, retirement or removal of any one or more of the TRUSTEES during the life of the settlor, the SETTLOR will have the right to appoint such other TRUSTEE or TRUSTEES in the place of the TRUSTEE or TRUSTEES so dying, retiring or removed. In case of inability or refusal on the part of any trustee to act as such trustee, the surviving trustee will be entitled to nominate a competent male member of the family of AB and if no such person is available, then and in such an event the vacancy shall be filled up by the court of competent jurisdiction: PROVIDED, however, that in case of acquisition of the trust properties or any portion thereof, the TRUSTEES or TRUSTEE shall invest the compensation money either in purchase of some other income-fetching property or properties or purchase some securities to be held by him or them on the same terms as to trust hereunder created and that the TRUSTEE or TRUSTEES so appointed will have the same powers and rights as if he or they was or were originally appointed the TRUSTEE or TRUSTEES under these presents.

The Schedule above referred to

IN WITNESS, etc.

Signed, sealed and delivered in the presence of:	AB CD EF

55
Wakf Property

Power of mutawalli to sell or mortgage. A mutawalli has no power, without the permission of the court, to mortgage, sell or exchange wakf property or any part thereof unless he is expressly empowered by the deed of wakf to do so[1] or authorised by the court but he is to obtain the previous sanction of the Board in all such cases.[2] The 1995 Act makes it clear that notwithstanding anything contained in the wakf deed, any gift, sale, exchange or mortgage of any immovable property which is wakf property shall be void unless such gift, sale, exchange or mortgage is effected with the prior sanction of the Board and that no mosque, dargah or khangah shall be gifted, sold, exchanged or mortgaged except in accordance with any law for the time being in force.[3]

The Board may accord sanction to such transaction if it is of opinion that such transaction is necessary or beneficial to the wakf, consistent with the objects of the wakf, the consideration thereof is reasonable and adequate.[3]

The following enactments relating to administration of trusts apply to wakfs:[4]

(*i*) Official Trustees Act II of 1913.

(*ii*) Charitable Endowments Act VI of 1890, ss. 2, 3, 4, 5, 6 and 8.

(*iii*) Religious Endowments Act XX of 1863, s. 14.

(*iv*) The Code of Civil Procedure 1908, ss. 92 and 93.

(*v*) Charitable and Religious Trusts Act XIV of 1920.

(*vi*) The Bombay Public Trusts Act 1950 (Bom. Act XXIX of 1950).

1 Mulla on *Principles of Mahomedan Law,* 19th Ed., p. 179.
2 Section 36A of the Central Wakf Act 1954 and s. 53 of the Bengal Wakf Act 1934.
3 Section 51 of the Wakf Act 1995.
4 *See* Mulla on *Principles of Mahomedan Law*, 19th Ed., pp. 201-202.

FORMS

Deed of Wakf

TO ALL TO WHOM these presents shall come I .... wife of .... a Mahomedan by faith and religion governed by *sunni/shia* school of Mahomedan Law etc. SEND GREETING WHEREAS I am of my free will and own accord desirous of permanently dedicating my properties, movable and immovable, fully mentioned and described in the schedule hereunder written for purposes recognised by the Mahomedan Law as religious, pious and/or charitable NOW KNOW YE and I hereby declare as follows:

1. I dedicate all the properties mentioned and described in the schedule hereunder written with all appurtenances and the rents, issues and profits thereof absolutely and permanently by way of wakf for the purposes as aforesaid with intent to extinguish all my rights and claim therein and vest the same in God and complete the same by delivery of possession to the mutawalli in the manner hereinafter mentioned.

2. The ultimate benefit under this wakf is reserved for purposes and objects recognised by the Hanafi or Sunni School of Mahomedan Law as religious, pious and/or charitable and indicated in the paragraph next succeeding.

3. The purposes and objects referred to in the last preceding paragraph are *inter alia* as follows:

(*i*) The payment of my just debts.

(*ii*) The maintenance and support of myself and my ....

(*iii*) The distribution of alms to poor and indigent persons on every Thursday in the week the amount or value of such weekly alms not to be less than Rupees ....

(*iv*) The observance of the tenth day of Mohurrum by distribution of milk and other food.

(*v*) The celebration of ceremonies known as Mound Shariff.

(*vi*) To help poor and meritorious students professing Islam faith and reading in any recognised institution.

(*vii*) The performance of the annual fateha of myself after my death and of my husband after his death and the members of ....

(*viii*) Other religious, pious and/or charitable purposes as may be thought fit by the mutawalli from time to time or a court of law including pecuniary reliefs or assistance to indigent members of my family and the family of my..........

4. The moneys which may be realized by execution of the decrees in the suits mentioned in the said schedule hereto shall, after payment therefrom of my debts, be invested in landed properties and such landed properties shall form a part of the estate hereby made wakf estate.

5. Out of the income of the said wakf estate the said .... shall each receive a monthly sum of not more than Rs .... only for the benefit of themselves and their respective families and descendants. As regards the respective amounts to be spent for the other purposes aforesaid, the mutawalli or mutawallis for the time being shall have absolute discretion.

6. For the appointment of mutawalli, the following rules are laid down:

(*i*) I shall be the mutawalli for my life.

(*ii*) After my death Sri AB and CD son of MN shall be joint mutawallis and each of them shall be at liberty to appoint one of his or her lineal male descendants as his or her successor failing which each shall be succeeded by his or her eldest lineal male descendant. All the mutawallis for the time being and each of them shall have the power of appointing their, his or her successors or successor.

7. The mutawalli or mutawallis for the time being (jointly if there are more than one) shall, as and by way of remuneration, be entitled to receive jointly one-fourth part of the net income of the wakf estate and to retain all expenses of management including the costs of all necessary litigations.

8. Notwithstanding anything herein contained, no mutawalli will directly or indirectly grant or extend any benefit out of the wakf estate to my .... or any descendants of theirs.

9. In cases of necessity and for the benefit of the wakf estate, the mutawalli or mutawallis for the time being shall after obtaining sanction of the Wakf Board Constituted under the Wakf Act 1995 and in accordance with its directions, be at liberty, to sell, mortgage, transfer, alienate, partition and/or demise the wakf properties mentioned in the said schedule hereto or any part thereof and to invest the moneys thereby raised and in the event of such sale, mortgage, transfer, alienation, partition and/or lease the proceeds thereof as well as such investments shall form part of the wakf estate but no purchaser, mortgagee, transferee, alienee, co-sharer or lessee of the said properties shall be concerned to enquire whether the respective sales, mortgages, transfers, alienations, partition or leases are necessary for or beneficial to the wakf estate or to see to the application of the proceeds thereof.

10. The dedication hereby made will bind my heirs, executors and representatives.

11. The properties hereby dedicated are valued at Rs. ....

The Schedule above referred to

Part I

Part II

IN WITNESS WHEREOF the said MR has executed these presents on this .... day of .... 1999 at Calcutta.

Signed, sealed and delivered
by MR in the presence of:

NOTE: *Wakf as defined by Mahomedan jurists.* The term 'wakf' literally means detention. The term wakf has defined by Justice Kader as the property vests in God Almighty and the income is applied to the objects.[5] The legal meaning of 'wakf', according to Abu Hanifa is the detention of a specific thing in the ownership of the wakif or appropriator, and the devoting or appropriating of its profits or usufruct "in charity on the poor or other good objects". According to the two disciples, Abu Yusuf and Muhammad, wakf signifies the extinction of the appropriator's ownership in the thing dedicated and the detention of the thing is the implied ownership of God in such a manner that its profits may revert to or be applied "for the benefit of mankind". Baillie, 557-558. See Hadaya, 231, 234. A wakf extinguishes the right of the wakif or dedicator and transfers ownership to God. The mutawalli is the manager of the wakf, but the property does not vest in him, as it would in a trustee in English law.[6] The expression "vested in trust" in s. 10 of the Limitation Act does not apply to the mutawalli. It is also for this reason that the Indian Trusts Act 1882, exempts from its scope the rules of law applicable to wakf.[7] A wakf, however, is a trust for the purposes of s. 92 of the Code of Civil Procedure.[8]

Deed of Wakf (Mahomedan)—Movables and Immovables

WHEREAS I, AB son of, etc., of, (hereinafter called the WAKIF), am solely and absolutely seized and possessed of or otherwise well and sufficiently entitled to the property fully mentioned and described in Schedule Y hereto, and also to the shares of the joint stock companies and other securities, and also to the moneys and other movable properties set out in Schedule Z hereto: AND WHEREAS I desire to make a wakf of the properties set out in Schedules Y and Z hereto to grant aid to the poor and meritorious students (Mahomedan) prosecuting studies in the school known as .... and in the event of abolition of the said school to apply the income for such public charitable purposes as are hereinafter mentioned: NOW THIS DEED WITNESSES that I, the WAKIF, divest myself of all ownership, possession and enjoyment

5 Kader: *The Law of Wakfs*, Ed. 1999, p. 40.
6 *Mahomed Rustom* v *Mustaq Hussain* 47 IA 224.
7 *Per Amir A.J. Vaidus* v *Balusami* (1921)48 IA 362.
8 *Md. Kuzim* v *Syed Ali* 136 IC 417; Mulla's *Mahomedan Law*, 19th Ed., p. 143.

of the same and vest the same in God so as to create an endowment thereof for the religious and charitable objects hereunder mentioned and deliver possession thereof to the mutawalli hereunder appointed to effectuate my said wish and desire.

1. I appoint myself as the first mutawalli for administration of this wakf for the term of my natural life, which shall all along be known and designated as the wakf of AB.

2. After my death, CD son of, etc., and EF son of, etc., shall be the successors in my office and act as mutawalli of this wakf if qualified for the office who shall select two among their descendants as their successors and the vacancy thus created by death shall be filled up by this process for generations.

3. In the event of the death without selecting his substitute or retirement of any mutawalli holding office, the continuing mutawalli will co-opt a mutawalli in the place of one dying or retiring in the first place out of my heirs and their descendants, both male and female, PROVIDED they are found competent in that behalf, but preference shall always be given to a male eligible for the purpose.

4. Should any of the mutawallis be deemed unfit to hold the office, he shall be liable to be removed from the office of mutawalli.

5. The mutawalli or mutawallis shall realize the income of the wakf property, and shall at the first instance pay the outgoings and expenses of management of the wakf property. After such payment, the surplus shall be distributed by the mutawalli or mutawallis for the time being once in every .... months amongst the beneficiaries hereinafter mentioned.

6. The mutawallis shall, out of the surplus income as aforesaid of the wakf estate, set apart a sum equivalent to 75% to be applied in granting aid or financial assistance to poor and meritorious students prosecuting studies in the school subject to increase or diminution as may be permitted or justified by the income for the time being and pay the residue to me, AB the WAKIF for the time of my natural life. After my death, such surplus income shall be paid to my descendants in accordance with their respective shares according to Mahomedan law. And in the event of my descendants becoming extinct, the mutawalli or the mutawallis for the time being shall hold the property for medical reliefs to the Mussalman poor belonging to .... school, and shall spend the surplus income for the benefit of the poor of the said school in such manner as the mutawalli or mutawallis for the time being in their discretion shall decide.

Schedule Y above referred to

Schedule Z above referred to

IN WITNESS, etc.

WITNESSES: AB

Appointment of Mutawalli

TO ALL TO WHOM these presents shall come I ...... son of ...... by faith ...... by occupation .... residing at .... SEND GREETING WHEREAS by a deed of Declaration of Wakf made by .... (hereinafter referred to as the WAKIF) on and bearing date the day of .... and registered by the Sub-Registrar of Assurance of .... in Book No. 1, volume ...., pages .... being, ... for the year .... the said WAKIF dedicated the properties therein and in the schedule hereto particularly mentioned and described absolutely by way of wakf, divested himself of the ownership thereof to all intents and purposes and intended that the said properties shall be held and so treated and the rents, issues and profits thereof shall at all times thereafter be appropriated for the objects and purposes as indicated therein the ultimate benefit under the said wakf being reserved for purposes recognized by Mahomedan law as religious, pious or charitable as appearing in clauses .... to .... thereof AND WHEREAS the said Deed is in full force and virtue and the income of the properties dedicated being utilised for the purposes mentioned therein AND WHEREAS by the said deed hereinbefore recited the said WAKIF laid down the following scheme for administration of the wakf and made provisions for the appointment of mutawalli, that is to say.

(*a*) ....

(*b*) ....

(*c*) ....

NOW KNOW YE ALL that in exercise of the powers, authorities and liberties given to and vested in me under by virtue of the deed hereinbefore recited and every and any other powers enabling me I the said .... do hereby nominate and appoint .... son of .... deceased at present residing at .... by faith .... by occupation .... a Mahomedan belonging the Sunni School of Mahomedan law as mutawalli to be my successor in office after my death and in the event of his death during my lifetime his sons/daughters named .... of the same place and caste as mutawalli or mutawallis next after me to administer the said Wakf estate.

IN WITNESS WHEREOF I the said .... have hereunto set and subscribed my hand and seal this .... day of .... 2000.

Signed, sealed and delivered at

Schedule of wakf properties

CHANGES IN THE LAW AS REGARDS*

Transfer of Wakf Property

In 1954 the Wakf Act was passed by the Parliament to provide for the better administration and supervision of Wakfs. The Act extended to whole of India

* See page 1292.

except the State of Jammu and Kashmir. In respect of States of Bihar, Uttar Pradesh and West Bengal the Act was enforceable only after the State Government recommended for its application and Central Government issued a notification making the provisions of the Act applicable to the State. The Wakf (Amendment) Act 1984 to a certain extent modified the Wakf Act 1954.

Wakf means the permanent dedication by a person professing Islam or any other person of any other religion of any movable or immovable property for any purpose recognised by the Muslim Law as pious, religious or charitable. It includes a wakf by user or by grant for any purpose recognised by Muslim Law as pious, religious or charitable and a Wakf-alal-auld. A Wakif means any person making such dedication. A wakf by user shall not cease to be a wakf by non-user for any length of period. In case of a dedication by a person not professing Islam the wakf or the dedication shall be void if on the death of such person any objection to such dedication is raised by any legal representative of such person.

Board of Wakfs. The State Government may by notification in the Official Gazette establish a Board of Wakfs. The Board shall be a body corporate having perpetual succession and a common seal with power to acquire and hold property and to transfer such property subject to such conditions and restrictions as may be prescribed. The Board may sue and be sued in its name.

Wakf Commissioner. There shall be in each State a Wakf Commissioner who shall be the Chief Executive Officer of the Board. The Wakf Commissioner shall look after the administration and do all such acts as may be necessary for the due control, maintenance and administration of wakfs.

Registration. Every wakf shall be registered at the office of the Wakf Commissioner who shall maintain a register which shall be open to inspection. Any change in the wakf shall be notified to the Wakf Commissioner.

Transfer of wakf property. Section 36A of the 1954 Act provides for alienation of wakf property. The provisions contained in the Walf Deed will be subject to the provisions of the Act. No gift, sale, exchange or hypothecation of any wakf immovable property shall be valid unless prior sanction of the Board is obtained. In granting sanction to such a transaction the Board must be of the opinion that the transaction is necessary or beneficial to the wakf, it is consistent with the objects of the wakf and the consideration is reasonable and adequate.

Sale. In case of sale of wakf immovable property prior sanction of the Board is to be obtained and thereafter the property is to be sold by public auction and again such auction sale has to be confirmed by the Board. However, the auction sale can be avoided only if the mutawalli or any other person aggrieved makes an application to the Tribunal set up by the State

Government for the State under s. 55 of the Act and after hearing the parties and for reasons to be recorded in writing the Tribunal permits such sale to be made otherwise than by public auction in the interest of the wakf.

Suits. No suit shall be instituted against the Board in respect of any act without giving two months notice in writing setting out the cause of action, the name, description and the residence of the plaintiff and the reliefs claimed. The plaint shall contain that such notice has been delivered or left at the office of the Board.

Lease. The provisions as regards gift, exchange or hypothecation applies to lease for a period of one year or more. The mutawalli can give a lease of his own without prior permission of the Board for a period of less than 12 months.

Notification bringing into force the provisions of the Act of 1954 in different States. The Act has been brought into force in Ajmer, Andaman, Andhra Pradesh, Assam, Bhopal, Bihar, Coorg, Dadra, Nagar Haveli, Delhi, Himachal Pradesh, Hyderabad, Kutch, Madhya Pradesh, Chennai, Manipur, Mysore, Nicobar Islands, Orissa, Patiala, Pondicherry, Punjab, Rajasthan, Travancore-Cochin, Tripura, Vindhya Pradesh.

Until the Wakfs Act 1954 was, by notification, brought into force the Mussulman Wakf Act 1923 would apply to Gujarat and Maharashtra, the Uttar Pradesh Muslim Wakfs Act 1960 would apply to Uttar Pradesh and the Bengal Wakfs Act 1934 would apply to West Bengal.

The Bengal Wakf Act 1934. Wakf-alal-aulad means a wakf under which not less than 75% of the net available income is for the time being payable to the wakif for himself or any member of his family or descendants. The property ultimately vests in favour of God Almighty.

Transfer of wakf property. Section 53 of the Bengal Wakfs Act 1934 provided that the mutawalli could enter into an agreement for transfer of wakf property if he is expressly empowered by the Wakf Deed but that a notice of the proposed transfer in prescribed form shall be sent to the Commissioner of Wakfs one month before the transfer was made. If there is no power to transfer in the Wakf Deed then with the previous sanction of the Board of Wakf the mutawalli may enter into agreement for transfer and may transfer any immovable property of the wakf by way of sale, gift, mortgage, exchange, lease or tenancy of any kind. The Board would give sanction if it was satisfied that the proposed transfer was for legal necessity.

In every suit or proceeding in respect of any wakf property or in respect of a mutawalli except for recovery of rent the court shall issue notice to the Commissioner of Wakf.

Agreement to transfer and conveyance. These have to be executed in accordance with the law applicable in the State where the wakf property is situated.

Wakf Act 1995 Passed by the Indian Parliament Came into Force from 1st January 1996

The Wakf Act 1995 by s. 112 has repealed the Wakf Act 1954 and the Wakf (Amendment) Act 1984. It has also repealed any corresponding law in force in any State.

The Act of 1995 extends to the whole of India except the State of Jammu & Kashmir.

It has created a Board consisting of members taken from the members of the Parliament, Legislature, Muslim religious organisations, prominent Muslim Jurists, Mutawallis, etc. The Board has been given power to control over the activity and administration of the wakfs.

Almost all the disputes are to be settled by the Tribunal set up under the Act in relation to wakf. The Board has been given power to recover any money due from any person as arrears of land revenue. In respect of matters within the jurisdiction of the Tribunal the Civil Court will have no jurisdiction. Matters which are not within the purview of the Tribunal are subject to the jurisdiction of the Civil Court. The Board and the State Government have been given wide powers over the wakf property and over the functions of the mutawallis.

The mutawallis cannot borrow any money without the previous sanction of the Board (s. 76).

Section 87 disqualifies a wakf which is not registered with the Wakf Board from filing any suit or taking any legal proceedings for determination of any right on behalf of any wakf and any pending proceedings shall not be proceeded with.

In any proceeding before the Tribunal or the court by wakf or the mutawallis or by any beneficiary, the Board shall be a necessary party or the Board shall be given notice of the proceedings. No legal proceeding or suit by or against the mutawallis shall be compromised without sanction of the Board.

Under s. 196 the State Government has been given the power to regulate the secular activities of the wakfs.

Subject to directions by the Central Government, the State Government may give general or special directions to the Board and the Board shall comply with such directions. In certain circumstances the State Government may supersede the Board.

Sections 13 and 14 envisage the setting-up of a Board of Wakfs in every State and the Union Territory of Delhi. It will function under the State Government. The members of the Board shall hold office for a term of five years.

Prior Sanction of Wakf Board is required for transfer of wakf property. Under s. 32 the general superintendence of all wakf in any State shall vest in the Board or the State. The function of the Board shall be, *inter alia*, to sanction any transfer of immovable property of a wakf by way of sale, gift, mortgage, exchange or lease in accordance with the provisions of the Act. No such sanction shall be given unless at least two-thirds of the members of the Board vote in favour of such transaction. The Board may utilise wakf land or property for development for a Shopping Centre, market, housing flats and the like. The Board shall give the mutawallis the first chance to do such development work, if they fail then the Board will take up the work. The Board will return the wakf property to the mutawallis after it realises all the costs of construction or such development work.

FORMS

Agreement to Lease Wakf Property

THIS AGREEMENT TO LEASE is made on this ...... day of .... 1999 BETWEEN Md. .... of .... representing .... (hereinafter referred to as the LESSOR) of the one part and AB & Co. of .... (hereinafter referred to as the LESSEE) of the other part.

WHEREAS by a Deed of Wakf dated .... Md. .... dedicated his immovable property being .... for pious and religious purposes mentioned in the said Deed.

AND WHEREAS the LESSOR has been appointed as the mutawalli under the said Wakf Deed and the LESSOR is managing and administering the said wakf property.

AND WHEREAS the wakf property requires urgent repairs and that the income from wakf property is inadequate to carry out the necessary repairs.

AND WHEREAS the front portion of the ground floor of the wakf property is not properly utilised and is not required for the objects and use of the beneficiaries under the said Wakf Deed and with slight renovation the front portion can be let out at reasonable rent which will be adequate for the maintenance and upkeep of the wakf property.

AND WHEREAS the LESSOR applied to the Wakf Board for the permission to enter into THESE PRESENTS for leasing out the said portion of the wakf property and a copy of these presents was furnished along with the application.

AND WHEREAS the Board has considered the matter and has recorded such leasing out is a legal necessity for maintenance and upkeep of the wakf property and has granted its consent for execution of these presents.

AND WHEREAS the LESSEE has inspected all relevant documents including the Wakf Deed, application to the Board and the Board's sanction and has satisfied itself as to the authority and power of the LESSOR to enter into these presents and the validity of the proposed lease and thereupon has agreed to take on lease the front portion of the wakf property at .... for a period of 21 years.

NOW THESE PRESENTS WITNESSETH and the parties hereto agree as follows:

1. The LESSOR agrees to demise to the LESSEE and the LESSEE agrees to take on lease three rooms on the ground-floor facing the road in the premises No. .... for a period of 21 years commencing from the date of Deed of Lease to be executed at an yearly rent of Rs. 1,20,000 to be paid in advance from the commencement of lease.

2. The LESSEE shall pay all present and future taxes, duties, rates, levies and outgoings in respect of the said demised premises to the Government or Municipal Corporation or any other local authority or public body.

3. The Deed of Lease will contain the usual covenants to be given by the LESSOR and LESSEE and the usual terms and conditions and subject to the provisions of the Statute applicable to the wakf property.

4. The draft of the Deed of Lease will be prepared by the Lessee's Advocate and will be approved by the Lessor's Advocate and subject to the sanction by the Board.

5. The LESSEE shall make necessary repairs and renovation without in any way damaging the structures or any portion of the construction and paint the entire building at its own costs.

6. The LESSEE shall bear and pay the requisite stamp duty and registration charges and other legal expenses in respect of the present agreement as also the said Deed of Lease to be executed.

7. It is understood that these presents are subject to obtaining the requisite permission or No Objection Certificate of the authorities concerned at the costs of the LESSOR.

8. If the requisite sanction, permission or the No Objection Certificate cannot be obtained or there be undue delay in obtaining such permission sanction or No Objection Certificate the LESSEE shall have the option to terminate this Agreement to Lease on giving three months' notice.

9. In consideration of the LESSOR agreeing to enter into this Agreement to Lease and by way of security deposit the LESSEE has paid to the lessor Rs. 1,20,000 which would remain free of interest and would be adjusted against the rent.

IN WITNESS WHEREOF the parties have executed these presents on the day, month and year first above-written.

Signed and delivered
by Md. ....
in the presence of:

For ....
Signature

1.

2.

Signed, sealed and delivered by Mr. .... pursuant to Board Resolution dated .... of AB & Co. in the presence of:

For AB & Co.

Signature

1.

2.

Deed of Lease of Wakf Property

THIS DEED OF LEASE is made on this .... day of .... 2000 BETWEEN Md. AB of .... representing CD Wakf (hereinafter referred to as the LESSOR) of the one part and EF Limited, a company registered under the Companies Act 1956 and having its Registered Office at .... (hereinafter referred to as the LESSEE) of the other part.

WHEREAS by Deed of Wakf dated .... 1980 Md. CD dedicated his immovable property being .... for pious and religious purposes mentioned in the said Deed.

AND WHEREAS the LESSOR has been appointed as the mutawalli under the said Wakf Deed and the LESSOR is acting as such mutawalli and is managing and administrating the said wakf property.

AND WHEREAS the LESSOR obtained permission from the Wakf Board for leasing out three rooms on the ground floor of .... facing the Street to the LESSEE at a yearly rent of Rs. 1,20,000.

AND WHEREAS with the permission, sanction and approval of the Wakf Board the LESSOR entered into an Agreement to Lease dated .... 1999 for granting lease of the said three rooms for a period of 21 years at a yearly rent of Rs. 1,20,000 payable in advance.

AND WHEREAS the LESSEE made enquiries and taken inspection of documents and has satisfied itself about the power and authority of the LESSOR to lease out the said three rooms to the LESSEE for the said period at the said rent.

AND WHEREAS the LESSEE hereby agrees that the LESSOr has not and does not give any warranty as to his title or power or authority or the validity of these presents save and except that the Wakf Deed and the permission of the Wakf Board are valid and genuine documents.

AND WHEREAS the parties have agreed to execute the Deed of Lease as contemplated in the said Agreement to Lease dated .... 1999.

NOW THESE PRESENTS WITNESSETH and the parties hereby agree as follows:

1. In pursuance of the said Agreement to Lease and in consideration of the rent hereby reserved and on the terms and conditions, covenants and agreements herein contained and on the part of the lessee to be observed and performed the LESSOR doth hereby demise unto the LESSEE all that the said three rooms each measuring 140 sq. ft. situate on the ground floor of premises No. .... of .... facing West having frontage on the .... to hold the said premises unto the LESSEE for a term of 21 years commencing from .... 2000 but subject to earlier determination as mentioned hereinafter.

2. The LESSEE shall pay by way of LESSEE rent a sum of Rs. 1,20,000 per year payable in advance by .... 2000 and thereafter within February each year.

3. The security deposit of Rs. 1,20,000 given by the LESSEE will be adjusted towards the lease rent of the last year.

4. The LESSEE shall pay all present and future municipal rates, taxes, duties and levies and other outgoings either statutory or otherwise payable to Municipalities or other authorities in respect of the said leasehold premises.

5. The LESSEE shall keep the leasehold premises in good and tenantable repairs but shall not carry out any additions or alterations to the said premises without the written permission of the LESSOR.

6. The LESSEE shall not use the said premises for any unlawful purpose or bring in the premises any inflammable or hazardous article or goods or store them.

7. The LESSEE agree to use the said premises only for the purposes of carrying on its business and in doing so undertakes not to create any nuisance or undue annoyance to the neighbours.

8. If the LESSEE makes any default in payment of any yearly lease rent and such default continues for more than three months or commits any breach of any of the terms herein then the LESSOR would have the liberty to terminate the lease and to re-enter the said premises.

9. The LESSEE shall not sub-lease or grant any leave or licence to any other person, firm or company or create any charge or mortgage over the said leasehold property without prior written consent of the LESSOR and the permission of the Wakf Board.

10. The LESSEE shall make arrangement for separate Meters for waters, electricity and gas at its own costs and any consent or permission, if required, in this respect will be given by the LESSOR.

11. The LESSEE agrees and on enquiry has satisfied itself that all necessary sanctions, permissions and No Objection Certificates have been obtained for the purpose of leasing out the said premises and execution of these presents.

12. The LESSEE agrees to bear and pay the requisite Stamp Duty and the Registration charges and other legal expenses in respect of the present Deed of Lease.

IN WITNESS WHEREOF the parties have executed these presents on the day, month and year first above-written.

Signed and delivered
by Md. AB in the
presence of: Signature
1.
2.

Signed, sealed and delivered by
Mr. ....
pursuant to Board Resolution
dated .... of EFLimited
in the presence of: Signature
1.
2.

Wakf-alal-Aulad

THIS DEED OF WAKF is made on this .... day of .... 1999 by Md. MAL of .... (hereinafter called the WAKIF).

WHEREAS the WAKIF is the owner and in possession of the immovable property mentioned in the schedule hereto.

AND WHEREAS the WAKIF has no debts and the dower debt of his wife also has been partly paid to her and partly relinquished by her by the deed dated .... 1998.

AND WHEREAS the WAKIF is entitled to and is desirous of making wakf of the said properties for the benefit and maintenance of himself, his own heirs and descendants and ultimately for the benefit of poor Muslims.

NOW THIS DEED OF wakf witnesseth as follows:

1. The WAKIF hereby makes a settlement by way of wakf of all his immovable properties mentioned in the schedule hereto and relinquishes all his right, title and interest in the said properties as owner thereof.

2. That the aforesaid property shall no longer be the private property of any one but shall be wakf property for the maintenance and support of the WAKIF, his family, children and descendants and in case of extinction of his line of descendants for the benefit of the poor of Park Circus area belonging to the Muslim faith.

3. That the WAKIF hereby appoints and constitutes himself the sole mutawalli of the said wakf during his lifetime with absolute power of management thereof and shall appropriate the income of the said property to his own use.

4. That after the death of WAKIF any person nominated by the WAKIF in his lifetime or failing such nomination his eldest son or failing him the eldest male descendant and failing a male descendant a female descendant of the WAKIF in the male line of descendant or failing her the eldest male descendant in the female line of the descendant and failing him the eldest female descendant shall be the mutawalli.

5. The second and subsequent mutawallis shall have power to nominate their successors and failing such nomination the descendants in the order given in cl. (4) shall be the mutawallis.

6. The mutawalli for the time being shall manage the wakf property to the best of his ability and in case he is a minor or person of unsound mind his guardian appointed by the court shall manage the property on his behalf.

7. That after the payment of revenue, cesses, rates, taxes and necessary expenses of management the surplus receipts of the said property shall be divided by the mutawalli amongst the WAKIF'S descendants according to their shares under the Mohammedan Law.

8. That the mutawalli shall have no power to sell, mortgage, transfer or charge the immovable property mentioned in the First Schedule hereto or any part thereof except by lease for a period not exceeding seven years at a time but he may call in and convert into cash the property mentioned in the said schedule hereto and deposit the money in any nationalised bank or invest it in such securities as he may deem fit or may purchase immovable property and all such moneys, securities and immovable properties into which the property mentioned in the said schedule may be so converted shall be deemed to be part of the wakf property as if the same were included in the first schedule hereto.

9. That the descendants of the WAKIF will have no right to transfer or charge in any manner their share of the income or profits of the wakf property.

10. That on the extinction of the line of descendants of the WAKIF the mutawalli for the time being shall use the income, profits or surplus of the aforesaid property for the sole use and benefit of the Mussalmans of the city of Calcutta in such manner as he shall think fit.

The Schedule

IN WITNESS WHEREOF the WAKIF has signed this deed on the day, month and year first above-written.

WITNESSES:

1.

2.

Sd/

Md. MAL

(WAKIF)

Deed of Wakf for Ultimate Religious and Charitable Purposes

THIS DEED OF WAKF is made on the ...... day of .... 1999 by Md. MAL of .... (hereinafter called the WAKIF).

WHEREAS the WAKIF is the owner and in possession of the assets and properties, movable and immovable, described and mentioned in the schedule hereunder.

AND WHEREAS the WAKIF of his free will and own accord is desirous of permanently settling the properties described in the schedule for purposes recognised by the Mohammedan Law as pious, religious and/or charitable.

NOW THEREFORE THIS DEED witnesseth as follows:

1. I, the WAKIF, hereby dedicate and transfer all my properties mentioned in the schedule hereunder with all rents, issues, profits thereof and appurtenances thereto absolutely and permanently by way of wakf for pious, religious and/or charitable purposes and divest myself of all rights and claims therein and vest the same in Allah and complete the same by delivery of possession to the mutawalli in the manner hereinafter mentioned.

2. The ultimate benefit under this wakf is reserved for purposes and objects recognised by the Hanafi (or Sunni) School of Mohammedan Law as religious, pious and/or charitable including the following:

(*a*) the payment of my just debts;

(*b*) the maintenance and support of myself, my wife and descendants;

(*c*) the distribution of alms to poor and indigent persons on every Friday the value of such weekly alms not being less than Rs. 100;

(*d*) the observance of the tenth day of Mohurrum by distribution of milk, etc. to the poor;

(*e*) the celebration of ceremonies known as Moulood Shariff;

(*f*) to help poor and meritorious students professing Islam faith and studying in any recognised institution;

(*g*) to perform the annual fateha of myself and after my death, the members of my family;

(*h*) other religious, pious and/or charitable purposes as may be thought fit by the mutawalli from time to time or directed by a Court of Law including pecuniary reliefs or assistance to indigent members of my family.

3. The moneys which may be realised from my debtors mentioned in the said schedule hereto shall after payment of my debts, be invested in landed properties and such landed properties shall form a part of the estate hereby made wakf properties.

4. From the income of the said estate my sons AB, DE, GH and JK shall each receive a monthly sum of not more than Rs. 1,000 for the benefit of themselves and their respective families and descendants. As regards the respective amounts to be spent for the other purposes aforesaid, the mutawalli for the time being shall have absolute discretion to decide.

5. As regards the appointment of mutawalli and succession thereof it is declared that:

(*a*) I shall be the first mutawalli for my life.

(b) After my death AB and DE my sons shall be joint mutawallis and each of them shall be at liberty to appoint one of his lineal male descendants. Each mutawalli for the time being shall have the power of appointing his successor.

6. The mutawalli for the time being shall, as and by way of remuneration, be entitled to receive 20% of the net income or surplus of the wakf estate and to retain all the expenses of the management including the costs of all litigations.

7. In case of legal necessity and for the benefit of the wakf estate the mutawalli for the time being shall be at liberty, at his discretion to sell, mortgage, transfer, alienate, partition, and/or demise the wakf properties mentioned in the said schedule hereto or any part thereof subject to the prior sanction of the Board of Wakfs for the State of West Bengal and to invest the moneys thereby raised shall form part of the wakf estate but no purchaser, mortgagee, transferee, alinee, co-sharer or lessee of the said properties shall be concerned to enquire whether the respective sales, mortgages, transfers, alienations, partition or leases are necessary for or beneficial to the wakf estate or to see to the application of the proceeds thereof.

8. The dedication hereby made will bind me, my heirs, executors and representatives.

9. The properties hereby dedicated are valued at Rs. 10,00,000.

The Schedule above referred to

Part I

Part II

IN WITNESS WHEREOF I have executed these presents on the day, month and year first above-written.

Signed: Md. MAL
(As WAKIF)

WITNESSES:

Accepted: Md. MAL
(As Mutawalli)

Deed of Wakf for Public Purposes

THIS DEED OF WAKF is made on the .... day of .... 1999 by Md. MAL of .... (hereinafter called the WAKIF).

WHEREAS the WAKIF is the owner and in possession of the properties described in the Schedule hereunder and is desirous of dedicating the said properties in the service of Allah and to be used for charitable purposes.

AND WHEREAS the WAKIF has no wife or children and the other properties belonging to him are sufficient for his maintenance during his lifetime.

NOW THIS DEED of wakf witnesses as follows:

1. That I, the WAKIF, hereby transfer, dedicate to Allah and declare as wakf all that property more particularly described in the schedule annexed hereto, the approximate value whereof is Rs. 20 lakhs.

2. That I shall be the first mutawalli of the wakf property with power to nominate the next mutawalli and/or acting mutawalli in my temporary absence from Calcutta on Haj Pilgrimage. If I die during such pilgrimage or do not return for three years, he shall continue to act as such mutawalli and shall be deemed to be the mutawalli with the like powers and subject to the like obligations and duties as myself. All acts done or deeds executed shall be valid and binding as if the same had been done, exercised, executed, taken or had by me or a duly appointed lifetime mutawalli. In case I return from the pilgrimage within three years I shall resume the office of the first mutawalli and such nominated mutawalli shall be deemed *ipso facto* to be removed.

3. Each mutawalli whether nominated by the preceding mutawalli or appointed in the manner prescribed in the succeeding clause shall exercise the similar powers and be subject to the same duties and obligations and enjoy the equivalent privileges as are applicable to me or any succeeding mutawalli.

4. In case of any vacancy arising in the office of the mutawalli which cannot be filled up by nomination as aforesaid, the principal Civil Court of original jurisdiction shall be entitled to appoint a fit person professing the Islam faith of Hanafi School, after hearing such objections as may be raised by any beneficiary or person professing the Islam faith of the said School.

5. The mutawalli shall manage the wakf property to the best of his ability and may for such purpose engage or employ managers, agents, contractors, accountants or other assistants as may be conductive to the carrying on of the objects of the wakf efficiently and economically. The mutawalli may delegate any of his functions to a committee of persons subject, however, to the retention of the supervisory control by the mutawalli whose decision in all matters affecting the wakf shall prevail.

6. The income of the wakf property after defraying the expenses of its upkeep, management, repair and renovation shall be utilised for, among others, the following objects:

(*a*) payment to poor and deserving Muslims to enable them to perform Haj pilgrimage;

(*b*) feeding of the poor Muslims;

(*c*) supporting the blind, disabled and/or poor Muslims who are unable to earn their livelihood except by begging;

(*d*) providing sanitary habitation for poor Muslim families living in bustees, shanties and footpath.

7. The mutawalli may accept donations, grants, presents, offerings and other moneys and properties for the purpose of carrying out the object of the wakf and convert any property into any other kind for more effectively carrying out the objects of the wakf, wherever necessary, with the consent of the Board of Wakf.

The Schedule

IN WITNESS WHEREOF I have declared, dedicated and transferred the property mentioned in Schedule as wakf property and I have accepted and assumed control thereof as mutawalli thereof and I have executed these presents on the day, month and year first above-written.

WITNESSES: Sd/- Md. MAL

1. (WAKIF)

2. Sd/- Md. MAL

(Mutawalli)

NOTE: Directions for conduct of 'Fateha' at the graveyard and to use the house for those purposes are valid objects of a Wakf. Where the offerings of prayers are not confined to prayers at the tombs of the grantor or his family members and the grant was by the head of the order and related to prayers at a number of tombs in the graveyard it must be held that a Wakf of a public nature was created—*Wali Mohammed* v *Rahmat Bee* AIR 1999 SC 1136.

56

Will*

Some recent legislations in India. The Hindu Adoptions and Maintenance Act 1956, has for the first time codified the duty of the heirs to provide for maintenance to the dependants of the deceased out of property inherited by them. A Hindu wife is entitled to separate residence and maintenance in cases coming under s. 18 of the Act. A widowed daughter-in-law, illegitimate children, infirm parents and others all come as dependants. But s. 30 of the Hindu Succession Act gives a Hindu power to dispose of his estate by will. Under s. 27 of the former Act, a claim for maintenance is not a charge on the estate; it can therefore be defeated by a will.

Consolidating Act. The Indian Succession Act of 1925 consolidated the law relating to testamentary and intestate succession. It repealed *inter alia* the following enactments: (*i*) the Indian Succession Act (Act X of 1865); (*ii*) the Parsi Intestate Succession Act (Act XXI of 1865); (*iii*) the Hindu Wills Act (Act XXI of 1870); (*iv*) the Married Women's Property Act (Act III of 1874), s. 2; (*v*) the Probate and Administration Act (Act V of 1881), (Act VI of 1889), (Act II of 1890) and (Act VIII of 1903); (*vi*) the Succession Certificate Act (Act VII of 1889); and (*vii*) the Native Christian Administration of Estate Act (Act VII of 1901). The Indian Succession Act applies to whole of India but not in all cases to Hindus, Mahomedans, Buddhists, Sikhs or Jainas, *e.g.* Part II on Domicile, Part III of Marriage, s. 118, s. 69 and other provisions. Section 212 of the Indian Succession Act makes it obligatory on the part of Europeans, Armenians, Jews, East Indians to obtain Letters of Administration to establish title to the property of the deceased, but the section has no application to Hindus, Mahomedans, Buddhists, Sikhs, Jainas, Indian Christians and Parsis.

* Testamentary matters dealing with Probate, Letters of Administration and Succession Certificate have been dealt with in Chapter 53 also.

Muslim law. Among the Mahomedans the leading authority on the subject of will is Hedaya which was composed by Shaik Burhan-ud-Din Ali in the twelfth century who belonged to the Hanafi school of Mahomedan law. The Fatawa Alamgiri is another authority compiled in the seventeenth century during the reign of Emperor Aurangzab. So the idea of will was known to the Mahomedans from very ancient times long before the arrival of the British in India. The Indian Succession Act 1925, does not apply to the Mahomedans. So a will is valid and effective in Mahomedan law even not attested.[1] In Mahomedan law no particular writing is necessary to make a valid will not even any particular form, so long the declaration is sufficiently clear. A letter by a testator shortly before his death containing directions as to disposal of his estate after death was held by the Privy Council as to constitute a valid will.[2] Another special feature of the Mahomedan will is that the testamentary power is limited to one-third of the surplus estate after payment of funeral expenses and debt and no bequest to any heir is valid in the absence of the consent of the other heirs after the death of the testator. A Mahomedan will is admissible in evidence after due proof although no probate has been obtained and further no Letters of Administration are necessary to establish any right to the estate of a deceased Mahomedan except as regards debts due to the same.[3] The executor of the will of a Mahomedan, if he accepts the office from the date of the testator's death, has power to alienate the estate for the purpose of administration. A child in the womb and a child, *i.e.* son adopted by the widow of a deceased after his death, are considered as persons in existence at the time of death in Hindu law, but in Mahomedan law a child in the womb loses the legacy unless born within six months from the date of the will.[4] Muslim law does not recognise adoption.

Characteristics of a will. In ascertaining whether a particular document is a will or not, one of the tests is whether it is a declaration of the intention of the testator as to disposal of his property after his death and secondly whether it is revocable or not. The irrevocability of a document is inconsistent with a will.[5]

Requisites of a valid will

(a) *Capacity of the testator.* The testator must be a person in full possession of his senses and power able to make a testament and not disabled for any special cause in respect of his person, mind, condition or the property concerning which the testament is to be made. Special disability of infants,

1 In re, *Abdus Satar* 7 Bom LR 558.
2 *Mazhar Husen* v *Bodha Bibi* (1898)21 All 91.
3 Section 212(2) of the Indian Succession Act.
4 Mulla: *Mahomedan Law,* 19th Ed., p. 107.
5 Section 62 of the Indian Succession Act; in re, *Marsland* (1939) WN 251; (1939)1 Ch 820.

lunatics and married women shall always be borne in mind.[6] A man cannot by will or otherwise dispose of his dead-body or that of any other person.[7]

(b) *Intention to dispose.* As it is the free mind and not the words that give life to a testament, so a free mind and clear conscience to dispose, rather a firm determination, are essential for validity of a will, *e.g.* if a man rashly, unadvisably, incidentally and not seriously write down something, that is no testament and is never so regarded. Mind must be free, conscience clear and not moved by fear, fraud and flattery or undue influence, solicitation of other or other unworthy motive.

(*c*) The form and order of law should be observed regarding signature, attestation, etc.

(*d*) If the will is in a language not known to the testator, the same should be read over and explained to him by some competent person so that he may fully understand the nature, contents and implication of the document and the person so explaining shall make an endorsement on the will to that effect.

Distinction—Executor and Trustee. The words "executor" and "trustee" are mostly synonymous. A trustee is regarded as an executor and an executor is regarded as a trustee.[8] Under s. 3 of the Indian Trusts Act II of 1882, a trustee is a person who enjoys the faith and confidence of the author of the "trust" and under s. 5 of the same Act a trust of any property may also be created even by the will of the author of the trust. So it follows that when a trust is created under the will of the testator where he appoints his executors also as the trustees of the trust or he appoints executors to administer his general estate and trustees to administer the trust estate. In cases where the residue of the estate is bequeathed on trust and separate trustees are appointed to administer the same the executors after administering the general estate hand over the residue to the trustees appointed by the will; but if however the executors are themselves appointed trustees, then and in such an event the executors become trustees when the estate is free and cleared off payment of the debts and discharge of legacies.[9] An application for his removal under s. 30 of the Indian Succession Act 1925, is not maintainable.[10] The other distinction between an executor and a trustee in this regard is that an executor after once accepting the office of an executor cannot retire by appointing someone in his place without fully administering the estate, but a trustee can retire by appointing a new trustee under s. 72 of

6 Section 59 of the Indian Succession Act.
7 Halsbury's *Laws of England*, 2nd Ed., vol. 15, p. 207.
8 In re, *Robinson* (1951)1 Ch 198.
9 In re, *Smith* 43 Ch D 302.
10 In goods of *Sarnath Sanyal* AIR 1949 All 93.

the Indian Trusts Act subject however to approval of the principal court of original jurisdiction.[11] An executor becomes a trustee after assenting to a legacy until delivery of possession.

Another distinction between an executor and a trustee is that an executor or an administrator may buy the property of the deceased. It is not a breach of trust provided a fair price is paid and the sale is an otherwise regular nevertheless it may be the subject to inquiry by a Court of Equity[12] which provides that the sale is voidable at the instance of a person interested in the property. Nevertheless such purchase is looked upon with suspicion.[13] This section does not admit any exception even though the sale is made with the sanction of the court. But a trustee for sale cannot buy the property at all. It is a breach of trust irrespective of the fact as to whether a fair price is paid or not. Section 52 of the Indian Trusts Act is explicit on this point. The above rule extends to dealings between a director and his company surviving partner and the share of the deceased person and to fiduciary relations. It was held by the Privy Council in *Raja Peary Mohon Mukherjee* v *Manohar Mukherjee,*[14] that a *shebait* also cannot purchase the property of the deity. The only protection afforded in such cases is by s. 96 of the Trust Act which is applicable to constructive trustees or resulting trustees as pointed out in *Raja of Mamnod* v *Arunachalam*.[15] Section 96 of the Indian Trust Act 1882, is controlled by and should be read subject to s. 59A of the Transfer of Property Act. It will not protect any person in cases of evasion of any law.[16] But a trustee for sale cannot buy the property at all. It is a breach of trust irrespective of the fact as to whether a fair price is paid or not. Section 52 of the Indian Trusts Act is explicit.

The property of the deceased testator vests in all the executors and if there are more than one executor, all of them together become legal representatives of the testator. The estate of the deceased cannot therefore be controlled or represented by one of the legal representatives of the deceased to the exclusion of other legal representatives.[17]

A further distinction is as regards accounts to be rendered by executors and trustees. In the case of an executor a suit for account of the estate is barred after three years under Art. 113 of the Limitation Act 1963. But there is no limitation against a trustee for following the trust property or proceeds

11 See also Lewin on *Trust,* 12th Ed., p. 932 and 15th Ed., p. 416.
12 Section 310 of the Indian Succession Act 1925.
13 Willams on *Executors*, 12th Ed., pp. 567 & 1207.
14 26 CWN 138.
15 38 Mad 321.
16 *Abdul Ghafoor* v *Md. Paharia* AIR 1957 Pat 136.
17 *K. Leelavathy* v *P.V. Gangadharan* AIR 1999 SC 1267.

thereof[18] or for an account of the trust property. Under s. 10 of the Limitation Act there is no bar of limitation even against an executor if he is a trustee for a specific purpose.

Will void. A will or any part of a will, the making of which has been caused by fraud or coercion, or undue influence or by such importunity as takes away the free agency of the testator, is void.[19]

Limited power of disposition. A man can only dispose of by a will his property which could be alienated by gift *inter vivos*. The right to perform religious services or the shebaitship of any religious endowment cannot be disposed of by will.[1] A Hindu governed by the Dayabhaga or Bengal School of Hindu law can make a will both in respect of his self-acquired and also ancestral estate, whereas a Hindu governed by the Mitakshara School of Hindu law could make a will only in respect of his self-acquired or separate estate until 1956. Section 30 of the Hindu Succession Act 1956, gave the right to such a person to make a will even in respect of his coparcenery interest. Under s. 14(1) of the Hindu Succession Act (Act XXX of 1956), any property possessed by a female Hindu whether acquired before or after the commencement of the Act is her absolute property. She is therefore fully competent to make any will unless of course the will, award or other instrument by virtue whereof she acquires the same, expressly provides for a restricted estate.[2] The Supreme Court held that if the acquisition is by virtue of, or in recognition of, any existing right, she will have an absolute estate notwithstanding the restrictive clause.[3]

A Mahomedan cannot dispose of his property by a will to an heir unless the other heirs consent to the bequest after the death of the testator, and if the bequest be to a non-heir, it will be valid only to the extent of one-third of the surplus of his estate after payment of funeral expenses and debts, and the bequest in excess of the legal third cannot take effect unless the heirs' consent thereto after the death of the testator. No absolute freedom, no will can deprive wife's right of maintenance.[4] Although a person not otherwise disqualified can dispose of his properties according to his wish and desire nevertheless he does not enjoy absolute freedom, in the matter inasmuch as certain things are prohibited in law as being against public policy though not punishable by law nor immoral, e.g. (*i*) he cannot convert an absolute estate into a life or limited estate as regards gifts with restraints on alienation (s. 138); (*ii*) gifts against bankruptcy laws;[5] (*iii*) condition opposed to the

18 Sections 62 and 63 of the Indian Trust Act.
19 Section 61 of the Indian Succession Act 1925.
1 *Angurbala* v *Debdutta* AIR 1947 Cal 278.
2 Section 14(2) of the Indian Succession Act.
3 *Vaddeboyina* v *Vaddeboyina* AIR 1977 SC 1944.
4 *Pritambhai* v *Sundermall* (1945)1 MLJ 58.
5 *Bilson* v *Crofts* LR 15 Eq 314.

policy of marriage laws—a condition restraining the marriage of the donee is void but not a partial restraint on marriage; (*iv*) conditions against public policy of administration.[6] Moreover he cannot create any estate unknown in law.[7] Furthermore he cannot create any estate in favour of an unborn person except to the extent permitted under ss. 112 and 113 of the Indian Succession Act nor any perpetuity except as provided under s. 114 of the said Act. It was held by the Supreme Court in *Bairang Bahadur Singh* v *Bakhtrey*,[8] that the restraint on the power of alienation depends upon the whole tenor of the will.

Revocation of wills—power of appointment.[9] A will is liable to be revoked or altered by the maker of it at any time when he is competent to dispose of his property by another will.

A will containing bequest in favour of charity or for religious use also stands revoked in case of death of the maker earlier than 12 months and who has a nephew or niece or other nearer relation.[10] Such a will is to be deposited with the Registrar.[11] This section, however, does not apply to Hindus.

A will made in exercise of a power of appointment, when the property over which the power of appointment is exercised would not, in default of such appointment, pass to his or her executor administrator, or to the person entitled in case of intestacy. Where a man is invested with power to determine the disposition of property of which he is not the owner, he is said to have power to appoint over such property.[12]

No other act, e.g. birth or adoption of a son which might influence the mind of a testator, operates as revocation of a will.[13] Even the gift or sale of the property disposed of under any will does not so operate, though it makes the will infructuous.[14]

Execution and attestation[15]

Execution. Every testator not being a soldier employed in an expedition or engaged in actual warfare, or an airman so employed or engaged, or a mariner at sea, must execute his will according to the following rules:

6 Sengupta's *Indian Succession Act*, 3rd Ed., p. 225.
7 *Tagore* v *Tagore* 18 WR 359 (PC).
8 AIR 1953 SC 7.
9 Sections 69 and 70 of the Indian Succession Act 1925.
10 Section 118 of the Indian Succession Act.
11 Part IX, ss. 42-48 of the Indian Registration Act.
12 Section 69 of the Indian Succession Act.
13 *Mir Syed Hossain* v *Taiyabba Begum* 26 IC 457.
14 *Asanand* v *Rozni* 2 Lah LJ 178.
15 Section 63 of the Indian Succession Act.

(1) The testator must sign in his own handwriting affix his mark to the will or it must be signed by some other person in his presence and by his direction.

(2) The signature or mark of the testator, or the signature of the person signing for him, must be so placed that it will appear that it was intended thereby to give effect to the writing as a will. In the event the testator though literate cannot sign the will in his own handwriting the person signing the will shall also sign an endorsement to that effect.[16]

(3) The will must be attested by two or more independent witnesses each of whom has seen the testator to sign the will in the presence and by the direction of the testator, or has received from the testator a personal acknowledgement of his signature or mark or of the signature of such other person; and each of the witnesses must sign the will in the presence of the testator; but it will not be necessary that more than one witness be present at the same time, and no particular form of attestation will be necessary. It is not necessary that any technical words or terms of art be used in a will, but only that the wording be such that the intention of the testator can be known therefrom. Wills made by Mahomedans may be oral. Even if in writing, no particular form is necessary so long the intention is clear.[17] A letter by a testator containing instructions as to disposition of his estate was held to constitute a valid will.[18]

A blind man is incapable of attesting a will.[19] A solicitor attesting a will will lose his fees for work to be done in connection with the estate where such fees are provided for in the will as he becomes a beneficiary in such a case.[20] This provision does not apply to India.

Registration of the will. It is not absolutely necessary that the will shall be registered; nevertheless it is also prudent to have the same registered. In case the original will is lost, probate may easily be obtained of a certified copy of the same.

A testator may deposit his will for safe custody with the Registrar[1] of which the court may require production. Then the Registrar will open it and send the same to the court after copying the contents in Book 3.[2] A will requires registration if it creates a family settlement of the properties of the testator.

16 Section 3(56) of the General Clauses Act.
17 *Mahomed Ali* v *Ahmed Buksh* (1876)25 WR 121 (PC).
18 *Mazhar Husen* v *Bodha Bibi* (1898)21 All 91 (PC).
19 Re, *Limond* (1915)2 Ch 240; 84 LJ Ch 833.
20 Re, *Pooley* 40 Ch D 1.
1 Section 46 of the Indian Registration Act.
2 Section 294 of the Indian Succession Act.

Obliteration, interlineation or alteration. No obliteration, interlineation or other alteration made in a will after the execution thereof can have effect, except so far as the words or meaning of the will have been rendered illegible or indiscernible, unless such alteration has been executed in like manner as hereinbefore is required for the execution of the will; provided that the will so altered will be deemed to be duly executed if the signature of the testator and of the witness be made in the margin or on some other part of the will opposite or near to such alteration, or at the foot or end of or opposite to a memorandum referring to such alteration, and written at the end or some other part of the will.[3]

Benefit to attesting witness. A will is not to be deemed to be insufficiently attested by reason of any benefit thereby given, either by way of bequest or by way of appointment, to any person attesting it, or to his or her wife or husband; but the bequest or appointment will be void so far as it concerns the person so attesting, or the wife or husband of such person, or any person claiming under either of them. In England, under s. 15 of the Wills Act 1837, a beneficial gift to an attesting witness or to his wife or her husband is also void though the will is in other respect good and valid.[4] A solicitor attesting a will, which provides for his professional charges for work to be done in respect of the estate, loses the same.[5] Section 67 of the Indian Succession Act does not apply to Hindus, Buddhists etc. So the above law is not applicable in their cases.[6]

A legatee under a will does not lose his legacy by attesting a codicil which confirms the will.[7]

Vesting of legacy. If a legacy is given in general terms without specifying the time when it is to be paid, the legatee has a vested interest in it from the day of the death of the testator and, if he dies without having received it, it will pass to his legal representatives.[8] The legacy vests in the legatee with effect from the death of the testator even though possession is postponed. In the result on the death of the legatee his legal representative gets the legacy.[9]

Residuary legatee. A residuary legatee can be constituted by words that show an intention on the part of the testator that the person designated shall take the surplus or residue of his property.

3 Section 71 of the Indian Succession Act 1925.
4 Re, *Craven* (1908)24 TLR 750.
5 Re, *Pooley* 40 Ch D 1.
6 *Bai Gangabai* v *Bhugwandas* 29 Bom 530.
7 Section 67 of the Indian Succession Act 1925.
8 Section 104 of the Indian Succession Act.
9 Section 119 of the Indian Succession Act.

Under a residuary bequest, the legatee is entitled to the property belonging to the testator at the time of his death, of which he has not made any testamentary disposition which is capable of taking effect.

When legacy lapses—when legacy does not lapse. A legacy vests in the legatee immediately upon the death of the testator no matter when it is to be paid or delivered unless the same is contingent. If the legatee is not the child of the testator or other lineal descendant[1] the legacy cannot take effect, but will lapse and form part of the residue of the testator's property, unless it appears by the will that the testator intended that the same would go to his heirs or some other person.[2] So the representatives of the legatee are not entitled to the legacy unless he (legatee) survived the testator. If a legacy is given to legatees in words which show that the testator intended to give them distinct share of it, then, if any legatee dies before the testator, so much of the legacy as was intended for him will fall into the residue of the testator's property. When a share which lapses is a part of general residue bequeathed by the will, that share will go as undisposed of. The doctrine of lapse applies to contingent legacy.[3] It lapses on the death of the legatee before the testator whether the contingency happens or not. It also applies to conditional legacy and power of appointment exercised by will. It was held that when an annuity is payable *putra pautradi krame,* the legacy lapses on the death of the legatee unless the same is charged on any specific property.[4]

If a legacy is given to two persons jointly and one of them dies before the testator, the other legatee takes the whole. Where a bequest has been made to any child or other lineal descendant of the testator, and the legatee dies in the lifetime of the testator, but any lineal descendant of his survives the testator, the bequest will not lapse, but it will take effect as if the death of the legatee had happened immediately after the death of the testator, unless a contrary intention appears by the will.[5] This section, *i.e.* s. 109 of the Indian Succession Act, is based on s. 33 of the original English Wills Act 1837 (1 Vict C 26) which prolongs the life of the testator by legal fiction for the limited purpose of giving effect to the will. The expression "lineal descendant" includes all descendants, male and female.[6] When a bequest is made to confer an absolute estate in the beneficiary any subsequent clause

1 Section 109 of the Indian Succession Act.
2 Section 105 of the Indian Succession Act—See also Williams on *Executor*, 13th Ed., p. 644.
3 Section 124 of the Indian Succession Act.
4 *Jagadish* v *Rai Pade* 22 Pat LT 396; AIR 1941 Pat 458.
5 Section 109 of the Indian Succession Act.
6 *Bhimnath* v *Tara* 33 CWN 837 (PC); AIR 1929 PC 162.

in the will as to bequest of any of the property to any other person in the event the first legatee dies without dealing with the same is inoperative.[7]

Where a bequest is made to one person for the benefit of another, the legacy does not lapse by the death, in the testator's lifetime, of the person to whom the bequest is made.[8]

Privileged will. Any soldier being in an expedition or engaged in actual warfare or an airman so employed or engaged, or any mariner at sea, if he has completed the age of 18 years, can dispose of his property by a *privileged will* made in accordance with the following rules:

(1) The will can be written wholly by the testator with his own hand. In such a case it need not be signed or attested.

(2) It can be written wholly or in part by another person and signed by the testator. In such a case it need not be attested.

(3) If the instrument purporting to be a will is written wholly or in part by another man and not signed by the testator, it will be deemed to be his will if it is shown that it was written by the testator's directions, or that he recognised it as his will.

(4) If it appears on the face of the instrument that the execution of it in the manner intended by the testator was not completed, the instrument will not, by reason of that circumstances, be invalid, provided that his non-execution of it can be reasonably ascribed to some cause other than the abandonment of the testamentary intentions expressed in the instrument.

(5) If the soldier, airman or mariner has written the instrument for the preparation of his will, but has died before it could be prepared and executed, such instructions will be considered to constitute his will.

(6) If the soldier, airman or mariner has, in the presence of two witnesses, given verbal instructions for the preparation of his will and they have been reduced into writing in his lifetime, but if he has died before the instrument could be prepared and executed, such instructions will be considered to constitute his will, although they may not have been reduced into writing in his presence, nor read over to him.

(7) The soldier, airman or mariner can make a will by word of mouth by declaring his intentions before two witnesses present at the same time.

(8) A will made by word of mouth will be null and void at the expiration of one month after the testator being still alive, has ceased to be entitled to make a privileged will.

Codicils. It is a maxim that no person can die with two testaments yet any number of instruments all clearly testamentary may be admitted into

7 *Lalit Mohon Mondal* v *Prafullo Kumar Mondal* 86 CWN 396.

8 Section 110 of the Indian Succession Act 1925.

probate.[9] So by a codicil a testator can appoint additional executor, replace the deceased executor, vary appointment and provide for omissions in the will. A codicil is defined in s. 2(*b*) of the Indian Succession Act.

A codicil means an instrument made in relation to a will and explaining altering or adding to its disposition and is deemed to form part of the will; the law applicable to wills is also applicable to codicil, except that a legatee under a will does not lose his legacy by attesting a codicil which confirms the will[10] and the rules governing the execution and attestation of both are the same.[11]

Void Bequests

Bequest to religious or charitable uses. No man having a nephew or niece or any nearer relative has power to bequeath any property to religious or charitable use except by a will executed not less than 12 months before the death and deposited within six months from its execution in some place provided by law for the safe custody of the wills of living persons.[12] The procedure for depositing will has been prescribed in Part X, ss. 42 to 46 of the Indian Registration Act (XVI of 1908).

This law is not applicable in the case of Hindu and Mahomedan bequests or religious or charitable uses. The court adopts a benevolent rule and allows more latitude in cases of gifts or bequest to charities, the rule being that (*i*) the organisation must be in existence; (*ii*) object definitely benevolent certain and clear.[13] The charitable objects must not be mixed up with other objects as otherwise the bequest will fail on account of uncertainty.[14] Another rule is that the court cannot make a will for the author of the trust if he has left the language vague or uncertain.[15]

Effect of direction for accumulation. Where the terms of a will direct that the income arising from any property shall be accumulated either wholly or in part during any period longer than a period of 18 years from the death of the testator, such direction will, save as hereinafter provided, be void to the extent to which the period during the accumulation is directed exceeds the aforesaid period and, at the end of such period of 18 years, the property

9 Williams on *Executors,* 11th Ed., vol. I, p. 116.
10 Section 67 of the Indian Succession Act does not apply to Hindus, Buddhists etc.
11 Prideaux's *Conveyancing,* 24th Ed., vol. 3, p. 589.
12 Section 118 of the Indian Succession Act and it is based upon the Statute of Mortmain (9 Geo 11 e 34) which has no application in India—*Mayor of Lyons* v *East India Co. Ltd.* 1 MIA 175.
13 Section 89 of the Indian Succession Act.
14 *Blair* v *Auncan* 1902 AC 37.
15 *Grimmond* v *Grimmond* 1905 AC 124. See also Tudor on *Charities,* 5th Ed., p. 11.

and the income thereof will be disposed of as if the period, during which the accumulation has been directed to be made, had elapsed.[16]

The above provision will not affect any direction for accumulation for the purposes of—

(*i*) The payment of debts of the testator or any other person taking any interest under the will, or

(*ii*) the provision of portions for children or remoter issue of the testator or of any other person taking any interest under the will, or

(*iii*) the preservation or maintenance of any property bequeathed and such direction can be made accordingly.

Rule against perpetuity. No bequest is valid whereby the vesting of the thing bequeathed may be delayed beyond the lifetime of one or more persons living at the testator's death and the minority of some persons who shall be in existence at the expiration of that period, and to whom, if he attains full age, the thing bequeathed is to belong.[17]

English legal policy always favoured the right of free alienation and has endeavoured to give effect to that principle in every department of law. Perpetuity means creation of an inalienable and indestructible interest, that is to say, an interest which does not vest until a remote period. It is not the same thing as a rule of possibility.[18] The Rule in *Shelley's* case[19] laid down that the expression "heirs in fee" or "in tail" in a conveyance or gift of a freehold estate are words of limitation to the estate of the purchaser or donee, *i.e.* "words which mark the estate to be given to the grantee" and not "words of gift conferring any interest upon his heirs". In India we are familiar with the expression "heirs, executors, administrators and representatives" and in Bengal *putra pautradi krame*. These do not confer, any benefit upon them. The rule has been abolished by s. 131 of the Law of Property Act 1925. The English Rule was modified with effect from 1st January 1926, by s. 163 of the Law of property Act 1925. As settled now, it fixes the life or lives in existence and 21 years thereafter.[1]

All charitable gifts create an inalienable and a permanent interest. So charitable trusts are not subject to rule against perpetuity if the vesting is not delayed beyond the statutory period.[2]

16 Section 117 of the Indian Succession Act.
17 Section 114 of the Indian Succession Act.
18 Section 114 of the Indian Succession Act.
19 *Shelley's* case 1 Rep. 94 (104); Williams on *Real Property*, 20th Ed., p. 336.
1 Grey on *Perpetuities*, 3rd Ed., p. 174.
2 *Colgan* v *Adm. General* 15 Mad 424.

Bequest to unborn persons. The law on this subject is that ordinarily a Hindu cannot make a bequest to a person not in existence at the time of his death. This was laid down in the *Tagore's* case.[3] It is no longer good law. The doctrine was modified by the three Acts—Hindu Transfer and Bequest Act (Act I of 1914), Hindu Disposal of Property Act of 1916 and lastly by Hindu Transfer of Bequests (City of Madras Act 1921). The legal position as it stood after the amendment was that no such bequest shall be invalid by reason of the fact that the proposed legatee was not in existence on the date of death of the testator. The above rule is subject to certain exceptions: (1) A child in the womb is considered a living person.[4] (2) Bequest to a person answering any particular description with reference to his relationship with the testator where possession is deferred until a time after the death by reason of a prior bequest provided he comes into existence meanwhile.[5] (3) Bequest to a person though not born at the time of the testator's death which is subject to a prior bequest is valid provided the same comprises the entire remaining interest.[6] Bequest unless hit by the rule against perpetuity.[7] An unborn person may be the beneficiary of a charitable trust created under a will.

Bequest in favour of an idol not in existence. The Calcutta High Court held that a Hindu cannot make a gift in favour of an idol not consecrated at the time of his death.[8] A Special Bench, however, held that a gift or devise in favour of an idol to be consecrated by the executor or other person who is in existence is not a gift or devise in favour of an unborn person and so is valid.[9]

Instructions for drawing a will. The draftsman of a will must be very cautious. He should keep and preserve the Instruction Notes made before starting with the preparation of the draft. It is always better to have the Instruction Notes signed by the party. In order to effect a valid disposition of property, which is the subject-matter of the will, it is necessary in so far as movables are concerned that it shall be in conformity with the law of the testator's domicile and, in the case of immovables, law of the country in which the property is situate.[10] The other factors to be considered are *inter alia* (*i*) testamentary capacity of the testator; (*ii*) his state of mind, readiness and willingness to make the will; (*iii*) power of understanding the nature, contents and effect of the will; (*iv*) heritable character of the property—whether the

3 18 WR 359, 371 (PC).
4 *Okhoymoney* v *Nilmony* 15 Cal 282.
5 Section 112 of the Indian Succession Act.
6 Section 113 of the Indian Succession Act.
7 Section 114 of the Indian Succession Act.
8 *Upendra* v *Hem Chandra* 25 Cal 405.
9 *Bhupati Nath Smrititirtha's* case 37 Cal 128.
10 Section 5 of the Indian Succession Act.

same is legally bequeathable; (*v*) legality of the interest created under the will; and (*vi*) legal competency of the devisees to accept the devises. An unprivileged will shall always be in writing, duly signed by the testator and attested by at least tow witnesses.[11] All erasures and alterations require the signatures of the testator and also the attesting witnesses.[12]

A will is a most solemn document. It is also a sacred one as by it a dead man entrusts to the living the carrying out of his wishes and desire.[13] The preparation of a will is an intelligent work on the part of the draftsman. He should, therefore, study carefully laws relating to Real Properties and the provisions of Part VI, ss. 57 to 120 of the Indian Succession Act and also Hindu Succession Act, Hindu Adoptions and Maintenance Act before drafting the will.

Although under s. 85 of the Indian Succession Act, the court always tries to give a rational construction to the words of a will as far as possible and lawful nevertheless it is the duty of the draftsman to avoid ambiguity and deficiency as under the rule of construction of wills, external evidence as to intention of the testator is not admissible.[14]

Probate. Probate of a will can be granted only to a person not being minor or a lunatic but not to any association[15] unless it satisfies the conditions prescribed by the rules made by the State Government. Probate or Letter of Administration can be granted to Banaras Hindu University.[16] Probate once granted authenticates the will against the world. It is a complete answer to the challenge of the authority of the executor as regards his dealings with the estate of the deceased in due course of administration.

Bequests and Devises to the Solicitor by his Client

GENERALLY

The burden of proof that a testator was capable of making a will, and knew and approved its contents, is in all cases upon the party propounding it; and though in general a presumption of capacity arises from the fact that the will is in ordinary form and of knowledge and approval from the fact of execution yet in the case of a solicitor or other person (for there is no special rule applicable to solicitors who prepare or procure a will under which he takes some benefit the court will require affirmative proof) which is to be most satisfactorily furnished by showing that the nature, contents and effects

11 Section 63 of the Indian Succession Act.

12 Section 71 of the Indian Succession Act.

13 *Ram Gopal Lal* v *Aipina Kumar* 49 IA 413 (417); see also 27 CWN 485.

14 In re, *Follett Barclays Bank Ltd.* v *Dovell* (1954)3 All ER 478.

15 Section 235 of the Indian Succession Act.

16 *Banaras Hindu University* v *Gouri Dutt* 1949 ALJ 523.

of the will were read over and explained to the testator the same having been prepared in accordance with his or her instructions and also of the testator's knowledge and approval.[17]

Where, therefore, the client is intending to give some benefit to the solicitor, it is always prudent that the latter should insist on the will being prepared by another solicitor, and should endeavour his best to ensure the preservation of evidences that the will was read over explained to and approved by the testator and of the instructions from which the will was prepared though other evidence may, of course, suffice.[18]

The court refused to decree specific performance in favour of a vendor whose title depended on a will drawn by a solicitor in favour of himself, until the validity of the will had been conclusively established[19] the purchaser had to bear the costs ultimately.

Certain general Rules to be followed.

(1) English rules or authorities have a persuasive value in India.

(2) No distinction in gifts, or wills, or inheritance between movable and immovable property is made in India.

In construing a will a benignant construction must be put. When there is an absolute grant of property repugnant restrictions are rejected. Where an estate of inheritance unknown to law is created it is not wholly void, it is enforceable to the extent allowed by law, namely, a life estate on the first taker can be given effect to. Life estate can be created by will.

(3) Under Dayabhaga School the extent of testamentary power extends to ancestral and acquired property movable and immovable. Even in the Mitakshara School one may alienate his undivided share for consideration or may make testamentary disposition thereof but cannot make a gift of undivided share.[20]

(4) A child expectant is considered to be in existence.

(5) The law of perpetuities cannot be violated by the bequests contained in the will.

(6) The intention of a testator must be gathered from the words of his will. Courts are not at liberty to invent for him a new will. Least trend of an intention in the will to create an ordinary estate of inheritance will be given effect to. But, where such intention is absent an estate of inheritance cannot be conferred on even the first taker of the life estate.

17 *Wintte* v *Nye* (1959)1 All ER 552 (HL).
18 In re, *Estate of Austin* (1929)73 Salgo 545.
19 *Grove* v *Bastard* (1848)2 Ph 619.
20 Section 30 of the Hindu Succession Act.

(7) Where there were strained relations between the testator and his relatives he would be justified in making the neighbours, who looked after him in his last days, beneficiaries and cannot be condemned as suspicious circumstance. Old persons usually put thumb impression instead of signature and this also cannot be a suspicious circumstance.[1] Where a will provided that on the death of the testator and his wife the properties would be enjoyed by their daughter and on the latter's death the properties would go to her children, the daughter gets only a life-estate.[2]

(8) Application to revoke probate or letters of administration is to be treated as a miscellaneous application and not a suit and can be disposed of summarily or after giving an opportunity to both the parties to adduce evidence and consideration thereof. If it is treated as a suit the applicant cannot prove the will and at the same time cannot contend that the will was not validly executed.[3]

(9) Non-mentioning of natural heirs in the will or any reason assigned for exclusion of natural heirs are no grounds for making the will suspicious. Attestation of will cannot be doubted on the ground that no person was called for from locality to witness the will.[4] Unrebutted testimony of attesting witness proving the will as validly executed entitled to probate.[5]

(10) Trial Court would be wrong if it directs a petition for probate to be a contested matter and to be registered as civil suit and court-fees deposited.[6]

When a man is married and still keeps company with another woman the status of the second woman, married to him or not, is that of a kept mistress and on the man's death, the first lady not having been divorced, the second woman cannot succeed to his estate and her application for Succession Certificate is not maintainable .[7]

(11) Proceeding for restoration of possession against licensee for restoration of possession under s. 41 of the Presidency Small Cause Courts Act 1882, will not abate on the death of the licensee as the cause of action is not personal and does not die with the death of the party.[8]

(12) Trusts of various kinds are recognised and acted on in India.

(13) A trust does not fail if one or more trustees decline to act.

1 *Misri Lal* v *Daulat Devi* AIR 1997 SC 3819.
2 *S. Rajagopal* v *Hamasaveni* AIR 1992 SC 704.
3 *Nalini Navin* v *Chandravadan* AIR 1997 SC 1055.
4 *Dhyan Chand* v *Savitri Devi* AIR 1998 HP 37.
5 *Surinder* v *State* AIR 1998 Del 140.
6 *Umesh Vashwani* v *Ratna* AIR 1998 Raj 84.
7 *Nimbamma* v *Rathnamma* AIR 1999 Kant 226.
8 *Ha Malbari* v *Nasiruddin* AIR 1998 SC 411.

FORMS

Will Bequeathing all Properties to One Person

THIS IS THE last will and/or codicil, notwithstanding any will made by me at any time heretofore made and I declare this to be my will. It will be effective after my death. It is my wish and desire that after my death my wife (or son), CD, shall be entitled to all my estate and effects thereof absolutely and forever.

I, accordingly, declare him/her as the sole beneficiary and universal legatee of my this will.

I hereby leave, give, devise and bequeath absolutely and forever to my said wife (or son), CD, her (or his) heirs, executors or administrators, for her (or his) use and benefit, absolutely and forever, all my property, assets and credits, both movable and immovable, of whatsoever character or wheresoever situate including all reversion, expectancy and future assets, if any, acquired by me and I hereby appoint her (or him), the said CD, sole executrix (or executor) of this my will who will be entitled to obtain probate without being required to furnish any security. Dated this .... day of .... 19......... .

IN WITNESS, I have hereunto set and subscribed my hand and signature this .... day of .... 19......... .

Signed[9] by the within-named testator as his last will and testament in our presence all being present at the same time. Thereafter at his request and in his presence and in the presence of one another we subscribed our respective names

Signature of witnesses

Will with Legacies, Residue to One Person

THIS IS THE LAST will and testament of me, AB, of etc., I hereby revoke all wills by me at any time heretofore made and declare this to be my last will. This will be effective after my death and carried out to its terms.

9 Section 63 of the Indian Succession Act as to execution and attestation of unprivileged wills.

(1) I appoint CD of, etc., to be sole executor of my this will and the trustee of my estate.

(2) I direct that my said executor shall so soon as convenient after obtaining probate pay for discharge and satisfy all testamentary expenses and my just debts and liabilities.

(3) I accordingly leave, bequeath and give a sum of Rupees .... to my grandson, EF and my gold watch and the whole of my library with its use and enjoyment to my friend, GH.

(4) Subject to the above specific legacies I give, leave and bequeath the rest and residue of my estate, movable and immovable, including future assets if any acquired by me hereafter absolutely and forever unto and to the use of my son XY, his heirs, executors, administrators or assigns.

IN WITNESS WHEREOF I have hereunto set and subscribed my hand and signature this .... day of .... 1999.

Signed by the within-named Testator as his last Will and Testament in our presence all being present at the same time. Thereafter at the request of the Testator and in his presence and in the presence of one another. We, XY and MN, subscribed our respective names

Signed, sealed and delivered by AB the TESTATOR

Signed by XY in the presence of AB the TESTATOR and MN

Signed by MN, in the presence of TESTATOR and XY

Will with Legacies for Children

THIS IS THE LAST will and testament of me, AB of, etc. This will be operative with effect from my death. I hereby revoke all wills and codicils by me heretofore made.

1. I hereby appoint CD of, etc., and EF of, etc., as the executors of my this will, trustees of my estate and also the guardians of the person and property of my minor children, GH and IJ, during the respective periods of their minority. In case any one of the executors fails to obtain probate or

act as trustee and guardian, the other shall act as the sole executor, trustee and guardian.

2. I direct my said executors or executor and trustees or trustee to pay out of my estate a sum of Rs. 1 lakh to X and a further sum of Rs.1 lakh to Y for their absolute use and benefit and I hereby give, leave and bequeath the same unto and in their favour absolutely. It is my further wish and desire that a sum of Rupees 1 lakh should be paid for the expenses of the marriage of MN of, etc., should I not celebrate *his* or *her* marriage during my lifetime and I direct my said executors or executor and trustees or trustee to pay the same accordingly on the occasion of *his* or *her* marriage.

3. Subject to what are hereinbefore stated, my said executors or executor and trustees or trustee shall, after defraying the costs, charges and expenses of administration, hold and possess the entire estate, both movable and immovable, in trust for my children for their maintenance and support until the youngest of them shall attain the age of 21 years.

4. My said executors or executor and trustees or trustee shall be entitled to convert the movables only into money which should be invested in the purchase of Government securities or trustees securities or in loans against the first mortgage of houses and lands or in any other good and sound investments with power to draw interest, dividends, etc. to alter and vary the same at their discretion such investment or investments into other investment or investments of the same or like nature, to be held upon trust as aforesaid.

5. My said executors or executor and trustees or trustee shall look after, manage and keep and maintain in good repair and develop all my properties, and realise the rents, profits and other income thereof.

6. I further direct that my said executors or executor and trustees or trustee shall after paying all my just debts, testamentary and other expenses and the legacies hereinbefore recited, and, after providing for the costs, charges and expenses of the management and development of the said properties and for payment of the revenue and taxes spend the surplus of the income for all the necessary expenses for maintenance and education of my said children during their minority and on my last child attaining the age 21 years shall divide the remaining property equally among all my children, when and in such an event the trust hereunder created shall come to an end.

Provided, however, they shall keep and maintain proper account of the estate and file the same in court once in every six months and get the same audited and passed.

Provided, however, further that in the event of acquisition or compulsory purchase of any property, the said executors and trustees shall invest the proceeds in purchase of some other suitable property or properties to be also held by them in trust as aforesaid.

IN WITNESS WHEREOF I have hereunto set and subscribed my hand and signature this .... day of .... 1999.

Signed by the within-named Testator as his last Will and Testament in our presence all being present at the same time. Thereafter at the request of the Testator and in his presence and in the presence of one another We XY and MN subscribed our respective names

Signed, sealed and delivered by AB the Testator

Signed by XY in the presence of AB the Testator and MN

Signed by MN in the presence of Testator and XY

Will with Legacies and Trust for Children and Continuation of Business

THIS IS THE last will and testament of me, AB of, etc., I hereby revoke all wills and codicil, if any heretofore made by me and declare this to be my last will. This will be operative after my death.

1. I appoint CD of, etc., and EF of, etc., (hereinafter called "my trustees"), to be the executors and trustees of this my will, and also to be the guardians of my children, GH, IJ and KL during the respective periods of their minority. In case any of them fails to act in any of the offices, the other will act solely to all intents and purposes.

2. I hereby give, leave and bequeath the following legacies to be paid out of my estate as soon as possible after my death, *viz*.,

(*a*) to MN Rs. 1,000 absolutely and forever,

(*b*) to XY my radio set and gold watch, also absolutely and forever.

3. Subject to what are hereinbefore stated, I hereby give leave and bequeath the rest and residue of my estate, movable and immovable, of whatever nature and wherever situate unto the said trustees upon trust, for the use and benefit of my children and I direct that my trustees shall

upon the youngest of my said children attaining majority divide the residue of the property among children after making several payments (as in previous precedent, cl. 6.)

4. My trustees may, in their absolute discretion, carry on and continue for such period as they shall think proper the business of, etc., at the date hereof carried on by me at, etc., either alone or in partnership with any partner or partners whom I may have admitted therein before my death, or who, in their discretion, may be admitted by them, without any detriment to the trust of my estate. And I declare that my trustees shall not be liable to my estate or any person interested therein for any loss incurred or suffered in carrying on my said business except on account of any wilful and/or *mala fide* act, default, negligence on their part or wrongful conversion or misappropriation of its funds and assets and not otherwise and that every trustee hereof shall be fully indemnified out of my estates against all liability which he may incur in connection therewith.

PROVIDED HOWEVER that they shall keep and maintain proper account of the estate and file the same in court once in every six months and get the same audited and passed.

PROVIDED HOWEVER further that in the event of acquisition or compulsory purchase of any property the said executors and trustees shall invest the proceeds in purchase of some other properties also to be held by them in trust as aforesaid.

IN WITNESS WHEREOF the said AB testator has executed these presents on the day, month and year mentioned hereinabove in the presence of OP and PQ.

Signed by testator AB

Signed and sealed by CD and EF

the trustees in token of acceptance
of the Office of Trustees

Signed by OP in the presence of
AB the testator and PQ

Signed by PQ in the presence of
AB the testator and OP

Codicil Substituting New Executor for Deceased One

THIS IS a codicil to the last will and testament made and published by me, AB of, etc., on the .... day of .... 2000.

WHEREAS in my said will I had appointed CD of, etc., to be one of the executors and trustees thereof. And whereas the said CD having died, on the day or lately (if the date of death is not known), I am desirous of substituting EF of, etc., as the executor and trustee of my said will in the place and instead of the said CD. Now by this codicil I revoke the appointment of the said CD and I do appoint EF to be one of the executors and trustees of my said will in the place of the said CD deceased, and I do hereby and hereunder declare that my said will shall be read interpreted and construed and understood throughout as if the name of the said EF had been inserted in my said will instead of the name of CD save as aforesaid. I do ratify and confirm my said will in all other respects.

IN WITNESS WHEREOF I have hereto set and subscribed my hand and signature this .... day of .... 2000.

Signed by the within-named Testator as his last will and Testament in our presence all being present at the same time. Thereafter at the request of Testator and in his presence and in the presence of one another we subscribe our respective names

Signed by AB the Testator

Signed by MN in the presence of AB and PQ

Singed by PQ in the presence of AB and MN

Codicil with New Bequests on Death of a Legatee

THIS IS A CODICIL to the last will made and published by me, AB of, etc., on the .... day of ...... 2000.

WHEREAS CD, one of the residuary legatees named in my said will having died since the date thereof (exact date to be given, if known), the legacy thereunder bequeathed unto and in his favour shall after my death fail and form a part of my general estate which was never intended by me. And whereas in the circumstances aforesaid it is my wish and desire that the said legacy shall go to his brother EF. Now by this codicil I do hereby give leave and bequeath the same unto and in favour of his brother, EF. Provided, however, and in case the said EF shall also predecease me, (which May God Forbid) then and in such an event the same shall pass unto and vest in GH and LJ, the two sons of the said EF, in equal shares absolutely and forever. And in all other respects I confirm my said will.

IN WITNESS WHEREOF I have hereunto set and subscribed my hand and signature this .... day of .... 2000.

Signed by the within-named Testator as his last Will and Testament at the same time. Thereafter at the request of Testator and in his presence and in the presence of one another we subscribe our respective names

Signed by AB the Testator

Signed by MN in the presence of AB and PQ

Signed by PQ in the presence of AB and MN

NOTE: Under s. 105 of the Indian Succession Act 1925, when the legatee does not survive the testator the legacy shall lapse unless otherwise provided for in the will. Section 109 also applies to Hindu which is an exception to the doctrine of lapse. It contemplates legacy in favour of any child or other lineal descendant of the testator. This section is based upon s. 33 of the English Wills Act.[10]

Bequest Absolute of Land in Trust for Religious uses with a Direction to Found a Temple and Carry out Maintenance of the Deity and other Expenses from the Money Raised from Sale of Property Existing at the Testator's Death

THIS IS THE LAST WILL and testament of AB, son of .... This will be effective after my death.

I hereby revoke all wills, codicils and other testamentary dispositions heretofore made by me and declare this to be my last will and testament. I appoint CD as the executor of my this will and the trustee of my estate. He will be entitled to obtain probate without being required to furnish any security. It is my wish and desire that my land situate at ...... fully mentioned and described in the schedule below shall be given to and utilised for the service of a deity to be named as .... to be consecrated and established after my death by the said executor and trustee in a temple also to be constructed by him for which purpose and in order to raise capital he will

10 1 Vic C 26.

sell and convert into money all the machinery, plants, stock-in-trade and other assets of my trade or business carried under the name and style of .... at ....

Accordingly I hereby leave and I bequeath my land situate at .... in the city of ...... in the district of .... and more particularly described in the schedule hereto and all the plants, machinery, stock-in-trade and other assets of my said trade or business at the time of my death, and also the goodwill thereof and all the book and other debts which shall then be due or owing to me on account of the said trade or business and all the moneys, securities, goods, credits and effects whether of the said trade or business or otherwise belonging to me at my death (subject to what I may otherwise dispose of during my lifetime or by any codicil hereto) unto and to the use of CD, son of etc.

TO HAVE AND TO HOLD the same upon trust with power to sell and convert into money all such parts thereof, except the said land. I direct that out of the money so realised and out of such money as I did possessed of at my death, the said CD shall at the first instance pay for discharge and satisfy all my funeral and testamentary expenses, death-bed charges and other just debts and liabilities and after payment thereof construct and build a temple on the said land and which, when completed, will be the property of the deity to be installed and named "Shree Shree Radharamanji Maharaj". I further direct that the said CD shall invest the surplus of the said moneys lying in his hands after the construction of the temple in such Government or other securities, shares and debentures all to be held by him in trust as aforesaid and shall, out of the interest or dividends etc. of such investments, carry out the worship or seva of the said "Shree Shree Radharamanji Maharaj". I appoint the said CD as also to act as *shebait* of the said deity when consecrated and established as aforesaid who shall have power to nominate and/or appoint his successor or successors in office and in the absence thereof his descendants shall act as trustees and *shebaits*. If the said CD shall die without nominating his successor and leaving no descendants or he or they refuse and/or neglect to perform the duties of the *shebait* or otherwise become unfit or personally incapable to act in the said trust, then, and in every such case, it shall be lawful for my heirs and legal representative to remove him or them from the office of the trustee and appoint another in his or their place and stead, failing which a new trustee shall be appointed by the court of competent jurisdiction.

Dated this .... day of .... 2000.

The Schedule above referred to

IN WITNESS, etc. (see first precedent)

Signed by etc. (see first precedent) AB

Codicil with Bequest and Authority to Widow to Adopt

THIS IS CODICIL of me, AB, of etc., to my last will and testament dated the .... day of .... and which I direct to be treated as part thereof.

1. I leave, give and bequeath the sum of Rupees .... to each son and Rupees .... to each daughter of my deceased daughter, CD living at the time of my death for their absolute use and benefit and I direct that the legacy hereby given to each such son or daughter, who shall have attained the age of 21 years or married under that age, shall be paid to him or her, as the case may be, as conveniently as possible after my death, and that the legacy hereby given to each and every such son or daughter, who shall not have attained the age of 21 years or married under that age, shall be invested in Government securities in the names or name of my trustees or trustee, who shall stand possessed thereof in trust to transfer, assign and make over the same to him or her, whose legacy is represented thereby, upon his or her attaining the age of 21 years or marrying under that age, and, in the meantime and until it is transferred, assigned and made over, in trust to receive the accumulated interest of the said legacy or Government securities investing such interest, from time to time as circumstances admit, in Government securities also. I direct that each of the bequests by me hereinbefore made shall be deemed and taken to have vested in the several legatees, to whom they are by me bequeathed, immediately upon my death, and that, out of the accumulated interest on the legacies aforesaid, shall be defrayed the expenses for education of those children, and that in case of any of the said legatees dying at any time after my death, his or her legacy shall be payable to his or her executor, administrator or heir.

2. I hereby give my wife, the said EF, authority, power, and liberty to adopt a suitable boy as my son; in the event of such adopted son dying without leaving a widow or male issue, to adopt another boy, and in the same way on the death of such adopted son without leaving a widow or male issue to adopt another boy successively.

3. Subject as aforesaid I confirm my said will.

IN WITNESS WHEREOF, I have hereunto set and subscribed my hand and signature this .... day of ...... 1999.

Signed by the within named Testator as his last Will and Testament in our presence all being present at the same time. Thereafter at the request of Testator and in the presence of one another we subscribe our respective names

Signed by AB the Testator

Signed by MN in the presence of
AB and PQ

Signed by PQ in the presence of
AB and MN

Codicil Revising Will and Providing for Wife and Future Children

THIS IS A CODICIL to the will of me, AB, of, etc., which bears date the .... day of ....

WHEREAS since the date of the said will I have married CD I hereby revise my said will.

NOW I HEREBY leave, give and bequeath to my said wife for her life the annual sum of Rs. ...., from the day of my death to be paid to her by equal monthly payments. And I declare that my child or children by her shall participate equally with my other children in my general movable and immovable property according to the trusts of my said will. Subject as aforesaid I confirm the said will.

IN WITNESS WHEREOF I have hereunto set and subscribed my hand and signature this .... day of .... 2000.

Signed by the within named Testator as his last will and Testament in our presence all being present at the same time. Thereafter at the request of Testator and in his presence and in the presence of one another we subscribe our respective names

Signed by AB the Testator

Signed by MN in the presence of
AB and PQ

Signed by PQ in the presence of
AB and MN

Will with Provision for Appointment of Trustee for a School

I, ... son of .... hereby declare this to be my last will thereby revoking all or any previous wills or codicils made by me and devise and bequeath my estate as follows:

After defraying the expenses of administration of my said estate and obtaining probate or letters of administration with the will annexed and after meeting all expenses of my funeral and construction of the *samadhi* as provided in the will and after paying off all debts or liabilities that may be owing from me to any other person or persons, I hereby bequeath and devise all my movable and immovable properties including choses-in-action and trade-mark and patent rights unto—

(1) Shri .... of ....

(2) Shri .... of ....

(3) Shri .... of ....

(4) Shri .... of ....

(5) Shri .... of ....

jointly as trustees of my said estate for the purpose of establishing and maintaining a school for the education of the children of poor persons specially those belonging to the scheduled castes and of beggars and unattached children.

The said trustees shall be entitled to convert all my properties and assets into any kind of Trustees' security and keep the same invested in such securities as they deem fit in order to carry out the purposes of the trust and change the same.

The school shall be named .... and shall consist of kindergarten, primary and secondary classes, so as to equip each child with an appropriate mode of living and becoming a good citizen of India having knowledge of arts and science suitable to the mental equipment of each such child and making him physically fit to bear the burden of life thereafter. The said school shall have attached residential boarding house where each child shall receive enough individual attention and shall be brought up in a decent and orderly way of life.

No fees shall be charged in the said school and the children shall be clothed and fed properly. For the purposes of carrying out the objects of the trust, the trustees may establish and maintain a dairy, a laundry, workshop and/or any other institution which they may consider suitable or advisable to assist them in the duties aforesaid.

In case State aid should become necessary, the trustees shall be entitled to apply for the same and observe the rules and regulations that may be imposed upon them by the State, which may override any of the instructions hereby given by me.

The trustees are directed to set apart a sum of Rs. .... to be utilized for the building of a *samadhi* in my name at any appropriate place, whereto should be attached small resting place for travellers which should be equipped with a well and other necessary amenities of life.

I have no wife nor any children. But in case any near relation of mine should on account of poverty be unable to maintain and educate his or her children, such children should be given preference in the admission to the aforesaid school.

IN WITNESS WHEREOF I have hereunto set and subscribed my hand and signature this .... day of 2000.

Signed by the within named Testator as his last Will and Testament in our presence all being present at the sametime. Thereafter at the request of Testator and in his presence and in the presence of one another we subscribe our respective names

Signed by AB the Testator

Signed by MN in the presence of AB and PQ

Signed by PQ in the presence of AB and MN

Court Proceedings. Application for Probate or Letters of Administration with the Will annexed has to be made by a petition. The petition has to be made in the court within whose jurisdiction the testator had permanent residence or within whose jurisdiction some properties covered by the Will are situated. A copy of the Will or a statement of contents of the Will is to be annexed to the petition. The petition must contain the date of the Testator's death, a statement that this was the last will and Testament, it was duly executed and attested and the amount and particulars of assets likely to come in the petitioner's hands and that the petitioner is the executor named in the Will. Particulars of value of assets lying in different places outside the jurisdiction of the court should also be stated.

If the Will has been lost or mislaid after the Testator's death or it has been accidentally destroyed then on the basis of a copy of a draft of the Will, the Probate may be granted for a limited period until the original or an authenticated copy of the Will is produced.

Revocation. The Probate or Letters of Administration may be revoked for a just cause. It will be revoked if the Probate proceeding was defective in substance or if the Probate was obtained fraudulently by making false suggestions or concealing any material fact from the court or by making untrue allegations or the grant has become useless or inoperative through circumstances or that the person obtaining the Probate exhibited incorrect inventory or accounts.

Caveat. A Caveat may be filed under s. 148A of the Code of Civil Procedure 1908 in any matter apprehended to be filed in court so that without notice to the Caveator no order would be made in such intended matter. This Caveat remains valid for 90 days but can be renewed from time to time by fresh Caveat. Caveat may be filed in case of probate proceedings before the same are started or after institution thereof. A Caveat before institution of such proceedings under s. 284 of the Indian Succession Act 1925 remains valid for an indefinite time. The question of limitation does not arise in case of it being filed in a pending proceeding. The form of Caveat in High Court is slightly different from the Form in the District Courts.

Petition for Revocation of Probate

In the Court of ....

Case No. 3 of 1999

AB of .... *Petitioner*

versus

XY of .... *Opposite Party*

Petition for revocation of Probate.
(Under s. 263 of the Indian Succession Act 1925)

The humble petition of the petitioner above-named

MOST RESPECTFULLY SHEWETH:

1. The opposite party XY by filing Case No. 3 of 1999 obtained a Probate/ Letters of Administration, by suppressing the material facts which if disclosed would have disentitled him from obtaining the Probate/Letters of Administration.

2. That the material facts are as follows:

(*a*) the proceedings were defective because of ....

(*b*) false suggestions were made and material facts were suppressed such as ....

(*c*) untrue allegations of a fact essential in point of law to justify grant was made.

3. That the applicant having practising fraud upon the Learned Court and by suppressing material facts have obtained the Probate/Letters of Administration of the Will which had been revoked. A later Will was made and has since been discovered.

The petitioner, therefore, prays that the Probate/Letters of Administration may kindly be revoked and further orders be passed as may deem fit and proper.

Signature

Verification

I, AB .... son of .... GB .... by occupation service do hereby solemnly affirm and say as follows:

1. I am the petitioner herein.

2. The statements in paragraphs 1, 2 and 3 of the foregoing petition are true to my knowledge as also based on information derived from records of the proceedings in this Learned Court and believed by me to be true.

3. The statements in the foregoing paragraphs are true to my knowledge.

I sign this verification on this .... day of October 1999 at the Court Premises at Alipore.

Before me — Identified by Clerk of Advocate

Commissioner of Oath
or as the officer may be

Advocate for Petitioner

Application for Revocation of Succession Certificate

In the Court of ....

Case No. 5 of 1999

Mrs. X wife of Late Mr. Z .... of .... *Petitioner*

versus

Mr. BC of .... *Opposite Party*

Petition for revocation of the Succession Certificate
(under s. 383 of the Indian Succession Act 1925)

The humble petition of the petitioner above-named

MOST RESPECTFULLY SHEWETH:

1. The opposite party filed an application for grant of Succession Certificate in Case No. 5 of 1999. The opposite party obtained a Succession Certificate in respect of the debts of the deceased Mr. Z on 5th May 2000.

2. Your petitioner is the widow of the deceased. As the nearest relation your petitioner was entitled to obtain the Succession Certificate for recovering the debts of the deceased.

3. That the opposite party is a step-son of the petitioner. He knew the petitioner being the nearest relation is entitled to be served with the notice of such application. However, the opposite party fraudulently suppressed

the name of the petitioner in the application and consequently no notice was issued to the petitioner by the Learned Court and the Succession Certificate was issued without hearing the petitioner.

By reasons of the aforesaid, it is humbly prayed that the Succession Certificate granted to the opposite party be revoked and further and consequential orders be passed as to this Learned Court may deem fit and proper.

Signature

Verification

I, Mrs. X wife of late Mr. Z residing at .... do hereby solemnly affirm and say as follows:

1. The statements in the paragraphs 1, 2 and 3 of the foregoing petition are true to my knowledge and also based on information derived from the records of the proceedings of this Learned Court and believed by me to be true.

2. The statements hereinabove in the verification are true to my knowledge.

I sign this verification on this .... day of October 1999 at the Court House at Alipore Judges' Court.

Before me — Deponent

Oath Commissioner — Identified by

or as the officer may be — Clerk of Advocate

Advocate of Petitioner

Objection to Petition for Grant of Probate

In the Court of the Civil Judge (Senior Division)

Alipore

Original Petition No. 5 of 1999

In the matter of:

The Will of S. Mohanta, the deceased

And

In the matter of:

A. Vaisnab, residing at 5 Brindaban Road, Calcutta

Plaintiff

versus

G. Avadhoot, residing at 6 Brindaban Road, Calcutta

Defendant

The humble petition of the defendant above-named most respectfully

SHEWETH:

1. The plaintiff claims to be the executor of an alleged Will of the said S. Mohanta dated 5th June 1985 and claims to have the said Will established.

2. The defendant disputes the validity of the said Will.

3. The defendant states that the said Will and Codicil of the deceased were not executed in accordance with the provisions of the Indian Succession Act 1925.

4. The deceased at the time of execution of the said Will and Codicil was not of sound mind, memory and understanding.

5. The defendant states that the execution of the said Will and Codicil was procured by undue influence by the plaintiff.

6. The plaintiff fraudulently obtained the signatures of the said deceased on the Will and Codicil by fraud representing to him that the said documents were required to be executed for the purpose of inducting tenant in the said premises. The said deceased due to failing eyesight was not in a position to read the documents and did not read or understand the said documents. The deceased did not understand the nature or the contents of the said Will and Codicil.

7. Ten years prior to the said purported Will and Codicil the said deceased in sound mind, memory and understanding and with full vision and eyesight executed a Will written by his own hand and duly executed the same in presence of two respectable witnesses appointing the defendant as the Executor thereof. A copy of the said Will dated 5th June 1975 is annexed hereto marked "A".

8. The defendant states that the Will and Codicil relied on by the plaintiff be declared null and void and the Probate granted to the plaintiff be cancelled.

In the premises the defendant claims:

(*a*) declaration that the said Will and Codicil of which the plaintiff obtained the Probate is null and void;

(*b*) delivery of the said Will and Codicil and Probate granted and on such delivery cancellation thereof;

(*c*) further and other reliefs.

Verification

I, G. Avadhoot son of late B. Avadhoot by occupation landlord residing at 6 Brindaban Road, Calcutta do hereby solemnly affirm and say as follows:

1. The statements in the paragraph Nos. 1 to 8 hereinabove are true to my knowledge derived from records maintained by me and the proceedings in this Learned Court and Mr. X and Mr. Z the witnesses to the said purported Will and Codicil on the basis of which the plaintiff obtained the Probate and believed by me to be true.

2. I sign this verification on this 5th day of January 2000 at the Court House at Alipore.

Sd/ G. Avodhoot
Identified by me

Advocate for the
Defendant

Petition of Consent to Grant of Succession Certificate

District: South 24-Parganas

In the Court of the Learned District Delegate at Alipore

Act 39 Case No. 363 of 1996

(Succession)

In the matter of:

Abdul Khalik since deceased of 2 Bagan Road, Calcutta 700 024, Police Station–Metiaburuz, District–South 24-Parganas, by faith Muslim and Nationality Citizen of India

And

In the matter of:

An application for grant of Succession Certificate in respect of Back Wages amount lying at the office "The Air Corporation of India Ltd." at 7 Roy Road, Calcutta 700 001 of Abdul Khalik since deceased under s. 372 of the Indian Succession Act 39 of 1925

And

In the matter of:
Jamina Bibi, widow of deceased Abdul Khalik residing at 2 Bagan Road, Calcutta 700 024, Police Station–Metiaburuz, District–South 24- Parganas
..................*Applicant*

The humble petition of:

(1) Abdul Manna

(2) Abdul Hanan

(3) Abdul Kanna

All sons of deceased Abdul Khalik residing at 2 Bagan Road, Calcutta 700 024, Police Station– Metiaburuz, District–South 24-Parganas

(4) Amina Khatoon, Married daughter of Abdul Khalik and wife of Late Md. Rahim, residing at 2 Bagan Road, Calcutta 700 024, Police Station–Metiaburuz, District–South 24- Parganas

(5) Khaira Banu, Unmarried daughter of deceased Abdul Khalik residing at 2 Bagan Road, Calcutta 700 024, Police Station–Metiaburuz, District–South 24-Parganas

MOST RESPECTFULLY SHEWETH:

1. That the deceased above-named died intestate on or about 10th day of July 1995 at about 11-30 p.m. at the Calcutta Medical College and Hospital, Calcutta, leaving behind him his widow Jamina Bibi three sons and two daughters and that the deceased left no other heirs and legal representatives.

2. That the applicant Jamina Bibi is the mother of your petitioners and she is one of the heirs and legal representatives of the deceased.

3. That your petitioner's said mother has applied for grant of the Succession Certificate in her name in respect of the goods and assets and securities and debts of our father Abdul Khalik since deceased.

4. That the petitioners above-named as the other heirs of the deceased do hereby give our consent to the grant of such Succession Certificate to the applicant Jamina Bibi and that your petitioners have no objection to the grant of the Succession Certificate to be issued in her favour by this Learned Court.

5. That this application is made *bona fide* and for the ends of justice.

Under the circumstances set forth above Your Honour would be graciously pleased to note and record the consent and no objection of your petitioners to the issue of Succession Certificate in favour of Jamina Bibi, widow of the deceased Abdul Khalik and pass such other order or orders as to Your Honour may seem fit and proper.

And your petitioners as in duty bound shall ever pray.

Verification

We, the petitioners above-named do hereby declare that the statements made in paragraphs 1 to 4 of the foregoing petition are true to our knowledge and the rest are our humble submission before this Learned Court. We sign this verification this the .... day of .... 1996 at our Advocate's Chamber.

Prepared in my office — Signatures

Read over and explained in Bengali and Hindi

1.
2.
3.
4.
5.

Advocate

Act 39 Case No. 363/96, granted on 18.6.97 (7th S.J.)

High Court Form No. (J) 55

Succession Certificate

Section 377 of the Indian Succession Act 1925

In the Court of the District Delegate at Alipore

Jamina Bibi, widow of Abdul Khalik residing at 2 Bagan Road, Calcutta 700 024, District–South 24-Parganas.

Whereas you applied on the 28th August 1996 for a certificate under Part X of the Indian Succession Act 1925 in the matter of the Estate of deceased, in respect of the following debts and securities, namely:

Abdul Khalik

Payment of back wages of Rs. 50,000 (Rupees fifty thousand) only with interest accrued thereon if any and lying at "The Air Corporation of India Ltd." having its office at 7 Roy Road, Calcutta 700 001 is standing to the credit in the name of deceased Abdul Khalik, in terms of its letter of 28th August 1995.

This Certificate is accordingly granted to you and empowers you to collect those debts and to receive interest or dividends on .... to negotiate or transfer .... both to receive interest or dividends on and to negotiate or transfer the same or any to them.

Succession Certificate issued on a
Stamp Duty of Rs. 1,400.

Dated this 19th day of June 1997 Sd/- District Judge or Delegate 7th

Sub-Judge 19th
June 1997

Seal

Seal of the Court of the District Delegate

South 24-Parganas, Alipore.

57

Registration of Documents

(The Registration Act 1908)

Compulsorily registrable. An instrument of gift of immovable property; a non-testamentary instrument which purports or operates to create, declare, assign, limit or extinguish in present or in future any right, title or interest, vested or contingent, in immovable property or which acknowledges receipt or payment of any consideration in relation thereto are compulsorily registrable. Leases of immovable property from year to year or for any term exceeding one year or for receiving yearly rent are compulsorily registrable. Non-testamentary instruments transferring or assigning any decree or order of a court or any award when such decree order or award purports or operates to create, declare, assign or limit or extinguish in present or in future any right, title or interest, vested or contingent, in any immovable property are compulsorily registrable.[1] An authority to adopt a son is compulsorily registrable.[2] The document is to be registered with the Registrar of Assurances or Sub-registrars.

Exceptions. Any document in itself NOT creating, declaring, assigning, limiting or extinguishing any right, title or interest in immovable property but merely creating a right to obtain another document which will when executed create, declare, assign, limit or extinguish any such right, title or interest is not compulsorily registrable. Agreements to sale, lease or transfer are not compulsorily registrable.[3] Any decree or order of a court even though relates to immovable property is not compulsorily registrable (unless it is a Compromise Decree and comprises immovable property which was not the subject-matter of the suit or proceeding).[4]

1 Section 17(1) of the Registration Act 1908.
2 Section 17(3) of the Registration Act 1908.
3 Section 17(2)(*v*) of the Registration Act 1908.
4 Section 17(2)(*vi*) of the Registration Act 1908.

An endorsement on a mortgage deed acknowledging payment of the whole or any part of the mortgage money and any other receipt for payment of money due under a mortgage when such receipt does not purport to extinguish the mortgage is not compulsorily registrable.[5] A certificate of sale granted to the purchaser of any property sold by public auction or by a Civil Court or Revenue Officer is not compulsorily registrable.[6]

An agreement for sale of immovable property though containing a recital of payment of earnest money or whole or part of purchase money is not compulsorily registrable.[7]

Documents of which registration is optional. The following Instruments are valid and effective without registration. However, these documents may be registered at the option of the parties.

(*a*) Instruments acknowledging receipt or payment of any consideration on account of creation, declaration, assignment, limitation or extinction of any right, title or interest in immovable property or lease of immovable property for a term not exceeding one year.

(*b*) Instruments other than Wills which purport or operate to create, declare, assign, limit or extinguish any right, title or interest to or in a *movable* property are not compulsorily registrable but may be registered at the option of the executants.

(*c*) Wills are not compulsorily registrable though it may cover immovable property. Such Wills which cover movable and/or immovable properties may be registered at the option of the parties.

(*d*) All documents which are not compulsorily registrable under s. 17 may be registered at the option of the parties.[8]

Requirements for registration by Registration Officer. If the document is in a language which the Registering Officer does not understand he may ask for a translation into a language commonly used in the district. The Registering Officer may ask for attestation of all interlineations, blanks, erasures and alterations in the document. The document to be registered should contain description of identity of the property and a Map or Plan. The houses and lands covered by the non-testamentary document should give references to the Government Maps and Surveys.[9]

Some states by amendments have provided that a document shall not be registered if the transaction is opposed to the public policy. In all land

5 Section 17(2)(*xi*) of the Registration Act 1908.
6 Section 17(2)(*xii*) of the Registration Act 1908.
7 Explanation to s. 17(2) of the Registration Act 1908.
8 Section 18 of the Registration Act 1908.
9 Sections 19-22 of the Registration Act 1908.

transactions in Salt Lake, Calcutta, the State Government must be made a party or prior permission of the Metropolitan Development Department, Government of West Bengal should be obtained.[10]

Time-limit for registration. A non-testamentary document shall be presented for registration to the proper officer within four months from the date of its execution. A Will can be presented for registration at any time. A copy of a Decree or an order is to be presented for registration within four months from the date when it became final.[11] In certain cases and in case of doubt as to the validity of registration, the document may be re-registered within four months from date when it became known that the registration is invalid or of doubtful validity.[12] Where a document is executed by several persons at different times, it should be presented for registration within four months of the first execution and within four months for re-registration of each subsequent execution.[13] If for unavoidable reasons the document cannot be presented within four months of its execution for registration, then on payment of fine not exceeding ten times the amount of proper registration fee, the document may be registered within another four months.[14] A document executed by all of any of the parties out of India may be accepted for registration if presented within four months after the date of arrival of the document in India.[15] A Will may be presented for registration at any time.[16]

Registration Officer. Normally the documents have to be registered at the Sub-registrar's Office within whose jurisdiction the immovable property is situate.[17] However, any Registrar may register any document registrable with a Sub-registrar subordinate to him. Further except in Gujarat, Orissa, Rajasthan, Uttar Pradesh and West Bengal the *Registrar of the Presidencey Towns* and the *Registrar of Delhi may register any document in respect of a property situate in any part of India.*[18] By a special arrangement in special circumstances, the Registering Officer may attend at the residence or office of the Executant for registration of document or to accept deposit of a Will.[19]

Executants or their authorised persons to present the documents for registration. Every instrument for registration is to be presented at the proper Registration Office by the person executing or claiming under the Decree or

10 Notification No. 452—Regn. R3M—25/87 dated 21st May 1988.
11 Section 23 of the Registration Act 1908.
12 Section 23A of the Registration Act 1908.
13 Section 24 of the Registration Act 1908.
14 Section 25 of the Registration Act 1908.
15 Section 26 of the Registration Act 1908.
16 Section 27 of the Registration Act 1908.
17 Section 28 of the Registration Act 1908.
18 Section 30 of the Registration Act 1908.
19 Section 31 of the Registration Act 1908.

document or by his representative or assign or duly authorised person under a Power of Attorney.[20]

A Power of Attorney for presentation of document for registration will be accepted if the Power of Attorney was executed and authenticated by the Registering Office within whose jurisdiction the Principal resides. If the Principal does not reside in India then the Power of Attorney should be executed before and authenticated by a Notary Public or any Court, Judge, Magistrate, Indian Consul or Vice-consul or the representative of Central Government. Such execution of Power of Attorney may be proved by production of it and no further evidence is necessary.[1]

An executant not appearing before the Registering Officer. Where one of the executants after execution of the document does not attend the Registering Office, the other party may compel the absenting party to attend through the process of the court and admit execution.[2] Wills and the authority to adopt may be presented for registration by the Testator or the Donor and after his death by executor or the Dones for registration.[3] A Will may be deposited with the Registrar in a sealed cover and such deposit may be through an agent. After death of the Testator, on an application of the interested persons the sealed envelope containing the Will is opened, contents of the Will are recorded in Book No. 3 maintained by the Registrar and the original Will is thereafter kept in the custody of the Registrar.[4]

Effect of registration. A registered document shall operate from the time from which it would have commenced to operate in terms thereof and not from the date of registration.[5] A non-testamentary document relating to movable or immovable property shall prevail over any oral agreement or declaration. However, if pursuant to any oral agreement or declaration, delivery of possession has been given and under any law it is a valid transfer, then such oral agreement will prevail over subsequent registered document. A mortgage by deposit of Title Deeds will prevail over a subsequent Registered Mortgage.[6]

Effect of non-registration. A document required to be compulsorily registered if not registered then it will not affect any immovable property comprised therein or confer any power to adopt. Such document will not

20 Section 32 of the Registration Act 1908.
1 Section 33 of the Registration Act 1908.
2 Sections 36-39 of the Registration Act 1908.
3 Sections 40-41 of the Registration Act 1908.
4 Sections 42-45 of the Registration Act 1908.
5 Section 47 of the Registration Act 1908.
6 Section 48 of the Registration Act 1908.

be received as evidence in any transaction affecting such property or conferring any power to adopt.[7]

However, the document compulsorily registrable, if not registered, may be received in evidence of a contract in a suit for specific performance or as evidence of part-performance of a contract or as evidence of any collateral transaction not required to be effected by a registered instrument.[8]

Endorsement on the document by Registering Officer. On admitting registration of a document, the Registering Officer should endorse on the document the admission of signature of the executants, the payment of money or consideration, the date and other particulars. If a person admitting the execution refused to endorsing the same, the Registering Officer shall nevertheless register it but shall endorse a note of such refusal. The Registering Officer shall endorse a Certificate on the Instrument containing the word "Registered" together with the Book No. and page No. of the Book on which the document has been copied. Such Certificate shall be signed sealed and dated by the Registering Officer. Such Certificate is thereafter admissible in evidence.[9] The endorsements and Certificate shall be copied in the margin of the Register and the copy of Plan or Map, if any, shall be filed in Book No. 1. The document then shall be returned to the person who presented the same for registration or to his nominee.[10]

Fees for registration. The fee payable for registering a document or for searching of the register or for obtaining of copies are fixed by the State Government by a Notification.[11]

Registration and Tax Clearance Certificate

(The Income-tax Act 1961)

Every transaction involving the allowing of possession of any immovable property to be taken or retained in part performance of a contract of the nature referred to in s. 53A of Transfer of Property Act 1882 was required to be in writing and registered with the Competent Authority (the then Deputy Commissioner of I.T. Department).

Every transaction other than sale, exchange or lease compulsorily registrable under the Registration Act whereby a person acquired any right in or with respect of any building or part of a building which had been

7 Section 49 of the Registration Act 1908.
8 Proviso to s. 49 of the Registration Act 1908.
9 Sections 58-60 of the Registration Act 1908.
10 Section 61 of the Registration Act 1908.
11 Sections 78-80 of the Registration Act 1908.

constructed or which was to be constructed was to be in writing and registered with the Competent Authority.[12]

With effect from 1.10.1986, the provisions of Chapter XXC, containing ss. 269U to 269UO, are operative. Section 269UC puts certain restrictions on transfer of immovable property and s. 269UL puts restrictions on registration, etc., of documents in respect of transfer of immovable property.

In respect of documents compulsorily registrable relating to immovable property of the value of Rs. 5 lakhs or more the Registering Officer shall not register the transaction unless a Tax Clearance Certificate under s. 230A of Income Tax Act is produced.

Notice to be given

[The Urban Land (Ceiling & Regulation) Act 1976]

(*Since repealed*)

No person holding vacant land within the ceiling limit shall transfer such land by way of sale, mortgage, gift, lease or otherwise except after giving notice in writing of the intended transfer to the Competent Authority.[13]

A document purporting to transfer by way of sale, mortgage, gift, lease or otherwise of any urban property shall not be registered by the Registering Officer unless evidence is produced that proper notice has been given at least 60 days before to the Competent Authority under the Act of 1976.[14]

Permission Required

[The West Bengal Government Land (Regulation of Transfer) Act 1993 w.e.f. 4.3.1997]

A Registering Authority shall not register any document relating to transfer of Government land held by any Lessee on lease in favour of any person without the permission of the Competent Authority. Transfer of such leasehold land in favour of State Government or a Government undertaking does not require any permission of Competent Authority.[15]

12 Section 269AB of the Income-tax Act 1961. It may be noted that Chapter XXA, containing ss. 269A to 269S, was not to apply to or in relation to the transfer of any immovable property made after 30.9.1986 as mendated by s. 269RR.

13 Section 26 of the Urban Land (Ceiling and Regulation) Act 1976.

14 Section 28 of the Urban Land (Ceiling and Regulation) Act 1976.

15 Section 4 of the West Bengal Government Land (Regulation of Transfer) Act 1993.

58

Computer Contracts*

To be very simple a contract is an agreement enforceable by law. In the eyes of law a contract will create rights and duties. In fact the very intention of entering into a contract is to protect the rights of respective parties. Normally we witness the signing of a contract in the following circumstances *i.e.* when the subject-matter is having considerable monetary worth, when a party has to perform a particular task within a specified time, when the parties are not familiar with each other, when there is a need to clarify the rights and duties of respective parties to show clearly where the respective parties stand, when a remedy has to be provided if any party suffers any loss because the other party failed to perform his part.

Normally while structuring a contract there is no hard and fast rule to be followed, depending upon the situation, legal rules have to be taken from the Indian Contract Act 1872 and Companies Act 1956. Thus to draft a contract relating to partnership, inputs from the Indian Partnership Act 1932 are crucial. Apart from the laws enacted on the subject, attention should be given to various judgements delivered on that particular subject.

Computer contracts can be divided into 3 distinct areas.

(*a*) Hardware contracts. As the name implies such contracts relate to the hardware *i.e.* the issues dealing with the selling, marketing, distribution, installation, servicing/maintenance of computers. In simple words they are concerned with various activities connected with the machine. Machine and the related items of a computer are generally called hardware. Just like any tangible property hardware can be subjected to various transactions like lease, sale etc.

(*b*) Software contracts. Such contracts refer to the computer programs. There are various activities revolving around a computer program, for e.g.

---

* Contributed by V.K. Unni, Faculty, NALSAR University of Law, Hyderabad.

like developing/writing the program, marketing that particular program, issuing licenses to use such programs etc. What we call software comprises of programs, which are in simple words, directions issued to the computer (hardware) to function in a particular manner. Depending upon the functions we can broadly classify software into 2 broad heads namely applications software and operating systems.

Applications software performs all the specialised tasks that computers are used for: for e.g. video editing, animation, computer aided design, airline reservations, email, chat etc, examples Adobe Photoshop, Corel Draw etc.

An operating system termed "OS" is the program that, manages all the other programs in a computer. Right from the moment a computer is switched on, the operating system is working; to interpret and manage the entire computer's other programs and resources, until the computer is shut down. In case the Computer is running 2 programs at the same time, the OS allocates computer's resources.

An operating system program, which should be present in all computers, controls various functions of hardware and allocates various resources of the computer. The OS also controls internal components, such as memory, external devices-monitors, modems, storage devices-and the look and feel of the user interface. Examples of Operating Systems are Windows 98, Windows XP, Linux etc.

(c) Net related contracts. They are called in popular terms as Net-ware or Web-ware contracts, they relate to contracts relating to Internet like e.g. hosting of a website, registration of a particular domain name, agreements on web server co-location etc. Any activity relating to the Internet needs certain devices like fax-modem, certain programs like Windows Explorer for net browsing, certain services like net connectivity, provided by Internet Service Providers like Sify, BSNL etc.

Issues involved in a hardware contract

Sale and installation. More often than not a hardware contract is for the delivery of machines (computers), these machines can be easily ascertained by referring to a distinctive code no. which is normally printed in the machine along with a model name or number. Such contracts may be for a complete computer system, or parts of such systems. Such contracts can envisage various payment options like outright sale, rental, lease etc. In such contracts, the manufacturer can enter into an agreement with the end user, or he can enter into a contract with another who can act as a supplier to end users.

The place of installation of the machine is very important in such contracts because the place of installation can influence the delivery, freight charges etc. Normally in outright sales delivery is made immediately on signing the contract. The duty of the manufacturer/supplier of the machines/hardware is to assemble the components, thoroughly test it, and safely transport and deliver the machines to the premises of the buyer. Normally a buyer may also require the supplier to test the machines/hardware after the machines are installed at the buyer's site before accepting the machines and making the payment.

Initially when the machine is ready the manufacturer/supplier will invite the customer to visit the manufacturer's office to see the tests, which are carried out on the machine. After such tests are carried out the machines are shipped to the premises of the customer and installed at the places earmarked for keeping the machine/computer. Thereafter the manufacturer/ supplier's engineers perform some standard tests in the presence of the customer's technical team. Once such a test is performed satisfactorily at the installation site the customer shall accept the machine and the purchase price shall be paid immediately. Just like any other equipment, the defects/ damages of a machine /computer will become noticeable only after a period of long usage; so the manufacturer/supplier shall guarantee such machine, for a limited period against faulty workmanship, materials etc. This period can range from 6 to 24 months.

Generally customer/buyer has the following duties:

- To pay the price stipulated in the contract;
- To prepare the installation site;
- To take care and maintain the machine.

Generally manufacturer/supplier has the following duties:

- To deliver the computer specified in the contract in working condition;
- To ensure confidentiality with respect to the information supplied by the client.

Just as in any other sale the title to the machine pass to the customer/ buyer after the final payment. It is a common practice for the manufacturer/ supplier to provide the customer an indemnity with respect to third party Intellectual property right violations.

In some cases the computers may be taken on rent and in such cases the contract commence from the date of delivery of the computer. In such contracts the title rests with the supplier of the computers

Marketing agreements. For the success of any product a well-oiled supply chain is a must and obviously the computer industry is no exception to this general rule. Some computer manufacturers appoint distributors while some appoint agents to market their products. The position of the distributor is that of an independent contractor and the distributor buys from the manufacturer and sells at a profit of the customers. This shows that the distributor is faced with some risks especially pertaining to bad loans.

The case of an agent is different because the agent acts as middleman between the manufacturer and customer. There is no personal liability on agent's part and the manufacturer shall indemnify the agent for any loss, which may arise in the ordinary course of business. Agents commonly are paid a commission, which can be a percentage of the net selling price of the computer.

Whatever be the type of the agreement, apart from creating a contractual relationship between parties, it also stipulates various roles assigned to both the parties with regard to manufacturing and packaging, licensing, publicity, maintenance/ customer support of the computer.

In contracts relating to distribution, price of the machine and the conditions of payment are very important. In some contracts the manufacturer may undertake to supply the computer to the distributor at a special price, which is less than the price charged from other distributors. Such agreements also may contain clauses that protect distributor from sudden price hikes by stipulating a notice period of atleast 2 months before increasing the price. It is common for the distribution agreement to clearly mention the geographical area where the distributor can operate.

Maintenance agreements. Maintenance can be of 2 types, preventive maintenance, which involves regular testing and adjusting various features relating to the computer to prevent any defect to the computer, and curative maintenance to cure or rectify any defect to the computer, which has arisen.

Thus the latter agreements shall include the proper definition of the circumstances, which require maintenance along with, configuration of the computer. It shall also specify the people who are competent to carryout maintenance. Another factor to be considered is the clause which shall guarantee quick response on the part of the service provider, so such agreements shall include a clause specifying the timeframe within which engineers of the service provider shall reach the place where computer is installed. The price for maintaining computers shall be charged annually, which may be paid in 2 or 3 instalments.

In ordinary circumstances a maintenance agreement is for a specific period wherein any party can terminate the agreement by giving a notice to the other party. Again there cannot be any change in equipment as mentioned in the agreement. Maintenance services have to be carried out in accordance with the time schedule provided in the agreement.

Customer has the following duties:

- To pay the maintenance price as fixed in the agreement;
- To take proper care of the equipment;
- To provide the service provider access to the place of computer installation.

The service provider has the following duties:

- To carryout maintenance of the computer specified in the contract with proper care;
- To ensure confidentiality with respect to the information supplied by the customer.

Contracts relating to employment Here one has to appreciate the fact that IT industry essentially depends upon the strength of its human resources. More often than not the main ingredient of this industry is intellectual capabilities of its employees; this is very true in the case of software where the final output is the collective commodification of intellect. Thus the agreements, which the companies enter with their employees should be drafted in a very professional manner because any addition or omission can have serious implications in case differences arise with them on a future date. Such a contract should be frame taking into account the interests of the employer and the legislations pertaining to the subject-matter.

As a matter of general principle, such contracts must contain crystal clear provisions regarding the ownership of inventions, which arise in the course of employment. A company or the firm engaged in software development should contain a specific clause that the copyright of the software produced during the course of employment will belong to the company. In many cases the employees will be having access to confidential information/ know-how and sufficient care should be taken to ensure that the said employee would be able to misappropriate or pass on that to a competitor.

IT industry is the one with very high attrition rates and retaining the best employees is a very difficult task for any employer. Thus it is not uncommon for the employer to include some provisions, which prohibit the employee from starting a competitive business. Such employments always stipulate clause, which preclude employees from starting competitive businesses for a specified period. But here care should be taken to make sure that the employer is not crossing the limits because if the clauses are very harsh the courts may view them as affecting the constitutional right of the employee to carry on any trade or profession. Thus care should be taken not to include unreasonable clauses that affect any constitutional right or provisions, which may in effect restrain business or trade.

Non-disclosure agreements. In many cases software companies work in a specific project for their client, which may be of much importance to the client. In such cases the clients may insist that the employees of the companies who work in that specific project execute a non-disclosure agreement regarding the project, which they are working upon. This would be in addition to the employment contracts, which the employees had signed at the time of their appointment. For example if Infosys is doing a special project for the Reserve Bank of India, (RBI), RBI can ask the employees of Infosys who work in that special project to sign a Non Disclosure Agreement.

Agreement with contractors. The concept of outsourcing has steadily gained ground in the software industry. Several large software companies in order to keep their overhead accounts low have started the practice of entrusting a portion of their work to some small or medium sized companies. This will alleviate their burden of keeping a large workforce, but here ample care should be taken to ensure that all the confidential information pertaining to the project is preserved to the maximum. Such contracts should contain specific provisions regarding the liability of the company to which the work is being outsourced. In case of any misappropriation of valuable information the company, which entrusts the work to the other company, should have adequate legal remedy and so specific clauses should be inserted in the agreement to protect the interests of the outsourcer.

Agreements with consultants. This is the era of consultants. Mostly companies engaged in developing software take the services of consultants because of their expertise in providing solutions tailor-made for a particular sector. But they are not the employees of the company and for that matter he may be eligible for some benefits like provident fund, gratuity etc. The company should draft the agreement, which specifies the ownership regarding all intellectual property developed by the consultants while the company engages their services. The consultant shall never be an agent of the company; he is dealing with the company on a principal-to-principal basis. All the products or know-how developed by the consultant when the company engages him should belong to the company. Agreements made by the company with the consultant should really take care of this issue and must contain specific clauses clarifying the right of the company.

Software contracts. Earlier the distinction between software and hardware was not that prevalent. People were buying a computer that included the price of hardware, i.e the processor, motherboard, hard disc, monitor etc. along with the built-in software. Thus in the earlier days software was considered as a thing which is given free with the hardware. Most of the major computer manufacturers were bundling the software along with the hardware. Finally by around 1970 some of the leading companies decided to charge their software separately as they were facing an anti trust litigation initiated by the Dept. of Justice, USA.

In the case of sale of software there is a very important distinction. Software is never sold as any other product; it is always viewed as an intangible property. It is only licensed and this is the most popular form of agreement being made in relation to software. Under this agreement the person who develops the software licenses certain rights in relation to the software. Thus the developer becomes the Licensor and the customer becomes the Licensee. The Licensor still remains the owner of the software and the Licensee is granted certain limited rights under the agreement and thus a lot will depend upon the terms and conditions of the agreement.

What these contracts normally grant is a non-exclusive and non-transferrable licence to run the software on a single computer at a time. The Licensee is not in any way empowered to transfer this right to any third party. Since the licence is non-exclusive in nature the Licensor can grant these rights to other parties, or in another words the Licensor can sell the software to other people. The Licensee has the limited right to use the software only on one computer at a given time and in case anybody loads the same software into his computer by making a copy from the Licensee then the Licensee is deemed to have violated the licence agreement.

Having stated the above these licences may permit the users to use the software on more than one computers located in a particular place, of course the licence fee would be calculated on the basis of the number of systems that use a particular software. In some cases a company or a firm may negotiate with a software company to grant a license to use particular software for the entire company or a particular division of the company. Most often the licences are granted forever but in some cases there may be tie period fixed in the terms of the licence agreement after which both the parties on the payment of an additional fee might renew it.

Shrink-wrap licences. These types of licence agreement intend to establish a binding legal agreement between the software vendor and the user. The agreement can be generally seen inside the box containing the software, printed on the envelope containing the CD-ROM or disks, or may be printed in the user manual. It always begins with a warning to the user not to open the software envelope or use the software unless and until he or she fully agrees with the terms and conditions of the agreement. Shrink-wrap licences have traditionally been widely used in the computer software industry in mass market transactions. When you purchase a copy of MS-Word, for example, you will notice that the packaging of the software, or the envelope inside the box containing the computer disks, have licence agreements printed on them, along with a provision stating that opening the envelope or box (or using the software) constitutes acceptance of the terms and conditions of the licence.

Making use of this type of agreement has become the legal licensing paradigm of the software industry, which caters to the consumer mass-market software. Infact the word "shrink-wrap" developed from the fact that such agreements used to be included on the outside of the software packaging, which was visible through the clear plastic shrink-wrap with which the package was sealed.

But whether such "shrink-wrap" agreements are enforceable against the user who breaches their terms is worth taking a look.

In *Step-Saver Data Systems* v *Wyse Technology*,[1] Step-Saver, creator of a multi-user IBM package integrating hardware and software, had an on going long standing relationship with Wyse, creator of an operating system that Step-Saver incorporated into its multi- user package. Based on the course of the parties' dealings and in reliance on Wyse's representations, Step-Saver acquired copies of Wyse's software. Printed on each package of the software was a shrink-wrap licence which, *inter alia*, disclaimed all express and implied warranties - which disclaimers were inconsistent with Wyse's prior representations and express warranties to Step-Saver. The court ruled that the shrink-wrap licence on Wyse's software, which substantially altered the allocation of risks between the parties and conflicted with Wyse's earlier representations — and which was not expressly accepted by Step-Saver — did not become part of the parties' agreement.

In *ProCD, Inc.* v *Zeidenberg*,[2] involved the CD-ROM product sold under the trade mark "Select Phone." It has a listing of over 95 million telephone numbers, bundled with the software that enables a user to access those numbers on his or her computer, and cost ProCD millions of dollars to develop. The defendant, a student living in Madison, Wisconsin, purchased copies of Select Phone. He then copied the telephone listings from the CD-ROM onto his computer, created a software search engine, and uploaded the whole thing onto a World Wide Website that soon generated over 20,000 hits a day. Naturally, ProCD sued, alleging copyright infringement, breach of the express terms of the shrink-wrap license agreement.

Whether Zeidenberg violate the terms of the shrink-wrap licence agreement, which expressly stated that copying of the software and the data (the telephone listings) may be done only for individual or personal use and that distribution, sub-licence or lease of the software or the data was prohibited? The court again said no. Copying of the data was clearly prohibited by the license agreement. But the court refused to enforce the agreement. The court stated that the terms of the Select Phone licence agreement were not presented to Zeidenberg or any other purchaser at the time of sale. The only reference to the agreement was a statement in small print at the bottom of the package that said users were subject to the terms and conditions of the enclosed licence agreement. Zeidenberg did not have the opportunity to inspect or consider the terms of the licence. The court did not think that mere reference to the terms at the time of the initial contract formation — forking over payment at the check-out counter —

1 939 F 2d 91 (3d Cir 1991).
2 908 F Supp 640 (WD Wis 1996).

presented Zeidenberg with an adequate opportunity to decide whether the licence terms were acceptable or not. Zeidenberg had to have been given the opportunity to read and consider the terms in their entirety at the time of initial contract formation, which the court said was the time the retail transaction was consummated. Under section 2-209 of the Uniform Commercial Code, the court held that the licence agreement terms contained inside the Select Phone package constituted additional terms to which Zeidenberg did not agree, nor have the opportunity to agree to, upon the initial agreement — payment at the check-out counter in exchange for the copy of the software. Further, the court held, even if the agreement were enforceable, copyright law would pre-empt the provision of the agreement prohibiting copying of the uncopyrightable telephone listings.

This case was then appealed before the U.S. Court of Appeals for the Seventh Circuit. The said court reversed the ruling and held in favour of ProCD emphasising the fact that the information provided on the box and under the shrink-wrapping gave ample notice to Ziedenberg about the existence of an agreement and had the agreement been unacceptable to him he could have prevented the formation of the contract by merely returning the CD to ProCD.

Click-wrap and browse-wrap licences. Most of us might have surfed the World Wide Web and to visit a web-site, purchase a product or service, or download a computer program/ "software". On such occasions it is very much possible that we are greeted by a reference to numerous lines of legal terms and provisions and a request or requirement for our consent to those terms. Here we are all experiencing a new form of contract presentation on the Internet that is commonly known as "click-wrap" or "browse-wrap." There are some differences between click-wrap and browse-wrap, but their purposes are usually the same. The distinctions, details and prime legal issues regarding these new forms of contracts, are worth discussing here.

What are click-wrap and browse-wrap? The advent of the Internet and the World Wide Web has given a new, electronic medium that facilitates the distribution of information, products, services, etc. that were previously distributed through physical mediums, such as personal meetings, hard-copies, and store-shelf packaging. With the arrival of this electronic medium, new means for providers to form contracts with consumers (or users), which shall govern the distribution of their offerings, has become imperative. Click-wrap and browse-wrap, as they are usually referred to, have emerged to provide this new means to form contracts over the Internet, particularly over the World Wide Web. Thus, the main purpose of click-wrap and browse-wrap is to enter into a contract (or agreement) between two or more parties where the terms and provisions of the agreement, and the consent to them, are communicated over the Internet. Infact the concept of click-wrap and browse-wrap evolved, to some extent, from the concept of "shrink-wrap," which is a continuing practice. As noted above these licences are primarily used for computer games and software providers, to present the terms and provisions associated with the use of a product within a sealed packaging (e.g., in a written or electronic format) that typically can only be accessed after the product has been purchased and unwrapped.

Click-wrap agreements normally consists of a presentation within a web-page of the terms and provisions of an agreement or contract along with a button, link, or other means that requires the reader, such as a user or consumer, to indicate the acceptance of the terms and provisions before proceeding with any further transactions. They are presented in a scrolling window (or scroll box) or a frame of a web-page, and a popular means to obtain consent from the reader is a button or link (*i.e.*, hyper-link) located near the agreement that is labelled "I Agree". These agreements are also called as "click-through" or "click" agreements.

Browse-wrap agreement when compared with click-wrap, contains a link, button, or other means within a web-page to direct a reader to a presentation of the terms and provisions of an agreement or contract. The presentation of the terms and provisions of a browse-wrap agreement is presented on another web-page or mostly in a remote location on the initial web-page, normally at the bottom of a long web-page. In most cases, the location of the presentation typically does not make it necessary for the terms and provisions to be read and agreed to prior to the user conducting further transactions. Furthermore, a user is typically presumed by implication to consent on the terms and conditions of a browse-wrap agreement by the mere act of browsing the associated web-site, regardless of whether those terms and conditions are actually reviewed by the user. Browse-wrap agreements are interchangeably called as "web-wrap" agreements.

What are the main differences between click-wrap and browse-wrap?
Based on the previous explanations of click-wrap and browse-wrap, some main differences can be recognized. One main difference is that a click-wrap agreement typically requires a reader to actively indicate his/her consent to the terms and provisions of the agreement before proceeding with further transactions, whereas a browse-wrap agreement does not have such a requirement. Another main distinguishing feature is that a click-wrap agreement typically presents the terms and provisions of the agreement forthright and in the same location or vicinity as the means for consent. In most of the click-wrap agreements, the terms and conditions are given above the buttons that can be clicked to accept or reject the agreement. Whereas, in contrast, a browse-wrap agreement typically presents the terms and provisions of the agreement in a location that is far from relevant initial references to the agreement and the means for acknowledgement of the

reader's consent. In such agreements, terms and provisions are displayed on a separate web-page.

Depending upon the previous differences, as well as other considerations, such as legalities and web-page aesthetics, there are many distinctions in the application of click-wrap and browse-wrap agreements, although some of these applications will likely change as laws and legal interpretations evolve. For example, click-wrap agreements are normally used to present and obtain consent to end user licence agreements for computer software and games that are purchased and or downloaded from the Internet. Whereas browse-wrap agreements are typically used to present terms of service contracts, for example, that applies to a service provided from an Internet web-site.

Legal issues regarding click-wrap and browse-wrap. There are many important legal issues regarding click-wrap and browse-wrap, which can really affect the enforceability of such agreements. These pertain to notice, consent, and fairness. These legal issues, and other related issues, will be discussed with respect to click-wrap and browse-wrap in the discussion below.

(a) Notice of click-wrap and browse-wrap. Notice is a very important legal issue with respect to the enforceability of click-wrap and browse-wrap agreements. This is because the enforceability of all agreements requires all parties who shall be bound by such agreements to knowingly agree to the terms and conditions of the agreements. Thus it is logical to assume that, the parties have notice of the existence of a click-wrap or browse-wrap agreement in order to agree to its terms and conditions.

Usually the notice of the existence of a click-wrap agreement is not a problem. If a user tries to get the service or product over the Internet that involves a click-wrap agreement, the click-wrap agreement is made available upfront to the user on an initial web-page before the user can proceed with the transaction. But notice of the existence of a browse-wrap agreement can be an issue atleast in some cases. This happens because, browse-wrap agreements are not presented to a user up-front on an initial web-page before the user can proceed with a transaction, but instead are presented on a separate web-page that can be reached by a link or other means of direction from the initial web-page. Apart from this, the link or other means of directing a user to the browse-wrap agreement is placed in a located in a manner which is not that easily noticeable on the initial web-page, normally at the bottom of the web-page. In most cases it is not visible on a screen unless the user scrolls down the page. Thus it is very much possible for a user not to receive any notice of the existence of a browse-wrap agreement.

Court decisions regarding notice and click-wrap. Forrest v *Verizon Communications, Inc.,*[3] deals with a dispute over notice of the forum selection clause of a click-wrap agreement between plaintiff *Forrest* and defendant *Verizon*. The argument of the plaintiff was that the forum selection clause was unenforceable because the click-wrap agreement did not provide adequate notice of the forum selection clause. The click-wrap text was placed in a scroll box (*i.e.*, a scrolling window), which included the statement "PLEASE READ THE FOLLOWING AGREEMENT CAREFULLY" at the top of the text.

Furthermore, the click-wrap agreement required a button labelled "I Accept," which was located below the scroll box, to be selected to complete the transaction with the defendant. Interestingly only a small portion of the click-wrap text was seen in the scroll box at one time, and the entire text of the agreement was very lengthy. The forum provision clause of the agreement was given at the end of the text and could only be seen after scrolling through most of the agreement. The court rejected the plaintiff's assertion of inadequate notice, relying on the traditional notion of contract law that "one who signs a contract is bound by a contract which he has an opportunity to read whether he does so or not." The court here compared the scroll box to the series of pages in a traditional contract and determined, therefore, that adequate notice of the forum selection clause was provided by the click-wrap agreement.

In *DeJohn* v *The TV Corporation International, et al,*[4] the plaintiff *DeJohn* tried to buy Internet domain names from defendant. *TV Corp.* through the website of defendant Register.com. For this transaction, the plaintiff entered into a click-wrap service agreement with defendant Register.com. A hyper-link on Register.com's web-page connected the plaintiff to a web-page containing the service agreement. To complete the purchase, DeJohn had to click a box, located just below the hyper-link, to indicate that he had read, understood, and agreed to the terms of the service agreement. While the dispute arose, DeJohn asserted that the click-wrap service agreement did not provide adequate notice of its terms, since the terms were only visible after following a link to a separate web-page. The court rejected this argument, finding that DeJohn was able to review the terms of the agreement by selecting the link.

Court decisions regarding notice and browse-wrap. Pollstar v *Gigmania Ltd.*,[5] involves a browse-wrap case, where the user was alerted to a license agreement by small grey print on a grey background. Furthermore clicking on the text did not take the user to the text of the agreement. Nevertheless,

3 805 A 2d 1007 (DC 2002).

4 245 F Supp 2d 913 (CD Ill 2003).

5 170 F Supp 2d 974, (ED Cal 2000).

the court decided that people sometimes enter into a contract by using a service without seeing the terms first. Using the analogy of a person purchasing an airline ticket stamped with terms and conditions, the court decided that even without obvious notice of the contract terms, a contract was formed. The enforceability of browse-wrap with respect to notice was one of first impression for the court in this case.

In *Register.com, Inc.* v *Verio, Inc.*[6] plaintiff Register.com, a registrar of Internet domain names, went to the court seeking an injunction against defendant Verio, a competitor and Internet service provider, for using automated software to access information on its web-site about its customers and compiling the information for mass-marketing purposes, such as sending "spam". Register.com contended that this involved breach of contract because its web-site contained a browse-wrap agreement that prohibited commercial use of any information obtained from its site. The browse-wrap agreement stated that using Register.com's web-site demonstrated assent to be bound by the terms and conditions of the agreement. However, Verio contended that there was no notice of such agreement provided to a user before the user became subject to the terms by using the web-site. The court, however, found that the "terms of use are clearly posted on Register's website.

(b) Consent to click-wrap and browse-wrap. Consent is a very important legal issue concerning the enforceability of click-wrap and browse-wrap agreements. As per the fundamentals of contract law, the parties to an agreement or contract must consent to the terms and conditions in order for the agreement to be binding upon them. Or in other words there should be mutual assent, or a "meeting of the minds." While it is always safe and advisable to have an explicit consent to an agreement, which of course is relied by courts in determining contract disputes, there can be circumstances in which consent can also be implied. For example, if a party knows the terms and conditions of an agreement and that party takes action that indicates the acceptance of them, a court may bind the party by its implied consent to the agreement, even thought the party never explicitly submitted consent. Having stated the above, a court may not hold a party bound to an agreement by implied consent, if the actions relied on for implied consent are unintentional or if the party had no notice of the agreement and, therefore, could not consent.

Click-wrap, as discussed above, always provides a means to indicate consent and requires the user to select the means before proceeding with a transaction. The presentation of a click-wrap agreement in a web-page may include a button or link that is labelled "I agree" or "I accept". Thus, click-wrap agreements usually provide a sufficient means for a user to indicate

6 126 F Supp 2d 238, (SDNY 2000).

consent to an agreement, although there is some legal dissension over the appropriate particulars for this means. Eventhough a click-wrap agreement provides a button or other means for a user to select to indicate consent, the legal validity of this consent may be questioned if there is no explicit acknowledgement in the click-wrap that selecting the button will indicate consent to the agreement. Thus, if the button or other means is located in a position such that the user can select it without seeing some, or may be even all, of the terms and conditions of the agreement, the legal validity of the consent may come into question.

While comparing with click-wrap, browse-wrap does not provide a means for a user to actively consent to an agreement. As discussed previously, browse-wrap does not even present the existence of the agreement to a user in an up-front and perceptible manner. On the other hand, browse-wrap agreements are typically framed in a manner to indicate that a user's consent is submitted by the act of the user browsing a web-site or conducting transactions within the web-site. Thus, browse-wrap agreements are typically based on the implied consent of a user, since the user's actions are used to indicate consent. As discussed above, this manner of obtaining implied consent may not be upheld in a legal dispute, particularly if a user was not provided with sufficient notice of the browse-wrap agreement.

Court decisions regarding consent and click-wrap. The case of *I. Lan Systems, Inc.* v *Netscout Service Level Corp.*,[7] was regarding the issue of whether the buyer of software was subject to the terms of a click wrap licence agreement which did not appear on the seller's web-site until after the purchase of the software was completed. I. Lan Systems made the payment for the software and was required either to accept or reject a license agreement within the software before proceeding further; I. Lan Systems selected the "I Agree" box. When the issue came before court, I. Lan Systems argued that it did not consent to the terms of the licence agreement, as they were not known to it at the time of the purchase and consequently the terms were not binding on him. The court rejected this argument and held that I. Lan Systems explicitly consented to the click wrap license agreement when it clicked on the box labelled "I Agree."

In *Moore* v *Microsoft Corp.*[8] the court held that the end-user licence agreement ("EULA") contained in defendant Microsoft's software program made it a validly binding contract between the parties which barred plaintiff Moore's claims. The court reasoned that the terms and conditions of the EULA were displayed prominently on the program user's computer screen before the installation of the software. Furthermore, the program's user was

7 183 F Supp 2d 328 (D Mass 2002).

8 293 AD 2d 587; 741 NYS 2d 91 (NYAD 2 Dept 2002).

required to express his consent to the EULA by clicking on the "I agree" icon before proceeding with the download of the software. Thus, the defendant offered a contract that the plaintiff agreed by using the software after having a chance to read the license. As a result, the court concluded, the plaintiff's claims were barred by the clear disclaimers, waivers of liability, and limitations of remedies contained in the EULA.

Court decisions regarding consent and browse-wrap. In the case of *Specht* v *Netscape Communications,*[9] visitors to a website who intended to download software were required to press a button to download the software. The issue was whether pressing the button, which was labelled "Download", amounted to consent to the licence agreement that included arbitration of disputes between plaintiff Specht and defendant Netscape Communications. The licence agreement terms were not visible when a web-site visitor, such as Specht, selected the "Download" button. But there was an invitation to read the terms of the licence agreement located at the bottom of the download web-page along with a link to the agreement on a separate web-page. A visitor was not asked to affirmatively indicate consent to this browse-wrap agreement before downloading the software. Therefore, the court held that the agreement, including the arbitration provision, was unenforceable, since there was nothing to show that the plaintiff had consented to it.

In *Ticketmaster Corp.* v *Tickets.com, Inc.*[10] a federal district court in the Central District of California turned down the plea of the plaintiff to enforce its browse-wrap agreement because the defendant had not agreed to be bound by its terms and conditions. The plaintiff, Ticketmaster Corp., operated a web-site where users could get details about upcoming events and purchase tickets online. Defendant Tickets.com using automated software obtained those details from the plaintiff's web-site on upcoming concerts and ticket vendor locations and posted the data on its own web-site. Plaintiff alleged that the defendant's actions were a breach of contract because Ticketmaster's browse-wrap agreement prohibited using any of the information obtained from its site for commercial use. Ticketmaster's browse-wrap agreement had a general statement that use of the site bound users to its terms and conditions. Next to this statement was a link to the full text of the Website's terms and conditions. The court held that Ticketmaster's browse-wrap agreement was unenforceable because it did not provide for sufficient proof of Tickets.com's consent to the agreement.

(c) Fairness of click-wrap and browse-wrap. Fairness is also a vital legal issue that may affect the enforceability of click-wrap and browse-wrap

9 306 F 3d 17 (2d Cir 2002).

10 2000 US Dist LEXIS 4553 (CD Cal 2000).

agreements. Fairness is a very broad term and this may include considerations of the conscionability of the terms and condition of the agreement as well as the amount of bargaining power that is shared by the parties in making the agreement. Just as the case with most forms of contracts, a court may find a click-wrap or browse-wrap agreement unenforceable to some extent if it contains terms or conditions that go against public policy or otherwise affect the conscience of the court. Again a court may limit the enforceability of a click-wrap or browse-wrap agreement if it finds that one or more of the parties was placed in the position of having an insufficient amount of bargaining power to affect the formation of a binding agreement or contract.

Fairness can be an issue with respect to both click-wrap and browse-wrap contracts. Court may feel that, the accepting party of a click-wrap or browse-wrap agreement, for e.g. a user, does not have the chance to negotiate the terms and conditions with the offering party of the agreement, such as the provider, because the click-wrap and browse-wrap agreements are presented over the Internet, instead of person to person. Thus more often than not, click-wrap and browse-wrap agreements contain terms and conditions that may be deemed unconscionable in view of the public policy of various jurisdictions. For e.g. some click-wrap and browse-wrap agreements may contain terms and conditions that confer the offering party the authority to freely invade the privacy of the accepting party, some click-wrap and browse-wrap agreements may include terms and conditions that completely shield the offering party from liability for knowingly providing a defective product or service but hold the user liable to the fullest extent for misuse of the product or service. In all such issues there is no parity of status between the parties and the agreement is always one-sided. If such is the case then the court will be forced to limit the enforceability of click-wrap or browse-wrap because of fairness issues.

Court decisions regarding fairness and click-wrap. In *Caspi* v *Microsoft Network, L.L.C.*[11] Caspi entered into a click-wrap agreement with Microsoft as an online subscriber to Microsoft's MSN network. The terms of Microsoft's MSN click-wrap membership agreement were displayed in a scrollable window. The subscriber had to click "I agree," to continue the registration process, or "I Don't Agree," which would discontinue the registration process. Caspi contended that Microsoft engaged in "unilateral negative option billing" by rolling subscribers into more expensive plans without their consent. Microsoft's click-wrap agreement had a forum selection clause requiring jurisdiction and venue in Microsoft's backyard, King County, Washington. Caspi also argued, that the forum selection clause of the click-

11 732 A 2d 528 (NJ App Div 1999).

wrap agreement was unenforceable because it lacked fairness. However, the court enforced the forum selection clause, finding that (1) there was no fraud or unfair bargaining power, (2) the clause did not violate public policy, and (3) it did not seriously inconvenience trial.

Court decisions regarding fairness and browse-wrap. In the case of *Comb* v *PayPal, Inc.*[12] the court rejected the validity of the terms in a browse-wrap agreement. PayPal was an on-line payment service provider. When some issues arose regarding its business, it tried to rely on the terms of its browse-wrap user agreement, which had a clause that provided for arbitration in case of any dispute. A link to the text of the browse-wrap user agreement was provided but the link need not be opened for the application to be processed. The agreement filled approximately 25 printed pages, and allegedly contained several overreaching and onerous provisions. The court noted that although the amount of the average transaction handled by PayPal was $55 the arbitration clause of the browse-wrap agreement required use of the more expensive commercial arbitration rules of the American Arbitration Association. Based on California law, the court found that the browse-wrap agreement was unconscionable and unfair in light of the cost of meeting the forum selection clause in comparison to the limited value of the average claim.

Developments and strategies regarding click-wrap and browse-wrap. The applications of click-wrap and browse-wrap are relatively new and may evolve considerably based on judicial, legislative, industry, and public opinions, among other influences. In that regard, some relevant developments and strategies concerning click-wrap and browse-wrap are discussed in the following sections. In India this concept is still in its infancy and there has been no judicial pronouncements regarding the enforceability of such contracts.

Emerging judicial opinions on enforceability of click-wrap and browse-wrap. Since click-wrap and browse-wrap are relatively new concepts, obviously there are very few published court decisions regarding such agreements. But over a period of time, as more and more cases are decided by the courts, the judicial opinions on the enforceability of click-wrap and browse-wrap will definitely take shape. If we analyse a recent court decision, it certainly indicates a change from the strict disapproval of browse-wrap indicated in the earlier case of *Comb* v *PayPal*.[13] In this more recent case of *Ticketmaster Corp.* v *Tickets.com, Inc.*[14] the court expressed its liking for a rule that required "unmistakable assent," such as by way of a

12 218 F Supp 2d 1165 (ND Cal 2002).
13 Ibid.
14 2003 US Dist. LEXIS 6484.

click-through agreement, before a contract could be formed. However, the court recognised that case law involving agreements for cruise tickets and parking tickets has established that unmistakable assent is not always necessary for contract formation. In that regard, the court accepted that knowledge or presumptive knowledge of the existence of browse-wrap terms may be a sufficient basis for contract formation where assent is defined as further use of a website. As a result, the court decided that with respect to browse-wrap, "a contract can be formed by proceeding into the interior web pages after knowledge or, in some cases, presumptive knowledge of the conditions accepted when doing so".[15]

Strategies for ensuring the enforceability of click-wrap and browse-wrap. Based on some of the unfavourable court decisions to product or service providers attempting to enforce click-wrap or browse-wrap agreements, several strategies can be suggested to ensure the enforceability of click-wrap and browse-wrap. Several steps have been recommended for ensuring the enforceability of click-wrap, which include: (1)displaying the terms and conditions of a click-wrap agreement in a highly noticeable location prior to the provision of any goods and services; (2) providing a highly visible and easily understood means to consent or decline the terms of a click-wrap agreement, preferably located at the bottom of the agreement; and (3) providing an eye-catching notice that an indication of acceptance of the click-wrap forms a legal contract binding both parties.

Thus steps can be suggested for ensuring the enforceability of browse-wrap, including: (1) making the link to the browse-wrap terms and conditions very noticeable and clearly indicative of its purpose (e.g., in some sites they use the words "THESE TERMS AND CONDITIONS GOVERN YOUR USE OF THIS SITE. YOU MUST CLICK HERE BEFORE PROCEEDING"); (2) providing a noticeable browse-wrap link consistently on each web-page and/or employing a persistent window that does not disappear as the web-site is navigated (e.g., on a web-site with multiple frames); and (3) clearly stating in the browse-wrap terms that the user agrees to be bound to the agreement by merely navigating the web-site.

With the rising use of click wrap and browse-wrap agreements over the Internet, issues pertaining to notice, consent, and fairness are likely to arise in legal disputes over these emerging forms of contracts. There are only a few published court decisions. Interestingly we can see that courts have typically upheld click-wrap agreements more consistently than browse-wrap agreements in such decisions. However, as more enterprises make use of the Internet as a medium for contract formation, it may become more

15 *Ibid.*

complex and challenging for users to dispute issues such as notice, consent, or fairness of browse-wrap, as well as of click-wrap. Further more the attitude of the courts may become more rigid in applying standards that are established for such issues of click-wrap and browse-wrap as the court decisions become more consistent. Thus it is in the interests of both providers and users to take adequate precautions to avoid disputes over the enforceability of click-wrap and browse-wrap agreements.

Issues in customised software agreements. While software licensing via the "shrink wrap" contracts contained on store-bought programs is applicable in the case of general software like MS-Office, licensing of customized software involves a lot of flexibility regarding negotiation. But of course there are some issues which needs to be negotiated very carefully.

Ownership issues. Clarity regarding ownership is a very important issue which one needs to focus. This should include terms regarding the owner of the customized software product and precisely what kind of a license the owner is getting. Unlike, other software, customized software is usually a joint project between a programmer/developer, and a client with specific needs.

Thus the agreement will contain clauses on who will own the software when it's completed and who will own its copyright. It may be the licensor (company creating the customized software), who will license the product to the user. It could be the user if the programmer is merely paid for his programming services. In some cases it could be jointly owned. Obviously, this has many implications and the best is to include a clause, which should contain one of the last two choices — that is, ownership by the user or joint ownership.

Duration of the licence. The second concern is regarding the duration of the licence. Here a number of factors are to be taken into account, like how long is the licence? Whether it is for a definite term or is it is, forever? Whether you are the only one who will have the right to use this software, or can variations or duplicates of it be licensed to other companies, like your competitors? How many licences one should have enable all those people who need to work with the software to do so. Whether there are any other limitations being placed on your use of the software.

The importance of source code. Another important aspect is the provision pertaining to source code. Source code and object code are the most frequently used terms in connection with a computer program. Thus it would be helpful to have a brief understanding of these terms.

Source code and object code denote the "before" and "after" versions of a computer program that is compiled before it is fit to be run in a computer. The source code contains the programming statements that are written by a programmer before being saved in a file. For example, a programmer using the C++ language types in a desired sequence of C++ language statements and thereafter saves them as a file. This file contains the source code. Thus Source code" is a human-readable text version of the program, which programmers can read and understand. But the computer cannot understand the source code and hence this source code should be converted into a format, which it can understand.

Thus after the source code is written it is compiled (or converted) with a C++ compiler so that the computer can understand the instructions. The resulting output, i.e. the compiled file, is referred to as object code. The object code consists of a sequence of instructions that the processor can understand and it is extremely difficult for a human to read or modify the object code. Thus when anybody buys an operating system or application software, it is mostly in the form of compiled object code and the source code is not included. Proprietary software companies like Microsoft and Adobe usually do not entertain any third party to access their source code although of late, there is a movement to develop software for e.g. Linux that is open to further improvement by anyone who wants to improve it, and here the source code is provided.

Having seen the importance of source code in a computer program, it is very much essential to include terms regarding access to the software's "source code". Without the source code, the user will land in trouble if the licensor fails or refuses to maintain the program or shuts shop because of some other reasons. Thus it is vital to negotiate either a complete license to the source code or access to it under certain agreed-upon conditions.

The best option would always be to get a license to the source code, but in case this is not possible then the user should make sure that the source code is available in cases of emergency by virtue of a concept termed "source code escrow." A "source code escrow" is a separate agreement entered into among the licensor, the licensee (user) and an independent, third party escrow agent. Under a standard source code escrow contract, the licensor deposits true copies of the software, including its object and source code and pertinent documentation, with the escrow agent, who will confirm its receipt in good order and release it to the beneficiary or its agents under certain designated circumstances. Usually this happens when there is a failure to maintain the software or the bankruptcy or other dissolution of the licensor's company.

Basically the escrow agreement is a trust agreement, where the source code is placed in trust with the third party, the licensor in these agreements is the party who settles or deposits the source code in trust and is often called the "Settler". The escrow agent is mostly referred to as the "Escrowee," "Escrow Agent," "Trust Agent" or some variation of these, to reinforce the notion that it is acting as a neutral in the transaction, holding the source code and supporting materials, which, themselves, are often referred to as the "Deposit." Finally the licensee (user) is termed as the "beneficiary" of the agreement, since it is the party that shall be given the access to the source code under certain defined conditions.

Although the precise terms of source code escrow agreements vary, there are certain aspects of these agreements that both licensors and licensees shall need to evaluate carefully before entering into such an agreement. The main issues always pertain to the duration and frequency of the deposit put in escrow along with degree of validation applied to it; clauses which specify the person who will be paying the cost of the escrow agent's services and of any administrative or litigation costs; the conditions under which the deposit may be released; and, lastly terms relating to title, confidentiality and warranty considerations. The features of a source code escrow agreement are discussed separately.

Payment, acceptance and maintenance. All customized software takes time to develop and usually consists of several modules or functional areas to it, it is always better to insist on progress payments in exchange for specific milestones. Furthermore clauses should be there to make sure that any modules developed in progress actually work, both independently and with the rest of the system.

Then there shall be provisions which relate to final acceptance of conditions, under which the licensor will be entitled to its full payment. Final acceptance criteria must be careful to clearly and comprehensively lay out performance standards as well as a certain test period for bug fixes before the software will be considered accepted. Another important clause is the one which pertains to maintenance and upgradation over time, here care should be taken to provide an affordable guaranteed maintenance contract, along with access to any upgrades that either the licensor or licensee may wish to incorporate into the software.

Warranties. Another important issue is regarding warranties. Warranties are the declarations that licensors make about how the software will perform and what will be done if it doesn't live up to those promises. The main issues here are the availability of refunds for software that doesn't perform as promised and the promptness on the part of the Licensor to repair or enhance the software in a timely manner. Other issues pertain to the licensor's responsibility for business damages sustained by the licensee because of non-functional software.

Confidentiality and trade secrets. Provisions relating to confidentiality and trade secrets are very important and should be properly addressed in the agreement. This is because in all customized software the user or his company is in a sense a co-creator of the software with the licensor. The software may reflect the user's proprietary methods, terminology, concepts, etc. along with the proprietary algorithms, techniques and expressions of ideas developed by the licensor. Both the parties should declare that they will not reveal the trade secrets and confidential information of the other party and this must be an important part of any software license.

The main features of a source code escrow agreement. To be simple the "deposit" clauses of a source code escrow agreement will specify the details to be given to the escrow agent, how it will be validated, and how frequently it will be updated. The escrowed materials will be released to the beneficiary only when the original programmer is no longer around to help. This would naturally involve new programmers, who are often unfamiliar with the program or its history.

For this reason, the agreement contains clauses that require the licensor or "Settlor" to deposit not only the source code, but also all materials sufficient for a trained computer programmer of general proficiency to maintain and support the software without further assistance from the Settlor. This normally consists of design notes, documentation, flow charts and instructions, etc. Furthermore there are clauses, which require the source code component of the deposit be accompanied by a running object code version submitted on virus-free magnetic media, compiled and ready to be read by a computer. This will really be helpful to the escrow agent so that he can verify that the contents of the deposit are in good working condition and certify the condition to the beneficiary.

Moreover, such agreements usually shall demand the settlor to deposit any maintenance modifications; updates, new releases or documentation related to the deposit materials that the licensee/beneficiary is entitled to receive under the licence agreement within a reasonable time of its delivery to the licensee. In order to facilitate the verification process the escrow agent has to make copies of the software, and for this the Settlor shall give the escrow agent a limited license to make such copies for the purposes set forth in the agreement. But the agreement should contain the clause that title to the deposit and all associated intellectual property rights remains with the Settlor.

Another clause deals with the level of verification the Escrow Agent will be called upon to apply to the deposit to certify it. The range here is significant; it can be from the most liberal one to the most stringent procedures, which allow validation of the integrity and completeness of the deposit, compared to the version of the software and documentation given to the licensee.

Of course from a licensee's viewpoint, the more stringent the procedures used, the safer it will feel, but this is usually balanced with the cost of performing such tests, since the cost is most often borne by the licensee.

Since the licensee is aptly considered the beneficiary of the trust, most of source code escrow agreements impose the overall cost of the storage and maintenance of the deposit, on the licensee/beneficiary.

If the deposit is made, verified and updated in good order, the most important issue pertains to the conditions under which the escrow agent is required to release it to the licensee/beneficiary or give it back to the Settlor. While some sample escrow agreements have certain conditions like bankruptcy or insolvency of the programmer, most common conditions that warrant the release of the source code pertains to certain major default provisions in the underlying software license agreement, which place the licensee at risk of irreparable injury. The most common illustrations, other than the programmer shutting shop, are failures to rectify or make the suitable modifications to the software within a certain period of time after notice; the programmer ceasing to further develop or support the software in general; failing to sign a maintenance agreement concerning the software, and similar contingencies.

Here, licensors insist on certain protections — and rightly so. First and foremost, licensors normally stipulate the licensee to make written demand to the escrow agent for release of the deposit, citing the "release event" contained in the escrow agreement. In turn, the escrow agent shall give notice of the demand to the licensor, who will typically have a certain amount of time in which to either agree to the release or dispute it. Failure on the part of the licensor to respond within a fixed period of time shall result in the release of the deposit. In case the licensor disputes the demand for the release, then there arises a serious issue. This is an area of contention since the conditions upon which the demand is made are often time-sensitive. In any case most licensees don't want to get into time consuming and expensive litigation to find out whether they had a right to get the code released.

Precisely because of this source code escrow agreements have provisions dealing with expedited arbitration and, sometimes, injunctive relief. In such cases a related provision must cover whether the licensor or licensee will cover the litigation or arbitration costs and expenses of the escrow agent, with the common compromise being either a 50-50 split between the licensor and licensee. In some other cases there may be provisions, which fix responsibility on the losing party to reimburse the costs completely. Another contentious issue is that of title and confidentiality. Although the Settlor gives a limited license to the escrow agent, title remains in the Settlor. Thus even in a scenario where the beneficiary is given access to the code and materials, still the title shall remain with the Settlor. Here the beneficiary is only granted the right of use, subject to strict limitations.

Of course there are some limitations being imposed upon the beneficiary getting access to the source code. The main limitation deals with the independent contractors, which the beneficiary may use in the event it gains access to the source code. Customized software is a highly competitive field, and it is highly probable that particular software contains some or most of the settlor's trade secret material. Here Licensors shall always include a list of competitors with whom the beneficiary is precluded from using as a replacement for the programming vendor. Generally, a prudent Licensor will stipulate that the beneficiary shall acknowledge the continuing trade-secret nature of the software. Furthermore there are clauses which require the beneficiary to obtain confidentiality agreements from all those who handle the code, and to assign back to the Licensor all intellectual property rights to any derivative works that may be created in the process of repairs or modifications.

Many source-code escrow agreements provide that, upon release of the source code, any warranties that originally applied to the software were void, upon the premise that the settlor should not be responsible for software once it's been tampered with by the beneficiary or its agents. It seems that this provision is a bit harsh on the licensee who is forced to obtain the source code due to inaction by the original licensor.

Website development agreements. Before concluding this chapter on computer contracts the main provisions of a website development agreement shall be discussed. As in any agreement here also the subject matter of the agreement must be described. Such an agreement should specify exactly what is to be developed and how it will be developed. That is, would the website development contain only writing the computer code for the website, or should it include the design and appearance of the site as well?

Whether it is only computer programming or more, the website developer normally retains title to the "work product." Thus in order for the client to rightfully utilize the product as its own, it must be licensed; much the same way as any other intellectual property is licensed. There can be licences which are quite restrictive; limiting the use of the product by the developer's client to the Internet and to the website created. This may not be in the interest of the organization for which the website is developed and it is always better to obtain title to the website software used to develop the site.

Again it is quite usual for the website developer to claim title to all materials created by him or her eventhough the costs of the development are borne by the client. This shall include all copyrights and other intellectual property rights. These, in turn, are licensed to the client as mentioned in the preceding paragraph. This is a norm in the technology industry where the development of a software program is often paid for by a single customer, while the website developer retains title to the program and licences the software to the customer/client. Usually the customer/client provides all the subject-matter to the website developer for use on the website. This subject-matter can range from product trademarks, product logos, literary information, or practically anything under the sun, owned by the client. Therefore, a clause is included to reaffirm the rights of the client in its own materials.

A website is truly a collection of components owned by multiple parties. Thus websites may include audio, as well video components; it is very much likely that the website includes the intellectual property of many parties. Thus there would be a clause which makes it clear that there is no transfer of third party rights or any of the components of the website.

It must be borne in mind that in a website development agreement which eventually leads to the publication of material, there is a mutuality of submissions by both the website developer and the client. The website developer will be contributing computer software that he/she develops whereas the client will be providing the content for the web page. Neither the client nor the developer, before entering into a website development agreement, will conduct any due diligence necessary to confirm that respective parties are the true owners of the materials they are providing so as to ensure there is no infringement of some third party's intellectual property rights. Thus the agreement should contain clauses which provide for mutual cross-indemnifications.

It is normal in software and website development contracts for the developer to include as a minimum a warranty that the work product will function in accordance with certain applicable specifications agreed to by the parties. Thus contracts will include a clause wherein the developer warrants the substantial conformance with acceptance criteria that have been approved, prior to contracting, between the parties.

Another important aspect to be remembered is that the World Wide Web is an international technology which rarely respects any frontiers. Thus the developer has to warrant that the use of his or her product will not violate any laws on the subject on a global basis. It is also common for developers to warrant that the contents supplied by them will in no way be scandalous, libelous or pornographic.

The website developer expects a similar warranty from the client. Thus the agreements contain clauses wherein the client warrants that it shall not violate any law or regulation nor post any defamatory or trade libellous; pornographic or obscene; content. Furthermore the client has to warrant that it has all the rights needed for the production, distribution, exhibition and exploitation of the Client Properties as part of the Work Product consistent with the license granted in this Agreement; and there is no outstanding contract, agreement to which Client is a party which conflicts with this Agreement or might limit restrict or impair the rights granted hereunder.

As is the case with all software development contracts and software licensing agreements, there shall be a clause normally at the end, which limits the liability of parties. Such a clause shall specify that neither party shall have any liability whatsoever for any cover or setoff nor for any indirect, consequential, exemplary, incidental or punitive damages, including lost profits, even if such party has been advised of the possibility of such damages. Normally such a clause is given in bold letters so that it become more noticeable.

Conclusion. This chapter has tried to shed some light on most of the agreements being used in the I.T. industry. Thus it is imperative for a user or a lawyer to understand, the concept of licensing which is prevalent in the software industry and how these licences are different from the general ones. The terms like shrink wrap, click wrap, browse wrap, object code, source code etc. might sound a bit strange to a conventional lawyer, but they are the standard terms which the I.T. industry is using. Thus an understanding of the basic concepts will help a long way in developing awareness and interest in this fast evolving field where developments are taking place at very rapid pace.

Forms

Hardware Sale and Installation Agreement

THIS AGREEMENT is made the .... day of .... 2004 by and BETWEEN (1) Eastern Computers Limited, a Company incorporated under the Companies Act 1956 (India) and having its administrative office at 54, Shakespeare Sarani, Kolkata 700 064 (herein after called "the SELLER", the expression unless repugnant to the context or specifically exempted shall include its successors and permitted assigns) of the first part AND (2) National Silk Foundation, a Society registered under the Societies Registration Act (XXI of 1860) having its administrative office at Bungalow No.1, Satellite Complex, Ashram Road, Ahmedabad 380015 (herein after called "the CUSTOMER", the expression unless repugnant to the context or specifically exempted shall include its successors and permitted assigns) of the second part.

The SELLER and the CUSTOMER are together called PARTIES.

WHEREAS the SELLER has agreed to sell and install certain computer equipment for the CUSTOMER upon the terms and conditions hereinafter contained.

THEREFORE IT IS HEREBY AGREED as follows:

1. Definitions

In this Agreement, unless the context otherwise requires, the following words shall have the following meanings:

(1) 'The Equipment' shall mean the computer equipment mentioned in the Schedule and any replacement equipment and /or parts provided as per clause 18 as the situation demands or the case may require;

(2) 'Essential Software' means the computer software embedded in or forming an essential part of the Equipment as specified in the Schedule;

(3) 'The Price' shall mean the price for the Equipment and the services to be provided hereunder as specified in the Schedule;

(4) 'The Off-Loading Point' shall mean the customer's off-loading point mentioned in the Schedule;

(5) 'The Location' shall mean the customer's room in which the Equipment shall be installed as mentioned in the Schedule;

(6) 'The Delivery Date' shall mean the delivery date specified in the Schedule, including any extended date applicable under Clause 12;

(7) 'The Commissioning Date' shall mean the date on which the Equipment is accepted by the customer pursuant to clause 11;

(8) 'Business day' means a day other than a Sunday or a public holiday.

2. Products and services to be provided

(1) The SELLER hereby agrees to:

(*a*) sell the Equipment to the CUSTOMER free from any encumbrances;

(*b*) deliver the Equipment to and install it at the Location on the Delivery Date;

(*c*) provide the other services hereinafter described upon the terms and conditions hereinafter contained.

(2) Floppy discs, CD-ROMs, stationery, printing cartridges and similar accessories shall not be supplied free as part of the Equipment.

3. Price and payment

(1) The Price shall be paid by the CUSTOMER as to 25 per cent upon the signing of this Agreement (by way of a deposit)) whereas the balance shall be paid within 3 days from the Commissioning Date.

(2) The Price and any extra charges payable under this Agreement are in conformity with the seller's standard price list in force on the date of this Agreement.

(3) The Price and any extra charges payable under this Agreement are exclusive of Taxes which shall be paid by the CUSTOMER at the rate and

in the manner for the time being prescribed by laws of the Republic of India.

(4) Any charges payable by the CUSTOMER under this Agreement in addition to the Price shall be paid within 3 days from the Commissioning Date.

(5) If the CUSTOMER defaults in making any payment under this Agreement, upon the expiry of 7 days from the date on which payment becomes due, the SELLER may charge interest on such sum on a day to day basis from the date or last date for payment thereof to the date of actual payment (both dates inclusive) at the rate of ...... per cent from time to time in force compounded half yearly. The CUSTOMER shall pay such interest on demand from the SELLER. This is without prejudice to the SELLER's other rights and remedies.

4. Title and risk

(1) The ownership of the Equipment shall pass to the CUSTOMER upon payment in full of the price mentioned in this Agreement and any other sums that may then be due under this Agreement.

(2) Once the Equipment is installed at the location of the CUSTOMER the risk in the Equipment shall pass to the CUSTOMER and accordingly the CUSTOMER shall be liable for insuring the Equipment against all normal risks with effect from the time risk passes.

(3) The Copyright, Patent, Trade Mark or other intellectual property rights in the Essential software are owned the Software Owner and have been licensed to the SELLER.

(4) The SELLER shall discharge its obligations under this Agreement on the following terms and conditions:

(*a*) The CUSTOMER is purchasing the media on which such Essential Software is recorded or embedded only.

(*b*) Nothing contained in clause 4(4) shall be construed as an assignment or transfer of any copyright, design right or other intellectual property rights in such Essential Software, all of which rights are owned by the Software Owner duly licensed to the SELLER.

(*c*) Except as provided by Clause 4(4)(*e*), the SELLER hereby grants to the CUSTOMER a non-exclusive and non-transferable licence, to use such Essential Software in the form in which it is embedded in the Equipment on the delivery date for use in conjunction with other parts of the Equipment on the condition that the Equipment shall be used for its intended purpose only.

(*d*) The CUSTOMER shall not rent, lease, sub-licence, copy, modify, adapt, merge, translate, reverse engineer, decompile, disassemble or create derivative works based on the whole or any part of such Essential Software or any part thereof in any manner.

(*e*) The CUSTOMER shall be entitled to transfer the benefit of the licence granted pursuant to clause 4(4)(*c*) to any purchaser of the Equipment on the condition that the purchaser gives in writing before making such purchase to be bound by the terms of clause 4(4) including the provisions of this paragraph (*e*). The Licence shall automatically terminate forthwith in case the purchaser does not accept such terms.

(*f*) The Licence shall remain effective without any limitation in time unless it is terminated in accordance with paragraph (*e*) or until the CUSTOMER shall terminate it by erasing or deleting such Essential Software. The Licence shall also terminate forthwith automatically if the CUSTOMER fails to abide by the terms of clause 4(4) of this Agreement. In case of such termination of the Licence, the CUSTOMER shall delete or otherwise destroy such Essential software and issue the SELLER, a written statement certifying that the Essential software has been destroyed.

(5) The price includes the right for the CUSTOMER to use the Essential software in terms of sub-clauses (3) and (4).

5. Location preparation

The SELLER shall in advance inform the CUSTOMER of the date of delivery of the Equipment and provide all assistance to enable the CUSTOMER to prepare the most suitable Location for the installation of the Equipment and for this purpose the SELLER shall depute a qualified technical person, free of charge, to advise the CUSTOMER. The CUSTOMER shall get the location ready, at its own expense and provide the required environmental and operational conditions prior to delivery

6. Information and access

(1) The CUSTOMER shall provide the SELLER promptly with any information, which the SELLER may reasonably require to carryout the performance of this Agreement without any delay.

(2) The CUSTOMER shall, for the purposes of this Agreement, provide to the authorized personnel of the SELLER during normal working hours

full and safe access to the Location along with sufficient working space and such other facilities as any be needed for the installation of the Equipment.

7. Pre-delivery tests

(1) The SELLER shall carryout standard works tests (hereinafter called TESTS) on the Equipment before delivery to the CUSTOMER, the results of which shall be given to the CUSTOMER on request, along with a certificate that the Equipment has passed the same.

(2) The CUSTOMER or its authorized representative may witness the TESTS. The SELLER shall give the CUSTOMER atleast 10 day's written notice of the date and time at which the SELLER intends to carry out the TESTS. The SELLER reserves the right to proceed with the TESTS without the CUSTOMER in case the CUSTOMER fails to attend the TESTS at the time and place specified in the notice.

8. Delivery

(*a*) When the Delivery Date is due the SELLER shall deliver the Equipment to the Off-Loading Point and then move the equipment to the Location.

(*b*) If the Equipment requires any removal of doors, widening of entrances or any other structural work of any description for the purpose of moving the Equipment from the Off-Loading Point to the Location, such work shall be undertaken by the CUSTOMER at its own expense prior to delivery.

(*c*) In the event of SELLER providing any special equipment, manpower or works necessary to move the equipment from the off-Loading point to the Location, the CUSTOMER shall reimburse the SELLER the reasonable costs incurred for doing so.

9. Installation

(1) The SELLER shall install the Equipment at the Location when the Delivery Date becomes due.

(2) In case it becomes necessary to remove, adjust, change or otherwise disconnect any of the customer's existing equipment at the Location in order to carry out the installation of the Equipment, then the CUSTOMER shall permit, and obtain all the required permission from the concerned authorities as may be required for such removal, adjustment, change or disconnection and shall give the SELLER all necessary help to carryout such work.

10. Post-delivery tests

(1) Not more than 10 days from the date of installation of the Equipment the SELLER shall, subject the Equipment to the seller's common installation tests (hereinafter called 'INSTALLATION TESTS') to make sure that the Equipment and every part thereof is in full working condition. Upon customer's request, the SELLER shall supply the CUSTOMER copies of the specification and results of the INSTALLATION TESTS.

(2) If any part of the Equipment fails to pass the INSTALLATION TESTS then, the INSTALLATION TESTS shall be repeated on such part of the Equipment within a reasonable period of time and if any part of the equipment fails to pass the second INSTALLATION TESTS, the SELLER shall, upon request made by the CUSTOMER, replace such part of the Equipment.

(3) The CUSTOMER or its Authorized representative reserves the right to witness the INSTALLATION TESTS. The SELLER shall give the CUSTOMER at least 48 hours written notice of the date and time at which the SELLER intends to carry out the INSTALLATION TESTS. The SELLER reserves the right to proceed with the INSTALLATION TESTS without the CUSTOMER in case the CUSTOMER fails to attend the TESTS at the time and date specified in the notice.

11. Acceptance

The CUSTOMER shall accept the Equipment after the Equipment and every part thereof has passed the INSTALLATION TESTS and the CUSTOMER shall, sign an Acceptance Certificate as given in the Annexure.

12. Force Majeure

Notwithstanding anything contained in this Agreement, neither party shall be responsible for any delay in performing its part hereunder in case such delay is caused by circumstances beyond its reasonable control provided the party so delaying promptly notifies the other party in writing of the reasons for the delay. Such party's obligations shall be suspended during the term that the said circumstances continue and such party shall be given a reasonable extension of time for performance taking into account the period of delay. Except where such delay is a result of an act or omission of the other party:

(1) any costs arising from such delay shall be borne by the party incurring the same;

(2) in case such delay persists for more than 45 days, either party reserves the right to terminate this Agreement forthwith to the other in which event neither party shall be liable to the other reason of such termination except that the CUSTOMER shall pay the SELLER a reasonable amount with respect to any work done before such termination and for that purpose the SELLER

reserves the right to deduct such sum from any amounts previously paid by the CUSTOMER under this Agreement.

13. Customer's default

In case the SELLER is prevented from performing its duties under this Agreement by reason of any act or omission of the CUSTOMER which is not covered by clause 13, then the SELLER reserves the right to charge from the CUSTOMER all reasonable costs, expenses and losses sustained or incurred by the SELLER as a result which may include, without limitation, the cost of storage and insurance of the Equipment. The SELLER shall promptly give in writing a notice to the CUSTOMER of any claim, which may arise under this Clause, by giving the necessary details of such act or omission.

14. Cancellation

The CUSTOMER may cancel this Agreement, for any reason not falling under Clause 15, in respect of all or any part of the Equipment, by giving a 20 days written notice prior to the Delivery Date and paying the SELLER cancellation charges: of a sum equal to 7.5 per cent of the price of the equipment cancelled.

15. Termination

(1) This Agreement may be terminated forthwith by either party by giving notice in writing to the other if the other party shall have a receiver or administrative receiver appointed or shall pass a resolution for winding-up, or a court of competent jurisdiction issuing an order to that effect, or shall enter into any voluntary arrangement with its creditors or shall cease or threaten to cease to carry on business.

(2) Any termination under sub-clause (1) shall discharge the parties' from further obligations under this Agreement and in the case of a termination by the SELLER shall entitle the SELLER to enter any of the customer's premises and take back any of the SELLER'S equipment and materials and also to be paid a reasonable amount for any work carried out by it prior to such termination and in the case of a termination by the CUSTOMER shall entitle the CUSTOMER to be repaid forthwith any amount previously paid under this Agreement, whether paid by way of a deposit or otherwise, and to recover from the SELLER the amount of any loss or damage sustained or incurred by the CUSTOMER as a consequence of such termination.

(3) Notwithstanding the termination of this Agreement, accrued rights or duties of either party shall remain unaffected. The termination shall have no effect on the coming into force or the continuance in force of any provision hereof which is expressly or by implication intended to come into or continue in force on or after such termination.

16. Seller's warranties

(1) (*a*) The SELLER warrants that the Equipment shall be free form defects in materials, workmanship and installation for a period of 18 months after the Commissioning Date ('the Warranty Period').

(*b*) In the event of a breach of the said warranty the CUSTOMER shall issue a written notice regarding the such breach to the SELLER who upon receiving such notice shall at its own expense and within 5 days after receiving such notice, repair or, at its option, replace the Equipment or such parts of it as are defective or otherwise rectify such defect provided that the SELLER shall have no liability or duty under the said warranty unless it shall have received written notice of the defect in question during the Warranty period. The legal and beneficial ownership of the Equipment or any defective parts shall revert to the SELLER upon the replacement of the Equipment or such defective parts whereupon the legal and beneficial ownership of the replacement equipment or parts shall vest in the CUSTOMER.

(*c*) The SELLER shall have no liability or duty as per the said warranty other than to rectify breaches thereof by the provision of materials and services within 5 days and without charges to the CUSTOMER. If the SELLER fails to discharge the said obligations the SELLER's shall be liable only to pay a sum equivalent to the price of the equipment or such parts as the case may be. The SELLER shall not be liable, whether in contract or tort, with respect to defects in the Equipment notified to it, without prejudice to liability under Clause.

(*d*) The said warranty shall not apply in case the CUSTOMER does not use the Equipment in a proper manner and if any part of the equipment has been modified, altered or repaired by any person other than the representative of the SELLER. Said warranty shall not apply if repairing is needed because of reasons other than ordinary use including without limitation accident, hazard, misuse or failure or fluctuation of electric power.

(2) The SELLER does not warrant that the Equipment is suitable for any particular function unless the CUSTOMER conveys that function to the SELLER in writing and the SELLER confirms in writing that the Equipment shall be suitable for that particular function.

(3) The SELLER does not give any warranty that the Equipment shall achieve any specific performance standard unless:

(*a*) the SELLER has specifically guaranteed such standard in writing subject to specified tolerances in an agreed sum as liquidated damages; and

(*b*) the environmental conditions stipulated by the SELLER are provided.

(4) With the exception of conditions and warranties specified by The Sale of Goods Act 1930, the express terms of this Agreement are in lieu of all warranties, obligations, conditions, terms, duties, and undertakings implied by statutory law, common law, trade usage, custom, course of dealing or otherwise, all of which are hereby excluded to the maximum extent permitted by law.

17. Confidentiality

Each party shall treat as confidential all facts/data/information obtained from the other as a result of this Agreement and shall not disclose such facts/ data /information to any person without the other party's prior written consent. This Clause shall not apply to any facts/information/data, which was legitimately possessed by such party prior to the signing of this Agreement or which forms part of public domain or shall become so at a future date, otherwise than as a result of a breach of this Clause, or which is trivial or obvious. Each party shall ensure that its employees, including sub-contractors, comply with the provisions of this Clause. The foregoing obligations as to confidentiality shall survive any termination of this Agreement.

18. Operating manuals and training

(1) The SELLER shall provide the CUSTOMER with 3 copies of operating manuals containing adequate information, which shall enable the CUSTOMER to operate the Equipment in a proper manner. Additional copies of operating manuals shall be provided to the CUSTOMER, on request, for which the SELLER may charge a reasonable fee.

(2) The SELLER shall train the customer's staff to use the Equipment as set out in the schedule. If the customer's staffs require any additional training the SELLER shall provide such training in conformity with its standard scale of charges applicable.

19. Removal of labels

The CUSTOMER shall not change, take off, alter or remove any labels, name plates, insignia, lettering or other markings which are on the Equipment at the time of installation thereof.

20. Maintenance

The parties shall enter into a maintenance agreement on the Commissioning Date in respect of the Equipment in the form of the draft annexed hereto.

21. Intellectual property rights indemnity

(1) The SELLER shall indemnify the CUSTOMER on demand, against all claims, costs, demands, allegations, charges, expenses and liabilities of whatsoever nature arising out of or in connection with any claim that the normal use or possession of the Equipment infringes the intellectual

property right, including without limitation any patent, copyright, registered design, design right or trademark of any third party, subject to the following condition:

(*a*) the CUSTOMER shall forthwith intimate the SELLER in writing of any allegations of infringement of which it has notice and shall not make any admissions without the seller's prior written consent;

(2) The indemnity under sub-clause (1) above shall not be applicable in case the infringement is a result of the use of the Equipment or any part thereof in conjunction with any equipment and /or computer programs not sold, supplied or authorized by the SELLER for use with the Equipment.

(3) If a Court of competent jurisdiction delivers any judgment to the effect that customer's normal use or possession of the Equipment constitutes an infringement of a third party's intellectual property rights then the SELLER shall promptly and at its own expense:

(*a*) obtain on behalf of the CUSTOMER the right to continue using and possessing the Equipment; or

(*b*) without deviating from its overall performance, replace the Equipment so as to avoid the infringement and also reimburse the CUSTOMER for the amount of any direct loss incurred by the CUSTOMER during such replacement or remove the Equipment from the Location and refund the price to the CUSTOMER.

22. Liability

(1) The SELLER shall indemnify the CUSTOMER on demand, against any loss, destruction or damage to any property or injury to or death of any person caused by any negligent act or omission or willful misconduct of the SELLER, its employees, agents or sub-contractors or by any defect in the design or workmanship of the Equipment.

(2) The CUSTOMER shall indemnify the SELLER on demand against, any loss destruction or damage of or damage to any property or injury to or death of any person caused by any negligent act or omission or willful misconduct of the CUSTOMER, its employees, agents or sub- contractors.

(3) Notwithstanding anything contained in this Agreement the SELLER shall not be liable to indemnify the CUSTOMER for loss or profits or contracts to other indirect or consequential loss whether arising from negligence, or breach of contract.

(4) The SELLER shall not be liable to the CUSTOMER for any damage/ destruction/loss of computer programs and/or data, arising out of any failure or lapse on the part of the CUSTOMER to follow the best computing practices.

23. Entire agreement

This Agreement supersedes all prior arrangements, agreements, and understandings entered between the parties relating to the subject-matter hereof. Any addition to or modification of any provision of this Agreement shall be binding only if the said addition or modification be made by a written instrument signed by a duly authorized representative of each of the parties.

24. Assignment

Except as specifically provided in this Agreement, neither party shall assign or otherwise transfer this Agreement or any of its rights and obligations hereunder whether in whole or in part without the prior written consent of the other.

25. Sub-contracts

The SELLER shall not, without the prior written consent of the CUSTOMER, enter into any sub-contract with any person for the performance of any part of this Agreement provided that his provision shall not apply to:

(*a*) the purchase by the SELLER of equipment and materials; and

(*b*) the sub-contracts (if any) specified in the schedule.

The SELLER shall be liable for all of its obligations under this Agreement notwithstanding any sub-contract by the SELLER for the performance of any part of this Agreement.

26. Notice

All notices which are required to be given hereunder shall be in writing and shall be sent to the address of the recipient set out in this Agreement or such other address in India as the recipient may designate by notice may be delivered personally or by express courier or facsimile transmission and shall be deemed to have been served if by hand when delivered, if by express courier 48 hours after posting and if by facsimile transmission when dispatched.

27. Interpretation

In this Agreement :

(1) reference to any statue or statutory provision shall include a reference to the statue or statutory provision as from time to time amended, extended or re-enacted;

(2) Words importing the singular include the plural, words importing any gender include every corporate and unincorporated; and (in each case) *vice versa*;

(*a*) Any reference to a party to this Agreement includes a reference its successors in title and permitted assigns;

(*b*) The headings to the Clauses are for ease of reference only and shall not affect the interpretation or construction of this Agreement.

(*c*) Nothing in this Agreement shall be construed to constitute a partnership, joint-venture or agency relationship between parties.

28. Governing Law

The Agreement shall be governed by and construed in accordance with the Laws of the Republic of India.

29. Disputes settlement

Any dispute or claim arising out of or in connection with this Agreement or the performance, breach or termination hereof, shall be finally settled by binding arbitration conducted in Kolkata (India) by a Panel consisting of three arbitrators, wherein one arbitrator shall be appointed by the SELLER, the other arbitrator shall be appointed by the CUSTOMER and the third arbitrator shall be appointed jointly by the PARTIES. The provisions of the Arbitration and Conciliation Act 1996 shall govern arbitration. The award of arbitration shall be binding and final.

30. Severability

In case the whole or any part of any provision term of this agreement is deemed to be illegal or unenforceable the other provisions of this Agreement and the remaining part of the provision in question shall remain in full force and effect.

31. Survival

The clauses of this Agreement, intended to survive the termination of this Agreement shall continue to remain in full force and effect after such termination.

IN WITNESS WHEREOF, each of the parties has caused this Agreement to be duly executed and delivered as of the day and year first above written.

Signed for and on behalf of:

By ....

Signature ....

Title ....

Witness ....

Signed for and on behalf of

By ....

Signature ....

Title ....

Witness ....

THE SCHEDULE

A. The equipment

The schedules must provide full description of each item, the number of such items and the price per item. The description shall also contain the manufacturer's reference number and also define the equipment to distinguish it from similar equipments from competitors.

B. Essential Software

Owned by third parties.

C. Price

The equipment price.

D. The off-loading point.

E. The location.

F. The delivery date.

G. Training.

H. Sub-contracts.

Hardware maintenance agreement

THIS AGREEMENT is made the .... day of .... 2003 by and BETWEEN Eastern Computers Services Limited, a Company incorporated under Companies Act 1956 (India) and having its administrative office at 54, Shakespeare Sarani , Kolkata 700 064 (herein after called "the SERVICE PROVIDER", the expression unless repugnant to the context or specifically exempted shall include its successors and permitted assigns of the first part) AND National Silk Foundation, a Society registered under the Societies Registration Act (Act XXI of 1860) having its administrative office at Bungalow No.1, Satellite Complex, Ashram Road, Ahmedabad 380015 (herein after called "the CUSTOMER", the expression unless repugnant to the context or specifically exempted shall include its successors and permitted assigns) of the second part.

The SERVICE PROVIDER and CUSTOMER are together called PARTIES.

Recital:

The SERVICE PROVIDER has agreed to maintain the CUSTOMER's computer equipment hereinafter described upon the terms and conditions hereinafter contained.

NOW IT IS HEREBY AGREED as follows:

1. Definitions

In this agreement, unless the context otherwise demands, the following expressions shall have the following meanings:

(*i*) 'The Equipment' shall mean the computer equipment mentioned in the Schedule and the Supplementary Equipment and such additions and changes thereto as shall from time to time be agreed in writing between the PARTIES.

(*ii*) 'The Supplementary Equipment' shall have the meaning attributed thereto in Clause 3(*iii*).

(*iii*) 'The Location' shall mean the CUSTOMER's computer room in which the Equipment has been installed as specified in the Schedule.

(*iv*) 'The Commencement Date' shall mean the date on which this agreement becomes operational as specified in the Schedule.

(*v*) 'The Initial Period' shall mean the initial period of this agreement as specified in the Schedule.

(*vi*) 'The Scheduled Maintenance' shall mean the maintenance services to be provided by the SERVICE PROVIDER in accordance with Clause 2.

(*vii*) 'The Emergency Maintenance Services shall mean the emergency maintenance services to be provided by the SERVICE PROVIDER in accordance with Clause 4.

(*viii*) 'The Maintenance Services' shall mean the Scheduled Maintenance Services and the Emergency Maintenance Services.

(*ix*) 'The Maintenance Charge' shall mean the periodic charge for the Scheduled Maintenance Services mentioned in the Schedule as varied from time to time be agreed in writing between the PARTIES.

(*x*) 'Maintenance Hours' shall mean the hours between 9.00 am and 6.00 pm each day excluding Sundays and public holidays.

2. Scheduled maintenance Services

As long as this agreement remains valid the SERVICE PROVIDER hereby agrees to provide the following maintenance services with respect to the Equipment:

(*i*) *Preventive maintenance.* The SERVICE PROVIDER shall visit the Location every 3 months to check the functions of the Equipment and make such adjustments as shall be necessary to keep the Equipment in good working condition. SERVICE PROVIDER shall make such visits only during Maintenance Hours by prior appointment with the CUSTOMER. If it is convenient in the opinion of the SERVICE PROVIDER to do so, such maintenance may be carried out at the same time as corrective maintenance.

(*ii*) *Corrective maintenance.* Upon receiving information from the CUSTOMER that the Equipment has failed or is not functioning properly the SERVICE PROVIDER shall during Maintenance Hours carry out such repairs and/or change the defective parts of the Equipment, as may be necessary, to restore the Equipment to its proper working condition.

(*iii*) *Response time.* Upon receiving a request for corrective maintenance the SERVICE PROVIDER shall endeavour its best to send a qualified service engineer to the Location within 6 hours.

3. Charges

(*i*) In consideration of the Scheduled Maintenance Services the CUSTOMER shall make payment of the Maintenance Charge periodically in advance as specified in the Schedule. The Maintenance Charge shall be paid with out prior demand. All payments shall be made in the manner specified in the Schedule.

(*ii*) Any charges payable by the CUSTOMER here under in addition to the Maintenance Charge shall be paid within 30 days from receiving the SERVICE PROVIDER's invoice.

(*iii*) When it becomes known to the SERVICE PROVIDER that any equipment at the Location which is not included in the Equipment and in respect of which the CUSTOMER requests any maintenance Services ('Supplementary Equipment') the SERVICE PROVIDER shall provide the Maintenance Services in respect of the supplementary Equipment in the same way as in respect of the Equipment and charge for it in accordance with the rate set out in the schedule.

(*iv*) The SERVICE PROVIDER shall at any time after the expiry of the Initial Period increase the Maintenance Charges by giving to the CUSTOMER not less than 60 day's prior written notice. Where such notice is given, the CUSTOMER shall have the right to terminate this Agreement as from the date on which such notice expires by giving to the SERVICE PROVIDER written notice of termination not less than 30 days' before such date.

(*v*) The Price and any extra charges payable under this agreement are exclusive of taxes which shall be paid by the CUSTOMER at the rate and in the manner for the time being prescribed by laws of the Republic of India.

(*vi*) If the CUSTOMER defaults in making any payment under this agreement, upon the expiry of 7 days from the date on which payment becomes due, the SERVICE PROVIDER may charge interest on such sum on a day to day basis from the last date for payment thereof to the date of actual payment, both dates inclusive, at the rate of ...... per cent from time to time in force compounded half yearly. The CUSTOMER shall pay such interest on demand from the SERVICE PROVIDER. This is without prejudice to the SERVICE PROVIDER's other rights and remedies.

4. Emergency Maintenance Services

Apart from the Scheduled Maintenance Services the SERVICE PROVIDER shall provide during the subsistence of this agreement emergency corrective maintenance service outside Maintenance Hours as far as practicable after the receiving a request made by the CUSTOMER during at the SERVICE PROVIDER's standard scale of charges for such service from time to time in force. Such charges shall operate from the first arrival of the SERVICE PROVIDER's engineer at the Location to his final departure there from.

5. Exceptions

(*i*) The Maintenance Services do not include any maintenance of the Equipment, which is necessitated as a result of any cause other than fair wear and tear or the SERVICE PROVIDER's negligence or default including without limitation:

(*a*) Failure or fluctuation of electric power, air conditioning, humidity control or other environmental conditions; or

(*b*) Accident, transportation, neglect, misuse, or default of the CUSTOMER, its employees or agents or any third party; or

(*c*) Any defect in any attachments or associated equipment which do not form part of the Equipment; or

(*d*) Act of God, fire, flood, war, act, of violence, or any other similar occurrence; or

(*e*) Any attempt by any person other than the SERVICE PROVIDER's personnel to repair or maintain the Equipment;

(*ii*) The SERVICE PROVIDER shall at the request and expense of the CUSTOMER rectify or replace any part of the Equipment which has failed due to a cause other than fair wear and tear or the SERVICE PROVIDER's negligence or default. In such cases the work shall commence only after the CUSTOMER accepts the written quotation of the SERVICE PROVIDER.

(*iii*) The Maintenance Services shall not include the following:

(*a*) service at any site other than at the Location specified in the schedule;

(*b*) repair of tapes, disk, printing cartridges or other consumable supplies;

(*c*) repair or support of the operating system of any computer;

(*d*) repair or support of any electrical work external to the Equipment;

(*e*) maintenance of any attachments or associated equipment which do not form part of the Equipment; or

(*f*) retrieval of any data or programs lost or destroyed as a result of any computer virus attack, breakdown of or fault in the Equipment.

6. Replacement

(*i*) The SERVICE PROVIDER shall reserve the right to replace the whole of the Equipment or any part or parts thereof which may be defective.

(*ii*) The SERVICE PROVIDER while making any such replacement shall not remove the Equipment or any part or parts thereof until the Replacement Equipment has been made ready for installation.

(*iii*) The SERVICE PROVIDER shall at the time of any such replacement intimate the CUSTOMER in writing of the serial numbers of the Replacement Equipment.

(*iv*) If the Replacement Equipment is not identical in all respects to the replaced equipment then this fact shall be communicated by the SERVICE PROVIDER to the CUSTOMER in writing at the time of replacement.

(*v*) Within 10 days of being communicated of replacement of non-identical equipment the CUSTOMER shall have the right to direct that the Replacement Equipment or any part thereof be removed and either the Equipment be put back or other equipment identical to the Equipment be installed and the SERVICE PROVIDER shall comply with such direction immediately.

(*vi*) The Replacement Equipment shall become the property of the owner of the Equipment. The Equipment or any part or parts thereof removed shall become the property of the SERVICE PROVIDER subject to the condition that the owner of the Equipment shall be the owner of equipment identical in value and performance to the Equipment.

(*vii*) The provisions of this agreement shall apply to all replacements and renewals of any part or parts of the Equipment made by the SERVICE PROVIDER during the subsistence of this agreement.

7. Service visits outside the Maintenance Services

The SERVICE PROVIDER shall make an additional charge, in accordance with its standard scale of charges from time in force, for service visits made at the request of the CUSTOMER by reason of any defect in the Equipment due to causes not covered by the Maintenance Services.

8. Duration

This agreement shall commence on the Commencement Date, shall continue for the Initial Period and shall remain in force thereafter until terminated by either party giving to the other not less than 6 months' written notice of termination issued on the last day of the Initial period or at any time thereafter but shall be subject to earlier termination as provided elsewhere in this agreement.

9. Customer's obligations

During the subsistence of this agreement the CUSTOMER shall:

(*i*) Make sure that appropriate environmental conditions are maintained for the Equipment and shall maintain in good condition the accommodation of the Equipment, the cables, wirings and fittings associated therewith and the electricity supply thereto.

(*ii*) Not make any modification to the Equipment without the SERVICE PROVIDER's prior written consent.

(*iii*) Operate the Equipment in a proper and prudent manner according to the manufacturer's operating instructions and ensure that only competent trained employees are permitted to operate the Equipment.

(*iv*) Not make any attempt to adjust, repair or maintain the Equipment and shall not direct, permit or authorize anyone other than the SERVICE PROVIDER to carry out any adjustments, repairs or maintenance of the Equipment.

(*v*) Use on the Equipment only such spare parts as the SERVICE PROVIDER shall recommend in writing.

(*vi*) Not remove the Equipment from the Location without the SERVICE PROVIDER's prior written consent.

(*vii*) Not use in conjunction with the Equipment any accessory, attachment or additional equipment other than that which has been supplied by or approved in writing by the SERVICE PROVIDER.

(*viii*) Provide the SERVICE PROVIDER with complete and safe access to the Equipment for the purposes of this agreement.

(*ix*) Provide sufficient working space around the Equipment for the use of the SERVICE PROVIDER's personnel and shall make available such reasonable facilities as may be requested from time to time by the SERVICE PROVIDER for storing safely the test equipment and spare parts.

(*x*) Promptly inform the SERVICE PROVIDER when the Equipment needs maintenance or is not working satisfactorily. CUSTOMER failure to intimate the SERVICE PROVIDER any failure or malfunctioning within 2 months of its occurrence shall free the SERVICE PROVIDER from all obligations to investigate or correct such failure or malfunctioning.

(*xi*) Subject to Clause 12(*ii*), provide the SERVICE PROVIDER such programs, operating manuals and information as may be necessary to enable the SERVICE PROVIDER to perform its obligation hereunder.

(*xii*) Make available to the SERVICE PROVIDER free of cost all facilities and services reasonably required by the SERVICE PROVIDER to perform the Maintenance Services including without limitation computer runs, print-outs, typing and photocopying.

10. Spare parts

(*i*) The CUSTOMER shall purchase from the SERVICE PROVIDER such spare parts as the SERVICE PROVIDER shall specify which shall be supplied at the SERVICE PROVIDER's list prices from time to time in force.

(*ii*) The SERVICE PROVIDER shall not be liable for any delay in performing its obligations hereunder if any of the specified spare parts are not available otherwise than due to the default of the SERVICE PROVIDER.

11. Termination

(*i*) Not with standing anything else contained herein, this agreement may be terminated:

(*a*) by the SERVICE PROVIDER forthwith on giving notice in writing to the CUSTOMER incase the CUSTOMER makes any default to pay any sum due under the terms of this Agreement otherwise than as a consequence of any default on the part of the SERVICE PROVIDER and such sum remains unpaid for 30 days after written notice from the SERVICE PROVIDER that such sum has not been paid; or

(*b*) by the CUSTOMER forthwith on giving notice in writing to the SERVICE PROVIDER if the Equipment is lost, stolen or destroyed or damaged beyond economic repair; or

(*c*) by either party forthwith on giving notice in writing to the other if the other commits any material breach of any term of this agreement other than any failure by the CUSTOMER to make any payment hereunder in which event the provisions of paragraph (a) above shall apply and in the case of a breach capable of being rectified shall have failed, within 30 days after the receipt of a request in writing from the other party so, to do, to rectify the breach; or

(*d*) by either party forthwith on giving notice in writing to the other if the other party becomes insolvent or an official liquidator appointed of it or over any part of its undertaking or assets or shall cease to carry on business.

(*ii*) Any termination of this agreement howsoever happened shall not affect any accrued rights or liabilities of either party nor shall it affect the coming into force or the continuance intended to come into or continue in force on or after such termination.

(*iii*) On the termination of this agreement the CUSTOMER shall be entitled to reimbursement of a pro-rata part of the Maintenance Charge paid in advance.

12. Confidentiality

(*i*) Each party shall treat as confidential all facts/data/information obtained from the other as a result of this agreement and shall not disclose such facts/data/information to any person without the other party's prior written consent. This clause shall not apply to any facts/information/data, which was legitimately possessed by such party prior to the signing of this agreement or which forms part of public domain or shall become so at a future date, otherwise than as a result of a breach of this clause, or which is trivial or obvious. Each party shall ensure that its employees, including sub contractors, comply with the provisions of this clause. The foregoing obligations as to confidentiality shall survive any termination of this agreement.

(*ii*) The CUSTOMER's obligations under clause 9(*xi*) to make available the information therein mentioned shall be subject to the SERVICE PROVIDER signing such confidentiality undertaking as may be required by or to protect any third party having in such information prior to the same being made available.

13. Force majeure

Neither party shall be liable for any delay in performing any of its obligations hereunder if such delay is caused by factors and/or circumstances beyond the reasonable control of the party so delaying and such party shall be entitled to a reasonable extension of time for the performance of such obligations.

14. Liability

(*i*) The SERVICE PROVIDER shall not be liable for any loss or damage sustained or incurred by the CUSTOMER or any third party including, without limitation, any loss of use of the Equipment or loss of or spoiling of the CUSTOMER's programs or data resulting from any breakdown of or fault in the Equipment unless such breakdown or fault is caused by the negligence or misconduct of the SERVICE PROVIDER, its employees, agents or sub-contractors or except to the extent that such loss or damage arises from any unreasonable delay by the SERVICE PROVIDER in providing the Maintenance Services.

(*ii*) The CUSTOMER shall indemnify the SERVICE PROVIDER on demand against, any loss destruction or damage of or damage to any property or injury to or death of any person caused by any negligent act or omission or willful misconduct of the CUSTOMER, its employees, agents or sub-contractors.

(*iii*) The SERVICE PROVIDER shall indemnify the CUSTOMER on demand against, any loss destruction or damage of or damage to any property or injury to or death of any person caused by any negligent act or omission or willful misconduct of the SERVICE PROVIDER, its employees, agents or sub-contractors.

(*iv*) Notwithstanding anything contained in this agreement the SERVICE PROVIDER shall not be liable to indemnify the CUSTOMER for any indirect or consequential loss whether arising from negligence, or breach of contract.

15. Entire agreement

This agreement supersedes all prior arrangements, agreements, and understandings entered between the parties relating to the subject-matter hereof. Any addition to or modification of any provision of this agreement shall be binding only if the said addition or modification be made by a written instrument signed by a duly authorized representative of each of the parties.

16. Assignment

Except as specifically provided in this agreement, neither party shall assign or otherwise transfer this agreement or any of its rights and obligations hereunder whether in whole or in part without the prior written consent of the other.

17. Sub-contracts

(*i*) The SERVICE PROVIDER shall not, without the prior written consent of the CUSTOMER, enter into any sub-contract with any person for the performance of any part of this agreement.

(*ii*) The SERVICE PROVIDER shall be liable for all of its obligations under this agreement notwithstanding any sub-contract by the SERVICE PROVIDER for the performance of any part of this agreement.

18. Notices

All notices which are required to be given hereunder shall be in writing and shall be sent to the address of the recipient set out in this agreement or such other address in India as the recipient may designate by notice may be delivered personally or by express courier or facsimile transmission and shall be deemed to have been served if by hand when delivered, if by express courier 48 hours after posting and if by facsimile transmission when dispatched.

19. Interpretation

In this agreement:

(*i*) reference to any statue or statutory provision shall include a reference to the statue or statutory provision as from time to time amended, extended or re-enacted;

(*ii*) Words importing the singular include the plural, words importing any gender include every corporate and unincorporated; and (in each case) *vice versa*;

(*a*) any reference to a party to this agreement includes a reference its successors in title and permitted assigns;

(*b*) the headings to the clauses are for ease of reference only and shall not affect the interpretation or construction of this agreement;

(*c*) nothing in this agreement shall be construed to constitute a partnership, joint-venture or agency relationship between PARTIES.

20. Governing Law

The agreement shall be governed by and construed in accordance with the Laws of the Republic of India.

21. Dispute Settlement

Any dispute or claim arising out of or in connection with this agreement or the performance, breach or termination hereof, shall be finally settled by binding arbitration conducted in Kolkata (India) by a Panel consisting of three arbitrators, wherein one arbitrator shall be appointed by the SERVICE PROVIDER, other arbitrator shall be appointed by the CUSTOMER and the third arbitrator shall be appointed jointly by the PARTIES. The provisions of the Arbitration and Conciliation Act 1996 shall govern arbitration. The award of arbitration shall be binding and final.

22. Severability

If any provision of this agreement is held to be invalid, illegal or unenforceable under present or future laws, such provision shall be struck from the agreement; however such invalidity or enforceability shall not affect the remaining provisions or conditions of this agreement. The parties shall remain legally bound by the remaining terms of this agreement and shall strive to reform the agreement in a manner consistent with the original intent of the parties.

IN WITNESS WHEREOF, each of the parties has caused this agreement to be duly executed and delivered as of the day and year first above written.

Signed for and on behalf of:

By ....

Signature ....

Title ....

Witness ....

Signed for and on behalf of:

By..

Signature ....

Title ....

Witness ....

THE SCHEDULE

A. The Equipment

B. The Location

C. Commencement Date

Date of the Agreement

D. The Initial Period

E. The Maintenance Charge

Total Charges:

Advance:

Balance payable:

F. Method of Payment.

Software Licence Agreement

THIS AGREEMENT is made the 28th day of May 2004 by and BETWEEN Eastern Computers Limited (A Company incorporated under Companies Act 1956 (India) and having its administrative office at 54 Park Street, Kolkata 700 017 (herein after called "the LICENSOR", the expression unless repugnant to the context or specifically exempted shall include its successors and permitted assigns) of the first part AND National Silk Foundation, a Society registered under the Societies Registration Act (Act XXI of 1860) having its administrative office at Bungalow No. 1, Satellite Complex, Ashram Road, Ahmedabad 380 009 (herein after called "the LICENSEE", the expression unless repugnant to the context or specifically exempted shall include its successors and permitted assigns) of the second part.

The LICENSOR and the LICENSEE are together called the PARTIES.

WHEREAS the LICENSOR has agreed to deliver to the LICENSEE and install on the LICENSEE's computer certain computer programs and to grant the LICENSEE a non-exclusive to use such programs and their associated documentation upon the terms and conditions hereinafter contained.

THEREFORE IT IS HEREBY AGREED as follows:

1. Definitions

In this Agreement, unless the context otherwise requires, the following words shall have the following meanings:

1. 'The Licence' shall mean the licence granted by the LICENSOR in accordance with provisions of Clause 7.

2. 'The Equipment' shall mean the LICENSEE's computer for which the Licence is granted, specified by type and serial number in the Schedule and using the "XXXX" operating system.

3. 'The Licensed Programs' shall mean the computer programs of the LICENSOR specified in the Schedule.

4. 'The Program Documentations' shall mean the operating manuals, user instructions, technical literature and all other related materials which is readable by the human eye supplied to the for helping the use of the Licensed Programs.

5. 'The Media' shall mean the media on which the Licensed Programs and the Program Documentation are printed or recorded as supplied to the LICENSEE by the LICENSOR.

6. 'Use the Licensed Programs' shall mean to install the Licensed Programs into and store and run them on the Equipment in accordance with the terms of this Agreement.

7. 'The Licence Fee' shall mean the fee for the licence and the services to be provided under this Agreement as specified in the Schedule.

8. 'The Delivery Date' shall mean the delivery date mentioned as per the Schedule or such extended date as may be granted in accordance with provisions of Clause 21.

9. 'The Location' shall mean the LICENSEE's computer room where the Equipment is kept as specified in the Schedule.

10. 'The Acceptance Date' shall mean the date on which the Licensed Programs are accepted or deemed to be accepted by the LICENSEE in accordance with the provisions of Clause 5.

2. Products and services to be provided

THE LICENSOR hereby agrees to:

(*i*) grant to the LICENSEE a non-exclusive licence to use the licensed program materials;

(*ii*) provide the licensed programs to the LICENSEE and load them on the Equipment;

(*iii*) hand over training and operating manuals to the LICENSEE;

(*iv*) provide the other services herein after described; as per the terms and conditions hereinafter contained.

3. Payment

(*i*) The Licence Fee shall be paid by the LICENSEE on the Acceptance Date.

(*ii*) Licence Fee and other charges payable under this Agreement are exclusive of taxes which shall be paid by the LICENSEE at the rate and in the manner for the time being prescribed by laws of the Republic of India.

(*iii*) Any amount payable by the LICENSEE hereunder in addition to the Licence Fee shall be paid within 45 days after the receipt by the LICENSEE of the LICENSOR's invoice regarding that amount.

(*iv*) If the LICENSEE defaults in making any payment under this Agreement, upon the expiry of 7 days from the date on which payment becomes due, the LICENSOR may charge interest on such sum on a day to day basis from the date or last date for payment thereof to the date of actual payment (both dates inclusive) at the rate of ...... per cent from time to time in force compounded half yearly. The LICENSEE shall pay such interest on demand from the LICENSOR. This is without prejudice to the LICENSOR's other rights and remedies.

4. Delivery and installation

Once the delivery date is due the LICENSOR shall deliver the Licensed Programs to the LICENSEE and load the same on the Equipment at the Location. The Licensed Programs shall contain one copy of the object code of the Licensed Programs in machine-readable form only, on the storage media mentioned in the Schedule.

5. Testing and acceptance

(*i*) After the Licensed Programs are loaded, the LICENSEE shall provide the LICENSOR the requisite test data which is appropriate to test the efficiency of the Licensed Programs along with the results expected to be attained by processing such test data using Licensed Programs. Upon receiving such data along with the expected results the LICENSOR shall process such data, in the presence of the LICENSEE or its authorised agent, on the Equipment using the Licensed Programs by way of acceptance test within 10 days after such receipt at a time mutually convenient to the PARTIES.

(*ii*) The LICENSEE shall accept the Licensed Programs forthwith after the LICENSOR has proved that the Licensed Programs have correctly processed the test data by attaining the expected results. The LICENSEE shall if required by the LICENSOR, sign an acceptance certificate in the form annexed hereto acknowledging such acceptance.

(*iii*) In case the LICENSEE fails to provide any test data as aforesaid or fails to attend the acceptance tests within the said period of 10 days then the LICENSEE shall be deemed to have accepted the Licensed Programs.

6. Warranty

I. (*a*) The LICENSOR warrants that the Licensed Programs shall after acceptance by the LICENSEE provide the facilities and functions set out in the Specification when properly used on the Equipment. The Program Documentation shall provide adequate information and instruction to enable the LICENSEE make appropriate use of such facilities and functions.

(*b*) Upon the LICENSOR receiving any written notice from the LICENSEE after the Acceptance Date of any breach of the said warranty then the LICENSOR shall at its own expense and within a reasonable time after receiving such notice remedy the defect or error in question. However the

LICENSOR shall have no liability or obligations under the said warranty unless the LICENSOR receives a written notice of the defect or error in question within 12 months from the Acceptance Date.

(*c*) The said warranty shall be applicable only if the LICENSEE complies with its obligations hereunder and to there having been made no alterations to the Licensed Programs by any person other than the LICENSOR. As far as possible the LICENSEE shall furnish the LICENSOR with a documented example of the defect or error.

II. The LICENSOR shall have no liability or obligations under the said warranty other than to rectify the breaches thereof by the provisions of materials and services within a reasonable time and without charge to the LICENSEE. If the LICENSOR shall fail to comply with such obligations its liability for such failure shall be limited to a sum equal to the Licence Fee. The foregoing states the entire liability of the LICENSOR, whether in contract or tort, for defects and errors in the Licensed Program Materials which are notified to the LICENSOR after Acceptance Date.

III. The LICENSEE acknowledges that the Licensed Programs have not been developed to suit the requirements of the LICENSEE and that it is therefore the responsibility of the LICENSEE to make sure that the facilities and functions described in the specification meet its requirements. THE LICENSOR shall have no liability for any failure of the Licensed Programs to provide any facility or function not specified in the specification.

IV. The express terms of this Agreement are in lieu of all warranties, obligations, conditions, terms, duties, and undertakings implied by statutory law, common law, trade usage, custom, course of dealing or otherwise, all of which are hereby excluded to the maximum extent permitted by law.

7. Licence

I. The LICENSOR hereby grants to the LICENSEE a non-exclusive licence to use the Licensed Program Materials subject to the terms and conditions hereinafter contained

II. The LICENSEE shall utilise the Licensed Program Materials for processing its own data for its own internal business only. The LICENSEE shall not allow any third party to use the Licensed Program Materials nor use the Licensed Program Materials for and on behalf of any third party in any manner possible.

III. The use of the Licensed Program Materials shall be limited to use on and in conjunction with the Equipment save that:

(*a*) In the case of any inability to use the Licensed Program Materials in conjunction with the Equipment because of it being inoperable for any reason then the Licence shall be temporarily extended without additional charge to use with any other equipment until such inability has been rectified provided that such equipment is under the direct control of the LICENSEE. It shall be the duty of the LICENSEE to immediately inform the LICENSOR such temporary use and of the commencement and cessation thereof;

(*b*) The Licence may with the prior written permission of the LICENSOR use the Licensed Program Materials on and in conjunction with any suitable replacement equipment, which shall be specified by type and serial number, if the use of the Licensed Program Materials on and in conjunction with the Equipment is permanently discontinued. Once such permission being granted the replacement equipment shall become the Equipment for the purposes of the Licence.

IV. The Licence shall not be deemed to extend to any programs or materials of the LICENSOR other than the Licensed Program Materials unless specifically agreed to in writing by the LICENSOR.

V. The LICENSEE hereby acknowledges that it is licensed to use the Licensed Program Materials strictly in accordance with the express terms of this Agreement and not further or otherwise.

8. Duration of Licence

The Licence shall have its force from the Acceptance Date and shall continue until terminated in accordance with clause .... or as otherwise provided in this Agreement.

9. Proprietary Rights

(*i*) The Licensed Program and the copyright and other intellectual property rights of nature in the Licensed Program Materials are and shall remain the property of the LICENSOR and the LICENSOR shall have the right to grant licence to use Licensed Program Materials to third parties.

(*ii*) In case the LICENSEE becomes aware of any unauthorized use of the whole or any part of the Licensed Program Materials by any person the LICENSEE shall notify the LICENSOR forthwith.

(*iii*) The LICENSEE shall allow the LICENSOR to check the use of the Licensed Program Materials at all reasonable occasions and for doing so the LICENSOR and / or its authorised agent shall have the right to enter any of the LICENSEE's premises.

10. Intellectual Property Rights Indemnity

The LICENSOR shall indemnify the LICENSEE against any claim that the normal use or possession of the Licensed Program Materials infringes the intellectual property rights of any third party provided that the LICENSOR is given immediate notice such claim, that the LICENSEE does not prejudice the LICENSOR's defence of such claim and that the claim does not arise as a result of the use of the Licensed Program Materials in conjunction with any equipment not approved by the LICENSOR. The LICENSOR shall have the right to replace, modify, change or alter all or any part of the Licensed Program Materials so as to avoid any infringement. The foregoing declares the entire liability if the LICENSOR to the LICENSEE in respect of the infringement of the intellectual property rights of any third party.

11. Confidentiality of Licensed Program Materials

(*i*) The LICENSEE hereby undertakes to treat as confidential all information contained or expressed in the Licensed Program Materials and the specification and all information, know-how conveyed to the LICENSEE by training (hereinafter called 'the INFORMATION').

(*ii*) The LICENSEE shall not without the prior written permission of the LICENSOR divulge any part of the INFORMATION to any person except:

(*a*) the LICENSEE's own employees who need to know the same;

(*b*) the LICENSEE's auditors and any other persons or bodies having a right, duty or obligation to know the business of the LICENSEE only in pursuance of such right, duty or obligation;

(*c*) any person who is from time to time appointed by the LICENSEE to maintain any equipment on which the Licensed Programs are being installed only to the extent necessary to enable such person properly to maintain such equipment.

(*iii*) The LICENSEE hereby undertakes to make sure that the persons and bodies mentioned in paragraphs (*a*), (*b*) and (*c*) of sub-clause (*ii*) have sufficient knowledge that the INFORMATION is confidential prior to the disclosure of any part of the INFORMATION and that they owe a duty of confidence to the LICENSOR, the LICENSEE hereby undertakes to indemnify the LICENSOR against any loss, destruction or damage which the LICENSOR may sustain as a result of any failure on the part of the LICENSEE to comply with such an undertaking.

(*iv*) Upon knowledge of any breach of confidence by any person to whom the LICENSEE divulges all or any part of the INFORMATION, the LICENSEE shall immediately notify the LICENSOR and shall provide the LICENSOR all reasonable assistance in connection with any proceedings, which the LICENSOR may institute against such person for breach of confidence.

(*v*) The foregoing obligations pertaining to confidentiality shall remain in full force and effect not with standing any termination of the Licence or this Agreement.

12. Copying

(*i*) The LICENSEE may make only so many copies of the Licensed Programs as are reasonably needed for operational security and use. All such copies and the media on which they are recorded shall belong to the LICENSOR and the LICENSEE shall have the obligation to make sure that all such copies bear the LICENSOR's proprietary notices. The Licence shall apply to all such copies as it applies to the Licensed Programs.

(*ii*) Only after obtaining the prior written consent of the LICENSOR, the LICENSEE shall make any copy of the Program Documentation.

13. Security

The LICENSEE shall during the continuation of the Licence:

(*i*) effect and maintain adequate security measures so that no unauthorized person can access or use the Licensed Program Materials;

(*ii*) have effective control over Licensed Program Materials and all copies thereof;

(*iii*) keep a full and accurate record of the LICENSEE's copying and disclosure of the Licensed Program Materials and shall produce such record to the LICENSOR whenever such a request is made.

14. Alterations

(*i*) The LICENSEE shall not modify, alter, change, adapt or translate the whole or any part of the Licensed Program Materials in any manner possible nor allow the whole or any part of the Licensed Program to be combined with or become included in any other computer programs nor decompile, disassemble or reverse engineer the same nor attempt to do any of such things, except to the extent and in the circumstances expressly required to be permitted by the LICENSOR by law.

(*ii*) To the extent that the Copyright Act, 1957 (India), grants the LICENSEE the right to decompile the Licensed Programs so as to obtain the details needed to make the Licensed Programs interoperable with other computer programs used by the LICENSEE, the LICENSOR hereby undertakes to provide such information readily available to the LICENSEE. The LICENSOR hereby reserves the right to impose reasonable conditions that may include a fee for doing so. The LICENSEE shall first give the LICENSOR sufficient details of the LICENSEE's objectives and the other software concerned. Requests for the sufficient information should be given by notice to the LICENSOR as per the terms and conditions of this Agreement.

15. Software Maintenance

Unless the LICENSEE enters into a software maintenance agreement with the LICENSOR on or before the Acceptance Date the LICENSOR shall not provide any maintenance in respect of the Licensed Program Materials. If on a subsequent date the LICENSEE desires to receive the then current release of the Licensed Program Materials or maintenance, then the LICENSOR may at its discretion provide the same if the LICENSEE enters into a new licence agreement in respect of such release and also enters into the LICENSOR's standard software maintenance agreement then in force.

16. Operating Manuals

The LICENSOR shall supply the LICENSEE with 3 copies of operating manuals for the Licensed Programs containing sufficient information so that all the facilities and functions set out in the specification can be properly utilised. If the LICENSEE needs further copies of such operating manuals then these may be obtained under licence from the LICENSOR after paying the standard scale of charges from time to time in force.

17. Training

(*i*) The LICENSOR shall impart training for the staff of the LICENSEE to use the Licensed Programs as set out in the Schedule.

(*ii*) Any additional training needed by the LICENSEE shall be provided by the LICENSOR as per the LICENSOR's standard scale of charges from time to time in force.

18. Licensee's Confidential Information

The LICENSOR shall consider as confidential all information provided by the LICENSEE under this Agreement which is designated as confidential by the LICENSEE or which is by its implication clearly confidential provided that this clause shall not extend to any information which was rightfully known to the LICENSOR prior to the commencement of the negotiations leading to this Agreement or which is already in public domain or becomes so at a future date, otherwise than as a result of a breach of this clause. The LICENSOR hereby undertakes not to divulge any confidential information to any person except to its own employees who need to know the same. The LICENSOR shall ensure that its employees are fully aware of and comply with the provisions of this Clause. The foregoing obligations shall survive any terminations of the Licence or this Agreement.

19. Termination

(*i*) The LICENSEE may terminate the Licence at any time by giving at least 45 day's prior written notice to the LICENSOR.

(*ii*) The LICENSOR may terminate the Licence forthwith by issuing notice in writing to the LICENSEE if:

(*a*) the LICENSEE commits any material breach of any term of this Agreement and in the case of a breach capable of being remedied, the LICENSEE has failed to remedy the breach and 30 days have expired after the receipt of a request in writing from the LICENSOR to that effect;

(*b*) the LICENSEE permanently discontinues the use of the Licensed Program Materials; or

(*c*) the LICENSEE becoming insolvent or an official liquidator appointed of it or over any part of its undertaking or assets or shall cease to carry on business.

(*iii*) Except as expressly provided in sub-clause (2) or elsewhere in this Agreement the Licence may not be terminated.

(*iv*) Immediately upon the termination of the Licence the LICENSEE shall return to the LICENSOR the Licensed Program Materials and all copies of the whole or any part thereof, in the alternative upon a request being made by the LICENSOR the LICENSEE shall destroy the same by deleting the Licensed Programs from the media on which they are stored and certify in writing to the LICENSOR that they have been destroyed. The LICENSEE shall also delete the Licensed Programs from the Equipment and shall certify to the LICENSOR that the same has been done.

(*v*) Any termination of the Licence or this Agreement shall have no effect on any of the accrued rights or liabilities of either party nor shall it affect the coming into force or the continuance in force of any provisions hereof which is expressly or by implication intended to come into or continue in force on or after such terminations.

20. Assignment

The LICENSEE shall not be entitled to assign, sub-license or otherwise transfer the Licence whether in whole or in part except that the LICENSEE shall be entitled to assign the entire benefit of the Licence to any company which is from time to time a holding company or a subsidiary of the LICENSEE, as defined under the relevant provisions of the Companies Act 1956 (India), subject to such company first entering into a legally binding covenant with the LICENSOR undertaking to comply with the terms and conditions hereof and provided that at the time of such assignment such company holds the exclusive possession of the Equipment for its own use and benefit.

21. Force Majeure

Notwithstanding anything contained in this Agreement, neither party shall be responsible for any delay in performing its part hereunder in case such delay is caused by circumstances beyond its reasonable control provided the party so delaying promptly notifies the other party in writing of the reasons for the delay. Such party's obligations shall be suspended during the term that the said circumstances continue and such party shall be given a reasonable extension of time for performance taking into account the period of delay. Except where such delay is a result of an act or omission of the other party:

(*a*) any costs arising from such delay shall be borne by the party incurring the same;

(*b*) in case such delay persists for more than 45 days, either party reserves the right to terminate this Agreement forthwith to the other in which event neither party shall be liable to the other reason of such termination except that the LICENSEE shall pay the LICENSOR a reasonable amount with respect to any work done before such termination and for that purpose the LICENSOR reserves the right to deduct such sum from any amounts previously paid by the LICENSEE under this Agreement.

22. Liability

(*i*) The LICENSOR shall indemnify the LICENSEE on demand, against any loss, destruction or damage to any property or injury to or death of any person caused by any negligent act or omission or willful misconduct of the LICENSOR, its employees, agents or sub-contractors or by any defect in the design or workmanship of the Licensed Program Material.

(*ii*) The LICENSEE shall indemnify the LICENSOR on demand against, any loss destruction or damage of or damage to any property or injury to or death of any person caused by any negligent act or omission or willful misconduct of the LICENSEE, its employees, agents or sub-contractors.

(*iii*) Notwithstanding anything contained in this Agreement the LICENSOR shall not be liable to indemnify the LICENSEE for loss or profits or contracts to other indirect or consequential loss whether arising from negligence, or breach of contract.

(*iv*) The LICENSOR shall not be liable to the LICENSEE for any damage/destruction/loss of computer programs and/or data, arising out of any failure or lapse on the part of the LICENSEE to follow the best computing practices.

23. Entire Agreement

This Agreement along with the schedules and exhibits, if any, comprises the whole and complete agreement and it shall supersede all prior arrangements, agreements, and understandings entered between the PARTIES relating to the subject-matter hereof. Any addition to or modification of any provision of this Agreement shall be binding only if the said addition or modification be made by a written instrument signed by a duly authorized representative of each of the parties.

24. Notice

All notices which are required to be given hereunder shall be in writing and shall be sent to the address of the recipient set out in this Agreement or such other address in India as the recipient may designate by notice may be delivered personally or by express courier or facsimile transmission and shall be deemed to have been served if by hand when delivered, if by express courier 48 hours after posting and if by facsimile transmission when dispatched.

25. Interpretation

In this Agreement:

(*a*) reference to any statue or statutory provision shall include a reference to the statue or statutory provision as from time to time amended, extended or re-enacted;

(*b*) words importing the singular include the plural, words importing any gender include every corporate and unincorporated; and (in each case) *vice versa*;

(*c*) any reference to a party to this Agreement includes a reference its successors in title and permitted assigns;

(*d*) the headings to the clauses are for ease of reference only and shall not affect the interpretation or construction of this Agreement;

(*e*) nothing in this Agreement shall be construed to constitute a partnership, joint-venture or agency relationship between PARTIES.

26. Governing Law

The Agreement shall be governed by and construed in accordance with the Laws of the Republic of India.

27. Dispute Settlement

Any dispute or claim arising out of or in connection with this Agreement or the performance, breach or termination hereof, shall be finally settled by binding arbitration conducted in Kolkata (India) by a Panel consisting of

Three arbitrators, wherein one arbitrator shall be appointed by the LICENSOR, other arbitrator shall be appointed by the LICENSEE and the third arbitrator shall be appointed jointly by the PARTIES. The arbitration shall be governed by the provisions of the Arbitration and Conciliation Act 1996. The award of arbitration shall be binding and final.

28. Severability

If any provision of this Agreement is held to be invalid, illegal or unenforceable under present or future laws, such provision shall be struck from the Agreement; however such invalidity or enforceability shall not affect the remaining provisions or conditions of this Agreement. The PARTIES shall remain legally bound by the remaining terms of this Agreement and shall strive to reform the Agreement in a manner consistent with the original intent of the PARTIES.

IN WITNESS WHEREOF, each of the PARTIES has caused this Agreement to be duly executed and delivered as of the day and year first above written.

Signed for and on behalf of:

By ....

Signature ....

Title ....

Witness ....

Signed for and on behalf of:

By ....

Signature ....

Title ....

Witness ....

The Schedule

A. Details of the Equipment.

B. Details of the Licensed Programs.

C. Licence Fees.

D. Delivery Date.

E. Location.

F. Storage.

G. Training:

(*i*) Total number of staff to be trained in total;

(*ii*) Duration of training needed;

(*iii*) Place of training;

(*iv*) Amount to be paid as T.A. / D.A.

ACCEPTANCE CERTIFICATE

To: Eastern Computers Limited

From: National Silk Foundation

Date: 1.7.2004

Dear Sirs,

This has reference to the agreement between our organisations dated 30th May 2004 ('the Agreement') pertaining to the installation and licensing of computer programs ('the Licensed Programs'). We wish to inform the following:

1. We have today accepted the Licensed Programs.

2. We have verified the Licensed Programs and found them to be conforming to the description contained in the Agreement and that the same have been installed on the Equipment (as defined in the Agreement) to our utmost satisfaction.

3. The Licensed Programs have successfully processed the test data referred to in clause 5 of the Agreement. We hereby attach a copy of such data and the results of such tests for your perusal.

Signed for and on behalf of:

National Silk Foundation

By ....

Signature ....

Title ....

Witness ....

General Index

(Chapterwise Index is in pages 1419-1448)

(Chapterwise Index is in pages 1419-1448)

(Chapterwise Index is in pages 1419-1448)

(Chapterwise Index is in pages 1419-1448)

(Chapterwise Index is in pages 1419-1448)

(Chapterwise Index is in pages 1419-1448)

(Chapterwise Index is in pages 1419-1448)

(Chapterwise Index is in pages 1419-1448)

(Chapterwise Index is in pages 1419-1448)

(Chapterwise Index is in pages 1419-1448)

(Chapterwise Index is in pages 1419-1448)

(Chapterwise Index is in pages 1419-1448)

Chapterwise Index

(General Index is in pages 1407-1418)

Adoption

Agreement

Agreement—*continued*

Apartment Ownership

(General Index is in pages 1407-1418)

Apprenticeship

Arbitration and Award

(General Index is in pages 1407-1418)

Arbitration and Award—*continued*

Assignment of Copyright etc.

Bail Petition

(General Index is in pages 1407-1418)

Bail Petition—*continued*

Bonds

Cancellation of Documents

(General Index is in pages 1407-1418)

Clubs and Societies

Companies

Construction Agreement

(General Index is in pages 1407-1418)

Consumer Protection Act

Co-operative Society, Registration of

Debutter Property

(General Index is in pages 1407-1418)

Development and Sale of Apartments

Disclaimer

Distributorship

(General Index is in pages 1407-1418)

Divorce–Nullity of Marriage and Judicial Separation

Endowment

(General Index is in pages 1407-1418)

Exchange

Foreign Collaboration and Joint Venture

Franchising

Gift

(General Index is in pages 1407-1418)

Guarantees and Indemnities

Guardianship

Hire-Purchase

(General Index is in pages 1407-1418)

Insolvency

Labour Laws

Leases

(General Index is in pages 1407-1418)

Leases—*continued*

Lease Financing of Equipment

Leave & Licence and Easement

(General Index is in pages 1407-1418)

Mentally ill Persons

Maintenance

Mortgages and Pledges

(General Index is in pages 1407-1418)

Mortgages and Pledges—*continued*

Negotiable Instruments

(General Index is in pages 1407-1418)

Negotiable Instruments—*continued*

Notice

(General Index is in pages 1407-1418)

Notice — *continued*

(General Index is in pages 1407-1418)

Partnership

Partition

(General Index is in pages 1407-1418)

Patents and Trade Marks

Power-of-Attorney

(General Index is in pages 1407-1418)

Promoters' Loan Agreement

Public Interest Litigation

Railways, Claims Against

(General Index is in pages 1407-1418)

Receipt and Acknowledgement

Rectification and Modification of Deeds

(General Index is in pages 1407-1418)

Release

Sales

(General Index is in pages 1407-1418)

Sales—*continued*

(General Index is in pages 1407-1418)

Sales—*continued*

Sole Selling Agency

Special Leave Petition to Appeal

(General Index is in pages 1407-1418)

Surrender

Testamentary Matters

PROBATE, LETTERS OF ADMINISTRATION AND SUCCESSION CERTIFICATE

(General Index is in pages 1407-1418)

Testamentary Matters—*continued*

Trust

(General Index is in pages 1407-1418)

Trust—*continued*

Wakf Property

(General Index is in pages 1407-1418)

Will

(General Index is in pages 1407-1418)

Registration of Documents

Computer Contacts

(General Index is in pages 1407-1418)

Computer Contacts—*continued*

(General Index is in pages 1407-1418)